Philips' Concise Atlas of the World

PHILIPS'

CONCISE ATLAS OF THE WORLD

LA LANTERNA
Chantal
DA MARIO

George Philip

London · Melbourne · Milwaukee

Edited by
B.M. Willett, B.A., Cartographic Editor, George Philip and Son Ltd
Consultant Cartographer Harold Fullard, M.Sc.
Maps prepared by George Philip Cartographic Services Ltd
under the direction of A.G. Poynter, M.A.,
Director of Cartography

Third Edition 1983 Reprinted 1984

British Library Cataloguing in Publication Data

Philips' concise atlas of the world – 3rd ed.
1. World – Atlases
912 G1021
ISBN 0 540 05451 8

Printed in Great Britain by George Philip Printers Ltd

Title-page illustration Portovenere on the Gulf of Genoa, Italy (Bruce Coleman Ltd)

Preface

The **Concise Atlas** has been devised as a useful reference book that will meet most people's needs. The map coverage of the world is comprehensive and at scales suitable to the area concerned. Each continental section is introduced with two maps, one to show the political divisions and one to show the relief of land. Within each continental section maps of the important political, cultural or geographical regions, such as Italy and the Balkans, precede those at larger scales of the individual countries and more densely populated regions.

The majority of the maps are coloured to the relief of the land, shown by layer colours with relief shading in grey. On this physical background are shown the patterns of settlement and communications.

Spellings of names are in the form given in the latest official lists and generally agree with the rules of the Permanent Committee on Geographical Names and the United States Board on Geographic Names. This means that for many well-known places the local spelling is used, with the English conventional form given in parentheses, for example, Roma (Rome) or Warszawa (Warsaw). The index refers the reader from the conventional form to the local form.

The index contains over 45,000 names and shows the map page number and the geographical coordinates for each entry.

B.M. Willett

Contents

1 **General Reference**
1 **The World—Physical** 1:150M
2-3 **The World—Political** 1:80M
4-5 **The Polar Regions** 1:35M
6-7 **The Atlantic Ocean**
Equatorial Scale 1:50M

Above Le Boitier in the Beaujolais district of France (Bruce Coleman Ltd)

Opposite above The Namib Desert, Namibia (Bruce Coleman Ltd)

Opposite below Darjeeling, India (Bruce Coleman Ltd)

Europe

8-9 **Europe—Physical** 1:17½M
European Organisations 1:40M
10 **Europe—Political** 1:20M
11 **The British Isles—Political** 1:4M
12-13 **England and Wales** 1:2M
14 **Scotland** 1:2M
15 **Ireland** 1:2M
16 **The Netherlands, Belgium and Luxembourg** 1:2½M
17 **France** 1:5M
18-19 **Northern France** 1:2½M
20-21 **Southern France** 1:2½M
22-23 **Central Europe** 1:5M
24-25 **Germany and Switzerland** 1:2½M
26-27 **Austria, Czechoslovakia and Hungary** 1:2½M
28 **Poland** 1:2½M
29 **Spain and Portugal** 1:5M
30-31 **Western Spain and Portugal** 1:2½M
32-33 **Eastern Spain** 1:2½M
34-35 **The Mediterranean Lands** 1:10M
36-37 **Italy and the Balkan States** 1:5M
Malta 1:1M
38-39 **Northern Italy and Western Yugoslavia** 1:2½M
40-41 **Southern Italy** 1:2½M
42-43 **Eastern Yugoslavia and Bulgaria** 1:2½M
44-45 **Greece and Albania** 1:2½M
46 **Romania** 1:2½M
47 **Southern Norway** 1:2½M
48-49 **Denmark and Southern Sweden** 1:2½M
50-51 **Scandinavia and the Baltic Lands** 1:5M
Iceland 1:5M
52-53 **The U.S.S.R. in Europe** 1:10M
54-55 **European Russia—Central** 1:5M
56-57 **European Russia—South** 1:5M

Asia

58-59 **The Union of Soviet Socialist Republics** 1:20M
60 **Asia—Physical** 1:50M
61 **Asia—Political** 1:50M
62 **Israel and West Jordan** 1:1M
63 **Arabia and The Horn of Africa** 1:15M
64-65 **The Near and Middle East** 1:10M
66-67 **South Asia** 1:10M
68-69 **The Indo-Gangetic Plain** 1:6M
S. Asia—Irrigation 1:40M
70 **Southern India and Sri Lanka** 1:6M
71 **Mainland South-East Asia** 1:10M
Pen. Malaysia & Singapore 1:6M
72-73 **The East Indies** 1:12½M
Java & Madura 1:7½M
74 **Japan** 1:10M
Southern Japan 1:5M
75 **China** 1:20M
76-77 **Eastern China and Korea** 1:10M

Africa

78 **Africa—Physical** 1:40M
79 **Africa—Political** 1:40M
80-81 **Northern Africa** 1:15M
82-83 **North-West Africa** 1:8M
84-85 **West Africa** 1:8M
86-87 **The Nile Valley** 1:8M
The Nile Delta 1:4M
88-89 **Central and South Africa** 1:15M
90-91 **East Africa** 1:8M
92-93 **Southern Africa** 1:8M
Madagascar 1:8M

Australasia

94-95 **The Pacific Ocean**
Equatorial Scale 1:60M
96-97 **Australia** 1:12M
Australasia – Physical 1:80M
98-99 **Eastern Australia** 1:7½M
Papua New Guinea 1:12M
100 **South-East Australia** 1:4½M
101 **New Zealand** 1:6M
Samoa 1:12M
Fiji and Tonga 1:12M
New Zealand and Dependencies 1:60M

Above Rain forest along the Blackwater River on the border between Guyana and Brazil (Bruce Coleman Ltd)

Top Sheep grazing on the Canterbury Plains, South Island, New Zealand, with the Southern Alps in the distance (Bruce Coleman Ltd)

The Americas

102-3 **North America – Physical** 1:30M
North America – Political 1:70M
104-5 **Canada** 1:15M
Alaska 1:30M
106-7 **Eastern Canada** 1:7M
108-9 **Western Canada** 1:7M
110-11 **The United States** 1:12M
Hawaii 1:10M
112-13 **North – Eastern United States** 1:2½M
114-15 **The Eastern United States** 1:6M
116-17 **The Middle United States** 1:6M
118-19 **The Western United States** 1:6M
120 **Mexico** 1:12M
Panama Canal 1:1M
121 **The West Indies** 1:12M
Bermuda 1:1M
Leeward Is. 1:8M
Windward Is. 1:8M
Trinidad and Tobago 1:8M
Jamaica 1:8M
122 **South America – Physical** 1:30M
123 **South America – Political** 1:30M
124-25 **Central South America** 1:8M
126-27 **South America – North** 1:16M
128 **South America – South** 1:16M

Index

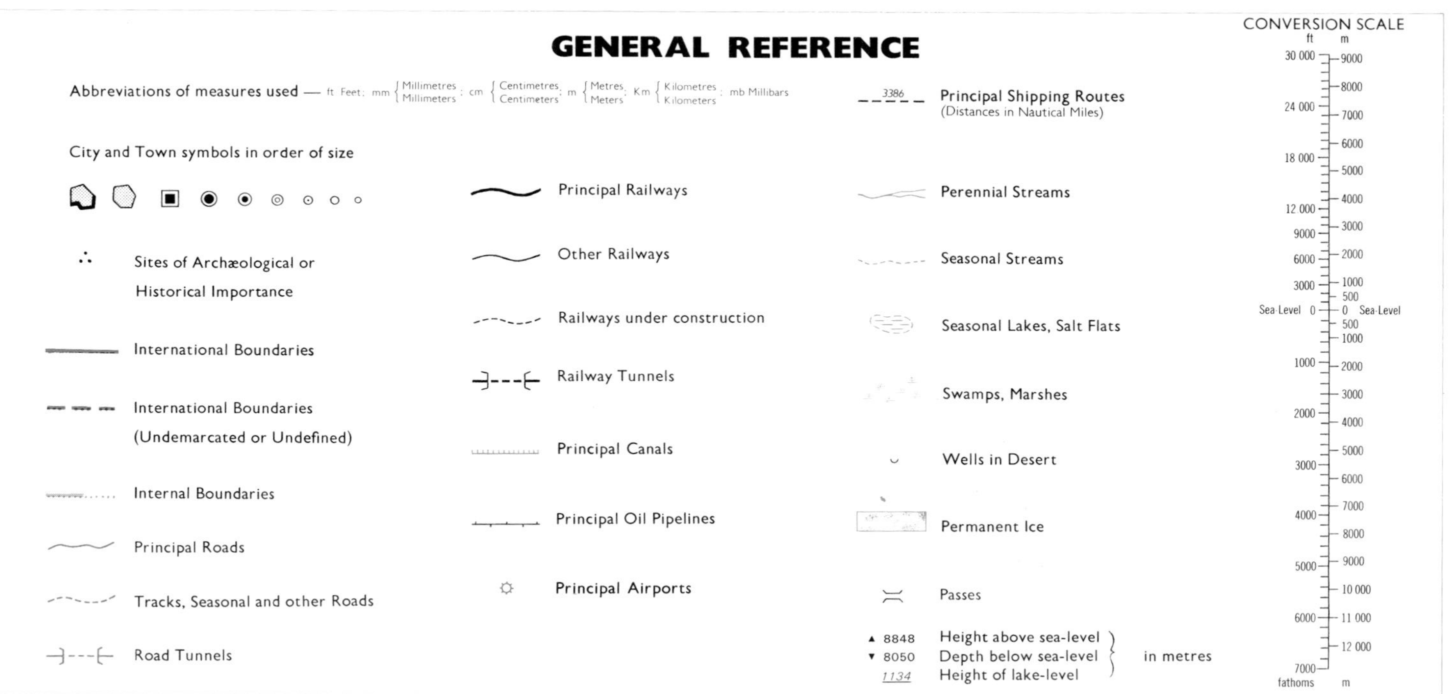

GENERAL REFERENCE
Abbreviations of measures used — ft Feet; mm Millimetres / Millimeters; cm Centimetres / Centimeters; m Metres / Meters; Km Kilometres / Kilometers; mb Millibars
City and Town symbols in order of size
Sites of Archæological or Historical Importance
International Boundaries
International Boundaries (Undemarcated or Undefined)
Internal Boundaries
Principal Roads
Tracks, Seasonal and other Roads
Road Tunnels
Principal Railways
Other Railways
Railways under construction
Railway Tunnels
Principal Canals
Principal Oil Pipelines
Principal Airports
3386
Principal Shipping Routes (Distances in Nautical Miles)
Perennial Streams
Seasonal Streams
Seasonal Lakes, Salt Flats
Swamps, Marshes
Wells in Desert
Permanent Ice
Passes
8848 Height above sea-level
8050 Depth below sea-level
1134 Height of lake-level
in metres
CONVERSION SCALE
ft m
30 000
24 000
18 000
12 000
9000
6000
3000
Sea-Level 0
1000
2000
3000
4000
5000
6000
7000
fathoms
9000
8000
7000
6000
5000
4000
3000
2000
1000
500
0 Sea-Level
500
1000
2000
3000
4000
5000
6000
7000
8000
9000
10 000
11 000
12 000
m

THE WORLD

Physical

1:150 000 000

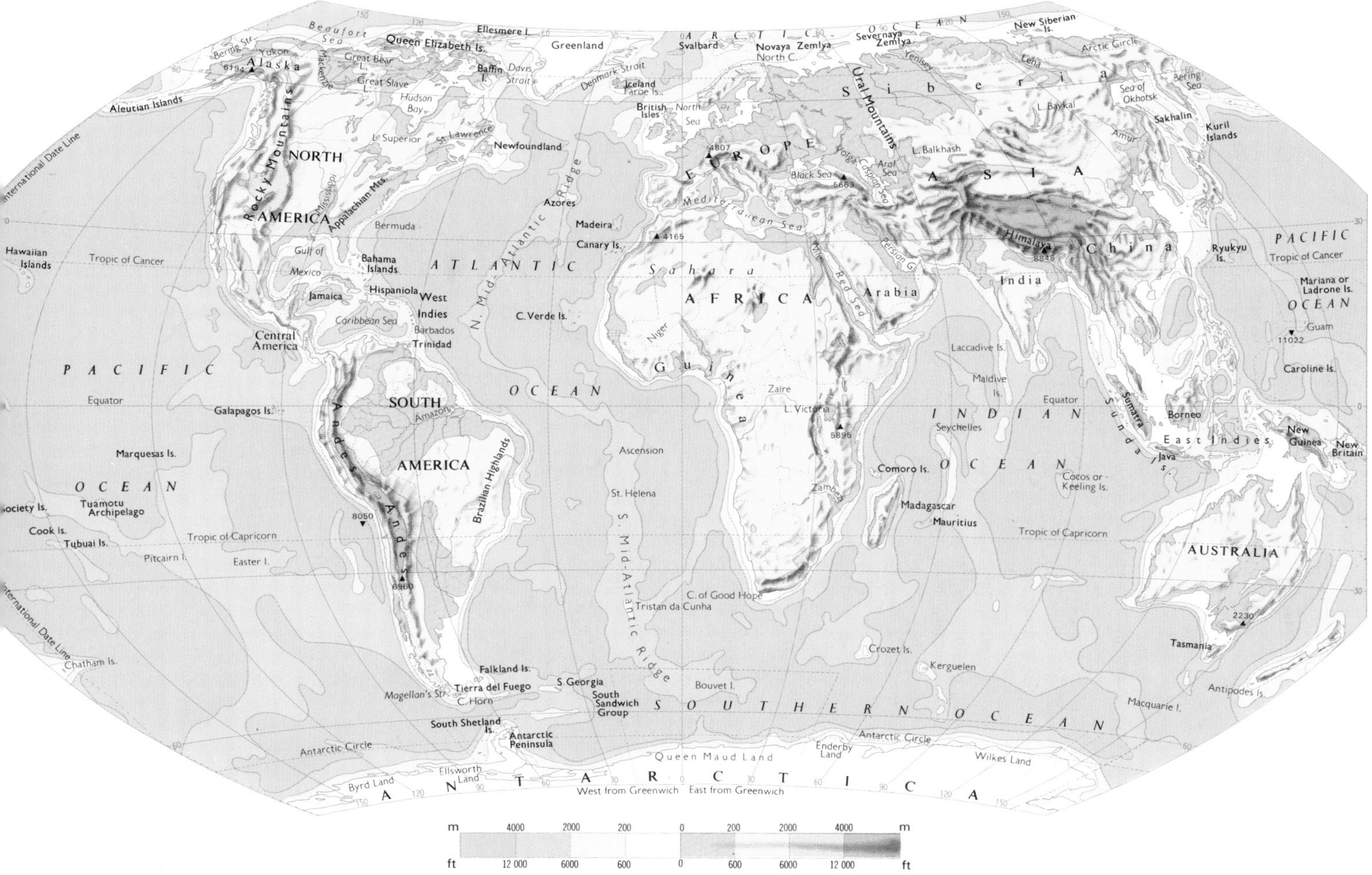

Beaufort Sea
Queen Elizabeth Is.
Ellesmere I.
Greenland
Svalbard
Novaya Zemlya
North C.
Severnaya Zemlya
New Siberian Is.
Arctic Circle
Bering Str.
Yukon
Alaska
6194
Great Bear L.
Great Slave L.
Baffin I.
Davis Strait
Denmark Strait
Iceland
Faroe Is.
Ural Mountains
Siberia
Lena
Sea of Okhotsk
Bering Sea
Aleutian Islands
Hudson Bay
British Isles
North Sea
L. Baykal
Sakhalin
Kuril Islands
Amur
Rocky Mountains
NORTH AMERICA
L. Superior
St. Lawrence
Newfoundland
4807
EUROPE
Volga
L. Balkhash
Black Sea
Aral Sea
Caspian Sea
5633
ASIA
International Date Line
Mississippi
Appalachian Mts.
Azores
Mediterranean Sea
Bermuda
Madeira
Canary Is.
4165
Himalaya
8848
China
Ryukyu Is.
PACIFIC
Hawaiian Islands
Tropic of Cancer
Gulf of Mexico
Bahama Islands
ATLANTIC
N. Mid-Atlantic Ridge
Sahara
Persian G.
Nile
Red Sea
Arabia
India
Mariana or Ladrone Is.
OCEAN
Jamaica
Hispaniola
West Indies
Caribbean Sea
Barbados
Trinidad
C. Verde Is.
AFRICA
Niger
Laccadive Is.
Guam
11022
Central America
PACIFIC
Guinea
Zaire
Maldive Is.
Caroline Is.
OCEAN
Equator
Galapagos Is.
SOUTH AMERICA
Amazon
L. Victoria
INDIAN
Seychelles
Sumatra
Borneo
Sunda Is.
East Indies
New Guinea
New Britain
5895
Java
Marquesas Is.
Andes
Brazilian Highlands
Ascension
Comoro Is.
OCEAN
Cocos or Keeling Is.
OCEAN
St. Helena
Zambezi
Society Is.
Tuamotu Archipelago
8050
Madagascar
Mauritius
Cook Is.
Tubuai Is.
Tropic of Capricorn
Pitcairn I.
Easter I.
S. Mid-Atlantic Ridge
AUSTRALIA
6960
C. of Good Hope
Tristan da Cunha
2230
Chatham Is.
Crozet Is.
Kerguelen
Tasmania
Falkland Is.
Tierra del Fuego
Magellan's Str.
C. Horn
S. Georgia
South Sandwich Group
Bouvet I.
SOUTHERN OCEAN
Antipodes Is.
Macquarie I.
South Shetland Is.
Antarctic Peninsula
Antarctic Circle
Queen Maud Land
Enderby Land
Wilkes Land
Byrd Land
Ellsworth Land
ANTARCTICA
West from Greenwich
East from Greenwich

m 4000 2000 200 0 200 2000 4000 m
ft 12 000 6000 600 0 600 6000 12 000 ft

Projection: Hammer Equal Area

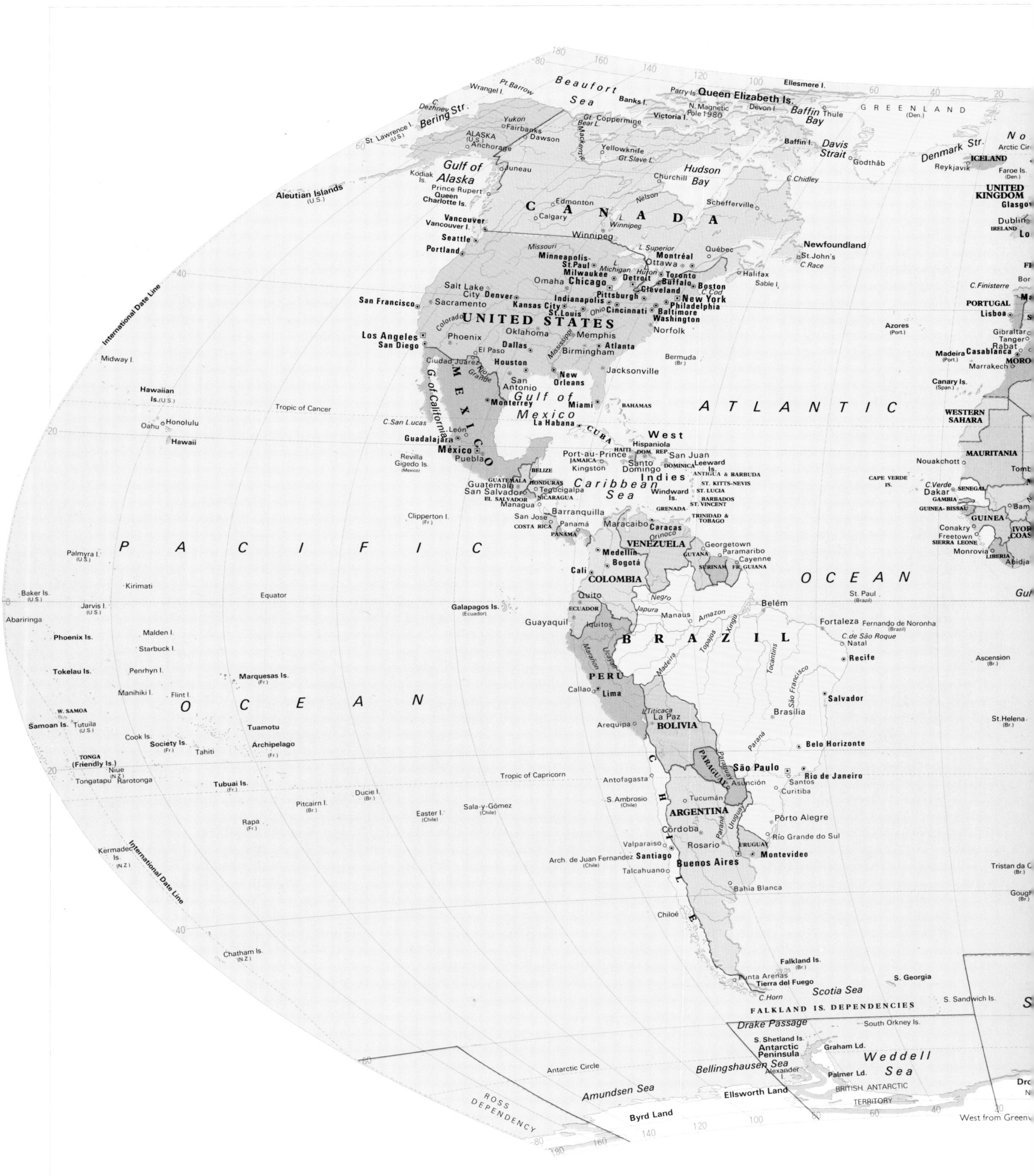
Beaufort Sea
Queen Elizabeth Is.
Ellesmere I.
Banks I.
Parry Is.
N. Magnetic Pole 1980
Devon I.
Baffin Bay
Thule
GREENLAND (Den.)
Wrangel I.
Pt. Barrow
C. Dezhnev
Bering Str.
St. Lawrence I. (U.S.)
Yukon
Fairbanks
Dawson
ALASKA (U.S.)
Anchorage
Gt. Bear L.
Coppermine
Mackenzie
Victoria I.
Yellowknife
Gt. Slave L.
Baffin I.
Davis Strait
Godthåb
Denmark Str.
ICELAND
Reykjavik
Faroe Is. (Den.)
Arctic Cir.
Gulf of Alaska
Juneau
Kodiak Is.
Prince Rupert
Queen Charlotte Is.
Aleutian Islands (U.S.)
Hudson Bay
Churchill
C. Chidley
Nelson
Edmonton
Calgary
CANADA
Schefferville
Vancouver
Vancouver I.
Winnipeg
L. Winnipeg
Seattle
Portland
UNITED KINGDOM
Glasgow
Dublin
IRELAND
L. Superior
Missouri
Minneapolis-St. Paul
Milwaukee
L. Michigan
L. Huron
Montréal
Ottawa
Québec
Newfoundland
St. John's
C. Race
Halifax
Sable I.
Toronto
Buffalo
Boston
C. Cod
Detroit
Chicago
Omaha
Cleveland
Salt Lake City
Denver
Pittsburgh
New York
Philadelphia
Baltimore
Washington
San Francisco
Sacramento
Kansas City
Indianapolis
Ohio
Cincinnati
St. Louis
C. Finisterre
PORTUGAL
Lisboa
Colorado
UNITED STATES
Norfolk
Los Angeles
San Diego
Phoenix
Oklahoma
Memphis
Mississippi
Dallas
Atlanta
Birmingham
El Paso
Ciudad Juárez
Rio Grande
Houston
Bermuda (Br.)
Jacksonville
Azores (Port.)
Gibraltar
Tanger
Rabat
Madeira (Port.)
Casablanca
Marrakech
International Date Line
Midway I.
San Antonio
New Orleans
MEXICO
G. of California
Monterrey
Gulf of Mexico
Miami
BAHAMAS
ATLANTIC
Canary Is. (Span.)
WESTERN SAHARA
Hawaiian Is. (U.S.)
Tropic of Cancer
Oahu
Honolulu
Hawaii
C. San Lucas
La Habana
CUBA
West Indies
Hispaniola
León
Guadalajara
México
Puebla
Revilla Gigedo Is. (Mexico)
Port-au-Prince
HAITI
DOM. REP.
San Juan
Leeward Is.
JAMAICA
Kingston
Santo Domingo
DOMINICA
ANTIGUA & BARBUDA
ST. KITTS-NEVIS
ST. LUCIA
BARBADOS
ST. VINCENT
GRENADA
TRINIDAD & TOBAGO
Windward Is.
BELIZE
GUATEMALA
Guatemala
HONDURAS
Tegucigalpa
San Salvador
EL SALVADOR
NICARAGUA
Managua
Caribbean Sea
MAURITANIA
Nouakchott
CAPE VERDE IS.
C. Verde
Dakar
SENEGAL
GAMBIA
GUINEA-BISSAU
GUINEA
Clipperton I. (Fr.)
San José
COSTA RICA
Panamá
PANAMA
Barranquilla
Maracaibo
Caracas
Orinoco
VENEZUELA
Georgetown
Paramaribo
Cayenne
GUYANA
SURINAM
FR. GUIANA
Conakry
Freetown
SIERRA LEONE
Monrovia
LIBERIA
Abidjan
Palmyra I. (U.S.)
PACIFIC
Medellín
Bogotá
Cali
COLOMBIA
OCEAN
Kirimati
Baker Is. (U.S.)
Equator
Jarvis I. (U.S.)
Galapagos Is. (Ecuador)
Quito
ECUADOR
Negro
Japura
Manaus
Amazon
Belém
St. Paul (Brazil)
Abariringa
Malden I.
Guayaquil
Iquitos
Fortaleza
Fernando de Noronha (Brazil)
C. de São Roque
Natal
Phoenix Is.
Starbuck I.
BRAZIL
Tapajos
Xingu
Tocantins
Recife
Ascension (Br.)
Tokelau Is.
Penrhyn I.
Marquesas Is. (Fr.)
Maranon
Ucayali
Madeira
São Francisco
Manihiki I.
Flint I.
PERU
Callao
Lima
Salvador
W. SAMOA
Samoan Is.
Tutuila (U.S.)
OCEAN
Tuamotu Archipelago (Fr.)
L. Titicaca
La Paz
BOLIVIA
Arequipa
Brasília
St. Helena (Br.)
Cook Is.
Society Is. (Fr.)
Tahiti
Paraná
Belo Horizonte
TONGA (Friendly Is.)
Niue (N.Z.)
Tongatapu
Rarotonga
Tubuai Is. (Fr.)
Tropic of Capricorn
PARAGUAY
Paraguay
São Paulo
Rio de Janeiro
Santos
Asunción
Curitiba
Antofagasta
CHILE
S. Ambrosio (Chile)
Tucumán
Pitcairn I. (Br.)
Ducie I. (Br.)
Easter I. (Chile)
Sala-y-Gómez (Chile)
ARGENTINA
Uruguay
Pôrto Alegre
Rapa (Fr.)
Córdoba
Paraná
Rio Grande do Sul
Valparaiso
Rosario
URUGUAY
Montevideo
Kermadec Is. (N.Z.)
Arch. de Juan Fernandez (Chile)
Santiago
Buenos Aires
Talcahuano
Tristan da Cunha (Br.)
Bahia Blanca
Gough I. (Br.)
Chiloé
Chatham Is. (N.Z.)
Falkland Is. (Br.)
Punta Arenas
Tierra del Fuego
S. Georgia
C. Horn
Scotia Sea
S. Sandwich Is.
FALKLAND IS. DEPENDENCIES
Drake Passage
South Orkney Is.
S. Shetland Is.
Antarctic Peninsula
Graham Ld.
Weddell Sea
Palmer Ld.
Alexander I.
Bellingshausen Sea
Antarctic Circle
Amundsen Sea
Ellsworth Land
BRITISH ANTARCTIC TERRITORY
ROSS DEPENDENCY
Byrd Land
West from Greenwich

Projection: *Hammer Equal Area*

ARCTIC OCEAN
Laptev Sea
East Siberian Sea
Barents Sea
Kara Sea
UNION OF SOVIET SOCIALIST REPUBLICS
Bering Sea
Sea of Okhotsk
MONGOLIA
CHINA
JAPAN
Sea of Japan
INDIA
PAKISTAN
IRAN (PERSIA)
SAUDI ARABIA
Arabian Sea
Bay of Bengal
South China Sea
PACIFIC OCEAN
INDIAN OCEAN
INDONESIA
AUSTRALIA
Arafura Sea
Timor Sea
Tasman Sea
NEW ZEALAND
MADAGASCAR
SOUTH AFRICA
ZAÏRE (CONGO)
ANGOLA
ETHIOPIA
SUDAN
CHAD
LIBYA
EGYPT
TRUST TERRITORY OF THE PACIFIC ISLANDS (U.S.)
SOUTHERN OCEAN
AUSTRALIAN DEPENDENCY
Tropic of Cancer
Tropic of Capricorn
Equator
Antarctic Circle
Ross Sea
Wilkes Land
Enderby Land
S. Magnetic Pole 1980
from Greenwich

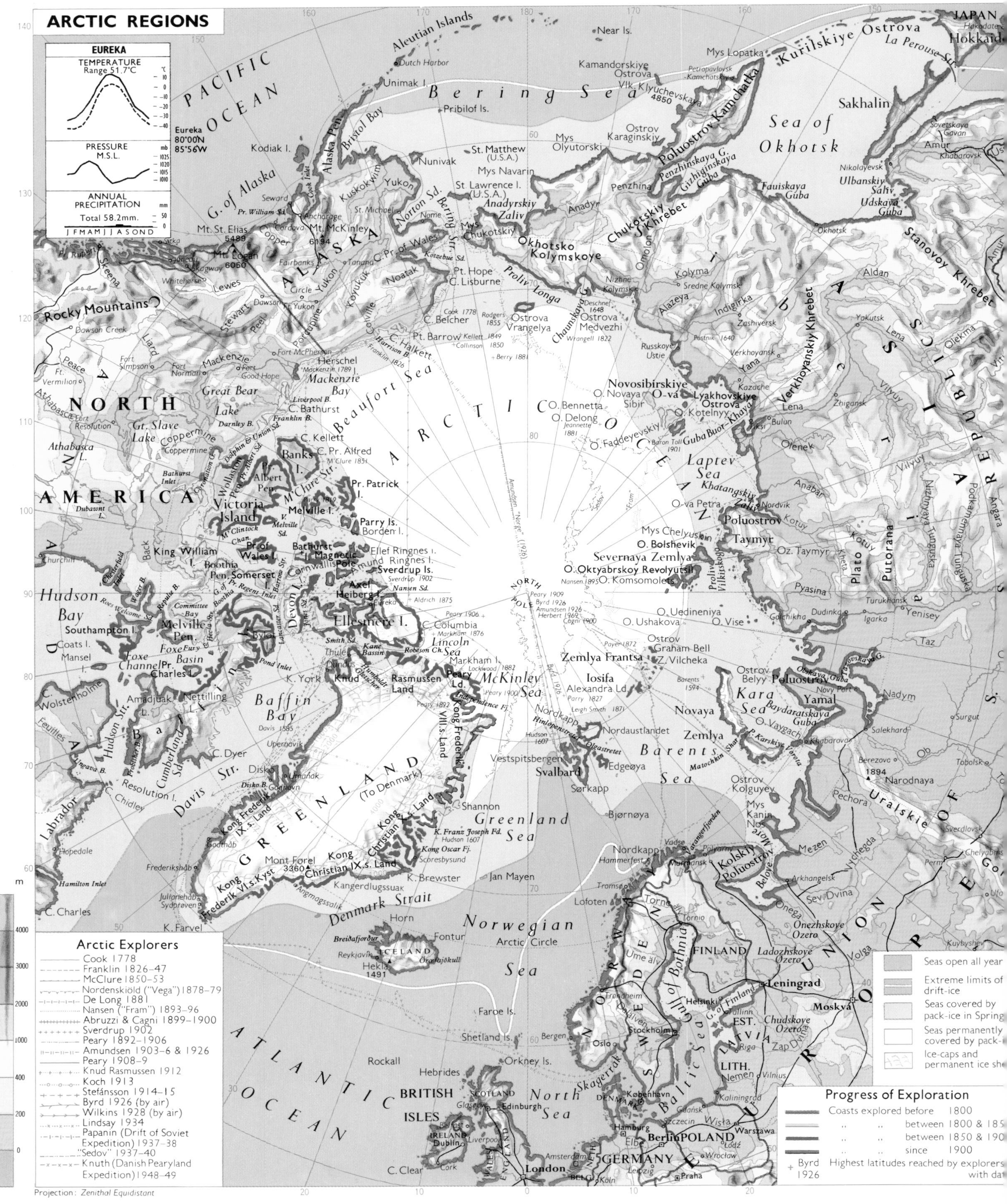
ARCTIC REGIONS
EUREKA
TEMPERATURE
Range 51.7°C
PRESSURE
M.S.L.
ANNUAL
PRECIPITATION
Total 58.2mm.
J F M A M J J A S O N D
Eureka
80°00'N
85°56'W
Arctic Explorers
Cook 1778
Franklin 1826–47
McClure 1850–53
Nordenskiöld ("Vega") 1878–79
De Long 1881
Nansen ("Fram") 1893–96
Abruzzi & Cagni 1899–1900
Sverdrup 1902
Peary 1892–1906
Amundsen 1903–6 & 1926
Peary 1908–9
Knud Rasmussen 1912
Koch 1913
Stefánsson 1914–15
Byrd 1926 (by air)
Wilkins 1928 (by air)
Lindsay 1934
Papanin (Drift of Soviet Expedition) 1937–38
"Sedov" 1937–40
Knuth (Danish Pearyland Expedition) 1948–49
Seas open all year
Extreme limits of drift-ice
Seas covered by pack-ice in Spring
Seas permanently covered by pack-
Ice-caps and permanent ice she
Progress of Exploration
Coasts explored before 1800
,, ,, between 1800 & 185
,, ,, between 1850 & 190
,, ,, since 1900
Byrd 1926 Highest latitudes reached by explorers with da
Projection: Zenithal Equidistant
ft m
12 000 4000
9000 3000
6000 2000
3000 1000
1200 400
600 200
0 0
PACIFIC OCEAN
Bering Sea
Sea of Okhotsk
ARCTIC OCEAN
Beaufort Sea
NORTH AMERICA
ALASKA
GREENLAND (To Denmark)
Baffin Bay
Hudson Bay
Greenland Sea
Norwegian Sea
Barents Sea
Kara Sea
Laptev Sea
ATLANTIC OCEAN
North Sea
NORTH POLE
ASIA
BRITISH ISLES
ICELAND
NORWAY
SWEDEN
FINLAND
GERMANY
POLAND
UNION OF SOVIET SOCIALIST REPUBLICS

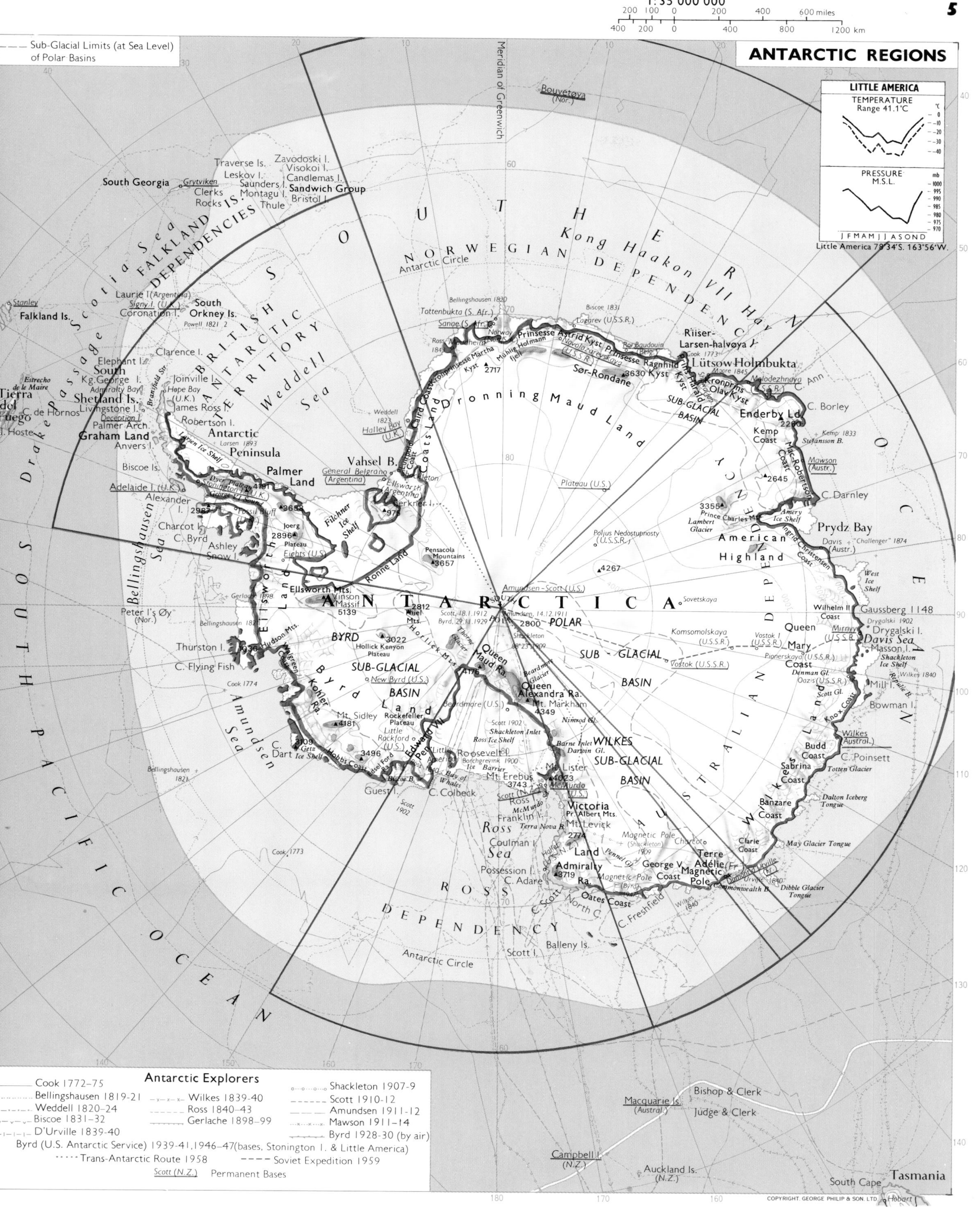

ANTARCTIC REGIONS
1:35 000 000
200 100 0 200 400 600 miles
400 200 0 400 800 1200 km
Sub-Glacial Limits (at Sea Level) of Polar Basins
LITTLE AMERICA
TEMPERATURE Range 41.1°C
PRESSURE M.S.L.
J F M A M J J A S O N D
Little America 78°34'S. 163°56'W.
Antarctic Explorers
Cook 1772-75
Bellingshausen 1819-21
Weddell 1820-24
Biscoe 1831-32
D'Urville 1839-40
Wilkes 1839-40
Ross 1840-43
Gerlache 1898-99
Shackleton 1907-9
Scott 1910-12
Amundsen 1911-12
Mawson 1911-14
Byrd 1928-30 (by air)
Byrd (U.S. Antarctic Service) 1939-41, 1946-47 (bases, Stonington I. & Little America)
Trans-Antarctic Route 1958
Soviet Expedition 1959
Scott (N.Z.) Permanent Bases
Meridian of Greenwich
SOUTHERN OCEAN
SOUTH PACIFIC OCEAN
ANTARCTICA
Antarctic Circle
NORWEGIAN DEPENDENCY
Kong Haakon VII Hav
AUSTRALIAN DEPENDENCY
ROSS DEPENDENCY
FALKLAND IS. DEPENDENCIES
BRITISH ANTARCTIC TERRITORY
Weddell Sea
Scotia Sea
Drake Passage
Bellingshausen Sea
Amundsen Sea
Ross Sea
Davis Sea
Prydz Bay
South Georgia
Falkland Is.
South Orkney Is.
South Shetland Is.
Sandwich Group
Tierra del Fuego
C. de Hornos
Graham Land
Antarctic Peninsula
Palmer Land
Dronning Maud Land
Enderby Ld.
American Highland
Wilkes Land
Victoria Land
Byrd Land
Ellsworth Land
Queen Mary Coast
Terre Adélie
George V Coast
Oates Coast
Filchner Ice Shelf
Ross Ice Shelf
Amery Ice Shelf
Vinson Massif 5139
Mt. Erebus 3743
Queen Alexandra Ra.
Queen Maud Ra.
Horlick Mts.
Pensacola Mountains
BYRD SUB-GLACIAL BASIN
POLAR SUB-GLACIAL BASIN
WILKES SUB-GLACIAL BASIN
Magnetic Pole
Bouvetøya (Nor.)
Peter I's Øy (Nor.)
Balleny Is.
Scott I.
Macquarie Is. (Austral.)
Campbell I. (N.Z.)
Auckland Is. (N.Z.)
Bishop & Clerk
Judge & Clerk
Tasmania
South Cape
Hobart
COPYRIGHT, GEORGE PHILIP & SON, LTD.

ARCTIC OCEAN
Svalbard
Zemlya Frantsa Iosifa
Novaya Zemlya
Barents Sea
Kara Sea
Severnaya Zemlya
Greenland Sea
Norwegian Sea
GREENLAND
ICELAND
Davis Strait
Baffin Bay
Baffin Island
Ellesmere Island
Queen Elizabeth Islands
Beaufort Sea
Hudson Bay
Labrador
Newfoundland
C A N A D A
UNITED STATES
Gulf of Mexico
Florida
CUBA
West Indies
Caribbean Sea
Sargasso Sea
North American Basin
Northern Mid-Atlantic Ridge
NORTH ATLANTIC OCEAN
Azores
Canary Basin
Cape Verde Basin
Madeira
Islas Canarias
Bay of Biscay
North Sea
Baltic Sea
Mediterranean Sea
UNITED KINGDOM
IRELAND
FRANCE
SPAIN
PORTUGAL
MOROCCO
ALGERIA
TUNISIA
LIBYA
Sahara
MAURITANIA
SENEGAL
NIGER
NIGERIA
CHAD
CAMEROON
WESTERN SAHARA
U.S.S.R.
FINLAND
SWEDEN
POLAND
ROMANIA
BULGARIA
GREECE
VENEZUELA
COLOMBIA
MEXICO
Tropic of Cancer
GUINEA CURRENT
NORTH EQUATORIAL CURRENT
LABRADOR COLD CURRENT
NORTH ATLANTIC DRIFT
GULF STREAM

SOUTH ATLANTIC OCEAN
PACIFIC OCEAN
SOUTHERN OCEAN
BRAZIL
BOLIVIA
PERU
ARGENTINA
PARAGUAY
URUGUAY
FALKLAND IS.
DEPENDENCIES
BRITISH ANTARCTIC TERRITORY
Weddell Sea
Ross Sea
Scotia Sea
Drake Passage
Dronning Maud Land
Enderby Land
Coats Land
Ellsworth Land
Byrd Land
Graham Land
Palmer Land
Antarctic Peninsula
Antarctic Circle
Tropic of Capricorn
Equatorial Limit of Icebergs
Southern Mid-Atlantic Ridge
Walvis Ridge
Atlantic Indian Ridge
Chile Rise
Brazil Basin
Angola Basin
Cape Basin
Agulhas Basin
Argentine Basin
South East Pacific Basin
Antarctic (Southern Pacific) Basin
Antarctic Basin
BENGUELA COLD CURRENT
PERUVIAN COLD CURRENT
EQUATORIAL CURRENT
BRAZIL CURRENT
WEST WIND DRIFT
CAPE HORN COLD CURRENT
Rio de Janeiro
São Paulo
Buenos Aires
Montevideo
Santiago
Lima
Cape Town
Salvador
Recife
Fortaleza
Belo Horizonte
Brasília
Pôrto Alegre
Córdoba
Rosario
Asunción
La Paz
Valparaíso
Tierra del Fuego
Falkland Is.
South Georgia
South Sandwich Is.
South Orkney Is.
South Shetland Is.
Tristan da Cunha
Gough I.
St. Helena
Ascension
Bouvetøya
Madeira – Cape Town 4677
Pampas
Mato Grosso
Direction of Currents
Principal Shipping Routes (Distances in Nautical Miles)
Projection: Mollweide

Arctic Circle
E.E.C. Members
E.F.T.A. Member
All E.F.T.A. and associated states have Free Trade Agreements with the E.E.C.
States with Association Agreement with E.E.C.
Associate Member of E.F.T.A.
States with Trading Agreement with E.E.C.
Warsaw Pact Countries
The E.E.C. has Trading Agreements with certain countries in the Mediterranean, Pacific and Latin American areas.
EUROPEAN ORGANIZATIONS
1 : 40 000 000
Iceland
Reykjavik
Hekla 1491
Öræfajökull 2119
3734
Arctic Circle
NORWEGIAN SEA
Faroe Is.
Rockall
St. Kilda
Hebrides
Shetland Is.
Orkney Is.
Lindesnes
British Isles
Ben Nevis 1343
Edinburgh
NORTH SEA
Ireland
Belfast
Irish Sea
Dublin
Great Britain
St. George's Channel
Snowdon 1085
Cardiff
Celtic Sea
Lands End
Scilly Is.
Thames
London
Frisian Is.
Amsterdam
Netherlands
C. Clear
English Channel
Channel Is.
Str. of Dover
Brussel
Rhine
Ardennes
Eifel
Meuse
Hunsrück
Brittany
Paris
Seine
Vosges
Black Forest
Loire
ATLANTIC OCEAN
Flores
Terceira
Pico
Azores
São Miguel
4861
Bay of Biscay
Gironde
Saône
Jura
Massif Central
Mt. Dore 1886
Mt. Blanc 4807
ALPS
C. Finisterre
Cantabrian Mts.
Garonne
Cevennes
Rhône
Old Castile
Maladetta 3404
Pyrenees
Iberian Peninsula
Douro
Ebro
G. of Lion
Riviera
Ligurian Sea
Lisboa
C. da Roca
Madrid
Tagus
New Castile
Corsica
Guadiana
Sierra Morena
Str. of Bonifacio
Sardinia
C. St. Vincent
6293
Madeira
Guadalquivir
Andalusia
Mulhacen 3478
Sa. Nevada
Balearic Is.
MEDITERRANEAN
Str. of Gibraltar
C. Trafalgar
Gibraltar
Er Rif
Casablanca
Alger
Maritime Atlas
Tunis
Plateau of the Shotts
Atlas
Saharan Atlas
Palma
Tenerife
Canary Is.
Toubkal 4165
Great Atlas
Gulf of Gabes
Gran Canaria
Fuerteventura
Tropic of Cancer
Sahara
ft m
12 000 4000
6000 2000
3000 1000
1200 400
600 200
0 0
200 600
2000 6000
4000 12 000
m ft
Projection: Bonne.
West from Greenwich
East from Greenwich

1:17 500 000

100 0 100 200 300 400 500 miles
100 0 200 400 600 800 km

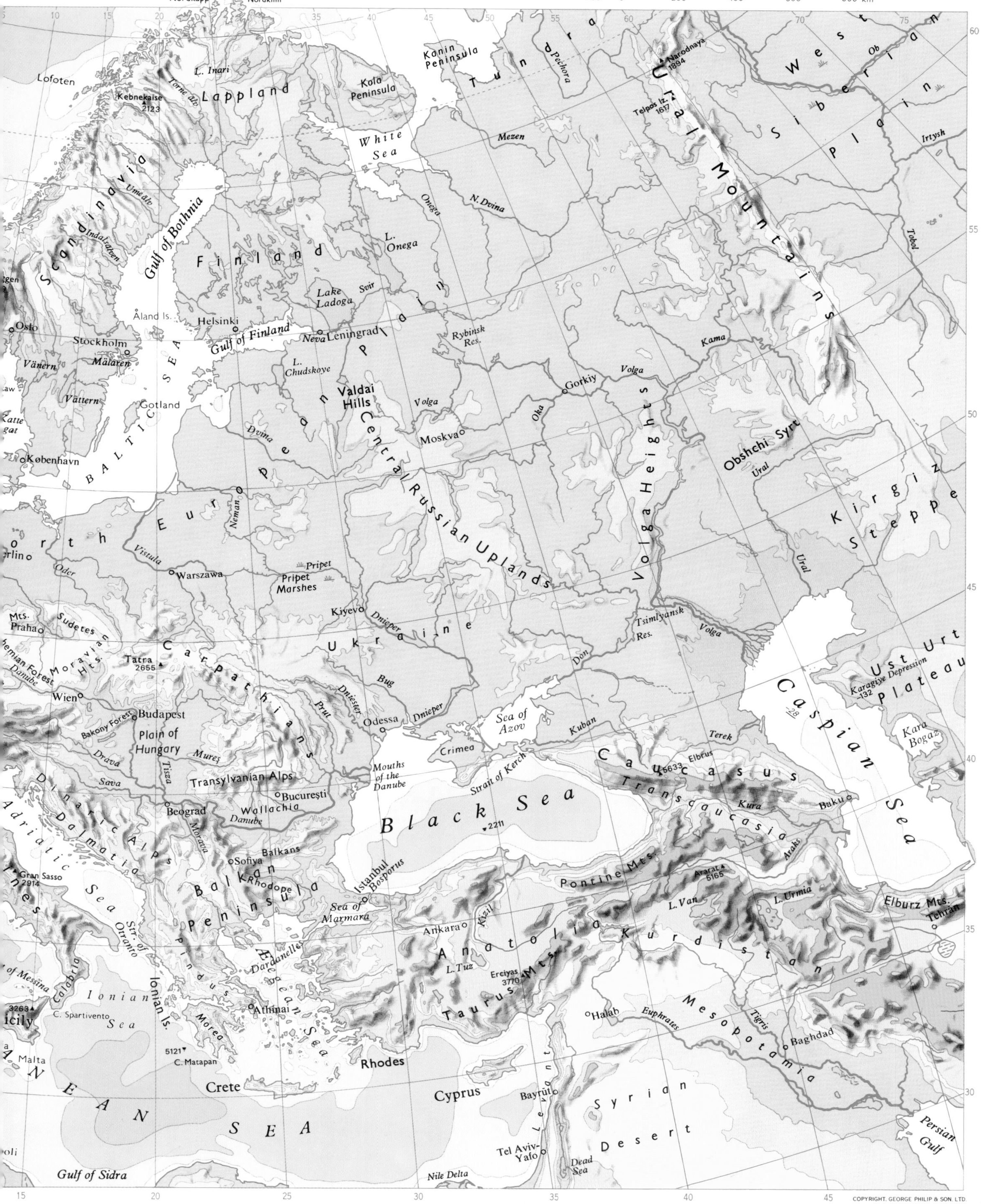

Nordkapp Nordkinn
Lofoten
L. Inari
Torne älv
Kebnekaise 2123
Lappland
Kola Peninsula
Kanin Peninsula
Tundra
Pechora
Narodnaya 1894
Telpos Iz. 1617
West Siberian Plain
Ob
Irtysh
White Sea
Mezen
Scandinavia
Umeälv
Gulf of Bothnia
Indalsälven
N. Dvina
Onega
L. Onega
Ural Mountains
Tobol
Finland
Lake Ladoga
Svir
Åland Is.
Helsinki
Oslo
Stockholm
Mälaren
Vänern
Vättern
Gulf of Finland
Neva
Leningrad
Rybinsk Res.
Kama
L. Chudskoye
Valdai Hills
Volga
Gorkiy
Gotland
BALTIC SEA
Kattegat
København
Dvina
Moskva
Oka
Volga Heights
Obshchi Syrt
Ural
Central Russian Uplands
North European Plain
Neman
Kirgiz Steppe
Berlin
Vistula
Oder
Warszawa
Pripet
Pripet Marshes
Ural
Mts.
Praha
Sudetes
Kiyevo
Dnieper
Ukraine
Tsimlyansk Res.
Volga
Ust Urt Plateau
Karagiye Depression -132
Bohemian Forest
Danube
Moravian Hts.
Tatra 2655
Carpathians
Don
Wien
Prut
Dniester
Bug
Caspian Sea
-28
Bakony Forest
Budapest
Plain of Hungary
Odessa
Dnieper
Sea of Azov
Kuban
Terek
Kara Bogaz
Drava
Mureș
Crimea
Elbrus 5633
Caucasus
Sava
Tisza
Transylvanian Alps
Mouths of the Danube
Strait of Kerch
Transcaucasia
Kura
Baku
Dinaric Alps
Beograd
Wallachia
București
Danube
Black Sea
2211
Adriatic Sea
Dalmatia
Morava
Balkans
Sofiya
Araks
Apennines
Gran Sasso 2914
Balkan Peninsula
Rhodope
Istanbul
Bosporus
Pontine Mts.
Ararat 5165
L. Urmia
Elburz Mts.
Tehrān
Sea of Marmara
L. Van
Str. of Otranto
Pindus
Ankara
Kizil
Anatolia
Kurdistan
Str. of Messina
Calabria
Dardanelles
L. Tuz
Erciyas 3770
Ionian Sea
Ionian Is.
Aegean Sea
Athinai
Taurus Mts.
Halab
Mesopotamia
Euphrates
Tigris
3263
Sicily
C. Spartivento
Morea
5121
C. Matapan
Baghdad
Malta
Rhodes
MEDITERRANEAN SEA
Crete
Cyprus
Bayrūt
Levant
Syrian Desert
Persian Gulf
Tel Aviv-Yafo
Dead Sea
Tripoli
Gulf of Sidra
Nile Delta

1:20 000 000

100 0 100 200 300 400 500 miles

100 0 200 400 600 800 km

UNION OF SOVIET SOCIALIST REPUBLICS
R. S. F. S. R.
UKRAINIAN S.S.R.
BYELORUSSIAN S.S.R.
LITHUANIAN S.S.R.
LATVIAN S.S.R.
ESTONIAN S.S.R.
MOLDAVIAN S.S.R.
GEORGIAN S.S.R.
ARMENIAN S.S.R.
AZERBAIJAN S.S.R.
KAZAKH S.S.R.
FINLAND
SWEDEN
NORWAY
DENMARK
POLAND
CZECHOSLOVAKIA
HUNGARY
ROMANIA
BULGARIA
YUGOSLAVIA
ALBANIA
GREECE
TURKEY
SYRIA
IRAQ
IRAN (PERSIA)
CYPRUS
AUSTRIA
SWITZERLAND
ITALY
FRANCE
SPAIN
PORTUGAL
BELGIUM
NETHERLANDS
UNITED KINGDOM
IRELAND
ICELAND
ALGERIA
TUNISIA
MOROCCO
MALTA
ATLANTIC OCEAN
NORTH SEA
BALTIC SEA
BLACK SEA
CASPIAN SEA
MEDITERRANEAN SEA
ADRIATIC SEA
BAY OF BISCAY
Tyrrhenian Sea
Ionian Sea
English Channel
Arctic Circle
MOSKVA
Leningrad
WARSZAWA
BERLIN
PRAHA
WIEN
BUDAPEST
BUCUREŞTI
BEOGRAD
SOFIYA
ATHINAI
ISTANBUL
Ankara
ROMA
PARIS
LONDON
Dublin
MADRID
STOCKHOLM
Oslo
KØBENHAVN
Helsinki

1: 4 000 000
20 0 20 40 60 miles
20 0 20 40 60 80 km
The DISTRICTS of Northern Ireland have been numbered and can be identified by reference to this table.
1 Londonderry
2 Limavady
3 Coleraine
4 Ballymoney
5 Moyle
6 Larne
7 Ballymena
8 Magherafelt
9 Cookstown
10 Strabane
11 Omagh
12 Fermanagh
13 Dungannon
14 Craigavon
15 Armagh
16 Newry & Mourne
17 Banbridge
18 Down
19 Lisburn
20 Antrim
21 Newtownabbey
22 Carrickfergus
23 North Down
24 Ards
25 Castlereagh
26 Belfast
1 Merseyside
2 Greater Manchester
3 West Yorkshire
4 South Yorkshire
5 West Glamorgan
6 Mid Glamorgan
7 South Glamorgan
Orkney Is.
ORKNEY
Shetland Is.
SHETLAND
HIGHLAND
ATLANTIC OCEAN
NORTH SEA
IRISH SEA
CELTIC SEA
ENGLISH CHANNEL
SCOTLAND
IRELAND
NORTHERN IRELAND
ENGLAND
WALES
Projection: Conical with two standard parallels
West from Greenwich
East from Greenwich
COPYRIGHT, GEORGE PHILIP & SON, LTD.

NORTH SEA
IRISH SEA
SCOTLAND
Southern Uplands
Pennines
Cheviot Hills
Cumbrian Mts.
North Channel
Firth of Clyde
Solway Firth
Firth of Forth
NORTHUMBERLAND
CUMBRIA
DURHAM
CLEVELAND
TYNE & WEAR
NORTH YORKSHIRE
HUMBERSIDE
LANCASHIRE
MERSEYSIDE
SOUTH YORKSHIRE
W. YORKSHIRE
CHESHIRE
DERBY
NOTTS
LINCOLN
CLWYD
GWYNEDD
ISLE OF MAN
Edinburgh
Glasgow
Newcastle
Sunderland
Middlesbrough
Carlisle
Leeds
Bradford
Manchester
Liverpool
Sheffield
Hull
York
Lancaster
Preston
Blackpool
Nottingham
Derby
Lincoln
Belfast
Douglas
Berwick-upon-Tweed
Scarborough
Hartlepool
Darlington
Dumfries
Ayr
Kilmarnock
Stirling
Falkirk
Dunfermline
Kirkcaldy
N. York Moors
Lincoln Wolds
The Wash
Anglesey
Arran
Kintyre
Holderness

ENGLISH CHANNEL
Bristol Channel
Bay
Channel Islands
Guernsey
St. Peter Port
Sark
Alderney
Jersey
St. Helier
C. de la Hague
Cherbourg
Barfleur
Quineville
Valognes
Barneville
Carentan
Périers
St-Lô
Isigny
Vierville
Arromanches
Bayeux
Caen
Lisieux
Pont l' Évêque
Honfleur
Trouville
Le Havre
C. de la Hève
Seine
Etretat
C. d' Antifer
Fécamp
St-Valery-en-Caux
Yvetot
Caudebec
Dieppe
Le Tréport
Rouen
Elbeuf
Louviers
Bernay
FRANCE
LONDON
Brighton
Hove
Hastings
Eastbourne
Beachy Hd.
Newhaven
Worthing
Littlehampton
Bognor Regis
Selsey Bill
Chichester
Portsmouth
Southampton
Bournemouth
Poole
Weymouth
Portland Bill
Exeter
Plymouth
Torquay (Torbay)
Paignton
Dartmoor
Exmoor
Penzance
St. Ives
Camborne
Truro
Falmouth
Lizard
Eddystone
CORNWALL
DEVON
DORSET
SOMERSET
AVON
WILTS
HANTS
BERKS
OXFORD
BUCKS
HERTFORD
ESSEX
KENT
SURREY
EAST SUSSEX
WEST SUSSEX
ISLE OF WIGHT
GLOUCESTER
WORCESTER
HEREFORD
WARWICK
NORTHAMPTON
BEDFORD
CAMBRIDGE
SUFFOLK
GWENT
MID GLAMORGAN
WEST GLAMORGAN
S. GLAMORGAN
DYFED
POWYS
WALES
Cardiff
Swansea
Newport
Bristol
Bath
Gloucester
Cheltenham
Oxford
Reading
Swindon
Salisbury
Winchester
Birmingham
Coventry
Northampton
Milton Keynes
Luton
Cambridge
Ipswich
Colchester
Southend
Canterbury
Dover
Folkestone
Margate
Ramsgate
Maidstone
Gillingham
SCILLY ISLES
On same Scale
St.Ives
Penzance
Land's End
Isles of Scilly
St. Mary's
1: 2 000 000
10 0 10 20 30 40 50 miles
10 0 10 20 30 40 50 60 70 80 km
ft m
3000 1000
1200 400
600 200
300 100
0 0
50 150
100 300
m ft
Projection: Conical with two standard parallels.
West from Greenwich
East from Greenwich
COPYRIGHT, GEORGE PHILIP & SON, LTD.

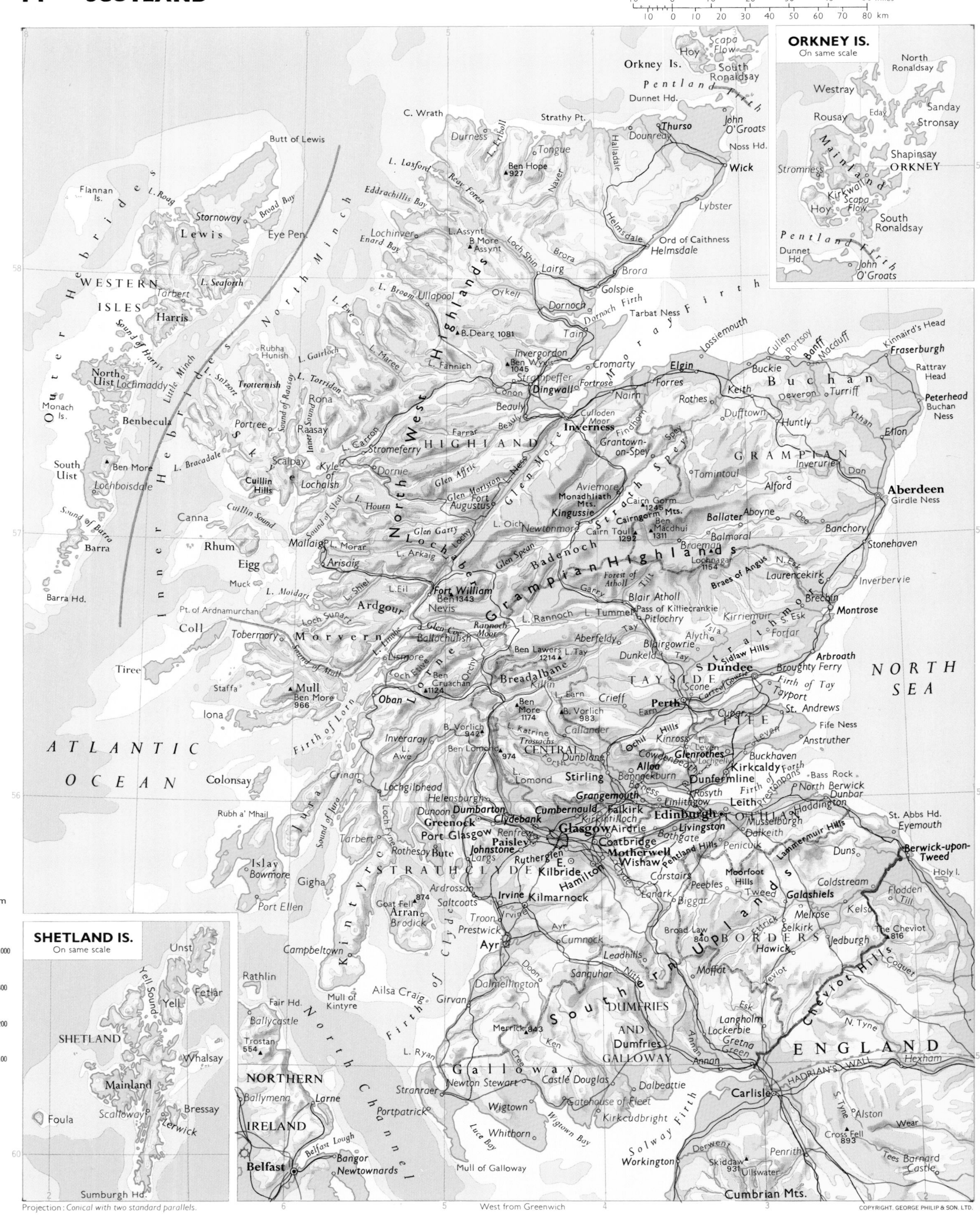
1:2 000 000
miles
km
ORKNEY IS.
On same scale
SHETLAND IS.
On same scale
Orkney Is.
Hoy
Scapa Flow
South Ronaldsay
Pentland Firth
Dunnet Hd.
C. Wrath
Strathy Pt.
Thurso
John O'Groats
Noss Hd.
Wick
Butt of Lewis
North Ronaldsay
Westray
Rousay
Eday
Sanday
Stronsay
Mainland
Shapinsay
ORKNEY
Stromness
Kirkwall
Durness
L. Eriboll
Tongue
Ben Hope
Dounreay
Halladale
Naver
L. Laxford
Reay Forest
Eddrachillis Bay
Flannan Is.
L. Roag
Stornoway
Broad Bay
Lewis
Eye Pen.
Lochinver
Enard Bay
L. Assynt
B. More Assynt
Loch Shin
Lybster
Helmsdale
Ord of Caithness
Brora
Lairg
Golspie
WESTERN ISLES
Outer Hebrides
Tarbert
L. Seaforth
Harris
Sound of Harris
North Minch
Little Minch
Inner Hebrides
L. Broom
Ullapool
Oykell
Dornoch
Dornoch Firth
Tarbat Ness
Tain
Moray Firth
L. Ewe
B. Dearg 1081
Rubha Hunish
L. Gairloch
L. Maree
Invergordon
Ben Wyvis
Cromarty
Lossiemouth
Elgin
Cullen
Portsoy
Banff
Macduff
Kinnaird's Head
Fraserburgh
North Uist
Lochmaddy
L. Snizort
Trotternish
L. Torridon
Rona
L. Fannich
Strathpeffer
Dingwall
Fortrose
Forres
Nairn
Buckie
Keith
Buchan
Rattray Head
Peterhead
Buchan Ness
Monach Is.
Benbecula
Portree
Raasay
Inner Sound
Sound of Raasay
North West Highlands
Conon
Beauly
Culloden Moor
Inverness
Findhorn
Rothes
Dufftown
Deveron
Turriff
Huntly
Ythan
Ellon
South Uist
Ben More
Lochboisdale
L. Bracadale
Skye
Scalpay
Kyle of Lochalsh
L. Carron
Stromeferry
Farrar
HIGHLAND
Glen Affric
Loch Ness
Glen More
Grantown-on-Spey
Spey
GRAMPIAN
Inverurie
Don
Aberdeen
Girdle Ness
Cuillin Hills
Dornie
Glen Moriston
Fort Augustus
Aviemore
Monadhliath Mts.
Kingussie
Strath Spey
Cairn Gorm 1245
Cairngorm Mts.
Tomintoul
Alford
Aboyne
Dee
Ballater
Banchory
Canna
Cuillin Sound
Sound of Sleat
L. Hourn
Glen Garry
L. Oich
Newtonmore
Cairn Toul 1292
Ben Macdhui 1311
Balmoral
Stonehaven
Sound of Barra
Barra
Rhum
Mallaig
L. Morar
Lochaber
L. Lochy
L. Arkaig
Glen Spean
Badenoch
Braemar
Lochnagar 1154
Grampian Highlands
N. Esk
Eigg
Arisaig
Forest of Atholl
Tilt
Garry
Braes of Angus
Laurencekirk
Inverbervie
Muck
L. Moidart
L. Shiel
L. Eil
Fort William
Ben Nevis 1343
Blair Atholl
Pass of Killiecrankie
Pitlochry
Brechin
Montrose
Barra Hd.
Ardgour
Pt. of Ardnamurchan
Loch Sunart
L. Rannoch
L. Tummel
Kirriemuir
S. Esk
Strathmore
Coll
Tobermory
Morvern
L. Linnhe
Glen Coe
Ballachulish
Rannoch Moor
Aberfeldy
Tay
Alyth
Isla
Forfar
Arbroath
Lismore
Sound of Mull
Ben Lawers 1214
L. Tay
Blairgowrie
Sidlaw Hills
Tiree
Loch Etive
Ben Cruachan 1124
Orchy
Breadalbane
Dunkeld
Dundee
Broughty Ferry
NORTH SEA
Mull
Ben More 966
Staffa
Oban
Lorne
Killin
TAYSIDE
Scone
Carse of Gowrie
Firth of Tay
Tayport
Iona
Firth of Lorn
B. Vorlich 942
Ben More 1174
L. Earn
B. Vorlich 983
Crieff
Perth
Earn
Cupar
FIFE
St. Andrews
Fife Ness
ATLANTIC OCEAN
Inveraray
L. Awe
L. Katrine
Trossachs
Callander
Ochil Hills
Kinross
Leven
Anstruther
Ben Lomond 974
CENTRAL
Dunblane
Glenrothes
Buckhaven
Colonsay
Crinan
L. Lomond
Stirling
Alloa
Cowdenbeath
Bannockburn
Kirkcaldy
Firth of Forth
Bass Rock
Lochgilphead
Helensburgh
Grangemouth
Bo'ness
Dunfermline
Rosyth
Prestonpans
North Berwick
Dunbar
Rubh' a' Mhail
Jura
Sound of Jura
Loch Fyne
Dunoon
Dumbarton
Cumbernauld
Falkirk
Linlithgow
Leith
Haddington
Greenock
Clydebank
Kirkintilloch
Edinburgh
LOTHIAN
Musselburgh
St. Abbs Hd.
Eyemouth
Port Glasgow
Renfrew
Glasgow
Airdrie
Livingston
Dalkeith
Lammermuir Hills
Tarbert
Paisley
Johnstone
Coatbridge
Bathgate
Penicuik
Berwick-upon-Tweed
Rothesay
Bute
Largs
Rutherglen
Motherwell
Wishaw
Pentland Hills
Duns
Islay
Bowmore
STRATHCLYDE
E. Kilbride
Hamilton
Carstairs
Moorfoot Hills
Holy I.
Gigha
Kintyre
Ardrossan
Lanark
Peebles
Tweed
Coldstream
Saltcoats
Irvine
Kilmarnock
Biggar
Galashiels
Flodden
Till
Port Ellen
Goat Fell 874
Arran
Brodick
Troon
Prestwick
Melrose
Kelso
Firth of Clyde
Ayr
Cumnock
Broad Law 840
Ettrick
Selkirk
BORDERS
Jedburgh
The Cheviot 816
Campbeltown
Leadhills
Hawick
Rathlin
Sanquhar
Nith
Southern Uplands
Moffat
Teviot
Cheviot Hills
Coquet
Ailsa Craig
Doon
Dalmellington
Fair Hd.
Mull of Kintyre
Girvan
DUMFRIES AND GALLOWAY
Esk
Langholm
Lockerbie
N. Tyne
Ballycastle
North Channel
Merrick 843
Ken
Dumfries
Annan
Gretna Green
Trostan 554
L. Ryan
Galloway
Cree
ENGLAND
Hexham
Hadrian's Wall
NORTHERN IRELAND
Ballymena
Larne
Stranraer
Newton Stewart
Castle Douglas
Dalbeattie
Carlisle
Portpatrick
Wigtown
Gatehouse of Fleet
Kirkcudbright
Solway Firth
S. Tyne
Alston
Wear
Belfast Lough
Luce Bay
Whithorn
Wigtown Bay
Cross Fell 893
Belfast
Bangor
Newtownards
Mull of Galloway
Workington
Derwent
Skiddaw 931
Ullswater
Penrith
Tees
Barnard Castle
Cumbrian Mts.
Unst
Yell Sound
Yell
Fetlar
SHETLAND
Whalsay
Mainland
Bressay
Foula
Scalloway
Lerwick
Sumburgh Hd.
ft
m
West from Greenwich

Projection: *Conical with two standard parallels.*

1:2 000 000

10 0 10 20 30 40 50 miles

10 0 10 20 30 40 50 60 70 80 km

ATLANTIC OCEAN
IRISH SEA
North Channel
St. George's Channel
Kintyre
Arran
Campbeltown
Rathlin I.
Fair Hd.
Mull of Kintyre
Ailsa Craig
Giant's Causeway
Portrush
Malin Hd.
Lough Swilly
Sheep Haven
Horn Hd.
Tory I.
Carndonagh
Inishowen Pen.
Moville
Buncrana
Bloody Foreland
Gweedore
Errigal 752
Derryveagh Mts.
Letterkenny
Aran I.
DONEGAL
Gweebarra B.
Loughros More B.
Glenties
Bluestack 676
Finn
Lifford
Strabane
Sperrin Mts.
Sawel 683
Magherafelt
Coleraine
Limavady
Londonderry
Ballymoney
Ballycastle
Trostan 554
Ballymena
Larne
Stranraer
I. Magee
Portpatrick
Carrickfergus
Antrim
Belfast L.
Bangor
Donaghadee
Newtownards
Belfast
Lisburn
L. Neagh 16
Cookstown
NORTHERN IRELAND
ULSTER
Omagh
Rossan Pt.
Rathlin O Birne I.
Killybegs
Donegal
Donegal Bay
Bundoran
Ballyshannon
L. Erne
Irvinestown
Dungannon
Portadown
Lurgan (Craigavon)
Armagh
Banbridge
Downpatrick
Strangford L.
Ards Pen.
Enniskillen
Dundrum
Slieve Donard 852
Newcastle
Mourne Mts.
Newry
Sl. Gullion 577
Warrenpoint
Dundrum Bay
Carlingford L.
Greenore
Downpatrick Hd.
Broad Haven
Killala B.
Erris Hd.
Belmullet
Mullet Peninsula
Blacksod Bay
Killala
Ballina
Sligo B.
Sligo
Collooney
Ox Mts.
SLIGO
LEITRIM
L. Allen
L. Arrow
Upper L. Erne
Clones
MONAGHAN
Monaghan
Castleblayney
Belturbet
Annalee
Cootehill
CAVAN
Cavan
Carrickmacross
Dundalk
Dundalk Bay
Louth
LOUTH
Ardee
Kingscourt
Achill Hd.
Achill
Achill I.
L. Conn
Nephin 806
MAYO
Leitrim
Boyle
Carrick-on-Shannon
Castlebar
Clew Bay
Clare I.
Westport
Croagh Patrick 765
Claremorris
Castlerea
ROSCOMMON
L. Gowna
Granard
Longford
L. Sheelin
Oldcastle
Ceanannas Mor (Kells)
An Uaimh (Navan)
Drogheda
Killary Harbour
Inishbofin
Mweelrea 819
L. Mask
CONNACHT
Robe
Roscommon
LONGFORD
L. Ree
Inny
Athboy
MEATH
Balbriggan
Ballinrobe
Tuam
Suck
Mullingar
Trim
Boyne
Swords
Lambay I.
Clifden
Twelve Pins
Connemara
L. Corrib
Slyne Hd.
Athlone
WESTMEATH
DUBLIN
Ireland's Eye
Howth Head
Dublin (Baile Atha Cliath)
Dublin Bay
Dun Laoghaire
Bray
GALWAY
IRELAND
Ballinasloe
Clara
Edenderry
Maynooth
Celbridge
Liffey
Galway
Clare
Athenry
Tullamore
Brosna
Daingean
OFFALY
Droichead Nua
Naas
Kippure 754
Kilkieran B.
Galway Bay
Inishmore
Aran Is.
Loughrea
Shannon
Slieve Aughty
Portumna
Gort
Birr
Portarlington
KILDARE
Kildare
Poulaphouca Res.
Mountmellick
Sl. Bloom
Port Laoise
LEINSTER
LAOIS
Athy
Barrow
WICKLOW
Wicklow
Wicklow Hd.
Wicklow Mts.
Lugnaquillia 923
Rathdrum
Hags Hd.
Ennistymon
Liscannor Bay
Mal Bay
CLARE
L. Derg
Roscrea
Miltown Malbay
Ennis
Nenagh
Carlow
Mizen Hd.
Arklow
Avoca
Killaloe
Ballina
Keeper 694
Templemore
Nore
Tullow
Shillelagh
Kilkee
Rineanna
Ardnacrusha
CARLOW
Muine Bheag
Gorey
Kilrush
Limerick
Thurles
Kilkenny
TIPPERARY
Mt. Leinster 796
Slaney
Loop Hd.
Foynes
Rathkeale
Vale
KILKENNY
Cashel
Suir
R. Shannon
Listowel
LIMERICK
Golden Vale
Tipperary
Callan
Enniscorthy
WEXFORD
Cahore Pt.
Kerry Hd.
Newcastle
Brandon Bay
Tralee Bay
Fenit
Feale
Rath Luirc (Charleville)
Galtymore 920
Galty Mts.
Caher
Slievenamon 722
Carrick-on-Suir
New Ross
Wexford
Wexford Harbour
Rosslare
Greenore Pt.
Tralee
MUNSTER
Clonmel
Tuskar Rock
Carnsore Pt.
Brandon 953
Dingle
Sl. Mish
Maine
Newmarket
Mitchelstown
Knockmealdown Mts.
Comeragh Mts.
Waterford
Tramore
Gt. Blasket I.
KERRY
Kanturk
Blackwater
Mallow
WATERFORD
Fermoy
Lismore
Dungarvan
Hook Hd.
Waterford Harbour
Saltee Is.
Dunmore Hd.
Dingle Bay
Laune
Killarney
Macgillycuddy's Reeks
Carrauntuohill 1040
Lakes of Killarney
Boggeragh Mts.
Dungarvan Bay
Valentia Harbour
Valentia I.
Cahirciveen
Kenmare
CORK
Blarney
Cork
Youghal
Macroom
Lee
Midleton
Youghal Harbour
St. David's Hd.
Skellig Rocks
Passage West
Cobh
Ballinskelligs B.
Kenmare River
Caha Mts.
Glengarriff
Bandon
Crosshaven
Kinsale
Cork Harbour
Castletown Bearhaven
Bantry
Clonakilty
Bear I.
Crow Hd.
Bantry Bay
Skull
Skibbereen
Clonakilty Bay
Old Head of Kinsale
Dunmanus Bay
Baltimore
Galley Hd.
Mizen Hd.
Fastnet Rock
Clear I.
C. Clear
Towns underlined in Northern Ireland give their names to the Districts in which they stand
The remaining Districts are:—
1 Fermanagh
2 Moyle
3 Newtownabbey
4 North Down
5 Castlereagh
6 Ards
7 Down
8 Newry & Mourne
ft m
3000 1000
1200 400
600 200
300 100
0 0
100 300
200 600
m ft
Projection: Conical with two standard parallels.
West from Greenwich

1:2 500 000

10 0 10 20 30 40 50 miles

10 0 10 20 30 40 50 60 70 80 km

Projection: Conical with two standard parallels

East from Greenwich

1:5 000 000

20 10 0 20 40 60 80 100 miles

40 20 0 40 80 120 160 km

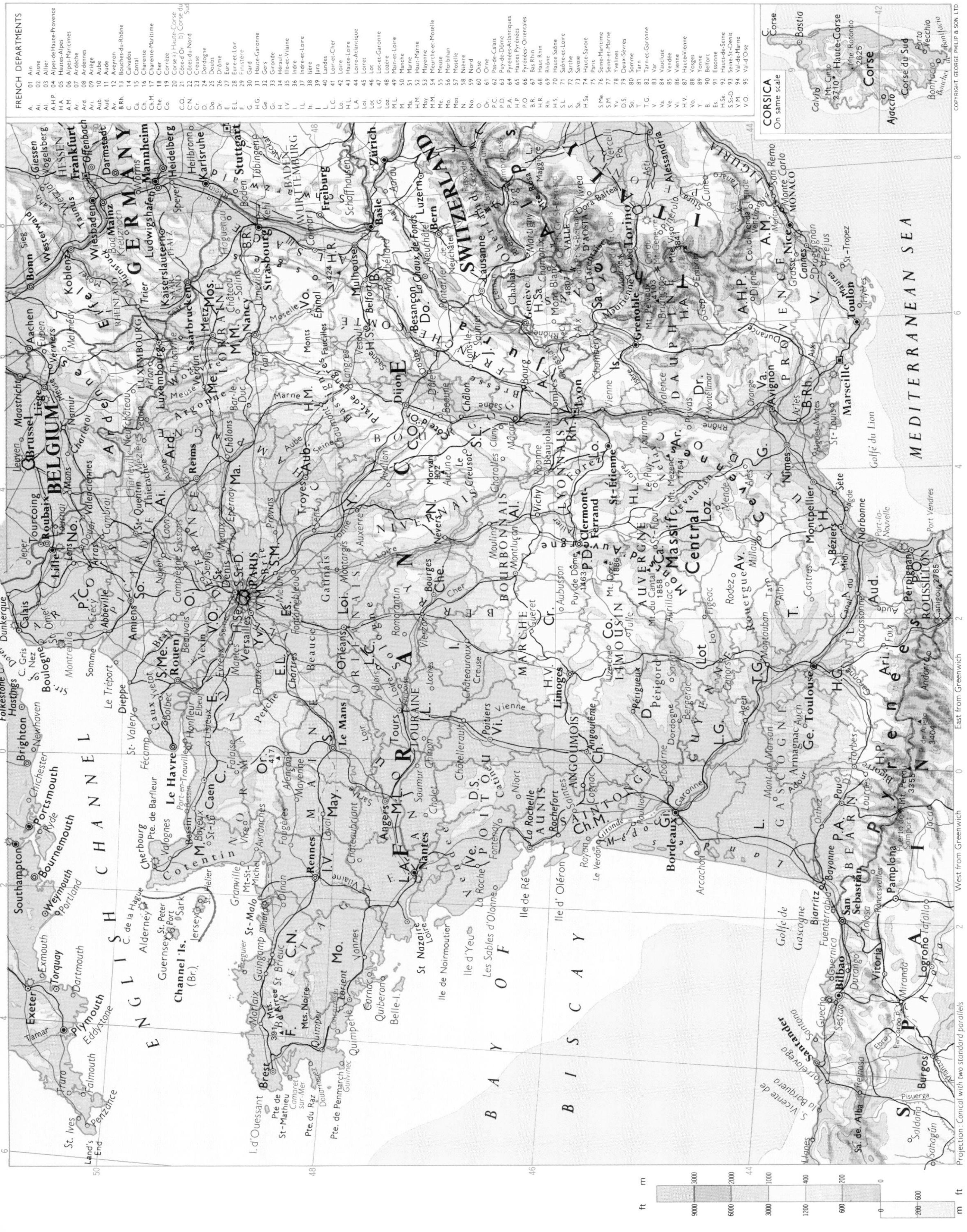

FRENCH DEPARTMENTS

Abbr.	No.	Department
A.	01	Ain
Ai.	02	Aisne
Al.	03	Allier
A.H.P.	04	Alpes-de Haute-Provence
H.A.	05	Hautes-Alpes
A.M.	06	Alpes-Maritimes
Ar.	07	Ardèche
Ard.	08	Ardennes
Ari.	09	Ariège
Aub.	10	Aube
Aud.	11	Aude
Av.	12	Aveyron
B.Rh.	13	Bouches-du-Rhône
C.	14	Calvados
Ca.	15	Cantal
Ch.	16	Charente
Ch.M.	17	Charente-Maritime
Che.	18	Cher
Co.	19	Corrèze
	20	Corse a) Haute-Corse b) Corse du Sud
C.O.	21	Côte-d'Or
C.N.	22	Côtes-du-Nord
Cr.	23	Creuse
D.	24	Dordogne
Do.	25	Doubs
Dr.	26	Drôme
E.	27	Eure
E.L.	28	Eure-et-Loir
F.	29	Finistère
G.	30	Gard
H.G.	31	Haute-Garonne
Ge.	32	Gers
Gi.	33	Gironde
H.	34	Hérault
I.V.	35	Ille-et-Vilaine
I.	36	Indre
I.L.	37	Indre-et-Loire
Is.	38	Isère
J.	39	Jura
L.	40	Landes
L.C.	41	Loir-et-Cher
Lo.	42	Loire
H.L.	43	Haute-Loire
L.A.	44	Loire-Atlantique
Loi.	45	Loiret
Lot	46	Lot
L.G.	47	Lot-et-Garonne
Loz.	48	Lozère
M.L.	49	Main-et-Loire
M.	50	Manche
Ma.	51	Marne
H.M.	52	Haut-Marne
May.	53	Mayenne
M.M.	54	Meurthe-et-Moselle
Me.	55	Meuse
Mo.	56	Morbihan
Mos.	57	Moselle
N.	58	Nièvre
No.	59	Nord
O.	60	Oise
Or.	61	Orne
P.C.	62	Pas-de-Calais
P.D.	63	Puy-de-Dôme
P.A.	64	Pyrénées-Atlantiques
H.P.	65	Hautes Pyrénées
P.O.	66	Pyrénées- Orientales
B.R.	67	Bas Rhin
H.R.	68	Haut Rhin
Rh.	69	Rhône
H.S.	70	Haute Saône
S.L.	71	Saône-et-Loire
S.	72	Sarthe
Sa.	73	Savoie
H.Sa.	74	Haute-Savoie
	75	Paris
S.Me.	76	Seine-Maritime
S.M.	77	Seine-et-Marne
Yv.	78	Yvelines
D.S.	79	Deux-Sèvres
So.	80	Somme
T.	81	Tarn
T.G.	82	Tarn-et-Garonne
V.	83	Var
Va.	84	Vaucluse
Ve.	85	Vendée
Vi.	86	Vienne
H.V.	87	Haute-Vienne
Vo.	88	Vosges
Y.	89	Yonne
B.	90	Belfort
Es.	91	Essonne
H.Se.	92	Hauts-de-Seine
S.St-D.	93	Seine-St-Denis
V.M.	94	Val-de-Marne
V.O.	95	Val-d'Oise

CORSICA
On same scale

ft	m
9000	3000
6000	2000
3000	1000
1200	400
600	200
0	0
200	600
ft	m

Projection: Conical with two standard parallels

West from Greenwich   East from Greenwich

ENGLAND
English Channel
CHANNEL ISLANDS
Alderney
Guernsey
St. Peter Port
Herm
Sark
Jersey
St. Helier
Casquets
Roches Douvres
Les Minquiers
Golfe de St-Malo
Baie de la Seine
Lyme Bay
Dartmoor
South Downs
Exeter
Plymouth
Torquay
Paignton
Southampton
Portsmouth
Bournemouth
Poole
Weymouth
Brighton
Worthing
Eastbourne
Hastings
Bexhill
Eastleigh
Yeovil
Penzance
Falmouth
Truro
St. Austell
Land's End
Lizard Pt.
Start Pt.
Portland Bill
Beachy Head
I. of Wight
Newport
Ryde
Cherbourg
Caen
Le Havre
Bayeux
Lisieux
Dieppe
Rouen
Évreux
Alençon
Le Mans
Laval
Rennes
Fougères
Mayenne
Angers
Tours
Nantes
St. Nazaire
Cholet
La Roche-sur-Yon
Niort
Poitiers
Châtellerault
La Rochelle
Rochefort
Saintes
Cognac
Angoulême
Brest
Morlaix
Quimper
Lorient
Vannes
St-Brieuc
St-Malo
Dinan
Douarnenez
Concarneau
Pontivy
Saumur
Bressuire
Parthenay
Royan
Ile d'Ouessant
Belle-Ile
Ile de Groix
Ile de Noirmoutier
Ile d'Yeu
Ile de Ré
Ile d'Oléron
Baie de Bourgneuf
Pertuis Breton
Pertuis d'Antioche
Mer d'Iroise
Monts d'Arrée
Montagne Noire
Collines de Normandie
Collines du Perche
BRETAGNE
NORMANDIE
MAINE
ANJOU
TOURAINE
POITOU
AUNIS
ANGOUMOIS
CALVADOS
CÔTES-DU-NORD
MORBIHAN
LOIRE-ATLANTIQUE
DEUX-SÈVRES
VIENNE
CHARENTE
CHARENTE-MARITIME
Plaines et Seuil du Poitou
F
R
DÉPARTEMENTS IN THE PARIS AREA
1 Ville de Paris
2 Seine-St-Denis
3 Val-de-Marne
4 Hauts-de-Seine
ft m
12 000 4000
9000 3000
6000 2000
4500 1500
3000 1000
1200 400
600 200
0 0
200 600
2000 6000
m ft
Projection: Conical with two standard parallels
West from Greenwich
East from Greenwich

1:2 500 000

10 0 10 20 30 40 50 miles

10 0 10 20 30 40 50 60 70 80 km

BELGIUM

LUXEMBOURG

GERMANY

FRANCE

SWITZERLAND

ITALY

ATLANTIC OCEAN
Golfe de Gascogne
FRANCE
SPAIN
ANDORRA
Bordeaux
Toulouse
Limoges
Poitiers
Angoulême
La Rochelle
Rochefort
Niort
Cholet
Châteauroux
Bourges
Nevers
Moulins
Montluçon
Clermont-Ferrand
Vichy
Périgueux
Brive-la-Gaillarde
Tulle
Aurillac
Rodez
Millau
Albi
Montauban
Agen
Cahors
Castres
Carcassonne
Narbonne
Béziers
Perpignan
Tarbes
Pau
Bayonne
Biarritz
San Sebastián
Pamplona
Huesca
Zaragoza
Lérida
Gerona
Figueras
Manresa
Ile de Noirmoutier
Ile d'Yeu
Ile de Ré
Ile d'Oléron
Pertuis Breton
Pertuis d'Antioche
Bassin d'Arcachon
Étang d'Hourtin et de Carcans
Étang de Lacanau
Étang de Cazaux
Étang de Biscarrosse
Étang de Leucate
POITOU
AUNIS
SAINTONGE
ANGOUMOIS
LIMOUSIN
MARCHE
BERRY
BOURBONNAIS
AUVERGNE
GUYENNE
GASCOGNE
LANGUEDOC
ROUSSILLON
BÉARN
NAVARRE
Plateau de Millevaches
Mts de Lacaune
Sierra de la Peña
Sierra de Guara
Pic de Vignemale 3303
Pic d'Aneto 3404
Pic de Montcalm 3080
Pic d'Estats 3141
Puy de Sancy 1886
Puy de Dôme 1463
ft m
12,000 4000
9000 3000
6000 2000
4500 1500
3000 1000
1200 400
600 200
0 0
200 600
2000 6000
m ft
Projection: Conical with two standard parallels
West from Greenwich
East from Greenwich

1:2 500 000

10 0 10 20 30 40 50 miles

10 0 10 20 30 40 50 60 70 80 km

SWITZERLAND
ITALY
CORSICA
LIGURIAN SEA
MEDITERRANEAN SEA
Golfo di Génova
Lion
Luzern
Schwyz
Bern
Neuchâtel
Fribourg
Lausanne
Genève
Lac Léman
Interlaken
Davos
Bergamo
Brescia
MILANO
(Milan)
Novara
Pavia
Cremona
Piacenza
Parma
TORINO
(Turin)
Alessandria
Asti
Cúneo
Savona
GENOVA
(Genoa)
La Spezia
Carrara
Massa
Livorno
San Remo
Impéria
MONACO
Monte-Carlo
Nice
Cannes
Antibes
Grasse
Fréjus
St-Raphaël
Toulon
MARSEILLE
Aix-en-Provence
Arles
Avignon
Nîmes
Valence
Grenoble
Chambéry
Annecy
LYON
Vienne
St-Étienne
Mâcon
Chalon-sur-Saône
Beaune
Dole
Besançon
Pontarlier
ILES D'HYÈRES
Hyères
Bastia
Ajaccio
Corte
Porto-Vecchio
Bonifacio
Sartène
Calvi
Elba
Capraia
Gorgona
Pianosa
Mont Blanc
4807
Matterhorn
4478
Monte Rosa
4634
Aosta
Gran Paradiso
4061
Massif du Pelvoux
4103
Briançon
Gap
Digne
ALPES-DE-HAUTE-PROVENCE
ALPES-MARITIMES
VAUCLUSE
PROVENCE
DAUPHINÉ
SAVOIE
HAUTE-SAVOIE
VALAIS
Alpes Valaisannes
Berner Alpen
Lago Maggiore
L. di Como
L. d'Iseo
L. d'Orta
Lac du Bourget
Rhône
Durance
Isère
Po
Camargue
Côte d'Azur
Riviera
Piemonte
Lombardia
CORSE DU SUD
HAUTE CORSE
Mont Cinto
2710
2940

NORTH SEA
BALTIC
NETHERLANDS
BELGIUM
LUX.
WEST GERMANY
EAST GERMANY
CZECHOSLOVAKIA
FRANCE
SWITZERLAND
AUSTRIA
ITALY
ADRIATIC SEA
Golfo di Génova
Golfo di Venézia
NIEDERSACHSEN
NORDRHEIN-WESTFALEN
RHEINLAND-PFALZ
SAARLAND
BADEN-WÜRTTEMBERG
BAYERN
SCHLESWIG-HOLSTEIN
LORRAINE
CHAMPAGNE
BOURGOGNE
FRANCHE-COMTÉ
DAUPHINÉ
PROVENCE
PIEMONTE
LOMBARDIA
EMILIA-ROMAGNA
TRENTINO-ALTO-ADIGE
FRIULI-VENEZIA GIULIA
TIROL
SALZBURG
KÄRNTEN
STEIERMARK
OBER-ÖSTERREICH
NIEDER-ÖSTERREICH
BURGENLAND
Hamburg
Bremen
Hannover
Kiel
Lübeck
Berlin
Potsdam
Magdeburg
Leipzig
Dresden
Karl-Marx-Stadt (Chemnitz)
Halle
Erfurt
Köln (Cologne)
Düsseldorf
Dortmund
Essen
Bonn
Frankfurt
Wiesbaden
Mainz
Mannheim
Stuttgart
Nürnberg
München (Munich)
Augsburg
Regensburg
Würzburg
Kassel
Amsterdam
Rotterdam
's-Gravenhage (The Hague)
Utrecht
Antwerpen
Brussel (Bruxelles)
Liège
Lille
Luxembourg
Reims
Metz
Nancy
Strasbourg
Dijon
Lyon
Genève
Lausanne
Bern
Basel
Zürich
Luzern
Innsbruck
Salzburg
Linz
Wien (Vienna)
Graz
Klagenfurt
Praha (Prague)
Plzeň (Pilsen)
Brno
Szczecin (Stettin)
Ljubljana
Zagreb
Rijeka
Trieste
Venézia (Venice)
Verona
Pádova (Padua)
Milano (Milan)
Torino (Turin)
Génova (Genoa)
Bologna
Parma
Firenze (Florence)
Grenoble
Marseille
Nice
Avignon
Mt. Blanc 4807
Matterhorn 4478
Gr. Glockner 3797
Ortles 3899
Mt. Viso 3851
Projection: Conical with two standard parallels
East from Greenwich

1:5 000 000

50 0 50 100 miles

50 0 50 100 150 km

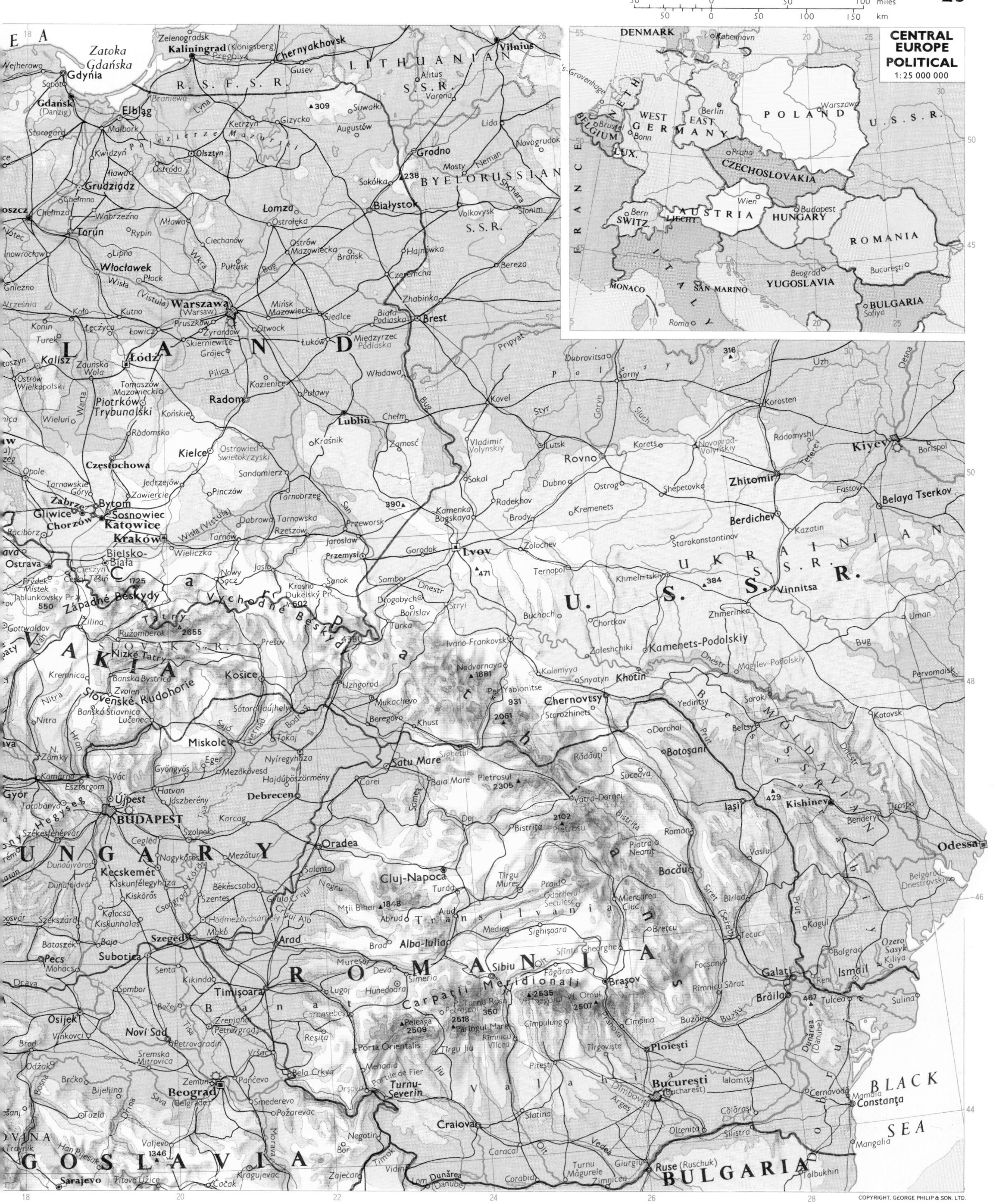
CENTRAL EUROPE POLITICAL
1:25 000 000
DENMARK
København
WEST GERMANY
EAST GERMANY
Berlin
Bonn
POLAND
Warszawa
U.S.S.R.
NETH.
BELGIUM
Brussel
LUX.
FRANCE
CZECHOSLOVAKIA
Praha
SWITZ.
Bern
LIECHT.
AUSTRIA
Wien
HUNGARY
Budapest
ROMANIA
Bucureşti
ITALY
MONACO
SAN MARINO
Roma
YUGOSLAVIA
Beograd
BULGARIA
Sofiya
Zatoka Gdańska
Gdynia
Gdańsk (Danzig)
Elbląg
Kaliningrad (Königsberg)
Chernyakhovsk
R. S. F. S. R.
Vilnius
LITHUANIAN S.S.R.
Grodno
BYELORUSSIAN S.S.R.
Białystok
Olsztyn
Grudziądz
Toruń
Włocławek
Warszawa (Warsaw)
Łódź
POLAND
Radom
Lublin
Brest
Kielce
Częstochowa
Katowice
Kraków
Lvov
Rovno
Zhitomir
Kiyev
Berdichev
Belaya Tserkov
Vinnitsa
U. S. S. R.
UKRAINIAN S.S.R.
Ostrava
Západné Beskydy
Vychodné Beskydy
Tatry
SLOVAK S.R.
Nízke Tatry
Slovenské Rudohorie
Košice
Miskolc
CZECHOSLOVAKIA
Karpaty
Uzhgorod
Ivano-Frankovsk
Chernovtsy
MOLDAVIAN S.S.R.
Kishinev
Odessa
Iaşi
Debrecen
BUDAPEST
HUNGARY
Győr
Kecskemét
Szeged
Oradea
Cluj-Napoca
Transilvania
Carpaţii Meridionali
ROMANIA
Timişoara
Arad
Sibiu
Braşov
Bacău
Galaţi
Brăila
Ploieşti
Bucureşti (Bucharest)
Craiova
Constanţa
BLACK SEA
Pécs
Subotica
Novi Sad
Beograd (Belgrade)
Osijek
Sarajevo
YUGOSLAVIA
BULGARIA
Ruse (Ruschuk)
Dunărea (Danube)

BALTIC SEA
NORTH SEA
POLAND
DENMARK
GERMANY
BERLIN
HAMBURG
BREMEN
HANNOVER
LEIPZIG
DRESDEN
MAGDEBURG
DORTMUND
DÜSSELDORF
KÖLN
ESSEN
DUISBURG
FRANKFURT
POTSDAM
SCHWERIN
ROSTOCK
Mecklenburger Bucht
Deutsche Bucht
NORDFRIESISCHE INSELN
OSTFRIESISCHE INSELN
WADDENEILANDEN
Elbe
Weser
Ems
Rhein
Oder

CZECHOSLOVAKIA
PRAHA (PRAGUE)
Plzeň
FRANKFURT
Wiesbaden
Mainz
Mannheim
Heidelberg
Karlsruhe
STUTTGART
Nürnberg
Regensburg
Augsburg
Ulm
MÜNCHEN (Munich)
Salzburg
Linz
Innsbruck
Bolzano
Trento
Udine
Strasbourg
Saarbrücken
LUXEMBOURG
Metz
Nancy
Mulhouse
Basel
Zürich
Bern
Lausanne
Genève
Como
SWITZERLAND
AUSTRIA
ITALY
FRANCE
YUGOSLAVIA
Conical with two standard parallels
East from Greenwich
COPYRIGHT GEORGE PHILIP & SON LTD.
ft 12 000 9000 6000 4500 3000 1200 600 0
m 4000 3000 2000 1500 1000 400 200 0
1:2 500 000
10 0 10 20 30 40 50 miles
10 0 10 20 30 40 50 60 70 80 km

DRESDEN
Karl-Marx-Stadt
(Chemnitz)
Erfurt
Weimar
Gotha
Jena
Gera
Zwickau
Plauen
Hof
Coburg
Bayreuth
Bamberg
Würzburg
Aschaffenburg
Schweinfurt
Erlangen
Fürth
Nürnberg
Regensburg
Ingolstadt
Augsburg
MÜNCHEN
(Munich)
Landshut
Passau
Ulm
Neu Ulm
STUTTGART
Esslingen
Heilbronn
Ludwigsburg
Göppingen
Memmingen
Kempten
Ravensburg
Friedrichshafen
Rosenheim
Salzburg
Linz
Urfahr
Wels
Steyr
Innsbruck
Garmisch-Partenkirchen
Kufstein
Dornbirn
Bregenz
Feldkirch
VORARLBERG
LIECHTENSTEIN
SWITZERLAND
Graz
Leoben
Kapfenberg
Bruck
Knittelfeld
Judenburg
Klagenfurt
Villach
Wörther See
Maribor
Celje
Ljubljana
Kranj
Jesenice
Gorizia
Trieste
Udine
Pordenone
Treviso
Vicenza
Bassano del Grappa
Rovereto
Trento
Bolzano
Merano
Bressanone
Brescia
Bergamo
PRAHA
(PRAGUE)
Plzeň
Kladno
Karlovy Vary
Cheb
Chomutov
Most
Teplice
Ústí nad Labem
Děčín
Liberec
Jablonec
Mladá Boleslav
Kolín
Jihlava
Tábor
Písek
České Budějovice
Český Krumlov
Klatovy
Strakonice
ZÁPADOČESKÝ
STŘEDOČESKÝ
SEVEROČESKÝ
JIHOČESKÝ
VÝCHODOČESKÝ
ČESKÁ SOCIALISTICKÁ
Vltava
Labe (Elbe)
Ohře
Berounka
Donau
(Danube)
Inn
Salzach
Enns
Mur
Drau
Drava
Isar
Lech
Main
Neckar
Bodensee
Chiemsee
Ammersee
Starnberger See
BAYERN
BADEN-WÜRTTEMBERG
HESSEN
Thüringer Wald
Fichtelgebirge
Fränkische Schweiz
Böhmer Wald
Oberpfälzer Wald
Bayerischer Wald
Schwäbische Alb
Erzgebirge
Lechtaler Alpen
Zillertaler Alpen
Hohe Tauern
Niedere Tauern
Karnische Alpen
Karawanken
Dolomiti
SALZBURG
KÄRNTEN
STEIERMARK
OBERÖSTERREICH
NIEDERÖSTERREICH
TRENTINO
ALTO ADIGE
FRIULI
VENEZIA GIULIA
LOMBARDIA
VENETO
ITALY
AUSTRIA
GERMANY
SLOVENIJA
YUGOSLAVIA
St. Pölten
Krems
Gross Glockner
3797
Ortles
3899
Marmolada
3342
Triglav
2863
Zugspitze
2968
ft
m
12,000
9000
6000
4500
3000
1200
600
0
4000
3000
2000
1500
1000
400
200
0

Projection: *Conical with two standard parallels*

1:2 500 000
10 0 10 20 30 40 50 miles
10 0 10 20 30 40 50 60 70 80 km

P O L A N D
C Z E C H O S L O V A K I A
H U N G A R Y
R O M A N I A
Y U G O S L A V I A
U. S. S. R.
Wrocław (Breslau)
Opole
Częstochowa
Kielce
Radomsko
Góry Świętokrzyskie
Katowice
Gliwice
Bytom
Zabrze
Sosnowiec
Chorzów
Kraków
Tarnów
Rzeszów
Przemyśl
Nowy Sącz
Ostrava
Karviná
Olomouc
Bielsko-Biała
Krosno
Zakopane
Tatry
Gerlachovka
2655
Žilina
Prešov
Košice
Uzhgorod
Mukachevo
Trenčín
Nitra
Trnava
Bratislava
WIEN (VIENNA)
Nové Zámky
Komárno
Győr
Esztergom
Vác
BUDAPEST
Kispest
Rákospalota
Újpest
Miskolc
Eger
Gyöngyös
Salgótarján
Nyíregyháza
Debrecen
Szolnok
Cegléd
Kecskemét
Szeged
Hódmezővásárhely
Békéscsaba
Oradea
Arad
Timişoara
Székesfehérvár
Veszprém
Balaton
Szombathely
Zalaegerszeg
Nagykanizsa
Kaposvár
Pécs
Baja
Subotica
Sombor
Osijek
Dunaújváros
Dunaj
Duna (Danube)
Tisza
Váh
Vistula
Dunajec
Slovenské Rudohorie
Nízke Tatry
Beskydy
Munţii Bihor
Satu Mare
East from Greenwich

1:2 500 000
10 0 10 20 30 40 50 miles
10 0 10 20 30 40 50 60 70 80 km
BALTIC SEA
POLAND
U. S. S. R.
CZECHOSLOVAKIA
WARSZAWA (WARSAW)
ŁÓDŹ
Kraków
Wrocław (Breslau)
Poznań
Gdańsk (Danzig)
Gdynia
Sopot
Szczecin (Stettin)
Bydgoszcz
Toruń
Białystok
Lublin
Kaliningrad (Königsberg)
Grodno
Brest
Frankfurt
Görlitz
Liberec
Częstochowa
Kielce
Radom
Olsztyn
Elbląg
Koszalin
Słupsk
Opole
Katowice
Zatoka Gdańska
Zalew Wiślany
Wisła
Odra (Oder)
Warta
Bug
Narew
Noteć
Pilica
Nysa
GÓRY ŚWIĘTOKRZYSKIE
m ft
1500 4500
1000 3000
400 1200
200 600
0 0

1:5 000 000

50 0 50 100 miles

50 0 50 100 150 km

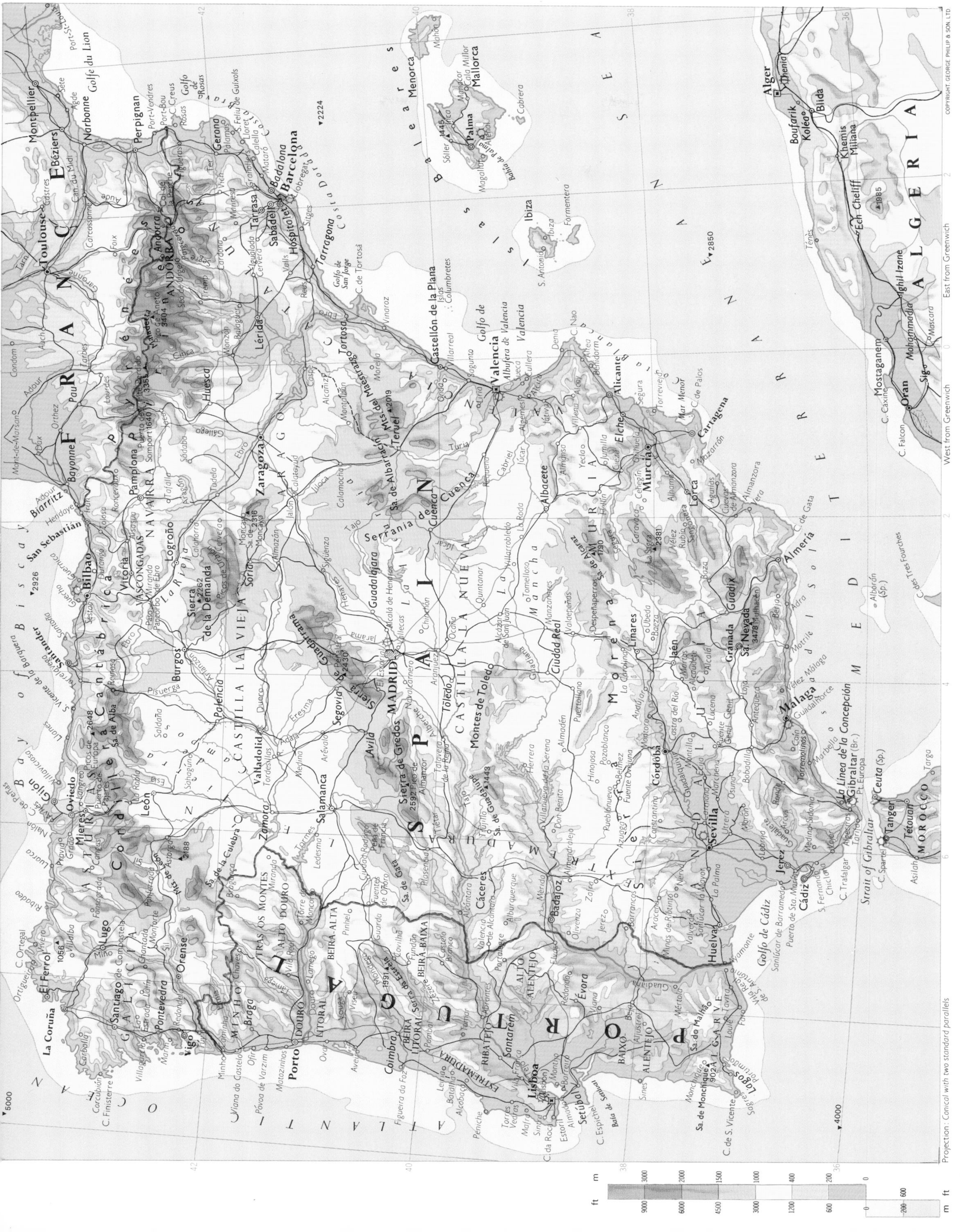

Projection: Conical with two standard parallels

West from Greenwich

East from Greenwich

m	ft
3000	9000
2000	6000
1500	4500
1000	3000
400	1200
200	600
0	0
200	600

BAY OF BISCAY
ATLANTIC OCEAN
San Sebastián
Bilbao
Santander
Gijón
Oviedo
La Coruña (Corunna)
El Ferrol
Santiago de Compostela
Vigo
Orense
Lugo
León
Burgos
Logroño
Vitoria
Palencia
Valladolid
Zamora
Salamanca
Segovia
Avila
MADRID
Guadalajara
Soria
Porto (Oporto)
Vila Nova de Gaia
Braga
Coimbra
Aveiro
Bragança
Ponferrada
Astorga
Benavente
Toro
Tordesillas
Medina del Campo
Ciudad Rodrigo
Béjar
Plasencia
Talavera de la Reina
Duero
Douro
Miño
Sil
Esla
Pisuerga
Tajo
Ebro
Picos de Europa
Sierra de Guadarrama
Sierra de Gredos
Sierra de Gata
Serra da Estrela
Sierra de la Demanda
Montañas de León
Cabo Ortegal
Cabo Finisterre
Cabo Mondego

1:2 500 000
10 0 10 20 30 40 50 miles
10 0 10 20 30 40 50 60 70 80 km
ft m
9000 3000
6000 2000
4500 1500
3000 1000
1200 400
600 200
0 0
200 600
2000 6000
m ft
Projection: Conical with two standard parallels
West from Greenwich
COPYRIGHT GEORGE PHILIP & SON, LTD.
MEDITERRANEAN SEA
MOROCCO
Golfo de Cádiz
Strait of Gibraltar
Costa del Sol
Algarve
LISBOA (LISBON)
Sevilla (Seville)
Córdoba
Granada
Málaga
Cádiz
Jerez de la Frontera
Huelva
Faro
Badajoz
Mérida
Évora
Setúbal
Almería
Gibraltar (Br.)
Algeciras
Ceuta (Sp.)
Tanger (Tangier)
Tétouan
Melilla (Sp.)
Alborán (Sp.)
Sierra Nevada
Sierra Morena
Montes de Toledo

BAY OF BISCAY
Golfe de Gascogne
Golfo de San Jorge
Menorca (Minorca)
Mallorca (Majorca)
ISLAS BALEARES
ANDORRA
ROUSSILLON
NAVARRE
BÉARN
VASCONGADAS
Toulouse
Montauban
Narbonne
Béziers
Perpignan
Carcassonne
Tarbes
Bayonne
Biarritz
San Sebastián
Bilbao
Santander
Vitoria
Pamplona
Logroño
Burgos
Soria
Zaragoza (Saragossa)
Huesca
Lérida
Tarragona
Reus
Manresa
Sabadell
Tarrasa
Badalona
BARCELONA
Hospitalet de Llobregat
Mataró
Gerona
Figueras
Teruel
Castellón de la Plana
Cuenca
Guadalajara
Alcalá de Henares
MADRID
Aranjuez
Sierra de la Demanda
Sa. de Moncayo
Sa. de Albarracín
Montes Universales
Mts. del Maestrazgo
Sierra de la Peña
Sa. de Guara
Sa. de Alcubierre
Los Monegros
Pico de Aneto 3404
Pico de Posets 3375
Monte Perdido 3355
Vignemale 3303
Pic de Montcalm 3080
Sa. del Montsech
Sa. de San Just
Sa. de Cantabria
Sa. de Cebollera
Sa. de Montsant
Jalón
Ebro
Duero
Tajo
Júcar
Cinca
Segre
Cabo de Creus
Cabo Tortosa
Islas Columbretes

1:2 500 000

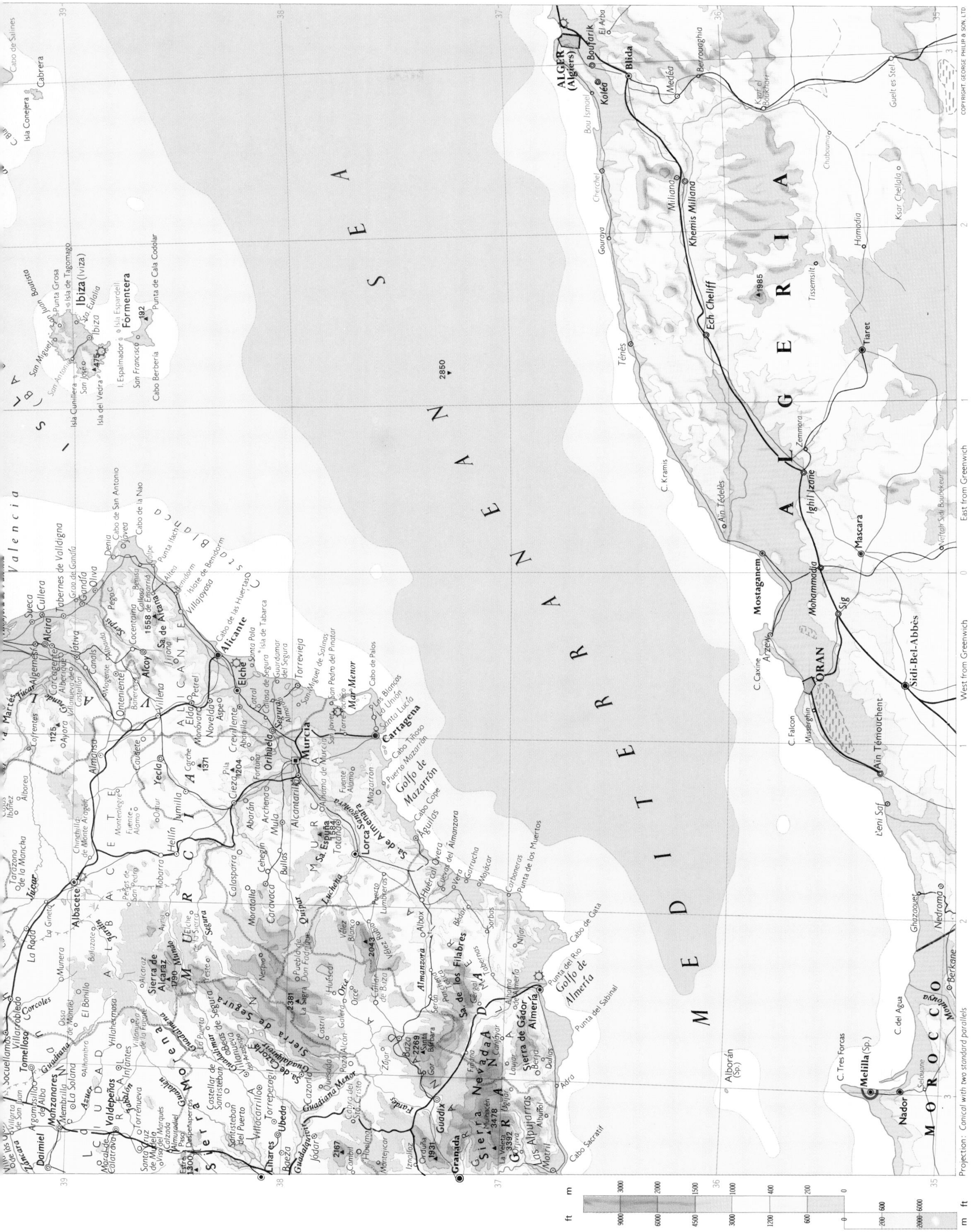

10 0 10 20 30 40 50 miles

10 0 10 20 30 40 50 60 70 80 km

MEDITERRANEAN SEA

ISLAS BALEARES

ALGERIA

MOROCCO

Ibiza (Iviza)

Formentera

Alicante

Murcia

Cartagena

Almería

Granada

ORAN

ALGER (Algiers)

Melilla (Sp.)

Projection: Conical with two standard parallels

West from Greenwich

East from Greenwich

m	ft
3000	9000
2000	6000
1500	4500
1000	3000
400	1200
200	600
0	0
200	600
2000	6000

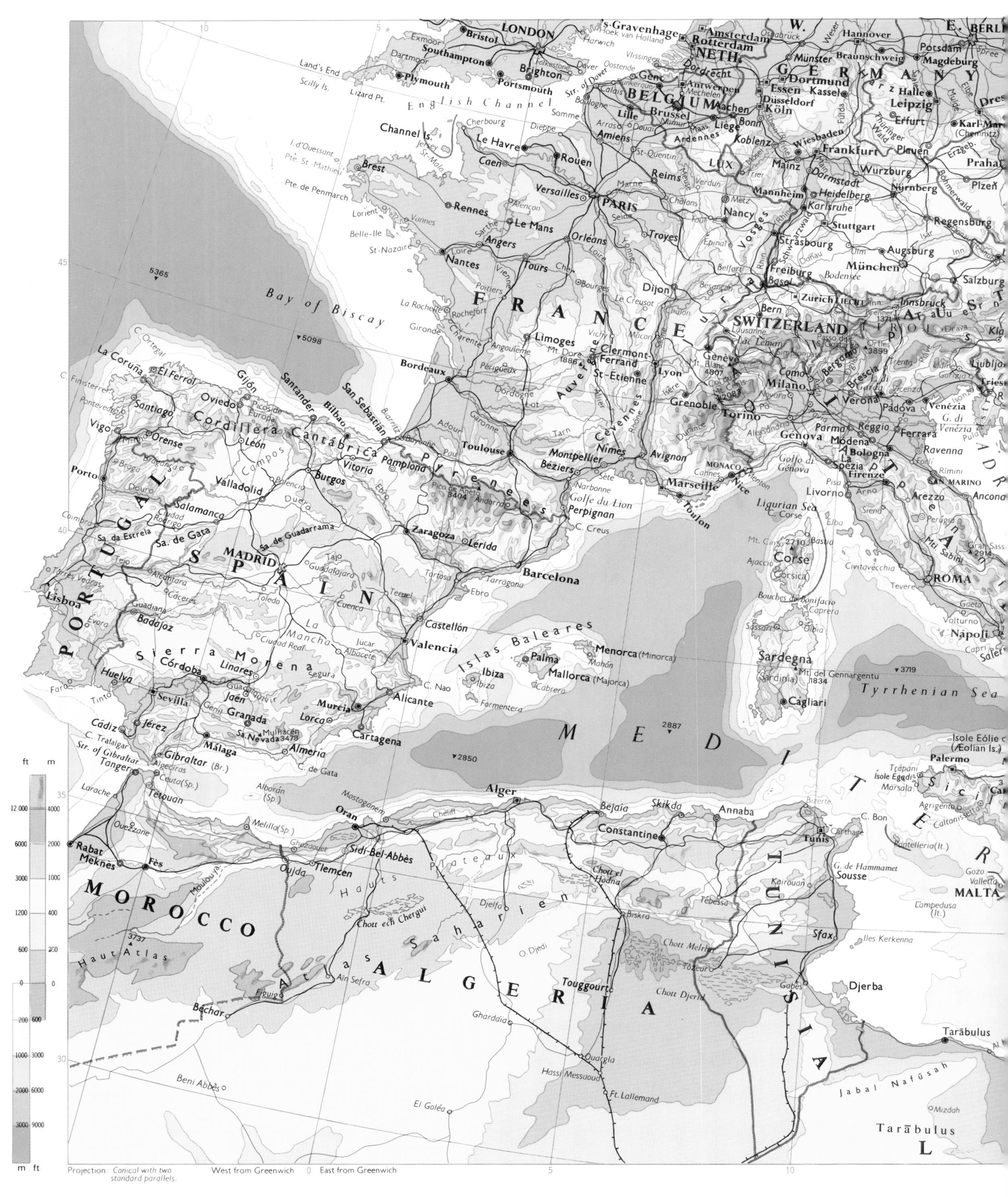

LONDON
Bristol
Southampton
Brighton
Portsmouth
Plymouth
Exmoor
Dartmoor
Land's End
Scilly Is.
Lizard Pt.
English Channel
Folkestone
Dover
Harwich
Str. of Dover
's-Gravenhage
Hoek van Holland
Amsterdam
Rotterdam
NETH.
Dordrecht
Vlissingen
Oostende
Gent
Antwerpen
Mechelen
BELGIUM
Brussel
Calais
Dunkerque
Boulogne
Lille
Arras
Douai
Amiens
Namur
Liège
Aachen
Maas
Ardennes
Osnabrück
Münster
Hannover
Braunschweig
Magdeburg
Potsdam
Spree
Dortmund
Essen
Kassel
Düsseldorf
Köln
Bonn
GERMANY
Harz
Halle
Leipzig
Erfurt
Thüringer Wald
Karl-Marx-Stadt (Chemnitz)
Erzgeb.
Praha
Plzeň
Weser
Fulda
Mulde
Elbe
Koblenz
Wiesbaden
Frankfurt
Plauen
Mainz
Main
Darmstadt
Würzburg
Mannheim
Heidelberg
Nürnberg
Böhmerwald
Karlsruhe
Regensburg
Stuttgart
Isar
Augsburg
Inn
Ulm
Donau
München
Salzburg
Bodensee
LUX.
Trier
Mosel
Verdun
Metz
Nancy
Vosges
Rhein
Schwarzwald
Strasbourg
Freiburg
Basel
Épinal
Belfort
Channel Is.
Jersey
St-Malo
Cherbourg
Dieppe
Somme
Le Havre
Rouen
Caen
I. d'Ouessant
Pte. St-Mathieu
Brest
Pte. de Penmarch
Lorient
Vannes
Rennes
Alençon
Versailles
PARIS
Marne
Reims
St-Quentin
Meuse
Châlons
Seine
Troyes
Le Mans
Sarthe
Angers
Orléans
Loire
Belle-Ile
St-Nazaire
Nantes
Tours
Cher
Bourges
Vienne
Poitiers
Dijon
Le Creusot
Besançon
Jura
Bern
Zürich
LIECHT.
Innsbruck
Lausanne
Lac Léman
SWITZERLAND
Simplon
Passo del S. Gottardo
Ortles 3899
Brenner 1371
TIROL
Drava
Genève
Mt. Blanc 4807
Col du Mt. Cenis 2083
Bay of Biscay
5365
5098
La Rochelle
Rochefort
Gironde
Charente
Angoulême
Limoges
Vichy
Mâcon
Saône
Mt. Dore 1886
Clermont-Ferrand
St-Étienne
Lyon
Périgueux
FRANCE
Bordeaux
Dordogne
Lot
Auvergne
Allier
Isère
Grenoble
Torino
Novara
Po
Como
Milano
Bergamo
Brescia
Garda
Verona
Trento
Vicenza
Padova
Venézia
Udine
Gorizia
Ljubljana
Trieste
G. di Venézia
Isonzo
Adige
Piave
Alessandria
Genova
Parma
Reggio
Modena
Ferrara
Bologna
Ravenna
Forlì
Rimini
SAN MARINO
Ancona
La Spezia
Firenze
Pisa
Livorno
Arno
Arezzo
Siena
Perugia
Gran Sasso 2914
Mti. Sabini
Golfo di Genova
MONACO
Cannes
Nice
Menton
Toulon
Marseille
Durance
Avignon
Rhône
Nîmes
Cévennes
Montpellier
Sète
Béziers
Narbonne
Golfe du Lion
Perpignan
C. Creus
Tarn
Garonne
Toulouse
Adour
Pau
Bayonne
Biarritz
Pyrenees
Pico de Aneto 3404
ANDORRA
C. Ortegal
La Coruña
El Ferrol
C. Finisterre
Santiago
Pontevedra
Vigo
Gijón
Oviedo
Picos de Europa
Cordillera Cantábrica
Santander
Bilbao
San Sebastián
Vitoria
Pamplona
Burgos
Ebro
León
Orense
Miño
Braga
Porto
Douro
Campos
Valladolid
Palencia
Duero
Salamanca
Ciudad Rodrigo
Coimbra
Sa. da Estrela
Sa. de Gata
Sa. de Guadarrama
MADRID
Zaragoza
Lérida
Barcelona
Tarragona
Tortosa
Teruel
Tajo
Guadalajara
Cuenca
Toledo
Tejo
Torres Vedras
Lisboa
Alcántara
Cáceres
Guadiana
Badajoz
Évora
PORTUGAL
SPAIN
La Mancha
Ciudad Real
Jucar
Albacete
Castellón
Valencia
Sierra Morena
Córdoba
Linares
Segura
Huelva
Tinto
Faro
Sevilla
Guadalquivir
Jaén
Granada
Genil
Sa. Nevada
Mulhacén 3478
Almería
Murcia
Lorca
Cartagena
Alicante
C. Nao
Cádiz
Jérez
Málaga
C. Trafalgar
Str. of Gibraltar
Gibraltar (Br.)
Algeciras
Tanger
Ceuta (Sp.)
Tétouan
Larache
C. de Gata
Alborán (Sp.)
Islas Baleares
Ibiza
Formentera
Palma
Mallorca (Majorca)
Cabrera
Menorca (Minorca)
Mahón
MEDITERRANEAN
2850
2887
3719
Ligurian Sea
C. Corse
Elba
Mt. Cinto 2710
Bastia
Ajaccio
Corse (Corsica)
Civitavecchia
Tevere
ROMA
Gaeta
Volturno
Nápoli
Capri
Salerno
Bouches de Bonifacio
Caprera
Sassari
Olbia
Sardegna (Sardinia)
Mt. del Gennargentu 1834
Cagliari
Tyrrhenian Sea
Isole Eólie (Æolian Is.)
Palermo
Trapani
Ísole Egadi
Marsala
Sicilia
Agrigento
Caltanissetta
Pantelleria (It.)
Gozo
Valletta
MALTA
Lampedusa (It.)
Alger
Mostaganem
Oran
Chéliff
Béjaïa
Skikda
Annaba
Bizerte
C. Bon
Tunis
Carthage
Constantine
G. de Hammamet
Sousse
Kairouan
Rabat
Meknès
Fès
Ouezzane
Melilla (Sp.)
Ghazaouet
Sidi-Bel-Abbès
Tlemcen
Oujda
Moulouya
MOROCCO
Hauts Plateaux
Chott el Hodna
Tébessa
Chott ech Chergui
Djelfa
Saharien Atlas
3737
Haut Atlas
ALGERIA
Biskra
Chott Melrhir
Tozeur
Chott Djerid
Gabès
Djerba
Sfax
Iles Kerkenna
TUNISIA
O. Djedi
Aïn Sefra
Figuig
Béchar
Touggourt
Ghardaïa
Ouargla
Hassi Messaoud
Ft. Lallemand
Beni Abbès
El Goléa
Jabal Nafūsah
Mizdah
Tarābulus
L
ft
m
12 000
6000
3000
1200
600
0
200
1000
2000
3000
4000
2000
1000
400
200
0
600
3000
6000
9000
m
ft
Projection: Conical with two standard parallels.
West from Greenwich
0
East from Greenwich
10
5
45
40
35
30

1:10 000 000

50 0 50 100 150 200 miles

50 0 100 200 300 km

Poznań
Warszawa
Brest
Pinsk
Polesye
Chernigov
Desna
Konotop
Sumy
Belgorod
Kazanskaya
Volgograd
Łódź
Radom
Lublin
Kielce
Wrocław
Bug
Pripyat
Styr
Goryn
Lutsk
Rovno
Zhitomir
Kiyev
Dnepr
Pereyaslav-Khmelnitskiy
Belaya Tserkov
Nezhin
Poltava
Kharkov
Slavyansk
Artemovsk
Voroshilovgrad
(Lugansk)
Kamensk-Shakhtinskiy
Tsimlyanskoye Vdkhr.
Donets
Shakhty
Don
Novocherkassk
Rostov
Manych
Oz. Manych Gudilo
Chorzów
Kraków
Tarnów
Przemyśl
Lvov
Berdichev
Vinnitsa
Uman
Cherkassy
Kremenchug
(Dnieper)
Pavlograd
Gorlovka
Makeyevka
Donetsk
Dneprodzerzhinsk
Dnepropetrovsk
Kirovograd
Krivoy Rog
Zaporozhye
Ostrava
Cieszyn
Jablunkovsky Pr.
Tatry
2655
Slavkov
Kamenets-Podol'skiy
Mogilev-Podolskiy
Pervomaysk
Voznesensk
Balta
Nikolayev
Kherson
Melitopol
Berdyansk
Zhdanov
(Mariupol)
Taganrog
Azov
Yeisk
Tikhoretsk
Stavropol
Armavir
Maykop
Krasnodar
Kuban
Kerch
Sea of Azov
Perekop
Karkinitskiy Zaliv
Krymskaya (Crimea)
Feodosiya
Novorossiysk
Tuapse
Sukhumi
Poti
Batumi
M. Tarkhankut
Yevpatoriya
Simferopol
1545
Yalta
Sevastopol
Balaklava
U. S. S. R.
U K R A I N I A N S. S. R.
MOLDAVIAN S.S.R.
Chernovtsy
Prut
Dnestr
Beltsy
Botoşani
Iaşi
Kishinev
Tiraspol
Bendery
Odessa
Belgorod Dnestrovskiy
Izmail
Sulina
Galaţi
Brăila
Siret
Kolomyya
Carpathians
Bratislava
Banská Štiavnica
Košice
Miskolc
Tokaj
Tisza
Budapest
HUNGARY
Kecskemét
Balaton
Szeged
Pécs
Hódmezővásárhely
Debrecen
Oradea
Someş
Pietrosul 2305
Pietrosu 2102
Cluj-Napoca
Körös
Arad
Mureş
R O M A N I A
Braşov
(Orasul Stalin)
Sibiu
Negoiu 2535
Carpaţii Meridionali
Ploieşti
Piteşti
Bucureşti
Constanţa
Subotica
Timişoara
Novi Sad
Petrovaradin
Sombor
Drava
Brod
Sava
Banja Luka
Beograd
Portile de Fier
Turnu-Severin
Orşova
Smederevo
Craiova
Dunărea (Danube)
Silistra
Tolbukhin
Ruse
Pleven
Vidin
Varna
Kragujevac
Morava
Niš
Sarajevo
Bosna
Drina
Mostar
Durmitor 2522
Novi Pazar
Dubrovnik (Ragusa)
Kotor
Cetinje
CRNA GORA
Shkodër
Tiranë
Durrësi
Elbasan
Sofiya
BULGARIA
Stara Planina
Shipchenski Pr.
Turnova
Sliven
Burgas
Musala 2925
Plovdiv
Maritsa
Rhodopi Planina
Edirne
Skopje
Vardar
Struma
2764
Bitola
ALBANIA
Vlorë
Sérrai
Kaválla
Alexandroúpolis
Thessaloníki
Aliákmon
Olimbos 2917
Lárisa
Vólos
Kérkira
Nótia Pindhos
GREECE
Levkás
Návpaktos
Kefallinía
Pátrai
Korinthiakós Kólpos
Thívai
Athínai
Piraiévs
Kórinthos
Návplion
Pelopónnisos
Olympia
Zákinthos
Kalamata
Spárti
Pílos
Ákra Taínaron
Kíthira
Andikíthira
Athos 2033
Límnos
Lésvos
Voríai Sporádhes
Évvoia
Aegean Sea
Khíos
Sámos
Ikaría
Síros
Ándros
Kikládhes
Náxos
Mílos
Íos
Thíra
Dhodhekánisos
Ródhos
Kárpathos
Kríti
Khaniá
Ídhi Oros 2456
Iráklion
Istanbul
Karadeniz Boğazı (Bosporus)
Üsküdar
İzmit
Tekirdağ
Marmara Denizi
Enez
Gelibolu (Gallipoli)
Çanakkale
Bandırma
Bursa
İznik Gölü
Bilecik
Sakarya
Eskişehir
Balıkesir
Ayvalık
Troy
Kütahya
Manisa
İzmir
Aydın
Denizli
Muğla
Afyon Karahisar
Bolvadin
Eğridir Gölü
Beyşehir Gölü
Isparta
Burdur
Antalya
Antalya Körfezi
Elmalı 3086
Konya
Karaman
Toros Dağları
Zonguldak
Ereğli
Bolu
Kastamonu
2565
Çankırı
Çorum
Kızıl Irmak
Ankara
Yozgat
Tuz Gölü
Kırşehir
Aksaray
Niğde
Kayseri
Erciyas Dağı 3770
TURKEY
İnebolu
İnce Burnu
Sinop
Samsun
Amasya
Tokat
Sivas
Giresun
Tirebolu
Trabzon
Rize
Kuzey Anadolu Dağları
Erzincan
Fırat
Keban
Gürün
Malatya
Maraş
Gaziantep
Osmaniye
Adana
Seyhan
Tarsus
Mersin
Silifke
İskenderun
İskenderun Körfezi
Antakya
Halab
SYRIA
Hamah
Al Lādhiqīyah
Bāniyās
Ḩims
Tarābulus
LEBANON
3083
Bayrūt (Beirut)
Saydā
Dimashq (Damascus)
Jabal ash Shaykh 2814
Jabal ad Durūz
Boşra
'Akko
Hefa (Haifa)
Jordan
ISRAEL
Tel Aviv-Yafo
Jerusalem
'Ammān
JORDAN
Dead Sea
Gaza
El 'Arîsh
Petra
Ma'ān
Eilat
Al 'Aqabah
Khalīj al 'Aqaba
Sinai 2637
Gebel el Tîh
CYPRUS
Nicosia
Famagusta
Morphou
Olympus 1951
Larnaca
Limassol
Ródhos
4486
Megiste (Kastellórizon)
BLACK SEA
2211
Ionian Sea
5121
4135
MEDITERRANEAN SEA
3174
Bari
Barletta
Brindisi
Táranto
Golfo di Táranto
Str. of Otranto
C. Sta. Maria di Leuca
La Sila 1929
Spartivento
Messina
Cyrene
Darnah
Al Marj (Barce)
Khalīj Bōmba
Tubruq
Banghāzī
Khalīj Surt
Barqa
LIBYA
Khalīg el Salûm
Salûm
Matrûh
El 'Alamein
El Iskandarîya
Rashîd
Bahra el Burullus
Dumyât
Bur Sa'îd
El Mahalla el Kubra
Tanta
El Qantara
Isma'ilîya
Suez Canal
El Suweis
Khalîg es Suweis
El Qâhira
El Faiyûm
Nile
Beni Suef
EGYPT

----- Division between Greeks and Turks in Cyprus; Turks to the north.

SWITZERLAND
Brenner 1371
Passo del S. Gottardo 2108
Genève
Lyon
Rhône
Sion
Brig
Domodossola
Matterhorn Mte. Rosa 4634
Mt. Blanc 4807
Gr. St. Bernard
Annecy
Chambéry
Vienne
Grenoble
Mt. Pelvoux 4103
Briançon
Col du Mt. Cenis 2083
Gran Paradiso 4061
V. D'AOSTA
Ivrea
Biella
Novara
Milano (Milan)
Como
Bérgamo
Bréscia
LOMBARDIA
Lugano
Lago Maggiore
L. di Como
Lecco
Busto Arsizio
Varese
Chiavenna
Bernina 4049
Ortles
Adamello 3554
Merano
Bolzano
Bressanone
TRENTINO ALTO ADIGE
Marmolada 3342
Trento
Lago di Garda
Rovereto
Riva
Belluno
Vittório Véneto
FRIULI VENEZIA GIULIA
Údine
Kobarid (Caporetto) 2863
Villach
Klagenfurt
Maribor
Drave
Karawanken
Ljubljana
Zagreb
Celje
Sava
Varaždin
Trieste
Gorízia
Postojna
Kočevje
Cerknica
Rijeka (Fiume)
Kupa
Karlovac
Sisak
Koper
Istra
Rovinj
Pula (Pola)
Rt. Kamenjak
Krk
Cres
Lošinj
Senj
Kvarner
Kvarnerić
Pag
Velebit Planina
Bihać
Gospić
Gračac
Zadar
Dugi Otok
Šibenik
Split
Brač
Hvar
Vis
Korčula
Lastovo
Palagruža (Yugoslavia)
Dinara Planina
Turin
Torino
Susa
Pinerolo
Monviso
Saluzzo
Cúneo
Mondovì
Asti
Alba
Alessándria
Casale
Vercelli
Chivasso
PIEMONTE
DAUPHINÉ
Valence
Montelimar
Embrun
Mt. Pelat 3052
Alpes Maritimes
Nyons
Orange
Avignon
Digne
PROVENCE
Durance
Aix
Marseille
Toulon
Draguignan
Grasse
Cannes
Antibes
Nice
MONACO
Menton
Monte Carlo
San Remo
Impéria
Fréjus
St-Tropez
Îles d'Hyères
Martigues
Savona
Génova (Genoa)
Riv. di Ponente
Riv. di Levante
Chiávari
Golfo di Génova
La Spézia
Pavia
Piacenza
Cremona
Mantova (Mantua)
Verona
Vicenza
Pádova (Padua)
Treviso
Venézia (Venice)
Chióggia
Golfo di Venézia
Rovigo
Adige
Po
Parma
Réggio
Módena
Ferrara
Bologna
EMILIA ROMAGNA
Mte. Cimone 2165
Imola
Faenza
Forlì
Ravenna
Comácchio
Cesena
Rubicone
Rímini
SAN MARINO
Pésaro
Fano
Urbino
Senigállia
Ancona
Loreto
Macerata
Civitanova
Fabriano
Carrara
Massa
Pistóia
Prato
Lucca
Pisa
Firenze (Florence)
Livorno (Leghorn)
Pontedera
Volterra
TOSCANA
Siena
Arezzo
Cortona
L. Trasimeno
Perúgia
Assisi
Foligno
Monti Vettore 2478
UMBRIA
Ascoli Piceno
San Benedetto
Amiata 1738
Chiusi
Orvieto
L. di Bolsena
Viterbo
Grosseto
Ombrone
Orbetello
Mte. Argentario
Fiora
Civitavécchia
L. di Bracciano
Spoleto
Terni
Rieti
Téramo
Gran Sasso 2914
L'Aquila
ABRUZZO
Pescara
Chieti
Ortona
Lanciano
Vasto
Mt. Amaro 2795
Términi
ROMA (Rome)
Tivoli
Ostia
Velletri
Frosinone
Anzio
Latina
Sabáudia
Terracina
Fondi
Gaeta
Ísole Ponziane
Garigliano
Volturno
Caserta
Aversa
Benevento
Avellino
Vesuvio 1277
Nápoli (Naples)
Ischia
Torre Annunziata
Capri
Sorrento
Castellammare
Nocera
Salerno
Éboli
Sele
MOLISE
Campobasso
S. Severo
Sannicandro
Monte Gargano 1056
Monte S. Ángelo
G. di Manfredónia
Fóggia
Cerignola
Barletta
Trani
Molfetta
Ándria
Ofanto
Corato
Spinazzola
Potenza
Matera
BASILICATA
Agri
Pisciotta
Sinni
2271
Corigliano
Cosenza
1929
Crotone
Sambiase
Nicastro
Catanzaro
Squillace
Pizzo
Palmi
Tauriánova
Réggio
C. Spartivento
Str. di Messina
Ligurian Sea
LIGURIAN SEA
C. Corse
Capraia
Piombino
Portoferráio
Elba
Bastia
Calvi
Mt. Cinto 2710
CORSE (CORSICA) (Fr.)
Ajaccio
Alèria
Sartène
Pto. Vecchio
Bonifacio
Bouches de Bonifacio
Maddalena
Caprera
Asinara
Golfo dell' Asinara
C. Falcone
Porto Torres
Sássari
Ólbia (Terranova)
Golfo Aranci
Alghero
Bosa
Coghinas
Núoro
Orosei
SARDEGNA (SARDINIA)
C. Mte. Santo
Mt. Gennargentu 1834
Arbatax
Sorgono
Tirso
Oristano
Golfo di Oristano
Terralba
Ierzu
Iglesias
Portoscuso
Carbonia
Cágliari
Golfo di Cágliari
G. di Palmas
C. Carbonara
C. Spartivento
2855
3719
TYRRHENIAN SEA
Ustica (It.)
Isole Eólie o Lípari
Strómboli
Salina
Lípari
Vulcano
Isole Égadi
Favignana
Trápani
Érice
Castellammare
Palermo
Alcamo
Segesta
Marsala
Castelvetrano
Selinunte
Menfi
Sciacca
Platani
Pto. Empédocle
Agrigento
Términi
Cefalù
Mistretta
Monti Nebrodi
Milazzo
Patti
Messina
C. Peloro
Etna 3340
Adrano
Giarre
Paternò
Catánia
Lentini
Augusta
Siracusa (Syracuse)
Enna
Caltanissetta
Piazza
Caltagirone
Favara
Licata
Salso
Gela
Vittória
Ragusa
Módica
Íspica
Noto
C. Passero
C. Bon
AFRICA
Pantelleria (Ital.)
1730
Lampedusa (Ital.)
Gozo
Comino
Valletta
Mdina
MALTA
MEDIT
C. S. Dimitri
Gozo (Ghawdex)
Victoria (Rabat)
Comino (Kemmuna)
St. Pauls Bay
239
Mosta
Sliema
Mdina
Hamrun
Valletta
Rabat
Luqa
Marsaxlokk
Zurrieq
Birzebbuga
MALTA 1:1 000 000
miles
km
S.E. EUROPE POLITICAL 1:25 000 000
FRANCE
SWITZ.
Bern
LIECHT.
AUSTRIA
Wien
HUNGARY
Budapest
U.S.S.R.
ROMANIA
București
Venezia
Trieste
SAN MARINO
YUGOSLAVIA
Beograd
ADRIATIC SEA
ITALY
Roma
Napoli
Corse (Fr.)
Sofija
BULGARIA
Tirana
ALBANIA
Thessaloniki
GREECE
Athínai
AEGEAN SEA
TURKEY
Sicilia
MALTA
Kríti
MEDITERRANEAN SEA
ft m
12,000 4000
9000 3000
6000 2000
4500 1500
3000 1000
1200 400
600 200
0 0
200 600
m ft
Projection: Conical with two standard parallels

1:5 000 000
50 0 50 100 miles
50 0 50 100 150 km
R O M A N I A
Transilvania
Carpaţii Meridionali
Carpathians
Banat
Valahia
Dunărea (Danube)
U. S. S. R.
Ismail
Bolgrad
Reni
Kagul
Ozero Sasyk
Kiliya
Sulina
Tulcea
Galaţi
Brăila
Bîrlad
Tecuci
Focşani
Rîmnicu Sărat
Buzău
Ploieşti
Bucureşti
(Bucharest)
Constanţa
Mamaia
Mangalia
Cernavodă
Călăraşi
Olteniţa
Giurgiu
Alexandria
Craiova
Caracal
Slatina
Piteşti
Tîrgovişte
Cîmpina
Braşov
Făgăraş
Sibiu
Mediaş
Sighişoara
Alba-Iulia
Deva
Arad
Timişoara
Lugoj
Caransebeş
Reşiţa
Petroşeni
Tîrgu Jiu
Rîmnicu Vîlcea
Cîmpulung
Turnu-Severin
Orşova
Bela Crkva
Calafat
Corabia
Turnu Măgurele
Zimnicea
Ruse (Ruschuk)
Silistra
Tutrakan
Tolbukhin
Balchik
Nos Kaliakra
Varna
Kolarovgrad (Shumen)
Razgrad
Türgovishte
Türnovo
Gabrovo
Kazanlŭk
Sliven
Aytos
Burgas
Polyanovgrad
Yambol
Elkhovo
Stara Zagora
Dimitrovgrad
Khaskovo
Plovdiv
Pazardzhik
Sofiya (Sofia)
Pernik
Radomir
Kyustendil
Stanke Dimitrov (Marek)
Musala 2925
Vratsa
Pleven
Svishtov
Lom
Oryakhovo
Vidin
Somovit
Teteven
Vezhen 2198
Shipka
Stara Planina
Rhodopi Planina
Smolyan
Zlatograd
Momchilgrad
Kŭrdzhali
Pirin Planina
Struma
Mesta
Petrich
B U L G A R I A
BLACK SEA
TURKEY
Edirne
Kırklareli
Istranca Dağlari 1018
Karadeniz Boğazi
Beykoz
İstanbul
Üsküdar
Tekirdağ
Marmara denizi
Marmara
İmralı
Bandırma
Bursa
2543
Gelibolu (Gallipoli)
Saros Körfezi
Enez
Çanakkale
Çanakkale Boğazi
Troy (Ilium)
Ida 1766
Edremit
Edremit Körfezi
Ayvalık
Bergama (Pergamum)
Kırkağaç
Akhisar
Balıkesir
Simav
Kirmasti
2181
Anadolu
Manisa
Gediz
Menemen
Turgutlu
İzmir (Smyrna)
Alaşehir
Sarıgöl
2157
Ephesus
Kuşadası
Aydın
Büyük Menderes
Çürüksu Çayi
2308
Muğla
2294
Mandalya Körfezi
Kerme Körfezi
Kos
Ródhos
4486
Kárpathos
1215
Kásos
Tílos
Sámos
Ikaría
Fournoi
Pátmos
Kálimnos
Khíos
Çeşme
Lésvos
Mitilíni
968
Límnos
Moúdhros
Bozcaada
Gökçeada
Samothráki 1600
Thásos
1127
Áyios Evstrátios
Baba Burun
THRÁKI
Alexandroúpolis
Komotiní
Xánthi
Dhidhimótikhon
Dráma
Philippi
Kaválla
Sérrai
Thessaloníki
Ákra Plati
Polýyiros
Áthos 2033
Ákra Pláka
Singitikós Kólpos
Toronaíos Kólpos
Thermaïkós Kólpos
Ákra Ámbelos
Ólimbos 2917 (Olympus)
Óssa 1978
Lárisa
Kateríni
Kozáni
Véroia
Yiannitsá
Édhessa
Flórina
Kastoría
Préspansko Jezero
Prespa
THESSALIA
Kalabáka
Tríkkala
Kardhítsa
Fársala
Vólos
Pagastikós Kólpos
Iliodhrómia
Voríai Sporádhes
Skíros
Évvoia
Khalkís
Dhírfis 1743
Lamía
Thermopílai
Gióna 2510
Parnassós 2457
STEREÁ ELLÁS
Náfpaktos
Agrínion
Mesolóngion
Patraïkós Kólpos
Pátrai
Korinthiakós Kólpos
Thívai
Marathón
Athínai (Athens)
Piraievs (Piraeus)
Megara
Salamís
Saronikós Kólpos
Mikínai
Mycenae
Kórinthos
Argos
Návplion
Argolikós Kólpos
Trípolis
Spárti
Kalamáta
Messíni
Pílos
Kiparissía
Kiparissiakós Kólpos
Filiatrá
Pírgos
Olympia
PELOPÓNNISOS
Erímanthos 2224
Killíni 2376
Taïyetos Óros
Messiniakós Kólpos
Lakonikós Kólpos
Yíthion
Ákra Taínaron
Ákra Maléa
Kíthira
Andikíthira
Ídhra
Lávrion
Kéa
Kíthnos
Sérifos
Sífnos
Mílos
Síros
Ermoúpolis
Tínos
Ándros
Míkonos
Rinía
Páros
Náxos
1001
Íos
Síkinos
Amorgós
Astipálaia
Thíra
KIKLÁDHES
DHODHEKÁNISOS
AEGEAN SEA
Ákra Kafirévs
1398
1297
Ákra Spátha
Kólpos Khaníon
Khaniá
Kólpos Soúdhas
Réthimnon
Ákra Stavros
Iráklion
Knossós
Kólpos Merabéllou
Lévka Óri 2452
Ídhi Óros 2456
Dhíkti 2148
Kára Sfakíon
Ierápetra
Ákra Líthinon
KRITI
5121
MEDITERRANEAN SEA
IONIAN SEA
Iónioi Nísoi
Kérkira (Corfu)
Levkás (Sta. Maura)
Kefallinía
Argostólion
Itháki
Zákinthos
Préveza
Árta
Ioánnina
Ípiros
Pindhos Óros
Smólikas 2637
G R E E C E
ALBANIA
Tiranë
Durrës
Elbasan
Shkumbini
Berat
Korçë
Vlorë
Vjosa
Gjirokastër
Sazan
Tomorrit 2480
Korab 2764
2259
Jablanica
Ohridsko Jezero
Ohrid
Debar
Bitola (Monastir)
Prilep
Crna
Vardar
MAKEDONIJA
Solunska 2540
Titov Veles
Tetovo
Skopje
Kumanovo
Štip
Kočani
Strumica
Dojran
Šar Pl. 2496
Prizren
Đakovica
Peć
Priština
Vranje
Kosovska Mitrovica
Kopaonik
Novi Pazar
Leskovac
Kuršumlija
Niš
Pirot
P. Dragoman
Suva Pl.
Južna Morava
Stara Planina 2168
Timok
Zaječar
Bor
Negotin
Kruševac
Kraljevo
Čačak
Kragujevac
Titovo Užice
Morava
SERBIA
YUGOSLAVIA
Smederevo
Požarevac
Beograd (Belgrade)
Zemun
Pančevo
Vršac
Zrenjanin
Novi Sad
Petrovaradin
Sremska Mitrovica
Vinkovci
Osijek
Bečej
Sombor
Subotica
Senta
Kikinda
Szeged
Hódmezővásárhely
Makó
Kiskunhalas
Kiskőrös
Szentes
Békéscsaba
Kalocsa
Baja
Szekszárd
Pécs
Mohács
Kaposvár
Bijeljina
Brčko
Tuzla
Drina
Sava
Bosna
Valjevo
Sarajevo
Han Pijesak
Višegrad
Konjic
Mostar
Stolac
Pljevlja
Durmitor 2522
Tara
Nikšić
Trebinje
CRNA GORA
Titograd (Podgorica)
Cetinje
Kotor
Hercegnovi
Bar
Ulcinj
Bojana
Skadarsko Jezero
Shkodër (Skoder)
Drin
Beli Drim
Crna Gora
Brindisi
Lecce
Galatina
Otranto
C. d'Otranto
Str. of Otranto
Capo Sta. Maria di Leuca
Mţii Bihor 1848
Abrud
Crişul
Mureş
Brad
Peleaga 2509
Parîngul Mare 2518
Negoiul 2535
Vf. Omul 2507
P. Turnu Roşu
Porţile de Fier
Gura Portiţei
Ialomiţa
Argeş
Dîmboviţa
Vedea
Olt
Jiu
Siret
Prut
Mehadia
Trajanova Vrata
Marica
Tundzha
Arda
Ergene
East from Greenwich
18 20 22 24 26 28
46 44 42 40 38 36

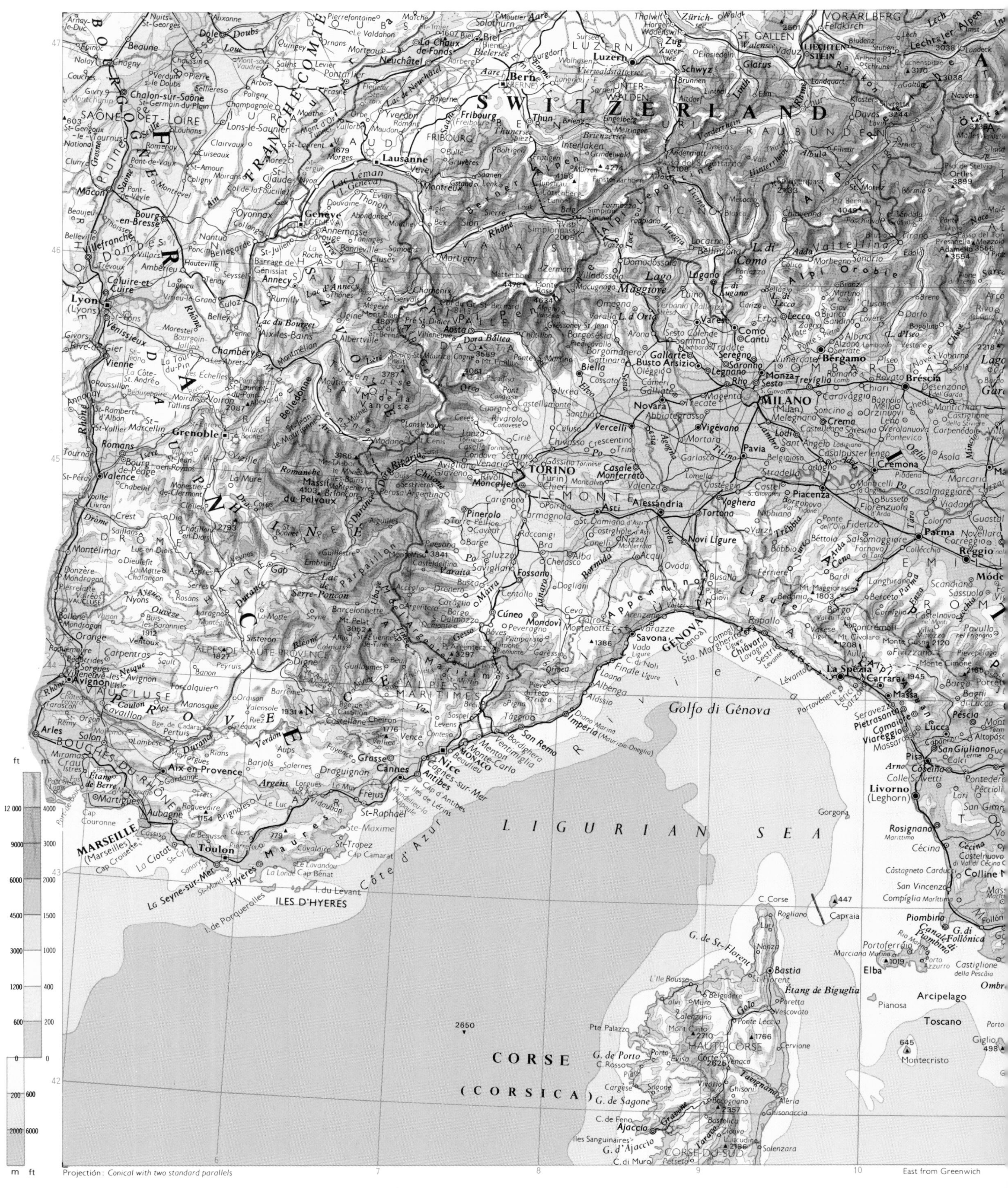
SWITZERLAND
FRANCE
LIGURIAN SEA
Golfo di Génova
CORSE
(CORSICA)
Côte d'Azur
ILES D'HYERES
Arcipelago
Toscano
MILANO
TORINO
(Turin)
GENOVA
(Genoa)
Lyon
(Lyons)
MARSEILLE
(Marseilles)
Grenoble
Lausanne
Genève
Bern
Luzern
Zürich
Nice
MONACO
Cannes
Toulon
Ajaccio
Bastia
Livorno
(Leghorn)
La Spezia
Bergamo
Bréscia
Cremona
Piacenza
Parma
Novara
Vercelli
Alessandria
Asti
Pavia
Savona
Sanremo
Avignon
Arles
Aix-en-Provence
Chambéry
Annecy
Lac Léman
(L. Genève)
Lago Maggiore
L. di Como
SAVOIE
HAUTE-SAVOIE
DRÔME
VAUCLUSE
BOUCHES-DU-RHÔNE
ALPES-DE-HAUTE-PROVENCE
ALPES-MARITIMES
HAUTE-CORSE
CORSE-DU-SUD
VALAIS
TICINO
GRAUBÜNDEN
ST. GALLEN
FRIBOURG
VORARLBERG
LIECHTENSTEIN
Projection: Conical with two standard parallels
East from Greenwich
ft
m

1: 2 500 000

10 0 10 20 30 40 50 miles

10 0 10 20 30 40 50 60 70 80 km

HUNGARY

YUGOSLAVIA

ADRIATIC SEA

Golfo di Venézia

SAN MARINO

ROMA (ROME)

Innsbruck
Hohe Tauern
Niedere Tauern
Zillertaler Alpen
Graz
Klagenfurt
Villach
Wörther See
Karawanken
Karnische Alpen
Maribor
Nagykanizsa
Zalaegerszeg
Keszthely
Balaton
Bakony
Rába
Dráva
Sava
Ljubljana
Zagreb
Karlovac
Bjelovar
Virovitica
Bilo Gora
Moslavačka Gora
Banja Luka
Bihać
Kupa
Una
Vrbas
Bosna
Gorizia
Trieste
Monfalcone
Údine
Pordenone
Treviso
Venézia (Venice)
Mestre
Chióggia
Pádova (Padua)
Rovigo
Ferrara
Foci del Po
Valli di Comácchio
Ravenna
Rímini
Pésaro
Ancona
Urbino
Arezzo
Perúgia
L. Trasimeno
Assisi
Foligno
Terni
Spoleto
Rieti
L'Aquila
Pescara
Chieti
Gran Sasso d'Italia
Avezzano
Sulmona
Vasto
Tévere (Tiber)
Civitavécchia
L. di Bolsena
L. di Bracciano
Tívoli
Frascati
Rijeka (Fiume)
Pula
Istra
Krk
Cres
Lošinj
Rab
Pag
Velebit Planina
Velika Kapela
Mala Kapela
Zadar
Šibenik
Split
Dinara Planina
Dugi Otok
Kornat
Brač
Hvar
Vis
Korčula
Lastovo
Mljet
Pelješac
Palagruža
Pianosa
Tremiti
L. di Lésina
L. di Varano
Vieste
Monte Sant'Ángelo
Tévere
UMBRIA
MARCHE
ABRUZZI
LAZIO
MOLISE
FRIULI
VENEZIA GIULIA
HERCEGOVINA
DALMACIJA

CORSE
CORSICA
CORSE-DU-SUD
G.d'Ajaccio
G. de Valinco
Bonifacio
Îles Cerbicales
Bouches de Bonifacio
Maddalena
Caprera
Costa Smeralda
Golfo dell' Asinara
Asinara
Pórto Torres
Sássari
Alghero
Tempio Pausania
Ólbia
G.di Ólbia
Tavolara
L.di Coghinas
Ozieri
Posada
Siniscola
C. Comino
Nuoro
Golfo di Orosei
Dorgali
SARDEGNA
SARDINIA
L.del Tirso
Monti del Gennargentu
1834
Oristano
Golfo di Oristano
C. Mannu
C. di Monte Santu
Arbatax
Lanusei
Tortolì
Flumendosa
Iglesias
Carbonia
San Pietro
Sant' Antíoco
Cágliari
Golfo di Cágliari
C. Ferrato
C. Carbonara
Serpentara
C. Spartivento
G.di Pálmas
TYRRHENIAN SEA
3719
3589
Vatican City
ROMA (Rome)
Tivoli
Fregene
Lido di Ostia (Lido di Roma)
Velletri
Frosinone
Latina
Ánzio
Nettuno
Terracina
Formia
Gaeta
Golfo di Gaeta
Monte Circeo 541
Palmarola
Ísole Ponziane
Ponza 283
Zannone
Ventotene
Ustica
C. San Vito
PALERMO
Bagheria
G. di Castellammare
Trápani
Érice
Levanzo
Ísole Égadi
Marettimo
Favignana
Marsala
Alcamo
Castelvetrano
Mazara del Vallo
Sciacca
Belice
Corleone
1613
Agrigento
Porto Empédocle
Sicilian Channel
Iles de la Galite
C. Serrat
Bizerte (Binzert)
C. Blanc
Cani
Menzel-Bourguiba
Plane
Zembra
Golfe de Tunis
C. Bon
TUNIS
Halq el Oued
Mateur
Tabarka
El Kala
ALGERIA
Béja
Bou Salem
Medjerda
Menzel-Temime
Kelibia
Soliman
Nabeul
Hammamet
Zaghouan
Téboursouk
TUNISIA
Pantelleria
836
1319
MEDITERRANEAN
ft m
9000 3000
6000 2000
4500 1500
3000 1000
1200 400
600 200
0 37 0
200 600
2000 6000
4000 12 000
m ft
East from Greenwich

Projection: Conical with two standard parallels

1:2 500 000
10 0 10 20 30 40 50 miles
10 0 10 20 30 40 50 60 70 80 km
ADRIATIC SEA
IONIAN SEA
RANEAN SEA
Strait of Otranto
Golfo di Táranto
G. di Manfredónia
G. di Salerno
G. di Policastro
Golfo di Sant'Eufémia
Golfo di Squillace
G. di Gióia
Golfo di Catánia
Str. di Messina
Isole Eólie o Lípari (Æolian Is.)
BASILICATA
CALABRIA
ALBANIA
Monte Sant'Ángelo
Manfredónia
Fóggia
Cerignola
Barletta
Trani
Bisceglie
Molfetta
Bari
Mola di Bari
Monopoli
Altamura
Gravina
Brindisi
Lecce
Táranto
Grottáglie
Manduria
Nardò
Galatina
Gallipoli
Otranto
C. d'Otranto
C. Santa Maria di Leuca
Potenza
Matera
Salerno
Benevento
Avellino
Campobasso
Lucera
Cosenza
Rossano
Crotone
C. delle Colonne
Catanzaro
Vibo Valéntia
Réggio di Calábria
Messina
C. Spartivento
Catánia
Siracusa
Augusta
Ragusa
Módica
Noto
Pachino
C. Passero
Vittória
Cómiso
Caltagirone
Enna
Milazzo
Taormina
Acireale
Monti Nebrodi
Strómboli
Lípari
Salina
Vulcano
Filicudi
Alicudi
Kérkira (Corfu)
Durrësi (Durazzo)
Tirana
Vlora (Valona)
Berati
Elbasani
Fieri
Karaburuni
Monte Pollino 2271
La Sila 1929
Aspromonte 1956
Etna 3340
3065
4116
15 16 17 18 19
37 38 39 40 41

HUNGARY
YUGOSLAVIA
ALBANIA
ADRIATIC SEA
TOLNA
SOMOGY
BARANYA
CSONGRÁD
BIHOR
ARAD
Autonomna Pokrajina Vojvodina
BOSNA
HERCEGOVINA
CRNA GORA (MONTENEGRO)
SRBIJA
Socijalistička Autonomna Pokrajina Kosovo
MAKEDONIJA
DALMACIJA
Nagykanizsa
Kaposvár
Pécs
Szekszárd
Baja
Kecel
Kiskunhalas
Kiskunmajsa
Hódmezővásárhely
Szeged
Orosháza
Gyula
Arad
Timişoara
Lugoj
Hunedoara
Reşiţa
Caransebeş
Subotica
Sombor
Osijek
Vukovar
Vinkovci
Novi Sad
Zrenjanin
Kikinda
Vršac
Pančevo
Beograd (Belgrade)
Zemun
Smederevo
Požarevac
Šabac
Valjevo
Kragujevac
Čačak
Kraljevo
Kruševac
Niš
Leskovac
Pirot
Vranje
Priština
Prizren
Peć
Skopje
Kumanovo
Tetovo
Titov Veles
Štip
Prilep
Bitola
Ohrid
Ohridsko Jezero (L. Ohrid)
Prespansko Jezero (L. Prespa)
Tirana
Durrësi (Durazzo)
Elbasani
Shkodra
Skadarsko Jezero
Titograd
Cetinje
Kotor
Dubrovnik
Mostar
Sarajevo
Zenica
Tuzla
Banja Luka
Bjelovar
Virovitica
Koprivnica
Slavonski Brod
Titovo Užice
Novi Pazar
Kosovska Mitrovica
Korčula
Lastovo
Mljet
Hvar
Sava
Drava
Dunav (Danube)
Tisa
Morava
Drina
Neretva
Vardar
Timok
Prokletije
Šar Planina
Kopaonik
Fruška Gora
Munţii Poiana Ruscă
Projection: Conical with two standard parallels
East from Greenwich
ft m
9000 3000
6000 2000
4500 1500
3000 1000
1200 400
600 200
0 0
200 600
2000 6000
m ft

1:2 500 000

10 0 10 20 30 40 50 miles

10 0 10 20 30 40 50 60 70 80 km

TRANSILVANIA

ROMANIA

U. S. S. R.

UKRAINIAN S.S.R.

VALAHIA (WALACHIA)

DOBROGEA

BULGARIA

TURKEY

GREECE

BLACK SEA

BUCUREŞTI (Bucharest)

Stara Planina (Balkan)

Karadeniz Boğazi (Bosporus)

Thessaloníki
Skopje
Tirana
Sofiya
Plovdiv
Stara Zagora
Pleven
Niš
Priština
Prizren
Bitola
Ohrid
Kavála
Lárisa
Kérkira
Durrësi
Shkodra
Thásos
Límnos
Samothráki
Thermaïkós Kólpos
Strimonikós Kólpos
Saros Körfezi
Evros
Axiós
Vardar
Maritsa
Mesta
Rodopi
Stara Planina
Sredna Gora
Ohridsko Jezero
Prespansko Jezero
Skadarsko Jezero
Çanakkale Boğazi

1:2 500 000

10 0 10 20 30 40 50 miles

10 0 10 20 30 40 50 60 70 80 km

SEA OF CRETE (Sea of Candia)

Continuation Eastwards on same scale

East from Greenwich

Projection: Conical with two standard parallels

m	ft
3000	9000
2000	6000
1500	4500
1000	3000
400	1200
200	600
0	0
200	600
2000	6000

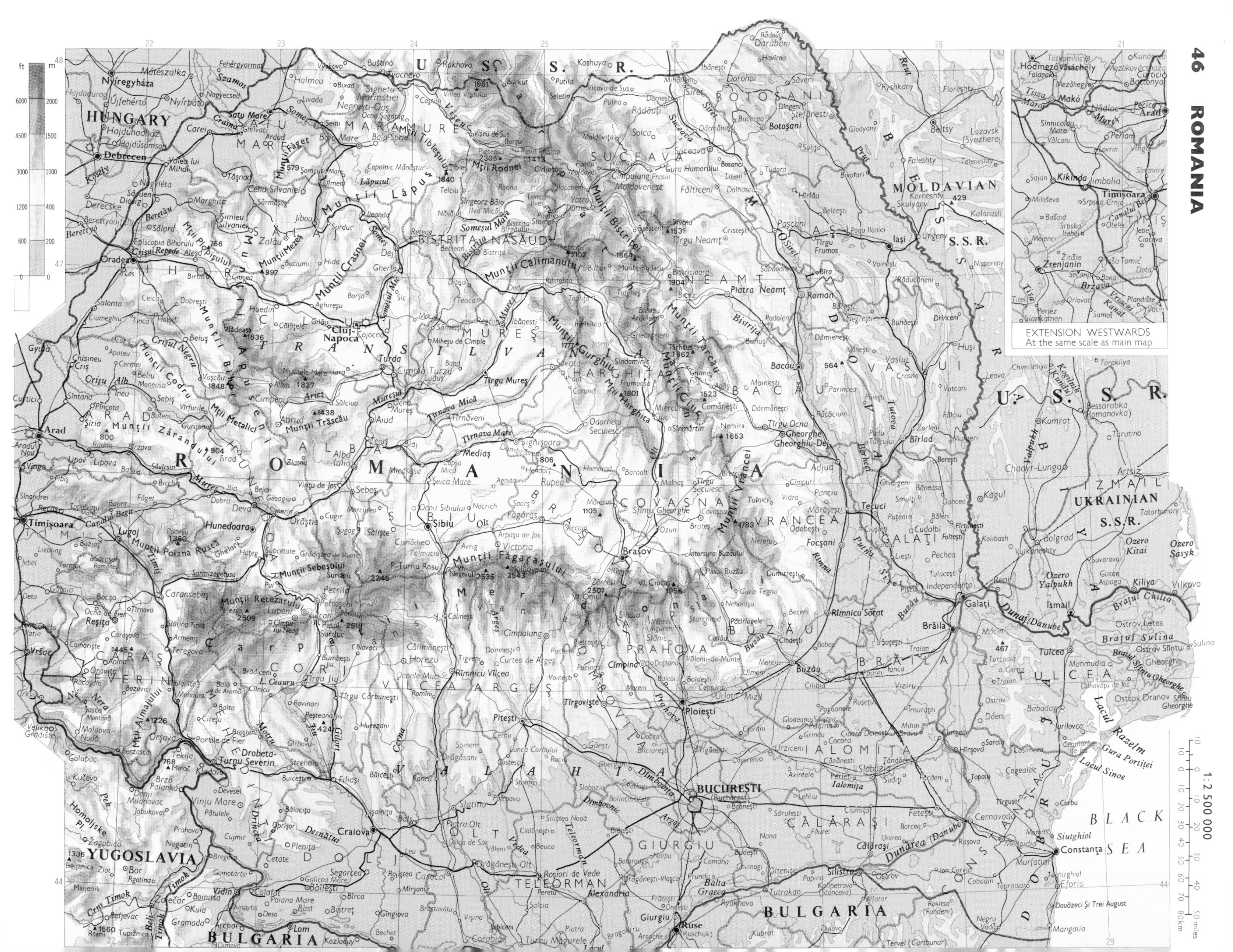
1:2 500 000
miles
km
EXTENSION WESTWARDS
At the same scale as main map
ROMANIA
BLACK SEA
BUCUREŞTI
BULGARIA
HUNGARY
YUGOSLAVIA
UKRAINIAN S.S.R.
MOLDAVIAN S.S.R.
U.S.S.R.

1:2 500 000

10 0 10 20 30 40 50 miles

10 0 10 20 30 40 50 60 70 80 km

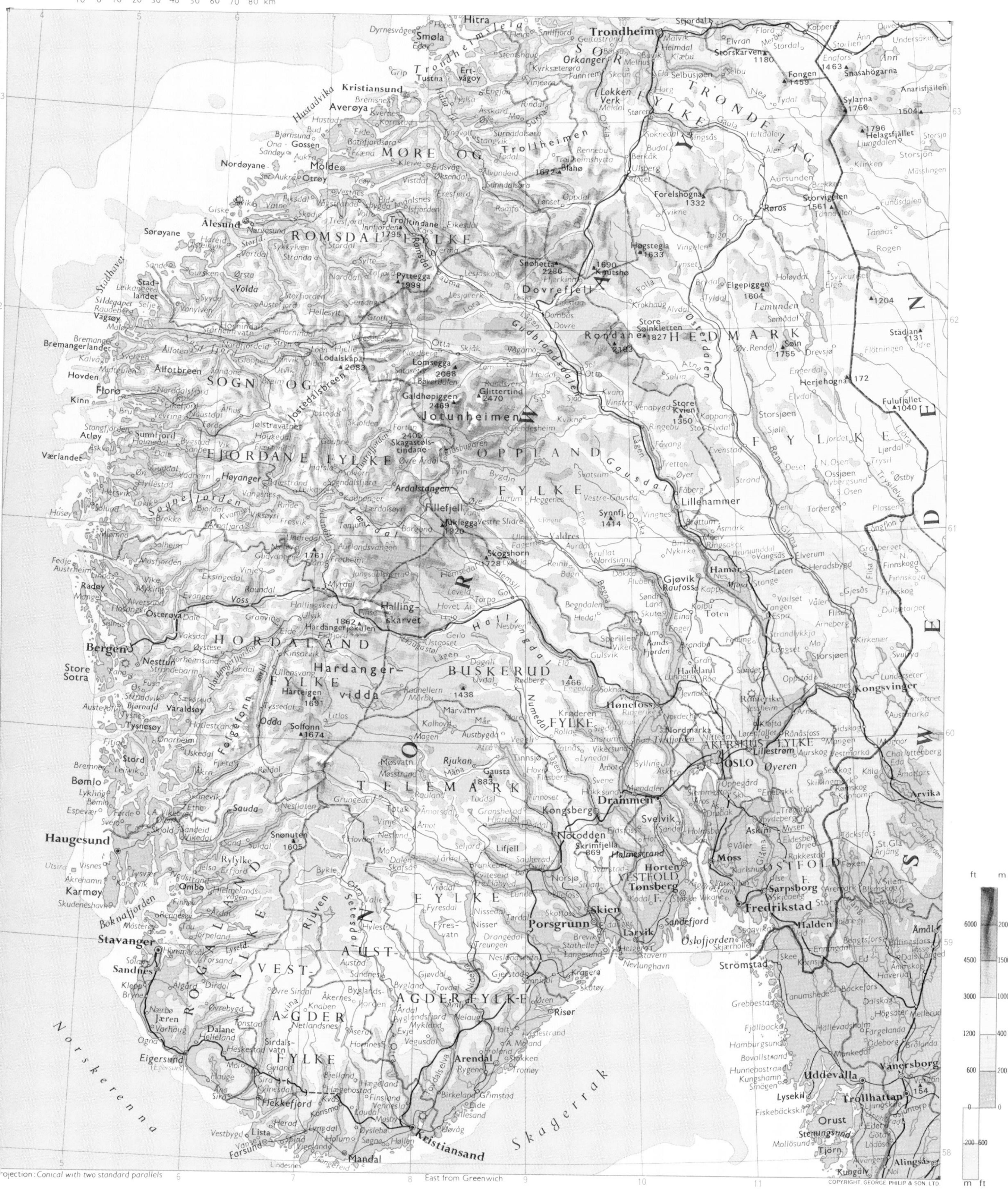
Hitra
Smøla
Trondheim
Stjørdal
Orkanger
SØR-TRØNDELAG FYLKE
Kristiansund
Averøya
Tustna
Ertvågøy
Trollheimen
Molde
Nordøyane
MØRE OG ROMSDAL FYLKE
Ålesund
Sørøyane
Stadlandet
Stadhavet
Sildegaper
Vågsøy
Bremangerlandet
Hovden
Florø
Kinn
Atløy
Værlandet
SOGN OG FJORDANE FYLKE
Jostedalsbreen
Lodalskåpa 2083
Jotunheimen
Galdhøpiggen 2469
Glittertind 2470
Skagastølstindane 2405
Dovrefjell
Snøhetta 2286
Rondane
Gudbrandsdalen
HEDMARK FYLKE
Røros
Forelshogna 1332
Høgstegla 1633
Storvigelen 1561
Elgepiggen 1604
Femunden
Sylarna 1766
Helagsfjället 1796
OPPLAND FYLKE
Lillehammer
Hamar
Gjøvik
Elverum
Kongsvinger
Ardalstangen
Høyanger
Sognefjorden
Voss
Bergen
Store Sotra
HORDALAND FYLKE
Hardangervidda
Hallingskarvet
Hardangerjøkulen
BUSKERUD FYLKE
Hønefoss
Drammen
Kongsberg
Rjukan
Gausta 1883
OSLO
Lillestrøm
AKERSHUS FYLKE
Øyeren
Moss
Sarpsborg
Fredrikstad
Halden
ØSTFOLD FYLKE
TELEMARK FYLKE
Skien
Porsgrunn
Larvik
Sandefjord
Tønsberg
Horten
VESTFOLD F.
Oslofjorden
Strömstad
Haugesund
Karmøy
Stord
Bømlo
Odda
Sauda
Stavanger
Sandnes
Jæren
ROGALAND FYLKE
VEST-AGDER FYLKE
AUST-AGDER FYLKE
Arendal
Grimstad
Risør
Kristiansand
Mandal
Flekkefjord
Farsund
Eigersund
Norskerenna
Skagerrak
Uddevalla
Trollhättan
Vänersborg
Orust
Tjörn
Alingsås
Arvika
SWEDEN
Projection: Conical with two standard parallels
East from Greenwich
COPYRIGHT GEORGE PHILIP & SON LTD

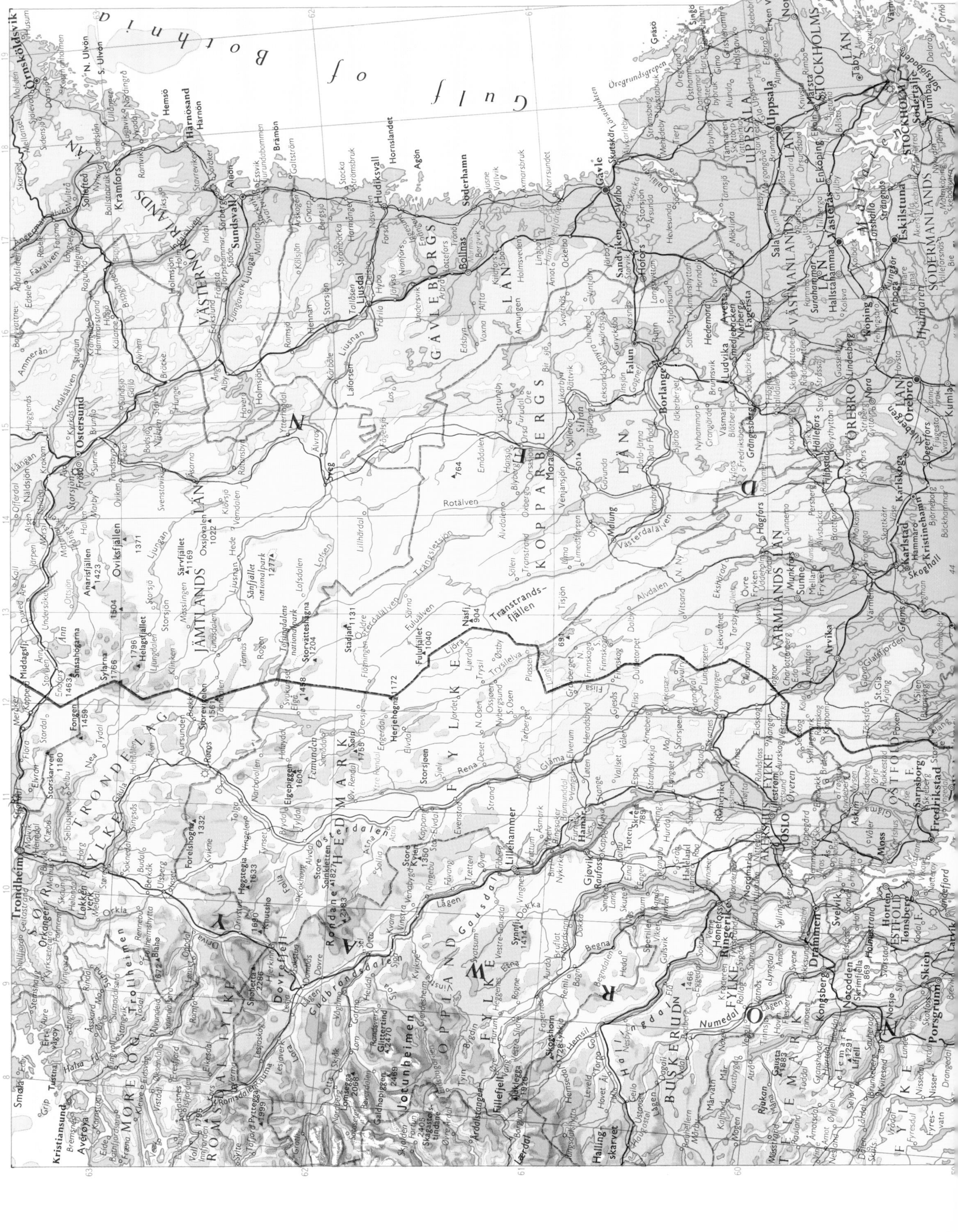

Gulf of Bothnia

VÄSTERNORRLANDS LÄN

JÄMTLANDS LÄN

GÄVLEBORGS LÄN

KOPPARBERGS LÄN

UPPSALA LÄN

STOCKHOLMS LÄN

VÄSTMANLANDS LÄN

SÖDERMANLANDS LÄN

ÖREBRO LÄN

VÄRMLANDS LÄN

SØR TRØNDELAG FYLKE

MØRE OG ROMSDAL FYLKE

HEDMARK FYLKE

OPPLAND FYLKE

BUSKERUD FYLKE

AKERSHUS FYLKE

ØSTFOLD FYLKE

VESTFOLD FYLKE

TELEMARK FYLKE

NORWAY

SWEDEN

1:2 500 000

miles	10	0	10	20	30	40	50			
km	10	0	10	20	30	40	50	60	70	80

ft	m
6000	2000
4500	1500
3000	1000
1200	400
600	200
0	0
200	600

BALTIC SEA

Skagerrak

Kattegat

DENMARK

POLAND

GERMANY

Projection: Conical with two standard parallels

East from Greenwich

ICELAND
on the same scale as general map
West from 18 Greenwich
Arctic Circle
Vatnajökull
Reykjavík
Keflavík
Akranes
Hafnarfjörður
Akureyri
Húsavík
Sauðárkrókur
Ísafjörður
Seyðisfjörður
Faxaflói
Breiðafjörður
Húnaflói
Langjökull
Hofsjökull
Mýrdalsjökull
Hekla 1491
Vestmannaeyjar
Surtsey
NORWEGIAN SEA
Lofoten
Vesterålen
Moskenstraumen
Vestfjorden
Tromsø
Narvik
Kiruna
Gällivare
Kebnekaise
Bodø
Mo
Mosjøen
Namsos
Steinkjer
Levanger
Trondheim
Kristiansund
Molde
Ålesund
Stadlandet
N.-TRØNDELAG
SØR-TRØNDELAG
NORRBOTTEN
VÄSTERBOTTEN
Luleå
Boden
Piteå
Skellefteå
Lycksele
Umeå
Örnsköldsvik
Härnösand
Kramfors
Sollefteå
Östersund
Storsjön
Storuman
Uddjaur
Storavan
Stora Lulevatten
Haparanda
Tornio
Kemi
Rovaniemi
Oulu
Oulujärvi
Kajaani
Iisalmi
Kuopio
Jyväskylä
Vaasa
Kokkola
Jakobstad
Kvarken
KESKI-SUOMEN
Inari
Nordkapp
Hammerfest
Lopphavet
Porsangen
Vadsø
Varangerfjorden
Tanafjorden
Laksefjorden
Kautokeino
Karasjok
Kirkenes
Nikel
Lotta

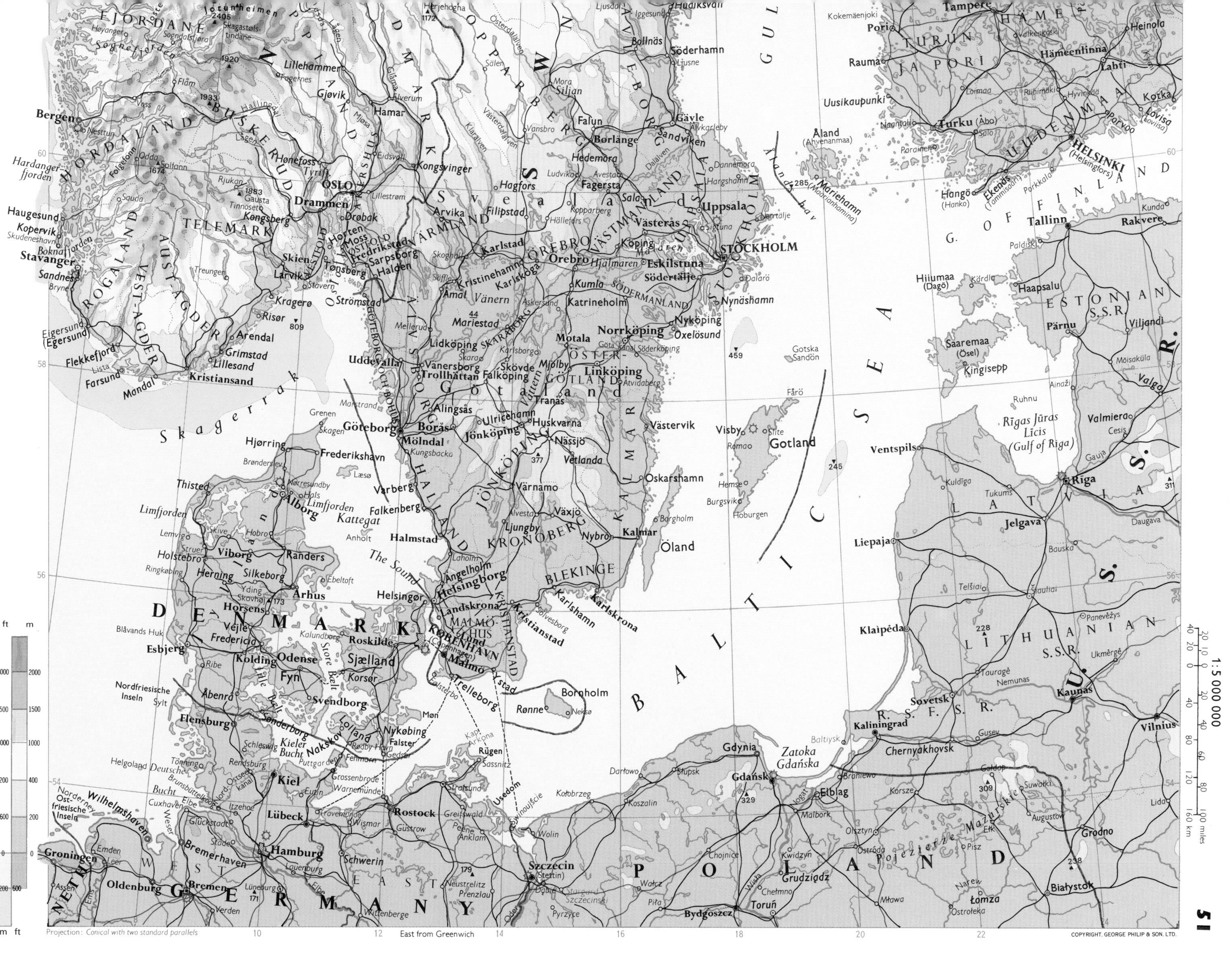
1:5 000 000
20 10 0 20 40 60 80 100 miles
40 20 0 40 80 120 160 km
East from Greenwich
Projection: Conical with two standard parallels
COPYRIGHT, GEORGE PHILIP & SON, LTD.
ft m
Skagerrak
Kattegat
The Sound
BALTIC SEA
G. OF FINLAND
Rīgas Jūras Licis (Gulf of Riga)
Zatoka Gdańska
DENMARK
POLAND
LITHUANIAN S.S.R.
ESTONIAN S.S.R.
WEST GERMANY
EAST
Bergen
Stavanger
Kristiansand
OSLO
Drammen
Göteborg
Malmö
KØBENHAVN (Copenhagen)
STOCKHOLM
Uppsala
Västerås
Örebro
Norrköping
Linköping
Jönköping
Kalmar
Karlskrona
Helsingborg
Halmstad
Ålborg
Århus
Odense
Esbjerg
Kiel
Lübeck
Hamburg
Bremen
Rostock
Szczecin (Stettin)
Gdańsk
Gdynia
Kaliningrad
Klaipėda
Liepaja
Ventspils
Riga
Jelgava
Tallinn
HELSINKI (Helsingfors)
Turku (Åbo)
Tampere
Vilnius
Kaunas
Białystok
Bydgoszcz
Toruń
Gotland
Öland
Bornholm
Sjælland
Fyn
Saaremaa (Ösel)
Hiiumaa (Dagö)
Åland (Ahvenanmaa)

Kolguyev
P-ov. Kanin
Cheshskaya Guba
Timanskiy Kryazh
Bolshezemelskaya Tundra
Malozemelskaya Tundra
Pechora
Arctic Circle
Beloye More (White Sea)
Kolskiy Poluostrov
Murmansk
Arkhangelsk (Archangel)
Onezhskaya Guba
Kandalakshskiy Zaliv
KARELIAN A.S.S.R.
Petrozavodsk
Onezhskoye Ozero
Ladozhskoye Ozero
LENINGRAD
Novgorod
Pskov
Vologda
Kotlas
Syktyvkar
Kirov
Perm
SVERDLOVSK
Izhevsk
Kazan
GORKIY
Yaroslavl
Rybinsk
Kostroma
Ivanovo
Vladimir
MOSKVA (Moscow)
Tula
Ryazan
Kaluga
Smolensk
Bryansk
Orel
Lipetsk
Tambov
Penza
Ulyanovsk
KUYBYSHEV
Orenburg
Ufa
Zlatoust
Miass
Magnitogorsk
Nizhniy Tagil
Serov
Krasnoturinsk
Vorkuta
Inta
Ukhta
Pechora
Sosnogorsk
Severnyye Uvaly
RUSSIAN SOVIET FEDERATIVE SOCIALIST REPUBLIC
UDMURT A.S.S.R.
MARI A.S.S.R.
CHUVASH A.S.S.R.
TATAR A.S.S.R.
BASHKIR A.S.S.R.
MORDOVIAN A.S.S.R.
Cheboksary
Yoshkar Ola
Saransk
Syzran
Togliatti
Novokuybyshevsk
Chapayevsk
Vitebsk
Mogilev
Gomel
Minsk
Bobruysk
BYELORUSSIAN S.S.R. (WHITE RUSSIA)
Polesye (Pripet-Marshes)
Brest
Grodno
Vilnius
Kaunas
LITHUANIAN S.S.R.
Klaipeda (Memel)
Kaliningrad (Königsberg)
R.S.F.S.R.
Riga
Daugavpils
LATVIAN S.S.R.
Liepaja
Ventspils
Tallinn
ESTONIAN S.S.R.
Tartu
Narva
Pärnu
Hiiumaa
Saaremaa
G. of Finland
Gulf of Bothnia
FINLAND
Helsinki
Tampere
Turku
Oulu
Kuopio
Lahti
Vyborg
Kronshtadt
Åland (Ahvenanmaa)
Stockholm
SWEDEN
NORWAY
Lappland
Inari
Luleå
Kemi
Tornio
Kiruna
Gällivare
Narvik
Bodø
Umeå
Härnösand
Sundsvall
Hudiksvall
POLAND
WARSZAWA (Warsaw)
Bialystok
Lublin
Dnepr
Volga
Kama
Belaya
Vychegda
Sev. Dvina
Mezen
Onega
Daugava
Neman
Rybinskoye Vdkhr.
Kamskoye Vdkhr.
Gorkovskoye Vdkhr.
Kuybyshevskoye Vdkhr.
Valdayskaya Vozvyshennost
Oz. Ilmen
Chudskoye Ozero
Cherepovets
Orekhovo-Zuyevo
Kolomna
Serpukhov
Podolsk
Kalinin
Kimry
Velikiye Luki
Orsha
Polotsk

1 Kabardino-Balkar A.S.S.R.
2 North Ossetian A.S.S.R.
3 Nakhichevan A.S.S.R. (Azer.)
4 Checheno-Ingush A.S.S.R.
C A S P I A N S E A
B L A C K S E A
M E D I T E R R A N E A N S E A
L e v a n t
Kara Bogaz Gol
Azovskoye More (Sea of Azov)
U K R A I N I A N S.S.R.
MOLDAVIAN S.S.R.
R O M A N I A
BULGARIA
T U R K E Y
S Y R I A
I R A Q
I R A N (P E R S I A)
CYPRUS
LEBANON
GEORGIAN S.S.R.
ARMENIAN S.S.R.
AZERBAIJAN S.S.R.
DAGESTAN
KALMYK A.S.S.R.
K A Z A K H S. S. R.
Steppe
Prikaspiyskaya Nizmennost
Ergeni Vozvyshennost
Privolzhsk
KHARKOV
Volgograd (Stalingrad)
Rostov
Donetsk
Zaporozhye
Dnepropetrovsk
Odessa
Kishinev
BUCUREŞTI (Bucharest)
ISTANBUL
Ankara
Izmir (Smyrna)
Tbilisi
Yerevan
BAKU
Astrakhan
TEHRAN
Baghdād
Dimashq (Damascus)
Bayrūt (Beirut)
Halab
Trabzon
Samsun
Sevastopol
Simferopol
Yalta
Kerch
Krasnodar
Sochi
Sukhumi
Batumi
Makhachkala
Groznyy
Tabrīz
Rasht
Hamadān
Qom
Kirkūk
Al Mawşil
Gaziantep
Adana
Konya
Bursa
Varna
Constanţa
Brăila
Galaţi
Ploieşti
Braşov
Ruse
Burgas
Marmara Denizi
Tuz Gölü
Van Gölü
Ozero Sevan
Dijlah (Tigris)
Nahr al Furāt
Volga
Don
Dnepr
Dnestr
Kura
Aras
Kuzey Anadolu Dağlari
Toros Dağlari
Bol'shoi Kavkaz
Alborz
Bādiyat ash Sham
Elbrus 5633
Kazbek 5047
Ararat 5165
Damāvand 5604
-28
Projection: Conical with two standard parallels
East from Greenwich
Division between Greeks and Turks in Cyprus; Turks to the North.
ft m
12 000 4000
6000 2000
3000 1000
1200 400
600 200
0 0
200 600
1000 3000
2000 6000
4000 12 000
m ft
1:10 000 000
100 50 0 50 100 150 200 miles
100 0 100 200 300 km

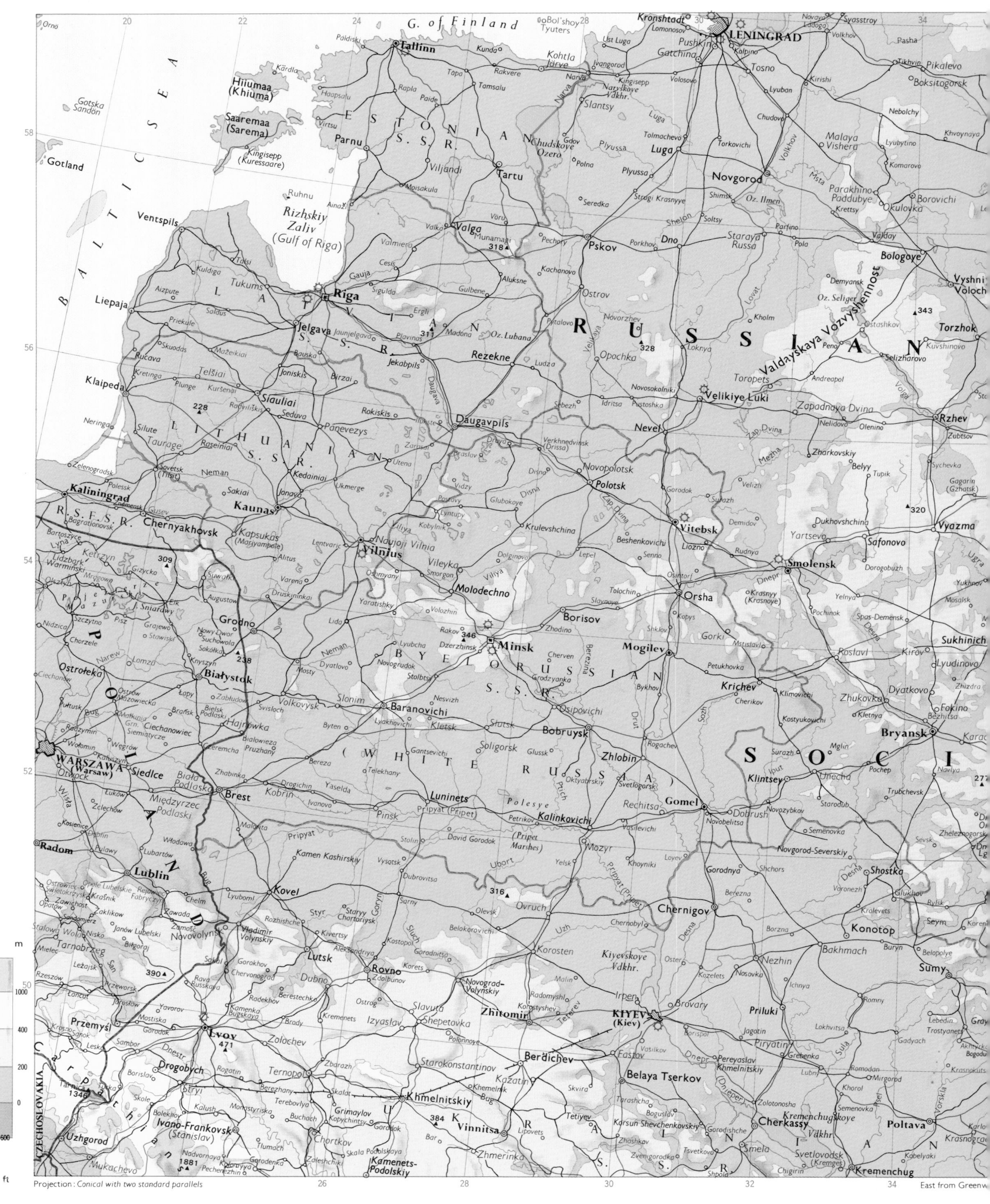
G. of Finland
Bol'shoy Tyuters
Kronshtadt
Lomonosov
LENINGRAD
Pushkin
Gatchina
Kolpino
Tosno
Lyuban
Kirishi
Volkhov
Syasstroy
Novaya Ladoga
Pasha
Tikhvin
Pikalevo
Boksitogorsk
Nebolchy
Khvoynaya
Lyubytino
Komarovo
Tallinn
Paldiski
Kunda
Kohtla Järve
Rakvere
Tapa
Tamsalu
Rapla
Paide
Haapsalu
Virtsu
Pärnu
Kärdla
Hiiumaa (Khiuma)
Saaremaa (Sarema)
Kingisepp (Kuressaare)
Gotska Sandön
Gotland
Ust Luga
Ivangorod
Narva
Kingisepp
Narvskoye Vdkhr.
Volosovo
Slantsy
Luga
Tolmachevo
Chudovo
Malaya Vishera
Torkovichi
ESTONIAN S.S.R.
Chudskoye Ozero
Gdov
Polna
Plyussa
Viljandi
Tartu
Ruhnu
Ainaži
Rizhskiy Zaliv (Gulf of Riga)
Mõisaküla
Ventspils
BALTIC SEA
Seredka
Strugi Krasnyye
Shimsk
Oz. Ilmen
Novgorod
Msta
Parakhino Paddubye
Okulovka
Borovichi
Krettsy
Soltsy
Shelon
Valka
Valga
Võru
Munamägi
318
Pechory
Pskov
Porkhov
Dno
Staraya Russa
Parfino
Pola
Valday
Bologoye
Vyshni Voloch
Valmiera
Cēsis
Gauja
Sigulda
Talsi
Kuldiga
Tukums
Aizpute
Liepaja
Riga
Jelgava
Saldus
Priekule
Ergli
Gulbene
Aluksne
Kachanovo
Ostrov
Demyansk
Oz. Seliger
Ostashkov
343
Torzhok
Kuvshinovo
Selizharovo
LATVIAN S.S.R.
Jaunjelgava
Plavinas
311
Madona
Oz. Lubana
Pytalovo
Novorzhev
328
Opochka
Loknya
Kholm
Valdayskaya Vozvyshennost
Peno
Andreapol
Toropets
RUSSIAN
Skuodas
Mažeikiai
Bauska
Jēkabpils
Daugava
Rēzekne
Ludza
Rucava
Klaipeda
Kretinga
Telšiai
Plunge
Kuršenai
Joniskis
Birzai
Šiauliai
Radviliškis
Šeduva
228
Rokiskis
Novosokolniki
Pustoshka
Idritsa
Sebezh
Velikiye Luki
Zapadnaya Dvina
Nelidovo
Olenino
Rzhev
Zubtsov
Volga
Neringa
Silute
Taurage
Raseiniai
Panevezys
Daugavpils
Ilukste
Zarasai
LITHUANIAN S.S.R.
Utena
Verkhnedvinsk (Drissa)
Nevel
Zap. Dvina
Zharkovskiy
Belyy
Tupik
Sychevka
Gagarin (Gzhatsk)
Zelenogradsk
Sovetsk (Tilsit)
Polessk
Neman
Kedainiai
Braslav
Drysa
Disna
Novopolotsk
Polotsk
Velizh
Gorodok
Surazh
Mezha
Kaliningrad
Sakiai
Ukmerge
Jonava
Vidzy
Postavy
Glubokoye
Kaunas
Gusev
R.S.F.S.R.
Chernyakhovsk
Bagrationovsk
Kapsukas (Mariyampole)
Lyntupy
Kobylnik
Krulevshchina
Vitebsk
Demidov
Dukhovshchina
Yartsevo
Safonovo
Vyazma
320
Bartoszyce
Lyna
Ketrzyn
Lidzbark Warminski
309
Gizycko
Mragowo
Olsztyn
Suwałki
Lentvaris
Naujoji Vilnia
Vilnius
Alytus
Vileyka
Vilnia
Dolginovo
Lepel
Beshenkovichi
Senno
Liozno
Rudnya
Smolensk
Dorogobuzh
Ugra
Yukhnov
Oshmyany
Smorgon
Varena
Druskininkai
Augustow
Ełk
Śniardwy
Pisz
Grajewo
Szczytno
Nidzica
Molodechno
Vilyia
Yaratishky
Volozhin
Tolochin
Slavnoye
Osintorf
Orsha
Dnepr
Krasnyy (Krasnoye)
Yelnya
Mosalsk
Pochinok
Spas-Demensk
Grodno
Nowy Dwór
Suchowola
Sokółka
Stawiski
238
Lida
Rakov
346
Minsk
Dzerzhinsk
Zhodino
Borisov
Kopys
Shklov
Gorki
Mstislavl
Desna
Sukhinich
Chorzele
Narew
Łomża
Kniszyn
Białystok
Ostrołęka
Ciechanów
Neman
Lyubcha
Novogrudok
Dyatlovo
Mosty
Stolbtsy
Cherven
Berezina
Mogilev
Roslavl
Kirov
Lyudinovo
BYELORUSSIAN S.S.R.
Grodzyanka
Petukhovka
Krichev
Klimovichi
Zhukovka
Dyatkovo
Zhizdra
Fokino
Bezhitsa
Ostrów Mazowiecka
Łapy
Zabłudów
Bielsk Podlaski
Brańsk
Volkovysk
Slonim
Nesvizh
Svisloch
Osipovichi
Bykhov
Cherikov
Kostyukovichi
Kletnya
Pułtusk
Bug
Małkinia
Ciechanowiec
Siemiatycze
Hajnówka
Białowieża
Pruzhany
Byten
Baranovichi
Lyakhovichi
Kletsk
Slutsk
Soligorsk
Glussk
Bobruysk
Zhlobin
Rogachev
Drut
Sozh
Surazh
Mglin
Bryansk
Karachev
SOVIET
Radzymin
Wołomin
Węgrów
Kałuszyn
Czeremcha
Gantsevichi
WARSZAWA (Warsaw)
Otwock
Siedlce
Biała Podlaska
Zhabinka
Telekhany
Oktyabrskiy
Svetlogorsk
Klintsey
Iput
Unecha
Pochep
Navlya
277
Wisła
Łuków
Zelechów
Międzyrzec Podlaski
Brest
Drogichin
Kobrin
Yaselda
Ivanovo
Luninets
Pinsk
Pripyat (Pripet)
Polesye
Petrikov
Kalinkovichi
Rechitsa
Gomel
Dobrush
Novozybkov
Starodub
Trubchevsk
Kozienice
Dęblin
Włodawa
Malorita
Radom
Puławy
Lubartów
POLAND
Pripyat
Stolin
David Gorodok
(Pripet Marshes)
Mozyr
Vasilevichi
Novobelitsa
Semenovka
Zheleznogorsk
Sevsk
Kamen Kashirskiy
Vysotsk
Dubrovitsa
Ubort
Yelsk
Khoyniki
Loyev
Novgorod-Severskiy
Shchors
Gorodnya
Shostka
Glukhov
Lublin
Ostrowiec Świętokrzyski
Opole Lubelskie
Kraśnik
Rejowiec Fabryczny
Chełm
Lyuboml
Kovel
Sarny
Goryn
316
Olevsk
Ovruch
Chernobyl
Chernigov
Berezna
Voronezh
Krolevets
Rylsk
Opatów
Zawichost
Zaklików
Sandomierz
Zawada
Zamość
Novovolynsk
Vladimir Volynskiy
Rozhishche
Styr
Staryy Chartoriysk
Sluch
Belokorovichi
Uzh
Kiyevskoye Vdkhr.
Borzna
Konotop
Seym
Stalowa Wola
Nisko
Janów Lubelski
Biłgoraj
Kivertsy
Kostopol
Aleksandriya
Gorodnitsa
Korosten
Oster
Bakhmach
Buryn
Belopolye
Mielec
Tarnobrzeg
San
Leżajsk
Rzeszów
Łańcut
Przeworsk
390
Sokal
Gorokhov
Chervonograd
Lutsk
Dubno
Rovno
Zdolbunov
Korets
Novograd-Volynskiy
Malin
Kozelets
Nosovka
Nezhin
Ichnya
Sumy
Rava Russkaya
Radekhov
Berestechko
Yaroslaw
Yavorov
Kamenka Bugskaya
Brody
Ostrog
Kremenets
Izyaslav
Slavuta
Shepetovka
Polonnoye
Radomyshl
Korostyshev
Teterev
Irpen
Zhitomir
KIYEV (Kiev)
Brovary
Priluki
Romny
Przemyśl
Krosno
Sanok
Lesko
Mostiska
Gorodok
Lvov
471
Zolochev
Sambor
Dnestr
Borispol
Jagotin
Piryatin
Lokhvitsa
Lebedin
Trostyanets
Grebenka
Sula
Gadyach
Akhtyrka
Bogodukhov
Drogobych
Borislav
Rogatin
Ternopol
Zbarazh
Starokonstantinov
Berdichev
Fastov
Vasilkov
Dnepr
Pereyaslav Khmelnitskiy
Lubny
Romodan
Mirgorod
Krasnokutsk
Tarnica
1346
Skole
Stryi
Kalush
Berezhany
Terebovlya
Skalat
Khmelnitskiy
Khmelnik
Kazatin
Skvira
Belaya Tserkov
(Dnieper)
Zolotonosha
Khorol
Semenovka
Psel
Vorskla
Bolekhov
Monastyriska
Buchach
Grimaylov
Kopychintsy
Bug
Tarashcha
Boguslav
Tetiyev
Korsun Shevchenkovskiy
Kremenchugskoye Vdkhr.
Cherkassy
Poltava
Karlovka
Krasnograd
Uzhgorod
Ivano-Frankovsk (Stanislav)
Chortkov
Gorodok
384
Vinnitsa
Lipovets
Zhashkov
Gorodishche
Smela
Kobelyaki
Nadvornaya
1881
Pechenezhin
Gorodenka
Tlumach
Zaleshchiki
Skala Podolskaya
Kamenets-Podolskiy
Bar
Zhmerinka
Zvenigorodka
Tsvetkovo
Shpola
Chigirin
Svetlovodsk (Kremges)
Kremenchug
Mukachevo
Carpathians
CZECHOSLOVAKIA
UKRAINIAN
Orno
20
22
24
26
28
30
32
34
58
56
54
52
50
ft
m
3000
1000
1200
400
600
200
0
200
600
Projection: Conical with two standard parallels
East from Greenw

1:5 000 000

50 0 50 100 miles

50 0 50 100 150 km

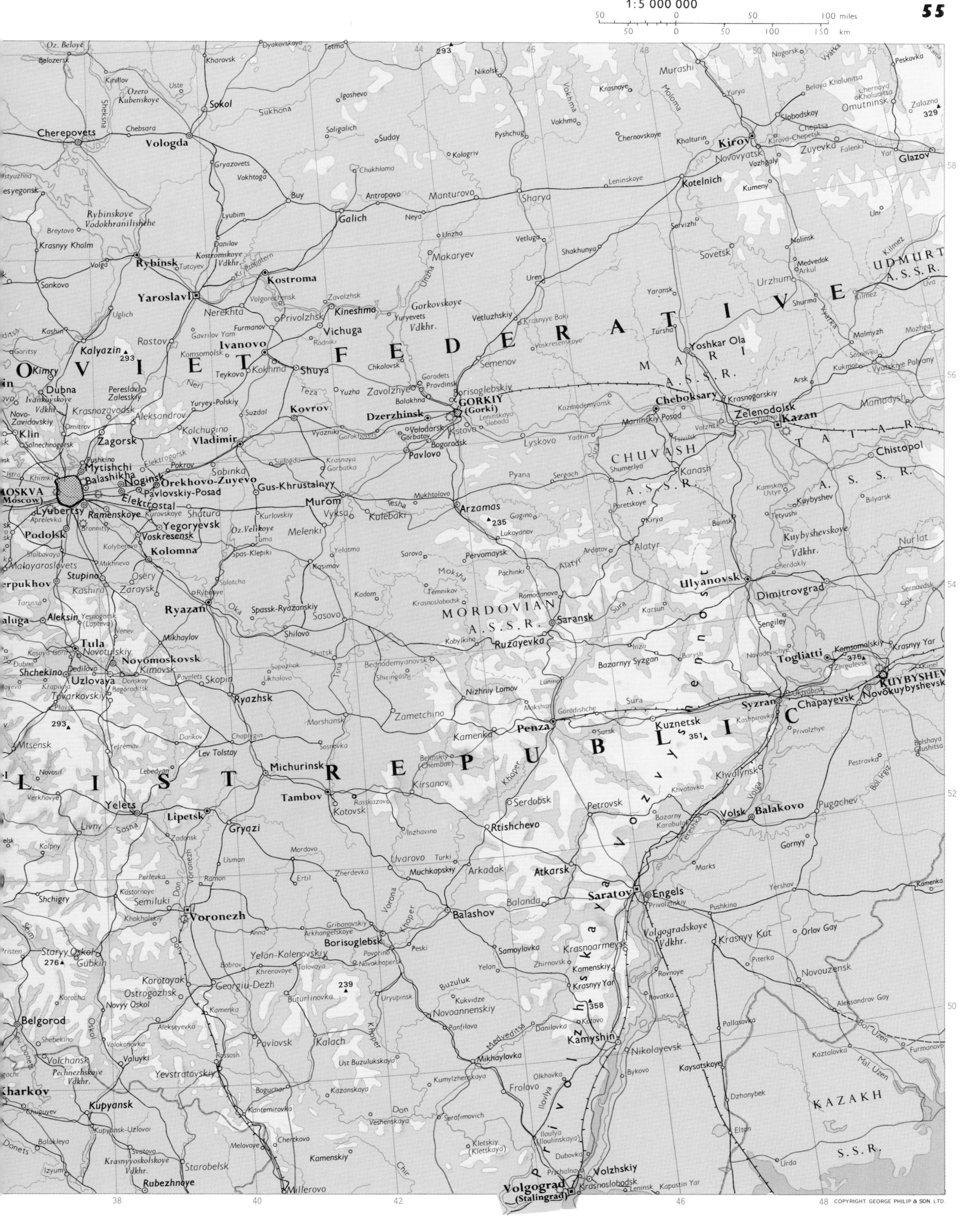

Oz. Beloye
Belozersk
Kharovsk
Dyakovskaya
Totma
Nikolsk
Murashi
Nagorsk
Peskovka
Kirillov
Ozero Kubenskoye
Uste
Sheksna
Sokol
Igoshevo
Sukhona
Vokhma
Moloma
Krasnoye
Yurya
Belaya Kholunitsa
Omutninsk
Zalazna
329
Cherepovets
Chebsara
Vologda
Soligalich
Suday
Pyshchug
Chernovskoye
Khalturin
Kirov
Slobodskoy
Kirovo-Chepetsk
Zuyevka
Falenki
Yar
Glazov
Kologriv
Novovyatsk
Vozhgaly
Gryazovets
Vokhtoga
Chukhloma
Leninskoye
Kotelnich
Kumeny
Buy
Antropovo
Manturovo
Sharya
Rybinskoye Vodokhranilishche
Lyubim
Galich
Neya
Uni
Breytovo
Danilov
Unzha
Vetluga
Sorvizhi
Nolinsk
Krasnyy Kholm
Kostromskoye Vdkhr.
Makaryev
Shakhunya
Sovetsk
Medvedok
Arkul
Kilmez
Volga
Rybinsk
Tutayev
Kostroma
Uren
Urzhum
UDMURT A.S.S.R.
Uva
Sonkovo
Yaroslavl
Volgorechensk
Zavolzhsk
Yaransk
Shurma
Vyatka
Uglich
Nerekhta
Kineshma
Gorkovskoye Vdkhr.
Yuryevets
Vetluzhskiy
Krasnyye Baki
Tursha
Yoshkar Ola
Malmyzh
Mozhga
Kashin
Rostov
Gavrilov Yam
Furmanov
Privolzhsk
Vichuga
Rodniki
Kalyazin
293
Ivanovo
Komsomolsk
Voskresenskoye
Teykovo
Kokhma
Shuya
Chkolovsk
Semenov
MARI A.S.S.R.
Kukmor
Vyatskiye Polyany
Sosnovka
Kimry
Dubna
Pereslavl Zalesskiy
Nerl
Teza
Yuzha
Zavolzhye
Gorodets
Pravdinsk
Balakhna
Borisoglebskiy
GORKIY (Gorki)
Arsk
Krasnogorskiy
Cheboksary
Zelenodolsk
Mamadysh
Ivankovskoye Vdkhr.
Yuryev-Polskiy
Krasnozavodsk
Aleksandrov
Suzdal
Kovrov
Dzerzhinsk
Leninskaya Sloboda
Kozmodemyansk
Mariinskiy Posad
Kazan
Novo-Zavidovskiy
Klin
Omitrov
Solnechnogorsk
Zagorsk
Kolchugino
Vladimir
Vyazniki
Gorokhovets
Volodarsk
Gorbatov
Kstovo
Bogorodsk
Lyskovo
Yadrin
Tsivilsk
Volzhsk
TATAR A.S.S.R.
Pushkino
Mytishchi
Elektrogorsk
Sudogda
Krasnaya Gorbatka
Pavlovo
CHUVASH A.S.S.R.
Chistopol
Istra
Khimki
Balashikha
Noginsk
Pokrov
Sobinka
Orekhovo-Zuyevo
Pyana
Sergach
Shumerlya
Kanash
MOSKVA (Moscow)
Pavlovskiy-Posad
Elektrostal
Gus-Khrustalnyy
Murom
Mukhtolovo
Kamskoye Ustye
Kuybyshev
Bilyarsk
Lyubertsy
Aprelevka
Ramenskoye
Kurovskoye
Shatura
Kurlovskiy
Vyksa
Tesha
Kulebaki
Arzamas
235
Poretskoye
Tetyushi
Podolsk
Bronnitsy
Yegoryevsk
Voskresensk
Oz. Velikoye
Tuma
Melenki
Gagino
Lukoyanov
Kirya
Buinsk
Kuybyshevskoye Vdkhr.
Nurlat
Stolbovaya
Maloyaroslavets
Kolybelskoye
Kolomna
Spas-Klepiki
Yelatma
Sarova
Pervomaysk
Ardatov
Alatyr
Serpukhov
Mikhnevo
Stupino
Kashira
Ozery
Zaraysk
Kasimov
Moksha
Pochinki
Cherdakly
Tarussa
Kaluga
Aleksin
Yasnogorsk (Laptevo)
Rybnoye
Spolotcha
Ryazan
Oka
Spassk-Ryazanskiy
Kadom
Temnikov
Krasnoslobodsk
Romodanovo
Ulyanovsk
Dimitrovgrad
Sernovodsk
Sok
Venev
Tula
Novotulskiy
Mikhaylov
Sasovo
Shilovo
MORDOVIAN A.S.S.R.
Saransk
Sura
Karsun
Sengiley
Kosaya Gora
Dubna
Shchekino
Dedilovo
Novomoskovsk
Kimovsk
Shatsk
Bednodemyanovsk
Kobylkino
Ruzayevka
Inza
Barysh
Novodevichye
Togliatti
Komsomolskiy
375
Krasnyy Yar
Zhigulevsk
KUYBYSHEV
Novokuybyshevsk
Kinel
Uzlovaya
Donskoy
Bogoroditsk
Pavelets
Skopin
Sapozhok
Likholovo
Shiringushi
Bazarnyy Syzgan
Lunino
Oktyabrsk
Krapivna
Tovarkovskiy
Plavsk
Ryazhsk
Tsna
Nizhniy Lomov
Mokshan
Gorodishche
Sura
Syzran
Chapayevsk
293
Morshansk
Zametchino
Kuznetsk
351
Kashpirovka
Mtsensk
Dankov
Chaplygin
Lev Tolstoy
Sosnovka
Kamenka
Penza
Sursk
Privolzhye
Bolshaya Glushitsa
Yefremov
Belinskiy (Chembar)
Khoper
Novosil
Lebedyan
Michurinsk
REPUBLIC
Pestravka
Khvalynsk
Bol. Irgiz
Verkhovye
Tambov
Rasskazovo
Kirsanov
Khvatovka
Volga
Yelets
Kotovsk
Serdobsk
Petrovsk
Bazarny Karabulak
Volsk
Balakovo
Pugachev
Livny
Sosna
Lipetsk
Gryazi
Inzhavino
Rtishchevo
Tereshka
Zadonsk
Gornyy
Yelsk
Kolpny
Usman
Mordovo
Uvarovo
Turki
Muchkapskiy
Arkadak
Atkarsk
Marks
Perlevka
Ramon
Voronezh
Ertil
Zherdevka
Vorona
Kastornoye
Don
Semiluki
Shchigry
Balanda
Saratov
Engels
Privolzhskiy
Yershov
Kamenka
Pushkino
Khokholskiy
Voronezh
Anna
Gribanovskiy
Arkhangelskoye
Borisoglebsk
Khoper
Balashov
Volgogradskoye Vdkhr.
Krasnyy Kut
Orlov Gay
Seim
Pristen
Staryy Oskol
276
Gubkin
Yelan-Kolenovskiy
Bobrov
Khrenovoye
Talovaya
Povorino
Novokhopersk
Peski
Samoylovka
Krasnoarmeysk
Piterka
Novouzensk
Korotoyak
Ostrogozhsk
Georgiu-Dezh
Yelan
Zhirnovsk
Kamenskiy
Krasnyy Yar
Rovnoye
Korocha
Novyy Oskol
239
Buturlinovka
Buzuluk
Uryupinsk
Kukvidze
Novoannenskiy
358
Lovatka
Aleksandrov Gay
Belgorod
Oskol
Kamenka
Panfilova
Medveditsa
Danilovka
Kamyshin
Kotovo
Pallasovka
Bol. Uzen
Furmanovo
Severskiy Donets
Shebekino
Volokonovka
Alekseyevka
Pavlovsk
Kalach
Khoper
Rossosh
Valuyki
Volchansk
Pechenezhskoye Vdkhr.
Yevstratovskiy
Ust Buzulukskaya
Mikhaylovka
Nikolayevsk
Kaysatskoye
Kaztalovka
Mal. Uzen
Kumylzhenskaya
Olkhovka
Bykovo
Kharkov
Boguchar
Kazanskaya
Frolovo
Ilovlya
Dzhanybek
KAZAKH S.S.R.
Chuguyev
Kupyansk
Kantemirovka
Don
Kupyansk-Uzlovoi
Veshenskaya
Serafimovich
Privolzhskaya Vozvyshennost
Balakleya
Donets
Svatovo
Melovoye
Chertkovo
Kletskiy (Kletskaya)
Ilovlya (Iloulinskaya)
Dubovka
Elton
Krasnyyoskolskoye Vdkhr.
Kamenskiy
Chir
Urda
Izyum
Starobelsk
Prichalnaya
Volzhskiy
Rubezhnoye
Millerovo
Volgograd (Stalingrad)
Krasnoslobodsk
Leninsk
Kapustin Yar
SOVIET FEDERATIVE SOCIALIST REPUBLIC
38
40
42
44
46
48
50
52
58
56
54
52
50

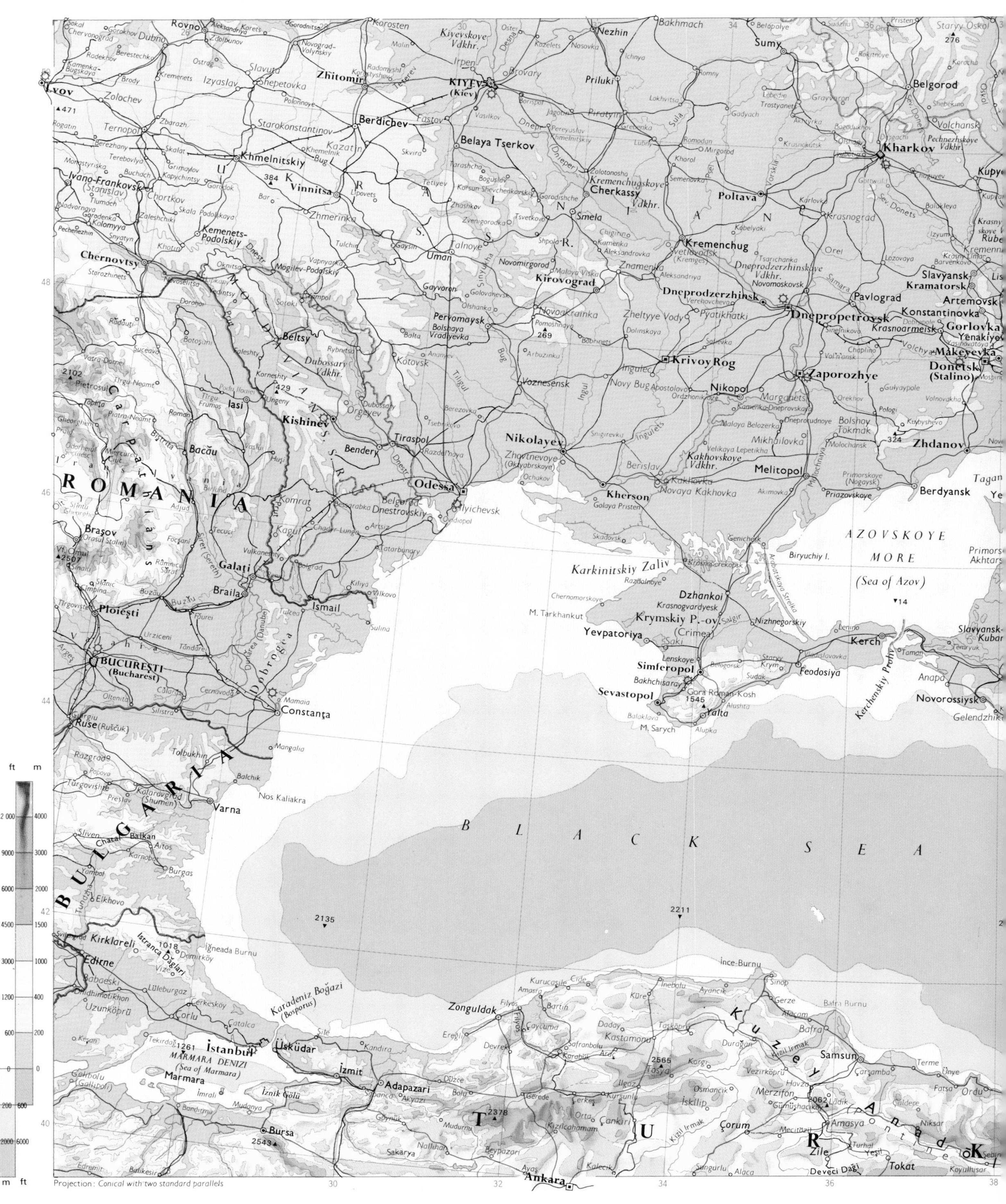

Rovno
Dubno
Korosten
Kiyevskoye Vdkhr.
Nezhin
Bakhmach
Sumy
Starvy Oskol
Lvov
Zhitomir
KIYEV (Kiev)
Brovary
Priluki
Belgorod
Shepetovka
Izyaslav
Slavuta
Zolochev
Berdichev
Fastov
Ternopol
Starokonstantinov
Belaya Tserkov
Kharkov
Volchansk
Khmelnitskiy
Vinnitsa
Cherkassy
Kremenchugskoye Vdkhr.
Poltava
Ivano-Frankovsk (Stanislav)
Chortkov
Zhmerinka
Smela
Krasnograd
Kamenets-Podolskiy
Uman
Talnoye
Kremenchug
Chernovtsy
Mogilev-Podolskiy
Kirovograd
Dneprodzerzhinsk
Dneprodzerzhinskoye Vdkhr.
Slavyansk
Kramatorsk
Artemovsk
Pavlograd
Dnepropetrovsk
Konstantinovka
Gorlovka
Pervomaysk
Beltsy
Dubossary Vdkhr.
Krivoy Rog
Zaporozhye
Donetsk (Stalino)
Makeyevka
Iasi
Kishinev
Voznesensk
Nikopol
Zhdanov
Tiraspol
Bendery
Nikolayev
Kakhovskoye Vdkhr.
Melitopol
Bacău
ROMANIA
Odessa
Kherson
Novaya Kakhovka
Berdyansk
Ilyichevsk
Belgorod-Dnestrovskiy
Braşov
Galaţi
Braila
Ismail
Karkinitskiy Zaliv
Dzhankoi
AZOVSKOYE MORE (Sea of Azov)
Ploieşti
Krymskiy P.-ov (Crimea)
Yevpatoriya
Kerch
BUCUREŞTI (Bucharest)
Simferopol
Feodosiya
Sevastopol
Gora Roman-Kosh
1545
Yalta
Constanţa
Anapa
Novorossiysk
Kerchenskiy Proliv
Ruse (Ruščuk)
Tolbukhin
Varna
BULGARIA
Nos Kaliakra
BLACK SEA
Burgas
2135
2211
Kirklareli
Edirne
İnce Burnu
Karadeniz Boğazi (Bosporus)
Zonguldak
Sinop
Samsun
Kuzey Anadolu
İstanbul
Üsküdar
MARMARA DENIZI (Sea of Marmara)
İzmit
Adapazari
Kastamonu
Merzifon
Amasya
Bursa
Çankiri
Çorum
Tokat
Ankara
TURK
Projection: Conical with two standard parallels
30
32
34
36
38
ft
m
12 000
9000
6000
4500
3000
1200
600
0
200
2000
4000
3000
2000
1500
1000
400
200
0
600
6000
m
ft

1:5 000 000

50 0 50 100 miles

50 0 50 100 150 km

Yelan-Kolenovskiy
Bobrov
Khrenovoye
Talovaya
Povorino
Peski
Novokhopersk
Samoylovka
Krasnoarmeysk
Zhirnovsk
Kamenskiy
Krasnyy Kut
Orlov Gay
Oz. Chalkar
Chalkar
Dzhambeyty
Georgiu-Dezh
Ostrogozhsk
Kamenka
Buturlinovka
239
Yelan
Uryupinsk
Buzuluk
Kukvidze
Krasnyy Yar
358
Rovnoye
Piterka
Novouzensk
Chapayevo
Novoannenskiy
Panfilovo
Vozyshennost
Kotovo
Novatka
Volgogradskoye
Vdkhr.
Aleksandrov Gay
Pavlovsk
Kalach
Medveditsa
Danilovka
Pallasovka
Mergenevskiy
Karsha
Rossosh
Ust Buzulukskaya
Mikhaylovka
Kamyshin
Nikolayevsk
Bol. Uzen
Furmanovo
Ural
Bazartobe
Boguchar
Kazanskaya
Kumylzhenskaya
Olkhovka
Bykovo
Kaysatskoye
Kaztalovka
Mal. Uzen
Antonovo
Kantemirovka
Frolovo
Ilovlya
Kulagino
Don
Veshenskaya
Serafimovich
Privolzhskaya
Dzhanybek
K A Z A K H
Melovoye
Chertkovo
Kletskiy (Kletskaya)
Ilovlya (Ilovlinskaya)
Elton
Inderborskiy
Kamenskiy
Dubovka
S. S. R.
Millerovo
Sovetskaya
Chir
Prichalnaya
Volzhskiy
Urda
Donetsk
Volgograd (Stalingrad)
Leninsk
Kapustin Yar
Kalach na Donu
Krasnoslobodsk
Shungay
Surovikino
Krasnoarmeysk
Vladimirovka
Zelënyy
Topoli
Voroshilovgrad (Lugansk)
Glubokiy
Chernyshkovskiy
Volga
Verkhniy Baskunchak
Kamensk-Shakhtinskiy
Morozovsk
Akhtubinsk (Petropavlovskiy)
Makhambet (Yamankhalinka)
Krasnodon
Sverdlovsk
Krasnyy Luch
Lenin
Tsimlyanskoye Vdkhr.
Likhovskoi
Gukovo
Belaya Kalitva
Krasnodonetskaya
Sinegorski
Novobogatinskoye
Rovenki
Krasny Sulin
Artemovski
Tsimlyansk
Kotelnikovo
Guryev
Shakhty
Ust-Donetskiy
Konstantinovski
Volgodonsk
Dubovskoye
Obilnoye
Kopanovka
Kamenolomni
Kurgan
Tuzlov
Novocherkassk
Yenotayevka
-28
Bolshaya Martynovka
Zavetnoye
Zimovniki
Rostov
Azov
Bataysk
Manych
Veselovskoye Vdkhr.
Kuberle
Mechetinskaya
K A L M Y K
A. S. S. R.
Ganyushkino
Krasnyy Yar
Zernograd
Yeya
Proletarskaya
Remontnoye
Astrakhan
Kushchevskaya
Yegorlykskaya
Gigant
Oz. Manych-Gudilo
Krasnoye
Kamyzyak
Stara-minskaya
Salsk
Elista (Stepnoi)
-28
Peschanokopskoye
Yegorlyk
Leninsk
Priyutnoye
Kirovskiy
Pavlovskaya
Belaya Glina
Krasnogvardeyskoye
Divnoye
Liman
Kaltay
Kalaus
Ipatovo
Prikaspiyskaya Nizmennost
Ergeni Vozyshennost
Tikhoretsk
Kaspiyskiy
Novaleksandrovskaya
Kropotkin
Izobil'nyy
Korenovsk
Svetlograd (Petrovskoye)
Arzgir
O. Kulaly
Mangyshlakskiy Zaliv
Blagodarnoye
Beloye Ozero
Kuma
Ust-Labinsk
M. Tyub Karagan
Fort Shevchenko
P-ov. Mangyshlak
Krasnodar
Armavir
Stavropol
Prikumsk
Staryy Biryuzyak
C A S P I A N
Kuban
831
Kurganinsk (Kurgannaya)
Vladimirovka
Tyuleniy
Maykop
Nevinnomyssk
Labinsk
Zelenokumsk (Vorontsovo-Aleksandrovskoye)
Bryanskoye
Khadyzhensk
Apsheronsk
Urup
Kursavka
Laba
Neftegorsk
Cherkessk
Mineralnyye Vody
O. Chechen
Aleksandriyskaya
Shevchenko
Dakhovskaya
Georgievsk
Lopatin
Yessentuki
Pyatigorsk
Kizlyar
Terek
Prokhladnyy
Mozdok
CHECHENO-
Kislovodsk
Mayskiy
Karachayevsk
Nartkala
Malgobek
INGUSH
Gudermes
Sulak
Sochi
Krasnaya Polyana
Nalchik
Kizil Yurt
Matsesta
Teberda
KABARDINO-BALKAR A.S.S.R.
Groznyy
A.S.S.R.
Khasavyurt
Makhachkala
Adler
Tyrnyauz
Elkhotovo
Beslan
Kumtorkala
Kaspiysk
Gagra
Elbrus
5633
Ordzhonikidze
Sayasan
Buynaksk
Bolshoy Kavkaz
ABKHAZ A.S.S.R.
Kodori
5203
N. OSSETIAN A.S.S.R.
Gudata
Novyy Afon
Inguri
Sadon
Izberbash
Sukhumi
Tkvarcheli
Kazbek
5047
Tebulos
4492
Khunzakh
Novokayakent
Ochamchire
Tsageri
Agvali
Kakhib
Akusha
Gali
Dzhvari
Zugdidi
Rioni
Oni
Tlyarata
Dagestanskiye Ogni
800
Anaklia
GEORGIA
Sachkhere
Kuli
Madzhalis
Derbent
Mikha-Tskhakaya
Kutaisi
Tkibuli
Chiatura
Tskhinvali (Staliniri)
DAGESTAN A.S.S.R.
Kasumkent
Zestafoni
Dusheti
Poti
Samtredia
Khashuri
Gori
Telavi
Kvareli
Lagodekhi
Mikhaylovka
Kaspi
Khachmas
S. S. R.
Mtskheta
Samur
Kobuleti
Makharadze
Borzhomi
Tbilisi
Gurdzhaani
Zakataly
Kuba
Divichi
Khulo
Signakhi
Citeli Ckaro
Alazan
Akhty
Batumi
ADZHAR A.S.S.R.
Akhaltsikhe
Khrami
Mirzaani
Bazar Dyuzi
4466
Siazan
Vale
Marneuli
Rustavi
Iori
Sheki (Nukha)
Akhalkalaki
Shaumyani
Mingechaurskoye Vdkhr.
Kutkashen
Baba dag
3629
Hopa
Borçka
Akstafa
Kura
Mashtaga
Pazar
Artvin
Ardahan
Çildir
Alaverdi
Tauz
Shamkhor
Yevlakh
Agdash
Shemakha
Surakhany
Artem
Görele
Akçaabat
Rize
Ardanuç
Kisir
3192
Kirovakan
Kirovabad
Mingechaur
Geokchay
Sumgait
Zyrya
Trabzon
Sürmene
Kaçkar
3937
Dilizhan
Chanlar
Lyaki
AZERBAIJAN S.S.R.
BAKU
Leninakan
Sevan
Dashkesan
Kyurdamir
Artik
Aragats
4090
Chambarak
Ozero Sevan
Mir-Bashir
Barda
Kazi Magomed
Çakirgöl
3063
Oltu
Şelim
Kars
Kamo
Terter
Sabirabad
Alyata
Gümüşane
Çoruh
İspir
Narman
Sarikamiş
Digor
ARMENIAN
Agdzhabedi
Ali-Bayramly
Doğu Karadeniz Dağlari
Bayburt
Tortum
Aras
Kağizman
Echmiadzin
Yerevan
Martuni
Agdam
Imishly
Karachala
M. Byandovan
TURKEY

from Greenwich 40 42 44 46 48 50

50 48 46 44 42 40

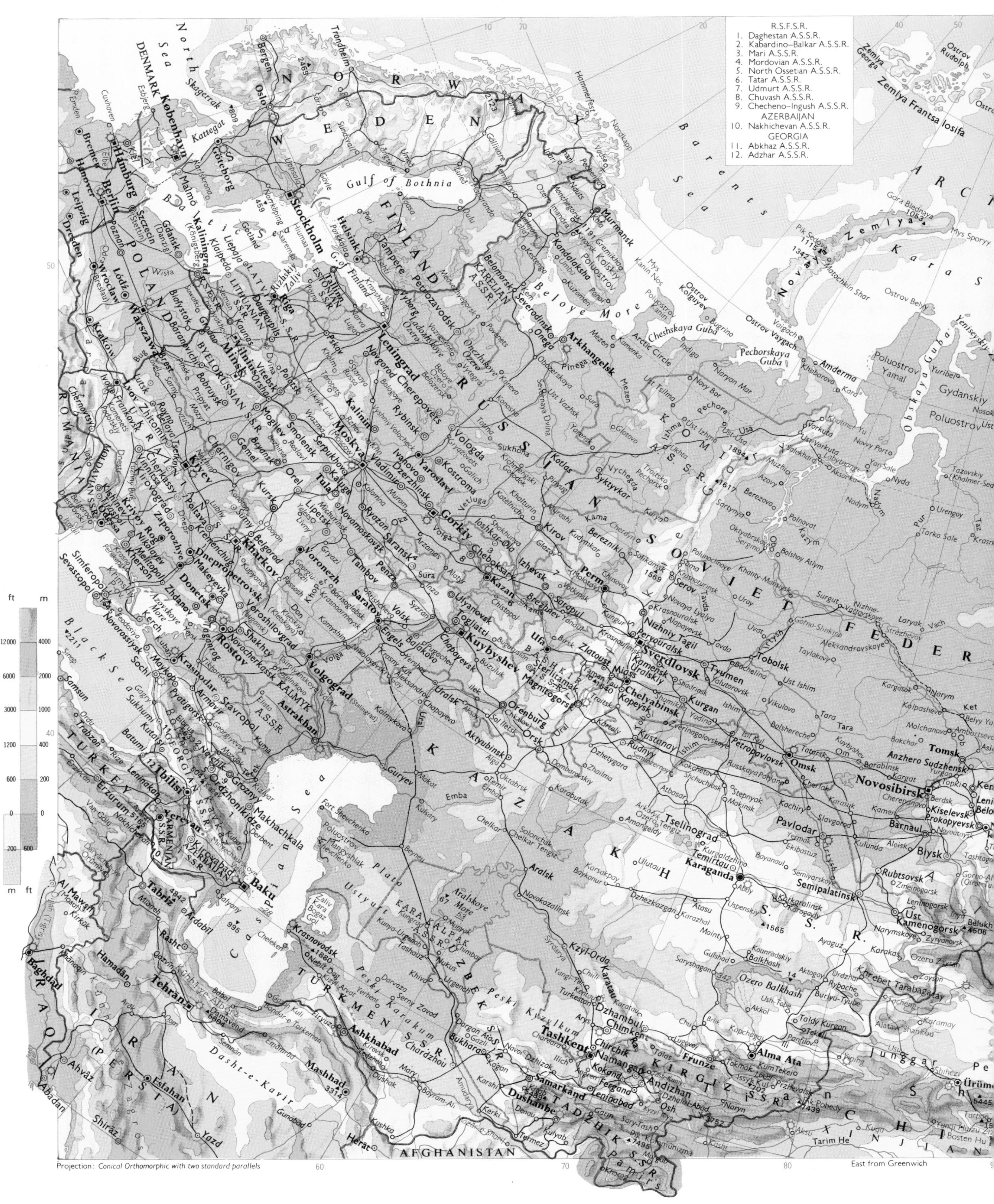
R.S.F.S.R.
1. Daghestan A.S.S.R.
2. Kabardino-Balkar A.S.S.R.
3. Mari A.S.S.R.
4. Mordovian A.S.S.R.
5. North Ossetian A.S.S.R.
6. Tatar A.S.S.R.
7. Udmurt A.S.S.R.
8. Chuvash A.S.S.R.
9. Checheno-Ingush A.S.S.R.
AZERBAIJAN
10. Nakhichevan A.S.S.R.
GEORGIA
11. Abkhaz A.S.S.R.
12. Adzhar A.S.S.R.
ft m
12000 4000
6000 2000
3000 1000
1200 400
600 200
0 0
200 600
m ft
Barents Sea
Beloye More
Gulf of Bothnia
Black Sea
Caspian Sea
Aralskoye More
NORWAY
SWEDEN
FINLAND
POLAND
DENMARK
ROMANIA
TURKEY
IRAN (PERSIA)
IRAQ
AFGHANISTAN
RUSSIAN SOVIET FEDERATIVE S.R.
KAZAKH S.S.R.
UKRAINIAN S.S.R.
BYELORUSSIAN S.S.R.
TURKMEN S.S.R.
UZBEK S.S.R.
KIRGIZ S.S.R.
TADZHIK S.S.R.
KARELIAN A.S.S.R.
KOMI A.S.S.R.
Moskva
Leningrad
Kiyev
Kharkov
Gorkiy
Kuybyshev
Sverdlovsk
Volgograd
Rostov
Tbilisi
Baku
Yerevan
Tashkent
Alma Ata
Frunze
Dushanbe
Ashkhabad
Novosibirsk
Omsk
Karaganda
Stockholm
Oslo
Helsinki
Warszawa
Berlin
Tehrān
Baghdād
Projection: Conical Orthomorphic with two standard parallels
East from Greenwich

1:20 000 000
100 0 100 200 300 400 500 miles
100 0 200 400 600 800 km
Boundaries of U.S.S.R.
Boundaries of S.S.R.
Boundaries of A.S.S.R.
COPYRIGHT, GEORGE PHILIP & SON, LTD.
OCEAN
Laptev Sea
East Siberian Sea
Chukotskoye More
Bering Sea
Sea of Okhotsk
Sea of Japan
Japan
Severnaya Zemlya
Ostrov Komsomolets
Ostrov Oktyabrskoy Revolyutsii
Ostrov Bolshevik
Proliv Vilskutskogo
Poluostrov Taymyr
Gory Byrranga
Novosibirskiye Ostrova
Ostrov Kotelnyy
Lyakhovskiye Ostrova
Proliv Dmitriya Lapteva
Ostrov Vrangelya
Ostrova Medvezhi
Chukotskiy Khrebet
Mys Dezhneva (East C.)
St. Lawrence I. (U.S.A.)
Anadyrskiy Zaliv
Koryakskiy Khrebet
Poluostrov Kamchatka
Petropavlovsk-Kamchatskiy
Komandorskiye Ostrova
Khrebet Cherskogo
Verkhoyanskiy Khrebet
Okhotsko Kolymskoye
Zaliv Shelikhova
Gizhiginskaya Guba
Penzhinskaya Guba
YAKUT A.S.S.R.
SOCIALIST REPUBLIC
Nordvik
Tiksi
Verkhoyansk
Srednekolymsk
Magadan
Okhotsk
Yakutsk
Vilyuysk
Olekminsk
Aldan
Stanovoy Khrebet
Khrebet Dzhugdzhur
Kirensk
Bratsk
Krasnoyarsk
Nizhneudinsk
Irkutsk
Angarsk
Cheremkhovo
Ulan Ude
Chita
Blagoveshchensk
Komsomolsk
Khabarovsk
Birobidzhan
Nikolayevsk-na-Am.
Sakhalin
Sovetskaya Gavan
Yuzhno-Sakhalinsk
Khrebet Sikhote Alin
Vladivostok
Nakhodka
Ussuriysk
Kurilskiye Ostrova
Hokkaido
Sapporo
Hakodate
Honshū
Nii-gata
Kanazawa
To-yama
Qiqihar
Harbin
Jilin
Changchun
Fushun
Shenyang
Anshan
Dandong
Yingkou
Lüda
Beijing
Zhangjiakou
Baotou
Chongjin
Wŏnsan
P'yongyang
Sŏul
Inch'on
Taejŏn
Pusan
NORTH KOREA
SOUTH KOREA
Ulaanbaatar (Ulan Bator)
Hangayn Nuruu
MONGOLIA
GOBI
REPUBLIC
Da Hinggan Ling
Hulun Nur
Arctic Circle

1:50 000 000

250 0 250 500 750 1000 miles

250 0 500 1000 1500 km

m	ft
6000	18 000
4000	12 000
2000	6000
1000	3000
400	1200
200	600
0	0
200	600
2000	6000
4000	12 000
6000	18 000
8000	24 000

1: 50 000 000

250 0 250 500 750 1000 miles

250 0 500 1000 1500 km

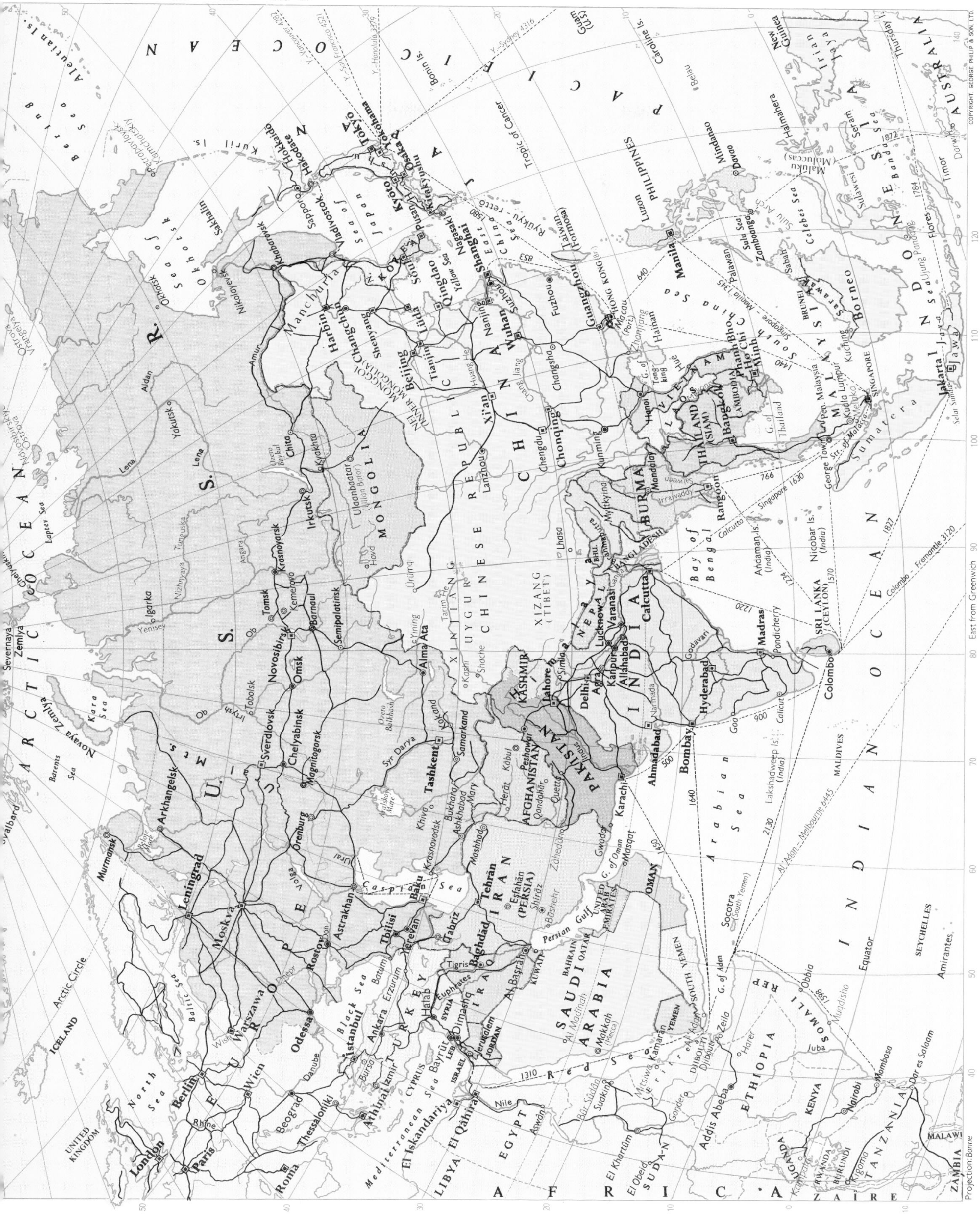

East from Greenwich

Projection: Bonne

1:1 000 000
miles
km
1949–1974 Armistice lines between Israel and the Arab States.
MEDITERRANEAN SEA
LEBANON
SYRIA
JORDAN
ISRAEL
Under Israeli Occupation
Gaza Strip
EGYPT
DEAD SEA
Hagalil (Galilee)
Shomron (Samaria)
Hanegev
Sur (Tyre)
Qiryat Shemona
Nahariyya
'Akko (Acre)
Qiryat Yam
HEFA (Haifa)
Tirat Karmel
Zefat
Terverya
Yam Kinneret (Sea of Galilee)
Nazerat (Nazareth)
'Afula
Hadera
Netanya
Tulkarm
Nabulus
Herzliyya
TEL AVIV-YAFO (Jaffa)
Ramat Gan
Petah Tiqwa
Bat Yam
Holon
Rishon le Ziyyon
Lod (Lydda)
Ramla
Rehovot
Ashdod
Ashqelon
Qiryat Gat
Gaza
Khan Yunis
Be'er Sheva'
JERUSALEM (Yerushalayim, Al Quds)
Ram Allah
Ariha (Jericho)
Bayt Lahm (Bethlehem)
Al Khalil (Hebron)
Irbid
Dar'a
Az Zarqa'
As Salt
'AMMAN
Al Mafraq
Cease Fire Line 1967
Continuation Southwards 1:2 500 000
Dimona
Elat
Al 'Aqabah
PETRA
Projection: Conical with two standard parallels
East from Greenwich
COPYRIGHT, GEORGE PHILIP & SON, LTD.

1:15 000 000

100 0 100 200 300 400 miles

100 0 100 200 300 400 500 600 km

SAUDI ARABIA

IRAN (PERSIA)

IRAQ

SYRIA

LEBANON

ISRAEL

JORDAN

EGYPT

SUDAN

ETHIOPIA

SOMALI REP.

DJIBOUTI

KENYA

UGANDA

YEMEN

SOUTH YEMEN

OMAN

UNITED ARAB EMIRATES (TRUCIAL STATES)

KUWAIT

QATAR

BAHRAIN

AFGHANISTAN

An Nafūd

Rub' al Khali

Red Sea

Persian Gulf

Gulf of Oman

Gulf of Aden

INDIAN OCEAN

Dasht-e Lūt

Bādiyat ash Shām

Ogaden

Socotra (South Yemen)

ft m

12 000 4000

9000 3000

6000 2000

4500 1500

3000 1000

1200 400

600 200

0 0

200 600

2000 6000

4000 12 000

m ft

Projection: Sanson-Flamsteed's Sinusoidal

35 40 East from Greenwich 45 50

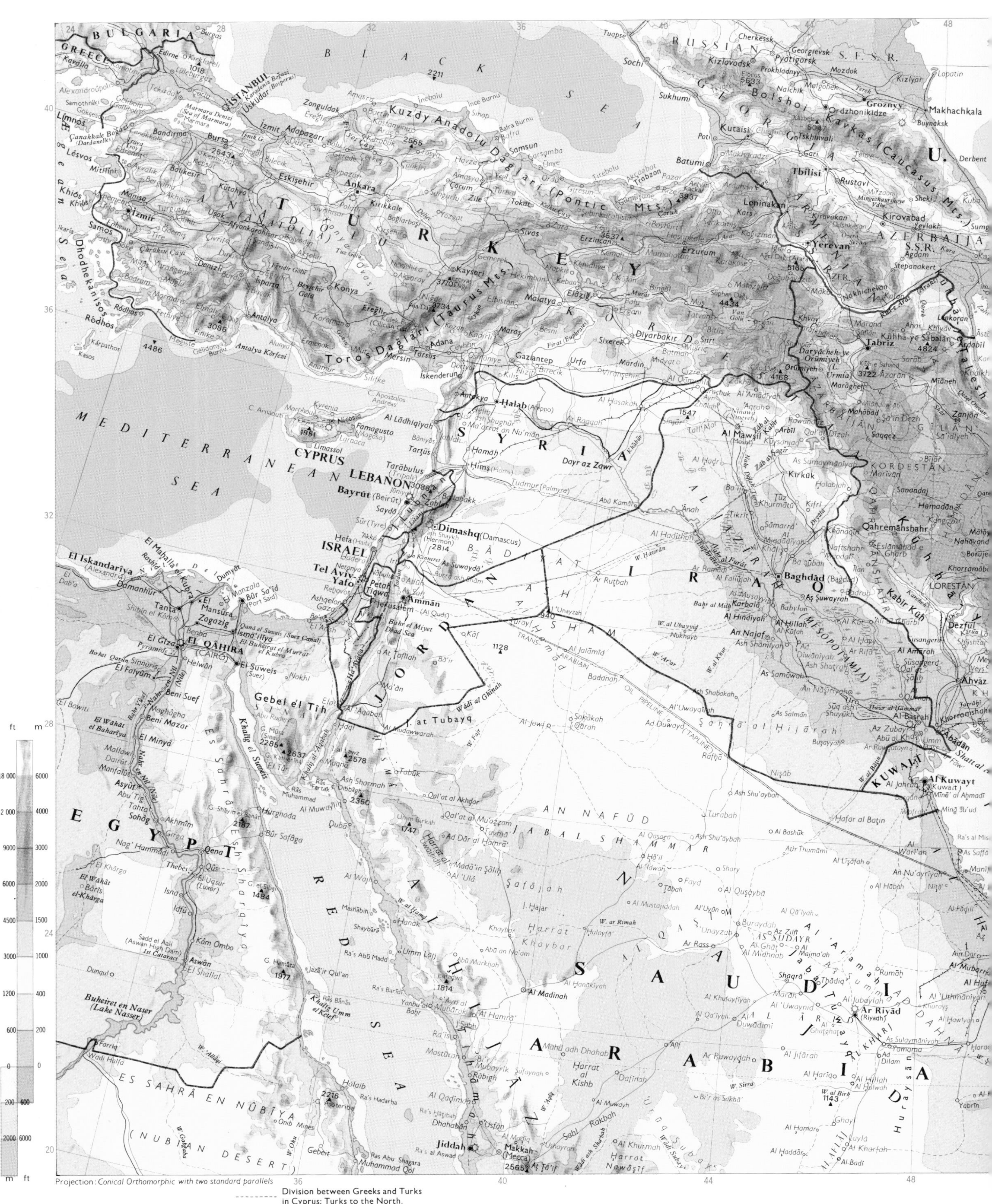

BULGARIA
GREECE
BLACK SEA
RUSSIAN S.F.S.R.
GEORGIA
Bolshoi Kavkas (Caucasus Mts.)
ARMENIAN S.S.R.
AZERBAIJAN S.S.R.
TURKEY
ANADOLU (ANATOLIA)
Kuzey Anadolu Dağlari (Pontic Mts.)
Toros Dağlari (Taurus Mts.)
İSTANBUL
Ankara
İzmir
Adana
Konya
Kayseri
Erzurum
Trabzon
Tbilisi
Yerevan
Baku
MEDITERRANEAN SEA
CYPRUS
Nicosia
SYRIA
Halab (Aleppo)
Dimashq (Damascus)
LEBANON
Bayrūt (Beirūt)
ISRAEL
Tel Aviv-Yafo
Jerusalem
JORDAN
'Ammān
IRAQ
Baghdād
Al Mawşil (Mosul)
Al Başrah
KUWAIT
Al Kuwayt (Kuwait)
Tabrīz
Kūh-ha-ye Zagros
EGYPT
El Qâhira (Cairo)
El Iskandarîya (Alexandria)
Bûr Sa'îd (Port Said)
El Suweis (Suez)
Aswân
Buheiret en Naser (Lake Nasser)
Es Sahrâ en Nûbîya (Nubian Desert)
RED SEA
SAUDI ARABIA
Al Madīnah
Makkah (Mecca)
Jiddah
Ar Riyāḍ (Riyadh)
AN NAFŪD
BĀDIYAT ASH SHAM
AL HIJĀZ
Ad Dahnā'
ft m
18 000 6000
12 000 4000
9000 3000
6000 2000
4500 1500
3000 1000
1200 400
600 200
0 0
200 600
2000 6000
m ft

Projection: *Conical Orthomorphic with two standard parallels*

Division between Greeks and Turks in Cyprus; Turks to the North.

1:10 000 000

100 0 100 200 300 miles

100 0 100 200 300 400 500 km

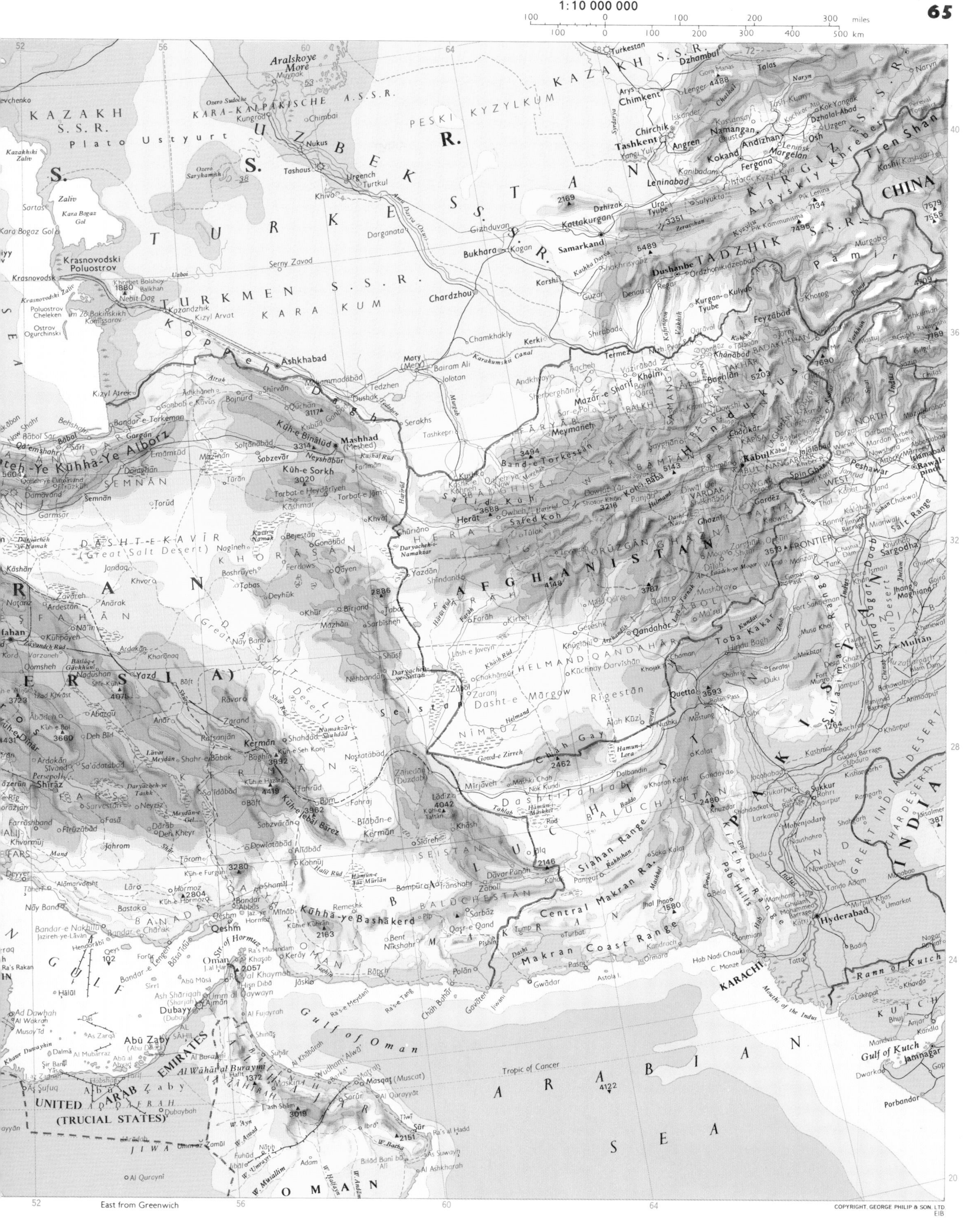

Aralskoye More
KAZAKH S.S.R.
Plato Ustyurt
KARA-KALPAKSKAYA A.S.S.R.
PESKI KYZYLKUM
UZBEK S.S.R.
TURKMEN S.S.R.
KARA KUM
Kara Bogaz Gol
Krasnovodskiy Poluostrov
Krasnovodsk
Nebit Dag
Kazandzhik
Kizyl Arvat
Nukus
Tashauz
Urgench
Khiva
Turtkul
Bukhara
Kagan
Samarkand
Kattakurgan
Dzhizak
Chardzhou
Karshi
Guzar
Chamkhakly
Kerki
Mary (Merv)
Bairam Ali
Iolotan
Tedzhen
Serakhs
Ashkhabad
Kopet Dagh
Karakumskiy Canal
Turkestan
Dzhambul
Talas
Arys
Chimkent
Chirchik
Tashkent
Yangi Yul
Angren
Namangan
Andizhan
Kokand
Fergana
Margelan
Osh
Leninabad
Kanibadam
Ura-Tyube
Dushanbe
Ordzhonikidzeabad
Regar
Denau
Kurgan-Tyube
Kulyab
Termez
TADZHIK S.S.R.
KIRGIZ S.S.R.
Alayskiy Khrebet
Pik Lenina 7134
Pik Kommunizma 7495
Pamir
Tien Shan
Kashi (Kashgar)
CHINA
Naryn
Dzhalal-Abad
Uzgen
Khorog
Feyzabad
BADAKHSHAN
Hindu Kush
Kunduz
Khanabad
Baghlan
Kholm
Mazar-e Sharif
Balkh
Sheberghan
Andkhvoy
Meymaneh
Band-e Torkestan
Herat
Safed Koh
Koh-i-Baba
Kabul
Jalalabad
Peshawar
Islamabad
Rawalpindi
NORTH WEST FRONTIER
Ghazni
Gardez
AFGHANISTAN
Qandahar
Farah
Shindand
Helmand
Dasht-e Margow
Rigestan
Chaghai Hills
Quetta
Bolan Pass
Zahedan (Duzdab)
Zabol
Seistan
Dasht-e Kavir (Great Salt Desert)
Dasht-e Lut (Great Sand Desert)
KHORASAN
Mashhad (Meshed)
Kuh-e Binalud
Neyshabur
Sabzevar
Bojnurd
Quchan
Shirvan
Torbat-e Heydariyeh
Torbat-e Jam
Kashmar
Gonabad
Ferdows
Qayen
Birjand
Tabas
Semnan
Damavand
Kuh-ha-ye Alborz
Gorgan
Babol
Sari
Kashan
Natanz
Ardestan
Anarak
Nain
Esfahan
Yazd
Bafq
Kerman
Rafsanjan
Sirjan
Bam
Shiraz
Fasa
Jahrom
Lar
Bandar Abbas
Qeshm
Minab
Kuh-ha-ye Bashakerd
BALUCHESTAN
Iranshahr
Khash
Taftan 4042
Jask
Chah Bahar
Gwadar
Pasni
Ormara
Makran Coast Range
Central Makran Ra.
Siahan Range
Kirthar Range
Pab Hills
Dasht-i-Tahlab
BALUCHISTAN
PAKISTAN
Karachi
Hyderabad
Kotri
Sukkur
Rohri
Shikarpur
Jacobabad
Larkana
Mohenjodaro
Nawabshah
SIND
Multan
Dera Ismail Khan
Dera Ghazi Khan
Sargodha
Sulaiman Range
Toba Kakar
Thal Desert
Sind Sagar Doab
Salt Range
THAR DESERT
GREAT INDIAN DESERT
INDIA
Jaisalmer
Rann of Kutch
Gulf of Kutch
Jamnagar
Dwarka
Porbandar
Mouths of the Indus
Ras Musandam
Str. of Hormuz
Oman
Al Khaymah
Umm al Qaywayn
Ash Shariqah (Sharjah)
Dubayy (Dubai)
Abu Zaby (Abu Dhabi)
UNITED ARAB EMIRATES (TRUCIAL STATES)
Al Buraymi
Suhar
Masqat (Muscat)
Sur
Ras al Hadd
OMAN
Gulf of Oman
Tropic of Cancer
ARABIAN SEA
Ad Dawhah
GULF
East from Greenwich

ft	m
18 000	6000
12 000	4000
9000	3000
6000	2000
4500	1500
3000	1000
1200	400
600	200
0	0
200	600
m	ft

Continuation Southwards on same scale

Projection: *Conical with two standard parallels*

1:10 000 000

50 0 50 100 150 200 miles

50 0 50 100 150 200 250 300 km

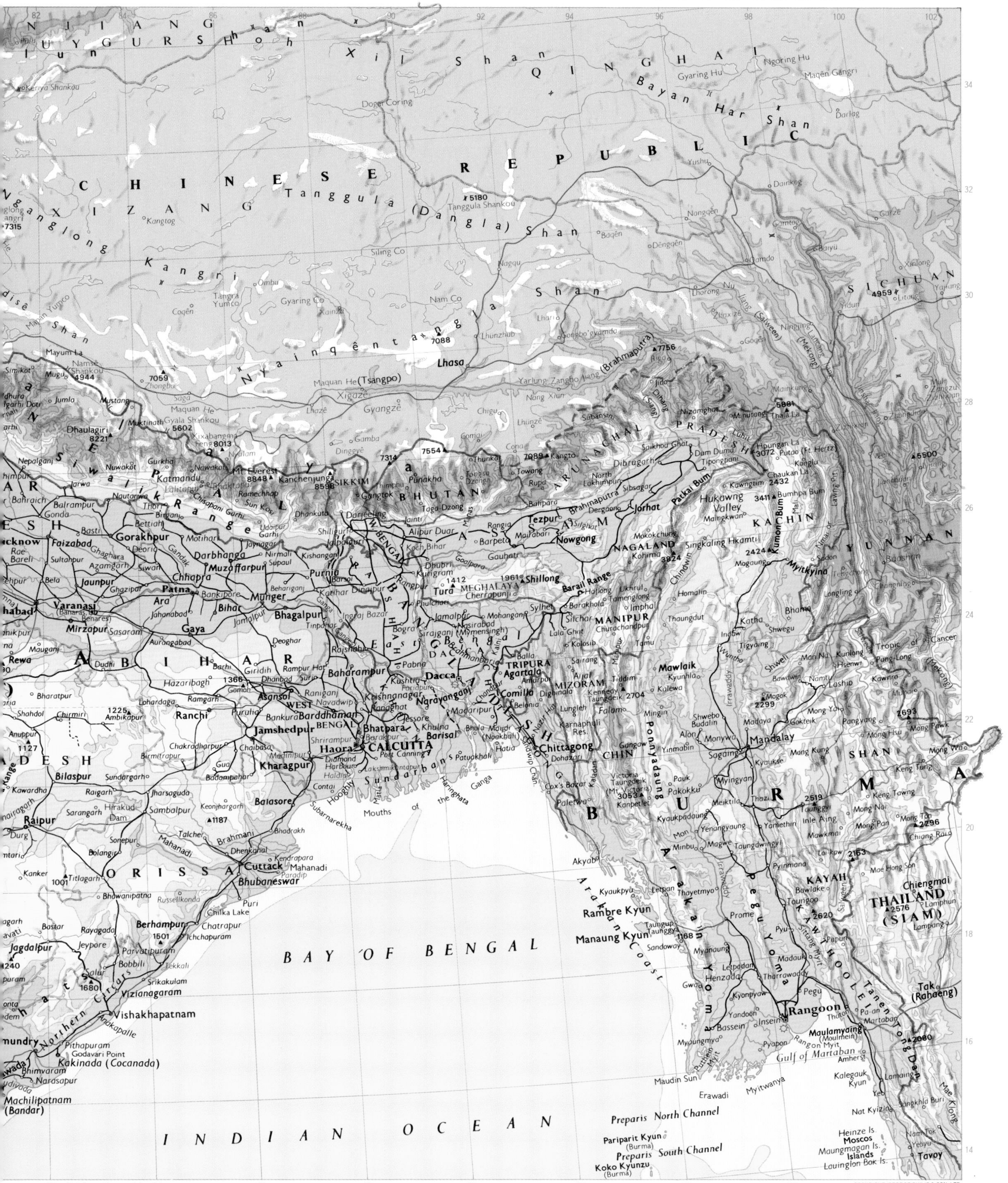

CHINESE REPUBLIC

XIZANG

QINGHAI

SICHUAN

YUNNAN

NEPAL

BHUTAN

SIKKIM

BANGLADESH

BURMA

THAILAND (SIAM)

BIHAR

ORISSA

WEST BENGAL

ASSAM

MEGHALAYA

ARUNACHAL PRADESH

NAGALAND

MANIPUR

MIZORAM

TRIPURA

BAY OF BENGAL

INDIAN OCEAN

Lhasa

CALCUTTA

Dacca

Rangoon

Mandalay

Mt. Everest 8848

Kanchenjunga 8598

Tanggula (Dangla) Shan

Nyainqêntanglha Shan

Bayan Har Shan

Xil Shan

Brahmaputra

Ganga

Irrawaddy

Mouths of the Ganga

Gulf of Martaban

Preparis North Channel

Preparis South Channel

Tropic of Cancer

East from Greenwich

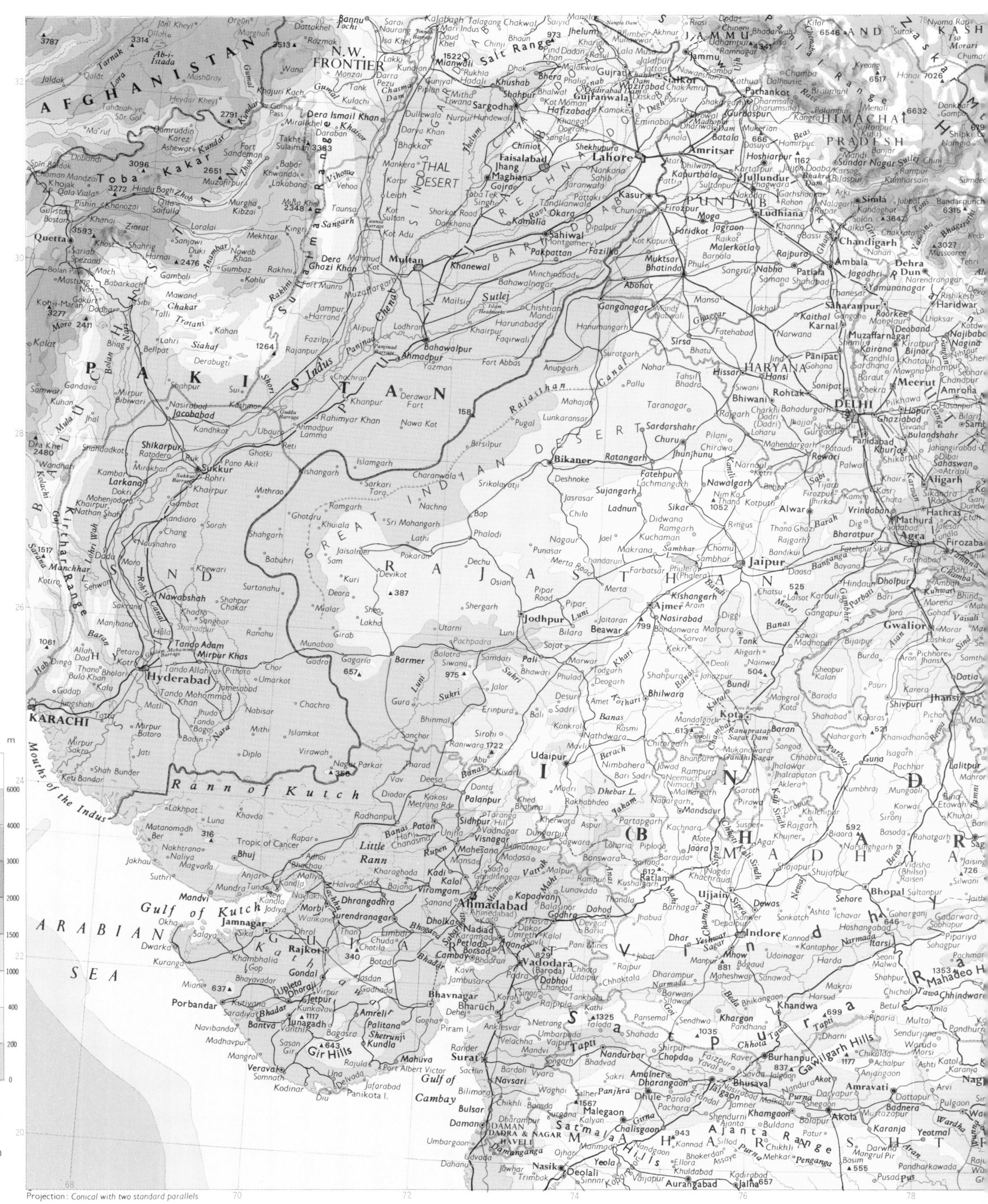
AFGHANISTAN
PAKISTAN
N.W. FRONTIER
THAL DESERT
Salt Range
PUNJAB
JAMMU
HIMACHAL PRADESH
HARYANA
DELHI
New Delhi
GREAT INDIAN DESERT
RAJASTHAN
SIND
INDIA
MADHYA PRADESH
GUJARAT
Rann of Kutch
Little Rann
Mouths of the Indus
Gulf of Kutch
Gulf of Cambay
ARABIAN SEA
Kirthar Range
Toba Kakar
Sulaiman Range
Satpura Range
Vindhya Range
Ajanta Range
Satmala Hills
Gawilgarh Hills
Gir Hills
Tropic of Cancer
Indus
Sutlej
Chenab
Jhelum
Ravi
Beas
Luni
Narmada
Tapti
Chambal
Rajasthan Canal
Quetta
Multan
Bahawalpur
Lahore
Amritsar
Faisalabad
Sargodha
Jhelum
Jammu
Sialkot
Gujranwala
Ludhiana
Jullundur
Simla
Chandigarh
Patiala
Ambala
Dehra Dun
Saharanpur
Meerut
Agra
Mathura
Aligarh
Gwalior
Jhansi
Bikaner
Jodhpur
Jaipur
Ajmer
Kota
Udaipur
Barmer
Sukkur
Larkana
Jacobabad
Shikarpur
Hyderabad
Mirpur Khas
KARACHI
Nawabshah
Dera Ismail Khan
Dera Ghazi Khan
Bhuj
Jamnagar
Rajkot
Porbandar
Junagadh
Bhavnagar
Ahmadabad
Vadodara (Baroda)
Surat
Daman
DADRA & NAGAR HAVELI
Indore
Ujjain
Bhopal
Ratlam
Khandwa
Burhanpur
Jalgaon
Bhusaval
Akola
Amravati
Nasik
Aurangabad
Jalna
Malegaon
Dhule
ft m
18 000 6000
12 000 4000
9000 3000
6000 2000
4500 1500
3000 1000
1200 400
600 200
0 0
200 600
2000 6000
m ft
Projection: Conical with two standard parallels

1:6 000 000

50 0 50 100 150 miles

50 0 50 100 150 200 250 km

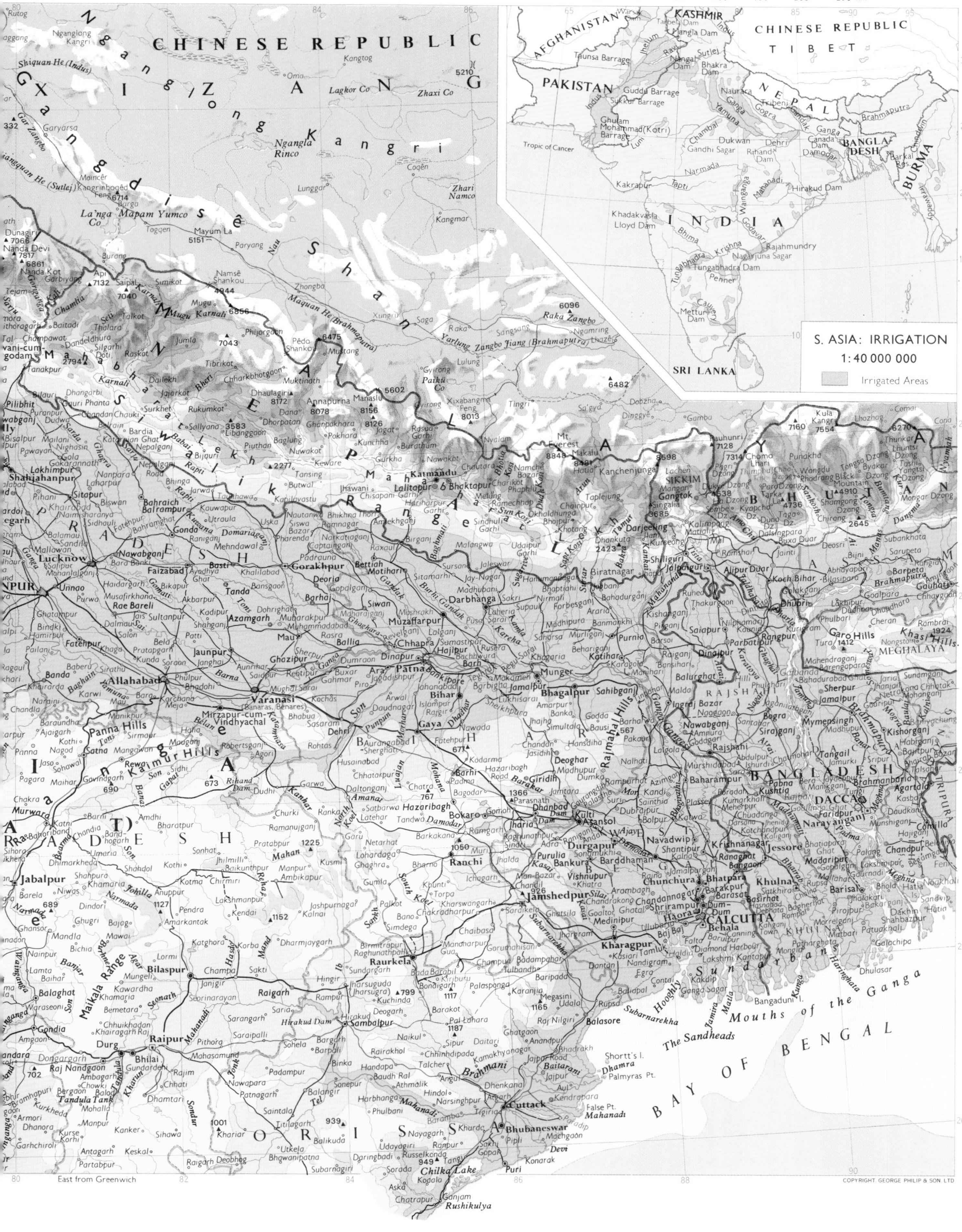

CHINESE REPUBLIC

X I Z A N G

Gangdisê Shan

Nganglong Kangri

N E P A L

U T T A R P R A D E S H

M A D H Y A P R A D E S H

B I H A R

W E S T B E N G A L

O R I S S A

BANGLADESH

B H U T A N

SIKKIM

MEGHALAYA

TRIPURA

BAY OF BENGAL

Mouths of the Ganga

The Sandheads

Sundarbans

Mt. Everest 8848

Kanchenjunga

Annapurna 8078

Dhaulagiri 8172

Manaslu 8156

Katmandu

Lucknow

Allahabad

Varanasi (Banaras, Benares)

Patna

Gaya

Ranchi

Jamshedpur

CALCUTTA

DACCA

Cuttack

Bhubaneswar

Puri

Jabalpur

Raipur

Bilaspur

Sambalpur

Darjeeling

Gangtok

Kaimur Hills

Rajmahal Hills

Maikala Range

Panna Hills

Garo Hills

Khasi Hills

Chilka Lake

Hirakud Dam

Shortt's I.

Palmyras Pt.

False Pt.

S. ASIA: IRRIGATION

1:40 000 000

Irrigated Areas

AFGHANISTAN

KASHMIR

PAKISTAN

CHINESE REPUBLIC

TIBET

NEPAL

INDIA

BANGLADESH

BURMA

SRI LANKA

Tropic of Cancer

Warsak Dam, Tarbela Dam, Mangla Dam, Taunsa Barrage, Nangal Dam, Bhakra Dam, Guddu Barrage, Sukkur Barrage, Ghulam Mohammad (Kotri) Barrage, Chambal, Gandhi Sagar, Rihand Dam, Dukwan, Dehri, Ganga, Canada Dam, Damodar, Narmada, Tapti, Kakrapur, Hirakud Dam, Khadakvasla, Lloyd Dam, Rajahmundry, Nagarjuna Sagar, Tungabhadra Dam, Mettur Dam

East from Greenwich

1:6 000 000

50 0 50 100 150 miles

50 0 50 100 150 200 250 km

SRI LANKA
On same scale

ft	m
6000	2000
4500	1500
3000	1000
1200	400
600	200
0	0
200	600
2000	6000
4000	12 000
m	ft

Projection: Conical with two standard parallels

East from Greenwich

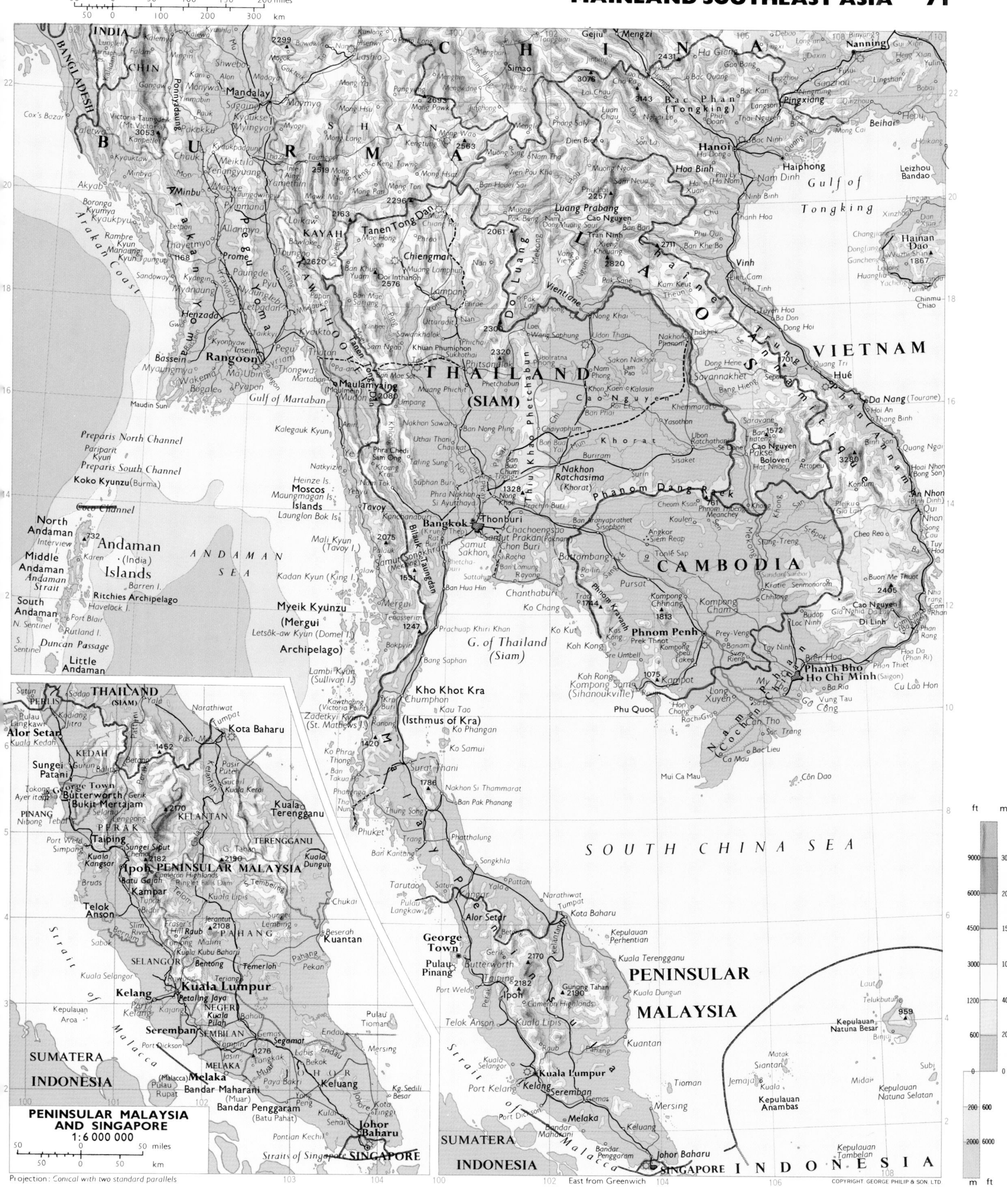
1:10 000 000
miles
km
INDIA
BANGLADESH
CHIN
Mandalay
Sagaing
Shwebo
Monywa
Maymyo
Lashio
Kyaukse
Meiktila
Myingyan
Pakokku
Cox's Bazar
Victoria Taungdeik (Mt Victoria) 3053
Kanpetlet
Paletwa
B U R M A
S H A N
Taunggyi
Yamethin
Minbu
Magwe
Pyinmana
Akyab
Boronga
Kyaukpyu
Ramree
Kyun
Thayetmyo
Prome
Sandoway
Arakan Coast
Arakan Yoma
Pegu Yoma
Irrawaddy
Henzada
Bassein
Rangoon
Pegu
Syriam
Thaton
Maulamyaing (Moulmein)
Martaban
Gulf of Martaban
KAYAH
Loikaw
Toungoo
Tanen Tong Dan
Dawna Range
Chiengmai
Doi Inthanon 2576
Lampang
Maudin Sun
Preparis North Channel
Preparis South Channel
Koko Kyunzu (Burma)
Coco Channel
North Andaman
Middle Andaman
South Andaman
Andaman (India) Islands
Andaman Strait
Ritchies Archipelago
Havelock I.
Port Blair
Rutland I.
N. Sentinel
S. Sentinel
Duncan Passage
Little Andaman
A N D A M A N S E A
Kalegauk Kyun
Heinze Is.
Moscos Islands
Launglon Bok Is
Tavoy
Mali Kyun (Tavoy I.)
Kadan Kyun (King I.)
Myeik Kyunzu (Mergui Archipelago)
Mergui
Letsôk-aw Kyun (Domel I.)
Tenasserim
Lambi Kyun (Sullivan I.)
Zadetkyi Kyun (St. Matthew's I.)
Victoria Point
C H I N A
Kunming
Gejiu
Mengzi
Simao
Nanning
Pingxiang
Beihai
Hainan Dao
Leizhou Bandao
Haiphong
Hanoi
Bac Phan (Tongking)
Dien Bien
Hoa Binh
Nam Dinh
Gulf of Tongking
Luang Prabang
Vientiane
L A O S
Doi Luang
Mekong
Vinh
Savannakhet
Hué
Da Nang (Tourane)
Quang Ngai
VIETNAM
Annamitique
Khorat
Nakhon Ratchasima (Khorat)
Ubon Ratchathani
Phanom Dang Raek
T H A I L A N D (SIAM)
Phitsanulok
Nakhon Sawan
Bangkok
Thonburi
Chao Phraya
Samut Prakan
Chon Buri
Gulf of Thailand (Siam)
Ko Chang
Chanthaburi
Prachuap Khiri Khan
Bang Saphan
Kho Khot Kra (Isthmus of Kra)
Chumphon
Ko Phangan
Ko Samui
Surat Thani
Nakhon Si Thammarat
Phuket
Trang
Songkhla
Pattani
Narathiwat
C A M B O D I A
Tonlé Sap
Battambang
Siem Reap
Kompong Chhnang
Kompong Cham
Phnom Penh
Kompong Som (Sihanoukville)
Kampot
Phu Quoc
Kratie
Stung-Treng
Buon Me Thuot
Kontum
Cao Nguyen
Da Lat
Di Linh
Phanh Bho Ho Chi Minh (Saigon)
Vung Tau
Cu Lao Hon
Can Tho
Soc Trang
Bac Lieu
Ca Mau
Mui Ca Mau
Côn Dao
Long Xuyen
My Tho
S O U T H C H I N A S E A
PENINSULAR MALAYSIA
Alor Setar
George Town
Pulau Pinang
Butterworth
Taiping
Ipoh
Cameron Highlands
Kota Baharu
Kuala Terengganu
Kepulauan Perhentian
Kuantan
Kuala Lumpur
Port Kelang
Seremban
Port Dickson
Melaka
Mersing
Tioman
Keluang
Johor Baharu
SINGAPORE
Strait of Malacca
SUMATERA
INDONESIA
I N D O N E S I A
Kepulauan Anambas
Kepulauan Natuna Besar
Kepulauan Natuna Selatan
Kepulauan Tambelan
PENINSULAR MALAYSIA AND SINGAPORE
1:6 000 000
THAILAND (SIAM)
PERLIS
KEDAH
PINANG
PERAK
KELANTAN
TERENGGANU
PAHANG
SELANGOR
NEGERI SEMBILAN
MELAKA
JOHOR
Sungei Patani
Bukit Mertajam
Telok Anson
Kelang
Petaling Jaya
Segamat
Muar
Bandar Maharani
Bandar Penggaram (Batu Pahat)
Kepulauan Aroa
Straits of Singapore
Projection: Conical with two standard parallels
East from Greenwich
COPYRIGHT GEORGE PHILIP & SON LTD
ft
m

BURMA
Rangoon
Moulmein
G. of Martaban
Thaton
Tavoy
Mergui
Victoria Point
THAILAND (SIAM)
Bangkok (Krung Thep)
Phra Nakhon Si Ayutthaya
Nakhon Ratchasima (Khorat)
Phitsanulok
Uttaradit
Udon Thani
Nong Khai
Ubon Ratchathani
Phnom Dangrek
Chumphon
Kho Khot Kra
Ranong
Surat Thani
Ko Samui
Nakhon Si Thammarat
Phuket
Songkhla (Singora)
Pattani
Gulf of Thailand (Siam)
LAOS
Savannakhet
Thakhek
Pakse
Attopeu
Saravane
CAMBODIA
Phnom Penh
Battambang
Siem Reap
Kompong Cham
Kampot
Kompong Som
Phu Quoc
VIET-NAM
Hue
Da Nang (Tourane)
Quang Ngai
Qui Nhon
Nha Trang
Phan Rang
Bien Hoa
PHANH BHO HO CHI MINH (Saigon)
Vung Tau
Can Tho
Ca Mau
Mui Bai Bung
Con Son
Mui Varella
Mui Ca Na
Hsisha
Chuntao
Spratly I.
Amboyna I.
Palawan
Islands (Philippines)
ANDAMAN SEA
SOUTH CHINA SEA
Strait of Malacca
MALAYSIA
PENINSULAR MALAYSIA
George Town
Kota Baharu
Kuala Terengganu
Ipoh
Taiping
Kuala Lumpur
Port Kelang
Seremban
Melaka
Kuantan
Johor Baharu
SINGAPORE
Kepulauan Natuna Besar
Kepulauan Anambas
SARAWAK
Kuching
Sibu
Bintulu
Miri
BRUNEI
Bandar Seri Begawan
SABAH
Kota Kinabalu (Jesselton)
Kinabalu 4101
Kudat
BORNEO
KALIMANTAN
Pontianak
Singkawang
Banjarmasin
Kotabaru
Pulau Laut
INDONESIA
SUMATERA
ACEH
Banda Aceh (Kutaraja)
Sabang
Medan
Belawan
Simeulue
Nias
Sibolga
Padang
Bukittinggi
Siberut
Kepulauan Mentawai
Pakanbaru
RIAU
Jambi
Palembang
Bengkulu
Enggano
LAMPUNG
Tanjungkarang
Telukbetung
Bangka
Pangkalpinang
Belitung (Billiton)
Kepulauan Riau
Kepulauan Lingga
Selat Karimata
JAVA SEA
Greater Sunda Islands
JAWA (JAVA)
JAKARTA
Bogor
Bandung
Cirebon
Semarang
Surakarta
Yogyakarta
Surabaya
Malang
Madura
BALI
Lombok
NUSA TENGG
INDIAN OCEAN
Java Trench
6650
6073
4424
Projection: Mercator
East from Greenwich

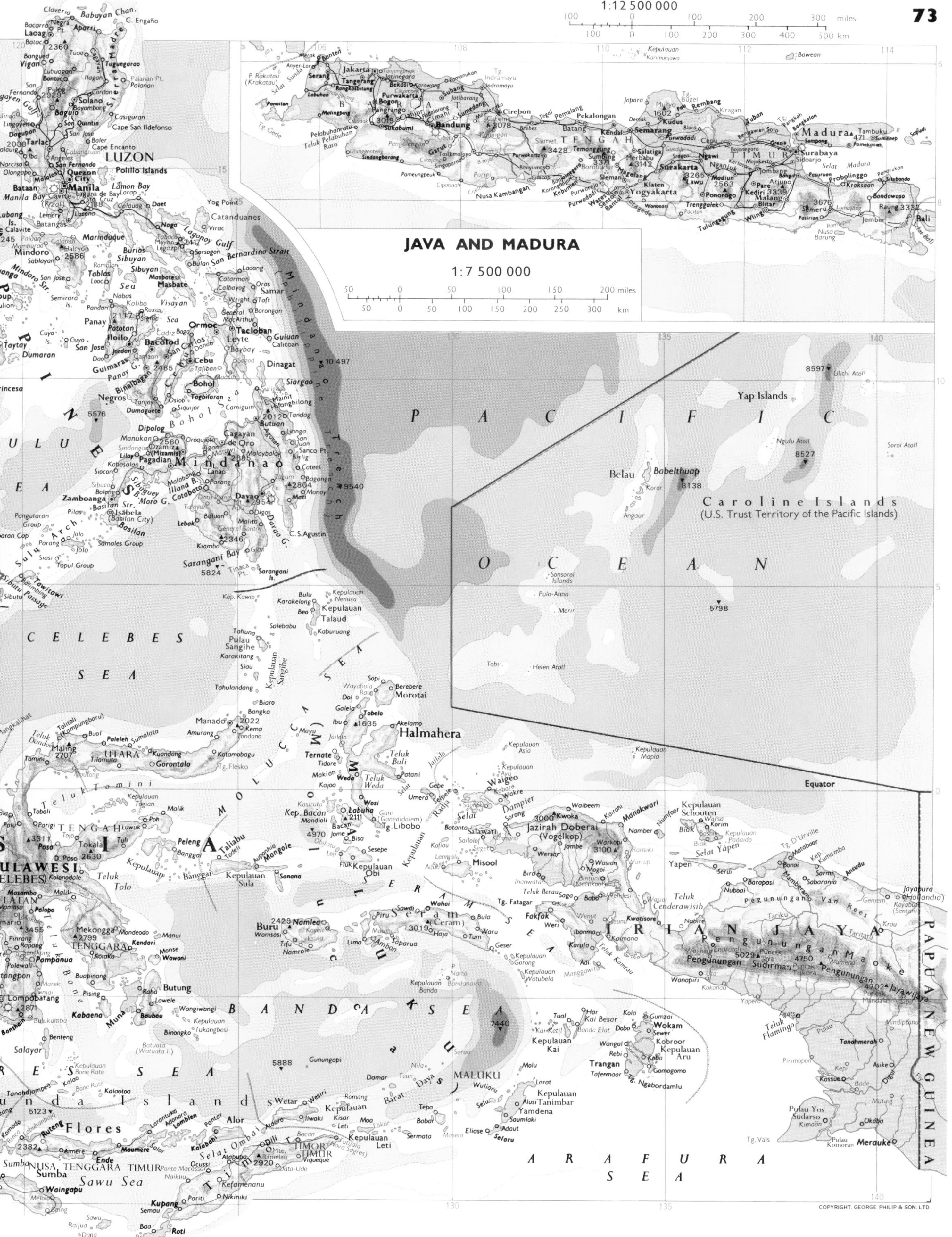
1:12 500 000
miles
km
JAVA AND MADURA
1:7 500 000
miles
km
LUZON
Polillo Islands
Manila
Lamon Bay
Manila Bay
Catanduanes
Marinduque
Mindoro
Sibuyan Sea
Masbate
Samar
Panay
Leyte
Negros
Cebu
Bohol
Dinagat
Siargao
Mindanao
Bohol Sea
Sulu Sea
Sulu Arch.
Celebes Sea
Mindanao (Philippine) Trench
10 497
9540
Pacific Ocean
Yap Islands
Belau
Babelthuap
Caroline Islands
(U.S. Trust Territory of the Pacific Islands)
Kepulauan Talaud
Molucca Sea
Morotai
Halmahera
Ternate
Teluk Tomini
Sulawesi
(Celebes)
Teluk Bone
Kepulauan Sula
Kepulauan Banggai
Buru
Seram
(Ceram)
Ceram Sea
Banda Sea
Flores
Flores Sea
Sumba
Sawu Sea
Nusa Tenggara Timur
Timor
Alor
Kepulauan Kai
Kepulauan Aru
Kepulauan Tanimbar
Maluku
Waigeo
Misool
Jazirah Doberai
(Vogelkop)
Teluk Cenderawasih
Irian Jaya
Pegunungan Sudirman
Pegunungan Jayawijaya
Puncak Jaya
5029
Jayapura
(Hollandia)
Merauke
Papua New Guinea
Arafura Sea
Equator
Jakarta
Bandung
Semarang
Yogyakarta
Surakarta
Surabaya
Madura
Malang
Bali

1:5 000 000

Projection: Conical with two standard parallels

East from Greenwich

Continuation Southwards on same scale

1:10 000 000

Projection: Bonne

East from Greenwich

REFERENCE TO PREFECTURES

HOKKAIDŌ DISTRICT	KINKI DISTRICT
1 Hokkaidō	24 Hyogo
TŌHOKU DISTRICT	25 Kyōto
2 Aomori	26 Shiga
3 Akita	27 Ōsaka
4 Iwate	28 Nara
5 Yamagata	29 Mie
6 Miyagi	30 Wakayama
7 Fukushima	CHŪGOKU DISTRICT
CHŪBU DISTRICT	31 Tottori
8 Niigata	32 Okayama
9 Ishikawa	33 Shimane
10 Toyama	34 Hiroshima
11 Fukui	35 Yamaguchi
12 Gifu	SHIKOKU DISTRICT
13 Nagano	36 Kagawa
14 Yamanashi	37 Tokushima
15 Aichi	38 Ehime
16 Shizuoka	39 Kōchi
KANTŌ DISTRICT	KYŪSHŪ DISTRICT
17 Gumma	40 Fukuoka
18 Tochigi	41 Saga
19 Saitama	42 Nagasaki
20 Ibaraki	43 Kumamoto
21 Tōkyō	44 Ōita
22 Chiba	45 Miyazaki
23 Kanagawa	46 Kagoshima

1:20 000 000

100 0 100 200 300 400 miles

100 0 100 200 300 400 500 600 km

UNION OF SOVIET SOCIALIST REPUBLICS

U. S. S. R.

MONGOLIA

CHINA

XIZANG (TIBET)

JAPAN

NORTH KOREA

SOUTH KOREA

TAIWAN (FORMOSA)

PHILIPPINES

VIETNAM

LAOS

THAILAND (SIAM)

BURMA

BANGLADESH

BHUTAN

NEPAL

INDIA

JAMMU & KASHMIR

KAZAKH S.S.R.

KIRGIZ S.S.R.

EAST CHINA SEA

YELLOW SEA

SOUTH CHINA SEA

BAY OF BENGAL

BEIJING

SHANGHAI

TIANJIN

Tropic of Cancer

East from Greenwich

Projection: Bonne

m 6000 4000 3000 2000 1500 1000 400 200 0 200 2000 4000 6000 m

ft 18 000 12 000 9000 6000 4500 3000 1200 600 0 600 6000 12 000 18 000 ft

U.S.S.R.
MONGOLIA
NEI MONGGOL ZIZHIQU
HEILONGJIANG
JILIN
LIAONING
HEBEI
NINGXIA HUIZU ZIZHIQU
Alxa Zuoqi (Bayan Hot)
NORTH KOREA
SOUTH KOREA
SEA OF JAPAN
YELLOW
Bo Hai (Gulf of Chihli)
Korea Bay
Cease Fire Line
HARBIN
CHANGCHUN
SHENYANG
BEIJING
TIANJIN
TAIYUAN
LÜDA
Qiqihar
Jilin
Fushun
Anshan
Dandong
Shijiazhuang
Baotou
Hohhot
Datong
Lanzhou
Pyŏngyang
SOUL (Seoul)
Inch'ŏn
Vladivostok
Khabarovsk
Blagoveshchensk
Chita
Ulan Ude
Irkutsk
Ulaanbaatar (Ulan Bator)
Hailar
THE GREAT WALL
Mu Us Shamo (Ordos)
Yablonovyy Khrebet
Borshchovochnyy Khrebet
Da Hinggan Ling
Xiao Hinggan Ling
Ozero Baikal

1:10 000 000

50 0 50 100 150 200 250 miles

50 0 50 100 150 200 250 300 350 400 km

EAST CHINA SEA
SOUTH CHINA SEA
PACIFIC OCEAN
JAPAN
Nansei-shotō
Ryūkyū-rettō
Okinawa
Naha
Kagoshima
Nagasaki
Fukuoka
Cheju Do (Quelpart)
Tropic of Cancer
Formosa Strait
TAIWAN (FORMOSA)
TAIBEI
Gaoxiong
Tainan
Taizhong
Penghu
Bashi Channel
Batan Is.
Babuyan Is.
Luzon
PHILIPPINES
SHANGHAI
Hangzhou
Ningbo
Suzhou
Wuxi
NANJING
Hefei
Xuzhou
Zhengzhou
Luoyang
Xi'an
WUHAN
Hankou
Hanyang
Changsha
Nanchang
Fuzhou
Xiamen
Shantou
GUANGZHOU (Canton)
Kowloon
Victoria
HONGKONG (Br.)
Macau (Port.)
Zhanjiang
Haikou
Hainan
CHONGQING
Guiyang
Nanning
Liuzhou
Guilin
HANOI
Haiphong
VIETNAM
Gulf of Tongking
JIANGSU
ANHUI
HENAN
HUBEI
HUNAN
JIANGXI
ZHEJIANG
FUJIAN
GUANGDONG
GUANGXI-ZHUANGZU ZIZHIQU
GUIZHOU
SICHUAN
CHINA
Projection: Lambert's Equivalent Azimuthal
East from Greenwich
COPYRIGHT GEORGE PHILIP & SON, LTD.

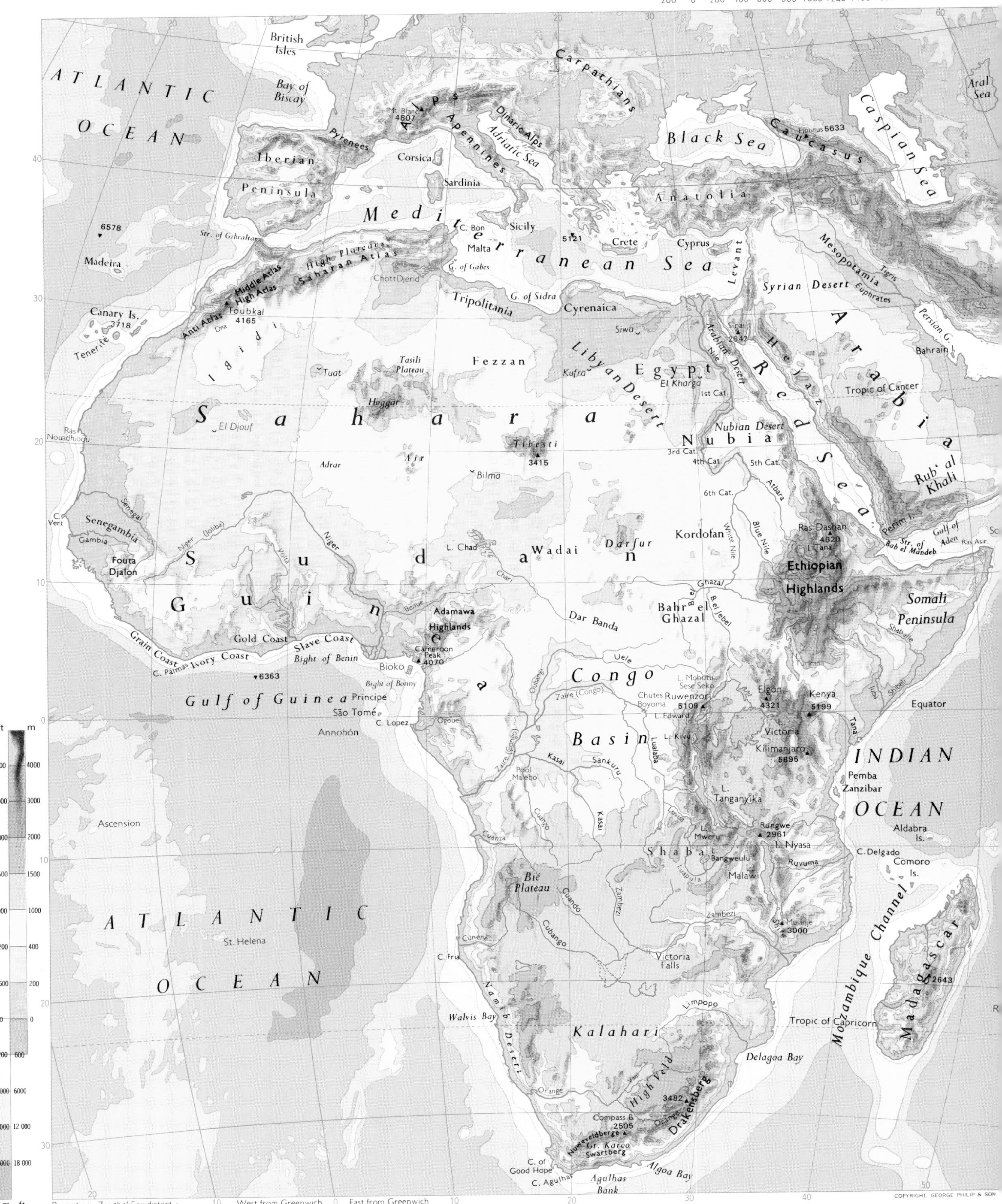
1:40 000 000
200 0 200 400 600 800 1000 miles
200 0 200 400 600 800 1000 1200 1400 1600 km
ATLANTIC OCEAN
British Isles
Bay of Biscay
Alps
Mt. Blanc 4807
Carpathians
Dinaric Alps
Apennines
Adriatic Sea
Pyrenees
Iberian Peninsula
Corsica
Sardinia
Black Sea
Caucasus
Elburus 5633
Caspian Sea
Aral Sea
Anatolia
Mediterranean Sea
6578
Madeira
Str. of Gibraltar
C. Bon
Sicily
Malta
5121
Crete
Cyprus
Levant
Mesopotamia
Tigris
Euphrates
Syrian Desert
High Plateaus
Saharan Atlas
Middle Atlas
High Atlas
Anti Atlas
Toubkal 4165
G. of Gabes
Chott Djerid
Tripolitania
G. of Sidra
Cyrenaica
Canary Is.
3718
Tenerife
Igidi
Siwa
Sinai 2642
Arabian Desert
Hejaz
Arabia
Persian G.
Bahrain
Tasili Plateau
Tuat
Fezzan
Libyan Desert
Kufra
Egypt
El Kharga
Nile
1st Cat.
Red Sea
Tropic of Cancer
Hoggar
Sahara
El Djouf
Ras Nouadhibou
Tibesti 3415
Nubian Desert
Nubia
3rd Cat.
4th Cat.
5th Cat.
Adrar
Air
Bilma
Atbara
6th Cat.
Rub' al Khali
C. Vert
Senegal
Senegambia
Gambia
Niger (Joliba)
Volta
Niger
L. Chad
Wadai
Darfur
Kordofan
White Nile
Blue Nile
Ras Dashan 4620
L. Tana
Perim I.
Str. of Bab el Mandeb
Gulf of Aden
Ras Asir
Fouta Djalon
Sudan
Chari
Ethiopian Highlands
Bahr el Ghazal
Bahr el Jebel
Somali Peninsula
Shabale
Guinea
Benue
Adamawa Highlands
Dar Banda
Grain Coast
Gold Coast
Slave Coast
Ivory Coast
C. Palmas
Bight of Benin
Cameroon Peak 4070
Bioko
Bight of Bonny
6363
Uele
Congo Basin
Turkana
L. Mobutu Sese Seko
Ruwenzori 5109
Elgon 4321
Kenya 5199
Juba
Shibeli
Equator
Gulf of Guinea
Principe
São Tomé
C. Lopez
Annobón
Ogooue
Oubangi
Zaïre (Congo)
Chutes Boyoma
L. Edward
L. Kivu
L. Victoria
Kilimanjaro 5895
Tana
Lualaba
Kasai
Sankuru
Pool Malebo
Zaïre (Congo)
Cuango
INDIAN OCEAN
Pemba
Zanzibar
L. Tanganyika
Ascension
Luvua
L. Mweru
Rungwe 2961
L. Nyasa
Aldabra Is.
Cuanza
Shaba
L. Bangweulu
L. Malawi
Ruvuma
C. Delgado
Comoro Is.
Bié Plateau
Cuando
Zambezi
Luapula
Mulanje 3000
Shire
Mozambique Channel
Madagascar
2643
ATLANTIC OCEAN
St. Helena
Cunene
Cubango
C. Fria
Victoria Falls
Namib Desert
Walvis Bay
Limpopo
Tropic of Capricorn
Kalahari
Delagoa Bay
High Veld
Vaal
Orange
3482
Drakensberg
Compass B. 2505
Nuweveldberge
Gt. Karoo
Swartberg
C. of Good Hope
C. Agulhas
Agulhas Bank
Algoa Bay
ft m
12 000 4000
9000 3000
6000 2000
4500 1500
3000 1000
1200 400
600 200
0 0
200 600
2000 6000
4000 12 000
6000 18 000
m ft
Projection: Zenithal Equidistant.
West from Greenwich
East from Greenwich

1:40 000 000

200 0 200 400 600 800 1000 miles

200 0 200 400 600 800 1000 1200 1400 1600 km

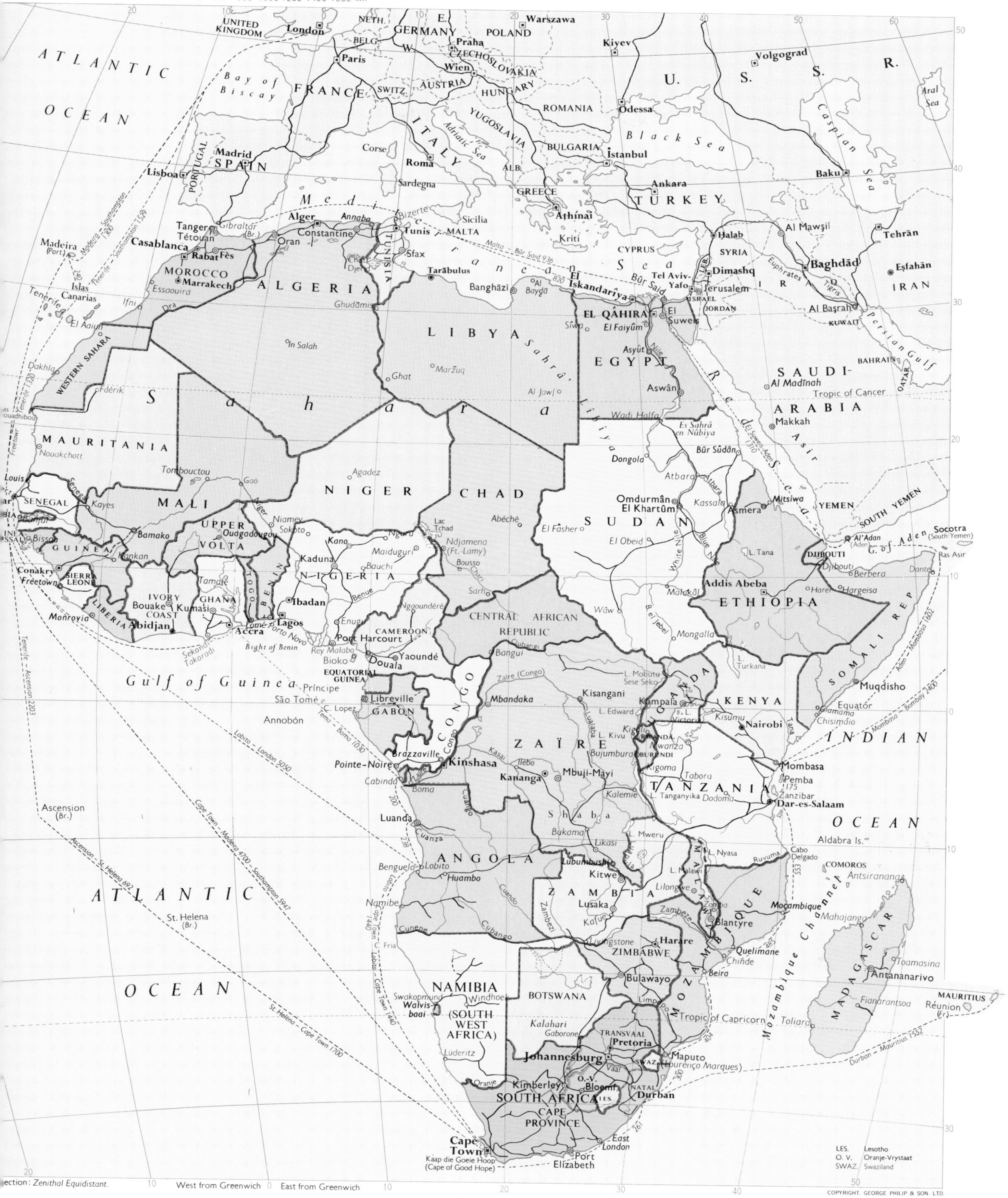

ATLANTIC OCEAN

UNITED KINGDOM London NETH. BELG. E. GERMANY W. GERMANY POLAND Warszawa Praha CZECHOSLOVAKIA Wien AUSTRIA HUNGARY Kiyev Volgograd U. S. S. R. Aral Sea Caspian Sea Paris FRANCE SWITZ. Bay of Biscay ROMANIA Odessa YUGOSLAVIA Adriatic Sea Black Sea ITALY BULGARIA İstanbul Baku Corse Roma ALB. Madrid SPAIN PORTUGAL Lisboa Sardegna GREECE Ankara TURKEY Athínai Sicilia MALTA Kriti CYPRUS Mediterranean Sea

Tanger Tétouan Gibraltar (Br.) Alger Annaba Constantine Oran Tunis Bizerte TUNISIA Sfax Djerba Casablanca Rabat Fès MOROCCO Marrakech Essaouira Ifni Dra ALGERIA Ghudāmis Tarābulus Banghāzi Al Baydā El Iskandarîya Bûr Saîd Tel Aviv-Yafo Jerusalem ISRAEL JORDAN LEB. Dimashq SYRIA Halab Al Mawşil Tehrān Baghdād Eşfahān IRAN IRAQ Euphrates Tigris Al Başrah KUWAIT Persian Gulf BAHRAIN QATAR

Madeira (Port.) Islas Canarias Tenerife El Aaiún WESTERN SAHARA Dakhla Fdérik Nouadhibou Sahara In Salah LIBYA Ghat Marzūq Al Jawf Sahrā' Lībīya EL QÂHIRA El Faiyûm Sîwa EL Suweis Asyût EGYPT Nile Aswân Wadi Halfa Es Sahrâ en Nûbîya Red Sea SAUDI ARABIA Al Madīnah Makkah Tropic of Cancer Asir

MAURITANIA Nouakchott Tombouctou Gao St. Louis SENEGAL Kayes Senegal MALI Agadez NIGER CHAD Dongola Bûr Sûdân Atbara Omdurmân El Khartûm Kassala Asmera Mitsiwa YEMEN SOUTH YEMEN Socotra (South Yemen) Al 'Adan (Aden) Gulf of Aden Ras Asir GAMBIA Banjul GUINEA-BISSAU Bissau GUINEA Kankan Conakry Freetown SIERRA LEONE Bamako UPPER VOLTA Ouagadougou Niamey Sokoto Kano Nguru Lac Tchad Ndjamena (Ft.-Lamy) Abéché El Fasher SUDAN El Obeid White Nile Blue Nile L. Tana DJIBOUTI Djibouti Berbera Dante

Kaduna Maiduguri Bauchi NIGERIA Bousso Chari Benue Tamale GHANA IVORY COAST Bouake Kumasi TOGO BENIN Ibadan Lagos Porto Novo Lomé Accra LIBERIA Monrovia Abidjan Sekondi Takoradi Bight of Benin Enugu Port Harcourt Ngaoundéré CAMEROON Sarh CENTRAL AFRICAN REPUBLIC Wâw Malakâl Bahr el Jebel Addis Abeba ETHIOPIA Harer Hargeisa SOMALI REP. Mongalla

Rey Malabo Bioko Douala Yaoundé EQUATORIAL GUINEA Bangui Ubangi Gulf of Guinea Príncipe São Tomé C. Lopez Annobón Libreville GABON CONGO Zaïre (Congo) Mbandaka L. Mobutu Sese Seko Kisangani UGANDA Kampala L. Turkana KENYA L. Victoria L. Edward Equator Kisumu Nairobi Tana Muqdisho Chisimaio Lualaba L. Kivu Kigali RWANDA BURUNDI Bujumbura Mwanza ZAÏRE Brazzaville Kinshasa Pointe-Noire Cabinda Boma Ilebo Kasai Kananga Mbuji-Mayi Kigoma Tabora TANZANIA Mombasa Pemba Zanzibar Dar-es-Salaam Kalemie L. Tanganyika Dodoma Cuango Luanda Cuanza Shaba Bukama L. Mweru Likasi Lubumbashi Kitwe L. Nyasa Ruvuma L. Malawi Cabo Delgado COMOROS Antsiranana Aldabra Is. INDIAN OCEAN

Benguela Lobito Huambo ANGOLA Namibe ZAMBIA Lusaka Kafue Lilongwe MALAWI Zomba Blantyre Moçambique Zambeze Zambezi Cuando Cubango Cunene Fria Livingstone Harare ZIMBABWE Quelimane Chinde Beira MOZAMBIQUE Mozambique Channel Mahajanga MADAGASCAR Toamasina Antananarivo Fianarantsoa Toliara MAURITIUS Réunion (Fr.)

NAMIBIA (SOUTH WEST AFRICA) Swakopmund Windhoek Walvis-baai BOTSWANA Bulawayo Limpopo Kalahari Gaborone TRANSVAAL Pretoria Tropic of Capricorn Johannesburg SWAZ. Maputo (Lourenço Marques) Vaal Lüderitz Oranje Kimberley O.V. Bloemf. NATAL Durban LES. SOUTH AFRICA CAPE PROVINCE East London Cape Town Port Elizabeth Kaap die Goeie Hoop (Cape of Good Hope)

Ascension (Br.) St. Helena (Br.) ATLANTIC OCEAN

Madeira – Southampton 1300; Tenerife – Southampton 1529; Malta – Bûr Saîd 936; Tenerife – Ascension 2203; Lobito – London 5050; Temo – Boma 1030; Cape Town – Madeira 4700 – Southampton 5947; Ascension – St. Helena 692; St. Helena – Cape Town 1700; Lobito – Cape Town 1440; Cape Town – Lobito 1460; Bûr Saîd – Aden 1310; Aden – Mombasa 1602; Mombasa – Bombay 2400; Durban – Mauritius 1552

LES. Lesotho
O. V. Oranje-Vrystaat
SWAZ. Swaziland

Projection: Zenithal Equidistant. West from Greenwich 0 East from Greenwich

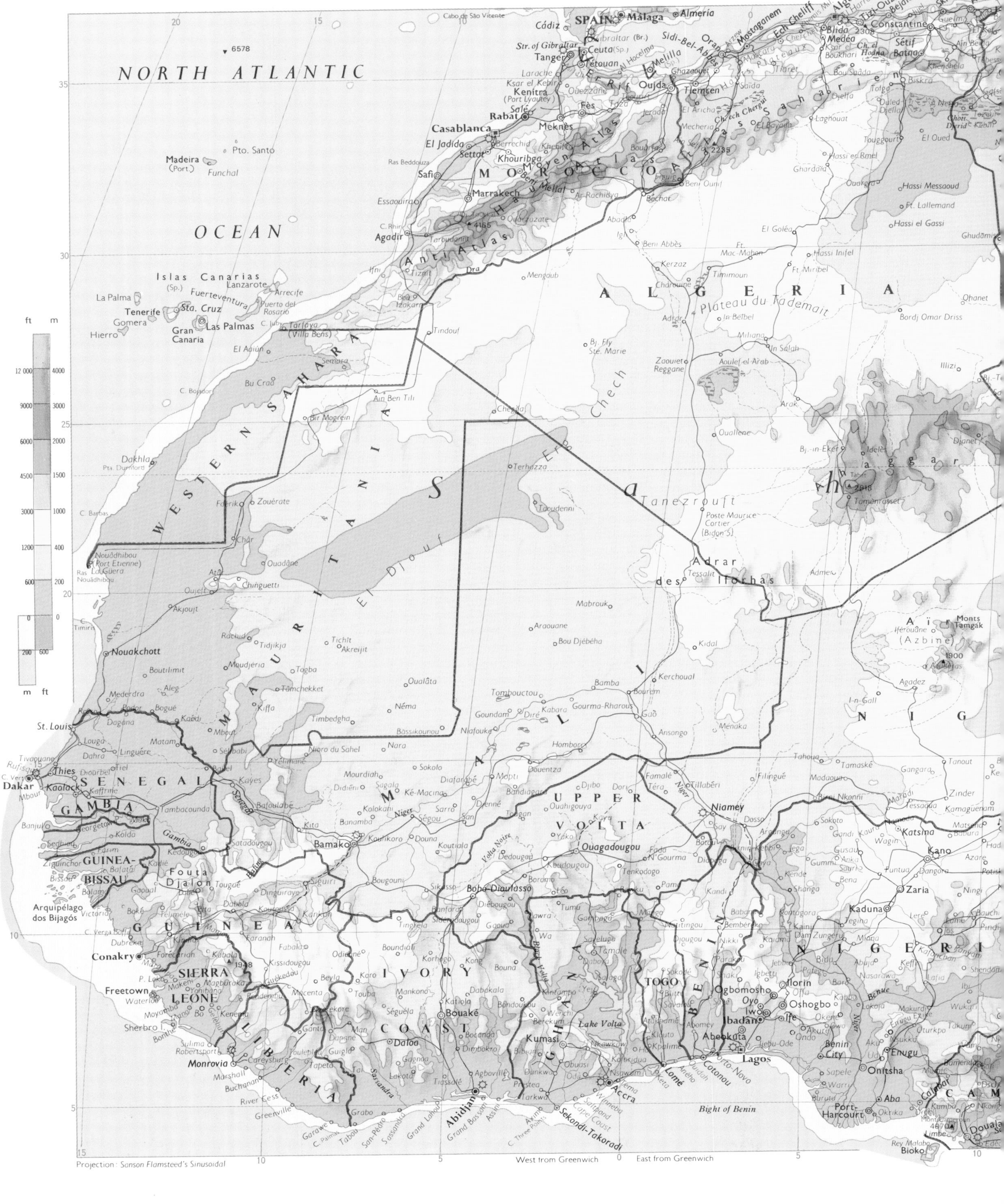

NORTH ATLANTIC OCEAN

SPAIN

MOROCCO

ALGERIA

WESTERN SAHARA

MAURITANIA

MALI

SENEGAL

GAMBIA

GUINEA-BISSAU

GUINEA

SIERRA LEONE

LIBERIA

IVORY COAST

UPPER VOLTA

GHANA

TOGO

BENIN

NIGERIA

Madeira (Port.)

Islas Canarias (Sp.)

Arquipélago dos Bijagós

Casablanca · Rabat · Marrakech · Agadir · Fès · Meknès · Oujda · Tlemcen · Alger (Algiers) · Constantine · Oran · Tanger · Ceuta · Melilla · Málaga · Almería · Cádiz

Dakar · St. Louis · Nouakchott · Banjul · Bamako · Conakry · Freetown · Monrovia · Abidjan · Ouagadougou · Niamey · Accra · Lomé · Cotonou · Porto-Novo · Lagos · Ibadan · Kano · Kaduna · Zaria · Kumasi · Bouaké · Tombouctou · Gao · Tindouf · Ouallene · Tamanrasset

Anti Atlas · Haut Atlas · Moyen Atlas · Plateau du Tademait · Tanezrouft · Adrar des Iforhas · El Djouf · Erg Chech · Ahaggar · Aïr (Azbine) · Fouta Djalon · Lake Volta · Bight of Benin

ft m

12 000 4000

9000 3000

6000 2000

4500 1500

3000 1000

1200 400

600 200

0 0

200 600

m ft

Projection: Sanson Flamsteed's Sinusoidal

West from Greenwich 0 East from Greenwich

20 15 10 5 0 5 10

35 30 25 20 15 10 5

1:15 000 000

100 0 100 200 300 400 miles

100 0 100 200 300 400 500 600 km

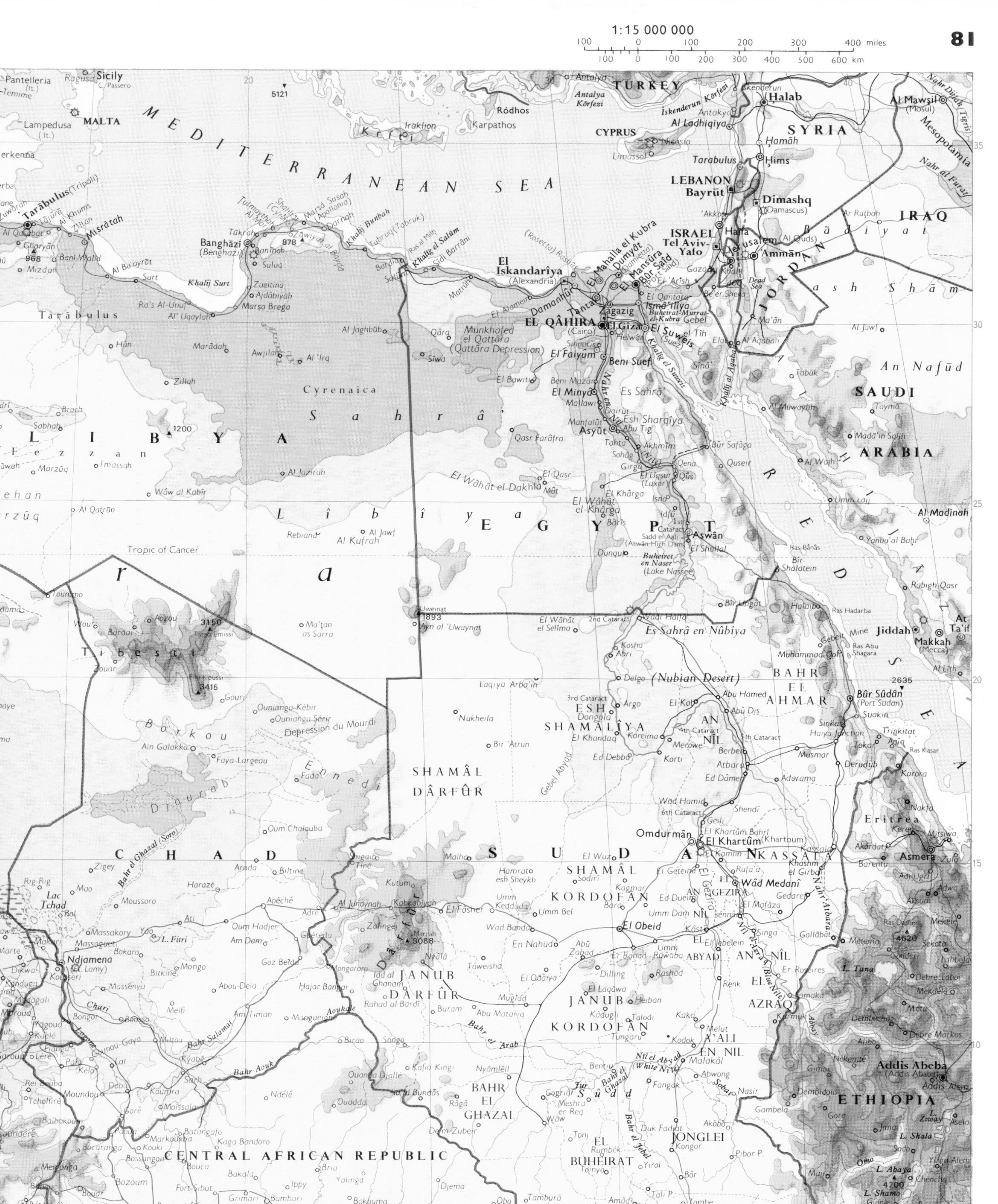
MEDITERRANEAN SEA
Sicily
MALTA
Pantelleria
Lampedusa
Kerkenna
Krítí
Iráklion
Karpathos
Ródhos
TURKEY
Antalya
Antalya Körfezi
CYPRUS
Limassol
Nicosia
İskenderun
İskenderun Körfezi
Antakya
Halab
Al Lādhiqīyah
SYRIA
Ḥamāh
Ḥimṣ
Tarābulus
LEBANON
Bayrūt
Dimashq
(Damascus)
Al Mawṣil
(Mosul)
Mesopotamia
Nahr Dijlah (Tigris)
Nahr al Furāt
IRAQ
Ar Ruṭbah
Bādiyat ash Shām
ISRAEL
Tel Aviv-Yafo
Haifa
Jerusalem (Al Quds)
'Ammān
JORDAN
Gaza
Dead Sea
Ma'ān
Al 'Aqabah
Tarābulus (Tripoli)
Miṣrātah
Tarābulus
Khalīj Surt
Banghāzī (Benghazi)
Ajdābiyah
Marsa Brega
Tubruq (Tobruk)
Cyrenaica
Al Jaghbūb
Awjilah
Zillah
Marādah
Hūn
LIBYA
Fezzan
Marzūq
Sabhah
Tmassah
Al Jazīrah
Wāw al Kabīr
Al Qaṭrūn
Ṣaḥrā' Lībīyah
Al Kufrah
Al Jawf
Rebiana
Tropic of Cancer
El Iskandarîya (Alexandria)
El Mahalla el Kubra
Dumyât (Damietta)
El Manṣûra
Bûr Sa'îd (Port Said)
Ṭanṭa
Zagazig
Damanhûr
Ismâ'ilîya
EL QÂHIRA (Cairo)
El Gîza
Helwân
El Suweis (Suez)
El Faiyûm
Beni Suef
El Minya
Mallawi
Asyût
Sohâg
Girga
Qena
El Uqsur (Luxor)
Isna
Idfu
Aswân
Sadd el Aali (Aswân High Dam)
Buheiret en Naser (Lake Nasser)
Munkhafed el Qaṭṭâra (Qaṭṭâra Depression)
Sîwa
Qâra
El Alamein
Maṭrûḥ
Es Sahrâ' Esh Sharqîya
El Wâḥât el-Dakhla
El Wâḥât el-Khârga
El Khârga
Qasr Farâfra
EGYPT
Es Sîna'
Khalîg el Suweis
Khalîg el 'Aqaba
Bûr Safâga
Quseir
Ras Bânâs
Bîr Shalatein
Halaib
Ras Hadarba
Wadi Halfa
Es Sahrâ en Nûbîya
(Nubian Desert)
Uweinat 1893
Ma'ṭan as Sarra
Tibesti
Tarso Emissi 3150
Emi Koussi 3415
Bardaï
Aozou
Borkou
Faya-Largeau
Ounianga-Kébir
Depression du Mourdi
Ennedi
Fada
Djourab
Oum Chalouba
CHAD
Lac Tchad
Ndjamena (Ft. Lamy)
Abéché
Biltine
Moussoro
Am Dam
Mongo
Chari
Bahr Salamat
Bahr Aouk
Sarh
Moundou
Bongor
Laï
Doba
Koumra
SHAMÂL DÂRFÛR
Laqiya Arba'în
Nukheila
Bir 'Atrun
Gebel Abyad
Kutum
Kabkabîyah
El Fasher
Jebel Marra 3088
Dârfûr
Nyâlâ
JANUB DÂRFÛR
Bahr el 'Arab
ESH SHAMÂLÎYA
Dongola
Merowe
Kareima
Karima
Ed Debba
Delgo
Abu Hamed
4th Cataract
5th Cataract
AN NÎL
Atbara
Berber
Ed Dâmer
Shendî
6th Cataract
BAHR EL AHMAR
Bûr Sûdân (Port Sudan)
Suakin
Tokar
Haiya Junction
Sinkat
Omdurmân
El Khartûm (Khartoum)
El Khartûm Bahrî
SUDAN
KASSALA
Kassala
Khashm el Girba
Nahr 'Atbara
Wad Medanî
GEZIRA
Gedaref
Sennâr
SHAMÂL KORDOFÂN
El Obeid
Umm Ruwaba
EL NÎL EL ABYAD
Kôstî
Ed Dueim
AN NÎL EL AZRAQ
Bahr el Azraq (Blue Nile)
Er Roseires
JANUB KORDOFÂN
Kadugli
Talodi
Kaka
Kodok
Malakâl
A'ALI EN NÎL
Nasir
Bahr el Ghazal
Nîl el Abyad (White Nile)
Sobat
BAHR EL GHAZAL
Wâw
Sudd
Bahr el Jebel
EL BUHEIRAT
Rumbek
JONGLEI
Bor
Pibor P.
GHARB EL ISTIWA'IYA
SHARQ EL ISTIWA'IYA
Juba
Torit
Kapoeta
Mongalla
Yei
Maridi
Tambura
Eritrea
Keren
Asmera
Mitsiwa
Akordat
Adwa
Aksum
Ras Dashen 4620
Gonder
L. Tana
Debre Markos
Dembecha
Nekemte
Addis Abeba
Addis Alem
ETHIOPIA
Gambela
Gore
Jima
L. Ziway
L. Shala
L. Abaya
L. Shamo
4200
Chew Bahir (L. Stefanie)
L. Turkana
Lokitaung
KENYA
Mega
Jiddah
Makkah (Mecca)
At Ta'if
SAUDI ARABIA
An Nafūd
Tabūk
Al Madīnah
Yanbu' al Baḥr
Rabigh
RED SEA
CENTRAL AFRICAN REPUBLIC
Bangui
Bouar
Bambari
Bria
Ndélé
Birao
Djema
Obo
ZAÏRE (CONGO)
Ubangi
Bomu
Uele
Bondo
Bambili
KENYA
15
20
25
30
35
40
5
10
15
20
25
30
35

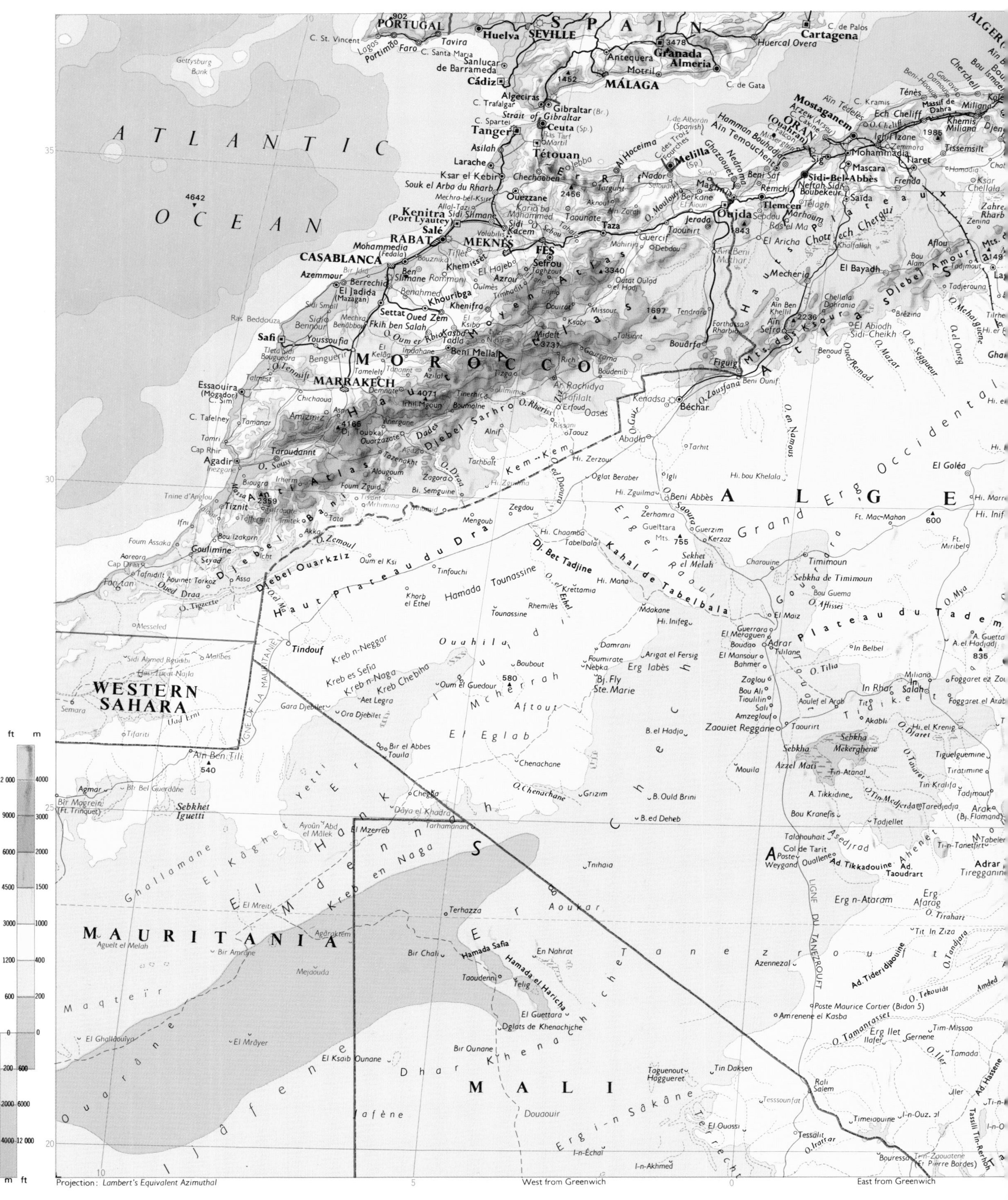
PORTUGAL
S P A I N
ALGERIA
C. St. Vincent
Lagos
Portimão
Faro
Tavira
C. Santa Maria
Huelva
SEVILLE
Sanlucar de Barrameda
Cádiz
Antequera
Granada
Almeria
Motril
MÁLAGA
C. de Gata
Huercal Overa
Cartagena
C. de Palos
Gettysburg Bank
Algeciras
C. Trafalgar
Gibraltar (Br.)
Strait of Gibraltar
C. Spartel
Tanger
Ceuta (Sp.)
Martil
Tétouan
Asilah
Larache
Ksar el Kebir
Souk el Arba du Rharb
Chechaouen
Ouezzane
Kenitra (Port Lyautey)
Salé
RABAT
Mohammedia (Fedala)
CASABLANCA
Azemmour
Berrechid
El Jadida (Mazagan)
MEKNÈS
FÈS
Sefrou
Taza
Al Hoceima
Melilla (Sp.)
Nador
Oujda
Jerada
Taourirt
Guercif
Ras Beddouza
Safi
Youssoufia
Benguerir
Khouribga
Khenifra
Oued Zem
Settat
Fkih ben Salah
Kasba Tadla
Beni Mellal
Midelt
M O R O C C O
MARRAKECH
Essaouira (Mogador)
C. Sim
C. Tafelney
Tamri
Cap Rhir
Agadir
Taroudannt
Ouarzazate
Zagora
Tiznit
Ifni
Goulimine
Tan-tan
Cap Draa
Oued Draa
H a u t A t l a s
M o y e n A t l a s
A n t i A t l a s
Djebel Sarhro
Djebel Bani
Djebel Ouarkziz
Er Rachidya
Erfoud
Boudenib
Figuig
Bouârfa
Kenadsa
Béchar
Abadla
Tindouf
Mostaganem
ORAN (OUAHRAN)
Arzew
Sidi-Bel-Abbès
Tlemcen
Maghnia
Nedroma
Mascara
Tiaret
Saïda
Mecheria
Aïn Sefra
El Bayadh
El Abiodh Sidi-Cheikh
Tissemsilt
Khemis Miliana
Cherchell
Ténès
Ech Cheliff
Aflou
Djebel Amour
Chott ech Chergui
Hauts Plateaux
Atlas Saharien
Mts. des Ksour
Beni Abbès
Kerzaz
Timimoun
Sebkha de Timimoun
Adrar
Reggane
Zaouiet Reggane
El Goléa
Grand Erg Occidental
Erg er Raoui
Kahal de Tabelbala
Tabelbala
Dj. Bet Tadjine
Haut Plateau du Dra
Hamada Tounassine
Ouahila
Erg Iabès
Erg Chech
El Eglab
Aftout
Plateau du Tademaït
Tidikelt
In Salah
Reg
Tanezrouft
Aoukar
El Mreyé
Erg Iguidi
WESTERN SAHARA
Semara
Tifariti
Aïn Ben Tili
Bir Moghreïn (Ft. Trinquet)
Sebkhet Iguetti
MAURITANIA
M A L I
Taoudenni
Hamada Safia
Hamada el Haricha
El Guettara
Erg Chech
Tessalit
Bordj Mokhtar
Poste Maurice Cortier (Bidon 5)
Ouallene
Ad. Tikkadouine
Erg n-Ataram
Azennezal
Ghallamane
El Kaghet
Mejaouda
Maqteïr
Ouarane
Ijâfene
Dhar
Erg i-n Sâkâne
Tin Daksen
Projection: Lambert's Equivalent Azimuthal
West from Greenwich
East from Greenwich
ft m
12 000 4000
9000 3000
6000 2000
4500 1500
3000 1000
1200 400
600 200
0 0
200 600
2000 6000
4000 12 000
m ft

1:8 000 000

50 0 50 100 150 200 miles

50 0 50 100 150 200 250 300 km

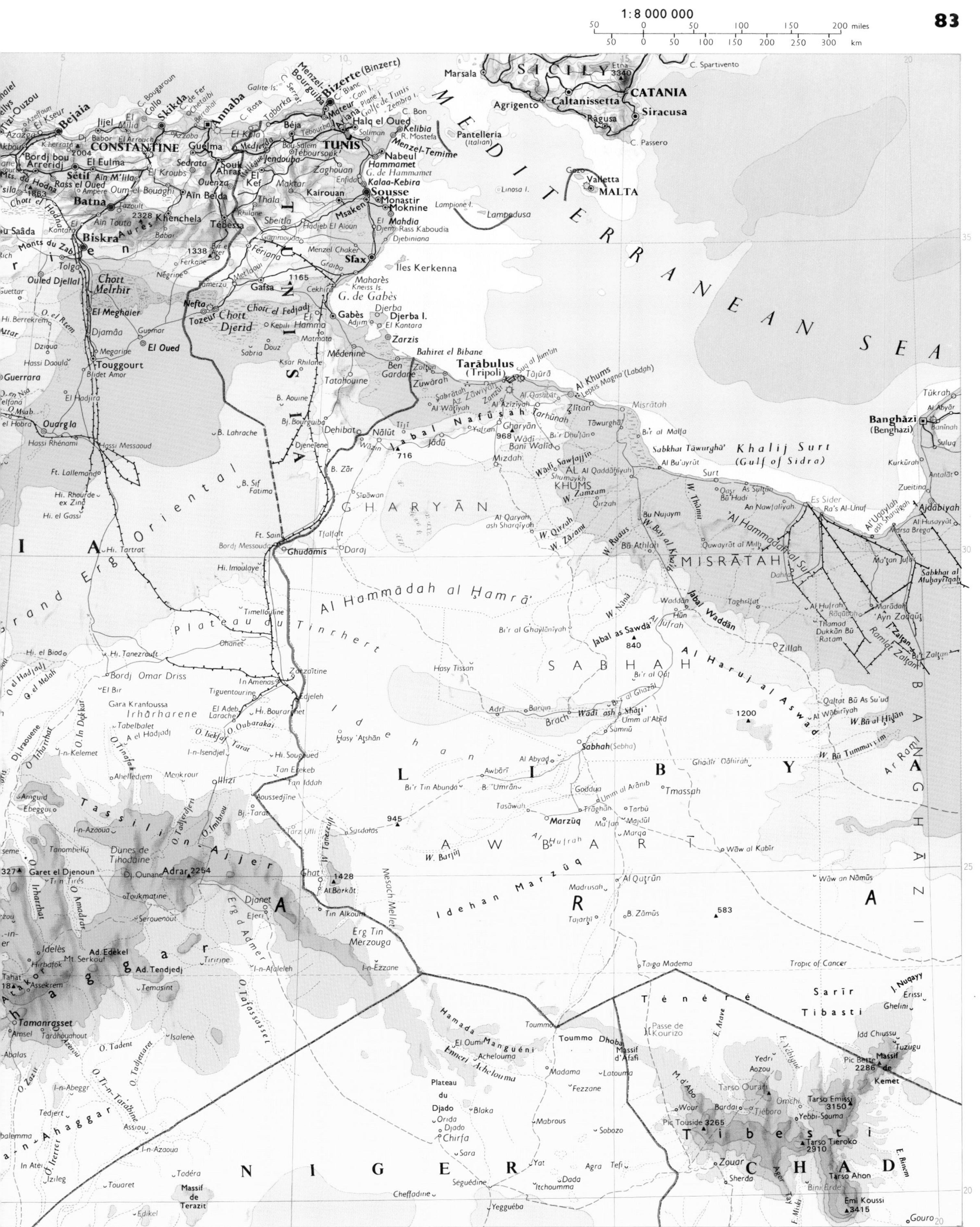

MEDITERRANEAN SEA
SICILY
Marsala
Agrigento
Caltanissetta
CATANIA
Siracusa
Ragusa
Etna 3340
C. Spartivento
C. Passero
Pantelleria (Italian)
Gozo
Valletta
MALTA
Linosa I.
Lampione I.
Lampedusa
Bizerte (Binzert)
Menzel-Bourguiba
Mateur
Ariana
Halq el Oued
TUNIS
Béja
Kelibia
C. Bon
Nabeul
Hammamet
G. de Hammamet
Menzel-Temime
Kalaa-Kebira
Sousse
Monastir
Moknine
Mahdia
Kairouan
Zaghouan
Enfida
Maktar
El Kef
Jendouba
Thala
Sbeitla
Kasserine
Feriana
Gafsa
Sfax
Iles Kerkenna
Maharès
G. de Gabès
Gabès
Djerba I.
Zarzis
Medenine
Ben Gardane
Tataouine
Kebili
Douz
Tozeur
Nefta
Chott Djerid
Chott el Fedjadj
TUNISIA
Annaba
Skikda
Jijel
Bejaia
CONSTANTINE
Guelma
Souk Ahras
Sétif
Bordj bou Arreridj
El Eulma
Batna
Aïn Beida
Khenchela
Tébessa
Biskra
Aurès 2328
Monts du Zab
Bou Saâda
Chott el Hodna
Tolga
Ouled Djellal
Chott Melrhir
El Meghaier
Djamâa
El Oued
Touggourt
Ouargla
Hassi Messaoud
Grand Erg Oriental
Plateau du Tinrhert
Bordj Omar Driss
In Amenas
Irharharene
Tassili n' Ajjer
Dunes de Tihodaine
Adrar 2254
Djanet
Erg d'Admer
Ahaggar
Tamanrasset
Assekrem
Ad. Tendjedj
Ad. Edekel
Idelès
ALGERIA
Tarābulus (Tripoli)
Zuwārah
Az Zāwiyah
Al Khums
Leptis Magna (Labdah)
Misrātah
Gharyān
Jabal Nafūsah
Nālūt
Ghudāmis
Al Hammādah al Hamrā'
Khalij Surt (Gulf of Sidra)
Surt
Banghāzi (Benghazi)
Ajdābiyah
Es Sider
Sabkhat Tawurghā'
Jabal Waddān
Waddān
Hūn
Al Jufrah
Jabal as Sawdā' 840
Al Harūj al Aswad
Sabhah (Sebha)
Marzūq
Ubari
Ghāt
Idehan Marzūq
Idehan
Zillah
Ramlat Zaltan
SABHAH
AWBĀRĪ
BANGHĀZI
MISRĀTAH
KHUMS
GHARYĀN
LIBYA
Tropic of Cancer
Sarīr Tibasti
Ténéré
Passe de Kourizo
Toummo
Massif d'Afafi
Hamada Manguéni
Plateau du Djado
Djado
Chirfa
Séguédine
Bilma
Dirkou
NIGER
Massif de Terazit
Tibesti
Pic Toussidé 3265
Tarso Emissi 3150
Tarso Tieroko 2910
Emi Koussi 3415
Pic Bette 2286
Massif de Kemet
Zouar
Bardaï
CHAD
Gouro

MAURITANIA
SENEGAL
GAMBIA
GUINEA-BISSAU
GUINEA
SIERRA LEONE
LIBERIA
IVORY COAST
Nouakchott
Akjoujt
DAKAR
St. Louis
Thiès
Kaolack
Ziguinchor
Bissau
Conakry
Freetown
Monrovia
Bamako
Abidjan
Bouaké
Kankan
Kindia
Labé
Kayes
Ségou
Mopti
Bobo Dioulasso
Tombouctou (Timbuktu)
Fouta Djalon
Arquipélago dos Bijagós
Grain Coast
Ivory Coast
NORTHERN
SOUTHERN
EASTERN
WESTERN
ft
m
12 000
9000
6000
4500
3000
1200
600
0
200
400
1000
1500
2000
3000
4000
6000
18 000

Projection: Lambert's Equivalent Azimuthal

1:8 000 000

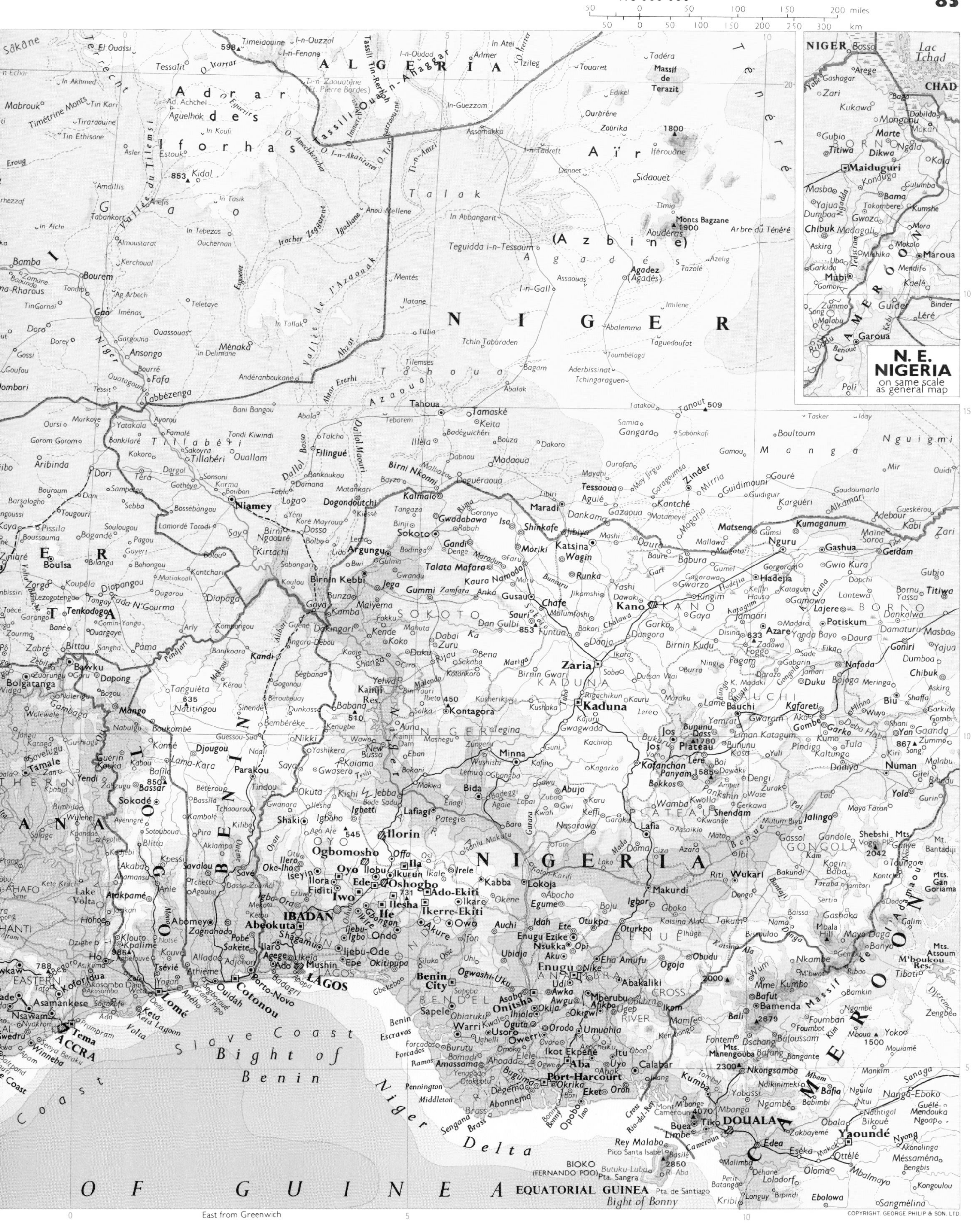
50 0 50 100 150 200 miles
50 0 50 100 150 200 250 300 km
N.E. NIGERIA
on same scale
as general map
A L G E R I A
N I G E R
N I G E R I A
B E N I N
T O G O
CAMEROON
EQUATORIAL GUINEA
CHAD
Lac Tchad
Adrar des Iforhas
Aïr (Azbine)
Ténéré
Tassili Ouan-n-Ahaggar
Massif de Terazit
Monts Bagzane
Agadez (Agadès)
Tahoua
Niamey
Maradi
Zinder
Sokoto
Kano
Katsina
Zaria
Kaduna
Jos
Plateau
Bauchi
Maiduguri
Ilorin
Ogbomosho
Oyo
Oshogbo
Ibadan
Abeokuta
Lagos
Porto-Novo
Cotonou
Lomé
Accra
Tema
Benin City
Onitsha
Enugu
Aba
Port-Harcourt
Calabar
Douala
Yaoundé
Buea
Rey Malabo
BIOKO (FERNANDO POO)
Slave Coast
Bight of Benin
Niger Delta
Bight of Bonny
OF GUINEA
East from Greenwich

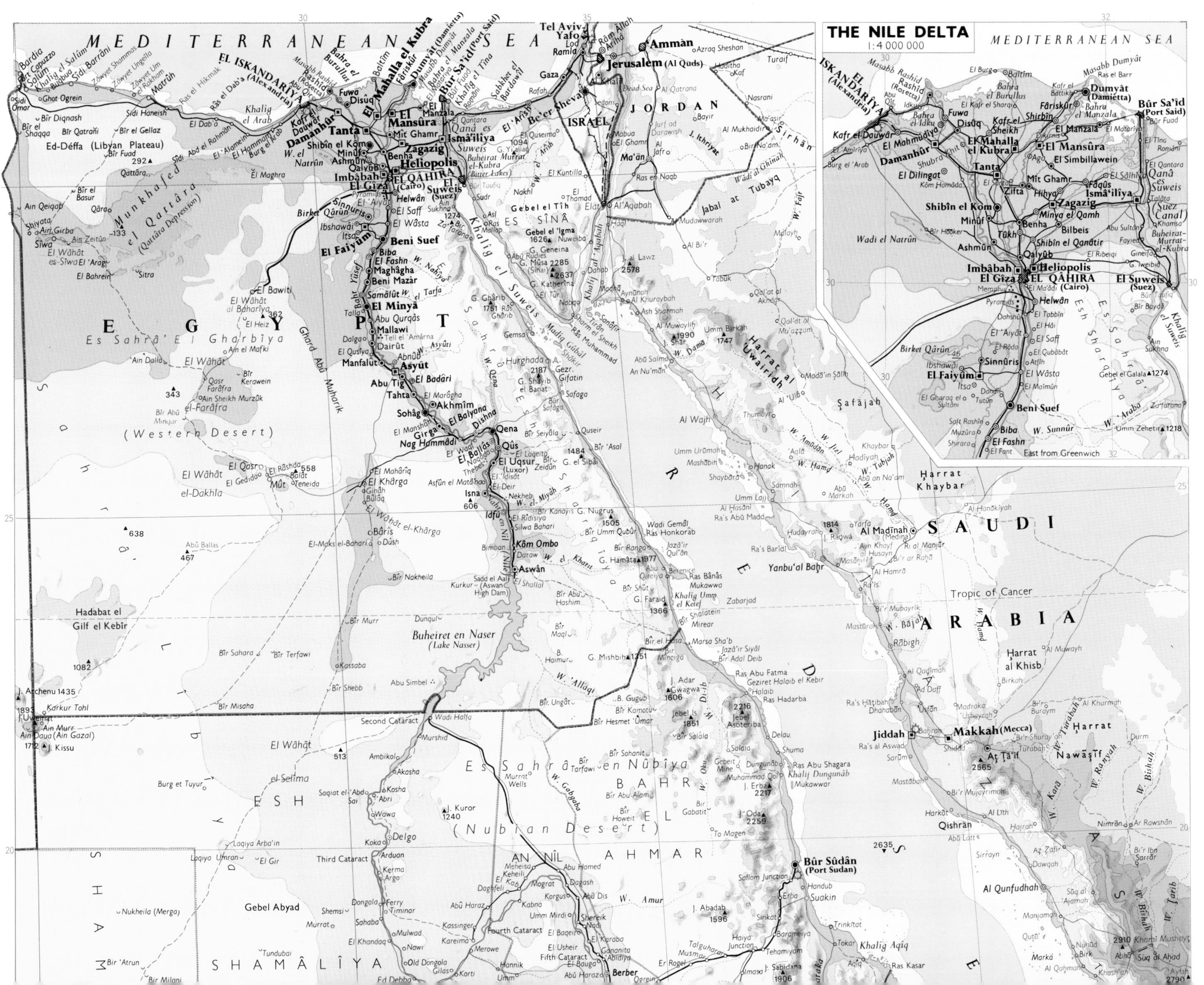
THE NILE DELTA
1:4 000 000
MEDITERRANEAN SEA
EL ISKANDARÎYA (Alexandria)
Bûr Sa'îd (Port Said)
Dumyât (Damietta)
El Mansûra
Tanta
Zagazig
Ismâ'ilîya
El Suweis (Suez)
EL QÂHIRA (Cairo)
Heliopolis
El Gîza
Helwân
Beni Suef
El Faiyûm
Birket Qârûn
Damanhûr
East from Greenwich
Tel Aviv-Yafo
Jerusalem (Al Quds)
Ammân
JORDAN
ISRAEL
Gaza
El Minyâ
Asyût
Sohâg
Qena
El Uqsur (Luxor)
Aswân
Buheiret en Naser (Lake Nasser)
Es Sahrâ' El Gharbîya (Western Desert)
Munkhafed el Qattâra (Qattâra Depression)
Hadabat el Gilf el Kebîr
Khalîg el Suweis
SAUDI ARABIA
Tropic of Cancer
Al Madînah (Medina)
Makkah (Mecca)
Jiddah
Bûr Sûdân (Port Sudan)
BAHR EL AHMAR
Es Sahrâ en Nûbîya (Nubian Desert)
Wadi Halfa
Second Cataract
Third Cataract
Fourth Cataract
Fifth Cataract
Old Dongola
Berber
Abu Hamed

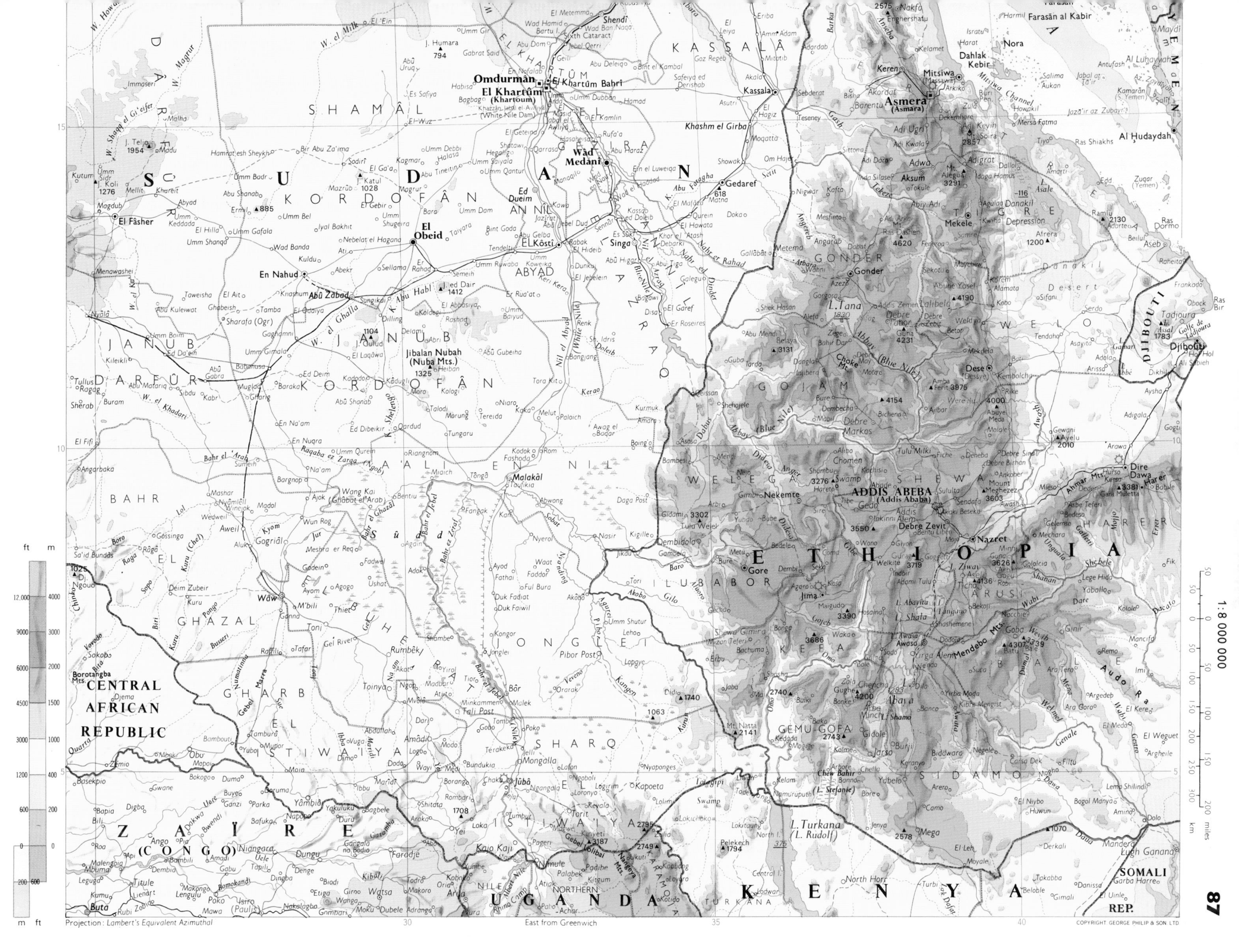
1:8 000 000
50 0 50 100 150 200 miles
50 0 50 100 150 200 250 300 km
ETHIOPIA
SUDAN
KENYA
UGANDA
ZAÏRE (CONGO)
CENTRAL AFRICAN REPUBLIC
SOMALI REP.
DJIBOUTI
YEMEN
ADDIS ABEBA (Addis Ababa)
Omdurmân
El Khartûm (Khartoum)
El Khartûm Bahri
Asmera (Asmara)
Djibouti
El Obeid
Wad Medanî
Gonder
Dese
Dire Dawa
Harer
Malakâl
Wâw
Jubâ
Kassala
El Fâsher
En Nahud
L. Tana
L. Turkana (L. Rudolf)
Danakil Depression
Jibalan Nubah (Nuba Mts.)
COPYRIGHT GEORGE PHILIP & SON LTD
East from Greenwich
Projection: Lambert's Equivalent Azimuthal
m 4000 3000 2000 1500 1000 400 200 0
ft 12 000 9000 6000 4500 3000 1200 600 0 200 600

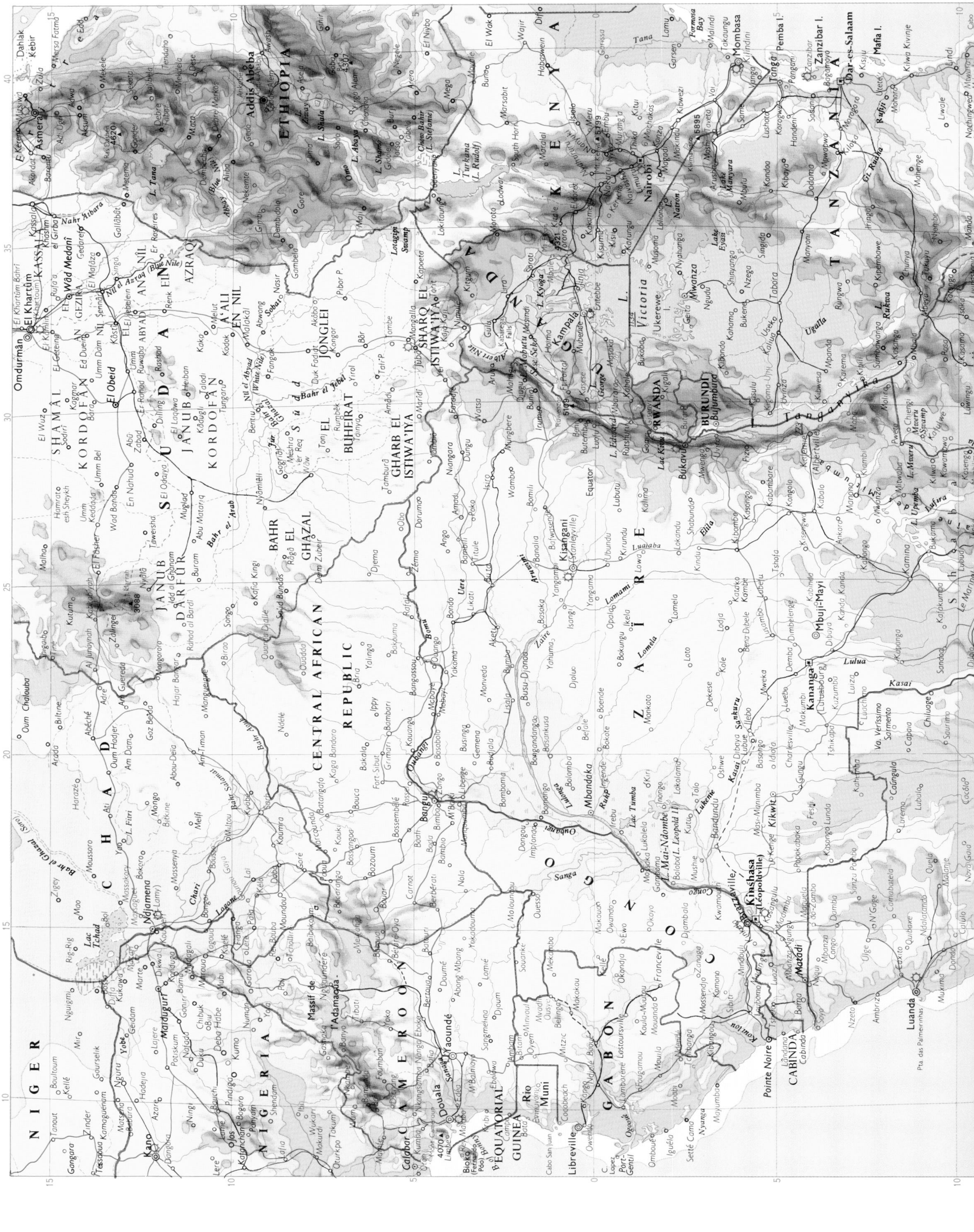
NIGER
CHAD
NIGERIA
CAMEROON
CENTRAL AFRICAN REPUBLIC
SUDAN
ETHIOPIA
KENYA
UGANDA
TANZANIA
RWANDA
BURUNDI
ZAÏRE
CONGO
GABON
EQUATORIAL GUINEA
Rio Muni
CABINDA
Addis Abeba
Khartoum
Omdurman
Nairobi
Mombasa
Dar-es-Salaam
Kampala
Kinshasa (Léopoldville)
Brazzaville
Bangui
Yaoundé
Douala
Libreville
Luanda
Ndjamena (Fort-Lamy)
Kisangani (Stanleyville)
Lac Tchad
L. Victoria
L. Tanganyika
L. Turkana (L. Rudolf)
Zanzibar I.
Pemba I.
Mafia I.

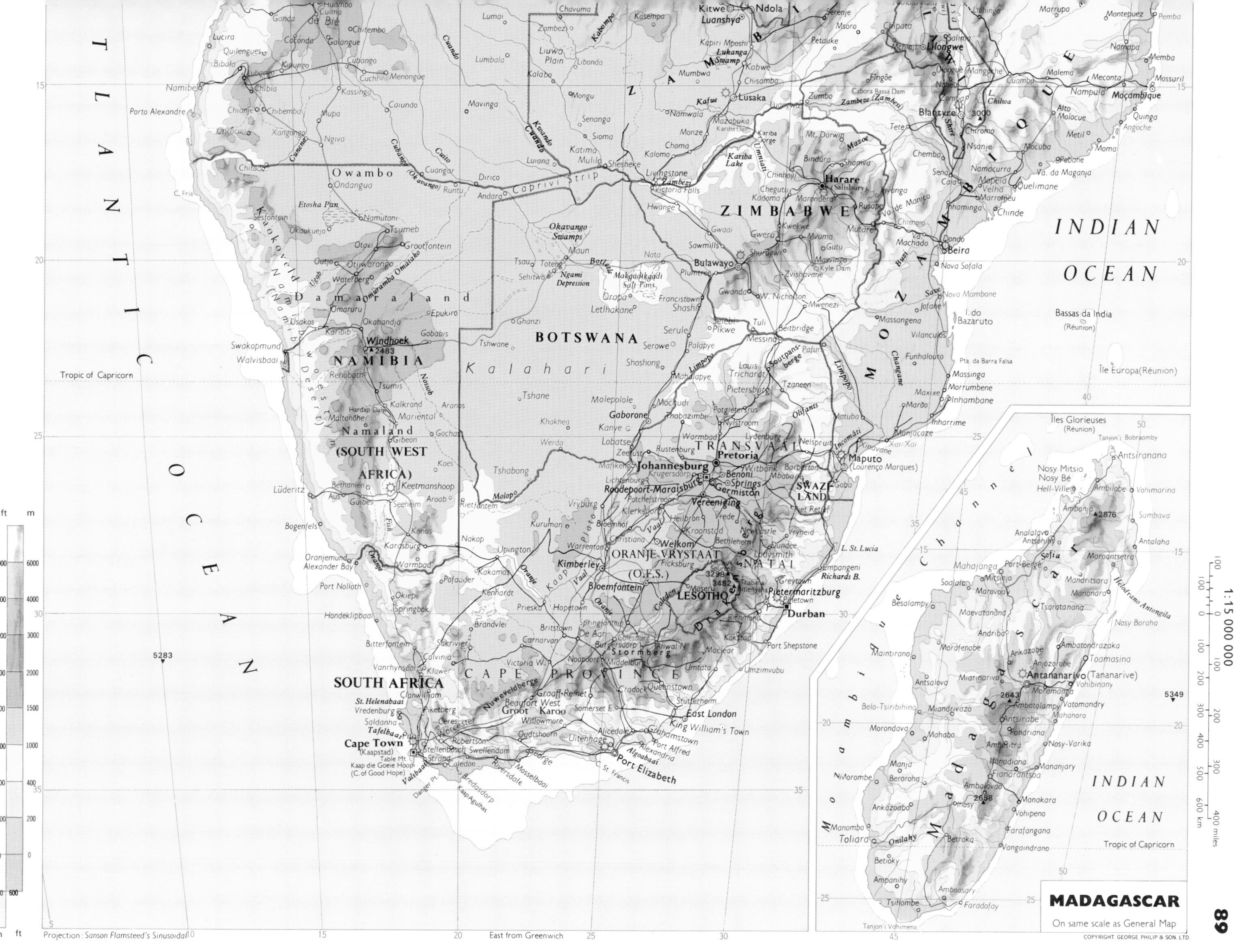

1:15 000 000
100 0 100 200 300 400 miles
100 0 100 200 300 400 500 600 km
MADAGASCAR
On same scale as General Map
COPYRIGHT GEORGE PHILIP & SON LTD
INDIAN OCEAN
ATLANTIC OCEAN
Mozambique Channel
MOZAMBIQUE
ZIMBABWE
BOTSWANA
Kalahari
NAMIBIA
(SOUTH WEST AFRICA)
SOUTH AFRICA
LESOTHO
SWAZILAND
TRANSVAAL
ORANJE-VRYSTAAT (O.F.S.)
NATAL
CAPE PROVINCE
Tropic of Capricorn
East from Greenwich
Projection: Sanson Flamsteed's Sinusoidal

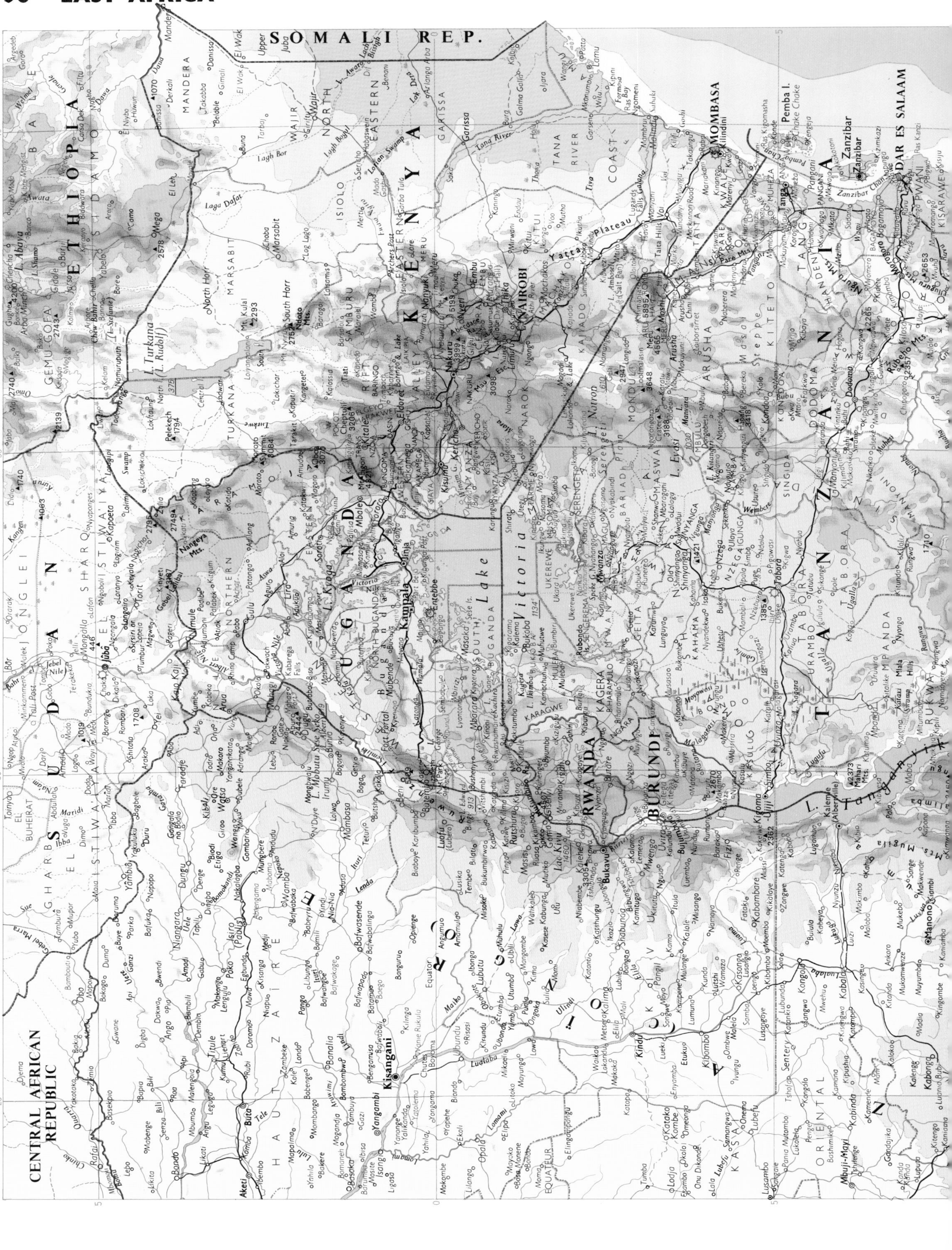

SOMALI REP.
ETHIOPIA
SUDAN
KENYA
UGANDA
TANZANIA
ZAIRE
RWANDA
BURUNDI
CENTRAL AFRICAN REPUBLIC
NAIROBI
MOMBASA
DAR ES SALAAM
Zanzibar
Pemba I.
Kampala
Kisangani
Lake Victoria
L. Turkana (L. Rudolf)
L. Tanganyika

1:8 000 000

50 0 50 100 150 200 miles
50 0 100 200 300 km

INDIAN OCEAN
ZAMBIA
ZIMBABWE
MOZAMBIQUE
MALAWI
BOTSWANA
ANGOLA
TRANSVAAL
HARARE (Salisbury)
Lusaka
Bulawayo
Beira
Blantyre
Lilongwe
Livingstone
Lubumbashi (Elisabethville)
Moçambique
Zambezi
Kariba Lake
Île de Juan de Nova (Réunion)
Projection: Lambert's Equivalent Azimuthal
East from Greenwich
COPYRIGHT, GEORGE PHILIP & SON, LTD.

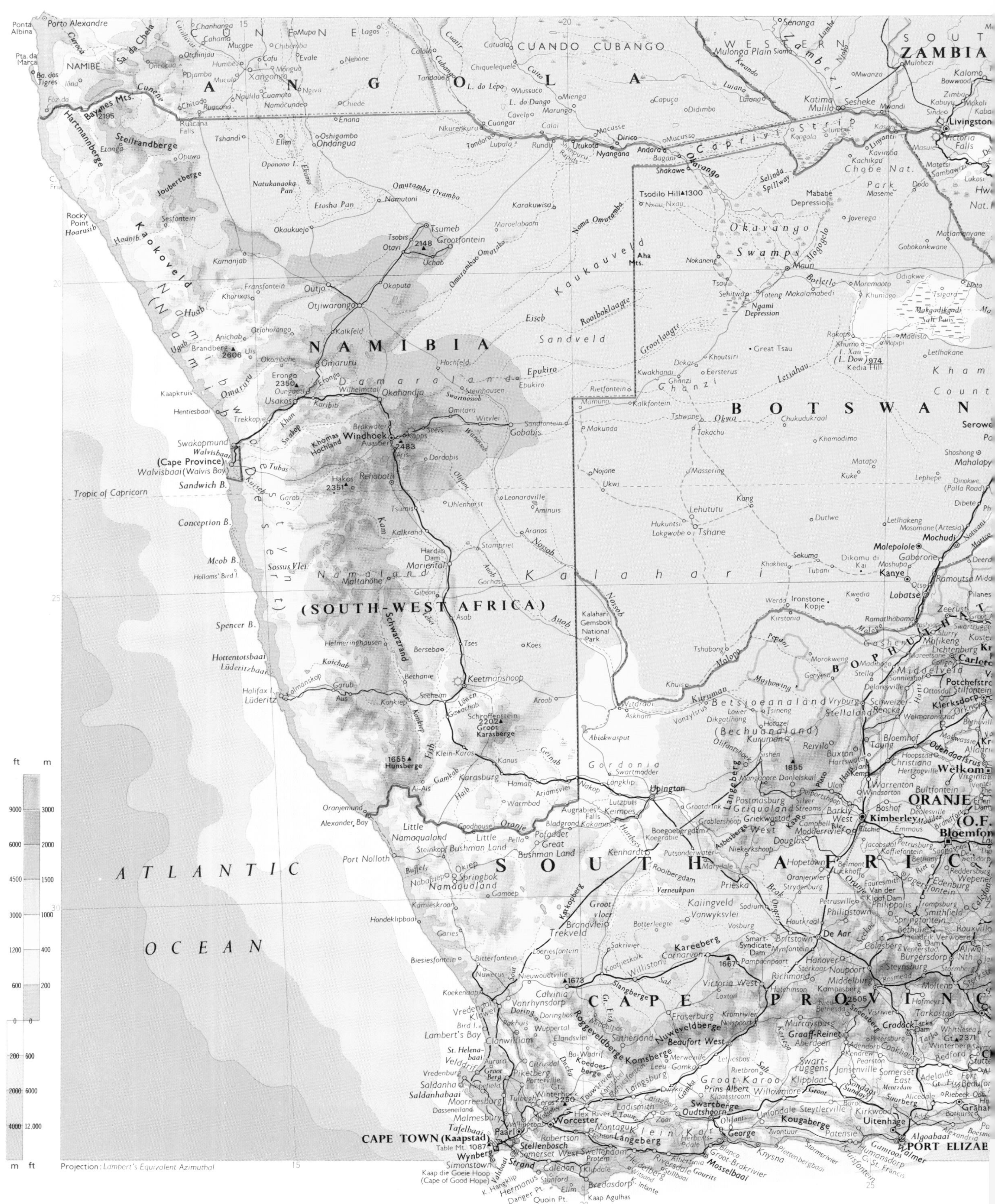
A N G O L A
CUNENE
CUANDO CUBANGO
NAMIBE
ZAMBIA
WESTERN
SOUTHERN
NAMIBIA
(SOUTH-WEST AFRICA)
BOTSWANA
SOUTH AFRICA
CAPE PROVINCE
ORANJE (O.F.S.)
BOPHUTHATSWANA
ATLANTIC OCEAN
Porto Alexandre
Ponta Albina
Pta. da Marca
Ba. dos Tigres
Foz do Cunene
Baynes Mts. 2195
Hartmannberge
Steilrandberge
Joubertberge
Kaokoveld
Rocky Point
Hoarusib
Sesfontein
Kamanjab
Namib Desert
Etosha Pan
Okaukuejo
Namutoni
Tsumeb
Otavi
Grootfontein
2148
Outjo
Otjiwarongo
Okaputa
Kalkfeld
Omaruru
Brandberg 2606
Erongo 2350
Usakos
Karibib
Okahandja
Damaraland
Swakopmund
Walvisbaai (Walvis Bay)
(Cape Province)
Sandwich B.
Tropic of Capricorn
Khomas Hochland
Windhoek
2483
Gobabis
Rehoboth
Hakos 2351
Conception B.
Meob B.
Hollams' Bird I.
Sossus Vlei
Namaland
Maltahöhe
Mariental
Hardap Dam
Gibeon
Schwarzrand
Spencer B.
Hottentotsbaai
Lüderitzbaai
Halifax I.
Lüderitz
Aus
Bethanie
Keetmanshoop
Seeheim
Schroffenstein 2202
Groot Karasberge
Hunsberge 1655
Karasburg
Oranjemund
Alexander Bay
Kalahari
Kalahari Gemsbok National Park
Okavango Swamps
Maun
Ngami Depression
Makgadikgadi Salt Pans
Tsodilo Hill 1300
Aha Mts.
Ghanzi
Kaukauveld
Sandveld
Caprivi Strip
Katima Mulilo
Livingstone
Victoria Falls
Chobe Nat. Park
Mababe Depression
Serowe
Mahalapye
Molepolole
Gaborone
Kanye
Lobatse
Mochudi
Kimberley
Bloemfontein
Welkom
Klerksdorp
Mafikeng
Upington
Augrabies Falls
Little Namaqualand
Bushman Land
Port Nolloth
Springbok
Kenhardt
Prieska
De Aar
Carnarvon
Victoria West
Beaufort West
Graaff-Reinet
Cradock
Calvinia
Vanrhynsdorp
Clanwilliam
Lambert's Bay
St. Helenabaai
Saldanha
Malmesbury
Paarl
Worcester
CAPE TOWN (Kaapstad)
Table Mt. 1087
Stellenbosch
Somerset West
Simonstown
Kaap die Goeie Hoop (Cape of Good Hope)
Hermanus
Danger Pt.
Quoin Pt.
Kaap Agulhas
Bredasdorp
Swellendam
Mosselbaai
George
Knysna
Oudtshoorn
Groot Karoo
Klein Karoo
Swartberge
Kougaberge
Uitenhage
PORT ELIZABETH
Algoabaai
Nuweveldberge
Roggeveldberge
Sneeuberg 2505
Kompasberg
1673
1667
Projection: Lambert's Equivalent Azimuthal
ft m
9000 3000
6000 2000
4500 1500
3000 1000
1200 400
600 200
0 0
200 600
2000 6000
4000 12,000
m ft

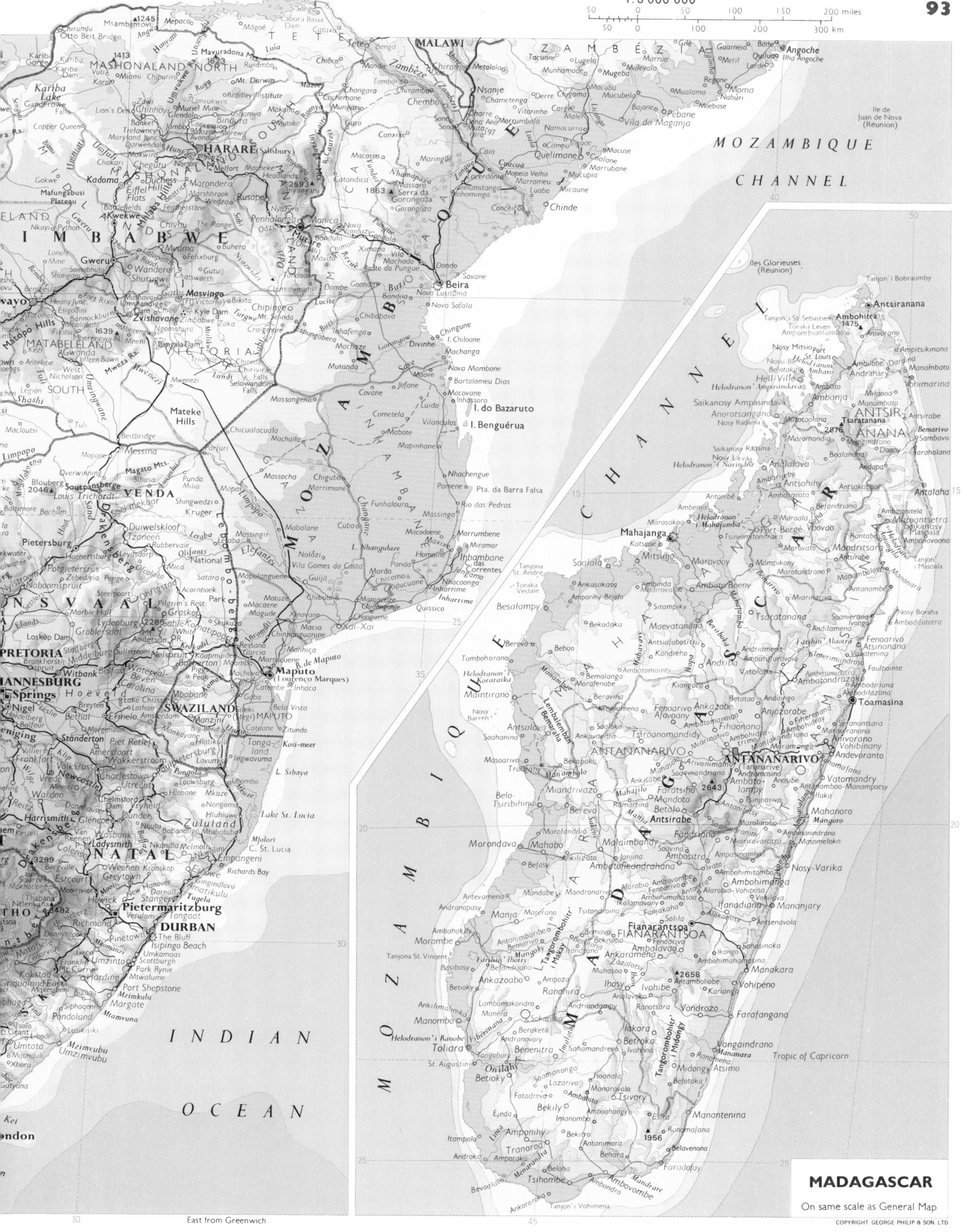

1:8 000 000
50 0 50 100 150 200 miles
50 0 100 200 300 km
MOZAMBIQUE CHANNEL
INDIAN OCEAN
MOZAMBIQUE
ZAMBÉZIA
MALAWI
TETE
MASHONALAND NORTH
ZIMBABWE
MATABELELAND
VICTORIA
VENDA
TRANSVAAL
SWAZILAND
MAPUTO
NATAL
Zululand
Tongaland
HARARE (Salisbury)
Kadoma
Gweru
Masvingo
Mutare
Beira
Quelimane
Chinde
Angoche
Tete
Inhambane
Maputo (Lourenço Marques)
Xai-Xai
I. do Bazaruto
I. Benguérua
Pta. da Barra Falsa
PRETORIA
JOHANNESBURG
Springs
Pietersburg
Pietermaritzburg
DURBAN
Richards Bay
Port Shepstone
Margate
Lake St. Lucia
Kosi-meer
L. Sibaya
Limpopo
Ile de Juan de Nova (Réunion)
Iles Glorieuses (Réunion)
MADAGASCAR
ANTANANARIVO
Antananarivo (Tananarive)
Antsiranana
Mahajanga
Toamasina
Antsirabe
Fianarantsoa
Toliara
Maintirano
Morondava
Mananjary
Manakara
Farafangana
Faradofay
Tsaratanana 2876
Ambohitra 1475
2643
2658
1956
Nosy Barren
Tropic of Capricorn
East from Greenwich

MADAGASCAR

On same scale as General Map

EUROPE
U. S. S. R.
Leningrad
Moskva
Sverdlovsk
Omsk
Novosibirsk
Tomsk
Barnaul
Irkutsk
Ozero Baykal
Chita
Ulan Ude
Semipalatinsk
Karaganda
L. Balkhash
Aral Sea
Alma Ata
Tashkent
Samarkand
Ürümqi
Hovd
Ulyasutay
Ulaanbaatar
MONGOLIA
Altai
ASIA
Manchuria
Harbin
Changchun
Shenyang
Vladivostok
Blagoveshchensk
Amur
Khabarovsk
Sakhalin
G. of Sakhalin
Sea of Okhotsk
Okhotsk
Kamchatka
Petropavlovsk
Komandorskie Is. (U.S.S.R.)
Near I.
Kiska I.
Aleutian Is.
Aleutian Trench
Kuril Is.
Kuril Trench
La Perouse Strait
Hakodate
Sendai
Sea of Japan
JAPAN
TŌKYŌ
Yokohama
Kyōto
Nagoya
Ōsaka
Fuji-san 3776
Shikoku
Kyūshū
Kitakyūshū
Nagasaki
Pusan
KOREA
N. KOREA
Sŏul
Antung
Lüda
Qingdao
Beijing
Tianjin
Jinan
Lanzhou
Xi'an
Huang He
Nanjing
Yellow Sea
SHANGHAI
Hangzhou
Wenzhou
East China Sea
Wuhan
Changsha
Chongqing
Chang Jiang
Fuzhou
Xiamen
Taibei
Taiwan (Formosa)
Guangzhou
MACAU (Port.)
HONG KONG
Hainan
Hanoi
Kunming
CHINA
Kunlun Shan
XIZANG (TIBET)
Lhasa
Mt. Everest 8848
Himalaya
NEPAL
Brahmaputra
AFGHANISTAN
Kabul
Srinagar
Lahore
PAKISTAN
Delhi
Agra
Kanpur
Varanasi
Ganges
Calcutta
BANGLADESH
Chittagong
Myitkyina
Mandalay
Irrawaddy
Salween
BURMA
INDIA
Cuttack
Hyderabad
Bay of Bengal
Rangoon
Madras
SRI LANKA
Colombo
Andaman Is.
Nicobar Is.
Mergui Arch.
Isthmus of Kra
THAILAND (SIAM)
Bangkok
Chiengmai
LAOS
VIETNAM
Mekong
CAMBODIA
Phnom Penh
Ho Chi Minh (Saigon)
Gulf of Thailand
C. Camau
South China Sea
Palawan
Mindoro
Manila
PHILIPPINES
Samar
10,497
Mindanao
Mindanao Trench
Sulu Sea
Kinabalu 4101
SABAH
BRUNEI
Labuan
SARAWAK
Natuna
George Town
PENINSULAR MALAYSIA
Kuala Lumpur
Melaka
SINGAPORE
Nias
Sumatra
Borneo
Celebes Sea
Celebes
Moluccas
Halmahera
Dampier Strait
Bangka
Palembang
Java Sea
Jakarta
Semarang
Surabaya
Java
Sunda Strait
Java Trench 7450
Bali
Lombok
Sumbawa
Flores
Flores Sea
Sumba
Timor
Ujung Pandang
Banda Sea
Buru
Ceram
Amboina
7440
Aru Is.
Tanimbar Is.
INDONESIA
Sunda Islands
Irian Jaya
5029
PAPUA NEW GUINEA
New Guinea
Madang
Rabaul
New Britain
New Ireland
Bismarck Arch.
Admiralty Is.
9103
Lae
Port Moresby
Louisiade Arch.
SOLOMON ISLANDS
Honiara
Guadalcanal
Christmas I. (Austral.)
Cocos (Keeling) Is. (Austral.)
Ashmore Is.
Arafura Sea
Torres Strait
Thursday I.
C. York
C. Arnhem
Darwin
G. of Carpentaria
Larrimah
Wyndham
Newcastle Waters
NORTHERN TERRITORY
Cairns
Townsville
Mt. Isa
Great Divide
Rockhampton
Longreach
QUEENSLAND
Maryborough
Brisbane
Ipswich
N.W. Cape
Onslow
AUSTRALIA
Alice Springs
WESTERN AUSTRALIA
Shark Bay
Oodnadatta
L. Eyre
SOUTH AUSTRALIA
Geraldton
Kalgoorlie
Perth
Fremantle
Geographe Bay
Albany
K. George Sd.
Great Australian Bight
F. - A. 1353
Adelaide
Darling
Murray
NEW SOUTH WALES
Sydney
Newcastle
Katoomba
Wollongong
Canberra
Mt. Kosciusko 2230
VICTORIA
Ballarat
Geelong
Melbourne
Encounter Bay
Bass Strait
Launceston
TASMANIA
Hobart
Coral Sea
Coral Sea Islands Territory
VANUATU
New Caledonia (Fr.)
Nouméa
Chesterfield Is.
Loyalty Is.
7570
Norfolk I. (Aust.)
Lord Howe I. (Aust.)
Lord Howe Rise
Tasman Sea
Auckland
Hamilton
NEW ZEALAND
Palmerston N.
Wellington
Cook Strait
Nelson
Mt. Cook 3764
Christchurch
Oamaru
Dunedin
Invercargill
Stewart I.
Bounty
Antipodes
Auckland Is. (N.Z.)
Campbell I. (N.Z.)
Macquarie Is. (Austral.)
10,047
East Australian Current
INDIAN OCEAN
Al 'Adan - Melbourne 6445
Colombo - Fremantle 3120
Cape Town - Fremantle 5615
Cape Town - Melbourne 5814
Cape Town - Hobart 5838
Amsterdam I. (Fr.)
St Paul I. (Fr.)
Mid-Oceanic Ridge
South-East Indian Ridge
Mid-Indian Ridge
Indian Rise
Indian-Antarctic Ridge
Crozet Is. (Fr.)
Kerguelen (Fr.)
Heard Is. (Aust.)
Japan Trench 10,542
10,554
Bonin Is.
Volcano Is.
Marcus I.
Marcus Necker Ridge
Wake I. (U.S.)
South Honshu Ridge
Ryūkyū Is.
Kuro Siwo
Emperor Seamount Chain
Yokohama - Vancouver 4280
7168
6603
3389
Midway
Northern Marianas
Mariana Trench
Guam (U.S.)
11,022
U.S. TRUST TERR. OF THE PACIFIC ISLANDS
Bikini Atoll
Eniwetok Atoll
Marshall Is.
Micronesia
Yap
Belau
Fed. States of Micronesia
Truk
Ponape
Caroline Islands
Equatorial
Jaluit
Butaritari
Gilbert Is.
NAURU
Banaba
Melanesia
International Date Line
TUVALU (Ellice Is.)
Funafuti
Sta. Cruz I.
9165
Wallis & Futuna (Fr.)
Rotuma
Vanua Levu
Viti Levu
Suva
FIJI
Projection: Mollweide's Homolographic
East from Greenwich
5615 Principal Shipping Routes (Distances in Nautical Miles)
ft
m

ALASKA
Gulf of Alaska
Juneau
Sitka
Prince of Wales I.
Dawson Creek
Prince Rupert
Kitimat
Queen Charlotte Is.
L. Athabaska
Churchill
Lynn Lake
Hudson Bay
Belcher Is.
GREENLAND
C. Farewell
CANADA
Edmonton
Prince Albert
Saskatoon
L. Winnipeg
James Bay
Schefferville
Hamilton Inlet
Labrador
Strait of Belle Isle
NORTH AMERICA
Rocky Mountains
Vancouver
Vancouver I.
Victoria
Calgary
Medicine Hat
Regina
Winnipeg
St. Lawrence
Anticosti
G. of St. Lawrence
Newfoundland
Pr. Edward I.
C. Race
C. Breton I.
Fredericton
Saint John
Southampton 3091
Seattle
Tacoma
Portland
Spokane
Helena
Butte
Boise
Snake
Bismarck
Missouri
Duluth
L. Superior
Sault Ste. Marie
Montréal
Québec
Ottawa
Toronto
L. Huron
L. Ontario
Michigan
St. Paul
Minneapolis
Milwaukee
CHICAGO
L. Erie
Buffalo
Boston
C. Sable
Sable I.
New York
NEW YORK
Philadelphia
Baltimore
Washington
Richmond
Norfolk
C. Hatteras
Pittsburgh
Detroit
Cincinnati
Indianapolis
C. Blanco
C. Mendocino
Mendocino Seascarp
Sacramento
Oakland
San Francisco
Salt Lake City
Cheyenne
Denver
Des Moines
Kansas
St. Louis
Colorado
UNITED STATES
Memphis
Appalachian Mts.
Oklahoma
Little Rock
Atlanta
Santa Fé
Dallas
Mississippi
Los Angeles
San Diego
El Paso
Ciudad Juárez
Austin
Savannah
Jacksonville
Houston
New Orleans
Mobile
Galveston
San Antonio
Tampa
Miami
Gulf of Mexico
Florida Strait
BAHAMAS
Bermuda (U.K.)
New York - Recife 3678
N.Y. - C. 1972
Panamá - Liverpool 4530
ATLANTIC OCEAN
NORTH
4418
6741
2419
2091
822
Murray Seascarp
Guadalupe
6225
Pto. Eugenia
CALIFORNIAN CURRENT
Sierra Madre
Gulf of California
MEXICO
Torreón
Monterrey
C. S. Lucas
Tampico
San Luis Potosí
Aguascalientes
Guadalajara
México
Veracruz
Puebla
5700
Acapulco
Mérida
Yucatan Channel
La Habana
CUBA
Hawaiian Is. (U.S.A.)
Ridge
Oahu
Honolulu
Hawaii
Tropic of Cancer
Clarion Fracture Zone
Revilla Gigedo Is. (Mexico)
(U.S.)
PACIFIC
3277
4711
West Indies
Hispaniola
9200
7680
JAMAICA
HAITI
DOM. REP.
St. Thomas (U.S.)
Virgin Is.
Leeward Is.
Kingston
Santo Domingo
PUERTO RICO
BELIZE
GUATEMALA
Guatemala
HONDURAS
Tegucigalpa
Caribbean Sea
Guadeloupe (Fr.)
Martinique (Fr.)
BARBADOS
Curaçao (Ne.)
Windward Is.
TRINIDAD & TOBAGO
EL SALVADOR
Salvador
NICARAGUA
Managua
CENTRAL AMERICA
San José
COSTA RICA
Barranquilla
Maracaibo
Caracas
Colón
Panamá
PANAMA
Canal
Orinoco
VENEZUELA
S.E. MONSOON DRIFT
Clipperton Fracture Zone
Clipperton I. (Fr.)
CURRENT
Palmyra Is. (U.S.)
Line Islands Ridge
Teraina
Tabuaeran
Kirimati
OCEAN
Jarvis I. (U.S.)
Equator
3666
Cocos I.
Medellín
Bogotá
Cali
COLOMBIA
835
C. S. Francisco
Galápagos (Ecuador)
Quito
ECUADOR
Guayaquil
Chimborazo 6267
Cuenca
Iquitos
Manaus
Amazon
Malden I.
Starbuck I.
Tahiti - Panamá 4570
C. Pariñas
BRAZIL
Marquesas Is.
Lobos I.
Chiclayo
Trujillo
SOUTH AMERICA
Tongareva
Penrhyn Is.
Manihiki
Caroline I.
Vostok I.
Flint I.
Suwarrow Is.
East Pacific Ridge
PERUVIAN CURRENT
706
PERU
6369
Lima
Callao
Cuzco
L. Titicaca
Illampu & Ancohuma 6550
La Paz
BOLIVIA
Arequipa
Arica
6866
Peru-Chile Trench
650
Leeward Is.
Society Is.
Tuamotu Archipelago
Auckland - Panamá 6510
Southeast Pacific Basin
Cook Islands (N.Z.)
1303
Windward Is.
Tahiti
Manuae
FRENCH POLYNESIA
Tuamotu Ridge
Austral Seamount Chain
Rarotonga
Tubuai Is. (Austral Is.)
Rapa Iti
Pitcairn I. (U.K.)
Ducie I.
Tropic of Capricorn
Iquique
8050
Antofagasta Trench
PARAGUAY
Salta
Asunción
Sala-y-Gomez (Chile)
Easter Is. (Chile)
San Félix (Chile)
San Ambrosio (Chile)
793
Tucumán
Corrientes
Paraná
Pto. Alegre
Córdoba
Santa Fe
Paysandú
Rosario
URUGUAY
Montevideo
Aconcagua
6960
Arch. de Juan Fernández (Chile)
Alejandro Selkirk
Robinson Crusoe
Valparaíso
Santiago
Buenos Aires
La Plata
Río de la Plata
Concepción
ARGENTINA
Mar del Plata
Neuquen
Pacific-Antarctic Ridge
Chile Rise
P.A. - Valparaiso 1414
1355
1295
Buenos Aires - Montevideo
SOUTH ATLANTIC OCEAN
Patagonia
Andes
Chonos Arch.
Pacific-Antarctic Basin
WEST WIND DRIFT
CAPE HORN CURRENT
G. of Penas
P. Deseado
Argentine Basin
6212
Wellington Is.
Sta. Cruz
P.A. - Punta Arenas
Falkland Is. (U.K.)
Stanley
Punta Arenas
Str. of Magellan
Tierra del Fuego
C. Horn
South Georgia
West from Greenwich
160
140
120
100
80
60
40
20

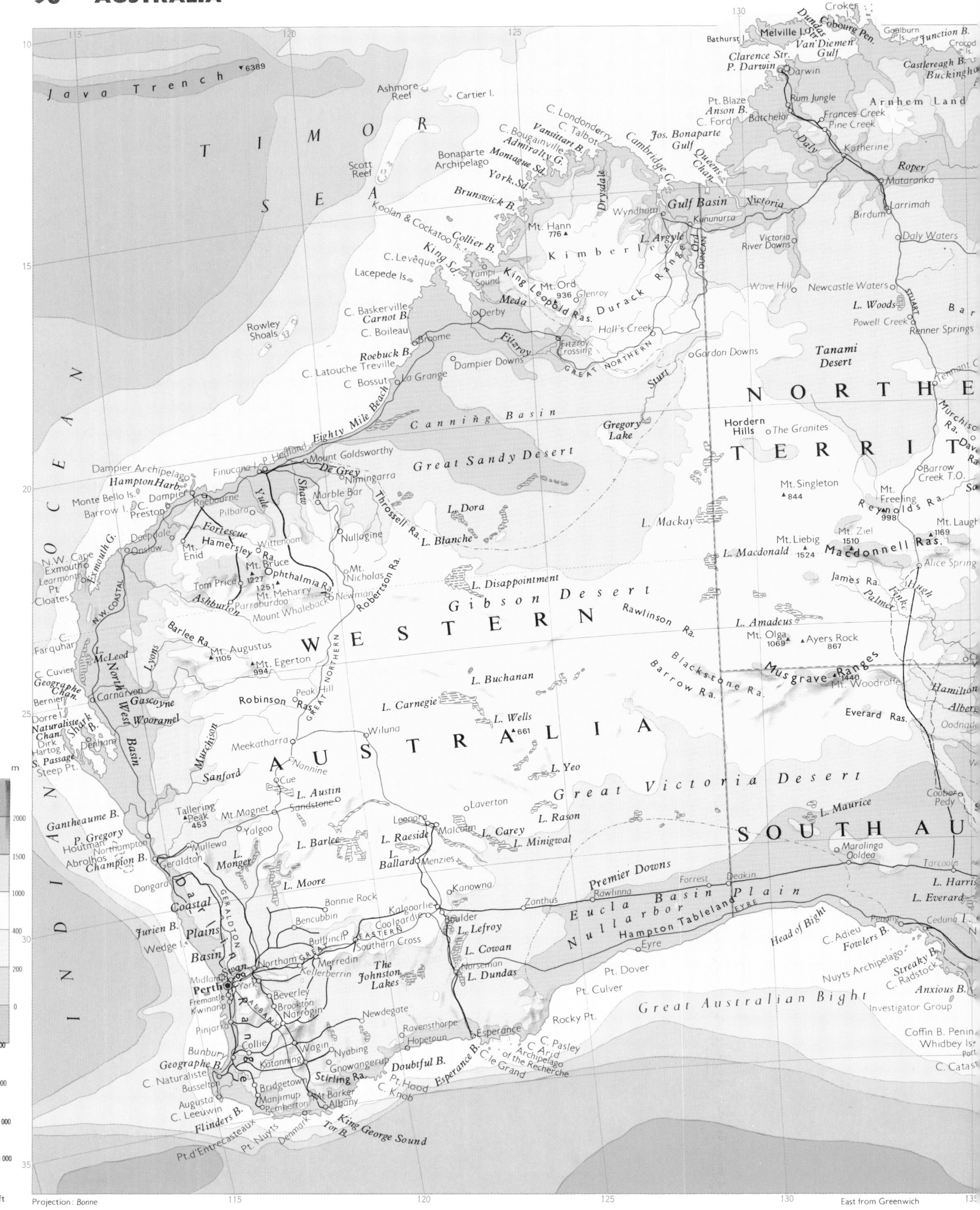

Java Trench
6389
TIMOR SEA
INDIAN OCEAN
WESTERN AUSTRALIA
NORTHERN TERRITORY
SOUTH AU
Ashmore Reef
Cartier I.
Scott Reef
Bonaparte Archipelago
Rowley Shoals
Melville I.
Bathurst I.
Dundas Str.
Cobourg Pen.
Van Diemen Gulf
Croker I.
Goulburn Is.
Junction B.
Croker Is.
Castlereagh B.
Buckingham
Clarence Str.
P. Darwin
Darwin
Rum Jungle
Arnhem Land
Pt. Blaze
Anson B.
C. Ford
Batchelor
Frances Creek
Pine Creek
Daly
Katherine
Roper
Mataranka
Larrimah
Birdum
Daly Waters
C. Londonderry
C. Talbot
Vansittart B.
C. Bougainville
Admiralty G.
Montague Sd.
York Sd.
Brunswick B.
Cambridge G.
Jos. Bonaparte Gulf
Queens Chan.
Drysdale
Wyndham
Gulf Basin
Victoria
Kununurra
Mt. Hann
776
L. Argyle
Ord
DUNCAN
Victoria River Downs
Koolan & Cockatoo Is.
Collier B.
King Sd.
C. Levêque
Lacepede Is.
Yampi Sound
Kimberley
King Leopold Ras.
Mt. Ord
936
Glenroy
Meda
Durack Range
Wave Hill
Newcastle Waters
STUART
L. Woods
Powell Creek
Renner Springs
C. Baskerville
Carnot B.
C. Boileau
Derby
Broome
Fitzroy
Fitzroy Crossing
Hall's Creek
GREAT NORTHERN
Gordon Downs
Tanami Desert
Roebuck B.
C. Latouche Treville
C. Bossut
La Grange
Dampier Downs
Sturt
Tennant C.
Eighty Mile Beach
Canning Basin
Gregory Lake
Hordern Hills
The Granites
Murchison Ra.
Davenport Ra.
Dampier Archipelago
Hampton Harb.
Finucane I.
P. Hedland
Mount Goldsworthy
De Grey
Nimingarra
Great Sandy Desert
Monte Bello Is.
Barrow I.
C. Dampier
C. Preston
Roebourne
Pilbara
Yule
Shaw
Marble Bar
Throssell Ra.
L. Dora
L. Mackay
Mt. Singleton
844
Barrow Creek T.O.
Mt. Freeling
Reynolds Ra.
998
Mt. Laughlen
1169
Exmouth G.
Deepdale
Onslow
Fortescue
Mt. Enid
Hamersley Ra.
Wittenoom
Nullagine
L. Blanche
Mt. Ziel
1510
Mt. Liebig
1524
Macdonnell Ras.
L. Macdonald
Alice Springs
N.W. Cape
Exmouth
Learmonth
Pt. Cloates
Mt. Bruce
1227
Ophthalmia Ra.
Mt. Nicholas
Robertson Ra.
Tom Price
1251
Mt. Meharry
Newman
Ashburton
Paraburdoo
Mount Whaleback
L. Disappointment
Gibson Desert
Rawlinson Ra.
James Ra.
Palmer
Finke
Hugh
N.W. COASTAL
C. Farquhar
Barlee Ra.
Mt. Augustus
1105
Mt. Egerton
994
Lyons
L. Amadeus
Mt. Olga
1069
Ayers Rock
867
L. McLeod
North West Basin
Blackstone Ra.
Barrow Ra.
Musgrave Ranges
1440
Mt. Woodroffe
C. Cuvier
Geographe Chan.
Bernier I.
Carnarvon
Gascoyne
Peak Hill
Robinson Ras.
GREAT NORTHERN
L. Buchanan
L. Carnegie
L. Wells
661
Everard Ras.
Hamilton
Alberga
Oodnadatta
Dorre I.
Naturaliste Chan.
Dirk Hartog I.
Shark B.
Denham
Wooramel
S. Passage
Steep Pt.
Murchison
Meekatharra
Wiluna
Nannine
Cue
L. Yeo
Sanford
L. Austin
Sandstone
Great Victoria Desert
Gantheaume B.
Tallering Peak
453
Mt. Magnet
Laverton
Yalgoo
L. Rason
Coober Pedy
L. Maurice
Leonora
Malcolm
L. Raeside
L. Carey
L. Minigwal
P. Gregory
Houtman Abrolhos
Northampton
Mullewa
Geraldton
Champion B.
L. Monger
L. Barlee
L. Ballard
Menzies
Maralinga
Ooldea
Tarcoola
Dongara
Dandaragan
L. Moore
Kanowna
Forrest
Deakin
Premier Downs
Rawlinna
Eucla Basin
Nullarbor Plain
EYRE
L. Harris
L. Everard
Coastal Plains Basin
GERALDTON
Bonnie Rock
Kalgoorlie
Coolgardie
Boulder
Zanthus
Hampton Tableland
Head of Bight
Penong
Ceduna
Jurien B.
Bencubbin
Bullfinch
EASTERN
GREAT
Southern Cross
L. Lefroy
C. Adieu
Fowlers B.
Wedge I.
L. Cowan
Eyre
Nuyts Archipelago
Streaky B.
C. Radstock
Merredin
Kellerberrin
The Johnston Lakes
Norseman
L. Dundas
Pt. Dover
Anxious B.
Swan
Northam
Midland
Perth
York
Fremantle
Kwinana
Beverley
Brookton
Narrogin
ALBANY
Darling Range
Pt. Culver
Great Australian Bight
Investigator Group
Newdegate
Rocky Pt.
Pinjarra
Ravensthorpe
Hopetoun
Esperance
C. Pasley
C. Arid
Archipelago of the Recherche
Coffin B. Penin.
Whidbey Is.
Bunbury
Collie
Wagin
Nyabing
Geographe B.
Katanning
Gnowangerup
Doubtful B.
Esperance B.
C. le Grand
C. Catastrophe
C. Naturaliste
Busselton
Bridgetown
Stirling Ra.
Pt. Hood
C. Knob
Augusta
C. Leeuwin
Manjimup
Pemberton
Mt Barker
Albany
Flinders B.
Pt. d'Entrecasteaux
Pt. Nuyts
Denmark
Tor B.
King George Sound
ft m
6000 2000
4500 1500
3000 1000
1200 400
600 200
0 0
200 600
2000 6000
4000 12 000
6000 18 000
m ft
10
15
20
25
30
35
115
120
125
130
135
Projection: Bonne
East from Greenwich

Boundaries of the artesian basins

1:12 000 000
100 0 100 200 miles
100 0 100 200 300 400 km
AUSTRALASIA
POLITICAL
1:80 000 000
INDONESIA
IRIAN JAYA
PAPUA NEW GUINEA
SOLOMON ISLANDS
INDIAN OCEAN
AUSTRALIA
WESTERN AUSTRALIA
NORTHERN TERRITORY
QUEENSLAND
SOUTH AUSTRALIA
NEW SOUTH WALES
VICTORIA
TASMANIA
PACIFIC OCEAN
SOUTHERN OCEAN
Tasman Sea
NEW ZEALAND
Tropic of Capricorn
International Date Line
Thursday I.
Banks I.
Prince of Wales I.
C. York
Newcastle B.
Endeavour Str.
P. Musgrave
Shelburne B.
C. Grenville
Cape York Peninsula
Temple B.
Duifken Pt.
Albatross B.
Weipa
Wenlock
C. Weymouth
C. Direction
Coral Sea Basin
Gulf of Carpentaria
Archer
C. Keer-Weer
Holroyd
Coen
Princess Charlotte B.
Bathurst B.
C. Melville
Osprey Rf.
Great Barrier Reef
Coleman
Normanby
C. Flattery
C. Bedford
Cooktown
Laura
Mornington I.
C. van Diemen
Wellesley Is.
Bentinck I.
Mitchell
C. Tribulation
Trinity Bay
Mossman
Gilbert
Chillagoe
Mareeba
Cairns
Atherton
Bartle Frere
Innisfail
C. Grafton
Burketown
Normanton
Georgetown
Croydon
Newcastle Ra.
Einasleigh
Forsayth
Gregory Ra.
Norman
Leichhardt
Hinchinbrook I.
Ingham
Palm Is.
Seaview Ra.
Greenvale
Halifax B.
Townsville
C. Cleveland
C. Bowling Green
Dobbyn
Camooweal
Kajabbi
Flinders
Ayr
Home Hill
Bowen
Mount Isa
Mary Kathleen
Cloncurry
Julia Cr.
Richmond
Pentland
Charters Towers
Proserpine
Whitsunday I.
Cumberland Is.
Selwyn Range
Selwyn
Duchess
Dajarra
Georgina
Hughenden
Mt. Dalrymple
Collinsville
Netherdale
Repulse B.
Mackay
C. Palmerston
Sarina
Denham Ra.
Broad Sd.
Connors Ra.
QUEENSLAND
Winton
Muttaburra
Boulia
Diamantina
Belyando
Blair Athol
Clermont
Isaac
Peak Ra.
Drummond Ra.
Great Dividing Range
Longreach
Ilfracombe
Barcaldine
Aramac
Alpha
Emerald
Nogoa
Mackenzie
Thomson
Bedourie
Eyre Cr.
L. Machattie
Jundah
Barcoo
Blackall
Springsure
Yaraka
Windorah
Warrego Ra.
Mt. Morgan
Rockhampton
Yeppoon
Keppel B.
C. Capricorn
Curtis I.
P. Curtis
Gladstone
Biloela
Bustard Head
Dawson
Expedition Ra.
Mt. Acland
Theodore
Moura
Birdsville
Augathella
Adavale
Charleville
Injune
Taroom
Gayndah
Bundaberg
Burnett
Hervey Bay
Maryborough
Childers
Sandy C.
Fraser I.
L. Yamma Yamma
Quilpie
Warburton
Cooper Creek
Strzelecki Cr.
Bulloo
Grey Range
Mitchell
Roma
Wandoan
Miles
Murgon
Wondai
Kingaroy
Nanango
Gympie
Nambour
Bribie I.
Moreton B.
Condamine
Maranoa
Balonne
Wyandra
Thargomindah
Cunnamulla
St. George
Moonie
Dalby
Toowoomba
Ipswich
Brisbane
Moreton I.
N. Stradbroke I.
Southport
L. Gregory
L. Blanche
L. Eyre (South)
L. Callabonna
L. Frome
Tibooburra
Paroo
Dirranbandi
Goondiwindi
Mungindi
Macintyre
Warwick
Stanthorpe
Murwillumbah
Mt. Barney
Sutherland Pt.
C. Byron
Lismore
Ballina
Casino
Tenterfield
Gwydir
Moree
Warialda
Inverell
Clarence
Grafton
Glen Innes
Bourke
Barwon
Walgett
Paroo Chan.
Barrier Ra.
Narrabri
The Round Mountain
Coffs Harbour
St. Mary Pk.
Hawker
Flinders Ranges
NEW SOUTH WALES
Coonamble
Liverpool Plains
Bogan
Macquarie
Castlereagh
New England Range
Armidale
Tamworth
Gunnedah
Macleay
Broken Hill
Wilcannia
Darling
Cobar
Nyngan
Gilgandra
Liverpool Ra.
Kempsey
Port Macquarie
Radium Hill
Menindee
Barrier
Taree
Barrington Tops
Peterborough
Jamestown
Burra
Ivanhoe
Narromine
Dubbo
Wellington
Mudgee
Muswellbrook
Singleton
Cessnock
Maitland
Sugarloaf Pt.
P. Stephens
Newcastle
Roto
Condobolin
Parkes
Hillston
L. Cargelligo
Forbes
Orange
Bathurst
Lithgow
Katoomba
Penrith
Hawkesbury R.
Murray River
Wentworth
Mildura
Lachlan
Cowal
Murrumbidgee Irrigation Area
Cowra
SYDNEY & Port Jackson
Renmark
Murray
Gawler
Elizabeth
Adelaide
Loxton
Balranald
Hay
Griffith
Leeton
Narrandera
Cootamundra
Young
Wollongong
Shellharbour
Nowra
Bowral
G. St. Vincent
Mt. Lofty
Murray Bridge
Pinnaroo
Ouyen
Swan Hill
Kerang
Murrumbidgee
Junee
Wagga Wagga
Yass
Goulburn
Jervis B.
Tasman Sea
Alexandrina
Coorong
Encounter B.
Wimmera
Riverina
Deniliquin
Echuca
Shepparton
Wangaratta
Albury
Tumut
Canberra
Queanbeyan
Bordertown
Horsham
Bendigo
L. Hume
Benalla
Mt. Bogong
Mt. Kosciusko
Cooma
Batemans B.
Kingston S.E.
Naracoorte
Stawell
VICTORIA
Ararat
Maryborough
Castlemaine
Bega
Penola
Millicent
Mt. Gambier
Hamilton
Ballarat
MELBOURNE
Australian Alps
Gippsland
Bombala
Twofold B.
Disaster B.
C. Howe
Mallacoota Inlet
C. Northumberland
Discovery B.
C. Bridgewater
Portland
Port Fairy
Warrnambool
Geelong
Colac
Moe
Sale
Yallourn
Morwell
Traralgon
Bairnsdale
Orbost
Snowy
Pt. Hicks
C. Otway
Port Phillip B.
Phillip I.
Wonthaggi
Ninety Mile Beach
Corner Inlet
Lihou Reef & Cays
Mellish Reef
CORAL SEA ISLANDS TERRITORY
Marion Reef
PACIFIC OCEAN
Îles Avon
Îles Chesterfield
Frederick Reef
Kenn Reef
Swain Rfs.
Saumarez Rf.
Bellona Rfs.
Wreck Reef
Bird I.
Cato I.
Tropic of Capricorn
C. Townshend
Townshend I.
Bass Strait
King I.
Wilsons Promontory
Flinders I.
Furneaux Group
Cape Barren I.
C. Portland
Clarke I.
Hunter I.
C. Grim
Devonport
Scottsdale
Launceston
Ben Lomond
Burnie
Ulverstone
Beaconsfield
Sandy C.
Zeehan
Mt. Ossa
St. Marys
Strahan
Great L.
Freycinet Penin.
Macquarie Harb.
Queenstown
TASMANIA
New Norfolk
Hobart
Low Rocky Pt.
Huonville
Tasman Penin.
P. Arthur
Storm B.
P. Davey
Bruny I.
S.E. Cape
on same scale
COPYRIGHT, GEORGE PHILIP & SON, LTD

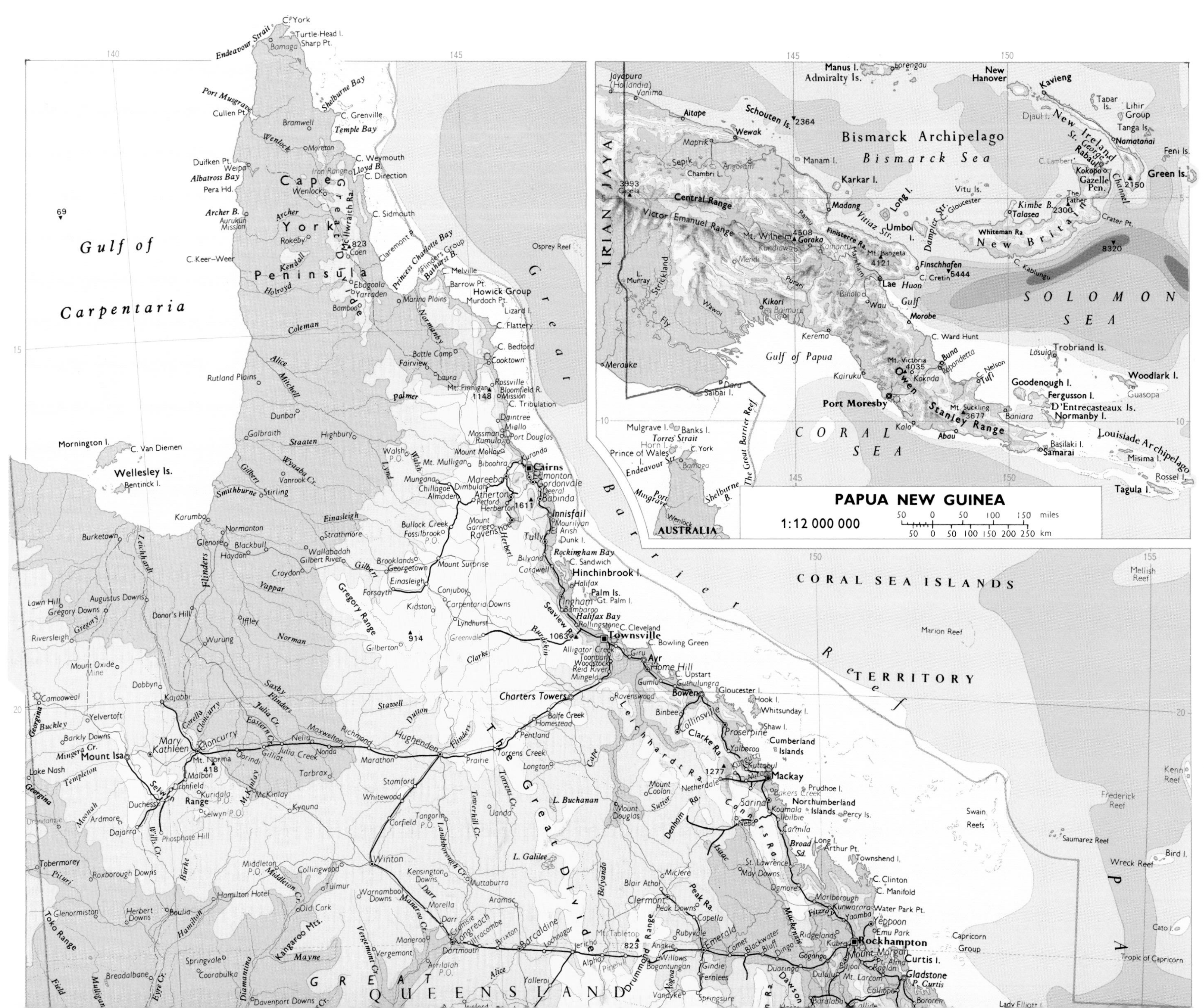
PAPUA NEW GUINEA
1:12 000 000
Bismarck Archipelago
Bismarck Sea
SOLOMON SEA
CORAL SEA
Gulf of Papua
New Ireland
New Britain
Owen Stanley Range
Central Range
Victor Emanuel Range
Port Moresby
Lae
Madang
Wewak
Rabaul
IRIAN JAYA
AUSTRALIA
Louisiade Archipelago
Trobriand Is.
Woodlark I.
D'Entrecasteaux Is.
Torres Strait
The Great Barrier Reef
CORAL SEA ISLANDS TERRITORY
Great Barrier Reef
Gulf of Carpentaria
Cape York Peninsula
Wellesley Is.
Mornington I.
Cairns
Townsville
Mackay
Rockhampton
Gladstone
Cooktown
Charters Towers
Mount Isa
Cloncurry
Hughenden
Winton
Longreach
Normanton
Burketown
Innisfail
Bowen
Ayr
Hinchinbrook I.
Whitsunday I.
Cumberland Islands
Northumberland Islands
Curtis I.
Capricorn Group
Swain Reefs
Tropic of Capricorn
The Great Divide
Gregory Range
Selwyn Range
Leichhardt Ra.
Clarke Ra.
Peak Ra.
Drummond Range
L. Buchanan
L. Galilee
Flinders
Leichhardt
Burdekin
Mitchell
Gilbert
Herbert
Diamantina
Dawson
Mackenzie
GREAT
QUEENSLAND

1:7 500 000
50 0 50 100 150 200 miles
50 0 50 100 150 200 250 300 km
FIC OCEAN
Tasman Sea
NEW SOUTH WALES
SOUTH AUSTRALIA
VICTORIA
TASMANIA
Bass Strait
Great Divide
The Great Divide
Flinders Ranges
Grey Range
BASIN
BRISBANE
SYDNEY
CANBERRA
MELBOURNE
ADELAIDE
Hobart
Launceston
Newcastle
Wollongong
Broken Hill
Dubbo
Wagga Wagga
Albury
Bendigo
Ballarat
Geelong
Mildura
Port Augusta
Port Pirie
Whyalla
Mount Gambier
Toowoomba
Ipswich
Lismore
Tamworth
Armidale
Coffs Harbour
Port Macquarie
Charleville
Roma
Bourke
Kangaroo I.
Spencer Gulf
Gulf St. Vincent
Flinders Island
King Island
Continuation Southwards
Projection: Bonne
East from Greenwich
COPYRIGHT. GEORGE PHILIP & SON. LTD.

1:4 500 000

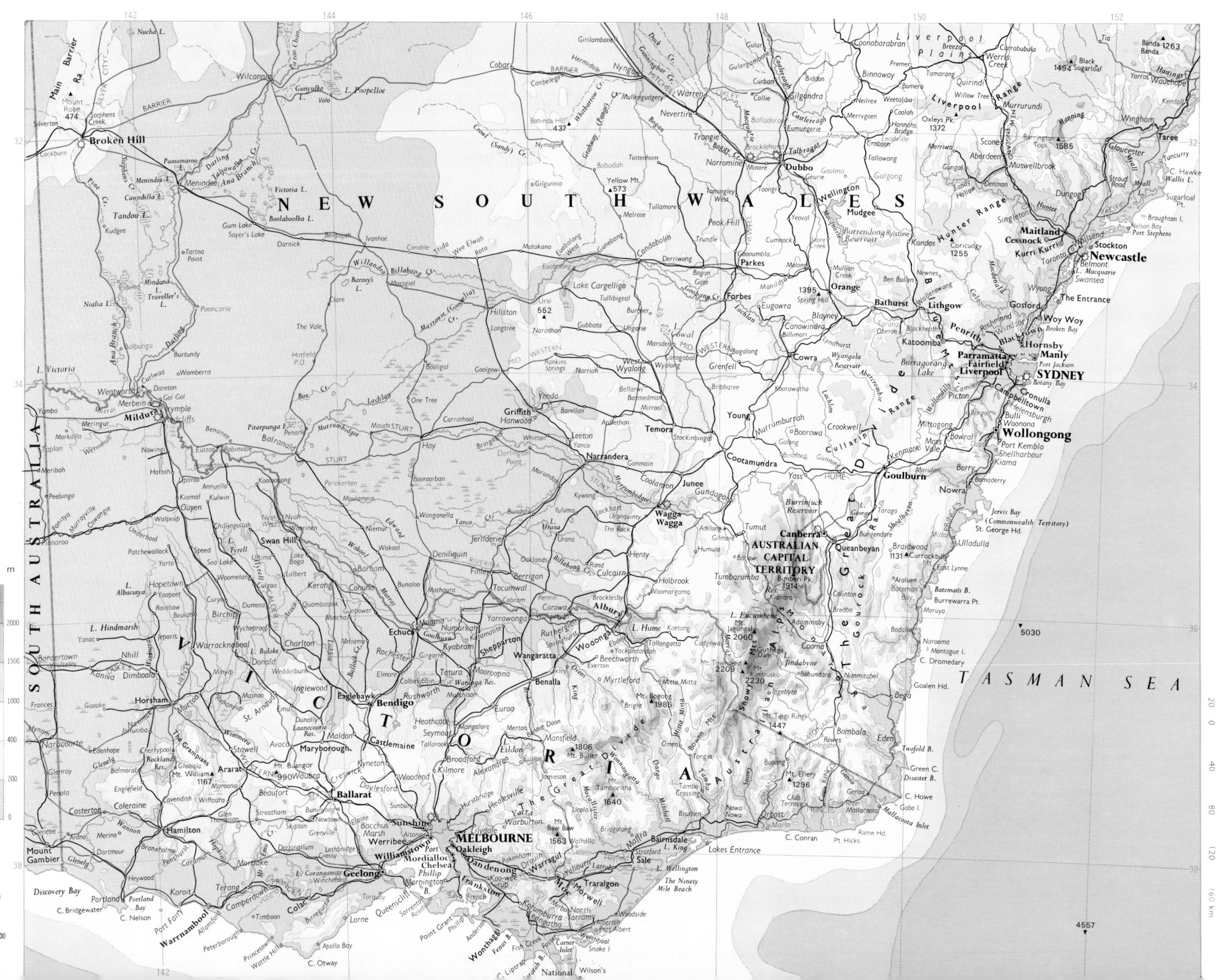
20 0 20 40 60 80 100 miles
20 0 40 80 120 160 km
NEW SOUTH WALES
VICTORIA
AUSTRALIAN CAPITAL TERRITORY
SOUTH AUSTRALIA
TASMAN SEA
SYDNEY
MELBOURNE
Canberra
Newcastle
Wollongong
Broken Hill
Mildura
Bendigo
Ballarat
Geelong
Albury
Wagga Wagga
Dubbo
Orange
Bathurst
Goulburn
Mount Gambier
Warrnambool
ft
m
6000
2000
4500
1500
3000
1000
1200
400
600
200
0
0
200
600
2000
6000
4000
12 000

1:6 000 000

20 0 20 40 60 80 100 miles

20 0 40 80 120 160 km

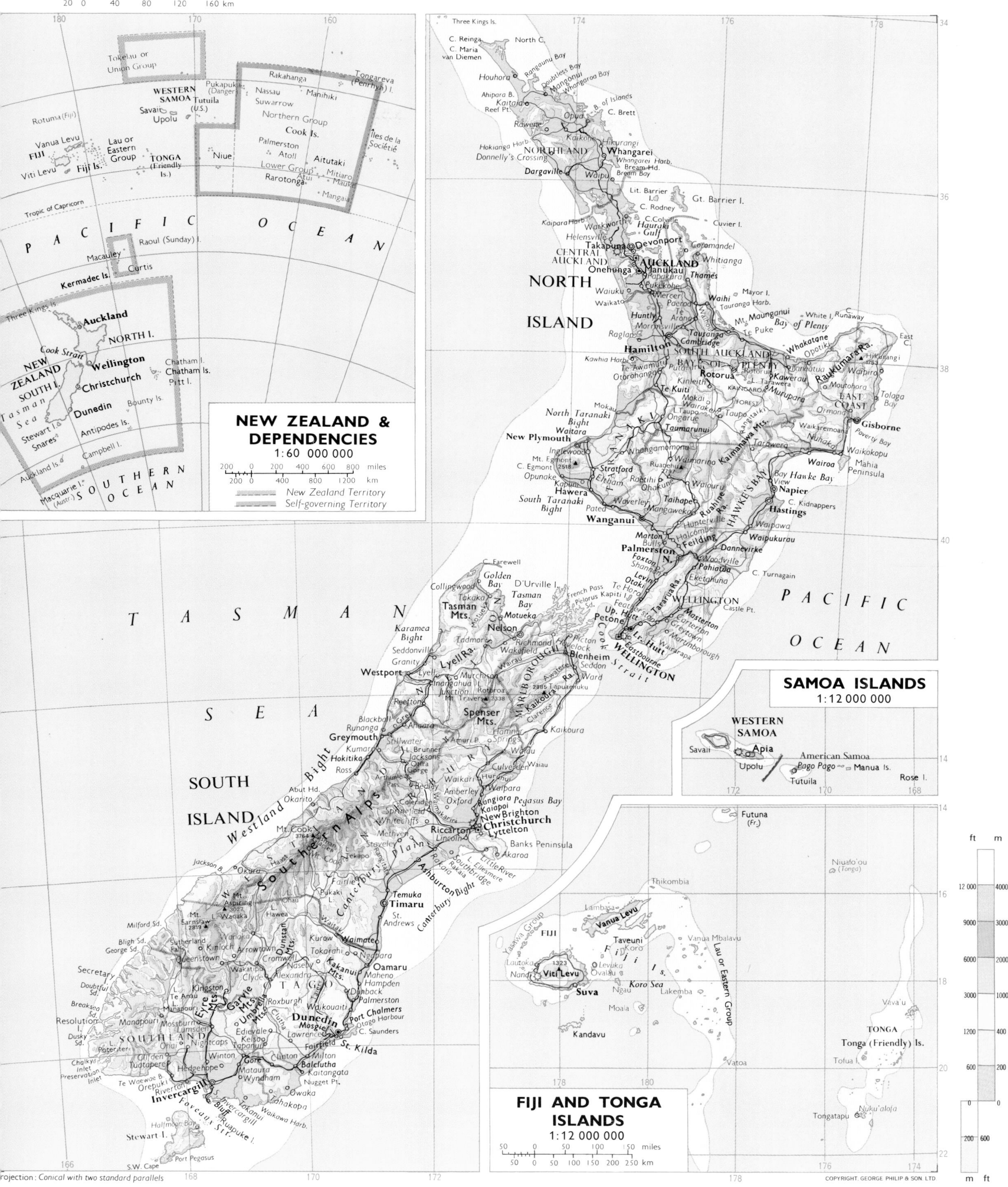
NEW ZEALAND & DEPENDENCIES
1:60 000 000
200 0 200 400 600 800 miles
200 0 400 800 1200 km
New Zealand Territory
Self-governing Territory
Tokelau or Union Group
WESTERN SAMOA
Savai'i
Upolu
Tutuila (U.S.)
Pukapuka (Danger)
Rakahanga
Manihiki
Nassau
Suwarrow
Northern Group
Tongareva (Penrhyn) I.
Cook Is.
Palmerston Atoll
Lower Group
Aitutaki
Atiu
Mitiaro
Mauke
Mangaia
Rarotonga
Niue
Îles de la Société
Rotuma (Fiji)
Vanua Levu
FIJI
Viti Levu
Fiji Is.
Lau or Eastern Group
TONGA (Friendly Is.)
Tropic of Capricorn
PACIFIC OCEAN
Raoul (Sunday) I.
Macauley I.
Curtis
Kermadec Is.
Three Kings Is.
Auckland
NORTH I.
Cook Strait
NEW ZEALAND
Wellington
SOUTH I.
Christchurch
Dunedin
Tasman Sea
Chatham I.
Chatham Is.
Pitt I.
Bounty Is.
Antipodes Is.
Stewart I.
Snares
Campbell I.
Auckland Is.
Macquarie I. (Austr.)
SOUTHERN OCEAN
NORTH ISLAND
SOUTH ISLAND
TASMAN SEA
PACIFIC OCEAN
NORTHLAND
CENTRAL AUCKLAND
SOUTH AUCKLAND BAY OF PLENTY
EAST COAST
HAWKE'S BAY
TARANAKI
WELLINGTON
NELSON
MARLBOROUGH
WESTLAND
CANTERBURY
OTAGO
SOUTHLAND
AUCKLAND
Whangarei
Dargaville
Hamilton
Rotorua
Taumarunui
New Plymouth
Gisborne
Napier
Hastings
Wanganui
Palmerston N.
Cook Strait
WELLINGTON
Nelson
Blenheim
Westport
Greymouth
Hokitika
Christchurch
Timaru
Oamaru
Dunedin
Invercargill
Southern Alps
Mt. Cook 3764
Canterbury Plains
Stewart I.
SAMOA ISLANDS
1:12 000 000
WESTERN SAMOA
Savaii
Apia
Upolu
American Samoa
Pago Pago
Tutuila
Manua Is.
Rose I.
FIJI AND TONGA ISLANDS
1:12 000 000
50 0 50 100 150 miles
50 0 50 100 150 200 250 km
Futuna (Fr.)
Niuafo'ou (Tonga)
Thikombia
Vanua Levu
Taveuni
Fiji Is.
Viti Levu
Suva
Koro Sea
Kandavu
Lau or Eastern Group
TONGA
Tonga (Friendly) Is.
Tongatapu
Nuku'alofa
Vava'u
ft m
12 000 4000
9000 3000
6000 2000
3000 1000
1200 400
600 200
0 0
200 600
m ft
Projection: Conical with two standard parallels
COPYRIGHT. GEORGE PHILIP & SON. LTD.

ARCTIC OCEAN
ATLANTIC
PACIFIC
Greenland
Greenland Sea
Denmark Strait
Iceland
Baffin Bay
Davis Strait
Baffin Island
Hudson Bay
Hudson Strait
James Bay
Labrador
Newfoundland
Laurentian Plateau
Ungava Peninsula
Southampton I.
Foxe Basin
Foxe Channel
Melville Pen.
Boothia Pen.
Gulf of Boothia
Cumberland Sound
Frobisher Bay
Ellesmere I.
Axel Heiberg Land
Sverdrup Is.
Queen Elizabeth Islands
Devon I.
Lancaster Sound
Parry Is.
Melville I.
Melville Sound
M'Clure Strait
Banks I.
Victoria I.
Prince of Wales I.
Kane Basin
Nares Str.
Thule
Beaufort Sea
Mackenzie Mts.
Great Bear L.
Great Slave L.
Athabasca L.
Lake Winnipeg
Brooks Range
Alaska
Alaska Range
Mt. McKinley 6194
Mt. St. Elias 5489
Mt. Logan 6050
Gulf of Alaska
Alexander Archipelago
Queen Charlotte Islands
Queen Charlotte Sound
Vancouver I.
Juan de Fuca Strait
Coast Mountains
Rocky Mountains
Selkirk Mts.
Great Plains
Cascade Range
Sierra Nevada
Coast Range
Great Basin
Wasatch Mountains
Colorado Plateau
Death Valley
Mt. Whitney 4418
Mt. Shasta 4317
Mt. Rainier 4392
Mt. Robson 3954
Mt. Waddington 3994
Mt. Elbert 4399
Blanca Pk. 4364
Appalachian Mts.
Allegheny Mts.
Blue Ridge 2037
Cumberland Plateau
Ozark Plateau
Bering Strait
Bering Sea
Aleutian Islands
Alaska Pen.
Kodiak I.
Nunivak I.
St. Lawrence I.
Wrangel I.
Asia
Mendocino Seascarp
Murray Seascarp
Gulf of St. Lawrence
Nova Scotia
Bay of Fundy
New York
Philadelphia
Washington
Chesapeake Bay
C. Hatteras
Bermuda
Montreal
Quebec
Ottawa
Toronto
Hamilton
Detroit
Chicago
St. Louis
Memphis
Atlanta
Kansas City
Minneapolis
Winnipeg
Regina
Edmonton
Calgary
Denver
Vancouver
Seattle
Portland
San Francisco
Los Angeles
Missouri
Mississippi
Ohio
Yukon
Mackenzie
Porcupine
Peace
Athabasca
N. Saskatchewan
S. Saskatchewan
Nelson
Churchill
Fraser
Columbia
Snake
Colorado
Great Salt Lake
L. Superior
L. Michigan
L. Huron
L. Erie
L. Ontario
Niagara Falls
Mt. Washington 1917
C. Farewell
Godthåb
Julianehåb
Hamilton Inlet
Belle Isle Strait
Anticosti
Resolution I.
Belcher Is.
Arctic Circle
C. Barrow
Kicking Horse Pass
Yellowhead Pass
Crowsnest Pass
Mt. Forel 3360
Gunnbjørns Field 3700
Petermann's Peak 2940
Llano Estacado

1:30 000 000

100 0 100 200 300 400 500 600 700 miles

100 0 200 400 600 800 1000 km

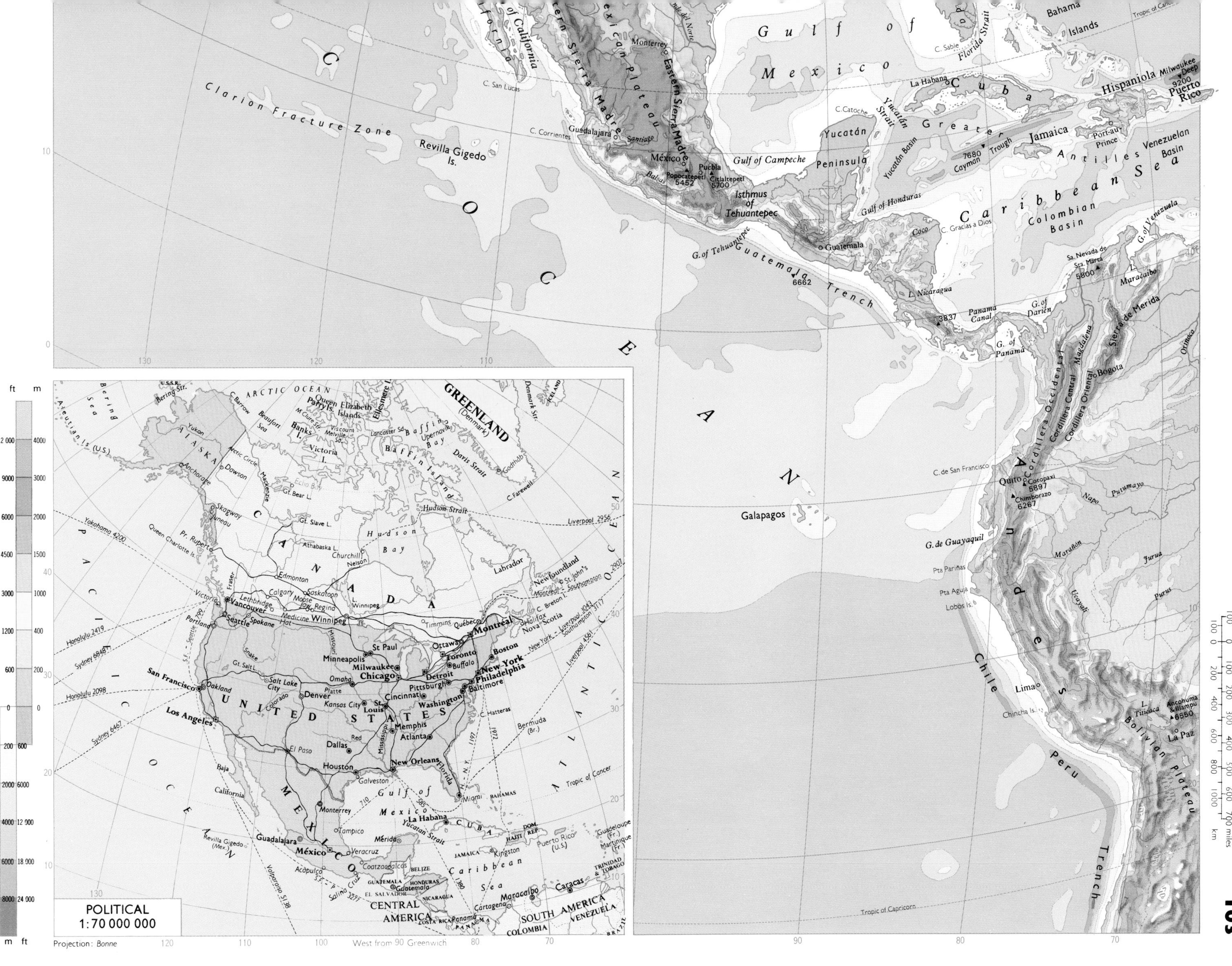

Gulf of Mexico
Caribbean Sea
Pacific Ocean
Cuba
Hispaniola
Jamaica
Puerto Rico
Bahama Islands
Greater Antilles
Yucatán Peninsula
Yucatán Strait
Gulf of Honduras
Gulf of Campeche
Isthmus of Tehuantepec
Eastern Sierra Madre
Mexican Plateau
México
Guatemala
Panama Canal
G. of Panama
Colombian Basin
Venezuelan Basin
Cayman Trough
Andes
Sierra de Merida
Cordillera Oriental
Cordillera Central
Cordillera Occidental
Bolivian Plateau
Peru Chile Trench
Guatemala Trench
Galapagos
Revilla Gigedo Is.
Clarion Fracture Zone
La Habana
Quito
Lima
La Paz
G. de Guayaquil
Tropic of Capricorn
GREENLAND (Denmark)
CANADA
UNITED STATES
MEXICO
CENTRAL AMERICA
SOUTH AMERICA
ALASKA
Hudson Bay
Baffin Island
ARCTIC OCEAN
ATLANTIC OCEAN
PACIFIC OCEAN
Tropic of Cancer
West from 90 Greenwich
POLITICAL 1:70 000 000
Projection: Bonne

PACIFIC OCEAN
ALASKA
YUKON TERRITORY
NORTHWEST TERRITORIES
INUVIK
MACKENZIE
FRANKLIN
KEEWATIN
CENTRAL ARCTIC
BRITISH COLUMBIA
ALBERTA
SASKATCHEWAN
MANITOBA
UNITED STATES
WASHINGTON
MONTANA
NORTH DAKOTA
SOUTH DAKOTA
MINNESOTA
NEBRASKA
WYOMING
Mackenzie Mountains
Rocky Mountains
Coast Mountains
Cassiar Mountains
Columbia Mountains
Selkirk Mts.
Cariboo Mts.
St. Elias Mts.
Wrangell Mts.
Franklin Mts.
Caribou Mts.
Banks Island
Victoria Island
Prince of Wales Island
Prince Albert Pen.
Wollaston Pen.
Amundsen Gulf
Coronation Gulf
Queen Maud Gulf
M'Clintock Channel
Viscount Melville Sound
Great Bear Lake
Great Slave L.
Lake Athabasca
Reindeer Lake
Lake Winnipeg
Lake Manitoba
Queen Charlotte Is.
Vancouver I.
Juan de Fuca Str.
Anchorage
Fairbanks
Whitehorse
Dawson
Inuvik
Yellowknife
Edmonton
Calgary
Vancouver
Victoria
Seattle
Tacoma
Spokane
Saskatoon
Regina
Moose Jaw
Prince Albert
Lethbridge
Medicine Hat
Winnipeg
St. Boniface
Minneapolis
Omaha
Prince George
Prince Rupert
Kamloops
Mt. Logan 6050
Mt. Robson 3954
Churchill Pk. 3200
Mt. Waddington 3994
Projection: Bonne
ALASKA
1:30 000 000
U.S.S.R.
BERING SEA
Aleutian Is.
GULF OF ALASKA
Brooks Range
Alaska Range
Seward Pen.
Alaska Peninsula
Kodiak I.
Nome
Juneau
Sitka
Ketchikan
West from Greenwich

1:15 000 000

100 50 0 100 200 300 400 miles

100 0 100 200 300 400 500 600 km

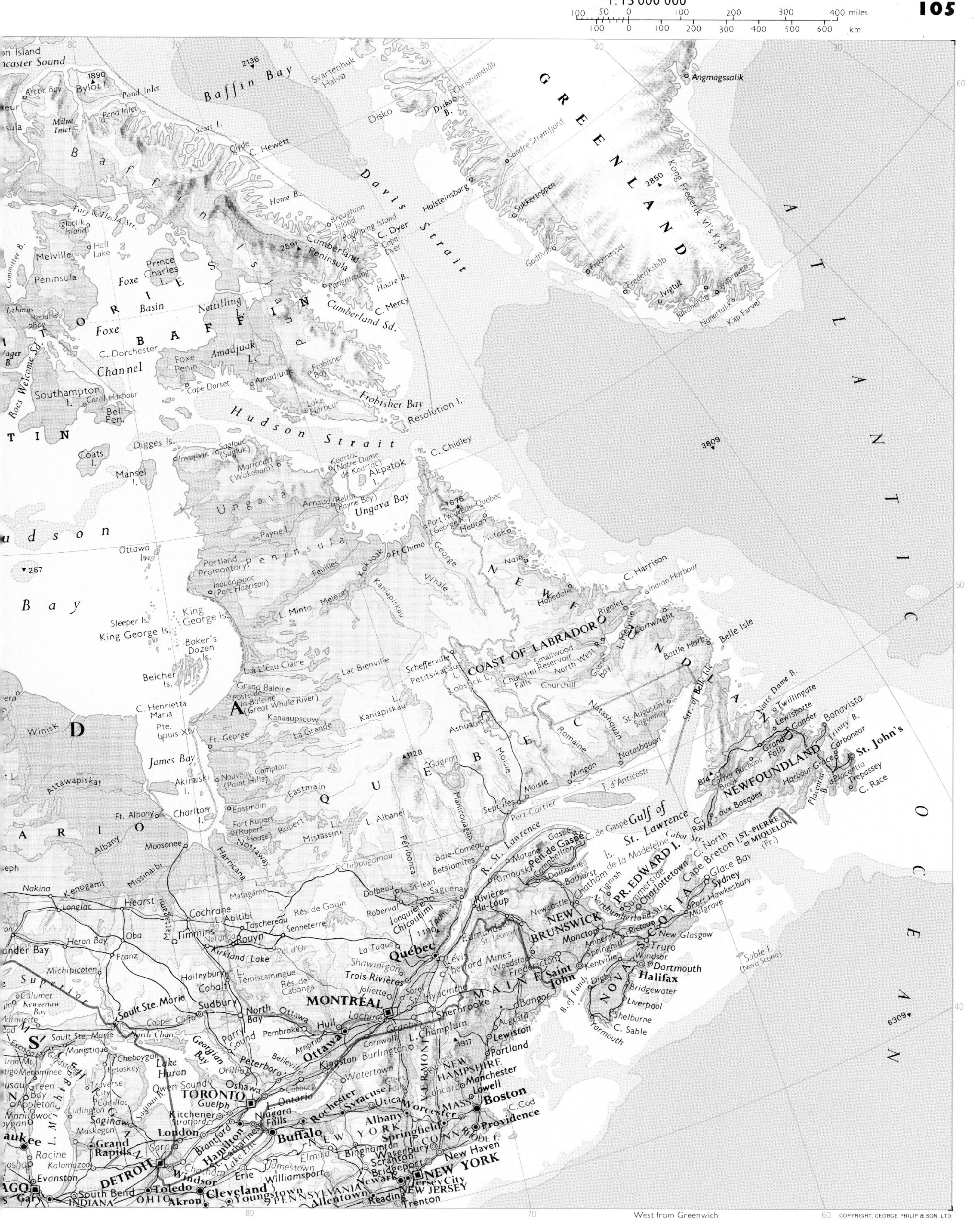
Baffin Bay
Davis Strait
GREENLAND
ATLANTIC OCEAN
Hudson Strait
Ungava Peninsula
Ungava Bay
Hudson Bay
James Bay
Foxe Basin
Foxe Channel
BAFFIN I.
COAST OF LABRADOR
NEWFOUNDLAND
QUEBEC
Gulf of St. Lawrence
NEW BRUNSWICK
NOVA SCOTIA
PR. EDWARD I.
ST. PIERRE et MIQUELON (Fr.)
MONTRÉAL
Québec
Ottawa
TORONTO
DETROIT
Boston
NEW YORK
Buffalo
Cleveland
Halifax
St. John's
Angmagssalik
Frobisher Bay
Resolution I.
Lake Huron
L. Ontario
Lake Erie
West from Greenwich

N. W TERRITORIES

MANITOBA

HUDSON BAY

JAMES BAY

ONTARIO

LAKE SUPERIOR

LAKE HURON

LAKE MICHIGAN

LAKE ERIE

LAKE ONTARIO

WISCONSIN

MICHIGAN

ILLINOIS

NEW YORK

ft	m
4500	1500
3000	1000
1200	400
600	200
0	0
200	600
2000	6000
4000	12 000
m	ft

Lambert's Equivalent Azimuthal

INDIANA OHIO PENNSYLVANIA

1:7 000 000

50 0 50 100 150 200 miles
50 0 50 100 150 200 250 300 km

COAST OF LABRADOR
NEWFOUNDLAND
QUEBEC
NEW BRUNSWICK
NOVA SCOTIA
PRINCE EDWARD ISLAND
MAINE
GULF OF ST. LAWRENCE
ATLANTIC OCEAN
Cabot Strait
Str. of Belle Isle
Bay of Fundy
St. Lawrence
Î. d'Anticosti
Dét. de Jacques-Cartier
Dét. d'Honguedo
Pén. de Gaspé
Mts. Chic-Chocs
Îs. de la Madeleine (Quebec)
Cape Breton Island
SAINT-PIERRE ET MIQUELON (Fr.)
Sable I. (Nova Scotia)
Smallwood Reservoir
Rés. Manicouagan
Mealy Mts.
Long Range Mts.
L. Melville
South Aulatsivik I.
Nain
Hopedale
Happy Valley
Goose Bay
North-West River
Churchill Falls
Schefferville
Labrador City
Wabush
Sept-Îles
Port-Cartier
Havre-St-Pierre
Baie-Comeau
Matane
Rimouski
Chicoutimi
Rivière-du-Loup
Gaspé
Campbellton
Dalhousie
Bathurst
Chatham
Newcastle
Moncton
Fredericton
Saint John
Edmundston
Charlottetown
Summerside
Amherst
Truro
New Glasgow
Halifax
Dartmouth
Yarmouth
Sydney
Glace Bay
New Waterford
Sydney Mines
Louisbourg
Corner Brook
Stephenville
Gander
Grand Falls
Botwood
Lewisporte
St. John's
Avalon Peninsula
Channel-Port aux Basques
St. Pierre
Miquelon
Bangor
Augusta
Waterville
Lewiston
Auburn
Portland
Rockland
Bath
Brunswick
Saco
Biddeford
Sanford
Portsmouth
Manchester
Nashua
Haverhill
Lawrence
Lynn
Gloucester
BOSTON
Brockton
Thetford Mines
Lac-Mégantic
Montmagny
Lauzon
Lévis
West from Greenwich

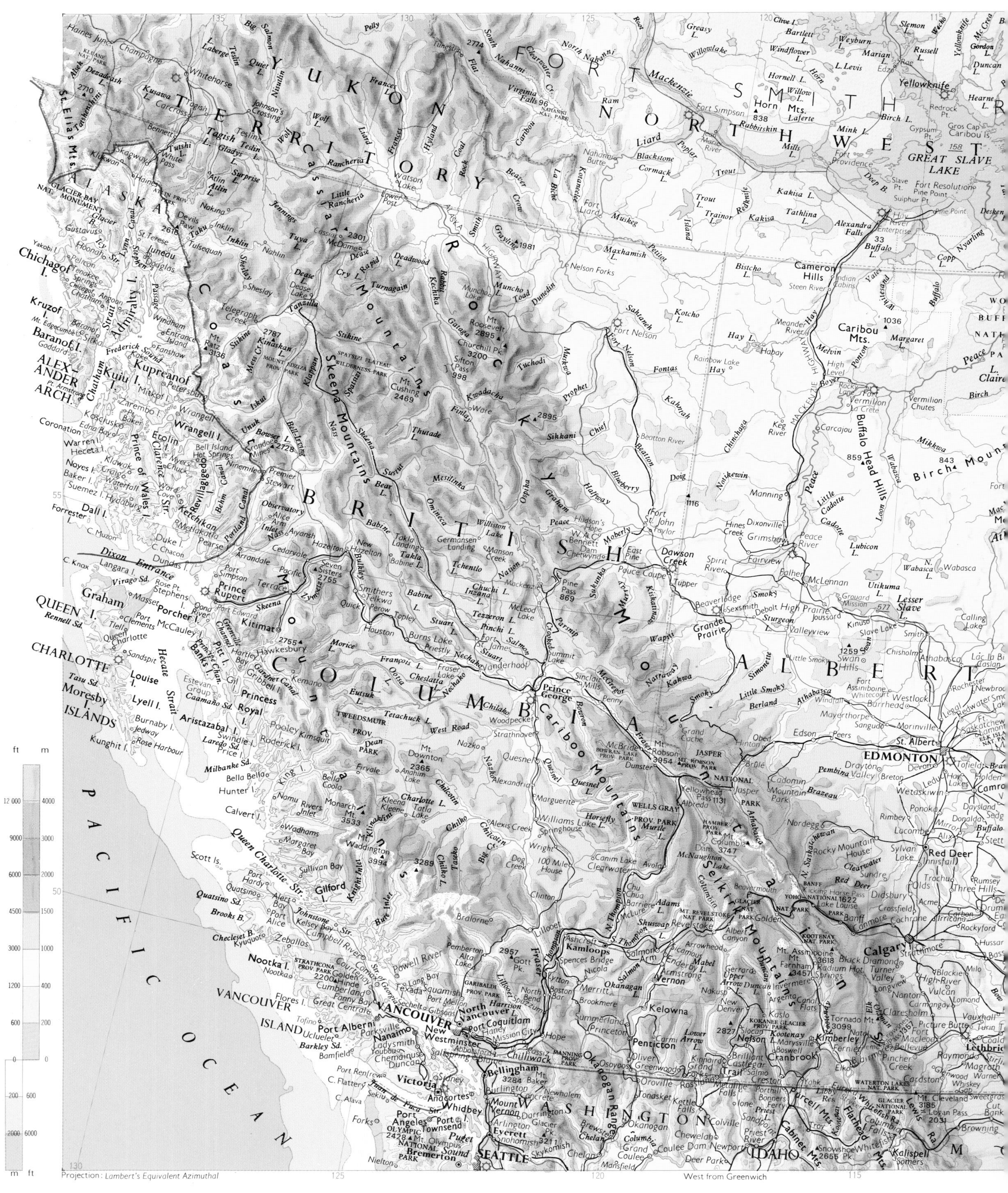
YUKON TERRITORY
NORTHWEST TERRITORIES
FORT SMITH
BRITISH COLUMBIA
ALBERTA
ALASKA
WASHINGTON
IDAHO
PACIFIC OCEAN
ROCKY MOUNTAINS
Cassiar Mountains
Coast Mountains
Skeena Mountains
Cariboo Mountains
Selkirk Mountains
Purcell Mts.
Cabinet Mts.
Caribou Mts.
Buffalo Head Hills
Birch Mountains
St. Elias Mts.
GREAT SLAVE LAKE
Lesser Slave L.
QUEEN CHARLOTTE ISLANDS
Graham I.
Moresby I.
VANCOUVER ISLAND
ALEXANDER ARCH.
Chichagof I.
Baranof I.
Kupreanof I.
Prince of Wales I.
Dixon Entrance
Queen Charlotte Str.
Whitehorse
Yellowknife
Fort Simpson
Fort Nelson
Fort St. John
Dawson Creek
Grande Prairie
Peace River
Prince Rupert
Kitimat
Prince George
Kamloops
Vernon
Kelowna
Penticton
Nelson
Cranbrook
Kimberley
Lethbridge
Calgary
Red Deer
EDMONTON
St. Albert
Jasper
Banff
VANCOUVER
North Vancouver
New Westminster
Victoria
Nanaimo
Port Alberni
Bellingham
Everett
SEATTLE
Bremerton
Port Angeles
Juneau
Skagway
Ketchikan
Wrangell
Petersburg
Mt. Robson 3954
Mt. Waddington 3994
Mt. Columbia 3747
Mt. Baker 3284
Mt. Olympus 2428
Yellowhead Pass 1131
Pine Pass 869
Projection: Lambert's Equivalent Azimuthal
West from Greenwich

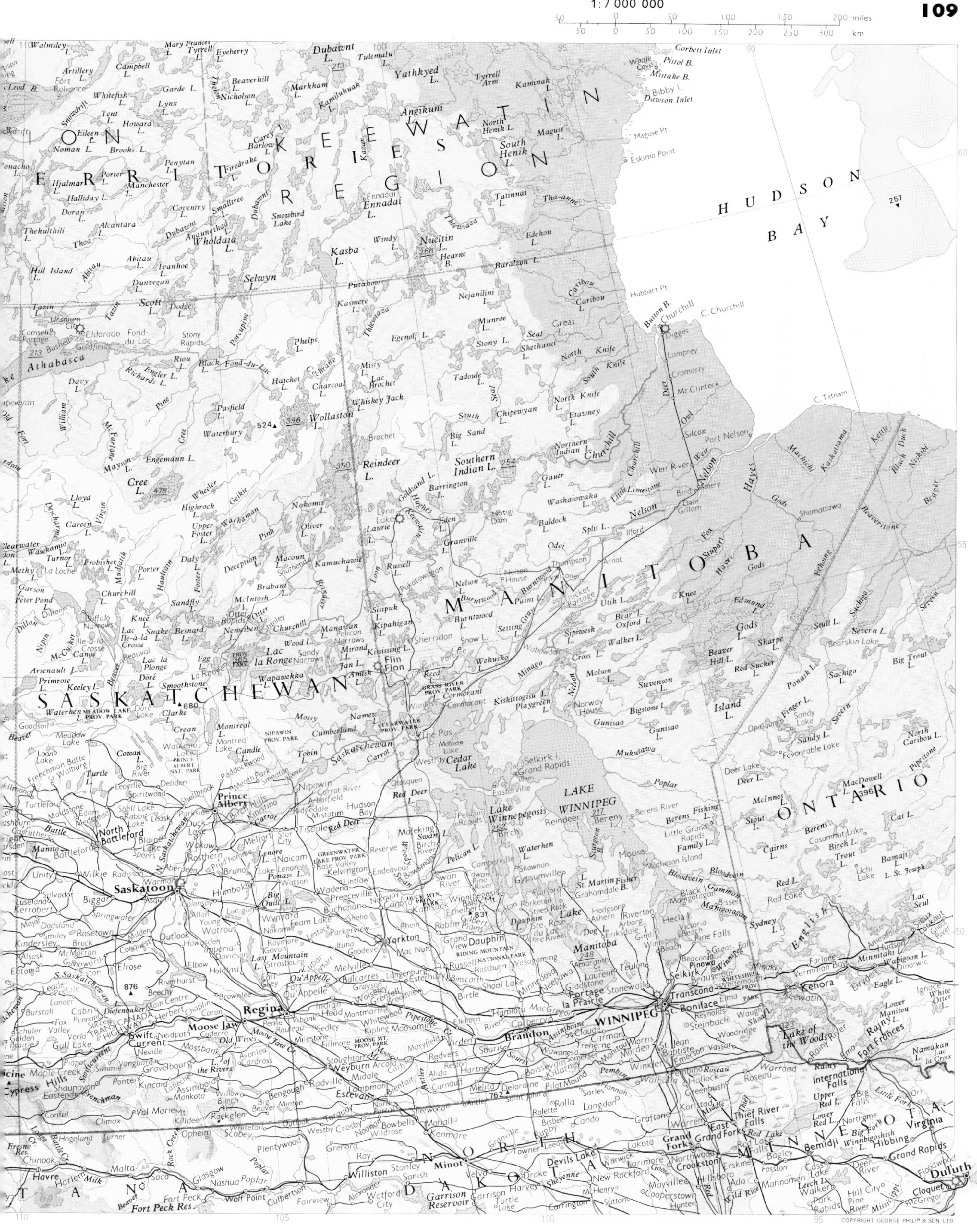

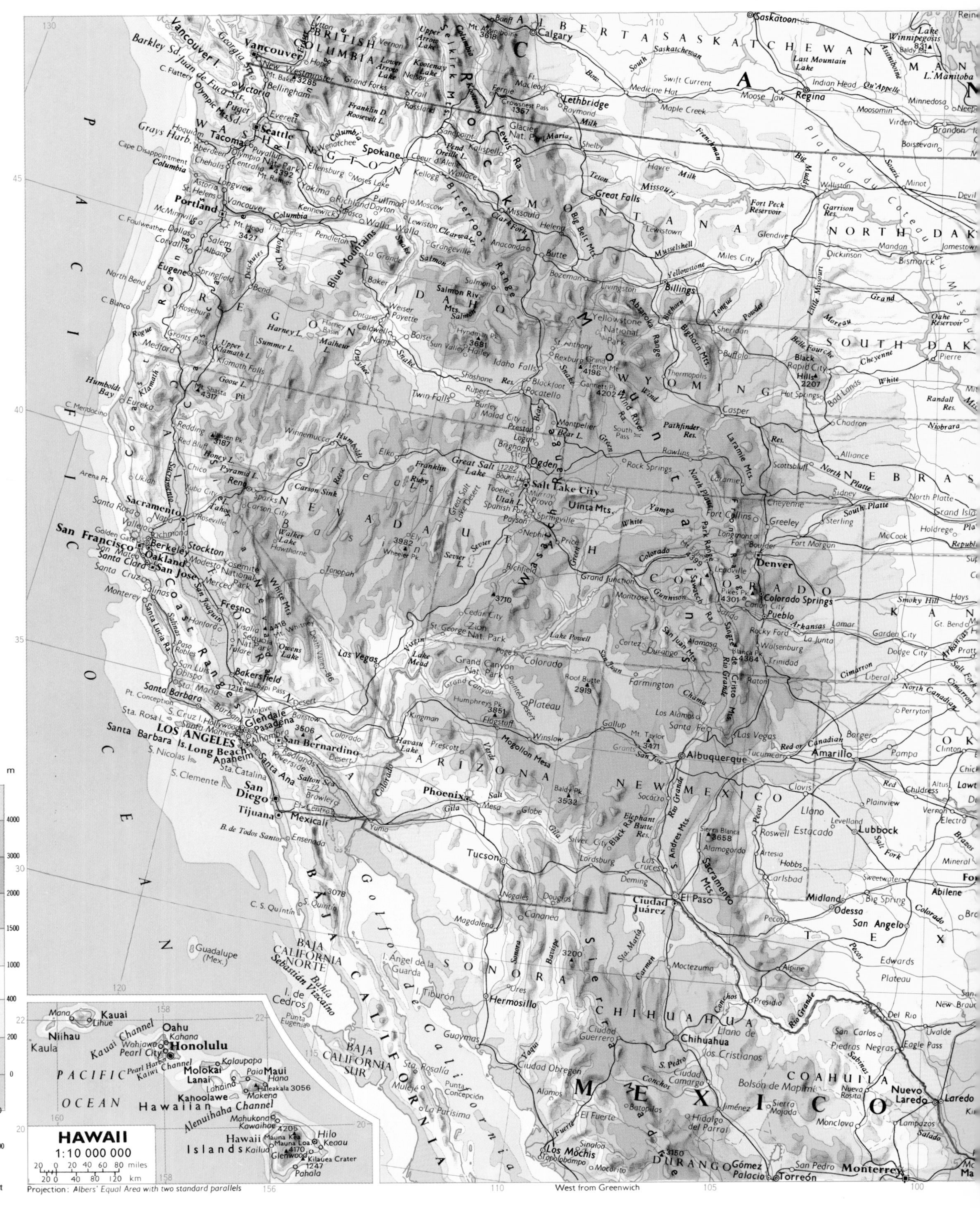
CANADA
ALBERTA
SASKATCHEWAN
BRITISH COLUMBIA
Vancouver
Vancouver I.
Victoria
Calgary
Saskatoon
Regina
Lethbridge
Moose Jaw
Medicine Hat
Swift Current
Seattle
Tacoma
Spokane
WASHINGTON
Portland
OREGON
Eugene
Salem
Mt. Rainier
Mt. Hood 3427
IDAHO
Boise
Idaho Falls
Pocatello
Twin Falls
MONTANA
Great Falls
Helena
Butte
Missoula
Billings
NORTH DAKOTA
Bismarck
SOUTH DAKOTA
Pierre
Rapid City
WYOMING
Casper
Cheyenne
Yellowstone National Park
Grand Teton Mt. 4196
Great Salt Lake
Salt Lake City
Ogden
Provo
UTAH
NEVADA
Reno
Carson City
Las Vegas
Great Basin
CALIFORNIA
Sacramento
San Francisco
Oakland
Berkeley
San Jose
Stockton
Fresno
Bakersfield
Santa Barbara
LOS ANGELES
Long Beach
Glendale
Pasadena
San Bernardino
San Diego
Tijuana
Mexicali
Mt. Whitney 4418
Death Valley
Mt. Shasta 4317
Lassen Pk. 3187
COLORADO
Denver
Colorado Springs
Pueblo
Pikes Pk. 4301
Grand Junction
NEBRASKA
North Platte
ARIZONA
Phoenix
Tucson
Flagstaff
Grand Canyon Nat. Park
NEW MEXICO
Albuquerque
Santa Fe
Las Cruces
El Paso
Ciudad Juárez
Amarillo
Lubbock
Midland
Odessa
San Angelo
Abilene
TEXAS
OKLAHOMA
KANSAS
MEXICO
SONORA
CHIHUAHUA
COAHUILA
DURANGO
BAJA CALIFORNIA
BAJA CALIFORNIA NORTE
BAJA CALIFORNIA SUR
Hermosillo
Chihuahua
Monterrey
Torreón
Nuevo Laredo
Laredo
Golfo de California
PACIFIC OCEAN
Sierra Madre
Rocky Mountains
Coast Ranges
Sierra Nevada
Cascade Range
Wasatch Range
Colorado Plateau
Mogollon Mesa
Snake
Columbia
Colorado
Rio Grande
Missouri
HAWAII
1:10 000 000
Kauai
Niihau
Oahu
Honolulu
Molokai
Lanai
Maui
Kahoolawe
Hawaii
Hilo
Mauna Kea 4205
Mauna Loa 4170
Haleakala 3056
Kauai Channel
Alenuihaha Channel
PACIFIC OCEAN
Hawaiian Islands
miles
km
ft
m
12 000
9000
6000
4500
3000
1200
600
0
200
2000
4000
3000
2000
1500
1000
400
200
0
600
6000
Projection: Albers' Equal Area with two standard parallels
West from Greenwich

1:12 000 000

50 0 50 100 150 200 250 300 miles

50 0 50 100 150 200 250 300 350 400 450 km

CANADA · MAINE · NEW BRUNSWICK · MINNESOTA · WISCONSIN · IOWA · ILLINOIS · INDIANA · OHIO · MISSOURI · KENTUCKY · TENNESSEE · ARKANSAS · MISSISSIPPI · ALABAMA · GEORGIA · LOUISIANA · FLORIDA · WEST VIRGINIA · VIRGINIA · NORTH CAROLINA · SOUTH CAROLINA · PENNSYLVANIA · NEW YORK · VERMONT · NEW HAMPSHIRE · MASSACHUSETTS · MARYLAND · NEW JERSEY · BAHAMAS

Major cities:

Winnipeg · Thunder Bay · Duluth · Minneapolis · St. Paul · MONTRÉAL · Ottawa · TORONTO · Buffalo · DETROIT · CHICAGO · Milwaukee · Grand Rapids · Cleveland · Cincinnati · Columbus · Indianapolis · St. Louis · Kansas City · Memphis · Nashville · Louisville · Little Rock · Birmingham · Atlanta · Montgomery · Jackson · New Orleans · Baton Rouge · Shreveport · Mobile · Jacksonville · Tampa · St. Petersburg · Orlando · Miami · West Palm Beach · Charlotte · Raleigh · Columbia · Charleston · Savannah · Richmond · Norfolk · Washington DC · Baltimore · PHILADELPHIA · NEW YORK · Newark · Boston · Providence · Hartford · Albany · Syracuse · Rochester · Pittsburgh · Des Moines · Québec · Sherbrooke

Water bodies:

Lake Superior · Lake Michigan · Lake Huron · Lake Erie · Lake Ontario · GULF OF MEXICO · ATLANTIC OCEAN · Chesapeake Bay · Delaware Bay · Tampa Bay · Lake Okeechobee · Lake Winnipeg · Lake Nipigon

COPYRIGHT GEORGE PHILIP & SON LTD

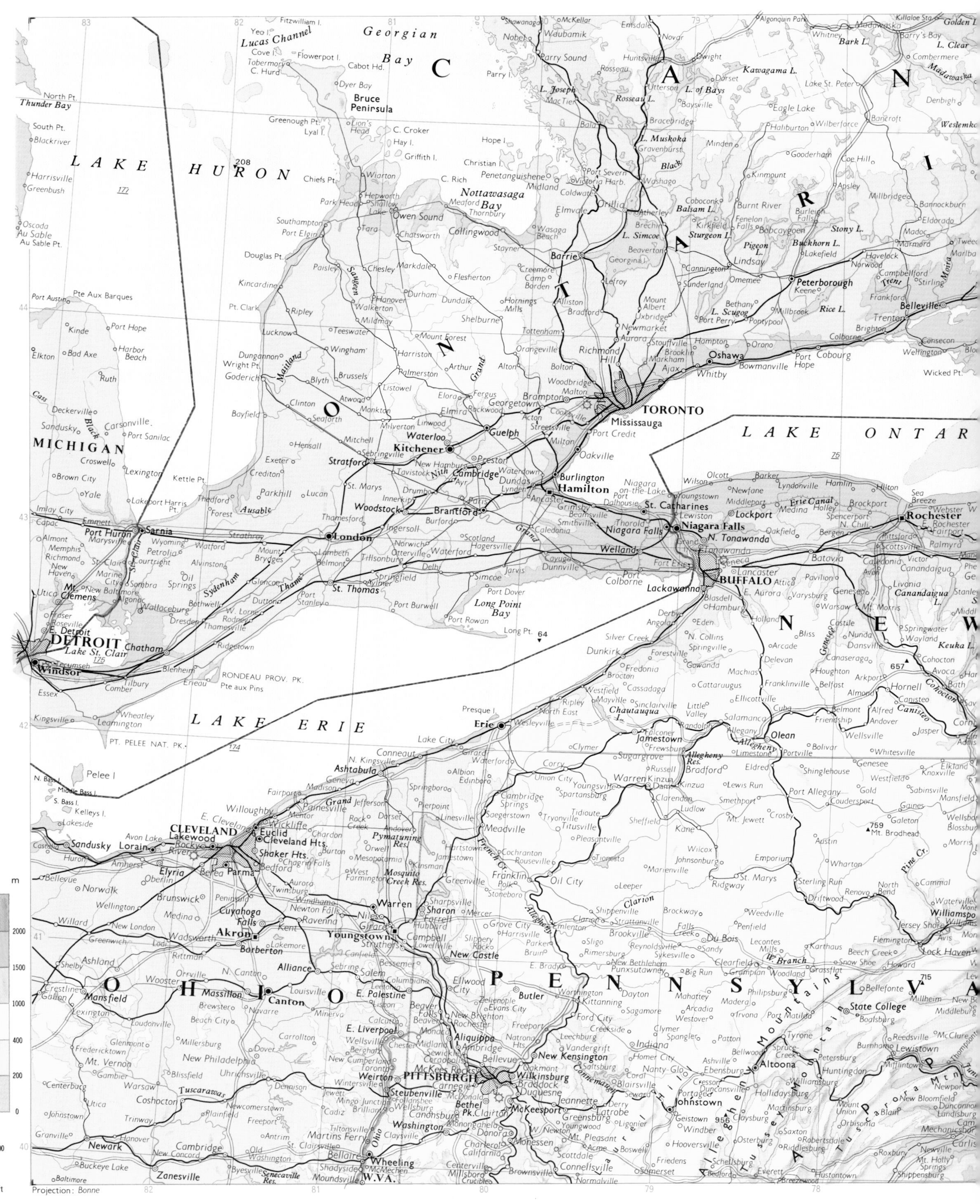
Georgian Bay
ONTARIO
LAKE HURON
LAKE ONTARIO
LAKE ERIE
MICHIGAN
OHIO
PENNSYLVANIA
NEW YORK
Bruce Peninsula
Nottawasaga Bay
Thunder Bay
Lucas Channel
TORONTO
Mississauga
Hamilton
Burlington
Oakville
Kitchener
Waterloo
Guelph
Cambridge
Brantford
London
Stratford
Woodstock
St. Thomas
Sarnia
Port Huron
DETROIT
Windsor
Chatham
Lake St. Clair
Barrie
Orillia
Owen Sound
Collingwood
Peterborough
Oshawa
Whitby
Belleville
Lindsay
L. Simcoe
L. Muskoka
Niagara Falls
St. Catharines
Welland
BUFFALO
Lackawanna
Lockport
Rochester
N. Tonawanda
Tonawanda
Erie Canal
Jamestown
Olean
Salamanca
Dunkirk
Erie
Ashtabula
CLEVELAND
Lakewood
Euclid
Cleveland Hts.
Shaker Hts.
Parma
Lorain
Elyria
Sandusky
Akron
Cuyahoga Falls
Barberton
Canton
Massillon
Youngstown
Warren
Alliance
Mansfield
Wooster
Steubenville
Weirton
Wheeling
W.VA.
PITTSBURGH
McKeesport
Wilkinsburg
New Kensington
Washington
Butler
New Castle
Sharon
Meadville
Oil City
Franklin
Bradford
Altoona
Johnstown
State College
Allegheny Res.
Pymatuning Res.
Mosquito Creek Res.
Long Point Bay
Pelee I.
PT. PELEE NAT. PK.
RONDEAU PROV. PK.
Projection: Bonne
ft
m
6000
2000
4500
1500
3000
1000
1200
400
600
200
0
0
200
600
m
ft

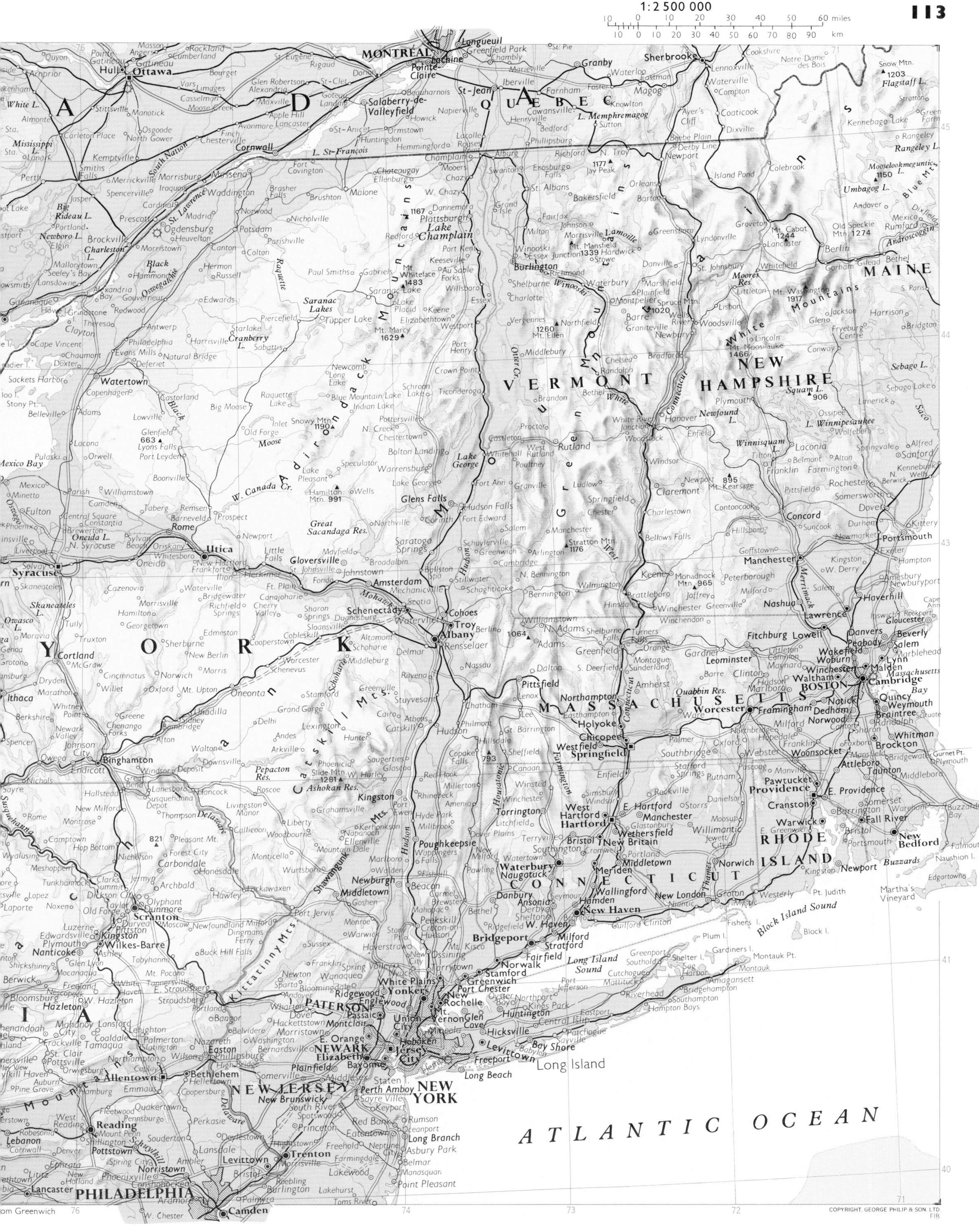
1:2 500 000
10 0 10 20 30 40 50 60 miles
10 0 10 20 30 40 50 60 70 80 90 km
MONTREAL
Ottawa
Hull
Sherbrooke
QUEBEC
CANADA
L. Memphremagog
Cornwall
L. St-François
Salaberry-de-Valleyfield
St-Jean
Granby
Magog
Plattsburgh
Lake Champlain
Burlington
Montpelier
Barre
Ogdensburg
Massena
Watertown
Adirondack Mountains
Mt. Marcy 1629
Mt. Mansfield 1339
Green Mountains
White Mountains
Mt. Washington 1917
VERMONT
NEW HAMPSHIRE
MAINE
Rutland
Lake George
Glens Falls
Saratoga Springs
Utica
Syracuse
Rome
Amsterdam
Schenectady
Troy
Albany
Cohoes
Rensselaer
Concord
Manchester
Nashua
Portsmouth
Lawrence
Haverhill
Lowell
Fitchburg
Worcester
BOSTON
Cambridge
Quincy
Brockton
Providence
Pawtucket
Cranston
Warwick
Fall River
New Bedford
Newport
RHODE ISLAND
MASSACHUSETTS
Pittsfield
Northampton
Holyoke
Chicopee
Springfield
Hartford
West Hartford
E. Hartford
New Britain
Meriden
Middletown
Waterbury
New Haven
Bridgeport
Stamford
Norwalk
Danbury
New London
CONNECTICUT
Catskill Mts.
Kingston
Poughkeepsie
Newburgh
Binghamton
Ithaca
Cortland
Scranton
Wilkes-Barre
Hazleton
Allentown
Bethlehem
Easton
Reading
Lancaster
Norristown
Trenton
Camden
PHILADELPHIA
NEW JERSEY
Paterson
Newark
Elizabeth
Jersey City
Yonkers
White Plains
NEW YORK
Long Island
Long Island Sound
Block Island Sound
Martha's Vineyard
Nantucket
ATLANTIC OCEAN
Montauk Pt.
Long Branch
Asbury Park
COPYRIGHT. GEORGE PHILIP & SON. LTD

QUÉBEC
CANADA
ONTARIO
LAKE SUPERIOR
LAKE HURON
LAKE ONTARIO
LAKE ERIE
LAKE MICHIGAN
Georgian Bay
North Channel
Manitoulin I.
Green Bay
MICHIGAN
WISCONSIN
ILLINOIS
INDIANA
OHIO
PENNSYLVANIA
NEW YORK
NEW JERSEY
MARYLAND
DELAWARE
WEST VIRGINIA
VIRGINIA
VERMONT
NEW HAMPSHIRE
MASS.
CONN.
R.I.
Chesapeake Bay
MONTREAL
Ottawa
TORONTO
Hamilton
Québec
Sudbury
Sault Ste. Marie
Kingston
BOSTON
NEW YORK
PHILADELPHIA
BALTIMORE
WASHINGTON D.C.
PITTSBURGH
CLEVELAND
DETROIT
CHICAGO
MILWAUKEE
INDIANAPOLIS
CINCINNATI
BUFFALO
PATERSON
NEWARK
Rochester
Syracuse
Albany
Richmond
Columbus
Dayton
Toledo
Louisville
Lexington
Grand Rapids
Lansing
Flint
Saginaw
Green Bay
Evansville

1:6 000 000
50 0 50 100 miles
50 0 50 100 150 km
Continuation Eastwards On same scale
ATLANTIC OCEAN
GULF OF MEXICO
BAHAMAS
TENNESSEE
NORTH CAROLINA
SOUTH CAROLINA
GEORGIA
ALABAMA
MAINE
NEW HAMPSHIRE
Nashville
Knoxville
Chattanooga
Asheville
Charlotte
Raleigh
Durham
Greensboro
Winston-Salem
Wilmington
Columbia
Charleston
Savannah
Augusta
ATLANTA
Macon
Columbus
Montgomery
Birmingham
Mobile
Pensacola
Tallahassee
Jacksonville
St. Augustine
Daytona Beach
Orlando
Tampa
St. Petersburg
Ft. Myers
MIAMI
Ft. Lauderdale
West Palm Beach
Portland
Bangor
Augusta
Great Abaco I.
Grand Bahama I.
Projection: Alber's Equal Area with two standard parallels
West from Greenwich
COPYRIGHT GEORGE PHILIP & SON LTD.
m ft

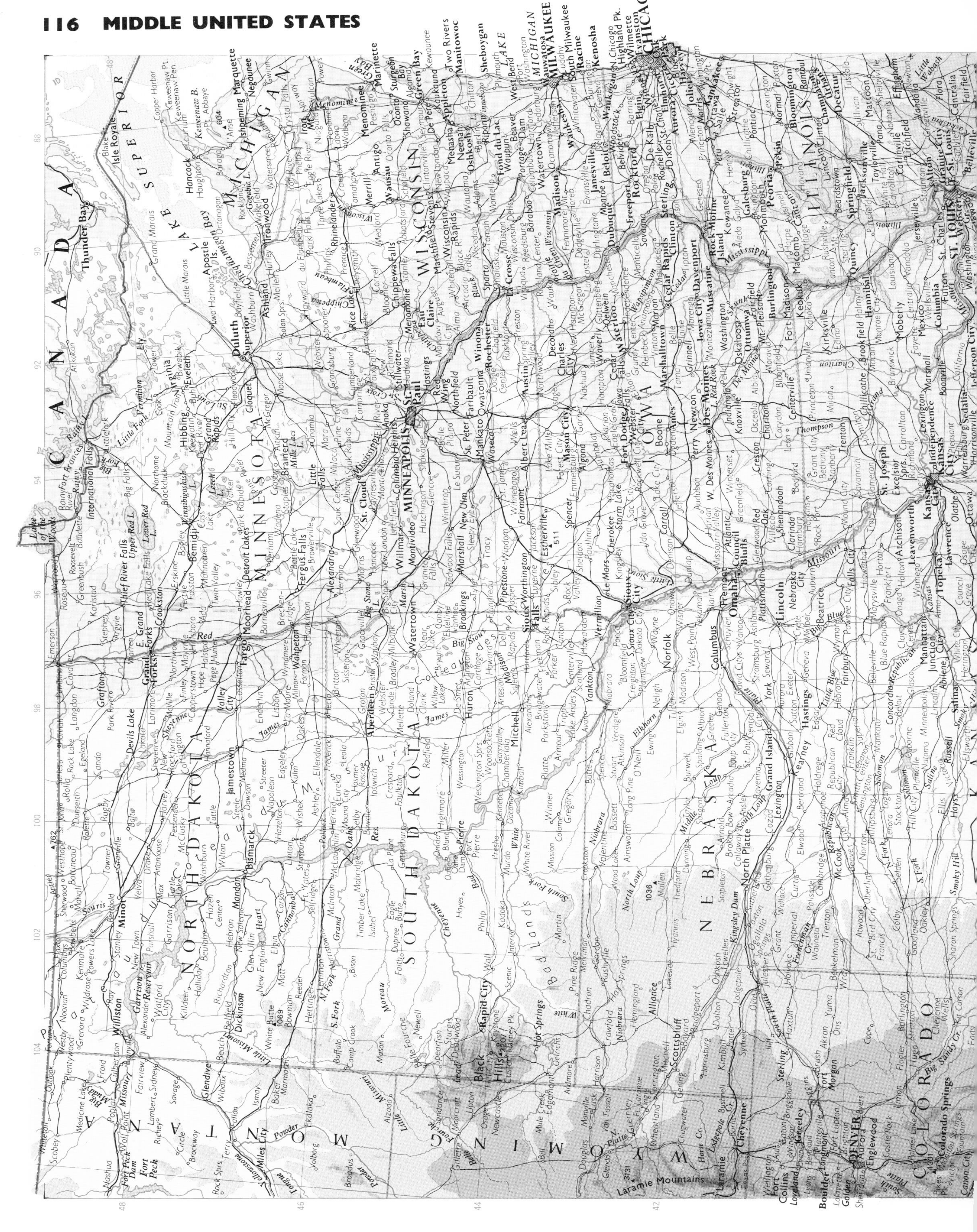
CANADA
LAKE SUPERIOR
LAKE MICHIGAN
NORTH DAKOTA
SOUTH DAKOTA
MINNESOTA
WISCONSIN
MICHIGAN
IOWA
ILLINOIS
NEBRASKA
COLORADO
MINNEAPOLIS
ST. PAUL
MILWAUKEE
CHICAGO
ST. LOUIS
DENVER
Omaha
Des Moines
Laramie Mountains

1:6 000 000
miles
km
NEW MEXICO
OKLAHOMA
ARKANSAS
TENNESSEE
MISSISSIPPI
LOUISIANA
TEXAS
MEXICO
COAHUILA
CHIHUAHUA
GULF OF MEXICO
Continuation Southwards on same scale
West from Greenwich
Projection: Albers' Equal Area with two standard parallels
COPYRIGHT GEORGE PHILIP & SON, LTD

1:6 000 000

50 0 50 100 miles

50 0 50 100 150 km

BRITISH COLUMBIA
ALBERTA
SASKATCHEWAN
CANADA
WASHINGTON
OREGON
IDAHO
MONTANA
WYOMING
NEVADA
Cascade Range
Coast Ranges
Bitterroot Range
Lemhi Range
Salmon River Mountains
Clearwater Mountains
Blue Mountains
Wallowa Mts.
Bighorn Mountains
Absaroka Range
Wind River Range
Uinta Mountains
Medicine Bow Range
Lewis Range
Cabinet Mountains
Sapphire Mts.
Little Belt Mts.
Big Belt Mts.
Crazy Mts.
Olympic Mts.
Ruby Mts.
Independence Mts.
Shoshone Mountains
Stillwater Mts.
Trinity Mts.
Klamath Mts.
Great Salt Lake Desert
GREAT SALT LAKE
VANCOUVER
SEATTLE
PORTLAND
Spokane
Boise
Salt Lake City
Reno
Sacramento
Columbia
Snake
Missouri
Yellowstone

NEW MEXICO
ARIZONA
TEXAS
CHIHUAHUA
SONORA
MEXICO
BAJA CALIFORNIA
Golfo de California
Colorado Plateau
Sangre de Cristo Mts.
San Juan Mts.
Sacramento Mts.
Santa Lucia Range
Grand Canyon
Painted Desert
Mojave Desert
Death Valley
Salton Sea
Sierra de Juarez
Albuquerque
Santa Fe
El Paso
Ciudad Juárez
Chihuahua
Tucson
Phoenix
Mesa
Flagstaff
Las Vegas
LOS ANGELES
SAN BERNARDINO
SAN DIEGO
Tijuana
Mexicali
Hermosillo
Nogales
Fresno
Bakersfield
Santa Barbara
SAN JOSE
Gulf of Santa Catalina
I. de Guadalupe (Mexico)
West from Greenwich
ft m
12 000 4000
9000 3000
6000 2000
4500 1500
3000 1000
1200 400
600 200
0 0
200 600
2000 6000
4000 12 000
m ft
COPYRIGHT, GEORGE PHILIP & SON, LTD.

1:12 000 000

100 0 100 200 miles

100 0 100 200 300 km

UNITED STATES

GULF OF MEXICO

PACIFIC OCEAN

MEXICO

GUATEMALA

BELIZE

HONDURAS

EL SALVADOR

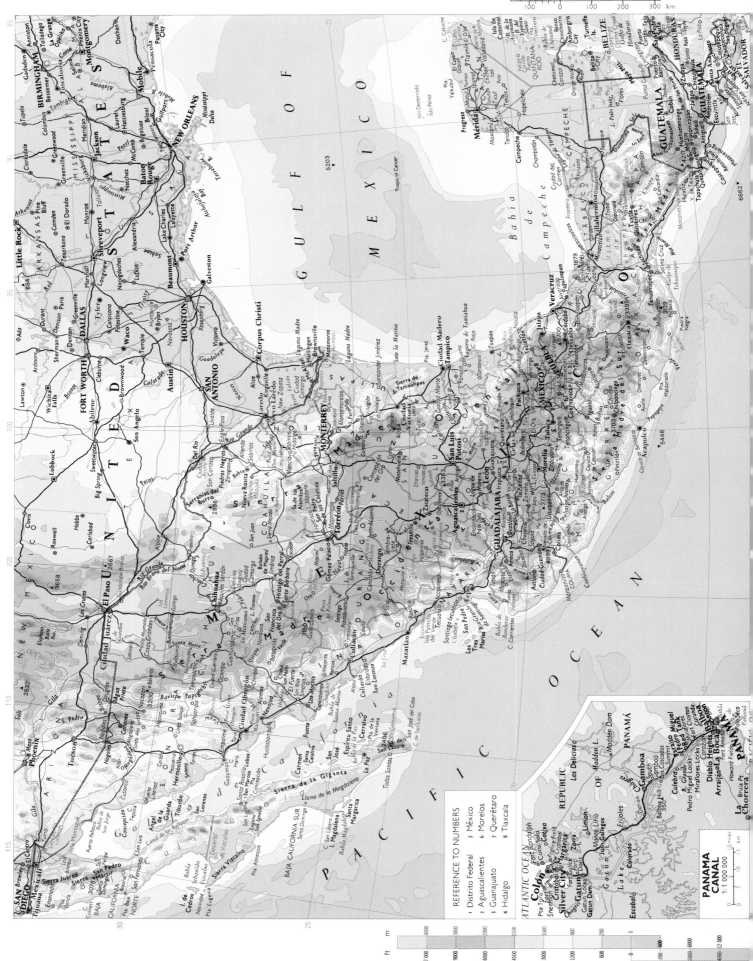

REFERENCE TO NUMBERS

1 Distrito Federal	5 México
2 Aguascalientes	6 Morelos
3 Guanajuato	7 Querétaro
4 Hidalgo	8 Tlaxcala

PANAMA CANAL

1:1 000 000

0 10 miles

0 5 10 15 km

m	ft
4000	12 000
3000	9000
2000	6000
1500	4500
1000	3000
400	1200
200	600
0	0
200	600
2000	6000
4000	12 000

1:12 000 000

100 0 100 200 miles

100 0 100 200 300 km

BERMUDA 1:1 000 000

LEEWARD ISLANDS 1:8 000 000

WINDWARD ISLANDS 1:8 000 000

JAMAICA 1:8 000 000

TRINIDAD & TOBAGO 1:8 000 000

GULF OF MEXICO

ATLANTIC OCEAN

CARIBBEAN SEA

PACIFIC OCEAN

GREATER ANTILLES

LESSER ANTILLES

BAHAMAS

CUBA

HISPANIOLA

HAITI

DOMINICAN REP.

PUERTO RICO

JAMAICA

MEXICO

HONDURAS

NICARAGUA

COSTA RICA

PANAMA

COLOMBIA

VENEZUELA

m	ft
6000	18 000
4000	12 000
3000	9000
2000	6000
1500	4500
1000	3000
400	1200
200	600
0	0
200	600
2000	6000
4000	12 000
6000	18 000
8000	24 000

West from Greenwich

Projection: Bi-polar oblique Conical Orthomorphic

1:30 000 000

ATLANTIC OCEAN
PACIFIC OCEAN
SOUTH ATLANTIC OCEAN
Trinidad
Caracas
Margarita
Tobago I.
Sa. Nevada de Santa Marta
Barranquilla
Maracaibo
L. Maracaibo
G. of Darien
Panama Canal
Gulf of Panamá
Cord. de Mérida
Medellín
Bogotá
Cali
Quito
Cotopaxi 5897
Chimborazo 6267
Guayaquil
G. of Guayaquil
C. de San Francisco
Pta. Pariñas
Pta. Aguja
Lobos Is.
Huascarán 6768
Lima
Chincha Is.
Llanos
Guiana Highlands
Roraima 2810
Sierra Pacaraima
Georgetown
C. Orange
Serra de Tumucumaque
Equator
Marajó I.
Belém
Manaus
Amazon
Selvas
Fortaleza
C. São Roque
C. Branco
Plateau of Borborema
Recife
Salvador
Brasília
Brazilian Highlands
Plateau of Mato Grosso
Abrolhos Bank
Belo Horizonte
Pico da Bandeira 2890
Serra da Mantiqueira
São Paulo
C. Frio
Rio de Janeiro
L. Titicaca
Ancohuma & Illampu 6550
La Paz
L. Poopó
Bolivian Plateau
Atacama Desert
Peru Trench
Tropic of Capricorn
S. Félix
S. Ambrosio
8050
Ojos del Salado 6863
Tucumán
Gran Chaco
Asunción
Iguaçu Falls
Salinas Grandes
Córdoba
L. Mar Chiquita
Sierra de Córdoba
Entre Rios
Porto Alegre
Lagoa dos Patos
Serra do Mar
Aconcagua 6960
Uspallata Pass
Santiago
Valparaíso
Arch. de Juan Fernández
Rosario
Buenos Aires
La Plata
Montevideo
Río de la Plata
Pampas
Pta. Mogotes
Bahía Blanca
G. of San Matías
Valdés Peninsula
Chile Rise
Chiloé I.
Chonos Archipelago
Taitao Peninsula
S. Valentín 4058
G. of Peñas
G. of San Jorge
Patagonia
Andes
Argentine Basin
6212
5994
Wellington I.
Madre de Dios I.
Falkland Islands
West Falkland
East Falkland
Magellan's Strait
Tierra del Fuego
Santa Inés I.
Staten I.
Cockburn Chan.
Beagle Chan.
C. Horn
Orinoco
Meta
Guaviare
Caquetá
Putumayo
Japurá
Napo
Marañón
Negro
Branco
Casiquiare
Essequibo
Courantyne
Pará
Tocantins
Xingu
Tapajós
Juruá
Purus
Madeira
Ucayali
Madre de Dios
Mamoré
Guaporé
Roosevelt
Aripuanã
Teles Pires
Arinos
Araguaia
Parnaíba
São Francisco
Paraguay
Paraná
Pilcomayo
Uruguay
Salado
Colorado
Negro
Chubut
Magdalena
Cordillera Occidental
Cordillera Central
Cordillera Oriental
Chile Peru Trench
ft m
18 000 6000
12 000 4000
9000 3000
6000 2000
3000 1000
1200 400
600 200
0 0
200 600
2000 6000
4000 12 000
6000 18 000
8000 24 000
m ft
Projection: Lambert's Equivalent Azimuthal
West from Greenwich

1:30 000 000

100 0 100 200 300 400 500 miles

100 0 200 400 600 800 km

Projection: Lambert's Equivalent Azimuthal

West from Greenwich

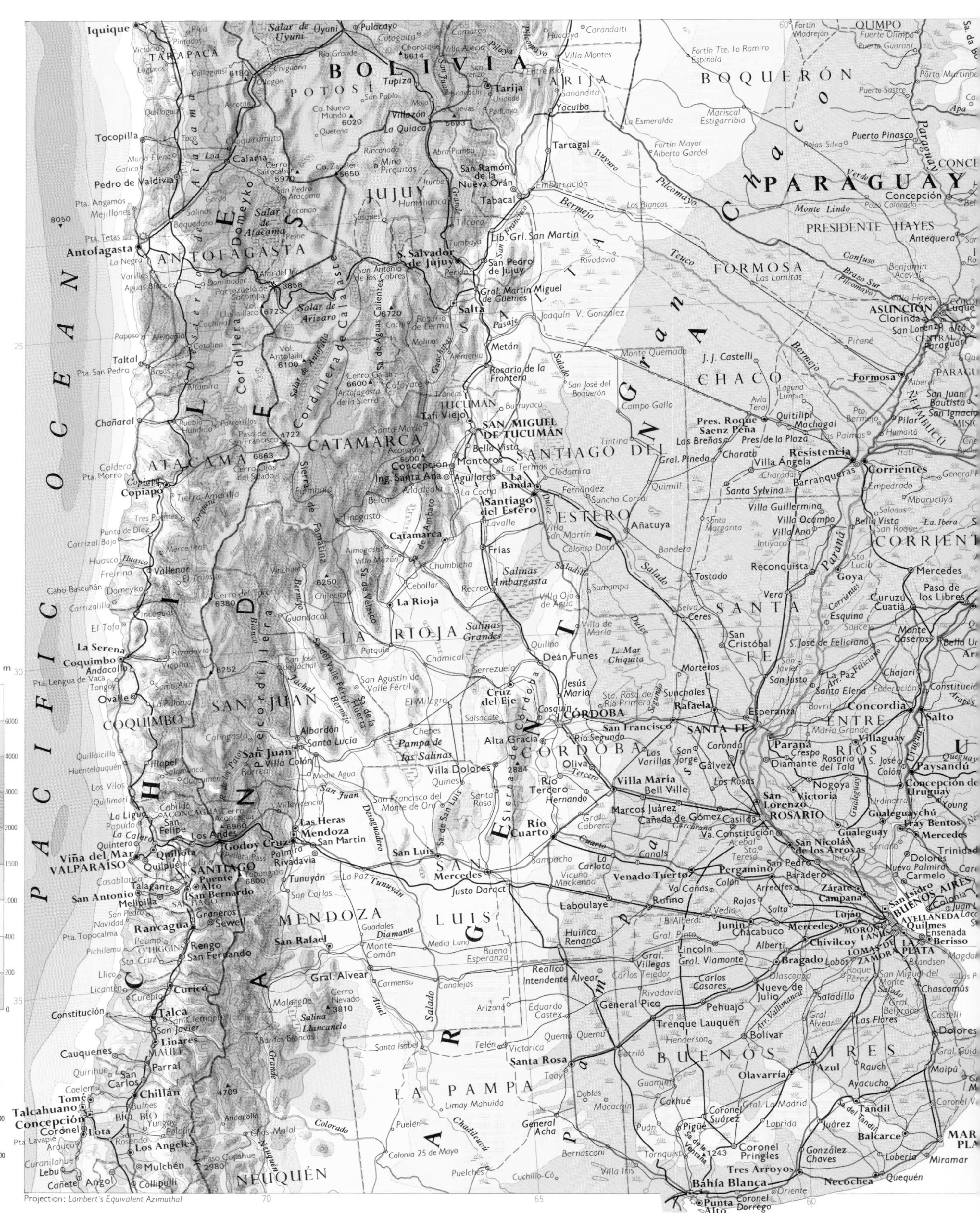
PACIFIC OCEAN
BOLIVIA
PARAGUAY
ARGENTINA
CHILE
ANDES
Gran Chaco
Chaco
Pampa
Desierto de Atacama
Cordillera Domeyko
Cordillera de Calalaste
Cordillera Blanca
Cordillera de Antofalla
Sierra de Famatina
Sierra de Córdoba
Salar de Uyuni
Salar de Atacama
Salar de Arizaro
Salinas Grandes
Salinas Ambargasta
Pampa de las Salinas
Salina Llancanelo
L. Mar Chiquita
TARAPACÁ
POTOSÍ
TARIJA
BOQUERÓN
JUJUY
ANTOFAGASTA
SALTA
FORMOSA
PRESIDENTE HAYES
CHACO
CATAMARCA
TUCUMÁN
SANTIAGO DEL ESTERO
ATACAMA
LA RIOJA
SANTA FE
CORRIENTES
COQUIMBO
SAN JUAN
CÓRDOBA
ENTRE RÍOS
ACONCAGUA
MENDOZA
SAN LUIS
O'HIGGINS
MAULE
BÍO BÍO
LA PAMPA
BUENOS AIRES
NEUQUÉN
Iquique
Pica
Pintados
Victoria
Lagunas
Collaguasi
6180
Ollagüe
Quillagua
Tocopilla
Toco
Chuquicamata
María Elena
Gatico
Loa
Calama
Pedro de Valdivia
Pta. Angamos
Mejillones
8050
Pta. Tetas
Antofagasta
La Negra
Baquedano
Salinas
Sierra Gorda
San Pedro de Atacama
Toconao
Peine
Varillas
Aguas Blancas
Paposo
Taltal
Pta. San Pedro
Chañaral
Caldera
Pta. Morro
Copiapó
Tierra Amarilla
Vallenar
Huasco
Freirina
Domeyko
Cabo Bascuñán
Carrizalillo
El Tofo
La Serena
Coquimbo
Andacollo
Vicuña
Pta. Lengua de Vaca
Tongoy
Ovalle
Illapel
Salamanca
Los Vilos
Quilimarí
La Ligua
Cabildo
San Felipe
Los Andes
La Calera
Quillota
Quintero
Viña del Mar
VALPARAÍSO
SANTIAGO
Puente Alto
San Bernardo
San Antonio
Melipilla
Rancagua
Sewell
Rengo
San Fernando
Pichilemu
Curicó
Licantén
Constitución
Talca
San Javier
Linares
Parral
Cauquenes
San Carlos
Chillán
Tomé
Talcahuano
Concepción
Coronel
Lota
Los Angeles
Mulchén
Lebu
Cañete
Angol
Collipulli
Pulacayo
Uyuni
Rio Grande
Tupiza
Villazón
La Quiaca
Tarija
Yacuiba
Villa Montes
Camargo
Pilcomayo
Tartagal
Embarcación
San Ramón de la Nueva Orán
Tabacal
Humahuaca
Lib. Grl. San Martín
S. Salvador de Jujuy
San Pedro de Jujuy
Gral. Martín Miguel de Güemes
Salta
Cafayate
Metán
Rosario de la Frontera
Tafí Viejo
SAN MIGUEL DE TUCUMÁN
Bella Vista
Monteros
Concepción
Aguilares
La Banda
Santiago del Estero
Añatuya
Catamarca
Belén
Tinogasta
Frías
La Rioja
Chilecito
Dean Funes
Jesús María
Cruz del Eje
Cosquín
CÓRDOBA
Alta Gracia
Villa Dolores
Río Tercero
Villa María
Bell Ville
Río Cuarto
San Francisco
Rafaela
Esperanza
SANTA FE
Paraná
Reconquista
Resistencia
Corrientes
Barranqueras
Presidencia Roque Sáenz Peña
Goya
Esquina
Concordia
Salto
Paysandú
Concepción del Uruguay
Gualeguaychú
Gualeguay
Fray Bentos
Mercedes
ROSARIO
San Lorenzo
Casilda
San Nicolás de los Arroyos
Pergamino
Venado Tuerto
Marcos Juárez
Zárate
Campana
Luján
BUENOS AIRES
Quilmes
La Plata
Ensenada
Berisso
Junín
Chacabuco
Chivilcoy
Mercedes
Bragado
Lincoln
Nueve de Julio
Pehuajó
Trenque Lauquen
Bolívar
Olavarría
Azul
Tandil
Balcarce
Necochea
Quequén
Tres Arroyos
Coronel Pringles
Bahía Blanca
Punta Alto
Coronel Dorrego
General Pico
Santa Rosa
General Acha
Laboulaye
Rufino
Huinca Renancó
San Luis
Mercedes
Villa Mercedes
San Juan
Mendoza
Godoy Cruz
San Martín
Las Heras
Tunuyán
San Rafael
Gral. Alvear
Malargüe
Cerro Nevado 3810
Aconcagua 6960
Tupungato 6800
Asunción
Luque
Concepción
Formosa
Pilar
Puerto Pinasco
Puerto Casado
J. J. Castelli
Projection: Lambert's Equivalent Azimuthal
ft
m
18 000
12 000
9000
6000
4500
3000
1200
600
0
6000
4000
3000
2000
1500
1000
400
200
0
200
2000
4000
6000
600
6000
12 000
18 000
70
65
60
25
30
35

Projection: *Lambert's Equivalent Azimuthal*

1:8 000 000
50 0 50 100 150 miles
50 0 50 100 150 200 km
BELO HORIZONTE
Lima
Itabirito
Vitória
Itaquari
Vila Velha
Guarapari
Castelo
Cachoeiro de Itapemirim
Três Lagoas
Andradina
Mirassol
S. José do Rio Prêto
Olímpia
Passos
Batatais
Oliveira
Congonhas
Cons. Lafaiete
Ouro Prêto
Ponte Nova
GROSSO
Xavantina
Mirandópolis
Araçatuba
Catanduva
Bebedouro
Ribeirão Prêto
São Seb. do Paraíso
Represa de Furnas
Campo Belo
São João del Rei
Carangola
Muriaé
Alegre
Ubá
Maracaju
Pardo
Panorama
Aguapeí
Birigui
Tietê
Taquaritinga
Novo Horizonte
Jaboticabal
Guaxupé
Três Pontas
Lavras
Barbacena
Cataguases
Itaperuna
SUL
Rio Brilhante
Pres. Epitácio
Adamantina
SÃO PAULO
Penápolis
Lins
Mogi Guaçu
Mococa
Casa Branca
Alfenas
Varginha
Santos Dumont
Leopoldina
Cambuci
Guarus
Dourados
Santo Anastácio
Ivinheima
Peixe
Tupã
Pirajuí
Araraquara
São Carlos
São João da Boa Vista
Poços de Caldas
Pouso Alegre
Três Corações
Juiz de Fora
Três Rios
Paraíba do Sul
CAMPOS
Cabo de São Tomé
Ponta Porã
Presidente Prudente
Martinópolis
Marília
Garça
Bariri
Jaú
Araras
Pinhal
São Lourenço
Mantiqueira
Além Paraíba
RIO DE JANEIRO
Pedro Juan Caballero
Paraná
Rancharia
Paranapanema
Paraguaçu Paulista
Bauru
Rio Claro
Limeira
Ouro Fino
Mogi-Mirim
Itajubá
2787
Volta Redonda
Barra do Piraí
Nova Friburgo
Pôrto São José
Centenário do Sul
Porecatu
Assis
Santa Cruz do Rio Pardo
Piracicaba
Americana
Serra da Mantiqueira
Cruzeiro
Petrópolis
Macaé
Paranavaí
Sertanópolis
Amambaí
Cambará
CAMPINAS
Bragança Paulista
Guaratinguetá
Barra Mansa
Mar
DUQUE DE CAXIAS
Amambal
Ivaí
Nova Esperança
Londrina
Rolândia
Ourinhos
Cornélio Procópio
Botucatu
Avaré
Jacarèzinho
Tietê
Itu
Jundiaí
Taubaté
Nova Iguaçu
SÃO GONÇALO
NITERÓI
RIO DE JANEIRO
Cabo Frio
La. de Araruama
Maringá
Cianorte
Arapongas
Tatuí
Sorocaba
S. J. dos Campos
Jacareí
Angra dos Reis
Ilha Grande
Baía da Ilha Grande
Pta. de Juatinga
Tropic of Capricorn
Cruzeiro do Oeste
Mandaguari
Apucarana
Joaquim Távora
Itapetininga
Itaporanga
SÃO PAULO
SANTO ANDRÉ
Mogi das Cruzes
Guaíra
Sa. dos Dourados
Campo Mourão
Ibaiti
Tibaji
Itapeva
Itararé
Jaguariaíva
Paranapiacaba
São Vicente
SANTOS
Guarujá
Ilha de São Sebastião
Pta. do Boi
Igatimi
Pto. Mendes
PARANÁ
Cândido de Abreu
Juquiá
Itanhaém
Registro
BRAZIL
Piquiri
Ivaí
Serra do Mar
ALTO PARANÁ
Cascavel
Sa. das Araras
Pitanga
Castro
Apiaí
Iguape
Ilha Comprida
Ponta Grossa
Prudentópolis
1889
Fernandarias
Itaipu Dam
Foz do Iguaçu
Guarapuava
Palmeira
CURITIBA
Antonina
Ilha do Cardoso
Iguaçu
Laranjeiras do Sul
Irati
Iguaçu Falls
Irala
Chopim
União da Vitória
Lapa
Paranaguá
Guaratuba
Bernardo de Irigoyen
Rio Negro
Mafra
São Francisco do Sul
Sa. da Fartura
Palmas
Clevelândia
Pto. União
Sa. do Espigão
Joinvile
Eldorado
San Pedro
Paraná
MISIONES
1340
Caçador
Blumenau
Itajaí
Santa Cecília
Uruguai
Chapecó
SANTA CATARINA
Brusque
Encarnación
Oberá
Montecarlo
Joaçaba
Campos Novos
Rio do Sul
Leandro N. Alem
Erechim
Ilha de Santa Catarina
Florianópolis
Santa Rosa
San Javier
Lajes
Pelotas
Santo Ângelo
Ijuí
Caràzinho
Passo Fundo
1808
São Luís Gonzaga
Coxilha Grande
Laguna
Sa. do Espinilho
Cruz Alta
Vacaria
Tubarão
Cabo Santa Marta Grande
Guaporé
Criciúma
RIO GRANDE
Bento Gonçalves
Araranguá
Santiago
Jacuí
Caxias do Sul
Taquari
Santa Maria
Santa Cruz do Sul
Montenegro
Nôvo Hamburgo
Taquara
São Leopoldo
Osorio
Alegrete
Cachoeira do Sul
Jacuí
Rio Pardo
DO SUL
PORTO ALEGRE
São Gabriel
Sa. Encantadas
Santana do Livramento
Caçapava do Sul
Camaquã
Dom Pedrito
Rivera
Santana
Camaquã
Mostardas
Bagé
Sa. do Canguçu
Canguçu
Lagoa dos Patos
Tacuarembó
URUGUAY
Pelotas
Rio Grande
ATLANTIC
Negro
Melo
Gregorio
Rio Branco
Jaguarão
Sta. Clara de Olimar
Lagoa Mirim
Chuy del Yi
Lagoa Mangueira
Treinta y Tres
José Batlle y Ordóñez
Lascano
Santa Vitória do Palmar
Aigua
Castillos
Minas
Rocha
San Carlos
Maldonado
MONTEVIDEO
OCEAN
5304
25
30
35
55
50
45
40
West from Greenwich

NICARAGUA
COSTA RICA
PANAMA
COLOMBIA
VENEZUELA
GUYANA
TRINIDAD & TOB
GRENADA
ECUADOR
PERU
BOLIVIA
ARGENTINA
PARAG
AMAZONAS
RORAIMA
RONDÔNIA
ACRE
CHILE
PACIFIC OCEAN
Cocos Ridge
Milne Edwards Trench
Peru Chile Trench
Krümmel Trench
Equator
Sierra Pacaraima
Pakaraima Mts.
Serra dos Pareceis
Chaco Boreal
Lago Titicaca
L. Poopó
Desierto de Sechura
Golfo de Panamá
G. de Guayaquil
Malpelo (Colombia)
Caracas
Bogotá
Quito
Lima
La Paz
Manaus
Maracaibo
Medellín
Cali
Guayaquil
Barranquilla
Cartagena
Panama
Port of Spain
Arequipa
Cuzco
Iquitos
Santa Cruz
Cochabamba
Sucre
Potosí
Porto Velho
Rio Branco
Mt. Roraima
ft
m
18 000
12 000
9000
6000
4500
3000
1200
600
0
200
6000
4000
3000
2000
1500
1000
400
200
0
200
2000
4000
6000
8000
600
6000
12 000
18 000
24 000
m ft
Projection: Sanson-Flamsteed's Sinusoidal

1:16 000 000

100 0 100 200 300 400 500 miles

100 0 100 200 300 400 500 600 700 800 km

ATLANTIC OCEAN
Equator
Paramaribo
Cayenne
FR. GUIANA
C.Orange
Oiapoque
AMAPÁ
Amapá
C.do Norte
Macapá
Estuario do Rio Amazonas
Ilha Caviana
Ilha de Marajó
Belém (Pará)
Santarém
PARÁ
São Luís (Maranhão)
Parnaíba
Fortaleza (Ceará)
Rocas
Fernando de Noronha (Braz.)
MARANHÃO
Bacabal
Caxias
Teresina
CEARÁ
RIO GRANDE DO NORTE
Natal
C. de São Roque
PARAÍBA
João Pessoa (Paraíba)
Campina Grande
PIAUÍ
PERNAMBUCO
RECIFE (Pernambuco)
ALAGOAS
Maceió
SERGIPE
Aracaju
BAHIA
Salvador (Bahia)
Feira de Santana
Alagoinhas
Santo Amaro
Ilhéus
Vitória da Conquista
GOIÁS
Brasília
Goiânia
Anápolis
MINAS GERAIS
Belo Horizonte
Montes Claros
Uberaba
Uberlândia
Juiz de Fora
ESPÍRITO SANTO
Vitória
Campos
Petrópolis
Niterói
RIO DE JANEIRO
SÃO PAULO
Campinas
Ribeirão Prêto
Campo Grande
Planalto do Mato Grosso
Planalto do Brasil
Trindade (Braz.)
6059

1:16 000 000

100 50 0 100 200 300 miles

100 0 100 200 300 400 km

PARAGUAY

URUGUAY

MATO GROSSO DO SUL

PARANÁ

SANTA CATARINA

RIO GRANDE DO SUL

SÃO PAULO

RIO DE JANEIRO

ARGENTINA

PATAGONIA

CHILE

SOUTH ATLANTIC OCEAN

Peru—Chile Trench

Richards Trench

Tropic of Capricorn

Asunción

Córdoba

Rosario

BUENOS AIRES

MONTEVIDEO

SANTIAGO

Valparaíso

Mendoza

San Juan

San Miguel de Tucumán

Salta

Antofagasta

Concepción

Talcahuano

Bahía Blanca

Mar del Plata

Pôrto Alegre

Curitiba

Florianópolis

Comodoro Rivadavia

Río Gallegos

Punta Arenas

Tierra del Fuego

Cabo de Hornos (C. Horn)

Estrecho de Magallanes (Magellan's Str.)

Golfo San Matías

Golfo San Jorge

Río de la Plata

Lagoa dos Patos

FALKLAND ISLANDS (Islas Malvinas) (Br.)

West Falkland

East Falkland

Stanley

South Georgia (Br.)

I. de Chiloé

Archipiélago de los Chonos

I. Wellington

Arch. Reina Adelaida

I. Santa Inés

I. de los Estados (Staten I.)

5830

ft m

18 000 6000

12 000 4000

9000 3000

6000 2000

4500 1500

3000 1000

1200 400

600 200

0 0

200 600

2000 6000

4000 12 000

6000 18 000

8000 24 000

m ft

Projection: Sanson-Flamsteed's Sinusoidal

60 West from Greenwich 55

INDEX

'he number printed in bold type against each entry indicates ıe map page where the feature can be found. This is followed y its geographical coordinates. The first coordinate indicates ıtitude, i.e. distance north or south of the Equator. The econd coordinate indicates longitude, i.e. distance east or west f the meridian of Greenwich in England (shown as 0° ongitude). Both latitude and longitude are measured in egrees and minutes (with 60 minutes in a degree), and appear n the map as horizontal and vertical gridlines respectively. 'hus the entry for Paris in France reads.

Paris, France **19** 48 50 N 2 20 E

'his entry indicates that Paris is on page 19, at latitude 48 egrees 50 minutes north (approximately five-sixths of the istance between horizontal gridlines 48 and 49, marked on ither side of the page) and at longitude 2 degrees 20 minutes ast (approximately one-third of the distance between vertical ridlines 2 and 3, marked at top and bottom of the page). Paris an be found where lines extended from these two points cross n the page. The geographical coordinates are sometimes only pproximate but are close enough for the place to be located. ivers have been indexed to their mouth or confluence.

An open square □ signifies that the name refers to an administrative subdivision of a country while a solid square ■ follows the name of a country. An arrow ⤳ follows the name of a river.

The alphabetical order of names composed of two or more words is governed primarily by the first word and then by the second. This rule applies even if the second word is a description or its abbreviation, R.,L.,I. for example. Names composed of a proper name (Gibraltar) and a description (Strait of) are positioned alphabetically by the proper name. If the same place name occurs twice or more times in the index and all are in the same country, each is followed by the name of the administrative subdivision in which it is located. The names are placed in the alphabetical order of the subdivisions. If the same place name occurs twice or more in the index and the places are in different countries they will be followed by their country names, the latter governing the alphabetical order. In a mixture of these situations the primary order is fixed by the alphabetical sequence of the countries and the secondary order by that of the country subdivisions.

'lease refer to the table at the end of the index for the recent place name changes in India, Iran, Mozambique and Zimbabwe.

bbreviations used in the index:

. R.–Autonomous Region
. S. S. R.–Autonomous Soviet Socialist Republic
fghan.–Afghanistan
fr.–Africa
la.–Alabama
las.–Alaska
lg.–Algeria
lta.–Alberta
mer.–America
nd. P.–Andhra Pradesh
rch.–Archipelago
rgent.–Argentina
riz.–Arizona
rk.–Arkansas
tl. Oc. – Atlantic Ocean
ustral. – Australia
. – Baie, Bahía, Bay, Bucht, Bugt
.A. – Buenos Aires
.C. – British Columbia
angla. – Bangladesh
arr. – Barrage
ay. – Bayern
elg. – Belgium
erks. – Berkshire
ol. – Bolshoi
oliv. – Bolivia
ots. – Botswana
r. – British
ri. – Bridge
t. – Bight
ucks. – Buckinghamshire
ulg. – Bulgaria
. – Cabo, Cap, Cape, Coast
Prov. – Cape Province
alif. – California
amb. – Cambodia
ambs. – Cambridgeshire
an. – Canada
ent. – Central
han. – Channel
o. – Country
olomb. – Colombia
olo. – Colorado
onn. – Connecticut
ord. – Cordillera
r. – Creek
umb. – Cumbria
zech. – Czechoslovakia
.C. – District of Columbia
el. – Delaware
ep. – Dependency
erby. – Derbyshire
es. – Desert
ist. – District
j. – Djebel
umf. & Gall. – Dumfries and Galloway
– East
ng. – England
ed. – Federal, Federation
a. – Florida
or. – Forest
. – France, French
s. – Falls
. – Fort
G. – Golfe, Golfo, Gulf, Guba
Ga. – Georgia
Ger. – Germany
Glam. – Glamorgan
Glos. – Gloucestershire
Gr. – Grande, Great, Greater, Group
H.K. – Hong Kong
H.P. – Himachal Pradesh
Hants. – Hampshire
Harb. – Harbor, Harbour
Hd. – Head
Here. & Worcs. – Hereford and Worcester
Herts. – Hertfordshire
Hts. – Heights
Hung. – Hungary
I.o.M. – Isle of Man
I.(s). – Île, Ilha, Insel, Isla, Island, Isle
Id. – Idaho
Ill. – Illinois
Ind. – Indiana
Ind. Oc. – Indian Ocean
Indon. – Indonesia
J. – Jabal, Jabel, Jazira
Junc. – Junction
K. – Kap, Kapp
K. – Kuala
Kal. – Kalmyk A.S.S.R.
Kans. – Kansas
Kep. – Kepulauan
Ky. – Kentucky
L. – Lac, Lacul, Lago, Lagoa, Lake, Limni, Loch, Lough
La. – Lousiana
Lancs. – Lancashire
Leb. – Lebanon
Leics. – Leicestershire
Lim. – Limerick
Lincs. – Lincolnshire
Lit. – Little
Lr. – Lower
Mad. P. – Madhya Pradesh
Madag. – Madagascar
Malay. – Malaysia
Man. – Manitoba
Manch. – Manchester
Maran. – Maranhão
Mass. – Massachusetts
Md. – Maryland
Me. – Maine
Mend. – Mendoza
Mér. – Méridionale
Mich. – Michigan
Mid. – Middle
Minn. – Minnesota
Miss. – Mississippi
Mo. – Missouri
Mong. – Mongolia
Mont. – Montana
Moroc. – Morocco
Mozam. – Mozambique
Mt.(e). – Mont, Monte, Monti, Montaña, Mountain
Mys. – Mysore
N. – Nord, Norte, North, Northern, Nouveau
N.B. – New Brunswick
N.C. – North Carolina
N.D. – North Dakota
N.H. – New Hampshire
N.I. – North Island
N.J. – New Jersey
N. Mex. – New Mexico
N.S. – Nova Scotia
N.S.W. – New South Wales
N.T. – Northern Territory
N.W.T. – North West Territory
N.Y. – New York
N.Z. – New Zealand
Nat. – National
Nat.Park. – National Park
Nebr. – Nebraska
Neth. – Netherlands
Nev. – Nevada
Newf. – Newfoundland
Nic. – Nicaragua
Northants. – Northamptonshire
Northumb. – Northumberland
Notts. – Nottinghamshire
O. – Oued, ouadi
Occ. – Occidentale
O.F.S. – Orange Free State
Okla. – Oklahoma
Ont. – Ontario
Or. – Orientale
Oreg. – Oregon
Os. – Ostrov
Oxon. – Oxfordshire
Oz. – Ozero
P. – Pass, Passo, Pasul, Pulau
P.E.I. – Prince Edward Island
P.N.G. – Papua New Guinea
P.O. – Post Office
P. Rico.–Puerto Rico
Pa. – Pennsylvania
Pac. Oc. – Pacific Ocean
Pak. – Pakistan
Parag. – Paraguay
Pass. – Passage
Pen. – Peninsula, Peninsule
Phil. – Philippines
Pk. – Peak
Plat. – Plateau
P-ov. – Poluostrov
Port. – Portugal, Portuguese
Prom. – Promontory
Prov. – Province, Provincial
Pt. – Point
Pta. – Ponta, Punta
Pte. – Pointe
Qué. – Québec
Queens. – Queensland
R. – Rio, River
R.I. – Rhode Island
R.S.F.S.R. – Russian Soviet Federative Socialist Republic
Ra.(s). – Range(s)
Raj. – Rajasthan
Reg. – Region
Rep. – Republic
Res. – Reserve, Reservoir
Rhld. – Pfz. – Rheinland–Pfalz
S. – San, South
S. Afr. – South Africa
S. Austral. – South Australia
S.C. – South Carolina
S.D. – South Dakota
S.-Holst. – Schleswig-Holstein
S.I. – South Island
S. Leone–Sierra Leone
S.S.R. – Soviet Socialist Republic
Sa. – Serra, Sierra
Sard. – Sardinia
Sask. – Saskatchewan
Scot. – Scotland
Sd. – Sound
Sept. – Septentrionale
Sev. – Severnaja
Sib. – Siberia
Som. – Somerset
Span. – Spanish
Sprs. – Springs
St. – Saint
Sta. – Santa, Station
Staffs. – Staffordshire
Ste. – Sainte
Sto. – Santo
Str. – Strait, Stretto
Switz. – Switzerland
T.O. – Telegraph Office
Tas. – Tasmania
Tenn. – Tennessee
Terr. – Territory
Tex. – Texas
Tg. – Tanjung
Thai. – Thailand
Tipp. – Tipperary
Trans. – Transvaal
U.K. – United Kingdom
U.S.A. – United States of America
U.S.S.R. – Union of Soviet Socialist Republics
Ukr. – Ukraine
Ut.P. – Uttar Pradesh
Utd. – United
V. – Vorota
Va. – Virginia
Vdkhr. – Vodokhranilishche
Venez. – Venezuela
Vic. – Victoria
Viet. – Vietnam
Vol. – Volcano
Vt. – Vermont
W. – Wadi, West
W.A. – Western Australia
W. Isles–Western Isles
W. Va. – West Virginia
Wash. – Washington
Wilts. – Wiltshire
Wis. – Wisconsin
Wlkp. – Wielkopolski
Wyo. – Wyoming
Yorks. – Yorkshire
Yug. – Yugoslavia
Zap. – Zapadnaja
Zimb. – Zimbabwe

A

Aachen 24 50 47N 6 4 E
Aâlâ en Nil □ 87 8 50N 29 55 E
Aalen 25 48 49N 10 6 E
Aalsmeer 16 52 17N 4 43 E
Aalst 16 50 56N 4 2 E
Aalten 16 51 56N 6 35 E
Aarau 25 47 23N 8 4 E
Aarberg 25 47 2N 7 16 E
Aare → 25 47 33N 8 14 E
Aargau □ 25 47 26N 8 10 E
Aarschot 16 50 59N 4 49 E
Aba, Nigeria 85 5 10N 7 19 E
Aba, Zaïre 90 3 58N 30 17 E
Âbâ, Jazîrat 87 13 30N 32 31 E
Ābādān 64 30 22N 48 20 E
Abade, Ethiopia 87 9 22N 38 3 E
Abade, Iran 65 31 8N 52 40 E
Abadin 30 43 21N 7 29W
Abadla 82 31 2N 2 45W
Abaetetuba 127 1 40 S 48 50W
Abagnar Qi 76 43 52N 116 2 E
Abai 125 25 58 S 55 54W
Abak 85 4 58N 7 50 E
Abakaliki 85 6 22N 8 2 E
Abakan 59 53 40N 91 10 E
Abal Nam 86 25 20N 38 37 E
Abalemma 85 16 12N 7 50 E
Abanilla 33 38 12N 1 3W
Abano Terme 39 45 22N 11 46 E
Abarán 33 38 12N 1 23W
Abarqū 65 31 10N 53 20 E
'Abasân 62 31 19N 34 21 E
Abashiri 74 44 0N 144 15 E
Abashiri-Wan 74 44 0N 144 30 E
Abau 98 10 11 S 148 46 E
Abaújszántó 27 48 16N 21 12 E
Abay 58 49 38N 72 53 E
Abaya L. 87 6 30N 37 50 E
Abaza 58 52 39N 90 6 E
Abbadia San Salvatore 39 42 53N 11 40 E
Abbay (Nîl el Azraq) → 87 15 38N 32 31 E
Abbaye, Pt. 114 46 58N 88 4W
Abbé, L. 87 11 8N 41 47 E
Abbeville, France 19 50 6N 1 49 E
Abbeville, La., U.S.A. 117 30 0N 92 7W
Abbeville, S.C., U.S.A. 115 34 12N 82 21W
Abbiategrasso 38 45 23N 8 55 E
Abbieglassie 99 27 15 S 147 28 E
Abbotsford, B.C., Can. 108 49 5N 122 20W
Abbotsford, Qué., Can. 113 45 25N 72 53W
Abbotsford, U.S.A. 116 44 55N 90 20W
Abbottabad 66 34 10N 73 15 E
Abd al Kūrī 63 12 5N 52 20 E
Abéché 81 13 50N 20 35 E
Abejar 32 41 48N 2 47W
Abekr 87 12 45N 28 50 E
Abêlessa 82 22 58N 4 47 E
Abengourou 84 6 42N 3 27W
Åbenrå 49 55 3N 9 25 E
Abensberg 25 48 49N 11 51 E
Abeokuta 85 7 3N 3 19 E
Aber 90 2 12N 32 25 E
Aberaeron 13 52 15N 4 16W
Aberayron = Aberaeron 13 52 15N 4 16W
Abercorn 99 25 12 S 151 5 E
Abercorn = Mbala 91 8 46 S 31 17 E
Abercrombie → 100 33 54 S 149 8 E
Aberdare 13 51 43N 3 27W
Aberdare Ra. 90 0 15 S 36 50 E
Aberdeen, Austral. 99 32 9 S 150 56 E
Aberdeen, Can. 109 52 20N 106 8W
Aberdeen, S. Afr. 92 32 28 S 24 2 E
Aberdeen, U.K. 14 57 9N 2 6W
Aberdeen, Ala., U.S.A. 115 33 49N 88 33W
Aberdeen, Idaho, U.S.A. 118 42 57N 112 50W
Aberdeen, S.D., U.S.A. 116 45 30N 98 30W
Aberdeen, Wash., U.S.A. 118 47 0N 123 50W
Aberdovey 13 52 33N 4 3W
Aberfeldy 14 56 37N 3 50W
Abergaria-a-Velha 30 40 41N 8 32W
Abergavenny 13 51 49N 3 1W
Abernathy 117 33 49N 101 49W
Abert L. 118 42 40N 120 8W
Aberystwyth 13 52 25N 4 6W
Abha 86 18 0N 42 34 E
Abhayapuri 69 26 24N 90 38 E
Abidiya 86 18 18N 34 3 E
Abidjan 84 5 26N 3 58W
Abilene, Kans., U.S.A. 116 39 0N 97 16W
Abilene, Texas, U.S.A. 117 32 22N 99 40W
Abingdon, U.K. 13 51 40N 1 17W
Abingdon, Ill., U.S.A. 116 40 53N 90 23W
Abingdon, Va., U.S.A. 115 36 46N 81 56W
Abitau → 109 59 53N 109 3W
Abitau L. 109 60 27N 107 15W
Abitibi L. 106 48 40N 79 40W
Abiy Adi 87 13 39N 39 3 E
Abkhaz A.S.S.R. □ 57 43 0N 41 0 E
Abkit 59 64 10N 157 10 E
Abnûb 86 27 18N 31 4 E
Åbo 51 60 28N 22 15 E
Abo, Massif d' 83 21 41N 16 8 E
Abocho 85 7 35N 6 56 E
Abohar 68 30 10N 74 10 E
Aboisso 84 5 30N 3 5W
Aboméy 85 7 10N 2 5 E
Abondance 21 46 18N 6 42 E
Abong-Mbang 88 4 0N 13 8 E
Abonnema 85 4 41N 6 49 E
Abony 27 47 12N 20 3 E
Aboso 84 5 23N 1 57W
Abou-Deïa 81 11 20N 19 20 E
Aboyne 14 57 4N 2 48W
Abra Pampa 124 22 43 S 65 42W
Abrantes 31 39 24N 8 7W
Abraveses 30 40 41N 7 55W
Abreojos, Pta. 120 26 50N 113 40W
Abreschviller 19 48 39N 7 6 E
Abrets, Les 21 45 32N 5 35 E
Abri, Esh Shimâliya, Sudan 86 20 50N 30 27 E
Abri, Janub Kordofân, Sudan 87 11 40N 30 21 E
Abrud 46 46 19N 23 5 E
Abruzzi □ 39 42 15N 14 0 E
Absaroka Ra. 118 44 40N 110 0W
Abū al Khaşīb 64 30 25N 48 0 E
Abū 'Alī 64 27 20N 49 27 E
Abu 'Arīsh 63 16 53N 42 48 E
Abû Ballas 86 24 26N 27 36 E
Abu Deleiq 87 15 57N 33 48 E
Abū Dhabī 65 24 28N 54 36 E
Abû Dîs 62 31 47N 35 16 E
Abû Dis 86 19 12N 33 38 E
Abû Dom 87 16 18N 32 25 E
Abû Gabra 87 11 2N 26 50 E
Abû Ghaush 62 31 48N 35 6 E
Abû Gubeiha 87 11 30N 31 15 E
Abu Habl, Khawr → 87 12 37N 31 0 E
Abû Hamed 86 19 32N 33 13 E
Abu Haraz 87 14 35N 33 30 E
Abû Haraz 86 19 8N 32 18 E
Abû Higar 87 12 50N 33 59 E
Abū Kamāl 64 34 30N 41 0 E
Abū Madd, Ra's 64 24 50N 37 7 E
Abû Markhah 64 25 4N 38 22 E
Abu Qir 86 31 18N 30 0 E
Abu Qireiya 86 24 5N 35 28 E
Abu Qurqâs 86 28 1N 30 44 E
Abû Rudies 86 29 0N 33 15 E
Abu Salama 86 27 10N 35 51 E
Abû Simbel 86 22 18N 31 40 E
Abu Tig 86 27 4N 31 15 E
Abu Tiga 87 12 47N 34 12 E
Abû Zabad 87 12 25N 29 10 E
Abū Zābī 65 24 28N 54 22 E
Abuja 85 9 16N 7 2 E
Abukuma-Gawa → 74 38 06N 140 52 E
Abunã 126 9 40 S 65 20W
Abunã → 126 9 41 S 65 20W
Aburo, Mt. 90 2 4N 30 53 E
Abut Hd. 101 43 7 S 170 15 E
Abwong 87 9 2N 32 14 E
Åby 49 58 40N 16 10 E
Aby, Lagune 84 5 15N 3 14W
Acámbaro 120 20 0N 100 40W
Acanthus 44 40 27N 23 47 E
Acaponeta 120 22 30N 105 20W
Acapulco 120 16 51N 99 56W
Acatlán 120 18 10N 98 3W
Acayucan 120 17 59N 94 58W
Accéglio 38 44 28N 6 59 E
Accomac 114 37 43N 75 40W
Accra 85 5 35N 0 6W
Accrington 12 53 46N 2 22W
Acebal 124 33 20 S 60 50W
Aceh □ 72 4 15N 97 30 E
Acerenza 41 40 50N 15 58 E
Acerra 41 40 57N 14 22 E
Aceuchal 31 38 39N 6 30W
Achalpur 68 21 22N 77 32 E
Achenkirch 26 47 32N 11 45 E
Achensee 26 47 26N 11 45 E
Acher 68 23 10N 72 32 E
Achern 25 48 37N 8 5 E
Achill 15 53 56N 9 55W
Achill Hd. 15 53 59N 10 15W
Achill I. 15 53 58N 10 5W
Achill Sound 15 53 53N 9 55W
Achim 24 53 1N 9 2 E
Achinsk 59 56 20N 90 20 E
Achol 87 6 35N 31 32 E
Acireale 41 37 37N 15 9 E
Ackerman 117 33 20N 89 8W
Acklins I. 121 22 30N 74 0W
Acland, Mt. 97 24 50 S 148 20 E
Acme 108 51 33N 113 30W
Aconcagua □, Argent. 124 32 50 S 70 0W
Aconcagua □, Chile 124 32 15 S 70 30W
Aconcagua, Cerro 124 32 39 S 70 0W
Aconquija, Mt. 124 27 0 S 66 0W
Açores, Is. dos = Azores 6 38 44N 29 0W
Acquapendente 39 42 45N 11 50 E
Acquasanta 39 42 46N 13 24 E
Acquaviva delle Fonti 41 40 53N 16 50 E
Acqui 38 44 40N 8 28 E
Acre = 'Akko 62 32 55N 35 4 E
Acre □ 126 9 1 S 71 0W
Acre → 126 8 45 S 67 22W
Acri 41 39 29N 16 23 E
Acs 27 47 42N 18 0 E
Actium 44 38 57N 20 45 E
Acton 112 43 38N 80 3W
Ad Dahnā 64 24 30N 48 10 E
Ad Dammām 64 26 20N 50 5 E
Ad Dār al Ḩamrā' 64 27 20N 37 45 E
Ad Dawhah 65 25 15N 51 35 E
Ad Dilam 64 23 55N 47 10 E
Ada, Ghana 85 5 44N 0 40 E
Ada, Minn., U.S.A. 116 47 20N 96 30W
Ada, Okla., U.S.A. 117 34 50N 96 45W
Ada, Yugo. 42 45 49N 20 9 E
Adaja → 30 41 32N 4 52W
Ådalslinden 48 63 27N 16 55 E
Adam 65 22 15N 57 28 E
Adamaoua, Massif de l' 85 7 20N 12 20 E
Adamawa Highlands = Adamaoua, Massif de l' 85 7 20N 12 20 E
Adamello, Mt. 38 46 10N 10 34 E
Adami Tulu 87 7 53N 38 41 E
Adaminaby 99 36 0 S 148 45 E
Adams, Mass., U.S.A. 113 42 38N 73 8W
Adams, N.Y., U.S.A. 114 43 50N 76 3W
Adams, Wis., U.S.A. 116 43 59N 89 50W
Adam's Bridge 70 9 15N 79 40 E
Adams Center 113 43 51N 76 1W
Adams L. 108 51 10N 119 40W
Adams, Mt. 118 46 10N 121 28W
Adam's Peak 70 6 48N 80 30 E
Adamuz 31 38 2N 4 32W
Adana 64 37 0N 35 16 E
Adanero 30 40 56N 4 36W
Adapazarı 64 40 48N 30 25 E
Adarama 87 17 10N 34 52 E
Adare, C. 5 71 0 S 171 0 E
Adaut 73 8 8 S 131 7 E
Adavale 97 25 52 S 144 32 E
Adda → 38 45 8N 9 53 E
Addis Ababa = Addis Abeba 87 9 2N 38 42 E
Addis Abeba 87 9 2N 38 42 E
Addis Alem 87 9 0N 38 17 E
Addison 112 42 9N 77 15W
Adebour 85 13 17N 11 50 E
Adel 115 31 10N 83 28W
Adelaide, Austral. 97 34 52 S 138 30 E
Adelaide, Madag. 93 32 42 S 26 20 E
Adelaide I. 5 67 15 S 68 30W
Adelaide Pen. 104 68 15N 97 30W
Adélie, Terre 5 68 0 S 140 0 E
Ademuz 32 40 5N 1 13W
Aden = Al 'Adan 63 12 45N 45 12 E
Aden, G. of 63 13 0N 50 0 E
Adendorp 92 32 25 S 24 30 E
Adgz 82 30 47N 6 30W
Adhoi 68 23 26N 70 32 E
Adi 73 4 15 S 133 30 E
Adi Daro 87 14 20N 38 14 E
Adi Keyih 87 14 51N 39 22 E
Adi Kwala 87 14 38N 38 48 E
Adi Ugri 87 14 58N 38 48 E
Adieu, C. 96 32 0 S 132 10 E
Adigala 87 10 24N 42 15 E
Adige → 39 45 9N 12 20 E
Adigrat 87 14 20N 39 26 E
Adilabad 70 19 33N 78 20 E
Adin 118 41 10N 121 0W
Adin Khel 65 32 45N 68 5 E
Adirampattinam 70 10 28N 79 20 E
Adirondack Mts. 114 44 0N 74 15W
Adjim 83 33 47N 10 50 E
Adjohon 85 6 41N 2 32 E
Adjud 46 46 7N 27 10 E
Adjumani 90 3 20N 31 50 E
Adlavik Is. 107 55 2N 57 45W
Adler 57 43 28N 39 52 E
Admer 83 20 21N 5 27 E
Admer, Erg d' 83 24 0N 9 5 E
Admiralty B. 5 62 0 S 59 0W
Admiralty G. 96 14 20 S 125 55 E
Admiralty I. 104 57 40N 134 35W
Admiralty Inlet 118 48 0N 122 40W
Admiralty Is. 94 2 0 S 147 0 E
Admiralty Ra. 5 72 0 S 164 0 E
Ado 85 6 36N 2 56 E
Ado Ekiti 85 7 38N 5 12 E
Adok 87 8 10N 30 20 E
Adola 87 11 14N 41 44 E
Adonara 73 8 15 S 123 5 E
Adoni 70 15 33N 77 18W
Adony 27 47 6N 18 52 E
Adour → 20 43 32N 1 32W
Adra, India 69 23 30N 86 42 E
Adra, Spain 33 36 43N 3 3W
Adrano 41 37 40N 14 49 E
Adrar 82 27 51N 0 11W
Adré 81 13 40N 22 20 E
Adrī 83 27 32N 13 2 E
Ádria 39 45 4N 12 3 E
Adrian, Mich., U.S.A. 114 41 55N 84 0W
Adrian, Tex., U.S.A. 117 35 19N 102 37W
Adriatic Sea 34 43 0N 16 0 E
Adua 73 1 45 S 129 50 E
Adur 70 9 8N 76 40 E
Adwa 87 14 15N 38 52 E
Adzhar A.S.S.R. □ 57 42 0N 42 0 E
Adzopé 84 6 7N 3 49W
Ægean Sea 35 37 0N 25 0 E
Æolian Is. = Eólie 41 38 30N 14 50 E
Aerht'ai Shan 75 46 40N 92 45 E
Ærø 49 54 52N 10 25 E
Ærøskøbing 49 54 53N 10 24 E
Aëtós 45 37 15N 21 50 E
Afafi, Massif d' 83 22 11N 15 10 E
Afándou 45 36 18N 28 12 E
Afarag, Erg 82 23 50N 2 47 E
Affreville = Khemis Miliania 82 36 11N 2 14 E
Afghanistan ■ 65 33 0N 65 0 E
Afgoi 63 2 7N 44 59 E
'Afif 64 23 53N 42 56 E
Afikpo 85 5 53N 7 54 E
Aflisses, O. → 82 28 40N 0 50 E
Aflou 82 34 7N 2 3 E
Afognak I. 104 58 10N 152 50W
Afragola 41 40 54N 14 15 E
Afrera 87 13 16N 41 5 E
Africa 78 10 0N 20 0 E
Afton 113 42 14N 75 31W
Aftout 82 26 50N 3 45W
Afuá 127 0 15 S 50 20W
Afula 62 32 37N 35 17 E
Afyonkarahisar 64 38 45N 30 33 E
Aga 86 30 55N 31 10 E
Agadès = Agadez 85 16 58N 7 59 E
Agadez 85 16 58N 7 59 E
Agadir 82 30 28N 9 35W
Agano → 74 37 57N 139 8 E
Agapa 59 71 27N 89 15 E
Agar 68 23 40N 76 2 E
Agaro 87 7 50N 36 38 E
Agartala 67 23 50N 91 23 E
Agăş 46 46 28N 26 15 E
Agassiz 108 49 14N 121 46W
Agats 73 5 33 S 138 0 E
Agattu I. 104 52 25N 172 30 E
Agbélouvé 85 6 35N 1 14 E
Agboville 84 5 55N 4 15W
Agdam 57 40 0N 46 58 E
Agdash 57 40 44N 47 22 E
Agde 20 43 19N 3 28 E
Agde, C. d' 20 43 16N 3 28 E
Agdzhabedi 57 40 5N 47 27 E
Agen 20 44 12N 0 38 E
Ager Tay 83 20 0N 17 41
Agersø 49 55 13N 11 12
Ageyevo 55 54 10N 36 27
Agger 49 56 47N 8 13
Ággius 40 40 56N 9 4
Aghil Mts. 69 36 0N 77 0
Aginskoye 59 51 6N 114 32
Agira 41 37 40N 14 30
Agly → 20 42 46N 3 3
Agnibilékrou 84 7 10N 3 11
Agnita 46 45 59N 24 40
Agnone 41 41 49N 14 20
Agofie 85 8 27N 0 15
Agogna → 38 45 4N 8 52
Agogo 87 7 50N 28 45
Agon 18 49 2N 1 34
Agön 48 61 34N 17 23
Ágordo 39 46 18N 12 2
Agout → 20 43 47N 1 41
Agra 68 27 17N 77 58
Agramunt 32 41 48N 1 6
Agreda 32 41 51N 1 55
Agri → 41 40 13N 16 44
Ağri Daği 64 39 50N 44 15
Ağri Karakose 64 39 44N 43 3
Agrigento 40 37 19N 13 33
Agrinion 45 38 37N 21 27
Agrópoli 41 40 23N 14 59
Água Clara 127 20 25 S 52 45
Agua Prieta 120 31 20N 109 32
Aguadas 126 5 40N 75 38
Aguadilla 121 18 27N 67 10
Aguanish 107 50 14N 62 2
Aguanus → 107 50 13N 62 5
Aguapey → 124 29 7 S 56 36
Aguaray Guazú → 124 24 47 S 57 19
Aguarico → 126 0 59 S 75 11
Aguas → 32 41 20N 0 30
Aguas Blancas 124 24 15 S 69 55
Aguas Calientes, Sierra de 124 25 26 S 66 40
Aguascalientes 120 21 53N 102 12
Aguascalientes □ 120 22 0N 102 20
Agudo 31 38 59N 4 52
Águeda 30 40 34N 8 27
Agueda → 30 41 2N 6 56
Aguié 85 13 31N 7 46
Aguilafuente 30 41 13N 4 7
Aguilar 31 37 31N 4 40
Aguilar de Campóo 30 42 47N 4 15
Aguilares 124 27 26 S 65 35
Aguilas 33 37 23N 1 35
Agulaa 87 13 40N 39 40
Agulhas, Kaap 92 34 52 S 20 0
Agung 72 8 20 S 115 28
'Agur 62 31 42N 34 55
Agur 90 2 28N 32 55
Agusan → 73 9 0N 125 30
Agvali 57 42 36N 46 8
Aha Mts. 92 19 45 S 21 0
Ahaggar 83 23 0N 6 30
Ahamansu 85 7 38N 0 35
Ahar 64 38 35N 47 0
Ahaus 24 52 4N 7 1
Ahelledjem 83 26 37N 6 58
Ahipara B. 101 35 5 S 173 5
Ahiri 70 19 30N 80 0
Ahlen 24 51 45N 7 52
Ahmadabad (Ahmedabad) 68 23 0N 72 40
Ahmadnagar (Ahmednagar) 70 19 7N 74 46
Ahmadpur 68 29 12N 71 10
Ahmar Mts. 87 9 20N 41 15
Ahoada 85 5 8N 6 36
Ahr → 24 50 33N 7 17
Ahrensbök 24 54 0N 10 34
Ahrweiler 24 50 31N 7 3
Aḩsā', Wāḩat al 64 25 50N 49 0
Ahuachapán 120 13 54N 89 52
Åhus 49 55 56N 14 18
Ahvāz 64 31 20N 48 40
Ahvenanmaa = Åland 51 60 15N 20 0
Ahwar 63 13 30N 46 40
Ahzar 85 15 30N 3 20
Aichach 25 48 28N 11 9
Aichi □ 74 35 0N 137 15
Aidone 41 37 26N 14 26
Aiello Cálabro 41 39 6N 16 12
Aigle 25 46 18N 6 58
Aigle, L' 18 48 46N 0 38
Aignay-le-Duc 19 47 40N 4 43
Aigre 20 45 54N 0
Aigua 125 34 13 S 54 46
Aigueperse 20 46 3N 3 13
Aigues-Mortes 21 43 35N 4 12
Aigues-Mortes, G. d' 21 43 31N 4 3
Aiguilles 21 44 47N 6 5
Aiguillon 20 44 18N 0 2
Aiguillon, L' 20 46 20N 1 16
Aigurande 20 46 27N 1 49
Aihui 75 50 10N 127 30
Aija 126 9 50 S 77 45
Aijal 67 23 40N 92 44
Aiken 115 33 34N 81 50
Aillant-sur-Tholon 19 47 52N 3 20
Aillik 107 55 11N 59 18
Ailly-sur-Noye 19 49 45N 2 20
Ailsa Craig 14 55 15N 5
'Ailūn 62 32 18N 35 47
Aim 59 59 0N 133 55
Aimere 73 8 45 S 121
Aimogasta 124 28 33 S 66 50
Aimorés 127 19 30 S 41
Ain □ 21 46 5N 5 20
Ain → 21 45 45N 5 11
Ain Banaiyan 65 23 0N 51
Aïn Beïda 83 35 50N 7
Ain ben Khellil 82 33 15N 0 49
Aïn Ben Tili 82 25 59N 9 27
Aïn Beni Mathar 82 34 1N 2
Aïn Benian 82 36 48N 2 55
Ain Dalla 86 27 20N 27 2
Ain Dar 64 25 55N 49 10
Ain el Mafki 86 27 30N 28 1

n Galakka **81** 18 10N 18 30 E
n Girba **86** 29 20N 25 14 E
'n M'lila **83** 36 2N 6 35 E
n Qeiqab **86** 29 42N 24 55 E
n-Sefra **82** 32 47N 0 37W
n Sheikh Murzûk **86** 26 47N 27 45 E
n Sukhna **86** 29 32N 32 20 E
n Tédelès **82** 36 0N 0 21 E
n-Témouchent **82** 35 16N 1 8W
n Touta **83** 35 26N 5 54 E
n Zeitûn **86** 29 10N 25 48 E
n Zorah **82** 34 37N 3 32W
nabo **63** 9 0N 46 25 E
naži **54** 57 50N 24 24 E
nos Óros **45** 38 10N 20 35 E
nsworth **116** 42 33N 99 52W
r **85** 18 30N 8 0 E
raines **19** 49 58N 1 55 E
rdrie **14** 55 53N 3 57W
re **19** 50 37N 2 22 E
re →, France **19** 49 18N 4 55 E
re →, U.K. **12** 53 42N 0 55W
re, I. del **32** 39 48N 4 16 E
re-sur-l'Adour **20** 43 42N 0 15W
rvault **18** 46 50N 0 8W
sch → **25** 49 46N 11 1 E
sne □ **19** 49 42N 3 40 E
sne → **19** 49 26N 2 50 E
ana, Sierra de **33** 38 35N 0 24W
ape **98** 3 11 S 142 22 E
kin **116** 46 32N 93 43W
olía Kai Akarnanía □ **45** 38 45N 21 18 E
olikón **45** 38 26N 21 21 E
ıd **46** 46 19N 23 44 E
x-en-Provence **21** 43 32N 5 27 E
x-la-Chapelle = Aachen **24** 50 47N 6 4 E
x-les-Bains **21** 45 41N 5 53 E
x-sur-Vienne **20** 45 48N 1 8 E
yansh **108** 55 17N 129 2W
yina **45** 37 45N 23 26 E
yínion **44** 40 28N 22 28 E
yion **45** 38 15N 22 5 E
zenay **18** 46 44N 1 38W
zpute **54** 56 43N 21 40 E
accio **21** 41 55N 8 40 E
accio, G. d' **21** 41 52N 8 40 E
anta Ra. **70** 20 28N 75 50 E
ax **112** 43 50N 79 1W
dâbiyah **83** 30 54N 20 4 E
dovščina **39** 45 54N 13 54 E
bar **87** 10 35N 38 36 E
ka **27** 47 4N 17 31 E
mān **65** 25 25N 55 30 E
mer **68** 26 28N 74 37 E
o **119** 32 18N 112 54W
ok **87** 9 15N 28 28 E
Dağ **64** 36 30N 30 0 E
aba **85** 8 10N 1 2 E
abli **82** 26 49N 1 31 E
aki Beseka **87** 8 55N 38 45 E
ala **87** 15 39N 36 13 E
aroa **101** 43 49 S 172 59 E
asha **86** 21 10N 30 32 E
ashi **74** 34 45N 135 0 E
bou **83** 36 31N 4 31 E
elamo **73** 1 35N 129 40 E
ernes **47** 58 45N 7 30 E
ershus fylke □ **47** 60 0N 11 10 E
eru → **70** 17 25N 80 0 E
eti **88** 2 38N 23 47 E
haïa □ **45** 38 5N 21 45 E
halkalaki **57** 41 27N 43 25 E
haltsikhe **57** 41 40N 43 0 E
harnaí **45** 38 5N 23 44 E
helóös → **45** 38 36N 21 14 E
hendria **45** 34 58N 25 16 E
héron → **44** 39 20N 20 29 E
hisar **64** 38 56N 27 48 E
hladhókambos **45** 37 31N 22 35 E
hmîm **86** 26 31N 31 47 E
htopol **43** 42 6N 27 56 E
htubinsk (Petropavlovskiy) **57** 48 13N 46 7 E
hty **57** 41 30N 47 45 E
htyrka **54** 50 25N 35 0 E
miski I. **106** 52 50N 81 30W
movka **56** 46 44N 35 0 E
rkeby **49** 55 4N 14 55 E
ita **74** 39 45N 140 7 E
ta □ **74** 39 40N 140 30 E
oujt **84** 19 45N 14 15W
ka **82** 29 22N 8 9W
ko **62** 32 55N 35 4 E
kol **58** 45 0N 75 39 E
köy **45** 37 30N 27 18 E
ampa **85** 8 15N 2 10 E
avik **104** 68 12N 135 0W
monte **31** 37 13N 6 38W
noul **82** 34 40N 3 55W
o **85** 10 19N 10 48 E
obo → **87** 7 48N 33 3 E
ola **68** 20 42N 77 2 E
onolinga **85** 3 50N 12 18 E
ordat **87** 15 30N 37 40 E
osombo Dam **85** 6 20N 0 5 E
ot, India **68** 21 10N 77 10 E
ot, Sudan **87** 6 31N 30 9 E
patok I. **105** 60 25N 68 8W
ranes **50** 64 19N 21 58W
rehamn **47** 59 15N 5 10 E
reïjit **84** 18 19N 9 11W
rítas Venétiko, Ákra **45** 36 43N 21 54 E
ron, Colo., U.S.A. **116** 40 13N 103 15W
ron, Ohio, U.S.A. **114** 41 7N 81 31W
rotíri, Ákra **44** 40 26N 25 27 E
sai Chih **69** 35 15N 79 55 E
saray **64** 38 25N 34 2 E
sarka **58** 66 31N 67 50 E
say **52** 51 11N 53 0 E
şehir **64** 38 18N 31 30 E
senovo Zilovskoye **59** 53 20N 117 40 E
stafa **57** 41 7N 45 27 E
u **75** 41 5N 80 10 E
Aksum **87** 14 5N 38 40 E
Aktogay **58** 46 57N 79 40 E
Aktyubinsk **53** 50 17N 57 10 E
Aku **85** 6 40N 7 18 E
Akure **85** 7 15N 5 5 E
Akureyri **50** 65 40N 18 6W
Akusha **57** 42 18N 47 30 E
Al Abyār **83** 32 9N 20 29 E
Al 'Adan **63** 12 45N 45 0 E
Al Amāda03yah **64** 37 5N 43 30 E
Al Amārah **64** 31 55N 47 15 E
Al 'Aqabah **62** 29 31N 35 0 E
Al 'Aramah **64** 25 30N 46 0 E
Al Ashkhara **65** 21 50N 59 30 E
Al 'Ayzarīyah (Bethany) **62** 31 47N 35 15 E
Al 'Azīzīyah **83** 32 30N 13 1 E
Al Badī' **64** 22 0N 46 35 E
Al Barkāt **83** 24 56N 10 14 E
Al Başrah **64** 30 30N 47 50 E
Al Bāzūrīyah **62** 33 15N 35 16 E
Al Bīrah **62** 31 55N 35 12 E
Al Bu'ayrāt **83** 31 24N 15 44 E
Al Buqay'ah **62** 32 15N 35 30 E
Al Dīwaniyah **64** 32 0N 45 0 E
Al Fallūjah **64** 33 20N 43 55 E
Al Fāw **64** 30 0N 48 30 E
Al Fujayrah **65** 25 7N 56 18 E
Al Ghatghaţ **64** 24 40N 46 15 E
Al Hābah **64** 27 10N 47 0 E
Al Haddār **64** 21 58N 45 57 E
Al Ḩadīthah **64** 34 0N 41 13 E
Al Hāmad **64** 31 30N 39 30 E
Al Ḩamar **64** 22 23N 46 6 E
Al Hammādah al Ḩamrā' **83** 29 30N 12 0 E
Al Hamrā **64** 24 2N 38 55 E
Al Ḩarīq **64** 23 29N 46 27 E
Al Harīr, W. → **62** 32 44N 35 59 E
Al Harūj al Aswad **83** 27 0N 17 10 E
Al Ḩasakah **64** 36 35N 40 45 E
Al Ḩawīyah **64** 24 40N 49 15 E
Al Ḩawrah **63** 13 50N 47 35 E
Al Ḩawţah **63** 16 5N 48 20 E
Al Ḩayy **64** 32 5N 46 5 E
Al Ḩillah, Iraq **64** 32 30N 44 25 E
Al Ḩillah, Si. Arab. **64** 23 35N 46 50 E
Al Hindīyah **64** 32 30N 44 10 E
Al Ḩişn **62** 32 29N 35 52 E
Al Hoceïma **82** 35 8N 3 58W
Al Ḩudaydah **63** 14 50N 43 0 E
Al Ḩufrah, Awbārī, Libya **83** 25 32N 14 1 E
Al Ḩufrah, Misrātah, Libya **83** 29 5N 18 3 E
Al Hūfūf **64** 25 25N 49 45 E
Al Ḩulwah **64** 23 24N 46 48 E
Al Husayyāt **83** 30 24N 20 37 E
Al 'Idwah **64** 27 15N 42 35 E
Al Irq **81** 29 5N 21 35 E
Al Ittihad = Madīnat ash Sha'b **63** 12 50N 45 0 E
Al Jāfūrah **64** 25 0N 50 15 E
Al Jaghbūb **81** 29 42N 24 38 E
Al Jahrah **64** 29 25N 47 40 E
Al Jalāmīd **64** 31 20N 39 45 E
Al Jawf, Libya **81** 24 10N 23 24 E
Al Jawf, Si. Arab. **64** 29 55N 39 40 E
Al Jazir **63** 18 30N 56 31 E
Al Jazirah, Libya **81** 26 10N 21 20 E
Al Jazirah, Si. Arab. **64** 33 30N 44 0 E
Al Jubayl **64** 27 0N 49 50 E
Al Jubaylah **64** 24 55N 46 25 E
Al Junaynah **81** 13 27N 22 45 E
Al Juwārah **63** 19 0N 57 13 E
Al Khābūrah **65** 23 57N 57 5 E
Al Khalīl = Hebron **62** 31 32N 35 6 E
Al Khalūf **63** 20 30N 58 13 E
Al Kharfah **64** 22 0N 46 35 E
Al Kharj **64** 24 0N 47 0 E
Al Khufayfīyah **64** 24 50N 44 35 E
Al Khums **83** 32 40N 14 17 E
Al Khums □ **83** 31 20N 14 10 E
Al Khurmah **64** 21 58N 42 3 E
Al Kufrah **81** 24 17N 23 15 E
Al Kūt **64** 32 30N 46 0 E
Al Kuwayt **64** 29 30N 47 30 E
Al Lādhiqīyah **64** 35 30N 35 45 E
Al Lidām **63** 20 33N 44 45 E
Al Līth **86** 20 9N 40 15 E
Al Lubban **62** 32 9N 35 14 E
Al Luḩayyah **63** 15 45N 42 40 E
Al Madīnah **64** 24 35N 39 52 E
Al-Mafraq **62** 32 17N 36 14 E
Al Majma'ah **64** 25 57N 45 22 E
Al Manāmāh **65** 26 10N 50 30 E
Al Marj **81** 32 25N 20 30 E
Al Maşirah **63** 20 25N 58 50 E
Al Matamma **63** 16 10N 44 30 E
Al Mawşil **64** 36 15N 43 5 E
Al Mazra **62** 31 16N 35 31 E
Al Midhnab **64** 25 50N 44 18 E
Al Miqdādīyah **64** 34 0N 45 0 E
Al Mish'āb **64** 28 12N 48 36 E
Al Mubarraz **64** 25 30N 49 40 E
Al Muḩarraq **65** 26 15N 50 40 E
Al Mukallā **63** 14 33N 49 2 E
Al Mukhā **63** 13 18N 43 15 E
Al Musayyib **64** 32 40N 44 25 E
Al Mustajiddah **64** 26 30N 41 50 E
Al Muwayliḩ **64** 27 40N 35 30 E
Al Qaddāhīyah **83** 31 15N 15 9 E
Al Qadīmah **64** 22 20N 39 13 E
Al Qāmishli **64** 37 10N 41 10 E
Al Qaryah ash Sharqīyah **83** 30 28N 13 40 E
Al Qaşabát **83** 32 39N 14 1 E
Al Qaţīf **64** 26 35N 50 0 E
Al Qaţrūn **83** 24 56N 15 3 E
Al Quaisūmah **64** 28 10N 46 20 E
Al Quds **62** 31 47N 35 10 E
Al Qunfidha **86** 19 3N 41 4 E
Al Quraiyat **65** 23 17N 58 53 E
Al Qurnah **64** 31 1N 47 25 E
Al 'Ulá **64** 26 35N 38 0 E
Al Uqaylah ash Sharqīgah **83** 30 12N 19 10 E
Al Uqayr **64** 25 40N 50 15 E
Al 'Uthmānīyahyah **64** 25 5N 49 22 E
Al 'Uwaynid **64** 24 50N 46 0 E
Al' 'Uwayqīlah ash Sharqīgah **64** 30 30N 42 10 E
Al 'Uyūn **64** 26 30N 43 50 E
Al Wajh **86** 26 10N 36 30 E
Al Wakrah **65** 25 10N 51 40 E
Al Wari'āh **64** 27 51N 47 25 E
Al Wātīyah **83** 32 28N 11 57 E
Al Yāmūn **62** 32 29N 35 14 E
Ala **38** 45 46N 11 0 E
Alabama □ **115** 33 0N 87 0W
Alabama → **115** 31 8N 87 57W
Alaçati **45** 38 16N 26 23 E
Alaejos **30** 41 18N 5 13W
Alagna Valsésia **38** 45 51N 7 56 E
Alagoa Grande **127** 7 3 S 35 35W
Alagoas □ **127** 9 0 S 36 0W
Alagoinhas **127** 12 7 S 38 20W
Alagón **32** 41 46N 1 12W
Alagón → **31** 39 44N 6 53W
Alajuela **121** 10 2N 84 8W
Alakamisy **93** 21 19 S 47 14 E
Alakurtti **52** 67 0N 30 30 E
Alameda, Spain **31** 37 12N 4 39W
Alameda, Idaho, U.S.A. **118** 43 2N 112 30W
Alameda, N. Mex., U.S.A. **119** 35 10N 106 43W
Alamitos, Sierra de los **120** 37 21N 115 10W
Alamo **119** 36 21N 115 10W
Alamogordo **119** 32 59N 106 0W
Alamos **120** 27 0N 109 0W
Alamosa **119** 37 30N 106 0W
Åland **51** 60 15N 20 0 E
Aland **70** 17 36N 76 35 E
Alandroal **31** 38 41N 7 24W
Alandur **70** 13 0N 80 15 E
Alange, Presa de **31** 38 45N 6 18W
Alanis **31** 38 3N 5 43W
Alanya **64** 36 38N 32 0 E
Alaotra, Farihin' **93** 17 30 S 48 30 E
Alapayevsk **58** 57 52N 61 42 E
Alar del Rey **30** 42 38N 4 20W
Alaraz **30** 40 45N 5 17W
Alaşehir **53** 38 23N 28 30 E
Alaska □ **104** 65 0N 150 0W
Alaska, G. of **104** 58 0N 145 0W
Alaska Highway **108** 60 0N 130 0W
Alaska Pen. **104** 56 0N 160 0W
Alaska Range **104** 62 50N 151 0W
Alássio **38** 44 1N 8 10 E
Alataw Shankou **75** 45 5N 81 57 E
Alatri **40** 41 44N 13 21 E
Alatyr **55** 54 45N 46 35 E
Alatyr → **55** 54 52N 46 36 E
Alausi **126** 2 0 S 78 50W
Álava □ **32** 42 48N 2 28W
Alava, C. **118** 48 10N 124 40W
Alaverdi **57** 41 15N 44 37 E
Alawoona **99** 34 45 S 140 30 E
Alayor **32** 39 57N 4 8 E
Alazan → **57** 41 5N 46 40 E
Alba **38** 44 41N 8 1 E
Alba □ **46** 46 10N 23 30 E
Alba de Tormes **30** 40 50N 5 30W
Alba Iulia **46** 46 8N 23 39 E
Albac **46** 46 28N 23 1 E
Albacete **33** 39 0N 1 50W
Albacete □ **33** 38 50N 2 0W
Albacutya, L. **99** 35 45 S 141 58 E
Albæk **49** 57 36N 10 25 E
Albæk Bucht **49** 57 35N 10 40 E
Albaida **33** 38 51N 0 31W
Albalate de las Nogueras **32** 40 22N 2 18W
Albalate del Arzobispo **32** 41 6N 0 31W
Albania ■ **44** 41 0N 20 0 E
Albano Laziale **40** 41 44N 12 40 E
Albany, Austral. **96** 35 1 S 117 58 E
Albany, Ga., U.S.A. **115** 31 40N 84 10W
Albany, Minn., U.S.A. **116** 45 37N 94 38W
Albany, N.Y., U.S.A. **114** 42 35N 73 47W
Albany, Oreg., U.S.A. **118** 44 41N 123 0W
Albany, Tex., U.S.A. **117** 32 45N 99 20W
Albany → **106** 52 17N 81 31W
Albardón **124** 31 20 S 68 30W
Albarracín **32** 40 25N 1 26W
Albarracín, Sierra de **32** 40 30N 1 30W
Albatross B. **97** 12 45 S 141 30 E
Albegna → **39** 42 30N 11 11 E
Albemarle **115** 35 27N 80 15W
Albemarle Sd. **115** 36 0N 76 30W
Albenga **38** 44 3N 8 12 E
Alberche → **30** 39 58N 4 46W
Alberdi **124** 26 14 S 58 20W
Alberes, Mts. **32** 42 28N 2 56 E
Alberique **33** 39 7N 0 31W
Albersdorf **24** 54 8N 9 19 E
Albert **19** 50 0N 2 38 E
Albert Canyon **108** 51 8N 117 41W
Albert L. **99** 35 30 S 139 10 E
Albert, L. = Mobutu Sese Seko, L. **90** 1 30N 31 0 E
Albert Lea **116** 43 32N 93 20W
Albert Nile → **90** 3 36N 32 2 E
Alberta □ **108** 54 40N 115 0W
Alberti **124** 35 1 S 60 16W
Albertinia **92** 34 11 S 21 34 E
Albertirsa **27** 47 14N 19 37 E
Alberton **107** 46 50N 64 0W
Albertville **21** 45 40N 6 22 E
Albertville = Kalemie **90** 5 55 S 29 9 E
Alberz, Reshteh-Ye Kūhhā-Ye **65** 36 0N 52 0 E
Albi **20** 43 56N 2 9 E
Albia **116** 41 0N 92 50W
Albina **127** 5 37N 54 15W
Albina, Ponta **92** 15 52 S 11 44 E
Albino **38** 45 47N 9 48 E
Albion, Idaho, U.S.A. **118** 42 21N 113 37W
Albion, Mich., U.S.A. **114** 42 15N 84 45W
Albion, Nebr., U.S.A. **116** 41 47N 98 0W
Albion, Pa., U.S.A. **112** 41 53N 80 21W
Albocácer **32** 40 21N 0 1 E
Alböke **49** 56 57N 16 47 E
Alborán **31** 35 57N 3 0W
Alborea **33** 39 17N 1 24W
Ålborg **49** 57 2N 9 54 E
Ålborg B. **49** 56 50N 10 35 E
Albox **33** 37 23N 2 8W
Albreda **108** 52 35N 119 10W
Albuera, La **31** 38 45N 6 49W
Albufeira **31** 37 5N 8 15W
Albula → **25** 46 38N 9 30 E
Albuñol **33** 36 48N 3 11W
Albuquerque **119** 35 5N 106 47W
Albuquerque, Cayos de **121** 12 10N 81 50W
Alburg **113** 44 58N 73 19W
Alburno, Mte. **41** 40 32N 15 15 E
Alburquerque **31** 39 15N 6 59W
Albury **97** 36 3 S 146 56 E
Alby **48** 62 30N 15 28 E
Alcácer do Sal **31** 38 22N 8 33W
Alcaçovas **31** 38 23N 8 9W
Alcalá de Chisvert **32** 40 19N 0 13 E
Alcalá de Guadaira **31** 37 20N 5 50W
Alcalá de Henares **32** 40 28N 3 22W
Alcalá de los Gazules **31** 36 29N 5 43W
Alcalá la Real **31** 37 27N 3 57W
Alcamo **40** 37 59N 12 55 E
Alcanadre **32** 42 24N 2 7W
Alcanadre → **32** 41 43N 0 12W
Alcanar **32** 40 33N 0 28 E
Alcanede **31** 39 25N 8 49W
Alcanena **31** 39 27N 8 40W
Alcañices **30** 41 41N 6 21W
Alcaníz **32** 41 2N 0 8W
Alcântara **127** 2 20 S 44 30W
Alcántara **31** 39 41N 6 57W
Alcantara L. **109** 60 57N 108 9W
Alcantarilla **33** 37 59N 1 12W
Alcaracejos **31** 38 24N 4 58W
Alcaraz **33** 38 40N 2 29W
Alcaraz, Sierra de **33** 38 40N 2 20W
Alcarria, La **32** 40 31N 2 45W
Alcaudete **31** 37 35N 4 5W
Alcázar de San Juan **33** 39 24N 3 12W
Alcira **33** 39 9N 0 30W
Alcoa **115** 35 50N 84 0W
Alcobaça **31** 39 32N 9 0W
Alcobendas **32** 40 32N 3 38W
Alcolea del Pinar **32** 41 2N 2 28W
Alcora **32** 40 5N 0 14W
Alcoutim **31** 37 25N 7 28W
Alcova **118** 42 37N 106 52W
Alcoy **33** 38 43N 0 30W
Alcubierre, Sierra de **32** 41 45N 0 22W
Alcublas **32** 39 48N 0 43W
Alcudia **32** 39 51N 3 7 E
Alcudia, B. de **32** 39 47N 3 15 E
Alcudia, Sierra de la **31** 38 34N 4 30W
Aldabra Is. **3** 9 22 S 46 28 E
Aldan **59** 58 40N 125 30 E
Aldan → **59** 63 28N 129 35 E
Aldeburgh **13** 52 9N 1 35 E
Aldeia Nova **31** 37 55N 7 24W
Alder **118** 45 27N 112 3W
Alderney **18** 49 42N 2 12W
Aldershot **13** 51 15N 0 43W
Aldersyde **108** 50 40N 113 53W
Aledo **116** 41 10N 90 50W
Alefa **87** 11 55N 36 55 E
Aleg **84** 17 3N 13 55W
Alegre **125** 20 50 S 41 30W
Alegrete **125** 29 40 S 56 0W
Aleisk **58** 52 40N 83 0 E
Alejandro Selkirk, I. **95** 33 50 S 80 15W
Aleksandriya, Ukraine S.S.R., U.S.S.R. **54** 50 37N 26 19 E
Aleksandriya, Ukraine S.S.R., U.S.S.R. **56** 48 42N 33 3 E
Aleksandriyskaya **57** 43 59N 47 0 E
Aleksandrov **55** 56 23N 38 44 E
Aleksandrovac, Srbija, Yugo. **42** 44 28N 21 13 E
Aleksandrovac, Srbija, Yugo. **42** 43 28N 21 3 E
Aleksandrovka **56** 48 55N 32 20 E
Aleksandrovo **43** 43 14N 24 51 E
Aleksandrovsk-Sakhaliniskiy **59** 50 50N 142 20 E
Aleksandrovskiy Zavod **59** 50 40N 117 50 E
Aleksandrovskoye **58** 60 35N 77 50 E
Aleksandrów Kujawski **28** 52 53N 18 43 E
Aleksandrów Łódźki **28** 51 49N 19 17 E
Alekseyevka **55** 50 43N 38 40 E
Aleksin **55** 54 31N 37 9 E
Aleksinac **42** 43 31N 21 42 E
Alèm Paraíba **125** 21 52 S 42 41W
Alemania, Argent. **124** 25 40 S 65 30W
Alemania, Chile **124** 25 10 S 69 55W
Ålen **47** 62 51N 11 17 E
Alençon **18** 48 27N 0 4 E
Alenuihaha Chan. **110** 20 25N 156 0W
Aleppo = Ḩalab **64** 36 10N 37 15 E
Aléria **21** 42 5N 9 26 E
Alert Bay **108** 50 30N 126 55W
Alès **21** 44 9N 4 5 E
Aleşd **46** 47 3N 22 22 E
Alessándria **38** 44 54N 8 37 E
Ålestrup **49** 56 42N 9 29 E
Ålesund **47** 62 28N 6 12 E
Alet-les-Bains **20** 43 0N 2 14 E
Aleutian Is. **104** 52 0N 175 0W
Aleutian Trench **94** 48 0N 180 0
Alexander **116** 47 51N 103 40W
Alexander Arch. **104** 57 0N 135 0W
Alexander B. **92** 28 36 S 16 33 E
Alexander City **115** 32 58N 85 57W
Alexander I. **5** 69 0 S 70 0W
Alexandra, Austral. **99** 37 8 S 145 40 E
Alexandra, N.Z. **101** 45 14 S 169 25 E
Alexandra Falls **108** 60 29N 116 18W
Alexandria, B.C., Can. **108** 52 35N 122 27W
Alexandria, Ont., Can. **106** 45 19N 74 38W
Alexandria, Romania **46** 43 57N 25 24 E
Alexandria, S. Afr. **92** 33 38 S 26 28 E
Alexandria, Ind., U.S.A. **114** 40 18N 85 40W
Alexandria, La., U.S.A. **117** 31 20N 92 30W
Alexandria, Minn., U.S.A. **116** 45 50N 95 20W
Alexandria, S.D., U.S.A. **116** 43 40N 97 45W
Alexandria, Va., U.S.A. **114** 38 47N 77 1W

Alexandria = El Iskandarîya 86 31 0N 30 0 E
Alexandria Bay 114 44 20N 75 52W
Alexandrina, L. 97 35 25 S 139 10 E
Alexandroúpolis 44 40 50N 25 54 E
Alexis → 107 52 33N 56 8W
Alexis Creek 108 52 10N 123 20W
Alfambra 32 40 33N 1 5W
Alfândega da Fé 30 41 20N 6 59W
Alfaro 32 42 10N 1 50W
Alfatar 43 43 59N 27 13 E
Alfeld 24 52 0N 9 49 E
Alfenas 125 21 20 S 46 10W
Alfiós → 45 37 40N 21 33 E
Alfonsine 39 44 30N 12 1 E
Alford 14 57 13N 2 42W
Alfred, Me., U.S.A. 113 43 28N 70 40W
Alfred, N.Y., U.S.A. 112 42 15N 77 45W
Alfreton 12 53 6N 1 22W
Alfta 48 61 21N 16 4 E
Alga 58 49 53N 57 20 E
Algaba, La 31 37 27N 6 1W
Algar 31 36 40N 5 39W
Ålgård 47 58 46N 5 53 E
Algarinejo 31 37 19N 4 9W
Algarve 31 36 58N 8 20W
Algeciras 31 36 9N 5 28W
Algemesí 33 39 11N 0 27W
Alger 82 36 42N 3 8 E
Algeria ■ 82 35 10N 3 11 E
Alghero 40 40 34N 8 20 E
Algiers = Alger 82 36 42N 3 8 E
Algoabaai 92 33 50 S 25 45 E
Algodonales 31 36 54N 5 24W
Algodor → 30 39 55N 3 53W
Algoma, Oreg., U.S.A. 118 42 25N 121 54W
Algoma, Wis., U.S.A. 114 44 35N 87 27W
Algona 116 43 4N 94 14W
Algonac 112 42 37N 82 32W
Alhama de Almería 33 36 57N 2 34W
Alhama de Aragón 32 41 18N 1 54W
Alhama de Granada 31 37 0N 3 59W
Alhama de Murcia 33 37 51N 1 25W
Alhambra, Spain 33 38 54N 3 4W
Alhambra, U.S.A. 119 34 2N 118 10W
Alhaurín el Grande 31 36 39N 4 41W
Alhucemas = Al-Hoceïma 82 35 8N 3 58W
'Alī al Gharbī 64 32 30N 46 45 E
Ali Bayramly 57 39 59N 48 52 E
Ali Sabieh 87 11 10N 42 44 E
Ália 40 37 47N 13 42 E
'Alīābād 65 28 10N 57 35 E
Aliaga 32 40 40N 0 42W
Aliákmon → 44 40 30N 22 36 E
Alibag 70 18 38N 72 56 E
Alibo 87 9 52N 37 5 E
Alibunar 42 45 5N 20 57 E
Alicante 33 38 23N 0 30W
Alicante □ 33 38 30N 0 37W
Alice, S. Afr. 92 32 48 S 26 55 E
Alice, U.S.A. 117 27 47N 98 1W
Alice →, Queens., Austral. 98 24 2 S 144 50 E
Alice →, Queens., Austral. 98 15 35 S 142 20 E
Alice Arm 108 55 29N 129 31W
Alice, Punta dell' 41 39 23N 17 10 E
Alice Springs 96 23 40 S 133 50 E
Alicedale 92 33 15 S 26 4 E
Aliceville 115 33 9N 88 10W
Alick Cr. → 98 20 55 S 142 20 E
Alicudi, I. 41 38 33N 14 20 E
Alida 109 49 25N 101 55W
Aligarh, Raj., India 68 25 55N 76 15 E
Aligarh, Ut. P., India 68 27 55N 78 10 E
Alīgūdarz 64 33 25N 49 45 E
Alijó 30 41 16N 7 27W
Alimena 41 37 42N 14 4 E
Alimnía 45 36 16N 27 43 E
Alingsås 49 57 56N 12 31 E
Alipur 68 29 25N 70 55 E
Alipur Duar 69 26 30N 89 35 E
Aliquippa 114 40 38N 80 18W
Aliste → 30 41 34N 5 58W
Alitus 54 54 24N 24 3 E
Alivérion 45 38 24N 24 2 E
Aliwal North 92 30 45 S 26 45 E
Alix 108 52 24N 113 11W
Aljezur 31 37 18N 8 49W
Aljustrel 31 37 55N 8 10W
Alkamari 85 13 27N 11 10 E
Alkmaar 16 52 37N 4 45 E
All American Canal 119 32 45N 115 0W
Allada 85 6 41N 2 9 E
Allah Dad 68 25 38N 67 34 E
Allahabad 69 25 25N 81 58 E
Allakh-Yun 59 60 50N 137 5 E
Allal Tazi 82 34 30N 6 20W
Allan 109 51 53N 106 4W
Allanche 20 45 14N 2 57 E
Allanmyo 67 19 30N 95 17 E
Allanridge 92 27 45 S 26 40 E
Allanwater 106 50 14N 90 10W
Allaqi, Wadi → 86 23 7N 32 47 E
Allariz 30 42 11N 7 50W
Allassac 20 45 15N 1 29 E
Allegan 114 42 32N 85 52W
Allegany 112 42 6N 78 30W
Allegheny → 114 40 27N 80 0W
Allegheny Mts. 114 38 0N 80 0W
Allegheny Res. 112 42 0N 78 55W
Allègre 20 45 12N 3 41 E
Allen, Bog of 15 53 15N 7 0W
Allen, L. 15 54 12N 8 5W
Allenby (Hussein) Bridge 62 31 53N 35 33 E
Allende 120 28 20N 100 50W
Allentown 114 40 36N 75 30W
Allensteig 26 48 41N 15 20 E
Alleppey 70 9 30N 76 28 E
Aller → 24 52 57N 9 10 E
Allevard 21 45 24N 6 5 E
Alliance, Nebr., U.S.A. 116 42 10N 102 50W
Alliance, Ohio, U.S.A. 114 40 53N 81 7W
Allier □ 20 46 25N 3 0 E
Allier → 19 46 57N 3 4 E
Allingåbro 49 56 28N 10 20 E
Allinge 49 55 17N 14 50 E
Alliston 106 44 9N 79 52W
Alloa 14 56 7N 3 49W
Allos 21 44 15N 6 38 E
Alma, Can. 107 48 35N 71 40W
Alma, Ga., U.S.A. 115 31 33N 82 28W
Alma, Kans., U.S.A. 116 39 1N 96 22W
Alma, Mich., U.S.A. 114 43 25N 84 40W
Alma, Nebr., U.S.A. 116 40 10N 99 25W
Alma, Wis., U.S.A. 116 44 19N 91 54W
'Almā ash Sha'b 62 33 7N 35 9 E
Alma Ata 58 43 15N 76 57 E
Almada 31 38 40N 9 9W
Almaden 98 17 22 S 144 40 E
Almadén 31 38 49N 4 52W
Almagro 31 38 50N 3 45W
Almanor, L. 118 40 15N 121 11W
Almansa 33 38 51N 1 5W
Almanza 30 42 39N 5 3W
Almanzor, Pico de 30 40 15N 5 18W
Almanzora → 33 37 14N 1 46W
Almarcha, La 32 39 41N 2 24W
Almaş, Mţii. 46 44 49N 22 12 E
Almazán 32 41 30N 2 30W
Almazora 32 39 57N 0 3W
Almeirim, Brazil 127 1 30 S 52 34W
Almeirim, Port. 31 39 12N 8 37W
Almelo 16 52 22N 6 42 E
Almenar 32 41 43N 2 12W
Almenara 32 39 46N 0 14W
Almenara, Sierra de 33 37 34N 1 32W
Almendralejo 31 38 41N 6 26W
Almería 33 36 52N 2 27W
Almería □ 33 37 20N 2 20W
Almería, G. de 33 36 41N 2 28W
Almirante 14 9 10N 82 30W
Almiropótamos 45 38 16N 24 11 E
Almirós 45 39 11N 22 45 E
Almodôvar 31 37 31N 8 2W
Almodóvar del Campo 31 38 43N 4 10W
Almogia 31 36 50N 4 32W
Almonaster la Real 31 37 52N 6 48W
Almont 112 42 53N 83 2W
Almonte 113 45 14N 76 12W
Almonte → 31 39 41N 6 28W
Almora 69 29 38N 79 40 E
Almoradi 33 38 7N 0 46W
Almorox 30 40 14N 4 24W
Almoustarat 85 17 35N 0 8 E
Älmult 49 56 33N 14 8 E
Almuñécar 31 36 43N 3 41W
Almunia de Doña Godina, La 32 41 29N 1 23W
Alnif 82 31 10N 5 8W
Alnwick 12 55 25N 1 42W
Aloi 90 2 16N 33 10 E
Alonsa 109 50 50N 99 0W
Alor 73 8 15 S 124 30 E
Alor Setar 71 6 7N 100 22 E
Alora 31 36 49N 4 46W
Alosno 31 37 33N 7 7W
Alougoum 82 30 17N 6 56W
Alpedrinha 30 40 6N 7 27W
Alpena 114 45 6N 83 24W
Alpes-de-Haute-Provence □ 21 44 8N 6 10 E
Alpes-Maritimes □ 21 43 55N 7 10 E
Alpha 97 23 39 S 146 37 E
Alpi Apuane 38 44 7N 10 14 E
Alpi Lepontine 25 46 22N 8 27 E
Alpi Orobie 38 46 7N 10 0 E
Alpi Retiche 25 46 30N 10 0 E
Alpiarça 31 39 15N 8 35W
Alpine, Ariz., U.S.A. 119 33 57N 109 4W
Alpine, Tex., U.S.A. 117 30 25N 103 35W
Alps 22 47 0N 8 0 E
Alpujarras, Las 33 36 55N 3 20W
Alrø 49 55 52N 10 5 E
Alsace 19 48 15N 7 25 E
Alsask 109 51 21N 109 59W
Alsásua 32 42 54N 2 10W
Alsen 48 63 23N 13 56 E
Alsfeld 24 50 44N 9 19 E
Alsónémedi 27 47 20N 19 15 E
Alsten 50 65 58N 12 40 E
Alta 50 69 57N 23 10 E
Alta Gracia 124 31 40 S 64 30W
Alta Lake 108 50 10N 123 0W
Alta, Sierra 32 40 31N 1 30W
Altaelva → 50 69 46N 23 45 E
Altafjorden 50 70 5N 23 5 E
Altagracia 126 10 45N 71 30W
Altai = Aerhatai Shan 75 46 40N 92 45 E
Altamaha → 115 31 19N 81 17W
Altamira, Brazil 127 3 12 S 52 10W
Altamira, Chile 124 25 47 S 69 51W
Altamira, Cuevas de 30 43 20N 4 5W
Altamont 113 42 43N 74 3W
Altamura 41 40 50N 16 33 E
Altanbulag 75 50 16N 106 30 E
Altar 120 30 40N 111 50W
Altata 120 24 30N 108 0W
Altavista 114 37 9N 79 22W
Altay 75 47 48N 88 10 E
Altdorf 25 46 52N 8 36 E
Alte Mellum 24 53 45N 8 6 E
Altea 33 38 38N 0 2W
Altenberg 24 50 46N 13 47 E
Altenbruch 24 53 48N 8 44 E
Altenburg 24 50 59N 12 28 E
Altenkirchen, Germ., E. 24 54 38N 13 20 E
Altenkirchen, Germ., W. 24 50 41N 7 38 E
Altenmarkt 26 47 43N 14 39 E
Altenteptow 24 53 42N 13 15 E
Alter do Chão 31 39 12N 7 40W
Altkirch 19 47 37N 7 15 E
Altmühl → 25 48 54N 11 54 E
Alto Adige = Trentino-Alto Adige 38 46 30N 11 0 E
Alto Araguaia 127 17 15 S 53 20W
Alto Chindio 91 16 19 S 35 25 E
Alto Cuchumatanes = Cuchumatanes, Sa. de los 120 15 30N 91 10W
Alto del Inca 124 24 10 S 68 10W
Alto Ligonha 91 15 30 S 38 11 E
Alto Molocue 91 15 50 S 37 35 E
Alto Paraná □ 125 25 0 S 54 50W
Alton, Can. 112 43 54N 80 5W
Alton, U.S.A. 116 38 55N 90 5W
Alton Downs 99 26 7 S 138 57 E
Altona, Austral. 100 37 51 S 144 50 E
Altona, Ger. 24 53 32N 9 56 E
Altoona 114 40 32N 78 24W
Altopáscio 38 43 50N 10 40 E
Altötting 25 48 14N 12 41 E
Altstätten 25 47 22N 9 33 E
Altun Shan 75 38 30N 88 0 E
Alturas 118 41 36N 120 37W
Altus 117 34 30N 99 25W
Alucra 57 40 22N 38 47 E
Aluksne 54 57 24N 27 3 E
Alùla 63 11 50N 50 45 E
Alupka 56 44 23N 34 2 E
Alushta 56 44 40N 34 25 E
Alusi 73 7 35 S 131 40 E
Alustante 32 40 36N 1 40W
Alva 117 36 50N 98 50W
Alvaiázere 30 39 49N 8 23W
Älvängen 49 57 58N 12 8 E
Alvarado, Mexico 120 18 40N 95 50W
Alvarado, U.S.A. 117 32 25N 97 15W
Alvaro Obregón, Presa 120 27 55N 109 52W
Alvdal 47 62 6N 10 37 E
Alvear 124 29 5 S 56 30W
Alverca 31 38 56N 9 1W
Alvesta 49 56 54N 14 35 E
Alvie 99 38 14 S 143 30 E
Alvin 117 29 23N 95 12W
Alvinston 113 42 49N 81 52W
Alvito 31 38 15N 8 0W
Älvros 48 62 3N 14 38 E
Älvsborgs län □ 49 58 30N 12 30 E
Älvsbyn 50 65 40N 21 0 E
Älvsered 49 57 14N 12 51 E
Alwar 68 27 38N 76 34 E
Alwaye 70 10 8N 76 24 E
Alxa Zuoqi 76 38 50N 105 40 E
Alyangula 97 13 55 S 136 30 E
Alyaskitovyy 59 64 45N 141 30 E
Alyata 57 39 58N 49 25 E
Alyth 14 56 38N 3 15W
Alzada 116 45 3N 104 22W
Alzano Lombardo 38 45 44N 9 43 E
Alzey 25 49 48N 8 4 E
Am Dam 81 12 40N 20 35 E
Am Géréda 81 12 53N 21 14 E
Am-Timan 81 11 0N 20 10 E
Amadeus, L. 96 24 54 S 131 0 E
Amâdi 87 5 29N 30 25 E
Amadi 90 3 40N 26 40 E
Amadjuak 105 64 0N 72 39W
Amadjuak L. 105 65 0N 71 8W
Amadora 31 38 45N 9 13W
Amagasaki 74 34 42N 135 20 E
Amager 49 55 37N 12 35 E
Amakusa-Shotō 74 32 15N 130 10 E
Åmål 48 59 3N 12 42 E
Amalapuram 70 16 35N 81 55 E
Amalfi 41 40 39N 14 34 E
Amaliás 45 37 47N 21 22 E
Amalner 68 21 5N 75 5 E
Amambaí 125 23 5 S 55 13W
Amambaí → 125 23 22 S 53 56W
Amambay □ 125 23 0 S 56 0W
Amambay, Cordillera de 125 23 0 S 55 45W
Amándola 39 42 59N 13 21 E
Amangeldy 58 50 10N 65 10 E
Amantea 41 39 8N 16 3 E
Amapá 127 2 5N 50 50W
Amapá □ 127 1 40N 52 0W
Amara 87 10 25N 34 10 E
Amarante, Brazil 127 6 14 S 42 50W
Amarante, Port. 30 41 16N 8 5W
Amaranth 109 50 36N 98 43W
Amaravati → 70 11 0N 78 15 E
Amareleja 31 38 12N 7 13W
Amargosa 127 13 2 S 39 36W
Amarillo 117 35 14N 101 46W
Amaro, Mt. 39 42 5N 14 6 E
Amarpur 69 25 5N 87 0 E
Amasra 64 41 45N 32 30 E
Amassama 85 5 1N 6 2 E
Amasya 64 40 40N 35 50 E
Amatikulu 93 29 3 S 31 33 E
Amatitlán 120 14 29N 90 38W
Amatrice 39 42 38N 13 16 E
Amazon = Amazonas → 127 0 5 S 50 0W
Amazonas □ 126 4 0 S 62 0W
Amazonas → 127 0 5 S 50 0W
Ambad 70 19 38N 75 50 E
Ambahakily 93 21 36 S 43 41 E
Ambala 68 30 23N 76 56 E
Ambalangoda 70 6 15N 80 5 E
Ambalapuzha 70 9 25N 76 25 E
Ambalavao 93 21 50 S 46 56 E
Ambam 88 2 20N 11 15 E
Ambanja 93 13 40 S 48 27 E
Ambarchik 59 69 40N 162 20 E
Ambarijeby 93 14 56 S 47 41 E
Ambarnath 70 19 12N 73 22 E
Ambaro, Helodranon' 93 13 23 S 48 38 E
Ambartsevo 58 57 30N 83 52 E
Ambasamudram 70 8 43N 77 25 E
Ambato 126 1 5 S 78 42W
Ambato Boeny 93 16 28 S 46 43 E
Ambato, Sierra de 124 28 25 S 66 10W
Ambatofinandrahana 93 20 33 S 46 48 E
Ambatolampy 93 19 20 S 47 35 E
Ambatondrazaka 93 17 55 S 48 28 E
Ambatosoratra 93 17 37 S 48 31 E
Ambenja 93 15 17 S 46 58 E
Amberg 25 49 25N 11 52 E
Ambergris Cay 120 18 0N 88 0W
Ambérieu-en-Bugey 21 45 57N 5 20 E
Amberley 101 43 9 S 172 44 E
Ambert 20 45 33N 3 4
Ambidédi 84 14 35N 11 4
Ambikapur 69 23 15N 83 1
Ambikol 86 21 20N 30 5
Ambinanindrano 93 20 5 S 48 2
Ambjörnarp 49 57 25N 13 1
Ambleside 12 54 26N 2 5
Ambo, Ethiopia 87 12 20N 37 3
Ambo, Peru 126 10 5 S 76 1
Ambodifototra 93 16 59 S 49 5
Ambodilazana 93 18 6 S 49 1
Ambohimahasoa 93 21 7 S 47 1
Ambohimanga 93 20 52 S 47 3
Ambon 73 3 35 S 128 2
Amboseli L. 90 2 40 S 37 1
Ambositra 93 20 31 S 47 2
Ambovombé 93 25 11 S 46
Amboy 119 34 33N 115 5
Amboyna I. 72 7 50N 112 5
Ambridge 112 40 36N 80 1
Ambriz 88 7 48 S 13
Ambur 70 12 48N 78 4
Amby 99 26 30 S 148 1
Amchitka I. 104 51 30N 179
Amderma 58 69 45N 61 3
Ameca 120 20 30N 104
Ameca → 120 20 40N 105 1
Amecameca 120 19 7N 98 4
Ameland 16 53 27N 5 4
Amélia 39 42 34N 12 2
Amélie-les-Bains-Palalda 20 42 29N 2 4
Amen 59 68 45N 180
Amendolaro 41 39 58N 16 3
American Falls 118 42 46N 112 5
American Falls Res. 118 43 0N 112 5
American Highland 5 73 0 S 75
American Samoa 101 14 20 S 170 4
Americana 125 22 45 S 47 2
Americus 115 32 0N 84 1
Amersfoort, Neth. 16 52 9N 5 2
Amersfoort, S. Afr. 93 26 59 S 29 5
Amery 109 56 34N 94
Amery Ice Shelf 5 69 30 S 72
Ames 116 42 0N 93 4
Amesbury 113 42 50N 70 5
Amesdale 109 50 2N 92 5
Amfiklia 45 38 38N 22 3
Amfilokhía 45 38 52N 21
Amfípolis 44 40 48N 23 5
Ámfissa 45 38 32N 22 2
Amga 59 60 50N 132
Amga → 59 62 38N 134 3
Amgu 59 45 45N 137 1
Amgun → 59 52 56N 139 3
Amherst, Burma 67 16 2N 97 2
Amherst, Can. 107 45 48N 64
Amherst, Mass., U.S.A. 113 42 21N 72 3
Amherst, Ohio, U.S.A. 112 41 23N 82 1
Amherst, Tex., U.S.A. 117 34 0N 102 2
Amherst I. 113 44 8N 76 4
Amherstburg 106 42 6N 83
Amiata, Mte. 39 42 54N 11 4
Amiens 19 49 54N 2 1
Amigdhalokefáli 45 35 23N 23 3
Amindaion 44 40 42N 21 4
Amirante Is. 3 6 0 S 53
Amisk L. 109 54 35N 102 1
Amite 117 30 47N 90 3
Amizmiz 82 31 12N 8 1
Åmli 47 58 45N 8 3
Amlwch 12 53 24N 4 2
Amm Adam 87 16 20N 36
'Ammān 62 31 57N 35 5
Ammanford 13 51 48N 4
Ammerån 48 63 9N 16 1
Ammerån → 48 63 9N 16 1
Ammersee 25 48 0N 11
Ammi'ad 62 32 55N 35 3
Amnéville 19 49 16N 6
Amorebieta 32 43 13N 2 4
Amorgós 45 36 50N 25 5
Amory 115 33 59N 88 2
Amos 106 48 35N 78
Åmot, Buskerud, Norway 47 59 54N 9 5
Åmot, Telemark, Norway 47 59 34N 8
Åmotsdal 47 59 37N 8 2
Amour, Djebel 82 33 42N 1 3
Amoy = Xiamen 76 24 25N 118
Ampanihy 93 24 40 S 44 4
Ampasindava, Helodranon' 93 13 40 S 48 1
Ampasindava, Saikanosy 93 13 42 S 47 5
Amper 85 9 25N 9 4
Amper → 25 48 30N 11 5
Ampère 83 35 44N 5 2
Ampezzo 39 46 25N 12 4
Amposta 32 40 43N 0 3
Ampotaka 93 25 3 S 44 4
Ampoza 93 22 20 S 44 4
Amqa 62 32 59N 35 1
Amqui 107 48 28N 67 2
Amraoti 68 20 55N 77 4
Amreli 68 21 35N 71 1
Amrenene el Kasba 82 22 10N 0 3
Amritsar 68 31 35N 74 5
Amroha 68 28 53N 78 3
Amrum 24 54 37N 8 2
Amsel 83 22 47N 5 2
Amsterdam, Neth. 16 52 23N 4 5
Amsterdam, U.S.A. 114 42 58N 74 1
Amsterdam, I. 3 37 30 S 77 3
Amstetten 26 48 7N 14 5
Amudarya → 58 43 40N 59
Amund Ringnes I. 4 78 20N 96 2
Amundsen Gulf 104 71 0N 124
Amundsen Sea 5 72 0 S 115
Amungen 48 61 10N 15 4
Amuntai 72 2 28 S 115 2
Amur → 59 52 56N 141 1
Amurang 73 1 5N 124 4
Amuri Pass 101 42 31 S 172 1
Amurrio 32 43 3N 3
Amursk 59 50 14N 136 5

Amurzet 59 47 50N 131 5 E
Amusco 30 42 10N 4 28W
Amvrakikós Kólpos 45 39 0N 20 55 E
Amvrosiyevka 57 47 43N 38 30 E
Amzeglouf 82 26 50N 0 1 E
An Nafūd 64 28 15N 41 0 E
An Najaf 64 32 3N 44 15 E
An Nāqūrah 62 33 7N 35 8 E
An Nāşirīyah 64 31 0N 46 15 E
An Nawfalīyah 83 30 54N 17 58 E
An Nhon (Binh Dinh) 71 13 55N 109 7 E
An Nîl □ 86 19 30N 33 0 E
An Nîl el Abyad □ 87 14 0N 32 15 E
An Nîl el Azraq □ 87 12 30N 34 30 E
An Nu'ayrīyah 64 27 30N 48 30 E
An Uaimh 15 53 39N 6 40W
Ana-Sira 47 58 17N 6 25 E
Anabar → 59 73 8N 113 36 E
'Anabtā 62 32 19N 35 7 E
Anaconda 118 46 7N 113 0W
Anacortes 118 48 30N 122 40W
Anadarko 117 35 4N 98 15W
Anadia 30 40 26N 8 27W
Anadolu 64 38 0N 30 0 E
Anadyr 59 64 35N 177 20 E
Anadyr → 59 64 55N 176 5 E
Anadyrskiy Zaliv 59 64 0N 180 0 E
Anáfi 45 36 22N 25 48 E
Anafópoulo 45 36 17N 25 50 E
Anagni 40 41 44N 13 8 E
'Ānah 64 34 25N 42 0 E
Anahim Lake 108 52 28N 125 18W
Anáhuac 120 27 14N 100 9W
Anai Mudi, Mt. 70 10 12N 77 4 E
Anaimalai Hills 70 10 20N 76 40 E
Anakapalle 70 17 42N 83 06 E
Anakie 98 23 32 S 147 45 E
Anaklia 57 42 22N 41 35 E
Analalava 93 14 35 S 48 0 E
Anambar → 68 30 15N 68 50 E
Anambas, Kepulauan 72 3 20N 106 30 E
Anamoose 116 47 55N 100 20W
Anamosa 116 42 7N 91 30W
Anamur 64 36 8N 32 58 E
Anan 74 33 54N 134 40 E
Anand 68 22 32N 72 59 E
Anandpur 69 21 16N 86 13 E
Anánes 45 36 33N 24 9 E
Anantapur 70 14 39N 77 42 E
Anantnag 69 33 45N 75 10 E
Ananyev 56 47 44N 29 47 E
Anapa 56 44 55N 37 25 E
Anápolis 127 16 15 S 48 50W
Anār 65 30 55N 55 13 E
Anārak 65 33 25N 53 40 E
Anatolia = Anadolu 64 38 0N 30 0 E
Anatone 118 46 9N 117 4W
Añatuya 124 28 20 S 62 50W
Anaunethad L. 109 60 55N 104 25W
Anaye 81 19 15N 12 50 E
Ancenis 18 47 21N 1 10W
Anchorage 104 61 10N 149 50W
Ancião 30 39 56N 8 27W
Ancohuma, Nevada 126 16 0 S 68 50W
Ancón 126 11 50 S 77 10W
Ancona 39 43 37N 13 30 E
Ancud 128 42 0 S 73 50W
Ancud, G. de 128 42 0 S 73 0W
Anda 76 46 24N 125 19 E
Andacollo, Argent. 124 37 10 S 70 42W
Andacollo, Chile 124 30 5 S 71 10W
Andalgalá 124 27 40 S 66 30W
Åndalsnes 47 62 35N 7 43 E
Andalucía 31 37 35N 5 0W
Andalusia 115 31 19N 86 30W
Andalusia = Andalucía 31 37 35N 5 0W
Andaman Is. 71 12 30N 92 30 E
Andaman Sea 72 13 0N 96 0 E
Andaman Str. 71 12 15N 92 20 E
Andara 92 18 2 S 21 9 E
Andelot 19 48 15N 5 18 E
Andelys, Les 18 49 15N 1 25 E
Andenne 16 50 30N 5 5 E
Andéranboukane 85 15 26N 3 2 E
Andermatt 25 46 38N 8 35 E
Andernach 24 50 24N 7 25 E
Andernos-les-Bains 20 44 44N 1 6W
Anderslöv 49 55 26N 13 19 E
Anderson, Calif., U.S.A. 118 40 30N 122 19W
Anderson, Ind., U.S.A. 114 40 5N 85 40W
Anderson, Mo., U.S.A. 117 36 43N 94 29W
Anderson, S.C., U.S.A. 115 34 32N 82 40W
Anderson → 104 69 42N 129 0W
Anderson, Mt. 93 25 5 S 30 42 E
Anderstorp 49 57 19N 13 39 E
Andes 126 5 40N 75 53W
Andes, Cord de los 126 20 0 S 68 0W
Andfjorden 50 69 10N 16 20 E
Andhra, L. 70 18 54N 73 32 E
Andhra Pradesh □ 70 16 0N 79 0 E
Andikíthira 45 35 52N 23 15 E
Andímilos 45 36 47N 24 12 E
Andíparos 45 37 0N 25 3 E
Andípaxoi 45 39 9N 20 13 E
Andípsara 45 38 30N 25 29 E
Andirrion 45 38 24N 21 46 E
Andizhan 58 41 10N 72 0 E
Andkhvoy 65 36 52N 65 8 E
Andol 70 17 51N 78 4 E
Andong 76 36 40N 128 43 E
Andorra ■ 32 42 30N 1 30 E
Andorra La Vella 32 42 31N 1 32 E
Andover, U.K. 13 51 13N 1 29W
Andover, N.Y., U.S.A. 112 42 11N 77 48W
Andover, Ohio, U.S.A. 112 41 35N 80 35W
Andrahary, Mt. 93 13 37 S 49 17 E
Andraitx 32 39 39N 2 25 E
Andramasina 93 19 11 S 47 35 E
Andranopasy 93 21 17 S 43 44 E
Andreanof Is. 104 52 0N 178 0W
Andreapol 54 56 40N 32 17 E
Andrespol 28 51 45N 19 34 E
Andrews, S.C., U.S.A. 115 33 29N 79 30W
Andrews, Tex., U.S.A. 117 32 18N 102 33W
Ándria 41 41 13N 16 17 E
Andriba 93 17 30 S 46 58 E
Andrijevica 42 42 45N 19 48 E
Andrítsaina 45 37 29N 21 52 E
Androka 93 24 58 S 44 2 E
Ándros 45 37 50N 24 57 E
Andros I. 121 24 30N 78 0W
Andros Town 121 24 43N 77 47W
Andrychów 27 49 51N 19 18 E
Andújar 31 38 3N 4 5W
Aneby 49 57 48N 14 49 E
Anegada I. 121 18 45N 64 20W
Anegada Passage 121 18 15N 63 45W
Anécho 85 6 12N 1 34 E
Anergane 82 31 4N 7 14W
Aneto, Pico de 32 42 37N 0 40 E
Ang Thong 71 14 35N 100 31 E
Angamos, Punta 124 23 1 S 70 32W
Ang'angxi 75 47 10N 123 48 E
Angara → 59 58 30N 97 0 E
Angarab 87 13 11N 37 7 E
Angarsk 59 52 30N 104 0 E
Angaston 99 34 30 S 139 8 E
Ånge 48 62 31N 15 35 E
Angel de la Guarda 120 29 30N 113 30W
Angeles 73 15 9N 120 33 E
Ängelholm 49 56 15N 12 58 E
Angellala 99 26 24 S 146 54 E
Angels Camp 119 38 8N 120 30W
Ängelsberg 48 59 58N 16 0 E
Anger → 87 9 37N 36 6 E
Angereb → 87 13 45N 36 40 E
Ångermanälven → 48 62 40N 18 0 E
Angermünde 24 53 1N 14 0 E
Angers, Can. 113 45 31N 75 29W
Angers, France 18 47 30N 0 35W
Angerville 19 48 19N 2 0 E
Ängesån → 50 66 50N 22 15 E
Anghiari 39 43 32N 12 3 E
Angikuni L. 109 62 0N 100 0W
Angkor 71 13 22N 103 50 E
Anglés 32 41 57N 2 38 E
Anglesey 12 53 17N 4 20W
Anglet 20 43 29N 1 31W
Angleton 117 29 12N 95 23W
Anglin → 20 46 42N 0 52 E
Anglure 19 48 35N 3 50 E
Angmagssalik 4 65 40N 37 20W
Ango 90 4 10N 26 5 E
Angoche 91 16 8 S 40 0 E
Angoche, I. 91 16 20 S 39 50 E
Angol 124 37 56 S 72 45W
Angola, Ind., U.S.A. 114 41 40N 85 0W
Angola, N.Y., U.S.A. 112 42 38N 79 2W
Angola ■ 89 12 0 S 18 0 E
Angoon 108 57 40N 134 40W
Angoram 98 4 4 S 144 4 E
Angoulême 20 45 39N 0 10 E
Angoumois 20 45 50N 0 25 E
Angra dos Reis 125 23 0 S 44 10W
Angren 58 41 1N 70 12 E
Angu 90 3 25N 24 28 E
Anguilla 121 18 14N 63 5W
Angus, Braes of 14 56 51N 3 10W
Anhanduí → 125 21 46 S 52 9W
Anholt 49 56 42N 11 33 E
Anhua 77 28 23N 111 12 E
Anhui □ 75 32 0N 117 0 E
Anhwei □ = Anhui □ 75 32 0N 117 0 E
Ánidhros 45 36 38N 25 43 E
Anie 85 7 42N 1 8 E
Animas 119 31 58N 108 58W
Ånimskog 49 58 53N 12 35 E
Anin 71 15 36N 97 50 E
Anina 42 45 6N 21 51 E
Anivorano 93 18 44 S 48 58 E
Anjangaon 68 21 10N 77 20 E
Anjar 68 23 6N 70 10 E
Anjidiv I. 70 14 40N 74 10 E
Anjou 18 47 20N 0 15W
Anjozorobe 93 18 22 S 47 52 E
Anju 76 39 36N 125 40 E
Anka 85 12 13N 5 58 E
Ankang 75 32 40N 109 1 E
Ankara 64 40 0N 32 54 E
Ankaramena 93 21 57 S 46 39 E
Ankazoabo 93 22 18 S 44 31 E
Ankazobe 93 18 20 S 47 10 E
Ankisabe 93 19 17 S 46 29 E
Anklam 24 53 48N 13 40 E
Anklesvar 68 21 38N 73 3 E
Ankober 87 9 35N 39 40 E
Ankoro 90 6 45 S 26 55 E
Anlu 77 31 15N 113 45 E
Ånn 48 63 19N 12 34 E
Ann Arbor 114 42 17N 83 45W
Ann C., Antarct. 5 66 30 S 50 30 E
Ann C., U.S.A. 114 42 39N 70 37W
Anna, U.S.A. 117 37 28N 89 10W
Anna, U.S.S.R. 55 51 28N 40 23 E
Annaba 83 36 50N 7 46 E
Annaberg-Buchholz 24 50 34N 12 58 E
Annalee → 15 54 3N 7 15W
Annam = Trung-Phan 71 16 30N 107 30 E
Annamitique, Chaîne 71 17 0N 106 0 E
Annan 14 55 0N 3 17W
Annan → 14 54 58N 3 18W
Annapolis 114 38 95N 76 30W
Annapolis Royal 107 44 44N 65 32W
Annapurna 69 28 34N 83 50 E
Anneberg 49 57 32N 12 6 E
Annecy 21 45 55N 6 8 E
Annecy, L. d' 21 45 52N 6 10 E
Annemasse 21 46 12N 6 16 E
Anning 75 24 55N 102 26 E
Anniston 115 33 45N 85 50W
Annobón 79 1 25 S 5 35 E
Annonay 21 45 15N 4 40 E
Annonciation, L' 106 46 25N 74 55W
Annot 21 43 58N 6 38 E
Annotto Bay 121 18 17N 77 3W
Annuello 99 34 53 S 142 55 E
Annville 113 40 18N 76 32W
Annweiler 25 49 12N 7 58 E
Áno Arkhánai 45 35 16N 25 11 E
Áno Porróia 44 41 17N 23 2 E
Áno Viánnos 45 35 2N 25 21 E
Anoka 116 45 10N 93 26W
Anorotsangana 93 13 56 S 47 55 E
Anqing 75 30 30N 117 3 E
Anren 77 26 43N 113 18 E
Ansāb 64 29 11N 44 43 E
Ansai 76 36 50N 109 20 E
Ansbach 25 49 17N 10 34 E
Anse au Loup, L' 107 51 32N 56 50W
Anse, L' 106 46 47N 88 28W
Anseba → 87 16 0N 38 30 E
Anshan 76 41 5N 122 58 E
Anshun 75 26 18N 105 57 E
Ansirabe 93 19 55 S 47 2 E
Ansley 116 41 19N 99 24W
Ansó 32 42 51N 0 48W
Anson 117 32 46N 99 54W
Anson B. 96 13 20 S 130 6 E
Ansongo 85 15 25N 0 35 E
Ansonia 113 41 21N 73 6W
Anstruther 14 56 14N 2 40W
Ansudu 73 2 11 S 139 22 E
Antabamba 126 14 40 S 73 0W
Antakya 64 36 14N 36 10 E
Antalaha 93 14 57 S 50 20 E
Antalya 64 36 52N 30 45 E
Antalya Körfezi 64 36 15N 31 30 E
Antananarivo 93 18 55 S 47 31 E
Antananarivo □ 93 19 0 S 47 0 E
Antanimbaribe 93 21 30 S 44 48 E
Antarctic Pen. 5 67 0 S 60 0W
Antarctica 5 90 0 S 0 0
Antelope 91 21 2 S 28 31 E
Antequera, Parag. 124 24 8 S 57 7W
Antequera, Spain 31 37 5N 4 33W
Antero Mt. 119 38 45N 106 15W
Anthemoús 44 40 31N 23 15 E
Anthony, Kans., U.S.A. 117 37 8N 98 2W
Anthony, N. Mex., U.S.A. 119 32 1N 106 37W
Anti Atlas, Mts. 82 30 0N 8 30W
Antibes 21 43 34N 7 6 E
Antibes, C. d' 21 43 31N 7 7 E
Anticosti, Î. d' 107 49 30N 63 0W
Antifer, C. d' 18 49 41N 0 10 E
Antigo 116 45 8N 89 5W
Antigonish 107 45 38N 61 58W
Antigua 120 14 34N 90 41W
Antigua & Barbuda ■ 121 17 0N 61 50W
Antilla 121 20 40N 75 50W
Antimony 119 38 7N 112 0W
Antioch 118 38 7N 121 45W
Antioche, Pertuis d' 20 46 6N 1 20W
Antioquia 126 6 40N 75 55W
Antipodes Is. 94 49 45 S 178 40 E
Antler 116 48 58N 101 18W
Antler → 109 49 8N 101 0W
Antlers 117 34 15N 95 35W
Antofagasta 124 23 50 S 70 30W
Antofagasta □ 124 24 0 S 69 0W
Antofagasta de la Sierra 124 26 5 S 67 20W
Antofalla 124 25 30 S 68 5W
Antofalla, Salar de 124 25 40 S 67 45W
Anton 117 33 49N 102 5W
Anton Chico 119 35 12N 105 5W
Antongila, Helodrano 93 15 30 S 49 50 E
Antonibé 93 15 7 S 47 24 E
Antonibé, Presqu'île d' 93 14 55 S 47 20 E
Antonina 125 25 26 S 48 42W
Antonito 119 37 4N 106 1W
Antonovo 57 49 25N 51 42 E
Antrain 18 48 28N 1 30W
Antrim 15 54 43N 6 13W
Antrim □ 15 54 55N 6 20W
Antrim, Mts. of 15 54 57N 6 8W
Antrodoco 39 42 25N 13 4 E
Antropovo 55 58 26N 42 51 E
Antsalova 93 18 40 S 44 37 E
Antsiranana 93 12 25 S 49 20 E
Antsohihy 93 14 50 S 47 59 E
Antwerp 113 44 12N 75 36W
Antwerp = Antwerpen 16 51 13N 4 25 E
Antwerpen 16 51 13N 4 25 E
Antwerpen □ 16 51 15N 4 40 E
Anupgarh 68 29 10N 73 10 E
Anuradhapura 70 8 22N 80 28 E
Anvers = Antwerpen 16 51 13N 4 25 E
Anvers I. 5 64 30 S 63 40W
Anvik 104 62 37N 160 20W
Anxi, Fujian, China 77 25 2N 118 12 E
Anxi, Gansu, China 75 40 30N 95 43 E
Anxious B. 96 33 24 S 134 45 E
Anyama 84 5 30N 4 3W
Anyang 76 36 5N 114 21 E
Anyer-Lor 73 6 6 S 105 56 E
Anyi, Jiangxi, China 77 28 49N 115 25 E
Anyi, Shanxi, China 77 35 2N 111 2 E
Anyuan 77 25 9N 115 21 E
'Anzah 62 32 22N 35 12 E
Anzhero-Sudzhensk 58 56 10N 86 0 E
Ánzio 40 41 28N 12 37 E
Aoiz 32 42 46N 1 22W
Aomori 74 40 45N 140 45 E
Aomori □ 74 40 45N 140 40 E
Aonla 68 28 16N 79 11 E
Aoreora 82 28 51N 10 53W
Aosta 38 45 43N 7 20 E
Aoudéras 85 17 45N 8 20 E
Aouinet Torkoz 82 28 31N 9 46W
Aoukar 82 23 50N 2 45W
Aouker 84 17 40N 10 0W
Aoulef el Arab 82 26 55N 1 2 E
Apa → 124 22 6 S 58 2W
Apache, Ariz., U.S.A. 119 31 46N 109 6W
Apache, Okla., U.S.A. 117 34 53N 98 22W
Apalachee B. 115 30 0N 84 0W
Apalachicola 115 29 40N 85 0W
Apapa 85 6 25N 3 25 E
Apaporis → 126 1 23 S 69 25W
Aparri 73 18 22N 121 38 E
Apateu 46 46 36N 21 47 E
Apatin 42 45 40N 19 0 E
Apàtity 52 67 34N 33 22 E
Apatzingán 120 19 0N 102 20W
Apeldoorn 16 52 13N 5 57 E
Apen 24 53 12N 7 47 E
Apenam 72 8 35 S 116 13 E
Apennines 9 44 20N 10 20 E
Apia 101 13 50 S 171 50W
Apiacás, Serra dos 126 9 50 S 57 0W
Apizaco 120 19 26N 98 9W
Aplao 126 16 0 S 72 40W
Apo, Mt. 73 6 53N 125 14 E
Apolda 24 51 1N 11 30 E
Apollo Bay 100 38 45 S 143 40 E
Apollonia 45 36 58N 24 43 E
Apollonia = Marsá Susah 81 32 52N 21 59 E
Apolo 126 14 30 S 68 30W
Apostle Is. 116 47 0N 90 30W
Apóstoles 125 28 0 S 56 0W
Apostolovo 56 47 39N 33 39 E
Apoteri 126 4 2N 58 32W
Appalachian Mts. 114 38 0N 80 0W
Appalachicola → 115 29 40N 85 0W
Appennini 41 41 0N 15 0 E
Appennino Ligure 38 44 30N 9 0 E
Appenzell-Ausser Rhoden □ 25 47 23N 9 23 E
Appenzell-Inner Rhoden □ 25 47 20N 9 25 E
Appiano 39 46 27N 11 17 E
Apple Hill 113 45 13N 74 46W
Appleby 12 54 35N 2 29W
Appleton 114 44 17N 88 25W
Approuague 127 4 20N 52 0W
Aprelevka, U.S.S.R. 55 55 33N 37 4 E
Aprelevka, U.S.S.R. 55 55 34N 37 4 E
Apricena 41 41 47N 15 25 E
Aprigliano 41 39 17N 16 19 E
Aprília 40 41 38N 12 38 E
Apsheronsk 57 44 28N 39 42 E
Apt 21 43 53N 5 24 E
Apucarana 125 23 55 S 51 33W
Apulia = Púglia 41 41 0N 16 30 E
Apure → 126 7 37N 66 25W
Apurimac → 126 12 17 S 73 56W
Apuseni, Munţii 46 46 30N 22 45 E
Aqabah = Al 'Aqabah 86 29 13N 35 0 E
'Aqabah, Khalīj al 64 28 15N 33 20 E
Āqcheh 65 37 0N 66 5 E
Aqīq 86 18 14N 38 12 E
Aqīq, Khalīg 86 18 20N 38 10 E
Aqrabā 62 32 9N 35 20 E
Aqrah 64 36 46N 43 45 E
Aquidauana 127 20 30 S 55 50W
Áquila, L' 39 42 21N 13 24 E
Aquiles Serdán 120 28 37N 105 54W
Ar Rachidiya 82 31 58N 4 20W
Ar Rafīd 62 32 57N 35 52 E
Ar Ramādī 64 33 25N 43 20 E
Ar Raml 83 26 45N 19 40 E
Ar Ramthā 62 32 34N 36 0 E
Ar Raqqah 64 36 0N 38 55 E
Ar Rass 64 25 50N 43 40 E
Ar Rifā'ī 64 31 50N 46 10 E
Ar Riyāḑ 64 24 41N 46 42 E
Ar Rummān 62 32 9N 35 48 E
Ar Ruţbah 64 33 0N 40 15 E
Ar Ruwayḑah 64 23 40N 44 40 E
Arab, Bahr el → 87 9 50N 29 0 E
Arab, Khalīg el 86 30 55N 29 0 E
Arab, Shatt al 64 30 0N 48 31 E
Arabatskaya Strelka 56 45 40N 35 0 E
Arabba 39 46 30N 11 51 E
Arabia 60 25 0N 45 0 E
Arabian Sea 60 16 0N 65 0 E
Arac 64 41 15N 33 21 E
Aracaju 127 10 55 S 37 4W
Aracataca 126 10 38N 74 9W
Aracati 127 4 30 S 37 44W
Araçatuba 125 21 10 S 50 30W
Aracena 31 37 53N 6 38W
Aracena, Sierra de 31 37 50N 6 50W
Araçuaí 127 16 52 S 42 4W
'Arad 62 31 15N 35 12 E
Arad 42 46 10N 21 20 E
Arad □ 42 46 20N 22 0 E
Arada 81 15 0N 20 20 E
Aradu Nou 42 46 8N 21 20 E
Arafura Sea 73 9 0 S 135 0 E
Aragats 57 40 30N 44 15 E
Aragón 32 41 25N 1 0W
Aragón → 32 42 13N 1 44W
Aragona 40 37 24N 13 36 E
Araguacema 127 8 50 S 49 20W
Araguaia → 127 5 21 S 48 41W
Araguari 127 18 38 S 48 11W
Araguari → 127 1 15N 49 55W
Arak 82 25 20N 3 45 E
Arāk 64 34 0N 49 40 E
Arakan Coast 67 19 0N 94 0 E
Arakan Yoma 67 20 0N 94 40 E
Arákhova 45 38 28N 22 35 E
Araks = Aras, Rūd-e → 64 39 10N 47 10 E
Aral Sea = Aralskoye More 58 44 30N 60 0 E
Aralsk 58 46 50N 61 20 E
Aralskoye More 58 44 30N 60 0 E
Aramā, Mţii. de 46 47 10N 22 30 E
Aramac 97 22 58 S 145 14 E
Arambagh 69 22 53N 87 48 E
Aran I. 15 55 0N 8 30W
Aran Is. 15 53 5N 9 42W
Aranda de Duero 32 41 39N 3 42W
Arandelovac 42 44 18N 20 27 E
Aranjuez 30 40 1N 3 40W
Aranos 92 24 9 S 19 7 E
Aransas Pass 117 27 55N 97 9W
Araouane 84 18 55N 3 30W
Arapahoe 116 40 22N 99 53W
Arapey Grande → 124 30 55 S 57 49W
Arapkir 64 39 5N 38 30 E

Arapongas 125 23 29 S 51 28W
Araranguá 125 29 0 S 49 30W
Araraquara 127 21 50 S 48 0W
Ararás, Serra das 125 25 0 S 53 10W
Ararat 97 37 16 S 143 0 E
Ararat, Mt. = Ağri Daği 64 39 50N 44 15 E
Araria 69 26 9N 87 33 E
Araripe, Chapada do 127 7 20 S 40 0W
Araruama, Lagoa de 125 22 53 S 42 12W
Aras, Rūd-e → 64 39 10N 47 10 E
Arauca 126 7 0N 70 40W
Arauca → 126 7 24N 66 35W
Arauco 124 37 16 S 73 25W
Arauco □ 124 37 40 S 73 25W
Arawa 87 9 57N 41 58 E
Araxá 127 19 35 S 46 55W
Araya, Pen. de 126 10 40N 64 0W
Arba Minch 87 6 0N 37 30 E
Arbatax 40 39 57N 9 42 E
Arbaza 59 52 40N 92 30 E
Arbīl 64 36 15N 44 5 E
Arboga 48 59 24N 15 52 E
Arbois 19 46 55N 5 46 E
Arbore 87 5 3N 36 50 E
Arborea 40 39 46N 8 34 E
Arborfield 109 53 6N 103 39W
Arborg 109 50 54N 97 13W
Arbrå 48 61 28N 16 22 E
Arbresle, L' 21 45 50N 4 26 E
Arbroath 14 56 34N 2 35W
Arbuckle 118 39 3N 122 2W
Arbus 40 39 30N 8 33 E
Arbuzinka 56 47 0N 31 59 E
Arc 19 47 28N 5 34 E
Arc → 21 45 34N 6 12 E
Arcachon 20 44 40N 1 10W
Arcachon, Bassin d' 20 44 42N 1 10W
Arcade 112 42 34N 78 25W
Arcadia, Fla., U.S.A. 115 27 20N 81 50W
Arcadia, La., U.S.A. 117 32 34N 92 53W
Arcadia, Nebr., U.S.A. 116 41 29N 99 4W
Arcadia, Pa., U.S.A. 112 40 46N 78 54W
Arcadia, Wis., U.S.A. 116 44 13N 91 29W
Arcata 118 40 55N 124 4W
Arcévia 39 43 29N 12 58 E
Archangel = Arkhangelsk 52 64 40N 41 0 E
Archar 42 43 50N 22 54 E
Archbald 113 41 30N 75 31W
Archena 33 38 9N 1 16W
Archer → 97 13 28 S 141 41 E
Archer B. 98 13 20 S 141 30 E
Archers Post 90 0 35N 37 35 E
Archidona 31 37 6N 4 22W
Arci, Monte 40 39 47N 8 44 E
Arcidosso 39 42 51N 11 30 E
Arcila = Asilah 82 35 29N 6 0W
Arcis-sur-Aube 19 48 32N 4 10 E
Arco, Italy 38 45 55N 10 54 E
Arco, U.S.A. 118 43 45N 113 16W
Arcola 109 49 40N 102 30W
Arcos 32 41 12N 2 16W
Arcos de los Frontera 31 36 45N 5 49W
Arcos de Valdevez 30 41 55N 8 22W
Arcot 70 12 53N 79 20 E
Arcoverde 127 8 25 S 37 4W
Arcs, Les 21 43 27N 6 29 E
Arctic Bay 105 73 1N 85 7W
Arctic Ocean 4 78 0N 160 0W
Arctic Red River 104 67 15N 134 0W
Arda →, Bulg. 43 41 40N 26 29 E
Arda →, Italy 38 44 53N 9 52 E
Ardabīl 64 38 15N 48 18 E
Ardahan 64 41 7N 42 41 E
Ardakān 65 30 20N 52 5 E
Årdal, Aust-Agder, Norway 47 58 42N 7 48 E
Årdal, Rogaland, Norway 47 59 9N 6 13 E
Ardales 31 36 53N 4 51W
Årdalstangen 47 61 14N 7 43 E
Ardatov 55 54 51N 46 15 E
Ardea 44 40 58N 22 3 E
Ardèche □ 21 44 42N 4 16 E
Ardèche → 21 44 16N 4 39 E
Ardee 15 53 51N 6 32W
Arden 112 44 43N 76 56W
Arden Stby. 49 56 46N 9 52 E
Ardennes 16 50 0N 5 10 E
Ardennes □ 19 49 35N 4 40 E
Ardentes 19 46 45N 1 50 E
Ardestān 65 33 20N 52 25 E
Ardgour 14 56 45N 5 25W
Ardhas → 44 41 36N 26 25 E
Ardila → 31 38 12N 7 28W
Ardino 43 41 34N 25 9 E
Ardjuno 73 7 49 S 112 34 E
Ardlethan 99 34 22 S 146 53 E
Ardmore, Austral. 98 21 39 S 139 11 E
Ardmore, Okla., U.S.A. 117 34 10N 97 5W
Ardmore, Pa., U.S.A. 113 39 58N 75 18W
Ardmore, S.D., U.S.A. 116 43 0N 103 40W
Ardnacrusha 15 52 43N 8 38W
Ardnamurchan, Pt. of 14 56 44N 6 14W
Ardore Marina 41 38 11N 16 10 E
Ardres 19 50 50N 2 0 E
Ardrossan, Austral. 99 34 26 S 137 53 E
Ardrossan, U.K. 14 55 39N 4 50W
Ards □ 15 54 35N 5 30W
Ards Pen. 15 54 30N 5 25W
Ardud 46 47 37N 22 52 E
Ardunac 57 41 8N 42 5 E
Åre 48 63 22N 13 15 E
Arecibo 121 18 29N 66 42W
Areia Branca 127 5 0 S 37 0W
Aremark 47 59 15N 11 42 E
Arenas 30 43 17N 4 50W
Arenas de San Pedro 30 40 12N 5 5W
Arendal 47 58 28N 8 46 E
Arendsee 24 52 52N 11 27 E
Arenys de Mar 32 41 35N 2 33 E
Arenzano 38 44 24N 8 40 E
Areópolis 45 36 40N 22 22 E
Arequipa 126 16 20 S 71 30W
Arero 87 4 41N 38 50 E
Arès 20 44 47N 1 8W
Arévalo 30 41 3N 4 43W
Arezzo 39 43 28N 11 50 E
Arga → 32 42 18N 1 47W
Argalasti 44 39 13N 23 13 E
Argamasilla de Alba 33 39 8N 3 5W
Arganda 32 40 19N 3 26W
Arganil 30 40 13N 8 3W
Argelès-Gazost 20 43 0N 0 6W
Argelès-sur-Mer 20 42 34N 3 1 E
Argens → 21 43 24N 6 44 E
Argent-sur-Sauldre 19 47 33N 2 25 E
Argenta, Can. 108 50 20N 116 55W
Argenta, Italy 39 44 37N 11 50 E
Argentan 18 48 45N 0 1W
Argentário, Mte. 39 42 23N 11 11 E
Argentat 20 45 6N 1 56 E
Argentera 38 44 23N 6 58 E
Argentera, Monte del 38 44 12N 7 5 E
Argenteuil 19 48 57N 2 14 E
Argentia 107 47 18N 53 58W
Argentiera, C. dell' 40 40 44N 8 8 E
Argentière, L' 21 44 47N 6 33 E
Argentina ■ 128 35 0 S 66 0W
Argentino, L. 128 50 10 S 73 0W
Argenton-Château 18 46 59N 0 27W
Argenton-sur-Creuse 20 46 36N 1 30 E
Argeş □ 46 45 0N 24 45 E
Argeş → 46 44 30N 25 50 E
Arghandab → 66 31 30N 64 15 E
Argo 86 19 28N 30 30 E
Argolikós Kólpos 45 37 20N 22 52 E
Argolis □ 45 37 38N 22 50 E
Argonne 19 49 0N 5 20 E
Árgos 45 37 40N 22 43 E
Árgos Orestikón 44 40 27N 21 26 E
Argostólion 45 38 12N 20 33 E
Arguedas 32 42 11N 1 36W
Arguello, Pt. 119 34 34N 120 40W
Argun → 59 53 20N 121 28 E
Argungu 85 12 40N 4 31 E
Argyle 116 48 23N 96 49W
Argyrádhes 44 39 27N 19 58 E
Århus 49 56 8N 10 11 E
Århus Amtskommune □ 49 56 15N 10 15 E
Ariamsvlei 92 28 9 S 19 51 E
Ariana 83 36 52N 10 12 E
Ariano Irpino 41 41 10N 15 4 E
Ariano nel Polèsine 39 44 56N 12 5 E
Aribinda 85 14 17N 0 52W
Arica, Chile 126 18 32 S 70 20W
Arica, Colomb. 126 2 0 S 71 50W
Arid, C. 96 34 1 S 123 10 E
Aridh 64 25 0N 46 0 E
Ariège □ 20 42 56N 1 30 E
Ariège → 20 43 30N 1 25 E
Arieş → 46 46 24N 23 20 E
Arilje 42 43 44N 20 7 E
Arima 121 10 38N 61 17W
Arinos → 126 10 25 S 58 20W
Ario de Rosales 120 19 12N 102 0W
Aripuanã 126 9 25 S 60 30W
Aripuanã → 126 5 7 S 60 25W
Ariquemes 126 9 55 S 63 6W
Arisaig 14 56 55N 5 50W
Arîsh, W. el → 86 31 9N 33 49 E
Arissa 87 11 10N 41 35 E
Aristazabal I. 108 52 40N 129 10W
Arivaca 119 31 37N 111 25W
Arivonimamo 93 19 1 S 47 11 E
Ariyalur 70 11 8N 79 8 E
Ariza 74 41 19N 2 3W
Arizaro, Salar de 124 24 40 S 67 50W
Arizona 124 35 45 S 65 25W
Arizona □ 119 34 20N 111 30W
Arizpe 120 30 20N 110 11W
Årjäng 48 59 24N 12 8 E
Arjeplog 50 66 3N 18 2 E
Arjona, Colomb. 126 10 14N 75 22W
Arjona, Spain 31 37 56N 4 4W
Arka 59 60 15N 142 0 E
Arkadak 55 51 58N 43 19 E
Arkadelphia 117 34 5N 93 0W
Arkadhía □ 45 37 30N 22 20 E
Arkaig, L. 14 56 58N 5 10W
Arkalyk 58 50 13N 66 50 E
Arkansas □ 117 35 0N 92 30W
Arkansas → 117 33 48N 91 4W
Arkansas City 117 37 4N 97 3W
Arkathos → 44 39 20N 21 4 E
Arkhángelos 45 36 13N 28 7 E
Arkhangelsk 52 64 40N 41 0 E
Arkhangelskoye 55 51 32N 40 58 E
Arkiko 87 15 33N 39 30 E
Arklow 15 52 48N 6 10W
Árkoi 45 37 24N 26 44 E
Arkona, Kap 24 54 41N 13 26 E
Arkonam 70 13 7N 79 43 E
Arkösund 49 58 29N 16 56 E
Arkoúdhi 45 38 33N 20 43 E
Arkticheskiy, Mys 59 81 10N 95 0 E
Arkul 55 57 17N 50 3 E
Arlanc 20 45 25N 3 42 E
Arlanza → 30 42 6N 4 9W
Arlanzón → 30 42 3N 4 17W
Arlberg Pass 25 47 9N 10 12 E
Arlee 118 47 10N 114 4W
Arles 21 43 41N 4 40 E
Arlington, S. Afr. 93 28 1 S 27 53 E
Arlington, Oreg., U.S.A. 118 45 48N 120 6W
Arlington, S.D., U.S.A. 116 44 25N 97 4W
Arlington, Va., U.S.A. 114 38 52N 77 5W
Arlington, Wash., U.S.A. 118 48 11N 122 4W
Arlon 16 49 42N 5 49 E
Arlöv 49 55 38N 13 5 E
Arly 85 11 35N 1 28 E
Armagh 15 54 22N 6 40W
Armagh □ 15 54 18N 6 37W
Armagnac 20 43 44N 0 10 E
Armançon → 19 47 59N 3 30 E
Armavir 57 45 2N 41 7 E
Armenia 126 4 35N 75 45W
Armenian S.S.R. □ 57 40 0N 44 0 E
Armeniş 46 45 13N 22 17 E
Armentières 19 50 40N 2 50 E
Armidale 97 30 30 S 151 40 E
Armour 116 43 20N 98 25W
Armstrong, B.C., Can. 108 50 25N 119 10W
Armstrong, Ont., Can. 106 50 18N 89 4W
Armstrong, U.S.A. 117 26 59N 97 48W
Armur 70 18 48N 78 16 E
Arnaía 44 40 30N 23 40 E
Arnaouti, C. 64 35 0N 32 20 E
Arnarfjörður 50 65 48N 23 40W
Arnaud → 105 60 0N 70 0W
Arnay-le-Duc 19 47 10N 4 27 E
Arnedillo 32 42 13N 2 14W
Arnedo 32 42 12N 2 5W
Årnes 50 66 1N 21 31W
Årnes 47 60 7N 11 28 E
Arnett 117 36 9N 99 44W
Arnhem 16 51 58N 5 55 E
Arnhem B. 96 12 20 S 136 10 E
Arnhem, C. 97 12 20 S 137 30 E
Arnhem Land 96 13 10 S 134 30 E
Arni 70 12 43N 79 19 E
Árnissa 44 40 47N 21 49 E
Arno → 38 43 41N 10 17 E
Arnold, Nebr., U.S.A. 116 41 29N 100 10W
Arnold, Pa., U.S.A. 112 40 36N 79 44W
Arnoldstein 26 46 33N 13 43 E
Arnon → 19 47 13N 2 1 E
Arnot 109 55 56N 96 41W
Arnøy 50 70 9N 20 40 E
Arnprior 106 45 26N 76 21W
Arnsberg 24 51 25N 8 2 E
Arnstadt 24 50 50N 10 56 E
Aroab 92 26 41 S 19 39 E
Aroánia Óri 45 37 56N 22 12 E
Aroche 31 37 56N 6 57W
Arolsen 24 51 23N 9 1 E
Aron → 19 46 50N 3 27 E
Arona 38 45 45N 8 32 E
Arosa, Ria de → 30 42 28N 8 57W
Arpajon, Cantal, France 20 44 54N 2 28 E
Arpajon, Essonne, France 19 48 37N 2 12 E
Arpino 40 41 40N 13 35 E
Arrabury 99 26 45 S 141 0 E
Arrah 69 25 35N 84 32 E
Arraiján 120 8 56N 79 36W
Arraiolos 31 38 44N 7 59W
Arran 14 55 34N 5 12W
Arrandale 108 54 57N 130 0W
Arras 19 50 17N 2 46 E
Arrats → 20 44 6N 0 52 E
Arreau 20 42 54N 0 22 E
Arrecife 80 28 57N 13 37W
Arrecifes 124 34 06 S 60 9W
Arrée, Mts. d' 18 48 26N 3 55W
Arriaga 120 21 55N 101 23W
Arrilalah P.O. 98 23 43 S 143 54 E
Arromanches-les-Bains 18 49 20N 0 38W
Arronches 31 39 8N 7 16W
Arros, R 20 43 40N 0 2W
Arrou 18 48 6N 1 8 E
Arrow, L. 15 54 3N 8 20W
Arrow Rock Res. 118 43 45N 115 50W
Arrowhead 108 50 40N 117 55W
Arrowtown 101 44 57 S 168 50 E
Arroyo de la Luz 31 39 30N 6 38W
Arroyo Grande 119 35 9N 120 32W
Års 49 56 48N 9 30 E
Ars 20 46 13N 1 30W
Ars-sur-Moselle 19 49 5N 6 4 E
Arsenault L. 109 55 6N 108 32W
Arsiero 39 45 49N 11 22 E
Arsikere 70 13 15N 76 15 E
Arsk 55 56 10N 49 50 E
Árta 45 39 8N 21 2 E
Artá 32 39 41N 3 21 E
Árta □ 44 39 15N 21 5 E
Arteaga 120 18 50N 102 20W
Arteijo 30 43 19N 8 29W
Artem, Ostrov 57 40 28N 50 20 E
Artemovsk, R.S.F.S.R., U.S.S.R. 59 54 45N 93 35 E
Artemovsk, Ukraine S.S.R., U.S.S.R. 56 48 35N 38 0 E
Artemovski 57 47 45N 40 16 E
Artenay 19 48 5N 1 50 E
Artern 24 51 22N 11 18 E
Artesa de Segre 32 41 54N 1 3 E
Artesia 117 32 55N 104 25W
Artesia Wells 117 28 17N 99 18W
Artesian 116 44 2N 97 54W
Arthez-de-Béarn 20 43 29N 0 38W
Arthington 84 6 35N 10 45W
Arthur → 99 41 2 S 144 40 E
Arthur Pt. 98 22 7 S 150 3 E
Arthur's Pass 101 42 54 S 171 35 E
Artigas 124 30 20 S 56 30W
Artik 57 40 38N 43 58 E
Artillery L. 109 63 9N 107 52W
Artois 19 50 20N 2 30 E
Artotína 45 38 42N 22 2 E
Artsiz 56 46 4N 29 26 E
Artvin 64 41 14N 41 44 E
Aru, Kepulauan 73 6 0 S 134 30 E
Aru Meru □ 90 3 20 S 36 50 E
Arua 90 3 1N 30 58 E
Aruanã 127 14 54 S 51 10W
Aruba 121 12 30N 70 0W
Arudy 20 43 7N 0 28W
Arun → 69 26 55N 87 10 E
Arunachal Pradesh □ 67 28 0N 95 0 E
Aruppukottai 70 9 31N 78 8 E
Arusha 90 3 20 S 36 40 E
Arusha □ 90 4 0 S 36 30 E
Arusha Chini 90 3 32 S 37 20 E
Arusi □ 87 7 45N 39 00 E
Aruvi → 70 8 48N 79 53 E
Aruwimi → 90 1 13N 23 36 E
Arvada 118 44 43N 106 6W
Arvakalu 70 8 20N 79 58 E
Arvayheer 75 46 15N 102 48 E
Arve → 21 46 11N 6 8 E
Arvi 68 20 59N 78 16 E
Arvida 107 48 25N 71 14W
Arvidsjaur 50 65 35N 19 10 E
Arvika 48 59 40N 12 36 E
Arxan 75 47 11N 119 57 E
Arys 58 42 26N 68 48 E
Arzachena 40 41 5N 9 27 E
Arzamas 55 55 27N 43 55 E
Arzew 82 35 50N 0 23W
Arzgir 57 45 18N 44 23 E
Arzignano 39 45 30N 11 20 E
Aš 26 50 13N 12 12 E
'As Saffānīyah 64 28 5N 48 50 E
Aş Şāfī 62 31 2N 35 28 E
As Salt 62 32 2N 35 43 E
As Samāwah 64 31 15N 45 15 E
As Samū' 62 31 24N 35 4 E
As Sanamayn 62 33 3N 36 10 E
As Sulaymānīyah 64 24 9N 47 18 E
As Sulṭan 83 31 4N 17 8 E
As Sumaymānīyah 64 35 35N 45 29 E
As Summān 64 25 0N 47 0 E
As Suwaih 65 22 10N 59 33 E
As Suwaydā' 64 32 40N 36 30 E
Aş Şuwayrah 64 32 55N 45 0 E
Asab 92 25 30 S 18 0 E
Asaba 85 6 12N 6 38 E
Asafo 84 6 20N 2 40W
Asahigawa 74 43 46N 142 22 E
Asale, L. 87 14 0N 40 20 E
Asamankese 85 5 50N 0 40W
Asansol 69 23 40N 87 1 E
Åsarna 48 62 39N 14 22 E
Asbe Teferi 87 9 4N 40 49 E
Asbesberge 92 29 0 S 23 0 E
Asbestos 107 45 47N 71 58W
Asbury Park 114 40 15N 74 1W
Ascensión, B. de la 120 19 50N 87 20W
Ascension I. 7 8 0 S 14 15W
Aschach 26 48 22N 14 2 E
Aschaffenburg 25 49 58N 9 8 E
Aschendorf 24 53 2N 7 22 E
Aschersleben 24 51 45N 11 28 E
Asciano 39 43 14N 11 32 E
Áscoli Piceno 39 42 51N 13 34 E
Áscoli Satriano 41 41 11N 15 32 E
Ascope 126 7 46 S 79 8W
Ascotán 124 21 45 S 68 17W
Aseb 87 13 0N 42 40 E
Åseda 49 57 10N 15 20 E
Asedjrad 82 24 51N 1 29 E
Asela 87 8 0N 39 0 E
Asenovgrad 43 42 1N 24 51 E
Aseral 47 58 37N 7 25 E
Asfeld 19 49 27N 4 5 E
Asfûn el Matâ'na 86 25 26N 32 30 E
Åsgårdstrand 47 59 22N 10 27 E
Ash Fork 119 35 14N 112 32W
Ash Grove 117 37 21N 93 36W
Ash Shām, Bādiyat 64 32 0N 40 0 E
Ash Shāmiyah 64 31 55N 44 35 E
Ash Shāriqah 65 25 23N 55 26 E
Ash Shaṭrah 64 31 30N 46 10 E
Ash Shu'aybah 64 27 53N 42 43 E
Ash Shu'bah 64 28 54N 44 44 E
Ash Shūnah ash Shamālīyah 62 32 37N 35 34 E
Asha 52 55 0N 57 16 E
Ashaira 86 21 40N 40 40 E
Ashanti □ 85 7 30N 1 30W
Ashburn 115 31 42N 83 40W
Ashburton 101 43 53 S 171 48 E
Ashburton → 96 21 40 S 114 56 E
Ashby-de-la-Zouch 12 52 45N 1 29W
Ashcroft 108 50 40N 121 20W
Ashdod 62 31 49N 34 35 E
Ashdot Yaaqov 62 32 39N 35 35 E
Asheboro 115 35 43N 79 46W
Asherton 117 28 25N 99 43W
Asheville 115 35 39N 82 30W
Asheweig → 106 54 17N 87 12W
Ashford, Austral. 99 29 15 S 151 3 E
Ashford, U.K. 13 51 8N 0 53 E
Ashford, U.S.A. 118 46 45N 122 2W
Ashikaga 74 36 28N 139 29 E
Ashizuri-Zaki 74 32 44N 133 0 E
Ashkhabad 58 38 0N 57 50 E
Ashland, Kans., U.S.A. 117 37 13N 99 43W
Ashland, Ky., U.S.A. 114 38 25N 82 40W
Ashland, Me., U.S.A. 107 46 34N 68 26W
Ashland, Mont., U.S.A. 118 45 41N 106 12W
Ashland, Nebr., U.S.A. 116 41 5N 96 27W
Ashland, Ohio, U.S.A. 114 40 52N 82 20W
Ashland, Oreg., U.S.A. 118 42 10N 122 38W
Ashland, Pa., U.S.A. 113 40 45N 76 22W
Ashland, Va., U.S.A. 114 37 46N 77 30W
Ashland, Wis., U.S.A. 116 46 40N 90 52W
Ashley, N.D., U.S.A. 116 46 3N 99 23W
Ashley, Pa., U.S.A. 113 41 12N 75 55W
Ashley Snow I. 5 73 35 S 77 6W
Ashmont 108 54 7N 111 35W
Ashmore Reef 96 12 14 S 123 5 E
Ashmûn 86 30 18N 30 55 E
Ashq'elon 62 31 42N 34 35 E
Ashtabula 114 41 52N 80 50W
Ashti 70 18 50N 75 15 E
Ashton, S. Afr. 92 33 50 S 20 5 E
Ashton, U.S.A. 118 44 6N 111 30W
Ashton-under-Lyne 12 53 30N 2 8W
Ashuanipi, L. 107 52 45N 66 15W
Asia 60 45 0N 75 0 E
Asia, Kepulauan 73 1 0N 131 13 E
Asiago 39 45 52N 11 30 E
Asifabad 70 19 20N 79 24 E
Asike 73 6 39 S 140 24 E
Asilah 82 35 29N 6 0W
Asinara, G. dell' 40 41 0N 8 30 E
Asinara I. 40 41 5N 8 15 E
Asino 58 57 0N 86 0 E
'Asīr □ 63 18 40N 42 30 E
Asir, Ras 63 11 55N 51 10 E
Aska 70 19 2N 84 42 E

Asker 47 59 50N 10 26 E
Askersund 49 58 53N 14 55 E
Askim 47 59 35N 11 10 E
Askja 50 65 3N 16 48W
Asl 86 29 33N 32 44 E
Asmār 65 35 10N 71 27 E
Asmera (Asmara) 87 15 19N 38 55 E
Asnæs 49 55 40N 11 0 E
Asni 82 31 17N 7 58W
Aso 74 33 0N 131 5 E
Asola 38 45 12N 10 25 E
Asoteriba, Jebel 86 21 51N 36 30 E
Asotin 118 46 20N 117 3W
Aspe 33 38 20N 0 40W
Aspen 119 39 12N 106 56W
Aspermont 117 33 11N 100 15W
Aspiring, Mt. 101 44 23 S 168 46 E
Aspres 21 44 32N 5 44 E
Aspromonte 41 38 10N 16 0 E
Aspur 68 23 58N 74 7 E
Asquith 109 52 8N 107 13W
Assa 82 28 35N 9 6W
Assâba 84 16 10N 11 45W
Assam □ 67 26 0N 93 0 E
Assamakka 85 19 21N 5 38 E
Asse 16 50 24N 4 10 E
Assekrem 83 23 16N 5 49 E
Assémini 40 39 18N 9 0 E
Assen 16 53 0N 6 35 E
Assens, Fyn, Denmark 49 56 41N 10 3 E
Assens, Fyn, Denmark 49 55 16N 9 55 E
Assini 84 5 9N 3 17W
Assiniboia 109 49 40N 105 59W
Assiniboine → 109 49 53N 97 8W
Assis 125 22 40 S 50 20W
Assisi 39 43 4N 12 36 E
Ássos 45 38 22N 20 33 E
Assus 44 39 32N 26 22 E
Assynt, L. 14 58 25N 5 15W
Astaffort 20 44 4N 0 40 E
Astakidha 45 35 53N 26 50 E
Astara 53 38 30N 48 50 E
Asti 38 44 54N 8 11 E
Astipálaia 45 36 32N 26 22 E
Astorga 30 42 29N 6 8W
Astoria 118 46 16N 123 50W
Åstorp 49 56 6N 12 55 E
Astrakhan 57 46 25N 48 5 E
Astrakhan-Bazàr 53 39 14N 48 30 E
Astudillo 30 42 12N 4 22W
Asturias 30 43 15N 6 0W
Asunción 124 25 10 S 57 30W
Asunción, La 126 11 2N 63 53W
Asutri 87 15 25N 35 45 E
Aswa → 90 3 43N 31 55 E
Aswad, Ras al 86 21 20N 39 0 E
Aswân 86 24 4N 32 57 E
Aswân High Dam = Sadd el Aali 86 24 5N 32 54 E
Asyût 86 27 11N 31 4 E
Asyûti, Wadi → 86 27 11N 31 16 E
Aszód 27 47 39N 19 28 E
At Ţafilah 64 30 45N 35 30 E
At Ta'if 86 21 5N 40 27 E
Aţ Ţur 62 31 47N 35 14 E
Aţ Ţurrah 62 32 39N 35 59 E
Atacama □ 124 27 30 S 70 0W
Atacama, Desierto de 124 24 0 S 69 20W
Atacama, Salar de 124 23 30N 68 20W
Atakor 83 23 27N 5 31 E
Atakpamé 85 7 31N 1 13 E
Atalándi 45 38 39N 22 58 E
Atalaya 126 10 45 S 73 50W
Atami 74 35 5N 139 4 E
Atapupu 73 9 0 S 124 51 E
Atâr 80 20 30N 13 5W
Atara 59 63 10N 129 10 E
Ataram, Erg n- 82 23 57N 2 0 E
Atarfe 31 37 13N 3 40W
Atascadero 119 35 32N 120 44W
Atasu 58 48 30N 71 0 E
Atauro 73 8 10 S 125 30 E
Atbara 86 17 42N 33 59 E
'Atbara → 86 17 40N 33 56 E
Atbasar 58 51 48N 68 20 E
Atchafalaya B. 117 29 30N 91 20W
Atchison 116 39 40N 95 10W
Atebubu 85 7 47N 1 0W
Ateca 32 41 20N 1 49W
Aterno → 39 42 11N 13 51 E
Atesine, Alpi 38 46 55N 11 30 E
Atessa 39 42 5N 14 27 E
Ath 16 50 38N 3 47 E
Ath Thāmāmi 64 27 45N 44 45 E
Athabasca 108 54 45N 113 20W
Athabasca → 109 58 40N 110 50W
Athabasca, L. 109 59 15N 109 15W
Athboy 15 53 37N 6 55W
Athenry 15 53 18N 8 45W
Athens, Can. 113 44 38N 75 57W
Athens, Ala., U.S.A. 115 34 49N 86 58W
Athens, Ga., U.S.A. 115 33 56N 83 24W
Athens, N.Y., U.S.A. 113 42 15N 73 48W
Athens, Ohio, U.S.A. 114 39 25N 82 6W
Athens, Pa., U.S.A. 113 41 57N 76 36W
Athens, Tenn., U.S.A. 115 35 45N 84 38W
Athens, Tex., U.S.A. 117 32 11N 95 48W
Athens = Athínai 45 37 58N 23 46 E
Atherley 112 44 37N 79 20W
Atherton 97 17 17 S 145 30 E
Athiéme 85 6 37N 1 40 E
Athínai 45 37 58N 23 46 E
Athlone 15 53 26N 7 57W
Athni 70 16 44N 75 6 E
Atholl, Forest of 14 56 51N 3 50W
Atholville 107 47 59N 66 43W
Áthos, Mt. 44 40 9N 24 22 E
Athy 15 53 0N 7 0W
Ati, Chad 81 13 13N 18 20 E
Ati, Sudan 87 13 5N 29 2 E
Atiak 90 3 12N 32 2 E
Atico 126 16 14 S 73 40W
Atienza 32 41 12N 2 52W
Atikokan 106 48 45N 91 37W
Atikonak L. 107 52 40N 64 32W
Atka 59 60 50N 151 48 E
Atkarsk 55 51 55N 45 2 E
Atkinson 116 42 35N 98 59W
Atlanta, Ga., U.S.A. 115 33 50N 84 24W
Atlanta, Tex., U.S.A. 117 33 7N 94 8W
Atlantic 116 41 25N 95 0W
Atlantic City 114 39 25N 74 25W
Atlantic Ocean 6 0 0 20 0W
Atlin 104 59 31N 133 41W
Atlin, L. 108 59 26N 133 45W
'Atlit 62 32 42N 34 56 E
Atløy 47 61 21N 4 58 E
Atmakur 70 14 37N 79 40 E
Atmore 115 31 2N 87 30W
Atna → 47 61 44N 10 49 E
Atoka 117 34 22N 96 10W
Átokos 45 38 28N 20 49 E
Atouguia 31 39 20N 9 20W
Atoyac → 120 16 30N 97 31W
Atrak → 65 37 50N 57 0 E
Ätran 49 57 7N 12 57 E
Atrauli 68 28 2N 78 20 E
Atri 39 42 35N 14 0 E
Atsbi 87 13 52N 39 50 E
Atsoum, Mts. 85 6 41N 12 57 E
Attalla 115 34 2N 86 5W
Attawapiskat 106 52 56N 82 24W
Attawapiskat → 106 52 57N 82 18W
Attawapiskat, L. 106 52 18N 87 54W
Attendorn 24 51 8N 7 54 E
Attersee 26 47 55N 13 32 E
Attica 114 40 20N 87 15W
Attichy 19 49 25N 3 3 E
Attigny 19 49 28N 4 35 E
Attikamagen L. 107 55 0N 66 30W
Attiki □ 45 38 10N 23 40 E
'Attīl 62 32 23N 35 4 E
Attleboro 114 41 56N 71 18W
Attock 66 33 52N 72 20 E
Attopeu 71 14 48N 106 50 E
Attur 70 11 35N 78 30 E
Atuel → 124 36 17 S 66 50W
Åtvidaberg 49 58 12N 16 0 E
Atwater 119 37 21N 120 37W
Atwood, Can. 112 43 40N 81 1W
Atwood, U.S.A. 116 39 52N 101 3W
Au Sable → 114 44 25N 83 20W
Au Sable Pt. 106 46 40N 86 10W
Aubagne 21 43 17N 5 37 E
Aube □ 19 48 15N 4 0 E
Aube → 19 48 34N 3 43 E
Aubenas 21 44 37N 4 24 E
Aubenton 19 49 50N 4 12 E
Aubigny-sur-Nère 19 47 30N 2 24 E
Aubin 20 44 33N 2 15 E
Aubrac, Mts. d' 20 44 38N 2 58 E
Auburn, Ala., U.S.A. 115 32 37N 85 30W
Auburn, Calif., U.S.A. 118 38 53N 121 4W
Auburn, Ind., U.S.A. 114 41 20N 85 0W
Auburn, N.Y., U.S.A. 114 42 57N 76 39W
Auburn, Nebr., U.S.A. 116 40 25N 95 50W
Auburn Range 99 25 15 S 150 30 E
Auburndale 115 28 5N 81 45W
Aubusson 20 45 57N 2 11 E
Auch 20 43 39N 0 36 E
Auchel 19 50 30N 2 29 E
Auchi 85 7 6N 6 13 E
Auckland 101 36 52 S 174 46 E
Auckland Is. 94 50 40 S 166 5 E
Aude □ 20 43 8N 2 28 E
Aude → 20 43 13N 3 14 E
Auden 106 50 14N 87 53W
Auderville 18 49 43N 1 57W
Audierne 18 48 1N 4 34W
Audincourt 19 47 30N 6 50 E
Audo Ra. 87 6 20N 41 50 E
Audubon 116 41 43N 94 56W
Aue 24 50 34N 12 43 E
Auerbach 24 50 30N 12 25 E
Auffay 18 49 43N 1 07 E
Augathella 97 25 48 S 146 35 E
Augrabies Falls 92 28 35 S 20 20 E
Augsburg 25 48 22N 10 54 E
Augusta, Italy 41 37 14N 15 12 E
Augusta, Ark., U.S.A. 117 35 17N 91 25W
Augusta, Ga., U.S.A. 115 33 29N 81 59W
Augusta, Kans., U.S.A. 117 37 40N 97 0W
Augusta, Me., U.S.A. 107 44 20N 69 46W
Augusta, Mont., U.S.A. 118 47 30N 112 29W
Augusta, Wis., U.S.A. 116 44 41N 91 8W
Augustenborg 49 54 57N 9 53 E
Augusto Cardosa 91 12 40 S 34 50 E
Augustów 28 53 51N 23 00 E
Augustus Downs 98 18 35 S 139 55 E
Augustus, Mt. 96 24 20 S 116 50 E
Aukan 87 15 29N 40 50 E
Aulla 38 44 12N 10 0 E
Aulnay 20 46 2N 0 22W
Aulne → 18 48 17N 4 16W
Aulnoye 19 50 12N 3 50 E
Ault 116 40 40N 104 42W
Ault-Onival 18 50 5N 1 29 E
Aulus-les-Bains 20 42 49N 1 19 E
Aumale 19 49 46N 1 46 E
Aumont-Aubrac 20 44 43N 3 17 E
Auna 85 10 9N 4 42 E
Aundh 70 17 33N 74 23 E
Aunis 20 46 5N 0 50W
Auponhia 73 1 58 S 125 27 E
Aups 21 43 37N 6 15 E
Auraiya 69 26 28N 79 33 E
Aurangabad, Bihar, India 69 24 45N 84 18 E
Aurangabad, Maharashtra, India 70 19 50N 75 23 E
Auray 18 47 40N 3 0W
Aurès 83 35 8N 6 30 E
Aurich 24 53 28N 7 30 E
Aurillac 20 44 55N 2 26 E
Aurlandsvangen 47 60 55N 7 12 E
Auronza 39 46 33N 12 27 E
Aurora, Can. 112 44 0N 79 28W
Aurora, S. Afr. 92 32 40 S 18 29 E
Aurora, Colo., U.S.A. 116 39 44N 104 55W
Aurora, Ill., U.S.A. 114 41 42N 88 12W
Aurora, Mo., U.S.A. 117 36 58N 93 42W
Aurora, Nebr., U.S.A. 116 40 55N 98 0W
Aurora, Ohio, U.S.A. 112 41 21N 81 20W
Aurskog 47 59 55N 11 26 E
Aurukun Mission 98 13 20 S 141 45 E
Aus 92 26 35 S 16 12 E
Aust-Agder fylke □ 47 58 55N 7 40 E
Austad 47 58 58N 7 37 E
Austerlitz = Slavkov 27 49 10N 16 52 E
Austevoll 47 60 5N 5 13 E
Austin, Minn., U.S.A. 116 43 37N 92 59W
Austin, Nev., U.S.A. 118 39 30N 117 1W
Austin, Pa., U.S.A. 112 41 40N 78 7W
Austin, Tex., U.S.A. 117 30 20N 97 45W
Austin, L. 96 27 40 S 118 0 E
Austral Downs 97 20 30 S 137 45 E
Austral Is. = Tubuai Is. 95 23 0 S 150 0W
Austral Seamount Chain 95 24 0 S 150 0W
Australia ■ 94 23 0 S 135 0 E
Australian Alps 97 36 30 S 148 30 E
Australian Cap. Terr. □ 97 35 30 S 149 0 E
Australian Dependency □ 5 73 0 S 90 0 E
Austria ■ 26 47 0N 14 0 E
Austvågøy 50 68 20N 14 40 E
Auterive 20 43 21N 1 29 E
Authie → 19 50 22N 1 38 E
Authon 18 48 12N 0 55 E
Autlán 120 19 40N 104 30W
Autun 19 46 58N 4 17 E
Auvergne 20 45 20N 3 15 E
Auvézère → 20 45 12N 0 50 E
Auxerre 19 47 48N 3 32 E
Auxi-le-Château 19 50 15N 2 8 E
Auxonne 19 47 10N 5 20 E
Auzances 20 46 2N 2 30 E
Auzat 20 45 27N 3 19 E
Avallon 19 47 30N 3 53 E
Avalon Pen. 107 47 30N 53 20W
Avalon Res. 117 32 30N 104 30W
Avanigadda 70 16 0N 80 56 E
Avaré 125 23 4 S 48 58W
Avas 44 40 57N 25 56 E
Aveiro, Brazil 127 3 10 S 55 5W
Aveiro, Port. 30 40 37N 8 38W
Aveiro □ 30 40 40N 8 35W
Åvej 64 35 40N 49 15 E
Avellaneda 124 34 50 S 58 10W
Avellino 41 40 54N 14 46 E
Averøya 47 63 0N 7 35 E
Aversa 41 40 58N 14 11 E
Avery 118 47 22N 115 56W
Aves, I. de 121 15 45N 63 55W
Aves, Is. de 121 12 0N 67 30W
Avesnes-sur-Helpe 19 50 8N 3 55 E
Avesta 48 60 9N 16 10 E
Aveyron □ 20 44 22N 2 45 E
Aveyron → 20 44 7N 1 5 E
Avezzano 39 42 2N 13 24 E
Avgó 45 35 33N 25 37 E
Aviá Terai 124 26 45 S 60 50W
Aviano 39 46 3N 12 35 E
Avigliana 38 45 7N 7 13 E
Avigliano 41 40 44N 15 41 E
Avignon 21 43 57N 4 50 E
Ávila 30 40 39N 4 43W
Ávila □ 30 40 30N 5 0W
Ávila, Sierra de 30 40 40N 5 0W
Avilés 30 43 35N 5 57W
Avionárion 45 38 31N 24 8 E
Avisio → 39 46 7N 11 5 E
Aviz 31 39 4N 7 53W
Avize 19 48 59N 4 0 E
Avoca, Austral. 100 37 5 S 143 26 E
Avoca, Ireland 15 52 52N 6 13W
Avoca, U.S.A. 112 42 24N 77 25W
Avoca → 100 35 40 S 143 43 E
Avola, Can. 108 51 45N 119 19W
Avola, Italy 41 36 56N 15 7 E
Avon, N.Y., U.S.A. 112 43 0N 77 42W
Avon, S.D., U.S.A. 116 43 0N 98 3W
Avon □ 13 51 30N 2 40W
Avon →, Avon, U.K. 13 51 30N 2 43W
Avon →, Hants., U.K. 13 50 44N 1 45W
Avon →, Warwick, U.K. 13 52 0N 2 9W
Avon Downs 97 19 58 S 137 25 E
Avon, Îles 97 19 37 S 158 17 E
Avon Lake 112 41 28N 82 3W
Avondale 91 17 43 S 30 58 E
Avonlea 109 50 0N 105 0W
Avonmore 113 45 10N 74 58W
Avonmouth 13 51 30N 2 42W
Avramov 43 42 45N 26 38 E
Avranches 18 48 40N 1 20W
Avre → 18 48 47N 1 22 E
Avrig 46 45 43N 24 21 E
Avrillé 20 46 28N 1 28W
Avtovac 42 43 9N 18 35 E
Awag el Baqar 87 10 10N 33 10 E
'Awālī 65 26 0N 50 30 E
Awarja → 70 17 5N 76 15 E
'Awartā 62 32 10N 35 17 E
Awasa, L. 87 7 0N 38 30 E
Awash 87 9 1N 40 10 E
Awash → 87 11 45N 41 5 E
Awaso 84 6 15N 2 22W
Awatere → 101 41 37 S 174 10 E
Awbārī 83 26 46N 12 57 E
Awbārī □ 83 26 35N 12 46 E
Awe, L. 14 56 15N 5 15W
Aweil 87 8 42N 27 20 E
Awgu 85 6 4N 7 24 E
Awjilah 81 29 8N 21 7 E
Ax-les-Thermes 20 42 44N 1 50 E
Axarfjörður 50 66 15N 16 45W
Axel Heiberg I. 4 80 0N 90 0W
Axim 84 4 51N 2 15W
Axintele 46 44 37N 26 47 E
Axiós → 44 40 57N 22 35 E
Axmarsbruk 48 61 3N 17 10 E
Axminster 13 50 47N 3 1W
Axstedt 24 53 26N 8 43 E
Axvall 49 58 23N 13 34 E
Ay 19 49 3N 4 0 E
Ayabaca 126 4 40 S 79 53W
Ayabe 74 35 20N 135 20 E
Ayacucho, Argent. 124 37 5 S 58 20W
Ayacucho, Peru 126 13 0 S 74 0W
Ayaguz 58 48 10N 80 0 E
Ayakudi 70 10 28N 77 56 E
Ayamonte 31 37 12N 7 24W
Ayan 59 56 30N 138 16 E
Ayancık 56 41 57N 34 18 E
Ayas 56 40 10N 32 14 E
Ayaviri 126 14 50 S 70 35W
Āybaq 65 36 15N 68 5 E
Ayenngré 85 8 40N 1 1 E
Ayeritam 71 5 24N 100 15 E
Ayer's Cliff 113 45 10N 72 3W
Ayers Rock 96 25 23 S 131 5 E
Aygues → 21 44 7N 4 43 E
Ayiá 44 39 43N 22 45 E
Ayía Ánna 45 38 52N 23 24 E
Ayía Marína 45 35 27N 26 53 E
Ayía Marína 45 37 11N 26 48 E
Ayía Paraskeví 44 39 14N 26 16 E
Ayía Rouméli 45 35 14N 23 58 E
Ayiássos 45 39 5N 26 23 E
Áyion Óros 44 40 25N 24 6 E
Áyios Andréas 45 37 21N 22 45 E
Áyios Evstrátios 44 39 34N 24 58 E
Áyios Evstrátios 44 39 30N 25 0 E
Áyios Ioannis, Ákra 45 35 20N 25 40 E
Áyios Kírikos 45 37 34N 26 17 E
Áyios Matthaíos 44 39 30N 19 47 E
Áyios Míronos 45 35 15N 25 1 E
Áyios Nikólaos 45 35 11N 25 41 E
Áyios Pétros 45 38 38N 20 33 E
Áyios Yeóryios 45 37 28N 23 57 E
Aykathonisi 45 37 28N 27 0 E
Aykin 52 62 15N 49 56 E
Aylesbury 13 51 48N 0 49W
Aylmer 112 42 46N 80 59W
Aylmer L. 104 64 0N 110 8W
'Ayn al Mubārak 64 24 10N 38 10 E
'Ayn 'Arīk 62 31 54N 35 8 E
'Ayn Zaqqūt 83 29 0N 19 30 E
Ayn Zhālah 64 36 45N 42 35 E
Ayna 33 38 34N 2 3W
Ayolas 124 27 10 S 56 59W
Ayom 87 7 49N 28 23 E
Ayon, Ostrov 59 69 50N 169 0 E
Ayora 33 39 3N 1 3W
Ayr, Austral. 97 19 35 S 147 25 E
Ayr, U.K. 14 55 28N 4 37W
Ayr → 14 55 29N 4 40W
Ayre, Pt. of 12 54 27N 4 21W
Aysha 87 10 50N 42 23 E
Aytos 43 42 42N 27 16 E
Aytoska Planina 43 42 45N 27 30 E
Ayu, Kepulauan 73 0 35N 131 5 E
Ayutla 120 16 58N 99 17W
Ayvalık 64 39 20N 26 46 E
Az Zāhirīyah 62 31 25N 34 58 E
Az Zahrān 64 26 10N 50 7 E
Az Zarqā 62 32 5N 36 4 E
Az Zāwiyah 83 32 52N 12 56 E
Az-Zilfī 64 26 12N 44 52 E
Az Zubayr 64 30 20N 47 50 E
Azambuja 31 39 4N 8 51W
Azamgarh 69 26 5N 83 13 E
Azaouak, Vallée de l' 85 15 50N 3 20 E
Āzārbāijān □ 64 37 0N 44 30 E
Azare 85 11 55N 10 10 E
Azay-le-Rideau 18 47 16N 0 30 E
Azazga 83 36 48N 4 22 E
Azbine = Aïr 85 18 0N 8 0 E
Azeffoun 83 36 51N 4 26 E
Azemmour 82 33 20N 9 20W
Azerbaijan S.S.R. □ 57 40 20N 48 0 E
Azezo 87 12 28N 37 15 E
Azilal, Beni Mallal 82 32 0N 6 30W
Azimganj 69 24 14N 88 16 E
Aznalcóllar 31 37 32N 6 17W
Azogues 126 2 35 S 78 0W
Azor 62 32 2N 34 48 E
Azores 6 38 44N 29 0W
Azov 57 47 3N 39 25 E
Azov Sea = Azovskoye More 56 46 0N 36 30 E
Azovskoye More 56 46 0N 36 30 E
Azovy 58 64 55N 64 35 E
Azpeitia 32 43 12N 2 19W
Azrou 82 33 28N 5 19W
Aztec 119 36 54N 108 0W
Azúa de Compostela 121 18 25N 70 44W
Azuaga 31 38 16N 5 39W
Azuara 32 41 15N 0 53W
Azuer → 31 39 8N 3 36W
Azuero, Pen. de 121 7 30N 80 30W
Azul 124 36 42 S 59 43W
Azzaba 83 36 48N 7 6 E
Azzano Décimo 39 45 53N 12 46 E

B

Ba Don 71 17 45N 106 26 E
Ba Ngoi = Cam Lam 71 11 50N 109 10 E
Ba Xian 76 39 8N 116 22 E
Baa 73 10 50 S 123 0 E
Baamonde 30 43 7N 7 44W
Baarle Nassau 16 51 27N 4 56 E
Baarn 16 52 12N 5 17 E
Bāb el Māndeb 63 12 35N 43 25 E
Baba 43 42 44N 23 59 E
Baba Burnu 44 39 29N 26 2 E
Baba dag 57 41 0N 48 19W
Babadag 46 44 53N 28 44 E
Babaeski 43 41 26N 27 6 E
Babahoyo 126 1 40 S 79 30W
Babana 85 10 31N 3 46 E

Babar, Alg. 83 35 10N 7 6 E
Babar, Indon. 73 8 0 S 129 30 E
Babar, Pak. 68 31 7N 69 32 E
Babarkach 68 29 45N 68 0 E
Babayevo 55 59 24N 35 55 E
Babb 118 48 56N 113 27W
Babenhausen 25 49 57N 8 56 E
Babia Gora 27 49 38N 19 38 E
Babile 87 9 16N 42 11 E
Babinda 98 17 20 S 145 56 E
Babine 108 55 22N 126 37W
Babine → 108 55 45N 127 44W
Babine L. 108 54 48N 126 0W
Babo 73 2 30 S 133 30 E
Babócsa 27 46 2N 17 21 E
Bābol 65 36 40N 52 50 E
Bābol Sar 65 36 45N 52 45 E
Baborów Kietrz 27 50 7N 18 1 E
Baboua 88 5 49N 14 58 E
Babuna 42 41 30N 21 40 E
Babura 85 12 51N 8 59 E
Babušnica 42 43 7N 22 27 E
Babuyan Chan. 73 19 10N 122 0 E
Babylon, Iraq 64 32 40N 44 30 E
Babylon, U.S.A. 113 40 42N 73 20W
Bač 42 45 29N 19 17 E
Bac Kan 71 22 5N 105 50 E
Bac Ninh 71 21 13N 106 4 E
Bac Phan 71 22 0N 105 0 E
Bac Quang 71 22 30N 104 48 E
Bacabal 127 4 15 S 44 45W
Bacan, Kepulauan 73 0 35 S 127 30 E
Bacan, Pulau 73 0 50 S 127 30 E
Bacarès, Le 20 42 47N 3 3 E
Bacarra 73 18 15N 120 37 E
Bacau 73 8 27 S 126 27 E
Bacău 46 46 35N 26 55 E
Bacău □ 46 46 30N 26 45 E
Baccarat 19 48 28N 6 42 E
Bacchus Marsh 100 37 43 S 144 27 E
Bacerac 120 30 18N 108 50W
Băceşti 46 46 50N 27 11 E
Bacharach 25 50 3N 7 46 E
Bachelina 58 57 45N 67 20 E
Bachuma 87 6 48N 35 53 E
Bačina 42 43 42N 21 23 E
Back → 104 65 10N 104 0W
Bačka Palanka 42 45 17N 19 27 E
Bačka Topola 42 45 49N 19 39 E
Bäckefors 49 58 48N 12 9 E
Bački Petrovac 42 45 29N 19 32 E
Backnang 25 48 57N 9 26 E
Backstairs Passage 97 35 40 S 138 5 E
Bacolod 73 10 40N 122 57 E
Bacqueville 18 49 47N 1 0 E
Bacs-Kiskun □ 27 46 43N 19 30 E
Bácsalmás 27 46 8N 19 17 E
Bad → 116 44 22N 100 22W
Bad Aussee 26 47 43N 13 45 E
Bad Axe 106 43 48N 82 59W
Bad Bergzabern 25 49 6N 8 0 E
Bad Bramstedt 24 53 56N 9 53 E
Bad Doberan 24 54 6N 11 55 E
Bad Driburg 24 51 44N 9 0 E
Bad Ems 25 50 22N 7 44 E
Bad Frankenhausen 24 51 21N 11 3 E
Bad Freienwalde 24 52 47N 14 3 E
Bad Godesberg 24 50 41N 7 4 E
Bad Hersfeld 24 50 52N 9 42 E
Bad Hofgastein 26 47 17N 13 6 E
Bad Homburg 25 50 17N 8 33 E
Bad Honnef 24 50 39N 7 13 E
Bad Ischl 26 47 44N 13 38 E
Bad Kissingen 25 50 11N 10 5 E
Bad Kreuznach 25 49 47N 7 47 E
Bad Lands 116 43 40N 102 10W
Bad Langensalza 24 51 6N 10 40 E
Bad Lauterberg 24 51 38N 10 29 E
Bad Leonfelden 26 48 31N 14 18 E
Bad Lippspringe 24 51 47N 8 46 E
Bad Mergentheim 25 49 29N 9 47 E
Bad Münstereifel 24 50 33N 6 46 E
Bad Muskau 24 51 33N 14 43 E
Bad Nauheim 25 50 24N 8 45 E
Bad Oeynhausen 24 52 16N 8 45 E
Bad Oldesloe 24 53 48N 10 22 E
Bad Orb 25 50 16N 9 21 E
Bad Pyrmont 24 51 59N 9 15 E
Bad Reichenhall 25 47 44N 12 53 E
Bad St.-Peter 24 54 23N 8 32 E
Bad Salzuflen 24 52 8N 8 44 E
Bad Segeberg 24 53 58N 10 16 E
Bad Tölz 25 47 43N 11 34 E
Bad Waldsee 25 47 56N 9 46 E
Bad Wildungen 24 51 7N 9 10 E
Bad Wimpfen 25 49 12N 9 10 E
Bad Windsheim 25 49 29N 10 25 E
Badagara 70 11 35N 75 40 E
Badagri 85 6 25N 2 55 E
Badajoz 31 38 50N 6 59W
Badajoz □ 31 38 40N 6 30W
Badakhshan □ 65 36 30N 71 0 E
Badalona 32 41 26N 2 15 E
Badalzai 66 29 50N 65 35 E
Badampahar 69 22 10N 86 10 E
Badanah 64 30 58N 41 30 E
Badas 72 4 33N 114 25 E
Badas, Kepulauan 72 0 45N 107 5 E
Baddo → 66 28 0N 64 20 E
Bade 73 7 10 S 139 35 E
Baden, Austria 27 48 1N 16 13 E
Baden, Can. 112 43 14N 80 40W
Baden, Switz. 25 47 28N 8 18 E
Baden-Baden 25 48 45N 8 15 E
Baden-Württemberg □ 25 48 40N 9 0 E
Badgastein 26 47 7N 13 9 E
Badger 107 49 0N 56 4W
Bādghīsāt □ 65 35 0N 63 0 E
Badia Polèsine 39 45 6N 11 30 E
Badin 68 24 38N 68 54 E
Badnera 68 20 48N 77 44 E
Badogo 84 11 2N 8 13W
Badong 77 31 1N 110 23 E
Badrinath 69 30 45N 79 30 E
Baduen 63 7 15N 47 40 E
Badulla 70 7 1N 81 7 E
Baena 31 37 37N 4 20W
Baeza 33 37 57N 3 25W
Bafa Gölü 45 37 30N 27 29 E
Bafang 85 5 9N 10 11 E
Bafatá 84 12 8N 14 40W
Baffin B. 4 72 0N 64 0W
Baffin I. 105 68 0N 75 0W
Bafia 88 4 40N 11 10 E
Bafilo 85 9 22N 1 22 E
Bafing → 84 13 49N 10 50W
Bafoulabé 84 13 50N 10 55W
Bafoussam 85 5 28N 10 25 E
Bafra 56 41 34N 35 54 E
Bafra, C. 56 41 44N 35 58 E
Bāft, Esfahān, Iran 65 31 40N 55 25 E
Bāft, Kermān, Iran 65 29 15N 56 38 E
Bafut 85 6 6N 10 2 E
Bafwasende 90 1 3N 27 5 E
Bagalkot 70 16 10N 75 40 E
Bagamoyo 90 6 28 S 38 55 E
Bagamoyo □ 90 6 20 S 38 30 E
Baganga 73 7 34N 126 33 E
Bagansiapiapi 72 2 12N 100 50 E
Bagasra 68 21 30N 71 0 E
Bagawi 87 12 20N 34 18 E
Bagdarin 59 54 26N 113 36 E
Bagé 125 31 20 S 54 15W
Bagenalstown = Muine Bheag 15 52 42N 6 57W
Baggs 118 41 8N 107 46W
Baghdād 64 33 20N 44 30 E
Bagherhat 69 22 40N 89 47 E
Bagheria 40 38 5N 13 30 E
Bāghīn 65 30 12N 56 45 E
Baghlān 65 36 12N 69 0 E
Baghlān □ 65 36 0N 68 30 E
Bagley 116 47 30N 95 22W
Bagnacavallo 39 44 25N 11 58 E
Bagnara Cálabra 41 38 16N 15 49 E
Bagnères-de-Bigorre 20 43 5N 0 9 E
Bagnères-de-Luchon 20 42 47N 0 38 E
Bagni di Lucca 38 44 1N 10 37 E
Bagno di Romagna 39 43 50N 11 59 E
Bagnoles-de-l'Orne 18 48 32N 0 25W
Bagnoli di Sopra 39 45 13N 11 55 E
Bagnolo Mella 38 45 27N 10 14 E
Bagnols-les-Bains 20 44 30N 3 40 E
Bagnols-sur-Cèze 21 44 10N 4 36 E
Bagnorégio 39 42 38N 12 7 E
Bagolino 38 45 49N 10 28 E
Bagotville 107 48 22N 70 54W
Bagrdan 42 44 5N 21 11 E
Baguio 73 16 26N 120 34 E
Bahabón de Esgueva 32 41 52N 3 43W
Bahadurgarh 68 28 40N 76 57 E
Bahama, Canal Viejo de 121 22 10N 77 30W
Bahamas ■ 121 24 0N 75 0W
Baharîya, El Wâhât al 86 28 0N 28 50 E
Bahau 71 2 48N 102 26 E
Bahawalnagar 68 30 0N 73 15 E
Bahawalpur 68 29 24N 71 40 E
† Bahawalpur □ 68 29 5N 71 3 E
Baheri 69 28 45N 79 34 E
Bahi 90 5 58 S 35 21 E
Bahi Swamp 90 6 10 S 35 0 E
Bahía = Salvador 127 13 0 S 38 30W
Bahía □ 127 12 0 S 42 0W
Bahía Blanca 124 38 35 S 62 13W
Bahía de Caráquez 126 0 40 S 80 27W
Bahía, Islas de la 121 16 45N 86 15W
Bahía Laura 128 48 10 S 66 30W
Bahía Negra 126 20 5 S 58 5W
Bahir Dar 87 11 37N 37 10 E
Bahmer 82 27 32N 0 10W
Bahönye 27 46 25N 17 28 E
Bahr Aouk → 88 8 40N 19 0 E
Bahr el Ahmar □ 86 20 0N 35 0 E
Bahr el Ghazâl □ 87 7 0N 28 0 E
Bahr el Jebel → 87 7 30N 30 30 E
Bahr Salamat → 81 9 20N 18 0 E
Bahr Yûsef → 86 28 25N 30 35 E
Bahra el Burullus 86 31 28N 30 48 E
Bahraich 69 27 38N 81 37 E
Bahrain ■ 65 26 0N 50 35 E
Bai 84 13 35N 3 28W
Baia Mare 46 47 40N 23 35 E
Baia-Sprie 46 47 41N 23 43 E
Baïbokoum 81 7 46N 15 43 E
Baicheng 76 45 38N 122 42 E
Băicoi 46 45 3N 25 52 E
Baidoa 63 3 8N 43 30 E
Baie Comeau 107 49 12N 68 10W
Baie-St-Paul 107 47 28N 70 32W
Baie Trinité 107 49 25N 67 20W
Baie Verte 107 49 55N 56 12W
Baignes 20 45 23N 0 25W
Baigneux-les-Juifs 19 47 31N 4 39 E
Ba'ījī 64 35 0N 43 30 E
Baikal, L. = Baykal, Oz. 59 53 0N 108 0 E
Bailadila, Mt. 70 18 43N 81 15 E
Baile Atha Cliath = Dublin 15 53 20N 6 18W
Bailei 87 6 44N 40 18 E
Bailén 31 38 8N 3 48W
Băileşti 46 44 01N 23 20 E
Bailhongal 70 15 55N 74 53 E
Bailleul 19 50 44N 2 41 E
Bailundo 89 12 10 S 15 50 E
Baimuru 98 7 35 S 144 51 E
Bain-de-Bretagne 18 47 50N 1 40W
Bainbridge, Ga., U.S.A. 115 30 53N 84 34W
Bainbridge, N.Y., U.S.A. 113 42 17N 75 29W
Baing 73 10 14 S 120 34 E
Bainville 116 48 8N 104 10W
Bā'ir 64 30 45N 36 55 E
Baird 117 32 25N 99 25W
Baird Mts. 104 67 10N 160 15W
Bairin Youqi 76 43 30N 118 35 E
Bairin Zuoqi 76 43 58N 119 15 E
Bairnsdale 97 37 48 S 147 36 E
Baise → 20 44 17N 0 18 E
Baissa 85 7 14N 10 38 E
Baitadi 69 29 35N 80 25 E
Baiyin 76 36 45N 104 14 E
Baiyu Shan 76 37 15N 107 30 E
Baiyuda 86 17 35N 32 07 E
Baja 27 46 12N 18 59 E
Baja California 120 31 10N 115 12W
Baja, Pta. 120 29 50N 116 0W
Bajah, Wadi → 86 23 14N 39 20 E
Bajana 68 23 7N 71 49 E
Bajimba, Mt. 99 29 17 S 152 6 E
Bajina Bašta 42 43 58N 19 35 E
Bajmok 42 45 57N 19 24 E
Bajo Nuevo 121 15 40N 78 50W
Bajoga 85 10 57N 11 20 E
Bajool 98 23 40 S 150 35 E
Bak 27 46 43N 16 51 E
Bakala 88 6 15N 20 20 E
Bakar 39 45 18N 14 32 E
Bakchav 58 57 1N 82 5 E
Bakel 84 14 56N 12 20W
Baker, Calif., U.S.A. 119 35 16N 116 8W
Baker, Mont., U.S.A. 116 46 22N 104 12W
Baker, Nev., U.S.A. 118 38 59N 114 7W
Baker, Oreg., U.S.A. 118 44 50N 117 55W
Baker I. 94 0 10N 176 35W
Baker, L. 104 64 0N 96 0W
Baker Lake 104 64 20N 96 3W
Baker Mt. 118 48 50N 121 49W
Baker's Dozen Is. 106 56 45N 78 45W
Bakersfield, Calif., U.S.A. 119 35 25N 119 0W
Bakersfield, Vt., U.S.A. 113 44 46N 72 48W
Bakhchisaray 56 44 40N 33 45 E
Bakhmach 54 51 10N 32 45 E
Bakhtiārī □ 64 32 0N 49 0 E
Bakinskikh Komissarov, im 26 64 39 20N 49 15 E
Bakırköy 43 40 59N 28 53 E
Bakkafjörður 50 66 2N 14 48W
Bakkagerði 50 65 31N 13 49W
Bakony → 27 47 35N 17 54 E
Bakony Forest = Bakony Hegység 27 47 10N 17 30 E
Bakony Hegység 27 47 10N 17 30 E
Bakori 85 11 34N 7 25 E
Bakouma 88 5 40N 22 56 E
Bakov 26 50 27N 14 55 E
Baku 57 40 25N 49 45 E
Bala 112 45 1N 79 37W
Bal'ā 62 32 20N 35 6 E
Bala, L. = Tegid, L. 12 52 53N 3 38W
Balabac I. 72 8 0N 117 0 E
Balabac, Str. 72 7 53N 117 5 E
Balabakk 64 34 0N 36 10 E
Balabalangan, Kepulauan 72 2 20 S 117 30 E
Bălăciţa 46 44 23N 23 8 E
Balaghat 69 21 49N 80 12 E
Balaghat Ra. 70 18 50N 76 30 E
Balaguer 32 41 50N 0 50 E
Balakhna 55 56 25N 43 32 E
Balaklava, Austral. 99 34 7 S 138 22 E
Balaklava, U.S.S.R. 56 44 30N 33 30 E
Balakleya 56 49 28N 36 55 E
Balakovo 55 52 4N 47 55 E
Balanda 55 51 30N 44 40 E
Balangir 69 20 43N 83 35 E
Balapur 68 20 40N 76 45 E
Balashikha 55 55 49N 37 59 E
Balashov 55 51 30N 43 10 E
Balasinor 68 22 57N 73 23 E
Balasore 69 21 35N 87 3 E
Balassagyarmat 27 48 4N 19 15 E
Balât 86 25 36N 29 19 E
Balaton 27 46 50N 17 40 E
Balatonfüred 27 46 58N 17 54 E
Balatonszentgyörgy 27 46 41N 17 19 E
Balazote 33 38 54N 2 09W
Balboa 120 9 0N 79 30W
Balboa Hill 120 9 6N 79 44W
Balbriggan 15 53 35N 6 10W
Balcarce 124 38 0 S 58 10W
Balcarres 109 50 50N 103 35W
Balchik 43 43 28N 28 11 E
Balclutha 101 46 15 S 169 45 E
Bald Knob 117 35 20N 91 35W
Baldock L. 109 56 33N 97 57W
Baldwin, Fla., U.S.A. 115 30 15N 82 10W
Baldwin, Mich., U.S.A. 114 43 54N 85 53W
Baldwinsville 114 43 10N 76 19W
Bale 39 45 4N 13 46 E
Bale □ 87 6 20N 41 30 E
Baleares □ 32 39 30N 3 0 E
Baleares, Islas 32 39 30N 3 0 E
Balearic Is. = Baleares, Islas 32 39 30N 3 0 E
Băleni 46 45 48N 27 51 E
Baler 73 15 46N 121 34 E
Balfe's Creek 98 20 12 S 145 55 E
Balfour 93 26 38 S 28 35 E
Balfouriyya 62 32 38N 35 18 E
Bali, Camer. 85 5 54N 10 0 E
Bali, Indon. 72 8 20 S 115 0 E
Bali □ 72 8 20 S 115 0 E
Bali, Selat 73 8 30 S 114 35 E
Baligród 27 49 20N 22 17 E
Balikesir 64 39 35N 27 58 E
Balikpapan 72 1 10 S 116 55 E
Balimbing 73 5 10N 120 3 E
Baling 71 5 41N 100 55 E
Balipara 67 26 50N 92 45 E
Baliza 127 16 0 S 52 20W
Balkan Mts. = Stara Planina 43 43 15N 23 0 E
Balkan Pen. 9 42 0N 22 0 E
Balkh 65 36 44N 66 47 E
Balkh □ 65 36 30N 67 0 E
Balkhash 58 46 50N 74 50 E
Balkhash, Ozero 58 46 0N 74 50 E
Ballachulish 14 56 40N 5 10W
Balladoran 100 31 52 S 148 39 E
Ballarat 97 37 33 S 143 50 E
Ballard, L. 96 29 20 S 120 10 E
Ballarpur 70 19 50N 79 23 E
Ballater 14 57 2N 3 2W
Ballenas, Canal de las 120 29 10N 113 45W
Balleny Is. 5 66 30 S 163 0 E
Ballia 69 25 46N 84 12 E
Ballina, Austral. 97 28 50 S 153 31 E
Ballina, Mayo, Ireland 15 54 7N 9 10W
Ballina, Tipp., Ireland 15 52 49N 8 27W
Ballinasloe 15 53 20N 8 12W
Ballinger 117 31 45N 99 58W
Ballinrobe 15 53 36N 9 13W
Ballinskelligs B. 15 51 46N 10 11W
Ballon 18 48 10N 0 14 E
Ballycastle 15 55 12N 6 15W
Ballymena 15 54 53N 6 18W
Ballymena □ 15 54 53N 6 18W
Ballymoney 15 55 5N 6 30W
Ballymoney □ 15 55 5N 6 23W
Ballyshannon 15 54 30N 8 10W
Balmaceda 128 46 0 S 71 50W
Balmazújváros 27 47 37N 21 21 E
Balmoral, Austral. 99 37 15 S 141 48 E
Balmoral, U.K. 14 57 3N 3 13W
Balmorhea 117 31 2N 103 41W
Balonne → 97 28 47 S 147 56 E
Balrampur 69 27 30N 82 20 E
Balranald 97 34 38 S 143 33 E
Balş 46 44 22N 24 5 E
Balsas → 120 17 55N 102 10W
Bålsta 48 59 35N 17 30 E
Balston Spa 113 43 0N 73 52W
Balta, Romania 46 44 54N 22 38 E
Balta, U.S.A. 116 48 12N 100 7W
Balta, R.S.F.S.R., U.S.S.R. 57 42 58N 44 32 E
Balta, Ukraine S.S.R., U.S.S.R. 56 48 2N 29 45 E
Baltanás 30 41 56N 4 15W
Baltic Sea 51 56 0N 20 0 E
Baltîm 86 31 35N 31 10 E
Baltimore, Ireland 15 51 29N 9 22W
Baltimore, U.S.A. 114 39 18N 76 37W
Baltrum 24 53 43N 7 25 E
Baluchistan □ 65 27 30N 65 0 E
Balurghat 69 25 15N 88 44 E
Balygychan 59 63 56N 154 12 E
Bam 65 29 7N 58 14 E
Bama 85 11 33N 13 41 E
Bamako 84 12 34N 7 55W
Bamba 85 17 5N 1 24W
Bambari 88 5 40N 20 35 E
Bamberg, Ger. 25 49 54N 10 53 E
Bamberg, U.S.A. 115 33 19N 81 1W
Bambesi 87 9 45N 34 40 E
Bambey 84 14 42N 16 28W
Bambili 90 3 40N 26 0 E
Bamboo 98 14 34 S 143 20 E
Bamenda 85 5 57N 10 11 E
Bamfield 108 48 45N 125 10W
Bāmīān □ 65 35 0N 67 0 E
Bamiancheng 76 43 15N 124 2 E
Bamkin 85 6 3N 11 27 E
Bampūr 65 27 15N 60 21 E
Ban Aranyaprathet 71 13 41N 102 30 E
Ban Ban 71 19 31N 103 30 E
Ban Bua Chum 71 15 11N 101 12 E
Ban Houei Sai 71 20 22N 100 32 E
Ban Khe Bo 71 19 10N 104 39 E
Ban Khun Yuam 71 18 49N 97 57 E
* Ban Me Thuot 71 12 40N 108 3 E
Ban Phai 71 16 4N 102 44 E
Ban Thateng 71 15 25N 106 27 E
Baña, Punta de la 32 40 33N 0 40 E
Banaba 94 0 45 S 169 50 E
Banadar Daryay Oman □ 65 27 30N 56 0 E
Banalia 90 1 32N 25 5 E
Banam 71 11 20N 105 17 E
Banamba 84 13 29N 7 22W
Banana 98 24 28 S 150 8 E
Bananal, I. do 127 11 30 S 50 30W
Banaras = Varanasi 69 25 22N 83 8 E
Banas →, Gujarat, India 68 23 45N 71 25 E
Banas →, Madhya Pradesh, India 69 24 15N 81 30 E
Bânâs, Ras. 86 23 57N 35 50 E
Banbridge 15 54 21N 6 17W
Banbridge □ 15 54 21N 6 16W
Banbury 13 52 4N 1 21W
Banchory 14 57 3N 2 30W
Bancroft 106 45 3N 77 51W
Band 43 46 30N 24 25 E
Band-e Torkestān 65 35 30N 64 0 E
Banda 68 25 30N 80 26 E
Banda Aceh 72 5 35N 95 20 E
Banda Banda, Mt. 99 31 10 S 152 28 E
Banda Elat 73 5 40 S 133 5 E
Banda, Kepulauan 73 4 37 S 129 50 E
Banda, La 124 27 45 S 64 10W
Banda Sea 73 6 0 S 130 0 E
Bandama → 84 6 32N 5 30W
Bandanaira 73 4 32 S 129 54 E
Bandanwara 68 26 9N 74 38 E
Bandar = Machilipatnam 70 16 12N 81 12 E
Bandār 'Abbās 65 27 15N 56 15 E
Bandar-e Būshehr 65 28 55N 50 55 E
Bandar-e Chārak 65 26 45N 54 20 E
Bandar-e Deylam 64 30 5N 50 10 E
Bandar-e Lengeh 65 26 35N 54 58 E
Bandar-e Ma'shur 64 30 35N 49 10 E
Bandar-e Nakhīlū 65 26 58N 53 30 E
Bandar-e Rīg 65 29 30N 50 45 E
Bandar-e Shāh 65 37 0N 54 10 E
Bandar-e Shāhpūr 64 30 30N 49 5 E
Bandar-i-Pahlavī 64 37 30N 49 30 E
Bandar Seri Begawan 72 4 52N 115 0 E
Bandawe 91 11 58 S 34 5 E
Bande 30 42 3N 7 58W
Bandeira, Pico da 125 20 26 S 41 47W
Bandera, Argent. 124 28 55 S 62 20W
Bandera, U.S.A. 117 29 45N 99 3W
Banderas, Bahía de 120 20 40N 105 30W
Bandia → 70 19 2N 80 28 E
Bandiagara 84 14 12N 3 29W
Bandırma 64 40 20N 28 0 E
Bandon 15 51 44N 8 45W
Bandon → 15 51 40N 8 41W
Bandula 91 19 0 S 33 7 E

† Now part of Punjab □

** Renamed Buon Me Thuot*

Name	Page	Lat.	Long.
ndundu	88	3 15 S	17 22 E
ndung	73	6 54 S	107 36 E
neasa	46	45 56N	27 55 E
ieres	33	38 44N	0 38W
nes	121	21 0N	75 42W
ieza, La	30	42 17N	5 54W
nff, Can.	108	51 10N	115 34W
nff, U.K.	14	57 40N	2 32W
nff Nat. Park	108	51 30N	116 15W
nfora	84	10 40N	4 40W
ng Hieng →	71	16 10N	105 10 E
ng Lamung	71	13 3N	100 56 E
ng Saphan	71	11 14N	99 28 E
ngala Dam	91	21 7 S	31 25 E
ngalore	70	12 59N	77 40 E
ngante	85	5 8N	10 32 E
ngaon	69	23 0N	88 47 E
ngassou	88	4 55N	23 7 E
ngeta, Mt.	98	6 21 S	147 3 E
nggai	73	1 40 S	123 30 E
nggi, P.	72	7 17N	117 12 E
nghāzī	83	32 11N	20 3 E
nghāzi □	83	32 7N	20 4 E
ngil	73	7 36 S	112 50 E
ngjang	87	11 23N	32 41 E
ngka, Pulau, Sulawesi, Indon.	73	1 50N	125 5 E
ngka, Pulau, Sumatera, Indon.	72	2 0 S	105 50 E
ngka, Selat	72	2 30 S	105 30 E
ngkalan	73	7 2 S	112 46 E
ngkinang	72	0 18N	101 5 E
ngko	72	2 5 S	102 9 E
ngkok = Krung Thep	71	13 45N	100 35 E
ngladesh ■	67	24 0N	90 0 E
ngolo	84	7 1N	7 29W
ngor, N. Ireland, U.K.	15	54 40N	5 40W
ngor, Wales, U.K.	12	53 13N	4 9W
ngor, Me., U.S.A.	107	44 48N	68 42W
ngor, Pa., U.S.A.	113	40 51N	75 13W
ngued	73	17 40N	120 37 E
ngui	88	4 23N	18 35 E
nguru	90	0 30N	27 10 E
ngweulu, L.	91	11 0 S	30 0 E
ngweulu Swamp	91	11 20 S	30 15 E
ni	121	18 16N	70 22W
ni →	84	14 30N	4 12W
ni Bangou	85	15 3N	2 42 E
ni, Djebel	82	29 16N	8 0W
nī Na'īm	62	31 31N	35 10 E
nī Suhaylah	62	31 21N	34 19 E
nia	84	9 4N	3 6W
niara	98	9 44 S	149 54 E
ninah	83	32 0N	20 12 E
niyās	64	35 10N	36 0 E
nja Luka	42	44 49N	17 11 E
njar	73	7 24 S	108 30 E
njarmasin	72	3 20 S	114 35 E
njarnegara	73	7 24 S	109 42 E
njul	84	13 28N	16 40W
nkeryd	49	57 53N	14 6 E
nket	91	17 27 S	30 19 E
nkilaré	85	14 35N	0 44 E
nkipore	69	25 35N	85 10 E
nks I., B.C., Can.	108	53 20N	130 0W
nks I., N.W.T., Can.	4	73 15N	121 30W
nks I., P.N.G.	97	10 10 S	142 15 E
nks Pen.	101	43 45 S	173 15 E
nks Str.	99	40 40 S	148 10 E
nkura	69	23 11N	87 18 E
nkya	42	42 43N	23 8 E
nn →, Down, U.K.	15	54 30N	6 31W
nn →, Londonderry, U.K.	15	55 10N	6 34W
nnalec	18	47 57N	3 42W
nning	119	33 58N	116 52W
nningville = Bandundu	88	3 15 S	17 22 E
nnockburn, Can.	112	44 39N	77 33W
nnockburn, U.K.	14	56 5N	3 55W
nnockburn, Zimb.	91	20 17 S	29 48 E
ñolas	32	42 16N	2 44 E
non	21	44 2N	5 38 E
ños de la Encina	31	38 10N	3 46W
ños de Molgas	30	42 15N	7 40W
novce	27	48 44N	18 16 E
nská Bystrica	27	48 46N	19 14 E
nská Štiavnica	27	48 25N	18 55 E
nsko	43	41 52N	23 28 E
nswara	68	23 32N	74 24 E
nten	73	6 5 S	106 8 E
ntry	15	51 40N	9 28W
ntry, B.	15	51 35N	9 50W
ntul	73	7 55 S	110 19 E
ntva	68	21 29N	70 12 E
ntval	70	12 55N	75 0 E
nya	43	42 33N	24 50 E
nyak, Kepulauan	72	2 10N	97 10 E
nyo	85	6 52N	11 45 E
nyuls	20	42 29N	3 8 E
nyumas	73	7 32 S	109 18 E
nyuwangi	73	8 13 S	114 21 E
nzare Coast	5	68 0 S	125 0 E
nzyville = Mobayi	88	4 15N	21 8 E
ocheng	77	33 12N	106 56 E
ode	76	39 1N	111 5 E
oding	76	38 50N	115 28 E
oji	77	34 20N	107 5 E
ojing	77	28 45N	109 41 E
okang	77	31 54N	111 12 E
oshan	76	25 10N	99 5 E
otou	76	40 32N	110 2 E
oying	77	33 17N	119 20 E
p	68	27 23N	72 18 E
patla	70	15 55N	80 30 E
paume	19	50 7N	2 50 E
qa el Gharbīyya	62	32 25N	35 2 E
'qūbah	64	33 45N	44 50 E
quedano	124	23 20 S	69 52W
r, U.S.S.R.	56	49 4N	27 40 E
r, Yugo.	42	42 8N	19 8 E
r Harbor	107	44 15N	68 20W
r-le-Duc	19	48 47N	5 10 E
r-sur-Aube	19	48 14N	4 40 E
r-sur-Seine	19	48 7N	4 20 E
rabai	72	2 32 S	115 34 E
Barabinsk	58	55 20N	78 20 E
Baraboo	116	43 28N	89 46W
Baracoa	121	20 20N	74 30W
Baradero	124	33 52 S	59 29W
Baraga	116	46 49N	88 29W
Barahona, Dom. Rep.	121	18 13N	71 7W
Barahona, Spain	32	41 17N	2 39W
Barail Range	67	25 15N	93 20 E
Baraka →	86	18 13N	37 35 E
Barakhola	67	25 0N	92 45 E
Barakot	69	21 33N	84 59 E
Barakula	99	26 30 S	150 33 E
Baralaba	98	24 13 S	149 50 E
Baralzon L.	109	60 0N	98 3W
Baramati	70	18 11N	74 33 E
Baramba	69	20 25N	85 23 E
Barameiya	86	18 32N	36 38 E
Baramula	69	34 15N	74 20 E
Baran	68	25 9N	76 40 E
Baranof I.	104	57 0N	135 10W
Baranovichi	54	53 10N	26 0 E
Baranów Sandomierski	28	50 29N	21 30 E
Baranya □	27	46 0N	18 15 E
Barão de Melgaço	126	11 50 S	60 45W
Baraolt	46	46 5N	25 34 E
Barapasi	73	2 15 S	137 5 E
Barasat	69	22 46N	88 31 E
Barat Daya, Kepulauan	73	7 30 S	128 0 E
Barataria B.	117	29 15N	89 45W
Baraut	68	29 13N	77 7 E
Barbacena	125	21 15 S	43 56W
Barbacoas	126	1 45N	78 0W
Barbados ■	121	13 0N	59 30W
Barban	39	45 5N	14 4 E
Barbastro	32	42 2N	0 5 E
Barbate	31	36 13N	5 56W
Barberino di Mugello	39	44 1N	11 15 E
Barberton, S. Afr.	93	25 42 S	31 2 E
Barberton, U.S.A.	114	41 0N	81 40W
Barbezieux	20	45 28N	0 9W
Barbigha	69	25 21N	85 47 E
Barbourville	115	36 57N	83 52W
Barbuda I.	121	17 30N	61 40W
Barca, La	120	20 20N	102 40W
Barcaldine	97	23 43 S	145 6 E
Barcarrota	31	38 31N	6 51W
Barcellona Pozzo di Gotto	41	38 8N	15 15 E
Barcelona, Spain	32	41 21N	2 10 E
Barcelona, Venez.	126	10 10N	64 40W
Barcelona □	32	41 30N	2 0 E
Barcelonette	21	44 23N	6 40 E
Barcelos	126	1 0 S	63 0W
Barcin	28	52 52N	17 55 E
Barcoo →	97	25 30 S	142 50 E
Barcs	27	45 58N	17 28 E
Barczewo	28	53 50N	20 42 E
Barda	57	40 25N	47 10 E
Bardai	83	21 25N	17 0 E
Bardas Blancas	124	35 49 S	69 45W
Bardejov	27	49 18N	21 15 E
Bardera	63	2 20N	42 27 E
Bardi	38	44 38N	9 43 E
Bardi, Ra's	64	24 17N	37 31 E
Bardia	81	31 45N	25 0 E
Bardo	28	50 31N	16 42 E
Bardoli	68	21 12N	73 5 E
Bardolino	38	45 33N	10 43 E
Bardsey I.	12	52 46N	4 47W
Bardstown	114	37 50N	85 29W
Bareilly	69	28 22N	79 27 E
Barentin	18	49 33N	0 58 E
Barenton	18	48 38N	0 50W
Barents Sea	4	73 0N	39 0 E
Barentu	87	15 2N	37 35 E
Barfleur	18	49 40N	1 17W
Barga, China	75	30 40N	81 20 E
Barga, Italy	38	44 5N	10 30 E
Bargal	63	11 25N	51 0 E
Bargara	98	24 50 S	152 25 E
Barge	38	44 43N	7 19 E
Barge, La	118	42 12N	110 4W
Bargnop	87	9 32N	28 25 E
Bargteheide	24	53 42N	10 13 E
Barguzin	59	53 37N	109 37 E
Barh	69	25 29N	85 46 E
Barhaj	69	26 18N	83 44 E
Barham	100	35 36 S	144 8 E
Barhi	69	24 15N	85 25 E
Bari, India	68	26 39N	77 39 E
Bari, Italy	41	41 6N	16 52 E
Bari Doab	68	30 20N	73 0 E
Bariadi □	90	2 45 S	34 40 E
Barīm	63	12 39N	43 25 E
Barinas	126	8 36N	70 15W
Baring C.	104	70 0N	117 30W
Baringo	90	0 47N	36 16 E
Baringo □	90	0 55N	36 0 E
Baringo, L.	90	0 47N	36 16 E
Baripada	69	21 57N	86 45 E
Bârîs	86	24 42N	30 31 E
Barisal	69	22 45N	90 20 E
Barisan, Bukit	72	3 30 S	102 15 E
Barito →	72	4 0 S	114 50 E
Barjac	21	44 20N	4 22 E
Barjols	21	43 34N	6 2 E
Barjūj, Wadi →	83	25 26N	12 12 E
Bark L.	112	45 27N	77 51W
Barka = Baraka →	87	18 13N	37 35 E
Barkalı	65	23 40N	58 0 E
Barker	112	43 20N	78 35W
Barkley Sound	108	48 50N	125 10W
Barkly Downs	98	20 30 S	138 30 E
Barkly East	92	30 58 S	27 33 E
Barkly Tableland	97	17 50 S	136 40 E
Barkly West	92	28 5 S	24 31 E
Barkol, Wadi →	86	17 40N	32 0 E
Barksdale	117	29 47N	100 2W
Barlee, L.	96	29 15 S	119 30 E
Barlee Ra.	96	23 30 S	116 0 E
Barletta	41	41 20N	16 17 E
Barleur, Pointe de	18	49 42N	1 16W
Barlinek	28	53 0N	15 15 E
Barlow L.	109	62 00N	103 0W
Barmedman	99	34 9 S	147 21 E
Barmer	68	25 45N	71 20 E
Barmera	99	34 15 S	140 28 E
Barmouth	12	52 44N	4 3W
Barmstedt	24	53 47N	9 46 E
Barnagar	68	23 7N	75 19 E
Barnard Castle	12	54 33N	1 55W
Barnato	99	31 38 S	145 0 E
Barnaul	58	53 20N	83 40 E
Barne Inlet	5	80 15 S	160 0 E
Barnes	99	36 2 S	144 47 E
Barnesville	115	33 6N	84 9W
Barnet	13	51 37N	0 15W
Barneveld, Neth.	16	52 7N	5 36 E
Barneveld, U.S.A.	113	43 16N	75 14W
Barneville	18	49 23N	1 46W
Barney, Mt.	97	28 17 S	152 44 E
Barngo	99	25 3 S	147 20 E
Barnhart	117	31 10N	101 8W
Barnsley	12	53 33N	1 29W
Barnstaple	13	51 5N	4 3W
Barnsville	116	46 43N	96 28W
Baro	85	8 35N	6 18 E
Baro →	87	8 26N	33 13 E
Baroda	68	25 29N	76 35 E
Baroda = Vadodara	68	22 20N	73 10 E
Barpali	69	21 11N	83 35 E
Barqin	83	27 33N	13 34 E
Barques, Pte. aux	114	44 5N	82 55W
Barquinha	31	39 28N	8 25W
Barquisimeto	126	10 4N	69 19W
Barr	19	48 25N	7 28 E
Barra, Brazil	127	11 5 S	43 10W
Barra, U.K.	14	57 0N	7 30W
Barra do Corda	127	5 30 S	45 10W
Barra do Piraí	125	22 30 S	43 50W
Barra Falsa, Pta. da	93	22 58 S	35 37 E
Barra Hd.	14	56 47N	7 40W
Barra Mansa	125	22 35 S	44 12W
Barra, Sd. of	14	57 4N	7 25W
Barraba	99	30 21 S	150 35 E
Barrackpur	69	22 44N	88 30 E
Barrafranca	41	37 22N	14 10 E
Barranca, Lima, Peru	126	10 45 S	77 50W
Barranca, Loreto, Peru	126	4 50 S	76 50W
Barrancabermeja	126	7 0N	73 50W
Barrancas	126	8 55N	62 5W
Barrancos	31	38 10N	6 58W
Barranqueras	124	27 30 S	59 0W
Barranquilla	126	11 0N	74 50W
Barras	127	4 15 S	42 18W
Barraute	106	48 26N	77 38W
Barre	114	44 15N	72 30W
Barreal	124	31 33 S	69 28W
Barreiras	127	12 8 S	45 0W
Barreirinhas	127	2 30 S	42 50W
Barreiro	31	38 40N	9 6W
Barreiros	127	8 49 S	35 12W
Barrême	21	43 57N	6 23 E
Barren I.	71	12 17N	93 50 E
Barren, Nosy	93	18 25 S	43 40 E
Barretos	127	20 30 S	48 35W
Barrhead	108	54 10N	114 24W
Barrie	106	44 24N	79 40W
Barrier Ra.	97	31 0 S	141 30 E
Barrière	108	51 12N	120 7W
Barrington, Ill., U.S.A.	114	42 8N	88 5W
Barrington, R.I., U.S.A.	113	41 43N	71 20W
Barrington L.	109	56 55N	100 15W
Barrington Tops	97	32 6 S	151 28 E
Barrow	104	71 16N	156 50W
Barrow →	15	52 10N	6 57W
Barrow Creek T.O.	96	21 30 S	133 55 E
Barrow I.	96	20 45 S	115 20 E
Barrow-in-Furness	12	54 8N	3 15W
Barrow Pt.	98	14 20 S	144 40 E
Barrow Ra.	96	26 0 S	127 40 E
Barrow Str.	4	74 20N	95 0W
Barruecopardo	30	41 4N	6 40W
Barruelo	30	42 54N	4 17W
Barry	13	51 23N	3 19W
Barry's Bay	106	45 29N	77 41W
Barsalogho	85	13 25N	1 3W
Barsi	70	18 10N	75 50 E
Barsø	49	55 7N	9 33 E
Barstow, Calif., U.S.A.	119	34 58N	117 2W
Barstow, Tex., U.S.A.	117	31 28N	103 24W
Barth	24	54 20N	12 36 E
Bartica	126	6 25N	58 40W
Bartin	64	41 38N	32 21 E
Bartle Frere, Mt.	97	17 27 S	145 50 E
Bartlesville	117	36 50N	95 58W
Bartlett	117	30 46N	97 30W
Bartlett, L.	108	63 5N	118 20W
Bartolomeu Dias	91	21 10 S	35 8 E
Barton-upon-Humber	12	53 41N	0 27W
Bartoszyce	28	54 15N	20 55 E
Bartow	115	27 53N	81 49W
Barumba	90	1 3N	23 37 E
Baruth	24	52 3N	13 31 E
Barvenkovo	56	48 57N	37 0 E
Barwani	68	22 2N	74 57 E
Barycz →	28	51 42N	16 15 E
Barysh	55	53 39N	47 8 E
Bas-Rhin □	19	48 40N	7 30 E
Bašaid	42	45 38N	20 25 E
Bāsa'idū	65	26 35N	55 20 E
Basankusa	88	1 5N	19 50 E
Bascuñán, C.	124	28 52 S	71 35W
Basel (Basle)	25	47 35N	7 35 E
Basel-Stadt □	25	47 35N	7 35 E
Baselland □	25	47 26N	7 45 E
Basento →	41	40 21N	16 50 E
Bashkir A.S.S.R. □	52	54 0N	57 0 E
Basilaki I.	98	10 35 S	151 0 E
Basilan	73	6 35N	122 0 E
Basilan Str.	73	6 50N	122 0 E
Basildon	13	51 34N	0 29 E
Basilicata □	41	40 30N	16 0 E
Basim	70	20 3N	77 0 E
Basin	118	44 22N	108 2W
Basingstoke	13	51 15N	1 5W
Basirhat	69	22 40N	88 54 E
Baška	39	44 58N	14 45 E
Baskatong, Rés.	106	46 46N	75 50W
Baskerville C.	96	17 10 S	122 15 E
Basle = Basel	25	47 35N	7 35 E
Basmat	70	19 15N	77 12 E
Basoda	68	23 52N	77 54 E
Basoka	90	1 16N	23 40 E
Basongo	88	4 15 S	20 20 E
Basque Provinces = Vascongadas	32	42 50N	2 45W
Basra = Al Başrah	64	30 30N	47 50 E
Bass Rock	14	56 5N	2 40W
Bass Str.	97	39 15 S	146 30 E
Bassano	108	50 48N	112 20W
Bassano del Grappa	39	45 45N	11 45 E
Bassar	85	9 19N	0 57 E
Basse Santa-Su	84	13 13N	14 15W
Basse-Terre	121	16 0N	61 40W
Bassée, La	19	50 31N	2 49 E
Bassein	70	19 26N	72 48 E
Basseterre	121	17 17N	62 43W
Bassett, Nebr., U.S.A.	116	42 37N	99 30W
Bassett, Va., U.S.A.	115	36 48N	79 59W
Bassi	68	30 44N	76 21 E
Bassigny	19	48 0N	5 10 E
Bassikounou	84	15 55N	6 1W
Bassum	24	52 50N	8 42 E
Båstad	49	56 25N	12 51 E
Bastak	65	27 15N	54 25 E
Bastar	70	19 15N	81 40 E
Basti	69	26 52N	82 55 E
Bastia	21	42 40N	9 30 E
Bastia Umbra	39	43 4N	12 34 E
Bastide-Puylaurent, La	20	44 35N	3 55 E
Bastogne	16	50 1N	5 43 E
Bastrop	117	30 5N	97 22W
Basuto	92	19 50 S	26 25 E
Bat Yam	62	32 2N	34 44 E
Bata, Eq. Guin.	88	1 57N	9 50 E
Bata, Romania	46	46 1N	22 4 E
Bataan	73	14 40N	120 25 E
Batabanó	121	22 40N	82 20W
Batabanó, G. de	121	22 30N	82 30W
Batac	73	18 3N	120 34 E
Batagoy	59	67 38N	134 38 E
Batak	43	41 57N	24 12 E
Batakan	72	4 5 S	114 38 E
Batalha	31	39 40N	8 50W
Batama	90	0 58N	26 33 E
Batamay	59	63 30N	129 15 E
Batang, China	75	30 1N	99 0 E
Batang, Indon.	73	6 55 S	109 40 E
Batangafo	88	7 25N	18 20 E
Batangas	73	13 35N	121 10 E
Batanta	73	0 55 S	130 40 E
Batatais	125	20 54 S	47 37W
Batavia	114	43 0N	78 10W
Bataysk	57	47 3N	39 45 E
Batchelor	96	13 4 S	131 1 E
Bateman's B.	97	35 40 S	150 12 E
Batemans Bay	99	35 44 S	150 11 E
Batesburg	115	33 54N	81 32W
Batesville, Ark., U.S.A.	117	35 48N	91 40W
Batesville, Miss., U.S.A.	117	34 17N	89 58W
Batesville, Tex., U.S.A.	117	28 59N	99 38W
Bath, U.K.	13	51 22N	2 22W
Bath, Maine, U.S.A.	107	43 50N	69 49W
Bath, N.Y., U.S.A.	114	42 20N	77 17W
Bathgate	14	55 54N	3 38W
Bathurst, Austral.	97	33 25 S	149 31 E
Bathurst, Can.	107	47 37N	65 43W
Bathurst = Banjul	84	13 28N	16 40W
Bathurst B.	97	14 16 S	144 25 E
Bathurst, C.	104	70 34N	128 0W
Bathurst Harb.	99	43 15 S	146 10 E
Bathurst I., Austral.	96	11 30 S	130 10 E
Bathurst I., Can.	4	76 0N	100 30W
Bathurst In.	104	68 10N	108 50W
Bathurst Inlet	104	66 50N	108 1W
Batie	84	9 53N	2 53W
Batinah	65	24 0N	56 0 E
Batlow	99	35 31 S	148 9 E
Batman	64	37 55N	41 5 E
Batna	83	35 34N	6 15 E
Batočina	42	44 7N	21 5 E
Batoka	91	16 45 S	27 15 E
Baton Rouge	117	30 30N	91 5W
Batopilas	120	27 0N	107 45W
Batouri	88	4 30N	14 25 E
Battambang	71	13 7N	103 12 E
Batticaloa	70	7 43N	81 45 E
Battipáglia	41	40 38N	15 0 E
Battīr	62	31 44N	35 8 E
Battle, Can.	109	52 58N	110 52W
Battle, U.K.	13	50 55N	0 30 E
Battle →	109	52 43N	108 15W
Battle Camp	98	15 20 S	144 40 E
Battle Creek	114	42 20N	85 6W
Battle Harbour	107	52 16N	55 35W
Battle Lake	116	46 20N	95 43W
Battle Mountain	118	40 45N	117 0W
Battlefields	91	18 37 S	29 47 E
Battleford	109	52 45N	108 15W
Battonya	27	46 16N	21 3 E
Batu	87	6 55N	39 45 E
Batu Gajah	71	4 28N	101 3 E
Batu, Kepulauan	72	0 30 S	98 25 E
Batu Pahat	71	1 50N	'02 56 E
Batuata	73	6 12 S	122 42 E
Batumi	57	41 30N	41 30 E
Baturaja	72	4 11 S	104 15 E
Baturité	127	4 28 S	38 45W
Bau	72	1 25N	110 9 E
Baubau	73	5 25 S	122 38 E
Bauchi	85	10 22N	9 48 E
Bauchi □	85	10 30N	10 0 E
Baud	18	47 52N	3 1W
Baudette	116	48 46N	94 35W
Baugé	18	47 31N	0 8W
Baule-Escoublac, La	18	47 18N	2 23W
Baume-les-Dames	19	47 22N	6 22 E

Baunatal 24 51 13N 9 25 E
Baunei 40 40 2N 9 41 E
Bauru 125 22 10 S 49 0W
Baús 127 18 22 S 52 47W
Bauska 54 56 24N 25 15 E
Bautzen 24 51 11N 14 25 E
Baux, Les 21 43 45N 4 51 E
Bavanište 42 44 49N 20 53 E
Bavaria = Bayern □ 25 49 7N 11 30 E
Båven 48 59 0N 16 56 E
Bavi Sadri 68 24 28N 74 30 E
Bavispe → 120 29 30N 109 11W
Baw Baw, Mt. 100 37 49 S 146 19 E
Bawdwin 67 23 5N 97 20 E
Bawean 72 5 46 S 112 35 E
Bawku 85 11 3N 0 19W
Bawlake 67 19 11N 97 21 E
Baxley 115 31 43N 82 23W
Baxter Springs 117 37 3N 94 45W
Bay Bulls 107 47 19N 52 50W
Bay City, Mich., U.S.A. 114 43 35N 83 51W
Bay City, Oreg., U.S.A. 118 45 45N 123 58W
Bay City, Tex., U.S.A. 117 28 59N 95 55W
Bay de Verde 107 48 5N 52 54W
Bay, Laguna de 73 14 20N 121 11 E
Bay Minette 115 30 54N 87 43W
Bay St. Louis 117 30 18N 89 22W
Bay Shore 114 40 44N 73 15W
Bay Springs 117 31 58N 89 18W
Bay View 101 39 25 S 176 50 E
Baya 91 11 53 S 27 25 E
Bayamo 121 20 20N 76 40W
Bayamón 121 18 24N 66 10W
Bayan 76 46 5N 127 24 E
Bayan Har Shan 75 34 0N 98 0 E
Bayan Hot = Alxa Zuoqi 76 38 50N 105 40 E
Bayan Obo 76 41 52N 109 59 E
Bayana 68 26 55N 77 18 E
Bayanaul 58 50 45N 75 45 E
Bayanhongor 75 46 8N 102 43 E
Bayard 116 41 48N 103 17W
Bayázeh 65 33 30N 54 40 E
Baybay 73 10 40N 124 55 E
Bayburt 64 40 15N 40 20 E
Bayerischer Wald 25 49 0N 13 0 E
Bayern □ 25 49 7N 11 30 E
Bayeux 18 49 17N 0 42W
Bayfield, Can. 112 43 34N 81 42W
Bayfield, U.S.A. 116 46 50N 90 48W
Baykal, Oz. 59 53 0N 108 0 E
Baykit 59 61 50N 95 50 E
Baykonur 58 47 48N 65 50 E
Baymak 52 52 36N 58 19 E
Baynes Mts. 92 17 15 S 13 0 E
Bayombong 73 16 30N 121 10 E
Bayon 19 48 30N 6 20 E
Bayona 30 42 6N 8 52W
Bayonne, France 20 43 30N 1 28W
Bayonne, U.S.A. 113 40 41N 74 7W
Bayovar 126 5 50 S 81 0W
Baypore → 70 11 10N 75 47 E
Bayram-Ali 58 37 37N 62 10 E
Bayreuth 25 49 56N 11 35 E
Bayrischzell 25 47 39N 12 1 E
Bayrūt 64 33 53N 35 31 E
Bayt Awlá 62 31 37N 35 2 E
Bayt Fajjār 62 31 38N 35 9 E
Bayt Fūrīk 62 32 11N 35 20 E
Bayt Ḩānūn 62 31 32N 34 32 E
Bayt Jālā 62 31 43N 35 11 E
Bayt Lahm 62 31 43N 35 12 E
Bayt Rīma 62 32 2N 35 6 E
Bayt Sāḩūr 62 31 42N 35 13 E
Bayt Ummar 62 31 38N 35 7 E
Bayt 'ūr al Taḩtā 62 31 54N 35 5 E
Baytīn 62 31 56N 35 14 E
Baytown 117 29 42N 94 57W
Baytūniyā 62 31 54N 35 10 E
Bayzo 85 13 52N 4 35 E
Baza 33 37 30N 2 47W
Bazar Dyuzi 57 41 12N 47 50 E
Bazarny Karabulak 55 52 15N 46 20 E
Bazarnyy Syzgan 55 53 45N 46 40 E
Bazartobe 57 49 26N 51 45 E
Bazaruto, I. do 93 21 40 S 35 28 E
Bazas 20 44 27N 0 13W
Bazhong 77 31 52N 106 46 E
Beach 116 46 57N 103 58W
Beach City 112 40 38N 81 35W
Beachport 99 37 29 S 140 0 E
Beachy Head 13 50 44N 0 16 E
Beacon 114 41 32N 73 58W
Beaconia 109 50 25N 96 31W
Beaconsfield 97 41 11 S 146 48 E
Beagle, Canal 128 55 0 S 68 30W
Bealanana 93 14 33N 48 44 E
Beamsville 112 43 12N 79 28W
Béar, C. 20 42 31N 3 8 E
Bear I. 15 51 38N 9 50W
Bear L., B.C., Can. 108 56 10N 126 52W
Bear L., Man., Can. 109 55 8N 96 0W
Bear L., U.S.A. 118 42 0N 111 20W
Bearcreek 118 45 11N 109 6W
Beardmore 106 49 36N 87 57W
Beardmore Glacier 5 84 30 S 170 0 E
Beardstown 116 40 0N 90 25W
Béarn 20 43 8N 0 36W
Bearpaw Mt. 118 48 15N 109 30W
Bearskin Lake 106 53 58N 91 2W
Beas de Segura 33 38 15N 2 53W
Beasain 32 43 3N 2 11W
Beata, C. 121 17 40N 71 30W
Beatrice, U.S.A. 116 40 20N 96 40W
Beatrice, Zimb. 91 18 15 S 30 55 E
Beatrice, C. 97 14 20 S 136 55 E
Beatton → 108 56 15N 120 45W
Beatton River 108 57 26N 121 20W
Beatty 119 36 58N 116 46W
Beaucaire 21 43 48N 4 39 E
Beauce, Plaine de la 19 48 10N 1 45 E
Beauceville 107 46 13N 70 46W
Beaudesert 99 27 59 S 153 0 E
Beaufort, Austral. 100 37 25 S 143 25 E
Beaufort, Malay. 72 5 30N 115 40 E
Beaufort, N.C., U.S.A. 115 34 45N 76 40W
Beaufort, S.C., U.S.A. 115 32 25N 80 40W
Beaufort Sea 4 72 0N 140 0W
Beaufort West 92 32 18 S 22 36 E
Beaugency 19 47 47N 1 38 E
Beauharnois 106 45 20N 73 52W
Beaujeu 21 46 10N 4 35 E
Beaulieu 20 44 59N 1 50 E
Beaulieu → 108 62 3N 113 11W
Beauly 14 57 29N 4 27W
Beauly → 14 57 26N 4 28W
Beaumaris 12 53 16N 4 7W
Beaumetz-les-Loges 19 50 15N 2 40 E
Beaumont, Dordogne, France 20 44 45N 0 46 E
Beaumont, Sarthe, France 18 48 13N 0 8 E
Beaumont, U.S.A. 117 30 5N 94 8W
Beaumont-de-Lomagne 20 43 53N 0 59 E
Beaumont-le-Roger 18 49 4N 0 47 E
Beaumont-sur-Oise 19 49 9N 2 17 E
Beaune 19 47 2N 4 50 E
Beaune-la-Rolande 19 48 4N 2 25 E
Beaupréau 18 47 12N 1 00W
Beauséjour 109 50 5N 96 35W
Beausset, Le 21 43 10N 5 46 E
Beauvais 19 49 25N 2 8 E
Beauval 109 55 9N 107 37W
Beauvoir 18 46 55N 2 1W
Beauvoir-sur-Niort 20 46 12N 0 30W
Beaver, Alaska, U.S.A. 104 66 20N 147 30W
Beaver, Okla., U.S.A. 117 36 52N 100 31W
Beaver, Pa., U.S.A. 112 40 40N 80 18W
Beaver, Utah, U.S.A. 119 38 20N 112 45W
Beaver →, B.C., Can. 108 59 52N 124 20W
Beaver →, Sask., Can. 109 55 26N 107 45W
Beaver City 116 40 13N 99 50W
Beaver Dam 116 43 28N 88 50W
Beaver Falls 114 40 44N 80 20W
Beaver I. 106 45 40N 85 31W
Beaver, R 106 55 55N 87 48W
Beaverhill L., Alta., Can. 108 53 27N 112 32W
Beaverhill L., Man., Can. 109 54 5N 94 50W
Beaverhill L., N.W.T., Can. 109 63 2N 104 22W
Beaverlodge 108 55 11N 119 29W
Beavermouth 108 51 32N 117 23W
Beaverstone → 106 54 59N 89 25W
Beaverton 112 44 26N 79 9W
Beawar 68 26 3N 74 18 E
Bebedouro 125 21 0 S 48 25W
Beboa 93 17 22 S 44 33 E
Bebra 24 50 59N 9 48 E
Beccles 13 52 27N 1 33 E
Bečej 42 45 36N 20 3 E
Beceni 46 45 23N 26 48 E
Becerreá 30 42 51N 7 10W
Béchar 82 31 38N 2 18W
Bechyně 26 49 17N 14 29 E
Beckley 114 37 50N 81 8W
Beckum 24 51 46N 8 3 E
Bécon 18 47 30N 0 50W
Bečva → 27 49 31N 17 40 E
Bédar 33 37 11N 1 59W
Bédarieux 20 43 37N 3 10 E
Bédarrides 21 44 2N 4 54 E
Beddouza, Ras 82 32 33N 9 9W
Bedele 87 8 31N 36 23 E
Bederkesa 24 53 37N 8 50 E
Bedeso 87 9 58N 40 52 E
Bedford, Can. 106 45 7N 72 59W
Bedford, S. Afr. 92 32 40 S 26 10 E
Bedford, U.K. 13 52 8N 0 29W
Bedford, Ind., U.S.A. 114 38 50N 86 30W
Bedford, Iowa, U.S.A. 116 40 40N 94 41W
Bedford, Ohio, U.S.A. 114 41 23N 81 32W
Bedford, Pa., U.S.A. 112 40 1N 78 30W
Bedford, Va., U.S.A. 114 37 25N 79 30W
Bedford □ 13 52 4N 0 28W
Bedford, C. 97 15 14 S 145 21 E
Będków 28 51 36N 19 44 E
Bednja → 39 46 12N 16 25 E
Bednodemyanovsk 55 53 55N 43 15 E
Bedónia 38 44 28N 9 36 E
Bedourie 97 24 30 S 139 30 E
Bedous 20 43 0 0 36W
Będzin 28 50 19N 19 7 E
Beech Grove 114 39 40N 86 2W
Beechworth 99 36 22 S 146 43 E
Beechy 109 50 53N 107 24W
Beelitz 24 52 14N 12 58 E
Beenleigh 99 27 43 S 153 10 E
Be'er Sheva' 62 31 15N 34 48 E
Be'er Sheva' → 62 31 12N 34 40 E
Be'er Toviyya 62 31 44N 34 42 E
Be'eri 62 31 25N 34 30 E
Be'erotayim 62 32 19N 34 59 E
Beersheba = Be'er Sheva' 62 31 15N 34 48 E
Beeskow 24 52 9N 14 14 E
Beeston 12 52 55N 1 11W
Beetzendorf 24 52 42N 11 6 E
Beeville 117 28 27N 97 44W
Befale 88 0 25N 20 45 E
Befotaka 93 23 49 S 47 0 E
Bega 97 36 41 S 149 51 E
Bega, Canalul 42 45 37N 20 46 E
Bégard 18 48 38N 3 18W
* Begemdir & Simen □ 87 12 55N 37 30 E
Bègles 20 44 45N 0 35W
Begna → 47 60 41N 10 0 E
Begonte 30 43 10N 7 40W
Begu-Sarai 69 25 24N 86 9 E
Behbehān 64 30 30N 50 15 E
Behror 68 27 51N 76 20 E
Behshahr 65 36 45N 53 35 E
Bei Jiang → 75 23 2N 112 58 E
Bei'an 75 48 10N 126 20 E
Beibei 75 29 47N 106 22 E
Beihai 75 21 28N 109 6 E
Beijing 76 39 55N 116 20 E
Beijing □ 76 39 55N 116 20 E
Beilen 16 52 52N 6 27 E
Beilngries 25 49 1N 11 27 E
Beilpajah 99 32 54 S 143 52 E
Beilul 87 13 2N 42 20 E
Beira 91 19 50 S 34 52 E
Beirut = Bayrūt 64 33 53N 35 31 E
Beit Lāhiyah 62 31 32N 34 30 E
Beitaolaizhao 76 44 58N 125 58 E
Beitbridge 91 22 12 S 30 0 E
Beiuş 46 46 40N 22 21 E
Beizhen 76 37 20N 118 2 E
Beja 31 38 2N 7 53W
Béja 83 36 43N 9 12 E
Beja □ 31 37 55N 7 55W
Bejaia 83 36 42N 5 2 E
Béjar 30 40 23N 5 46W
Bejestān 65 34 30N 58 5 E
Bekasi 73 6 20 S 107 0 E
Békés 27 46 47N 21 9 E
Békés □ 27 46 45N 21 0 E
Békéscsaba 27 46 40N 21 5 E
Bekily 93 24 13 S 45 19 E
Bekoji 87 7 40N 39 17 E
Bekok 71 2 20N 103 7 E
Bekwai 85 6 30N 1 34W
Bela, India 69 25 50N 82 0 E
Bela, Pak. 66 26 12N 66 20 E
Bela Crkva 42 44 55N 21 27 E
Bela Palanka 42 43 13N 22 17 E
Bela Vista, Brazil 124 22 12 S 56 20W
Bela Vista, Mozam. 93 26 10 S 32 44 E
Bélâbre 20 46 34N 1 8 E
Belalcázar 31 38 35N 5 10W
Belanovica 42 44 15N 20 23 E
Belavenona 93 24 50 S 47 4 E
Belawan 72 3 33N 98 32 E
Belaya → 52 56 0N 54 32 E
Belaya Glina 57 46 5N 40 48 E
Belaya Kalitva 57 48 13N 40 50 E
Belaya Kholunitsa 55 58 41N 50 13 E
Belaya, Mt. 87 11 25N 36 8 E
Belaya Tserkov 54 49 45N 30 10 E
Belceşti 46 47 19N 27 7 E
Bełchatów 28 51 21N 19 22 E
Belcher, C. 4 71 0N 161 0W
Belcher Is. 106 56 15N 78 45W
Belchite 32 41 18N 0 43W
Belebey 52 54 7N 54 7 E
Belém (Pará) 127 1 20 S 48 30W
Belén, Argent. 124 27 40 S 67 5W
Belén, Parag. 124 23 30 S 57 6W
Belen 119 34 40N 106 50W
Belene 43 43 39N 25 10 E
Bélesta 20 42 55N 1 56 E
Belet Uen 63 4 30N 45 5 E
Belev 55 53 50N 36 5 E
Belfast, S. Afr. 93 25 42 S 30 2 E
Belfast, U.K. 15 54 35N 5 56W
Belfast, Maine, U.S.A. 107 44 30N 69 0W
Belfast, N.Y., U.S.A. 112 42 21N 78 9W
Belfast □ 15 54 35N 5 56W
Belfast, L. 15 54 40N 5 50W
Belfield 116 46 54N 103 11W
Belfort 19 47 38N 6 50 E
Belfort □ 19 47 38N 6 52 E
Belfry 118 45 10N 109 2W
Belgaum 70 15 55N 74 35 E
Belgioioso 38 45 9N 9 21 E
Belgium ■ 16 50 30N 5 0 E
Belgorod 56 50 35N 36 35 E
Belgorod-Dnestrovskiy 56 46 11N 30 23 E
Belgrade 118 45 50N 111 10W
Belgrade = Beograd 42 44 50N 20 37 E
Belhaven 115 35 34N 76 35W
Beli Drim → 42 42 6N 20 25 E
Beli Manastir 42 45 45N 18 36 E
Beli Timok → 42 43 53N 22 14 E
Belice → 40 37 35N 12 55 E
Belin 20 44 30N 0 47W
Belinga 88 1 10N 13 2 E
Belingwe 91 20 29 S 29 57 E
Belingwe, N. 91 20 37 S 29 55 E
Belinskiy (Chembar) 55 53 0N 43 25 E
Belinţ 42 45 48N 21 54 E
Belinyu 72 1 35 S 105 50 E
Belitung, P. 72 3 10 S 107 50 E
Beliu 46 46 30N 22 0 E
Belize ■ 120 17 0N 88 30W
Belize City 120 17 25N 88 0W
Beljanica 42 44 08N 21 43 E
Belkovskiy, Ostrov 59 75 32N 135 44 E
Bell → 106 49 48N 77 38W
Bell Bay 99 41 6 S 146 53 E
Bell I. 107 50 46N 55 35W
Bell-Irving → 108 56 12N 129 5W
Bell Peninsula 105 63 50N 82 0W
Bell Ville 124 32 40 S 62 40W
Bella Bella 108 52 10N 128 10W
Bella Coola 108 52 25N 126 40W
Bella Unión 124 30 15 S 57 40W
Bella Vista, Corrientes, Argent. 124 28 33 S 59 0W
Bella Vista, Tucuman, Argent. 124 27 10 S 65 25W
Bellac 20 46 7N 1 3 E
Bellágio 38 45 59N 9 15 E
Bellaire 114 40 1N 80 46W
Bellary 70 15 10N 76 56 E
Bellata 99 29 53 S 149 46 E
Belle Fourche 116 44 43N 103 52W
Belle Fourche → 116 44 25N 102 19W
Belle Glade 115 26 43N 80 38W
Belle-Île 18 47 20N 3 10W
Belle Isle 107 51 57N 55 25W
Belle-Isle-en-Terre 18 48 33N 3 23W
Belle Isle, Str. of 107 51 30N 56 30W
Belle, La 115 26 45N 81 22W
Belle Plaine, Iowa, U.S.A. 116 41 51N 92 18W
Belle Plaine, Minn., U.S.A. 116 44 35N 93 48W
Belle Yella 84 7 24N 10 0W
Belledonne 21 45 30N 6 10 E
Belledune 107 47 55N 65 50W
Bellefontaine 114 40 20N 83 45W
Bellefonte 114 40 56N 77 45W
Bellegarde, Ain, France 21 46 4N 5 49 E
Bellegarde, Creuse, France 20 45 59N 2 18 E
Bellegarde, Loiret, France 19 48 0N 2 2
Bellême 18 48 22N 0 3
Belleoram 107 47 31N 55 2
Belleville, Can. 106 44 10N 77 2
Belleville, Rhône, France 21 46 7N 4 4
Belleville, Vendée, France 18 46 48N 1 2
Belleville, Ill., U.S.A. 116 38 30N 90
Belleville, Kans., U.S.A. 116 39 51N 97 3
Belleville, N.Y., U.S.A. 113 43 46N 76 1
Bellevue, Can. 108 49 35N 114 2
Bellevue, Idaho, U.S.A. 118 43 25N 114 2
Bellevue, Ohio, U.S.A. 112 41 20N 82 4
Bellevue, Pa., U.S.A. 112 40 29N 80
Belley 21 45 46N 5 4
Bellin (Payne Bay) 105 60 0N 70
Bellingen 99 30 25 S 152 5
Bellingham 118 48 45N 122 2
Bellingshausen Sea 5 66 0 S 80
Bellinzona 25 46 11N 9
Bellona Reefs 97 21 26 S 159
Bellows Falls 114 43 10N 72 3
Bellpat 68 29 0N 68
Bellpuig 32 41 37N 1
Belluno 39 46 8N 12 1
Bellville 117 29 58N 96 1
Bellwood 112 40 36N 78 2
Belmar 113 40 10N 74
Bélmez 31 38 17N 5 1
Belmont, Austral. 99 33 4 S 151 4
Belmont, Can. 112 42 53N 81
Belmont, U.S.A. 112 42 14N 78
Belmonte, Brazil 127 16 0 S 39
Belmonte, Port. 30 40 21N 7 2
Belmonte, Spain 32 39 34N 2 4
Belmopan 120 17 18N 88 3
Belmullet 15 54 13N 9 5
Belo Horizonte 127 19 55 S 43 5
Belo-sur-Mer 93 20 42 S 44
Belo-Tsiribihina 93 19 40 S 44 3
Belogorsk, R.S.F.S.R., U.S.S.R. 59 51 0N 128 2
Belogorsk, Ukraine S.S.R., U.S.S.R. 56 45 3N 34 3
Belogradchik 42 43 53N 22 1
Belogradets 43 43 22N 27 1
Beloha 93 25 10 S 45
Beloit, Kans., U.S.A. 116 39 32N 98
Beloit, Wis., U.S.A. 116 42 35N 89
Belokorovichi 54 51 7N 28
Belomorsk 52 64 35N 34 3
Belonia 67 23 15N 91 3
Belopolye 54 51 14N 34 2
Beloretsk 52 53 58N 58 24
Belovo 58 54 30N 86
Beloye More 52 66 30N 38
Beloye, Oz. 52 60 10N 37 3
Beloye Ozero 57 45 15N 46 5
Belozem 43 42 12N 25
Belozersk 55 60 0N 37 3
Belpasso 41 37 37N 15
Belsito 40 37 50N 13 47
Beltana 99 30 48 S 138 25
Belterra 127 2 45 S 55
Beltinci 39 46 37N 16 20
Belton, S.C., U.S.A. 115 34 31N 82 3
Belton, Tex., U.S.A. 117 31 4N 97 3
Belton Res. 117 31 8N 97 3
Beltsy 56 47 48N 28 0
Belturbet 15 54 6N 7 2
Belukha 58 49 50N 86 50
Beluran 72 5 48N 117 35
Beluša 27 49 5N 18 27
Belušić 42 43 50N 21 10
Belvedere Maríttimo 41 39 37N 15 52
Belvès 20 44 46N 1 0
Belvidere, Ill., U.S.A. 116 42 15N 88 5
Belvidere, N.J., U.S.A. 113 40 48N 75 5
Belvis de la Jara 31 39 45N 4 57
Belyando → 97 21 38 S 146 50
Belyy 54 55 48N 32 51
Belyy, Ostrov 58 73 30N 71 0
Belyy Yar 58 58 26N 84 39
Belzig 24 52 8N 12 36
Belzoni 117 33 12N 90 30
Bełżyce 28 51 11N 22 17
Bemaraha, Lembalemban' i 93 18 40 S 44 45
Bemarivo 93 21 45 S 44 45
Bemarivo → 93 15 27 S 47 40
Bemavo 93 21 33 S 45 25
Bembéréke 85 10 11N 2 43
Bembesi 91 20 0 S 28 58
Bembesi → 91 18 57 S 27 47
Bembézar → 31 37 45N 5 13
Bemidji 116 47 30N 94 50
Ben 'Ammi 62 33 0N 35 7
Ben Cruachan 14 56 26N 5 8
Ben Dearg 14 57 47N 4 58
Ben Gardane 83 33 11N 11 11
Ben Hope 14 58 24N 4 36
Ben Lawers 14 56 33N 4 13
Ben Lomond, Austral. 97 41 38 S 147 42
Ben Lomond, U.K. 14 56 12N 4 39
Ben Macdhui 14 57 4N 3 40
Ben Mhor 14 57 16N 7 21
Ben More, Central, U.K. 14 56 23N 4 31
Ben More, Strathclyde, U.K. 14 56 26N 6 2
Ben More Assynt 14 58 7N 4 51
Ben Nevis 14 56 48N 5 0
Ben Slimane 82 33 38N 7 7
Ben Vorlich 14 56 22N 4 15
Ben Wyvis 14 57 40N 4 35
Bena 85 11 20N 5 50
Bena Dibele 88 4 4 S 22 50
Benagalbón 31 36 45N 4 15
Benagerie 99 31 25 S 140 22
Benahmed 82 33 4N 7 9
Benalla 97 36 30 S 146 0
Benambra, Mt. 100 36 31 S 147 34
Benamejí 31 37 16N 4 33
Benanee 99 34 31 S 142 52
Benares = Varanasi 69 25 22N 83 8
Bénat, C. 21 43 5N 6 22
Benavente, Port. 31 38 59N 8 49

* Renamed Gonder □

Name	Page	Lat.	Long.
ıavente, Spain	30	42 2N	5 43W
ıavides, Spain	30	42 30N	5 54W
ıavides, U.S.A.	117	27 35N	98 28W
ıbecula	14	57 26N	7 21W
ıcubbin	96	30 48 S	117 52 E
ıd	118	44 2N	121 15W
ıdel □	85	6 0N	6 0 E
ıder Beila	63	9 30N	50 48 E
ıdery	56	46 50N	29 30 E
ıdigo	97	36 40 S	144 15 E
ıdorf	24	50 26N	7 34 E
ıē Beraq, Israel	62	32 6N	34 51 E
ıē Beraq, Israel	62	32 6N	34 51 E
ıéna	84	13 9N	4 17W
ıenitra	93	23 27 S	45 5 E
ıešöv	26	49 46N	14 41 E
ıestroff	19	48 54N	6 45 E
ıet	20	46 22N	0 35W
ıevento	41	41 7N	14 45 E
ıfeld	19	48 22N	7 34 E
ıga	91	16 11 S	33 40 E
ıgal, Bay of	60	15 0N	90 0 E
ıgawan Solo →	73	7 5 S	112 35 E
ıgbu	75	32 58N	117 20 E
ıghazi = Banghāzī	83	32 11N	20 3 E
ıgkalis	72	1 30N	102 10 E
ıgkulu	72	3 50 S	102 12 E
ıgkulu □	72	3 48 S	102 16 E
ıgough	109	49 25N	105 10W
ıguela	89	12 37 S	13 25 E
ıguerir	82	32 16N	7 56W
ıguérua, I.	93	21 58 S	35 28 E
ıha	86	30 26N	31 8 E
ıi	90	0 30N	29 27 E
ıi →	126	10 23 S	65 24W
ıi Abbès	82	30 5N	2 5W
ıi-Haoua	82	36 30N	1 30 E
ıi Mazâr	86	28 32N	30 44 E
ıi Mellal	82	32 21N	6 21W
ıi Ounif	82	32 0N	1 10W
ıi Saf	82	35 17N	1 15W
ıi Suef	86	29 5N	31 6 E
ıiah L.	108	63 23N	112 17W
ıicarló	32	40 23N	0 23 E
ıidorm	33	38 33N	0 9W
ıidorm, Islote de	33	38 31N	0 9W
ıin ■	85	10 0N	2 0 E
ıin, Bight of	85	5 0N	3 0 E
ıin City	85	6 20N	5 31 E
ıisa	33	38 43N	0 03 E
ıjamin Aceval	124	24 58 S	57 34W
ıjamin Constant	126	4 40 S	70 15W
ıkelman	116	40 7N	101 32W
ıkovac	39	44 2N	15 37 E
ılidi	98	24 35 S	144 50 E
ınett	108	59 56N	134 53W
ınett, Ostrov	59	76 21N	148 56 E
ınettsville	115	34 38N	79 39W
ınington	114	42 52N	73 12W
ıoa	72	8 50 S	115 20 E
ıodet	18	47 53N	4 7W
ıoni	93	26 11 S	28 18 E
ıoud	82	32 20N	0 16 E
ısheim	25	49 40N	8 38 E
ıson	119	31 59N	110 19W
ıt	65	26 20N	59 31 E
ıteng	73	6 10 S	120 30 E
ıtinck I.	97	17 3 S	139 35 E
ıtiu	87	9 10N	29 55 E
ıto Gonçalves	125	29 10 S	51 31W
ıton, Ark., U.S.A.	117	34 30N	92 35W
ıton, Ill., U.S.A.	116	38 0N	88 55W
ıton Harbor	114	42 10N	86 28W
ıtong	71	3 31N	101 55 E
ıtu Liben	87	8 32N	38 21 E
ıue □	85	7 30N	7 30 E
ıue →	85	7 48N	6 46 E
ıxi	76	41 20N	123 48 E
ı	73	4 25N	126 50 E
ıgrad	42	44 50N	20 37 E
ıwawe	118	40 35N	116 30W
ıpu	74	33 15N	131 30 E
·ati	44	40 43N	19 59 E
·au, Teluk	73	2 30 S	132 30 E
·ber	86	18 0N	34 0 E
·bera	63	10 30N	45 2 E
·bérati	88	4 15N	15 40 E
·beria, C. del	33	38 39N	1 24 E
·bice →	126	6 20N	57 32W
·ceto	38	44 30N	10 0 E
·chtesgaden	25	47 37N	12 58 E
·ck-sur-Mer	19	50 25N	1 36 E
·dichev	56	49 57N	28 30 E
·dsk	58	54 47N	83 2 E
·dyansk	56	46 45N	36 50 E
·ea, Ky., U.S.A.	114	37 35N	84 18W
·ea, Ohio, U.S.A.	112	41 21N	81 50W
·ebere	73	2 25N	128 45 E
·eda	63	11 45N	51 0 E
·ekum	84	7 29N	2 34W
·enice	86	24 2N	35 25 E
·ens →	109	52 25N	97 2W
·ens I.	109	52 18N	97 18W
·ens River	109	52 25N	97 0W
·estechko	54	50 22N	25 5 E
·eşti	46	46 6N	27 50 E
·etău →	46	46 59N	21 7 E
·ettyo →	27	46 59N	21 7 E
·ettyóújfalu	27	47 13N	21 33 E
·evo, Majunga, Madag.	93	17 14 S	44 17 E
·evo, Tuléar, Madag.	93	19 44 S	44 58 E
·eza	54	52 31N	24 51 E
·ezhany	54	49 26N	24 58 E
·ezina →	54	52 33N	30 14 E
·ezna	55	51 35N	31 46 E
·ezniki	58	59 24N	56 46 E
·ezovka	56	47 14N	30 55 E
·ezovo	58	64 0N	65 0 E
·g	47	59 10N	11 18 E
·ga, Spain	32	42 6N	1 48 E
·ga, Sweden	49	57 14N	16 3 E
·gama	64	39 8N	27 15 E
Bérgamo	38	45 42N	9 40 E
Bergantiños	30	43 20N	8 40W
Bergedorf	24	53 28N	10 12 E
Bergen, Ger.	24	54 24N	13 26 E
Bergen, Neth.	16	52 40N	4 43 E
Bergen, Norway	47	60 23N	5 20 E
Bergen, U.S.A.	112	43 5N	77 56W
Bergen-op-Zoom	16	51 30N	4 18 E
Bergerac	20	44 51N	0 30 E
Bergheim	24	50 57N	6 38 E
Bergisch-Gladbach	24	50 59N	7 9 E
Bergkvara	49	56 23N	16 5 E
Bergsjö	48	61 59N	17 3 E
Bergues	19	50 58N	2 24 E
Bergum	16	53 13N	5 59 E
Bergvik	48	61 16N	16 50 E
Berhala, Selat	72	1 0 S	104 15 E
Berhampore	69	24 2N	88 27 E
Berhampur	70	19 15N	84 54 E
Berheci →	46	46 7N	27 19 E
Bering Sea	94	58 0N	167 0 E
Bering Str.	104	66 0N	170 0W
Beringen	16	51 3N	5 14 E
Beringovskiy	59	63 3N	179 19 E
Berislav	56	46 50N	33 30 E
Berisso	124	34 56 S	57 50W
Berja	33	36 50N	2 56W
Berkane	82	34 52N	2 20W
Berkeley	13	51 41N	2 28W
Berkeley Springs	114	39 38N	78 12W
Berkner I.	5	79 30 S	50 0W
Berkovitsa	43	43 16N	23 8 E
Berkshire □	13	51 30N	1 20W
Berland →	108	54 0N	116 50W
Berlanga	31	38 17N	5 50W
Berleburg	24	51 3N	8 22 E
Berlenga, Ilhas	31	39 25N	9 30W
Berlin, Ger.	24	52 32N	13 24 E
Berlin, Md., U.S.A.	114	38 19N	75 12W
Berlin, N.H., U.S.A.	114	44 29N	71 10W
Berlin, Wis., U.S.A.	114	43 58N	88 55W
Berlin, E. □	24	52 30N	13 30 E
Berlin, W. □	24	52 30N	13 20 E
Bermeja, Sierra	31	36 30N	5 11W
Bermejo →, Formosa, Argent.	124	26 51 S	58 23W
Bermejo →, San Juan, Argent.	124	32 30 S	67 30W
Bermeo	32	43 25N	2 47W
Bermillo de Sayago	30	41 22N	6 8W
Bermuda ■	121	32 45N	65 0W
Bern (Berne)	25	46 57N	7 28 E
Bern (Berne) □	25	46 45N	7 40 E
Bernado	119	34 30N	106 53W
Bernalda	41	40 24N	16 44 E
Bernalillo	119	35 17N	106 37W
Bernam →	71	3 45N	101 5 E
Bernardo de Irigoyen	125	26 15 S	53 40W
Bernasconi	124	37 55 S	63 44W
Bernau, Germ., E.	24	52 40N	13 35 E
Bernau, Germ., W.	25	47 45N	12 20 E
Bernay	18	49 5N	0 35 E
Bernburg	24	51 40N	11 42 E
Berndorf	26	47 59N	16 1 E
Berne = Bern	25	46 57N	7 28 E
Berneck	25	51 3N	11 40 E
Berner Alpen	25	46 27N	7 35 E
Bernese Oberland = Oberland	25	46 27N	7 35 E
Bernier I.	96	24 50 S	113 12 E
Bernina, Piz	25	46 20N	9 54 E
Bernkastel-Kues	25	49 55N	7 04 E
Beror Hayil	62	31 34N	34 38 E
Béroubouay	85	10 34N	2 46 E
Beroun	26	49 57N	14 5 E
Berounka →	26	50 0N	13 47 E
Berovo	42	41 38N	22 51 E
Berrahal	83	36 54N	7 33 E
Berre, Étang de	21	43 27N	5 5 E
Berrechid	82	33 18N	7 36W
Berri	99	34 14 S	140 35 E
Berriane	82	32 50N	3 46 E
Berrigan	100	35 38 S	145 49 E
Berrouaghia	82	36 10N	2 53 E
Berry, Austral.	99	34 46 S	150 43 E
Berry, France	19	47 0N	2 0 E
Berry Is.	121	25 40N	77 50W
Berryville	117	36 23N	93 35W
Bersenbrück	24	52 33N	7 56 E
Berthold	116	48 19N	101 45W
Berthoud	116	40 21N	105 5W
Bertincourt	19	50 5N	2 58 E
Bertoua	88	4 30N	13 45 E
Bertrand	116	40 35N	99 38W
Berufjörður	50	64 48N	14 29W
Berwick	114	41 4N	76 17W
Berwick-upon-Tweed	12	55 47N	2 0W
Berwyn Mts.	12	52 54N	3 26W
Berzasca	42	44 39N	21 58 E
Berzence	27	46 12N	17 11 E
Besalampy	93	16 43 S	44 29 E
Besançon	19	47 15N	6 0 E
Besar	72	2 40 S	116 0 E
Beserah	71	3 50N	103 21 E
Beshenkovichi	54	55 2N	29 29 E
Beška	42	45 8N	20 6 E
Beskydy	27	49 35N	18 40 E
Beslan	57	43 15N	44 28 E
Besna Kobila	42	42 31N	22 10 E
Besnard L.	109	55 25N	106 0W
Besni	64	37 41N	37 52 E
Besor, N. →	62	31 28N	34 22 E
Beşparmak Dağı	45	37 32N	27 30 E
Bessarabiya	46	47 0N	28 10 E
Bessarabka	56	46 21N	28 58 E
Bessèges	21	44 18N	4 8 E
Bessemer, Ala., U.S.A.	115	33 25N	86 57W
Bessemer, Mich., U.S.A.	116	46 27N	90 0W
Bessin	18	49 21N	1 0W
Bessines-sur-Gartempe	20	46 6N	1 22 E
Bet Alfa	62	32 31N	35 25 E
Bet Dagan	62	32 1N	34 49 E
Bet Guvrin	62	31 37N	34 54 E
Bet Ha'Emeq	62	32 58N	35 8 E
Bet Hashitta	62	32 31N	35 27 E
Bet Qeshet	62	32 41N	35 21 E
Bet She'an	62	32 30N	35 30 E
Bet Shemesh	62	31 44N	35 0 E
Bet Tadjine, Djebel	82	29 0N	3 30W
Bet Yosef	62	32 34N	35 33 E
Betafo	93	19 50 S	46 51 E
Betanzos	30	43 15N	8 12W
Bétaré Oya	88	5 40N	14 5 E
Bétera	32	39 35N	0 28W
Bethal	93	26 27 S	29 28 E
Bethanien	92	26 31 S	17 8 E
Bethany, S. Afr.	92	29 34 S	25 59 E
Bethany, U.S.A.	116	40 18N	94 0W
Bethany = Al Ayzarīyah	62	31 47N	35 15 E
Bethel, Alaska, U.S.A.	104	60 50N	161 50W
Bethel, Pa., U.S.A.	112	40 20N	80 2W
Bethel, Vt., U.S.A.	113	43 50N	72 37W
Bethlehem, S. Afr.	93	28 14 S	28 18 E
Bethlehem, U.S.A.	114	40 39N	75 24W
Bethlehem = Bayt Lahm	62	31 43N	35 12 E
Bethulie	92	30 30 S	25 59 E
Béthune	19	50 30N	2 38 E
Béthune →	18	49 53N	1 9 E
Betioky	93	23 48 S	44 20 E
Beton Bazoches	19	48 42N	3 15 E
Betong, Malay.	72	1 24N	111 31 E
Betong, Thai.	71	5 45N	101 5 E
Betoota	99	25 45 S	140 42 E
Betroka	93	23 16 S	46 0 E
Betsiamites	107	48 56N	68 40W
Betsiamites →	107	48 56N	68 38W
Betsiboka →	93	16 3 S	46 36 E
Betsjoeanaland	92	26 30 S	22 30 E
Bettiah	69	26 48N	84 33 E
Béttola	38	44 42N	9 32 E
Betul	68	21 58N	77 59 E
Betzdorf	24	50 47N	7 53 E
Beuca	46	44 14N	24 56 E
Beuil	21	44 6N	6 59 E
Beulah	116	47 18N	101 47W
Bevensen	24	53 5N	10 34 E
Beverley, Austral.	96	32 9 S	116 56 E
Beverley, U.K.	12	53 52N	0 26W
Beverly, Mass., U.S.A.	113	42 32N	70 50W
Beverly, Wash., U.S.A.	118	46 55N	119 59W
Beverly Hills	119	34 4N	118 29W
Beverwijk	16	52 28N	4 38 E
Bex	25	46 15N	7 0 E
Beyin	84	5 1N	2 41W
Beykoz	43	41 8N	29 7 E
Beyla	84	8 30N	8 38W
Beynat	20	45 8N	1 44 E
Beyneu	58	45 10N	55 3 E
Beypazarı	64	40 10N	31 56 E
Beyşehir Gölü	64	37 40N	31 45 E
Bezdan	42	45 50N	18 57 E
Bezet	62	33 4N	35 8 E
Bezhetsk	55	57 47N	36 39 E
Bezhitsa	54	53 19N	34 17 E
Béziers	20	43 20N	3 12 E
Bezwada = Vijayawada	70	16 31N	80 39 E
Bhadra →	70	14 0N	75 20 E
Bhadrakh	69	21 10N	86 30 E
Bhadravati	70	13 49N	75 40 E
Bhagalpur	69	25 10N	87 0 E
Bhaisa	70	19 10N	77 58 E
Bhakkar	68	31 40N	71 5 E
Bhakra Dam	68	31 30N	76 45 E
Bhamo	67	24 15N	97 15 E
Bhamragarh	70	19 30N	80 40 E
Bhandara	69	21 5N	79 42 E
Bhanrer Ra.	68	23 40N	79 45 E
Bharatpur	68	27 15N	77 30 E
Bharuch	68	21 47N	73 0 E
Bhatghar L.	70	18 10N	73 48 E
Bhatiapara Ghat	69	23 13N	89 42 E
Bhatinda	68	30 15N	74 57 E
Bhatkal	70	13 58N	74 35 E
Bhatpara	69	22 50N	88 25 E
Bhattiprolu	70	16 7N	80 45 E
Bhaun	68	32 55N	72 40 E
Bhaunagar = Bhavnagar	68	21 45N	72 10 E
Bhavani	70	11 27N	77 43 E
Bhavani →	70	11 0N	78 15 E
Bhavnagar	68	21 45N	72 10 E
Bhawanipatna	70	19 55N	80 10 E
Bhera	68	32 29N	72 57 E
Bhilsa = Vidisha	68	23 28N	77 53 E
Bhilwara	68	25 25N	74 38 E
Bhima →	70	16 25N	77 17 E
Bhimavaram	70	16 30N	81 30 E
Bhind	68	26 30N	78 46 E
Bhir	70	19 4N	75 46 E
Bhiwandi	70	19 20N	73 0 E
Bhiwani	68	28 50N	76 9 E
Bhola	69	22 45N	90 35 E
Bhongir	70	17 30N	78 56 E
Bhopal	68	23 20N	77 30 E
Bhor	70	18 12N	73 53 E
Bhubaneswar	69	20 15N	85 50 E
Bhuj	68	23 15N	69 49 E
Bhumibol Dam	72	17 15N	98 58 E
Bhusaval	68	21 3N	75 46 E
Bhutan ■	69	27 25N	90 30 E
Biafra, B. of = Bonny, Bight of	85	3 30N	9 20 E
Biak	73	1 10 S	136 6 E
Biała	28	50 24N	17 40 E
Biała →, Białystok, Poland	28	53 11N	23 4 E
Biała →, Tarnów, Poland	27	50 3N	20 55 E
Biała Piska	28	53 37N	22 5 E
Biała Podlaska	28	52 4N	23 6 E
Biała Podlaska □	28	52 0N	23 0 E
Biała Rawska	28	51 48N	20 29 E
Białobrzegi	28	52 27N	21 3 E
Białogard	28	54 2N	15 58 E
Białowieża	28	52 41N	23 49 E
Biały Bór	28	53 53N	16 51 E
Białystok	28	53 10N	23 10 E
Białystok □	28	53 9N	23 10 E
Biancavilla	41	37 39N	14 50 E
Biaro	73	2 5N	125 26 E
Biarritz	20	43 29N	1 33W
Biasca	25	46 22N	8 58 E
Biba	86	28 55N	31 0 E
Bibala	89	14 44 S	13 24 E
Bibane, Bahiret el	83	33 16N	11 13 E
Bibbiena	39	43 43N	11 50 E
Bibby I.	109	61 55N	93 0W
Biberach	25	48 5N	9 49 E
Bibey →	30	42 24N	7 13W
Bibiani	84	6 30N	2 8W
Bibile	70	7 10N	81 25 E
Biboohra	98	16 56 S	145 25 E
Bibungwa	90	2 40 S	28 15 E
Bic	107	48 20N	68 41W
Bicaj	44	42 0N	20 25 E
Bicaz	46	46 53N	26 5 E
Biccari	41	41 23N	15 12 E
Biche, La →	108	59 57N	123 50W
Bichena	87	10 28N	38 10 E
Bicknell, Ind., U.S.A.	114	38 50N	87 20W
Bicknell, Utah, U.S.A.	119	38 16N	111 35W
Bida	85	9 3N	5 58 E
Bidar	70	17 55N	77 35 E
Biddeford	107	43 30N	70 28W
Biddiyā	62	32 7N	35 4 E
Biddū	62	31 50N	35 8 E
Biddwara	87	5 11N	38 34 E
Bideford	13	51 1N	4 13W
Bidor	71	4 6N	101 15 E
Bié, Planalto de	89	12 0 S	16 0 E
Bieber	118	41 4N	121 6W
Biebrza →	28	53 13N	22 25 E
Biecz	27	49 44N	21 15 E
Biel (Bienne)	25	47 8N	7 14 E
Bielawa	28	50 43N	16 37 E
Bielé Karpaty	27	49 5N	18 0 E
Bielefeld	24	52 2N	8 31 E
Bielersee	25	47 6N	7 5 E
Biella	38	45 33N	8 3 E
Bielsk Podlaski	28	52 47N	23 12 E
Bielsko-Biała	27	49 50N	19 2 E
Bielsko-Biała □	27	49 45N	19 15 E
Bien Hoa	71	10 57N	106 49 E
Bienfait	109	49 10N	102 50W
Bienne = Biel	25	47 8N	7 14 E
Bienvenida	31	38 18N	6 12W
Bienville, L.	106	55 5N	72 40W
Biescas	32	42 37N	0 20W
Biese →	24	52 53N	11 46 E
Biesiesfontein	92	30 57 S	17 58 E
Bietigheim	25	48 57N	9 8 E
Biferno →	41	41 59N	15 2 E
Big →	107	54 50N	58 55W
Big B.	107	55 43N	60 35W
Big Beaver	109	49 10N	105 10W
Big Belt Mts.	118	46 50N	111 30W
Big Bend	93	26 50 S	32 2 E
Big Bend Nat. Park	117	29 15N	103 15W
Big Black →	117	32 0N	91 5W
Big Blue →	116	39 11N	96 40W
Big Cr. →	108	51 42N	122 41W
Big Cypress Swamp	115	26 12N	81 10W
Big Falls	116	48 11N	93 48W
Big Fork →	116	48 31N	93 43W
Big Horn	118	46 11N	107 25W
Big Horn Mts. = Bighorn Mts.	118	44 30N	107 30W
Big Lake	117	31 12N	101 25W
Big Moose	113	43 49N	74 58W
Big Muddy →	116	48 8N	104 36W
Big Pine	119	37 12N	118 17W
Big Piney	118	42 32N	110 3W
Big Quill L.	109	51 55N	104 50W
Big Rapids	114	43 42N	85 27W
Big River	109	53 50N	107 0W
Big Run	112	40 57N	78 55W
Big Sable Pt.	114	44 5N	86 30W
Big Sand L.	109	57 45N	99 45W
Big Sandy	118	48 12N	110 9W
Big Sandy Cr. →	116	38 6N	102 29W
Big Sioux →	116	42 30N	96 25W
Big Spring	117	32 10N	101 25W
Big Springs	116	41 4N	102 3W
Big Stone City	116	45 20N	96 30W
Big Stone Gap	115	36 52N	82 45W
Big Stone L.	116	45 30N	96 35W
Big Trout L.	106	53 40N	90 0W
Biganos	20	44 39N	0 59W
Bigfork	118	48 3N	114 2W
Biggar, Can.	109	52 4N	108 0W
Biggar, U.K.	14	55 38N	3 31W
Biggenden	99	25 31 S	152 4 E
Bighorn →	118	46 9N	107 28W
Bighorn Mts.	118	44 30N	107 30W
Bignona	84	12 52N	16 14W
Bigorre	20	43 6N	0 5 E
Bigstone L.	109	53 42N	95 44W
Bigtimber	118	45 53N	110 0W
Bigwa	90	7 10 S	39 10 E
Bihać	39	44 49N	15 57 E
Bihar	69	25 5N	85 40 E
Bihar □	69	25 0N	86 0 E
Biharamulo	90	2 25 S	31 25 E
Biharamulo □	90	2 30 S	31 20 E
Biharkeresztes	27	47 8N	21 44 E
Bihor □	46	47 0N	22 10 E
Bihor, Munţii	46	46 29N	22 47 E
Bijagós, Arquipélago dos	84	11 15N	16 10W
Bijaipur	68	26 2N	77 20 E
Bijapur, Mad. P., India	70	18 50N	80 50 E
Bijapur, Mysore, India	70	16 50N	75 55 E
Bījār	64	35 52N	47 35 E
Bijeljina	42	44 46N	19 17 E
Bijelo Polje	42	43 1N	19 45 E
Bijie	77	27 20N	105 16 E
Bijnor	68	29 27N	78 11 E
Bikaner	68	28 2N	73 18 E
Bikapur	69	26 30N	82 7 E
Bikin	59	46 50N	134 20 E
Bikini Atoll	94	12 0N	167 30 E
Bikoué	85	3 55N	11 50 E
Bilād Banī Bū 'Ali	65	22 0N	59 20 E
Bilara	68	26 14N	73 53 E
Bilaspur, Mad. P., India	69	22 2N	82 15 E

Bilaspur, Punjab, India 68 31 19N 76 50 E
Bilauk Taung dan 71 13 0N 99 0 E
Bilbao 32 43 16N 2 56W
Bilbeis 86 30 25N 31 34 E
Bilbor 46 47 6N 25 30 E
Bildudalur 50 65 41N 23 36W
Bileća 42 42 53N 18 27 E
Bilecik 64 40 5N 30 5 E
Biłgoraj 28 50 33N 22 42 E
Bilibino 59 68 3N 166 20 E
Bilibiza 91 12 30S 40 20 E
Bilir 59 65 40N 131 20 E
Bilishti 44 40 37N 21 2 E
Bill 116 43 18N 105 18W
Billabong Creek 100 35 5S 144 2 E
Billingham 12 54 36N 1 18W
Billings 118 45 43N 108 29W
Billingsfors 48 58 59N 12 15 E
Billiton Is = Belitung 72 3 10S 107 50 E
Billom 20 45 43N 3 20 E
Bilma 81 18 50N 13 30 E
Bilo Gora 42 45 53N 17 15 E
Biloela 97 24 24S 150 31 E
Biloxi 117 30 24N 88 53W
Bilpa Morea Claypan 99 25 0S 140 0 E
Biltine 81 14 40N 20 50 E
Bilyana 98 18 5S 145 50 E
Bilyarsk 55 54 58N 50 22 E
Bima 73 8 22S 118 49 E
Bimban 86 24 24N 32 54 E
Bimberi Peak 100 35 44S 148 51 E
Bimbila 85 8 54N 0 5 E
Bimbo 88 4 15N 18 33 E
Bimini Is. 121 25 42N 79 25W
Bin Xian 77 35 2N 108 4 E
Bina-Etawah 68 24 13N 78 14 E
Binalbagan 73 10 12N 122 50 E
Binalong 100 34 40S 148 39 E
Binalud, Kuh-e 65 36 30N 58 30 E
Binatang 72 2 10N 111 40 E
Binche 16 50 26N 4 10 E
Binda 99 27 52S 147 21 E
Bindle 99 27 40S 148 45 E
Bindura 91 17 18S 31 18 E
Bingara, N.S.W., Austral. 99 29 52S 150 36 E
Bingara, Queens., Austral. 99 28 10S 144 37 E
Bingen 25 49 57N 7 53 E
Bingerville 84 5 18N 3 49W
Bingham 107 45 5N 69 50W
Bingham Canyon 118 40 31N 112 10W
Binghamton 114 42 9N 75 54W
Bingöl 64 38 53N 40 29 E
Binh Dinh = An Nhon 71 13 55N 109 7 E
Binh Son 71 15 20N 108 40 E
Binjai 72 3 20N 98 30 E
Binnaway 99 31 28S 149 24 E
Binongko 73 5 55S 123 55 E
Binscarth 109 50 37N 101 17W
Bint Jubayl 62 33 8N 35 25 E
Bintan 72 1 0N 104 0 E
Bintulu 72 3 10N 113 0 E
Bintuni (Steenkool) 73 2 7S 133 32 E
Binyamina 62 32 32N 34 56 E
Binyang 77 23 12N 108 47 E
Binz 24 54 23N 13 37 E
Binzert = Bizerte 83 37 15N 9 50 E
Bio Bio □ 124 37 35S 72 0W
Biograd 39 43 56N 15 29 E
Biokovo 42 43 23N 17 0 E
Biougra 82 30 15N 9 14W
Biq'at Bet Netofa 62 32 49N 35 22 E
Bîr Abu Hashim 86 23 42N 34 6 E
Bîr Abu M'nqar 86 26 33N 27 33 E
Bîr Adal Deib 86 22 35N 36 10 E
Bi'r al Malfa 83 31 58N 15 18 E
Bir Aouine 83 32 25N 9 18 E
Bîr 'Asal 86 25 55N 34 20 E
Bir Autrun 81 18 15N 26 40 E
Bi'r Dhu'fān 83 31 59N 14 32 E
Bîr Diqnash 86 31 3N 25 23 E
Bir el Abbes 82 26 7N 6 9W
Bir el Ater 83 34 46N 8 3 E
Bîr el Basur 86 29 51N 25 49 E
Bîr el Gellaz 86 30 50N 26 40 E
Bîr el Shaqqa 86 30 54N 25 1 E
Bîr Fuad 86 30 35N 26 28 E
Bîr Haimur 86 22 45N 33 40 E
Bîr Jdid 82 33 26N 8 0W
Bîr Kanayis 86 24 59N 33 15 E
Bîr Kerawein 86 27 10N 28 25 E
Bîr Lahrache 83 32 1N 8 12 E
Bîr Maql 86 23 7N 33 40 E
Bîr Misaha 86 22 13N 27 59 E
Bir Mogrein 82 25 10N 11 25W
Bi'r Mubayrīk 64 23 22N 39 8 E
Bîr Murr 86 23 28N 30 10 E
Bi'r Nabālā 62 31 52N 35 12 E
Bîr Nakheila 86 24 1N 30 50 E
Bîr Qatrani 86 30 55N 26 10 E
Bîr Ranga 86 24 25N 35 15 E
Bir, Ras 87 12 0N 43 20 E
Bîr Sahara 86 22 54N 28 40 E
Bîr Seiyâla 86 26 10N 33 50 E
Bir Semguine 82 30 1N 5 39W
Bîr Shalatein 86 23 5N 35 25 E
Bîr Shebb 86 22 25N 29 40 E
Bîr Shût 86 23 50N 35 15 E
Bîr Terfawi 86 22 57N 28 55 E
Bîr Umm Qubûr 86 24 35N 34 2 E
Bîr Ungât 86 22 8N 33 48 E
Bîr Za'farâna 86 29 10N 32 40 E
Bîr Zāmūs 83 24 16N 15 6 E
Bi'r Zayt 62 31 59N 35 11 E
Bîr Zeidûn 86 25 45N 33 40 E
Bira 73 2 3S 132 2 E
Bîra 46 47 2N 27 3 E
Birak Sulaymān 62 31 42N 35 7 E
Biramféro 84 11 40N 9 10W
Birao 81 10 20N 22 47 E
Birawa 90 2 20S 28 48 E
Bîrca 46 43 59N 23 36 E
Birch Hills 109 52 59N 105 25W
Birch I. 109 52 26N 99 54W
Birch L., N.W.T., Can. 108 62 4N 116 33W
Birch L., Ont., Can. 106 51 23N 92 18W
Birch L., U.S.A. 106 47 48N 91 43W
Birch Mts. 108 57 30N 113 10W
Birch River 109 52 24N 101 6W
Birchip 99 35 56S 142 55 E
Birchiş 46 45 58N 22 9 E
Bird 109 56 30N 94 13W
Bird City 116 39 48N 101 33W
Bird I., Austral. 97 22 10S 155 28 E
Bird I., S. Afr. 92 32 3S 18 17 E
Bird I. = Aves, I. de 121 12 0N 67 30W
Birdlip 13 51 50N 2 7W
Birdsville 97 25 51S 139 20 E
Birdum 96 15 39S 133 13 E
Birecik 64 37 0N 38 0 E
Bireuen 72 5 14N 96 39 E
Birifo 84 13 30N 14 0W
Birigui 125 21 18S 50 16W
Birk 86 18 8N 41 30 E
Birka 86 22 11N 40 38 E
Birkenfeld 25 49 39N 7 11 E
Birkenhead 12 53 24N 3 1W
Birket Qârûn 86 29 30N 30 40 E
Birkfeld 26 47 21N 15 45 E
Birkhadem 82 36 43N 3 3 E
Birlad 46 46 15N 27 38 E
Birmingham, U.K. 13 52 30N 1 55W
Birmingham, U.S.A. 115 33 31N 86 50W
Birmitrapur 69 22 24N 84 46 E
Birni Ngaouré 85 13 5N 2 51 E
Birni Nkonni 85 13 55N 5 15 E
Birnin Gwari 85 11 0N 6 45 E
Birnin Kebbi 85 12 32N 4 12 E
Birnin Kudu 85 11 30N 9 29 E
Birobidzhan 59 48 50N 132 50 E
Birqīn 62 32 27N 35 15 E
Birr 15 53 7N 7 55W
Birrie → 99 29 43S 146 37 E
Birsilpur 68 28 11N 72 15 E
Birsk 52 55 25N 55 30 E
Birtin 46 46 59N 22 31 E
Birtle 109 50 30N 101 5W
Biryuchiy 56 46 10N 35 0 E
Birzai 54 56 11N 24 45 E
Bîrzava 46 46 7N 21 59 E
Bisa 73 1 15S 127 28 E
Bisáccia 41 41 0N 15 20 E
Bisacquino 40 37 42N 13 13 E
Bisalpur 69 28 14N 79 48 E
Bisbal, La 32 41 58N 3 2 E
Bisbee 119 31 30N 110 0W
Biscarrosse, Étang de 20 44 21N 1 10W
Biscay, B. of 6 45 0N 2 0W
Biscayne B. 115 25 40N 80 12W
Bisceglie 41 41 14N 16 30 E
Bischofshofen 26 47 26N 13 14 E
Bischofswerda 24 51 8N 14 11 E
Bischwiller 19 48 41N 7 50 E
Biscoe Bay 5 77 0S 152 0W
Biscoe I. 5 66 0S 67 0W
Biscostasing 106 47 18N 82 9W
Biševo 39 42 57N 16 3 E
Bisha 87 15 30N 37 31 E
Bisha, Wadi → 86 21 24N 43 26 E
Bishop, Calif., U.S.A. 119 37 20N 118 26W
Bishop, Tex., U.S.A. 117 27 35N 97 49W
Bishop Auckland 12 54 40N 1 40W
Bishop's Falls 107 49 2N 55 30W
Bishop's Stortford 13 51 52N 0 11 E
Bisignano 41 39 30N 16 17 E
Bisina, L. 90 1 38N 33 56 E
Biskra 83 34 50N 5 44 E
Biskupiec 28 53 53N 20 58 E
Bislig 73 8 15N 126 27 E
Bismarck 116 46 49N 100 49W
Bismarck Arch. 94 2 30S 150 0 E
Bismarck Sea 98 4 10S 146 50 E
Bismark 24 52 39N 11 31 E
Biso 90 1 44N 31 26 E
Bison 116 45 34N 102 28W
Bispfors 50 63 1N 16 37 E
Bispgården 48 63 2N 16 40 E
Bissagos = Bijagós, Arquipélago
dos 84 11 15N 16 10W
Bissau 84 11 45N 15 45W
Bissett 109 51 2N 95 41W
Bissikrima 84 10 50N 10 58W
Bistcho L. 108 59 45N 118 50W
Bistreţu 46 43 54N 23 23 E
Bistrica = Ilirska-Bistrica 39 45 34N 14 14 E
Bistriţa 46 47 9N 24 35 E
Bistriţa → 46 46 30N 26 57 E
Bistriţa Năsăud □ 46 47 15N 24 30 E
Bistriţei, Munţii 46 47 15N 25 40 E
Biswan 69 27 29N 81 2 E
Bisztynek 28 54 8N 20 53 E
Bitam 88 2 5N 11 25 E
Bitburg 25 49 58N 6 32 E
Bitche 19 49 2N 7 25 E
Bitkine 81 11 59N 18 13 E
Bitlis 64 38 20N 42 3 E
Bitola (Bitolj) 42 41 5N 21 10 E
Bitonto 41 41 7N 16 40 E
Bitter Creek 118 41 39N 108 36W
Bitter L. = Buheirat-Murrat-el-
Kubra 86 30 15N 32 40 E
Bitterfeld 24 51 36N 12 20 E
Bitterfontein 92 31 0S 18 32 E
Bitterroot → 118 46 52N 114 6W
Bitterroot Range 118 46 0N 114 20W
Bitti 40 40 29N 9 20 E
Bittou 85 11 17N 0 18W
Biu 85 10 40N 12 3 E
Bivolari 46 47 31N 27 27 E
Bivolu 46 47 16N 25 58 E
Biwa-Ko 74 35 15N 136 10 E
Biwabik 116 47 33N 92 19W
Bixad 46 47 56N 23 28 E
Biyang 77 32 38N 113 21 E
Biysk 58 52 40N 85 0 E
Bizana 93 30 50S 29 52 E
Bizerte (Binzert) 83 37 15N 9 50 E
Bjargtangar 50 65 30N 24 30W
Bjelasica 42 42 50N 19 40 E
Bjelašnica 42 43 43N 18 9 E
Bjelovar 42 45 56N 16 49 E
Bjerringbro 49 56 23N 9 39 E
Björbo 48 60 27N 14 44 E
Björneborg 48 59 14N 14 16 E
Bjørnøya 4 74 30N 19 0 E
Bjuv 49 56 5N 12 55 E
Blace 42 43 18N 21 17 E
Blachownia 28 50 49N 18 56 E
Black →, Can. 112 44 42N 79 19W
Black →, Ark., U.S.A. 117 35 38N 91 19W
Black →, N.Y., U.S.A. 113 43 59N 76 4W
Black →, Wis., U.S.A. 116 43 52N 91 22W
Black Diamond 108 50 45N 114 14W
Black Forest = Schwarzwald 25 48 0N 8 0 E
Black Hills 116 44 0N 103 50W
Black I. 109 51 12N 96 30W
Black L., Can. 109 59 12N 105 15W
Black L., U.S.A. 114 45 28N 84 15W
Black Mesa, Mt. 117 36 57N 102 55W
Black Mt. = Mynydd Du 13 51 45N 3 45W
Black Mts. 13 51 52N 3 5W
Black Range 119 33 30N 107 55W
Black River 121 18 0N 77 50W
Black River Falls 116 44 23N 90 52W
Black Sea 9 43 30N 35 0 E
Black Sugarloaf, Mt. 100 31 18S 151 35 E
Black Volta → 84 8 41N 1 33W
Black Warrior → 115 32 32N 87 51W
Blackall 97 24 25S 145 45 E
Blackball 101 42 22S 171 26 E
Blackbull 98 17 55S 141 45 E
Blackburn 12 53 44N 2 30W
Blackduck 116 47 43N 94 32W
Blackfoot 118 43 13N 112 12W
Blackfoot → 118 46 52N 113 53W
Blackfoot River Res. 118 43 0N 111 35W
Blackie 108 50 36N 113 37W
Blackpool 12 53 48N 3 3W
Blackriver 112 44 46N 83 17W
Blacks Harbour 107 45 3N 66 49W
Blacksburg 114 37 17N 80 23W
Blacksod B. 15 54 6N 10 0W
Blackstone 114 37 6N 78 0W
Blackstone → 108 61 5N 122 55W
Blackstone Ra. 96 26 00S 129 00 E
Blackville 107 46 44N 65 50W
Blackwater 98 23 35S 148 53 E
Blackwater →, Ireland 15 51 55N 7 50W
Blackwater →, U.K. 15 54 31N 6 35W
Blackwater Cr. → 99 25 56S 144 30 E
Blackwell 117 36 55N 97 20W
Blaenau Ffestiniog 12 53 0N 3 57W
Blagaj 42 43 16N 17 55 E
Blagodarnoye 57 45 7N 43 37 E
Blagoevgrad (Gorna Dzhumayo) 42 42 2N 23 5 E
Blagoveshchensk 59 50 20N 127 30 E
Blain 18 47 29N 1 45W
Blaine 118 48 59N 122 43W
Blaine Lake 109 52 51N 106 52W
Blainville 19 48 33N 6 23 E
Blair 116 41 38N 96 10W
Blair Athol 97 22 42S 147 31 E
Blair Atholl 14 56 46N 3 50W
Blairgowrie 14 56 36N 3 20W
Blairmore 108 49 40N 114 25W
Blairsville 112 40 27N 79 15W
Blaj 46 46 10N 23 57 E
Blake Pt. 116 48 12N 88 27W
Blakely 115 31 22N 85 0W
Blâmont 19 48 35N 6 50 E
Blanc, C. 83 37 15N 9 56 E
Blanc, Le 20 46 37N 1 3 E
Blanc, Mont 21 45 48N 6 50 E
Blanca, Bahía 128 39 10S 61 30W
Blanca Peak 119 37 35N 105 29W
Blanchard 117 35 8N 97 40W
Blanche L., S. Austral., Austral. 97 29 15S 139 40 E
Blanche L., W. Austral., Austral. 96 22 25S 123 17 E
Blanco, S. Afr. 92 33 55S 22 23 E
Blanco, U.S.A. 117 30 7N 98 30W
Blanco → 124 30 20S 68 42W
Blanco, C., C. Rica 121 9 34N 85 8W
Blanco, C., Spain 33 39 21N 2 51 E
Blanco, C., U.S.A. 118 42 50N 124 40W
Blanda → 50 65 20N 19 40W
Blandford Forum 13 50 52N 2 10W
Blanding 119 37 35N 109 30W
Blanes 32 41 40N 2 48 E
Blanice → 26 49 10N 14 5 E
Blankenberge 16 51 20N 3 9 E
Blankenburg 24 51 46N 10 56 E
Blanquefort 20 44 55N 0 38W
Blanquillo 125 32 53S 55 37W
Blansko 27 49 22N 16 40 E
Blantyre 91 15 45S 35 0 E
Blarney 15 51 57N 8 35W
Błaski 28 51 38N 18 30 E
Blatná 26 49 25N 13 52 E
Blatnitsa 43 43 41N 28 32 E
Blato 39 42 56N 16 48 E
Blaubeuren 25 48 24N 9 47 E
Blaydon 12 54 56N 1 47W
Blaye 20 45 8N 0 40W
Blaye-les-Mines 20 44 1N 2 8 E
Blayney 99 33 32S 149 14 E
Blaze, Pt. 96 12 56S 130 11 E
Błażowa 27 49 53N 22 7 E
Bleckede 24 53 18N 10 43 E
Bled 39 46 27N 14 7 E
Blednaya, Gora 58 76 20N 65 0 E
Bleiburg 26 46 35N 14 49 E
Blejeşti 46 44 19N 25 27 E
Blekinge län □ 49 56 20N 15 20 E
Blenheim, Can. 112 42 20N 82 0W
Blenheim, N.Z. 101 41 38S 173 57 E
Bléone → 21 44 5N 6 0 E
Bletchley 13 51 59N 0 44W
Bleymard, Le 20 44 30N 3 4
Blida 82 36 30N 2 4
Blidet Amor 83 32 59N 5 5
Blidö 48 59 37N 18 5
Blidsberg 49 57 56N 13 3
Bligh Sound 101 44 47S 167 3
Blind River 106 46 10N 82 5
Blinishti 44 41 52N 19 5
Blitar 73 8 5S 112 1
Blitta 85 8 23N 1
Block I. 114 41 11N 71 3
Block Island Sd. 113 41 17N 71 3
Bloemfontein 92 29 6S 26 1
Bloemhof 92 27 38S 25 3
Blois 18 47 35N 1 2
Blomskog 48 59 16N 12
Blönduós 50 65 40N 20 1
Błonie 28 52 12N 20 3
Bloodvein → 109 51 47N 96 4
Bloody Foreland 15 55 10N 8 1
Bloomer 116 45 8N 91 3
Bloomfield, Can. 112 43 59N 77 1
Bloomfield, Iowa, U.S.A. 116 40 44N 92 2
Bloomfield, N. Mexico, U.S.A. 119 36 46N 107 5
Bloomfield, Nebr., U.S.A. 116 42 38N 97 4
Bloomfield River Mission 98 15 56S 145 2
Bloomington, Ill., U.S.A. 116 40 27N 89
Bloomington, Ind., U.S.A. 114 39 10N 86 3
Bloomsburg 114 41 0N 76 3
Blora 73 6 57S 111 2
Blossburg 112 41 40N 77
Blouberg 93 23 8S 29
Blountstown 115 30 28N 85
Bludenz 26 47 10N 9 5
Blue Island 114 41 40N 87 4
Blue Lake 118 40 53N 124
Blue Mesa Res. 119 38 30N 107 1
Blue Mts., Austral. 97 33 40S 150
Blue Mts., Ore., U.S.A. 118 45 15N 119
Blue Mts., Pa., U.S.A. 114 40 30N 76 3
Blue Mud B. 97 13 30S 136
Blue Nile = An Nîl el Azraq □ 87 12 30N 34 3
Blue Nile = Nîl el Azraq → 87 15 38N 32 3
Blue Rapids 116 39 41N 96 3
Blue Ridge Mts. 115 36 30N 80 1
Blue Stack Mts. 15 54 46N 8
Blueberry → 108 56 45N 120 4
Bluefield 114 37 18N 81 1
Bluefields 121 12 20N 83 5
Bluff, Austral. 98 23 35S 149
Bluff, N.Z. 101 46 37S 168 2
Bluff, U.S.A. 119 37 17N 109 3
Bluffton 114 40 43N 85
Blumenau 125 27 0S 49
Blumenthal 24 53 5N 8 2
Blunt 116 44 32N 100
Bly 118 42 23N 121
Blyberg 48 61 9N 14 1
Blyth, Can. 112 43 44N 81 2
Blyth, U.K. 12 55 8N 1 3
Blythe 119 33 40N 114 3
Blytheswood 112 42 8N 82 3
Bø 47 59 25N 9
Bo 84 7 55N 11 5
Bo Duc 71 11 58N 106 5
Bo Hai 76 39 0N 120
Bo Xian 77 33 50N 115 4
Boa Vista 126 2 48N 60 3
Boaco 121 12 29N 85 3
Boal 30 43 25N 6 4
Boatman 99 27 16S 146 5
Bobai 77 22 17N 109 5
Bobbili 70 18 35N 83 3
Bóbbio 38 44 47N 9 2
Bobcaygeon 106 44 33N 78 3
Böblingen 25 48 41N 9 1
Bobo-Dioulasso 84 11 8N 4 1
Boboc 43 45 13N 26 5
Bobolice 28 53 58N 16 37
Boboshevo 42 42 9N 23 0
Bobov Dol 42 42 20N 23 0
Bóbr → 28 52 4N 15 4
Bobraomby, Tanjon' i 93 12 40S 49 10
Bobrinets 56 48 4N 32 5
Bobrov 55 51 5N 40 2
Bobruysk 54 53 10N 29 15
Bôca do Acre 126 8 50S 67 27
Boca, La 120 8 56N 79 30
Boca Raton 115 26 21N 80 5
Bocaiúva 127 17 7S 43 49
Bocanda 84 7 5N 4 31
Bocaranga 88 7 0N 15 35
Bocas del Toro 121 9 15N 82 20
Boceguillas 32 41 20N 3 39
Bochnia 27 49 58N 20 27
Bocholt 24 51 50N 6 35
Bochov 26 50 9N 13 3
Bochum 24 51 28N 7 12
Bockenem 24 52 1N 10 8
Boćki 28 52 39N 23 3
Bocşa Montană 42 45 21N 21 47
Boda 88 4 19N 17 26
Böda 49 57 15N 17 3
Bodafors 49 57 48N 14 23
Bodaybo 59 57 50N 114 0
Boden 50 65 50N 21 42
Bodensee 25 47 35N 9 25
Bodenteich 24 52 49N 10 41
Bodhan 70 18 40N 77 44
Bodinayakkanur 70 10 2N 77 10
Bodinga 85 12 58N 5 10
Bodmin 13 50 28N 4 44
Bodmin Moor 13 50 33N 4 36
Bodrog → 27 48 15N 21 35
Bodrum 64 37 5N 27 30
Bódva → 27 48 19N 20 45
Boegoebergdam 92 29 7S 22 9
Boën 21 45 44N 4 0
Boende 88 0 24S 21 12
Boerne 117 29 48N 98 41
Boffa 84 10 16N 14 3
Bogalusa 117 30 50N 89 55

Bogan → 97 29 59 S 146 17 E
Bogan Gate 99 33 7 S 147 49 E
Bogantungan 98 23 41 S 147 17 E
Bogata 117 33 26N 95 10W
Bogatić 42 44 51N 19 30 E
Bogenfels 92 27 25 S 15 25 E
Bogense 49 55 34N 10 5 E
Boggabilla 99 28 36 S 150 24 E
Boggabri 99 30 45 S 150 0 E
Boggeragh Mts. 15 52 2N 8 55W
Bognor Regis 13 50 47N 0 40W
Bogø 49 54 55N 12 2 E
Bogo 73 11 3N 124 0 E
Bogodukhov 54 50 9N 35 33 E
Bogong, Mt. 97 36 47 S 147 17 E
Bogor 73 6 36 S 106 48 E
Bogoroditsk 55 53 47N 38 8 E
Bogorodsk 55 56 4N 43 30 E
Bogorodskoye 59 52 22N 140 30 E
Bogoso 84 5 38N 2 3W
Bogota 126 4 34N 74 0W
Bogotol 58 56 15N 89 50 E
Bogra 69 24 51N 89 22 E
Boguchany 59 58 40N 97 30 E
Boguchar 57 49 55N 40 32 E
Bogué 84 16 45N 14 10W
Boguslav 56 49 47N 30 53 E
Boguszów 28 50 45N 16 12 E
Bohain 19 49 59N 3 28 E
Bohemia 26 50 0N 14 0 E
Bohemian Forest = Böhmerwald 25 49 30N 12 40 E
Bohena Cr. → 99 30 17 S 149 42 E
Bohinjska Bistrica 39 46 17N 14 1 E
Böhmerwald 25 49 30N 12 40 E
Bohmte 24 52 24N 8 20 E
Bohol 73 9 50N 124 10 E
Bohotleh 63 8 20N 46 25 E
Boi 85 9 35N 9 27 E
Boi, Pta. de 125 23 55 S 45 15W
Boiano 41 41 28N 14 29 E
Boileau, C. 96 17 40 S 122 7 E
Boinitsa 42 43 58N 22 32 E
Boise 118 43 43N 116 9W
Boise City 117 36 45N 102 30W
Boissevain 109 49 15N 100 5W
Boite → 39 46 5N 12 5 E
Boitzenburg 24 53 16N 13 36 E
Boizenburg 24 53 22N 10 42 E
Bojador C. 80 26 0N 14 30W
Bojana → 42 41 52N 19 22 E
Bojanowo 28 51 43N 16 42 E
Bojnūrd 65 37 30N 57 20 E
Bojonegoro 73 7 11 S 111 54 E
Boju 85 7 22N 7 55 E
Boka 42 45 22N 20 52 E
Boka Kotorska 42 42 23N 18 32 E
Bokala 84 8 31N 4 33W
Boké 84 10 56N 14 17W
Bokhara → 99 29 55 S 146 42 E
Bokkos 85 9 17N 9 1 E
Boknafjorden 47 59 14N 5 40 E
Bokoro 81 12 25N 17 14 E
Bokote 88 0 12 S 21 8 E
Bokpyin 71 11 18N 98 42 E
Boksitogorsk 54 59 32N 33 56 E
Bokungu 88 0 35 S 22 50 E
Bol, Chad 81 13 30N 15 0 E
Bol, Yugo. 39 43 18N 16 38 E
Bolama 84 11 30N 15 30W
Bolan Pass 66 29 50N 67 20 E
Bolaños → 120 21 14N 104 8W
Bolbec 18 49 30N 0 30 E
Boldeşti 46 45 3N 26 2 E
Bole, China 75 45 11N 81 37 E
Bole, Ethiopia 87 6 36N 37 20 E
Bolekhov 54 49 0N 24 0 E
Bolesławiec 28 51 17N 15 37 E
Bolgatanga 85 10 44N 0 53W
Bolgrad 56 45 40N 28 32 E
Boli, China 76 45 46N 130 31 E
Boli, Sudan 87 6 2N 28 48 E
Bolinao C. 73 16 23N 119 55 E
Bolívar, Argent. 124 36 15 S 60 53W
Bolívar, Colomb. 126 2 0N 77 0W
Bolivar, Mo., U.S.A. 117 37 38N 93 22W
Bolivar, Tenn., U.S.A. 117 35 14N 89 0W
Bolivia ■ 126 17 6 S 64 0W
Boljevac 42 43 51N 21 58 E
Bolkhov 55 53 25N 36 0 E
Bollène 21 44 18N 4 45 E
Bollnäs 48 61 21N 16 24 E
Bollon 99 28 2 S 147 29 E
Bollstabruk 48 63 1N 17 40 E
Bollullos 31 37 19N 6 32W
Bolmen 49 56 55N 13 40 E
Bolobo 88 2 6 S 16 20 E
Bologna 39 44 30N 11 20 E
Bologne 19 48 10N 5 8 E
Bologoye 54 57 55N 34 0 E
Bolomba 88 0 35N 19 0 E
Bolong 73 7 6N 122 16 E
Boloven, Cao Nguyen 71 15 10N 106 30 E
Bolpur 69 23 40N 87 45 E
Bolsena 39 42 40N 11 58 E
Bolsena, L. di 39 42 35N 11 55 E
Bolshaya Glushitsa 55 52 24N 50 29 E
Bolshaya Martynovka 57 47 12N 41 46 E
Bolshaya Vradiyevka 56 47 50N 30 40 E
Bolshereche 58 56 4N 74 45 E
Bolshevik, Ostrov 59 78 30N 102 0 E
Bolshezemelskaya Tundra 52 67 0N 56 0 E
Bolshoi Kavkas 57 42 50N 44 0 E
Bolshoy Anyuy → 59 68 30N 160 49 E
Bolshoy Atlym 58 62 25N 66 50 E
Bolshoy Begichev, Ostrov 59 74 20N 112 30 E
Bolshoy Lyakhovskiy, Ostrov 59 73 35N 142 0 E
Bolshoy Tokmak 56 47 16N 35 42 E
Bol'shoy Tyuters, Ostrov 54 59 51N 27 13 E
Bolsward 16 53 3N 5 32 E
Boltaña 32 42 28N 0 4 E
Boltigen 25 46 38N 7 24 E
Bolton, Can. 112 43 54N 79 45W
Bolton, U.K. 12 53 35N 2 26W
Bolu 64 40 45N 31 35 E
Bolvadin 64 38 45N 31 4 E
Bolzano (Bozen) 39 46 30N 11 20 E
Bom Despacho 127 19 43 S 45 15W
Bom Jesus da Lapa 127 13 15 S 43 25W
Boma 88 5 50 S 13 4 E
Bomaderry 99 34 52 S 150 37 E
Bombala 97 36 56 S 149 15 E
Bombarral 31 39 15N 9 9W
Bombay 70 18 55N 72 50 E
Bomboma 88 2 25N 18 55 E
Bombombwa 90 1 40N 25 40 E
Bomi Hills 84 7 1N 10 38W
Bomili 90 1 45N 27 5 E
Bomokandi → 90 3 39N 26 8 E
Bomongo 88 1 27N 18 21 E
Bomu → 88 4 40N 23 30 E
Bon C. 83 37 1N 11 2 E
Bonaire 121 12 10N 68 15W
Bonang 99 37 11 S 148 41 E
Bonanza 121 13 54N 84 35W
Bonaparte Archipelago 96 14 0 S 124 30 E
Boñar 30 42 52N 5 19W
Bonaventure 107 48 5N 65 32W
Bonavista 107 48 40N 53 5W
Bonavista, C. 107 48 42N 53 5W
Bondeno 39 44 53N 11 22 E
Bondo 88 3 55N 23 53 E
Bondoukou 84 8 2N 2 47W
Bondowoso 73 7 56 S 113 49 E
Bone Rate 73 7 25 S 121 5 E
Bone Rate, Kepulauan 73 6 30 S 121 10 E
Bone, Teluk 73 4 10 S 120 50 E
Bonefro 41 41 42N 14 55 E
Bo'ness 14 56 0N 3 38W
Bong Son = Hoai Nhon 71 14 28N 109 1 E
Bongandanga 88 1 24N 21 3 E
Bongor 81 10 35N 15 20 E
Bongouanou 84 6 42N 4 15W
Bonham 117 33 30N 96 10W
Bonifacio 21 41 24N 9 10 E
Bonifacio, Bouches de 40 41 12N 9 15 E
Bonin Is. 94 27 0N 142 0 E
Bonke 87 6 5N 37 16 E
Bonn 24 50 43N 7 6 E
Bonnat 20 46 20N 1 54 E
Bonne Terre 117 37 57N 90 33W
Bonners Ferry 118 48 38N 116 21W
Bonnétable 18 48 11N 0 25 E
Bonneuil-Matours 18 46 41N 0 34 E
Bonneval 18 48 11N 1 24 E
Bonneville 21 46 5N 6 24 E
Bonney, L. 99 37 50 S 140 20 E
Bonnie Rock 96 30 29 S 118 22 E
Bonny, France 19 47 34N 2 50 E
Bonny, Nigeria 85 4 25N 7 13 E
Bonny → 85 4 20N 7 10 E
Bonny, Bight of 85 3 30N 9 20 E
Bonnyville 109 54 20N 110 45W
Bonoi 73 1 45 S 137 41 E
Bonorva 40 40 25N 8 47 E
Bontang 72 0 10N 117 30 E
Bonthain 73 5 34 S 119 56 E
Bonthe 84 7 30N 12 33W
Bontoc 73 17 7N 120 58 E
Bonyeri 84 5 1N 2 46W
Bonyhád 27 46 18N 18 32 E
Booker 117 36 29N 100 30W
Boolaboolka, L. 99 32 38 S 143 10 E
Booligal 99 33 58 S 144 53 E
Boom 16 51 6N 4 20 E
Boonah 99 27 58 S 152 41 E
Boone, Iowa, U.S.A. 116 42 5N 93 53W
Boone, N.C., U.S.A. 115 36 14N 81 43W
Booneville, Ark., U.S.A. 117 35 10N 93 54W
Booneville, Miss., U.S.A. 115 34 39N 88 34W
Boonville, Ind., U.S.A. 114 38 3N 87 13W
Boonville, Mo., U.S.A. 116 38 57N 92 45W
Boonville, N.Y., U.S.A. 114 43 31N 75 20W
Boorindal 99 30 22 S 146 11 E
Boorowa 99 34 28 S 148 44 E
Boothia, Gulf of 105 71 0N 90 0W
Boothia Pen. 104 71 0N 94 0W
Bootle, Cumb., U.K. 12 54 17N 3 24W
Bootle, Merseyside, U.K. 12 53 28N 3 1W
Booué 88 0 5 S 11 55 E
Bopeechee 99 29 36 S 137 22 E
Bophuthatswana □ 92 26 0 S 26 0 E
Boppard 25 50 13N 7 36 E
Boquete 121 8 49N 82 27W
Bor 26 49 41N 12 45 E
Bôr 87 6 10N 31 40 E
Bor, Sweden 49 57 9N 14 10 E
Bor, Yugo. 42 44 8N 22 7 E
Borah, Mt. 118 44 19N 113 46W
Borama 63 9 55N 43 7 E
Borang 87 4 50N 30 59 E
Borås 49 57 43N 12 56 E
Borāzjān 65 29 22N 51 10 E
Borba, Brazil 126 4 12 S 59 34W
Borba, Port. 31 38 50N 7 26W
Borçka 57 41 25N 41 41 E
Bordeaux 20 44 50N 0 36W
Borden 107 46 18N 63 47W
Borden I. 4 78 30N 111 30W
Borders □ 14 55 35N 2 50W
Bordertown 97 36 19 S 140 45 E
Borđeyri 50 65 12N 21 6W
Bordighera 38 43 47N 7 40 E
Bordj bou Arreridj 83 36 4N 4 45 E
Bordj Bourguiba 83 32 12N 10 2 E
Bordj el Hobra 83 32 9N 4 51 E
Bordj Fly Ste. Marie 82 27 19N 2 32W
Bordj-in-Eker 83 24 9N 5 3 E
Bordj Menaiel 83 36 46N 3 43 E
Bordj Messouda 83 30 12N 9 25 E
Bordj Nili 82 33 28N 3 2 E
Bordj Omar Driss 83 28 10N 6 40 E
Bordj Zelfana 83 32 27N 4 15 E
Borek Wielkopolski 28 51 54N 17 11 E
Borensberg 49 58 34N 15 17 E
Borgarnes 50 64 32N 21 55W
Børgefjellet 50 65 20N 13 45 E
Borger, Neth. 16 52 54N 6 44 E
Borger, U.S.A. 117 35 40N 101 20W
Borghamn 49 58 23N 14 41 E
Borgholm 49 56 52N 16 39 E
Bórgia 41 38 50N 16 30 E
Borgo San Dalmazzo 38 44 19N 7 29 E
Borgo San Lorenzo 39 43 57N 11 21 E
Borgo Valsugano 39 46 3N 11 27 E
Borgomanero 38 45 41N 8 28 E
Borgonovo Val Tidone 38 45 1N 9 28 E
Borgorose 39 42 12N 13 14 E
Borgosésia 38 45 43N 8 17 E
Borgvattnet 48 63 26N 15 48 E
Borislav 54 49 18N 23 28 E
Borisoglebsk 55 51 27N 42 5 E
Borisoglebskiy 55 56 28N 43 59 E
Borisov 54 54 17N 28 28 E
Borispol 54 50 21N 30 59 E
Borja, Peru 126 4 20 S 77 40W
Borja, Spain 32 41 48N 1 34W
Borjas Blancas 32 41 31N 0 52 E
Borken 24 51 51N 6 52 E
Borkou 81 18 15N 18 50 E
Borkum 24 53 36N 6 42 E
Borlänge 48 60 29N 15 26 E
Borley, C. 5 66 15 S 52 30 E
Bormida → 38 44 23N 8 13 E
Bórmio 38 46 28N 10 22 E
Borna 24 51 8N 12 31 E
Borneo 72 1 0N 115 0 E
Bornholm 49 55 10N 15 0 E
Bornholmsgattet 49 55 15N 14 20 E
Borno □ 85 12 30N 12 30 E
Bornos 31 36 48N 5 42W
Bornu Yassa 85 12 14N 12 25 E
Borobudur 73 7 36 S 110 13 E
Borodino 54 55 31N 35 40 E
Borogontsy 59 62 42N 131 8 E
Boromo 84 11 45N 2 58W
Borongan 73 11 37N 125 26 E
Bororen 98 24 13 S 151 33 E
Borotangba Mts. 87 6 30N 25 0 E
Borovan 43 43 27N 23 45 E
Borovichi 54 58 25N 33 55 E
Borovsk 55 55 12N 36 24 E
Borrby 49 55 27N 14 10 E
Borriol 32 40 4N 0 4W
Borroloola 97 16 4 S 136 17 E
Borşa 46 47 41N 24 50 E
Borsod-Abaúj-Zemplén □ 27 48 20N 21 0 E
Bort-les-Orgues 20 45 24N 2 29 E
Borth 13 52 29N 4 3W
Borujerd 64 33 55N 48 50 E
Borzhomi 57 41 48N 43 28 E
Borzna 54 51 18N 32 26 E
Borzya 59 50 24N 116 31 E
Bosa 40 40 17N 8 32 E
Bosanska Brod 42 45 10N 18 0 E
Bosanska Dubica 39 45 10N 16 50 E
Bosanska Gradiška 42 45 10N 17 15 E
Bosanska Kostajnica 39 45 11N 16 33 E
Bosanska Krupa 39 44 53N 16 10 E
Bosanski Novi 39 45 2N 16 22 E
Bosanski Samac 42 45 3N 18 29 E
Bosansko Grahovo 39 44 12N 16 26 E
Bosansko Petrovac 39 44 35N 16 21 E
Bosaso 63 11 12N 49 18 E
Boscastle 13 50 42N 4 42W
Boscotrecase 41 40 46N 14 28 E
Bose 77 23 53N 106 35 E
Boshan 76 36 28N 117 49 E
Boshoek 92 25 30 S 27 9 E
Boshof 92 28 31 S 25 13 E
Boshrūyeh 65 33 50N 57 30 E
Bosilegrad 42 42 30N 22 27 E
Boskovice 27 49 29N 16 40 E
Bosna → 42 45 4N 18 29 E
Bosna i Hercegovina □ 42 44 0N 18 0 E
Bosnia = Bosna □ 42 44 0N 18 0 E
Bosnik 73 1 5 S 136 10 E
Bōsō-Hantō 74 35 20N 140 20 E
Bosobolo 88 4 15N 19 50 E
Bosporus = Karadeniz Boğazı 64 41 10N 29 10 E
Bossangoa 88 6 35N 17 30 E
Bossekop 50 69 57N 23 15 E
Bossembélé 81 5 25N 17 40 E
Bossier City 117 32 28N 93 48W
Bosso 85 13 43N 13 19 E
Bossut C. 96 18 42 S 121 35 E
Bosten Hu 75 41 55N 87 40 E
Boston, U.K. 12 52 59N 0 2W
Boston, U.S.A. 114 42 20N 71 0W
Boston Bar 108 49 52N 121 30W
Bosut → 42 45 20N 19 0 E
Boswell, Can. 108 49 28N 116 45W
Boswell, Okla., U.S.A. 117 34 1N 95 50W
Boswell, Pa., U.S.A. 112 40 9N 79 2W
Botad 68 22 15N 71 40 E
Botevgrad 43 42 55N 23 47 E
Bothaville 92 27 23 S 26 34 E
Bothnia, G. of 50 63 0N 20 0 E
Bothwell, Austral. 99 42 20 S 147 1 E
Bothwell, Can. 112 42 38N 81 52W
Boticas 30 41 41N 7 40W
Botletle → 92 20 10 S 23 15 E
Botoroaga 46 44 8N 25 32 E
Botoşani 46 47 42N 26 41 E
Botoşani □ 46 47 50N 26 50 E
Botro 84 7 51N 5 19W
Botswana ■ 92 22 0 S 24 0 E
Bottineau 116 48 49N 100 25W
Bottrop 24 51 34N 6 59 E
Botucatu 125 22 55 S 48 30W
Botwood 107 49 6N 55 23W
Bou Alam 82 33 50N 1 26 E
Bou Ali 82 27 11N 0 4W
Bou Djébéha 84 18 25N 2 45W
Bou Guema 82 28 49N 0 19 E
Bou Ismael 82 36 38N 2 42 E
Bou Izakarn 82 29 12N 9 46W
Bou Saâda 83 35 11N 4 9 E
Bou Salem 83 36 45N 9 2 E
Bouaké 84 7 40N 5 2W
Bouar 88 6 0N 15 40 E
Bouârfa 82 32 32N 1 58 E
Bouca 88 6 45N 18 25 E
Boucau 20 43 32N 1 29W
Bouches-du-Rhône □ 21 43 37N 5 2 E
Bouda 82 27 50N 0 27W
Boudenib 82 31 59N 3 31W
Boufarik 82 36 34N 2 58 E
Bougainville C. 96 13 57 S 126 4 E
Bougaroun, C. 83 37 6N 6 30 E
Bougie = Bejaia 83 36 42N 5 2 E
Bougouni 84 11 30N 7 20W
Bouillon 16 49 44N 5 3 E
Bouïra 83 36 20N 3 59 E
Boulder, Austral. 96 30 46 S 121 30 E
Boulder, Colo., U.S.A. 116 40 3N 105 10W
Boulder, Mont., U.S.A. 118 46 14N 112 4W
Boulder City 119 36 0N 114 50W
Boulder Dam = Hoover Dam 119 36 0N 114 45W
Bouli 84 15 17N 12 18W
Boulia 97 22 52 S 139 51 E
Bouligny 19 49 17N 5 45 E
Boulogne → 18 47 12N 1 47W
Boulogne-sur-Gesse 20 43 18N 0 38 E
Boulogne-sur-Mer 19 50 42N 1 36 E
Bouloire 18 47 58N 0 33 E
Boulsa 85 12 39N 0 34W
Boultoum 85 14 45N 10 25 E
Boumalne 82 31 25N 6 0W
Bouna 84 9 10N 3 0W
Boundiali 84 9 30N 6 20W
Bountiful 118 40 57N 111 58W
Bounty I. 94 48 0 S 178 30 E
Bourbon-Lancy 20 46 37N 3 45 E
Bourbon-l'Archambault 20 46 36N 3 4 E
Bourbonnais 20 46 28N 3 0 E
Bourbonne-les-Bains 19 47 59N 5 45 E
Bourem 85 17 0N 0 24W
Bourg 20 45 3N 0 34W
Bourg-Argental 21 45 18N 4 32 E
Bourg-de-Péage 21 45 2N 5 3 E
Bourg-en-Bresse 21 46 13N 5 12 E
Bourg-St.-Andéol 21 44 23N 4 39 E
Bourg-St.-Maurice 21 45 35N 6 46 E
Bourganeuf 20 45 57N 1 45 E
Bourges 19 47 9N 2 25 E
Bourget 113 45 26N 75 9W
Bourget, L. du 21 45 44N 5 52 E
Bourgneuf, B. de 18 47 3N 2 10W
Bourgneuf-en-Retz 18 47 2N 1 58W
Bourgneuf-la-Fôret, Le 18 48 10N 0 59W
Bourgogne 19 47 0N 4 30 E
Bourgoin-Jallieu 21 45 36N 5 17 E
Bourgueil 18 47 17N 0 10 E
Bourke 97 30 8 S 145 55 E
Bournemouth 13 50 43N 1 53W
Bourriot-Bergonce 20 44 7N 0 14W
Bouscat, Le 20 44 53N 0 32W
Boussac 20 46 22N 2 13 E
Boussens 20 43 12N 0 58 E
Bousso 81 10 34N 16 52 E
Boutilimit 84 17 45N 14 40W
Boutonne → 20 45 55N 0 43 E
Bouvet I. = Bouvetøya 7 54 26 S 3 24 E
Bouvetøya 7 54 26 S 3 24 E
Bouznika 82 33 46N 7 6W
Bouzonville 19 49 17N 6 32 E
Bova Marina 41 37 59N 15 56 E
Bovalino Marina 41 38 9N 16 10 E
Bovec 39 46 20N 13 33 E
Bovigny 16 50 12N 5 55 E
Bovill 118 46 58N 116 27W
Bovino 41 41 15N 15 20 E
Bow Island 108 49 50N 111 23W
Bowbells 116 48 47N 102 19W
Bowdle 116 45 30N 99 40W
Bowen 97 20 0 S 148 16 E
Bowen → 98 20 24 S 147 20 E
Bowen Mts. 99 37 0 S 148 0 E
Bowie, Ariz., U.S.A. 119 32 15N 109 30W
Bowie, Tex., U.S.A. 117 33 33N 97 50W
Bowland, Forest of 12 54 0N 2 30W
Bowling Green, Ky., U.S.A. 114 37 0N 86 25W
Bowling Green, Ohio, U.S.A. 114 41 22N 83 40W
Bowling Green, C. 97 19 19 S 147 25 E
Bowman 116 46 12N 103 21W
Bowman I. 5 65 0 S 104 0 E
Bowmans 99 34 10 S 138 17 E
Bowmanville 106 43 55N 78 41W
Bowmore 14 55 45N 6 18W
Bowral 97 34 26 S 150 27 E
Bowraville 99 30 37 S 152 52 E
Bowron → 108 54 3N 121 50W
Bowser L. 108 56 30N 129 30W
Bowsman 109 52 14N 101 12W
Bowwood 91 17 5 S 26 20 E
Boxelder Cr. → 118 47 20N 108 30W
Boxholm 49 58 12N 15 3 E
Boxtel 16 51 36N 5 20 E
Boyabat 56 41 28N 34 42 E
Boyce 117 31 25N 92 39W
Boyer → 108 58 27N 115 57W
Boyle 15 53 58N 8 19W
Boyne → 15 53 43N 6 15W
Boyne City 114 45 13N 85 1W
Boyni Qara 65 36 20N 67 0 E
Boynton Beach 115 26 31N 80 3W
Bozburun 45 36 43N 28 8 E
Bozcaada 44 39 49N 26 3 E
Bozeman 118 45 40N 111 0W
Bozen = Bolzano 39 46 30N 11 20 E
Božepole Wielkopolski 28 54 33N 17 56 E
Boževac 42 44 32N 21 24 E
Bozouls 20 44 28N 2 43 E
Bozoum 88 6 25N 16 35 E
Bozovici 46 44 56N 22 1 E
Bra 38 44 41N 7 50 E
Brabant □ 16 50 46N 4 30 E
Brabant L. 109 55 58N 103 43W

Brabrand 49 56 9N 10 7 E
Brač 39 43 20N 16 40 E
Bracadale, L. 14 57 20N 6 30W
Bracciano 39 42 6N 12 10 E
Bracciano, L. di 39 42 8N 12 11 E
Bracebridge 106 45 2N 79 19W
Brach 83 27 31N 14 20 E
Bracieux 19 47 30N 1 30 E
Bräcke 48 62 45N 15 26 E
Brackettville 117 29 21N 100 20W
Bracki Kanal 39 43 24N 16 40 E
Brad 46 46 10N 22 50 E
Brădano → 41 40 23N 16 51 E
Braddock 112 40 24N 79 51W
Bradenton 115 27 25N 82 35W
Bradford, Can. 112 44 7N 79 34W
Bradford, U.K. 12 53 47N 1 45W
Bradford, Pa., U.S.A. 114 41 58N 78 41W
Bradford, Vt., U.S.A. 113 43 59N 72 9W
Brădiceni 46 45 3N 23 4 E
Bradley, Ark., U.S.A. 117 33 7N 93 39W
Bradley, S.D., U.S.A. 116 45 10N 97 40W
Bradley Institute 91 17 7S 31 25 E
Bradore Bay 107 51 27N 57 18W
Bradshaw 97 15 21S 130 16 E
Brady 117 31 8N 99 25W
Brædstrup 49 55 58N 9 37 E
Braeside 113 45 28N 76 24W
Braga 30 41 35N 8 25W
Braga □ 30 41 30N 8 30W
Bragado 124 35 2S 60 27W
Bragança, Brazil 127 1 0S 47 2W
Bragança, Port. 30 41 48N 6 50W
Bragança □ 30 41 30N 6 45W
Bragança Paulista 125 22 55S 46 32W
Brahmanbaria 69 23 58N 91 15 E
Brahmani → 69 20 39N 86 46 E
Brahmaputra → 67 24 2N 90 59 E
Braich-y-pwll 12 52 47N 4 46W
Braidwood 99 35 27S 149 49 E
Brăila 46 45 19N 27 59 E
Brăila □ 46 45 5N 27 30 E
Brainerd 116 46 20N 94 10W
Braintree, U.K. 13 51 53N 0 34 E
Braintree, U.S.A. 113 42 11N 71 0W
Brak → 92 29 35S 22 55 E
Brake, Niedersachsen, Ger. 24 53 19N 8 30 E
Brake, Nordrhein, Ger. 24 51 43N 9 12 E
Bräkne-Hoby 49 56 14N 15 6 E
Brakwater 92 22 28S 17 3 E
Brålanda 49 58 34N 12 21 E
Bralorne 108 50 50N 123 45W
Bramberg 25 50 6N 10 40 E
Bramminge 49 55 28N 8 42 E
Brämön 48 62 14N 17 40 E
Brampton 106 43 45N 79 45W
Bramsche 24 52 25N 7 58 E
Bramwell 98 12 8S 142 37 E
Branco → 126 1 20S 61 50W
Brande 49 55 57N 9 8 E
Brandenburg 24 52 24N 12 33 E
Brandfort 92 28 40S 26 30 E
Brandon, Can. 109 49 50N 99 57W
Brandon, U.S.A. 113 43 48N 73 4W
Brandon B. 15 52 17N 10 8W
Brandon, Mt. 15 52 15N 10 15W
Brandsen 124 35 10S 58 15W
Brandval 47 60 19N 12 1 E
Brandvlei 92 30 25S 20 30 E
Brandýs 26 50 10N 14 40 E
Branford 113 41 15N 72 48W
Braniewo 28 54 25N 19 50 E
Bransfield Str. 5 63 0S 59 0W
Brańsk 28 52 44N 22 51 E
Branson, Colo., U.S.A. 117 37 4N 103 53W
Branson, Mo., U.S.A. 117 36 40N 93 18W
Brantford 106 43 10N 80 15W
Brantôme 20 45 22N 0 39 E
Branxholme 99 37 52S 141 49 E
Branzi 38 46 0N 9 46 E
Bras d'or, L. 107 45 50N 60 50W
Brasiléia 126 11 0S 68 45W
Brasília 127 15 47S 47 55 E
Braslav 54 55 38N 27 0 E
Braslovce 39 46 21N 15 3 E
Braşov 46 45 38N 25 35 E
Braşov □ 46 45 45N 25 15 E
Brass 85 4 35N 6 14 E
Brass → 85 4 15N 6 13 E
Brassac-les-Mines 20 45 24N 3 20 E
Brasschaat 16 51 19N 4 27 E
Brassey, Banjaran 72 5 0N 117 15 E
Brasstown Bald, Mt. 115 34 54N 83 45W
Bratislava 27 48 10N 17 7 E
Bratsigovo 43 42 1N 24 22 E
Bratsk 59 56 10N 101 30 E
Brattleboro 114 42 53N 72 37W
Braţul Chilia → 46 45 25N 29 20 E
Braţul Sfîntu Gheorghe → 46 45 0N 29 20 E
Braţul Sulina → 46 45 10N 29 20 E
Bratunac 42 44 13N 19 21 E
Braunau 26 48 15N 13 3 E
Braunschweig 24 52 17N 10 28 E
Braunton 13 51 6N 4 9W
Brava 63 1 20N 44 8 E
Bråviken 48 58 38N 16 32 E
Bravo del Norte → 120 25 57N 97 9W
Brawley 119 32 58N 115 30W
Bray 15 53 12N 6 6W
Bray, Pays de 19 49 46N 1 26 E
Bray-sur-Seine 19 48 25N 3 14 E
Brazeau → 108 52 55N 115 14W
Brazil 114 39 32N 87 8W
Brazil ■ 127 10 0S 50 0W
Brazilian Highlands = Brasil, Planalto 122 18 0S 46 30W
Brazo Sur → 124 25 21S 57 42W
Brazos → 117 28 53N 95 23W
Brazzaville 88 4 9S 15 12 E
Brčko 42 44 54N 18 46 E
Brda → 28 53 8N 18 8 E
Breadalbane, Austral. 98 23 50S 139 35 E
Breadalbane, U.K. 14 56 30N 4 15W
Breaksea Sd. 101 45 35S 166 35 E
Bream Bay 101 35 56S 174 28 E
Bream Head 101 35 51S 174 36 E
Breas 124 25 29S 70 24W
Brebes 73 6 52S 109 3 E
Brechin, Can. 112 44 32N 79 10W
Brechin, U.K. 14 56 44N 2 40W
Breckenridge, Colo., U.S.A. 118 39 30N 106 2W
Breckenridge, Minn., U.S.A. 116 46 20N 96 36W
Breckenridge, Tex., U.S.A. 117 32 48N 98 55W
Břeclav 27 48 46N 16 53 E
Brecon 13 51 57N 3 23W
Brecon Beacons 13 51 53N 3 27W
Breda 16 51 35N 4 45 E
Bredaryd 49 57 10N 13 45 E
Bredasdorp 92 34 33S 20 2 E
Bredbo 99 35 58S 149 10 E
Bredstedt 24 54 37N 8 59 E
Bregalnica → 42 41 43N 22 9 E
Bregenz 26 47 30N 9 45 E
Bregovo 42 44 9N 22 39 E
Bréhal 18 48 53N 1 30W
Bréhat, I. de 18 48 51N 3 0W
Breiðafjörður 50 65 15N 23 15W
Breil 21 43 56N 7 31 E
Breisach 25 48 2N 7 37 E
Brejo 127 3 41S 42 47W
Brekke 47 61 1N 5 26 E
Breloux-la-Crèche 20 46 23N 0 19W
Bremangerlandet 47 61 51N 5 0 E
Bremen 24 53 4N 8 47 E
Bremen □ 24 53 6N 8 46 E
Bremerhaven 24 53 34N 8 35 E
Bremerton 118 47 30N 122 38W
Bremervörde 24 53 28N 9 10 E
Bremnes 47 59 47N 5 8 E
Bremsnes 47 63 6N 7 40 E
Brenes 31 37 32N 5 54W
Brenham 117 30 5N 96 27W
Brenner Pass 26 47 0N 11 30 E
Breno 38 45 57N 10 20 E
Brent, Can. 106 46 2N 78 29W
Brent, U.K. 13 51 33N 0 18W
Brenta → 39 45 11N 12 18 E
Brentwood 13 51 37N 0 19 E
Bréscia 38 45 33N 10 13 E
Breskens 16 51 23N 3 33 E
Breslau = Wrocław 28 51 5N 17 5 E
Bresle → 18 50 4N 1 22 E
Bresles 19 49 25N 2 13 E
Bressanone 39 46 43N 11 40 E
Bressay I. 14 60 10N 1 5W
Bresse, La 19 48 0N 6 53 E
Bresse, Plaine de 19 46 50N 5 10 E
Bressuire 18 46 51N 0 30W
Brest, France 18 48 24N 4 31W
Brest, U.S.S.R. 54 52 10N 23 40 E
Bretagne 18 48 0N 3 0W
Bretçu 46 46 7N 26 18 E
Breteuil, Eur, France 18 48 50N 0 53 E
Breteuil, Oise, France 19 49 38N 2 18 E
Breton 108 53 7N 114 28W
Breton, Pertuis 20 46 17N 1 25W
Breton Sd. 117 29 40N 89 12W
Brett, C. 101 35 10S 174 20 E
Bretten 25 49 2N 8 43 E
Brevard 115 35 19N 82 42W
Brevik 47 59 4N 9 42 E
Brewarrina 99 30 0S 146 51 E
Brewer 107 44 43N 68 50W
Brewster, N.Y., U.S.A. 113 41 23N 73 37W
Brewster, Wash., U.S.A. 118 48 10N 119 51W
Brewster, Kap 4 70 7N 22 0W
Brewton 115 31 9N 87 2W
Breyten 93 26 16S 30 0 E
Breytovo 55 58 18N 37 50 E
Brežice 39 45 54N 15 35 E
Brézina 82 33 4N 1 14 E
Březnice 26 49 32N 13 57 E
Breznik 42 42 44N 22 50 E
Brezno 27 48 50N 19 40 E
Brezovo 43 42 21N 25 5 E
Bria 88 6 30N 21 58 E
Briançon 21 44 54N 6 39 E
Briare 19 47 38N 2 45 E
Bribie I. 97 27 0S 152 58 E
Bricon 19 48 5N 5 0 E
Bricquebec 18 49 28N 1 38W
Bridgehampton 113 40 56N 72 19W
Bridgend 13 51 30N 3 35W
Bridgeport, Calif., U.S.A. 119 38 14N 119 15W
Bridgeport, Conn., U.S.A. 114 41 12N 73 12W
Bridgeport, Nebr., U.S.A. 116 41 42N 103 10W
Bridgeport, Tex., U.S.A. 117 33 15N 97 45W
Bridger 118 45 20N 108 58W
Bridgeton 114 39 29N 75 10W
Bridgetown, Austral. 96 33 58S 116 7 E
Bridgetown, Barbados 121 13 0N 59 30W
Bridgetown, Can. 107 44 55N 65 18W
Bridgewater, Can. 107 44 25N 64 31W
Bridgewater, Mass., U.S.A. 113 41 59N 70 56W
Bridgewater, S.D., U.S.A. 116 43 34N 97 29W
Bridgewater, C. 97 38 23S 141 23 E
Bridgnorth 13 52 33N 2 25W
Bridgton 113 44 5N 70 41W
Bridgwater 13 51 7N 3 0W
Bridlington 12 54 6N 0 11W
Bridport, Austral. 99 40 59S 147 23 E
Bridport, U.K. 13 50 43N 2 45W
Brie-Comte-Robert 19 48 40N 2 35 E
Brie, Plaine de la 19 48 35N 3 10 E
Briec 18 48 6N 4 0W
Brienne-le-Château 19 48 24N 4 30 E
Brienon 19 48 0N 3 35 E
Brienz 25 46 46N 8 2 E
Brienzersee 25 46 44N 7 53 E
Briey 19 49 14N 5 57 E
Brig 25 46 18N 7 59 E
Brigg 12 53 33N 0 30W
Briggsdale 116 40 40N 104 20W
Brigham City 118 41 30N 112 1W
Bright 99 36 42S 146 56 E
Brighton, Austral. 99 35 5S 138 30 E
Brighton, Can. 106 44 2N 77 44W
Brighton, U.K. 13 50 50N 0 9W
Brighton, U.S.A. 116 39 59N 104 50W
Brignogan-Plage 18 48 40N 4 20W
Brignoles 21 43 25N 6 5 E
Brihuega 32 40 45N 2 52W
Brikama 84 13 15N 16 45W
Brilliant, Can. 108 49 19N 117 38W
Brilliant, U.S.A. 112 40 15N 80 39W
Brilon 24 51 23N 8 32 E
Brindisi 41 40 39N 17 55 E
Brinje 39 45 0N 15 9 E
Brinkley 117 34 55N 91 15W
Brinkworth 99 33 42S 138 26 E
Brion, Î. 107 47 46N 61 26W
Brionne 18 49 11N 0 43 E
Brionski 39 44 55N 13 45 E
Brioude 20 45 18N 3 24 E
Briouze 18 48 42N 0 23W
Brisbane 97 27 25S 153 2 E
Brisbane → 99 27 24S 153 9 E
Brisighella 39 44 14N 11 46 E
Bristol, U.K. 13 51 26N 2 35W
Bristol, Conn., U.S.A. 114 41 44N 72 57W
Bristol, Pa., U.S.A. 113 40 6N 74 52W
Bristol, R.I., U.S.A. 113 41 40N 71 15W
Bristol, S.D., U.S.A. 116 45 25N 97 43W
Bristol, Tenn., U.S.A. 115 36 36N 82 11W
Bristol B. 104 58 0N 160 0W
Bristol Channel 13 51 18N 4 30W
Bristol I. 5 58 45S 28 0W
Bristol L. 119 34 23N 116 50W
Bristow 117 35 55N 96 28W
British Antarctic Territory □ 5 66 0S 45 0W
British Columbia □ 108 55 0N 125 15W
British Guiana = Guyana ■ 126 5 0N 59 0W
British Honduras = Belize ■ 120 17 0N 88 30W
British Isles 8 55 0N 4 0W
Brits 93 25 37S 27 48 E
Britstown 92 30 37S 23 30 E
Britt 106 45 46N 80 34W
Brittany = Bretagne 18 48 0N 3 0W
Britton 116 45 50N 97 47W
Brive-la-Gaillarde 20 45 10N 1 32 E
Briviesca 32 42 32N 3 19W
Brixton 98 23 32S 144 57 E
Brlik 58 44 0N 74 5 E
Brno 27 49 10N 16 35 E
Bro 48 59 31N 17 38 E
Broach = Bharuch 68 21 47N 73 0 E
Broad → 115 33 59N 82 39W
Broad B. 14 58 14N 6 16W
Broad Haven 15 54 20N 9 55W
Broad Law 14 55 30N 3 22W
Broad Sd. 97 22 0S 149 45 E
Broadford 100 37 14S 145 4 E
Broads, The 12 52 45N 1 30 E
Broadsound Ra. 97 22 50S 149 30 E
Broadus 116 45 28N 105 27W
Broadview 109 50 22N 102 35W
Broager 49 54 53N 9 40 E
Broaryd 49 57 7N 13 15 E
Brochet 109 57 53N 101 40W
Brochet, L. 109 58 36N 101 35W
Brock 109 51 26N 108 43W
Brocken 24 51 48N 10 40 E
Brockport 114 43 12N 77 56W
Brockton 113 42 8N 71 2W
Brockville 106 44 35N 75 41W
Brockway, Mont., U.S.A. 116 47 18N 105 46W
Brockway, Pa., U.S.A. 112 41 14N 78 48W
Brocton 112 42 25N 79 26W
Brod 42 41 35N 21 17 E
Brodarevo 42 43 14N 19 44 E
Brodeur Pen. 105 72 30N 88 10W
Brodick 14 55 34N 5 9W
Brodnica 28 53 15N 19 25 E
Brody 54 50 5N 25 10 E
Brogan 118 44 14N 117 32W
Broglie 18 49 0N 0 30 E
Brok 28 52 43N 21 52 E
Broken → 100 36 24S 145 24 E
Broken Bay 100 33 30S 151 15 E
Broken Bow, Nebr., U.S.A. 116 41 25N 99 35W
Broken Bow, Okla., U.S.A. 117 34 2N 94 43W
Broken Hill 97 31 58S 141 29 E
Broken Hill = Kabwe 91 14 27S 28 28 E
Brokind 49 58 13N 15 42 E
Bromfield 13 52 25N 2 45W
Bromley 13 51 20N 0 5 E
Bromölla 49 56 5N 14 28 E
Brønderslev 49 57 16N 9 57 E
Brong-Ahafo 84 7 50N 2 0W
Bronkhorstspruit 93 25 46S 28 45 E
Bronnitsy 55 55 27N 38 10 E
Bronte, Italy 41 37 48N 14 49 E
Bronte, U.S.A. 117 31 54N 100 18W
Bronte Park 99 42 8S 146 30 E
Brookfield 116 39 50N 93 4W
Brookhaven 117 31 40N 90 25W
Brookings, Oreg., U.S.A. 118 42 4N 124 10W
Brookings, S.D., U.S.A. 116 44 20N 96 45W
Brooklands 98 18 10S 144 0 E
Brooklin 112 43 55N 78 55W
Brookmere 108 49 52N 120 53W
Brooks 108 50 35N 111 55W
Brooks B. 108 50 15N 127 55W
Brooks L. 109 61 55N 106 35W
Brooks Ra. 104 68 40N 147 0W
Brooksville 115 28 32N 82 21W
Brookton 96 32 22S 117 1 E
Brookville 114 39 25N 85 0W
Brooloo 99 26 30S 152 43 E
Broom, L. 14 57 55N 5 15W
Broome 96 18 0S 122 15 E
Broons 18 48 20N 2 16W
Brora 14 58 0N 3 50W
Brora → 14 58 4N 3 52W
Brösarp 49 55 43N 14 6 E
Brosna → 15 53 8N 8 0W
Broşteni 46 47 14N 25 43 E
Brothers 118 43 56N 120 39W
Brøttum 47 61 2N 10 34 E
Brou 18 48 13N 1 11 E
Brouage 20 45 52N 1 4W
Broughton Island 105 67 33N 63 0W
Broughty Ferry 14 56 29N 2 50W
Broumov 27 50 35N 16 20 E
Brouwershaven 16 51 45N 3 55 E
Brovary 54 50 34N 30 48 E
Brovst 49 57 6N 9 31 E
Browerville 116 46 3N 94 50W
Brown Willy 13 50 35N 4 34W
Brownfield 117 33 10N 102 15W
Browning 118 48 35N 113 0W
Brownlee 109 50 43N 106 1W
Brownsville, Oreg., U.S.A. 118 44 29N 123 0W
Brownsville, Tenn., U.S.A. 117 35 35N 89 15W
Brownsville, Tex., U.S.A. 117 25 56N 97 25W
Brownwood 117 31 45N 99 0W
Brownwood, L. 117 31 51N 98 35W
Brozas 31 39 37N 6 47W
Bru 47 61 32N 5 11 E
Bruas 71 4 31N 100 46 E
Bruay-en-Artois 19 50 29N 2 33 E
Bruce, Mt. 96 22 37S 118 8 E
Bruce Pen. 112 45 0N 81 30W
Bruche → 19 48 34N 7 43 E
Bruchsal 25 49 9N 8 39 E
Bruck an der Leitha 27 48 1N 16 47 E
Bruck an der Mur 26 47 24N 15 16 E
Brückenau 25 50 17N 9 48 E
Brue → 13 51 10N 2 59W
Bruges = Brugge 16 51 13N 3 13 E
Brugg 25 47 29N 8 11 E
Brugge 16 51 13N 3 13 E
Brühl 24 50 49N 6 51 E
Brûlé 108 53 15N 117 58W
Brûlon 18 47 58N 0 15W
Brumado 127 14 14S 41 40W
Brumath 19 48 43N 7 40 E
Brumunddal 47 60 53N 10 56 E
Brundidge 115 31 43N 85 45W
Bruneau 118 42 57N 115 55W
Bruneau → 118 42 57N 115 58W
Brunei = Bandar Seri Begawan 72 4 52N 115 0 E
Brunei ■ 72 4 50N 115 0 E
Brunflo 48 63 5N 14 50 E
Brunico 39 46 50N 11 55 E
Brunkeberg 47 59 26N 8 28 E
Brunna 48 59 52N 17 25 E
Brunnen 25 46 59N 8 37 E
Brunner 101 42 27S 171 20 E
Brunner, L. 101 42 37S 171 27 E
Brunnsvik 48 60 12N 15 8 E
Bruno 109 52 20N 105 30W
Brunsbüttelkoog 24 53 52N 9 13 E
Brunswick, Ga., U.S.A. 115 31 10N 81 30W
Brunswick, Md., U.S.A. 114 39 20N 77 38W
Brunswick, Me., U.S.A. 107 43 53N 69 50W
Brunswick, Mo., U.S.A. 116 39 26N 93 10W
Brunswick, Ohio, U.S.A. 112 41 15N 81 50W
Brunswick = Braunschweig 24 52 17N 10 28 E
Brunswick B. 96 15 15S 124 50 E
Brunswick, Pen. de 128 53 30S 71 30W
Bruntál 27 50 0N 17 27 E
Bruny I. 97 43 20S 147 15 E
Brusartsi 42 43 40N 23 5 E
Brush 116 40 17N 103 33W
Brushton 113 44 50N 74 62W
Brusio 25 46 14N 10 8 E
Brusque 125 27 5S 49 0W
Brussel 16 50 51N 4 21 E
Brussels, Can. 112 43 45N 81 25W
Brussels, Ont., Can. 112 43 44N 81 15W
Brussels = Bruxelles 16 50 51N 4 21 E
Bruthen 99 37 42S 147 50 E
Bruxelles 16 50 51N 4 21 E
Bruyères 19 48 10N 6 40 E
Brwinów 28 52 9N 20 40 E
Bryagovo 43 41 58N 25 8 E
Bryan, Ohio, U.S.A. 114 41 30N 84 30W
Bryan, Texas, U.S.A. 117 30 40N 96 27W
Bryan, Mt. 99 33 30S 139 0 E
Bryanka 57 48 32N 38 45 E
Bryansk 54 53 13N 34 25 E
Bryanskoye 57 44 20N 47 10 E
Bryant 116 44 35N 97 28W
Bryne 47 58 44N 5 38 E
Bryson City 115 35 28N 83 25W
Brza Palanka 42 44 28N 22 27 E
Brzava → 42 45 21N 20 45 E
Brzeg 28 50 52N 17 30 E
Brzeg Din 28 51 16N 16 41 E
Brześć Kujawski 28 52 36N 18 55 E
Brzesko 27 49 59N 20 34 E
Brzeszcze 27 49 59N 19 10 E
Brzeziny 28 51 49N 19 42 E
Brzozów 27 49 41N 22 3 E
Bū Athlah 83 30 9N 15 39 E
Bu Craa 80 26 45N 12 50W
Bua Yai 71 15 33N 102 26 E
Buabuq 86 31 29N 25 29 E
Buapinang 73 4 40S 121 30 E
Buayan 73 6 3N 125 6 E
Buba 84 11 40N 14 59W
Bubanza 90 3 6S 29 23 E
Bucak 64 37 28N 30 36 E
Bucaramanga 126 7 0N 73 0W
Bucchiánico 39 42 20N 14 10 E
Bucecea 46 47 47N 26 28 E
Buchach 54 49 5N 25 25 E
Buchan 14 57 32N 2 8W
Buchan Ness 14 57 29N 1 48W
Buchanan, Can. 109 51 40N 102 45W
Buchanan, Liberia 84 5 57N 10 2W
Buchanan, L., Queens., Austral. 98 21 35S 145 52 E
Buchanan, L., W. Australia, Austral. 96 25 33S 123 2 E
Buchanan, L., U.S.A. 117 30 50N 98 25W
Buchans 107 48 50N 56 52W
Bucharest = Bucureşti 46 44 27N 26 10 E

chholz 24 53 19N 9 51 E
chloe 25 48 3N 10 45 E
ckeburg 24 52 16N 9 2 E
ckeye 119 33 28N 112 40W
ckhannon 114 39 2N 80 10W
ckhaven 14 56 10N 3 2W
ckie 14 57 40N 2 58W
ckingham, Can. 106 45 37N 75 24W
ckingham, U.K. 13 52 0N 0 59W
ckingham □ 13 51 50N 0 55W
ckingham B. 97 12 10 S 135 40 E
ckingham Can. 70 14 0N 80 5 E
ckinguy 99 31 3 S 147 30 E
ckland Newton 13 50 45N 2 25W
ckley 118 47 10N 122 2W
cklin 117 37 37N 99 40W
cquoy 19 50 9N 2 43 E
ctouche 107 46 30N 64 45W
cureşti 46 44 27N 26 10 E
cyrus 114 40 48N 83 0W
dafok 27 47 26N 19 2 E
dalin 67 22 20N 95 10 E
dapest 27 47 29N 19 5 E
daun 68 28 5N 79 10 E
dd Coast 5 68 0 S 112 0 E
ddusò 40 40 35N 9 18 E
de 13 50 49N 4 33W
deşti 46 44 13N 26 30 E
dge Budge 69 22 30N 88 5 E
ðareyri 50 65 2N 14 13W
ðir 50 64 49N 23 23W
dia 32 40 38N 2 46W
djala 88 2 50N 19 40 E
drio 39 44 31N 11 31 E
dva 42 42 17N 18 50 E
dzyń 28 52 54N 16 59 E
ea 85 4 10N 9 9 E
ena Vista, Colo., U.S.A. 119 38 56N 106 6W
ena Vista, Va., U.S.A. 114 37 47N 79 23W
ena Vista L. 119 35 15N 119 21W
enaventura, Colomb. 126 3 53N 77 4W
enaventura, Mexico 120 29 50N 107 30W
endía, Pantano de 32 40 25N 2 43W
enos Aires 124 34 30 S 58 20W
enos Aires □ 124 36 30 S 60 0W
enos Aires, Lago 128 46 35 S 72 30W
ffalo, Mo., U.S.A. 117 37 40N 93 5W
ffalo, N.Y., U.S.A. 114 42 55N 78 50W
ffalo, Okla., U.S.A. 117 36 55N 99 42W
ffalo, S.D., U.S.A. 116 45 39N 103 31W
ffalo, Wyo., U.S.A. 118 44 25N 106 50W
ffalo → 108 60 5N 115 5W
ffalo Head Hills 108 57 25N 115 55W
ffalo L. 108 52 27N 112 54W
ffalo Narrows 109 55 51N 108 29W
ffels → 92 29 36 S 17 15 E
ford 115 34 5N 84 0W
g →, Poland 28 52 31N 21 5 E
g →, U.S.S.R. 56 46 59N 31 58 E
ga 126 4 0N 76 15W
ganda □ 90 0 0N 31 30 E
ganga 90 0 3 S 32 0 E
geat 20 45 36N 1 55 E
gel, Tanjung 72 6 26 S 111 3 E
gojno 42 44 2N 17 25 E
gsuk 72 8 15N 117 15 E
gt 76 48 47N 121 56 E
gue, Le 20 44 55N 0 56 E
gulma 52 54 33N 52 48 E
guma 85 4 42N 6 55 E
guruslan 52 53 39N 52 26 E
hăeşti 46 46 47N 27 32 E
heirat-Murrat-el-Kubra 86 30 15N 32 40 E
hl, Idaho, U.S.A. 118 42 35N 114 54W
hl, Minn., U.S.A. 116 47 30N 92 46W
huşi 46 46 41N 26 45 E
ick 117 37 38N 91 2W
ilth Wells 13 52 10N 3 26W
insk 55 55 0N 48 18 E
ir Nur 75 47 50N 117 42 E
is-les-Baronnies 21 44 17N 5 16 E
itrago 30 41 0N 3 38W
jalance 31 37 54N 4 23W
ján 30 42 59N 8 36W
janovac 42 42 28N 21 44 E
jaraloz 32 41 29N 0 10W
je 39 45 24N 13 39 E
jumbura (Usumbura) 90 3 16 S 29 18 E
k 27 47 22N 16 45 E
k 28 52 21N 16 30 E
kachacha 59 52 55N 116 50 E
kama 91 9 10 S 25 50 E
kavu 90 2 20 S 28 52 E
kene 90 4 15 S 32 48 E
khara 58 39 48N 64 25 E
kima 90 1 50 S 33 25 E
kittinggi 72 0 20 S 100 20 E
kkapatnam 70 14 14N 77 46 E
koba 90 1 20 S 31 49 E
koba □ 90 1 30 S 32 0 E
kowno 27 50 17N 19 35 E
kuru 85 9 42N 8 48 E
kuya 90 0 40N 31 52 E
la, Guin.-Biss. 84 12 7N 15 43W
la, Indon. 73 3 6 S 130 30 E
lan 73 12 40N 123 52 E
landshahr 68 28 28N 77 51 E
lâq 86 25 10N 30 38 E
lawayo 91 20 7 S 28 32 E
ldana 68 20 30N 76 18 E
lgan 75 48 45N 103 34 E
lgaria ■ 43 42 35N 25 30 E
lgroo 99 25 47 S 143 58 E
lhar 63 10 25N 44 30 E
li, Teluk 73 1 5N 128 25 E
liluyan, C. 72 8 20N 117 15 E
lki 87 6 11N 36 31 E
lkley → 108 55 15N 127 40W
ll Shoals L. 117 36 40N 93 5W
llaque → 31 38 59N 4 17W
llas 33 38 2N 1 40W
lle 25 46 37N 7 3 E
Buller, Mt. 100 37 10 S 146 28 E
Bullfinch 96 30 58 S 119 3 E
Bulli 99 34 15 S 150 57 E
Bullock Creek 98 17 43 S 144 31 E
Bulloo → 97 28 43 S 142 30 E
Bulloo Downs 99 28 31 S 142 57 E
Bulloo L. 99 28 43 S 142 25 E
Bulls 101 40 10 S 175 24 E
Bully-les-Mines 19 50 27N 2 44 E
Bulnes 124 36 42 S 72 19W
Bulo Burti 63 3 50N 45 33 E
Bulolo 98 7 10 S 146 40 E
Bulqiza 44 41 30N 20 21 E
Bulsar 68 20 40N 72 58 E
Bultfontein 92 28 18 S 26 10 E
Bulu Karakelong 73 4 35N 126 50 E
Bulukumba 73 5 33 S 120 11 E
Bulun 59 70 37N 127 30 E
Bumba 88 2 13N 22 30 E
Bumbiri I. 90 1 40 S 31 55 E
Bumble Bee 119 34 8N 112 18W
Bumhpa Bum 67 26 51N 97 14 E
Bumi → 91 17 0 S 28 20 E
Buna, Kenya 90 2 58N 39 30 E
Buna, P.N.G. 98 8 42 S 148 27 E
Bunazi 90 1 3 S 31 23 E
Bunbah, Khalīj 81 32 20N 23 15 E
Bunbury 96 33 20 S 115 35 E
Buncrana 15 55 8N 7 28W
Bundaberg 97 24 54 S 152 22 E
Bünde 24 52 11N 8 33 E
Bundi 68 25 30N 75 35 E
Bundoran 15 54 24N 8 17W
Bundukia 87 5 14N 30 55 E
Bundure 100 35 10 S 146 1 E
Bungendore 100 35 14 S 149 30 E
Bungo-Suidō 74 33 0N 132 15 E
Bungoma 90 0 34N 34 34 E
Bungu 90 7 35 S 39 0 E
Bungun Shara 75 49 0N 104 0 E
Bunia 90 1 35N 30 20 E
Bunji 69 35 45N 74 40 E
Bunju 72 3 35N 117 50 E
Bunkerville 119 36 47N 114 6W
Bunkie 117 31 1N 92 12W
Bunnell 115 29 28N 81 12W
Buñol 33 39 25N 0 47W
Buntok 72 1 40 S 114 58 E
Bununu 85 9 51N 9 32 E
Bununu Dass 85 10 0N 9 31 E
Bunza 85 12 8N 4 0 E
Buol 73 1 15N 121 32 E
Buorkhaya, Mys 59 71 50N 132 40 E
Buqayq 64 26 0N 49 45 E
Buqei'a 62 32 58N 35 20 E
Bur Acaba 63 3 12N 44 20 E
Bûr Fuad 86 31 15N 32 20 E
Bûr Safâga 86 26 43N 33 57 E
Bûr Sa'îd 86 31 16N 32 18 E
Bûr Sûdân 86 19 32N 37 9 E
Bûr Taufiq 86 29 54N 32 32 E
Bura 90 1 4 S 39 58 E
Buraimī, Al Wāhāt al 65 24 10N 55 43 E
Burao 63 9 32N 45 32 E
Buras 117 29 20N 89 33W
Buraydah 64 26 20N 44 8 E
Burbank 119 34 9N 118 23W
Burcher 99 33 30 S 147 16 E
Burdekin → 98 19 38 S 147 25 E
Burdett 108 49 50N 111 32W
Burdur 64 37 45N 30 22 E
Burdwan 69 23 14N 87 39 E
Bure 87 10 40N 37 4 E
Bure → 12 52 38N 1 45 E
Bureba, La 32 42 36N 3 24W
Büren 24 51 33N 8 34 E
Bureya → 59 49 27N 129 30 E
Burford 112 43 7N 80 27W
Burg, Magdeburg, Ger. 24 52 16N 11 50 E
Burg, Schleswig-Holstein, Ger. 24 54 25N 11 10 E
Burg el Arab 86 30 54N 29 32 E
Burg et Tuyur 86 20 55N 27 56 E
Burgas 43 42 33N 27 29 E
Burgaski Zaliv 43 42 30N 27 39 E
Burgdorf, Ger. 24 52 27N 10 0 E
Burgdorf, Switz. 25 47 3N 7 37 E
Burgenland □ 27 47 20N 16 20 E
Burgeo 107 47 37N 57 38W
Burgersdorp 92 31 0 S 26 20 E
Burghausen 25 48 10N 12 50 E
Búrgio 40 37 35N 13 18 E
Burglengenfeld 25 49 11N 12 2 E
Burgo de Osma 32 41 35N 3 4W
Burgohondo 30 40 26N 4 47W
Burgos 32 42 21N 3 41W
Burgos □ 32 42 21N 3 42W
Burgstädt 24 50 55N 12 49 E
Burgsteinfurt 24 52 9N 7 23 E
Burgsvik 49 57 3N 18 19 E
Burguillos del Cerro 31 38 23N 6 35W
Burgundy = Bourgogne 19 47 0N 4 30 E
Burhanpur 68 21 18N 76 14 E
Burhou 18 49 45N 2 15W
Buri Pen. 87 15 25N 39 55 E
Burias 73 12 55N 123 5 E
Burica, Pta. 121 8 3N 82 51W
Burigi, L. 90 2 2 S 31 22 E
Burin 107 47 1N 55 14W
Būrīn 62 32 11N 35 15 E
Buriram 71 15 0N 103 0 E
Burji 87 5 29N 37 51 E
Burkburnett 117 34 7N 98 35W
Burke 118 47 31N 115 56W
Burke → 98 23 12 S 139 33 E
Burketown 97 17 45 S 139 33 E
Burk's Falls 106 45 37N 79 24W
Burley 118 42 37N 113 55W
Burlington, Can. 112 43 18N 79 45W
Burlington, Colo., U.S.A. 116 39 21N 102 18W
Burlington, Iowa, U.S.A. 116 40 50N 91 5W
Burlington, Kans., U.S.A. 116 38 15N 95 47W
Burlington, N.C., U.S.A. 115 36 7N 79 27W
Burlington, N.J., U.S.A. 114 40 5N 74 50W
Burlington, Vt., U.S.A. 114 44 27N 73 14W
Burlington, Wash., U.S.A. 118 48 29N 122 19W
Burlington, Wis., U.S.A. 114 42 41N 88 18W
Burlyu-Tyube 58 46 30N 79 10 E
Burma ■ 67 21 0N 96 30 E
Burnaby I. 108 52 25N 131 19W
Burnet 117 30 45N 98 11W
Burnett → 97 24 45 S 152 23 E
Burney 118 40 56N 121 41W
Burnham 112 40 37N 77 34W
Burnie 97 41 4 S 145 56 E
Burnley 12 53 47N 2 15W
Burns, Oreg., U.S.A. 118 43 40N 119 4W
Burns, Wyo., U.S.A. 116 41 13N 104 18W
Burns Lake 108 54 20N 125 45W
Burnside → 104 66 51N 108 4W
Burnt River 112 44 41N 78 42W
Burntwood → 109 56 8N 96 34W
Burntwood L. 109 55 22N 100 26W
Burqā 62 32 18N 35 11 E
Burqān 64 29 0N 47 57 E
Burqin 75 47 43N 87 0 E
Burra 97 33 40 S 138 55 E
Burragorang, L. 100 33 52 S 150 37 E
Burreli 44 41 36N 20 1 E
Burrendong, L. 100 32 45 S 149 10 E
Burrewarra Pt. 100 35 50 S 150 15 E
Burriana 32 39 50N 0 4W
Burrinjuck Dam 100 35 0 S 148 34 E
Burrinjuck Res. 99 35 0 S 148 36 E
Burro, Serranías del 120 29 0N 102 0W
Burruyacú 124 26 30 S 64 40W
Burry Port 13 51 41N 4 17W
Bursa 64 40 15N 29 5 E
Burseryd 49 57 12N 13 17 E
Burstall 109 50 39N 109 54W
Burton L. 106 54 45N 78 20W
Burton-upon-Trent 12 52 48N 1 39W
Burtundy 99 33 45 S 142 15 E
Buru 73 3 30 S 126 30 E
Burullus, Bahra el 86 31 25N 31 0 E
Burundi ■ 90 3 15 S 30 0 E
Burung 72 0 24N 103 33 E
Bururi 90 3 57 S 29 37 E
Burutu 85 5 20N 5 29 E
Burwell 116 41 49N 99 8W
Bury 12 53 36N 2 19W
Bury St. Edmunds 13 52 15N 0 42 E
Buryat A.S.S.R. □ 59 53 0N 110 0 E
Buryn 54 51 13N 33 50 E
Burzenin 28 51 28N 18 47 E
Busalla 38 44 34N 8 58 E
Busango Swamp 91 14 15 S 25 45 E
Buşayyah 64 30 0N 46 10 E
Busca 38 44 31N 7 29 E
Bushati 44 41 58N 19 34 E
Bushell 109 59 31N 108 45W
Bushenyi 90 0 35 S 30 10 E
Bushnell, Ill., U.S.A. 116 40 32N 90 30W
Bushnell, Nebr., U.S.A. 116 41 18N 103 50W
Busia □ 90 0 25N 34 6 E
Busie 84 10 29N 2 22W
Businga 88 3 16N 20 59 E
Buskerud fylke □ 47 60 13N 9 0 E
Busko Zdrój 28 50 28N 20 42 E
Busoga □ 90 0 5N 33 30 E
Busovača 42 44 6N 17 53 E
Busra ash Shām 64 32 30N 36 25 E
Bussang 19 47 50N 6 50 E
Busselton 96 33 42 S 115 15 E
Busseto 38 44 59N 10 2 E
Bussum 16 52 16N 5 10 E
Bustard Hd. 97 24 0 S 151 48 E
Busto Arsizio 38 45 40N 8 50 E
Busto, C. 30 43 34N 6 28W
Busu-Djanoa 88 1 43N 21 23 E
Busuanga 73 12 10N 120 0 E
Büsum 24 54 7N 8 50 E
Buta 90 2 50N 24 53 E
Butare 90 2 31 S 29 52 E
Bute 14 55 48N 5 2W
Bute Inlet 108 50 40N 124 53W
Butemba 90 1 9N 31 37 E
Butembo 90 0 9N 29 18 E
Butera 41 37 10N 14 10 E
Butha Qi 75 48 0N 122 32 E
Butiaba 90 1 50N 31 20 E
Butler, Mo., U.S.A. 116 38 17N 94 18W
Butler, Pa., U.S.A. 114 40 52N 79 52W
Butom Odrzánski 28 51 44N 15 48 E
Butte, Mont., U.S.A. 118 46 0N 112 31W
Butte, Nebr., U.S.A. 116 42 56N 98 54W
Butterworth 71 5 24N 100 23 E
Button B. 109 58 45N 94 23W
Butuan 73 8 57N 125 33 E
Butuku-Luba 85 3 29N 8 33 E
Butung 73 5 0 S 122 45 E
Buturlinovka 55 50 50N 40 35 E
Butzbach 24 50 24N 8 40 E
Bützow 24 53 51N 11 59 E
Buxar 69 25 34N 83 58 E
Buxton, S. Afr. 92 27 38 S 24 42 E
Buxton, U.K. 12 53 16N 1 54W
Buxy 19 46 44N 4 40 E
Buy 55 58 28N 41 28 E
Buyaga 59 59 50N 127 0 E
Buynaksk 57 42 48N 47 7 E
Büyük Çekmece 43 41 2N 28 35 E
Büyük Kemikli Burun 44 40 20N 26 15 E
Buzançais 18 46 54N 1 25 E
Buzău 46 45 10N 26 50 E
Buzău □ 46 45 20N 26 30 E
Buzău → 46 45 10N 27 20 E
Buzău, Pasul 46 45 35N 26 12 E
Buzaymah 81 24 50N 22 2 E
Buzen 74 33 35N 131 5 E
Buzet 39 45 24N 13 58 E
Buzi → 91 19 50 S 34 43 E
Buziaş 42 45 38N 21 36 E
Buzuluk 52 52 48N 52 12 E
Buzuluk → 55 50 15N 42 7 E
Buzzards Bay 114 41 45N 70 38W
Bwana Mkubwe 91 13 8 S 28 38 E
Byala, Ruse, Bulg. 43 43 28N 25 44 E
Byala, Varna, Bulg. 43 42 53N 27 55 E
Byala Slatina 43 43 26N 23 55 E
Byandovan, Mys 57 39 45N 49 28 E
Bychawa 28 51 1N 22 36 E
Byczyna 28 51 7N 18 12 E
Bydgoszcz 28 53 10N 18 0 E
Bydgoszcz □ 28 53 16N 17 33 E
Byelorussian S.S.R. □ 54 53 30N 27 0 E
Byers 116 39 46N 104 13W
Byesville 112 39 56N 81 32W
Bygland 47 58 50N 7 48 E
Byglandsfjord 47 58 40N 7 50 E
Byglandsfjorden 47 58 44N 7 50 E
Byhalia 117 34 53N 89 41W
Bykhov 54 53 31N 30 14 E
Bykle 47 59 20N 7 22 E
Bykovo 57 49 50N 45 25 E
Bylas 119 33 11N 110 9W
Bylderup 49 54 57N 9 6 E
Bylot I. 105 73 13N 78 34W
Byrd, C. 5 69 38 S 76 7W
Byrd Land 5 79 30 S 125 0W
Byrd Sub-Glacial Basin 5 82 0 S 120 0W
Byrock 99 30 40 S 146 27 E
Byron, C. 97 28 38 S 153 40 E
Byrranga, Gory 59 75 0N 100 0 E
Byrum 49 57 16N 11 0 E
Byske 50 64 57N 21 11 E
Byske älv → 50 64 57N 21 13 E
Bystrzyca →, Lublin, Poland 28 51 21N 22 46 E
Bystrzyca →, Wrocław, Poland 28 51 12N 16 55 E
Bystrzyca Kłodzka 28 50 19N 16 39 E
Byten 54 52 50N 25 27 E
Bytom 28 50 25N 18 54 E
Bytów 28 54 10N 17 30 E
Byumba 90 1 35 S 30 4 E
Bzenec 27 48 58N 17 18 E
Bzura → 28 52 25N 20 15 E

C

Ca Mau 71 9 7N 105 8 E
Ca Mau, Mui = Bai Bung 71 8 35N 104 42 E
Caacupé 124 25 23 S 57 5W
Caála 89 12 46 S 15 30 E
Caamano Sd. 108 52 55N 129 25W
Caazapá 124 26 8 S 56 19W
Caazapá □ 125 26 10 S 56 0W
Caballeria, C. de 32 40 5N 4 5 E
Cabañaquinta 30 43 10N 5 38W
Cabanatuan 73 15 30N 120 58 E
Cabanes 32 40 9N 0 2 E
Cabano 107 47 40N 68 56W
Čabar 39 45 36N 14 39 E
Cabedelo 127 7 0 S 34 50W
Cabeza del Buey 31 38 44N 5 13W
Cabildo 124 32 30 S 71 5W
Cabimas 126 10 23N 71 25W
Cabinda 88 5 33 S 12 11 E
Cabinda □ 88 5 0 S 12 30 E
Cabinet Mts. 118 48 0N 115 30W
Cabo Blanco 128 47 15 S 65 47W
Cabo Frio 125 22 51 S 42 3W
Cabo Pantoja 126 1 0 S 75 10W
Cabonga, Réservoir 106 47 20N 76 40W
Cabool 117 37 10N 92 8W
Caboolture 99 27 5 S 152 58 E
Cabora Bassa Dam 91 15 20 S 32 50 E
Caborca (Heroica) 120 30 40N 112 10W
Cabot, Mt. 113 44 30N 71 25W
Cabot Strait 107 47 15N 59 40W
Cabra 31 37 30N 4 28W
Cabra del Santo Cristo 33 37 42N 3 16W
Cábras 40 39 57N 8 30 E
Cabrera, I. 33 39 8N 2 57 E
Cabrera, Sierra 30 42 12N 6 40W
Cabri 109 50 35N 108 25W
Cabriel → 33 39 14N 1 3W
Cacabelos 30 42 36N 6 44W
Čačak 42 43 54N 20 20 E
Cáceres, Brazil 126 16 5 S 57 40W
Cáceres, Spain 31 39 26N 6 23W
Cáceres □ 31 39 45N 6 0W
Cache Bay 106 46 22N 80 0W
Cachepo 31 37 20N 7 49W
Cachéu 84 12 14N 16 8W
Cachi 124 25 5 S 66 10W
Cachimbo, Serra do 127 9 30 S 55 0W
Cachoeira 127 12 30 S 39 0W
Cachoeira de Itapemirim 125 20 51 S 41 7W
Cachoeira do Sul 125 30 3 S 52 53W
Cachopo 31 37 20N 7 49W
Cacólo 88 10 9 S 19 21 E
Caconda 89 13 48 S 15 8 E
Cadarache, Barrage de 21 43 42N 5 47 E
Čadca 27 49 26N 18 45 E
Caddo 117 34 8N 96 18W
Cader Idris 12 52 43N 3 56W
Cadí, Sierra del 32 42 17N 1 42 E
Cadillac, Can. 106 48 14N 78 23W
Cadillac, France 20 44 38N 0 20W
Cadillac, U.S.A. 114 44 16N 85 25W
Cadiz 73 10 57N 123 15 E
Cádiz 31 36 30N 6 20W
Cadiz 112 40 13N 81 0W
Cádiz □ 31 36 36N 5 45W
Cádiz, G. de 31 36 40N 7 0W
Cadomin 108 53 2N 117 20W
Cadotte → 108 56 43N 117 10W
Cadours 20 43 44N 1 2 E
Caen 18 49 10N 0 22W
Caernarfon 12 53 8N 4 17W
Caernarfon B. 12 53 4N 4 40W
Caernarvon = Caernarfon 12 53 8N 4 17W
Caerphilly 13 51 34N 3 13W
Caesarea 62 32 30N 34 53 E
Caeté 127 19 55 S 43 40W

Caetité 127 13 50S 42 32W
Cafayate 124 26 2S 66 0W
Cafu 92 16 30S 15 8E
Cagayan 73 9 39N 121 16E
Cagayan → 73 18 25N 121 42E
Cagayan de Oro 73 8 30N 124 40E
Cagli 39 43 32N 12 38E
Cágliari 40 39 15N 9 6E
Cágliari, G. di 40 39 8N 9 10E
Cagnano Varano 41 41 49N 15 47E
Cagnes-sur-Mer 21 43 40N 7 9E
Caguas 121 18 14N 66 4W
Caha Mts. 15 51 45N 9 40W
Cahama 92 16 17S 14 19E
Caher 15 52 23N 7 56W
Cahersiveen 15 51 57N 10 13W
Cahore Pt. 15 52 34N 6 11W
Cahors 20 44 27N 1 27E
Cahuapanas 126 5 15S 77 0W
Caianda 91 11 2S 23 31E
Caibarién 121 22 30N 79 30W
Caicara 126 7 38N 66 10W
Caicó 127 6 20S 37 0W
Caicos Is. 121 21 40N 71 40W
Caicos Passage 121 22 45N 72 45W
Cainsville 112 43 9N 80 15W
Caird Coast 5 75 0S 25 0W
Cairn Gorm 14 57 7N 3 40W
Cairn Toul 14 57 3N 3 44W
Cairngorm Mts. 14 57 6N 3 42W
Cairns 97 16 57S 145 45E
Cairo, Ga., U.S.A. 115 30 52N 84 12W
Cairo, Illinois, U.S.A. 117 37 0N 89 10W
Cairo = El Qâhira 86 30 1N 31 14E
Cairo Montenotte 38 44 23N 8 16E
Caithness, Ord of 14 58 9N 3 37W
Caiundo 89 15 50S 17 28E
Caiza 126 20 2S 65 40W
Cajamarca 126 7 5S 78 28W
Cajarc 20 44 29N 1 50E
Cajàzeiras 127 6 52S 38 30W
Čajetina 42 43 47N 19 42E
Čajniče 42 43 34N 19 5E
Çakirgol 57 40 33N 39 40E
Čakovec 39 46 23N 16 26E
Cala 31 37 59N 6 21W
Cala → 31 37 38N 6 5W
Cala Cadolar, Punta de 33 38 38N 1 35E
Calabar 85 4 57N 8 20E
Calábria □ 41 39 24N 16 30E
Calaburras, Pta. de 31 36 30N 4 38W
Calaceite 32 41 1N 0 11E
Calafat 46 43 58N 22 59E
Calafate 128 50 19S 72 15W
Calahorra 32 42 18N 1 59W
Calais, France 19 50 57N 1 56E
Calais, U.S.A. 107 45 11N 67 20W
Calais, Pas de 19 50 57N 1 20E
Calalaste, Cord. de 124 25 0S 67 0W
Calama, Brazil 126 8 0S 62 50W
Calama, Chile 124 22 30S 68 55W
Calamar, Bolívar, Colomb. 126 10 15N 74 55W
Calamar, Vaupés, Colomb. 126 1 58N 72 32W
Calamian Group 73 11 50N 119 55E
Calamocha 32 40 50N 1 17W
Calañas 31 37 40N 6 53W
Calanda 32 40 56N 0 15W
Calang 72 4 37N 95 37E
Calangiánus 40 40 56N 9 12E
Calapan 73 13 25N 121 7E
Călăraşi 46 44 12N 27 20E
Calasparra 33 38 14N 1 41W
Calatafimi 40 37 56N 12 50E
Calatayud 32 41 20N 1 40W
Calauag 73 13 55N 122 15E
Calavà, C. 41 38 11N 14 55E
Calavite, Cape 73 13 26N 120 20E
Calbayog 73 12 4N 124 38E
Calbe 24 51 57N 11 47E
Calca 126 13 22S 72 0W
Calcasieu L. 117 30 0N 93 17W
Calci 38 43 44N 10 31E
Calcutta 69 22 36N 88 24E
Caldaro 39 46 23N 11 15E
Caldas da Rainha 31 39 24N 9 8W
Caldas de Reyes 30 42 36N 8 39W
Calder → 12 53 44N 1 21W
Caldera 124 27 5S 70 55W
Caldwell, Idaho, U.S.A. 118 43 45N 116 42W
Caldwell, Kans., U.S.A. 117 37 5N 97 37W
Caldwell, Texas, U.S.A. 117 30 30N 96 42W
Caledon 92 34 14S 19 26E
Caledon → 92 30 31S 26 5E
Caledon B. 97 12 45S 137 0E
Caledonia, Can. 112 43 7N 79 58W
Caledonia, U.S.A. 112 42 57N 77 54W
Calella 32 41 37N 2 40E
Calemba 92 16 0S 15 44E
Calera, La 124 32 50S 71 10W
Calexico 119 32 40N 115 33W
Calf of Man 12 54 4N 4 48W
Calgary 108 51 0N 114 10W
Calhoun 115 34 30N 84 55W
Cali 126 3 25N 76 35W
Calicoan 73 10 59N 125 50E
Calicut (Kozhikode) 70 11 15N 75 43E
Caliente 119 37 36N 114 34W
California, Mo., U.S.A. 116 38 37N 92 30W
California, Pa., U.S.A. 112 40 5N 79 55W
California □ 119 37 25N 120 0W
California, Baja, T.N. □ 120 30 0N 115 0W
California, Baja, T.S. □ 120 25 50N 111 50W
California, Golfo de 120 27 0N 111 0W
California, Lr. = California, Baja 120 25 50N 111 50W
Călimăneşti 46 45 14N 24 20E
Călimani, Munţii 46 47 12N 25 0E
Călineşti 46 45 21N 24 18E
Calingasta 124 31 15S 69 30W
Calipatria 119 33 8N 115 30W
Calistoga 118 38 36N 122 32W
Calitri 41 40 54N 15 25E
Callabonna, L. 97 29 40S 140 5E
Callac 18 48 25N 3 27W
Callan 15 52 33N 7 25W
Callander 14 56 15N 4 14W
Callao 126 12 0S 77 0W
Callaway 116 41 20N 99 56W
Callide 98 24 18S 150 28E
Calling Lake 108 55 15N 113 12W
Callosa de Ensarriá. 33 38 40N 0 8W
Callosa de Segura 33 38 7N 0 53W
Calne 12 51 26N 2 0W
Calola 92 16 25S 17 48E
Calore → 41 41 11N 14 28E
Caloundra 99 26 45S 153 10E
Calpe 33 38 39N 0 3E
Calstock 106 49 47N 84 9W
Caltabellotta 40 37 36N 13 11E
Caltagirone 41 37 13N 14 30E
Caltanissetta 41 37 30N 14 3E
Caluire-et-Cuire 21 45 49N 4 51E
Calulo 88 10 1S 14 56E
Calumet 114 47 14N 88 27W
Calunda 89 12 7S 23 36E
Caluso 38 45 18N 7 52E
Calvados □ 18 49 5N 0 15W
Calvert 117 30 59N 96 40W
Calvert I. 108 51 30N 128 0W
Calvinia 92 31 28S 19 45E
Calw 25 48 43N 8 44E
Calzada Almuradiel 33 38 32N 3 28W
Calzada de Calatrava 31 38 42N 3 46W
Cam → 13 52 21N 0 16E
Cam Lam 71 11 54N 109 10E
Cam Ranh 71 11 54N 109 12E
Camabatela 88 8 20S 15 26E
Camacupa 89 11 58S 17 22E
Camagüey 121 21 20N 78 0W
Camaiore 38 43 57N 10 18E
Camaná 126 16 30S 72 50W
Camaquã → 125 31 17S 51 47W
Camarat, C. 21 43 12N 6 41E
Camaret 18 48 16N 4 37W
Camargo 126 20 38S 65 15E
Camargue 21 43 34N 4 34E
Camariñas 30 43 8N 9 12W
Camarón, C. 121 16 0N 85 0W
Camarones 128 44 50S 65 40W
Camas 118 45 35N 122 24W
Camas Valley 118 43 0N 123 46W
Cambados 30 42 31N 8 49W
Cambará 125 23 2S 50 5W
Cambay 68 22 23N 72 33E
Cambay, G. of 68 20 45N 72 30E
Cambil 33 37 40N 3 33W
Cambo-les-Bains 20 43 22N 1 23W
Cambodia ■ 71 12 15N 105 0E
Camborne 13 50 13N 5 18W
Cambrai 19 50 11N 3 14E
Cambria 119 35 39N 121 6W
Cambrian Mts. 13 52 25N 3 52W
Cambridge, Can. 106 43 23N 80 15W
Cambridge, N.Z. 101 37 54S 175 29E
Cambridge, U.K. 13 52 13N 0 8E
Cambridge, Idaho, U.S.A. 118 44 36N 116 40W
Cambridge, Mass., U.S.A. 114 42 20N 71 8W
Cambridge, Md., U.S.A. 114 38 33N 76 2W
Cambridge, Minn., U.S.A. 116 45 34N 93 15W
Cambridge, N.Y., U.S.A. 113 43 2N 73 22W
Cambridge, Nebr., U.S.A. 116 40 20N 100 12W
Cambridge, Ohio, U.S.A. 114 40 1N 81 35W
Cambridge Bay 104 69 10N 105 0W
Cambridge Gulf 96 14 55S 128 15E
Cambridge Springs 112 41 47N 80 4W
Cambridgeshire □ 13 52 12N 0 7E
Cambrils 32 41 8N 1 3E
Cambuci 125 21 35S 41 55W
Camden, Ala., U.S.A. 115 31 59N 87 15W
Camden, Ark., U.S.A. 117 33 40N 92 50W
Camden, Me., U.S.A. 107 44 14N 69 6W
Camden, N.J., U.S.A. 114 39 57N 75 7W
Camden, S.C., U.S.A. 115 34 17N 80 34W
Camdenton 117 38 0N 92 45W
Camembert 18 48 53N 0 10E
Cámeri 38 45 30N 8 40E
Camerino 39 43 10N 13 4E
Cameron, Ariz., U.S.A. 119 35 55N 111 31W
Cameron, La., U.S.A. 117 29 50N 93 18W
Cameron, Mo., U.S.A. 116 39 42N 94 14W
Cameron, Tex., U.S.A. 117 30 53N 97 0W
Cameron Falls 106 49 8N 88 19W
Cameron Highlands 71 4 27N 101 22E
Cameron Hills 108 59 48N 118 0W
Cameroon ■ 88 6 0N 12 30E
Camerota 41 40 2N 15 21E
Cameroun → 85 4 0N 9 35E
Cameroun, Mt. 88 4 13N 9 10E
Cametá 127 2 12S 49 30W
Camiguin 73 8 55N 123 55E
Caminha 30 41 50N 8 50W
Camino 118 38 47N 120 40W
Camira Creek 99 29 15S 152 58E
Cammal 112 41 24N 77 28W
Camocim 127 2 55S 40 50W
Camogli 38 44 21N 9 9E
Camooweal 97 19 56S 138 7E
Camopi → 127 3 10N 52 20W
Camp Crook 116 45 36N 103 59W
Camp Wood 117 29 41N 100 0W
Campagna 41 40 40N 15 5E
Campana 124 34 10S 58 55W
Campana, I. 128 48 20S 75 20W
Campanario 31 38 52N 5 36W
Campania □ 41 40 50N 14 45E
Campbell 112 41 5N 80 36W
Campbell I. 94 52 30S 169 0E
Campbell L. 109 63 14N 106 55W
Campbell River 108 50 5N 125 20W
Campbell Town 99 41 52S 147 30E
Campbellford 112 44 18N 77 48W
Campbellsville 114 37 23N 85 21W
Campbellton 107 47 57N 66 43W
Campbelltown 99 34 4S 150 49E
Campbeltown 14 55 25N 5 36W
Campeche 120 19 50N 90 32W
Campeche □ 120 19 50N 90 32W
Campeche, Bahía de 120 19 30N 93 0W
Camperdown 99 38 14S 143 9E
Camperville 109 51 59N 100 9W
Campi Salentina 41 40 22N 18 2E
Campidano 40 39 30N 8 40E
Campillo de Altobuey 32 39 36N 1 49W
Campillo de Llerena 31 38 30N 5 50W
Campillos 31 37 4N 4 51W
Campina Grande 127 7 20S 35 47W
Campiña, La 31 37 45N 4 45W
Campinas 125 22 50S 47 0W
Campli 39 42 44N 13 40E
Campo, Camer. 88 2 22N 9 50E
Campo, Spain 32 42 25N 0 24E
Campo Belo 127 20 52S 45 16W
Campo de Criptana 33 39 24N 3 7W
Campo de Gibraltar 31 36 15N 5 25W
Campo Formoso 127 10 30S 40 20W
Campo Grande 127 20 25S 54 40W
Campo Maíor 127 4 50S 42 12W
Campo Maior 31 38 59N 7 7W
Campo Túres 39 46 53N 11 55E
Campoalegre 126 2 41N 75 20W
Campobasso 41 41 34N 14 40E
Campobello di Licata 40 37 16N 13 55E
Campobello di Mazara 40 37 38N 12 45E
Campofelice 40 37 54N 13 53E
Camporeale 40 37 53N 13 3E
Campos 125 21 50S 41 20W
Campos Belos 127 13 10S 47 3W
Campos del Puerto 33 39 26N 3 1E
Campos Novos 125 27 21S 51 50W
Camprodón 32 42 19N 2 23E
Campuya → 126 1 40S 73 30W
Camrose 108 53 0N 112 50W
Camsell Portage 109 59 37N 109 15W
Can Tho 71 10 2N 105 46E
Canaan 113 42 1N 73 20W
Canada ■ 104 60 0N 100 0W
Cañada de Gómez 124 32 40S 61 30W
Canadian 117 35 56N 100 25W
Canadian → 117 35 27N 95 3W
Canakkale 44 40 8N 26 30E
Canakkale Boğazi 44 40 0N 26 0E
Canal Flats 108 50 10N 115 48W
Canal latéral à la Garonne 20 44 25N 0 15E
Canalejas 124 35 15S 66 34W
Canals, Argent. 124 33 35S 62 53W
Canals, Spain 33 38 58N 0 35W
Canandaigua 114 42 55N 77 18W
Cananea 120 31 0N 110 20W
Canarias, Islas 80 28 30N 16 0W
Canarreos, Arch. de los 121 21 35N 81 40W
Canary Is. = Canarias, Islas 80 29 30N 17 0W
Canaveral, C. 115 28 28N 80 31W
Cañaveras 32 40 27N 2 24W
Canavieiras 127 15 39S 39 0W
Canbelego 99 31 32S 146 18E
Canberra 97 35 15S 149 8E
Canby, Calif., U.S.A. 118 41 26N 120 58W
Canby, Minn., U.S.A. 116 44 44N 96 15W
Canby, Ore., U.S.A. 118 45 16N 122 42W
Cancale 18 48 40N 1 50W
Canche → 19 50 31N 1 39E
Candala 63 11 30N 49 58E
Candas 30 43 35N 5 45W
Candé 18 47 34N 1 0W
Candela 41 41 8N 15 31E
Candelaria 125 27 29S 55 44W
Candelaria, Pta. de la 30 43 45N 8 0W
Candeleda 30 40 10N 5 14W
Candelo 99 36 47S 149 43E
Candia = Iráklion 45 35 20N 25 12E
Candia, Sea of = Crete, Sea of 45 36 0N 25 0E
Candle L. 109 53 50N 105 18W
Candlemas I. 5 57 3S 26 40W
Cando 116 48 30N 99 14W
Canea = Khaniá 45 35 30N 24 4E
Canelli 38 44 44N 8 18E
Canelones 125 34 32S 56 17W
Canet-Plage 20 42 41N 3 2E
Cañete, Chile 124 37 50S 73 30W
Cañete, Peru 126 13 8S 76 30W
Cañete, Spain 32 40 3N 1 54W
Cañete de las Torres 31 37 53N 4 19W
Canfranc 32 42 42N 0 31W
Cangas 30 42 16N 8 47W
Cangas de Narcea 30 43 10N 6 32W
Cangas de Onís 30 43 21N 5 8W
Canguaretama 127 6 20S 35 5W
Canguçu 125 31 22S 52 43W
Cangxi 77 31 47N 105 59E
Cangzhou 76 38 19N 116 52E
Cani, I. 83 36 21N 10 5E
Canicattì 40 37 21N 13 50E
Canicattini 41 37 1N 15 3E
Canim Lake 108 51 47N 120 54W
Canipaan 72 8 33N 117 15E
Canisteo 112 42 17N 77 37W
Canisteo → 112 42 15N 77 30W
Cañiza, La 30 42 13N 8 16W
Cañizal 30 41 12N 5 22W
Canjáyar 33 37 1N 2 44W
Çankırı 64 40 40N 33 37E
Cankuzo 90 3 10S 30 31E
Canmore 108 51 7N 115 18W
Cann River 99 37 35S 149 7E
Canna 14 57 3N 6 33W
Cannanore 70 11 53N 75 27E
Cannes 21 43 32N 7 0E
Canning Basin 96 19 50S 124 0E
Canning Town 69 22 23N 88 40E
Cannington 112 44 20N 79 2W
Cannock 12 52 42N 2 2W
Cannon Ball → 116 46 20N 100 38W
Canoe L. 109 55 10N 108 15W
Canon City 116 38 27N 105 14W
Canora 109 51 40N 102 30W
Canosa di Púglia 41 41 13N 16 4E
Canourgue, Le 20 44 26N 3 13E
Canowindra 99 33 35S 148 38
Canso 107 45 20N 61 0W
Cantabria, Sierra de 32 42 40N 2 30W
Cantabrian Mts. = Cantábrica, Cordillera 30 43 0N 5 10W
Cantábrica, Cordillera 30 43 0N 5 10W
Cantal □ 20 45 4N 2 45
Cantanhede 30 40 20N 8 36W
Cantavieja 32 40 31N 0 25W
Čantavir 42 45 55N 19 46
Canterbury, Austral. 99 25 23S 141 53
Canterbury, U.K. 13 51 17N 1 5
Canterbury □ 101 43 45S 171 19
Canterbury Bight 101 44 16S 171 55
Canterbury Plains 101 43 55S 171 22
Cantillana 31 37 36N 5 50W
Canton, Ga., U.S.A. 115 34 13N 84 29W
Canton, Ill., U.S.A. 116 40 32N 90 0W
Canton, Mass., U.S.A. 113 42 8N 71 8W
Canton, Miss., U.S.A. 117 32 40N 90 1W
Canton, Mo., U.S.A. 116 40 10N 91 33W
Canton, N.Y., U.S.A. 114 44 32N 75 3W
Canton, Ohio, U.S.A. 114 40 47N 81 22W
Canton, Okla., U.S.A. 117 36 5N 98 36W
Canton, S.D., U.S.A. 116 43 20N 96 35W
Canton = Guangzhou 75 23 5N 113 10
• Canton I. 94 2 50S 171 40W
Canton L. 117 36 12N 98 40W
Cantù 38 45 44N 9 8
Canudos 126 7 13S 58 5W
Canutama 126 6 30S 64 20W
Canutillo 119 31 58N 106 36W
Canyon, Texas, U.S.A. 117 35 0N 101 57W
Canyon, Wyo., U.S.A. 118 44 43N 110 36W
Canyonlands Nat. Park 119 38 25N 109 30W
Canyonville 118 42 55N 123 14W
Canzo 38 45 54N 9 18
Cao Xian 77 34 50N 115 35
Cáorle 39 45 36N 12 51
Cap-aux-Meules 107 47 23N 61 52W
Cap-Chat 107 49 6N 66 40W
Cap-de-la-Madeleine 106 46 22N 72 31W
Cap-Haïtien 121 19 40N 72 20W
Capa Stilo 41 38 25N 16 35
Capáccio 41 40 26N 15 4
Capaia 88 8 27S 20 13
Capanaparo → 126 7 1N 67 7W
Capbreton 20 43 39N 1 26W
Capdenac 20 44 34N 2 5
Cape → 98 20 49S 146 51
Cape Barren I. 97 40 25S 148 15
Cape Breton Highlands Nat. Park 107 46 50N 60 40W
Cape Breton I. 107 46 0N 60 30W
Cape Charles 114 37 15N 75 59W
Cape Coast 85 5 5N 1 15W
Cape Dorset 105 64 14N 76 32W
Cape Dyer 105 66 30N 61 22W
Cape Fear → 115 34 30N 78 25W
Cape Girardeau 117 37 20N 89 30W
Cape May 114 39 1N 74 53W
Cape Montague 107 46 5N 62 25W
Cape Palmas 84 4 25N 7 49W
Cape Province □ 92 32 0S 23 0
Cape Tormentine 107 46 8N 63 47W
Cape Town (Kaapstad) 92 33 55S 18 22
Cape Verde Is. ■ 6 17 10N 25 20W
Cape Vincent 113 44 9N 76 21W
Cape York Peninsula 97 12 0S 142 30
Capela 127 10 30S 37 0W
Capella 98 23 2S 148 1
Capella, Mt. 98 5 4S 141 8
Capelle, La 19 49 59N 3 50
Capendu 20 43 11N 2 31
Capernaum = Kefar Nahum 62 32 54N 35 32
Capestang 20 43 20N 3 2
Capim → 127 1 40S 47 47W
Capitan 119 33 33N 105 41W
Capizzi 41 37 50N 14 26
Čapljina 42 43 10N 17 43
Capoche → 91 15 35S 33 0
Capraia 38 43 2N 9 50
Caprarola 39 42 21N 12 11
Capreol 106 46 43N 80 56W
Caprera 40 41 12N 9 28
Capri 41 40 34N 14 15
Capricorn, C. 97 23 30S 151 13
Capricorn Group 98 23 30S 151 55
Caprino Veronese 38 45 37N 10 47
Caprivi Strip 92 18 0S 23 0
Captainganj 69 26 55N 83 45
Captain's Flat 99 35 35S 149 27
Captieux 20 44 18N 0 16W
Cápua 41 41 7N 14 15
Capulin 117 36 48N 103 59W
Caquetá → 126 1 15S 69 15W
Caracal 46 44 8N 24 22
Caracas 126 10 30N 66 55W
Caracol 127 9 15S 43 22W
Caradoc 99 30 35S 143 5
Caráglio 38 44 25N 7 25
Carajás, Serra dos 127 6 0S 51 30W
Carangola 125 20 44S 42 5W
Caransebeş 46 45 28N 22 18
Carantec 18 48 40N 3 55W
Carapelle → 41 41 3N 15 55
Caraş Severin □ 42 45 10N 22 10
Caraşova 42 45 11N 21 51
Caratasca, Laguna 121 15 20N 83 40W
Caratinga 127 19 50S 42 10W
Caraúbas 127 5 43S 37 33W
Caravaca 33 38 8N 1 52W
Caravággio 38 45 30N 9 39
Caravelas 127 17 45S 39 15W
Caraveli 126 15 45S 73 25W
Caràzinho 125 28 16S 52 46W
Carballino 30 42 26N 8 5W
Carballo 30 43 13N 8 41W
Carberry 109 49 50N 99 25W
Carbia 30 42 48N 8 14W
Carbó 120 29 42N 110 58W
Carbon 108 51 30N 113 9W

• *Renamed Abariringa*

arbonara, C. 40 39 8N 9 30 E
arbondale, Colo, U.S.A. 118 39 30N 107 10W
arbondale, Ill., U.S.A. 117 37 45N 89 10W
arbondale, Pa., U.S.A. 114 41 37N 75 30W
arbonear 107 47 42N 53 13W
arboneras 33 37 0N 1 53W
arboneras de Guadazaón 32 39 54N 1 50W
arbonia 40 39 10N 8 30 E
arcabuey 31 37 27N 4 17W
arcagente 33 39 8N 0 28W
arcajou 108 57 47N 117 6W
arcans, Étang d' 20 45 6N 1 7W
arcasse, C. 121 18 30N 74 28W
arcassonne 20 43 13N 2 20 E
arche 33 38 26N 1 9W
arcross 104 60 13N 134 45W
ardamom Hills 70 9 30N 77 15 E
árdenas, Cuba 121 23 0N 81 30W
árdenas, San Luis Potosí, Mexico 120 22 0N 99 41W
árdenas, Tabasco, Mexico 120 17 59N 93 21W
ardenete 32 39 46N 1 41W
ardiff 13 51 28N 3 11W
ardigan 13 52 6N 4 41W
ardigan B. 13 52 30N 4 30W
ardinal 113 44 47N 75 23W
ardona, Spain 32 41 56N 1 40 E
ardona, Uruguay 124 33 53 S 57 18W
ardoner → 32 41 41N 1 51 E
ardross 109 49 50N 105 40W
ardston 108 49 15N 113 20W
ardwell 98 18 14 S 146 2 E
areen L. 109 57 0N 108 11W
arei 46 47 40N 22 29 E
areme 73 6 55 S 108 27 E
arentan 18 49 19N 1 15W
arey, Idaho, U.S.A. 118 43 19N 113 58W
arey, Ohio, U.S.A. 114 40 58N 83 22W
arey, L. 96 29 0 S 122 15 E
arey L. 109 62 12N 102 55W
areysburg 84 6 34N 10 30W
argados Garajos 3 17 0 S 59 0 E
argèse 21 42 7N 8 35 E
arhaix-Plouguer 18 48 18N 3 36W
arhué 124 37 10 S 62 50W
aribbean Sea 121 15 0N 75 0W
ariboo Mts. 108 53 0N 121 0W
aribou 107 46 55N 68 0W
aribou →, Man., Can. 109 59 20N 94 44W
aribou →, N.W.T., Can. 108 61 27N 125 45W
aribou I. 106 47 22N 85 49W
aribou Is. 108 61 55N 113 15W
aribou L., Man., Can. 109 59 21N 96 10W
aribou L., Ont., Can. 106 50 25N 89 5W
aribou Mts. 108 59 12N 115 40W
arignan 19 49 38N 5 10 E
arignano 38 44 55N 7 40 E
arinda 99 30 28 S 147 41 E
ariñena 32 41 20N 1 13W
arinhanha 127 14 15 S 44 46W
arini 40 38 9N 13 10 E
arinola 40 41 11N 13 58 E
arinthia □ = Kärnten 26 46 52N 13 30 E
aripito 126 10 8N 63 6W
aritianas 126 9 20 S 63 6W
arlbrod = Dimitrovgrad 42 43 0N 22 48 E
arlentini 41 37 15N 15 2 E
arleton Place 106 45 8N 76 9W
arletonville 92 26 23 S 27 22 E
arlin 118 40 44N 116 5W
arlingford, L. 15 54 0N 6 5W
arlinville 116 39 20N 89 55W
arlisle, U.K. 12 54 54N 2 55W
arlisle, U.S.A. 114 40 12N 77 10W
arlitte, Pic 20 42 35N 1 55 E
arloforte 40 39 10N 8 18 E
arlos Casares 124 35 32 S 61 20W
arlos Tejedor 124 35 25 S 62 25W
arlota, La 124 33 30 S 63 20W
arlow 15 52 50N 6 58W
arlow □ 15 52 43N 6 50W
arlsbad, Calif., U.S.A. 119 33 11N 117 25W
arlsbad, N. Mex., U.S.A. 117 32 20N 104 14W
arlyle, Can. 109 49 40N 102 20W
arlyle, U.S.A. 116 38 38N 89 23W
armacks 104 62 5N 136 16W
armagnola 38 44 50N 7 42 E
arman 109 49 30N 98 0W
armangay 108 50 10N 113 10W
armanville 107 49 23N 54 19W
armarthen 13 51 52N 4 20W
armarthen B. 13 51 40N 4 30W
armaux 20 44 3N 2 10 E
armel 113 41 25N 73 38W
armel-by-the-Sea 119 36 38N 121 55W
armel Mt. 62 32 45N 35 3 E
armelo 124 34 0 S 58 20W
armen, Colomb. 126 9 43N 75 8W
armen, Parag. 125 27 13 S 56 12W
armen de Patagones 128 40 50 S 63 0W
armen, I. 120 26 0N 111 20W
armenes 30 42 58N 5 34W
armensa 124 35 15 S 67 40W
armi 114 38 6N 88 10W
armila 98 21 55 S 149 24 E
armona 31 37 28N 5 42W
arnarvon, Queens., Austral. 98 24 48 S 147 45 E
arnarvon, W. Austral., Austral. 96 24 51 S 113 42 E
arnarvon, S. Afr. 92 30 56 S 22 8 E
arnarvon Ra. 99 25 15 S 148 30 E
arnaxide 31 38 43N 9 14W
rndonagh 15 55 15N 7 16W
rnduff 109 49 10N 101 50W
rnegie 112 40 24N 80 4W
rnegie, L. 96 26 5 S 122 30 E
rnic Alps = Karnische Alpen 26 46 36N 13 0 E
rnot 88 4 59N 15 56 E
rnot B. 96 17 20 S 121 30 E
rnsore Pt. 15 52 10N 6 20W
ro 114 43 29N 83 27W
rol City 115 25 5N 80 16W
rolina, Brazil 127 7 10 S 47 30W

Carolina, S. Afr. 93 26 5 S 30 6 E
Carolina, La 31 38 17N 3 38W
Caroline I. 95 9 15 S 150 3W
Caroline Is. 94 8 0N 150 0 E
Caron 109 50 30N 105 50W
Caroni → 126 8 21N 62 43W
Carovigno 41 40 42N 17 40 E
Carpathians 46 49 50N 21 0 E
Carpații Meridionali 46 45 30N 25 0 E
Carpenédolo 38 45 22N 10 25 E
Carpentaria Downs 98 18 44 S 144 20 E
Carpentaria, G. of 97 14 0 S 139 0 E
Carpentras 21 44 3N 5 2 E
Carpi 38 44 47N 10 52 E
Carpino 41 41 50N 15 51 E
Carpinteria 119 34 25N 119 31W
Carpio 30 41 13N 5 7W
Carrabelle 115 29 52N 84 40W
Carrara 38 44 5N 10 7 E
Carrascosa del Campo 32 40 2N 2 45W
Carrauntohill, Mt. 15 52 0N 9 49W
Carrick-on-Shannon 15 53 57N 8 7W
Carrick-on-Suir 15 52 22N 7 30W
Carrickfergus 15 54 43N 5 50W
Carrickfergus □ 15 54 43N 5 49W
Carrickmacross 15 54 0N 6 43W
Carrieton 99 32 25 S 138 31 E
Carrington 116 47 30N 99 7W
Carrión → 30 41 53N 4 32W
Carrión de los Condes 30 42 20N 4 37W
Carrizal Bajo 124 28 5 S 71 20W
Carrizalillo 124 29 5 S 71 30W
Carrizo Cr. 117 36 30N 103 40W
Carrizo Springs 117 28 28N 99 50W
Carrizozo 119 33 40N 105 57W
Carroll 116 42 2N 94 55W
Carrollton, Ga., U.S.A. 115 33 36N 85 5W
Carrollton, Ill., U.S.A. 116 39 20N 90 25W
Carrollton, Ky., U.S.A. 114 38 40N 85 10W
Carrollton, Mo., U.S.A. 116 39 19N 93 24W
Carrollton, Ohio, U.S.A. 112 40 31N 81 9W
Carron → 14 57 30N 5 30W
Carron, L. 14 57 22N 5 35W
Carrot → 109 53 50N 101 17W
Carrot River 109 53 17N 103 35W
Carrouges 18 48 34N 0 10W
Carruthers 109 52 52N 109 16W
Çarşamba 64 41 15N 36 45 E
Carse of Gowrie 14 56 30N 3 10W
Carsoli 39 42 7N 13 3 E
Carson 116 46 27N 101 29W
Carson City 118 39 12N 119 46W
Carson Sink 118 39 50N 118 40W
Carsonville 114 43 25N 82 39W
Carstairs 14 55 42N 3 41W
Cartagena, Colomb. 126 10 25N 75 33W
Cartagena, Spain 33 37 38N 0 59W
Cartago, Colomb. 126 4 45N 75 55W
Cartago, C. Rica 121 9 50N 85 52W
Cartaxo 31 39 10N 8 47W
Cartaya 31 37 16N 7 9W
Carteret 18 49 23N 1 47W
Cartersville 115 34 11N 84 48W
Carterton 101 41 2 S 175 31 E
Carthage, Ark., U.S.A. 117 34 4N 92 32W
Carthage, Ill., U.S.A. 116 40 25N 91 10W
Carthage, Mo., U.S.A. 117 37 10N 94 20W
Carthage, N.Y., U.S.A. 114 43 59N 75 37W
Carthage, S.D., U.S.A. 116 44 14N 97 38W
Carthage, Texas, U.S.A. 117 32 8N 94 20W
Cartier I. 96 12 31 S 123 29 E
Cartwright 107 53 41N 56 58W
Caruaru 127 8 15 S 35 55W
Carúpano 126 10 39N 63 15W
Caruthersville 117 36 10N 89 40W
Carvin 19 50 30N 2 57 E
Carvoeiro 126 1 30 S 61 59W
Carvoeiro, Cabo 31 39 21N 9 24W
Casa Branca 31 38 29N 8 12W
Casa Grande 119 32 53N 111 51W
Casa Nova 127 9 25 S 41 5W
Casablanca, Chile 124 33 20 S 71 25W
Casablanca, Moroc. 82 33 36N 7 36W
Casacalenda 41 41 45N 14 50 E
Casal di Principe 41 41 0N 14 8 E
Casalbordino 39 42 10N 14 34 E
Casale Monferrato 38 45 8N 8 28 E
Casalmaggiore 38 44 59N 10 25 E
Casalpusterlengo 38 45 10N 9 40 E
Casamance → 84 12 33N 16 46W
Casamássima 41 40 58N 16 55 E
Casarano 41 40 0N 18 10 E
Casares 31 36 27N 5 16W
Casas Grandes 120 30 22N 108 0W
Casas Ibañez 33 39 17N 1 30W
Casasimarro 33 39 22N 2 3W
Casatejada 30 39 54N 5 40W
Casavieja 30 40 17N 4 46W
Cascade, Idaho, U.S.A. 118 44 30N 116 2W
Cascade, Mont., U.S.A. 118 47 16N 111 46W
Cascade Locks 118 45 44N 121 54W
Cascade Ra. 102 47 0N 121 30W
Cascais 31 38 41N 9 25W
Cáscina 38 43 40N 10 32 E
Caselle Torinese 38 45 12N 7 39 E
Caserta 41 41 5N 14 20 E
Cashel 15 52 31N 7 53W
Cashmere 118 47 31N 120 30W
Casiguran 73 16 22N 122 7 E
Casilda 124 33 10 S 61 10W
Casimcea 46 44 45N 28 23 E
Casino 97 28 52 S 153 3 E
Casiquiare → 126 2 1N 67 7W
Caslan 108 54 38N 112 31W
Čáslav 26 49 54N 15 22 E
Casma 126 9 30 S 78 20W
Casola Valsenio 39 44 12N 11 40 E
Cásoli 39 42 7N 14 18 E
Caspe 32 41 14N 0 1W
Casper 118 42 52N 106 20W
Caspian Sea 53 43 0N 50 0 E
Casquets 18 49 46N 2 15W

Cass City 114 43 34N 83 24W
Cass Lake 116 47 23N 94 38W
Cassá de la Selva 32 41 53N 2 52 E
Cassano Iónio 41 39 47N 16 20 E
Cassel 19 50 48N 2 30 E
Casselman 113 45 19N 75 5W
Casselton 116 47 0N 97 15W
Cassiar 108 59 16N 129 40W
Cassiar Mts. 108 59 30N 130 30W
Cassino 40 41 30N 13 50 E
Cassis 21 43 14N 5 32 E
Cassville 117 36 45N 93 52W
Cástagneto Carducci 38 43 9N 10 36 E
Castéggio 38 45 1N 9 8 E
Castejón de Monegros 32 41 37N 0 15W
Castel di Sangro 39 41 47N 14 6 E
Castel San Giovanni 38 45 4N 9 25 E
Castel San Pietro 39 44 23N 11 30 E
Castelbuono 41 37 56N 14 4 E
Casteldelfino 38 44 35N 7 4 E
Castelfiorentino 38 43 36N 10 58 E
Castelfranco Emília 38 44 37N 11 2 E
Castelfranco Véneto 39 45 40N 11 56 E
Casteljaloux 20 44 19N 0 6 E
Castellabate 41 40 18N 14 55 E
Castellammare del Golfo 40 38 2N 12 53 E
Castellammare di Stábia 41 40 47N 14 29 E
Castellammare, G. di 40 38 5N 12 55 E
Castellamonte 38 45 23N 7 42 E
Castellana Grotte 41 40 53N 17 10 E
Castellane 21 43 50N 6 31 E
Castellaneta 41 40 40N 16 57 E
Castellar de Santisteban 33 38 16N 3 8W
Castelleone 38 45 19N 9 47 E
Castelli 124 36 7 S 57 47W
Castelló de Ampurias 32 42 15N 3 4 E
Castellón □ 32 40 15N 0 5W
Castellón de la Plana 32 39 58N 0 3W
Castellote 32 40 48N 0 15W
Castelltersol 32 41 45N 2 8 E
Castelmáuro 41 41 50N 14 40 E
Castelnau-de-Médoc 20 45 2N 0 48W
Castelnaudary 20 43 20N 1 58 E
Castelnovo ne' Monti 38 44 27N 10 26 E
Castelnuovo di Val di Cécina 38 43 12N 10 54 E
Castelo 125 20 33 S 41 14 E
Castelo Branco 30 39 50N 7 31W
Castelo Branco □ 30 39 52N 7 45W
Castelo de Paiva 30 41 2N 8 16W
Castelo de Vide 31 39 25N 7 27W
Castelsarrasin 20 44 2N 1 7 E
Casteltérmini 40 37 32N 13 38 E
Castelvetrano 40 37 40N 12 46 E
Casterton 99 37 30 S 141 30 E
Castets 20 43 52N 1 6W
Castiglione del Lago 39 43 7N 12 3 E
Castiglione della Pescáia 38 42 46N 10 53 E
Castiglione della Stiviere 38 45 23N 10 30 E
Castiglione Fiorentino 39 43 20N 11 55 E
Castilblanco 31 39 17N 5 5W
Castilla La Nueva 31 39 45N 3 20W
Castilla La Vieja 30 41 55N 4 0W
Castilla, Playa de 31 37 0N 6 33W
Castille = Castilla 30 40 0N 3 30W
Castillon, Barrage de 21 43 53N 6 33 E
Castillon-en-Couserans 20 42 56N 1 1 E
Castillon-la-Bataille 20 44 51N 0 2W
Castillonès 20 44 39N 0 37 E
Castillos 125 34 12 S 53 52W
Castle Dale 118 39 11N 111 1W
Castle Douglas 14 54 57N 3 57W
Castle Harbour 121 32 17N 64 44W
Castle Point 101 40 54 S 176 15 E
Castle Rock, Colo., U.S.A. 116 39 26N 104 50W
Castle Rock, Wash., U.S.A. 118 46 20N 122 58W
Castlebar 15 53 52N 9 17W
Castleblaney 15 54 7N 6 44W
Castlegar 108 49 20N 117 40W
Castlegate 118 39 45N 110 57W
Castlemaine 97 37 2 S 144 12 E
Castlereagh 15 53 47N 8 30W
Castlereagh □ 15 54 33N 5 53W
Castlereagh → 97 30 12 S 147 32 E
Castlereagh B. 96 12 10 S 135 10 E
Castletown 12 54 4N 4 40W
Castletown Bearhaven 15 51 40N 9 54W
Castlevale 98 24 30 S 146 48 E
Castor 108 52 15N 111 50W
Castres 20 43 37N 2 13 E
Castries 121 14 0N 60 50W
Castril 33 37 48N 2 46W
Castro, Brazil 125 24 45 S 50 0W
Castro, Chile 128 42 30 S 73 50W
Castro Alves 127 12 46 S 39 33W
Castro del Río 31 37 41N 4 29W
Castro Marim 31 37 13N 7 26W
Castro Urdiales 32 43 23N 3 11W
Castro Verde 31 37 41N 8 4W
Castrojeriz 30 42 17N 4 9W
Castropol 30 43 32N 7 0W
Castroreale 41 38 5N 15 15 E
Castrovillari 41 39 49N 16 11 E
Castroville 117 29 20N 98 53W
Castuera 31 38 43N 5 37W
Casummit Lake 106 51 29N 92 22W
Cat I., Bahamas 121 24 30N 75 30W
Cat I., U.S.A. 117 30 15N 89 7W
Cat L. 106 51 40N 91 50W
Čata 27 47 58N 18 38 E
Catacáos 126 5 20 S 80 45W
Cataguases 125 21 23 S 42 39W
Catahoula L. 117 31 30N 92 5W
Catalão 127 18 10 S 47 57W
Catalina 107 48 31N 53 4W
Catalonia = Cataluña 32 41 40N 1 15 E
Cataluña 32 41 40N 1 15 E
Catamarca 124 28 30 S 65 50W
Catamarca □ 124 27 0 S 65 50W
Catanduanes 73 13 50N 124 20 E
Catanduva 125 21 5 S 48 58W
Catánia 41 37 31N 15 4 E
Catánia, G. di 41 37 25N 15 8 E

Catanzaro 41 38 54N 16 38 E
Catarman 73 12 28N 124 35 E
Catastrophe C. 96 34 59 S 136 0 E
Cateau, Le 19 50 6N 3 30 E
Cateel 73 7 47N 126 24 E
Cathcart 92 32 18 S 27 10 E
Cathlamet 118 46 12N 123 23W
Catio 84 11 17N 15 15W
Cativa 120 9 21N 79 49W
Catlettsburg 114 38 23N 82 38W
Cato I. 97 23 15 S 155 32 E
Catoche, C. 120 21 40N 87 8W
Catral 33 38 10N 0 47W
Catria, Mt. 39 43 28N 12 42 E
Catrimani 126 0 27N 61 41W
Catskill 114 42 14N 73 52W
Catskill Mts. 114 42 15N 74 15W
Cattaraugus 112 42 22N 78 52W
Cattólica 39 43 58N 12 43 E
Cattólica Eraclea 40 37 27N 13 24 E
Catuala 92 16 25 S 19 2 E
Catur 91 13 45 S 35 30 E
Cauca → 126 8 54N 74 28W
Caucaia 127 3 40 S 38 35W
Caucasus Mts. = Bolshoi Kavkas 57 42 50N 44 0 E
Caudebec-en-Caux 18 49 30N 0 42 E
Caudete 33 38 42N 1 2W
Caudry 19 50 7N 3 22 E
Caulnes 18 48 18N 2 10W
Caulónia 41 38 23N 16 25 E
Caúngula 88 8 26 S 18 38 E
Cauquenes 124 36 0 S 72 22W
Caura → 126 7 38N 64 53W
Cauresi → 91 17 8 S 33 0 E
Causapscal 107 48 19N 67 12W
Caussade 20 44 10N 1 33 E
Cauterets 20 42 52N 0 8W
Caux, Pays de 18 49 38N 0 35 E
Cava dei Tirreni 41 40 42N 14 42 E
Cávado → 30 41 32N 8 48W
Cavaillon 21 43 50N 5 2 E
Cavalaire-sur-Mer 21 43 10N 6 33 E
Cavalerie, La 20 44 0N 3 10 E
Cavalese 39 46 17N 11 29 E
Cavalier 116 48 50N 97 39W
Cavallo, Île de 21 41 22N 9 16 E
Cavally → 84 4 22N 7 32W
Cavan 15 54 0N 7 22W
Cavan □ 15 53 58N 7 10W
Cavárzere 39 45 8N 12 6 E
Cave City 114 37 13N 85 57W
Cavendish 99 37 31 S 142 2 E
Caviana, I. 127 0 10N 50 10W
Cavite 73 14 29N 120 55 E
Cavour 38 44 47N 7 22 E
Cavtat 42 42 35N 18 13 E
Cawndilla, L. 99 32 30 S 142 15 E
Cawnpore = Kanpur 69 26 28N 80 20 E
Caxias 127 4 55 S 43 20W
Caxias do Sul 125 29 10 S 51 10W
Caxine, C. 82 35 56N 0 27W
Caxito 88 8 30 S 13 30 E
Cay Sal Bank 121 23 45N 80 0W
Cayambe 126 0 3N 78 8W
Cayce 115 33 59N 81 10W
Cayenne 127 5 0N 52 18W
Cayes, Les 121 18 15N 73 46W
Cayeux-sur-Mer 19 50 10N 1 30 E
Caylus 20 44 15N 1 47 E
Cayman Is. 121 19 40N 80 30W
• Cayo 120 17 10N 89 0W
Cayo Romano 121 22 0N 78 0W
Cayuga, Can. 112 42 59N 79 50W
Cayuga, U.S.A. 113 42 54N 76 44W
Cayuga L. 114 42 45N 76 45W
Cazalla de la Sierra 31 37 56N 5 45W
Căzăneşti 46 44 36N 27 3 E
Cazaux et de Sanguinet, Étang de 20 44 29N 1 10W
Cazères 20 43 13N 1 5 E
Cazin 39 44 57N 15 57 E
Čazma 39 45 45N 16 39 E
Čazma → 39 45 35N 16 29 E
Cazombo 89 11 54 S 22 56 E
Cazorla 33 37 55N 3 2W
Cazorla, Sierra de 33 38 5N 2 55W
Cea → 30 42 0N 5 36W
Ceamurlia de Jos 43 44 43N 28 47 E
Ceanannus Mor 15 53 42N 6 53W
Ceará = Fortaleza 127 3 43 S 38 35W
Ceará □ 127 5 0 S 40 0W
Ceará Mirim 127 5 38 S 35 25W
Ceauru, L. 46 44 58N 23 11 E
Cebollar 124 29 10 S 66 35W
Cebollera, Sierra de 32 42 0N 2 30W
Cebreros 30 40 27N 4 28W
Cebu 73 10 18N 123 54 E
Ceccano 40 41 34N 13 18 E
Cece 27 46 46N 18 39 E
Cechi 84 6 15N 4 25W
Cecil Plains 99 27 30 S 151 11 E
Cécina 38 43 19N 10 33 E
Cécina → 38 43 19N 10 29 E
Ceclavin 30 39 50N 6 45W
Cedar → 116 41 17N 91 21W
Cedar City 119 37 41N 113 3W
Cedar Creek Res. 117 32 4N 96 5W
Cedar Falls 116 42 39N 92 29W
Cedar Key 115 29 9N 83 5W
Cedar L. 109 53 10N 100 0W
Cedar Rapids 116 42 0N 91 38W
Cedarburg 114 43 18N 87 55W
Cedartown 115 34 1N 85 15W
Cedarvale 108 55 1N 128 22W
Cedarville 118 41 37N 120 13W
Cedeira 30 43 39N 8 2W
Cedral 120 23 50N 100 42W
Cedrino → 40 40 23N 9 44 E
Cedro 127 6 34 S 39 3W
Cedros, I. de 120 28 10N 115 20W
Ceduna 96 32 7 S 133 46 E
Cedynia 28 52 53N 14 12 E
Cefalù 41 38 3N 14 1 E

named N'gage

• *Renamed San Ignacio*

HIA

Cega → 30 41 33N 4 46W
Cegléd 27 47 11N 19 47 E
Céglie Messápico 41 40 39N 17 31 E
Cehegín 33 38 6N 1 48W
Cehu-Silvaniei 46 47 24N 23 9 E
Ceiba, La 121 15 40N 86 50W
Ceica 46 46 53N 22 10 E
Ceira → 30 40 13N 8 16W
Cekhira 83 34 20N 10 5 E
Celano 39 42 6N 13 30 E
Celanova 30 42 9N 7 58W
Celaya 120 20 31N 100 37W
Celbridge 15 53 20N 6 33W
Celebes = Sulawesi 73 2 0S 120 0 E
Celebes Sea 73 3 0N 123 0 E
Čelić 42 44 43N 18 47 E
Celina 114 40 32N 84 31W
Celje 39 46 16N 15 18 E
Celldömölk 27 47 16N 17 10 E
Celle 24 52 37N 10 4 E
Celorico da Beira 30 40 38N 7 24W
Cement 117 34 56N 98 8W
Cengong 77 27 13N 108 44 E
Cenis, Col du Mt. 21 45 15N 6 55 E
Ceno → 38 44 4N 10 5 E
Cenon 20 44 50N 0 33W
Centallo 38 44 30N 7 35 E
Center, N.D., U.S.A. 116 47 9N 101 17W
Center, Texas, U.S.A. 117 31 50N 94 10W
Centerfield 119 39 9N 111 56W
Centerville, Ala., U.S.A. 115 32 55N 87 7W
Centerville, Iowa, U.S.A. 116 40 45N 92 57W
Centerville, Miss., U.S.A. 117 31 10N 91 3W
Centerville, Pa., U.S.A. 112 40 3N 79 59W
Centerville, S.D., U.S.A. 116 43 10N 96 58W
Centerville, Tenn., U.S.A. 115 35 46N 87 29W
Centerville, Tex., U.S.A. 117 31 15N 95 56W
Cento 39 44 43N 11 16 E
Central 119 32 46N 108 9W
Central □, Kenya 90 0 30S 37 30 E
Central □, Malawi 91 13 30S 33 30 E
Central □, U.K. 14 56 10N 4 30W
Central □, Zambia 91 14 25S 28 50 E
Central African Republic ■ 88 7 0N 20 0 E
Central City, Ky., U.S.A. 114 37 20N 87 7W
Central City, Nebr., U.S.A. 116 41 8N 98 0W
Central, Cordillera, Colomb. 126 5 0N 75 0W
Central, Cordillera, C. Rica 121 10 10N 84 5W
Central I. 90 3 30N 36 0 E
Central Islip 113 40 49N 73 13W
Central Makran Range 65 26 30N 64 15 E
Central Patricia 106 51 30N 90 9W
Central Ra. 98 5 0S 143 0 E
Central Russian Uplands 9 54 0N 36 0 E
Central Siberian Plateau 59 65 0N 105 0 E
Centralia, Ill., U.S.A. 116 38 32N 89 5W
Centralia, Mo., U.S.A. 116 39 12N 92 6W
Centralia, Wash., U.S.A. 118 46 46N 122 59W
Centúripe 41 37 37N 14 41 E
Cephalonia = Kefallinía 45 38 15N 20 30 E
Cepin 42 45 32N 18 34 E
Ceprano 40 41 33N 13 30 E
Ceptura 46 45 1N 26 21 E
Cepu 73 7 12S 111 31 E
Ceram = Seram 73 3 10S 129 0 E
Ceram Sea = Seram Sea 73 2 30S 128 30 E
Cerbère 20 42 26N 3 10 E
Cerbicales, Îles 21 41 33N 9 22 E
Cerbu 46 44 46N 24 46 E
Cercal 31 37 48N 8 40W
Cercemaggiore 41 41 27N 14 43 E
Cerdaña 32 42 22N 1 35 E
Cerdedo 30 42 33N 8 23W
Cère → 20 44 55N 1 49 E
Cerea 39 45 12N 11 13 E
Ceres, Argent. 124 29 55S 61 55W
Ceres, Italy 38 45 19N 7 22 E
Ceres, S. Afr. 92 33 21S 19 18 E
Céret 20 42 30N 2 42 E
Cerignola 41 41 17N 15 53 E
Cerigo = Kíthira 45 36 15N 23 0 E
Cérilly 20 46 37N 2 50 E
Cerisiers 19 48 8N 3 30 E
Cerizay 18 46 50N 0 40W
Çerkeş 64 40 49N 32 52 E
Cerknica 39 45 48N 14 21 E
Cermerno 42 43 35N 20 25 E
Cerna 46 45 4N 28 17 E
Cerna → 46 44 45N 24 0 E
Cernavodă 46 44 22N 28 3 E
Cernay 19 47 44N 7 10 E
Cernik 42 45 17N 17 22 E
Cerralvo 120 24 20N 109 45 E
Cerreto Sannita 41 41 17N 14 34 E
Cerritos 120 22 27N 100 20W
Cerro 119 36 47N 105 36W
Certaldo 38 43 32N 11 2 E
Cervaro → 41 41 30N 15 52 E
Cervera 32 41 40N 1 16 E
Cervera de Pisuerga 30 42 51N 4 30W
Cervera del Río Alhama 32 42 2N 1 58W
Cérvia 39 44 15N 12 20 E
Cervignano del Friuli 39 45 49N 13 20 E
Cervinara 41 41 2N 14 36 E
Cervione 21 42 20N 9 29 E
Cervo 30 43 40N 7 24W
Cesaro 41 37 50N 14 38 E
Cesena 39 44 9N 12 14 E
Cesenático 39 44 12N 12 22 E
Cēsis 54 57 17N 25 28 E
Česká Lípa 26 50 45N 14 30 E
Česka Socialistická Republika □ 26 49 30N 14 40 E
Česká Třebová 27 49 54N 16 27 E
České Budějovice 26 48 55N 14 25 E
České Velenice 26 48 45N 15 1 E
Ceskomoravská Vrchovina 26 49 30N 15 40 E
Český Brod 26 50 4N 14 52 E
Český Krumlov 26 48 43N 14 21 E
Český Těšin 27 49 45N 18 39 E
Çeşme 45 38 20N 26 23 E
Cessnock 97 32 50S 151 21 E
Cestas 20 44 44N 0 41W
Cestos → 84 5 40N 9 10W
Cetate 46 44 7N 23 2 E
Cétin Grad 39 45 9N 15 45 E
Cetina → 39 43 26N 16 42 E
Cetinje 42 42 23N 18 59 E
Cetraro 41 39 30N 15 56 E
Ceuta 82 35 52N 5 18W
Ceva 38 44 23N 8 3 E
Cévennes 20 44 10N 3 50 E
Ceyhan 64 37 4N 35 47 E
Ceylon = Sri Lanka ■ 70 7 30N 80 50 E
Cèze → 21 44 13N 4 43 E
Cha Pa 71 22 20N 103 47 E
Chabeuil 21 44 54N 5 1 E
Chablais 21 46 20N 6 36 E
Chablis 19 47 47N 3 48 E
Chabounia 82 35 30N 2 38 E
Chacabuco 124 34 40S 60 27W
Chachapoyas 126 6 15S 77 50W
Chachro 68 25 5N 70 15 E
Chaco □ 124 26 30S 61 0W
Chad ■ 81 15 0N 17 15 E
Chad, L. = Tchad, L. 81 13 30N 14 30 E
Chadan 59 51 17N 91 35 E
Chadileuvú → 124 37 46S 66 0W
Chadiza 91 14 45S 32 27 E
Chadron 116 42 50N 103 0W
Chadyr-Lunga 56 46 3N 28 51 E
Chagda 59 58 45N 130 38 E
Chagny 19 46 57N 4 45 E
Chagoda 54 59 10N 35 15 E
Chagos Arch. 60 6 0S 72 0 E
Chágres → 120 9 10N 79 40W
Chāh Bahār 65 25 20N 60 40 E
Chāh Gay Hills 65 29 30N 64 0 E
Chaillé-les-Marais 20 46 25N 1 2W
Chaise-Dieu, La 20 45 20N 3 40 E
Chaize-le-Vicomte, La 18 46 40N 1 18W
Chaj Doab 68 32 15N 73 0 E
Chajari 124 30 42S 58 0W
Chake Chake 90 5 15S 39 45 E
Chakhansur 65 31 10N 62 0 E
Chakhansur □ 65 30 0N 62 0 E
Chakonipau, L. 107 56 18N 68 30W
Chakradharpur 69 22 45N 85 40 E
Chakwal 68 32 56N 72 53 E
Chala 126 15 48S 74 20W
Chalais 20 45 16N 0 3 E
Chalakudi 70 10 18N 76 20 E
Chalcis = Khalkís 45 38 27N 23 42 E
Chaleur B. 107 47 55N 65 30W
Chalhuanca 126 14 15S 73 15W
Chalindrey 19 47 48N 5 26 E
Chaling 77 26 58N 113 30 E
Chalisgaon 70 20 30N 75 10 E
Chalkar 57 50 35N 51 52 E
Chalkar Oz. 57 50 33N 51 45 E
Chalky Inlet 101 46 3S 166 31 E
Challans 18 46 50N 1 52W
Challapata 126 18 53S 66 50W
Challerange 19 49 18N 4 46 E
Challis 118 44 32N 114 25W
Chalna 69 22 36N 89 35 E
Chalon-sur-Saône 19 46 48N 4 50 E
Chalonnes 18 47 20N 0 45W
Châlons-sur-Marne 19 48 58N 4 20 E
Châlus 20 45 39N 0 58 E
Cham 25 49 12N 12 40 E
Chama 119 36 54N 106 35W
Chaman 66 30 58N 66 25 E
Chamarajnagar-Ramasamudram 70 11 52N 76 52 E
Chamartín de la Rosa 32 40 28N 3 40W
Chamba 68 32 35N 76 10 E
Chambal → 69 26 29N 79 15 E
Chamberlain 116 43 50N 99 21W
Chambers 119 35 13N 109 30W
Chambersburg 114 39 53N 77 41W
Chambéry 21 45 34N 5 55 E
Chambly 113 45 27N 73 17W
Chambois 18 48 48N 0 6 E
Chambon-Feugerolles, Le 21 45 24N 4 18 E
Chambord 107 48 25N 72 6W
Chambri L. 98 4 15S 143 10 E
Chamical 124 30 22S 66 27W
Chamonix 21 45 55N 6 51 E
Champa 69 22 2N 82 43 E
Champagne, Can. 108 60 49N 136 30W
Champagne, France 19 49 0N 4 40 E
Champagne, Plaine de 19 49 0N 4 30 E
Champagnole 19 46 45N 5 55 E
Champaign 114 40 8N 88 14W
Champaubert 19 48 50N 3 45 E
Champdeniers 20 46 29N 0 25W
Champeix 20 45 37N 3 8 E
Champion B. 96 28 44S 114 36 E
Champlain, Can. 106 46 27N 72 24W
Champlain, U.S.A. 114 44 59N 73 27W
Champlain, L. 114 44 30N 73 20W
Champotón 120 19 20N 90 50W
Chamusca 31 39 21N 8 29W
Chañaral 124 26 23S 70 40W
Chanasma 68 23 44N 72 5 E
Chandalar 104 67 30N 148 35W
Chandannagar 69 22 52N 88 24 E
Chandausi 68 28 27N 78 49 E
Chandeleur Is. 117 29 48N 88 51W
Chandeleur Sd. 117 29 58N 88 40W
Chandigarh 68 30 43N 76 47 E
Chandler, Can. 107 48 18N 64 46W
Chandler, Ariz., U.S.A. 119 33 20N 111 56W
Chandler, Okla., U.S.A. 117 35 43N 96 53W
Chandmani 75 45 22N 98 2 E
Chandpur, Bangla. 69 23 8N 90 45 E
Chandpur, India 68 29 8N 78 19 E
Chandrapur 70 19 57N 79 25 E
Chang 68 26 59N 68 30 E
Chang Jiang →, Jiangsu, China 75 31 48N 121 10 E
Chang Jiang →, Shanghai, China 75 31 35N 121 15 E
Changanacheri 70 9 25N 76 31 E
Changbai 76 41 25N 128 5 E
Changbai Shan 76 42 20N 129 0 E
Changchiak'ou = Zhangjiakou 76 40 48N 114 55 E
Ch'angchou = Changzhou 75 31 47N 119 58 E
Changchun 76 43 57N 125 17 E
Changde 75 29 4N 111 35 E
Changfeng 77 32 28N 117 10 E
Changhai = Shanghai 75 31 15N 121 26 E
Changjiang 75 19 20N 108 55 E
Changjin-chŏsuji 76 40 30N 127 15 E
Changle 77 25 59N 119 27 E
Changli 76 39 40N 119 13 E
Changning 77 26 28N 112 22 E
Changping 76 40 14N 116 12 E
Changsha 75 28 12N 113 0 E
Changshou 77 29 51N 107 8 E
Changshu 77 31 38N 120 43 E
Changshun 77 26 3N 106 25 E
Changtai 77 24 35N 117 42 E
Changting 75 25 50N 116 22 E
Changyang 77 30 30N 111 10 E
Changzhi 76 36 10N 113 6 E
Changzhou 75 31 47N 119 58 E
Chanhanga 92 16 0S 14 8 E
Chanlar 57 40 25N 46 10 E
Channapatna 70 12 40N 77 15 E
Channel Is., U.K. 18 49 30N 2 40W
Channel Is., U.S.A. 119 33 55N 119 26W
Channel-Port aux Basques 107 47 30N 59 9W
Channing, Mich., U.S.A. 114 46 9N 88 1W
Channing, Tex., U.S.A. 117 35 45N 102 20W
Chantada 30 42 36N 7 46W
Chanthaburi 71 12 38N 102 12 E
Chantilly 19 49 12N 2 29 E
Chantonnay 18 46 40N 1 3W
Chantrey Inlet 104 67 48N 96 20W
Chanute 117 37 45N 95 25W
Chanza → 31 37 32N 7 30W
Chao Hu 77 31 30N 117 30 E
Chao Phraya → 71 13 32N 100 36 E
Chao'an 75 23 42N 116 32 E
Chaoyang, Guangdong, China 75 23 17N 116 30 E
Chaoyang, Liaoning, China 76 41 35N 120 22 E
Chapala 91 15 50S 37 35 E
Chapala, Lago de 120 20 10N 103 20W
Chapayevo 57 50 25N 51 10 E
Chapayevsk 55 53 0N 49 40 E
Chapecó 125 27 14S 52 41W
Chapel Hill 115 35 53N 79 3W
Chapelle-d'Angillon, La 19 47 21N 2 25 E
Chapelle-Glain, La 18 47 38N 1 11W
Chapleau 106 47 50N 83 24W
Chaplin 109 50 28N 106 40W
Chaplino 56 48 8N 36 15 E
Chaplygin 55 53 15N 40 0 E
Chapra 69 25 48N 84 44 E
Châr 80 21 32N 12 45 E
Chara 59 56 54N 118 20 E
Charadai 124 27 35S 60 0W
Charagua 126 19 45S 63 10W
Charaña 126 17 30S 69 25W
Charata 124 27 13S 61 14W
Charcas 120 23 10N 101 20W
Charcoal L. 109 58 49N 102 22W
Charcot I. 5 70 0S 75 0W
Chard 13 50 52N 2 59W
Chardara 58 41 16N 67 59 E
Chardon 112 41 34N 81 17W
Chardzhou 58 39 6N 63 34 E
Charente 20 45 40N 0 5 E
Charente □ 20 45 50N 0 16 E
Charente → 20 45 57N 1 5W
Charente-Maritime □ 20 45 30N 0 35W
Charentsavan 57 40 35N 44 41 E
Chārīkār 65 35 0N 69 10 E
Charité, La 19 47 10N 3 0 E
Chariton → 116 39 19N 92 58W
Charkhari 69 25 24N 79 45 E
Charkhi Dadri 68 28 37N 76 17 E
Charleroi 16 50 24N 4 27 E
Charlerol 112 40 8N 79 54W
Charles, C. 114 37 10N 75 59W
Charles City 116 43 2N 92 41W
Charles L. 109 59 50N 110 33W
Charles Town 114 39 20N 77 50W
Charleston, Ill., U.S.A. 114 39 30N 88 10W
Charleston, Miss., U.S.A. 117 34 2N 90 3W
Charleston, Mo., U.S.A. 117 36 52N 89 20W
Charleston, S.C., U.S.A. 115 32 47N 79 56W
Charleston, W. Va., U.S.A. 114 38 24N 81 36W
Charleston Harb. 115 32 46N 79 55W
Charlestown, S. Afr. 93 27 26S 29 53 E
Charlestown, U.S.A. 114 38 29N 85 40W
Charlesville 88 5 27S 20 59 E
Charleville 97 26 24S 146 15 E
Charleville = Rath Luirc 15 52 21N 8 40W
Charleville-Mézières 19 49 44N 4 40 E
Charlevoix 114 45 19N 85 14W
Charlieu 21 46 10N 4 10 E
Charlotte, Mich., U.S.A. 114 42 36N 84 48W
Charlotte, N.C., U.S.A. 115 35 16N 80 46W
Charlotte Amalie 121 18 22N 64 56W
Charlotte Harbor 115 26 58N 82 4W
Charlotte Waters 96 25 56S 134 54 E
Charlottenberg 48 59 54N 12 17 E
Charlottesville 114 38 1N 78 30W
Charlottetown 107 46 14N 63 8W
Charlton, Austral. 99 36 16S 143 24 E
Charlton, U.S.A. 116 40 59N 93 20W
Charlton I. 106 52 0N 79 20W
Charmes 19 48 22N 6 17 E
Charny 107 46 43N 71 15W
Charolles 21 46 27N 4 16 E
Charost 19 47 0N 2 7 E
Charouine 82 29 0N 0 15W
Charre 91 17 13S 35 10 E
Charroux 20 46 9N 0 25 E
Charters Towers 97 20 5S 146 13 E
Chartre, La 18 47 42N 0 34 E
Chartres 18 48 29N 1 30 E
Chascomús 124 35 30S 58 0W
Chasefu 91 11 55S 33 8 E
Chasovnya-Uchurskaya 59 57 15N 132 50 E
Chasseneuil-sur-Bonnieure 20 45 52N 0 29 E
Chata 68 27 42N 77 30 E
Châtaigneraie, La 18 46 38N 0 4
Chatal Balkan = Udvoy Balkan 43 42 50N 26 5
Château-Chinon 19 47 4N 3 5
Château-du-Loir 18 47 40N 0 2
Château-Gontier 18 47 50N 0 4
Château-la-Vallière 18 47 30N 0 2
Château-Landon 19 48 8N 2 4
Château, Le 20 45 52N 1 1
Château-Porcien 19 49 31N 4 1
Château-Renault 18 47 36N 0 5
Château-Salins 19 48 50N 6 3
Château-Thierry 19 49 3N 3 2
Châteaubourg 18 48 7N 1 2
Châteaubriant 18 47 43N 1 2
Châteaudun 18 48 3N 1 2
Châteaugiron 18 48 3N 1 3
Châteauguay 113 45 23N 73 4
Châteaulin 18 48 11N 4
Châteaumeillant 20 46 35N 2 1
Châteauneuf 18 48 35N 1 1
Châteauneuf-du-Faou 18 48 11N 3 5
Châteauneuf-sur-Charente 20 45 36N 0
Châteauneuf-sur-Cher 19 46 52N 2 1
Châteauneuf-sur-Loire 19 47 52N 2 1
Châteaurenard 21 43 53N 4 5
Châteauroux 19 46 50N 1 4
Châteaux-Arnoux 21 44 6N 6
Châtelaillon-Plage 20 46 5N 1
Châtelaudren 18 48 33N 2 5
Châtelet, Le, Cher, France 20 46 40N 2 2
Châtelet, Le, Seine-et-Marne, France 19 48 30N 2 4
Châtelguyon 20 45 55N 3
Châtellerault 18 46 50N 0 3
Châtelus-Malvaleix 20 46 18N 2
Chatfield 116 43 15N 91 5
Chatham, N.B., Can. 107 47 2N 65 2
Chatham, Ont., Can. 106 42 24N 82 1
Chatham, U.K. 13 51 22N 0 3
Chatham, La., U.S.A. 117 32 22N 92 2
Chatham, N.Y., U.S.A. 113 42 21N 73 3
Chatham Is. 94 44 0S 176 4
Chatham Str. 108 57 0N 134 4
Châtillon, Loiret, France 19 47 36N 2 4
Châtillon, Marne, France 19 49 5N 3 4
Chatillon 38 45 45N 7 4
Châtillon-Coligny 19 47 50N 2 5
Châtillon-en-Bazois 19 47 3N 3 3
Châtillon-en-Diois 21 44 41N 5 2
Châtillon-sur-Indre 18 46 59N 1 1
Châtillon-sur-Seine 19 47 50N 4 3
Châtillon-sur-Sèvre 18 46 56N 0 4
Chatmohar 69 24 15N 89 1
Chatra 69 24 12N 84 5
Chatrapur 69 19 22N 85
Châtre, La 20 46 35N 1 5
Chats, L. des 113 45 30N 76 2
Chatsworth, Can. 112 44 27N 80 5
Chatsworth, Zimb. 91 19 38S 31 1
Chattahoochee 115 30 43N 84 5
Chattanooga 115 35 2N 85 1
Chaudanne, Barrage de 21 43 51N 6 3
Chaudes-Aigues 20 44 51N 3
Chauffailles 21 46 13N 4 2
Chauk 67 20 53N 94 4
Chaukan La 67 27 0N 97 1
Chaulnes 19 49 48N 2 4
Chaumont, France 19 48 7N 5
Chaumont, U.S.A. 113 44 4N 76
Chaumont-en-Vexin 19 49 16N 1 5
Chaumont-sur-Loire 18 47 29N 1 1
Chaunay 20 46 13N 0
Chauny 19 49 37N 3 1
Chausey, Îs. 18 48 52N 1 4
Chaussin 19 46 59N 5 2
Chautauqua 112 42 17N 79 3
Chauvigny 18 46 34N 0 3
Chauvin 109 52 45N 110 1
Chaux-de-Fonds, La 25 47 7N 6 5
Chaves, Brazil 127 0 15S 49 5
Chaves, Port. 30 41 45N 7 3
Chavuma 89 13 4S 22 4
Chaykovskiy 52 56 47N 54
Chazelles-sur-Lyon 21 45 39N 4 2
Chazy 113 44 52N 73 2
Cheb (Eger) 26 50 9N 12 2
Cheboksary 55 56 8N 47 1
Cheboygan 114 45 38N 84 2
Chebsara 55 59 10N 38 5
Chech, Erg 82 25 0N 2 1
Chechaouen 82 35 9N 5 1
Chechen, Os. 57 43 59N 47 4
Checheno-Ingush A.S.S.R. □ 57 43 30N 45 2
Chęciny 28 50 46N 20 2
Checleset B. 108 50 5N 127 3
Checotah 117 35 31N 95 3
Chedabucto B. 107 45 25N 61
Cheduba I. 67 18 45N 93 4
Cheepie 99 26 33S 145 1
Chef-Boutonne 20 46 7N 0
Chegdomyn 59 51 7N 133 1
Chegga 82 25 27N 5 4
Chehalis 118 46 44N 122 5
Cheiron 21 43 49N 6 5
Cheju Do 77 33 29N 126 3
Chekalin 55 54 10N 36 1
Chekiang = Zhejiang □ 75 29 0N 120
Chela, Sa. da 92 16 20S 13 2
Chelan 118 47 49N 120
Chelan, L. 108 48 5N 120 3
Cheleken 53 39 26N 53
Chelforó 128 39 0S 66 3
Chéliff, O. → 82 36 0N 0
Chelkar 58 47 48N 59 3
Chelkar Tengiz, Solonchak 58 48 0N 62 3
Chellala Dahrania 82 33 2N 0
Chelles 19 48 52N 2 3
Chełm 28 51 8N 23 3
Chełm □ 28 51 15N 23 3
Chełmek 27 50 6N 19 1
Chełmno 28 53 20N 18 3
Chelmsford 13 51 44N 0 29

elmsford Dam 93 27 55 S 29 59 E
elmża 28 53 10N 18 39 E
elsea, Austral. 100 38 5 S 145 8 E
elsea, Can. 113 45 30N 75 47W
elsea, Okla., U.S.A. 117 36 35N 95 35W
elsea, Vt., U.S.A. 113 43 59N 72 27W
eltenham 13 51 55N 2 5W
elva 32 39 45N 1 0W
elyabinsk 58 55 10N 61 24 E
emainus 108 48 55N 123 42W
emillé 18 47 14N 0 45W
emnitz = Karl-Marx-Stadt 24 50 50N 12 55 E
emult 118 43 14N 121 47W
en, Gora 59 65 16N 141 50 E
en Xian 75 25 47N 113 1 E
enab → 68 30 23N 71 2 E
enachane, O. → 82 25 20N 3 20W
enango Forks 113 42 15N 75 51W
encha 87 6 15N 37 32 E
enchiang = Zhenjiang 75 32 12N 119 24 E
eney 118 47 29N 117 34W
engbu 77 26 18N 110 16 E
engcheng 77 35 8N 109 56 E
engde 76 40 59N 117 58 E
engdu 75 30 38N 104 2 E
enggu 77 33 10N 107 21 E
engjiang 75 24 39N 103 0 E
'engtu = Chengdu 75 30 38N 104 2 E
engyang 76 36 18N 120 21 E
enxi 77 28 2N 110 12 E
eo Reo 71 13 25N 108 28 E
eom Ksan 71 14 13N 104 56 E
epelare 43 41 44N 24 40 E
epén 126 7 15 S 79 23W
epes 124 31 20 S 66 35W
epo 121 9 10N 79 6W
eptsa → 55 58 36N 50 4 E
eptulil, Mt. 90 1 25N 35 35 E
equamegon B. 116 46 40N 90 30W
er □ 19 47 10N 2 30 E
er → 18 47 21N 0 29 E
eran 69 25 45N 90 44 E
erasco 38 44 39N 7 50 E
eraw 115 34 42N 79 54W
erbourg 18 49 39N 1 40W
erchell 82 36 35N 2 12 E
erdakly 55 54 25N 48 50 E
erdyn 52 60 24N 56 29 E
eremkhovo 59 53 8N 103 1 E
erepanovo 58 54 15N 83 30 E
erepovets 55 59 5N 37 55 E
ergui, Chott ech 82 34 21N 0 25 E
erikov 54 53 32N 31 20 E
erkassy 56 49 27N 32 4 E
erkessk 57 44 15N 42 5 E
erlak 58 54 15N 74 55 E
ernaya Kholunitsa 55 58 51N 51 52 E
erni 43 42 35N 23 18 E
ernigov 54 51 28N 31 20 E
ernikovsk 52 54 48N 56 8 E
ernobyl 54 51 13N 30 15 E
ernogorsk 59 53 49N 91 18 E
ernomorskoye 56 45 31N 32 40 E
ernovskoye 55 58 48N 47 20 E
ernovtsy 56 48 15N 25 52 E
ernoye 59 70 30N 89 10 E
ernyakhovsk 54 54 36N 21 48 E
ernyshkovskiy 57 48 30N 42 13 E
ernyshovskiy 59 63 0N 112 30 E
erokee, Iowa, U.S.A. 116 42 40N 95 30W
erokee, Okla., U.S.A. 117 36 45N 98 25W
erokees, L. O'The 117 36 50N 95 12W
erquenco 128 38 35 S 72 0W
errapunji 67 25 17N 91 47 E
erry Creek 118 39 50N 114 58W
erryvale 117 37 20N 95 33W
erskiy 59 68 45N 161 18 E
erskogo Khrebet 59 65 0N 143 0 E
ertkovo 57 49 25N 40 19 E
erven 54 53 45N 28 28 E
erven-Bryag 43 43 17N 24 7 E
ervonograd 54 50 25N 24 10 E
erwell → 13 51 46N 1 18W
esapeake 114 36 43N 76 15W
esapeake Bay 114 38 0N 76 12W
eshire □ 12 53 14N 2 30W
eshskaya Guba 52 67 20N 47 0 E
eslatta L. 108 53 49N 125 20W
esley 112 44 17N 81 5W
esne, Le 19 49 30N 4 45 E
este 33 39 30N 0 41W
ester, U.K. 12 53 12N 2 53W
ester, Calif., U.S.A. 118 40 22N 121 14W
ester, Ill., U.S.A. 117 37 58N 89 50W
ester, Mont., U.S.A. 118 48 31N 111 0W
ester, N.Y., U.S.A. 113 41 22N 74 16W
ester, Pa., U.S.A. 114 39 54N 75 20W
ester, S.C., U.S.A. 115 34 44N 81 13W
esterfield 12 53 14N 1 26W
esterfield, Îles 94 19 52 S 158 15 E
esterfield In. 104 63 25N 90 45W
esterfield Inlet 104 63 30N 90 45W
esterton Range 99 25 30 S 147 27 E
esterville 113 45 6N 75 14W
esuncook L. 107 46 0N 69 10W
etaibi 83 37 1N 7 20 E
éticamp 107 46 37N 60 59W
etumal 120 18 30N 88 20W
etumal, Bahía de 120 18 40N 88 10W
etwynd 108 55 45N 121 36W
evanceaux 20 45 18N 0 14W
eviot Hills 12 55 20N 2 30W
eviot Ra. 99 25 20 S 143 45 E
eviot, The 12 55 29N 2 8W
ew Bahir 87 4 40N 36 50 E
ewelah 118 48 17N 117 43W
eyenne, Okla., U.S.A. 117 35 35N 99 40W
eyenne, Wyo., U.S.A. 116 41 9N 104 49W
eyenne → 116 44 40N 101 15W
eyenne Wells 116 38 51N 102 10W
eylard, Le 21 44 55N 4 25 E
iabra 68 24 40N 76 54 E
Chhatarpur 69 24 55N 79 35 E
Chhindwara 68 22 2N 78 59 E
Chhlong 71 12 15N 105 58 E
Chi → 71 15 11N 104 43 E
Chiamis 73 7 20 S 108 21 E
Chiamussu = Jiamusi 75 46 40N 130 26 E
Chiang Mai 71 18 47N 98 59 E
Chiange 89 15 35 S 13 40 E
Chiapa → 120 16 42N 93 0W
Chiapas □ 120 17 0N 92 45W
Chiaramonte Gulfi 41 37 1N 14 41 E
Chiaravalle 39 43 38N 13 17 E
Chiaravalle Centrale 41 38 41N 16 25 E
Chiari 38 45 31N 9 55 E
Chiatura 57 42 15N 43 17 E
Chiávari 38 44 20N 9 20 E
Chiavenna 38 46 18N 9 23 E
Chiba 74 35 30N 140 7 E
Chiba □ 74 35 30N 140 20 E
Chibabava 93 20 17 S 33 35 E
Chibatu 73 7 6 S 107 59 E
Chibemba, Angola 89 15 48 S 14 8 E
Chibemba, Angola 92 16 20 S 15 20 E
Chibia 89 15 10 S 13 42 E
Chibougamau 106 49 56N 74 24W
Chibougamau L. 106 49 50N 74 20W
Chibuk 85 10 52N 12 50 E
Chic-Chocs, Mts. 107 48 55N 66 0W
Chicacole = Srikakulam 70 18 14N 84 4 E
Chicago 114 41 53N 87 40W
Chicago Heights 114 41 29N 87 37W
Chichagof I. 108 58 0N 136 0W
Chichaoua 82 31 32N 8 44W
Chichén Itzá 120 20 40N 88 32W
Chichester 13 50 50N 0 47W
Chichibu 74 36 5N 139 10 E
Ch'ich'ihaerh = Qiqihar 75 47 26N 124 0 E
Chickasha 117 35 0N 98 0W
Chiclana de la Frontera 31 36 26N 6 9W
Chiclayo 126 6 42 S 79 50W
Chico 118 39 45N 121 54W
Chico →, Chubut, Argent. 128 44 0 S 67 0W
Chico →, Santa Cruz, Argent. 128 50 0 S 68 30W
Chicomo 93 24 31 S 34 6 E
Chicopee 114 42 6N 72 37W
Chicoutimi 107 48 28N 71 5W
Chidambaram 70 11 20N 79 45 E
Chidenguele 93 24 55 S 34 11 E
Chidley C. 105 60 23N 64 26W
Chiede 92 17 15 S 16 22 E
Chiefs Pt. 112 44 41N 81 18W
Chiemsee 25 47 53N 12 27 E
Chiengi 91 8 45 S 29 10 E
Chienti → 39 43 18N 13 45 E
Chieri 38 45 0N 7 50 E
Chiers → 19 49 39N 5 0 E
Chiese → 38 45 8N 10 25 E
Chieti 39 42 22N 14 10 E
Chifeng 76 42 18N 118 58 E
Chigirin 56 49 4N 32 38 E
Chignecto B. 107 45 30N 64 40W
Chiguana 124 21 0 S 67 58W
Chihli, G. of = Bo Hai 76 39 0N 120 0 E
Chihuahua 120 28 40N 106 3W
Chihuahua □ 120 28 40N 106 3W
Chiili 58 44 20N 66 15 E
Chik Bollapur 70 13 25N 77 45 E
Chikhli 68 20 20N 76 18 E
Chikmagalur 70 13 15N 75 45 E
Chikodi 70 16 26N 74 38 E
Chikwawa 91 16 2 S 34 50 E
Chilako → 108 53 53N 122 57W
Chilanga 91 15 33 S 28 16 E
Chilapa 120 17 40N 99 11W
Chilas 69 35 25N 74 5 E
Chilcotin → 108 51 44N 122 23W
Childers 97 25 15 S 152 17 E
Childress 117 34 30N 100 15W
Chile ■ 128 35 0 S 72 0W
Chile Rise 95 38 0 S 92 0W
Chilecito 124 29 10 S 67 30W
Chilete 126 7 10 S 78 50W
Chililabombwe 91 12 18 S 27 43 E
Chilin = Jilin 76 43 55N 126 30 E
Chilka L. 69 19 40N 85 25 E
Chilko → 108 52 0N 123 40W
Chilko, L. 108 51 20N 124 10W
Chillagoe 97 17 7 S 144 33 E
Chillán 124 36 40 S 72 10W
Chillicothe, Ill., U.S.A. 116 40 55N 89 32W
Chillicothe, Mo., U.S.A. 116 39 45N 93 30W
Chillicothe, Ohio, U.S.A. 114 39 20N 82 58W
Chilliwack 108 49 10N 121 54W
Chilo 68 27 25N 73 32 E
Chiloane, I. 93 20 40 S 34 55 E
Chiloé, I. de 128 42 30 S 73 50W
Chilpancingo 120 17 30N 99 30W
Chiltern Hills 13 51 44N 0 42W
Chilton 114 44 1N 88 12W
Chiluage 88 9 30 S 21 50 E
Chilubula 91 10 14 S 30 51 E
Chilumba 91 10 28 S 34 12 E
Chilwa, L. 91 15 15 S 35 40 E
Chimacum 118 48 1N 122 46W
Chimay 16 50 3N 4 20 E
Chimbay 58 42 57N 59 47 E
Chimborazo 126 1 29 S 78 55W
Chimbote 126 9 0 S 78 35W
Chimishliya 46 46 34N 28 44 E
Chimkent 58 42 18N 69 36 E
Chimoio 91 19 4 S 33 30 E
Chimpembe 91 9 31 S 29 33 E
Chin □ 67 22 0N 93 0 E
Chin Ling Shan = Qinling Shandi 77 33 50N 108 10 E
China 120 25 40N 99 20W
China ■ 75 30 0N 110 0 E
Chinan = Jinan 76 36 38N 117 1 E
Chinandega 121 12 35N 87 12W
Chinati Pk. 117 30 0N 104 25W
Chincha Alta 126 13 25 S 76 7W
Chinchilla 99 26 45 S 150 38 E
Chinchilla de Monte Aragón 33 38 53N 1 40W
Chinchón 32 40 9N 3 26W
Chinchorro, Banco 120 18 35N 87 20W
Chinchou = Jinzhou 76 41 5N 121 3 E
Chincoteague 114 37 58N 75 21W
Chinde 91 18 35 S 36 30 E
Chindwin → 67 21 26N 95 15 E
Chinga 91 15 13 S 38 35 E
Chingleput 70 12 42N 79 58 E
Chingola 91 12 31 S 27 53 E
Chingole 91 13 4 S 34 17 E
Ch'ingtao = Qingdao 76 36 5N 120 20 E
Chinguetti 80 20 25N 12 24W
Chingune 93 20 33 S 35 0 E
Chinhae 76 35 9N 128 47 E
Chinhanguanine 93 25 21 S 32 30 E
Chiniot 68 31 45N 73 0 E
Chinju 76 35 12N 128 2 E
Chinle 119 36 14N 109 38W
Chinnamanur 70 9 50N 77 24 E
Chinnampo 76 38 52N 125 10 E
Chinnur 70 18 57N 79 49 E
Chino Valley 119 34 54N 112 28W
Chinon 18 47 10N 0 15 E
Chinook, Can. 109 51 28N 110 59W
Chinook, U.S.A. 118 48 35N 109 19W
Chinsali 91 10 30 S 32 2 E
Chintamani 70 13 26N 78 3 E
Chióggia 39 45 13N 12 15 E
Chios = Khíos 45 38 27N 26 9 E
* Chipai L. 106 52 56N 87 53W
Chipata 91 13 38 S 32 28 E
Chipatujah 73 7 45 S 108 0 E
Chipewyan L. 109 58 0N 98 27W
Chipinga 91 20 13 S 32 28 E
Chipiona 31 36 44N 6 26W
Chipley 115 30 45N 85 32W
Chiplun 70 17 31N 73 34 E
Chipman 107 46 6N 65 53W
Chipoka 91 13 57 S 34 28 E
Chippawa 112 43 5N 79 2W
Chippenham 13 51 27N 2 7W
Chippewa → 116 44 25N 92 10W
Chippewa Falls 116 44 55N 91 22W
Chiprovtsi 42 43 24N 22 52 E
Chiquián 126 10 10 S 77 0W
Chiquimula 120 14 51N 89 37W
Chiquinquira 126 5 37N 73 50W
Chir → 57 48 30N 43 0 E
Chirala 70 15 50N 80 26 E
Chiramba 91 16 55 S 34 39 E
Chirawa 68 28 14N 75 42 E
Chirayinkil 70 8 41N 76 49 E
Chirchik 58 41 29N 69 35 E
Chirfa 83 20 55N 12 22 E
Chiricahua Pk. 119 31 53N 109 14W
Chirikof I. 104 55 50N 155 40W
Chiriquí, Golfo de 121 8 0N 82 10W
Chiriquí, Lago de 121 9 10N 82 0W
† Chiriquí, Vol. de 121 8 55N 82 35W
Chirivira Falls 91 21 10 S 32 12 E
Chirnogi 46 44 7N 26 32 E
Chirpan 43 42 10N 25 19 E
Chirripó Grande, Cerro 121 9 29N 83 29W
Chisamba 91 14 55 S 28 20 E
Chisholm 108 54 55N 114 10W
Chishtian Mandi 68 29 50N 72 55 E
Chisimaio 79 0 22 S 42 32 E
Chisimba Falls 91 10 12 S 30 56 E
Chisineu Criş 42 46 32N 21 37 E
Chisone → 38 44 49N 7 25 E
Chisos Mts. 117 29 20N 103 15W
Chistopol 55 55 25N 50 38 E
Chita 59 52 0N 113 35 E
Chitapur 70 17 10N 77 5 E
Chitembo 89 13 30 S 16 50 E
Chitipa 91 9 41 S 33 19 E
Chitokoloki 89 13 50 S 23 13 E
Chitorgarh 68 24 52N 74 38 E
Chitrakot 70 19 10N 81 40 E
Chitral 66 35 50N 71 56 E
Chitravati → 70 14 45N 78 15 E
Chitré 121 7 59N 80 27W
Chittagong 67 22 19N 91 48 E
Chittagong □ 67 24 5N 91 0 E
Chittoor 70 13 15N 79 5 E
Chittur 70 10 40N 76 45 E
Chiusa 39 46 38N 11 34 E
Chiusi 39 43 1N 11 58 E
Chiva 33 39 27N 0 41W
Chivasso 38 45 10N 7 52 E
Chivilcoy 124 34 55 S 60 0W
Chiwanda 91 11 23 S 34 55 E
Chizela 91 13 10 S 25 0 E
Chkalov = Orenburg 52 52 0N 55 5 E
Chkolovsk 55 56 50N 43 10 E
Chlumec 26 50 9N 15 29 E
Chmielnik 28 50 37N 20 43 E
Choba 90 2 30N 38 5 E
Chobe National Park 92 18 0 S 25 0 E
Chocianów 28 51 27N 15 55 E
Chociwel 28 53 29N 15 21 E
Chodaków 28 52 16N 20 18 E
Chodavaram 70 17 50N 82 57 E
Chodecz 28 52 24N 19 2 E
Chodziez 28 52 58N 16 58 E
Choele Choel 128 39 11 S 65 40W
Choisy-le-Roi 19 48 45N 2 24 E
Choix 120 26 40N 108 23W
Chojna 28 52 58N 14 25 E
Chojnice 28 53 42N 17 32 E
Chojnów 28 51 18N 15 58 E
Choke Mts. 87 11 18N 37 15 E
Chokurdakh 59 70 38N 147 55 E
Cholet 18 47 4N 0 52W
Choluteca 121 13 20N 87 14W
Choma 91 16 48 S 26 59 E
Chomen Swamp 87 9 20N 37 10 E
Chomu 68 27 15N 75 40 E
Chomutov 26 50 28N 13 23 E
Chon Buri 71 13 21N 101 1 E
Chonan 76 36 48N 127 9 E
Chone 126 0 40 S 80 0W
Chong'an 77 27 45N 118 0 E
Chongde 77 30 32N 120 26 E
Chongjin 76 41 47N 129 50 E
Chŏngju 76 39 40N 125 5 E
Chŏngju 76 36 39N 127 27 E
Chongli 76 40 58N 115 15 E
Chongqing 75 29 35N 106 25 E
Chongzuo 77 22 23N 107 20 E
Chŏnju 76 35 50N 127 4 E
Chonming Dao 77 31 40N 121 30 E
Chonos, Arch. de los 128 45 0 S 75 0W
Chopda 68 21 20N 75 15 E
Chopim → 125 25 35 S 53 5W
Chorley 12 53 39N 2 39W
Chorolque, Cerro 124 20 59 S 66 5W
Choroszcz 28 53 10N 22 59 E
Chorrera, La 120 8 50N 79 50W
Chortkov, U.S.S.R. 54 49 2N 25 46 E
Chortkov, U.S.S.R. 56 49 1N 25 42 E
Chŏrwŏn 76 38 15N 127 10 E
Chorzele 28 53 15N 20 55 E
Chorzów 28 50 18N 18 57 E
Chos-Malal 124 37 20 S 70 15W
Chosan 76 40 50N 125 47 E
Chōshi 74 35 45N 140 51 E
Choszczno 28 53 7N 15 25 E
Choteau 118 47 50N 112 10W
Chotila 68 22 23N 71 15 E
Chowchilla 119 37 11N 120 12W
Choybalsan 75 48 4N 114 30 E
Christchurch, N.Z. 101 43 33 S 172 47 E
Christchurch, U.K. 13 50 44N 1 33W
Christian I. 112 44 50N 80 12W
Christiana 92 27 52 S 25 8 E
Christiansfeld 49 55 21N 9 29 E
Christie B. 109 62 32N 111 10W
Christina → 109 56 40N 111 3W
Christmas I., Ind. Oc. 94 10 30 S 105 40 E
* Christmas I., Pac. Oc. 95 1 58N 157 27W
Chrudim 26 49 58N 15 43 E
Chrzanów 27 50 10N 19 21 E
Chtimba 91 10 35 S 34 13 E
Chu 58 43 36N 73 42 E
Chu → 71 19 53N 105 45 E
Chu Chua 108 51 22N 120 10W
Ch'uanchou = Quanzhou 75 24 55N 118 34 E
Chūbu □ 74 36 45N 137 30 E
Chubut → 128 43 20 S 65 5W
Chuchi L. 108 55 12N 124 30W
Chudovo 54 59 10N 31 41 E
Chudskoye, Oz. 54 58 13N 27 30 E
Chūgoku □ 74 35 0N 133 0 E
Chūgoku-Sanchi 74 35 0N 133 0 E
Chuguyev 56 49 55N 36 45 E
Chugwater 116 41 48N 104 47W
Chukai 71 4 13N 103 25 E
Chukhloma 55 58 45N 42 40 E
Chukotskiy Khrebet 59 68 0N 175 0 E
Chukotskoye More 59 68 0N 175 0W
Chula Vista 119 32 39N 117 8W
Chulman 59 56 52N 124 52 E
Chulucanas 126 5 8 S 80 10W
Chulym → 58 57 43N 83 51 E
Chumbicha 124 29 0 S 66 10W
Chumerna 43 42 45N 25 55 E
Chumikan 59 54 40N 135 10 E
Chumphon 71 10 35N 99 14 E
Chumuare 91 14 31 S 31 50 E
Chuna → 59 57 47N 94 37 E
Chun'an 77 29 35N 119 3 E
Chunchŏn 76 37 58N 127 44 E
Chunga 91 15 0 S 26 2 E
Chungking = Chongqing 75 29 35N 106 25 E
Chunian 68 30 57N 74 0 E
Chunya 91 8 30 S 33 27 E
Chunya □ 90 7 48 S 33 0 E
Chuquibamba 126 15 47 S 72 44W
Chuquicamata 124 22 15 S 69 0W
Chuquisaca □ 126 23 30 S 63 30W
Chur 25 46 52N 9 32 E
Churachandpur 67 24 20N 93 40 E
Churchill 109 58 47N 94 11W
Churchill →, Man., Can. 109 58 47N 94 12W
Churchill →, Newf., Can. 107 53 19N 60 10W
Churchill, C. 109 58 46N 93 12W
Churchill Falls 107 53 36N 64 19W
Churchill L. 109 55 55N 108 20W
Churchill Pk. 108 58 10N 125 10W
Churu 68 28 20N 74 50 E
Chushal 69 33 40N 78 40 E
Chusovoy 52 58 15N 57 40 E
Chuvash A.S.S.R. □ 55 55 30N 47 0 E
Ci Xian 76 36 20N 114 25 E
Ciacova 42 45 35N 21 10 E
Cianjur 73 6 51 S 107 7 E
Cibadok 73 6 53 S 106 47 E
Cibatu 73 7 8 S 107 59 E
Cicero 114 41 48N 87 48W
Cidacos → 32 42 21N 1 38W
Cide 56 41 53N 33 1 E
Ciechanów 28 52 52N 20 38 E
Ciechanów □ 28 53 0N 20 30 E
Ciechanowiec 28 52 40N 22 31 E
Ciechocinek 28 52 53N 18 45 E
Ciego de Avila 121 21 50N 78 50W
Ciénaga 126 11 1N 74 15W
Cienfuegos 121 22 10N 80 30W
Cieplice Śląskie Zdrój 28 50 50N 15 40 E
Cierp 20 42 55N 0 40 E
Cies, Islas 30 42 12N 8 55W
Cieszanów 28 50 14N 23 8 E
Cieszyn 27 49 45N 18 35 E
Cieza 33 38 17N 1 23W
Cifuentes 32 40 47N 2 37W
Cijara, Pantano de 31 39 18N 4 52W
Cijulang 73 7 42 S 108 27 E
Cikajang 73 7 25 S 107 48 E
Cikampek 73 6 23 S 107 28 E
Cilacap 73 7 43 S 109 0 E
Çıldır 57 41 10N 43 20 E
Cilician Gates P. 64 37 20N 34 52 E

* *Renamed Wapikopa, L.*

† *Renamed Barú, Vol.*

* *Renamed Kirimati*

Cîlnicu	46	44 54N	23 4 E
Cimahi	73	6 53 S	107 33 E
Cimarron, Kans., U.S.A.	117	37 50N	100 20W
Cimarron, N. Mex., U.S.A.	117	36 30N	104 52W
Cimarron →	117	36 10N	96 17W
Cimone, Mte.	38	44 10N	10 40 E
Cîmpic Turzii	46	46 34N	23 53 E
Cîmpina	46	45 10N	25 45 E
Cîmpulung, Argeş, Romania	46	45 17N	25 3 E
Cîmpulung, Moldovenesc, Romania	46	47 32N	25 30 E
Cîmpuri	43	46 0N	26 50 E
Cinca →	32	41 26N	0 21 E
Cincer	42	43 55N	17 5 E
Cincinnati	114	39 10N	84 26W
Cîndeşti	46	45 15N	26 42 E
Ciney	16	50 18N	5 5 E
Cíngoli	39	43 23N	13 10 E
Cinigiano	39	42 53N	11 23 E
Cinto, Mt.	21	42 24N	8 54 E
Ciorani	46	44 45N	26 25 E
Ciotat, La	21	43 12N	5 36 E
Čiovo	39	43 30N	16 17 E
Circeo, Monte	40	41 14N	13 3 E
Circle, Alaska, U.S.A.	104	65 50N	144 10W
Circle, Montana, U.S.A.	116	47 26N	105 35W
Circleville, Ohio, U.S.A.	114	39 35N	82 57W
Circleville, Utah, U.S.A.	119	38 12N	112 24W
Cirebon	73	6 45 S	108 32 E
Cirencester	13	51 43N	1 59W
Cireşu	46	44 47N	22 31 E
Cirey-sur-Vezouze	19	48 35N	6 57 E
Ciriè	38	45 14N	7 35 E
Cirò	41	39 23N	17 3 E
Cisco	117	32 25N	99 0W
Cislău	46	45 14N	26 20 E
Cisna	27	49 12N	22 20 E
Cisnădie	46	45 42N	24 9 E
Cisterna di Latina	40	41 35N	12 50 E
Cisternino	41	40 45N	17 26 E
Citeli-Ckaro	57	41 33N	46 0 E
Citlaltépetl	120	19 0N	97 20W
Citrusdal	92	32 35 S	19 0 E
Città della Pieve	39	42 57N	12 0 E
Città di Castello	39	43 27N	12 14 E
Città Sant' Angelo	39	42 32N	14 5 E
Cittadella	39	45 39N	11 48 E
Cittaducale	39	42 24N	12 58 E
Cittanova	41	38 22N	16 5 E
Ciuc, Munţii	46	46 25N	26 5 E
Ciucaş	46	45 31N	25 56 E
Ciudad Acuña	120	29 20N	100 58W
Ciudad Altamirano	120	18 20N	100 40W
Ciudad Bolívar	126	8 5N	63 36W
Ciudad Camargo	120	27 41N	105 10W
Ciudad de Valles	120	22 0N	99 0W
Ciudad del Carmen	120	18 38N	91 50W
Ciudad Delicias = Delicias	120	28 10N	105 30W
Ciudad Guayana	126	8 0N	62 30W
Ciudad Guerrero	120	28 33N	107 28W
Ciudad Guzmán	120	19 40N	103 30W
Ciudad Juárez	120	31 40N	106 28W
Ciudad Madero	120	22 19N	97 50W
Ciudad Mante	120	22 50N	99 0W
Ciudad Obregón	120	27 28N	109 59W
Ciudad Real	31	38 59N	3 55W
Ciudad Real □	31	38 50N	4 0W
Ciudad Rodrigo	30	40 35N	6 32W
Ciudad Trujillo = Sto. Domingo	121	18 30N	70 0W
Ciudad Victoria	120	23 41N	99 9W
Ciudadela	32	40 0N	3 50 E
Ciulniţa	46	44 26N	27 22 E
Cividale del Friuli	39	46 6N	13 25 E
Cívita Castellana	39	42 18N	12 24 E
Civitanova Marche	39	43 18N	13 41 E
Civitavécchia	39	42 6N	11 46 E
Civitella del Tronto	39	42 48N	13 40 E
Civray	20	46 10N	0 17 E
Çivril	64	38 20N	29 43 E
Cixerri →	40	39 20N	8 40 E
Cizre	64	37 19N	42 10 E
Clacton-on-Sea	13	51 47N	1 10 E
Clain →	18	46 47N	0 33 E
Claire, L.	108	58 35N	112 5W
Clairemont	117	33 9N	100 44W
Clairton	112	40 18N	79 54W
Clairvaux-les-Lacs	21	46 35N	5 45 E
Claise →	18	46 56N	0 42 E
Clamecy	19	47 28N	3 30 E
Clanton	115	32 48N	86 36W
Clanwilliam	92	32 11 S	18 52 E
Clara	15	53 20N	7 38W
Clare, Austral.	99	33 50 S	138 37 E
Clare, U.S.A.	114	43 47N	84 45W
Clare □	15	52 20N	9 0W
Clare →	15	53 22N	9 5W
Clare I.	15	53 48N	10 0W
Claremont	114	43 23N	72 20W
Claremont Pt.	98	14 1 S	143 41 E
Claremore	117	36 40N	95 37W
Claremorris	15	53 45N	9 0W
Clarence →, Austral.	97	29 25 S	153 22 E
Clarence →, N.Z.	101	42 10 S	173 56 E
Clarence I.	5	61 10 S	54 0W
Clarence, I.	128	54 0 S	72 0W
Clarence Str., Austral.	96	12 0 S	131 0 E
Clarence Str., U.S.A.	108	55 40N	132 10W
Clarendon, Ark., U.S.A.	117	34 41N	91 20W
Clarendon, Tex., U.S.A.	117	34 58N	100 54W
Clarenville	107	48 10N	54 1W
Claresholm	108	50 0N	113 33W
Clarie Coast	5	68 0 S	135 0 E
Clarinda	116	40 45N	95 0W
Clarion, Iowa, U.S.A.	116	42 41N	93 46W
Clarion, Pa., U.S.A.	112	41 12N	79 22W
Clarion →	112	41 9N	79 41W
Clarion Fracture Zone	95	20 0N	120 0W
Clark	116	44 55N	97 45W
Clark Fork	118	48 9N	116 9W
Clark Fork →	118	48 9N	116 15W
Clark Hill Res.	115	33 45N	82 20W
Clark, Pt.	112	44 4N	81 45W
Clarkdale	119	34 53N	112 3W
Clarke City	107	50 12N	66 38W
Clarke, I.	97	40 32 S	148 10 E
Clarke L.	109	54 24N	106 54W
Clarke Ra.	98	20 45 S	148 20 E
Clark's Fork →	118	45 39N	108 43W
Clark's Harbour	107	43 25N	65 38W
Clarks Summit	113	41 31N	75 44W
Clarksburg	114	39 18N	80 21W
Clarksdale	117	34 12N	90 33W
Clarkston	118	46 28N	117 2W
Clarksville, Ark., U.S.A.	117	35 29N	93 27W
Clarksville, Tenn., U.S.A.	115	36 32N	87 20W
Clarksville, Tex., U.S.A.	117	33 37N	94 59W
Clatskanie	118	46 9N	123 12W
Claude	117	35 8N	101 22W
Claveria	73	18 37N	121 4 E
Clay Center	116	39 27N	97 9W
Clayette, La	21	46 17N	4 19 E
Claypool	119	33 27N	110 55W
Claysville	112	40 5N	80 25W
Clayton, Idaho, U.S.A.	118	44 12N	114 31W
Clayton, N. Mex., U.S.A.	117	36 30N	103 10W
Cle Elum	118	47 15N	120 57W
Clear L.	118	39 5N	122 47W
Clear, C.	15	51 26N	9 30W
Clear I.	15	51 26N	9 30W
Clear Lake, S.D., U.S.A.	116	44 48N	96 41W
Clear Lake, Wash., U.S.A.	118	48 27N	122 15W
Clear Lake Res.	118	41 55N	121 10W
Clearfield, Pa., U.S.A.	114	41 0N	78 27W
Clearfield, Utah, U.S.A.	118	41 10N	112 0W
Clearmont	118	44 43N	106 29W
Clearwater, Can.	108	51 38N	120 2W
Clearwater, U.S.A.	115	27 58N	82 45W
Clearwater →, Alta., Can.	108	52 22N	114 57W
Clearwater →, Alta., Can.	109	56 44N	111 23W
Clearwater Cr.	108	61 36N	125 30W
Clearwater, Mts.	118	46 20N	115 30W
Clearwater Prov. Park	109	54 0N	101 0W
Cleburne	117	32 18N	97 25W
Clécy	18	48 55N	0 29W
Cleethorpes	12	53 33N	0 2W
Cleeve Cloud	13	51 56N	2 0W
Clelles	21	44 50N	5 38 E
Clerks Rocks	5	56 0 S	34 30W
Clermont, Austral.	97	22 49 S	147 39 E
Clermont, France	19	49 23N	2 24 E
Clermont-en-Argonne	19	49 5N	5 4 E
Clermont-Ferrand	20	45 46N	3 4 E
Clermont-l'Hérault	20	43 38N	3 26 E
Clerval	19	47 25N	6 30 E
Clervaux	16	50 4N	6 2 E
Cléry-Saint-André	19	47 50N	1 46 E
Cles	38	46 21N	11 4 E
Cleveland, Austral.	99	27 30 S	153 15 E
Cleveland, Miss., U.S.A.	117	33 43N	90 43W
Cleveland, Ohio, U.S.A.	114	41 28N	81 43W
Cleveland, Okla., U.S.A.	117	36 21N	96 33W
Cleveland, Tenn., U.S.A.	115	35 9N	84 52W
Cleveland, Tex., U.S.A.	117	30 18N	95 0W
Cleveland □	12	54 35N	1 8 E
Cleveland, C.	97	19 11 S	147 1 E
Cleveland Heights	112	41 32N	81 30W
Clevelândia	125	26 24 S	52 23W
Clew B.	15	53 54N	9 50W
Clewiston	115	26 44N	80 50W
Clifden, Ireland	15	53 30N	10 2W
Clifden, N.Z.	101	46 1 S	167 42 E
Cliff	119	33 0N	108 36W
Clifton, Austral.	99	27 59 S	151 53 E
Clifton, Ariz., U.S.A.	119	33 8N	109 23W
Clifton, Tex., U.S.A.	117	31 46N	97 35W
Clifton Forge	114	37 49N	79 51W
Climax	109	49 10N	108 20W
Clinch →	115	36 0N	84 29W
Clingmans Dome	115	35 35N	83 30W
Clint	119	31 37N	106 11W
Clinton, B.C., Can.	108	51 6N	121 35W
Clinton, Ont., Can.	106	43 37N	81 32W
Clinton, N.Z.	101	46 12 S	169 23 E
Clinton, Ark., U.S.A.	117	35 37N	92 30W
Clinton, Ill., U.S.A.	116	40 8N	89 0W
Clinton, Ind., U.S.A.	114	39 40N	87 22W
Clinton, Iowa, U.S.A.	116	41 50N	90 12W
Clinton, Mass., U.S.A.	114	42 26N	71 40W
Clinton, Mo., U.S.A.	116	38 20N	93 46W
Clinton, N.C., U.S.A.	115	35 5N	78 15W
Clinton, Okla., U.S.A.	117	35 30N	99 0W
Clinton, S.C., U.S.A.	115	34 30N	81 54W
Clinton, Tenn., U.S.A.	115	36 6N	84 10W
Clinton C.	98	22 30 S	150 45 E
Clinton Colden L.	104	63 58N	107 27W
Clintonville	116	44 35N	88 46W
Clipperton Fracture Zone	95	19 0N	122 0W
Clipperton, I.	95	10 18N	109 13W
Clisson	18	47 5N	1 16W
Clive L.	108	63 13N	118 54W
Cloates, Pt.	96	22 43 S	113 40 E
Clocolan	93	28 55 S	27 34 E
Clodomira	124	27 35 S	64 14W
Clonakilty	15	51 37N	8 53W
Clonakilty B.	15	51 33N	8 50W
Cloncurry	97	20 40 S	140 28 E
Cloncurry →	98	18 37 S	140 40 E
Clones	15	54 10N	7 13W
Clonmel	15	52 22N	7 42W
Cloppenburg	24	52 50N	8 3 E
Cloquet	116	46 40N	92 30W
Clorinda	124	25 16 S	57 45W
Cloud Peak	118	44 23N	107 10W
Cloudcroft	119	33 0N	105 48W
Cloverdale	118	38 49N	123 0W
Clovis, Calif., U.S.A.	119	36 47N	119 45W
Clovis, N. Mex., U.S.A.	117	34 20N	103 10W
Cloyes	18	48 0N	1 14 E
Cluj-Napoca	46	46 47N	23 38 E
Cluj □	46	46 45N	23 30 E
Clunes	99	37 20 S	143 45 E
Cluny	21	46 26N	4 38 E
Cluses	21	46 5N	6 35 E
Clusone	38	45 54N	9 58 E
Clutha →	101	46 20 S	169 49 E
Clwyd □	12	53 5N	3 20W
Clwyd →	12	53 20N	3 30W
Clyde, Can.	105	70 30N	68 30W
Clyde, N.Z.	101	45 12 S	169 20 E
Clyde, U.S.A.	112	43 8N	76 52W
Clyde →	14	55 56N	4 29W
Clyde, Firth of	14	55 20N	5 0W
Clydebank	14	55 54N	4 25W
Clymer	112	42 3N	79 39W
Côa →	30	41 5N	7 6W
Coachella	119	33 44N	116 13W
Coahoma	117	32 17N	101 20W
Coahuayana →	120	18 41N	103 45W
Coahuila de Zaragoza □	120	27 0N	103 0W
Coal →	108	59 39N	126 57W
Coalane	91	17 48 S	37 2 E
Coalcomán	120	18 40N	103 10W
Coaldale	108	49 45N	112 35W
Coalgate	117	34 35N	96 13W
Coalinga	119	36 10N	120 21W
Coalville, U.K.	12	52 43N	1 21W
Coalville, U.S.A.	118	40 58N	111 24W
Coari	126	4 8 S	63 7W
Coast □	90	2 40 S	39 45 E
Coast Mts.	108	55 0N	129 0W
Coast Ranges	102	41 0N	123 0W
Coastal Plains Basin	96	30 10 S	115 30 E
Coatbridge	14	55 52N	4 2W
Coatepeque	120	14 46N	91 55W
Coatesville	114	39 59N	75 55W
Coaticook	107	45 10N	71 46W
Coats I.	105	62 30N	83 0W
Coats Land	5	77 0 S	25 0W
Coatzacoalcos	120	18 7N	94 25W
Cobadin	46	44 5N	28 13 E
Cobalt	106	47 25N	79 42W
Cobán	120	15 30N	90 21W
Cobar	97	31 27 S	145 48 E
Cóbh	15	51 50N	8 18W
Cobija	126	11 0 S	68 50W
Cobleskill	114	42 40N	74 30W
Coboconk	112	44 39N	78 48W
Cobourg	106	43 58N	78 10W
Cobourg Pen.	96	11 20 S	132 15 E
Cobram	99	35 54 S	145 40 E
Cobre	118	41 6N	114 25W
Coburg	25	50 15N	10 58 E
Coca	30	41 13N	4 32W
Cocanada = Kakinada	70	16 50N	82 11 E
Cocentaina	33	38 45N	0 27W
Cocha, La	124	27 50 S	65 40W
Cochabamba	126	17 26 S	66 10W
Cochem	25	50 8N	7 7 E
Cochemane	91	17 0 S	32 54 E
Cochin	70	9 59N	76 22 E
Cochin China = Nam-Phan	71	10 30N	106 0 E
Cochise	119	32 6N	109 58W
Cochran	115	32 25N	83 23W
Cochrane, Alta., Can.	108	51 11N	114 30W
Cochrane, Ont., Can.	106	49 0N	81 0W
Cochrane →	109	59 0N	103 40W
Cochrane, L.	128	47 10 S	72 0W
Cockatoo I.	96	16 6 S	123 37 E
Cockburn	99	32 5 S	141 0 E
Cockburn, Canal	128	54 30 S	72 0W
Cockburn I.	106	45 55N	83 22W
Coco →	121	15 0N	83 8W
Coco Chan.	71	13 50N	93 25 E
Coco Solo	120	9 22N	79 53W
Cocoa	115	28 22N	80 40W
Cocobeach	88	0 59N	9 34 E
Cocora	46	44 45N	27 3 E
Cocos I.	95	5 25N	87 55W
Cocos Is.	94	12 10 S	96 55 E
Cod, C.	111	42 8N	70 10W
Codajás	126	3 55 S	62 0W
Coderre	109	50 11N	106 31W
Codigoro	39	44 50N	12 5 E
Codó	127	4 30 S	43 55W
Codogno	38	45 10N	9 42 E
Codróipo	39	45 57N	13 0 E
Codru, Munţii	46	46 30N	22 15 E
Cody	118	44 35N	109 0W
Coe Hill	106	44 52N	77 50W
Coelemu	124	36 30 S	72 48W
Coen	97	13 52 S	143 12 E
Coesfeld	24	51 56N	7 10 E
Coeur d'Alene	118	47 45N	116 51W
Cœur d'Alene L.	118	47 32N	116 48W
Coevorden	16	52 40N	6 44 E
Coffeyville	117	37 0N	95 40W
Coffs Harbour	97	30 16 S	153 5 E
Cofrentes	33	39 13N	1 5W
Cogealac	46	44 36N	28 36 E
Coghinas →	40	40 55N	8 48 E
Coghinas, L. di	40	40 46N	9 3 E
Cognac	20	45 41N	0 20W
Cogne	38	45 37N	7 21 E
Cogolludo	32	40 59N	3 10W
Cohagen	118	47 2N	106 36W
Cohoes	114	42 47N	73 42W
Cohuna	99	35 45 S	144 15 E
Coiba, I.	121	7 30N	81 40W
Coig →	128	51 0 S	69 10W
Coihaique	128	45 30 S	71 45W
Coimbatore	70	11 2N	76 59 E
Coimbra, Brazil	126	19 55 S	57 48W
Coimbra, Port.	30	40 15N	8 27W
Coimbra □	30	40 12N	8 25W
Coín	31	36 40N	4 48W
Cojimies	126	0 20N	80 0W
Cojocna	46	46 45N	23 50 E
Cojutepequé	120	13 41N	88 54W
Čoka	42	45 57N	20 12 E
Cokeville	118	42 4N	111 0W
Col di Tenda	38	44 7N	7 36 E
Colaba Pt.	70	18 54N	72 47 E
Colac	97	38 21 S	143 35 E
Colachel	70	8 10N	77 15 E
Colares	31	38 48N	9 30W
Colbeck, C.	5	77 6 S	157 48W
Colbinabbin	99	36 38 S	144 4
Colborne	112	44 0N	77 5
Colby	116	39 27N	101
Colchagua □	124	34 30 S	71
Colchester	13	51 54N	0 5
Coldstream	14	55 39N	2 1
Coldwater, Can.	112	44 42N	79 4
Coldwater, U.S.A.	117	37 18N	99 2
Colebrook, Austral.	99	42 31 S	147 2
Colebrook, U.S.A.	114	44 54N	71 2
Coleman, Can.	108	49 40N	114 3
Coleman, U.S.A.	117	31 52N	99 3
Coleman →	97	15 6 S	141 3
Colenso	93	28 44 S	29 5
Coleraine, Austral.	99	37 36 S	141 4
Coleraine, U.K.	15	55 8N	6 4
Coleraine □	15	55 8N	6 4
Coleridge, L.	101	43 17 S	171 3
Coleroon →	70	11 25N	79 5
Colesberg	92	30 45 S	25
Colfax, La., U.S.A.	117	31 35N	92 3
Colfax, Wash., U.S.A.	118	46 57N	117 2
Colhué Huapi, L.	128	45 30 S	69
Cólico	38	46 8N	9 2
Coligny	93	26 17 S	26 1
Colima	120	19 10N	103 4
Colima □	120	19 10N	103 4
Colima, Nevado de	120	19 35N	103 4
Colina	124	33 13 S	70 4
Colina do Norte	84	12 28N	15
Colinas	127	6 0 S	44 1
Colinton	100	35 50 S	149 1
Coll	14	56 40N	6 3
Collaguasi	124	21 5 S	68 4
Collarada, Peña	32	42 43N	0 2
Collarenebri	99	29 33 S	148 3
Collbran	119	39 16N	107 5
Colle di Val d'Elsa	39	43 25N	11
Colle Salvetti	38	43 34N	10 2
Colle Sannita	41	41 22N	14 4
Collécchio	38	44 45N	10 1
Colleen Bawn	91	21 0 S	29 1
College Park	115	33 42N	84 2
Collette	107	46 40N	65 3
Collie	96	33 22 S	116
Collier B.	96	16 10 S	124 1
Colline Metallifere	38	43 10N	11
Collingwood, Austral.	98	22 20 S	142 3
Collingwood, Can.	106	44 29N	80 1
Collingwood, N.Z.	101	40 41 S	172 4
Collins	106	50 17N	89 2
Collinsville	97	20 30 S	147 5
Collipulli	124	37 55 S	72 3
Collo	83	36 58N	6 3
Collonges	21	46 9N	5 5
Collooney	15	54 11N	8 2
Colmar	19	48 5N	7 2
Colmars	21	44 11N	6 3
Colmenar	31	36 54N	4 2
Colmenar de Oreja	32	40 6N	3 2
Colmenar Viejo	30	40 39N	3 4
Colne	12	53 51N	2 1
Colo →	99	33 25 S	150 5
Cologna Véneta	39	45 19N	11 2
Cologne = Köln	24	50 56N	9 5
Colomb-Béchar = Béchar	82	31 38N	2 1
Colombey-les-Belles	19	48 32N	5 5
Colombey-les-Deux-Églises	19	48 13N	4 5
Colômbia	127	20 10 S	48 4
Colombia ■	126	3 45N	73
Colombo	70	6 56N	79 5
Colombus	119	31 54N	107 4
Colome	116	43 20N	99 4
Colón, Argent.	124	32 12 S	58 1
Colón, Cuba	121	22 42N	80 5
Colón, Panama	120	9 20N	79 5
Colonella	39	42 52N	13 5
Colonia	124	34 25 S	57 5
Colonia Dora	124	28 34 S	62 5
Colonial Hts.	114	37 19N	77 2
Colonne, C. delle	41	39 2N	17 1
Colonsay, Can.	109	51 59N	105 5
Colonsay, U.K.	14	56 4N	6 1
Colorado □	110	37 40N	106
Colorado →, Argent.	128	39 50 S	62
Colorado →, Calif., U.S.A.	119	34 45N	114 4
Colorado →, Tex., U.S.A.	117	28 36N	95 5
Colorado City	117	32 25N	100 5
Colorado Desert	110	34 20N	116
Colorado, I.	120	9 12N	79 5
Colorado Plateau	119	36 40N	110 3
Colorado R. Aqueduct	119	34 17N	114 1
Colorado Springs	116	38 55N	104 5
Colorno	38	44 55N	10 2
Colton, N.Y., U.S.A.	113	44 34N	74 5
Colton, Wash., U.S.A.	118	46 41N	117
Columbia, La., U.S.A.	117	32 7N	92
Columbia, Miss., U.S.A.	117	31 16N	89 5
Columbia, Mo., U.S.A.	116	38 58N	92 2
Columbia, Pa., U.S.A.	114	40 2N	76 3
Columbia, S.C., U.S.A.	115	34 0N	81
Columbia, Tenn., U.S.A.	115	35 40N	87
Columbia →	118	46 15N	124
Columbia Basin	118	47 30N	118 3
Columbia, C.	4	83 0N	70
Columbia City	114	41 8N	85 3
Columbia, District of □	114	38 55N	77
Columbia Falls	118	48 25N	114 1
Columbia Heights	116	45 5N	93 1
Columbia, Mt.	108	52 8N	117 2
Columbiana	112	40 53N	80 4
Columbretes, Is.	32	39 50N	0 5
Columbus, Ga., U.S.A.	115	32 30N	84 5
Columbus, Ind., U.S.A.	114	39 14N	85 5
Columbus, Kans., U.S.A.	117	37 15N	94 3
Columbus, Miss., U.S.A.	115	33 30N	88 2
Columbus, Mont., U.S.A.	118	45 38N	109 1
Columbus, N.D., U.S.A.	116	48 52N	102 4
Columbus, Nebr., U.S.A.	116	41 30N	97 2
Columbus, Ohio, U.S.A.	114	39 57N	83
Columbus, Tex., U.S.A.	117	29 42N	96 3
Columbus, Wis., U.S.A.	116	43 20N	89

Name	Page	Lat.	Long.
Colunga	**30**	43 29N	5 16W
Colusa	**118**	39 15N	122 1W
Colville	**118**	48 33N	117 54W
Colville ⤳	**104**	70 25N	151 0W
Colville, C.	**101**	36 29 S	175 21 E
Colwyn Bay	**12**	53 17N	3 44W
Coma	**87**	8 29N	36 53 E
Comácchio	**39**	44 41N	12 10 E
Comallo	**128**	41 0 S	70 5W
Comana	**46**	44 10N	26 10 E
Comanche, Okla., U.S.A.	**117**	34 27N	97 58W
Comanche, Tex., U.S.A.	**117**	31 55N	98 35W
Comăneşti	**46**	46 25N	26 26 E
Combahee ⤳	**115**	32 30N	80 31W
Combeaufontaine	**19**	47 38N	5 54 E
Comber	**112**	42 14N	82 33W
Comblain-au-Pont	**16**	50 29N	5 35 E
Combles	**19**	50 0N	2 50 E
Combourg	**18**	48 25N	1 46W
Combronde	**20**	45 58N	3 5 E
Comeragh Mts.	**15**	52 17N	7 35W
Comet	**98**	23 36 S	148 38 E
Comilla	**69**	23 28N	91 10 E
Comino, C.	**40**	40 28N	9 47 E
Comino I.	**36**	36 0N	14 20 E
Cómiso	**41**	36 57N	14 35 E
Comitán	**120**	16 18N	92 9W
Commentry	**20**	46 20N	2 46 E
Commerce, Ga., U.S.A.	**115**	34 10N	83 25W
Commerce, Tex., U.S.A.	**117**	33 15N	95 50W
Commercy	**19**	48 46N	5 34 E
Committee B.	**105**	68 30N	86 30W
Commonwealth B.	**5**	67 0 S	144 0 E
Commoron Cr. ⤳	**99**	28 22 S	150 8 E
Communism Pk. = Kommunisma, Pic	**65**	38 40N	72 0 E
Como	**38**	45 48N	9 5 E
Como, L. di	**38**	46 5N	9 17 E
Comodoro Rivadavia	**128**	45 50 S	67 40W
Comorin, C.	**70**	8 3N	77 40 E
Comorişte	**42**	45 10N	21 35 E
Comoro Is.	**3**	12 10 S	44 15 E
Comox	**108**	49 42N	124 55W
Compiègne	**19**	49 24N	2 50 E
Compíglia Maríttima	**38**	43 4N	10 37 E
Comporta	**31**	38 22N	8 46W
Comprida, I.	**125**	24 50 S	47 42W
Compton Downs	**99**	30 28 S	146 30 E
Côn Dao	**71**	8 45N	106 45 E
Conakry	**84**	9 29N	13 49W
Conara Junction	**99**	41 50 S	147 26 E
Concarneau	**18**	47 52N	3 56W
Conceição	**91**	18 47 S	36 7 E
Conceição da Barra	**127**	18 35 S	39 45W
Conceição do Araguaia	**127**	8 0 S	49 2W
Concepción, Argent.	**124**	27 20 S	65 35W
Concepción, Boliv.	**126**	16 15 S	62 8W
Concepción, Chile	**124**	36 50 S	73 0W
Concepción, Parag.	**124**	23 22 S	57 26W
Concepción □	**124**	37 0 S	72 30W
Concepción ⤳	**120**	30 32N	113 2W
Concepción del Oro	**120**	24 40N	101 30W
Concepción del Uruguay	**124**	32 35 S	58 20W
Concepción, L.	**126**	17 20 S	61 20W
Concepción, La = Ri-Aba	**85**	3 28N	8 40 E
Concepcion, Pt.	**119**	34 27N	120 27W
Concepción, Punta	**120**	26 55N	111 59W
Conception B.	**92**	23 55 S	14 22 E
Conception I.	**121**	23 52N	75 9W
Conception, Pt.	**119**	34 30N	120 34W
Concession	**91**	17 27 S	30 56 E
Conchas Dam	**117**	35 25N	104 10W
Conche	**107**	50 55N	55 58W
Conches	**18**	48 51N	2 43 E
Concho	**119**	34 32N	109 43W
Concho ⤳	**117**	31 30N	99 45W
Conchos ⤳	**120**	29 32N	104 25W
Concord, N.C., U.S.A.	**115**	35 28N	80 35W
Concord, N.H., U.S.A.	**114**	43 12N	71 30W
Concordia	**124**	31 20 S	58 2W
Concórdia	**126**	4 36 S	66 36W
Concordia	**116**	39 35N	97 40W
Concordia, La	**120**	16 8N	92 38W
Concots	**20**	44 26N	1 40 E
Concrete	**118**	48 35N	121 49W
Condamine ⤳	**97**	27 7 S	149 48 E
Condat	**20**	45 21N	2 46 E
Condé	**19**	50 26N	3 34 E
Conde	**116**	45 13N	98 5W
Condé-sur-Noireau	**18**	48 51N	0 33W
Condeúba	**127**	14 52 S	42 0W
Condobolin	**99**	33 4 S	147 6 E
Condom	**20**	43 57N	0 22 E
Condon	**118**	45 15N	120 8W
Condove	**38**	45 8N	7 19 E
Conegliano	**39**	45 53N	12 18 E
Conejera, I.	**33**	39 11N	2 58 E
Conflans-en-Jarnisy	**19**	49 10N	5 52 E
Confolens	**20**	46 2N	0 40 E
Confuso ⤳	**124**	25 9 S	57 34W
Congleton	**12**	53 10N	2 12W
Congo = Zaïre ⤳	**88**	1 30N	28 0 E
Congo ■	**88**	1 0 S	16 0 E
Congo Basin	**78**	0 10 S	24 30 E
Congonhas	**125**	20 30 S	43 52W
Congress	**119**	34 11N	112 56W
Conil	**31**	36 17N	6 10W
Coniston	**106**	46 29N	80 51W
Conjeevaram = Kanchipuram	**70**	12 52N	79 45 E
Conjuboy	**98**	18 35 S	144 35 E
Conklin	**109**	55 38N	111 5W
Conlea	**99**	30 7 S	144 35 E
Conn, L.	**15**	54 3N	9 15W
Connacht	**15**	53 23N	8 40W
Conneaut	**114**	41 55N	80 32W
Connecticut □	**114**	41 40N	72 40W
Connecticut ⤳	**114**	41 17N	72 21W
Connell	**118**	46 36N	118 51W
Connellsville	**114**	40 3N	79 32W
Connemara	**15**	53 29N	9 45W
Connemaugh ⤳	**112**	40 38N	79 42W
Conner, La	**118**	48 22N	122 27W
Connerré	**18**	48 3N	0 30 E
Connersville	**114**	39 40N	85 10W
Connors Ra.	**98**	21 40 S	149 10 E
Conoble	**99**	32 55 S	144 33 E
Conon ⤳	**14**	57 33N	4 28W
Cononaco ⤳	**126**	1 32 S	75 35W
Cononbridge	**14**	57 32N	4 30W
Conquest	**109**	51 32N	107 14W
Conquet, Le	**18**	48 21N	4 46W
Conrad	**118**	48 11N	112 0W
Conran, C.	**99**	37 49 S	148 44 E
Conroe	**117**	30 15N	95 28W
Conselheiro Lafaiete	**125**	20 40 S	43 48W
Conshohocken	**113**	40 5N	75 18W
Consort	**109**	52 1N	110 46W
Constance = Konstanz	**25**	47 39N	9 10 E
Constance, L. = Bodensee	**25**	47 35N	9 25 E
Constanţa	**46**	44 14N	28 38 E
Constanţa □	**46**	44 15N	28 15 E
Constantina	**31**	37 51N	5 40W
Constantine	**83**	36 25N	6 42 E
Constiiución, Chile	**124**	35 20 S	72 30W
Constitución, Uruguay	**124**	42 0 S	57 50W
Consucgra	**31**	39 28N	3 36W
Consui	**109**	49 20N	109 30W
Contact	**118**	41 50N	114 56W
Contai	**69**	21 54N	87 46 E
Contamana	**126**	7 19 S	74 55W
Contarina	**39**	45 2N	12 13 E
Contas ⤳	**127**	14 17 S	39 1W
Contes	**21**	43 49N	7 19 E
Contoocook	**113**	43 13N	71 45W
Contra Costa	**93**	25 9 S	33 30 E
Contres	**18**	47 24N	1 26 E
Contrexéville	**19**	48 6N	5 53 E
Conversano	**41**	40 57N	17 8 E
Conway, Ark., U.S.A.	**117**	35 5N	92 30W
Conway, N.H., U.S.A.	**114**	43 58N	71 8W
Conway, S.C., U.S.A.	**115**	33 49N	79 2W
Conway = Conwy	**12**	53 17N	3 50W
Conwy	**12**	53 17N	3 50W
Conwy ⤳	**12**	53 18N	3 50W
Coober Pedy	**96**	29 1 S	134 43 E
Cooch Behar	**69**	26 22N	89 29 E
Cook	**116**	47 49N	92 39W
Cook, Bahía	**128**	55 10 S	70 0W
Cook Inlet	**104**	59 0N	151 0W
Cook Is.	**95**	17 0 S	160 0W
Cook, Mt.	**101**	43 36 S	170 9 E
Cook Strait	**101**	41 15 S	174 29 E
Cookeville	**115**	36 12N	85 30W
Cookhouse	**92**	32 44 S	25 47 E
Cookshire	**113**	45 25N	71 38W
Cookstown	**15**	54 40N	6 43W
Cookstown □	**15**	54 40N	6 43W
Cooksville	**112**	43 36N	79 35W
Cooktown	**97**	15 30 S	145 16 E
Coolabah	**99**	31 1 S	146 43 E
Cooladdi	**99**	26 37 S	145 23 E
Coolah	**99**	31 48 S	149 41 E
Coolamon	**99**	34 46 S	147 8 E
Coolangatta	**99**	28 11 S	153 29 E
Coolgardie	**96**	30 55 S	121 8 E
Coolidge	**119**	33 1N	111 35W
Coolidge Dam	**119**	33 10N	110 30W
Cooma	**97**	36 12 S	149 8 E
Coonabarabran	**99**	31 14 S	149 18 E
Coonamble	**97**	30 56 S	148 27 E
Coondapoor	**70**	13 42N	74 40 E
Coongie	**99**	27 9 S	140 8 E
Coongoola	**99**	27 43 S	145 51 E
Cooninie, L.	**99**	26 4 S	139 59 E
Coonoor	**70**	11 21N	76 45 E
Cooper	**117**	33 20N	95 40W
Cooper ⤳	**115**	33 0N	79 55W
Coopers Cr. ⤳	**97**	28 29 S	137 46 E
Cooperstown, N.D., U.S.A.	**116**	47 30N	98 6W
Cooperstown, N.Y., U.S.A.	**114**	42 42N	74 57W
Coorabulka	**98**	23 41 S	140 20 E
Coorong, The	**97**	35 50 S	139 20 E
Cooroy	**99**	26 22 S	152 54 E
Coos Bay	**118**	43 26N	124 7W
Cootamundra	**97**	34 36 S	148 1 E
Cootehill	**15**	54 5N	7 5W
Cooyar	**99**	26 59 S	151 51 E
Cooyeana	**98**	24 29 S	138 45 E
Copahue Paso	**124**	37 49 S	71 8W
Copainalá	**120**	17 8N	93 11W
Cope	**116**	39 44N	102 50W
Cope, Cabo	**33**	37 26N	1 28W
Copenhagen = København	**49**	55 41N	12 34 E
Copertino	**41**	40 17N	18 2 E
Copiapó	**124**	27 30 S	70 20W
Copiapó ⤳	**124**	27 19 S	70 56W
Copley	**99**	30 36 S	138 26 E
Copp L.	**108**	60 14N	114 40W
Copparo	**39**	44 52N	11 49 E
Copper Center	**104**	62 10N	145 25W
Copper Cliff	**106**	46 28N	81 4W
Copper Harbor	**114**	47 31N	87 55W
Copper Queen	**91**	17 29 S	29 18 E
Copperbelt □	**91**	13 15 S	27 30 E
Coppermine	**104**	67 50N	115 5W
Coppermine ⤳	**104**	67 49N	116 4W
Coquet ⤳	**12**	55 18N	1 45W
Coquilhatville = Mbandaka	**88**	0 1N	18 18 E
Coquille	**118**	43 15N	124 12W
Coquimbo	**124**	30 0 S	71 20W
Coquimbo □	**124**	31 0 S	71 0W
Corabia	**46**	43 48N	24 30 E
Coracora	**126**	15 5 S	73 45W
Coradi, Is.	**41**	40 27N	17 10 E
Coral Gables	**115**	25 45N	80 16W
Coral Harbour	**105**	64 8N	83 10W
Coral Sea	**94**	15 0 S	150 0 E
Coral Sea Islands Terr.	**97**	20 0 S	155 0 E
Corangamite, L.	**100**	38 0 S	143 30 E
Coraopolis	**112**	40 30N	80 10W
Corato	**41**	41 12N	16 22 E
Corbeil-Essonnes	**19**	48 36N	2 26 E
Corbie	**19**	49 54N	2 30 E
Corbières	**20**	42 55N	2 35 E
Corbigny	**19**	47 16N	3 40 E
Corbin	**114**	37 0N	84 3W
Corbones ⤳	**31**	37 36N	5 39W
Corby	**13**	52 49N	0 31W
Corcoles ⤳	**33**	39 40N	3 18W
Corcoran	**119**	36 6N	119 35W
Corcubión	**30**	42 56N	9 12W
Cordele	**115**	31 55N	83 49W
Cordell	**117**	35 18N	99 0W
Cordenons	**39**	45 59N	12 42 E
Cordes	**20**	44 5N	1 57 E
Córdoba, Argent.	**124**	31 20 S	64 10W
Córdoba, Mexico	**120**	18 50N	97 0W
Córdoba, Spain	**31**	37 50N	4 50W
Córdoba □, Argent.	**124**	31 22 S	64 15W
Córdoba □, Spain	**31**	38 5N	5 0W
Córdoba, Sierra de	**124**	31 10 S	64 25W
Cordon	**73**	16 42N	121 32 E
Cordova, Ala., U.S.A.	**115**	33 45N	87 12W
Cordova, Alaska, U.S.A.	**104**	60 36N	145 45W
Corella	**32**	42 7N	1 48W
Corella ⤳	**98**	19 34 S	140 47 E
Corfield	**98**	21 40 S	143 21 E
Corfu = Kérkira	**44**	39 38N	19 50 E
Corgo	**30**	42 56N	7 25W
Cori	**40**	41 39N	12 53 E
Coria	**30**	40 0N	6 33W
Coricudgy, Mt.	**100**	32 51 S	150 24 E
Corigliano Cálabro	**41**	39 36N	16 31 E
Corinna	**99**	41 35 S	145 10 E
Corinth, Miss., U.S.A.	**115**	34 54N	88 30W
Corinth, N.Y., U.S.A.	**113**	43 15N	73 50W
Corinth = Kórinthos	**45**	38 19N	22 24 E
Corinth Canal	**45**	37 58N	23 0 E
Corinth, G. of = Korinthiakós	**45**	38 16N	22 30 E
Corinto, Brazil	**127**	18 20 S	44 30W
Corinto, Nic.	**121**	12 30N	87 10W
Corj □	**46**	45 5N	23 25 E
Cork	**15**	51 54N	8 30W
Cork □	**15**	51 50N	8 50W
Cork Harbour	**15**	51 46N	8 16W
Corlay	**18**	48 20N	3 5W
Corleone	**40**	37 48N	13 16 E
Corleto Perticara	**41**	40 23N	16 2 E
Çorlu	**43**	41 11N	27 49 E
Cormack L.	**108**	60 56N	121 37W
Cormóns	**39**	45 58N	13 29 E
Cormorant	**109**	54 14N	100 35W
Cormorant L.	**109**	54 15N	100 50W
Corn Is. = Maiz, Is. del	**121**	12 0N	83 0W
Cornélio Procópio	**125**	23 7 S	50 40W
Cornell	**116**	45 10N	91 8W
Corner Brook	**107**	48 57N	57 58W
Corner Inlet	**97**	38 45 S	146 20 E
Corníglio	**38**	44 29N	10 5 E
Corning, Ark., U.S.A.	**117**	36 27N	90 34W
Corning, Calif., U.S.A.	**118**	39 56N	122 9W
Corning, Iowa, U.S.A.	**116**	40 57N	94 40W
Corning, N.Y., U.S.A.	**114**	42 10N	77 3W
Corno, Monte	**39**	42 28N	13 34 E
Cornwall, Austral.	**99**	41 33 S	148 7 E
Cornwall, Can.	**106**	45 2N	74 44W
Cornwall □	**13**	50 26N	4 40W
Cornwallis I.	**4**	75 8N	95 0W
Corny Pt.	**99**	34 55 S	137 0 E
Coro	**126**	11 25N	69 41W
Coroatá	**127**	4 8 S	44 0W
Corocoro	**126**	17 15 S	68 28W
Coroico	**126**	16 0 S	67 50W
Coromandel	**101**	36 45 S	175 31 E
Coromandel Coast	**70**	12 30N	81 0 E
Corona, Austral.	**99**	31 16 S	141 24 E
Corona, Calif., U.S.A.	**119**	33 49N	117 36W
Corona, N. Mex., U.S.A.	**119**	34 15N	105 32W
Coronada	**119**	32 45N	117 9W
Coronado, Bahía de	**121**	9 0N	83 40W
Coronation	**108**	52 5N	111 27W
Coronation Gulf	**104**	68 25N	110 0W
Coronation I., Antarct.	**5**	60 45 S	46 0W
Coronation I., U.S.A.	**108**	55 52N	134 20W
Coronda	**124**	31 58 S	60 56W
Coronel	**124**	37 0 S	73 10W
Coronel Bogado	**124**	27 11 S	56 18W
Coronel Dorrego	**124**	38 40 S	61 10W
Coronel Oviedo	**124**	25 24 S	56 30W
Coronel Pringles	**124**	38 0 S	61 30W
Coronel Suárez	**124**	37 30 S	61 52W
Coronel Vidal	**124**	37 28 S	57 45W
Çorovoda	**44**	40 31N	20 14 E
Corowa	**99**	35 58 S	146 21 E
Corozal, Belize	**120**	18 23N	88 23W
Corozal, Panama	**120**	8 59N	79 34W
Corps	**21**	44 50N	5 56 E
Corpus	**125**	27 10 S	55 30W
Corpus Christi	**117**	27 50N	97 28W
Corpus Christi L.	**117**	28 5N	97 54W
Corque	**126**	18 20 S	67 41W
Corral de Almaguer	**32**	39 45N	3 10W
Corréggio	**38**	44 46N	10 47 E
Correntes, C. das	**93**	24 6 S	35 34 E
Corrèze □	**20**	45 20N	1 45 E
Correze ⤳	**20**	45 10N	1 28 E
Corrib, L.	**15**	53 5N	9 10W
Corrientes	**124**	27 30 S	58 45W
Corrientes □	**124**	28 0 S	57 0W
Corrientes ⤳, Argent.	**124**	30 42 S	59 38W
Corrientes ⤳, Peru	**126**	3 43 S	74 35W
Corrientes, C., Colomb.	**126**	5 30N	77 34W
Corrientes, C., Cuba	**121**	21 43N	84 30W
Corrientes, C., Mexico	**120**	20 25N	105 42W
Corrigan	**117**	31 0N	94 48W
Corry	**114**	41 55N	79 39W
Corse	**21**	42 0N	9 0 E
Corse, C.	**21**	43 1N	9 25 E
Corse-du-Sud □	**21**	41 45N	9 0 E
Corsica = Corse	**21**	42 0N	9 0 E
Corsicana	**117**	32 5N	96 30W
Corté	**21**	42 19N	9 11 E
Corte do Pinto	**31**	37 42N	7 29W
Cortegana	**31**	37 52N	6 49W
Cortez	**119**	37 24N	108 35W
Cortina d'Ampezzo	**39**	46 32N	12 9 E
Cortland	**114**	42 35N	76 11W
Cortona	**39**	43 16N	12 0 E
Coruche	**31**	38 57N	8 30W
Çorum	**64**	40 30N	34 57 E
Corumbá	**126**	19 0 S	57 30W
Corumbá de Goiás	**127**	16 0 S	48 50W
Coruña, La	**30**	43 20N	8 25W
Coruña, La □	**30**	43 10N	8 30W
Corund	**46**	46 30N	25 13 E
Corunna = La Coruña	**30**	43 20N	8 25W
Corvallis	**118**	44 36N	123 15W
Corvette, L. de la	**106**	53 25N	74 3W
Corydon	**116**	40 42N	93 22W
Cosalá	**120**	24 28N	106 40W
Cosamaloapan	**120**	18 23N	95 50W
Cosenza	**41**	39 17N	16 14 E
Coşereni	**46**	44 38N	26 35 E
Coshocton	**114**	40 17N	81 51W
Cosne-sur-Loire	**19**	47 24N	2 54 E
Cospeito	**30**	43 12N	7 34W
Cosquín	**124**	31 15 S	64 30W
Cossato	**38**	45 34N	8 10 E
Cossé-le-Vivien	**18**	47 57N	0 54W
Cosson ⤳	**19**	47 30N	1 15 E
Costa Blanca	**33**	38 25N	0 10W
Costa Brava	**32**	41 30N	3 0 E
Costa del Sol	**31**	36 30N	4 30W
Costa Dorada	**32**	40 45N	1 15 E
Costa Rica ■	**121**	10 0N	84 0W
Costa Smeralda	**40**	41 5N	9 35 E
Costigliole d'Asti	**38**	44 48N	8 11 E
Costilla	**119**	37 0N	105 30W
Coştiui	**46**	47 53N	24 2 E
Coswig	**24**	51 52N	12 31 E
Cotabato	**73**	7 14N	124 15 E
Cotagaita	**124**	20 45 S	65 40W
Côte d'Azur	**21**	43 25N	6 50 E
Côte d'Or	**19**	47 10N	4 50 E
Côte-d'Or □	**19**	47 30N	4 50 E
Côte-St.-André, La	**21**	45 24N	5 15 E
Coteau des Prairies	**116**	44 30N	97 0W
Coteau du Missouri, Plat. du	**116**	47 0N	101 0W
Coteau Landing	**113**	45 15N	74 13W
Cotentin	**18**	49 30N	1 30W
Côtes de Meuse	**19**	49 15N	5 22 E
Côtes-du-Nord □	**18**	48 25N	2 40W
Cotiella	**32**	42 31N	0 19 E
Cotina ⤳	**42**	43 36N	18 50 E
Cotonou	**85**	6 20N	2 25 E
Cotopaxi, Vol.	**126**	0 40 S	78 30W
Cotronei	**41**	39 9N	16 45 E
Cotswold Hills	**13**	51 42N	2 10W
Cottage Grove	**118**	43 48N	123 2W
Cottbus	**24**	51 44N	14 20 E
Cottbus □	**24**	51 43N	13 30 E
Cottonwood	**119**	34 48N	112 1W
Cotulla	**117**	28 26N	99 14W
Coubre, Pte. de la	**20**	45 42N	1 15W
Couches	**19**	46 53N	4 30 E
Couço	**31**	38 59N	8 17W
Coudersport	**114**	41 45N	77 40W
Couëron	**18**	47 13N	1 44W
Couesnon ⤳	**18**	48 38N	1 32W
Couhe-Vérac	**20**	46 18N	0 12 E
Coulanges	**19**	47 30N	3 30 E
Coulee City	**118**	47 36N	119 18W
Coulman I.	**5**	73 35 S	170 0 E
Coulommiers	**19**	48 50N	3 3 E
Coulon ⤳	**21**	43 51N	5 0 E
Coulonge ⤳	**106**	45 52N	76 46W
Coulonges	**20**	46 28N	0 35W
Council, Alaska, U.S.A.	**104**	64 55N	163 45W
Council, Idaho, U.S.A.	**118**	44 44N	116 26W
Council Bluffs	**116**	41 20N	95 50W
Council Grove	**116**	38 41N	96 30W
Courantyne ⤳	**126**	5 55N	57 5W
Courçon	**20**	46 15N	0 50W
Couronne, C.	**21**	43 19N	5 3 E
Cours	**21**	46 7N	4 19 E
Coursan	**20**	43 14N	3 4 E
Courseulles	**18**	49 20N	0 29W
Courtenay	**108**	49 45N	125 0W
Courtine, La	**20**	45 43N	2 16 E
Courtrai = Kortrijk	**16**	50 50N	3 17 E
Courtright	**112**	42 49N	82 28W
Courville	**18**	48 28N	1 15 E
Coushatta	**117**	32 0N	93 21W
Coutances	**18**	49 3N	1 28W
Couterne	**18**	48 30N	0 25W
Coutras	**20**	45 3N	0 8W
Coutts	**108**	49 0N	111 57W
Covarrubias	**32**	42 4N	3 31W
Covasna	**46**	45 50N	26 10 E
Covasna □	**46**	45 50N	26 0 E
Coventry	**13**	52 25N	1 31W
Coventry L.	**109**	61 15N	106 15W
Covilhã	**30**	40 17N	7 31W
Covington, Ga., U.S.A.	**115**	33 36N	83 50W
Covington, Ky., U.S.A.	**114**	39 5N	84 30W
Covington, Okla., U.S.A.	**117**	36 21N	97 36W
Covington, Tenn., U.S.A.	**117**	35 34N	89 39W
Cowal, L.	**97**	33 40 S	147 25 E
Cowan	**109**	52 5N	100 45W
Cowan, L.	**96**	31 45 S	121 45 E
Cowan L.	**109**	54 0N	107 15W
Cowangie	**99**	35 12 S	141 26 E
Cowansville	**113**	45 14N	72 46W
Cowarie	**99**	27 45 S	138 15 E
Cowdenbeath	**14**	56 7N	3 20W
Cowes	**13**	50 45N	1 18W
Cowra	**97**	33 49 S	148 42 E
Coxim	**127**	18 30 S	54 55W
Cox's Bazar	**67**	21 26N	91 59 E
Cox's Cove	**107**	49 7N	58 5W
Coyuca de Benítez	**120**	17 1N	100 8W
Coyuca de Catalan	**120**	18 18N	100 41W
Cozad	**116**	40 55N	99 57W
Cozumel, Isla de	**120**	20 30N	86 40W
Craboon	**99**	32 3 S	149 30 E
Cracow	**99**	25 17 S	150 17 E
Cracow = Kraków	**27**	50 4N	19 57 E
Cradock	**92**	32 8 S	25 36 E

Craig, Alaska, U.S.A. 108 55 30N 133 5W
Craig, Colo., U.S.A. 118 40 32N 107 33W
Craigavon = Lurgan 15 54 28N 6 20W
Craigmore 91 20 28 S 32 50 E
Crailsheim 25 49 7N 10 5 E
Craiova 46 44 21N 23 48 E
Cramsie 98 23 20 S 144 15 E
Cranberry Portage 109 54 35N 101 23W
Cranbrook, Austral. 99 42 0 S 148 5 E
Cranbrook, Can. 108 49 30N 115 46W
Crandon 116 45 32N 88 52W
Crane, Oregon, U.S.A. 118 43 21N 118 39W
Crane, Texas, U.S.A. 117 31 26N 102 27W
Cranston 113 41 47N 71 27W
Craon 18 47 50N 0 58W
Craonne 19 49 27N 3 46 E
Craponne 20 45 20N 3 51 E
Crasna 46 46 32N 27 51 E
Crasna → 46 47 44N 22 35 E
Crasnei, Munţii 46 47 0N 23 20 E
Crater, L. 118 42 55N 122 3W
Crater Pt. 98 5 25 S 152 9 E
Crateús 127 5 10 S 40 39W
Crati → 41 39 41N 16 30 E
Crato, Brazil 127 7 10 S 39 25W
Crato, Port. 31 39 16N 7 39W
Crau 21 43 32N 4 40 E
Crawford 116 42 40N 103 25W
Crawfordsville 114 40 2N 86 51W
Crawley 13 51 7N 0 10W
Crazy Mts. 118 46 14N 110 30W
Crean L. 109 54 5N 106 9W
Crécy-en-Brie 19 48 50N 2 53 E
Crécy-en-Ponthieu 19 50 15N 1 53 E
Crediton 112 43 17N 81 33W
Cree →, Can. 109 58 57N 105 47W
Cree →, U.K. 14 54 51N 4 24W
Cree L. 109 57 30N 106 30W
Creede 119 37 56N 106 59W
Creel 120 27 45N 107 38W
Creighton 116 42 30N 97 52W
Creil 19 49 15N 2 34 E
Crema 38 45 21N 9 40 E
Cremona 38 45 8N 10 2 E
Crepaja 42 45 1N 20 38 E
Crépy 19 49 37N 3 32 E
Crépy-en-Valois 19 49 14N 2 54 E
Cres 39 44 58N 14 25 E
Cresbard 116 45 13N 98 57W
Crescent, Okla., U.S.A. 117 35 58N 97 36W
Crescent, Oreg., U.S.A. 118 43 30N 121 37W
Crescent City 118 41 45N 124 12W
Crescentino 38 45 11N 8 7 E
Crespino 39 44 59N 11 51 E
Crespo 124 32 2 S 60 19W
Cressy 99 38 2 S 143 40 E
Crest 21 44 44N 5 2 E
Crested Butte 119 38 57N 107 0W
Crestline 112 40 46N 82 45W
Creston, Can. 108 49 10N 116 31W
Creston, Iowa, U.S.A. 116 41 0N 94 20W
Creston, Wash., U.S.A. 118 47 47N 118 36W
Creston, Wyo., U.S.A. 118 41 46N 107 50W
Crestview 115 30 45N 86 35W
Creswick 100 37 25 S 143 58 E
Crete 116 40 38N 96 58W
Crete = Kríti 45 35 15N 25 0 E
Crete, La 108 58 11N 116 24W
Crete, Sea of 45 36 0N 25 0 E
Cretin, C. 98 6 40 S 147 53 E
Creus, C. 32 42 20N 3 19 E
Creuse □ 20 46 0N 2 0 E
Creuse → 20 47 0N 0 34 E
Creusot, Le 19 46 50N 4 24 E
Creuzburg 24 51 3N 10 15 E
Crevalcore 39 44 41N 11 10 E
Crèvecœur-le-Grand 19 49 37N 2 5 E
Crevillente 33 38 12N 0 48W
Crewe 12 53 6N 2 28W
Crib Point 99 38 22 S 145 13 E
Criciúma 125 28 40 S 49 23W
Crieff 14 56 22N 3 50W
Crikvenica 39 45 11N 14 40 E
Crimea = Krymskaya 56 45 0N 34 0 E
Crimmitschau 24 50 48N 12 23 E
Crinan 14 56 6N 5 34W
Cristeşti 46 47 15N 26 33 E
Cristóbal 120 9 19N 79 54W
Crişul Alb → 42 46 42N 21 17 E
Crişul Negru → 46 46 38N 22 26 E
Crişul Repede → 46 46 55N 20 59 E
Crivitz 24 53 35N 11 39 E
Crna Gora 42 42 10N 21 30 E
Crna Gora □ 42 42 40N 19 20 E
Crna Reka → 42 41 33N 21 59 E
Crna Trava 42 42 49N 22 19 E
Crni Drim → 42 41 17N 20 40 E
Crni Timok → 42 43 53N 22 15 E
Crnoljeva Planina 42 42 20N 21 0 E
Črnomelj 39 45 33N 15 10 E
Croaghpatrick 15 53 46N 9 40W
Croatia = Hrvatska □ 39 45 20N 16 0 E
Crocker, Barisan 72 5 40N 116 30 E
Crocker I. 96 11 12 S 132 32 E
Crockett 117 31 20N 95 30W
Crocodile = Krokodil → 93 25 26 S 32 0 E
Crocodile Is. 96 12 3 S 134 58 E
Crocq 20 45 52N 2 21 E
Croisette, C. 21 43 13N 5 20 E
Croisic, Le 18 47 18N 2 30W
Croisic, Pte. du 18 47 19N 2 31W
Croix, La, L. 106 48 20N 92 15W
Cromarty, Can. 109 58 3N 94 9W
Cromarty, U.K. 14 57 40N 4 2W
Cromer 12 52 56N 1 18 E
Cromwell 101 45 3 S 169 14 E
Cronat 19 46 43N 3 40 E
Cronulla 100 34 3 S 151 8 E
Crooked →, Can. 108 54 50N 122 54W
Crooked →, U.S.A. 118 44 30N 121 16W
Crooked I. 121 22 50N 74 10W
Crookston, Minn., U.S.A. 116 47 50N 96 40W
Crookston, Nebr., U.S.A. 116 42 56N 100 45W
Crooksville 114 39 45N 82 8W
Crookwell 99 34 28 S 149 24 E
Crosby, Minn., U.S.A. 116 46 28N 93 57W
Crosby, N.D., U.S.A. 109 48 55N 103 18W
Crosby, Pa., U.S.A. 112 41 45N 78 23W
Crosbyton 117 33 37N 101 12W
Cross → 85 4 42N 8 21 E
Cross City 115 29 35N 83 5W
Cross Fell 12 54 44N 2 29W
Cross L. 109 54 45N 97 30W
Cross Plains 117 32 8N 99 7W
Cross River □ 85 6 0N 8 0 E
Cross Sound 104 58 20N 136 30W
Crosse, La, Kans., U.S.A. 116 38 33N 99 20W
Crosse, La, Wis., U.S.A. 116 43 48N 91 13W
Crossett 117 33 10N 91 57W
Crossfield 108 51 25N 114 0W
Crosshaven 15 51 48N 8 19W
Croton-on-Hudson 113 41 12N 73 55W
Crotone 41 39 5N 17 6 E
Crow → 108 59 41N 124 20W
Crow Agency 118 45 40N 107 30W
Crow Hd. 15 51 34N 10 9W
Crowell 117 33 59N 99 45W
Crowley 117 30 15N 92 20W
Crown Point 114 41 24N 87 23W
Crows Nest 99 27 16 S 152 4 E
Crowsnest Pass 108 49 40N 114 40W
Croydon, Austral. 97 18 13 S 142 14 E
Croydon, U.K. 13 51 18N 0 5W
Crozet Is. 3 46 27 S 52 0 E
Crozon 18 48 15N 4 30W
Cruz Alta 125 28 45 S 53 40W
Cruz, C. 121 19 50N 77 50W
Cruz del Eje 124 30 45 S 64 50W
Cruz, La 120 23 55N 106 54W
Cruzeiro 125 22 33 S 45 0W
Cruzeiro do Oeste 125 23 46 S 53 4W
Cruzeiro do Sul 126 7 35 S 72 35W
Cry L. 108 58 45N 129 0W
Crystal Brook 99 33 21 S 138 12 E
Crystal City, Mo., U.S.A. 116 38 15N 90 23W
Crystal City, Tex., U.S.A. 117 28 40N 99 50W
Crystal Falls 114 46 9N 88 11W
Crystal River 115 28 54N 82 35W
Crystal Springs 117 31 59N 90 25W
Csongrád 27 46 43N 20 12 E
Csongrád □ 27 46 32N 20 15 E
Csorna 27 47 38N 17 18 E
Csurgo 27 46 16N 17 9 E
Cu Lao Hon 71 10 54N 108 18 E
Cuácua → 91 17 54 S 37 0 E
Cuamato 92 17 2 S 15 7 E
Cuamba 91 14 45 S 36 22 E
Cuando → 89 14 0 S 19 30 E
Cuando Cubango □ 92 16 25 S 20 0 E
Cuangar 92 17 36 S 18 39 E
Cuarto → 124 33 25 S 63 2W
Cuba, Port. 31 38 10N 7 54W
Cuba, N. Mex., U.S.A. 119 36 0N 107 0W
Cuba, N.Y., U.S.A. 112 42 12N 78 18W
Cuba ■ 121 22 0N 79 0W
Cubango → 92 18 50 S 22 25 E
Cuchi 89 14 37 S 16 58 E
Cúcuta 126 7 54N 72 31W
Cudahy 114 42 54N 87 50W
Cudalbi 46 45 46N 27 41 E
Cuddalore 70 11 46N 79 45 E
Cuddapah 70 14 30N 78 47 E
Cuddapan, L. 99 25 45 S 141 26 E
Cudgewa 99 36 10 S 147 42 E
Cudillero 30 43 33N 6 9W
Cue 96 27 25 S 117 54 E
Cuéllar 30 41 23N 4 21W
Cuenca, Ecuador 126 2 50 S 79 9W
Cuenca, Spain 32 40 5N 2 10W
Cuenca □ 32 40 0N 2 0W
Cuenca, Serranía de 32 39 55N 1 50W
Cuerda del Pozo, Pantano de la 32 41 51N 2 44W
Cuernavaca 120 18 50N 99 20W
Cuero 117 29 5N 97 17W
Cuers 21 43 14N 6 5 E
Cuervo 117 35 5N 104 25W
Cuevas del Almanzora 33 37 18N 1 58W
Cuevo 126 20 15 S 63 30W
Cugir 46 45 48N 23 25 E
Cuiabá 127 15 30 S 56 0W
Cuiabá → 127 17 5 S 56 36W
Cuillin Hills 14 57 14N 6 15W
Cuillin Sd. 14 57 4N 6 20W
Cuiluan 76 47 51N 128 32 E
Cuima 89 13 25 S 15 45 E
Cuiseaux 21 46 30N 5 22 E
Cuito → 92 18 1 S 20 48 E
Cuitzeo, L. de 120 19 55N 101 5W
Cujmir 46 44 13N 22 57 E
Culan 20 46 34N 2 20 E
Culbertson 116 48 9N 104 30W
Culcairn 99 35 41 S 147 3 E
Culebra, Sierra de la 30 41 55N 6 20W
Culgoa → 99 29 56 S 146 20 E
Culiacán 120 24 50N 107 23W
Culion 73 11 54N 120 1 E
Cúllar de Baza 33 37 35N 2 34W
Cullarin Range 99 34 30 S 149 30 E
Cullen 14 57 45N 2 50W
Cullen Pt. 98 11 57 S 141 54 E
Cullera 33 39 9N 0 17W
Cullman 115 34 13N 86 50W
Culloden Moor 14 57 29N 4 7W
Culoz 21 45 47N 5 46 E
Culpeper 114 38 29N 77 59W
Culuene → 127 12 56 S 52 51W
Culver, Pt. 96 32 54 S 124 43 E
Culverden 101 42 47 S 172 49 E
Cumali 45 36 42N 27 28 E
Cumaná 126 10 30N 64 5W
Cumberland, B.C., Can. 108 49 40N 125 0W
Cumberland, Qué., Can. 113 45 30N 75 24W
Cumberland, Md., U.S.A. 114 39 40N 78 43W
Cumberland, Wis., U.S.A. 116 45 32N 92 3W
Cumberland → 115 36 15N 87 0W
Cumberland I. 115 30 52N 81 30W
Cumberland Is. 97 20 35 S 149 10 E
Cumberland L. 109 54 3N 102 18W
Cumberland Pen. 105 67 0N 64 0W
Cumberland Plat. 115 36 0N 84 30W
Cumberland Sd. 105 65 30N 66 0W
Cumborah 99 29 40 S 147 45 E
Cumbres Mayores 31 38 4N 6 39W
Cumbria □ 12 54 35N 2 55W
Cumbrian Mts. 12 54 30N 3 0W
Cumbum 70 15 40N 79 10 E
Cumnock, Austral. 99 32 59 S 148 46 E
Cumnock, U.K. 14 55 27N 4 18W
Cuncumén 124 31 53 S 70 38W
Cunene → 92 17 20 S 11 50 E
Cúneo 38 44 23N 7 31 E
Cunillera, I. 33 38 59N 1 13 E
Cunlhat 20 45 38N 3 32 E
Cunnamulla 97 28 2 S 145 38 E
Cuorgnè 38 45 23N 7 39 E
Cupar, Can. 109 50 57N 104 10W
Cupar, U.K. 14 56 20N 3 0W
Cupica, Golfo de 126 6 25N 77 30W
Ćuprija 42 43 57N 21 26 E
Curaçao 121 12 10N 69 0W
Curanilahue 124 37 29 S 73 28W
Curaray → 126 2 20 S 74 5W
Cure → 19 47 40N 3 41 E
Curepto 124 35 8 S 72 1W
Curiapo 126 8 33N 61 5W
Curicó 124 34 55 S 71 20W
Curicó □ 124 34 50 S 71 15W
Curitiba 125 25 20 S 49 10W
Currabubula 99 31 16 S 150 44 E
Currais Novos 127 6 13 S 36 30W
Curralinho 127 1 45 S 49 46W
Currant 118 38 51N 115 32W
Curraweena 99 30 47 S 145 54 E
Currawilla 99 25 10 S 141 20 E
Current → 117 37 15N 91 10W
Currie, Austral. 99 39 56 S 143 53 E
Currie, U.S.A. 118 40 16N 114 45W
Currie, Mt. 93 30 29 S 29 21 E
Currituck Sd. 115 36 20N 75 50W
Currockbilly Mt. 100 35 25 S 150 0 E
Curtea de Argeş 46 45 12N 24 42 E
Curtis, Spain 30 43 7N 8 4W
Curtis, U.S.A. 116 40 41N 100 32W
Curtis I. 97 23 35 S 151 10 E
Curuápanema → 127 2 25 S 55 2W
Curuçá 127 0 43 S 47 50W
Curuguaty 125 24 31 S 55 42W
Çürüksu Çayi → 53 37 27N 27 11 E
Curundu 120 8 59N 79 38W
Curup 72 4 26 S 102 13 E
Cururupu 127 1 50 S 44 50W
Curuzú Cuatiá 124 29 50 S 58 5W
Curvelo 127 18 45 S 44 27W
Cushing 117 35 59N 96 46W
Cushing, Mt. 108 57 35N 126 57W
Cusihuiriáchic 120 28 10N 106 50W
Cusna, Monte 38 44 13N 10 25 E
Cusset 20 46 8N 3 28 E
Custer 116 43 45N 103 38W
Cut Bank 118 48 40N 112 15W
Cuthbert 115 31 47N 84 47W
Cutro 41 39 1N 16 58 E
Cuttaburra → 99 29 43 S 144 22 E
Cuttack 69 20 25N 85 57 E
Cuvier, C. 96 23 14 S 113 22 E
Cuvier I. 101 36 27 S 175 50 E
Cuxhaven 24 53 51N 8 41 E
Cuyahoga Falls 114 41 8N 81 30W
Cuyo 73 10 50N 121 5 E
Cuzco, Boliv. 126 20 0 S 66 50W
Cuzco, Peru 126 13 32 S 72 0W
Čvrsnica 42 43 36N 17 35 E
Cwmbran 13 51 39N 3 0W
Cyangugu 90 2 29 S 28 54 E
Cybinka 28 52 12N 14 46 E
Cyclades = Kikladhes 45 37 20N 24 30 E
Cygnet 99 43 8 S 147 1 E
Cynthiana 114 38 23N 84 10W
Cypress Hills 109 49 40N 109 30W
Cyprus ■ 64 35 0N 33 0 E
Cyrenaica 81 27 0N 23 0 E
Cyrene = Shaḥḥāt 81 32 40N 21 35 E
Czaplinek 28 53 34N 16 14 E
Czar 109 52 27N 110 50W
Czarna →, Piotrkow Trybunalski, Poland 28 51 18N 19 55 E
Czarna →, Tarnobrzeg, Poland 28 50 3N 21 21 E
Czarna Woda 28 53 51N 18 6 E
Czarne 28 53 42N 16 58 E
Czarnków 28 52 55N 16 38 E
Czechoslovakia ■ 27 49 0N 17 0 E
Czechowice-Dziedzice 27 49 54N 18 59 E
Czeladz 28 50 16N 19 2 E
Czempiń 28 52 9N 16 33 E
Czeremcha 28 52 31N 23 21 E
Czersk 28 53 46N 17 58 E
Czerwieńsk 28 52 1N 15 13 E
Czerwionka 27 50 7N 18 37 E
Częstochowa 28 50 49N 19 7 E
Częstochowa □ 28 50 45N 19 0 E
Człopa 28 53 6N 16 6 E
Człuchów 28 53 41N 17 22 E
Czyzew 28 52 48N 22 19 E

D

Da → 71 21 15N 105 20 E
Da Hinggan Ling 75 48 0N 121 0 E
Da Lat 71 11 56N 108 25 E
Da Nang 71 16 4N 108 13 E
Da Qaidam 75 37 50N 95 15 E
Da Yunhe, Jiangsu, China 77 34 25N 120 5 E
Da Yunhe, Zhejiang, China 77 30 45N 120 35 E
Da'an 76 45 30N 124 7 E
Dab'a, Râs el 86 31 3N 28 31 E
Daba Shan 75 32 0N 109 0 E
Dabai 85 11 25N 5 15 E
Dabakala 84 8 15N 4 20W
Dabbūrīya 62 32 42N 35 22 E
Dabhoi 68 22 10N 73 20 E
Dąbie, Poland 28 53 27N 14 45 E
Dąbie, Poland 28 52 5N 18 50 E
Dabo 72 0 30 S 104 33 E
Dabola 84 10 50N 11 5W
Dabou 84 5 20N 4 23W
Daboya 85 9 30N 1 20W
Dabrowa Górnicza 28 50 15N 19 10 E
Dabrowa Tarnówska 27 50 10N 20 59 E
Dąbrówno 28 53 27N 20 2 E
Dabus → 87 10 48N 35 10 E
Dacato → 87 7 25N 42 40 E
Dacca 69 23 43N 90 26 E
Dacca □ 69 24 25N 90 25 E
Dachau 25 48 16N 11 27 E
Dadanawa 126 2 50N 59 30W
Daday 56 41 28N 33 27 E
Dade City 115 28 20N 82 12W
Dades, Oued → 82 30 58N 6 44W
Dadiya 85 9 35N 11 24 E
Dadra and Nagar Haveli □ 68 20 5N 73 0 E
Dadri = Charkhi Dadri 68 28 37N 76 17 E
Dadu 68 26 45N 67 45 E
Dăeni 46 44 51N 28 10 E
Daet 73 14 2N 122 55 E
Dafang 77 27 9N 105 39 E
Dagana 84 16 30N 15 35W
Dagash 86 19 19N 33 25 E
Dagestan A.S.S.R. □ 57 42 30N 47 0 E
Dagestanskiye Ogni 57 42 6N 48 12 E
Daghfeli 86 19 18N 32 40 E
Dagö = Hiiumaa 54 58 50N 22 45 E
Dagupan 73 16 3N 120 20 E
Dahab 86 28 30N 34 31 E
Dahlak Kebir 87 15 50N 40 10 E
Dahlenburg 24 53 11N 10 43 E
Dahlonega 115 34 35N 83 59W
Dahme, Germ., E. 24 51 51N 13 25 E
Dahme, Germ., W. 24 54 13N 11 5 E
Dahomey = Benin ■ 85 10 0N 2 0 E
Dahra 84 15 22N 15 30W
Dahra, Massif de 82 36 7N 1 21 E
Dai Shan 77 30 25N 122 10 E
Dai Xian 76 39 4N 112 58 E
Daimiel 33 39 5N 3 35W
Daingean 15 53 18N 7 15W
Daintree 98 16 20 S 145 20 E
Daiō-Misaki 74 34 15N 136 45 E
Dairût 86 27 34N 30 43 E
Daitari 69 21 10N 85 46 E
Dajarra 97 21 42 S 139 30 E
Dakar 84 14 34N 17 29W
Dakhla 80 23 50N 15 53W
Dakhla, El Wâhât el- 86 25 30N 28 50 E
Dakhovskaya 57 44 13N 40 13 E
Dakingari 85 11 37N 4 1 E
Dakor 68 22 45N 73 11 E
Dakoro 85 14 31N 6 46 E
Dakota City 116 42 27N 96 28W
Đakovica 42 42 22N 20 26 E
Đakovo 42 45 19N 18 24 E
Dalaba 84 10 42N 12 15W
Dalachi 76 36 48N 105 0 E
Dalai Nur 76 43 20N 116 45 E
Dalandzadgad 75 43 27N 104 30 E
Dalbandin 65 29 0N 64 23 E
Dalbeattie 14 54 55N 3 50W
Dalbosjön 49 58 40N 12 45 E
Dalby, Austral. 97 27 10 S 151 17 E
Dalby, Sweden 49 55 40N 13 22 E
Dale 47 61 22N 5 23 E
Dalen 47 59 26N 8 0 E
Dalga 86 27 39N 30 41 E
Dalhart 117 36 10N 102 30W
Dalhousie, Can. 107 48 5N 66 26W
Dalhousie, India 68 32 38N 76 0 E
Dali, Shaanxi, China 77 34 48N 109 58 E
Dali, Yunnan, China 75 25 40N 100 10 E
Daliang Shan 75 28 0N 102 45 E
Dalias 33 36 49N 2 52W
Dāliyat el Karmel 62 32 43N 35 2 E
Dalj 42 45 29N 18 59 E
Dalkeith 14 55 54N 3 5W
Dall I. 108 54 59N 133 25W
Dallarnil 99 25 19 S 152 2 E
Dallas, Oregon, U.S.A. 118 45 0N 123 15W
Dallas, Texas, U.S.A. 117 32 50N 96 50W
Dallol 87 14 14N 40 17 E
Dalmacija □ 42 43 20N 17 0 E
Dalmatia = Dalmacija □ 42 43 20N 17 0 E
Dalmellington 14 55 20N 4 25W
Dalneretchensk 59 45 50N 133 40 E
Daloa 84 7 0N 6 30W
Dalrymple, Mt. 97 21 1 S 148 39 E
Dalsjöfors 49 57 46N 13 5 E
Dalskog 49 58 44N 12 18 E
Dalton, Can. 106 48 11N 84 1W
Dalton, Ga., U.S.A. 115 34 47N 84 58W
Dalton, Mass., U.S.A. 113 42 28N 73 11W
Dalton, Nebr., U.S.A. 116 41 27N 103 0W
Dalton Iceberg Tongue 5 66 15 S 121 30 E
Daltonganj 69 24 0N 84 4 E
Dalvík 50 65 58N 18 32W
Daly → 96 13 35 S 130 19 E
Daly L. 109 56 32N 105 39W
Daly Waters 96 16 15 S 133 24 E
Dama, Wadi → 86 27 12N 35 50 E
Daman 68 20 25N 72 57 E
Daman □ 68 20 25N 72 58 E
Damanhûr 86 31 0N 30 30 E
Damar 73 7 7 S 128 40 E
Damaraland 92 21 0 S 17 0 E
Damascus = Dimashq 64 33 30N 36 18 E
Damaturu 85 11 45N 11 55 E
Damāvand 65 35 47N 52 0 E
Damāvand, Qolleh-ye 65 35 56N 52 10 E
Damba 88 6 44 S 15 20 E

Dāmghān 65 36 10N 54 17 E
Dămienesti 46 46 44N 27 1 E
Damietta = Dumyât 86 31 24N 31 48 E
Daming 76 36 15N 115 6 E
Dāmīya 62 32 6N 35 34 E
Dammarie 19 48 20N 1 30 E
Dammartin 19 49 3N 2 41 E
Damme 24 52 32N 8 12 E
Damodar → 69 23 17N 87 35 E
Damoh 69 23 50N 79 28 E
Damous 82 36 31N 1 42 E
Dampier 96 20 41 S 116 42 E
Dampier Arch. 96 20 38 S 116 32 E
Dampier Downs 96 18 24 S 123 5 E
Dampier, Selat 73 0 40 S 131 0 E
Dampier Str. 98 5 50 S 148 0 E
Damville 18 48 51N 1 5 E
Damvillers 19 49 20N 5 21 E
Dan-Gulbi 85 11 40N 6 15 E
Dan Xian 77 19 31N 109 33 E
Dana 73 11 0 S 122 52 E
Dana, Lac 106 50 53N 77 20W
Danakil Depression 87 12 45N 41 0 E
Danao 73 10 31N 124 1 E
Danbury 114 41 23N 73 29W
Danby L. 119 34 17N 115 0W
Dandeldhura 69 29 20N 80 35 E
Dandenong 99 38 0 S 145 15 E
Dandong 76 40 10N 124 20 E
Danforth 107 45 39N 67 57W
Danger Is. 95 10 53 S 165 49W
Danger Pt. 92 34 40 S 19 17 E
Dangla 87 11 18N 36 56 E
Dangora 85 11 30N 8 7 E
Dangshan 77 34 27N 116 22 E
Dangtu 77 31 32N 118 25 E
Dangyang 77 30 52N 111 44 E
Daniel 118 42 56N 110 2W
Daniel's Harbour 107 50 13N 57 35W
Danielskull 92 28 11 S 23 33 E
Danielson 113 41 50N 71 52W
Danilov 55 58 16N 40 13 E
Danilovgrad 42 42 38N 19 9 E
Danilovka 55 50 25N 44 12 E
Danissa 90 3 15N 40 58 E
Danja 85 11 21N 7 30 E
Dankalwa 85 11 52N 12 12 E
Dankama 85 13 20N 7 44 E
Dankov 55 53 20N 39 5 E
Danli 121 14 4N 86 35W
Dannemora, Sweden 48 60 12N 17 51 E
Dannemora, U.S.A. 114 44 41N 73 44W
Dannenberg 24 53 7N 11 4 E
Dannevirke 101 40 12 S 176 8 E
Dannhauser 93 28 0 S 30 3 E
Danshui 77 25 12N 121 25 E
Dansville 114 42 32N 77 41W
Dantan 69 21 57N 87 20 E
Dante 63 10 25N 51 26 E
Danube → 43 45 20N 29 40 E
Danukandi 69 23 32N 90 43 E
Danvers 113 42 34N 70 55W
Danville, Ill., U.S.A. 114 40 10N 87 40W
Danville, Ky., U.S.A. 114 37 40N 84 45W
Danville, Va., U.S.A. 115 36 40N 79 20W
Danzhai 77 26 11N 107 48 E
Danzig = Gdańsk 28 54 22N 18 40 E
Dao 73 10 30N 121 57 E
Dão → 30 40 20N 8 11W
Dao Xian 77 25 36N 111 31 E
Daosa 68 26 52N 76 20 E
Daoud = Aïn Beïda 83 35 44N 7 22 E
Daoulas 18 48 22N 4 17W
Dapong 85 10 55N 0 16 E
Daqing Shan 76 40 40N 111 0 E
Daqu Shan 77 30 25N 122 20 E
Dar al Hamrā, Ad 64 27 22N 37 43 E
Dar es Salaam 90 6 50 S 39 12 E
Dar'ā 62 32 36N 36 7 E
Dārāb 65 28 50N 54 30 E
Darabani 46 48 10N 26 39 E
Daraj 83 30 10N 10 28 E
Daravica 42 42 32N 20 8 E
Daraw 86 24 22N 32 51 E
Darazo 85 11 1N 10 24 E
Darband 66 34 20N 72 50 E
Darbhanga 69 26 15N 85 55 E
Darby 118 46 2N 114 7W
Darda 42 45 40N 18 41 E
Dardanelle 117 35 12N 93 9W
Dardanelles = Canakkale Boğazi 44 40 0N 26 0 E
Darfo 38 45 52N 10 11 E
Dargai 66 34 25N 71 55 E
Dargan Ata 58 40 29N 62 10 E
Dargaville 101 35 57 S 173 52 E
Darhan Muminggan Lianheqi 76 41 40N 110 28 E
Dari 87 5 48N 30 26 E
Darien 120 9 7N 79 46W
Darién, G. del 126 9 0N 77 0W
Darjeeling 69 27 3N 88 18 E
Dark Cove 107 48 47N 54 13W
Darling → 97 34 4 S 141 54 E
Darling Downs 99 27 30 S 150 30 E
Darling Ra. 96 32 30 S 116 0 E
Darlington, U.K. 12 54 33N 1 33W
Darlington, S.C., U.S.A. 115 34 18N 79 50W
Darlington, Wis., U.S.A. 116 42 43N 90 7W
Darlington Point 100 34 37 S 146 1 E
Darłowo 28 54 25N 16 25 E
Dărmănești 46 46 21N 26 33 E
Darmstadt 25 49 51N 8 40 E
Darnah 81 32 40N 22 35 E
Darnall 93 29 23 S 31 18 E
Darnétal 18 49 25N 1 10 E
Darney 19 48 5N 6 0 E
Darnick 100 32 48 S 143 38 E
Darnley B. 104 69 30N 123 30W
Darnley, C. 5 68 0 S 69 0 E
Daroca 32 41 9N 1 25W
Darr 98 23 13 S 144 7 E
Darr → 98 23 39 S 143 50 E
Darrington 118 48 14N 121 37W
Renamed Pakapuka
Darror → 63 10 30N 50 0 E
Darsana 69 23 35N 88 48 E
Darsi 70 15 46N 79 44 E
Darsser Ort 24 54 29N 12 31 E
Dart → 13 50 24N 3 36W
Dart, C. 5 73 6 S 126 20W
Dartmoor 13 50 36N 4 0W
Dartmouth, Austral. 98 23 31 S 144 44 E
Dartmouth, Can. 107 44 40N 63 30W
Dartmouth, U.K. 13 50 21N 3 35W
Dartmouth, L. 99 26 4 S 145 18 E
Dartuch, C. 32 39 55N 3 49 E
Daru 98 9 3 S 143 13 E
Daruvar 42 45 35N 17 14 E
Darvaza 58 40 11N 58 24 E
Darwha 68 20 15N 77 45 E
Darwin 96 12 25 S 130 51 E
Darwin Glacier 5 79 53 S 159 0 E
Daryacheh-ye-Sistan 65 31 0N 61 0 E
Daryapur 68 20 55N 77 20 E
Das 65 25 20N 53 30 E
Dashkesan 57 40 40N 46 0 E
Dasht → 65 25 10N 61 40 E
Dasht-e Kavīr 65 34 30N 55 0 E
Dasht-e Lūt 65 31 30N 58 0 E
Dasht-e Mārgow 65 30 40N 62 30 E
Daska 68 32 20N 74 20 E
Dassa-Zoume 85 7 46N 2 14 E
Dasseneiland 92 33 25 S 18 3 E
Datça 45 36 46N 27 40 E
Datia 68 25 39N 78 27 E
Datian 77 25 40N 117 50 E
Datong, Anhui, China 77 30 48N 117 44 E
Datong, Shanxi, China 76 40 6N 113 18 E
Dattapur 68 20 45N 78 15 E
Datu Piang 73 7 2N 124 30 E
Datu, Tanjung 72 2 5N 109 39 E
Daugava → 54 57 4N 24 3 E
Daugavpils 54 55 53N 26 32 E
Daulatabad 70 19 57N 75 15 E
Daun 25 50 10N 6 53 E
Dauphin 109 51 9N 100 5W
Dauphin I. 115 30 16N 88 10W
Dauphin L. 109 51 20N 99 45W
Dauphiné 21 45 15N 5 25 E
Dauqa 86 19 30N 41 0 E
Daura, Borno, Nigeria 85 11 31N 11 24 E
Daura, Kaduna, Nigeria 85 13 2N 8 21 E
Davangere 70 14 25N 75 55 E
Davao 73 7 0N 125 40 E
Davao, G. of 73 6 30N 125 48 E
Dāvar Panāh 65 27 25N 62 15 E
Davenport, Iowa, U.S.A. 116 41 30N 90 40W
Davenport, Wash., U.S.A. 118 47 40N 118 5W
Davenport Downs 98 24 8 S 141 7 E
Davenport Ra. 96 20 28 S 134 0 E
David 121 8 30N 82 30W
David City 116 41 18N 97 10W
David Gorodok 54 52 4N 27 8 E
Davidson 109 51 16N 105 59W
Davis, Antarct. 5 68 34 S 77 55 E
Davis, U.S.A. 118 38 33N 121 44W
Davis Dam 119 35 11N 114 35W
Davis Inlet 107 55 50N 60 59W
Davis Mts. 117 30 42N 104 15W
Davis Sea 5 66 0 S 92 0 E
Davis Str. 105 65 0N 58 0W
Davos 25 46 48N 9 49 E
Davy L. 109 58 53N 108 18W
Dawa → 87 4 11N 42 6 E
Dawaki, Bauchi, Nigeria 85 9 25N 9 33 E
Dawaki, Kano, Nigeria 85 12 5N 8 23 E
Dawes Ra. 98 24 40 S 150 40 E
Dawson, Can. 104 64 10N 139 30W
Dawson, Ga., U.S.A. 115 31 45N 84 28W
Dawson, N.D., U.S.A. 116 46 56N 99 45W
Dawson → 97 23 25 S 149 45 E
Dawson Creek 108 55 45N 120 15W
Dawson, I. 128 53 50 S 70 50W
Dawson Inlet 109 61 50N 93 25W
Dawson Range 98 24 30 S 149 48 E
Dax 20 43 44N 1 3W
Daxian 75 31 15N 107 23 E
Daxin 77 22 50N 107 11 E
Daxue Shan 75 30 30N 101 30 E
Daye 77 30 6N 114 58 E
Daylesford 100 37 21 S 144 9 E
Dayong 77 29 11N 110 30 E
Dayr Abū Sa'īd 62 32 30N 35 42 E
Dayr al-Ghuṣūn 62 32 21N 35 4 E
Dayr az Zawr 64 35 20N 40 5 E
Dayr Dirwān 62 31 55N 35 15 E
Daysland 108 52 50N 112 20W
Dayton, Ohio, U.S.A. 114 39 45N 84 10W
Dayton, Pa., U.S.A. 112 40 54N 79 18W
Dayton, Tenn., U.S.A. 115 35 30N 85 1W
Dayton, Wash., U.S.A. 118 46 20N 118 10W
Daytona Beach 115 29 14N 81 0W
Dayu 77 25 24N 114 22 E
Dayville 118 44 33N 119 37W
Dazhu 77 30 41N 107 15 E
Dazu 77 29 40N 105 42 E
De Aar 92 30 39 S 24 0 E
De Funiak Springs 115 30 42N 86 10W
De Grey 96 20 12 S 119 12 E
De Land 115 29 1N 81 19W
De Leon 117 32 9N 98 35W
De Pere 114 44 28N 88 1W
De Queen 117 34 3N 94 24W
De Quincy 117 30 30N 93 27W
De Ridder 117 30 48N 93 15W
De Smet 116 44 25N 97 35W
De Soto 116 38 7N 90 33W
De Tour 114 45 59N 83 56W
De Witt 117 34 19N 91 20W
Dead Sea = Miyet, Bahr el 64 31 30N 35 30 E
Deadwood 116 44 23N 103 44W
Deadwood L. 108 59 10N 128 30W
Deakin 96 30 46 S 128 0 E
Deal 13 51 13N 1 25 E
Dealesville 92 28 41 S 25 44 E
Dean, Forest of 13 51 50N 2 35W
Deán Funes 124 30 20 S 64 20W
Dearborn 106 42 18N 83 15W
Dease → 108 59 56N 128 32W
Dease L. 108 58 40N 130 5W
Dease Lake 108 58 25N 130 6W
Death Valley 119 36 19N 116 52W
Death Valley Junc. 119 36 21N 116 30W
Death Valley Nat. Monument 119 36 30N 117 0W
Deauville 18 49 23N 0 2 E
Deba Habe 85 10 14N 11 20 E
Debaltsevo 56 48 22N 38 26 E
Debao 77 23 21N 106 46 E
Debar 42 41 31N 20 30 E
Debden 109 53 30N 106 50W
Debdou 82 33 59N 3 0W
Dębica 27 50 2N 21 25 E
Dęblin 28 51 34N 21 50 E
Debno 28 52 44N 14 41 E
Débo, L. 84 15 14N 4 15W
Debolt 108 55 12N 118 1W
Debrc 42 44 38N 19 53 E
Debre Birhan 87 9 41N 39 31 E
Debre Markos 87 10 20N 37 40 E
Debre May 87 11 20N 37 25 E
Debre Sina 87 9 51N 39 50 E
Debre Tabor 87 11 50N 38 26 E
Debre Zebit 87 11 48N 38 30 E
Debrecen 27 47 33N 21 42 E
Dečani 42 42 30N 20 10 E
Decatur, Ala., U.S.A. 115 34 35N 87 0W
Decatur, Ga., U.S.A. 115 33 47N 84 17W
Decatur, Ill., U.S.A. 116 39 50N 89 0W
Decatur, Ind., U.S.A. 114 40 50N 84 56W
Decatur, Texas, U.S.A. 117 33 15N 97 35W
Decazeville 20 44 34N 2 15 E
Deccan 70 18 0N 79 0 E
Deception I. 5 63 0 S 60 15W
Deception L. 109 56 33N 104 13W
Děčín 26 50 47N 14 12 E
Decize 19 46 50N 3 28 E
Deckerville 112 43 33N 82 46W
Decollatura 41 39 2N 16 21 E
Decorah 116 43 20N 91 50W
Deda 46 46 56N 24 50 E
Dedéagach = Alexandroúpotis 44 40 50N 25 54 E
Dedham 113 42 14N 71 10W
Dedilovo 55 53 59N 37 50 E
Dédougou 84 12 30N 3 25W
Deduru Oya 70 7 32N 79 50 E
Dedza 91 14 20 S 34 20 E
Dee →, Scot., U.K. 14 57 4N 2 7W
Dee →, Wales, U.K. 12 53 15N 3 7W
Deep B. 108 61 15N 116 35W
Deepdale 96 21 42 S 116 10 E
Deepwater 99 29 25 S 151 51 E
Deer → 109 58 23N 94 13W
Deer Lake, Newf., Can. 107 49 11N 57 27W
Deer Lake, Ontario, Can. 109 52 36N 94 20W
Deer Lodge 118 46 25N 112 40W
Deer Park 118 47 55N 117 21W
Deer River 116 47 21N 93 44W
Deeral 98 17 14 S 145 55 E
Deerdepoort 92 24 37 S 26 27 E
Deesa 68 24 18N 72 10 E
Deferiet 113 44 2N 75 41W
Defiance 114 41 20N 84 20W
Deganya 62 32 43N 35 34 E
Degebe → 31 38 13N 7 29W
Degeh Bur 63 8 11N 43 31 E
Degema 85 4 50N 6 48 E
Deggendorf 25 48 49N 12 59 E
Degloor 70 18 34N 77 33 E
Deh Bīd 65 30 39N 53 11 E
Deh Kheyr 65 28 45N 54 40 E
Dehibat 83 32 0N 10 47 E
Dehiwala 70 6 50N 79 51 E
Dehkareqan 64 37 43N 45 55 E
Dehra Dun 68 30 20N 78 4 E
Dehri 69 24 50N 84 15 E
Dehui 76 44 30N 125 40 E
Deinze 16 50 59N 3 32 E
Dej 46 47 10N 23 52 E
Deje 48 59 35N 13 29 E
Dekalb 116 41 55N 88 45W
Dekemhare 87 15 6N 39 0 E
Dekese 88 3 24 S 21 24 E
Del Norte 119 37 40N 106 27W
Del Rio 117 29 23N 100 50W
Delagua 117 37 21N 104 35W
Delai 86 17 21N 36 6 E
Delano 119 35 48N 119 13W
Delareyville 92 26 41 S 25 26 E
Delavan 116 42 40N 88 39W
Delaware 114 40 20N 83 0W
Delaware □ 114 39 0N 75 40W
Delaware → 114 39 20N 75 25W
Delčevo 42 41 58N 22 46 E
Delegate 99 37 4 S 148 56 E
Delémont 25 47 22N 7 20 E
Delft 16 52 1N 4 22 E
Delft I. 70 9 30N 79 40 E
Delfzijl 16 53 20N 6 55 E
Delgado, C. 91 10 45 S 40 40 E
Delgo 86 20 6N 30 40 E
Delhi, Can. 112 42 51N 80 30W
Delhi, India 68 28 38N 77 17 E
Delhi, U.S.A. 113 42 17N 74 56W
Deli Jovan 42 44 13N 22 9 E
Delia 108 51 38N 112 23W
Delice → 64 39 45N 34 15 E
Delicias 120 28 10N 105 30W
Delitzsch 24 51 32N 12 22 E
Dell City 119 31 58N 105 19W
Dell Rapids 116 43 53N 96 44W
Delle 19 47 30N 7 2 E
Dellys 83 36 57N 3 57 E
Delmar 113 42 37N 73 47W
Delmenhorst 24 53 3N 8 37 E
Delmiro Gouveia 127 9 24 S 38 6W
Delnice 39 45 23N 14 50 E
Delong, Ostrova 59 76 40N 149 20 E
Deloraine, Austral. 99 41 30 S 146 40 E
Deloraine, Can. 109 49 15N 100 29W
Delorme, L. 107 54 31N 69 52W
Delphi, Greece 45 38 28N 22 30 E
Delphi, U.S.A. 114 40 37N 86 40W
Delphos 114 40 51N 84 17W
Delportshoop 92 28 22 S 24 20 E
Delray Beach 115 26 27N 80 4W
Delsbo 48 61 48N 16 32 E
Delta, Colo., U.S.A. 119 38 44N 108 5W
Delta, Utah, U.S.A. 118 39 21N 112 29W
Delungra 99 29 39 S 150 51 E
Delvina 44 39 59N 20 4 E
Delvinákion 44 39 57N 20 32 E
Demanda, Sierra de la 32 42 15N 3 0W
Demba 88 5 28 S 22 15 E
Dembecha 87 10 32N 37 30 E
Dembi 87 8 5N 36 25 E
Dembia 90 3 33N 25 48 E
Dembidolo 87 8 34N 34 50 E
Demer → 16 50 57N 4 42 E
Demetrias 44 39 22N 23 1 E
Demidov 54 55 16N 31 30 E
Deming 119 32 10N 107 50W
Demini → 126 0 46 S 62 56W
Demmin 24 53 54N 13 2 E
Demnate 82 31 44N 6 59W
Demonte 38 44 18N 7 18 E
Demopolis 115 32 30N 87 48W
Dempo, Mt. 72 4 2 S 103 15 E
Demyansk 54 57 40N 32 27 E
Den Burg 16 53 3N 4 47 E
Den Haag = 's Gravenhage 16 52 7N 4 17 E
Den Helder 16 52 57N 4 45 E
Den Oever 16 52 56N 5 2 E
Denain 19 50 20N 3 22 E
Denau 58 38 16N 67 54 E
Denbigh 12 53 12N 3 26W
Dendang 72 3 7 S 107 56 E
Dendermonde 16 51 2N 4 5 E
Deneba 87 9 47N 39 10 E
Deng Xian 77 32 34N 112 4 E
Denge 85 12 52N 5 21 E
Dengi 85 9 25N 9 55 E
Denham 96 25 56 S 113 31 E
Denham Ra. 97 21 55 S 147 46 E
Denia 33 38 49N 0 8 E
Deniliquin 97 35 30 S 144 58 E
Denison, Iowa, U.S.A. 116 42 0N 95 18W
Denison, Texas, U.S.A. 117 33 50N 96 40W
Denison Range 97 28 30 S 136 5 E
Denizli 64 37 42N 29 2 E
Denman Glacier 5 66 45 S 99 25 E
Denmark 96 34 59 S 117 25 E
Denmark ■ 49 55 30N 9 0 E
Denmark Str. 6 66 0N 30 0W
Dennison 112 40 21N 81 21W
Denpasar 72 8 45 S 115 14 E
Denton, Mont., U.S.A. 118 47 25N 109 56W
Denton, Texas, U.S.A. 117 33 12N 97 10W
D'Entrecasteaux Is. 98 9 0 S 151 0 E
D'Entrecasteaux Pt. 96 34 50 S 115 57 E
Denu 85 6 4N 1 8 E
Denver 116 39 45N 105 0W
Denver City 117 32 58N 102 48W
Deoband 68 29 42N 77 43 E
Deobhog 70 19 53N 82 44 E
Deogarh 69 21 22N 84 45 E
Deoghar 69 24 30N 86 42 E
Deolali 70 19 58N 73 50 E
Deoli 68 25 50N 75 20 E
Deoria 69 26 31N 83 48 E
Deosai Mts. 69 35 40N 75 0 E
Depew 112 42 55N 78 43W
Deping 76 37 25N 116 58 E
Deposit 113 42 5N 75 23W
Deputatskiy 59 69 18N 139 54 E
Dêqên 75 28 34N 98 51 E
Deqing 77 23 8N 111 42 E
Dera Ghazi Khan 68 30 5N 70 43 E
Dera Ismail Khan 68 31 50N 70 50 E
* Dera Ismail Khan □ 68 32 30N 70 0 E
Derbent 56 42 5N 48 4 E
Derby, Austral. 96 17 18 S 123 38 E
Derby, U.K. 12 52 55N 1 28W
Derby, Conn., U.S.A. 113 41 20N 73 5W
Derby, N.Y., U.S.A. 112 42 40N 78 59W
Derby □ 12 52 55N 1 28W
Derecske 27 47 20N 21 33 E
Derg → 15 54 42N 7 26W
Derg, L. 15 53 0N 8 20W
Dergachi 55 50 9N 36 11 E
Dergaon 67 26 45N 94 0 E
Dermantsi 43 43 8N 24 17 E
Dernieres Isles 117 29 0N 90 45W
Derryveagh Mts. 15 55 0N 8 40W
Derudub 86 17 31N 36 7 E
Derval 18 47 40N 1 41W
Dervéni 45 38 8N 22 25 E
Derventa 42 44 59N 17 55 E
Derwent 109 53 41N 110 58W
Derwent →, Derby, U.K. 12 52 53N 1 17W
Derwent →, N. Yorks., U.K. 12 53 45N 0 57W
Derwentwater, L. 12 54 35N 3 9W
Des Moines, Iowa, U.S.A. 116 41 35N 93 37W
Des Moines, N. Mex., U.S.A. 117 36 50N 103 51W
Des Moines → 116 40 23N 91 25W
Desaguadero →, Argent. 124 34 30 S 66 46W
Desaguadero →, Boliv. 126 18 24 S 67 5W
Deschaillons 107 46 32N 72 7W
Descharme → 109 56 51N 109 13W
Deschutes → 118 45 30N 121 0W
Dese 87 11 5N 39 40 E
Desenzano del Gardo 38 45 28N 10 32 E
Desert Center 119 33 45N 115 27W
Deskenatlata L. 108 60 55N 112 3W
Desna → 54 50 33N 30 32 E
Desnătui → 46 44 15N 23 27 E
Desolación, I. 128 53 0 S 74 0W
Despeñaperros, Paso 33 38 24N 3 30W
Despotovac 42 44 6N 21 30 E
Dessau 24 51 49N 12 15 E
Dessye = Dese 87 11 5N 39 40 E

* Now part of North West Frontier □

D'Estrees B. 99 35 55 S 137 45 E
Desuri 68 25 18N 73 35 E
Desvrès 19 50 40N 1 48 E
Deta 42 45 24N 21 13 E
Detinja → 42 43 51N 19 45 E
Detmold 24 51 55N 8 50 E
Detour Pt. 114 45 37N 86 35W
Detroit, Mich., U.S.A. 106 42 23N 83 5W
Detroit, Tex., U.S.A. 117 33 40N 95 10W
Detroit Lakes 116 46 50N 95 50W
Dett 91 18 38 S 26 50 E
Deurne, Belg. 16 51 12N 4 24 E
Deurne, Neth. 16 51 27N 5 49 E
Deutsche Bucht 24 54 10N 7 51 E
Deutschlandsberg 26 46 49N 15 14 E
Deux-Sèvres □ 18 46 35N 0 20W
Deva 46 45 53N 22 55 E
Devakottai 70 9 55N 78 45 E
Devaprayag 68 30 13N 78 35 E
Dévaványa 27 47 2N 20 59 E
Deveci Daği 56 40 10N 36 0 E
Devecser 27 47 6N 17 26 E
Deventer 16 52 15N 6 10 E
Deveron → 14 57 40N 2 31W
Devesel 46 44 28N 22 41 E
Devgad Baria 68 22 40N 73 55 E
Devgad, I. 70 14 48N 74 5 E
Devils Lake 116 48 5N 98 50W
Devils Paw 108 58 47N 134 0W
Devil's Pt. 70 9 26N 80 6 E
Devin 43 41 44N 24 24 E
Devizes 13 51 21N 2 0W
Devnya 43 43 13N 27 33 E
Devolii → 44 40 57N 20 15 E
Devon 108 53 24N 113 44W
Devon I. 4 75 10N 85 0W
Devonport, Austral. 97 41 10 S 146 22 E
Devonport, N.Z. 101 36 49 S 174 49 E
Devonport, U.K. 13 50 23N 4 11W
Devonshire □ 13 50 50N 3 40W
Dewas 68 22 59N 76 3 E
Dewetsdorp 92 29 33 S 26 39 E
Dewsbury 12 53 42N 1 38W
Dexter, Mo., U.S.A. 117 36 50N 90 0W
Dexter, N. Mex., U.S.A. 117 33 15N 104 25W
Deyhūk 65 33 15N 57 30 E
Deyyer 65 27 55N 51 55 E
Dezadeash L. 108 60 28N 136 58W
Dezfūl 64 32 20N 48 30 E
Dezh Shāhpūr 64 35 30N 46 25 E
Dezhneva, Mys 59 66 5N 169 40W
Dezhou 76 37 26N 116 18 E
Dháfni 45 37 48N 22 1 E
Dhafra 65 23 20N 54 0 E
Dhahaban 86 21 58N 39 3 E
Dhahira 65 23 40N 57 0 E
Dhahiriya = Aẓ Ẓāhirīyah 62 31 25N 34 58 E
Dhahran = Aẓ Ẓahrān 64 26 18N 50 10 E
Dhamar 63 14 30N 44 20 E
Dhamási 44 39 43N 22 11 E
Dhampur 68 29 19N 78 33 E
Dhamtari 69 20 42N 81 35 E
Dhanbad 69 23 50N 86 30 E
Dhankuta 69 26 55N 87 40 E
Dhanora 69 20 20N 80 22 E
Dhar 68 22 35N 75 26 E
Dharampur, Gujarat, India 70 20 32N 73 17 E
Dharampur, Mad. P., India 68 22 13N 75 18 E
Dharapuram 70 10 45N 77 34 E
Dharmapuri 70 12 10N 78 10 E
Dharmavaram 70 14 29N 77 44 E
Dharmsala (Dharamsala) 68 32 16N 76 23 E
Dhaulagiri 69 28 39N 83 28 E
Dhebar, L. 68 24 10N 74 0 E
Dhenkanal 69 20 45N 85 35 E
Dhenoúsa 45 37 8N 25 48 E
Dheskáti 44 39 55N 21 49 E
Dhespotikó 45 36 57N 24 58 E
Dhestina 45 38 25N 22 31 E
Dhidhimótikhon 44 41 22N 26 29 E
Dhikti 45 35 8N 25 22 E
Dhilianáta 45 38 15N 20 34 E
Dhílos 45 37 23N 25 15 E
Dhimitsána 45 37 36N 22 3 E
Dhírfis 45 38 40N 23 54 E
Dhodhekánisos 45 36 35N 27 0 E
Dhokós 45 37 20N 23 20 E
Dholiana 44 39 54N 20 32 E
Dholka 68 22 44N 72 29 E
Dholpur 68 26 45N 77 59 E
Dhomokós 45 39 10N 22 18 E
Dhond 70 18 26N 74 40 E
Dhoraji 68 21 45N 70 37 E
Dhoxáton 44 41 9N 24 16 E
Dhragonísi 45 37 27N 25 29 E
Dhrangadhra 68 22 59N 71 31 E
Dhriopís 45 37 25N 24 35 E
Dhrol 68 22 33N 70 25 E
Dhubaibah 65 23 25N 54 35 E
Dhubri 69 26 2N 89 59 E
Dhula 63 15 10N 47 30 E
Dhulia 68 20 58N 74 50 E
Dhurm → 86 20 18N 42 53 E
Di Linh, Cao Nguyen 71 11 30N 108 0 E
Dia 45 35 26N 25 13 E
Diablo Heights 120 8 58N 79 34W
Diafarabé 84 14 9N 4 57W
Diala 84 14 10N 10 0W
Dialakoro 84 12 18N 7 54W
Diallassagou 84 13 47N 3 41W
Diamante 124 32 5 S 60 40W
Diamante → 124 34 30 S 66 46W
Diamantina 127 18 17 S 43 40W
Diamantina → 97 26 45 S 139 10 E
Diamantino 127 14 30 S 56 30W
Diamond Harbour 69 22 11N 88 14 E
Diamond Mts. 118 40 0N 115 58W
Diamondville 118 41 51N 110 30W
Diancheng 77 21 30N 111 4 E
Diano Marina 38 43 55N 8 3 E
Dianra 84 8 45N 6 14W
Diapaga 85 12 5N 1 46 E
Diapangou 85 12 5N 0 10 E
Diariguila 84 10 35N 10 2W
Dibaya 88 6 30 S 22 57 E
Dibaya-Lubue 88 4 12 S 19 54 E
Dibbi 87 4 10N 41 52 E
Dibble Glacier Tongue 5 66 8 S 134 32 E
Dibete 92 23 45 S 26 32 E
Dibrugarh 67 27 29N 94 55 E
Dickinson 116 46 50N 102 48W
Dickson 115 36 5N 87 22W
Dickson City 113 41 29N 75 40W
Dickson (Dikson) 58 73 40N 80 5 E
Dicomano 39 43 53N 11 30 E
Didesa, W. → 87 10 2N 35 32 E
Didiéni 84 13 53N 8 6W
Didsbury 108 51 35N 114 10W
Didwana 68 27 23N 17 36 E
Die 21 44 47N 5 22 E
Diébougou 84 11 0N 3 15W
Diefenbaker L. 109 51 0N 106 55W
Diego Garcia 3 7 50 S 72 50 E
Diekirch 16 49 52N 6 10 E
Diélette 18 49 33N 1 52W
Diéma 84 14 32N 9 12W
Diémbéring 84 12 29N 16 47W
Dien Bien 71 21 20N 103 0 E
Diepholz 24 52 37N 8 22 E
Dieppe 18 49 54N 1 4 E
Dieren 16 52 3N 6 6 E
Dierks 117 34 9N 94 0W
Diest 16 50 58N 5 4 E
Dieulefit 21 44 32N 5 4 E
Dieuze 19 48 49N 6 43 E
Differdange 16 49 31N 5 54 E
Dig 68 27 28N 77 20 E
Digba 90 4 25N 25 48 E
Digby 107 44 38N 65 50W
Digges 109 58 40N 94 0W
Digges Is. 105 62 40N 77 50W
Dighinala 67 23 15N 92 5 E
Dighton 116 38 30N 100 26W
Digne 21 44 5N 6 12 E
Digoin 20 46 29N 3 58 E
Digos 73 6 45N 125 20 E
Digranes 50 66 4N 14 44 E
Digras 70 20 6N 77 45 E
Digul → 73 7 7 S 138 42 E
Dihang → 67 27 48N 95 30 E
Dijlah, Nahr → 64 31 0N 47 25 E
Dijon 19 47 20N 5 0 E
Dikala 87 4 45N 31 28 E
Dikkil 87 11 8N 42 20 E
Dikomu di Kai 92 24 58 S 24 36 E
Diksmuide 16 51 2N 2 52 E
Dikwa 85 12 4N 13 30 E
Dila 87 6 21N 38 22 E
Dili 73 8 39 S 125 34 E
Dilizhan 57 40 46N 44 57 E
Dilj 42 45 29N 18 1 E
Dillenburg 24 50 44N 8 17 E
Dilley 117 28 40N 99 12W
Dilling 87 12 3N 29 35 E
Dillingen 25 48 32N 10 29 E
Dillon, Can. 109 55 56N 108 35W
Dillon, Mont., U.S.A. 118 45 9N 112 36W
Dillon, S.C., U.S.A. 115 34 26N 79 20W
Dillon → 109 55 56N 108 56W
Dilston 99 41 22 S 147 10 E
Dimashq 64 33 30N 36 18 E
Dimbokro 84 6 45N 4 46W
Dimboola 99 36 28 S 142 7 E
Dîmbovița □ 46 45 0N 25 30 E
Dîmbovița → 46 44 14N 26 13 E
Dîmbovnic → 46 44 28N 25 18 E
Dimbulah 98 17 8 S 145 4 E
Dimitrovgrad, Bulg. 43 42 5N 25 35 E
Dimitrovgrad, U.S.S.R. 55 54 14N 49 39 E
Dimitrovgrad, Yugo. 42 43 0N 22 48 E
Dimitrovo = Pernik 42 42 35N 23 2 E
Dimmitt 117 34 36N 102 16W
Dimo 87 5 19N 29 10 E
Dimona 62 31 2N 35 1 E
Dimovo 42 43 43N 22 50 E
Dinagat 73 10 10N 125 40 E
Dinajpur 69 25 33N 88 43 E
Dinan 18 48 28N 2 2W
Dinant 16 50 16N 4 55 E
Dinapur 69 25 38N 85 5 E
Dinar 64 38 5N 30 15 E
Dinara Planina 39 43 50N 16 35 E
Dinard 18 48 38N 2 6W
Dinaric Alps = Dinara Planina 9 43 50N 16 35 E
Dinder, Nahr ed → 87 14 6N 33 40 E
Dindi → 70 16 24N 78 15 E
Dindigul 70 10 25N 78 0 E
Ding Xian 76 38 30N 114 59 E
Dingbian 76 37 35N 107 32 E
Dingelstädt 24 51 19N 10 19 E
Dinghai 77 30 1N 122 6 E
Dingle 15 52 9N 10 17W
Dingle B. 15 52 3N 10 20W
Dingmans Ferry 113 41 13N 74 55W
Dingnan 77 24 45N 115 0 E
Dingo 98 23 38 S 149 19 E
Dingolfing 25 48 38N 12 30 E
Dingtao 77 35 5N 115 35 E
Dinguiraye 84 11 18N 10 49W
Dingwall 14 57 36N 4 26W
Dingxi 76 35 30N 104 33 E
Dingxiang 76 38 30N 112 58 E
Dinokwe (Palla Road) 92 23 29 S 26 37 E
Dinosaur National Monument 118 40 30N 108 58W
Dinuba 119 36 31N 119 22W
Dio 49 56 37N 14 15 E
Diósgyör 27 48 7N 20 43 E
Diosig 46 47 18N 22 2 E
Diourbel 84 14 39N 16 12W
Diplo 68 24 35N 69 35 E
Dipolog 73 8 36N 123 20 E
Dipşa 46 46 58N 24 27 E
Dir 66 35 08N 71 59 E
Diré 84 16 20N 3 25W
Dire Dawa 87 9 35N 41 45 E
Direction, C. 97 12 51 S 143 32 E
Diriamba 121 11 51N 86 19W
Dirk Hartog I. 96 25 50 S 113 5 E
Dirranbandi 97 28 33 S 148 17 E
Disa 87 12 5N 34 15 E
Disappointment, C. 118 46 20N 124 0W
Disappointment L. 96 23 20 S 122 40 E
Disaster B. 97 37 15 S 150 0 E
Discovery B. 97 38 10 S 140 40 E
Disentis 25 46 42N 8 50 E
Dishna 86 26 9N 32 32 E
Disina 85 11 35N 9 50 E
Disko 4 69 45N 53 30W
Disko Bugt 4 69 10N 52 0W
Disna 54 55 32N 28 11 E
Disna → 54 55 34N 28 12 E
Distrito Federal □ 127 15 45 S 47 45W
Disûq 86 31 8N 30 35 E
Diu 68 20 45N 70 58 E
Dives → 18 49 18N 0 7W
Dives-sur-Mer 18 49 18N 0 8W
Divi Pt. 70 15 59N 81 9 E
Divichi 57 41 15N 48 57 E
Divide 118 45 48N 112 47W
Divinópolis 127 20 10 S 44 54W
Divnoye 57 45 55N 43 21 E
Divo 84 5 48N 5 15W
Diwal Kol 66 34 23N 67 52 E
Dixie 118 45 37N 115 27W
Dixon, Ill., U.S.A. 116 41 50N 89 30W
Dixon, Mont., U.S.A. 118 47 19N 114 25W
Dixon, N. Mex., U.S.A. 119 36 15N 105 57W
Dixon Entrance 108 54 30N 132 0W
Dixonville 108 56 32N 117 40W
Diyarbakir 64 37 55N 40 18 E
Diz Chah 65 35 30N 55 30 E
Djado 83 21 4N 12 14 E
Djado, Plateau du 83 21 29N 12 21 E
Djakarta = Jakarta 73 6 9 S 106 49 E
Djamâa 83 33 32N 5 59 E
Djamba 92 16 45 S 13 58 E
Djambala 88 2 32 S 14 30 E
Djanet 83 24 35N 9 32 E
Djaul I. 98 2 58 S 150 57 E
Djawa = Jawa 73 7 0 S 110 0 E
Djebiniana 83 35 1N 11 0 E
Djelfa 82 34 40N 3 15 E
Djema 90 6 3N 25 15 E
Djendel 82 36 15N 2 25 E
Djeneïene 83 31 45N 10 9 E
Djenné 84 14 0N 4 30W
Djenoun, Garet el 83 25 4N 5 31 E
Djerba 83 33 52N 10 51 E
Djerba, Île de 83 33 56N 11 0 E
Djerid, Chott 83 33 42N 8 30 E
Djibo 85 14 9N 1 35W
Djibouti 87 11 30N 43 5 E
Djibouti ■ 63 12 0N 43 0 E
Djolu 88 0 35N 22 5 E
Djorong 72 3 58 S 114 56 E
Djougou 85 9 40N 1 45 E
Djoum 88 2 41N 12 35 E
Djourab 81 16 40N 18 50 E
Djugu 90 1 55N 30 35 E
Djúpivogur 50 64 39N 14 17W
Djursholm 48 59 25N 18 6 E
Djursland 49 56 27N 10 45 E
Dmitriev-Lgovskiy 54 52 10N 35 0 E
Dmitriya Lapteva, Proliv 59 73 0N 140 0 E
Dmitrov 55 56 25N 37 32 E
Dmitrovsk-Orlovskiy 54 52 29N 35 10 E
Dneiper = Dnepr → 56 46 30N 32 18 E
Dnepr → 56 46 30N 32 18 E
Dneprodzerzhinsk 56 48 32N 34 37 E
Dneprodzerzhinskoye Vdkhr. 56 49 0N 34 0 E
Dnepropetrovsk 56 48 30N 35 0 E
Dneprorudnoye 56 47 21N 34 58 E
Dnestr → 56 46 18N 30 17 E
Dnestrovski = Belgorod 56 50 35N 36 35 E
Dniester = Dnestr → 56 46 18N 30 17 E
Dno 54 57 50N 29 58 E
Doba 81 8 40N 16 50 E
Dobbiaco 39 46 44N 12 13 E
Dobbyn 97 19 44 S 139 59 E
Dobczyce 27 49 52N 20 25 E
Döbeln 24 51 7N 13 10 E
Doberai, Jazirah 73 1 25 S 133 0 E
Dobiegniew 28 52 59N 15 45 E
Doblas 124 37 5 S 64 0W
Dobo 73 5 45 S 134 15 E
Doboj 42 44 46N 18 6 E
Dobra, Konin, Poland 28 51 55N 18 37 E
Dobra, Szczecin, Poland 28 53 34N 15 20 E
Dobra, Dîmbovita, Romania 43 44 52N 25 40 E
Dobra, Hunedoara, Romania 46 45 54N 22 36 E
Dobre Miasto 28 53 58N 20 26 E
Dobrinishta 43 41 49N 23 34 E
Dobříš 26 49 46N 14 10 E
Dobrodzień 28 50 45N 18 25 E
Dobropole 56 48 25N 37 2 E
Dobruja 46 44 30N 28 15 E
Dobrush 55 52 28N 30 19 E
Dobrzyń nad Wisłą 28 52 39N 19 22 E
Dobtong 87 6 25N 31 40 E
Dodecanese = Dhodhekánisos 45 36 35N 27 0 E
Dodge Center 116 44 1N 92 50W
Dodge City 117 37 42N 100 0W
Dodge L. 109 59 50N 105 36W
Dodgeville 116 42 55N 90 8W
Dodo 87 5 10N 29 57 E
Dodola 87 6 59N 39 11 E
Dodoma 90 6 8 S 35 45 E
Dodoma □ 90 6 0 S 36 0 E
Dodona 44 39 40N 20 46 E
Dodsland 109 51 50N 108 45W
Dodson 118 48 23N 108 16W
Doetinchem 16 51 59N 6 18 E
Doftana 46 45 11N 25 45 E
Dog Creek 108 51 35N 122 14W
Dog L., Man., Can. 109 51 2N 98 31W
Dog L., Ont., Can. 106 48 18N 89 30W
Doğanbey 45 37 40N 27 10 E
Dogliani 38 44 35N 7 55 E
Dogondoutchi 85 13 38N 4 2 E
Dogran 68 31 48N 73 35 E
Doguéraoua 85 14 0N 5 31 E
Dohad 68 22 50N 74 15 E
Dohazari 67 22 10N 92 5 E
Doi 73 2 14N 127 49 E
Doi Luang 71 18 30N 101 0 E
Doig → 108 56 25N 120 40W
Dois Irmãos, Sa. 127 9 0 S 42 30W
Dojransko Jezero 42 41 13N 22 44 E
Dokka 47 60 49N 10 7 E
Dokka → 47 61 7N 10 0 E
Dokkum 16 53 20N 5 59 E
Dokri 68 27 25N 68 7 E
Dol-de-Bretagne 18 48 34N 1 47W
Doland 116 44 55N 98 5W
Dolbeau 107 48 53N 72 18W
Dole 19 47 7N 5 31 E
Doleib, Wadi → 87 12 10N 33 15 E
Dolgellau 12 52 44N 3 53W
Dolgelley = Dolgellau 12 52 44N 3 53W
Dolginovo 54 54 39N 27 29 E
Dolianova 40 39 23N 9 11 E
Dolinskaya 56 48 6N 32 46 E
Dolj □ 46 44 10N 23 30 E
Dollart 16 53 20N 7 10 E
Dolna Banya 43 42 18N 23 44 E
Dolni Dŭbnik 43 43 24N 24 26 E
Dolo, Ethiopia 87 4 11N 42 3 E
Dolo, Italy 39 45 25N 12 4 E
Dolomites = Dolomiti 39 46 30N 11 40 E
Dolomiti 39 46 30N 11 40 E
Dolores, Argent. 124 36 20 S 57 40W
Dolores, Uruguay 124 33 34 S 58 15W
Dolores, Colo., U.S.A. 119 37 30N 108 30W
Dolores, Tex., U.S.A. 117 27 40N 99 38W
Dolores → 119 38 49N 108 17W
Đolovo 42 44 55N 20 52 E
Dolphin and Union Str. 104 69 5N 114 45W
Dolphin C. 128 51 10 S 59 0W
Dolsk 28 51 59N 17 3 E
Dom Pedrito 125 31 0 S 54 40W
Doma 85 8 25N 8 18 E
Domasi 91 15 15 S 35 22 E
Domazlice 26 49 28N 13 0 E
Dombarovskiy 58 50 46N 59 32 E
Dombasle 19 48 38N 6 21 E
Dombes 21 46 3N 5 0 E
Dombóvár 27 46 21N 18 9 E
Dombrád 27 48 13N 21 54 E
Domburg 16 51 34N 3 30 E
Domel I. = Letsok-aw Kyun 71 11 30N 98 25 E
Domérat 20 46 21N 2 32 E
Domeyko 124 29 0 S 71 0W
Domeyko, Cordillera 124 24 30 S 69 0W
Domfront 18 48 37N 0 40W
Dominador 124 24 21 S 69 20W
Dominica ■ 121 15 20N 61 20W
Dominican Rep. ■ 121 19 0N 70 30W
Dömitz 24 53 9N 11 13 E
Domme 20 44 48N 1 12 E
Domo 63 7 50N 47 10 E
Domodóssola 38 46 6N 8 19 E
Dompaire 19 48 14N 6 14 E
Dompierre-sur-Besbre 20 46 31N 3 41 E
Dompim 84 5 10N 2 5W
Domrémy 19 48 26N 5 40 E
Domsjö 48 63 16N 18 41 E
Domville, Mt. 99 28 1 S 151 15 E
Domvraina 45 38 15N 22 59 E
Domžale 39 46 9N 14 35 E
Don →, India 70 16 20N 76 15 E
Don →, Eng., U.K. 12 53 41N 0 51W
Don →, Scot., U.K. 14 57 14N 2 5W
Don →, U.S.S.R. 57 47 4N 39 18 E
Don Benito 31 38 53N 5 51W
Don Martín, Presa de 120 27 30N 100 50W
Dona Ana 91 17 25 S 35 5 E
Donaghadee 15 54 38N 5 32W
Donald 99 36 23 S 143 0 E
Donalda 108 52 35N 112 34W
Donaldsonville 117 30 2N 91 0W
Donalsonville 115 31 3N 84 52W
Donau → 23 48 10N 17 0 E
Donaueschingen 25 47 57N 8 30 E
Donauwörth 25 48 42N 10 47 E
Donawitz 26 47 22N 15 4 E
Doncaster 12 53 31N 1 9W
Dondo, Angola 88 9 45 S 14 25 E
Dondo, Mozam. 91 19 33 S 34 46 E
Dondo, Teluk 73 0 29N 120 30 E
Dondra Head 70 5 55N 80 40 E
Donegal 15 54 39N 8 8W
Donegal □ 15 54 53N 8 0W
Donegal B. 15 54 30N 8 35W
Donets → 57 47 33N 40 55 E
Donetsk 56 48 0N 37 45 E
Donga 85 7 45N 10 2 E
Dongara 96 29 14 S 114 57 E
Dongargarh 69 21 10N 80 40 E
Donges 18 47 18N 2 4W
Dongfang 77 18 50N 108 33 E
Donggala 73 0 30 S 119 40 E
Donggou 76 39 52N 124 10 E
Dongguan 77 22 58N 113 44 E
Dongguang 76 37 50N 116 30 E
Dongjingcheng 76 44 0N 129 10 E
Donglan 77 24 30N 107 21 E
Dongliu 77 30 13N 116 55 E
Dongola 86 19 9N 30 22 E
Dongou 88 2 0N 18 5 E
Dongping 76 35 55N 116 20 E
Dongshan 77 23 43N 117 30 E
Dongsheng 76 39 50N 110 0 E
Dongtai 77 32 51N 120 21 E
Dongting Hu 75 29 18N 112 45 E
Dongxing 75 21 34N 108 0 E
Dongyang 77 29 13N 120 15 E
Doniphan 117 36 40N 90 50W
Donja Stubica 39 45 59N 16 0 E

onji Dušnik 42 43 12N 22 5 E
onji Miholjac 42 45 45N 18 10 E
onji Milanovac 42 44 28N 22 6 E
onji Vakuf 42 44 8N 17 24 E
onjon, Le 20 46 22N 3 48 E
onna 50 66 6N 12 30 E
onna 117 26 12N 98 2W
onnaconna 107 46 41N 71 41W
onnelly's Crossing 101 35 42S 173 38 E
onora 112 40 11N 79 50W
onor's Hills 98 18 42S 140 33 E
onskoy 55 53 55N 38 15 E
onya Lendava 39 46 35N 16 25 E
onzère-Mondragon 21 44 28N 4 43 E
onzère-Mondragon, Barrage de 21 44 13N 4 42 E
onzy 19 47 20N 3 6 E
oon → 14 55 26N 4 41W
or (Tantûra) 62 32 37N 34 55 E
ora Báltea → 38 45 11N 8 5 E
ora, L. 96 22 0S 123 0 E
ora Riparia → 38 45 5N 7 44 E
orada, La 126 5 30N 74 40W
oran L. 109 61 13N 108 6W
orat, Le 20 46 14N 1 5 E
orchester 21 50 42N 2 28W
orchester, C. 105 65 27N 77 27W
ordogne □ 20 45 5N 0 40 E
ordogne → 20 45 2N 0 36W
ordrecht, Neth. 16 51 48N 4 39 E
ordrecht, S. Afr. 92 31 20S 27 3 E
ore → 20 45 50N 3 35 E
oré L. 109 54 46N 107 17W
oré Lake 109 54 38N 107 36W
ore, Mt. 20 45 32N 2 50 E
orfen 25 48 16N 12 10 E
orgali 40 40 18N 9 35 E
ori 85 14 3N 0 2W
oring → 92 31 54S 18 39 E
orion 106 45 23N 74 3W
ormaa-Ahenkro 84 7 15N 2 52W
ormo, Ras 87 13 14N 42 35 E
ornberg 39 55 45N 13 50 E
ornbirn 26 47 25N 9 45 E
ornes 19 46 48N 3 18 E
ornoch 14 57 52N 4 0W
ornoch Firth 14 57 52N 4 0W
oro 85 16 9N 0 51W
orog 27 47 42N 18 45 E
orogobuzh 54 54 50N 33 18 E
orohoi 46 47 56N 26 30 E
öröö Nuur 75 48 0N 93 0 E
orre I. 96 25 13S 113 12 E
orrigo 99 30 20S 152 44 E
orris 118 41 59N 121 58W
orset, Can. 112 45 14N 78 54W
orset, U.S.A. 112 41 4N 80 40W
orset □ 13 50 48N 2 25W
orsten 24 51 40N 6 55 E
ortmund 24 51 32N 7 28 E
örtyol 64 36 52N 36 12 E
orum 24 53 40N 8 33 E
oruma 90 4 42N 27 33 E
os Bahías, C. 128 44 58S 65 32W
os Cabezas 119 32 10N 109 37W
os Hermanas 31 37 16N 5 55W
osso 85 13 0N 3 13 E
othan 115 31 10N 85 25W
ouai 19 50 21N 3 4 E
ouala 88 4 0N 9 45 E
ouaouir 82 20 45N 3 0W
ouarnenez 18 48 6N 4 21W
ouăzeci Şi Trei August 46 43 55N 28 40 E
ouble Island Pt. 99 25 56S 153 11 E
oubrava → 26 49 40N 15 30 E
oubs □ 19 47 10N 6 20 E
oubs → 19 46 53N 5 1 E
oubtful B. 96 34 15S 119 28 E
oubtful Sd. 101 45 20S 166 49 E
oubtless B. 101 34 55S 173 26 E
oudeville 18 49 43N 0 47 E
oué 18 47 11N 0 20W
ouentza 84 14 58N 2 48W
ouglas, S. Afr. 92 29 4S 23 46 E
ouglas, U.K. 12 54 9N 4 29W
ouglas, Alaska, U.S.A. 108 58 23N 134 24W
ouglas, Ariz., U.S.A. 119 31 21N 109 30W
ouglas, Ga., U.S.A. 115 31 32N 82 52W
ouglas, Wyo., U.S.A. 116 42 45N 105 20W
ouglastown 107 48 46N 64 24W
ouglasville 115 33 46N 84 43W
ouirat 82 33 2N 4 11W
oukáton, Ákra 45 38 34N 20 30 E
oulevant 19 48 22N 4 53 E
oullens 19 50 10N 2 20 E
oumé 88 4 15N 13 25 E
ouna 84 13 13N 6 0W
ounreay 14 58 34N 3 44W
ourados 125 22 9S 54 50W
ourados → 125 21 58S 54 18W
ourdan 19 48 30N 2 0 E
ouro → 30 41 8N 8 40W
ouvaine 21 46 19N 6 16 E
ouz 83 33 25N 9 0 E
ouze → 20 43 54N 0 30W
ove → 12 52 51N 1 36W
ove Creek 119 37 46N 108 59W
over, Austral. 99 43 18S 147 2 E
over, U.K. 13 51 7N 1 19 E
over, Del., U.S.A. 114 39 10N 75 31W
over, N.H., U.S.A. 114 43 12N 70 51W
over, N.J., U.S.A. 113 40 53N 74 34W
over, Ohio, U.S.A. 114 40 32N 81 30W
over-Foxcroft 107 45 14N 69 14W
over Plains 113 41 43N 73 35W
over, Pt. 96 32 32S 125 32 E
over, Str. of 18 51 0N 1 30 E
ovey → 13 52 32N 4 0W
ovrefjell 47 62 15N 9 33 E
owa 81 13 38S 33 58 E
owagiac 114 42 0N 86 8W
owlat Yār 65 34 30N 65 45 E
owlatabad 65 28 20N 56 40W
Down □ 15 54 20N 6 0W
Downey 118 42 29N 112 3W
Downham Market 13 52 36N 0 22 E
Downieville 118 39 34N 120 50W
Downpatrick 15 54 20N 5 43W
Downpatrick Hd. 15 54 20N 9 21W
Dowshī 65 35 35N 68 43 E
Doylestown 113 40 21N 75 10W
Draa, C. 82 28 47N 11 0W
Draa, Oued → 82 30 29N 6 1W
Drac → 21 45 13N 5 41 E
Drachten 16 53 7N 6 5 E
Drăgăneşti 46 44 9N 24 32 E
Drăgăneşti-Viaşca 46 44 5N 25 33 E
Dragaš 42 42 5N 20 35 E
Drăgăşani 46 44 39N 24 17 E
Dragina 42 44 30N 19 25 E
Dragocvet 42 44 0N 21 15 E
Dragoman, Prokhod 42 43 0N 22 53 E
Dragonera, I. 32 39 35N 2 19 E
Dragovishtitsa (Perivol) 42 42 22N 22 39 E
Draguignan 21 43 30N 6 27 E
Drain 118 43 45N 123 17W
Drake, Austral. 99 28 55S 152 25 E
Drake, U.S.A. 116 47 56N 100 21W
Drake Passage 5 58 0S 68 0W
Drakensberg 93 31 0S 28 0 E
Dráma 44 41 9N 24 10 E
Dráma □ 44 41 20N 24 0 E
Drammen 47 59 42N 10 12 E
Drangajökull 50 66 9N 22 15W
Drangedal 47 59 6N 9 3 E
Dranov, Ostrov 46 44 55N 29 30 E
Drau = Drava → 26 46 32N 14 58 E
Drava → 42 45 33N 18 55 E
Draveil 19 48 41N 2 25 E
Dravograd 39 46 36N 15 5 E
Drawa → 28 52 52N 15 59 E
Drawno 28 53 13N 15 46 E
Drawsko Pomorskie 28 53 35N 15 50 E
Drayton Valley 108 53 12N 114 58W
Dren 42 43 8N 20 44 E
Drenthe □ 16 52 52N 6 40 E
Dresden, Can. 112 42 35N 82 11W
Dresden, Ger. 24 51 2N 13 45 E
Dresden □ 24 51 12N 14 0 E
Dreux 18 48 44N 1 23 E
Drezdenko 28 52 50N 15 49 E
Driffield 12 54 0N 0 25W
Driftwood 112 41 22N 78 9W
Driggs 118 43 50N 111 8W
Drin i zi → 44 41 37N 20 28 E
Drina → 42 44 53N 19 21 E
Drincea → 46 44 20N 22 55 E
Drînceni 46 46 49N 28 10 E
Drini → 44 42 20N 20 0 E
Drinjača → 42 44 15N 19 8 E
Driva → 47 62 33N 9 38 E
Drivstua 47 62 26N 9 47 E
Drniš 39 43 51N 16 10 E
Drøbak 47 59 39N 10 39 E
Drobin 28 52 42N 19 58 E
Drogheda 15 53 45N 6 20W
Drogichin 54 52 15N 25 8 E
Drogobych 54 49 20N 23 30 E
Drohiczyn 28 52 24N 22 39 E
Droichead Nua 15 53 11N 6 50W
Droitwich 13 52 16N 2 10W
Drôme □ 21 44 38N 5 15 E
Drôme → 21 44 46N 4 46 E
Dromedary, C. 99 36 17S 150 10 E
Dronero 38 44 29N 7 22 E
Dronfield 98 21 12S 140 3 E
Dronne → 20 45 2N 0 9W
Dronning Maud Land 5 72 30S 12 0 E
Dronninglund 49 57 10N 10 19 E
Dropt → 20 44 35N 0 6W
Drosendorf 26 48 52N 15 37 E
Drouzhba 43 43 15N 28 0 E
Drumbo 112 43 16N 80 35W
Drumheller 108 51 25N 112 40W
Drummond 118 46 40N 113 4W
Drummond I. 106 46 0N 83 40W
Drummond Ra. 97 23 45S 147 10 E
Drummondville 106 45 55N 72 25W
Drumright 117 35 59N 96 38W
Druskininkai 54 54 3N 23 58 E
Drut → 54 53 3N 30 42 E
Druya 54 55 45N 27 28 E
Druzhina 59 68 14N 145 18 E
Drvar 39 44 21N 16 23 E
Drvenik 39 43 27N 16 3 E
Drwęca → 28 53 0N 18 42 E
Dry Tortugas 121 24 38N 82 55W
Dryanovo 43 42 59N 25 28 E
Dryden, Can. 109 49 47N 92 50W
Dryden, U.S.A. 117 30 3N 102 3W
Drygalski I. 5 66 0S 92 0 E
Drysdale → 96 13 59S 126 51 E
Drzewiczka → 28 51 36N 20 36 E
Dschang 85 5 32N 10 3 E
Du Bois 114 41 8N 78 46W
Du Quoin 116 38 0N 89 10W
Duanesburg 113 42 45N 74 11W
Duaringa 98 23 42S 149 42 E
Ḍubā 64 27 10N 35 40 E
Dubai = Dubayy 65 25 18N 55 20 E
Dubawnt → 109 64 33N 100 6W
Dubawnt, L. 109 63 4N 101 42W
Dubayy 65 25 18N 55 20 E
Dubbo 97 32 11S 148 35 E
Dubele 90 2 56N 29 35 E
Dubica 39 45 11N 16 48 E
Dublin, Ireland 15 53 20N 6 18W
Dublin, Ga., U.S.A. 115 32 30N 82 34W
Dublin, Tex., U.S.A. 117 32 0N 98 20W
Dublin □ 15 53 24N 6 20W
Dublin B. 15 53 18N 6 5W
Dubna, U.S.S.R. 55 54 8N 36 59 E
Dubna, U.S.S.R. 55 56 44N 37 10 E
Dubno 54 50 25N 25 45 E
Dubois 118 44 7N 112 9W
Dubossary 56 47 15N 29 10 E
Dubossasy Vdkhr. 56 47 30N 29 0 E
Dubovka 57 49 5N 44 50 E
Dubovskoye 57 47 28N 42 46 E
Dubrajpur 69 23 48N 87 25 E
Dubrėka 84 9 46N 13 31W
Dubrovitsa 54 51 31N 26 35 E
Dubrovnik 42 42 39N 18 6 E
Dubrovskoye 59 58 55N 111 10 E
Dubuque 116 42 30N 90 41W
Duchang 77 29 18N 116 12 E
Duchesne 118 40 14N 110 22W
Duchess 97 21 20S 139 50 E
Ducie I. 95 24 40S 124 48W
Duck Lake 109 52 50N 106 16W
Duck Mt. Prov. Parks 109 51 45N 101 0W
Duderstadt 24 51 30N 10 15 E
Dudinka 59 69 30N 86 13 E
Dudley 13 52 30N 2 5W
Dudna → 70 19 17N 76 54 E
Dueñas 30 41 52N 4 33W
Dueodde 49 54 59N 15 4 E
Duero → 30 41 8N 8 40W
Duff Is. 94 9 53S 167 8 E
Dufftown 14 57 26N 3 9W
Dugi 39 44 0N 15 0 E
Dugo Selo 39 45 51N 16 18 E
Duifken Pt. 97 12 33S 141 38 E
Duisburg 24 51 27N 6 42 E
Duiwelskloof 93 23 42S 30 10 E
Dukati 44 40 16N 19 32 E
Duke I. 108 54 50N 131 20W
Dukelsky průsmyk 27 49 25N 21 42 E
Dukhān 65 25 25N 50 50 E
Dukhovshchina 54 55 15N 32 27 E
Dukla 27 49 30N 21 35 E
Duku, Bauchi, Nigeria 85 10 43N 10 43 E
Duku, Sokoto, Nigeria 85 11 11N 4 55 E
Dulce → 124 30 32S 62 33W
Dulce, Golfo 121 8 40N 83 20W
Dŭlgopol 43 43 3N 27 22 E
Dullewala 68 31 50N 71 25 E
Dülmen 24 51 49N 7 18 E
Dulovo 43 43 48N 27 9 E
Dululu 98 23 48S 150 15 E
Duluth 116 46 48N 92 10W
Dum Dum 69 22 39N 88 33 E
Dum Duma 67 27 40N 95 40 E
Dum Hadjer 81 13 18N 19 41 E
Dumaguete 73 9 17N 123 15 E
Dumai 72 1 35N 101 28 E
Dumaran 73 10 33N 119 50 E
Dumaring 73 1 46N 118 10 E
Dumas, Ark., U.S.A. 117 33 52N 91 30W
Dumas, Tex., U.S.A. 117 35 50N 101 58W
Dumbarton 14 55 58N 4 35W
Dumbrăveni 46 46 14N 24 34 E
Dumfries 14 55 4N 3 37W
Dumfries & Galloway □ 14 55 0N 4 0W
Dumka 69 24 12N 87 15 E
Dümmersee 24 52 30N 8 21 E
Dumoine → 106 46 13N 77 51W
Dumoine L. 106 46 55N 77 55W
Dumraon 69 25 33N 84 8 E
Dumyât 86 31 24N 31 48 E
Dumyât, Masabb 86 31 28N 31 51 E
Dun Laoghaire 15 53 17N 6 9W
Dun-le-Palestel 20 46 18N 1 39 E
Dun-sur-Auron 19 46 53N 2 33 E
Duna → 27 45 51N 18 48 E
Dunaföldvár 27 46 50N 18 57 E
Dunaj → 27 48 5N 17 10 E
Dunajec → 27 50 15N 20 44 E
Dunajska Streda 27 48 0N 17 37 E
Dunapatai 27 46 39N 19 4 E
Dunărea → 46 45 30N 8 15 E
Dunaszekcsö 27 46 6N 18 45 E
Dunaújváros 27 47 0N 18 57 E
Dunav → 42 44 47N 21 20 E
Dunavtsi 42 43 57N 22 53 E
Dunback 101 45 23S 170 36 E
Dunbar, Austral. 98 16 0S 142 22 E
Dunbar, U.K. 14 56 0N 2 32W
Dunblane 14 56 10N 3 58W
Duncan, Can. 108 48 45N 123 40W
Duncan, Ariz., U.S.A. 119 32 46N 109 6W
Duncan, Okla., U.S.A. 117 34 25N 98 0W
Duncan L. 108 62 51N 113 58W
Duncan, L. 106 53 29N 77 58W
Duncan Pass. 71 11 0N 92 30 E
Duncan Town 121 22 15N 75 45W
Duncannon 112 40 23N 77 2W
Dundalk, Can. 112 44 10N 80 24W
Dundalk, Ireland 15 54 1N 6 25W
Dundalk Bay 15 53 55N 6 15W
Dundas 106 43 17N 79 59W
Dundas I. 108 54 30N 130 50W
Dundas, L. 96 32 35S 121 50 E
Dundas Str. 96 11 15S 131 35 E
Dundee, S. Afr. 93 28 11S 30 15 E
Dundee, U.K. 14 56 29N 3 0W
Dundoo 99 27 40S 144 37 E
Dundrum 15 54 17N 5 50W
Dundrum B. 15 54 12N 5 40W
Dundwara 68 27 48N 79 9 E
Dunedin, N.Z. 101 45 50S 170 33 E
Dunedin, U.S.A. 115 28 1N 82 45W
Dunedin → 108 59 30N 124 5W
Dunfermline 14 56 5N 3 28W
Dungannon, Can. 112 43 51N 81 36W
Dungannon, U.K. 15 54 30N 6 47W
Dungannon □ 15 54 30N 6 55W
Dungarpur 68 23 52N 73 45 E
Dungarvan 15 52 6N 7 40W
Dungarvan Bay 15 52 5N 7 35W
Dungeness 13 50 54N 0 59 E
Dungo, L. do 92 17 15S 19 0 E
Dungog 99 32 22S 151 46 E
Dungu 90 3 40N 28 32 E
Dungunâb 86 21 10N 37 9 E
Dungunâb, Khalij 86 21 5N 37 12 E
Dunhinda Falls 70 7 5N 81 6 E
Dunhua 76 43 20N 128 14 E
Dunhuang 75 40 8N 94 36 E
Dunières 21 45 13N 4 20 E
Dunk I. 98 17 59S 146 29 E
Dunkeld 14 56 34N 3 36W
Dunkerque 19 51 2N 2 20 E
Dunkery Beacon 13 51 15N 3 37W
Dunkirk 114 42 30N 79 18W
Dunkirk = Dunkerque 19 51 2N 2 20 E
Dunkuj 87 12 50N 32 49 E
Dunkwa, Central, Ghana 84 6 0N 1 47W
Dunkwa, Central, Ghana 85 5 30N 1 0W
Dunlap 116 41 50N 95 36W
Dunmanus B. 15 51 31N 9 50W
Dunmore 114 41 27N 75 38W
Dunmore Hd. 15 52 10N 10 35W
Dunn 115 35 18N 78 36W
Dunnellon 115 29 4N 82 28W
Dunnet Hd. 14 58 38N 3 22W
Dunning 116 41 52N 100 4W
Dunnville 112 42 54N 79 36W
Dunolly 99 36 51S 143 44 E
Dunoon 14 55 57N 4 56W
Dunqul 86 23 26N 31 37 E
Duns 14 55 47N 2 20W
Dunseith 116 48 49N 100 2W
Dunsmuir 118 41 10N 122 18W
Dunstable 13 51 53N 0 31W
Dunstan Mts. 101 44 53S 169 35 E
Dunster 108 53 8N 119 50W
Dunvegan L. 109 60 8N 107 10W
Duolun 76 42 12N 116 28 E
Dupree 116 45 4N 101 35W
Dupuyer 118 48 11N 112 31W
Duque de Caxias 125 22 45S 43 19W
Duquesne 112 40 22N 79 55W
Dūrā 62 31 31N 35 1 E
Durack Range 96 16 50S 127 40 E
Durance → 21 43 55N 4 45 E
Durand 114 42 54N 83 58W
Durango, Mexico 120 24 3N 104 39W
Durango, Spain 32 43 13N 2 40W
Durango, U.S.A. 119 37 16N 107 50W
Durango □ 120 25 0N 105 0W
Durant 117 34 0N 96 25W
Duratón → 30 41 37N 4 7W
Durazno 124 33 25S 56 31W
Durazzo = Durrësi 44 41 19N 19 28 E
Durban, France 20 43 0N 2 49 E
Durban, S. Afr. 93 29 49S 31 1 E
Dúrcal 31 37 0N 3 34W
Đurđevac 42 46 2N 17 3 E
Düren 24 50 48N 6 30 E
Durg 69 21 15N 81 22 E
Durgapur 69 23 30N 87 20 E
Durham, Can. 106 44 10N 80 49W
Durham, U.K. 12 54 47N 1 34W
Durham, U.S.A. 115 36 0N 78 55W
Durham □ 12 54 42N 1 45W
Durmitor 34 43 10N 19 0 E
Durness 14 58 34N 4 45W
Durrës 44 41 19N 19 28 E
Durrësi 44 41 19N 19 28 E
Durrie 99 25 40S 140 15 E
Durtal 18 47 40N 0 18W
Duru 90 4 14N 28 50 E
D'Urville I. 101 40 50S 173 55 E
D'Urville, Tanjung 73 1 28S 137 54 E
Duryea 113 41 20N 75 45W
Dusa Mareb 63 5 30N 46 15 E
Dûsh 86 24 35N 30 41 E
Dushak 58 37 13N 60 1 E
Dushan 77 25 48N 107 30 E
Dushanbe 58 38 33N 68 48 E
Dusheti 57 42 10N 44 42 E
Dusky Sd. 101 45 47S 166 30 E
Düsseldorf 24 51 15N 6 46 E
Duszniki-Zdrój 28 50 24N 16 24 E
Dutch Harbor 104 53 54N 166 35W
Dutlhe 92 23 58S 23 46 E
Dutsan Wai 85 10 50N 8 10 E
Dutton 112 42 39N 81 30W
Dutton → 98 20 44S 143 10 E
Duved 48 63 24N 12 55 E
Duvno 42 43 42N 17 13 E
Duwādimi 64 24 35N 44 15 E
Duyun 77 26 18N 107 29 E
Duzce 64 40 50N 31 10 E
Duzdab = Zāhedān 65 29 30N 60 50 E
Dve Mogili 43 43 35N 25 55 E
Dvina, Sev. 52 64 32N 40 30 E
Dvinsk = Daugavpils 54 55 53N 26 32 E
Dvinskaya Guba 52 65 0N 39 0 E
Dvor 39 45 4N 16 22 E
Dvorce 27 49 50N 17 34 E
Dvur Králové 26 50 27N 15 50 E
Dwarka 68 22 18N 69 8 E
Dwight, Can. 112 45 20N 79 1W
Dwight, U.S.A. 114 41 5N 88 25W
Dyakovskoya 55 60 5N 41 12 E
Dyatkovo 54 53 40N 34 27 E
Dyatlovo 54 53 28N 25 28 E
Dyer, C. 105 66 40N 61 0W
Dyer Plateau 5 70 45S 65 30W
Dyersburg 117 36 2N 89 20W
Dyfed □ 13 52 0N 4 30W
Dyje → 27 48 37N 16 56 E
Dynevor Downs 99 28 10S 144 20 E
Dynów 27 49 50N 22 11 E
Dysart 109 50 57N 104 2W
Dzamin Üüd 75 43 50N 111 58 E
Dzerzhinsk, Byelorussian S.S.R., U.S.S.R. 54 53 40N 27 1 E
Dzerzhinsk, R.S.F.S.R., U.S.S.R. 55 56 14N 43 30 E
Dzhalal-Abad 58 40 56N 73 0 E
Dzhalinda 59 53 26N 124 0 E
Dzhambeyty 57 50 15N 52 30 E
Dzhambul 58 42 54N 71 22 E
Dzhankoi 56 45 40N 34 20 E
Dzhanybek 57 49 25N 46 50 E
Dzhardzhan 59 68 10N 124 10 E
Dzhelinde 59 70 0N 114 20 E

Dzhetygara 58 52 11N 61 12 E
Dzhezkazgan 58 47 44N 67 40 E
Dzhikimde 59 59 1N 121 47 E
Dzhizak 58 40 6N 67 50 E
Dzhugdzur, Khrebet 59 57 30N 138 0 E
Dzhungarskiye Vorota 58 45 0N 82 0 E
Dzhvari 57 42 42N 42 4 E
Działdowo 28 53 15N 20 15 E
Działoszyce 28 50 22N 20 20 E
Działoszyn 28 51 6N 18 50 E
Dzierzgoń 28 53 58N 19 20 E
Dzierzoniów 28 50 45N 16 39 E
Dzioua 83 33 14N 5 14 E
Dziwnów 28 54 2N 14 45 E
Dzungarian Gate = Alataw Shankou 75 45 5N 81 57 E
Dzuumod 75 47 45N 106 58 E

E

Eabamet, L. 106 51 30N 87 46W
Eads 116 38 30N 102 46W
Eagle, Alaska, U.S.A. 104 64 44N 141 7W
Eagle, Colo., U.S.A. 118 39 39N 106 55W
Eagle → 107 53 36N 57 26W
Eagle Butt 116 45 1N 101 12W
Eagle Grove 116 42 37N 93 53W
Eagle L., Calif., U.S.A. 118 40 35N 120 50W
Eagle L., Me., U.S.A. 107 46 23N 69 22W
Eagle Lake 117 29 35N 96 21W
Eagle Nest 119 36 33N 105 13W
Eagle Pass 117 28 45N 100 35W
Eagle River 116 45 55N 89 17W
Eaglehawk 99 36 39 S 144 16 E
Ealing 13 51 30N 0 19W
Earl Grey 109 50 57N 104 43W
Earle 117 35 18N 90 26W
Earlimart 119 35 53N 119 16W
Earn → 14 56 20N 3 19W
Earn, L. 14 56 23N 4 14W
Earnslaw, Mt. 101 44 32 S 168 27 E
Earth 117 34 18N 102 30W
Easley 115 34 52N 82 35W
East Angus 107 45 30N 71 40W
East Aurora 112 42 46N 78 38W
East B. 117 29 2N 89 16W
East Bengal 67 24 0N 90 0 E
East Beskids = Vychodné Beskydy 27 49 30N 22 0 E
East Brady 112 40 59N 79 36W
East C. 101 37 42 S 178 35 E
East Chicago 114 41 40N 87 30W
East China Sea 75 30 5N 126 0 E
East Coulee 108 51 23N 112 27W
East Falkland 128 51 30 S 58 30W
East Grand Forks 116 47 55N 97 5W
East Greenwich 113 41 39N 71 27W
East Hartford 113 41 45N 72 39W
East Helena 118 46 37N 111 58W
East Indies 72 0 0 120 0 E
East Jordan 114 45 10N 85 7W
East Kilbride 14 55 46N 4 10W
East Lansing 114 42 44N 84 29W
East Liverpool 114 40 39N 80 35W
East London 93 33 0 S 27 55 E
East Orange 114 40 46N 74 13W
East Pacific Ridge 95 15 0 S 110 0W
East Pakistan = Bangladesh ■ 67 24 0N 90 0 E
East Palestine 112 40 50N 80 32W
East Pine 108 55 48N 120 12W
East Pt. 107 46 27N 61 58W
East Point 115 33 40N 84 28W
East Providence 113 41 48N 71 22W
East Retford 12 53 19N 0 55W
East St. Louis 116 38 37N 90 4W
East Schelde → = Oosterschelde 16 51 38N 3 40 E
East Siberian Sea 59 73 0N 160 0 E
East Stroudsburg 113 41 1N 75 11W
East Sussex □ 13 51 0N 0 20 E
East Tawas 114 44 17N 83 31W
Eastbourne, N.Z. 101 41 19 S 174 55 E
Eastbourne, U.K. 13 50 46N 0 18 E
Eastend 109 49 32N 108 50W
Easter I. 95 27 8 S 109 23W
Easter Islands 95 27 0 S 109 0W
Eastern □, Kenya 90 0 0 S 38 30 E
Eastern □, Uganda 90 1 50N 33 45 E
Eastern Cr. → 98 20 40 S 141 35 E
Eastern Ghats 70 14 0N 78 50 E
Eastern Province □ 84 8 15N 11 0W
Easterville 109 53 8N 99 49W
Easthampton 113 42 15N 72 41W
Eastland 117 32 26N 98 45W
Eastleigh 13 50 58N 1 21W
Eastmain → 106 52 27N 78 26W
Eastmain (East Main) 106 52 10N 78 30W
Eastman, Can. 113 45 18N 72 19W
Eastman, U.S.A. 115 32 13N 83 20W
Easton, Md., U.S.A. 114 38 47N 76 7W
Easton, Pa., U.S.A. 114 40 41N 75 15W
Easton, Wash., U.S.A. 118 47 14N 121 8W
Eastport 107 44 57N 67 0W
Eaton 116 40 35N 104 42W
Eatonia 109 51 13N 109 25W
Eatonton 115 33 22N 83 24W
Eatontown 113 40 18N 74 7W
Eau Claire, S.C., U.S.A. 115 34 5N 81 2W
Eau Claire, Wis., U.S.A. 116 44 46N 91 30W
Eauze 20 43 53N 0 7 E
Ebagoola 98 14 15 S 143 12 E
Eban 85 9 40N 4 50 E
Ebbw Vale 13 51 47N 3 12W
Ebeggui 83 26 2N 6 0 E
Ebensburg 112 40 29N 78 43W
Ebensee 26 47 48N 13 46 E
Eberbach 25 49 27N 8 59 E
Eberswalde 24 52 49N 13 50 E
Ebingen 25 48 13N 9 1 E
Eboli 41 40 39N 15 2 E
Ebolowa 88 2 55N 11 10 E
Ebrach 25 49 50N 10 30 E
Ébrié, Lagune 84 5 12N 4 26W
Ebro → 32 40 43N 0 54 E
Ebro, Pantano del 30 43 0N 3 58W
Ebstorf 24 53 2N 10 23 E
Eceabat 44 40 11N 26 21 E
Éceuillé 18 47 10N 1 19 E
Echelles, Les 21 45 27N 5 45 E
Echmiadzin 57 40 12N 44 19 E
Echo Bay 106 46 29N 84 4W
Echo Bay (Port Radium) 104 66 05N 117 55W
Echoing → 109 55 51N 92 5W
Echternach 16 49 49N 6 25 E
Echuca 100 36 10 S 144 20 E
Ecija 31 37 30N 5 10W
Eckernförde 24 54 26N 9 50 E
Écommoy 18 47 50N 0 17 E
Écos 19 49 9N 1 35 E
Écouché 18 48 42N 0 10W
Ecuador ■ 126 2 0 S 78 0W
Ed 49 58 55N 11 55 E
Ed Dabbura 86 17 40N 34 15 E
Ed Dâmer 86 17 27N 34 0 E
Ed Debba 86 18 0N 30 51 E
Ed-Déffa 86 30 40N 26 30 E
Ed Deim 87 10 10N 28 20 E
Ed Dueim 87 14 0N 32 10 E
Edam, Can. 109 53 11N 108 46W
Edam, Neth. 16 52 31N 5 3 E
Edaplly 70 11 19N 78 3 E
Eday 14 59 11N 2 47W
Edd 87 14 0N 41 38 E
Eddrachillis B. 14 58 16N 5 10W
Eddystone 13 50 11N 4 16W
Eddystone Pt. 99 40 59 S 148 20 E
Ede, Neth. 16 52 4N 5 40 E
Ede, Nigeria 85 7 45N 4 29 E
Édea 88 3 51N 10 9 E
Edehon L. 109 60 25N 97 15W
Edekel, Adrar 83 23 56N 6 47 E
Eden, Austral. 99 37 3 S 149 55 E
Eden, N.C., U.S.A. 115 36 29N 79 53W
Eden, N.Y., U.S.A. 112 42 39N 78 55W
Eden, Tex., U.S.A. 117 31 16N 99 50W
Eden, Wyo., U.S.A. 118 42 2N 109 27W
Eden → 12 54 57N 3 2W
Eden L. 109 56 38N 100 15W
Edenburg 92 29 43 S 25 58 E
Edenderry 15 53 21N 7 3W
Edenton 115 36 5N 76 36W
Edenville 93 27 37 S 27 34 E
Eder → 24 51 15N 9 25 E
Ederstausee 24 51 11N 9 0 E
Edgar 116 40 25N 98 0W
Edgartown 113 41 22N 70 28W
Edge Hill 13 52 7N 1 28W
Edgefield 115 33 50N 81 59W
Edgeley 116 46 27N 98 41W
Edgemont 116 43 15N 103 53W
Edgeøya 4 77 45N 22 30 E
Edhessa 44 40 48N 22 5 E
Edievale 101 45 49 S 169 22 E
Edina, Liberia 84 6 0N 10 10W
Edina, U.S.A. 116 40 6N 92 10W
Edinburg 117 26 22N 98 10W
Edinburgh 14 55 57N 3 12W
Edirne 43 41 40N 26 34 E
Edithburgh 99 35 5 S 137 43 E
Edjeleh 83 28 38N 9 50 E
Edmeston 113 42 42N 75 15W
Edmond 117 35 37N 97 30W
Edmonds 118 47 47N 122 22W
Edmonton, Austral. 98 17 2 S 145 46 E
Edmonton, Can. 108 53 30N 113 30W
Edmund L. 109 54 45N 93 17W
Edmundston 107 47 23N 68 20W
Edna 117 29 0N 96 40W
Edna Bay 108 55 55N 133 40W
Edolo 38 46 10N 10 21 E
Edremit 64 39 34N 27 0 E
Edsbyn 48 61 23N 15 49 E
Edsel Ford Ra. 5 77 0 S 143 0W
Edsele 48 63 25N 16 32 E
Edson 108 53 35N 116 28W
Eduardo Castex 124 35 50 S 64 18W
Edward → 99 35 0 S 143 30 E
Edward I. 106 48 22N 88 37W
Edward, L. 90 0 25 S 29 40 E
Edward VII Pen. 5 80 0 S 150 0W
Edwards Plat. 117 30 30N 101 5W
Edwardsville 113 41 15N 75 56W
Edzo 108 62 49N 116 4W
Eekloo 16 51 11N 3 33 E
Ef'e, Nahal 62 31 9N 35 13 E
Eferding 26 48 18N 14 1 E
Efferi 83 24 30N 9 28 E
Effingham 114 39 8N 88 30W
Eforie Sud 46 44 1N 28 37 E
Ega → 32 42 19N 1 55W
Égadi, Ìsole 40 37 55N 12 16 E
Eganville 106 45 32N 77 5W
Egeland 116 48 42N 99 6W
Egenolf L. 109 59 3N 100 0W
Eger 27 47 53N 20 27 E
Eger → 27 47 38N 20 50 E
Egersund 47 58 26N 6 1 E
Egerton, Mt. 96 24 42 S 117 44 E
Egg L. 109 55 5N 105 30W
Eggenburg 26 48 38N 15 50 E
Eggenfelden 25 48 24N 12 46 E
Égletons 20 45 24N 2 3 E
Egmont, C. 101 39 16 S 173 45 E
Egmont, Mt. 101 39 17 S 174 5 E
Eğridir 64 37 52N 30 51 E
Eğridir Gölü 64 37 53N 30 50 E
Egtved 49 55 38N 9 18 E
Egume 85 7 30N 7 14 E
Éguzon 20 46 27N 1 33 E
Egvekinot 59 66 19N 179 50W
Egyek 27 47 39N 20 52 E
Egypt ■ 86 28 0N 31 0 E
Eha Amufu 85 6 30N 7 46 E
Ehime □ 74 33 30N 132 40 E
Ehingen 25 48 16N 9 43 E
Ehrwald 26 47 24N 10 56 E
Eibar 32 43 11N 2 28W
Eichstatt 25 48 53N 11 12 E
Eida 47 60 32N 6 43 E
Eider → 24 54 19N 8 58 E
Eidsvold 99 25 25 S 151 12 E
Eifel 25 50 10N 6 45 E
Eiffel Flats 91 18 20 S 30 0 E
Eigg 14 56 54N 6 10W
Eighty Mile Beach 96 19 30 S 120 40 E
Eil 63 8 0N 49 50 E
Eil, L. 14 56 50N 5 15W
Eildon, L. 99 37 10 S 146 0 E
Eileen L. 109 62 16N 107 37W
Eilenburg 24 51 28N 12 38 E
Ein el Luweiqa 87 14 5N 33 50 E
Einasleigh 97 18 32 S 144 5 E
Einasleigh → 98 17 30 S 142 17 E
Einbeck 24 51 48N 9 50 E
Eindhoven 16 51 26N 5 30 E
Einsiedeln 25 47 7N 8 46 E
Eiriksjökull 50 64 46N 20 24W
Eirunepé 126 6 35 S 69 53W
Eisenach 24 50 58N 10 18 E
Eisenberg 24 50 59N 11 50 E
Eisenerz 26 47 32N 14 54 E
Eisenhüttenstadt 24 52 9N 14 41 E
Eisenkappel 26 46 29N 14 36 E
Eisenstadt 27 47 51N 16 31 E
Eiserfeld 24 50 50N 7 59 E
Eisfeld 24 50 25N 10 54 E
Eisleben 24 51 31N 11 31 E
Ejby 49 55 25N 9 56 E
Eje, Sierra del 30 42 24N 6 54W
Ejea de los Caballeros 32 42 7N 1 9W
Ekalaka 116 45 55N 104 30W
Eket 85 4 38N 7 56 E
Eketahuna 101 40 38 S 175 43 E
Ekhinos 44 41 16N 25 1 E
Ekibastuz 58 51 50N 75 10 E
Ekimchan 59 53 0N 133 0W
Ekoli 90 0 23 S 24 13 E
Eksjö 49 57 40N 14 58W
Ekwan → 106 53 12N 82 15W
Ekwan Pt. 106 53 16N 82 7W
El Aaiún 80 27 9N 13 12W
El Aat 62 32 50N 35 45 E
El Abiodh-Sidi-Cheikh 82 32 53N 0 31 E
El Aïoun 82 34 33N 2 30W
El 'Aiyat 86 29 36N 31 15 E
El Alamein 86 30 48N 28 58 E
El 'Arag 86 28 40N 26 20 E
El Arahal 31 37 15N 5 33W
El Arba 82 36 37N 3 12 E
El Aricha 82 34 13N 1 10W
El Arîhã 62 31 52N 35 27 E
El Arish 98 17 35 S 146 1 E
El 'Arîsh 86 31 8N 33 50 E
El Arrouch 83 36 37N 6 53 E
• El Asnam 82 36 10N 1 20 E
El Astillero 30 43 24N 3 49W
El Badâri 86 27 4N 31 25 E
El Bahrein 86 28 30N 26 25 E
El Ballâs 86 26 2N 32 43 E
El Balyana 86 26 10N 32 3 E
El Baqeir 86 18 40N 33 40 E
El Barco de Ávila 30 40 21N 5 31W
El Barco de Valdeorras 30 42 23N 7 0W
El Bauga 86 18 18N 33 52 E
El Bawiti 86 28 25N 28 45 E
El Bayadh 82 33 40N 1 1 E
El Bierzo 30 42 45N 6 30W
El Bluff 121 11 59N 83 40W
El Bonillo 33 38 57N 2 35W
El Cajon 119 32 49N 117 0W
El Callao 126 7 18N 61 50W
El Camp 32 41 5N 1 10 E
El Campo 117 29 10N 96 20W
El Castillo 31 37 41N 6 19W
El Centro 119 32 50N 115 40W
El Cerro, Boliv. 126 17 30 S 61 40W
El Cerro, Spain 31 37 45N 6 57W
El Coronil 31 37 5N 5 38W
El Cuy 128 39 55 S 68 25W
El Cuyo 120 21 30N 87 40W
El Dab'a 86 31 0N 28 27 E
El Deir 86 25 25N 32 20 E
El Dere 63 3 50N 47 8 E
El Dias 120 20 40N 87 20W
El Dilingat 86 30 50N 30 31 E
El Diviso 126 1 22N 78 14W
El Djem 83 35 18N 10 42 E
El Djouf 84 20 0N 11 30 E
El Dorado, Ark., U.S.A. 117 33 10N 92 40W
El Dorado, Kans., U.S.A. 117 37 55N 96 56W
El Dorado, Venez. 126 6 55N 61 37W
El Dorado Springs 117 37 54N 93 59W
El Eglab 82 26 20N 4 30W
El Escorial 30 40 35N 4 7W
El Eulma 83 36 9N 5 42 E
El Faiyûm 86 29 19N 30 50 E
El Fâsher 87 13 33N 25 26 E
El Fashn 86 28 50N 30 54 E
El Ferrol 30 43 29N 8 15W
El Fifi 87 10 4N 25 0 E
El Fuerte 120 26 30N 108 40W
El Gal 63 10 58N 50 20 E
El Gebir 87 13 40N 29 40 E
El Gedida 86 25 40N 28 30 E
El Geteina 87 14 50N 32 27 E
El Gezira □ 87 15 0N 33 0 E
El Gîza 86 30 0N 31 10 E
El Goléa 82 30 30N 2 50 E
El Guettar 83 34 5N 4 38 E
El Hadjira 83 32 36N 5 30 E
El Hagiz 87 15 15N 35 50 E
El Hajeb 82 33 43N 5 13W
El Hammam 86 30 52N 29 25 E
El Hank 82 24 30N 7 0W
El Harrache 80 36 45N 3 5 E
El Hawata 87 13 25N 34 42
El Heiz 86 27 50N 28 40
El 'Idisât 86 25 30N 32 35
El Iskandarîya 86 31 0N 30 0
El Istwâ'ya □ 87 5 0N 30 0
El Jadida 80 33 11N 8 17
El Jebelein 81 12 40N 32 55
El Kab 86 19 27N 32 46
El Kala 83 36 50N 8 30
El Kalâa 82 32 4N 7 27
El Kamlin 87 15 3N 33 11
El Kantara, Alg. 83 35 14N 5 45
El Kantara, Tunisia 83 33 45N 10 58
El Karaba 86 18 32N 33 41
El Kef 83 36 12N 8 47
El Khandaq 86 18 30N 30 30
El Khârga 86 25 30N 30 33
El Khartûm 87 15 31N 32 35
El Khartûm □ 87 16 0N 33 0
El Khartûm Bahrî 87 15 40N 32 31
El-Khroubs 83 36 10N 6 55
El Khureiba 86 28 3N 35 10
El Kseur 83 36 46N 4 49
El Ksiba 82 32 45N 6 1
El Kuntilla 86 30 1N 34 45
El Laqâwa 81 11 25N 29 1
El Laqeita 86 25 50N 33 15
El Leiya 87 16 15N 35 28
El Mafâza 87 13 38N 34 30
El Mahalla el Kubra 86 31 0N 31 0
El Mahârîq 86 25 35N 30 35
El Mahmûdîya 86 31 10N 30 32
El Maiz 82 28 19N 0 9
El-Maks el-Bahari 86 24 30N 30 40
El Manshâh 86 26 26N 31 50
El Mansour 82 27 47N 0 14
El Mansûra 86 31 0N 31 19
El Manzala 86 31 10N 31 50
El Marâgha 86 26 35N 31 10
El Masid 87 15 15N 33 0
El Matariya 86 31 15N 32 0
El Meghaier 83 33 55N 5 58
El Meraguen 82 28 0N 0 7
El Metemma 87 16 50N 33 10
El Milagro 124 30 59 S 65 59
El Milia 83 36 51N 6 13
El Minyâ 86 28 7N 30 33
El Molar 32 40 42N 3 45
El Mreyye 84 18 0N 6 0
El Obeid 87 13 8N 30 10
El Odaiya 81 12 8N 28 12
El Oro 120 19 48N 100 8
El Oro = Sta. María del Oro 120 25 50N 105 20
El Oued 83 33 20N 6 58
El Palmito, Presa 120 25 40N 105 30
El Panadés 32 41 10N 1 30
El Pardo 30 40 31N 3 47
El Paso 119 31 50N 106 30
El Pedernoso 33 39 29N 2 45
El Pedroso 31 37 51N 5 45
El Pobo de Dueñas 32 40 46N 1 39
El Portal 119 37 44N 119 49
El Prat de Llobregat 32 41 18N 2 3
El Progreso 120 15 26N 87 51
El Provencío 33 39 23N 2 35
El Pueblito 120 29 3N 105 4
El Qâhira 86 30 1N 31 14
El Qantara 86 30 51N 32 20
El Qasr 86 25 44N 28 42
El Quseima 86 30 40N 34 15
El Qusîya 86 27 29N 30 44
El Râshda 86 25 36N 28 57
El Reno 117 35 30N 98 0
El Ribero 30 42 30N 8 30
El Rîdisiya 86 24 56N 32 51
El Ronquillo 31 37 44N 6 10
El Rubio 31 37 22N 5 0
El Saff 86 29 34N 31 16
El Salvador ■ 120 13 50N 89 0
El Sancejo 31 37 4N 5 6
El Sauce 121 13 0N 86 40
El Shallal 86 24 0N 32 53
El Simbillawein 86 30 48N 31 13
El Suweis 86 29 58N 32 31
El Thamad 86 29 40N 34 28
El Tigre 126 8 44N 64 15
El Tocuyo 126 9 47N 69 48
El Tofo 124 29 22 S 71 18
El Tránsito 124 28 52 S 70 17
El Tûr 86 28 14N 33 36
El Turbio 128 51 45 S 72 5
El Uqsur 86 25 41N 32 38
El Vado 32 41 2N 3 18
El Vallés 32 41 35N 2 20
El Vigía 126 8 38N 71 39
El Wak 90 2 49N 40 56
El Waqf 86 25 45N 32 15
El Wâsta 86 29 19N 31 12
El Weguet 87 5 28N 42 17
El Wuz 81 15 0N 30 7
Elafónisos 45 36 29N 22 56
Elamanchili = Yellamanchilli 70 17 26N 82 50
Elandsvlei 92 32 19 S 19 31
Élassa 45 35 18N 26 21
Elassón 44 39 53N 22 12
Elat 62 29 30N 34 56
Eláthia 45 38 37N 22 46
Elâzığ 64 38 37N 39 14
Elba, Italy 38 42 48N 10 15
Elba, U.S.A. 115 31 27N 86 4
Elbasani 44 41 9N 20 9
Elbasani-Berati □ 44 40 58N 20 0
Elbe → 24 53 50N 9 0
Elbert, Mt. 119 39 5N 106 27
Elberta 114 44 35N 86 14
Elberton 115 34 7N 82 51
Elbeuf 18 49 17N 1 2
Elbidtan 64 38 13N 37 12
Elbing = Elbląg 28 54 10N 19 25
Elbląg 28 54 10N 19 25
Elbląg □ 28 54 15N 19 30
Elbow 109 51 7N 106 35

* *Renamed Ech Cheliff*

brus 57 43 21N 42 30 E
burg 16 52 26N 5 50 E
burz Mts. = Alborz 65 36 0N 52 0 E
che 33 38 15N 0 42 W
che de la Sierra 33 38 27N 2 3W
cho I. 97 11 55 S 135 45 E
da 33 38 29N 0 47W
don 116 38 20N 92 38W
dora 116 42 20N 93 5W
dorado, Argent. 125 26 28 S 54 43W
dorado, Can. 109 59 35N 108 30W
dorado, Mexico 120 24 20N 107 22W
dorado, Ill., U.S.A. 114 37 50N 88 25W
dorado, Tex., U.S.A. 117 30 52N 100 35W
doret 90 0 30N 35 17 E
dred 112 41 57N 78 24W
ectra 117 34 0N 99 0W
efantes → 93 24 10 S 32 40 E
ektrogorsk 55 55 56N 38 50 E
ektrostal 55 55 41N 38 32 E
ele 85 5 5N 6 50 E
ena 43 42 55N 25 53 E
ephant Butte Res. 119 33 45N 107 30W
ephant I. 5 61 0 S 55 0W
ephant Pass 70 9 35N 80 25 E
eshnitsa 43 41 52N 23 36 E
euthera 121 25 0N 76 20W
evsis 45 38 4N 23 26 E
evtheroúpolis 44 40 52N 24 20 E
gepiggen 47 62 10N 11 21 E
geyo-Marakwet □ 90 0 45N 35 30 E
gin, N.B., Can. 107 45 48N 65 10W
gin, Ont., Can. 113 44 36N 76 13W
gin, U.K. 14 57 39N 3 20W
gin, Ill., U.S.A. 114 42 0N 88 20W
gin, N.D., U.S.A. 116 46 24N 101 46W
gin, Nebr., U.S.A. 116 41 58N 98 3W
gin, Nev., U.S.A. 119 37 21N 114 20W
gin, Oreg., U.S.A. 118 45 37N 118 0W
gin, Texas, U.S.A. 117 30 21N 97 22W
gon, Mt. 90 1 10N 34 30 E
ase 73 8 21 S 130 48 E
da 117 33 56N 103 41W
kón, Mt. 45 38 18N 22 45 E
n Pelin 43 42 40N 23 36 E
sabethville = Lubumbashi 91 11 40 S 27 28 E
sta 57 46 16N 44 14 E
zabeth, Austral. 97 34 42 S 138 41 E
zabeth, U.S.A. 114 40 37N 74 12W
zabeth City 115 36 18N 76 16W
zabethton 115 36 20N 82 13W
zabethtown, Ky., U.S.A. 114 37 40N 85 54W
zabethtown, N.Y., U.S.A. 113 44 13N 73 36W
zabethtown, Pa., U.S.A. 113 40 8N 76 36W
zondo 32 43 12N 1 30W
k 28 53 50N 22 21 E
k → 28 53 41N 22 28 E
k City 117 35 25N 99 25W
k Island Nat. Park 108 53 35N 112 59W
k Lake 106 47 40N 80 25W
k Point 109 53 54N 110 55W
k River, Idaho, U.S.A. 118 46 50N 116 8W
k River, Minn., U.S.A. 116 45 17N 93 34W
khart, Ind., U.S.A. 114 41 42N 85 55W
khart, Kans., U.S.A. 117 37 3N 101 54W
khorn 109 49 59N 101 14W
khorn → 116 41 7N 98 15W
khotovo 57 43 19N 44 15 E
khovo 43 42 10N 26 40 E
kin 115 36 17N 80 50W
kins 114 38 53N 79 53W
ko, Can. 108 49 20N 115 10W
ko, U.S.A. 118 40 50N 115 50W
ef Ringnes I. 4 78 30N 102 2W
en, Mt. 119 38 4N 110 56W
endale 116 46 3N 98 30W
ensburg 118 47 0N 120 30W
enville 114 41 42N 74 23W
ery, Mt. 99 37 28 S 148 47 E
esmere I. 4 79 30N 80 0W
esworth Land 5 76 0 S 89 0W
ice Is. = Tuvalu ■ 94 8 0 S 176 0 E
inwood 116 38 27N 98 37W
iot 93 31 22 S 27 48 E
iot Lake 106 46 25N 82 35W
is 116 39 0N 99 39W
isville 117 31 38N 89 12W
on 14 57 21N 2 5W
ore = Eluru 70 16 48N 81 8 E
s → 108 57 18N 111 40W
sworth 116 38 47N 98 15W
sworth Land 5 76 0 S 89 0W
sworth Mts. 5 78 30 S 85 0W
wangen 25 48 57N 10 9 E
wood City 114 40 52N 80 19W
n 25 46 54N 9 10 E
na, Can. 109 49 52N 95 55W
na, U.S.A. 118 47 0N 123 30 E
nalı 64 36 44N 29 56 E
nhurst 114 41 52N 87 58W
nina 85 5 5N 1 21W
nira, Can. 112 43 36N 80 33W
nira, U.S.A. 114 42 8N 76 49W
nore 99 36 30 S 144 37 E
nshorn 24 53 44N 9 40 E
nvale 112 44 35N 79 52W
e 20 42 36N 2 58 E
ra 112 43 41N 80 26W
s 45 36 46N 22 43 E
y 119 32 46N 111 33W
yes 19 48 6N 6 36 E
ose 109 51 12N 108 0W
as 106 48 32N 82 55W
inore, Cal., U.S.A. 119 33 40N 117 15W
inore, Utah, U.S.A. 119 38 40N 112 2W
pe 24 51 10N 8 1 E
ter → 24 51 25N 11 57 E
erwerda 24 51 27N 13 32 E
ham 101 39 26 S 174 19 E
on 57 49 5N 46 52 E
ru 70 16 48N 81 8 E
as 31 38 50N 7 10W
Elven 18 47 44N 2 36W
Elverum 47 60 53N 11 34 E
Elvo → 38 45 23N 8 21 E
Elvran 47 63 24N 11 3 E
Elwood, Ind., U.S.A. 114 40 20N 85 50W
Elwood, Nebr., U.S.A. 116 40 38N 99 51W
Ely, U.K. 13 52 24N 0 16 E
Ely, Minn., U.S.A. 116 47 54N 91 52W
Ely, Nev., U.S.A. 118 39 10N 114 50W
Elyashiv 62 32 23N 34 55 E
Elyria 114 41 22N 82 8W
Elyrus 45 35 15N 23 45 E
Elz → 25 48 21N 7 45 E
Emådalen 48 61 20N 14 44 E
Emba 58 48 50N 58 8 E
Emba → 58 45 25N 52 30 E
Embarcación 124 23 10 S 64 0W
Embarras Portage 109 58 27N 111 28W
Embóna 45 36 13N 27 51 E
Embrun 21 44 34N 6 30 E
Embu 90 0 32 S 37 38 E
Embu □ 90 0 30 S 37 35 E
Emden 24 53 22N 7 12 E
'Emeq Yizre'el 62 32 35N 35 12 E
Emerald 97 23 32 S 148 10 E
Emerson 109 49 0N 97 10W
Emery 119 38 59N 111 17W
Emery Park 119 32 10N 110 59W
Emi Koussi 83 20 0N 18 55 E
Emilia-Romagna □ 38 44 33N 10 40 E
Emilius, Mte. 38 45 41N 7 23 E
Eminabad 68 32 2N 74 8 E
Emine, Nos 43 42 40N 27 56 E
Emlenton 112 41 11N 79 41W
Emlichheim 24 52 37N 6 51 E
Emmaboda 49 56 37N 15 32 E
Emme → 25 47 0N 7 42 E
Emmeloord 16 52 44N 5 46 E
Emmen 16 52 48N 6 57 E
Emmendingen 25 48 7N 7 51 E
Emmental 25 47 0N 7 35 E
Emmerich 24 51 50N 6 12 E
Emmet 98 24 45 S 144 30 E
Emmetsburg 116 43 3N 94 40W
Emmett 118 43 51N 116 33W
Emöd 27 47 57N 20 47 E
Emona 43 42 43N 27 53 E
Empalme 120 28 1N 110 49W
Empangeni 93 28 50 S 31 52 E
Empedrado 124 28 0 S 58 46W
Emperor Seamount Chain 94 40 0N 170 0 E
Empoli 38 43 43N 10 57 E
Emporia, Kans., U.S.A. 116 38 25N 96 10W
Emporia, Va., U.S.A. 115 36 41N 77 32W
Emporium 114 41 30N 78 17W
Empress 109 50 57N 110 0W
Ems → 24 52 37N 9 26 E
Emsdale 112 45 32N 79 19W
Emsdetten 24 52 11N 7 31 E
Emu 76 43 40N 128 6 E
Emu Park 98 23 13 S 150 50 E
En Gedi 62 31 28N 35 25 E
En Gev 62 32 47N 35 38 E
En Harod 62 32 33N 35 22 E
'En Kerem 62 31 47N 35 6 E
En Nahud 87 12 45N 28 25 E
Enafors 48 63 17N 12 20 E
Enana 92 17 30 S 16 23 E
Enånger 48 61 30N 17 9 E
Enaratoli 73 3 55 S 136 21 E
Enard B. 14 58 5N 5 20W
Encantadas, Serra 125 30 40 S 53 0W
Encanto, C. 73 15 45N 121 38 E
Encarnación 125 27 15 S 55 50W
Encarnación de Diaz 120 21 30N 102 13W
Enchi 84 5 53N 2 48W
Encinal 117 28 3N 99 25W
Encino 119 34 38N 105 40W
Encounter B. 97 35 45 S 138 45 E
Endau 71 2 40N 103 38 E
Endau → 71 2 30N 103 30 E
Ende 73 8 45 S 121 40 E
Endeavour 109 52 10N 102 39W
Endeavour Str. 97 10 45 S 142 0 E
Endelave 49 55 46N 10 18 E
Enderbury I. 94 3 8 S 171 5W
Enderby 108 50 35N 119 10W
Enderby Land 5 66 0 S 53 0 E
Enderlin 116 46 37N 97 41W
Endicott, N.Y., U.S.A. 114 42 6N 76 2W
Endicott, Wash., U.S.A. 118 47 0N 117 45W
Endröd 27 46 55N 20 47 E
Enez 44 40 45N 26 5 E
Enfida 83 36 6N 10 28 E
Enfield 13 51 39N 0 4W
Engadin = Engiadina 25 46 51N 10 18 E
Engaño, C., Dom. Rep. 121 18 30N 68 20W
Engaño, C., Phil. 73 18 35N 122 23 E
Engelberg 25 46 48N 8 26 E
Engels 55 51 28N 46 6 E
Engemann L. 109 58 0N 106 55W
Enger 47 60 35N 10 20 E
Enggano 72 5 20 S 102 40 E
Enghien 16 50 37N 4 2 E
Engiadina 25 46 51N 10 18 E
Engil 82 33 12N 4 32W
Engkilili 72 1 3N 111 42 E
England 117 34 30N 91 58W
England □ 11 53 0N 2 0W
Englee 107 50 45N 56 5W
Englehart 106 47 49N 79 52W
Engler L. 109 59 8N 106 52W
Englewood, Colo., U.S.A. 116 39 40N 105 0W
Englewood, Kans., U.S.A. 117 37 7N 99 59W
Englewood, N.J., U.S.A. 113 40 54N 73 59W
English → 109 50 35N 93 30W
English Bazar 69 24 58N 88 10 E
English Channel 18 50 0N 2 0W
English River 106 49 14N 91 0W
Enid 117 36 26N 97 52W
Enipévs → 44 39 22N 22 17 E
Eniwetok 94 11 30N 162 15 E
Enkeldoorn 91 19 2 S 30 52 E
Enkhuizen 16 52 42N 5 17 E
Enköping 48 59 37N 17 4 E
Enna 41 37 34N 14 15 E
Ennadai 109 61 8N 100 53W
Ennadai L. 109 61 0N 101 0W
Ennedi 81 17 15N 22 0 E
Enngonia 99 29 21 S 145 50 E
Ennis, Ireland 15 52 51N 8 59W
Ennis, Mont., U.S.A. 118 45 20N 111 42W
Ennis, Texas, U.S.A. 117 32 15N 96 40W
Enniscorthy 15 52 30N 6 35W
Enniskillen 15 54 20N 7 40W
Ennistimon 15 52 56N 9 18W
Enns 26 48 12N 14 28 E
Enns → 26 48 14N 14 32 E
Enontekiö 50 68 23N 23 37 E
Enping 77 22 16N 112 21 E
Enriquillo, L. 121 18 20N 72 5W
Enschede 16 52 13N 6 53 E
Ensenada, Argent. 124 34 55 S 57 55W
Ensenada, Mexico 120 31 50N 116 50W
Enshi 77 30 18N 109 29 E
Ensisheim 19 47 50N 7 20 E
Entebbe 90 0 4N 32 28 E
Enterprise, Can. 108 60 47N 115 45W
Enterprise, Oreg., U.S.A. 118 45 30N 117 18W
Enterprise, Utah, U.S.A. 119 37 37N 113 36W
Entre Ríos, Boliv. 124 21 30 S 64 25W
Entre Ríos, Mozam. 91 14 57 S 37 20 E
Entre Ríos □ 124 30 30 S 58 30W
Entrecasteaux, Pt. d' 96 34 50 S 115 56 E
Entrepeñas, Pantano de 32 40 34N 2 42W
Enugu 85 6 20N 7 30 E
Enugu Ezike 85 7 0N 7 29 E
Enumclaw 118 47 12N 122 0W
Envermeières 18 49 54N 1 16 E
Envermeu 18 49 53N 1 15 E
Enz → 25 49 1N 9 6 E
Enza → 38 44 54N 10 31 E
Eólie, I. 41 38 30N 14 50 E
Epanomí 44 40 25N 22 59 E
Epe, Neth. 16 52 21N 5 59 E
Epe, Nigeria 85 6 36N 3 59 E
Épernay 19 49 3N 3 56 E
Épernon 19 48 35N 1 40 E
Ephesus, Turkey 45 37 50N 27 33 E
Ephesus, Turkey 64 38 0N 27 19 E
Ephraim 118 39 21N 111 37W
Ephrata 118 47 20N 119 32W
Epidaurus Limera 45 36 46N 23 0 E
Épila 32 41 36N 1 17W
Épinac-les-Mines 19 46 59N 4 31 E
Épinal 19 48 10N 6 27 E
Episcopia Bihorului 46 47 12N 21 55 E
Epitálion 45 37 37N 21 30 E
Epping 13 51 42N 0 8 E
Epukiro 92 21 40 S 19 9 E
Equatorial Guinea ■ 88 2 0 S 8 0 E
Er Rahad 87 12 45N 30 32 E
Er Rif 82 35 1N 4 1W
Er Roseires 87 11 55N 34 30 E
Er Yébigué 83 22 30N 17 30 E
Erandol 68 20 56N 75 20 E
Erāwadī Myit = Irrawaddy → 67 15 50N 95 6 E
Erba, Italy 38 45 49N 9 12 E
Erba, Sudan 86 19 5N 36 51 E
Ercha 59 69 45N 147 20 E
Erciyaş Dağı 64 38 30N 35 30 E
Erdao Jiang → 76 43 0N 127 0 E
Erding 25 48 18N 11 55 E
Erdre → 18 47 13N 1 32W
Erebus, Mt. 5 77 35 S 167 0 E
Erechim 125 27 35 S 52 15W
Ereğli, Turkey 64 41 15N 31 30 E
Ereğli, Turkey 64 37 31N 34 4 E
Erei, Monti 41 37 20N 14 20 E
Erenhot 76 43 48N 111 59 E
Eresma → 30 41 26N 40 45W
Eressós 45 39 11N 25 57 E
Erfenis Dam 92 28 30 S 26 50 E
Erfjord 47 59 20N 6 14 E
Erfoud 82 31 30N 4 15W
Erft → 24 51 11N 6 44 E
Erfurt 24 50 58N 11 2 E
Erfurt □ 24 51 10N 10 30 E
Ergani 64 38 17N 39 49 E
Ergene → 43 41 1N 26 22 E
Ergeni Vozyshennost 57 47 0N 44 0 E
Ergli 54 56 54N 25 38 E
Ergun Zuoqi 76 50 47N 121 31 E
Eria → 30 42 3N 5 44W
Eriba 87 16 40N 36 10 E
Eriboll, L. 14 58 28N 4 41W
Érice 40 38 4N 12 34 E
Erie 114 42 10N 80 7W
Erie Canal 112 43 15N 78 0W
Erie, L. 112 42 15N 81 0W
Erieau 112 42 16N 81 57W
Erigavo 63 10 35N 47 20 E
Erikoúsa 44 39 55N 19 14 E
Eriksdale 109 50 52N 98 7W
Erikslund 48 62 31N 15 54 E
Erímanthos 45 37 57N 21 50 E
Erimo-misaki 74 41 50N 143 15 E
Erithraí 45 38 13N 23 20 E
Eritrea □ 87 14 0N 41 0 E
Erjas → 31 39 40N 7 1W
Erlangen 25 49 35N 11 0 E
Ermelo, Neth. 16 52 18N 5 35 E
Ermelo, S. Afr. 93 26 31 S 29 59 E
Ermenak 64 36 38N 33 0 E
Ermióni 45 37 23N 23 15 E
Ermoúpolis = Síros 45 37 28N 24 57 E
Ernakulam = Cochin 70 9 59N 76 22 E
Erne → 15 54 30N 8 16W
Erne, Lough 15 54 26N 7 46W
Ernée 18 48 18N 0 56W
Ernstberg 25 50 14N 6 46 E
Erode 70 11 24N 77 45 E
Eromanga 99 26 40 S 143 11 E
Erongo 92 21 39 S 15 58 E
Erquy 18 48 38N 2 29W
Erquy, Cap d' 18 48 39N 2 29W
Erramala Hills 70 15 30N 78 15 E
Errer → 87 7 32N 42 35 E
Errigal, Mt. 15 55 2N 8 8W
Erris Hd. 15 54 19N 10 0W
Erseka 44 40 22N 20 40 E
Erskine 116 47 37N 96 0W
Erstein 19 48 25N 7 38 E
Ertil 55 51 55N 40 50 E
Ertvågøy 47 63 13N 8 26 E
Eruwa 85 7 33N 3 26 E
Ervy-le-Châtel 19 48 2N 3 55 E
Erwin 115 36 10N 82 28W
Erzgebirge 24 50 25N 13 0 E
Erzin 59 50 15N 95 10 E
Erzincan 64 39 46N 39 30 E
Erzurum 64 39 57N 41 15 E
Es Sahrâ' Esh Sharqîya 86 26 0N 33 30 E
Es Sînâ' 86 29 0N 34 0 E
Es Sûkî 87 13 20N 33 58 E
Esambo 90 3 48 S 23 30 E
Esan-Misaki 74 41 40N 141 10 E
Esbjerg 49 55 29N 8 29 E
Escalante 119 37 47N 111 37W
Escalante → 119 37 17N 110 53W
Escalón 120 26 46N 104 20W
Escalona 30 40 9N 4 29W
Escambia → 115 30 32N 87 15W
Escanaba 114 45 44N 87 5W
Esch-sur-Alzette 16 49 32N 6 0 E
Eschallens 25 46 39N 6 38 E
Eschede 24 52 44N 10 13 E
Eschwege 24 51 10N 10 3 E
Eschweiler 24 50 49N 6 14 E
Escobal 120 9 6N 80 1W
Escondido 119 33 9N 117 4W
Escuinapa 120 22 50N 105 50W
Escuintla 120 14 20N 90 48W
Eséka 85 3 41N 10 44 E
Esens 24 53 40N 7 35 E
Esera → 32 42 6N 0 15 E
Eşfahān 65 33 0N 53 0 E
Esgueva → 30 41 40N 4 43W
Esh Sham = Dimashq 64 33 30N 36 18 E
Esh Shamâlîya □ 86 19 0N 29 0 E
Eshowe 93 28 50 S 31 30 E
Eshta' ol 62 31 47N 35 0 E
Esiama 84 4 56N 2 25W
Esino → 39 43 39N 13 22 E
Esk →, Dumfries, U.K. 14 54 58N 3 4W
Esk →, N. Yorks., U.K. 12 54 27N 0 36W
Eskifjörður 50 65 3N 13 55W
Eskilstuna 48 59 22N 16 32 E
Eskimo Pt. 109 61 10N 94 15W
Eskişehir 64 39 50N 30 35 E
Esla → 30 41 29N 6 3W
Esla, Pantano del 30 41 29N 6 3W
Eslöv 49 55 50N 13 20 E
Esmeralda, La 124 22 16 S 62 33W
Esmeraldas 126 1 0N 79 40W
Espalion 20 44 32N 2 47 E
Espalmador, I. 33 38 47N 1 26 E
Espanola 106 46 15N 81 46W
Espardell, I. del 33 38 48N 1 29 E
Esparraguera 32 41 33N 1 52 E
Espejo 31 37 40N 4 34W
Esperance 96 33 45 S 121 55 E
Esperance B. 96 33 48 S 121 55 E
Esperanza 124 31 29 S 61 3W
Espéraza 20 42 56N 2 14 E
Espevær 47 59 35N 5 7 E
Espichel, C. 31 38 22N 9 16W
Espiel 31 38 11N 5 1W
Espigão, Serra do 125 26 35 S 50 30W
Espinal 126 4 9N 74 53W
Espinhaço, Serra do 127 17 30 S 43 30W
Espinho 30 41 1N 8 38W
Espinilho, Serra do 125 28 30 S 55 0W
Espinosa de los Monteros 30 43 5N 3 34W
Espírito Santo □ 127 20 0 S 40 45W
Espíritu Santo, B. del 120 19 15N 87 0W
Espíritu Santo, I. 120 24 30N 110 23W
Espluga de Francolí 32 41 24N 1 7 E
Espuña, Sierra 33 37 51N 1 35W
Espungabera 93 20 29 S 32 45 E
Esquel 128 42 55 S 71 20W
Esquina 124 30 0 S 59 30W
Essaouira (Mogador) 82 31 32N 9 48W
Essarts, Les 18 46 47N 1 12W
Essebie 90 2 58N 30 40 E
Essen, Belg. 16 51 28N 4 28 E
Essen, Ger. 24 51 28N 6 59 E
Essequibo → 126 6 50N 58 30W
Essex, Can. 112 42 10N 82 49W
Essex, U.S.A. 113 44 17N 73 21W
Essex □ 13 51 48N 0 30 E
Esslingen 25 48 43N 9 19 E
Essonne □ 19 48 30N 2 20 E
Essvik 48 62 18N 17 24 E
Estaca, Pta. del 30 43 46N 7 42W
Estadilla 32 42 4N 0 16 E
Estados, I. de Los 128 54 40 S 64 30W
Estagel 20 42 47N 2 40 E
Estância 127 11 16 S 37 26W
Estancia 119 34 50N 106 1W
Estarreja 30 40 45N 8 35W
Estats, Pic d' 32 42 40N 1 24 E
Estcourt 93 28 58 S 29 53 E
Este 39 45 12N 11 40 E
Esteban 30 43 33N 6 5W
Estelí 121 13 9N 86 22W
Estella 32 42 40N 2 0W
Estelline, S.D., U.S.A. 116 44 39N 96 52W
Estelline, Texas, U.S.A. 117 34 35N 100 27W
Estena → 31 39 23N 4 44W
Estepa 31 37 17N 4 52W
Estepona 31 36 24N 5 7W
Esterhazy 109 50 37N 102 5W
Esternay 19 48 44N 3 33 E
Esterri de Aneu 32 42 38N 1 5 E
Estevan 109 49 10N 102 59W

Name	Page	Lat.	Long.
Estevan Group	**108**	53 3N	129 38W
Estherville	**116**	43 25N	94 50W
Estissac	**19**	48 16N	3 48 E
Eston	**109**	51 8N	108 40W
Estonian S.S.R. □	**54**	58 30N	25 30 E
Estoril	**31**	38 42N	9 23W
Estouk	**85**	18 14N	1 2 E
Estrada, La	**30**	42 43N	8 27W
Estrêla, Serra da	**30**	40 10N	7 45W
Estrella	**33**	38 25N	3 35W
Estremoz	**31**	38 51N	7 39W
Estrondo, Serra do	**127**	7 20S	48 0W
Esztergom	**27**	47 47N	18 44 E
Et Tidra	**84**	19 45N	16 20W
Et Ţira	**62**	32 14N	34 56 E
Étables-sur-Mer	**18**	48 38N	2 51W
Etah	**68**	27 35N	78 40 E
Étain	**19**	49 13N	5 38 E
Etamamu	**107**	50 18N	59 59W
Étampes	**19**	48 26N	2 10 E
Étang	**19**	46 52N	4 10 E
Etanga	**92**	17 55S	13 00 E
Étaples	**19**	50 30N	1 39 E
Etawah	**68**	26 48N	79 6 E
Etawah →	**115**	34 20N	84 15W
Etawney L.	**109**	57 50N	96 50W
Eteh	**85**	7 2N	7 28 E
Ethel, Oued el →	**82**	28 31N	3 37W
Ethelbert	**109**	51 32N	100 25W
Ethiopia ■	**63**	8 0N	40 0 E
Ethiopian Highlands	**78**	10 0N	37 0 E
Etive, L.	**14**	56 30N	5 12W
Etna, Mt.	**41**	37 45N	15 0 E
Etne	**47**	59 40N	5 56 E
Etoile	**91**	11 33S	27 30 E
Etolin I.	**108**	56 5N	132 20W
Etosha Pan	**92**	18 40S	16 30 E
Etowah	**115**	35 20N	84 30W
Étrépagny	**18**	49 18N	1 36 E
Étretat	**18**	49 42N	0 12 E
Étroits, Les	**107**	47 24N	68 54W
Etropole	**43**	42 50N	24 0 E
Ettlingen	**25**	48 58N	8 25 E
Ettrick Water	**14**	55 31N	2 55W
Etuku	**90**	3 42S	25 45 E
Etzatlán	**120**	20 48N	104 5W
Eu	**18**	50 3N	1 26 E
Euabalong West	**100**	33 3S	146 23 E
Euboea = Évvoia	**45**	38 40N	23 40 E
Eucla Basin	**96**	31 19S	126 9 E
Euclid	**114**	41 32N	81 31W
Eucumbene, L.	**99**	36 2S	148 40 E
Eudora	**117**	33 5N	91 17W
Eufaula, Ala., U.S.A.	**115**	31 55N	85 11W
Eufaula, Okla., U.S.A.	**117**	35 20N	95 33W
Eufaula, L.	**117**	35 15N	95 28W
Eugene	**118**	44 0N	123 8W
Eugenia, Punta	**120**	27 50N	115 5W
Eugowra	**99**	33 22S	148 24 E
Eulo	**99**	28 10S	145 3 E
Eunice, La., U.S.A.	**117**	30 35N	92 28W
Eunice, N. Mex., U.S.A.	**117**	32 30N	103 10W
Eupen	**16**	50 37N	6 3 E
Euphrates = Furāt, Nahr al →	**64**	31 0N	47 25 E
Eure □	**18**	49 6N	1 0 E
Eure →	**18**	49 18N	1 12 E
Eure-et-Loir □	**18**	48 22N	1 30 E
Eureka, Can.	**4**	80 0N	85 56W
Eureka, Calif., U.S.A.	**118**	40 50N	124 0W
Eureka, Kans., U.S.A.	**117**	37 50N	96 20W
Eureka, Mont., U.S.A.	**118**	48 53N	115 6W
Eureka, Nev., U.S.A.	**118**	39 32N	116 2W
Eureka, S.D., U.S.A.	**116**	45 49N	99 38W
Eureka, Utah, U.S.A.	**118**	40 0N	112 9W
Euroa	**99**	36 44S	145 35 E
Europa, Picos de	**30**	43 10N	4 49W
Europa Pt. = Europa, Pta. de	**31**	36 3N	5 21W
Europa, Pta. de	**31**	36 3N	5 21W
Europe	**8**	50 0N	20 0 E
Europoort	**16**	51 57N	4 10 E
Euskirchen	**24**	50 40N	6 45 E
Eustis	**115**	28 54N	81 36W
Eutin	**24**	54 7N	10 38 E
Eutsuk L.	**108**	53 20N	126 45W
Eval	**62**	32 15N	35 15 E
Evale	**92**	16 33S	15 44 E
Evanger	**47**	60 39N	6 7 E
Evans	**116**	40 25N	104 43W
Evans Head	**99**	29 7S	153 27 E
Evans L.	**106**	50 50N	77 0W
Evans Mills	**113**	44 6N	75 48W
Evans Pass	**116**	41 0N	105 35W
Evanston, Ill., U.S.A.	**114**	42 0N	87 40W
Evanston, Wyo., U.S.A.	**118**	41 10N	111 0W
Evansville, Ind., U.S.A.	**114**	38 0N	87 35W
Evansville, Wis., U.S.A.	**116**	42 47N	89 18W
Évaux-les-Bains	**20**	46 12N	2 29 E
Eveleth	**116**	47 29N	92 46W
Even Yahuda	**62**	32 16N	34 53 E
Evensk	**59**	62 12N	159 30 E
Evenstad	**47**	61 25N	11 7 E
Everard, L.	**96**	31 30S	135 0 E
Everard Ras.	**96**	27 5S	132 28 E
Everest, Mt.	**69**	28 5N	86 58 E
Everett, Pa., U.S.A.	**112**	40 2N	78 24W
Everett, Wash., U.S.A.	**118**	48 0N	122 10W
Everglades, Fla., U.S.A.	**115**	26 0N	80 30W
Everglades, Fla., U.S.A.	**115**	25 52N	81 23W
Everglades Nat. Park.	**115**	25 27N	80 53W
Evergreen	**115**	31 28N	86 55W
Everson	**118**	48 57N	122 22W
Evesham	**13**	52 6N	1 57W
Evian-les-Bains	**21**	46 24N	6 35 E
Evinayong	**88**	1 26N	10 35 E
Évinos →	**45**	38 27N	21 40 E
Evisa	**21**	42 15N	8 48 E
Evje	**47**	58 36N	7 51 E
Évora	**31**	38 33N	7 57W
Évora □	**31**	38 33N	7 50W
Évreux	**18**	49 0N	1 8 E
Evritania □	**45**	39 5N	21 30 E
Évron	**18**	48 10N	0 24W
Évros □	**44**	41 10N	26 0 E
Evrótas →	**45**	36 50N	22 40 E
Évvoia	**45**	38 30N	24 0 E
Évvoia □	**45**	38 40N	23 40 E
Ewe, L.	**14**	57 49N	5 38W
Ewing	**116**	42 18N	98 22W
Ewo	**88**	0 48S	14 45 E
Exaltación	**126**	13 10S	65 20W
Excelsior Springs	**116**	39 20N	94 10W
Excideuil	**20**	45 20N	1 4 E
Exe →	**13**	50 38N	3 27W
Exeter, Can.	**112**	43 21N	81 29W
Exeter, U.K.	**13**	50 43N	3 31W
Exeter, Calif., U.S.A.	**119**	36 17N	119 9W
Exeter, N.H., U.S.A.	**113**	43 0N	70 58W
Exeter, Nebr., U.S.A.	**116**	40 43N	97 30W
Exmes	**18**	48 45N	0 10 E
Exmoor	**13**	51 10N	3 59W
Exmouth, Austral.	**96**	21 54S	114 10 E
Exmouth, U.K.	**13**	50 37N	3 26W
Exmouth G.	**96**	22 15S	114 15 E
Expedition Range	**97**	24 30S	149 12 E
Extremadura	**31**	39 30N	6 5W
Exuma Sound	**121**	24 30N	76 20W
Eyasi, L.	**90**	3 30S	35 0 E
Eyeberry L.	**109**	63 8N	104 43W
Eyemouth	**14**	55 53N	2 5W
Eygurande	**20**	45 40N	2 26 E
Eyjafjörður	**50**	66 15N	18 30W
Eymet	**20**	44 40N	0 25 E
Eymoutiers	**20**	45 40N	1 45 E
Eyrarbakki	**50**	63 52N	21 9W
Eyre	**96**	32 15S	126 18 E
Eyre Cr. →	**97**	26 40S	139 0 E
Eyre, L.	**97**	29 30S	137 26 E
Eyre Mts.	**101**	45 25S	168 25 E
Eyre (North), L.	**97**	28 30S	137 20 E
Eyre Pen.	**96**	33 30S	137 17 E
Eyre (South), L.	**99**	29 18S	137 25 E
Eyzies, Les	**20**	44 56N	1 1 E
Ez Zeidab	**86**	17 25N	33 55 E
Ezcaray	**32**	42 19N	3 0W
Ezine	**44**	39 48N	26 12 E
F			
Fabens	**119**	31 30N	106 8W
Fåborg	**49**	55 6N	10 15 E
Fabriano	**39**	43 20N	12 52 E
Făcăeni	**46**	44 32N	27 53 E
Facatativá	**126**	4 49N	74 22W
Fachi	**80**	18 6N	11 34 E
Facture	**20**	44 39N	0 58W
Fada	**81**	17 13N	21 34 E
Fada-n-Gourma	**85**	12 10N	0 30 E
Fadd	**27**	46 28N	18 49 E
Faddeyevskiy, Ostrov	**59**	76 0N	150 0 E
Fāḑilī	**64**	26 55N	49 10 E
Fadlab	**86**	17 42N	34 2 E
Faenza	**39**	44 17N	11 53 E
Fafa	**85**	15 22N	0 48 E
Fafe	**30**	41 27N	8 11W
Fagam	**85**	11 1N	10 1 E
Făgăras	**46**	45 48N	24 58 E
Făgăras, Munţii	**46**	45 40N	24 40 E
Fågelsjö	**48**	61 50N	14 35 E
Fagerhult	**49**	57 8N	15 40 E
Fagersta	**48**	60 1N	15 46 E
Făget	**46**	45 52N	22 10 E
Făget, Munţii	**46**	47 40N	23 10 E
Fagnano Castello	**41**	39 31N	16 4 E
Fagnano, L.	**128**	54 30S	68 0W
Fagnières	**19**	48 58N	4 20 E
Fahraj	**65**	29 0N	59 0 E
Fahūd	**65**	22 18N	56 28 E
Fair Hd.	**15**	55 14N	6 10W
Fair Isle	**11**	59 30N	1 40W
Fairbank	**119**	31 44N	110 12W
Fairbanks	**104**	64 50N	147 50W
Fairbury	**116**	40 5N	97 5W
Fairfax	**117**	36 37N	96 45W
Fairfield, Austral.	**100**	33 53S	150 57 E
Fairfield, Ala., U.S.A.	**115**	33 30N	87 0W
Fairfield, Calif., U.S.A.	**118**	38 14N	122 1W
Fairfield, Conn., U.S.A.	**113**	41 8N	73 16W
Fairfield, Idaho, U.S.A.	**118**	43 21N	114 46W
Fairfield, Ill., U.S.A.	**114**	38 20N	88 20W
Fairfield, Iowa, U.S.A.	**116**	41 0N	91 58W
Fairfield, Mont., U.S.A.	**118**	47 40N	112 0W
Fairfield, Texas, U.S.A.	**117**	31 40N	96 0W
Fairford	**109**	51 37N	98 38W
Fairhope	**115**	30 35N	87 50W
Fairlie	**101**	44 5S	170 49 E
Fairmont, Minn., U.S.A.	**116**	43 37N	94 30W
Fairmont, W. Va., U.S.A.	**114**	39 29N	80 10W
Fairmont Hot Springs	**108**	50 20N	115 56W
Fairplay	**119**	39 9N	105 40W
Fairport, N.Y., U.S.A.	**114**	43 8N	77 29W
Fairport, Ohio, U.S.A.	**112**	41 45N	81 17W
Fairview, Austral.	**98**	15 31S	144 17 E
Fairview, Can.	**108**	56 5N	118 25W
Fairview, N. Dak., U.S.A.	**116**	47 49N	104 7W
Fairview, Okla., U.S.A.	**117**	36 19N	98 30W
Fairview, Utah, U.S.A.	**118**	39 50N	111 0W
Fairweather, Mt.	**104**	58 55N	137 45W
Faith	**116**	45 2N	102 4W
Faizabad	**69**	26 45N	82 10 E
Faizpur	**68**	21 14N	75 49 E
Fajardo	**121**	18 20N	65 39W
Fakfak	**73**	3 0S	132 15 E
Fakiya	**43**	42 10N	27 6 E
Fakobli	**84**	7 23N	7 23W
Fakse	**49**	55 15N	12 8 E
Fakse B.	**49**	55 11N	12 15 E
Fakse Ladeplads	**49**	55 11N	12 9 E
Faku	**76**	42 32N	123 21 E
Falaise	**18**	48 54N	0 12W
Falakrón Óros	**44**	41 15N	23 58 E
Falam	**67**	23 0N	93 45 E
Falces	**32**	42 24N	1 48W
Fălciu	**46**	46 17N	28 7 E
Falcon, C.	**82**	35 50N	0 50W
Falcon Dam	**117**	26 50N	99 20W
Falconara Marittima	**39**	43 37N	13 23 E
Falconer	**112**	42 7N	79 13W
Faléa	**84**	12 16N	11 17W
Falenki	**55**	58 22N	51 35 E
Faleshty	**56**	47 32N	27 44 E
Falfurrias	**117**	27 14N	98 8W
Falher	**108**	55 44N	117 15W
Falkenberg, Ger.	**24**	51 34N	13 13 E
Falkenberg, Sweden	**49**	56 54N	12 30 E
Falkensee	**24**	52 35N	13 6 E
Falkenstein	**24**	50 27N	12 24 E
Falkirk	**14**	56 0N	3 47W
Falkland Is.	**128**	51 30S	59 0W
Falkland Is. Dependency □	**5**	57 0S	40 0W
Falkland Sd.	**128**	52 0S	60 0W
Falkonéra	**45**	36 50N	23 52 E
Falköping	**49**	58 12N	13 33 E
Fall Brook	**119**	33 25N	117 12W
Fall River	**114**	41 45N	71 5W
Fall River Mills	**118**	41 1N	121 30W
Fallon, Mont., U.S.A.	**116**	46 52N	105 8W
Fallon, Nev., U.S.A.	**118**	39 31N	118 51W
Falls City, Nebr., U.S.A.	**116**	40 0N	95 40W
Falls City, Oreg., U.S.A.	**118**	44 54N	123 29W
Falls Creek	**112**	41 8N	78 49W
Falmouth, Jamaica	**121**	18 30N	77 40W
Falmouth, U.K.	**13**	50 9N	5 5W
Falmouth, U.S.A.	**114**	38 40N	84 20W
False Divi Pt.	**70**	15 43N	80 50 E
Falset	**32**	41 7N	0 50 E
Falso, C.	**121**	15 12N	83 21W
Falster	**49**	54 45N	11 55 E
Falsterbo	**49**	55 23N	12 50 E
Fălticeni	**46**	47 21N	26 20 E
Falun	**48**	60 37N	15 37 E
Famagusta	**64**	35 8N	33 55 E
Famatina, Sierra, de	**124**	27 30S	68 0W
Family L.	**109**	51 54N	95 27W
Fan Xian	**76**	35 55N	115 38 E
Fana, Mali	**84**	13 0N	6 56W
Fana, Norway	**47**	60 16N	5 20 E
Fanárion	**44**	39 24N	21 47 E
Fandriana	**93**	20 14S	47 21 E
Fang Xian	**77**	32 3N	110 40 E
Fangchang	**77**	31 5N	118 4 E
Fangcheng	**77**	33 18N	112 59 E
Fangliao	**77**	22 22N	120 38 E
Fangzheng	**76**	49 50N	128 48 E
Fani i Madh →	**44**	41 56N	20 16 E
Fanjiatun	**76**	43 40N	125 0 E
Fannich, L.	**14**	57 40N	5 0W
• Fanning I.	**95**	3 51N	159 22W
Fanny Bay	**108**	49 27N	124 48W
Fanø	**49**	55 25N	8 25 E
Fano	**39**	43 50N	13 0 E
Fanshaw	**108**	57 11N	133 30W
Fao (Al Fāw)	**64**	30 0N	48 30 E
Faqirwali	**68**	29 27N	73 0 E
Fara in Sabina	**39**	42 13N	12 44 E
Faradje	**90**	3 50N	29 45 E
Faradofay	**93**	25 2S	47 0 E
Farafangana	**93**	22 49S	47 50 E
Farâfra, El Wâhât el-	**86**	27 15N	28 20 E
Farāh	**65**	32 20N	62 7 E
Farāh □	**65**	32 25N	62 10 E
Farahalana	**93**	14 26S	50 10 E
Faraid, Gebel	**86**	23 33N	35 19 E
Faramana	**84**	11 56N	4 45W
Faranah	**84**	10 3N	10 45W
Farasān, Jazā'ir	**63**	16 45N	41 55 E
Faratsiho	**93**	19 24S	46 57 E
Fardes →	**33**	37 35N	3 0W
Fareham	**13**	50 52N	1 11W
Farewell, C.	**101**	40 29S	172 43 E
Farewell C. = Farvel, K.	**4**	59 48N	43 55W
Fargo	**116**	46 52N	96 40W
Fari'a →	**62**	32 12N	35 27 E
Faribault	**116**	44 15N	93 19W
Faridkot	**68**	30 44N	74 45 E
Faridpur	**69**	23 15N	89 55 E
Fārila	**48**	61 48N	15 50 E
Farim	**84**	12 27N	15 9W
Farīmān	**65**	35 40N	59 49 E
Farina	**99**	30 3S	138 15 E
Faringe	**48**	59 55N	18 7 E
Fâriskûr	**86**	31 20N	31 43 E
Farmakonisi	**45**	37 17N	27 8 E
Farmerville	**117**	32 48N	92 23W
Farmington, N. Mex., U.S.A.	**119**	36 45N	108 28W
Farmington, N.H., U.S.A.	**113**	43 25N	71 7W
Farmington, Utah, U.S.A.	**118**	41 0N	111 12W
Farmington →	**113**	41 51N	72 38W
Farmville	**114**	37 19N	78 22W
Farnborough	**13**	51 17N	0 46W
Farne Is.	**12**	55 38N	1 37W
Farnham	**113**	45 17N	72 59W
Faro, Brazil	**127**	2 10S	56 39W
Faro, Port.	**31**	37 2N	7 55W
Faro □	**31**	37 12N	8 10W
Faroe Is.	**8**	62 0N	7 0W
Farquhar, C.	**96**	23 50S	113 36 E
Farrar →	**14**	57 30N	4 30W
Farrars, Cr. →	**98**	25 35S	140 43 E
Farrāshband	**65**	28 57N	52 5 E
Farrell	**114**	41 13N	80 29W
Farrell Flat	**99**	33 48S	138 48 E
Farrukhabad-cum-Fatehgarh	**69**	27 30N	79 32 E
Fars □	**65**	29 30N	55 0 E
Fársala	**44**	39 17N	22 23 E
Farsø	**49**	56 46N	9 19 E
Farsund	**47**	58 5N	6 55 E
Fartak, Râs	**64**	28 5N	34 34 E
Fartura, Serra da	**125**	26 21S	52 52W
Faru	**85**	12 48N	6 12 E
Farum	**49**	55 49N	12 21 E
Farvel, Kap	**4**	59 48N	43 55W
Farwell	**117**	34 25N	103 0W
Faryab □	**65**	36 0N	65 0 E
Fasā	**65**	29 0N	53 39 E
Fasano	**41**	40 50N	17 20
Fashoda	**87**	9 50N	32 2
Fastnet Rock	**15**	51 22N	9 37
Fastov	**54**	50 7N	29 57
Fatagar, Tanjung	**73**	2 46S	131 57
Fatehgarh	**69**	27 25N	79 35
Fatehpur, Raj., India	**68**	28 0N	74 40
Fatehpur, Ut. P., India	**69**	25 56N	81 13
Fatesh	**55**	52 8N	35 57
Fatick	**84**	14 19N	16 27
Fatima	**107**	47 24N	61 53
Fátima	**31**	39 37N	8 39
Fatoya	**84**	11 37N	9 10
Faucille, Col de la	**21**	46 22N	6 2
Faucilles, Monts	**19**	48 5N	5 50
Faulkton	**116**	45 4N	99 8
Faulquemont	**19**	49 3N	6 36
Fauquembergues	**19**	50 36N	2 5
Făurei	**46**	45 6N	27 19
Fauresmith	**92**	29 44S	25 17
Fauske	**50**	67 17N	15 25
Fåvang	**47**	61 27N	10 11
Favara	**40**	37 19N	13 39
Favignana	**40**	37 56N	12 18
Favignana, I.	**40**	37 56N	12 18
Favone	**21**	41 47N	9 26
Favourable Lake	**106**	52 50N	93 39
Fawn →	**106**	52 22N	88 20
Faxaflói	**50**	64 29N	23 0
Faya-Largeau	**81**	17 58N	19 6
Fayd	**64**	27 1N	42 52
Fayence	**21**	43 38N	6 42
Fayette, Ala., U.S.A.	**115**	33 40N	87 50
Fayette, Mo., U.S.A.	**116**	39 10N	92 40
Fayette, La	**114**	40 22N	86 52
Fayetteville, Ark., U.S.A.	**117**	36 0N	94 5
Fayetteville, N.C., U.S.A.	**115**	35 0N	78 58
Fayetteville, Tenn., U.S.A.	**115**	35 8N	86 30
Fayón	**32**	41 15N	0 20
Fazilka	**68**	30 27N	74 2
Fazilpur	**68**	29 18N	70 29
Fdérik	**80**	22 40N	12 45
Feale →	**15**	52 26N	9 40
Fear, C.	**115**	33 51N	78 0
Feather →	**118**	38 47N	121 36
Featherston	**101**	41 6S	175 20
Featherstone	**91**	18 42S	30 55
Fécamp	**18**	49 45N	0 22
Fedala = Mohammedia	**82**	33 44N	7 21
Federación	**124**	31 0S	57 55
Fedjadj, Chott el	**83**	33 52N	9 14
Fedje	**47**	60 47N	4 43
Fehérgyarmat	**27**	48 0N	22 30
Fehmarn	**24**	54 26N	11 10
Fei Xian	**77**	35 18N	117 59
Feilding	**101**	40 13S	175 35
Feira de Santana	**127**	12 15S	38 57
Fejér □	**27**	47 9N	18 30
Fejø	**49**	54 55N	11 30
Fekete →	**27**	45 47N	18 15
Felanitx	**33**	39 28N	3 9
Feldbach	**26**	46 57N	15 52
Feldberg, Germ., E.	**24**	53 20N	13 26
Feldberg, Germ., W.	**25**	47 51N	7 58
Feldkirch	**26**	47 15N	9 37
Feldkirchen	**26**	46 44N	14 6
Felipe Carrillo Puerto	**120**	19 38N	88 3
Felixstowe	**13**	51 58N	1 22
Felletin	**20**	45 53N	2 11
Feltre	**39**	46 1N	11 55
Femø	**49**	54 58N	11 53
Femunden	**47**	62 10N	11 53
Fen He →	**76**	35 36N	110 42
Fenelon Falls	**112**	44 32N	78 45
Feneroa	**87**	13 5N	39 3
Feng Xian, Jiangsu, China	**77**	34 43N	116 35
Feng Xian, Shaanxi, China	**77**	33 54N	106 40
Fengári	**44**	40 25N	25 32
Fengcheng, Jiangxi, China	**77**	28 12N	115 48
Fengcheng, Liaoning, China	**76**	40 28N	124 5
Fengdu	**77**	29 55N	107 41
Fengfeng	**76**	36 28N	114 8
Fenghua	**77**	29 40N	121 25
Fenghuang	**77**	27 57N	109 29
Fengjie	**75**	31 5N	109 36
Fengkai	**77**	23 24N	111 30
Fengle	**77**	31 29N	112 29
Fengning	**76**	41 10N	116 33
Fengtai	**76**	39 50N	116 18
Fengxian	**77**	30 55N	121 26
Fengxiang	**77**	34 29N	107 25
Fengxin	**77**	28 41N	115 18
Fengyang	**77**	32 51N	117 29
Fengzhen	**76**	40 25N	113 2
Feni Is.	**98**	4 0S	153 40
Fenit	**15**	52 17N	9 51
Fennimore	**116**	42 58N	90 41
Fenny	**69**	22 55N	91 32
Feno, C. de	**21**	41 58N	8 33
Fenoarivo Afovoany	**93**	18 26S	46 34
Fenoarivo Atsinanana	**93**	17 22S	49 25
Fens, The	**12**	52 45N	0 2
Fenton	**114**	42 47N	83 44
Fenyang	**76**	37 18N	111 48
Feodosiya	**56**	45 2N	35 28
Fer, C. de	**83**	37 3N	7 10
Ferdow	**65**	33 58N	58 2
Fère-Champenoise	**19**	48 45N	4 0
Fère-en-Tardenois	**19**	49 10N	3 30
Fère, La	**19**	49 40N	3 20
Ferentino	**40**	41 42N	13 14
Ferfer	**63**	5 4N	45 9
Fergana	**58**	40 23N	71 19
Fergus	**106**	43 43N	80 24
Fergus Falls	**116**	46 18N	96 7
Fergusson I.	**98**	9 30S	150 45
Fériana	**83**	34 59N	8 33
Feričanci	**42**	45 32N	18 0
Ferkane	**83**	34 37N	7 26
Ferkéssédougou	**84**	9 35N	5 6
Ferlach	**26**	46 32N	14 18
Ferland	**106**	50 19N	88 27

• *Renamed Tabuaeran*

Ferlo, Vallée du 84 15 15N 14 15W
Fermanagh □ 15 54 21N 7 40W
Fermo 39 43 10N 13 42 E
Fermoselle 30 41 19N 6 27W
Fermoy 15 52 4N 8 18W
Fernán Nuñéz 31 37 40N 4 44W
Fernández 124 27 55 S 63 50W
Fernandina Beach 115 30 40N 81 30W
Fernando de Noronha 127 4 0 S 33 10W
Fernando Póo = Bioko 85 3 30N 8 40 E
Ferndale, Calif., U.S.A. 118 40 37N 124 12W
Ferndale, Wash., U.S.A. 118 48 51N 122 41W
Fernie 108 49 30N 115 5W
Fernlees 98 23 51 S 148 7 E
Fernley 118 39 36N 119 14W
Feroke 70 11 9N 75 46 E
Ferozepore 68 30 55N 74 40 E
Férrai 44 40 53N 26 10 E
Ferrandina 41 40 30N 16 28 E
Ferrara 39 44 50N 11 36 E
Ferrato, C. 40 39 18N 9 39 E
Ferreira do Alentejo 31 38 4N 8 6W
Ferreñafe 126 6 42 S 79 50W
Ferret, C. 20 44 38N 1 15W
Ferrette 19 47 30N 7 20 E
Ferriday 117 31 35N 91 33W
Ferrières 19 48 5N 2 48 E
Ferriete 38 44 40N 9 30 E
Ferron 119 39 3N 111 3W
Ferryland 107 47 2N 52 53W
Ferté-Bernard, La 18 48 10N 0 40 E
Ferté, La 19 48 57N 3 6 E
Ferté-Mace, La 18 48 35N 0 21W
Ferté-St.-Aubin, La 19 47 42N 1 57 E
Ferté-Vidame, La 18 48 37N 0 53 E
Fertile 116 47 31N 96 18W
Fertília 40 40 37N 8 13 E
Fertöszentmiklós 27 47 35N 16 53 E
Fès 82 34 0N 5 0W
Feshi 88 6 8 S 18 10 E
Fessenden 116 47 42N 99 38W
Feteşti 46 44 22N 27 51 E
Fethiye 64 36 36N 29 10 E
Fetlar 14 60 36N 0 52W
Feuilles → 105 58 47N 70 4W
Feurs 21 45 45N 4 13 E
Feyzābād 65 37 7N 70 33 E
Fezzan 81 27 0N 15 0 E
Ffestiniog 12 52 58N 3 56W
Fiambalá 124 27 45 S 67 37W
Fianarantsoa 93 21 26 S 47 5 E
Fianarantsoa □ 93 19 30 S 47 0 E
Fianga 81 9 55N 15 9 E
Fibiş 42 45 57N 21 26 E
Fichtelgebirge 25 50 10N 12 0 E
Ficksburg 93 28 51 S 27 53 E
Fidenza 38 44 51N 10 3 E
Field 106 46 31N 80 1W
Field → 98 23 48 S 138 0 E
Fieri 44 40 43N 19 33 E
Fife □ 14 56 13N 3 2W
Fife Ness 14 56 17N 2 35W
Fifth Cataract 86 18 22N 33 50 E
Figeac 20 44 37N 2 2 E
Figline Valdarno 39 43 37N 11 28 E
Figtree 91 20 22 S 28 20 E
Figueira Castelo Rodrigo 30 40 57N 6 58W
Figueira da Foz 30 40 7N 8 54W
Figueiró dos Vinhos 30 39 55N 8 16W
Figueras 32 42 18N 2 58 E
Figuig 82 32 5N 1 11W
Fihaonana 93 18 36 S 47 12 E
Fiherenana 93 18 29 S 48 24 E
Fiherenana → 93 23 19 S 43 37 E
Fiji ■ 101 17 20 S 179 0 E
Fika 85 11 15N 11 13 E
Filabres, Sierra de los 33 37 13N 2 20W
Filadélfia 41 38 47N 16 17 E
Fil'akovo 27 48 17N 19 50 E
Filchner Ice Shelf 5 78 0 S 60 0W
Filer 118 42 30N 114 35W
Filey 12 54 13N 0 18W
Filiaşi 46 44 32N 23 31 E
Filiátes 44 39 38N 20 16 E
Filiatrá 45 37 9N 21 35 E
Filicudi 41 38 35N 14 33 E
Filiourí → 44 41 15N 25 40 E
Filipów 28 54 11N 22 37 E
Filipstad 48 59 43N 14 9 E
Filisur 25 46 41N 9 40 E
Fillmore, Can. 109 49 50N 103 25W
Fillmore, Calif., U.S.A. 119 34 23N 118 58W
Fillmore, Utah, U.S.A. 119 38 58N 112 20W
Filottrano 39 43 28N 13 20 E
Filyos 56 41 34N 32 4 E
Filyos → 64 41 35N 32 10 E
Finale Ligure 38 44 10N 8 21 E
Finale nell' Emília 39 44 50N 11 18 E
Fiñana 33 37 10N 2 50W
Finch 113 45 11N 75 7W
Findhorn → 14 57 38N 3 38W
Findlay 114 41 0N 83 41W
Finger L. 109 53 33N 124 18W
Fingõe 91 15 12 S 31 50 E
Finike 64 36 21N 30 10 E
Finistère □ 18 48 20N 4 0W
Finisterre 30 42 54N 9 16W
Finisterre, C. 30 42 50N 9 19W
Finisterre Ra. 98 6 0 S 146 30 E
Finke → 96 27 0 S 136 10 E
Finland ■ 52 63 0N 27 0 E
Finland, G. of 52 60 0N 26 0 E
Finlay → 108 57 0N 125 10W
Finley, Austral. 99 35 38 S 145 35 E
Finley, U.S.A. 116 47 35N 97 50W
Finn → 15 54 50N 7 55W
Finnigan, Mt. 98 15 49 S 145 17 E
Finnmark fylke □ 50 69 30N 25 0 E
Finschhafen 98 6 33 S 147 50 E
Finse 47 60 36N 7 30 E
Finsteraarhorn 25 46 31N 8 10 E
Finsterwalde 24 51 37N 13 42 E
Finucane I. 96 20 19 S 118 30 E
Fiora → 39 42 20N 11 35 E
Fiorenzuola d'Arda 38 44 56N 9 54 E
Fiq 62 32 46N 35 41 E
Fire River 106 48 47N 83 21W
Firebag → 109 57 45N 111 21W
Firedrake L. 109 61 25N 104 30W
Firenze 39 43 47N 11 15 E
Firminy, Aveyron, France 20 44 32N 2 19 E
Firminy, Loire, France 21 45 23N 4 18 E
Firozabad 68 27 10N 78 25 E
Fīrūzābād 65 28 52N 52 35 E
Fīrūzkūh 65 35 50N 52 50 E
Firvale 108 52 27N 126 13W
Fish → 92 28 7 S 17 45 E
Fisher B. 109 51 35N 97 13W
Fishguard 13 51 59N 4 59W
Fishing L. 109 52 10N 95 24W
Fismes 19 49 20N 3 40 E
Fitchburg 114 42 35N 71 47W
Fitero 32 42 4N 1 52W
Fitjar 47 59 55N 5 17 E
Fitri, L. 81 12 50N 17 28 E
Fitz Roy 128 47 0 S 67 0W
Fitzgerald, Can. 108 59 51N 111 36W
Fitzgerald, U.S.A. 115 31 45N 83 16W
Fitzroy →, Queens., Austral. 98 23 32 S 150 52 E
Fitzroy →, W. Australia, Austral. 96 17 31 S 123 35 E
Fitzroy Crossing 96 18 9 S 125 38 E
Fitzwilliam I. 112 45 30N 81 45W
Fiume = Rijeka 39 45 20N 14 27 E
Fiumefreddo Brúzio 41 39 14N 16 4 E
Fivizzano 38 44 12N 10 11 E
Fizi 90 4 17 S 28 55 E
Fjæra 47 59 52N 6 22 E
Fjellerup 49 56 29N 10 34 E
Fjerritslev 49 57 5N 9 15 E
Fkih ben Salah 82 32 32N 6 45W
Flå, Buskerud, Norway 47 60 25N 9 28 E
Flå, Sør-Trøndelag, Norway 47 63 13N 10 18 E
Flagler 116 39 20N 103 4W
Flagstaff 119 35 10N 111 40W
Flaherty I. 106 56 15N 79 15W
Flambeau → 116 45 18N 91 15W
Flamborough Hd. 12 54 8N 0 4W
Flaming Gorge Dam 118 40 50N 109 46W
Flaming Gorge L. 118 41 15N 109 30W
Flamingo, Teluk 73 5 30 S 138 0 E
Flanders = Flandres 16 51 10N 3 15 E
Flandre Occidental □ 16 51 0N 3 0 E
Flandre Orientale □ 16 51 0N 4 0 E
Flandreau 116 44 5N 96 38W
Flandres, Plaines des 16 51 10N 3 15 E
Flannan Is. 11 58 9N 7 52W
Flåsjön 50 64 5N 15 40 E
Flat → 108 61 51N 128 0W
Flat River 117 37 50N 90 30W
Flatey, Barðastrandarsýsla, Iceland 50 66 10N 17 52W
Flatey, Suður-Þingeyjarsýsla, Iceland 50 65 22N 22 56W
Flathead L. 118 47 50N 114 0W
Flattery, C., Austral. 98 14 58 S 145 21 E
Flattery, C., U.S.A. 118 48 21N 124 43W
Flavy-le-Martel 19 49 43N 3 12 E
Flaxton 116 48 52N 102 24W
Flèche, La 18 47 42N 0 5W
Fleetwood 12 53 55N 3 1W
Flekkefjord 47 58 18N 6 39 E
Flemington 112 41 7N 77 28W
Flensborg Fjord 49 54 50N 9 40 E
Flensburg 24 54 46N 9 28 E
Flers 18 48 47N 0 33W
Flesherton 112 44 16N 80 33W
Flesko, Tanjung 73 0 29N 124 30 E
Fletton 13 52 34N 0 13W
Fleurance 20 43 52N 0 40 E
Fleurier 25 46 54N 6 35 E
Flin Flon 109 54 46N 101 53W
Flinders → 97 17 36 S 140 36 E
Flinders B. 96 34 19 S 115 19 E
Flinders Group 98 14 11 S 144 15 E
Flinders I. 97 40 0 S 148 0 E
Flinders Ranges 97 31 30 S 138 30 E
Flint, U.K. 12 53 15N 3 7W
Flint, U.S.A. 114 43 5N 83 40W
Flint → 115 30 52N 84 38W
Flint, I. 95 11 26 S 151 48W
Flinton 99 27 55 S 149 32 E
Fliseryd 49 57 6N 16 15 E
Flix 32 41 14N 0 32 E
Flixecourt 19 50 0N 2 5 E
Flodden 12 55 37N 2 8W
Floodwood 116 46 55N 92 55W
Flora, Norway 47 63 27N 11 22 E
Flora, U.S.A. 114 38 40N 88 30W
Florac 20 44 20N 3 37 E
Florala 115 31 0N 86 20W
Florence, Ala., U.S.A. 115 34 50N 87 40W
Florence, Ariz., U.S.A. 119 33 0N 111 25W
Florence, Colo., U.S.A. 116 38 26N 105 0W
Florence, Oreg., U.S.A. 118 44 0N 124 3W
Florence, S.C., U.S.A. 115 34 12N 79 44W
Florence = Firenze 39 43 47N 11 15 E
Florence, L. 99 28 53 S 138 9 E
Florennes 16 50 15N 4 35 E
Florensac 20 43 23N 3 28 E
Florenville 16 49 40N 5 19 E
Flores, Azores 8 39 13N 31 13W
Flores, Guat. 120 16 59N 89 50W
Flores, Indon. 73 8 35 S 121 0 E
Flores I. 108 49 20N 126 10W
Flores Sea 72 6 30 S 124 0 E
Floresville 117 29 10N 98 10W
Floriano 127 6 50 S 43 0W
Florianópolis 125 27 30 S 48 30W
Florida, Cuba 121 21 32N 78 14W
Florida, Uruguay 125 34 7 S 56 10W
Florida □ 115 28 30N 82 0W
Florida B. 121 25 0N 81 20W
Florida Keys 121 25 0N 80 40W
Florida, Straits of 121 25 0N 80 0W
Florídia 41 37 6N 15 9 E
Floridsdorf 27 48 14N 16 22 E
Flórina 44 40 48N 21 26 E
Flórina □ 44 40 45N 21 20 E
Florø 47 61 35N 5 1 E
Flower Sta. 113 45 10N 76 41W
Flower's Cove 107 51 14N 56 46W
Floydada 117 33 58N 101 18W
Fluk 73 1 42 S 127 44 E
Flumen → 32 41 43N 0 9W
Flumendosa → 40 39 26N 9 38 E
Fluminimaggiore 40 39 25N 8 30 E
Flushing = Vlissingen 16 51 26N 3 34 E
Fluviá → 32 42 12N 3 7 E
Fly → 94 8 25 S 143 0 E
Flying Fish, C. 5 72 6 S 102 29W
Foam Lake 109 51 40N 103 32W
Foča 42 43 31N 18 47 E
Focşani 46 45 41N 27 15 E
Fogang 77 23 52N 113 30 E
Foggaret el Arab 82 27 13N 2 49 E
Foggaret ez Zoua 82 27 20N 2 53 E
Fóggia 41 41 28N 15 31 E
Foggo 85 11 21N 9 57 E
Foglia → 39 43 55N 12 54 E
Fogo 107 49 43N 54 17W
Fogo I. 107 49 40N 54 5W
Fohnsdorf 26 47 12N 14 40 E
Föhr 24 54 40N 8 30 E
Foia 31 37 19N 8 37W
Foix 20 42 58N 1 38 E
Foix □ 20 43 0N 1 30 E
Fojnica 42 43 59N 17 51 E
Fokino 54 53 30N 34 22 E
Fokis □ 45 38 30N 22 15 E
Fokstua 47 62 7N 9 17 E
Folda, Nord-Trøndelag, Norway 50 64 41N 10 50 E
Folda, Nordland, Norway 50 67 38N 14 50 E
Földeák 27 46 19N 20 30 E
Folégandros 45 36 40N 24 55 E
Folette, La 115 36 23N 84 9W
Foleyet 106 48 15N 82 25W
Folgefonn 47 60 3N 6 23 E
Foligno 39 42 58N 12 40 E
Folkestone 13 51 5N 1 11 E
Folkston 115 30 55N 82 0W
Follett 117 36 30N 100 12W
Follónica 38 42 55N 10 45 E
Follónica, Golfo di 38 42 50N 10 40 E
Folsom 118 38 41N 121 7W
Fond-du-Lac 109 59 19N 107 12W
Fond du Lac 116 43 46N 88 26W
Fond-du-Lac → 109 59 17N 106 0W
Fonda 113 42 57N 74 23W
Fondi 40 41 21N 13 25 E
Fonfría 30 41 37N 6 9W
Fongen 47 63 11N 11 38 E
Fonni 40 40 5N 9 16 E
Fonsagrada 30 43 8N 7 4W
Fonseca, G. de 120 13 10N 87 40W
Fontaine-Française 19 47 32N 5 21 E
Fontainebleau 19 48 24N 2 40 E
Fontas → 108 58 14N 121 48W
Fonte Boa 126 2 33 S 66 0W
Fontem 85 5 32N 9 52 E
Fontenay-le-Comte 20 46 28N 0 48W
Fontur 50 66 23N 14 32W
Fonyód 27 46 44N 17 33 E
Foochow = Fuzhou 75 26 5N 119 16 E
Foping 77 33 41N 108 0 E
Foppiano 38 46 21N 8 24 E
Föra 49 57 1N 16 51 E
Forbach 19 49 10N 6 52 E
Forbes 97 33 22 S 148 0 E
Forbesganj 69 26 17N 87 18 E
Forcados 85 5 26N 5 26 E
Forcados → 85 5 25N 5 19 E
Forcall → 32 40 51N 0 16W
Forcalquier 21 43 58N 5 47 E
Forchheim 25 49 42N 11 4 E
Ford City 112 40 47N 79 31W
Førde 47 61 27N 5 53 E
Ford's Bridge 99 29 41 S 145 29 E
Fordyce 117 33 50N 92 20W
Forécariah 84 9 28N 13 10W
Forel, Mt. 4 66 52N 36 55W
Foremost 108 49 26N 111 34W
Forenza 41 40 50N 15 50 E
Forest, Can. 112 43 6N 82 0W
Forest, U.S.A. 117 32 21N 89 27W
Forest City, Iowa, U.S.A. 116 43 12N 93 39W
Forest City, N.C., U.S.A. 115 35 23N 81 50W
Forest City, Pa., U.S.A. 113 41 39N 75 29W
Forest Grove 118 45 31N 123 4W
Forestburg 108 52 35N 112 1W
Forestier Pen. 99 43 0 S 148 0 E
Forestville, Can. 107 48 48N 69 2W
Forestville, U.S.A. 114 44 41N 87 29W
Forez, Mts. du 20 45 40N 3 50 E
Forfar 14 56 40N 2 53W
Forges-les-Eaux 19 49 37N 1 30 E
Forks 118 47 56N 124 23W
Forlì 39 44 14N 12 2 E
Forman 116 46 9N 97 43W
Formazza 38 46 23N 8 26 E
Formby Pt. 12 53 33N 3 7W
Formentera 33 38 43N 1 27 E
Formentor, C. de 32 39 58N 3 13 E
Fórmia 40 41 15N 13 34 E
Formigine 38 44 37N 10 51 E
Formiguères 20 42 37N 2 5 E
Formosa 124 26 15 S 58 10W
Formosa = Taiwan ■ 75 24 0N 121 0 E
Formosa □ 124 25 0 S 60 0W
Formosa Bay 90 2 40 S 40 20 E
Formosa, Serra 127 12 0 S 55 0W
Fornells 32 40 3N 4 7 E
Fornos de Algodres 30 40 38N 7 32W
Fornovo di Taro 38 44 42N 10 7 E
Forres 14 57 37N 3 38W
Forrest 99 38 33 S 143 47 E
Forrest City 117 35 0N 90 50W
Fors 48 60 14N 16 20 E
Forsa 48 61 44N 16 55 E
Forsand 47 58 54N 6 5 E
Forsayth 97 18 33 S 143 34 E
Forserum 49 57 42N 14 30 E
Forshaga 48 59 33N 13 29 E
Forskacka 48 60 39N 16 54 E
Forsmo 48 63 16N 17 11 E
Forst 24 51 43N 14 37 E
Forster 99 32 12 S 152 31 E
Forsyth, Ga., U.S.A. 115 33 4N 83 55W
Forsyth, Mont., U.S.A. 118 46 14N 106 37W
Fort Albany 106 52 15N 81 35W
Fort Amador 120 8 56N 79 32W
Fort Apache 119 33 50N 110 0W
Fort Assiniboine 108 54 20N 114 45W
Fort Augustus 14 57 9N 4 40W
Fort Beaufort 92 32 46 S 26 40 E
Fort Benton 118 47 50N 110 40W
Fort Bragg 118 39 28N 123 50W
Fort Bridger 118 41 22N 110 20W
Fort Chimo 105 58 6N 68 15W
Fort Chipewyan 109 58 42N 111 8W
Fort Clayton 120 9 0N 79 35W
Fort Collins 116 40 30N 105 4W
Fort-Coulonge 106 45 50N 76 45W
Fort Davis, Panama 120 9 17N 79 56W
Fort Davis, U.S.A. 117 30 38N 103 53W
Fort-de-France 121 14 36N 61 2W
Fort de Possel = Possel 88 5 5N 19 10 E
Fort Defiance 119 35 47N 109 4W
Fort Dodge 116 42 29N 94 10W
Fort Edward 113 43 16N 73 35W
Fort Frances 109 48 36N 93 24W
Fort Franklin 104 65 10N 123 30W
Fort Garland 119 37 28N 105 30W
Fort George 106 53 50N 79 0W
Fort Good-Hope 104 66 14N 128 40W
Fort Hancock 119 31 19N 105 56W
Fort Hertz (Putao) 67 27 28N 97 30 E
Fort Hope 106 51 30N 88 0W
Fort Huachuca 119 31 32N 110 30W
Fort Jameson = Chipata 91 13 38 S 32 28 E
Fort Kent 107 47 12N 68 30W
Fort Klamath 118 42 45N 122 0W
Fort Lallemand 83 31 13N 6 17 E
Fort-Lamy = Ndjamena 81 12 4N 15 8 E
Fort Laramie 116 42 15N 104 30W
Fort Lauderdale 115 26 10N 80 5W
Fort Liard 108 60 14N 123 30W
Fort Liberté 121 19 42N 71 51W
Fort Lupton 116 40 8N 104 48W
Fort Mackay 108 57 12N 111 41W
Fort McKenzie 107 57 20N 69 0W
Fort Macleod 108 49 45N 113 30W
Fort MacMahon 82 29 43N 1 45 E
Fort McMurray 108 56 44N 111 7W
Fort McPherson 104 67 30N 134 55W
Fort Madison 116 40 39N 91 20W
Fort Meade 115 27 45N 81 45W
Fort Miribel 82 29 25N 2 55 E
Fort Morgan 116 40 10N 103 50W
Fort Myers 115 26 39N 81 51W
Fort Nelson 108 58 50N 122 44W
Fort Nelson → 108 59 32N 124 0W
Fort Norman 104 64 57N 125 30W
Fort Payne 115 34 25N 85 44W
Fort Peck 118 48 1N 106 30W
Fort Peck Dam 118 48 0N 106 38W
Fort Peck L. 118 47 40N 107 0W
Fort Pierce 115 27 29N 80 19W
Fort Pierre 116 44 25N 100 25W
Fort Pierre Bordes = Ti-n-Zaouatene 82 20 0N 2 55 E
Fort Plain 113 42 56N 74 39W
Fort Portal 90 0 40N 30 20 E
Fort Providence 108 61 3N 117 40W
Fort Qu'Appelle 109 50 45N 103 50W
Fort Randolph 120 9 23N 79 53W
Fort Resolution 108 61 10N 113 40W
Fort Rixon 91 20 2 S 29 17 E
Fort Roseberry = Mansa 91 11 10 S 28 50 E
Fort Rupert (Rupert House) 106 51 30N 78 40W
Fort Saint 83 30 19N 9 31 E
Fort St. James 108 54 30N 124 10W
Fort St. John 108 56 15N 120 50W
Fort Sandeman 68 31 20N 69 31 E
Fort Saskatchewan 108 53 40N 113 15W
Fort Scott 117 37 50N 94 40W
Fort Severn 106 56 0N 87 40W
Fort Sherman 120 9 22N 79 56W
Fort Shevchenko 57 43 40N 51 20 E
Fort-Sibut 88 5 46N 19 10 E
Fort Simpson 108 61 45N 121 15W
Fort Smith, Can. 108 60 0N 111 51W
Fort Smith, U.S.A. 117 35 25N 94 25W
Fort Stanton 119 33 33N 105 36W
Fort Stockton 117 30 54N 102 54W
Fort Sumner 117 34 24N 104 16W
Fort Thomas 119 33 2N 109 59W
Fort Trinquet = Bir Mogrein 80 25 10N 11 35W
Fort Valley 115 32 33N 83 52W
Fort Vermilion 108 58 24N 116 0W
• Fort Victoria 91 20 8 S 30 49 E
Fort Walton Beach 115 30 25N 86 40W
Fort Wayne 114 41 5N 85 10W
Fort William 14 56 48N 5 8W
Fort Worth 117 32 45N 97 25W
Fort Yates 116 46 8N 100 38W
Fort Yukon 104 66 35N 145 20W
Fortaleza 127 3 45 S 38 35W
Forteau 107 51 28N 56 58W
Fortescue → 96 21 20 S 116 5 E
Forth, Firth of 14 56 5N 2 55W
Forthassa Rharbia 82 32 52N 1 18W
Fortore → 39 41 55N 15 17 E
Fortrose 14 57 35N 4 10W
Fortuna, Spain 33 38 11N 1 7W
Fortuna, Cal., U.S.A. 118 40 38N 124 8W
Fortuna, N.D., U.S.A. 116 48 55N 103 48W

• *Renamed Masvingo*

Place	Page	Lat.	Long.
Fortune B.	**107**	47 30N	55 22W
Forūr	**65**	26 20N	54 30 E
Fos	**21**	43 26N	4 56 E
Foshan	**75**	23 4N	113 5 E
Fossacesia	**39**	42 15N	14 30 E
Fossano	**38**	44 33N	7 40 E
Fossil	**118**	45 0N	120 9W
Fossilbrook P.O.	**98**	17 47 S	144 29 E
Fossombrone	**39**	43 41N	12 49 E
Fosston	**116**	47 33N	95 39W
Foster	**113**	45 17N	72 30W
Foster →	**109**	55 47N	105 49W
Fostoria	**114**	41 8N	83 25W
Fougamou	**88**	1 16 S	10 30 E
Fougères	**18**	48 21N	1 14W
Foul Pt.	**70**	8 35N	81 18 E
Foulness I.	**13**	51 36N	0 55 E
Foulness Pt.	**13**	51 36N	0 59 E
Foulpointe	**93**	17 41 S	49 31 E
Foum Assaka	**82**	29 8N	10 24W
Foum Zguid	**82**	30 2N	6 59W
Foumban	**85**	5 45N	10 50 E
Foundiougne	**84**	14 5N	16 32W
Fountain, Colo., U.S.A.	**116**	38 42N	104 40W
Fountain, Utah, U.S.A.	**118**	39 41N	111 37W
Fourchambault	**19**	47 0N	3 3 E
Fourchu	**107**	45 43N	60 17W
Fourmies	**19**	50 1N	4 2 E
Fournás	**45**	39 3N	21 52 E
Foúrnoi, Greece	**45**	37 36N	26 32 E
Foúrnoi, Greece	**45**	37 36N	26 28 E
Fours	**19**	46 50N	3 42 E
Fouta Djalon	**84**	11 20N	12 10W
Foux, Cap-à-	**121**	19 43N	73 27W
Foveaux Str.	**101**	46 42 S	168 10 E
Fowey	**13**	50 20N	4 39W
Fowler, Calif., U.S.A.	**119**	36 41N	119 41W
Fowler, Colo., U.S.A.	**116**	38 10N	104 0W
Fowler, Kans., U.S.A.	**117**	37 28N	100 7W
Fowlerton	**117**	28 26N	98 50W
Fownhope	**13**	52 0N	2 37W
Fox →	**109**	56 3N	93 18W
Fox Valley	**109**	50 30N	109 25W
Foxe Basin	**105**	68 30N	77 0W
Foxe Channel	**105**	66 0N	80 0W
Foxe Pen.	**105**	65 0N	76 0W
Foxen, L.	**48**	59 25N	11 55 E
Foxpark	**118**	41 4N	106 6W
Foxton	**101**	40 29 S	175 18 E
Foyle, Lough	**15**	55 6N	7 8W
Foynes	**15**	52 37N	9 5W
Foz	**30**	43 33N	7 20W
Fôz do Cunene	**92**	17 15 S	11 48 E
Foz do Gregório	**126**	6 47 S	70 44W
Foz do Iguaçu	**125**	25 30 S	54 30W
Frackville	**113**	40 46N	76 15W
Fraga	**32**	41 32N	0 21 E
Framingham	**113**	42 18N	71 26W
Frampol	**28**	50 41N	22 40 E
Franca	**127**	20 33 S	47 30W
Francavilla al Mare	**39**	42 25N	14 16 E
Francavilla Fontana	**41**	40 32N	17 35 E
France ■	**17**	47 0N	3 0 E
Frances	**99**	36 41 S	140 55 E
Frances →	**108**	60 16N	129 10W
Frances L.	**108**	61 23N	129 30W
Franceville	**88**	1 40 S	13 32 E
Franche-Comté	**19**	46 30N	5 50 E
Francisco I. Madero, Coahuila, Mexico	**120**	25 48N	103 18W
Francisco I. Madero, Durango, Mexico	**120**	24 32N	104 22W
Francofonte	**41**	37 13N	14 50 E
François, Can.	**107**	47 35N	56 45W
François, Mart.	**121**	14 38N	60 57W
François L.	**108**	54 0N	125 30W
Franeker	**16**	53 12N	5 33 E
Frankado	**87**	12 30N	43 12 E
Frankenberg	**24**	51 3N	8 47 E
Frankenthal	**25**	49 32N	8 21 E
Frankenwald	**25**	50 18N	11 36 E
Frankfort, Madag.	**93**	27 17 S	28 30 E
Frankfort, Ind., U.S.A.	**114**	40 20N	86 33W
Frankfort, Kans., U.S.A.	**116**	39 42N	96 26W
Frankfort, Ky., U.S.A.	**114**	38 12N	84 52W
Frankfort, Mich., U.S.A.	**114**	44 38N	86 14W
Frankfurt □	**24**	52 30N	14 0 E
Frankfurt am Main	**25**	50 7N	8 40 E
Frankfurt an der Oder	**24**	52 50N	14 31 E
Fränkische Alb	**25**	49 20N	11 30 E
Fränkische Rezal →	**25**	49 11N	11 1 E
Fränkische Saale →	**25**	50 30N	9 42 E
Fränkische Schweiz	**25**	49 45N	11 10 E
Franklin, Ky., U.S.A.	**115**	36 40N	86 30W
Franklin, La., U.S.A.	**117**	29 45N	91 30W
Franklin, Mass., U.S.A.	**113**	42 4N	71 23W
Franklin, N.H., U.S.A.	**114**	43 28N	71 39W
Franklin, N.J., U.S.A.	**113**	41 9N	74 38W
Franklin, Nebr., U.S.A.	**116**	40 9N	98 55W
Franklin, Pa., U.S.A.	**114**	41 22N	79 45W
Franklin, Tenn., U.S.A.	**115**	35 54N	86 53W
Franklin, Va., U.S.A.	**115**	36 40N	76 58W
Franklin, W. Va., U.S.A.	**114**	38 38N	79 21W
• Franklin □	**105**	71 0N	99 0W
Franklin B.	**104**	69 45N	126 0W
Franklin D. Roosevelt L.	**118**	48 30N	118 16W
Franklin I.	**5**	76 10 S	168 30 E
Franklin, L.	**118**	40 20N	115 26W
Franklin Mts.	**104**	65 0N	125 0W
Franklin Str.	**104**	72 0N	96 0W
Franklinton	**117**	30 53N	90 10W
Franklinville	**112**	42 21N	78 28W
Franks Peak	**118**	43 50N	109 5W
Frankston	**99**	38 8 S	145 8 E
Fränsta	**48**	62 30N	16 11 E
Frantsa Josifa, Zemlya	**58**	82 0N	55 0 E
Franz	**106**	48 25N	84 30W
Franz Josef Land = Frantsa Josifa	**58**	79 0N	62 0 E
Franzburg	**24**	54 9N	12 52 E
Frascati	**40**	41 48N	12 41 E
Fraser →, B.C., Can.	**108**	49 7N	123 11W
Fraser →, Newf., Can.	**107**	56 39N	62 10W
Fraser I.	**97**	25 15 S	153 10 E
Fraser Lake	**108**	54 0N	124 50W
Fraserburg	**92**	31 55 S	21 30 E
Fraserburgh	**14**	57 41N	2 0W
Fraserdale	**106**	49 55N	81 37W
Frashëri	**44**	40 23N	20 26 E
Frasne	**19**	46 50N	6 10 E
Frauenfeld	**25**	47 34N	8 54 E
Fray Bentos	**124**	33 10 S	58 15W
Frechilla	**30**	42 8N	4 50W
Fredericia	**49**	55 34N	9 45 E
Frederick, Md., U.S.A.	**114**	39 25N	77 23W
Frederick, Okla., U.S.A.	**117**	34 22N	99 0W
Frederick, S.D., U.S.A.	**116**	45 55N	98 29W
Frederick Reef	**97**	20 58 S	154 23 E
Frederick Sd.	**108**	57 10N	134 0W
Fredericksburg, Tex., U.S.A.	**117**	30 17N	98 55W
Fredericksburg, Va., U.S.A.	**114**	38 16N	77 29W
Frederickstown	**117**	37 35N	90 15W
Fredericton	**107**	45 57N	66 40W
Fredericton Junc.	**107**	45 41N	66 40W
Frederikshavn	**49**	57 28N	10 31 E
Frederikssund	**49**	55 50N	12 3 E
Fredonia, Ariz., U.S.A.	**119**	36 59N	112 36W
Fredonia, Kans., U.S.A.	**117**	37 34N	95 50W
Fredonia, N.Y., U.S.A.	**114**	42 26N	79 20W
Fredrikstad	**47**	59 13N	10 57 E
Freehold	**113**	40 15N	74 18W
Freeland	**113**	41 3N	75 48W
Freeling, Mt.	**96**	22 35 S	133 06 E
Freels, C.	**107**	49 15N	53 30W
Freeman	**116**	43 25N	97 20W
Freeport, Bahamas	**121**	26 30N	78 47W
Freeport, Can.	**107**	44 15N	66 20W
Freeport, Ill., U.S.A.	**116**	42 18N	89 40W
Freeport, N.Y., U.S.A.	**114**	40 39N	73 35W
Freeport, Tex., U.S.A.	**117**	28 55N	95 22W
Freetown	**84**	8 30N	13 17W
Frégate, L.	**106**	53 15N	74 45W
Fregenal de la Sierra	**31**	38 10N	6 39W
Fregene	**40**	41 50N	12 12 E
Fregeneda, La	**30**	40 58N	6 54W
Fréhel, C.	**18**	48 40N	2 20W
Frei	**47**	63 4N	7 48 E
Freiberg	**24**	50 55N	13 20 E
Freibourg = Fribourg	**25**	46 49N	7 9 E
Freiburg, Baden, Ger.	**25**	48 0N	7 52 E
Freiburg, Niedersachsen, Ger.	**24**	53 49N	9 17 E
Freire	**128**	38 54 S	72 38W
Freirina	**124**	28 30 S	71 10W
Freising	**25**	48 24N	11 47 E
Freistadt	**26**	48 30N	14 30 E
Freital	**24**	51 0N	13 40 E
Fréjus	**21**	43 25N	6 44 E
Fremantle	**96**	32 7 S	115 47 E
Fremont, Mich., U.S.A.	**114**	43 29N	85 59W
Fremont, Nebr., U.S.A.	**116**	41 30N	96 30W
Fremont, Ohio, U.S.A.	**114**	41 20N	83 5W
Fremont →	**119**	38 15N	110 20W
Fremont, L.	**118**	43 0N	109 50W
French →	**114**	41 30N	80 2W
French Guiana ■	**127**	4 0N	53 0W
French I.	**100**	38 20 S	145 22 E
French Terr. of Afars & Issas = Djibouti ■	**87**	11 30N	42 15 E
Frenchglen	**118**	42 48N	119 0W
Frenchman →	**118**	48 24N	107 5W
Frenchman Butte	**109**	53 35N	109 38W
Frenchman Creek →	**116**	40 13N	100 50W
Frenda	**82**	35 2N	1 1 E
Fresco →	**127**	7 15 S	51 30W
Freshfield, C.	**5**	68 25 S	151 10 E
Fresnay	**18**	48 17N	0 1 E
Fresnillo	**120**	23 10N	103 0W
Fresno	**119**	36 47N	119 50W
Fresno Alhandiga	**30**	40 42N	5 37W
Fresno Res.	**118**	48 40N	110 0W
Freudenstadt	**25**	48 27N	8 25 E
Frévent	**19**	50 15N	2 17 E
Freycinet Pen.	**97**	42 10 S	148 25 E
Freyung	**25**	48 48N	13 33 E
Fria	**84**	10 27N	13 38W
Fria, C.	**92**	18 0 S	12 0 E
Frias	**124**	28 40 S	65 5W
Fribourg	**25**	46 49N	7 9 E
Fribourg □	**25**	46 40N	7 0 E
Fridafors	**49**	56 25N	14 39 E
Friedberg, Bayern, Ger.	**25**	48 21N	10 59 E
Friedberg, Hessen, Ger.	**25**	50 21N	8 46 E
Friedland	**24**	53 40N	13 33 E
Friedrichshafen	**25**	47 39N	9 29 E
Friedrichskoog	**24**	54 1N	8 52 E
Friedrichsort	**24**	54 24N	10 11 E
Friedrichstadt	**24**	54 23N	9 6 E
Friendly (Tonga) Is.	**101**	22 0 S	173 0W
Friesach	**26**	46 57N	14 24 E
Friesack	**24**	52 43N	12 35 E
Friesland □	**16**	53 5N	5 50 E
Friesoythe	**24**	53 1N	7 51 E
Frijoles	**120**	9 11N	79 48W
Frillesås	**49**	57 20N	12 12 E
Frinnaryd	**49**	57 55N	14 50 E
Frio →	**117**	28 30N	98 10W
Friona	**117**	34 40N	102 42W
Frisian Is.	**24**	53 30N	6 0 E
Fristad	**49**	57 50N	13 0 E
Fritch	**117**	35 40N	101 35W
Fritsla	**49**	57 33N	12 47 E
Fritzlar	**24**	51 8N	9 19 E
Friuli-Venezia Giulia □	**39**	46 0N	13 0 E
Friville-Escarbotin	**19**	50 5N	1 33 E
Frobisher B.	**105**	62 30N	66 0W
Frobisher Bay	**105**	63 44N	68 31W
Frobisher L.	**109**	56 20N	108 15W
Frohavet	**50**	63 50N	9 35 E
Froid	**116**	48 20N	104 29W
Frolovo	**57**	49 45N	43 40 E
Fromberg	**118**	42 25N	108 58W
Frombork	**28**	54 21N	19 41 E
Frome	**13**	51 16N	2 17W
Frome, L.	**97**	30 45 S	139 45 E
Fromentine	**18**	46 53N	2 9W
Frómista	**30**	42 16N	4 25W
Front Range	**118**	40 0N	105 40W
Front Royal	**114**	38 55N	78 10W
Fronteira	**31**	39 3N	7 39W
Frontera	**120**	18 30N	92 40W
Frontignan	**20**	43 27N	3 45 E
Frosinone	**40**	41 38N	13 20 E
Frosolone	**41**	41 34N	14 27 E
Frostburg	**114**	39 43N	78 57W
Frostisen	**50**	68 14N	17 10 E
Frouard	**19**	48 47N	6 8 E
Frövi	**48**	59 28N	15 24 E
Frøya	**47**	63 43N	8 40 E
Fruges	**19**	50 30N	2 8 E
Frumoasa	**46**	46 28N	25 48 E
Frunze	**58**	42 54N	74 46 E
Fruška Gora	**42**	45 7N	19 30 E
Frutal	**127**	20 0 S	49 0W
Frutigen	**25**	46 35N	7 38 E
Frýdek-Místek	**27**	49 40N	18 20 E
Frýdlant, Severočeský, Czech.	**26**	50 56N	15 9 E
Frýdlant, Severomoravsky, Czech.	**27**	49 35N	18 20 E
Fryvaldov = Jeseník	**27**	50 0N	17 8 E
Fthiótis □	**45**	38 50N	22 25 E
Fu Xian, Liaoning, China	**76**	39 38N	121 58 E
Fu Xian, Shaanxi, China	**76**	36 0N	109 20 E
Fucécchio	**38**	43 44N	10 51 E
Fucheng	**76**	37 50N	116 10 E
Fuchou = Fuzhou	**75**	26 5N	119 16 E
Fuchuan	**77**	24 50N	111 5 E
Fuchun Jiang →	**77**	30 5N	120 5 E
Fúcino, Conca del	**39**	42 1N	13 31 E
Fuding	**77**	27 20N	120 12 E
Fuencaliente	**31**	38 25N	4 18W
Fuengirola	**31**	36 32N	4 41W
Fuente Álamo	**33**	38 44N	1 24W
Fuente Álamo	**33**	37 42N	1 6W
Fuente de Cantos	**31**	38 15N	6 18W
Fuente de San Esteban, La	**30**	40 49N	6 15W
Fuente del Maestre	**31**	38 31N	6 28W
Fuente el Fresno	**31**	39 14N	3 46W
Fuente Ovejuna	**31**	38 15N	5 25W
Fuentes de Andalucía	**31**	37 28N	5 20W
Fuentes de Ebro	**32**	41 31N	0 38W
Fuentes de León	**31**	38 5N	6 32W
Fuentes de Oñoro	**30**	40 33N	6 52W
Fuentesaúco	**30**	41 15N	5 30W
Fuerte →	**120**	25 50N	109 25W
Fuerte Olimpo	**124**	21 0 S	57 51W
Fuerteventura	**80**	28 30N	14 0W
Fûget, Munţii	**46**	45 50N	22 9 E
Fugløysund	**50**	70 15N	20 20 E
Fugou	**77**	34 3N	114 25 E
Fuhai	**75**	47 2N	87 25 E
Fuji-no-miya	**74**	35 10N	138 40 E
Fuji-San	**74**	35 22N	138 44 E
Fujian □	**75**	26 0N	118 0 E
Fujin	**76**	47 16N	132 1 E
Fujisawa	**74**	35 22N	139 29 E
Fukien = Fujian □	**75**	26 0N	118 0 E
Fukuchiyama	**74**	35 19N	135 9 E
Fukui	**74**	36 0N	136 10 E
Fukui □	**74**	36 0N	136 12 E
Fukuoka	**74**	33 39N	130 21 E
Fukuoka □	**74**	33 30N	131 0 E
Fukushima	**74**	37 44N	140 28 E
Fukushima □	**74**	37 30N	140 15 E
Fukuyama	**74**	34 35N	133 20 E
Fulda	**24**	50 32N	9 41 E
Fulda →	**24**	51 27N	9 40 E
Fuling	**77**	29 40N	107 20 E
Fullerton, Calif., U.S.A.	**119**	33 52N	117 58W
Fullerton, Nebr., U.S.A.	**116**	41 25N	98 0W
Fulton, Mo., U.S.A.	**116**	38 50N	91 55W
Fulton, N.Y., U.S.A.	**114**	43 20N	76 22W
Fulton, Tenn., U.S.A.	**115**	36 31N	88 53W
Fuluälven	**48**	61 18N	13 4 E
Fulufjället	**48**	61 32N	12 41 E
Fumay	**19**	50 0N	4 40 E
Fumel	**20**	44 30N	0 58 E
Funabashi	**74**	35 45N	140 0 E
Funafuti	**94**	8 30 S	179 0 E
Funchal	**80**	32 38N	16 54W
Fundación	**126**	10 31N	74 11W
Fundão	**30**	40 8N	7 30W
Fundy, B. of	**107**	45 0N	66 0W
Funing, Jiangsu, China	**77**	33 45N	119 50 E
Funing, Yunnan, China	**77**	23 35N	105 45 E
Funiu Shan	**77**	33 30N	112 20 E
Funsi	**84**	10 21N	1 54W
Funtua	**85**	11 30N	7 18 E
Fuping	**76**	38 48N	114 12 E
Fuqing	**77**	25 41N	119 21 E
Fur	**49**	56 50N	9 0 E
Furāt, Nahr al →	**64**	31 0N	47 25 E
Furmanov	**55**	57 10N	41 9 E
Furmanovo	**57**	49 42N	49 25 E
Furnas, Reprêsa de	**125**	20 50 S	45 0W
Furneaux Group	**97**	40 10 S	147 50 E
Furness, Pen.	**12**	54 12N	3 10W
Fürstenau	**24**	52 32N	7 40 E
Fürstenberg	**24**	53 11N	13 9 E
Fürstenfeld	**26**	47 3N	16 3 E
Fürstenfeldbruck	**25**	48 10N	11 15 E
Fürstenwalde	**24**	52 20N	14 3 E
Fürth	**25**	49 29N	11 0 E
Furth im Wald	**25**	49 19N	12 51 E
Furtwangen	**25**	48 3N	8 14 E
Furudal	**48**	61 10N	15 11 E
Furusund	**48**	59 40N	18 55 E
Fury and Hecla Str.	**105**	69 56N	84 0W
Fusa	**47**	60 12N	5 37 E
Fusagasuga	**126**	4 21N	74 22W
Fuscaldo	**41**	39 25N	16 1 E
Fushan	**76**	37 30N	121 15 E
Fushë Arrëzi	**44**	42 4N	20 2 E
Fushun	**76**	41 50N	123 56 E
Fusong	**76**	42 20N	127 15 E
Füssen	**25**	47 35N	10 43 E
Fusui	**77**	22 40N	107 56 E
Futuna	**94**	14 25 S	178 20 E
Fuwa	**86**	31 12N	30 33 E
Fuxin	**76**	42 5N	121 48 E
Fuyang, Anhui, China	**77**	33 0N	115 48 E
Fuyang, Zhejiang, China	**77**	30 5N	119 57 E
Fuyu	**76**	45 12N	124 43 E
Fuyuan	**75**	48 20N	134 5 E
Füzesgyarmat	**27**	47 6N	21 14 E
Fuzhou, Fujian, China	**75**	26 5N	119 16 E
Fuzhou, Jiangxi, China	**75**	28 0N	116 25 E
Fylde	**12**	53 50N	2 58W
Fyn	**49**	55 20N	10 30 E
Fyne, L.	**14**	56 0N	5 20W
Fyns Amtskommune □	**49**	55 15N	10 30 E
Fyresvatn	**47**	59 6N	8 10 E

G

Place	Page	Lat.	Long.
Gaanda	**85**	10 10N	12 27 E
Gabarin	**85**	11 8N	10 27 E
Gabas →	**20**	43 46N	0 42W
Gabela	**88**	11 0 S	14 24 E
Gabès	**83**	33 53N	10 2 E
Gabès, Golfe de	**83**	34 0N	10 30 E
Gabgaba, W.	**86**	22 10N	33 5 E
Gabin	**28**	52 23N	19 41 E
Gabon ■	**88**	0 10 S	10 0 E
Gaborone	**92**	24 45 S	25 57 E
Gabriels	**113**	44 26N	74 12W
Gabrovo	**43**	42 52N	25 19 E
Gacé	**18**	48 49N	0 20 E
Gach Sārān	**65**	30 15N	50 45 E
Gacko	**42**	43 10N	18 33 E
Gadag-Batgeri	**70**	15 30N	75 45 E
Gadamai	**87**	17 11N	36 10 E
Gadap	**68**	25 5N	67 28 E
Gadarwara	**68**	22 50N	78 50 E
Gadebusch	**24**	53 41N	11 6 E
Gadein	**87**	8 10N	28 45 E
Gadhada	**68**	22 0N	71 35 E
Gádor, Sierra de	**33**	36 57N	2 45W
Gadsden, Ala., U.S.A.	**115**	34 1N	86 0W
Gadsden, Ariz., U.S.A.	**119**	32 35N	114 47W
Gadwal	**70**	16 10N	77 50 E
Gadyach	**54**	50 21N	34 0 E
Găeşti	**46**	44 48N	25 19 E
Gaeta	**40**	41 12N	13 35 E
Gaeta, G. di	**40**	41 0N	13 25 E
Gaffney	**115**	35 3N	81 40W
Gafsa	**83**	32 24N	8 43 E
Gagarin (Gzhatsk)	**54**	55 38N	35 0 E
Gagetown	**107**	45 46N	66 10W
Gagino	**55**	55 15N	45 1 E
Gagliano del Capo	**41**	39 50N	18 23 E
Gagnef	**48**	60 36N	15 5 E
Gagnoa	**84**	6 56N	5 16W
Gagnon	**107**	51 50N	68 5W
Gagnon, L.	**109**	62 3N	110 27W
Gagra	**57**	43 20N	40 10 E
Gahini	**90**	1 50 S	30 30 E
Gahmar	**69**	25 27N	83 49 E
Gai Xian	**76**	40 22N	122 20 E
Gaibanda	**69**	25 20N	89 36 E
Gaïdhouronisi	**45**	34 53N	25 41 E
Gail	**117**	32 48N	101 25W
Gail →	**26**	46 36N	13 53 E
Gaillac	**20**	43 54N	1 54 E
Gaillon	**18**	49 10N	1 20 E
Gaines	**112**	41 46N	77 35W
Gainesville, Fla., U.S.A.	**115**	29 38N	82 20W
Gainesville, Ga., U.S.A.	**115**	34 17N	83 47W
Gainesville, Mo., U.S.A.	**117**	36 35N	92 26W
Gainesville, Tex., U.S.A.	**117**	33 40N	97 10W
Gainsborough	**12**	53 23N	0 46W
Gairdner L.	**96**	31 30 S	136 0 E
Gairloch, L.	**14**	57 43N	5 45W
Gaj	**42**	45 28N	17 3 E
Gal Oya Res.	**70**	7 5N	81 30 E
Galachipa	**69**	22 8N	90 26 E
Galán, Cerro	**124**	25 55 S	66 52W
Galana →	**90**	3 9 S	40 8 E
Galangue	**89**	13 42 S	16 9 E
Galanta	**27**	48 11N	17 45 E
Galápagos	**95**	0 0	89 0W
Galas →	**71**	4 55N	101 57 E
Galashiels	**14**	55 37N	2 50W
Galatás	**45**	37 30N	23 26 E
Galaţi	**46**	45 27N	28 2 E
Galaţi □	**46**	45 45N	27 30 E
Galatina	**41**	40 10N	18 10 E
Galátone	**41**	40 8N	18 3 E
Galax	**115**	36 42N	80 57W
Galaxídhion	**45**	38 22N	22 23 E
Galbraith	**98**	16 25 S	141 30 E
Galcaio	**63**	6 30N	47 30 E
Galdhøpiggen	**47**	61 38N	8 18 E
Galela	**73**	1 50N	127 49 E
Galera	**33**	37 45N	2 33W
Galesburg	**116**	40 57N	90 23W
Galeton	**112**	41 43N	77 40W
Gali	**57**	42 37N	41 46 E
Galicea Mare	**46**	44 4N	23 19 E
Galich	**55**	58 23N	42 12 E
Galiche	**43**	43 34N	23 50 E
Galicia	**30**	42 43N	7 45W
Galilee = Hagalil	**62**	32 53N	35 18 E
Galilee, L.	**98**	22 20 S	145 50 E
Galion	**112**	40 43N	82 48W
Galite, Is. de la	**83**	37 30N	8 59 E
Galiuro Mts.	**119**	32 40N	110 30W
Gallabat	**81**	12 58N	36 11 E
Gallarate	**38**	45 40N	8 48 E
Gallardon	**19**	48 32N	1 47 E
Gallatin	**115**	36 24N	86 27W
Galle	**70**	6 5N	80 10 E
Gállego →	**32**	41 39N	0 51W
Gallegos →	**128**	51 35 S	69 0W
Galley Hd.	**15**	51 32N	8 56W

* *Now part of Central Arctic and Baffin* □

Galliate 38 45 27N 8 44 E
Gallinas, Pta. 126 12 28N 71 40W
Gallípoli 41 40 8N 18 0 E
Gallipoli = Gelibolu 44 40 28N 26 43 E
Gallipolis 114 38 50N 82 10W
Gällivare 50 67 9N 20 40 E
Gallo, C. 40 38 13N 13 19 E
Gallocanta, Laguna de 32 40 58N 1 30W
Galloway 14 55 0N 4 25W
Galloway, Mull of 14 54 38N 4 50W
Gallup 119 35 30N 108 45W
Gallur 32 41 52N 1 19W
Gal'on 62 31 38N 34 51 E
Galong 99 34 37S 148 34 E
Galtström 48 62 10N 17 30 E
Galtür 26 46 58N 10 11 E
Galty Mts. 15 52 22N 8 10W
Galtymore 15 52 22N 8 12W
Galva 116 41 10N 90 0W
Galve de Sorbe 32 41 13N 3 10W
Galveston 117 29 15N 94 48W
Galveston B. 117 29 30N 94 50W
Gálvez, Argent. 124 32 0S 61 14W
Gálvez, Spain 31 39 42N 4 16W
Galway 15 53 16N 9 4W
Galway □ 15 53 16N 9 3W
Galway B. 15 53 10N 9 20W
Gamari, L. 87 11 32N 41 40 E
Gamawa 85 12 10N 10 31 E
Gambaga 85 10 30N 0 28W
Gambat 68 27 17N 68 26 E
Gambela 87 8 14N 34 38 E
Gambia ■ 84 13 25N 16 0W
Gambia → 84 13 28N 16 34W
Gamboa 120 9 8N 79 42W
Gamboli 68 29 53N 68 24 E
Gambos 89 14 37S 14 40 E
Gamerco 119 35 33N 108 56W
Gammon → 109 51 24N 95 44W
Gammouda 83 35 3N 9 39 E
Gan 20 43 12N 0 27W
Gan Goriama, Mts. 85 7 44N 12 45 E
Gan Jiang → 75 29 15N 116 0 E
Gan Shemu'el 62 32 28N 34 56 E
Gan Yavne 62 31 48N 34 42 E
Ganado, Ariz., U.S.A. 119 35 46N 109 41W
Ganado, Tex., U.S.A. 117 29 4N 96 31W
Gananoque 106 44 20N 76 10W
Ganaveh 65 29 35N 50 35 E
Gancheng 77 18 51N 108 37 E
Gand = Gent 16 51 2N 3 42 E
Ganda 89 13 3S 14 35 E
Gandak → 69 25 39N 85 13 E
Gandava 68 28 32N 67 32 E
Gander 107 48 58N 54 35W
Gander L. 107 48 58N 54 35W
Ganderowe Falls 91 17 20S 29 10 E
Gandesa 32 41 3N 0 26 E
Gandhi Sagar 68 24 40N 75 40 E
Gandi 85 12 55N 5 49 E
Gandía 33 38 58N 0 9W
Gandino 38 45 50N 9 52 E
Gandole 85 8 28N 11 35 E
Ganedidalem = Gani 73 0 48S 128 14 E
Ganetti 86 18 0N 31 10 E
Ganga → 69 23 20N 90 30 E
Ganga, Mouths of the 69 21 30N 90 0 E
Ganganagar 68 29 56N 73 56 E
Gangapur 68 26 32N 76 49 E
Gangara 85 14 35N 8 29 E
Gangavati 70 15 30N 76 36 E
Gangaw 67 22 5N 94 5 E
Gangdisê Shan 67 31 20N 81 0 E
Ganges 20 43 56N 3 42 E
Ganges = Ganga → 69 23 20N 90 30 E
Gangoh 68 29 46N 77 18 E
Gangtok 69 27 20N 88 37 E
Gani 73 0 48S 128 14 E
Ganj 68 27 45N 78 57 E
Gannat 20 46 7N 3 11 E
Gannett Pk. 118 43 15N 109 38W
Gannvalley 116 44 3N 98 57W
Ganquan 76 36 20N 109 20 E
Gänserdorf 27 48 20N 16 43 E
Gansu □ 75 36 0N 104 0 E
Ganta (Gompa) 84 7 15N 8 59W
Ganteaume B. 96 27 40S 114 10 E
Ganteaume, C. 99 36 4S 137 32 E
Gantsevichi 54 52 49N 26 30 E
Ganyu 77 34 50N 119 8 E
Ganyushkino 57 46 35N 49 20 E
Ganzhou 75 25 51N 114 56 E
Gao □ 85 18 0N 1 0 E
Gao Bang 72 22 37N 106 18 E
Gao'an 77 28 26N 115 17 E
Gaomi 76 36 20N 119 42 E
Gaoping 76 35 45N 112 55 E
Gaoua 84 10 20N 3 8W
Gaoual 84 11 45N 13 25W
Gaoxiong 75 22 38N 120 18 E
Gaoyou 77 32 47N 119 26 E
Gaoyou Hu 77 32 45N 119 20 E
Gaoyuan 76 37 8N 117 58 E
Gap 21 44 33N 6 5 E
Gar 75 32 10N 79 58 E
Garachiné 121 8 0N 78 12W
Garanhuns 127 8 50S 36 30W
Garawe 84 4 35N 8 0W
Garba Tula 90 0 30N 38 32 E
Garber 117 36 30N 97 36W
Garberville 118 40 11N 123 50W
Gard 63 9 30N 49 6 E
Gard □ 21 44 2N 4 10 E
Gard → 21 43 51N 4 37 E
Garda, L. di 38 45 40N 10 40 E
Gardala 81 5 40N 37 25 E
Gardanne 21 43 27N 5 27 E
Garde L. 109 62 50N 106 13W
Gardelegen 24 52 32N 11 21 E
Garden City, Kans., U.S.A. 117 38 0N 100 45W
Garden City, Tex., U.S.A. 117 31 52N 101 28W
Gardez 66 33 37N 69 9 E
Gardhíki 45 38 50N 21 55 E
Gardiner 118 45 3N 110 42W
Gardiners I. 113 41 4N 72 5W
Gardner 114 42 35N 72 0W
Gardner Canal 108 53 27N 128 8W
Gardnerville 118 38 59N 119 47W
Gardno, Jezioro 28 54 40N 17 7 E
Garešnica 42 45 36N 16 56 E
Garéssio 38 44 12N 8 1 E
Garfield 118 47 3N 117 8W
Gargaliánoi 45 37 4N 21 38 E
Gargano, Mte. 41 41 43N 15 43 E
Gargans, Mt. 20 45 37N 1 39 E
Gargouna 85 15 56N 0 13 E
Garhshankar 68 31 13N 76 11 E
Garibaldi Prov. Park 108 49 50N 122 40W
Garies 92 30 32S 17 59 E
Garigliano → 40 41 13N 13 44 E
Garissa 90 0 25S 39 40 E
Garissa □ 90 0 20S 40 0 E
Garkida 85 10 27N 12 36 E
Garko 85 11 45N 8 53 E
Garland 118 41 47N 112 10W
Garlasco 38 45 11N 8 55 E
Garm 58 39 0N 70 20 E
Garmisch-Partenkirchen 25 47 30N 11 5 E
Garmsār 65 35 20N 52 25 E
Garner 116 43 4N 93 37W
Garnett 116 38 18N 95 12W
Garo Hills 69 25 30N 90 30 E
Garob 92 26 37S 16 0 E
Garoe 63 8 25N 48 33 E
Garonne → 20 45 2N 0 36W
Garoua (Garwa) 85 9 19N 13 21 E
Garrel 24 52 58N 7 59 E
Garrigues 20 43 40N 3 30 E
Garrison, Mont., U.S.A. 118 46 30N 112 56W
Garrison, N.D., U.S.A. 116 47 39N 101 27W
Garrison, Tex., U.S.A. 117 31 50N 94 28W
Garrison Res. 116 47 30N 102 0W
Garrovillas 31 39 40N 6 33W
Garrucha 33 37 11N 1 49W
Garry → 14 56 47N 3 47W
Garry L. 104 65 58N 100 18W
Garsen 90 2 20S 40 5 E
Garson → 109 56 20N 110 1W
Garson L. 109 56 19N 110 2W
Gartempe → 20 46 47N 0 49 E
Gartz 24 53 12N 14 23 E
Garu 85 10 55N 0 11W
Garut 73 7 14S 107 53 E
Garvão 31 37 42N 8 21W
Garvie Mts. 101 45 30S 168 50 E
Garwa 69 24 11N 83 47 E
Garwolin 28 51 55N 21 38 E
Gary 114 41 35N 87 20W
Garz 24 54 17N 13 21 E
Garzê 75 31 39N 99 58 E
Garzón 126 2 10N 75 40W
Gasan Kuli 58 37 40N 54 20 E
Gascogne 20 43 45N 0 20 E
Gascogne, G. de 32 44 0N 2 0W
Gascony = Gascogne 20 43 45N 0 20 E
Gascoyne → 96 24 52S 113 37 E
Gascueña 32 40 18N 2 31W
Gash, Wadi → 87 16 48N 35 51 E
Gashaka 85 7 20N 11 29 E
Gashua 85 12 54N 11 0 E
Gaspé 107 48 52N 64 30W
Gaspé, C. 107 48 48N 64 7W
Gaspé, Pén. de 107 48 45N 65 40W
Gaspésie, Parc Prov. de la 107 48 55N 65 50W
Gassaway 114 38 42N 80 43W
Gássino Torinese 38 45 8N 7 50 E
Gassol 85 8 34N 10 25 E
Gastonia 115 35 17N 81 10W
Gastoúni 45 37 51N 21 15 E
Gastoúri 44 39 34N 19 54 E
Gastre 128 42 20S 69 15W
Gata, C. de 33 36 41N 2 13W
Gata, Sierra de 30 40 20N 6 45W
Gataga → 108 58 35N 126 59W
Gătaia 42 45 26N 21 30 E
Gatchina 54 59 35N 30 9 E
Gateshead 12 54 57N 1 37W
Gatesville 117 31 29N 97 45W
Gaths 91 20 2S 30 32 E
Gatico 124 22 29S 70 20W
Gâtinais 19 48 5N 2 40 E
Gâtine, Hauteurs de 20 46 35N 0 45W
Gatineau 113 45 29N 75 39W
Gatineau → 106 45 27N 75 42W
Gatineau, Parc de la 106 45 40N 76 0W
• Gatooma 91 18 20S 29 52 E
Gattinara 38 45 37N 8 22 E
Gatun 120 9 16N 79 55W
Gatun Dam 120 9 16N 79 55W
Gatun, L. 120 9 7N 79 56W
Gatun Locks 120 9 16N 79 55W
Gaucín 31 36 31N 5 19W
Gauer L. 109 57 0N 97 50W
Gauhati 67 26 10N 91 45 E
Gauja → 54 57 10N 24 16 E
Gaula → 47 63 21N 10 14 E
Gaussberg 5 66 45S 89 0 E
Gausta 47 59 50N 8 37 E
Gavá 32 41 18N 2 0 E
Gavarnie 20 42 44N 0 3W
Gavāter 65 25 10N 61 31 E
Gavdhopoúla 45 34 56N 24 0 E
Gávdhos 45 34 50N 24 5 E
Gavião 31 39 28N 7 56W
Gävle 48 60 40N 17 9 E
Gävleborgs län □ 48 61 30N 16 15 E
Gavorrano 38 42 55N 10 49 E
Gavray 18 48 55N 1 20W
Gavrilov Yam 55 57 18N 39 49 E
Gávrion 45 37 54N 24 44 E
Gawachab 92 27 4S 17 55 E
Gawilgarh Hills 68 21 15N 76 45 E
Gawler 97 34 30S 138 42 E
Gawler Ranges 96 32 30S 135 45 E
Gaxun Nur 75 42 22N 100 30 E
Gay 52 51 27N 58 27 E
Gaya, India 69 24 47N 85 4 E
Gaya, Niger 85 11 52N 3 28 E
Gaya, Nigeria 85 11 57N 9 0 E
Gaylord 114 45 1N 84 41W
Gayndah 97 25 35S 151 32 E
Gaysin 56 48 57N 28 25 E
Gayvoron 56 48 22N 29 52 E
Gaza 62 31 30N 34 28 E
Gaza □ 93 23 10S 32 45 E
Gaza Strip 62 31 29N 34 25 E
Gazaoua 85 13 32N 7 55 E
Gazelle Pen. 98 4 40S 152 0 E
Gazi 90 1 3N 24 30 E
Gaziantep 64 37 6N 37 23 E
Gazli 58 40 14N 63 24 E
Gbarnga 84 7 19N 9 13W
Gbekebo 85 6 20N 4 56 E
Gboko 85 7 17N 9 4 E
Gbongan 85 7 28N 4 20 E
Gcuwa 93 32 20S 28 11 E
Gdańsk 28 54 22N 18 40 E
Gdańsk □ 28 54 10N 18 30 E
Gdańska, Zatoka 28 54 30N 19 20 E
Gdov 54 58 48N 27 55 E
Gdynia 28 54 35N 18 33 E
Ge'a 62 31 38N 34 37 E
Gebe 73 0 5N 129 25 E
Gebeit Mine 86 21 3N 36 29 E
Gebel Mûsa 86 28 32N 33 59 E
Gecha 87 7 30N 35 18 E
Gedaref 87 14 2N 35 28 E
Gede, Tanjung 72 6 46S 105 12 E
Gedera 62 31 49N 34 46 E
Gedo 87 9 2N 37 25 E
Gèdre 20 42 47N 0 2 E
Gedser 49 54 35N 11 55 E
Gedser Odde 49 54 30N 11 58 E
Geelong 97 38 10S 144 22 E
Geestenseth 24 53 31N 8 51 E
Geesthacht 24 53 25N 10 20 E
Geidam 85 12 57N 11 57 E
Geikie → 109 57 45N 103 52W
Geili 87 16 1N 32 37 E
Geilo 47 60 32N 8 14 E
Geinica 27 48 51N 20 55 E
Geisingen 25 47 55N 8 37 E
Geislingen 25 48 37N 9 51 E
Geita 90 2 48S 32 12 E
Geita □ 90 2 50S 32 10 E
Gejiu 75 23 20N 103 10 E
Gel → 87 7 5N 29 10 E
Gel River 87 7 5N 29 10 E
Gela 41 37 6N 14 18 E
Gela, Golfo di 41 37 0N 14 8 E
Geladi 63 6 59N 46 30 E
Gelderland □ 16 52 5N 6 10 E
Geldermalsen 16 51 53N 5 17 E
Geldern 24 51 32N 6 18 E
Geldrop 16 51 25N 5 32 E
Geleen 16 50 57N 5 49 E
Gelehun 84 8 20N 11 40W
Gelendzhik 56 44 33N 38 10 E
Gelibolu 44 40 28N 26 43 E
Gelnhausen 25 50 12N 9 12 E
Gelsenkirchen 24 51 30N 7 5 E
Gelting 24 54 43N 9 53 E
Gemas 71 2 37N 102 36 E
Gembloux 16 50 34N 4 43 E
Gemena 88 3 13N 19 48 E
Gemerek 64 39 15N 36 10 E
Gemona del Friuli 39 46 16N 13 7 E
Gemsa 86 27 39N 33 35 E
Gemu-Gofa □ 87 5 40N 36 40 E
Gemünden 25 50 3N 9 43 E
Gen He → 76 50 16N 119 32 E
Genale 87 6 0N 39 30 E
Gençay 20 46 23N 0 23 E
Gendringen 16 51 52N 6 21 E
Geneina, Gebel 86 29 2N 33 55 E
General Acha 124 37 20S 64 38W
General Alvear, Buenos Aires, Argent. 124 36 0S 60 0W
General Alvear, Mendoza, Argent. 124 35 0S 67 40W
General Artigas 124 26 52S 56 16W
General Belgrano 124 36 35S 58 47W
General Cabrera 124 32 53S 63 52W
General Guido 124 36 40S 57 50W
General Juan Madariaga 124 37 0S 57 0W
General La Madrid 124 37 17S 61 20W
General MacArthur 73 11 18N 125 28 E
General Martin Miguel de Güemes 124 24 35S 65 0W
General Paz 124 27 45S 57 36W
General Pico 124 35 45S 63 50W
General Pinedo 124 27 15S 61 20W
General Pinto 124 34 45S 61 50W
General Santos 73 6 5N 125 14 E
General Toshevo 43 43 42N 28 6 E
General Trías 120 28 21N 106 22W
General Viamonte 124 35 1S 61 3W
General Villegas 124 35 0S 63 0W
Genesee, Idaho, U.S.A. 118 46 31N 116 59W
Genesee, Pa., U.S.A. 112 42 0N 77 54W
Genesee → 114 42 35N 78 0W
Geneseo, Ill., U.S.A. 116 41 25N 90 10W
Geneseo, Kans., U.S.A. 116 38 32N 98 8W
Geneseo, N.Y., U.S.A. 112 42 49N 77 49W
Geneva, Ala., U.S.A. 115 31 2N 85 52W
Geneva, N.Y., U.S.A. 114 42 53N 77 0W
Geneva, Nebr., U.S.A. 116 40 35N 97 35W
Geneva, Ohio, U.S.A. 114 41 49N 80 58W
Geneva = Genève 25 46 12N 6 9 E
Geneva, L. 114 42 38N 88 30W
Geneva, L. = Léman, Lac 25 46 26N 6 30 E
Genève 25 46 12N 6 9 E
Genève □ 25 46 10N 6 10 E
Gengenbach 25 48 25N 8 0 E
Genichesk 56 46 12N 34 50 E
Genil → 31 37 42N 5 19W
Génissiat, Barrage de 21 46 1N 5 48 E
Genjem 73 2 46S 140 12 E
Genk 16 50 58N 5 32 E
Genlis 19 47 15N 5 12 E
Gennargentu, Mti. del 40 40 0N 9 10 E
Gennep 16 51 41N 5 59 E
Gennes 18 47 20N 0 17W
Genoa, Austral. 99 37 29S 149 35 E
Genoa, N.Y., U.S.A. 113 42 40N 76 32W
Genoa, Nebr., U.S.A. 116 41 31N 97 44W
Genoa = Génova 38 44 24N 8 57 E
Génova 38 44 24N 8 56 E
Génova, Golfo di 38 44 0N 9 0 E
Gent 16 51 2N 3 42 E
Genthin 24 52 24N 12 10 E
Geographe B. 96 33 30S 115 15 E
Geographe Chan. 96 24 30S 113 0 E
Geokchay 57 40 42N 47 43 E
Georga, Zemlya 58 80 30N 49 0 E
George 92 33 58S 22 29 E
George → 107 58 49N 66 10W
George, L., N.S.W., Austral. 99 35 10S 149 25 E
George, L., S. Austral., Austral. 99 37 25S 140 0 E
George, L., Uganda 90 0 5N 30 10 E
George, L., Fla., U.S.A. 115 29 15N 81 35W
George, L., N.Y., U.S.A. 113 43 30N 73 30W
George River = Port Nouveau 105 58 30N 65 50W
George Sound 101 44 52S 167 25 E
George Town, Austral. 99 41 5S 146 49 E
George Town, Bahamas 121 23 33N 75 47W
George Town, Malay. 71 5 25N 100 15 E
George V Coast 5 69 0S 148 0 E
George VI Sound 5 71 0S 68 0W
George West 117 28 18N 98 5W
Georgetown, Austral. 97 18 17S 143 33 E
Georgetown, Ont., Can. 106 43 40N 79 56W
Georgetown, P.E.I., Can. 107 46 13N 62 24W
Georgetown, Gambia 84 13 30N 14 47W
Georgetown, Guyana 126 6 50N 58 12W
Georgetown, Colo., U.S.A. 118 39 46N 105 49W
Georgetown, Ky., U.S.A. 114 38 13N 84 33W
Georgetown, Ohio, U.S.A. 114 38 50N 83 50W
Georgetown, S.C., U.S.A. 115 33 22N 79 15W
Georgetown, Tex., U.S.A. 117 30 40N 97 45W
Georgi Dimitrov 43 42 15N 23 54 E
Georgi Dimitrov, Yazovir 43 42 37N 25 18 E
Georgia □ 115 32 0N 82 0W
Georgia, Str. of 108 49 25N 124 0W
Georgian B. 106 45 15N 81 0W
Georgian S.S.R. □ 57 42 0N 43 0 E
Georgievsk 57 44 12N 43 28 E
Georgina → 97 23 30S 139 47 E
Georgiu-Dezh 55 51 3N 39 30 E
Gera 24 50 53N 12 11 E
Gera □ 24 50 45N 11 45 E
Geraardsbergen 16 50 45N 3 53 E
Geral de Goiás, Serra 127 12 0S 46 0W
Geral, Serra 125 26 25S 50 0W
Geraldine 118 47 36N 110 18W
Geraldton, Austral. 96 28 48S 114 32 E
Geraldton, Can. 106 49 44N 86 59W
Gérardmer 19 48 3N 6 50 E
Gerede 56 40 45N 32 10 E
Gereshk 65 31 47N 64 35 E
Gérgal 33 37 7N 2 31W
Gerik 71 5 25N 101 0 E
Gering 116 41 51N 103 30W
Gerizim 62 32 13N 35 15 E
Gerlach 118 40 43N 119 27W
Gerlachovka 27 49 11N 20 7 E
Gerlogubi 63 6 53N 45 3 E
German Planina 42 42 20N 22 0 E
Germansen Landing 108 55 43N 124 40W
Germany, East ■ 24 52 0N 12 0 E
Germany, West ■ 24 52 0N 9 0 E
Germersheim 25 49 13N 8 20 E
Germiston 93 26 15S 28 10 E
Gernsheim 25 49 44N 8 29 E
Gerolstein 25 50 12N 6 40 E
Gerolzhofen 25 49 54N 10 21 E
Gerona 32 41 58N 2 46 E
Gerona □ 32 42 11N 2 30 E
Gerrard 108 50 30N 117 17W
Gers □ 20 43 35N 0 38 E
Gers → 20 44 9N 0 39 E
Gersfeld 24 50 27N 9 57 E
Gersoppa Falls 70 14 12N 74 46 E
Gerufa 92 19 17S 26 0 E
Geseke 24 51 38N 8 29 E
Geser 73 3 50S 130 54 E
Gesso → 38 44 24N 7 33 E
Gestro, Wabi → 87 4 12N 42 2 E
Getafe 30 40 18N 3 44W
Gethsémani 107 50 13N 60 40W
Gettysburg, Pa., U.S.A. 114 39 47N 77 18W
Gettysburg, S.D., U.S.A. 116 45 3N 99 56W
Getz Ice Shelf 5 75 0S 130 0W
Gévaudan 20 44 40N 3 40 E
Gevgelija 42 41 9N 22 30 E
Gévora → 31 38 53N 6 57W
Gex 21 46 21N 6 3 E
Geyikli 44 39 50N 26 12 E
Geyser 118 47 17N 110 30W
Geysir 50 64 19N 20 18W
Ghaghara → 69 25 45N 84 40 E
Ghalla, Wadi el → 87 10 25N 27 32 E
Ghana ■ 85 6 0N 1 0W
Ghansor 69 22 39N 80 1 E
Ghanzi 92 21 50S 21 34 E
Ghanzi □ 92 21 50S 21 45 E
Gharbîya, Es Sahrâ el 86 27 40N 26 30 E
Ghard Abû Muharik 86 26 50N 30 0 E
Ghardaïa 82 32 20N 3 37 E
Ghârib, G. 86 28 6N 32 54 E
Ghârib, Râs 86 28 6N 33 18 E
Gharyān 83 32 10N 13 0 E
Gharyān □ 83 30 35N 12 0 E
Ghat 83 24 59N 10 11 E
Ghatal 69 22 40N 87 46 E
Ghatampur 69 26 8N 80 13 E
Ghatprabha → 70 16 15N 75 20 E
Ghayl 64 21 40N 46 20 E

Renamed Kipungo

• Renamed Kadoma

Name	Map	Lat.	Long.
Ghazal, Bahr el →	**81**	15 0N	17 0 E
Ghazâl, Bahr el →	**87**	9 31N	30 25 E
Ghazaouet	**82**	35 8N	1 50W
Ghaziabad	**68**	28 42N	77 26 E
Ghazipur	**69**	25 38N	83 35 E
Ghazni	**66**	33 30N	68 28 E
Ghaznī □	**65**	33 0N	68 0 E
Ghedi	**38**	45 24N	10 16 E
Ghelari	**46**	45 38N	22 45 E
Ghèlinsor	**63**	6 28N	46 39 E
Ghent = Gand	**16**	51 2N	3 42 E
Gheorghe Gheorghiu-Dej	**46**	46 17N	26 47 E
Gheorgheni	**46**	46 43N	25 41 E
Ghergani	**46**	44 37N	25 37 E
Gherla	**46**	47 0N	23 57 E
Ghilarza	**40**	40 8N	8 50 E
Ghisonaccia	**21**	42 1N	9 26 E
Ghod →	**70**	18 30N	74 35 E
Ghot Ogrein	**86**	31 10N	25 20 E
Ghotaru	**68**	27 20N	70 1 E
Ghotki	**68**	28 5N	69 21 E
Ghowr □	**65**	34 0N	64 20 E
Ghudāmis	**83**	30 11N	9 29 E
Ghugri	**69**	22 39N	80 41 E
Ghugus	**70**	19 58N	79 12 E
Ghulam Mohammad Barrage	**68**	25 30N	68 20 E
Ghūrīān	**65**	34 17N	61 25 E
Gia Nghia	**71**	12 0N	107 42 E
Gian	**73**	5 45N	125 20 E
Giannutri	**38**	42 16N	11 5 E
Giant Mts. = Krkonoše	**26**	50 50N	16 10 E
Giant's Causeway	**15**	55 15N	6 30W
Giarre	**41**	37 44N	15 10 E
Giaveno	**38**	45 3N	7 20 E
Gibara	**121**	21 9N	76 11W
Gibbon	**116**	40 49N	98 45W
Gibe →	**87**	7 20N	37 36 E
Gibellina	**40**	37 48N	13 0 E
Gibeon	**92**	25 7 S	17 45 E
Gibraléon	**31**	37 23N	6 58W
Gibraltar	**31**	36 7N	5 22W
Gibraltar, Str. of	**31**	35 55N	5 40W
Gibson Des.	**96**	24 0 S	126 0 E
Gibsons	**108**	49 24N	123 32W
Giddalur	**70**	15 20N	78 57 E
Giddings	**117**	30 11N	96 58W
Gidole	**87**	5 40N	37 25 E
Gien	**19**	47 40N	2 36 E
Giessen	**24**	50 34N	8 40 E
Gifatin, Geziret	**86**	27 10N	33 50 E
Gifhorn	**24**	52 29N	10 32 E
Gifu	**74**	35 30N	136 45 E
Gifu □	**74**	35 40N	137 0 E
Gigant	**57**	46 28N	41 20 E
Giganta, Sa. de la	**120**	25 30N	111 30W
Gigen	**43**	43 40N	24 28 E
Gigha	**14**	55 42N	5 45W
Giglio	**38**	42 20N	10 52 E
Gignac	**20**	43 39N	3 32 E
Gigüela →	**33**	39 8N	3 44W
Gijón	**30**	43 32N	5 42W
Gil I.	**108**	53 12N	129 15W
Gila →	**119**	32 43N	114 33W
Gila Bend	**119**	33 0N	112 46W
Gila Bend Mts.	**119**	33 15N	113 0W
Gilan □	**64**	37 0N	48 0 E
Gilău	**46**	46 45N	23 23 E
Gilbert →	**97**	16 35 S	141 15 E
Gilbert Is.	**94**	1 0N	176 0 E
Gilbert Plains	**109**	51 9N	100 28W
Gilbert River	**98**	18 9 S	142 52 E
Gilberton	**98**	19 16 S	143 35 E
Gilf el Kebîr, Hadabat el	**86**	23 50N	25 50 E
Gilford I.	**108**	50 40N	126 30W
Gilgandra	**97**	31 43 S	148 39 E
Gilgil	**90**	0 30 S	36 20 E
Gilgit	**69**	35 50N	74 15 E
Giljeva Planina	**42**	43 9N	20 0 E
Gillam	**109**	56 20N	94 40W
Gilleleje	**49**	56 8N	12 19 E
Gillette	**116**	44 20N	105 30W
Gilliat	**98**	20 40 S	141 28 E
Gillingham	**13**	51 23N	0 34 E
Gilmer	**117**	32 44N	94 55W
Gilmore	**99**	35 20 S	148 12 E
Gilmour	**106**	44 48N	77 37W
Gilo →	**87**	8 10N	33 15 E
Gilort →	**46**	44 38N	23 32 E
Gilroy	**119**	37 1N	121 37W
Gimbi	**87**	9 3N	35 42 E
Gimigliano	**41**	38 58N	16 32 E
Gimli	**109**	50 40N	97 0W
Gimo	**48**	60 11N	18 12 E
Gimone →	**20**	44 0N	1 6 E
Gimont	**20**	43 38N	0 52 E
Gimzo	**62**	31 56N	34 56 E
Gin →	**70**	6 5N	80 7 E
Gin Gin	**99**	25 0 S	151 58 E
Ginâh	**86**	25 21N	30 30 E
Gindie	**98**	23 44 S	148 8 E
Gineta, La	**33**	39 8N	2 1W
Gîngiova	**46**	43 54N	23 50 E
Ginir	**87**	7 6N	40 40 E
Ginosa	**41**	40 35N	16 45 E
Ginzo de Limia	**30**	42 3N	7 47W
Giohar	**63**	2 48N	45 30 E
Gióia del Colle	**41**	40 49N	16 55 E
Gióia, G. di	**41**	38 30N	15 50 E
Gióia Táuro	**41**	38 26N	15 53 E
Gioiosa Iónica	**41**	38 20N	16 19 E
Gióna, Óros	**45**	38 38N	22 14 E
Giong, Teluk	**73**	4 50N	118 20 E
Giovi, Passo dei	**38**	44 33N	8 57 E
Giovinazzo	**41**	41 10N	16 40 E
Gippsland	**97**	37 45 S	147 15 E
Gir Hills	**68**	21 0N	71 0 E
Girab	**68**	26 2N	70 38 E
Giraltovce	**27**	49 7N	21 32 E
Girard, Kans., U.S.A.	**117**	37 30N	94 50W
Girard, Ohio, U.S.A.	**112**	41 10N	80 42W
Girard, Pa., U.S.A.	**112**	42 1N	80 21W
Girardot	**126**	4 18N	74 48W
Girdle Ness	**14**	57 9N	2 2W
Giresun	**64**	40 55N	38 30 E
Girga	**86**	26 17N	31 55 E
Giridih	**69**	24 10N	86 21 E
Girifalco	**41**	38 49N	16 25 E
Girilambone	**99**	31 16 S	146 57 E
Giro	**85**	11 7N	4 42 E
Giromagny	**19**	47 44N	6 50 E
Gironde □	**20**	44 45N	0 30W
Gironde →	**20**	45 32N	1 7W
Gironella	**32**	42 2N	1 53 E
Giru	**98**	19 30 S	147 5 E
Girvan	**14**	55 15N	4 50W
Gisborne	**101**	38 39 S	178 5 E
Gisenyi	**90**	1 41 S	29 15 E
Giske	**47**	62 30N	6 3 E
Gislaved	**49**	57 19N	13 32 E
Gisors	**19**	49 15N	1 47 E
Gitega (Kitega)	**90**	3 26 S	29 56 E
Giuba →	**63**	1 30N	42 35 E
Giugliano in Campania	**41**	40 55N	14 12 E
Giulianova	**39**	42 45N	13 58 E
Giurgeni	**46**	44 45N	27 48 E
Giurgiu	**46**	43 52N	25 57 E
Giv'at Brenner	**62**	31 52N	34 47 E
Giv'atayim	**62**	32 4N	34 49 E
Give	**49**	55 51N	9 13 E
Givet	**19**	50 8N	4 49 E
Givors	**21**	45 35N	4 45 E
Givry	**19**	46 41N	4 46 E
Giyon	**87**	8 33N	38 1 E
Giza = El Gîza	**86**	30 1N	31 11 E
Gizhiga	**59**	62 3N	160 30 E
Gizhiginskaya, Guba	**59**	61 0N	158 0 E
Giżycko	**28**	54 2N	21 48 E
Gizzeria	**41**	38 57N	16 10 E
Gjegjan	**44**	41 58N	20 3 E
Gjerstad	**47**	58 54N	9 0 E
Gjirokastra	**44**	40 7N	20 10 E
Gjoa Haven	**104**	68 20N	96 8W
Gjøl	**49**	57 4N	9 42 E
Gjøvik	**47**	60 47N	10 43 E
Glace Bay	**107**	46 11N	59 58W
Glacier B.	**108**	58 30N	136 10W
Glacier Nat. Park, Can.	**108**	51 15N	117 30W
Glacier Nat. Park, U.S.A.	**118**	48 35N	113 40W
Glacier Park	**118**	48 30N	113 18W
Glacier Peak Mt.	**118**	48 7N	121 7W
Gladewater	**117**	32 30N	94 58W
Gladstone, Austral.	**99**	33 15 S	138 22 E
Gladstone, Can.	**109**	50 13N	98 57W
Gladstone, U.S.A.	**114**	45 52N	87 1W
Gladwin	**114**	43 59N	84 29W
Gladys L.	**108**	59 50N	133 0W
Glafsfjorden	**48**	59 30N	12 37 E
Głagów Małapolski	**27**	50 10N	21 56 E
Gláma	**50**	65 48N	23 0W
Glåma →	**47**	59 12N	10 57 E
Glamoč	**39**	44 3N	16 51 E
Glan	**49**	58 37N	16 0 E
Glarus	**25**	47 3N	9 4 E
Glasco, Kans., U.S.A.	**116**	39 25N	97 50W
Glasco, N.Y., U.S.A.	**113**	42 3N	73 57W
Glasgow, U.K.	**14**	55 52N	4 14W
Glasgow, Ky., U.S.A.	**114**	37 2N	85 55W
Glasgow, Mont., U.S.A.	**118**	48 12N	106 35W
Glastonbury, U.K.	**13**	51 9N	2 42W
Glastonbury, U.S.A.	**113**	41 42N	72 27W
Glauchau	**24**	50 50N	12 33 E
Glazov	**55**	58 9N	52 40 E
Gleisdorf	**26**	47 6N	15 44 E
Gleiwitz = Gliwice	**28**	50 22N	18 41 E
Glen	**113**	44 7N	71 10W
Glen Affric	**14**	57 15N	5 0W
Glen Canyon Dam	**119**	37 0N	111 25W
Glen Canyon Nat. Recreation Area	**119**	37 30N	111 0W
Glen Coe	**12**	56 40N	5 0W
Glen Cove	**113**	40 51N	73 37W
Glen Garry	**14**	57 3N	5 7W
Glen Innes	**97**	29 44 S	151 44 E
Glen Lyon	**113**	41 10N	76 7W
Glen Mor	**14**	57 12N	4 37 E
Glen Moriston	**14**	57 10N	4 58W
Glen Orchy	**14**	56 27N	4 52W
Glen Spean	**14**	56 53N	4 40W
Glen Ullin	**116**	46 48N	101 46W
Glénans, Îles. de	**18**	47 42N	4 0W
Glenburnie	**100**	37 51 S	140 50 E
Glencoe, Can.	**112**	42 45N	81 43W
Glencoe, S. Afr.	**93**	28 11 S	30 11 E
Glencoe, U.S.A.	**116**	44 45N	94 10W
Glendale, Ariz., U.S.A.	**119**	33 40N	112 8W
Glendale, Calif., U.S.A.	**119**	34 7N	118 18W
Glendale, Oreg., U.S.A.	**118**	42 44N	123 29W
Glendale, Zimb.	**91**	17 22 S	31 5 E
Glendive	**116**	47 7N	104 40W
Glendo	**116**	42 30N	105 0W
Glenelg	**99**	34 58 S	138 31 E
Glenelg →	**99**	38 4 S	140 59 E
Glengarriff	**15**	51 45N	9 33W
Glengyle	**98**	24 48 S	139 37 E
Glenmora	**117**	31 1N	92 34W
Glenmorgan	**99**	27 14 S	149 42 E
Glenns Ferry	**118**	43 0N	115 15W
Glenorchy	**99**	42 49 S	147 18 E
Glenore	**98**	17 50 S	141 12 E
Glenormiston	**98**	22 55 S	138 50 E
Glenreagh	**99**	30 2 S	153 1 E
Glenrock	**118**	42 53N	105 55W
Glenrothes	**14**	56 12N	3 11W
Glens Falls	**114**	43 20N	73 40W
Glenties	**15**	54 48N	8 18W
Glenville	**114**	38 56N	80 50W
Glenwood, Alta., Can.	**108**	49 21N	113 31W
Glenwood, Newf., Can.	**107**	49 0N	54 58W
Glenwood, Ark., U.S.A.	**117**	34 20N	93 30W
Glenwood, Hawaii, U.S.A.	**110**	19 29N	155 10W
Glenwood, Iowa, U.S.A.	**116**	41 7N	95 41W
Glenwood, Minn., U.S.A.	**116**	45 38N	95 21W
Glenwood Sprs.	**118**	39 39N	107 21W
Glina	**39**	45 20N	16 6 E
Glinojeck	**28**	52 49N	20 21 E
Glittertind	**47**	61 40N	8 32 E
Gliwice	**28**	50 22N	18 41 E
Globe	**119**	33 25N	110 53W
Glodeanu Siliştea	**46**	44 50N	26 48 E
Glödnitz	**26**	46 53N	14 7 E
Glodyany	**46**	47 45N	27 31 E
Gloggnitz	**26**	47 41N	15 56 E
Głogów	**28**	51 37N	16 5 E
Głogowek	**28**	50 21N	17 53 E
Glorieuses, Îles	**93**	11 30 S	47 20 E
Glossop	**12**	53 27N	1 56W
Gloucester, Austral.	**99**	32 0 S	151 59 E
Gloucester, U.K.	**13**	51 52N	2 15W
Gloucester, U.S.A.	**113**	42 38N	70 39W
Gloucester, C.	**98**	5 26 S	148 21 E
Gloucester I.	**98**	20 0 S	148 30 E
Gloucestershire □	**13**	51 44N	2 10W
Gloversville	**114**	43 5N	74 18W
Glovertown	**107**	48 40N	54 03W
Głowno	**28**	51 59N	19 42 E
Głubczyce	**27**	50 13N	17 52 E
Glubokiy	**57**	48 35N	40 25 E
Glubokoye	**54**	55 10N	27 45 E
Glŭbovo	**43**	42 8N	25 55 E
Głuchołazy	**28**	50 19N	17 24 E
Glücksburg	**24**	54 48N	9 34 E
Glückstadt	**24**	53 46N	9 28 E
Glukhov	**54**	51 40N	33 58 E
Glussk	**54**	52 53N	28 41 E
Glyngøre	**49**	56 46N	8 52 E
Gmünd, Kärnten, Austria	**26**	46 54N	13 31 E
Gmünd, Niederösterreich, Austria	**26**	48 45N	15 0 E
Gmunden	**26**	47 55N	13 48 E
Gnarp	**48**	62 3N	17 16 E
Gnesta	**48**	59 3N	17 17 E
Gniew	**28**	53 50N	18 50 E
Gniewkowo	**28**	52 54N	18 25 E
Gniezno	**28**	52 30N	17 35 E
Gnjilane	**42**	42 28N	21 29 E
Gnoien	**24**	53 58N	12 41 E
Gnosjö	**49**	57 22N	13 43 E
Gnowangerup	**96**	33 58 S	117 59 E
Go Cong	**71**	10 22N	106 40 E
Goa	**70**	15 33N	73 59 E
Goa □	**70**	15 33N	73 59 E
Goageb	**92**	26 49 S	17 15 E
Goalen Hd.	**99**	36 33 S	150 4 E
Goalpara	**69**	26 10N	90 40 E
Goalundo Ghat	**69**	23 50N	89 47 E
Goaso	**84**	6 48N	2 30W
Goat Fell	**14**	55 37N	5 11W
Goba	**87**	7 1N	39 59 E
Gobabis	**92**	22 30 S	19 0 E
Gobi	**75**	44 0N	111 0 E
Gobichettipalayam	**70**	11 31N	77 21 E
Gobo	**87**	5 40N	31 10 E
Goch	**24**	51 40N	6 9 E
Gochas	**92**	24 59 S	18 55 E
Godavari →	**70**	16 25N	82 18 E
Godavari Point	**70**	17 0N	82 20 E
Godbout	**107**	49 20N	67 38W
Godda	**69**	24 50N	87 13 E
Goddua	**83**	26 26N	14 19 E
Godech	**42**	43 1N	23 4 E
Godegård	**49**	58 43N	15 8 E
Goderich	**106**	43 45N	81 41W
Goderville	**18**	49 38N	0 22 E
Godhavn	**4**	69 15N	53 38W
Godhra	**68**	22 49N	73 40 E
Gödöllö	**27**	47 38N	19 25 E
Godoy Cruz	**124**	32 56 S	68 52W
Gods →	**109**	56 22N	92 51W
Gods L.	**109**	54 40N	94 15W
Godthåb	**4**	64 10N	51 35W
Godwin Austen (K2)	**69**	36 0N	77 0 E
Goeie Hoop, Kaap die	**92**	34 24 S	18 30 E
Goéland, L. au	**106**	49 50N	76 48W
Goeree	**16**	51 50N	4 0 E
Goes	**16**	51 30N	3 55 E
Gogama	**106**	47 35N	81 43W
Gogango	**98**	23 40 S	150 2 E
Gogebic, L.	**116**	46 20N	89 34W
Gogha	**68**	21 40N	72 20 E
Gogolin	**28**	50 30N	18 0 E
Gogra = Ghaghara →	**67**	26 0N	84 20 E
Gogriâl	**87**	8 30N	28 8 E
Goiânia	**127**	16 43 S	49 20W
Goiás	**127**	15 55 S	50 10W
Goiás □	**127**	12 10 S	48 0W
Góis	**30**	40 10N	8 6W
Goisern	**26**	47 38N	13 38 E
Gojam □	**87**	10 55N	36 30 E
Gojeb, Wabi →	**87**	7 12N	36 40 E
Gojra	**68**	31 10N	72 40 E
Gokak	**70**	16 11N	74 52 E
Gokarannath	**69**	27 57N	80 39 E
Gokarn	**70**	14 33N	74 17 E
Gökçeada	**44**	40 10N	25 50 E
Gokteik	**67**	22 26N	97 0 E
Gokurt	**68**	29 40N	67 26 E
Gola	**69**	28 3N	80 32 E
Golakganj	**69**	26 8N	89 52 E
Golaya Pristen	**56**	46 29N	32 32 E
Golchikha	**4**	71 45N	83 30 E
Golconda	**118**	40 58N	117 32W
Gold Beach	**118**	42 25N	124 25W
Gold Coast, Austral.	**99**	28 0 S	153 25 E
Gold Coast, W. Afr.	**85**	4 0N	1 40W
Gold Hill	**118**	42 28N	123 2W
Gold River	**108**	49 46N	126 3 E
Gołdap	**28**	54 19N	22 18 E
Goldberg	**24**	53 34N	12 6 E
Golden, Can.	**108**	51 20N	117 59W
Golden, U.S.A.	**116**	39 42N	105 15W
Golden Bay	**101**	40 40 S	172 50 E
Golden Gate	**118**	37 54N	122 30W
Golden Hinde	**108**	49 40N	125 44W
Golden Lake	**112**	45 34N	77 21W
Golden Prairie	**109**	50 13N	109 37W
Golden Rock	**70**	10 45N	78 48 E
Golden Vale	**15**	52 33N	8 17
Goldendale	**118**	45 53N	120 48
Goldfield	**119**	37 45N	117 13
Goldfields	**109**	59 28N	108 29
Goldsand L.	**109**	57 2N	101 8
Goldsboro	**115**	35 24N	77 59
Goldsmith	**117**	32 0N	102 40
Goldthwaite	**117**	31 25N	98 32
Golegã	**31**	39 24N	8 29
Golęniów	**28**	53 35N	14 50
Golfito	**121**	8 41N	83 5
Golfo Aranci	**40**	41 0N	9 35
Goliad	**117**	28 40N	97 22
Golija, Crna Gora, Yugo.	**42**	43 5N	18 45
Golija, Srbija, Yugo.	**42**	43 22N	20 15
Golina	**28**	52 15N	18 4
Göllersdorf	**27**	48 29N	16 7
Golo →	**21**	42 31N	9 32
Golovanevsk	**56**	48 25N	30 30
Golspie	**14**	57 58N	3 58
Golub Dobrzyń	**28**	53 7N	19 2
Golubac	**42**	44 38N	21 38
Golyam Perelik	**43**	41 36N	24 33
Golyama Kamchiya →	**43**	43 10N	27 55
Goma, Rwanda	**90**	2 11 S	29 18
Goma, Zaîre	**90**	1 37 S	29 10
Gomare	**92**	19 25 S	22 8
Gomati →	**69**	25 32N	83 11
Gombari	**90**	2 45N	29 3
Gombe	**85**	10 19N	11 2
Gombe →	**90**	4 38 S	31 40
Gombi	**85**	10 12N	12 30
Gomel	**54**	52 28N	31 0
Gomera	**80**	28 7N	17 14
Gómez Palacio	**120**	25 40N	104 0
Gommern	**24**	52 5N	11 47
Gomogomo	**73**	6 39 S	134 43
Gomotartsi	**42**	44 6N	22 57
Gomphoi	**44**	39 31N	21 27
Gonābād	**65**	34 15N	58 45
Gonaïves	**121**	19 20N	72 42
Gonâve, G. de la	**121**	19 29N	72 42
Gonbab-e Kāvūs	**65**	37 20N	55 25
Gönc	**27**	48 28N	21 14
Gonda	**69**	27 9N	81 58
Gondal	**68**	21 58N	70 52
Gonder	**87**	12 39N	37 30
Gondia	**69**	21 23N	80 10
Gondola	**91**	19 10 S	33 37
Gondomar, Port.	**30**	41 10N	8 35
Gondomar, Spain	**30**	42 7N	8 45
Gondrecourt-le-Château	**19**	48 26N	5 30
Gonghe	**75**	36 18N	100 32
Gongola □	**85**	8 0N	12 0
Gongola →	**85**	9 30N	12 4
Goniadz	**28**	53 30N	22 44
Goniri	**85**	11 30N	12 15
Gonnesa	**40**	39 17N	8 27
Gónnos	**44**	39 52N	22 29
Gonnosfanadiga	**40**	39 30N	8 39
Gonzales, Calif., U.S.A.	**119**	36 35N	121 30
Gonzales, Tex., U.S.A.	**117**	29 30N	97 30
González Chaves	**124**	38 02 S	60 05
Good Hope, C. of = Goeie Hoop, K. die	**92**	34 24 S	18 30
Goodenough I.	**98**	9 20 S	150 15
Gooderham	**106**	44 54N	78 21
Goodeve	**109**	51 4N	103 10
Gooding	**118**	43 0N	114 44
Goodland	**116**	39 22N	101 44
Goodnight	**117**	35 4N	101 13
Goodooga	**99**	29 3 S	147 28
Goodsoil	**109**	54 24N	109 13
Goodsprings	**119**	35 51N	115 30
Goole	**12**	53 42N	0 52
Goolgowi	**99**	33 58 S	145 41
Goombalie	**99**	29 59 S	145 26
Goonda	**91**	19 48 S	33 57
Goondiwindi	**97**	28 30 S	150 21
Goor	**16**	52 13N	6 33
Gooray	**99**	28 25 S	150 2
Goose →	**107**	53 20N	60 35
Goose Bay	**107**	53 15N	60 20
Goose L.	**118**	42 0N	120 30
Gooty	**70**	15 7N	77 41
Gopalganj, Bangla.	**69**	23 1N	89 50
Gopalganj, India	**69**	26 28N	84 30
Göppingen	**25**	48 42N	9 40
Gor	**33**	37 23N	2 58
Góra, Leszno, Poland	**28**	51 40N	16 31
Góra, Płock, Poland	**28**	52 39N	20 6
Góra Kalwaria	**28**	51 59N	21 14
Gorakhpur	**69**	26 47N	83 23
Goražde	**42**	43 38N	18 58
Gorbatov	**55**	56 12N	43 2
Gorbea, Peña	**32**	43 1N	2 50
Gorda, Punta	**121**	14 20N	83 10
Gordon, Austral.	**99**	32 7 S	138 20
Gordon, U.S.A.	**116**	42 49N	102 12
Gordon →	**99**	42 27 S	145 30
Gordon Downs	**96**	18 48 S	128 33
Gordon L., Alta., Can.	**109**	56 30N	110 25
Gordon L., N.W.T., Can.	**108**	63 5N	113 11
Gordonia	**92**	28 13 S	21 10
Gordonvale	**98**	17 5 S	145 50
Gore	**99**	28 17 S	151 30
Goré	**81**	7 59N	16 31
Gore, Ethiopia	**87**	8 12N	35 32
Gore, N.Z.	**101**	46 5 S	168 58
Gore Bay	**106**	45 57N	82 28
Gorey	**15**	52 41N	6 18
Gorgān	**65**	36 55N	54 30
Gorgona	**38**	43 27N	9 52
Gorgona, I.	**126**	3 0N	78 10
Gorgora	**87**	12 15N	37 17
Gorham	**113**	44 23N	71 10
Gori	**57**	42 0N	44 7
Gorinchem	**16**	51 50N	4 59
Goritsy	**55**	57 4N	36 43
Gorízia	**39**	45 56N	13 37
Górka	**28**	51 39N	16 58
Gorki	**54**	54 17N	30 59

orki = Gorkiy 55 56 20N 44 0 E
orkiy 55 56 20N 44 0 E
orkovskoye Vdkhr. 55 57 2N 43 4 E
orlev 49 55 30N 11 15 E
orlice 27 49 35N 21 11 E
örlitz 24 51 10N 14 59 E
orlovka 56 48 19N 38 5 E
orman 117 32 15N 98 43W
orna Oryakhovitsa 43 43 7N 25 40 E
ornja Radgona 39 46 40N 16 2 E
ornja Tuzla 42 44 35N 18 46 E
ornji Grad 39 46 20N 14 52 E
ornji Milanovac 42 44 00N 20 29 E
ornji Vakuf 42 43 57N 17 34 E
orno Ablanovo 43 43 37N 25 43 E
orno-Altaysk 58 51 50N 86 5 E
orno Slinkino 58 60 5N 70 0 E
ornyatski 52 67 32N 64 3 E
ornyy 55 51 50N 48 30 E
orodenka 56 48 41N 25 29 E
orodets 55 56 38N 43 28 E
orodische 55 53 13N 45 40 E
orodishche 56 49 17N 31 27 E
orodnitsa 54 50 46N 27 19 E
orodnya 54 51 55N 31 33 E
orodok, Byelorussia, U.S.S.R. 54 55 30N 30 3 E
orodok, Ukraine, U.S.S.R. 54 49 46N 23 32 E
oroka 98 6 7 S 145 25 E
orokhov 54 50 30N 24 45 E
orokhovets 55 56 13N 42 39 E
orom Gorom 85 14 26N 0 14W
oromonzi 91 17 52 S 31 22 E
orong, Kepulauan 73 4 5 S 131 25 E
orongosa, Sa. da 91 18 27 S 34 2 E
orongose → 93 20 30 S 34 40 E
orontalo 73 0 35N 123 5 E
oronyo 85 13 29N 5 39 E
órowo Iławeckie 28 54 17N 20 30 E
orron 18 48 25N 0 50W
ort 15 53 4N 8 50W
orumahisani 69 22 20N 86 24 E
orzkowice 28 51 13N 19 36 E
orzno 28 53 12N 19 38 E
orzów Śląski 28 51 3N 18 22 E
orzów Wielkopolski 28 52 43N 15 15 E
orzów Wielkopolski □ 28 52 45N 15 30 E
osford 99 33 23 S 151 18 E
oshen, S. Afr. 92 25 50 S 25 0 E
oshen, Ind., U.S.A. 114 41 36N 85 46W
oshen, N.Y., U.S.A. 113 41 23N 74 21W
oslar 24 51 55N 10 23 E
ospič 39 44 35N 15 23 E
osport 13 50 48N 1 8W
ostivar 42 41 48N 20 57 E
ostyń 28 51 50N 17 3 E
ostynin 28 52 26N 19 29 E
öta älv → 49 57 42N 11 54 E
öteborg 49 57 43N 11 59 E
ötene 49 58 32N 13 30 E
otha 24 50 56N 10 42 E
othenburg 116 40 58N 100 8W
otland 49 57 30N 18 33 E
otō-Rettō 74 32 55N 129 5 E
otse Delchev (Nevrokop) 43 41 43N 23 46 E
öttingen 24 51 31N 9 55 E
ottwaldov (Zlin) 27 49 14N 17 40 E
oubangzi 76 41 20N 121 52 E
ouda 16 52 1N 4 42 E
oudiry 84 14 15N 12 45W
ough I. 7 40 10 S 9 45W
ouin Rés. 106 48 35N 74 40W
ouitafla 84 7 30N 5 53W
oula Touila 82 21 50N 1 57W
oulburn 97 34 44 S 149 44 E
oulburn → 100 36 6 S 144 55 E
oulburn Is. 96 11 40 S 133 20 E
oulia 84 10 1N 7 11W
oulimine 82 28 56N 10 0W
oulmina 82 31 41N 4 57W
ouménissa 44 40 56N 22 37 E
ounou-Gaya 81 9 38N 15 31 E
oúra 45 37 56N 22 20 E
ourara 82 29 0N 0 30 E
ouraya 82 36 31N 1 56 E
ourdon 20 44 44N 1 23 E
ouré 85 14 0N 10 10 E
ouri 81 19 36N 19 36 E
ourits → 92 34 21 S 21 52 E
ourma Rharous 85 16 55N 1 50W
ournay-en-Bray 19 49 29N 1 44 E
ourock Ra. 99 36 0 S 149 25 E
oursi 84 12 42N 2 37W
ouverneur 113 44 18N 75 30W
ouzon 20 46 12N 2 14 E
ovan 109 51 20N 105 0W
ove 97 12 25 S 136 55 E
overnador Valadares 127 18 15 S 41 57W
owan Ra. 98 25 0 S 145 0 E
owanda 114 42 29N 78 58W
owd-e Zirreh 65 29 45N 62 0 E
ower, The 13 51 35N 4 10W
owna, L. 15 53 52N 7 35W
owrie, Carse of 14 56 30N 3 10W
oya 124 29 10 S 59 10W
oyllarisquisga 126 10 31 S 76 24W
oz Beïda 81 12 10N 21 20 E
oz Regeb 87 16 3N 35 33 E
ozdnica 28 51 28N 15 4 E
ozo (Ghawdex) 36 36 0N 14 13 E
raaff-Reinet 92 32 13 S 24 32 E
rabow 24 53 17N 11 31 E
rabów 28 51 31N 18 7 E
račac 39 44 18N 15 57 E
račanica 42 44 43N 18 18 E
raçay 19 47 10N 1 50 E
race 118 38 38N 111 46W
raceville 116 45 36N 96 23W
racias a Dios, C. 121 15 0N 83 10W
radačac 42 44 52N 18 26 E
radeška Planina 42 41 30N 22 15 E
radets 43 42 46N 26 30 E
rado, Italy 39 45 40N 13 20 E
Grado, Spain 30 43 23N 6 4W
Gradule 99 28 32 S 149 15 E
Grady 117 34 52N 103 15W
Graeca, Lacul 46 44 5N 26 10 E
Graénalon, L. 50 64 10N 17 20W
Grafenau 25 48 51N 13 24 E
Gräfenberg 25 49 39N 11 15 E
Grafton, Austral. 97 29 38 S 152 58 E
Grafton, U.S.A. 116 48 30N 97 25W
Grafton, C. 97 16 51 S 146 0 E
Gragnano 41 40 42N 14 30 E
Graham, Can. 106 49 20N 90 30W
Graham, N.C., U.S.A. 115 36 5N 79 22W
Graham, Tex., U.S.A. 117 33 7N 98 38W
Graham → 108 56 31N 122 17W
Graham Bell, Os. 58 80 5N 70 0 E
Graham I. 108 53 40N 132 30W
Graham Land 5 65 0 S 64 0W
Graham Mt. 119 32 46N 109 58W
Grahamdale 109 51 23N 98 30W
Grahamstown 92 33 19 S 26 31 E
Grahovo 42 42 40N 18 40 E
Graïba 83 34 30N 10 13 E
Graie, Alpi 38 45 30N 7 10 E
Grain Coast 84 4 20N 10 0W
Grajaú 127 5 50 S 46 4W
Grajaú → 127 3 41 S 44 48W
Grajewo 28 53 39N 22 30 E
Gral. Martin Miguel de Gäemes 124 24 50 S 65 0W
Gramada 42 43 49N 22 39 E
Gramat 20 44 48N 1 43 E
Grammichele 41 37 12N 14 37 E
Grámmos, Óros 44 40 18N 20 47 E
Grampian □ 14 57 0N 3 0W
Grampian Mts. 14 56 50N 4 0W
Grampians, Mts. 99 37 0 S 142 20 E
Gran Canaria 80 27 55N 15 35W
Gran Chaco 124 25 0 S 61 0W
Gran Paradiso 38 45 33N 7 17 E
Gran Sasso d'Italia 39 42 25N 13 30 E
Granada, Nic. 121 11 58N 86 0W
Granada, Spain 33 37 10N 3 35W
Granada, U.S.A. 117 38 5N 102 20W
Granada □ 31 37 18N 3 0W
Granard 15 53 47N 7 30W
Granbury 117 32 28N 97 48W
Granby 106 45 25N 72 45W
Grand →, Mo., U.S.A. 116 39 23N 93 6W
Grand →, Mo., U.S.A. 116 39 23N 93 6W
Grand →, S.D., U.S.A. 116 45 40N 100 32W
Grand Bahama 121 26 40N 78 30W
Grand Bank 107 47 6N 55 48W
Grand Bassam 84 5 10N 3 49W
Grand Bérébу 84 4 38N 6 55W
Grand-Bourge 121 15 53N 61 19W
Grand Canyon 119 36 3N 112 9W
Grand Canyon National Park 119 36 15N 112 20W
Grand Cayman 121 19 20N 81 20W
Grand Cess 84 4 40N 8 12W
Grand-Combe, La 21 44 13N 4 2 E
Grand Coulee 118 47 48N 119 1W
Grand Coulee Dam 118 48 0N 118 50W
Grand Erg Occidental 82 30 20N 1 0 E
Grand Erg Oriental 83 30 0N 6 30 E
Grand Falls 107 48 56N 55 40W
Grand Forks, Can. 108 49 0N 118 30W
Grand Forks, U.S.A. 116 48 0N 97 3W
Grand-Fougeray 18 47 44N 1 43W
Grand Haven 114 43 3N 86 13W
Grand I. 106 46 30N 86 40W
Grand Island 116 40 59N 98 25W
Grand Isle 117 29 15N 89 58W
Grand Junction 119 39 0N 108 30W
Grand L., N.B., Can. 107 45 57N 66 7W
Grand L., Newf., Can. 107 53 40N 60 30W
Grand L., Newf., Can. 107 49 0N 57 30W
Grand L., U.S.A. 117 29 55N 92 45W
Grand Lac Victoria 106 47 35N 77 35W
Grand Lahou 84 5 10N 5 0W
Grand Lake 118 40 20N 105 54W
Grand-Lieu, Lac de 18 47 6N 1 40W
Grand-Luce, Le 18 47 52N 0 28 E
Grand Manan I. 107 44 45N 66 52W
Grand Marais, Can. 116 47 45N 90 25W
Grand Marais, U.S.A. 114 46 39N 85 59W
Grand Mère 106 46 36N 72 40W
Grand Popo 85 6 15N 1 57 E
Grand Portage 106 47 58N 89 41W
Grand-Pressigny, Le 18 46 55N 0 48 E
Grand Rapids, Can. 109 53 12N 99 19W
Grand Rapids, Mich., U.S.A. 114 42 57N 86 40W
Grand Rapids, Minn., U.S.A. 116 47 15N 93 29W
Grand St.-Bernard, Col. du 25 45 53N 7 11 E
Grand Teton 118 43 54N 111 50W
Grand Valley 118 39 30N 108 2W
Grand View 109 51 10N 100 42W
Grandas de Salime 30 43 13N 6 53W
Grande →, Jujuy, Argent. 124 24 20 S 65 2W
Grande →, Mendoza, Argent. 124 36 52 S 69 45W
Grande →, Boliv. 126 15 51 S 64 39W
Grande →, Bahia, Brazil 127 11 30 S 44 30W
Grande →, Minas Gerais, Brazil 127 20 6 S 51 4W
Grande →, Spain 33 39 6N 0 48W
Grande →, U.S.A. 117 25 57N 97 9W
Grande, B. 128 50 30 S 68 20W
Grande Baie 107 48 19N 70 52W
Grande Baleine → 106 55 20N 77 50W
Grande Cache 108 53 53N 119 8W
Grande, Coxilha 125 28 18 S 51 30W
Grande de Santiago → 120 21 20N 105 50W
Grande-Entrée 107 47 30N 61 40W
Grande, La 118 45 15N 118 0W
Grande-Motte, La 21 43 23N 4 3 E
Grande Prairie 108 55 10N 118 50W
Grande-Rivière 107 48 26N 64 30W
Grande-Saulde → 19 47 22N 1 55 E
Grande-Vallée 107 49 14N 65 8W
Grandes-Bergeronnes 107 48 16N 69 35W
Grandfalls 117 31 21N 102 51W
Grandoe Mines 108 56 29N 129 54W
Grândola 31 38 12N 8 35W
Grandpré 19 49 20N 4 50 E
Grandview 118 46 13N 119 58W
Grandvilliers 19 49 40N 1 57 E
Graneros 124 34 5 S 70 45W
Grange, La, Ga., U.S.A. 115 33 4N 85 0W
Grange, La, Ky., U.S.A. 114 38 20N 85 20W
Grange, La, Tex., U.S.A. 117 29 54N 96 52W
Grangemouth 14 56 1N 3 43W
Granger, U.S.A. 118 46 25N 120 5W
Granger, Wyo., U.S.A. 118 41 35N 109 58W
Grängesberg 48 60 6N 15 1 E
Grangeville 118 45 57N 116 4W
Granite City 116 38 45N 90 3W
Granite Falls 116 44 45N 95 35W
Granite Pk. 118 45 8N 109 52W
Granity 101 41 39 S 171 51 E
Granja 127 3 7 S 40 50W
Granja de Moreruela 30 41 48N 5 44W
Granja de Torrehermosa 31 38 19N 5 35W
Gränna 49 58 1N 14 28 E
Granollers 32 41 39N 2 18 E
Gransee 24 53 0N 13 10 E
Grant 116 40 53N 101 42W
Grant City 116 40 30N 94 25W
Grant, Mt. 118 38 34N 118 48W
Grant, Pt. 100 38 32 S 145 6 E
Grant Range Mts. 119 38 30N 115 30W
Grantham 12 52 55N 0 39W
Grantown-on-Spey 14 57 19N 3 36W
Grants 119 35 14N 107 51W
Grants Pass 118 42 30N 123 22W
Grantsburg 116 45 46N 92 44W
Grantsville 118 40 35N 112 32W
Granville, France 18 48 50N 1 35W
Granville, N.D., U.S.A. 116 48 18N 100 48W
Granville, N.Y., U.S.A. 114 43 24N 73 16W
Granville L. 109 56 18N 100 30W
Grao de Gandía 33 39 0N 0 7W
Grapeland 117 31 30N 95 31W
Gras, L. de 104 64 30N 110 30W
Graskop 93 24 56 S 30 49 E
Gräsö 48 60 28N 18 35 E
Grass → 109 56 3N 96 33W
Grass Range 118 47 0N 109 0W
Grass River Prov. Park 109 54 40N 100 50W
Grass Valley, Calif., U.S.A. 118 39 18N 121 0W
Grass Valley, Oreg., U.S.A. 118 45 22N 120 48W
Grassano 41 40 38N 16 17 E
Grasse 21 43 38N 6 56 E
Graubünden (Grisons) □ 25 46 45N 9 30 E
Graulhet 20 43 45N 1 58 E
Graus 32 42 11N 0 20 E
Grave, Pte. de 20 45 34N 1 4W
Gravelbourg 109 49 50N 106 35W
Gravelines 19 51 0N 2 10 E
's-Gravenhage 16 52 7N 4 17 E
Gravenhurst 112 44 52N 79 20W
Gravesend, Austral. 99 29 35 S 150 20 E
Gravesend, U.K. 13 51 25N 0 22 E
Gravina di Púglia 41 40 48N 16 25 E
Gravois, Pointe-à- 121 16 15N 73 56W
Gravone → 21 41 58N 8 45 E
Gray 19 47 27N 5 35 E
Grayling 114 44 40N 84 42W
Grayling → 108 59 21N 125 0W
Grays Harbor 118 46 55N 124 8W
Grays L. 118 43 8N 111 30W
Grayson 109 50 45N 102 40W
Graz 26 47 4N 15 27 E
Grazalema 31 36 46N 5 23W
Grdelica 42 42 55N 22 3 E
Greasy L. 108 62 55N 122 12W
Great Abaco I. 121 26 25N 77 10W
Great Australia Basin 97 26 0 S 140 0 E
Great Australian Bight 96 33 30 S 130 0 E
Great Bahama Bank 121 23 15N 78 0W
Great Barrier I. 101 36 11 S 175 25 E
Great Barrier Reef 97 18 0 S 146 50 E
Great Barrington 113 42 11N 73 22W
Great Basin 118 40 0N 116 30W
Great Bear → 104 65 0N 124 0W
Great Bear L. 104 65 30N 120 0W
Great Bena 113 41 57N 75 45W
Great Bend 116 38 25N 98 55W
Great Blasket I. 15 52 5N 10 30W
Great Britain 8 54 0N 2 15W
Great Bushman Land 92 29 20 S 19 20 E
Great Central 108 49 20N 125 10W
Great Divide, The 100 35 0 S 149 17 E
Great Dividing Ra. 97 23 0 S 146 0 E
Great Exuma I. 121 23 30N 75 50W
Great Falls, Can. 109 50 27N 96 1W
Great Falls, U.S.A. 118 47 27N 111 12W
Great Fish →, C. Prov., S. Afr. 92 31 30 S 20 16 E
Great Fish →, C. Prov., S. Afr. 92 33 28 S 27 5 E
Great Guana Cay 121 24 0N 76 20W
Great Harbour Deep 107 50 25N 56 32W
Great I. 109 58 53N 96 35W
Great Inagua I. 121 21 0N 73 20W
Great Indian Desert = Thar Desert 68 28 0N 72 0 E
Great Lake 97 41 50 S 146 40 E
Great Orme's Head 12 53 20N 3 52W
Great Ouse → 12 52 47N 0 22 E
Great Palm I. 98 18 45 S 146 40 E
Great Plains 102 47 0N 105 0W
Great Ruaha → 90 7 56 S 37 52 E
Great Salt Lake 102 41 0N 112 30W
Great Salt Lake Desert 118 40 20N 113 50W
Great Salt Plains Res. 117 36 40N 98 15W
Great Sandy Desert 96 21 0 S 124 0 E
Great Scarcies → 84 9 0N 13 0W
Great Slave L. 108 61 23N 115 38W
Great Smoky Mt. Nat. Park 115 35 39N 83 30W
Great Stour → 13 51 15N 1 20 E
Great Victoria Des. 96 29 30 S 126 30 E
Great Wall 76 38 30N 109 30 E
Great Whernside 12 54 9N 1 59W
Great Winterhoek 92 33 07 S 19 10 E
Great Yarmouth 12 52 40N 1 45 E
Greater Antilles 121 17 40N 74 0W
Greater London □ 13 51 30N 0 5W
Greater Manchester □ 12 53 30N 2 15W
Greater Sunda Is. 72 7 0 S 112 0 E
Grebbestad 49 58 42N 11 15 E
Grebenka 54 50 9N 32 22 E
Greco, Mte. 40 41 48N 14 0 E
Gredos, Sierra de 30 40 20N 5 0W
Greece ■ 44 40 0N 23 0 E
Greeley, Colo., U.S.A. 116 40 30N 104 40W
Greeley, Nebr., U.S.A. 116 41 36N 98 32W
Green →, Ky., U.S.A. 114 37 54N 87 30W
Green →, Utah, U.S.A. 119 38 11N 109 53W
Green B. 114 45 0N 87 30W
Green Bay 114 44 30N 88 0W
Green C. 99 37 13 S 150 1 E
Green Cove Springs 115 29 59N 81 40W
Green Is. 98 4 35 S 154 10 E
Green Island 101 45 55 S 170 26 E
Green River 119 38 59N 110 10W
Greenbush, Mich., U.S.A. 112 44 35N 83 19W
Greenbush, Minn., U.S.A. 116 48 46N 96 10W
Greencastle 114 39 40N 86 48W
Greene 113 42 20N 75 45W
Greenfield, Ind., U.S.A. 114 39 47N 85 51W
Greenfield, Iowa, U.S.A. 116 41 18N 94 28W
Greenfield, Mass., U.S.A. 114 42 38N 72 38W
Greenfield, Miss., U.S.A. 117 37 28N 93 50W
Greenfield Park 113 45 29N 73 29W
Greenland □ 4 66 0N 45 0W
Greenland Sea 4 73 0N 10 0W
Greenock 14 55 57N 4 46W
Greenore 15 54 2N 6 8W
Greenore Pt. 15 52 15N 6 20W
Greenport 113 41 5N 72 23W
Greensboro, Ga., U.S.A. 115 33 34N 83 12W
Greensboro, N.C., U.S.A. 115 36 7N 79 46W
Greensburg, Ind., U.S.A. 114 39 20N 85 30W
Greensburg, Kans., U.S.A. 117 37 38N 99 20W
Greensburg, Pa., U.S.A. 114 40 18N 79 31W
Greenville, Liberia 84 5 1N 9 6W
Greenville, Ala., U.S.A. 115 31 50N 86 37W
Greenville, Calif., U.S.A. 118 40 8N 121 0W
Greenville, Ill., U.S.A. 116 38 53N 89 22W
Greenville, Me., U.S.A. 107 45 30N 69 32W
Greenville, Mich., U.S.A. 114 43 12N 85 14W
Greenville, Miss., U.S.A. 117 33 25N 91 0W
Greenville, N.C., U.S.A. 115 35 37N 77 26W
Greenville, Ohio, U.S.A. 114 40 5N 84 38W
Greenville, Pa., U.S.A. 114 41 23N 80 22W
Greenville, S.C., U.S.A. 115 34 54N 82 24W
Greenville, Tenn., U.S.A. 115 36 13N 82 51W
Greenville, Tex., U.S.A. 117 33 5N 96 5W
Greenwater Lake Prov. Park 109 52 32N 103 30W
Greenwich, U.K. 13 51 28N 0 0
Greenwich, Conn., U.S.A. 113 41 1N 73 38W
Greenwich, N.Y., U.S.A. 113 43 2N 73 36W
Greenwich, Ohio, U.S.A. 112 41 1N 82 32W
Greenwood, Can. 108 49 10N 118 40W
Greenwood, Miss., U.S.A. 117 33 30N 90 4W
Greenwood, S.C., U.S.A. 115 34 13N 82 13W
Gregory 116 43 14N 99 20W
Gregory → 98 17 53 S 139 17 E
Gregory Downs 98 18 35 S 138 45 E
Gregory, L. 97 28 55 S 139 0 E
Gregory Lake 96 20 10 S 127 30 E
Gregory Ra. 97 19 30 S 143 40 E
Greiffenberg 24 53 6N 13 57 E
Greifswald 24 54 6N 13 23 E
Greifswalder Bodden 24 54 12N 13 35 E
Greifswalder Oie 24 54 15N 13 55 E
Grein 26 48 14N 14 51 E
Greiner Wald 26 48 30N 15 0 E
Greiz 24 50 39N 12 12 E
Gremikha 52 67 50N 39 40 E
Grenå 49 56 25N 10 53 E
Grenada 117 33 45N 89 50W
Grenada ■ 121 12 10N 61 40W
Grenade 20 43 47N 1 17 E
Grenadines 121 12 40N 61 20W
Grenen 49 57 44N 10 40 E
Grenfell, Austral. 99 33 52 S 148 8 E
Grenfell, Can. 109 50 30N 102 56W
Grenoble 21 45 12N 5 42 E
Grenora 116 48 38N 103 54W
Grenville, C. 97 12 0 S 143 13 E
Grenville Chan. 108 53 40N 129 46W
Gréoux-les-Bains 21 43 45N 5 52 E
Gresham 118 45 30N 122 25W
Gresik 73 7 13 S 112 38 E
Grèssoney St. Jean 38 45 49N 7 47 E
Gretna Green 14 55 0N 3 3W
Greven 24 52 7N 7 36 E
Grevená 44 40 4N 21 25 E
Grevená □ 44 40 2N 21 25 E
Grevenbroich 24 51 6N 6 32 E
Grevenmacher 16 49 41N 6 26 E
Grevesmühlen 24 53 51N 11 10 E
Grevie 49 56 22N 12 46 E
Grey → 101 42 27 S 171 12 E
Grey, C. 97 13 0 S 136 35 E
Grey Range 97 27 0 S 143 30 E
Grey Res. 107 48 20N 56 30W
Greybull 118 44 30N 108 3W
Greytown, N.Z. 101 41 5 S 175 29 E
Greytown, S. Afr. 93 29 1 S 30 36 E
Gribanovskiy 55 51 28N 41 50 E
Gribbell I. 108 53 23N 129 0W
Gridley 118 39 27N 121 47W
Griekwastad 92 28 49 S 23 15 E
Griffin 115 33 17N 84 14W
Griffith 97 34 18 S 146 2 E
Grillby 48 59 38N 17 15 E
Grim, C. 97 40 45 S 144 45 E
Grimari 88 5 43N 20 6 E
Grimaylov 54 49 20N 26 5 E
Grimma 24 51 14N 12 44 E
Grimmen 24 54 6N 13 2 E
Grimsby 112 43 12N 79 34W
Grimsby,Greater 12 53 35N 0 5W
Grimsey 50 66 33N 18 0W
Grimshaw 108 56 10N 117 40W
Grimstad 47 58 22N 8 35 E
Grindelwald 25 46 38N 8 2 E
Grindsted 49 55 46N 8 55 E

Grindu 46 44 44N 26 50 E
Grinnell 116 41 45N 92 43W
Griñón 30 40 13N 3 51W
Grintavec 39 46 22N 14 32 E
Grip 47 63 16N 7 37 E
Griqualand East 93 30 30 S 29 0 E
Griqualand West 92 28 40 S 23 30 E
Grisolles 20 43 49N 1 19 E
Grisslehamn 48 60 5N 18 49 E
Griz Nez, C. 19 50 50N 1 35 E
Grmeč Planina 39 44 43N 16 16 E
Groais I. 107 50 55N 55 35W
Groblersdal 93 25 15 S 29 25 E
Grobming 26 47 27N 13 54 E
Grocka 42 44 40N 20 42 E
Gródek 28 53 6N 23 40 E
Grodkow 28 50 43N 17 21 E
Grodno 54 53 42N 23 52 E
Grodzisk Mázowiecki 28 52 7N 20 37 E
Grodzisk Wielkopolski 28 52 15N 16 22 E
Grodzyanka 54 53 31N 28 42 E
Groesbeck 117 31 32N 96 34W
Groix 18 47 38N 3 29W
Groix, I. de 18 47 38N 3 28W
Grójec 28 51 50N 20 58 E
Gronau, Niedersachsen, Ger. 24 52 5N 9 47 E
Gronau, Nordrhein-Westfalen, Ger. 24 52 13N 7 2 E
Grong 50 64 25N 12 8 E
Groningen 16 53 15N 6 35 E
Groningen □ 16 53 16N 6 40 E
Grönskåra 49 57 5N 15 43 E
Groom 117 35 12N 100 59W
Groot → 92 33 45 S 24 36 E
Groot Berg → 92 32 47 S 18 8 E
Groot-Brakrivier 92 34 2 S 22 18 E
Groot Karoo 92 32 35 S 23 0 E
Groote Eylandt 97 14 0 S 136 40 E
Grootfontein 92 19 31 S 18 6 E
Grootlaagte → 92 20 55 S 21 27 E
Gros C. 108 61 59N 113 32W
Grosa, P. 33 39 6N 1 36 E
Grósio 38 46 18N 10 17 E
Grosne → 21 46 42N 4 56 E
Gross Glockner 26 47 5N 12 40 E
Gross Ottersleben 24 52 5N 11 33 E
Grossenbrode 24 54 21N 11 4 E
Grossenhain 24 51 17N 13 32 E
Grosseto 38 42 45N 11 7 E
Grossgerungs 26 48 34N 14 57 E
Groswater B. 107 54 20N 57 40W
Groton, Conn., U.S.A. 113 41 22N 72 12W
Groton, S.D., U.S.A. 116 45 27N 98 6W
Grottáglie 41 40 32N 17 25 E
Grottaminarda 41 41 5N 15 4 E
Grottammare 39 42 59N 13 52 E
Grouard Mission 108 55 33N 116 9W
Grouin, Pointe du 18 48 43N 1 51W
Groundhog → 106 48 45N 82 58W
Grouse Creek 118 41 44N 113 57W
Grove City 112 41 10N 80 5W
Groveton, N.H., U.S.A. 114 44 34N 71 30W
Groveton, Tex., U.S.A. 117 31 5N 95 4W
Grožnjan 39 45 22N 13 43 E
Groznyy 57 43 20N 45 45 E
Grubišno Polje 42 45 44N 17 12 E
Grudovo 43 42 21N 27 10 E
Grudusk 28 53 3N 20 38 E
Grudziądz 28 53 30N 18 47 E
Gruissan 20 43 8N 3 7 E
Grumo Áppula 41 41 2N 16 43 E
Grums 48 59 22N 13 5 E
Grünberg 24 50 37N 8 55 E
Grundy Center 116 42 22N 92 45W
Grungedal 47 59 44N 7 43 E
Gruver 117 36 19N 101 20W
Gruyères 25 46 35N 7 4 E
Gruža 42 43 54N 20 46 E
Gryazi 55 52 30N 39 58 E
Gryazovets 55 58 50N 40 10 E
Grybów 27 49 36N 20 55 E
Grycksbo 48 60 40N 15 29 E
Gryfice 28 53 55N 15 13 E
Gryfino 28 53 16N 14 29 E
Gryfow Sl. 28 51 2N 15 24 E
Grythyttan 48 59 41N 14 32 E
Grytviken 5 53 50 S 37 10W
Gstaad 25 46 28N 7 18 E
Guacanayabo, G. de 121 20 40N 77 20W
Guachípas → 124 25 40 S 65 30W
Guadajoz → 31 37 50N 4 51W
Guadalajara, Mexico 120 20 40N 103 20W
Guadalajara, Spain 32 40 37N 3 12W
Guadalajara □ 32 40 47N 3 0W
Guadalcanal, Solomon Is. 94 9 32 S 160 12 E
Guadalcanal, Spain 31 38 5N 5 52W
Guadalén → 31 38 5N 3 32W
Guadales 124 34 30 S 67 55W
Guadalete → 31 36 35N 6 13W
Guadalhorce → 31 36 41N 4 27W
Guadalimar → 33 38 5N 3 28W
Guadalmena → 33 38 19N 2 56W
Guadalmez → 31 38 46N 5 4W
Guadalope → 32 41 15N 0 3W
Guadalquivir → 31 36 47N 6 22W
Guadalupe, Spain 31 39 27N 5 17W
Guadalupe, U.S.A. 119 34 59N 120 33W
Guadalupe → 117 28 30N 96 53W
Guadalupe Bravos 120 31 20N 106 10W
Guadalupe I. 95 21 20N 118 50W
Guadalupe Pk. 119 31 50N 105 30W
Guadalupe, Sierra de 31 39 28N 5 30W
Guadarrama, Sierra de 30 41 0N 4 0W
Guadeloupe 121 16 20N 61 40W
Guadeloupe Passage 121 16 50N 62 15W
Guadiamar → 31 36 55N 6 24W
Guadiana → 31 37 14N 7 22W
Guadiana Menor → 33 37 56N 3 15W
Guadiaro → 31 36 17N 5 17W
Guadiato → 31 37 48N 5 5W
Guadiela → 32 40 22N 2 49W
Guadix 33 37 18N 3 11W
Guafo, Boca del 128 43 35 S 74 0W
Guaíra 125 24 5 S 54 10W
Guaira, La 126 10 36N 66 56W
Guaitecas, Islas 128 44 0 S 74 30W
Guajará-Mirim 126 10 50 S 65 20W
Guajira, Pen. de la 126 12 0N 72 0W
Gualdo Tadino 39 43 14N 12 46 E
Gualeguay 124 33 10 S 59 14W
Gualeguaychú 124 33 3 S 59 31W
Guam 94 13 27N 144 45 E
Guaminí 124 37 1 S 62 28W
Guamúchil 120 25 25N 108 3W
Guan Xian 75 31 2N 103 38 E
Guanabacoa 121 23 8N 82 18W
Guanacaste, Cordillera del 121 10 40N 85 4W
Guanaceví 120 25 40N 106 0W
Guanahani = San Salvador, I. 121 24 0N 74 40W
Guanajay 121 22 56N 82 42W
Guanajuato 120 21 0N 101 20W
Guanajuato □ 120 20 40N 101 20W
Guanare 126 8 42N 69 12W
Guandacol 124 29 30 S 68 40W
Guane 121 22 10N 84 7W
Guang'an 77 30 28N 106 35 E
Guangde 77 30 54N 119 25 E
Guangdong □ 75 23 0N 113 0 E
Guanghua 75 32 22N 111 38 E
Guangshun 77 26 8N 106 21 E
Guangxi Zhuangzu Zizhiqu □ 75 24 0N 109 0 E
Guangyuan 77 32 26N 105 51 E
Guangze 77 27 30N 117 12 E
Guangzhou 75 23 5N 113 10 E
Guanipa → 126 9 56N 62 26W
Guantánamo 121 20 10N 75 14W
Guantao 76 36 42N 115 25 E
Guanyun 77 34 20N 119 18 E
Guápiles 121 10 10N 83 46W
Guaporé → 126 11 55 S 65 4W
Guaqui 126 16 41 S 68 54W
Guara, Sierra de 32 42 19N 0 15W
Guarapari 125 20 40 S 40 30W
Guarapuava 125 25 20 S 51 30W
Guaratinguetá 125 22 49 S 45 9W
Guaratuba 125 25 53 S 48 38W
Guarda 30 40 32N 7 20W
Guarda □ 30 40 40N 7 20W
Guardafui, C. = Asir, Ras 63 11 55N 51 16 E
Guardamar del Segura 33 38 5N 0 39W
Guardavalle 41 38 31N 16 30 E
Guardia, La 30 41 56N 8 52W
Guardiagrele 39 42 11N 14 11 E
Guardo 30 42 47N 4 50W
Guareña 31 38 51N 6 6W
Guareña → 30 41 29N 5 23W
Guaria □ 124 25 45 S 56 30W
Guarujá 125 24 2 S 46 25W
Guarus 125 21 44 S 41 20W
Guasdualito 126 7 15N 70 44W
Guasipati 126 7 28N 61 54W
Guastalla 38 44 55N 10 40 E
Guatemala 120 14 40N 90 22W
Guatemala ■ 120 15 40N 90 30W
Guatire 126 10 28N 66 32W
Guaviare → 126 4 3N 67 44W
Guaxupé 125 21 10 S 47 5W
Guayama 121 17 59N 66 7W
Guayaquil 126 2 15 S 79 52W
Guayaquil, G. de 126 3 10 S 81 0W
Guaymas 120 27 59N 110 54W
Guazhou 77 32 17N 119 21 E
Guba 91 10 38 S 26 27 E
Gûbâl 86 27 30N 34 0 E
Gúbbio 39 43 20N 12 34 E
Gubin 28 51 57N 14 43 E
Gubio 85 12 30N 12 42 E
Gubkin 55 51 17N 37 32 E
Guča 42 43 46N 20 15 E
Guchil 71 5 35N 102 10 E
Gudalur 70 11 30N 76 29 E
Gudata 57 43 7N 40 10 E
Gudenå 49 56 27N 9 40 E
Gudermes 57 43 24N 46 5 E
Gudhjem 49 55 12N 14 58 E
Gudiña, La 30 42 4N 7 8W
Gudivada 70 16 30N 81 3 E
Gudiyatam 70 12 57N 78 55 E
Gudur 70 14 12N 79 55 E
Guebwiller 19 47 55N 7 12 E
Guecho 32 43 21N 2 59W
Guékédou 84 8 40N 10 5W
Guelma 83 36 25N 7 29 E
Guelph 106 43 35N 80 20W
Guelt es Stel 82 35 12N 3 1 E
Guelttara 82 29 23N 2 10W
Guemar 83 33 30N 6 49 E
Guéméné-Penfao 18 47 38N 1 50W
Guéméné-sur-Scorff 18 48 4N 3 13W
Guéné 85 11 44N 3 16 E
Guer 18 47 54N 2 8W
Güera, La 80 20 51N 17 0W
Guérande 18 47 20N 2 26W
Guerche, La 18 47 57N 1 16W
Guerche-sur-l'Aubois, La 19 46 58N 2 56 E
Guercif 82 34 14N 3 21W
Guéréda 81 14 31N 22 5 E
Guéret 20 46 11N 1 51 E
Guérigny 19 47 6N 3 10 E
Guernica 32 43 19N 2 40W
Guernsey, Chan. Is. 18 49 30N 2 35W
Guernsey, U.S.A. 116 42 19N 104 45W
Guerrara, Oasis, Alg. 83 32 51N 4 22 E
Guerrara, Saoura, Alg. 82 28 5N 0 8W
Guerrero □ 120 17 30N 100 0W
Guerzim 82 29 39N 1 40W
Guest I. 5 76 18 S 148 0W
Gueugnon 21 46 36N 4 4 E
Gueydan 117 30 3N 92 30W
Guglionesi 41 41 55N 14 54 E
Gui Jiang → 77 23 30N 111 15 E
Gui Xian 77 23 8N 109 35 E
Guia Lopes da Laguna 125 21 26 S 56 7W
Guichi 77 30 39N 117 27 E
Guider 85 9 56N 13 57 E
Guidimouni 85 13 42N 9 31 E
Guidong 77 26 7N 113 57 E
Guiglo 84 6 45N 7 30W
Guijo de Coria 30 40 6N 6 28W
Guildford 13 51 14N 0 34W
Guilford 107 45 12N 69 25W
Guilin 75 25 18N 110 15 E
Guillaumes 21 44 5N 6 52 E
Guillestre 21 44 39N 6 40 E
Guilvinec 18 47 48N 4 17W
Guimarães, Braz. 127 2 9 S 44 42W
Guimarães, Port. 30 41 28N 8 24W
Guimaras 73 10 35N 122 37 E
Guinea ■ 84 10 20N 10 0W
Guinea-Bissau ■ 84 12 0N 15 0W
Guinea, Gulf of 85 3 0N 2 30 E
Güines 121 22 50N 82 0W
Guingamp 18 48 34N 3 10W
Guipavas 18 48 26N 4 29W
Guiping 75 23 21N 110 2 E
Guipúzcoa □ 32 43 12N 2 15W
Guir, O. → 82 31 29N 2 17W
Güiria 126 10 32N 62 18W
Guiscard 19 49 40N 3 0 E
Guise 19 49 52N 3 35 E
Guitiriz 30 43 11N 7 50W
Guiuan 73 11 5N 125 55 E
Guixi 77 28 16N 117 15 E
Guiyang, Guizhou, China 75 26 32N 106 40 E
Guiyang, Hunan, China 77 25 46N 112 42 E
Guizhou □ 75 27 0N 107 0 E
Gujan-Mestras 20 44 38N 1 4W
Gujarat □ 68 23 20N 71 0 E
Gujranwala 68 32 10N 74 12 E
Gujrat 68 32 40N 74 2 E
Gukovo 57 48 1N 39 58 E
Gulargambone 100 31 20 S 148 30 E
Gulbarga 70 17 20N 76 50 E
Gulbene 54 57 8N 26 52 E
Guledgud 70 16 3N 75 48 E
Gulf Basin 96 15 20 S 129 0 E
Gulfport 117 30 21N 89 3W
Gulgong 99 32 20 S 149 49 E
Gulistan 68 30 30N 66 35 E
Gull Lake 109 50 10N 108 29W
Gullringen 49 57 48N 15 44 E
Gulma 85 12 40N 4 23 E
Gülpinar 44 39 32N 26 10 E
Gulshad 58 46 45N 74 25 E
Gulsvik 47 60 24N 9 38 E
Gulu 90 2 48N 32 17 E
Gulwe 90 6 30 S 36 25 E
Gulyaypole 56 47 45N 36 21 E
Gum Lake 99 32 42 S 143 9 E
Gumal → 68 31 40N 71 50 E
Gumbaz 68 30 2N 69 0 E
Gumel 85 12 39N 9 22 E
Gumiel de Hizán 32 41 46N 3 41W
Gumlu 98 19 53 S 147 41 E
Gumma □ 74 36 30N 138 20 E
Gummersbach 24 51 2N 7 32 E
Gummi 85 12 4N 5 9 E
Gümüsane 64 40 30N 39 30 E
Gümüşhaciköy 56 40 50N 35 18 E
Gumzai 73 5 28 S 134 42 E
Guna 68 24 40N 77 19 E
Guna Mt. 87 11 50N 37 40 E
Gundagai 99 35 3 S 148 6 E
Gundelfingen 25 48 33N 10 22 E
Gundih 73 7 10 S 110 56 E
Gundlakamma → 70 15 30N 80 15 E
Gungu 88 5 43 S 19 20 E
Gunisao → 109 53 56N 97 53W
Gunisao L. 109 53 33N 96 15W
Gunnedah 97 30 59 S 150 15 E
Gunning 100 34 47 S 149 14 E
Gunnison, Colo., U.S.A. 119 38 32N 106 56W
Gunnison, Utah, U.S.A. 118 39 11N 111 48W
Gunnison → 119 39 3N 108 30W
Guntakal 70 15 11N 77 27 E
Guntersville 115 34 18N 86 16W
Guntur 70 16 23N 80 30 E
Gunung-Sitoli 72 1 15N 97 30 E
Gunungapi 73 6 45 S 126 30 E
Gunupur 70 19 5N 83 50 E
Günz → 25 48 27N 10 16 E
Gunza 88 10 50 S 13 50 E
Günzburg 25 48 27N 10 16 E
Gunzenhausen 25 49 6N 10 45 E
Guo He → 77 32 59N 117 10 E
Guoyang 77 33 32N 116 12 E
Gupis 69 36 15N 73 20 E
Gura 68 25 12N 71 39 E
Gura Humorului 46 47 35N 25 53 E
Gura-Teghii 46 45 30N 26 25 E
Gurag 87 8 20N 38 20 E
Gürchan 64 34 55N 49 25 E
Gurdaspur 68 32 5N 75 31 E
Gurdon 117 33 55N 93 10W
Gurdzhaani 57 41 43N 45 52 E
Gurgaon 68 28 27N 77 1 E
Gurghiu, Munţii 46 46 41N 25 15 E
Gurk → 26 46 35N 14 31 E
Gurkha 69 28 5N 84 40 E
Gurley 99 29 45 S 149 48 E
Gurun 71 5 49N 100 27 E
Gurupá 127 1 25 S 51 35W
Gurupá, I. Grande de 127 1 25 S 51 45W
Gurupi → 127 1 13 S 46 6W
Guryev 57 47 5N 52 0 E
Gus-Khrustalnyy 55 55 42N 40 44 E
Gusau 85 12 12N 6 40 E
Gusev 54 54 35N 22 10 E
Gushan 76 39 50N 123 35 E
Gushi 77 32 11N 115 41 E
Gushiago 85 9 55N 0 15W
Gusinje 42 42 35N 19 50 E
Gúspini 40 39 32N 8 38 E
Gusselby 48 59 38N 15 14 E
Güssing 27 47 3N 16 20 E
Gustanj 39 46 36N 14 49 E
Gustine 119 37 14N 121 0
Güstrow 24 53 47N 12 12
Gusum 49 58 16N 16 30
Guta = Kalárovo 27 47 54N 18 0
Gütersloh 24 51 54N 8 25
Guthalongra 98 19 52 S 147 50
Guthega Dam 100 36 20 S 148 27
Guthrie 117 35 55N 97 30
Guttenberg 116 42 46N 91 10
Guyana ■ 126 5 0N 59 0
Guyang 76 41 0N 110 5
Guyenne 20 44 30N 0 40
Guymon 117 36 45N 101 30
Guyra 99 30 15 S 151 40
Guyuan 76 36 0N 106 20
Guzhen 77 33 22N 117 18
Guzmán, Laguna de 120 31 25N 107 25
Gwa 67 17 36N 94 34
Gwaai 91 19 15 S 27 45
Gwabegar 99 30 31 S 149 0
Gwadabawa 85 13 28N 5 15
Gwādar 66 25 10N 62 18
Gwagwada 85 10 15N 7 15
Gwalior 68 26 12N 78 10
Gwanda 91 20 55 S 29 0
Gwandu 85 12 30N 4 41
Gwane 90 4 45N 25 48
Gwaram 85 10 15N 10 25
Gwarzo 85 12 20N 8 55
Gwda → 28 53 3N 16 44
Gweebarra B. 15 54 52N 8 21
Gweedore 15 55 4N 8 15
• Gwelo 91 19 28 S 29 45
Gwent □ 13 51 45N 2 55
Gwi 85 9 0N 7 10
Gwinn 114 46 15N 87 29
Gwio Kura 85 12 40N 11 2
Gwol 84 10 58N 1 59
Gwoza 85 11 5N 13 40
Gwydir → 97 29 27 S 149 48
Gwynedd □ 12 53 0N 4 0
Gyaring Hu 75 34 50N 97 40
Gydanskiy P-ov. 58 70 0N 78 0
Gyland 47 58 24N 6 45
Gympie 97 26 11 S 152 38
Gyoda 74 36 10N 139 30
Gyoma 27 46 56N 20 50
Gyöngyös 27 47 48N 20 0
Györ 27 47 41N 17 40
Györ-Sopron □ 27 47 40N 17 20
Gypsum Pt. 108 61 53N 114 35
Gypsumville 109 51 45N 98 40
Gyttorp 48 59 31N 14 58
Gyula 27 46 38N 21 17
Gzhatsk = Gagarin 54 55 30N 35 0

H

Ha 'Arava 62 30 50N 35 20
Haag 25 48 11N 12 12
Haapamäki 50 62 18N 24 28
Haapsalu 54 58 56N 23 30
Haarlem 16 52 23N 4 39
Haast → 101 43 50 S 169 2
Hab Nadi Chauki 66 25 0N 66 50
Habana, La 121 23 8N 82 22
Habaswein 90 1 2N 39 30
Habay 108 58 50N 118 44
Habiganj 69 24 24N 91 30
Hablingbo 49 57 12N 18 16
Habo 49 57 55N 14 6
Hachenburg 24 50 40N 7 49
Hachijō-Jima 74 33 5N 139 45
Hachinohe 74 40 30N 141 29
Hachiōji 74 35 40N 139 20
Hadali 68 32 16N 72 11
Hadarba, Ras 86 22 4N 36 51
Hadd, Ras al 65 22 35N 59 50
Haddington 14 55 57N 2 48
Hadejia 85 12 30N 10 5
Hadejia → 85 12 50N 10 51
Haden 99 27 13 S 151 54
Hadera 62 32 27N 34 55
Hadera, N. → 62 32 28N 34 52
Haderslev 49 55 15N 9 30
Hadhra 86 20 10N 41 5
Hadhramaut = Haḍramawt 63 15 30N 49 30
Hadibu 63 12 35N 54 2
Hadjeb El Aïoun 83 35 21N 9 32
Haḍramawt 63 15 30N 49 30
Hadrians Wall 12 55 0N 2 30
Hadsten 49 56 19N 10 3
Hadsund 49 56 44N 10 8
Haeju 76 38 3N 125 45
Haerhpin = Harbin 76 45 48N 126 40
Ḥafar al Bāṭin 64 28 25N 46 0
Hafizabad 68 32 5N 73 40
Haflong 67 25 10N 93 5
Hafnarfjörður 50 64 4N 21 57
Haft-Gel 64 31 30N 49 32
Hafun, Ras 63 10 29N 51 30
Hagalil 62 32 53N 35 18
Hagari → 70 15 40N 77 0
Hagen 24 51 21N 7 29
Hagenow 24 53 25N 11 10
Hagerman 117 33 5N 104 22
Hagerstown 114 39 39N 77 46
Hagetmau 20 43 39N 0 37
Hagfors 48 60 3N 13 45
Häggenås 48 63 24N 14 55
Hagi, Iceland 50 65 28N 23 25
Hagi, Japan 74 34 30N 131 22
Hagolan 62 33 0N 35 45
Hags Hd. 15 52 57N 9 30
Hague, C. de la 18 49 44N 1 56
Hague, The = s'-Gravenhage 16 52 7N 4 17
Haguenau 19 48 49N 7 47
Hai □ 90 3 10 S 37 10
Haicheng 76 40 50N 122 45
Haifeng 77 22 58N 115 10

• *Renamed Gweru*

aiger 24 50 44N 8 12 E
aikang 77 20 52N 110 8 E
aikou 75 20 1N 110 16 E
ā'il 64 27 28N 41 45 E
ailar 75 49 10N 119 38 E
ailar He → 76 49 30N 117 50 E
ailey 118 43 30N 114 15W
aileybury 106 47 30N 79 38W
ailin 76 44 37N 129 30 E
ailing Dao 77 21 35N 111 47 E
ailong 76 42 32N 125 40 E
ailun 75 47 28N 126 50 E
ailuoto 50 65 3N 24 45 E
aimen 77 31 52N 121 10 E
ainan 77 19 0N 110 0 E
ainan Dao 75 19 0N 109 30 E
ainaut □ 16 50 30N 4 0 E
ainburg 27 48 9N 16 56 E
aines 118 44 51N 117 59W
aines City 115 28 6N 81 35W
aines Junction 108 60 45N 137 30W
ainfeld 26 48 3N 15 48 E
aining 77 30 28N 120 40 E
aiphong 71 20 47N 106 41 E
aiti ■ 121 19 0N 72 30W
aiya Junction 86 18 20N 36 21 E
aiyan 77 30 28N 120 58 E
aiyang 76 36 47N 121 9 E
aiyuan 76 36 35N 105 52 E
aja 73 3 19 S 129 37 E
ajar Bangar 81 10 40N 22 45 E
ajar, Jabal 64 26 5N 39 10 E
ajdú-Bihar □ 27 47 30N 21 30 E
ajdúböszörmény 27 47 40N 21 30 E
ajdúdurog 27 47 48N 21 30 E
ajdúhadház 27 47 40N 21 40 E
ajdúnánás 27 47 50N 21 26 E
ajdúsámson 27 47 37N 21 42 E
ajdúszobaszló 27 47 27N 21 22 E
ajipur 69 25 45N 85 13 E
ajówka 28 52 47N 23 35 E
ajr 65 24 0N 56 34 E
akansson, Mts. 91 8 40 S 25 45 E
åkantorp 49 58 18N 12 55 E
akken-Zan 74 34 10N 135 54 E
akodate 74 41 45N 140 44 E
alab = Aleppo 64 36 10N 37 15 E
alabjah 64 35 10N 45 58 E
alaib 86 22 12N 36 30 E
albe 86 19 40N 42 15 E
alberstadt 24 51 53N 11 2 E
alcombe 101 40 8 S 175 30 E
alcyon, Mt. 73 13 0N 121 30 E
alden 47 59 9N 11 23 E
aldensleben 24 52 17N 11 30 E
aldia 67 22 5N 88 3 E
aldwani-cum-Kathgodam 69 29 31N 79 30 E
aleakala Crater 110 20 43N 156 12W
aleyville 115 34 15N 87 40W
alf Assini 84 5 1N 2 50W
alfway 118 44 56N 117 8W
alfway → 108 56 12N 121 32W
alḥul 62 31 35N 35 7 E
ali, Si. Arab. 86 18 40N 41 15 E
ali, Yemen 63 18 30N 41 30 E
aliburton 106 45 3N 78 30W
alicarnassus 45 37 3N 27 30 E
alifax, Austral. 98 18 32 S 146 22 E
alifax, Can. 107 44 38N 63 35W
alifax, U.K. 12 53 43N 1 51W
alifax B. 97 18 50 S 147 0 E
alifax I. 92 26 38 S 15 4 E
alīl Rūd → 65 27 40N 58 30 E
all 26 47 17N 11 30 E
all Beach 105 68 46N 81 12W
allabro 49 56 22N 15 5 E
allands län □ 49 56 50N 12 50 E
allands Väderö 49 56 27N 12 34 E
allandsås 49 56 22N 13 0 E
alle, Belg. 16 50 44N 4 13 E
alle, Halle, Ger. 24 51 29N 12 0 E
alle, Nordrhein-Westfalen,
Ger. 24 52 4N 8 20 E
alle □ 24 51 28N 11 58 E
illefors 48 59 47N 14 31 E
illefors 49 59 46N 14 30 E
allein 26 47 40N 13 5 E
illekis 49 58 38N 13 27 E
allett 99 33 25 S 138 55 E
allettsville 117 29 28N 96 57W
illevadsholm 49 58 35N 11 33 E
alley Bay 5 75 31 S 26 36W
allia → 70 16 55N 79 20 E
alliday 116 47 20N 102 25W
alliday L. 109 61 21N 108 56W
allingskeid 47 60 40N 7 17 E
illnäs 50 64 19N 19 36 E
allock 109 48 47N 97 0W
alls Creek 96 18 16 S 127 38 E
allsberg 48 59 5N 15 7 E
allstahammar 48 59 38N 16 15 E
allstatt 26 47 33N 13 38 E
allstavik 48 60 5N 18 37 E
allstead 113 41 56N 75 45W
almahera 73 0 40N 128 0 E
almeu 46 47 57N 23 2 E
almstad 49 56 41N 12 52 E
alq el Oued 83 36 53N 10 18 E
als 49 56 59N 10 18 E
alsa 47 63 3N 8 14 E
alsafjorden 47 63 5N 8 10 E
ilsingborg = Helsingborg 49 56 3N 12 42 E
alstad 116 47 21N 96 50W
altdalen 47 62 56N 11 8 E
altern 24 51 44N 7 10 E
alul 65 25 40N 52 40 E
am 19 49 45N 3 4 E
amab 92 28 7 S 19 16 E
amad 87 15 20N 33 32 E
amada 74 34 56N 132 4 E
amadān 64 34 52N 48 32 E
amadān □ 64 35 0N 49 0 E
Hamadia 82 35 28N 1 57 E
Hamāh 64 35 5N 36 40 E
Hamamatsu 74 34 45N 137 45 E
Hamar 47 60 48N 11 7 E
Hamarøy 50 68 5N 15 38 E
Hamâta, Gebel 86 24 17N 35 0 E
Hamber Prov. Park 108 52 20N 118 0W
Hamburg, Ger. 24 53 32N 9 59 E
Hamburg, Ark., U.S.A. 117 33 15N 91 47W
Hamburg, Iowa, U.S.A. 116 40 37N 95 38W
Hamburg, N.Y., U.S.A. 112 42 44N 78 50W
Hamburg, Pa., U.S.A. 113 40 33N 76 0W
Hamburg □ 24 53 30N 10 0 E
Hamden 113 41 21N 72 56W
Hamdh, W. → 86 24 55N 36 20 E
Hämeen lääni □ 51 61 24N 24 10 E
Hämeenlinna 50 61 0N 24 28 E
Hamélé 84 10 56N 2 45W
Hameln 24 52 7N 9 24 E
Hamer Koke 87 5 15N 36 45 E
Hamersley Ra. 96 22 0 S 117 45 E
Hamhung 76 39 54N 127 30 E
Hami 75 42 55N 93 25 E
Hamilton, Austral. 97 37 45 S 142 2 E
Hamilton, Berm. 121 32 15N 64 45W
Hamilton, Can. 106 43 15N 79 50W
Hamilton, N.Z. 101 37 47 S 175 19 E
Hamilton, U.K. 14 55 47N 4 2W
Hamilton, Mo., U.S.A. 116 39 45N 93 59W
Hamilton, Mont., U.S.A. 118 46 20N 114 6W
Hamilton, N.Y., U.S.A. 114 42 49N 75 31W
Hamilton, Ohio, U.S.A. 114 39 20N 84 35W
Hamilton, Tex., U.S.A. 117 31 40N 98 5W
Hamilton → 98 23 30 S 139 47 E
Hamilton Hotel 98 22 45 S 140 40 E
Hamilton Inlet 107 54 0N 57 30W
Hamiota 109 50 11N 100 38W
Hamlet 115 34 56N 79 40W
Hamley Bridge 99 34 17 S 138 35 E
Hamlin, N.Y., U.S.A. 112 43 17N 77 55W
Hamlin, Tex., U.S.A. 117 32 58N 100 8W
Hamm 24 51 40N 7 49 E
Hammam Bouhadjar 82 35 23N 0 58W
Hammamet 83 36 24N 10 38 E
Hammamet, G. de 83 36 10N 10 48 E
Hammarstrand 48 63 7N 16 20 E
Hammel 49 56 16N 9 52 E
Hammelburg 25 50 7N 9 54 E
Hammeren 49 55 18N 14 47 E
Hammerfest 50 70 39N 23 41 E
Hammond, Ind., U.S.A. 114 41 40N 87 30W
Hammond, La., U.S.A. 117 30 32N 90 30W
Hammonton 114 39 40N 74 47W
Hamneda 49 56 41N 13 51 E
Hamoyet, Jebel 86 17 33N 38 2 E
Hampden 101 45 18 S 170 50 E
Hampshire □ 13 51 3N 1 20W
Hampshire Downs 13 51 10N 1 10W
Hampton, Ark., U.S.A. 117 33 35N 92 29W
Hampton, Iowa, U.S.A. 116 42 42N 93 12W
Hampton, N.H., U.S.A. 113 42 56N 70 48W
Hampton, S.C., U.S.A. 115 32 52N 81 2W
Hampton, Va., U.S.A. 114 37 4N 76 18W
Hampton Harbour 96 20 30 S 116 30 E
Hampton Tableland 96 32 0 S 127 0 E
Hamrat esh Sheykh 87 14 38N 27 55 E
Han Jiang → 77 23 25N 116 40 E
Han Shui → 77 30 35N 114 18 E
Hana 110 20 45N 155 59W
Hanak 86 25 32N 37 0 E
Hanang 90 4 30 S 35 25 E
Hanau 25 50 8N 8 56 E
Hancheng 76 35 31N 110 25 E
Hancock, Mich., U.S.A. 116 47 10N 88 40W
Hancock, Minn., U.S.A. 116 45 26N 95 46W
Hancock, Pa., U.S.A. 113 41 57N 75 19W
Handa, Japan 74 34 53N 137 0 E
Handa, Somalia 63 10 37N 51 2 E
Handan 76 36 35N 114 28 E
Handen 48 59 12N 18 12 E
Handeni 90 5 25 S 38 2 E
Handeni □ 90 5 30 S 38 0 E
Handlová 27 48 45N 18 35 E
Handub 86 19 15N 37 16 E
Hanegev 62 30 50N 35 0 E
Haney 108 49 12N 122 40W
Hanford 119 36 23N 119 39W
Hangang → 76 37 50N 126 30 E
Hangayn Nuruu 75 47 30N 100 0 E
Hangchou = Hangzhou 75 30 18N 120 11 E
Hanggin Houqi 76 40 58N 107 4 E
Hangklip, K. 92 34 26 S 18 48 E
Hangö 51 59 50N 22 57 E
Hangu 76 39 18N 117 53 E
Hangzhou 75 30 18N 120 11 E
Hangzhou Wan 75 30 15N 120 45 E
Ḥanish J. 63 13 45N 42 46 E
Haniska 27 48 37N 21 15 E
Hanita 62 33 5N 35 10 E
Hankinson 116 46 9N 96 58W
Hanko 51 59 59N 22 57 E
Hankou 77 30 35N 114 30 E
Hanksville 119 38 19N 110 45W
Hanmer 101 42 32 S 172 50 E
Hann, Mt. 96 16 0 S 126 0 E
Hanna 108 51 40N 111 54W
Hannaford 116 47 23N 98 11W
Hannah 116 48 58N 98 42W
Hannah B. 106 51 40N 80 0W
Hannibal 116 39 42N 91 22W
Hannik 86 18 12N 32 20 E
Hannover 24 52 23N 9 43 E
Hanö 49 56 2N 14 50 E
Hanöbukten 49 55 35N 14 30 E
Hanoi 71 21 5N 105 55 E
Hanover, Can. 112 44 9N 81 2W
Hanover, S. Afr. 92 31 4 S 24 29 E
Hanover, N.H., U.S.A. 114 43 43N 72 17W
Hanover, Ohio, U.S.A. 112 40 5N 82 17W
Hanover, Pa., U.S.A. 114 39 46N 76 59W
Hanover = Hannover 24 52 23N 9 43 E
Hanover, I. 128 51 0 S 74 50W
Hansi 68 29 10N 75 57 E
Hansjö 48 61 10N 14 40 E
Hanson Range 96 27 0 S 136 30 E
Hanwood 100 34 22 S 146 2 E
Hanyang 77 30 35N 114 2 E
Hanyin 77 32 54N 108 28 E
Hanzhong 75 33 10N 107 1 E
Hanzhuang 77 34 33N 117 23 E
Haparanda 50 65 52N 24 8 E
Happy 117 34 47N 101 50W
Happy Camp 118 41 52N 123 22W
Happy Valley 107 53 15N 60 20W
Hapur 68 28 45N 77 45 E
Ḥaql 86 29 10N 35 0 E
Har 73 5 16 S 133 14 E
Har Hu 75 38 20N 97 38 E
Har Us Nuur 75 48 0N 92 0 E
Har Yehuda 62 31 35N 34 57 E
Ḥaraḍ 64 24 22N 49 0 E
Haraisan Plateau 64 23 0N 47 40 E
Haramsøya 47 62 39N 6 12 E
Harardera 63 4 33N 47 38 E
Harat 87 16 5N 39 26 E
Harazé, Chad 81 14 20N 19 12 E
Harazé, Chad 81 9 57N 20 48 E
Harbin 76 45 48N 126 40 E
Harboør 49 56 38N 8 10 E
Harbor Beach 114 43 50N 82 38W
Harbor Springs 114 45 28N 85 0W
Harbour Breton 107 47 29N 55 50W
Harbour Grace 107 47 40N 53 22W
Harburg 24 53 27N 9 58 E
Hårby 49 55 13N 10 7 E
Harcourt 98 24 17 S 149 55 E
Harda 68 22 27N 77 5 E
Hardangerfjorden 47 60 15N 6 0 E
Hardangerjøkulen 47 60 30N 7 0 E
Hardangervidda 47 60 20N 7 20 E
Hardap Dam 92 24 32 S 17 50 E
Hardenberg 16 52 34N 6 37 E
Harderwijk 16 52 21N 5 38 E
Hardin 118 45 44N 107 35W
Harding 93 30 35 S 29 55 E
Hardisty 108 52 40N 111 18W
Hardman 118 45 12N 119 40W
Hardoi 69 27 26N 80 6 E
Hardwar 68 29 58N 78 9 E
Hardwick 113 44 30N 72 20W
Hardy 117 36 20N 91 30W
Hardy, Pen. 128 55 30 S 68 20W
Hare B. 107 51 15N 55 45W
Hare Gilboa 62 32 31N 35 25 E
Hare Meron 62 32 59N 35 24 E
Haren 24 52 47N 7 18 E
Harer 87 9 20N 42 8 E
Harer □ 87 7 12N 42 0 E
Hareto 87 9 23N 37 6 E
Harfleur 18 49 30N 0 10 E
Hargeisa 63 9 30N 44 2 E
Harghita □ 46 46 30N 25 30 E
Harghita, Mţii 46 46 25N 25 35 E
Hargshamn 48 60 12N 18 30 E
Hari → 72 1 16 S 104 5 E
Haricha, Hamada el 82 22 40N 3 15W
Harihar 70 14 32N 75 44 E
Haringhata → 69 22 0N 89 58 E
Haripad 70 9 14N 76 28 E
Harīrūd 65 35 0N 61 0 E
Harīrūd → 65 34 20N 62 30 E
Harkat 86 20 25N 39 40 E
Harlan, Iowa, U.S.A. 116 41 37N 95 20W
Harlan, Tenn., U.S.A. 115 36 50N 83 20W
Harlech 12 52 52N 4 7W
Harlem 118 48 29N 108 47W
Harlingen, Neth. 16 53 11N 5 25 E
Harlingen, U.S.A. 117 26 20N 97 50W
Harlowton 118 46 30N 109 54W
Harmånger 48 61 55N 17 20 E
Harmil 87 16 30N 40 10 E
Harney Basin 118 43 30N 119 0W
Harney L. 118 43 0N 119 0W
Harney Pk. 116 43 52N 103 33W
Härnön 48 62 36N 18 0 E
Härnösand 48 62 38N 18 0 E
Haro 32 42 35N 2 55W
Haro, C. 120 27 50N 110 55W
Harp L. 107 55 5N 61 50W
Harpanahalli 70 14 47N 76 2 E
Harpe, La 116 40 30N 91 0W
Harper 84 4 25N 7 43W
Harplinge 49 56 45N 12 45 E
Harrand 68 29 28N 70 3 E
Ḥarrat al Kishb 64 22 30N 40 15 E
Harrat al 'Uwairidh 64 26 50N 38 0 E
Harrat Khaibar 86 25 45N 40 0 E
Harrat Nawāsīf 86 21 30N 42 0 E
Harriman 115 36 0N 84 35W
Harrington Harbour 107 50 31N 59 30W
Harris 14 57 50N 6 55W
Harris L. 96 31 10 S 135 10 E
Harris, Sd. of 14 57 44N 7 6W
Harrisburg, Ill., U.S.A. 117 37 42N 88 30W
Harrisburg, Nebr., U.S.A. 116 41 36N 103 46W
Harrisburg, Oreg., U.S.A. 118 44 16N 123 10W
Harrisburg, Pa., U.S.A. 114 40 18N 76 52W
Harrismith 93 28 15 S 29 8 E
Harrison, Ark., U.S.A. 117 36 10N 93 4W
Harrison, Idaho, U.S.A. 118 47 30N 116 51W
Harrison, Nebr., U.S.A. 116 42 42N 103 52W
Harrison B. 104 70 25N 151 30W
Harrison, C. 107 54 55N 57 55W
Harrison L. 108 49 33N 121 50W
Harrisonburg 114 38 28N 78 52W
Harrisonville 116 38 39N 94 21W
Harriston 106 43 57N 80 53W
Harrisville 106 44 40N 83 19W
Harrogate 12 53 59N 1 32W
Harrow, Can. 112 42 2N 82 55W
Harrow, U.K. 13 51 35N 0 15W
Harsefeld 24 53 26N 9 31 E
Harstad 50 68 48N 16 30 E
Hart 114 43 42N 86 21W
Hartbees → 92 28 45 S 20 32 E
Hartberg 26 47 17N 15 58 E
Hartford, Conn., U.S.A. 114 41 47N 72 41W
Hartford, Ky., U.S.A. 117 37 26N 86 50W
Hartford, S.D., U.S.A. 116 43 40N 96 58W
Hartford, Wis., U.S.A. 116 43 18N 88 25W
Hartford City 114 40 22N 85 20W
Hartland 107 46 20N 67 32W
Hartland Pt. 13 51 2N 4 32W
Hartlepool 12 54 42N 1 11W
Hartley 91 18 10 S 30 14 E
Hartley Bay 108 53 25N 129 15W
Hartmannberge 92 17 0 S 13 0 E
Hartney 109 49 30N 100 35W
Hartselle 115 34 25N 86 55W
Hartshorne 117 34 51N 95 30W
Hartsville 115 34 23N 80 2W
Hartwell 115 34 21N 82 52W
Harunabad 68 29 35N 73 8 E
Harur 70 12 3N 78 29 E
Harvey, Ill., U.S.A. 114 41 40N 87 40W
Harvey, N.D., U.S.A. 116 47 50N 99 58W
Harwich 13 51 56N 1 18 E
Haryana □ 68 29 0N 76 10 E
Harz 24 51 40N 10 40 E
Harzgerode 24 51 38N 11 8 E
Hasa 64 26 0N 49 0 E
Hasaheisa 87 14 44N 33 20 E
Hasani 86 25 0N 37 8 E
Hasanpur 68 28 43N 78 17 E
Haselünne 24 52 40N 7 30 E
Hasharon 62 32 12N 34 49 E
Hashefela 62 31 30N 34 43 E
Håsjö 48 63 1N 16 5 E
Haskell, Okla., U.S.A. 117 35 51N 95 40W
Haskell, Tex., U.S.A. 117 33 10N 99 45W
Haslach 25 48 16N 8 7 E
Hasle 49 55 11N 14 44 E
Haslev 49 55 18N 11 57 E
Hasparren 20 43 24N 1 18W
Hasselt 16 50 56N 5 21 E
Hassene, Ad. 82 21 0N 4 0 E
Hassfurt 25 50 2N 10 30 E
Hassi Berrekrem 83 33 45N 5 16 E
Hassi bou Khelala 82 30 17N 0 18W
Hassi Daoula 83 33 4N 5 38 E
Hassi Djafou 82 30 55N 3 35 E
Hassi el Abiod 82 31 47N 3 37 E
Hassi el Biod 83 28 30N 6 0 E
Hassi el Gassi 83 30 52N 6 5 E
Hassi el Hadjar 83 31 28N 4 45 E
Hassi er Rmel 82 32 56N 3 17 E
Hassi Imoulaye 83 29 54N 9 10 E
Hassi Inifel 82 29 50N 3 41 E
Hassi Marroket 82 30 10N 3 0 E
Hassi Messaoud 83 31 43N 6 8 E
Hassi Rhénami 83 31 50N 5 58 E
Hassi Tartrat 83 30 5N 6 28 E
Hassi Zerzour 82 30 51N 3 56W
Hastings, Can. 112 44 18N 77 57W
Hastings, N.Z. 101 39 39 S 176 52 E
Hastings, U.K. 13 50 51N 0 36 E
Hastings, Mich., U.S.A. 114 42 40N 85 20W
Hastings, Minn., U.S.A. 116 44 41N 92 51W
Hastings, Nebr., U.S.A. 116 40 34N 98 22W
Hastings Ra. 99 31 15 S 152 14 E
Hästveda 49 56 17N 13 55 E
Hat Nhao 71 14 46N 106 32 E
Hatch 119 32 45N 107 8W
Hatches Creek 96 20 56 S 135 12 E
Hatchet L. 109 58 36N 103 40W
Haţeg 46 45 36N 22 55 E
Haţeg, Mţii. 46 45 25N 23 0 E
Hatfield P.O. 99 33 54 S 143 49 E
Hatgal 75 50 26N 100 9 E
Hathras 68 27 36N 78 6 E
Hattah 99 34 48 S 142 17 E
Hatteras, C. 115 35 10N 75 30W
Hattiesburg 117 31 20N 89 20W
Hatvan 27 47 40N 19 45 E
Hau Bon = Cheo Reo 71 13 25N 108 28 E
Haug 47 60 23N 10 26 E
Haugastøl 47 60 30N 7 50 E
Haugesund 47 59 23N 5 13 E
Haultain → 109 55 51N 106 46W
Hauraki Gulf 101 36 35 S 175 5 E
Hauran 62 32 50N 36 15 E
Hausruck 26 48 6N 13 30 E
Haut Atlas 82 32 30N 5 0W
Haut-Rhin □ 19 48 0N 7 15 E
Haut Zaïre □ 90 2 20N 26 0 E
Hautah, Wahāt al 64 23 40N 47 0 E
Haute-Corse □ 21 42 30N 9 30 E
Haute-Garonne □ 20 43 28N 1 30 E
Haute-Loire □ 20 45 5N 3 50 E
Haute-Marne □ 19 48 10N 5 20 E
Haute-Saône □ 19 47 45N 6 10 E
Haute-Savoie □ 21 46 0N 6 20 E
Haute-Vienne □ 20 45 50N 1 10 E
Hauterive 107 49 10N 68 16W
Hautes-Alpes □ 21 44 42N 6 20 E
Hautes-Pyrénées □ 20 43 0N 0 10 E
Hauteville 21 45 58N 5 36 E
Hautmont 19 50 15N 3 55 E
Hauts-de-Seine □ 19 48 52N 2 15 E
Hauts Plateaux 82 34 14N 1 0 E
Hauzenberg 25 48 39N 13 38 E
Havana 116 40 19N 90 3W
Havana = La Habana 121 23 8N 82 22W
Havasu, L. 119 34 18N 114 28W
Havdhem 49 57 10N 18 20 E
Havelange 16 50 23N 5 15 E
Havelock, N.B., Can. 107 46 2N 65 24W
Havelock, Ont., Can. 106 44 26N 77 53W
Havelock, N.Z. 101 41 17 S 173 48 E
Havelock I. 71 11 55N 93 2 E
Haverfordwest 13 51 48N 4 59W
Haverhill 114 42 50N 71 2W
Haveri 70 14 53N 75 24 E
Havering 13 51 33N 0 20 E
Haverstraw 113 41 12N 73 58W
Håverud 49 58 50N 12 28 E

Havîrna 46 48 4N 26 43 E
Havlíčkův Brod 26 49 36N 15 33 E
Havneby 49 55 5N 8 34 E
Havre 118 48 34N 109 40W
Havre -St.-Pierre 107 50 18N 63 33W
Havre-Aubert 107 47 12N 61 56W
Havre, Le 18 49 30N 0 5 E
Havza 64 41 0N 35 35 E
Haw → 115 35 36N 79 3W
Hawaii □ 110 20 30N 157 0W
Hawaii 110 20 0N 155 0W
Hawaiian Is. 110 20 30N 156 0W
Hawaiian Ridge 95 24 0N 165 0W
Hawarden, Can. 109 51 25N 106 36W
Hawarden, U.S.A. 116 43 2N 96 28W
Hawea Lake 101 44 28 S 169 19 E
Hawera 101 39 35 S 174 19 E
Hawick 14 55 25N 2 48W
Hawk Junction 106 48 5N 84 38W
Hawke B. 101 39 25 S 177 20 E
Hawke, C. 100 32 13 S 152 34 E
Hawker 97 31 59 S 138 22 E
Hawke's Bay □ 101 39 45 S 176 35 E
Hawkesbury 106 45 37N 74 37W
Hawkesbury → 97 33 30 S 151 10 E
Hawkesbury I. 108 53 37N 129 3W
Hawkinsville 115 32 17N 83 30W
Hawkwood 99 25 45 S 150 50 E
Hawley 116 46 58N 96 20W
Hawrān 62 32 45N 36 15 E
Hawthorne 118 38 31N 118 37W
Hawzen 87 13 58N 39 28 E
Haxtun 116 40 40N 102 39W
Hay, Austral. 97 34 30 S 144 51 E
Hay, U.K. 13 52 4N 3 9W
Hay →, Austral. 97 25 14 S 138 0 E
Hay →, Can. 108 60 50N 116 26W
Hay L. 108 58 50N 118 50W
Hay Lakes 108 53 12N 113 2W
Hay River 108 60 51N 115 44W
Hay Springs 116 42 40N 102 38W
Hayange 19 49 20N 6 2 E
Hayden, Ariz., U.S.A. 119 33 2N 110 48W
Hayden, Colo., U.S.A. 118 40 30N 107 22W
Haydon 98 18 0 S 141 30 E
Haye-Descartes, La 18 46 58N 0 42 E
Haye-du-Puits, La 18 49 17N 1 33W
Hayes 116 44 22N 101 1W
Hayes → 109 57 3N 92 12W
Haynesville 117 33 0N 93 7W
Hays, Can. 108 50 6N 111 48W
Hays, U.S.A. 116 38 55N 99 25W
Hayward 116 46 2N 91 30W
Hayward's Heath 13 51 0N 0 5W
Hazard 114 37 18N 83 10W
Hazaribagh 69 23 58N 85 26 E
Hazaribagh Road 69 24 12N 85 57 E
Hazebrouck 19 50 42N 2 31 E
Hazelton, Can. 108 55 20N 127 42W
Hazelton, U.S.A. 116 46 30N 100 15W
Hazen, N.D., U.S.A. 116 47 18N 101 38W
Hazen, Nev., U.S.A. 118 39 37N 119 2W
Hazlehurst, Ga., U.S.A. 115 31 50N 82 35W
Hazlehurst, Miss., U.S.A. 117 31 52N 90 24W
Hazleton 114 40 58N 76 0W
Ḥazor 62 33 2N 35 32 E
He Xian 77 24 27N 111 30 E
Head of Bight 96 31 30 S 131 25 E
Headlands 91 18 15 S 32 2 E
Healdsburg 118 38 33N 122 51W
Healdton 117 34 16N 97 31W
Healesville 99 37 35 S 145 30 E
Heanor 12 53 1N 1 20W
Heard I. 3 53 0 S 74 0 E
Hearne 117 30 54N 96 35W
Hearne B. 109 60 10N 99 10W
Hearne L. 108 62 20N 113 10W
Hearst 106 49 40N 83 41W
Heart → 116 46 40N 100 51W
Heart's Content 107 47 54N 53 27W
Heath Pt. 107 49 8N 61 40W
Heath Steele 107 47 17N 66 5W
Heavener 117 34 54N 94 36W
Hebbronville 117 27 20N 98 40W
Hebei □ 76 39 0N 116 0 E
Hebel 99 28 58 S 147 47 E
Heber Springs 117 35 29N 91 59W
Hebert 109 50 30N 107 10W
Hebgen, L. 118 44 50N 111 15W
Hebi 76 35 57N 114 7 E
Hebrides 14 57 30N 7 0W
Hebrides, Inner Is. 14 57 20N 6 40W
Hebrides, Outer Is. 14 57 30N 7 40W
Hebron, Can. 105 58 5N 62 30W
Hebron, N.D., U.S.A. 116 46 56N 102 2W
Hebron, Nebr., U.S.A. 116 40 15N 97 33W
Hebron = Al Khalil 62 31 32N 35 6 E
Heby 48 59 56N 16 53 E
Hecate Str. 108 53 10N 130 30W
Hechi 75 24 40N 108 2 E
Hechingen 25 48 20N 8 58 E
Hechuan 75 30 2N 106 12 E
Hecla 116 45 56N 98 8W
Hecla I. 109 51 10N 96 43W
Heddal 47 59 36N 9 9 E
Hédé 18 48 18N 1 49W
Hede 48 62 23N 13 30 E
Hedemora 48 60 18N 15 58 E
Hedley 117 34 53N 100 39W
Hedmark fylke □ 47 61 17N 11 40 E
Hedrum 47 59 7N 10 5 E
Heemstede 16 52 22N 4 37 E
Heerde 16 52 24N 6 2 E
Heerenveen 16 52 57N 5 55 E
Heerlen 16 50 55N 6 0 E
Hefa 62 32 46N 35 0 E
Hefei 75 31 52N 117 18 E
Hegang 75 47 20N 130 19 E
Hegyalja 27 48 25N 21 25 E
Heide 24 54 10N 9 7 E
Heidelberg, Ger. 25 49 23N 8 41 E
Heidelberg, C. Prov., S. Afr. 92 34 6 S 20 59 E
Heidelberg, Trans., S. Afr. 93 26 30 S 28 23 E
Heidenheim 25 48 40N 10 10 E
Heilbron 93 27 16 S 27 59 E
Heilbronn 25 49 8N 9 13 E
Heiligenblut 26 47 2N 12 51 E
Heiligenhafen 24 54 21N 10 58 E
Heiligenstadt 24 51 22N 10 9 E
Heilongjiang □ 75 48 0N 126 0 E
Heilunkiang = Heilongjiang □ 75 48 0N 126 0 E
Heim 47 63 26N 9 5 E
Heinola 51 61 13N 26 2 E
Heinze Is. 71 14 25N 97 45 E
Hejaz = Ḥijāz 64 26 0N 37 30 E
Hejian 76 38 25N 116 5 E
Hejiang 77 28 43N 105 46 E
Hekimhan 64 38 50N 38 0 E
Hekla 50 63 56N 19 35W
Hekou 75 22 30N 103 59 E
Hel 28 54 37N 18 47 E
Helagsfjället 48 62 54N 12 25 E
Helan Shan 76 39 0N 105 55 E
Helechosa 31 39 22N 4 53W
Helena, Ark., U.S.A. 117 34 30N 90 35W
Helena, Mont., U.S.A. 118 46 40N 112 0W
Helensburgh, Austral. 100 34 11 S 151 1 E
Helensburgh, U.K. 14 56 0N 4 44W
Helensville 101 36 41 S 174 29 E
Helez 62 31 36N 34 39 E
Helgasjön 49 57 0N 14 50 E
Helgeroa 47 59 0N 9 45 E
Helgoland 24 54 10N 7 51 E
Heligoland = Helgoland 24 54 10N 7 51 E
Heliopolis 86 30 6N 31 17 E
Hell-Ville 93 13 25 S 48 16 E
Hellebæk 49 56 4N 12 32 E
Helleland 47 58 33N 6 7 E
Hellendoorn 16 52 24N 6 27 E
Hellevoetsluis 16 51 50N 4 8 E
Hellín 33 38 31N 1 40W
Helmand □ 65 31 20N 64 0 E
Helmand → 66 31 12N 61 34 E
Helmand, Hamun 65 31 15N 61 15 E
Helme → 24 51 40N 11 20 E
Helmond 16 51 29N 5 41 E
Helmsdale 14 58 7N 3 40W
Helmstedt 24 52 16N 11 0 E
Helnæs 49 55 9N 10 0 E
Helper 118 39 44N 110 56W
Helsingborg 49 56 3N 12 42 E
Helsinge 49 56 2N 12 12 E
Helsingfors 51 60 15N 25 3 E
Helsingør 49 56 2N 12 35 E
Helsinki 51 60 15N 25 3 E
Helska, Mierzeja 28 54 45N 18 40 E
Helston 13 50 7N 5 17W
Helvellyn 12 54 31N 3 1W
Helwân 86 29 50N 31 20 E
Hemavati → 70 12 30N 76 20 E
Hemet 119 33 45N 116 59W
Hemingford 116 42 21N 103 4W
Hemphill 117 31 21N 93 49W
Hempstead 117 30 5N 96 5W
Hemse 49 57 15N 18 22 E
Hemsö 48 62 43N 18 5 E
Henan □ 75 34 0N 114 0 E
Henares → 32 40 24N 3 30W
Hendaye 20 43 23N 1 47W
Henderson, Argent. 124 36 18 S 61 43W
Henderson, Ky., U.S.A. 114 37 50N 87 38W
Henderson, N.C., U.S.A. 115 36 20N 78 25W
Henderson, Nev., U.S.A. 119 36 2N 115 0W
Henderson, Pa., U.S.A. 115 35 25N 88 40W
Henderson, Tex., U.S.A. 117 32 5N 94 49W
Hendersonville 115 35 21N 82 28W
Hendon 99 28 5 S 151 50 E
Hendorf 46 46 4N 24 55 E
Heng Xian 77 22 40N 109 17 E
Hengdaohezi 76 44 52N 129 0 E
Hengelo 16 52 3N 6 19 E
Hengshan, Hunan, China 77 27 16N 112 45 E
Hengshan, Shaanxi, China 76 37 58N 109 5 E
Hengshui 76 37 41N 115 40 E
Hengyang 75 26 52N 112 33 E
Hénin-Beaumont 19 50 25N 2 58 E
Henlopen, C. 114 38 48N 75 5W
Hennan, L. 48 62 3N 55 46 E
Hennebont 18 47 49N 3 19W
Hennenman 92 27 59 S 27 1 E
Hennessy 117 36 8N 97 53W
Hennigsdorf 24 52 38N 13 13 E
Henrichemont 19 47 20N 2 30 E
Henrietta 117 33 50N 98 15W
Henrietta Maria C. 106 55 9N 82 20W
Henrietta, Ostrov 59 77 6N 156 30 E
Henry 116 41 5N 89 20W
Henryetta 117 35 30N 96 0W
Hensall 112 43 26N 81 30W
Hentiyn Nuruu 75 48 30N 108 30 E
Henty 99 35 30 S 147 0 E
Henzada 67 17 38N 95 26 E
Hephaestia 44 39 55N 25 14 E
Heping 77 24 29N 115 0 E
Heppner 118 45 21N 119 34W
Hepu 77 21 40N 109 12 E
Hepworth 112 44 37N 81 9W
Herad 47 58 8N 6 47 E
Héraðsflói 50 65 42N 14 12W
Héraðsvötn → 50 65 45N 19 25W
Herāt 65 34 20N 62 7 E
Herāt □ 65 35 0N 62 0 E
Hérault □ 20 43 34N 3 15 E
Hérault → 20 43 17N 3 26 E
Herbault 18 47 36N 1 8 E
Herbert → 98 18 31 S 146 17 E
Herbert Downs 98 23 7 S 139 9 E
Herberton 98 17 20 S 145 25 E
Herbiers, Les 18 46 52N 1 0W
Herbignac 18 47 27N 2 18W
Herborn 24 50 40N 8 19 E
Herby 28 50 45N 18 50 E
Hercegnovi 42 42 30N 18 33 E
Herðubreið 50 65 11N 16 21W
Hereford, U.K. 13 52 4N 2 42W
Hereford, U.S.A. 117 34 50N 102 28W
Hereford and Worcester □ 13 52 10N 2 30W
Herefoss 47 58 32N 8 23 E
Herentals 16 51 12N 4 51 E
Herfølge 49 55 26N 12 9 E
Herford 24 52 7N 8 40 E
Héricourt 19 47 32N 6 45 E
Herington 116 38 43N 97 0W
Herisau 25 47 22N 9 17 E
Hérisson 20 46 32N 2 42 E
Herkimer 114 43 0N 74 59W
Herm 18 49 30N 2 28W
Hermagor 26 46 38N 13 23 E
Herman 116 45 51N 96 8W
Hermann 116 38 40N 91 25W
Hermannsburg 24 52 49N 10 6 E
Hermanus 92 34 27 S 19 12 E
Herment 20 45 45N 2 24 E
Hermidale 99 31 30 S 146 42 E
Hermiston 118 45 50N 119 16W
Hermitage 101 43 44 S 170 5 E
Hermite, I. 128 55 50 S 68 0W
Hermon, Mt. = Ash Shaykh, J. 64 33 20N 35 51 E
Hermosillo 120 29 10N 111 0W
Hernad → 27 47 56N 21 8 E
Hernandarias 125 25 20 S 54 40W
Hernando, Argent. 124 32 28 S 63 40W
Hernando, U.S.A. 117 34 50N 89 59W
Herne 24 51 33N 7 12 E
Herne Bay 13 51 22N 1 8 E
Herning 49 56 8N 8 58 E
Heroica Nogales = Nogales 120 31 20N 110 56W
Heron Bay 106 48 40N 86 25W
Herowābād 64 38 37N 48 32 E
Herreid 116 45 53N 100 5W
Herrera 31 37 26N 4 55W
Herrera de Alcántar 31 39 39N 7 25W
Herrera de Pisuerga 30 42 35N 4 20W
Herrera del Duque 31 39 10N 5 3W
Herrick 99 41 5 S 147 55 E
Herrin 117 37 50N 89 0W
Herrljunga 49 58 5N 13 1 E
Hersbruck 25 49 30N 11 25 E
Herstal 16 50 40N 5 38 E
Hersvik 47 61 10N 4 53 E
Hertford 13 51 47N 0 4W
Hertford □ 13 51 51N 0 5W
's-Hertogenbosch 16 51 42N 5 17 E
Hertzogville 92 28 9 S 25 30 E
Hervás 30 40 16N 5 52W
Hervey B. 97 25 0 S 152 52 E
* Hervey Is. 95 19 30 S 159 0W
Herzberg, Cottbus, Ger. 24 51 40N 13 13 E
Herzberg, Niedersachsen, Ger. 24 51 38N 10 20 E
Herzliyya 62 32 10N 34 50 E
Herzogenburg 26 48 17N 15 41 E
Hesdin 19 50 21N 2 0 E
Hesel 24 53 18N 7 36 E
Heskestad 47 58 28N 6 22 E
Hespeler 112 43 26N 80 19W
Hesse = Hessen 24 50 40N 9 20 E
Hessen □ 24 50 40N 9 20 E
Hettinger 116 46 0N 102 38W
Hettstedt 24 51 39N 11 30 E
Hève, C. de la 18 49 30N 0 5 E
Heves □ 27 47 50N 20 0 E
Hevron → 62 31 12N 34 42 E
Hewett, C. 105 70 16N 67 45W
Hex River 92 33 30 S 19 35 E
Hexham 12 54 58N 2 7W
Hexigten Qi 76 43 18N 117 30 E
Heyfield 100 37 59 S 146 47 E
Heysham 12 54 5N 2 53W
Heywood 99 38 8 S 141 37 E
Hi-no-Misaki 74 35 26N 132 38 E
Hialeach 115 25 49N 80 17W
Hiawatha, Kans., U.S.A. 116 39 55N 95 33W
Hiawatha, Utah, U.S.A. 118 39 29N 111 1W
Hibbing 116 47 30N 93 0W
Hickman 117 36 35N 89 8W
Hickory 115 35 46N 81 17W
Hicks Pt. 97 37 49 S 149 17 E
Hicksville 113 40 46N 73 30W
Hida 46 47 10N 23 19 E
Hida-Sammyaku 74 36 30N 137 40 E
Hidalgo 120 24 15N 99 26W
Hidalgo del Parral 120 26 58N 105 40W
Hidalgo, Presa M. 120 26 30N 108 35W
Hiddensee 24 54 30N 13 6 E
Hieflau 26 47 36N 14 46 E
Hiendelaencina 32 41 5N 3 0W
Hierro 80 27 44N 18 0 E
Higashiōsaka 74 34 40N 135 37 E
Higgins 117 36 9N 100 1W
High Atlas = Haut Atlas 82 32 30N 5 0W
High I. 107 56 40N 61 10W
High Island 117 29 32N 94 22W
High Level 108 58 31N 117 8W
High Point 115 35 57N 79 58W
High Prairie 108 55 30N 116 30W
High River 108 50 30N 113 50W
High Springs 115 29 50N 82 40W
High Tatra 27 49 30N 20 00 E
High Wycombe 13 51 37N 0 45W
Highbury 98 16 25 S 143 9 E
Highland □ 14 57 30N 5 0W
Highland Park 114 42 10N 87 50W
Highmore 116 44 35N 99 26W
Highrock L. 109 57 5N 105 32W
Higley 119 33 27N 111 46W
Hihya 86 30 40N 31 36 E
Hiiumaa 54 58 50N 22 45 E
Hijar 32 41 10N 0 27W
Ḥijārah, Şaḥrā' al 64 30 25N 44 30 E
Hiko 119 37 30N 115 13W
Hikone 74 35 15N 136 10 E
Hildburghhausen 25 50 24N 10 43 E
Hildesheim 24 52 9N 9 55 E
Hill City, Idaho, U.S.A. 118 43 20N 115 2W
Hill City, Kans., U.S.A. 116 39 25N 99 51W
Hill City, Minn., U.S.A. 116 46 57N 93 35W
Hill City, S.D., U.S.A. 116 43 58N 103 35W
Hill Island L. 109 60 30N 109 50W
Hillared 49 57 37N 13 10 E
Hillegom 16 52 18N 4 35 E
Hillerød 49 55 56N 12 19 E
Hillerstorp 49 57 20N 13 52 E
Hillingdon 13 51 33N 0 29W
Hillman 114 45 5N 83 52W
Hillmond 109 53 26N 109 41W
Hillsboro, Kans., U.S.A. 116 38 22N 97 10W
Hillsboro, N. Mex., U.S.A. 119 33 0N 107 35W
Hillsboro, N.D., U.S.A. 116 47 23N 97 9W
Hillsboro, N.H., U.S.A. 114 43 8N 71 56W
Hillsboro, Oreg., U.S.A: 118 45 31N 123 0W
Hillsboro, Tex., U.S.A. 117 32 0N 97 10W
Hillsdale, Mich., U.S.A. 114 41 55N 84 40W
Hillsdale, N.Y., U.S.A. 113 42 11N 73 30W
Hillsport 106 49 27N 85 34W
Hillston 97 33 30 S 145 31 E
Hilo 110 19 44N 155 5W
Hilonghilong 73 9 10N 125 45 E
Hilton 112 43 16N 77 48W
Hilversum 16 52 14N 5 10 E
Himachal Pradesh □ 68 31 30N 77 0 E
Himalaya 67 29 0N 84 0 E
Himara 44 40 8N 19 43 E
Himeji 74 34 50N 134 40 E
Himi 74 36 50N 137 0 E
Himmerland 49 56 45N 9 30 E
Ḥimş 64 34 40N 36 45 E
Hinako, Kepulauan 72 0 50N 97 20 E
Hinchinbrook I. 97 18 20 S 146 15 E
Hinckley, U.K. 13 52 33N 1 21W
Hinckley, U.S.A. 118 39 18N 112 41W
Hindås 49 57 42N 12 27 E
Hindaun 68 26 44N 77 5 E
Hindmarsh L. 99 36 5 S 141 55 E
Hindol 69 20 40N 85 10 E
Hindsholm 49 55 30N 10 40 E
Hindu Bagh 68 30 56N 67 50 E
Hindu Kush 65 36 0N 71 0 E
Hindupur 70 13 49N 77 32 E
Hines Creek 108 56 20N 118 40W
Hinganghat 68 20 30N 78 52 E
Hingham 118 48 34N 110 29W
Hingoli 70 19 41N 77 15 E
Hinlopenstretet 4 79 35N 18 40 E
Hinna 85 10 25N 11 35 E
Hinojosa del Duque 31 38 30N 5 9W
Hinsdale 118 48 26N 107 2W
Hinterrhein → 25 46 40N 9 25 E
Hinton, Can. 108 53 26N 117 34W
Hinton, U.S.A. 114 37 40N 80 51W
Hippolytushoef 16 52 54N 4 58 E
Hirakud 69 21 32N 83 51 E
Hirakud Dam 69 21 32N 83 45 E
Hiratsuka 74 35 19N 139 21 E
Hirhafok 83 23 49N 5 45 E
Hîrlău 46 47 23N 27 0 E
Hirosaki 74 40 34N 140 28 E
Hiroshima 74 34 24N 132 30 E
Hiroshima □ 74 34 50N 133 0 E
Hirsoholmene 49 57 30N 10 36 E
Hirson 19 49 55N 4 4 E
Hîrşova 46 44 40N 27 59 E
Hirtshals 49 57 36N 9 57 E
Ḥişn Dibā 65 25 45N 56 16 E
Hispaniola 121 19 0N 71 0W
Hissar 68 29 12N 75 45 E
Hita 74 33 20N 130 58 E
Hitachi 74 36 36N 140 39 E
Hitchin 13 51 57N 0 16W
Hitoyoshi 74 32 13N 130 45 E
Hitra 47 63 30N 8 45 E
Hitzacker 24 53 9N 11 1 E
Ḥiyyon, N. → 62 30 25N 35 10 E
Hjalmar L. 109 61 33N 109 25W
Hjälmare kanal 48 59 20N 15 59 E
Hjälmaren 48 59 18N 15 40 E
Hjartdal 47 59 37N 8 41 E
Hjerkinn 47 62 13N 9 33 E
Hjørring 49 57 29N 9 59 E
Hjorted 49 57 37N 16 19 E
Hjortkvarn 49 58 54N 15 26 E
Hlinsko 26 49 45N 15 54 E
Hlohovec 27 48 26N 17 49 E
Hńak 4 70 40N 52 10W
Ho 85 6 37N 0 27 E
Ho Chi Minh, Phanh Bho 71 10 58N 106 40 E
Hoa Binh 71 20 50N 105 20 E
Hoai Nhon (Bon Son) 71 14 28N 109 1 E
Hoare B. 105 65 17N 62 30W
Hobart, Austral. 97 42 50 S 147 21 E
Hobart, U.S.A. 117 35 0N 99 5W
Hobbs 117 32 40N 103 3W
Hobbs Coast 5 74 50 S 131 0W
Hoboken, Belg. 16 51 11N 4 21 E
Hoboken, U.S.A. 113 40 45N 74 4W
Hobro 49 56 39N 9 46 E
Hoburgen 49 56 55N 18 7 E
Hochatown 117 34 11N 94 39W
Hochschwab 26 47 35N 15 0 E
Höchst 25 50 6N 8 33 E
Höchstadt 25 49 42N 10 48 E
Hockenheim 25 49 18N 8 33 E
Hodgson 109 51 13N 97 36W
Hódmezövásárhely 27 46 28N 20 22 E
Hodna, Chott el 83 35 30N 5 0 E
Hodna, Monts du 83 35 52N 4 42 E
Hodonín 27 48 50N 17 10 E
Hoëdic 18 47 21N 2 52W
Hoek van Holland 16 52 0N 4 7 E
Hoëveld 93 26 30 S 30 0 E
Hof, Ger. 25 50 18N 11 55 E
Hof, Iceland 50 64 33N 14 40W
Höfðakaupstaður 50 65 50N 20 19W
Hofgeismar 24 51 29N 9 23 E
Hofors 48 60 31N 16 15 E
Hofsjökull 50 64 49N 18 48W
Hofsós 50 65 53N 19 26W
Hōfu 74 34 3N 131 34 E
Hogansville 115 33 14N 84 50W

* *Renamed Manuae*

Place	Page	Lat.	Long.
Hogeland	**118**	48 51N	108 40W
Hogenakai Falls	**70**	12 6N	77 50 E
Högfors	**48**	59 58N	15 3 E
Högsäter	**49**	58 38N	12 5 E
Högsby	**49**	57 10N	16 1 E
Högsjö	**48**	59 4N	15 44 E
Hoh Xil Shan	**75**	35 0N	89 0 E
Hohe Rhön	**25**	50 24N	9 58 E
Hohe Tauern	**26**	47 11N	12 40 E
Hohe Venn	**16**	50 30N	6 5 E
Hohenau	**27**	48 36N	16 55 E
Hohenems	**26**	47 22N	9 42 E
Hohenstein Ernstthal	**24**	50 48N	12 43 E
Hohenwald	**115**	35 35N	87 30W
Hohenwestedt	**24**	54 6N	9 30 E
Hohhot	**76**	40 52N	111 40 E
Hohoe	**85**	7 8N	0 32 E
Hoi An	**71**	15 30N	108 19 E
Hoi Xuan	**71**	20 25N	105 9 E
Hoisington	**116**	38 33N	98 50W
Højer	**49**	54 58N	8 42 E
Hok	**49**	57 31N	14 16 E
Hökensås	**49**	58 0N	14 5 E
Hökerum	**49**	57 51N	13 16 E
Hokianga Harbour	**101**	35 31 S	173 22 E
Hokitika	**101**	42 42 S	171 0 E
Hokkaidō □	**74**	43 30N	143 0 E
Hokksund	**47**	59 44N	9 59 E
Hol-Hol	**87**	11 20N	42 50 E
Holbæk	**49**	55 43N	11 43 E
Holbrook, Austral.	**99**	35 42 S	147 18 E
Holbrook, U.S.A.	**119**	35 54N	110 10W
Holden, Can.	**108**	53 13N	112 11W
Holden, U.S.A.	**118**	39 0N	112 26W
Holdenville	**117**	35 5N	96 25W
Holderness	**12**	53 45N	0 5W
Holdfast	**109**	50 58N	105 25W
Holdrege	**116**	40 26N	99 22W
Hole	**47**	60 6N	10 12 E
Hole-Narsipur	**70**	12 48N	76 16 E
Holešov	**27**	49 20N	17 35 E
Holguín	**121**	20 50N	76 20W
Holíč	**27**	48 49N	17 10 E
Hollabrunn	**26**	48 34N	16 5 E
Hollams Bird I.	**92**	24 40 S	14 30 E
Holland	**114**	42 47N	86 7W
Hollandia = Jayapura	**73**	2 28 S	140 38 E
Höllen	**47**	58 6N	7 49 E
Hollfeld	**25**	49 56N	11 18 E
Hollick Kenyon Plateau	**5**	82 0 S	110 0W
Hollidaysburg	**114**	40 26N	78 25W
Hollis	**117**	34 45N	99 55W
Hollister, Calif., U.S.A.	**119**	36 51N	121 24W
Hollister, Idaho, U.S.A.	**118**	42 21N	114 40W
Holly	**116**	38 7N	102 7W
Holly Hill	**115**	29 15N	81 3W
Holly Springs	**117**	34 45N	89 25W
Hollywood, Calif., U.S.A.	**110**	34 7N	118 25W
Hollywood, Fla., U.S.A.	**115**	26 0N	80 9W
Holm	**48**	62 40N	16 40 E
Holman Island	**104**	70 42N	117 41W
Hólmavík	**50**	65 42N	21 40W
Holmedal	**47**	61 22N	5 11 E
Holmegil	**48**	59 10N	11 44 E
Holmestrand	**47**	59 31N	10 14 E
Holmsbu	**47**	59 32N	10 27 E
Holmsjön	**48**	62 26N	15 20 E
Holmsland Klit	**49**	56 0N	8 5 E
Holmsund	**50**	63 41N	20 20 E
Holod	**46**	46 49N	22 8 E
Holon	**62**	32 2N	34 47 E
Holroyd →	**97**	14 10 S	141 36 E
Holstebro	**49**	56 22N	8 37 E
Holsworthy	**13**	50 48N	4 21W
Holt	**50**	63 33N	19 48W
Holte	**49**	55 50N	12 29 E
Holton, Can.	**107**	54 31N	57 12W
Holton, U.S.A.	**116**	39 28N	95 44W
Holtville	**119**	32 50N	115 27W
Holum	**47**	58 6N	7 32 E
Holwerd	**16**	53 22N	5 54 E
Holy Cross	**104**	62 10N	159 52W
Holy I., England, U.K.	**12**	55 42N	1 48W
Holy I., Wales, U.K.	**12**	53 17N	4 37W
Holyhead	**12**	53 18N	4 38W
Holyoke, Colo., U.S.A.	**116**	40 39N	102 18W
Holyoke, Mass., U.S.A.	**114**	42 14N	72 37W
Holyrood	**107**	47 27N	53 8W
Holzkirchen	**25**	47 53N	11 42 E
Holzminden	**24**	51 49N	9 31 E
Homa Bay	**90**	0 36 S	34 30 E
Homa Bay □	**90**	0 50 S	34 30 E
Homalin	**67**	24 55N	95 0 E
Homberg	**24**	51 2N	9 20 E
Hombori	**85**	15 20N	1 38W
Homburg	**25**	49 19N	7 21 E
Home B.	**105**	68 40N	67 10W
Home Hill	**97**	19 43 S	147 25 E
Homedale	**118**	43 42N	116 59W
Homer, Alaska, U.S.A.	**104**	59 40N	151 35W
Homer, La., U.S.A.	**117**	32 50N	93 4W
Homestead, Austral.	**98**	20 20 S	145 40 E
Homestead, Fla., U.S.A.	**115**	25 29N	80 27W
Homestead, Oreg., U.S.A.	**118**	45 5N	116 57W
Hominy	**117**	36 26N	96 24W
Homnabad	**70**	17 45N	77 11 E
Homoine	**93**	23 55 S	35 8 E
Homoljske Planina	**42**	44 10N	21 45 E
Homorod	**46**	46 5N	25 15 E
Homs = Ḥimş	**64**	34 40N	36 45 E
Hon Chong	**71**	10 25N	104 30 E
Honan = Henan □	**75**	34 0N	114 0 E
Honda	**126**	5 12N	74 45W
Hondeklipbaai	**92**	30 19 S	17 17 E
Hondo	**117**	29 22N	99 6W
Hondo →	**120**	18 25N	88 21W
Honduras ■	**121**	14 40N	86 30W
Honduras, Golfo de	**120**	16 50N	87 0W
Honesdale	**113**	41 34N	75 17W
Honey L.	**118**	40 13N	120 14W
Honfleur	**18**	49 25N	0 13 E
Hong Kong ■	**75**	22 11N	114 14 E
Hong'an	**77**	31 20N	114 40 E
Hongha →	**71**	22 0N	104 0 E
Honghai Wan	**77**	22 40N	115 0 E
Honghu	**77**	29 50N	113 30 E
Hongjiang	**75**	27 7N	109 59 E
Hongshui He →	**75**	23 48N	109 30 E
Hongtong	**76**	36 16N	111 40 E
Honguedo, Détroit d'	**107**	49 15N	64 0W
Hongze Hu	**75**	33 15N	118 35 E
Honiara	**94**	9 27 S	159 57 E
Honiton	**13**	50 48N	3 11W
Honkorâb, Ras	**86**	24 35N	35 10 E
Honolulu	**110**	21 19N	157 52W
Honshū	**74**	36 0N	138 0 E
Hontoria del Pinar	**32**	41 50N	3 10W
Hood Mt.	**118**	45 24N	121 41W
Hood, Pt.	**96**	34 23 S	119 34 E
Hood River	**118**	45 45N	121 31W
Hoodsport	**118**	47 24N	123 7W
Hooge	**24**	54 31N	8 36 E
Hoogeveen	**16**	52 44N	6 30 E
Hoogezand	**16**	53 11N	6 45 E
Hooghly →	**69**	21 56N	88 4 E
Hooghly-Chinsura	**69**	22 53N	88 27 E
Hook Hd.	**15**	52 8N	6 57W
Hook I.	**98**	20 4 S	149 0 E
Hook of Holland = Hoek van Holland	**16**	52 0N	4 7 E
Hooker	**117**	36 55N	101 10W
Hoopeston	**114**	40 30N	87 40W
Hoopstad	**92**	27 50 S	25 55 E
Hoorn	**16**	52 38N	5 4 E
Hoover Dam	**119**	36 0N	114 45W
Hooversville	**112**	40 8N	78 57W
Hop Bottom	**113**	41 41N	75 47W
Hopà	**57**	41 28N	41 30 E
Hope, Can.	**108**	49 25N	121 25 E
Hope, Ark., U.S.A.	**117**	33 40N	93 36W
Hope, N.D., U.S.A.	**116**	47 21N	97 42W
Hope Bay	**5**	65 0 S	55 0W
Hope, L.	**99**	28 24 S	139 18 E
Hope Pt.	**104**	68 20N	166 50W
Hope Town	**121**	26 35N	76 57W
Hopedale	**107**	55 28N	60 13W
Hopefield	**92**	33 3 S	18 22 E
Hopei = Hebei □	**76**	39 0N	116 0 E
Hopelchén	**120**	19 46N	89 50W
Hopen	**47**	63 27N	8 2 E
Hopetoun, Vic., Austral.	**99**	35 42 S	142 22 E
Hopetoun, W. Australia, Austral.	**100**	33 57 S	120 7 E
Hopetown	**92**	29 34 S	24 3 E
Hopkins	**116**	40 31N	94 45W
Hopkins →	**100**	38 25 S	142 30 E
Hopkinsville	**115**	36 52N	87 26W
Hopland	**118**	39 0N	123 7W
Hoptrup	**49**	55 11N	9 28 E
Hoquiam	**118**	46 50N	123 55W
Horazdovice	**26**	49 19N	13 42 E
Horcajo de Santiago	**32**	39 50N	3 1W
Hordaland fylke □	**47**	60 25N	6 15 E
Horden Hills	**96**	20 40 S	130 20 E
Horezu	**46**	45 6N	24 0 E
Horgen	**25**	47 15N	8 35 E
Horgoš	**42**	46 10N	20 0 E
Horice	**26**	50 21N	15 39 E
Horlick Mts.	**5**	84 0 S	102 0W
Hormoz	**65**	27 35N	55 0 E
Hormoz, Jaz. ye	**65**	27 8N	56 28 E
Hormuz Str.	**65**	26 30N	56 30 E
Horn, Austria	**26**	48 39N	15 40 E
Horn, Ísafjarðarsýsla, Iceland	**50**	66 28N	22 28W
Horn, Suður-Múlasýsla, Iceland	**50**	65 10N	13 31W
Horn →	**108**	61 30N	118 1W
Horn, Cape = Hornos, Cabo de	**128**	55 50 S	67 30W
Horn Head	**15**	55 13N	8 0W
Horn, I.	**115**	30 17N	88 40W
Horn Mts.	**108**	62 15N	119 15W
Hornachuelos	**31**	37 50N	5 14W
Hornavan	**50**	66 15N	17 30 E
Hornbæk	**49**	56 5N	12 26 E
Hornbeck	**117**	31 22N	93 20W
Hornbrook	**118**	41 58N	122 37W
Hornburg	**24**	52 2N	10 36 E
Horncastle	**12**	53 13N	0 8W
Horndal	**48**	60 18N	16 23 E
Hornell	**114**	42 23N	77 41W
Hornell L.	**108**	62 20N	119 25W
Hornepayne	**106**	49 14N	84 48W
Hornindal	**47**	61 58N	6 30 E
Hornnes	**47**	58 34N	7 45 E
Hornos, Cabo de	**128**	55 50 S	67 30W
Hornoy	**19**	49 50N	1 54 E
Hornsby	**99**	33 42 S	151 2 E
Hornsea	**12**	53 55N	0 10W
Hornslandet	**48**	61 35N	17 37 E
Hornslet	**49**	56 18N	10 19 E
Hörnum	**24**	54 44N	8 18 E
Horovice	**26**	49 48N	13 53 E
Horqin Youyi Qianqi	**75**	46 5N	122 3 E
Horqueta	**124**	23 15 S	56 55W
Horra, La	**30**	41 44N	3 53W
Horred	**49**	57 22N	12 28 E
Horse Cr. →	**116**	41 57N	103 58W
Horse Is.	**107**	50 15N	55 50W
Horsefly L.	**108**	52 25N	121 0W
Horsens	**49**	55 52N	9 51 E
Horsens Fjord	**49**	55 50N	10 0 E
Horseshoe Dam	**119**	33 45N	111 35W
Horsham, Austral.	**97**	36 44 S	142 13 E
Horsham, U.K.	**13**	51 4N	0 20W
Horšovský Týn	**26**	49 31N	12 58 E
Horten	**47**	59 25N	10 32 E
Hortobágy →	**27**	47 30N	21 6 E
Horton	**116**	39 42N	95 30W
Horton →	**104**	69 56N	126 52W
Hörvik	**49**	56 2N	14 45 E
Horwood, L.	**106**	48 5N	82 20W
Hosaina	**87**	7 30N	37 47 E
Hosdurga	**70**	13 49N	76 17 E
Hose, Pegunungan	**72**	2 5N	114 6 E
Hoshangabad	**68**	22 45N	77 45 E
Hoshiarpur	**68**	31 30N	75 58 E
Hosmer	**116**	45 36N	99 29W
Hospet	**70**	15 15N	76 20 E
Hospitalet de Llobregat	**32**	41 21N	2 6 E
Hospitalet, L'	**20**	42 36N	1 47 E
Hoste, I.	**128**	55 0 S	69 0W
Hostens	**20**	44 30N	0 40W
Hot	**71**	18 8N	98 29 E
Hot Creek Ra.	**118**	39 0N	116 0W
Hot Springs, Ari., U.S.A.	**117**	34 30N	93 0W
Hot Springs, S.D., U.S.A.	**116**	43 25N	103 30W
Hotagen	**50**	63 50N	14 30 E
Hotan	**75**	37 25N	79 55 E
Hotazel	**92**	27 17 S	23 00 E
Hotchkiss	**119**	38 47N	107 47W
Hoting	**50**	64 8N	16 15 E
Hotolishti	**44**	41 10N	20 25 E
Hottentotsbaai	**92**	26 8 S	14 59 E
Houat	**18**	47 24N	2 58W
Houck	**119**	35 15N	109 15W
Houdan	**19**	48 48N	1 35 E
Houffalize	**16**	50 8N	5 48 E
Houghton	**116**	47 9N	88 39W
Houghton L.	**114**	44 20N	84 40W
Houghton-le-Spring	**12**	54 51N	1 28W
Houhora	**101**	34 49 S	173 9 E
Houlton	**107**	46 5N	67 50W
Houma	**117**	29 35N	90 44W
Houndé	**84**	11 34N	3 31W
Hourtin	**20**	45 11N	1 4W
Hourtin, Étang d'	**20**	45 10N	1 6W
Houston, Can.	**108**	54 25N	126 39W
Houston, Mo., U.S.A.	**117**	37 20N	92 0W
Houston, Tex., U.S.A.	**117**	29 50N	95 20W
Houtman Abrolhos	**96**	28 43 S	113 48 E
Hov	**49**	55 55N	10 15 E
Hova	**49**	58 53N	14 14 E
Høvåg	**47**	58 10N	8 16 E
Hovd (Jargalant)	**75**	48 2N	91 37 E
Hovden	**47**	59 33N	7 22 E
Hove	**13**	50 50N	0 10W
Hovmantorp	**49**	56 47N	15 7 E
Hövsgöl Nuur	**75**	51 0N	100 30 E
Hovsta	**48**	59 22N	15 15 E
Howakil	**87**	15 10N	40 16 E
Howar, Wadi →	**87**	17 30N	27 8 E
Howard, Austral.	**99**	25 16 S	152 32 E
Howard, Kans., U.S.A.	**117**	37 30N	96 16W
Howard, Pa., U.S.A.	**112**	41 0N	77 40W
Howard, S.D., U.S.A.	**116**	44 2N	97 30W
Howard L.	**109**	62 15N	105 57W
Howe	**118**	43 48N	113 0W
Howe, C.	**97**	37 30 S	150 0 E
Howell	**114**	42 38N	83 56W
Howick, Can.	**113**	45 11N	73 51W
Howick, S. Afr.	**93**	29 28 S	30 14 E
Howick Group	**98**	14 20 S	145 30 E
Howitt, L.	**99**	27 40 S	138 40 E
Howley	**107**	49 12N	57 2W
Howrah	**69**	22 37N	88 20 E
Howth Hd.	**15**	53 21N	6 0W
Höxter	**24**	51 45N	9 26 E
Hoy I.	**14**	58 50N	3 15W
Hoya	**24**	52 47N	9 10 E
Hoyerswerda	**24**	51 26N	14 14 E
Hoyos	**30**	40 9N	6 45W
Hpungan Pass	**67**	27 30N	96 55 E
Hrádec Králové	**26**	50 15N	15 50 E
Hrádek	**27**	48 46N	16 16 E
Hranice	**27**	49 34N	17 45 E
Hron →	**27**	47 49N	18 45 E
Hrubieszów	**28**	50 49N	23 51 E
Hrubý Nízký Jeseník	**27**	50 7N	17 10 E
Hrvatska	**39**	45 20N	16 0 E
Hrvatska □	**42**	45 20N	18 0 E
Hsenwi	**67**	23 22N	97 55 E
Hsiamen = Xiamen	**75**	24 25N	118 4 E
Hsian = Xi'an	**77**	34 15N	109 0 E
Hsinhailien = Lianyungang	**77**	34 40N	119 11 E
Hsüchou = Xuzhou	**77**	34 18N	117 18 E
Hua Hin	**71**	12 34N	99 58 E
Hua Xian, Henan, China	**77**	35 30N	114 30 E
Hua Xian, Shaanxi, China	**77**	34 30N	109 48 E
Huacheng	**77**	24 4N	115 37 E
Huacho	**126**	11 10 S	77 35W
Huachón	**126**	10 35 S	76 0W
Huachuan	**76**	46 50N	130 21 E
Huade	**76**	41 55N	113 59 E
Huadian	**76**	43 0N	126 40 E
Huai He →	**75**	33 0N	118 30 E
Huai'an	**77**	33 30N	119 10 E
Huaide	**76**	43 30N	124 40 E
Huainan	**75**	32 38N	116 58 E
Huaiyang	**77**	33 40N	114 52 E
Huaiyuan	**77**	24 31N	108 22 E
Huajianzi	**76**	41 23N	125 20 E
Huajuapan de Leon	**120**	17 50N	97 48W
Hualian	**77**	23 59N	121 37 E
Huallaga →	**126**	5 0 S	75 30W
Hualpai Pk.	**119**	35 8N	113 58W
Huambo	**89**	12 42 S	15 54 E
Huan Jiang →	**76**	34 28N	109 0 E
Huan Xian	**76**	36 33N	107 7 E
Huancabamba	**126**	5 10 S	79 15W
Huancane	**126**	15 10 S	69 44W
Huancapi	**126**	13 40 S	74 0W
Huancavelica	**126**	12 50 S	75 5W
Huancayo	**126**	12 5 S	75 12W
Huang He	**75**	37 55N	118 50 E
Huangchuan	**77**	32 15N	115 10 E
Huangliu	**75**	18 20N	108 50 E
Huanglong	**76**	35 30N	109 59 E
Huangshi	**75**	30 10N	115 3 E
Huangyan	**77**	28 38N	121 19 E
Huánuco	**126**	9 55 S	76 15W
Huaraz	**126**	9 30 S	77 32W
Huarmey	**126**	10 5 S	78 5W
Huascarán	**126**	9 8 S	77 36W
Huasco	**124**	28 30 S	71 15W
Huasco →	**124**	28 27 S	71 13W
Huatabampo	**120**	26 50N	109 50W
Huay Namota	**120**	21 56N	104 30W
Huayllay	**126**	11 03 S	76 21W
Hubbard	**117**	31 50N	96 50W
Hubbart Pt.	**109**	59 21N	94 41W
Hubei □	**75**	31 0N	112 0 E
Hubli	**70**	15 22N	75 15 E
Hückelhoven-Ratheim	**24**	51 6N	6 13 E
Huczwa →	**28**	50 49N	23 58 E
Huddersfield	**12**	53 38N	1 49W
Hudi	**86**	17 43N	34 18 E
Hudiksvall	**48**	61 43N	17 10 E
Hudson, Can.	**109**	50 6N	92 09W
Hudson, Mass., U.S.A.	**113**	42 23N	71 35W
Hudson, Mich., U.S.A.	**114**	41 50N	84 20W
Hudson, N.Y., U.S.A.	**114**	42 15N	73 46W
Hudson, Wis., U.S.A.	**116**	44 57N	92 45W
Hudson, Wyo., U.S.A.	**118**	42 54N	108 37W
Hudson →	**114**	40 42N	74 2W
Hudson Bay, Can.	**105**	60 0N	86 0W
Hudson Bay, Sask., Can.	**109**	52 51N	102 23W
Hudson Falls	**114**	43 18N	73 34W
Hudson Hope	**108**	56 0N	121 54W
Hudson Mts.	**5**	74 32 S	99 20W
Hudson Str.	**105**	62 0N	70 0W
Hue	**71**	16 30N	107 35 E
Huebra →	**30**	41 2N	6 48W
Huedin	**46**	46 52N	23 2 E
Huelgoat	**18**	48 22N	3 46W
Huelma	**33**	37 39N	3 28W
Huelva	**31**	37 18N	6 57W
Huelva □	**31**	37 40N	7 0W
Huelva →	**31**	37 27N	6 0W
Huentelauquén	**124**	31 38 S	71 33W
Huércal Overa	**33**	37 23N	1 57W
Huerta, Sa. de la	**124**	31 10 S	67 30W
Huertas, C. de las	**33**	38 21N	0 24W
Huerva →	**32**	41 39N	0 52W
Huesca	**32**	42 8N	0 25W
Huesca □	**32**	42 20N	0 1 E
Huéscar	**33**	37 44N	2 35W
Huetamo	**120**	18 36N	100 54W
Huete	**32**	40 10N	2 43W
Hugh →	**96**	25 1 S	134 1 E
Hughenden	**97**	20 52 S	144 10 E
Hughes	**104**	66 0N	154 20W
Hugo	**116**	39 12N	103 27W
Hugoton	**117**	37 11N	101 22W
Hui Xian	**76**	35 27N	113 12 E
Hui'an	**77**	25 1N	118 43 E
Huichang	**77**	25 32N	115 45 E
Huichapán	**120**	20 24N	99 40W
Huihe	**76**	48 12N	119 17 E
Huila, Nevado del	**126**	3 0N	76 0W
Huilai	**77**	23 0N	116 18 E
Huimin	**76**	37 27N	117 28 E
Huinan	**76**	42 40N	126 2 E
Huinca Renancó	**124**	34 51 S	64 22W
Huining	**76**	35 38N	105 0 E
Huinong	**76**	39 5N	106 35 E
Huisne →	**18**	47 59N	0 11 E
Huize	**75**	26 24N	103 15 E
Huizhou	**77**	23 0N	114 23 E
Hukawng Valley	**67**	26 30N	96 30 E
Hukou	**77**	29 45N	116 21 E
Hukuntsi	**92**	23 58 S	21 45 E
Hula	**87**	6 33N	38 30 E
Hulan	**75**	46 1N	126 37 E
Ḥulayfā'	**64**	25 58N	40 45 E
Huld	**75**	45 5N	105 30 E
Ḥulda	**62**	31 50N	34 51 E
Hulin	**76**	45 48N	132 59 E
Hull, Can.	**106**	45 25N	75 44W
Hull, U.K.	**12**	53 45N	0 20W
Hull →	**12**	53 43N	0 25W
Hulst	**16**	51 17N	4 2 E
Hultsfred	**49**	57 30N	15 52 E
Hulun Nur	**75**	49 0N	117 30 E
Huma	**76**	51 43N	126 38 E
Huma He →	**76**	51 42N	126 42 E
Humahuaca	**124**	23 10 S	65 25W
Humaitá, Brazil	**126**	7 35 S	63 1W
Humaitá, Parag.	**124**	27 2 S	58 31W
Humansdorp	**92**	34 2 S	24 46 E
Humbe	**92**	16 40 S	14 55 E
Humber →	**12**	53 40N	0 10W
Humberside □	**12**	53 50N	0 30W
Humble	**117**	29 59N	93 18W
Humboldt, Can.	**109**	52 15N	105 9W
Humboldt, Iowa, U.S.A.	**116**	42 42N	94 15W
Humboldt, Tenn., U.S.A.	**117**	35 50N	88 55W
Humboldt →	**118**	40 2N	118 31W
Humboldt Gletscher	**4**	79 30N	62 0W
Hume, L.	**97**	36 0 S	147 0 E
Humenné	**27**	48 55N	21 50 E
Humphreys Pk.	**119**	35 24N	111 38W
Humpolec	**26**	49 31N	15 20 E
Hün	**83**	29 2N	16 0 E
Húnaflói	**50**	65 50N	20 50W
Hunan □	**75**	27 30N	112 0 E
Hunchun	**76**	42 52N	130 28 E
Hundested	**49**	55 58N	11 52 E
Hundred Mile House	**108**	51 38N	121 18W
Hunedoara	**46**	45 40N	22 50 E
Hunedoara □	**46**	45 50N	22 54 E
Hünfeld	**24**	50 40N	9 47 E
Hungary ■	**27**	47 20N	19 20 E
Hungary, Plain of	**9**	47 0N	20 0 E
Hungerford	**99**	28 58 S	144 24 E
Hŭngnam	**76**	39 49N	127 45 E
Huni Valley	**84**	5 33N	1 56W
Hunsberge	**92**	27 45 S	17 12 E
Hunsrück	**25**	49 30N	7 0 E
Hunstanton	**12**	52 57N	0 30 E
Hunsur	**70**	12 16N	76 16 E
Hunte →	**24**	52 30N	8 19 E
Hunter, N.D., U.S.A.	**116**	47 12N	97 17W
Hunter, N.Y., U.S.A.	**113**	42 13N	74 13W
Hunter →	**100**	32 52 S	151 46 E
Hunter I., Austral.	**97**	40 30 S	144 45 E
Hunter I., Can.	**108**	51 55N	128 0W
Hunter Ra.	**99**	32 45 S	150 15 E
Hunters Road	**91**	19 9 S	29 49 E
Hunterton	**99**	26 12 S	148 30 E
Hunterville	**101**	39 56 S	175 35 E

Renamed South Nyanza

Huntingburg 114 38 20N 86 58W
Huntingdon, Can. 106 45 6N 74 10W
Huntingdon, U.K. 13 52 20N 0 11W
Huntingdon, U.S.A. 114 40 28N 78 1W
Huntington, Ind., U.S.A. 114 40 52N 85 30W
Huntington, N.Y., U.S.A. 113 40 52N 73 25W
Huntington, Oreg., U.S.A. 118 44 22N 117 21W
Huntington, Ut., U.S.A. 118 39 24N 111 1W
Huntington, W. Va., U.S.A. 114 38 20N 82 30W
Huntington Beach 119 33 40N 118 0W
Huntington Park 119 33 58N 118 15W
Huntly, N.Z. 101 37 34S 175 11 E
Huntly, U.K. 14 57 27N 2 48W
Huntsville, Can. 106 45 20N 79 14W
Huntsville, Ala., U.S.A. 115 34 45N 86 35W
Huntsville, Tex., U.S.A. 117 30 45N 95 35W
Hunyani → 91 15 57S 30 39 E
Huo Xian 76 36 36N 111 42 E
Huon, G. 98 7 0S 147 30 E
Huonville 97 43 0S 147 5 E
Huoqiu 77 32 20N 116 12 E
Huoshao Dao 77 22 40N 121 30 E
Hupeh □ = Hubei □ 75 31 0N 112 0 E
Hurbanovo 27 47 51N 18 11 E
Hure Qi 76 42 45N 121 45 E
Hurezani 46 44 49N 23 40 E
Hurghada 86 27 15N 33 50 E
Hurley, N. Mex., U.S.A. 119 32 45N 108 7W
Hurley, Wis., U.S.A. 116 46 26N 90 10W
Huron, Ohio, U.S.A. 112 41 22N 82 34W
Huron, S.D., U.S.A. 116 44 22N 98 12W
Huron, L. 112 45 0N 83 0W
Hurricane 119 37 10N 113 12W
Hurso 87 9 35N 41 33 E
Hurum, Buskerud, Norway 47 59 36N 10 23 E
Hurum, Oppland, Norway 47 61 9N 8 46 E
Hurunui → 101 42 54S 173 18 E
Hurup 49 56 46N 8 25 E
Húsavík 50 66 3N 17 21W
Huşi 46 46 41N 28 7 E
Huskvarna 49 57 47N 14 15 E
Husøy 47 61 3N 4 44 E
Hussar 108 51 3N 112 41W
Hustopéce 27 48 57N 16 43 E
Husum, Ger. 24 54 27N 9 3 E
Husum, Sweden 48 63 21N 19 12 E
Hutchinson, Kans., U.S.A. 117 38 3N 97 59W
Hutchinson, Minn., U.S.A. 116 44 50N 94 22W
Hutou 76 45 58N 133 38 E
Huttenberg 26 46 56N 14 33 E
Hüttental 24 50 52N 8 1 E
Huttig 117 33 5N 92 10W
Hutton, Mt. 99 25 51S 148 20 E
Huwun 87 4 23N 40 6 E
Ḩuwwārah 62 32 9N 35 15 E
Huy 16 50 31N 5 15 E
Hvaler 47 59 4N 11 1 E
Hvammur 50 65 13N 21 49W
Hvar 39 43 11N 16 28 E
Hvarski Kanal 39 43 15N 16 35 E
Hvítá 50 64 40N 21 5W
Hvítá → 50 64 0N 20 58W
Hvítárvatn 50 64 37N 19 50W
Hvitsten 47 59 35N 10 42 E
Hwang Ho = Huang He → 76 37 50N 118 50 E
Hyannis 116 42 0N 101 45W
Hyargas Nuur 75 49 0N 93 0 E
Hyatts 114 38 59N 76 55W
Hybo 48 61 49N 16 15 E
Hyderabad, India 70 17 22N 78 29 E
Hyderabad, Pak. 68 25 23N 68 24 E
* Hyderabad □ 68 25 3N 68 24 E
Hyères 21 43 8N 6 9 E
Hyères, Îles d' 21 43 0N 6 28 E
Hyesan 76 41 20N 128 10 E
Hyland → 108 59 52N 128 12W
Hylestad 47 59 6N 7 29 E
Hyltebruk 49 56 59N 13 15 E
Hyndman Pk. 118 43 50N 114 10W
Hyōgo □ 74 35 15N 135 0 E
Hyrum 118 41 35N 111 56W
Hysham 118 46 21N 107 11W
Hythe 13 51 4N 1 5 E
Hyvinkää 51 60 38N 24 50 E

I

I-n-Azaoua 83 20 45N 7 31 E
I-n-Échaï 82 20 10N 2 5W
I-n-Gall 85 16 51N 7 1 E
I-n-Tabedog 82 19 48N 1 11 E
Iabès, Erg 82 27 30N 2 2W
Iaco → 126 9 3S 68 34W
Iacobeni 46 47 25N 25 20 E
Iakora 93 23 6S 46 40 E
Ialomiţa □ 46 44 30N 27 30 E
Ialomiţa → 46 44 42N 27 51 E
Ianca 46 45 6N 27 29 E
Iara 46 46 31N 23 35 E
Iaşi 46 47 20N 27 0 E
Iba 73 15 22N 120 0 E
Ibadan 85 7 22N 3 58 E
Ibagué 126 4 20N 75 20W
Iballja 44 42 12N 20 0 E
Ibăneşti 46 46 45N 24 50 E
Ibar → 42 43 43N 20 45 E
Ibaraki □ 74 36 10N 140 10 E
Ibarra 126 0 21N 78 7W
Ibba 87 4 49N 29 2 E
Ibba, Bahr el 87 5 30N 28 55 E
Ibbenbüren 24 52 16N 7 41 E
Ibembo 90 2 35N 23 35 E
Ibera, Laguna 124 28 30S 57 9W
Iberian Peninsula 8 40 0N 5 0W
Iberville 106 45 19N 73 17W
Iberville, Lac d' 106 55 55N 73 15W
Ibi 85 8 15N 9 44 E
Ibiá 127 19 30S 46 30W
Ibicuy 124 33 55S 59 10W
Ibioapaba, Sa. da 127 4 0S 41 30W
Ibiza 33 38 54N 1 26 E
Íblei, Monti 41 37 15N 14 45 E
Ibo 91 12 22S 40 40 E
Ibonma 73 3 29S 133 31 E
Ibotirama 127 12 13S 43 12W
İbriktepe 44 41 2N 26 33 E
Ibshawâi 86 29 21N 30 40 E
Ibu 73 1 35N 127 33 E
Iburg 24 52 10N 8 3 E
Icá 126 14 0S 75 48W
Iça → 126 2 55S 67 58W
Içana 126 0 21N 67 19W
Iceland ■ 50 65 0N 19 0W
Icha 59 55 30N 156 0 E
Ich'ang = Yichang 75 30 40N 111 20 E
Ichchapuram 70 19 10N 84 40 E
Ichihara 74 35 28N 140 5 E
Ichihawa 74 35 44N 139 55 E
Ichilo → 126 15 57S 64 50W
Ichinomiya 74 35 18N 136 48 E
Ichnya 54 50 52N 32 24 E
Icht 82 29 6N 8 54W
Icy Str. 108 58 20N 135 30W
Ida Grove 116 42 20N 95 25W
Idabel 117 33 53N 94 50W
Idaga Hamus 87 14 13N 39 48 E
Idah 85 7 5N 6 40 E
Idaho □ 118 44 10N 114 0W
Idaho City 118 43 50N 115 52W
Idaho Falls 118 43 30N 112 1W
Idaho Springs 118 39 49N 105 30W
Idanha-a-Nova 30 39 50N 7 15W
Idar-Oberstein 25 49 43N 7 19 E
Idd el Ghanam 81 11 30N 24 19 E
Iddan 63 6 10N 48 55 E
Idehan 83 27 10N 11 30 E
Idehan Marzūq 83 24 50N 13 51 E
Idelès 83 23 50N 5 53 E
Idfû 86 25 0N 32 49 E
Ídhi Óros 45 35 15N 24 45 E
Ídhra 45 37 20N 23 28 E
Idi 72 5 2N 97 37 E
Idi Amin Dada, L. = Edward, L. 90 0 25S 29 40 E
Idiofa 88 4 55S 19 42 E
Idkerberget 48 60 22N 15 15 E
Idku, Bahra el 86 31 18N 30 18 E
Idlip 64 35 55N 36 38 E
Idna 62 31 34N 34 58 E
Idrija 39 46 0N 14 5 E
Idritsa 54 56 25N 28 30 E
Idstein 25 50 13N 8 17 E
Idutywa 93 32 8S 28 18 E
Ieper 16 50 51N 2 53 E
Ierápetra 45 35 0N 25 44 E
Ierissós 44 40 22N 23 52 E
Ierissóu Kólpos 44 40 27N 23 57 E
Ierzu 40 39 48N 9 32 E
Iesi 39 43 32N 13 12 E
Ifach, Punta 33 38 38N 0 5 E
Ifanadiana 93 21 19S 47 39 E
Ife 85 7 30N 4 31 E
Iférouâne 85 19 5N 8 24 E
Iffley 98 18 53S 141 12 E
Ifni 82 29 29N 10 12W
Ifon 85 6 58N 5 40 E
Iforas, Adrar des 85 19 40N 1 40 E
Ifrane 82 33 33N 5 7W
Iganga 90 0 37N 33 28 E
Igarapava 127 20 3S 47 47W
Igarapé Açu 127 1 4S 47 33W
Igarka 59 67 30N 86 33 E
Igatimi 125 24 5S 55 40W
Igatpuri 70 19 40N 73 35 E
Igbetti 85 8 44N 4 8 E
Igbo-Ora 85 7 29N 3 15 E
Igboho 85 8 53N 3 50 E
Iggesund 48 61 39N 17 10 E
Ighil Izane 82 35 44N 0 31 E
Iglene 82 22 57N 4 58 E
Iglésias 40 39 19N 8 27 E
Igli 82 30 25N 2 19W
Igloolik 105 69 20N 81 49W
Igma 82 29 9N 6 24W
Igma, Gebel el 86 28 55N 34 0 E
Ignace 106 49 30N 91 40W
Igoshevo 55 59 25N 42 35 E
Igoumenítsa 44 39 32N 20 18 E
Iguaçu → 125 25 36S 54 36W
Iguaçu, Cat. del 125 25 41S 54 26W
Iguala 120 18 20N 99 40W
Igualada 32 41 37N 1 37 E
Iguassu = Iguaçu 125 25 41N 54 26W
Iguatu 127 6 20S 39 18W
Iguéla 88 2 0S 9 16 E
Igunga □ 90 4 20S 33 45 E
Ihiala 85 5 51N 6 55 E
Ihosy 93 22 24S 46 8 E
Ihotry, L. 93 21 56S 43 41 E
Ii 50 65 19N 25 22 E
Iida 74 35 35N 137 50 E
Iijoki → 50 65 20N 25 20 E
Iisalmi 50 63 32N 27 10 E
Iizuka 74 33 38N 130 42 E
Ijebu-Igbo 85 6 56N 4 1 E
Ijebu-Ode 85 6 47N 3 58 E
IJmuiden 16 52 28N 4 35 E
IJssel → 16 52 35N 5 50 E
IJsselmeer 16 52 45N 5 20 E
Ijuí → 125 27 58S 55 20W
Ikale 85 7 40N 5 37 E
Ikare 85 7 32N 5 40 E
Ikaría 45 37 35N 26 10 E
Ikast 49 56 8N 9 10 E
Ikeja 85 6 36N 3 23 E
Ikela 88 1 6S 23 6 E
Ikerre-Ekiti 85 7 25N 5 19 E
Ikhtiman 43 42 27N 23 48 E
Iki 74 33 45N 129 42 E
Ikimba L. 90 1 30S 31 20 E
Ikire 85 7 23N 4 15 E
Ikom 85 6 0N 8 42 E
Ikopa → 93 16 45S 46 40 E
Ikot Ekpene 85 5 12N 7 40 E
Ikungu 90 1 33S 33 42 E
Ikurun 85 7 54N 4 40 E
Ila 85 8 0N 4 39 E
Ilagan 73 17 7N 121 53 E
Ilam 69 26 58N 87 58 E
Ilanskiy 59 56 14N 96 3 E
Ilaro 85 6 53N 3 3 E
Iława 28 53 36N 19 34 E
Ilayangudi 70 9 34N 78 37 E
Ilbilbie 98 21 45S 149 20 E
Île-à-la Crosse 109 55 27N 107 53W
Île-à-la-Crosse, Lac 109 55 40N 107 45W
Île-Bouchard, L' 18 47 7N 0 26 E
Île-de-France 19 49 0N 2 20 E
Île-sur-le-Doubs, L' 19 47 26N 6 34 E
Ilebo 88 4 17S 20 55 E
Ileje □ 91 9 30S 33 25 E
Ilek 58 51 32N 53 21 E
Ilek → 52 51 30N 53 22 E
Ilero 85 8 0N 3 20 E
Ilesha, Oyo, Nigeria 85 7 37N 4 40 E
Ilesha, Oyo, Nigeria 85 8 57N 3 28 E
Ilford 109 56 4N 95 35W
Ilfov □ 46 44 20N 26 0 E
Ilfracombe, Austral. 97 23 30S 144 30 E
Ilfracombe, U.K. 13 51 13N 4 8W
Ílhavo 30 40 33N 8 43W
Ilhéus 127 14 49S 39 2W
Ilia 46 45 57N 22 40 E
Ilia □ 45 37 45N 21 35 E
Ilich 58 40 50N 68 27 E
Iliff 116 40 50N 103 3W
Iligan 73 8 12N 124 13 E
Ilikí, L. 45 38 24N 23 15 E
Iliodhrómia 44 39 12N 23 50 E
Ilion 114 43 0N 75 3W
Ilirska-Bistrica 39 45 34N 14 14 E
Ilkal 70 15 57N 76 8 E
Ilkeston 12 52 59N 1 19W
Illana B. 73 7 35N 123 45 E
Illapel 124 32 0S 71 10W
'Illār 62 32 23N 35 7 E
Ille 20 42 40N 2 37 E
Ille-et-Vilaine □ 18 48 10N 1 30W
Iller → 25 48 23N 9 58 E
Illescas 30 40 8N 3 51W
Illiers 18 48 18N 1 15 E
Illimani 126 16 30S 67 50W
Illinois □ 111 40 15N 89 30W
Illinois → 111 38 55N 90 28W
Illium = Troy 44 39 57N 26 12 E
Illizi 83 26 31N 8 32 E
Illora 31 37 17N 3 53W
Ilm → 24 51 7N 11 45 E
Ilmen, Oz. 54 58 15N 31 10 E
Ilmenau 24 50 41N 10 55 E
Ilo 126 17 40S 71 20W
Ilobu 85 7 45N 4 25 E
Iloilo 73 10 45N 122 33 E
Ilok 42 45 15N 19 20 E
Ilora 85 7 45N 3 50 E
Ilorin 85 8 30N 4 35 E
Iloulya 57 49 15N 44 2 E
Ilovatka 55 50 30N 45 50 E
Ilovlya → 57 49 14N 43 54 E
Iłowa 28 51 30N 15 10 E
Ilubabor □ 87 7 25N 35 0 E
Ilukste 54 55 55N 26 20 E
Ilva Mică 46 47 17N 24 40 E
Ilwaki 73 7 55S 126 30 E
Ilyichevsk 56 46 10N 30 35 E
Iłża 28 51 10N 21 15 E
Iłżanka → 28 51 14N 21 48 E
Imabari 74 34 4N 133 0 E
Imaloto → 93 23 27S 45 13 E
Imandra, Oz. 52 67 30N 33 0 E
Imari 74 33 15N 129 52 E
Imasa 86 18 0N 36 12 E
Imathía □ 44 40 30N 22 15 E
Imbâbah 86 30 5N 31 12 E
Imbler 118 45 31N 118 0W
Imdahane 82 32 8N 7 0W
imeni 26 Bakinskikh Komissarov (Neft-chala) 53 39 19N 49 12 E
imeni 26 Bakinskikh Komissarov (Vyshzha) 53 39 22N 54 10 E
Imeni Poliny Osipenko 59 52 30N 136 29 E
Imeri, Serra 126 0 50N 65 25W
Imerimandroso 93 17 26S 48 35 E
Imi (Hinna) 87 6 28N 42 10 E
Imishly 57 39 49N 48 4 E
Imitek 82 29 43N 8 10W
Imlay 118 40 45N 118 9W
Imlay City 112 43 0N 83 2W
Immenstadt 25 47 34N 10 13 E
Immingham 12 53 37N 0 12W
Immokalee 115 26 25N 81 26W
Imo □ 85 5 15N 7 20 E
Imola 39 44 20N 11 42 E
Imotski 42 43 27N 17 12 E
Imperatriz 127 5 30S 47 29W
Impéria 38 43 52N 8 0 E
Imperial, Can. 109 51 21N 105 28W
Imperial, Calif., U.S.A. 119 32 52N 115 34W
Imperial, Nebr., U.S.A. 116 40 38N 101 39W
Imperial Dam 119 32 50N 114 30W
Impfondo 88 1 40N 18 0 E
Imphal 67 24 48N 93 56 E
Imphy 19 46 56N 3 15 E
İmroz = Gökçeada 44 40 10N 25 50 E
Imst 26 47 15N 10 44 E
Imuruan B. 73 10 40N 119 10 E
In Belbel 82 27 55N 1 12 E
In Delimane 85 15 52N 1 31 E
In Rhar 82 27 10N 1 59 E
In Salah 82 27 10N 2 32 E
In Tallak 85 16 19N 3 15 E
Ina 74 35 50N 138 0 E
Ina-Bonchi 74 35 45N 137 58 E
Inangahua Junc. 101 41 52S 171 59 E
Inanwatan 73 2 10S 132 14 E
Iñapari 126 11 0S 69 40W
Inari 50 68 54N 27 5 E
Inarijärvi 50 69 0N 28 0 E
Inawashiro-Ko 74 37 29N 140 6 E
Inca 32 39 43N 2 54 E
Incaguasi 124 29 12S 71 5W
İnce-Burnu 56 42 7N 34 56 E
Inchon 76 37 27N 126 40 E
Incio 30 42 39N 7 21W
Incomáti → 93 25 46S 32 43 E
Incudine, L' 21 41 50N 9 12 E
Inda Silase 87 14 10N 38 15 E
Indalsälven → 48 62 36N 17 30 E
Indaw 67 24 15N 96 5 E
Indbir 87 8 7N 37 52 E
Independence, Calif., U.S.A. 119 36 51N 118 14W
Independence, Iowa, U.S.A. 116 42 27N 91 52W
Independence, Kans., U.S.A. 117 37 10N 95 43W
Independence, Mo., U.S.A. 116 39 3N 94 25W
Independence, Oreg., U.S.A. 118 44 53N 123 12W
Independence Fjord 4 82 10N 29 0W
Independence Mts. 118 41 30N 116 2W
Independenţa 46 45 25N 27 42 E
Inderborskiy 57 48 30N 51 42 E
India ■ 3 20 0N 78 0 E
Indian → 115 27 59N 80 34W
Indian-Antarctic Ridge 94 49 0S 120 0 E
Indian Cabins 108 59 52N 117 40W
Indian Harbour 107 54 27N 57 13W
Indian Head 109 50 30N 103 41W
Indian Ocean 3 5 0S 75 0 E
Indiana 114 40 38N 79 9W
Indiana □ 114 40 0N 86 0W
Indianapolis 114 39 42N 86 10W
Indianola, Iowa, U.S.A. 116 41 20N 93 32W
Indianola, Miss., U.S.A. 117 33 27N 90 40W
Indiga 52 67 50N 48 50 E
Indigirka → 59 70 48N 148 54 E
Indija 42 45 6N 20 7 E
Indio 119 33 46N 116 15W
Indonesia ■ 72 5 0S 115 0 E
Indore 68 22 42N 75 53 E
Indramayu 73 6 21S 108 20 E
Indramayu, Tg. 73 6 20S 108 20 E
Indravati → 70 19 20N 80 20 E
Indre □ 19 46 50N 1 39 E
Indre → 18 47 16N 0 19 E
Indre-et-Loire □ 18 47 12N 0 40 E
Indus → 68 24 20N 67 47 E
Indus, Mouth of the 68 24 00N 68 00 E
İnebolu 64 41 55N 33 40 E
İnegöl 64 40 5N 29 31 E
Ineu 42 46 26N 21 51 E
Inezgane 82 30 25N 9 29W
Infante, Kaap 92 34 27S 20 51 E
Infantes 33 38 43N 3 1W
Infiernillo, Presa del 120 18 9N 102 0W
Infiesto 30 43 21N 5 21W
Ingende 88 0 12S 18 57 E
Ingenio Santa Ana 124 27 25S 65 40W
Ingersoll 112 43 4N 80 55W
Ingham 97 18 43S 146 10 E
Ingleborough 12 54 11N 2 23W
Inglewood, Queensland, Austral. 99 28 25S 151 2 E
Inglewood, Vic., Austral. 99 36 29S 143 53 E
Inglewood, N.Z. 101 39 9S 174 14 E
Inglewood, U.S.A. 119 33 58N 118 21W
Ingólfshöfði 50 63 48N 16 39W
Ingolstadt 25 48 45N 11 26 E
Ingomar 118 46 35N 107 21W
Ingonish 107 46 42N 60 18W
Ingore 84 12 24N 15 48W
Ingrid Christensen Coast 5 69 30S 76 00 E
Ingul → 56 46 50N 32 15 E
Ingulec 56 47 42N 33 14 E
Ingulets → 56 46 41N 32 48 E
Inguri →, U.S.S.R. 57 42 38N 41 35 E
Inguri →, U.S.S.R. 57 42 15N 41 48 E
Inhaca, I. 93 26 1S 32 57 E
Inhafenga 93 20 36S 33 53 E
Inhambane 93 23 54S 35 30 E
Inhambane □ 93 22 30S 34 20 E
Inhaminga 91 18 26S 35 0 E
Inharrime 93 24 30S 35 0 E
Inharrime → 93 24 30S 35 0 E
Iniesta 33 39 27N 1 45W
Ining = Yining 75 43 58N 81 10 E
Inirida → 126 3 55N 67 52W
Inishbofin 15 53 35N 10 12W
Inishmore 15 53 8N 9 45W
Inishowen 15 55 14N 7 15W
Injune 97 25 53S 148 32 E
Inklin 108 58 56N 133 5W
Inklin → 108 58 50N 133 10W
Inkom 118 42 51N 112 15W
Inle L. 67 20 30N 96 58 E
Inn → 25 48 35N 13 28 E
Innamincka 99 27 44S 140 46 E
Inner Hebrides 14 57 0N 6 30W
Inner Mongolia = Nei Monggol Zizhiqu □ 76 42 0N 112 0 E
Inner Sound 14 57 30N 5 55W
Innerkip 112 43 13N 80 42W
Innerste → 24 52 45N 9 40 E
Innetalling I. 106 56 0N 79 0W
Innisfail, Austral. 97 17 33S 146 5 E
Innisfail, Can. 108 52 0N 113 57W
Innsbruck 26 47 16N 11 23 E
Inny → 15 53 30N 7 50W
Inongo 88 1 55S 18 30 E
Inoucdjouac (Port Harrison) 105 58 25N 78 15W
Inowrocław 28 52 50N 18 12 E
Inquisivi 126 16 50S 67 10W
Insein 67 16 50N 96 5 E
Însurăţei 46 44 50N 27 40 E
Inta 52 66 5N 60 8 E
Intendente Alvear 124 35 12S 63 32W
Interior 116 43 46N 101 59W
Interlaken 25 46 41N 7 50 E
International Falls 116 48 36N 93 25W
Interview I. 71 12 55N 92 42 E
Inthanon, Doi 71 18 35N 98 29 E

* Now part of Sind □

Intiyaco **124** 28 43 S 60 5W
Inútil, B. **128** 53 30 S 70 15W
Inuvik **104** 68 16N 133 40W
Inveraray **14** 56 13N 5 5W
Inverbervie **14** 56 50N 2 17W
Invercargill **101** 46 24 S 168 24 E
Inverell **97** 29 45 S 151 8 E
Invergordon **14** 57 41N 4 10W
Invermere **108** 50 30N 116 2W
Inverness, Can. **107** 46 15N 61 19W
Inverness, U.K. **14** 57 29N 4 12W
Inverness, U.S.A. **115** 28 50N 82 20W
Inverurie **14** 57 15N 2 21W
Investigator Group **96** 34 45 S 134 20 E
Investigator Str. **97** 35 30 S 137 0 E
Invona **112** 40 46N 78 35W
Inya **58** 50 28N 86 37 E
Inyanga **91** 18 12 S 32 40 E
Inyangani **91** 18 5 S 32 50 E
Inyantue **91** 18 30 S 26 40 E
Inyazura **91** 18 40 S 32 16 E
Inyo Range **119** 37 0N 118 0W
Inyokern **119** 35 38N 117 48W
Inza **55** 53 55N 46 25 E
Inzhavino **55** 52 22N 42 30 E
Ioánnina **44** 39 42N 20 47 E
Ioánnina (Janiná) □ **44** 39 39N 20 57 E
Iola **117** 38 0N 95 20W
Ion Corvin **46** 44 7N 27 50 E
Iona **14** 56 20N 6 25W
Ione, Calif., U.S.A. **118** 38 20N 120 56W
Ione, Wash., U.S.A. **118** 48 44N 117 29W
Ionia **114** 42 59N 85 7W
Ionian Is. = Iónioi Nísoi **45** 38 40N 20 0 E
Ionian Sea **35** 37 30N 17 30 E
Iónioi Nísoi **45** 38 40N 20 0 E
Iori → **57** 41 3N 46 17 E
Íos **45** 36 41N 25 20 E
Iowa □ **116** 42 18N 93 30W
Iowa City **116** 41 40N 91 35W
Iowa Falls **116** 42 30N 93 15W
Ipala **90** 4 30 S 32 52 E
Ipameri **127** 17 44 S 48 9W
Ipáti **45** 38 52N 22 14 E
Ipatovo **57** 45 45N 42 50 E
Ipel → **27** 48 10N 19 35 E
Ipiales **126** 0 50N 77 37W
Ipin = Yibin **75** 28 45N 104 32 E
Ípiros □ **44** 39 30N 20 30 E
Ipixuna **126** 7 0 S 71 40W
Ipoh **71** 4 35N 101 5 E
Ippy **88** 6 5N 21 7 E
İpsala **44** 40 55N 26 23 E
Ipsárion Óros **44** 40 40N 24 40 E
Ipswich, Austral. **97** 27 35 S 152 40 E
Ipswich, U.K. **13** 52 4N 1 9 E
Ipswich, Mass., U.S.A. **113** 42 40N 70 50W
Ipswich, S.D., U.S.A. **116** 45 28N 99 1W
Ipu **127** 4 23 S 40 44W
Iput → **54** 52 26N 31 2 E
Iquique **126** 20 19 S 70 5W
Iquitos **126** 3 45 S 73 10W
Iracoubo **127** 5 30N 53 10W
Iráklia **45** 36 50N 25 28 E
Iráklion **45** 35 20N 25 12 E
Iráklion □ **45** 35 10N 25 10 E
Irala **125** 25 55 S 54 35W
Iramba □ **90** 4 30 S 34 30 E
Iran ■ **65** 33 0N 53 0 E
Iran, Pegunungan **72** 2 20N 114 50 E
Iranamadu Tank **70** 9 23N 80 29 E
Īrānshahr **65** 27 15N 60 40 E
Irapuato **120** 20 40N 101 30W
Iraq ■ **64** 33 0N 44 0 E
Irarrar, O. → **82** 20 0N 1 30 E
Irati **125** 25 25 S 50 38W
Irbid **62** 32 35N 35 48 E
Irebu **88** 0 40 S 17 46 E
Iregua → **32** 42 27N 2 24 E
Ireland ■ **15** 53 0N 8 0W
Ireland I. **121** 32 16N 64 50W
Ireland's Eye **15** 53 25N 6 4W
Irele **85** 7 40N 5 40 E
Iret **59** 60 3N 154 20 E
Irgiz, Bol. **55** 52 10N 49 10 E
Irhârharene **83** 27 37N 7 30 E
Irharrhar, O. → **83** 28 3N 6 15 E
Irherm **82** 30 7N 8 18W
Irhil Mgoun **82** 31 30N 6 28W
Irian Jaya □ **73** 4 0S 137 0 E
Irié **84** 8 15N 9 10W
Iringa **90** 7 48 S 35 43 E
Iringa □ **90** 7 48 S 35 43 E
Irinjalakuda **70** 10 21N 76 14 E
Iriri → **127** 3 52 S 52 37W
Irish Sea **12** 54 0N 5 0W
Irkineyeva **59** 58 30N 96 49 E
Irkutsk **59** 52 18N 104 20 E
Irma **109** 52 55N 111 14W
Iroise, Mer d' **18** 48 15N 4 45W
Iron Baron **99** 32 58 S 137 11 E
Iron Gate = Portile de Fier **46** 44 42N 22 30 E
Iron Knob **97** 32 46 S 137 8 E
Iron Mountain **114** 45 49N 88 4W
Iron River **116** 46 6N 88 40W
Ironbridge **13** 52 38N 2 29W
Ironstone Kopje **92** 25 17 S 24 5 E
Ironton, Mo., U.S.A. **117** 37 40N 90 40W
Ironton, Ohio, U.S.A. **114** 38 35N 82 40W
Ironwood **116** 46 30N 90 10W
Iroquois Falls **106** 48 46N 80 41W
Irpen **54** 50 30N 30 15 E
Irrara Cr. → **99** 29 35 S 145 31 E
Irrawaddy □ **67** 17 0N 95 0 E
Irrawaddy → **67** 15 50N 95 6 E
Irsina **41** 40 45N 16 15 E
Irtysh → **58** 61 4N 68 52 E
Irumu **90** 1 32N 29 53 E
Irún **32** 43 20N 1 52W
Irurzun **32** 42 55N 1 50W
Irvine, Can. **109** 49 57N 110 16W
Irvine, U.K. **14** 55 37N 4 40W
Irvine, U.S.A. **114** 37 42N 83 58W
Irvinestown **15** 54 28N 7 38W
Irymple **99** 34 14 S 142 8 E
Is-sur-Tille **19** 47 30N 5 10 E
Isa **85** 13 14N 6 24 E
Isaac → **97** 22 55 S 149 20 E
Isabel **116** 45 27N 101 22W
Isabela, I. **120** 21 51N 105 55W
Isabella, Cord. **121** 13 30N 85 25W
Ísafjarðardjúp **50** 66 10N 23 0W
Ísafjörður **50** 66 5N 23 9W
Isagarh **68** 24 48N 77 51 E
Isaka **90** 3 56 S 32 59 E
Isangi **88** 0 52N 24 10 E
Isar → **25** 48 49N 12 58 E
Isarco → **39** 46 57N 11 18 E
Ísari **45** 37 22N 22 0 E
Isbergues **19** 50 36N 2 24 E
Isbiceni **46** 43 45N 24 40 E
Íschia **40** 40 45N 13 51 E
Ise **74** 34 25N 136 45 E
Ise-Wan **74** 34 43N 136 43 E
Isefjord **49** 55 53N 11 50 E
Iseo **38** 45 40N 10 3 E
Iseo, L. d' **38** 45 45N 10 3 E
Iseramagazi **90** 4 37 S 32 10 E
Isère □ **21** 45 15N 5 40 E
Isère → **21** 44 59N 4 51 E
Iserlohn **24** 51 22N 7 40 E
Isérnia **41** 41 35N 14 12 E
Iseyin **85** 8 0N 3 36 E
Ishikari-Wan (Otaru-Wan) **74** 43 25N 141 1 E
Ishikawa □ **74** 36 30N 136 30 E
Ishim **58** 56 10N 69 30 E
Ishim → **58** 57 45N 71 10 E
Ishinomaki **74** 38 32N 141 20 E
Ishmi **44** 41 33N 19 34 E
Ishpeming **114** 46 30N 87 40W
Isigny-sur-Mer **18** 49 19N 1 6W
Isil Kul **58** 54 55N 71 16 E
Isiolo **90** 0 24N 37 33 E
Isiolo □ **90** 2 30N 37 30 E
Isipingo Beach **93** 30 00 S 30 57 E
Isiro **90** 2 53N 27 40 E
Isisford **98** 24 15 S 144 21 E
İskenderun **64** 36 32N 36 10 E
İskilip **56** 40 50N 34 20 E
Iskŭr → **43** 43 45N 24 25 E
Iskŭr, Yazovir **43** 42 23N 23 30 E
Iskut → **108** 56 45N 131 49W
Isla → **14** 56 32N 3 20W
Isla Cristina **31** 37 13N 7 17W
Islamabad **66** 33 40N 73 10 E
Islamkot **68** 24 42N 70 13 E
Islampur **70** 17 2N 74 20 E
Island → **108** 60 25N 121 12W
Island Falls, Can. **106** 49 35N 81 20W
Island Falls, U.S.A. **107** 46 0N 68 16W
Island L. **109** 53 47N 94 25W
Island Pond **114** 44 50N 71 50W
Islands, B. of, Can. **107** 49 11N 58 15W
Islands, B. of, N.Z. **101** 35 20 S 174 20 E
Islay **14** 55 46N 6 10W
Isle → **20** 44 55N 0 15W
Isle-Adam, L' **19** 49 6N 2 14 E
Isle aux Morts **107** 47 35N 59 0W
Isle-Jourdain, L', Gers, France **20** 43 36N 1 5 E
Isle-Jourdain, L', Vienne, France **20** 46 13N 0 31 E
Isle of Wight □ **13** 50 40N 1 20W
Isle Royale **116** 48 0N 88 50W
Isleta **119** 34 58N 106 46W
Ismail **56** 45 22N 28 46 E
Ismâ'ilîya **86** 30 37N 32 18 E
Ismaning **25** 48 14N 11 41 E
Ismay **116** 46 33N 104 44W
Isna **86** 25 17N 32 30 E
Isola del Gran Sasso d'Italia **39** 42 30N 13 40 E
Ísola del Liri **40** 41 39N 13 32 E
Ísola della Scala **38** 45 16N 11 0 E
Ísola di Capo Rizzuto **41** 38 56N 17 5 E
Isparta **64** 37 47N 30 30 E
Isperikh **43** 43 43N 26 50 E
Íspica **41** 36 47N 14 53 E
İspir **57** 40 40N 40 50 E
Israel ■ **62** 32 0N 34 50 E
Issia **84** 6 33N 6 33W
Issoire **20** 45 32N 3 15 E
Issoudun **19** 46 57N 2 0 E
Issyk-Kul, Ozero **58** 42 25N 77 15 E
Ist **39** 44 17N 14 47 E
İstanbul **64** 41 0N 29 0 E
Istiaía **45** 38 57N 23 9 E
Istok **42** 42 45N 20 24 E
Istokpoga, L. **115** 27 22N 81 14W
Istra, U.S.S.R. **55** 55 55N 36 50 E
Istra, Yugo. **39** 45 10N 14 0 E
Istranca Dağları **43** 41 48N 27 30 E
Istres **21** 43 31N 4 59 E
Istria = Istra **39** 45 10N 14 0 E
Itá **124** 25 29 S 57 21W
Itabaiana **127** 7 18 S 35 19W
Itaberaba **127** 12 32 S 40 18W
Itabira **127** 19 37 S 43 13W
Itabirito **125** 20 15 S 43 48W
Itabuna **127** 14 48 S 39 16W
Itaituba **127** 4 10 S 55 50W
Itajaí **125** 27 50 S 48 39W
Itajubá **125** 22 24 S 45 30W
Itaka **91** 8 50 S 32 49 E
Italy ■ **36** 42 0N 13 0 E
Itampolo **93** 24 41 S 43 57 E
Itapecuru-Mirim **127** 3 24 S 44 20W
Itaperuna **127** 21 10 S 41 54W
Itapetininga **125** 23 36 S 48 7W
Itapeva **125** 23 59 S 48 59W
Itapicuru →, Bahia, Brazil **127** 11 47 S 37 32W
Itapicuru →, Maranhão, Brazil **127** 2 52 S 44 12W
Itapuá □ **125** 26 40 S 55 40W
Itaquari **125** 20 20 S 40 25W
Itaquatiara **126** 2 58 S 58 30W
Itaquí **124** 29 8 S 56 30W
Itararé **125** 24 6 S 49 23W
Itarsi **68** 22 36N 77 51 E
Itatí **124** 27 16 S 58 15W
Itatuba **126** 5 46 S 63 20W
Itchen → **13** 50 57N 1 20W
Itéa **45** 38 25N 22 25 E
Ithaca **114** 42 25N 76 30W
Ithaca = Itháki **45** 38 25N 20 43 E
Itháki **45** 38 25N 20 40 E
Ito **74** 34 58N 139 5 E
Itoman **77** 26 7N 127 40 E
Iton → **18** 49 9N 1 12 E
Itonamas → **126** 12 28 S 64 24W
Itsa **86** 29 15N 30 47 E
Íttiri **40** 40 38N 8 32 E
Itu, Brazil **125** 23 17 S 47 15W
Itu, Nigeria **85** 5 10N 7 58 E
Ituaçu **127** 13 50 S 41 18W
Ituiutaba **127** 19 0 S 49 25W
Itumbiara **127** 18 20 S 49 10W
Ituna **109** 51 10N 103 24W
Itunge Port **91** 9 40 S 33 55 E
Iturbe **124** 23 0 S 65 25W
Ituri → **90** 1 40N 27 1 E
Iturup, Ostrov **59** 45 0N 148 0 E
Ituyuro → **124** 22 40 S 63 50W
Itzehoe **24** 53 56N 9 31 E
Ivaí → **125** 23 18 S 53 42W
Ivalo **50** 68 38N 27 35 E
Ivalojoki → **50** 68 40N 27 40 E
Ivangorod **54** 59 37N 28 40 E
Ivangrad **42** 42 51N 19 52 E
Ivanhoe **97** 32 56 S 144 20 E
Ivanhoe L. **109** 60 25N 106 30W
Ivanić Grad **39** 45 41N 16 25 E
Ivanjica **42** 43 35N 20 12 E
Ivanjšcice **39** 46 12N 16 13 E
Ivankoyskoye Vdkhr. **55** 56 37N 36 32 E
Ivano-Frankovsk **56** 48 56N 24 43 E
Ivano-Frankovsk (Stanislav) **54** 48 40N 24 40 E
Ivanovo, Byelorussia, U.S.S.R. **54** 52 7N 25 29 E
Ivanovo, R.S.F.S.R., U.S.S.R. **55** 57 5N 41 0 E
Ivato **93** 20 37 S 47 10 E
Ivaylovgrad **43** 41 32N 26 8 E
Ivdel **52** 60 42N 60 24 E
Ivinheima → **125** 23 14 S 53 42W
Iviza = Ibiza **33** 39 0N 1 30 E
Ivohibe **93** 22 31 S 46 57 E
Ivory Coast ■ **84** 7 30N 5 0W
Ivösjön **49** 56 8N 14 25 E
Ivrea **38** 45 30N 7 52 E
Ivugivik, (N.D. d'Ivugivic) **105** 62 24N 77 55W
Iwahig **72** 8 35N 117 32 E
Iwaki **74** 37 3N 140 55 E
Iwakuni **74** 34 15N 132 8 E
Iwata **74** 34 42N 137 51 E
Iwate □ **74** 39 30N 141 30 E
Iwate-San **74** 39 51N 141 0 E
Iwo **85** 7 39N 4 9 E
IwoniczZdrój **27** 49 37N 21 47 E
Ixiamas **126** 13 50 S 68 5W
Ixopo **93** 30 11 S 30 5 E
Ixtepec **120** 16 32N 95 10W
Ixtlán de Juárez **120** 17 23N 96 28W
Ixtlán del Río **120** 21 5N 104 21W
Izabal, L. de **120** 15 30N 89 10W
Izamal **120** 20 56N 89 1W
Izberbash **57** 42 35N 47 52 E
Izbica **28** 50 53N 23 10 E
Izbica Kujawska **28** 52 25N 18 30 E
Izegem **16** 50 55N 3 12 E
Izgrev **43** 43 36N 26 58 E
Izhevsk **52** 56 51N 53 14 E
İzmir (Smyrna) **53** 38 25N 27 8 E
İzmit **64** 40 45N 29 50 E
Iznajar **31** 37 15N 4 19W
Iznalloz **33** 37 24N 3 30W
Izobil'nyy **57** 45 25N 41 44 E
Izola **39** 45 32N 13 39 E
Izra **62** 32 51N 36 15 E
Izra' **62** 32 52N 36 5 E
Iztochni Rodopi **43** 41 45N 25 30 E
Izumi-sano **74** 34 23N 135 18 E
Izumo **74** 35 20N 132 46 E
Izyaslav **54** 50 5N 26 50 E
Izyum **56** 49 12N 37 19 E

J

Jaba **87** 6 20N 35 7 E
Jaba' **62** 32 20N 35 13 E
Jabal el Awlîya **87** 15 10N 32 31 E
Jabalón → **31** 38 53N 4 5W
Jabalpur **69** 23 9N 79 58 E
Jabālyah **62** 31 32N 34 27 E
Jablah **64** 35 20N 36 0 E
Jablanac **39** 44 42N 14 56 E
Jablonec **26** 50 43N 15 10 E
Jablonica **27** 48 37N 17 26 E
Jabłonowo **28** 53 23N 19 10 E
Jaboticabal **125** 21 15 S 48 17W
Jabukovac **42** 44 22N 22 21 E
Jaburu **126** 5 30 S 64 0W
Jaca **32** 42 35N 0 33W
Jacareí **125** 23 20 S 46 0W
Jacarèzinho **125** 23 5 S 50 0W
Jáchymov **26** 50 22N 12 55 E
Jackman **107** 45 35N 70 17W
Jacksboro **117** 33 14N 98 15W
Jackson, Austral. **99** 26 39 S 149 39 E
Jackson, Ala., U.S.A. **115** 31 32N 87 53W
Jackson, Calif., U.S.A. **118** 38 19N 120 47W
Jackson, Ky., U.S.A. **114** 37 35N 83 22W
Jackson, Mich., U.S.A. **114** 42 18N 84 25W
Jackson, Minn., U.S.A. **116** 43 35N 95 0W
Jackson, Miss., U.S.A. **117** 32 20N 90 10W
Jackson, Ohio, U.S.A. **114** 39 0N 82 40W
Jackson, Tenn., U.S.A. **117** 35 40N 88 50W
Jackson, Wyo., U.S.A. **118** 43 30N 110 49W
Jackson Bay **101** 43 58 S 168 42 E
Jackson, L. **118** 43 55N 110 40W
Jacksons **101** 42 46 S 171 32 E
Jacksonville, Ala., U.S.A. **115** 33 49N 85 45W
Jacksonville, Fla., U.S.A. **115** 30 15N 81 38W
Jacksonville, Ill., U.S.A. **116** 39 42N 90 15W
Jacksonville, N.C., U.S.A. **115** 34 50N 77 29W
Jacksonville, Oreg., U.S.A. **118** 42 19N 122 56W
Jacksonville, Tex., U.S.A. **117** 31 58N 95 19W
Jacksonville Beach **115** 30 19N 81 26W
Jacmel **121** 18 14N 72 32W
Jacob Lake **119** 36 45N 112 12W
Jacobabad **68** 28 20N 68 29 E
Jacobina **127** 11 11 S 40 30W
Jacob's Well **62** 32 13N 35 13 E
Jacques-Cartier, Mt. **107** 48 57N 66 0W
Jacqueville **84** 5 12N 4 25W
Jacuí → **125** 30 2 S 51 15W
Jacundá → **127** 1 57 S 50 26W
Jade **24** 53 22N 8 14 E
Jadebusen **24** 53 30N 8 15 E
Jadotville = Likasi **91** 10 55 S 26 48 E
Jadovnik **42** 43 20N 19 45 E
Jadów **28** 52 28N 21 38 E
Jadraque **32** 40 55N 2 55W
Jādū **83** 32 0N 12 0 E
Jaén, Peru **126** 5 25 S 78 40W
Jaén, Spain **31** 37 44N 3 43W
Jaén □ **31** 37 50N 3 30W
Jaerens Rev **47** 58 45N 5 45 E
Jafène **82** 20 35N 5 30W
Jaffa = Tel Aviv-Yafo **62** 32 4N 34 48 E
Jaffa, C. **99** 36 58 S 139 40 E
Jaffna **70** 9 45N 80 2 E
Jagadhri **68** 30 10N 77 20 E
Jagadishpur **69** 25 30N 84 21 E
Jagdalpur **70** 19 3N 82 0 E
Jagersfontein **92** 29 44 S 25 27 E
Jagst → **25** 49 14N 9 11 E
Jagtial **70** 18 50N 79 0 E
Jaguariaíva **125** 24 10 S 49 50W
Jaguaribe → **127** 4 25 S 37 45W
Jagüey Grande **121** 22 35N 81 7W
Jahangirabad **68** 28 19N 78 4 E
Jahrom **65** 28 30N 53 31 E
Jailolo **73** 1 5N 127 30 E
Jailolo, Selat **73** 0 5N 129 5 E
Jainti **69** 26 45N 89 40 E
Jaipur **68** 27 0N 75 50 E
Jajce **42** 44 19N 17 17 E
Jajpur **69** 20 53N 86 22 E
Jakarta **73** 6 9 S 106 49 E
Jakobstad (Pietarsaari) **50** 63 40N 22 43 E
Jakupica **42** 41 45N 21 22 E
Jal **117** 32 8N 103 8W
Jalai Nur **76** 49 27N 117 42 E
Jalalabad, Afghan. **66** 34 30N 70 29 E
Jalalabad, India **69** 27 41N 79 42 E
Jalalpur Jattan **68** 32 38N 74 11 E
Jalapa, Guat. **120** 14 39N 89 59W
Jalapa, Mexico **120** 19 30N 96 56W
Jalas, Jabal al **64** 27 30N 36 30 E
Jalaun **69** 26 8N 79 25 E
Jaleswar **69** 26 38N 85 48 E
Jalgaon, Maharashtra, India **68** 21 0N 75 42 E
Jalgaon, Maharashtra, India **68** 21 2N 76 31 E
Jalingo **85** 8 55N 11 25 E
Jalisco □ **120** 20 0N 104 0W
Jallas → **30** 42 54N 9 8W
Jalna **70** 19 48N 75 38 E
Jalón → **32** 41 47N 1 4W
Jalpa **120** 21 38N 102 58W
Jalpaiguri **69** 26 32N 88 46 E
Jalq **65** 27 35N 62 46 E
Jaluit I. **94** 6 0N 169 30 E
Jamaari **85** 11 44N 9 53 E
Jamaica ■ **121** 18 10N 77 30W
Jamalpur, Bangla. **69** 24 52N 89 56 E
Jamalpur, India **69** 25 18N 86 28 E
Jamalpurganj **69** 23 2N 88 1 E
Jamanxim → **127** 4 43 S 56 18W
Jambe **73** 1 15 S 132 10 E
Jambi **72** 1 38 S 103 30 E
Jambi □ **72** 1 30 S 102 30 E
Jambusar **68** 22 3N 72 51 E
James → **116** 42 52N 97 18W
James B. **106** 51 30N 80 0W
James Range **96** 24 10 S 132 30 E
James Ross I. **5** 63 58 S 57 50W
Jamestown, Austral. **97** 33 10 S 138 32 E
Jamestown, S. Afr. **92** 31 6 S 26 45 E
Jamestown, Ky., U.S.A. **114** 37 0N 85 5W
Jamestown, N.D., U.S.A. **116** 46 54N 98 42W
Jamestown, N.Y., U.S.A. **114** 42 5N 79 18W
Jamestown, Pa., U.S.A. **112** 41 32N 80 27W
Jamestown, Tenn., U.S.A. **115** 36 25N 85 0W
Jamkhandi **70** 16 30N 75 15 E
Jammā'īn **62** 32 8N 35 12 E
Jammalamadugu **70** 14 51N 78 25 E
Jammerbugt **49** 57 15N 9 20 E
Jammu **68** 32 43N 74 54 E
Jammu & Kashmir □ **66** 34 25N 77 0 E
Jamnagar **68** 22 30N 70 6 E
Jamner **68** 20 45N 75 52 E
Jampur **68** 29 39N 70 40 E
Jamrud Fort **66** 33 59N 71 24 E
Jamshedpur **69** 22 44N 86 12 E
Jamtara **69** 23 59N 86 49 E
Jämtlands län □ **48** 62 40N 13 50 E
Jan Kemp **92** 27 55 S 24 51 E
Jan L. **109** 54 56N 102 55W
Jan Mayen Is. **4** 71 0N 9 0W
Jand **66** 33 30N 72 6 E
Janda, Laguna de la **31** 36 15N 5 45W
Jandaq **65** 34 3N 54 22 E
Jandola **66** 32 20N 70 9 E
Jandowae **99** 26 45 S 151 7 E
Jándula → **31** 38 3N 4 6W
Janesville **116** 42 39N 89 1W
Janga **85** 10 5N 1 0W
Jangaon **70** 17 44N 79 5 E
Jangeru **72** 2 20 S 116 29 E
Janikowo **28** 52 45N 18 7 E

Janīn 62 32 28N 35 18 E
Janja 42 44 40N 19 17 E
Janjevo 42 42 35N 21 19 E
Janjina 42 42 58N 17 25 E
Jánoshalma 27 46 18N 19 21 E
Jánosháza 27 47 8N 17 12 E
Jánossomorja 27 47 47N 17 11 E
Janów 28 50 44N 19 27 E
Janów Lubelski 28 50 48N 22 23 E
Janów Podlaski 28 52 11N 23 11 E
Janowiec Wielkopolski 28 52 45N 17 30 E
Januária 127 15 25 S 44 25W
Janub Dârfûr □ 87 11 0N 25 0 E
Janub Kordofân □ 87 12 0N 30 0 E
Janville 19 48 10N 1 50 E
Janzé 18 47 55N 1 28W
Jaora 68 23 40N 75 10 E
Japan ■ 74 36 0N 136 0 E
Japan, Sea of 74 40 0N 135 0 E
Japan Trench 94 32 0N 142 0 E
Japara 73 6 30 S 110 40 E
Japen = Yapen 73 1 50 S 136 0 E
Japurá → 126 3 8 S 64 46W
Jaque 126 7 27N 78 8W
Jara, La 119 37 16N 106 0W
Jaraicejo 31 39 40N 5 49W
Jaraiz 30 40 4N 5 45W
Jarales 119 34 39N 106 51W
Jarama → 32 40 2N 3 39W
Jarandilla 30 40 8N 5 39W
Jaranwala 68 31 15N 73 26 E
Jarash 62 32 17N 35 54 E
Jarbidge 118 41 56N 115 27W
Jardim 124 21 28 S 56 2W
Jardin → 33 38 50N 2 10W
Jardines de la Reina, Is. 121 20 50N 78 50W
Jargalant (Kobdo) 75 48 2N 91 37 E
Jargeau 19 47 50N 2 1 E
Jarmen 24 53 56N 13 20 E
Jarnac 20 45 40N 0 11W
Jarny 19 49 9N 5 53 E
Jarocin 28 51 59N 17 29 E
Jaroměr 26 50 22N 15 52 E
Jarosław 27 50 2N 22 42 E
Järpås 49 58 23N 12 57 E
Järpen 48 63 21N 13 26 E
Jarso 87 5 15N 37 30 E
Jarvis 112 42 53N 80 6W
Jarvis I. 95 0 15 S 159 55W
Jarvornik 27 50 23N 17 2 E
Jarwa 69 27 38N 82 30 E
Jaša Tomić 42 45 26N 20 50 E
Jasien 28 51 46N 15 0 E
Jasin 71 2 20N 102 26 E
Jāsk 65 25 38N 57 45 E
Jasło 27 49 45N 21 30 E
Jasper, Alta., Can. 108 52 55N 118 5W
Jasper, Ont., Can. 113 44 52N 75 57W
Jasper, Ala., U.S.A. 115 33 48N 87 16W
Jasper, Fla., U.S.A. 115 30 31N 82 58W
Jasper, Minn., U.S.A. 116 43 52N 96 22W
Jasper, Tex., U.S.A. 117 30 59N 93 58W
Jasper Nat. Park 108 52 50N 118 8W
Jassy = Iaşi 46 47 10N 27 40 E
Jastrebarsko 39 45 41N 15 39 E
Jastrowie 28 53 26N 16 49 E
Jastrzębie Zdrój 27 49 57N 18 35 E
Jászapáti 27 47 32N 20 10 E
Jászárokszállás 27 47 39N 20 1 E
Jászberény 27 47 30N 19 55 E
Jászkiser 27 47 27N 20 20 E
Jászladány 27 47 23N 20 10 E
Jataí 127 17 58 S 51 48W
Jati 68 24 20N 68 19 E
Jatibarang 73 6 28 S 108 18 E
Jatinegara 73 6 13 S 106 52 E
Játiva 33 39 0N 0 32W
Jatobal 127 4 35 S 49 33W
Jatt 62 32 24N 35 2 E
Jaú 125 22 10 S 48 30W
Jauja 126 11 45 S 75 15W
Jaunjelgava 54 56 35N 25 0 E
Jaunpur 69 25 46N 82 44 E
Java = Jawa 73 7 0 S 110 0 E
Java Sea 72 4 35 S 107 15 E
Java Trench 94 10 0 S 110 0W
Javadi Hills 70 12 40N 78 40 E
Jávea 33 38 48N 0 10 E
Javhlant = Ulyasutay 75 47 56N 97 28 E
Javla 70 17 18N 75 9 E
Javron 18 48 25N 0 25W
Jawa 73 7 0 S 110 0 E
Jawor 28 51 4N 16 11 E
Jaworzno 27 50 13N 19 11 E
Jay 117 36 25N 94 46W
Jaya, Puncak 73 3 57 S 137 17 E
Jayapura 73 2 28 S 140 38 E
Jayawijaya, Pegunungan 73 5 0 S 139 0 E
Jayton 117 33 17N 100 35W
Jean 119 35 47N 115 20W
Jean Marie River 104 61 32N 120 38W
Jean Rabel 121 19 50N 73 5W
Jeanerette 117 29 52N 91 38W
Jeanette, Ostrov 59 76 43N 158 0 E
Jeannette 112 40 20N 79 36W
Jebba, Moroc. 82 35 11N 4 43W
Jebba, Nigeria 85 9 9N 4 48 E
Jebel, Bahr el → 81 15 38N 32 31 E
Jebel Qerri 87 16 16N 32 50 E
Jedburgh 14 55 28N 2 33W
Jedlicze 27 49 43N 21 40 E
Jedlnia-Letnisko 28 51 25N 21 19 E
Jędrzejów 28 50 35N 20 15 E
Jedwabne 28 53 17N 22 18 E
Jedway 108 52 17N 131 14W
Jeetze → 24 53 9N 11 6 E
Jefferson, Iowa, U.S.A. 116 42 3N 94 25W
Jefferson, Ohio, U.S.A. 112 41 40N 80 46W
Jefferson, Tex., U.S.A. 117 32 45N 94 23W
Jefferson, Wis., U.S.A. 116 43 0N 88 49W
Jefferson City, Mo., U.S.A. 116 38 34N 92 10W
Jefferson City, Tenn., U.S.A. 115 36 8N 83 30W
Jefferson, Mt., Nev., U.S.A. 118 38 51N 117 0W
Jefferson, Mt., Oreg., U.S.A. 118 44 45N 121 50W
Jeffersonville 114 38 20N 85 42W
Jega 85 12 15N 4 23 E
Jekabpils 54 56 29N 25 57 E
Jelenia Góra 28 50 50N 15 45 E
Jelenia Góra □ 28 51 0N 15 30 E
Jelgava 54 56 41N 23 49 E
Jelica 42 43 50N 20 17 E
Jelli 87 5 25N 31 45 E
Jellicoe 106 49 40N 87 30W
Jelšava 27 48 37N 20 15 E
Jemaja 72 3 5N 105 45 E
Jember 73 8 11 S 113 41 E
Jembongan 72 6 45N 117 20 E
Jemeppe 16 50 37N 5 30 E
Jemnice 26 49 1N 15 34 E
Jena, Ger. 24 50 56N 11 33 E
Jena, U.S.A. 117 31 41N 92 7W
Jenbach 26 47 24N 11 47 E
Jendouba 83 36 29N 8 47 E
Jenkins 114 37 13N 82 41W
Jennings 117 30 10N 92 45W
Jennings → 108 59 38N 132 5W
Jenny 49 57 47N 16 35 E
Jeparit 99 36 8 S 142 1 E
Jequié 127 13 51 S 40 5W
Jequitinhonha 127 16 30 S 41 0W
Jequitinhonha → 127 15 51 S 38 53W
Jerada 82 34 17N 2 10W
Jerantut 71 3 56N 102 22 E
Jérémie 121 18 40N 74 10W
Jerez de García Salinas 120 22 39N 103 0W
Jerez de la Frontera 31 36 41N 6 7W
Jerez de los Caballeros 31 38 20N 6 45W
Jerez, Punta 120 22 58N 97 40W
Jericho 98 23 38 S 146 6 E
Jericho = El Arīḥā 62 31 52N 35 27 E
Jerichow 24 52 30N 12 2 E
Jerilderie 99 35 20 S 145 41 E
Jermyn 113 41 31N 75 31W
Jerome 119 34 50N 112 0W
Jerrobert 109 51 56N 109 8W
Jersey City 114 40 41N 74 8W
Jersey, I. 18 49 13N 2 7W
Jersey Shore 114 41 17N 77 18W
Jerseyville 116 39 5N 90 20W
Jerusalem 62 31 47N 35 10 E
Jervis B. 97 35 8 S 150 46 E
Jesenice 39 46 28N 14 3 E
Jeseník 27 50 0N 17 8 E
Jesenske 27 48 20N 20 10 E
Jesselton = Kota Kinabalu 72 6 0N 116 4 E
Jessnitz 24 51 42N 12 19 E
Jessore 69 23 10N 89 10 E
Jesup 115 31 36N 81 54W
Jesús María 124 30 59 S 64 5W
Jetmore 117 38 10N 99 57W
Jetpur 68 21 45N 70 10 E
Jevnaker 47 60 15N 10 26 E
Jewett, Ohio, U.S.A. 112 40 22N 81 2W
Jewett, Tex., U.S.A. 117 31 20N 96 8W
Jewett City 113 41 36N 72 0W
Jeypore 70 18 50N 82 38 E
Jeziorak, Jezioro 28 53 40N 19 35 E
Jeziorany 28 53 58N 20 46 E
Jeziorka → 28 51 59N 20 57 E
Jhajjar 68 28 37N 76 42 E
Jhal Jhao 66 26 20N 65 35 E
Jhalawar 68 24 40N 76 10 E
Jhang Maghiana 68 31 15N 72 22 E
Jhansi 68 25 30N 78 36 E
Jharia 69 23 45N 86 26 E
Jharsuguda 69 21 56N 84 5 E
Jhelum 68 33 0N 73 45 E
Jhelum → 68 31 20N 72 10 E
Jhunjhunu 68 28 10N 75 30 E
Ji Xian 76 36 7N 110 40 E
Jia Xian 76 38 12N 110 28 E
Jiamusi 75 46 40N 130 26 E
Ji'an 75 27 6N 114 59 E
Jianchuan 75 26 38N 99 55 E
Jiande 77 29 23N 119 15 E
Jiangbei 77 29 40N 106 34 E
Jiange 77 32 4N 105 32 E
Jiangjin 77 29 14N 106 14 E
Jiangling 75 30 25N 112 12 E
Jiangmen 75 22 32N 113 0 E
Jiangshan 77 28 40N 118 37 E
Jiangsu □ 75 33 0N 120 0 E
Jiangxi □ 75 27 30N 116 0 E
Jiangyin 77 31 54N 120 17 E
Jiangyong 77 25 20N 111 22 E
Jiangyou 77 31 44N 104 43 E
Jianning 77 26 50N 116 50 E
Jian'ou 75 27 3N 118 17 E
Jianshi 77 30 37N 109 38 E
Jianshui 75 23 36N 102 43 E
Jianyang 77 27 20N 118 5 E
Jiao Xian 76 36 18N 120 1 E
Jiaohe 76 38 2N 116 20 E
Jiaozhou Wan 76 36 5N 120 10 E
Jiaozuo 77 35 16N 113 12 E
Jiawang 77 34 28N 117 26 E
Jiaxing 75 30 49N 120 45 E
Jiayi 75 23 30N 120 24 E
Jibāl 63 22 10N 56 8 E
Jibiya 85 13 5N 7 12 E
Jibou 46 47 15N 23 17 E
Jibuti = Djibouti ■ 63 12 0N 43 0 E
Jičín 26 50 25N 15 28 E
Jiddah 64 21 29N 39 10 E
Jido 67 29 2N 94 58 E
Jifnā 62 31 58N 35 13 E
Jihlava 26 49 28N 15 35 E
Jihlava → 26 48 55N 16 36 E
Jihočeský □ 26 49 8N 14 35 E
Jihomoravský □ 27 49 5N 16 30 E
Jijel 83 36 52N 5 50 E
Jijiga 63 9 20N 42 50 E
Jijona 33 38 34N 0 30W
Jikamshi 85 12 12N 7 45 E
Jilin 76 43 44N 126 30 E
Jilin □ 76 44 0N 124 0 E
Jiloca → 32 41 21N 1 39W
Jilong 75 25 8N 121 42 E
Jílové 26 49 52N 14 29 E
Jima 87 7 40N 36 47 E
Jimbolia 42 45 47N 20 43 E
Jimena de la Frontera 31 36 27N 5 24W
Jiménez 120 27 10N 104 54W
Jimo 76 36 23N 120 30 E
Jin Xian 76 38 55N 121 42 E
Jinan 76 36 38N 117 1 E
Jincheng 76 35 29N 112 50 E
Jind 68 29 19N 76 22 E
Jindabyne 99 36 25 S 148 35 E
Jindabyne L. 100 36 20 S 148 38 E
Jindrichuv Hradeç 26 49 10N 15 2 E
Jing He → 77 34 27N 109 4 E
Jing Xian 77 26 33N 109 40 E
Jingchuan 76 35 20N 107 20 E
Jingdezhen 75 29 20N 117 11 E
Jinggu 75 23 35N 100 41 E
Jinghai 76 38 55N 116 55 E
Jingle 76 38 20N 111 55 E
Jingmen 77 31 0N 112 10 E
Jingning 76 35 30N 105 43 E
Jingshan 77 31 1N 113 7 E
Jingtai 76 37 10N 104 6 E
Jingxi 75 23 8N 106 27 E
Jingyu 76 42 25N 126 45 E
Jingyuan 76 36 30N 104 40 E
Jingziguan 77 33 15N 111 0 E
Jinhe 76 51 18N 121 32 E
Jinhua 75 29 8N 119 38 E
Jining, Nei Mongol Zizhiqu, China 76 41 5N 113 0 E
Jining, Shandong, China 77 35 22N 116 34 E
Jinja 90 0 25N 33 12 E
Jinjini 84 7 26N 3 42W
Jinmen Dao 77 24 25N 118 25 E
Jinnah Barrage 65 32 58N 71 33 E
Jinotega 121 13 6N 85 59W
Jinotepe 121 11 50N 86 10W
Jinshi 75 29 40N 111 50 E
Jinxiang 77 35 5N 116 22 E
Jinzhou 76 41 5N 121 3 E
Jiparaná (Machado) → 126 8 3 S 62 52W
Jipijapa 126 1 0 S 80 40W
Jiquilpan 120 19 57N 102 42W
Jishou 77 28 21N 109 43 E
Jisr al Ḥusayn (Allenby) Br. 62 31 53N 35 33 E
Jisr ash Shughūr 64 35 49N 36 18 E
Jitra 71 6 16N 100 25 E
Jiu → 46 44 40N 23 25 E
Jiudengkou 76 39 56N 106 40 E
Jiujiang 75 29 42N 115 58 E
Jiuling Shan 77 28 40N 114 40 E
Jiuquan 75 39 50N 98 20 E
Jixi 76 45 20N 130 50 E
Jizera → 26 50 10N 14 43 E
Jizl Wadi 86 25 30N 38 30 E
Joaçaba 125 27 5 S 51 31W
João Pessoa 127 7 10 S 34 52W
Joaquín V. González 124 25 10 S 64 0W
Jobourg, Nez de 18 49 41N 1 57W
Jódar 33 37 50N 3 21W
Jodhpur 68 26 23N 73 8 E
Joensuu 52 62 37N 29 49 E
Jœuf 19 49 12N 6 1 E
Joggins 107 45 42N 64 27W
Jogjakarta = Yogyakarta 73 7 49 S 110 22 E
Johannesburg 93 26 10 S 28 2 E
Johansfors 49 56 42N 15 32 E
John Day 118 44 25N 118 57W
John Day → 118 45 44N 120 39W
John H. Kerr Res. 115 36 20N 78 30W
John o' Groats 14 58 39N 3 3W
Johnson 117 37 35N 101 48W
Johnson City, N.Y., U.S.A. 114 42 7N 75 57W
Johnson City, Tenn., U.S.A. 115 36 18N 82 21W
Johnson City, Tex., U.S.A. 117 30 15N 98 24W
Johnsonburg 112 41 30N 78 40W
Johnson's Crossing 108 60 29N 133 18W
Johnston Falls = Mambilima Falls 91 10 31 S 28 45 E
Johnston I. 95 17 10N 169 8W
Johnstone Str. 108 50 28N 126 0W
Johnstown, N.Y., U.S.A. 114 43 1N 74 20W
Johnstown, Pa., U.S.A. 114 40 19N 78 53W
Johor □ 71 2 5N 103 20 E
Joigny 19 48 0N 3 20 E
Joinvile 125 26 15 S 48 55 E
Joinville 19 48 27N 5 10 E
Joinville I. 5 65 0 S 55 30W
Jokkmokk 50 66 35N 19 50 E
Jökulsá á Brú → 50 65 40N 14 16W
Jökulsá Fjöllum → 50 66 10N 16 30W
Joliet 114 41 30N 88 0W
Joliette 106 46 3N 73 24W
Jolo 73 6 0N 121 0 E
Jombang 73 7 33 S 112 14 E
Jome 73 1 16 S 127 30 E
Jomfruland 49 58 52N 9 36 E
Jönåker 49 58 44N 16 40 E
Jonava 54 55 8N 24 12 E
Jones Sound 4 76 0N 85 0W
Jonesboro, Ark., U.S.A. 117 35 50N 90 45W
Jonesboro, Ill., U.S.A. 117 37 26N 89 18W
Jonesboro, La., U.S.A. 117 32 15N 92 41W
Jonesport 107 44 32N 67 38W
Jonglei 87 6 25N 30 50 E
Joniskis 54 56 13N 23 35 E
Jönköping 49 57 45N 14 10 E
Jönköpings län □ 49 57 30N 14 30 E
Jonquière 107 48 27N 71 14W
Jonsberg 49 58 30N 16 48 E
Jonsered 49 57 45N 12 10 E
Jonzac 20 45 27N 0 28W
Joplin 117 37 0N 94 31W
Jordan, Phil. 73 10 41N 122 38 E
Jordan, U.S.A. 118 47 25N 106 58W
Jordan ■ 64 31 0N 36 0 E
Jordan → 62 31 48N 35 32 E
Jordan Valley 118 43 0N 117 2W
Jordanów 27 49 41N 19 49 E
Jorhat 67 26 45N 94 12 E
Jorm 65 36 50N 70 52 E
Jörn 50 65 4N 20 1 E
Jørpeland 47 59 3N 6 1 E
Jorquera → 124 28 3 S 69 58W
Jos 85 9 53N 8 51 E
Jošanička Banja 42 43 24N 20 47 E
José Batlle y Ordóñez 125 33 20 S 55 10W
Joseni 46 46 42N 25 29 E
Joseph 118 45 27N 117 13W
Joseph Bonaparte G. 96 14 35 S 128 50 E
Joseph City 119 35 0N 110 16W
Joseph, L., Newf., Can. 107 52 45N 65 18W
Joseph, L., Ont., Can. 112 45 10N 79 44W
Josselin 18 47 57N 2 33W
Jostedal 47 61 35N 7 15 E
Jotunheimen 47 61 35N 8 25 E
Jourdanton 117 28 54N 98 32W
Joussard 108 55 22N 115 50W
Jovellanos 121 22 40N 81 10W
Jowzjān □ 65 36 10N 66 0 E
Joyeuse 21 44 29N 4 16 E
Józefów 28 52 10N 21 11 E
Ju Xian 77 36 35N 118 20 E
Juan Aldama 120 24 20N 103 23W
Juan Bautista 119 36 55N 121 33W
Juan Bautista Alberdi 124 34 26 S 61 48W
Juan de Fuca Str. 118 48 15N 124 0W
Juan de Nova 93 17 3 S 43 45 E
Juan Fernández, Arch. de 95 33 50 S 80 0W
Juan José Castelli 124 25 27 S 60 57W
Juan L. Lacaze 124 34 26 S 57 25W
Juárez 124 37 40 S 59 43W
Juárez, Sierra de 120 32 0N 116 0W
Juàzeiro 127 9 30 S 40 30W
Juàzeiro do Norte 127 7 10 S 39 18W
Jubbulpore = Jabalpur 69 23 9N 79 58 E
Jübek 24 54 31N 9 24 E
Jubga 57 44 19N 38 48 E
Juby, C. 80 28 0N 12 59W
Júcar → 33 39 5N 0 10W
Juchitán 120 16 27N 95 5W
Judaea = Yehuda 62 31 35N 34 57 E
Judenburg 26 47 12N 14 38 E
Judith → 118 47 44N 109 38W
Judith Gap 118 46 40N 109 46W
Judith Pt. 113 41 20N 71 30W
Jugoslavia = Yugoslavia ■ 37 44 0N 20 0 E
Juigalpa 121 12 6N 85 26W
Juillac 20 45 20N 1 19 E
Juist 24 53 40N 7 0 E
Juiz de Fora 127 21 43 S 43 19W
Jujuy □ 124 23 20 S 65 40W
Julesberg 116 41 0N 102 20W
Juli 126 16 10 S 69 25W
Julia Cr. → 98 20 0 S 141 11 E
Julia Creek 97 20 39 S 141 44 E
Juliaca 126 15 25 S 70 10W
Julian 119 33 4N 116 38W
Julian Alps = Julijske Alpe 39 46 15N 14 1 E
Julianehåb 4 60 43N 46 0W
Jülich 24 50 55N 6 20 E
Julijske Alpe 39 46 15N 14 1 E
Jullundur 68 31 20N 75 40 E
Julu 76 37 15N 115 2 E
Jumbo 91 17 30 S 30 58 E
Jumentos Cays 121 23 0N 75 40 E
Jumet 16 50 27N 4 25 E
Jumilla 33 38 28N 1 19W
Jumla 69 29 15N 82 13 E
Jumna = Yamuna → 68 25 30N 81 53 E
Junagadh 68 21 30N 70 30 E
Junction, Tex., U.S.A. 117 30 29N 99 48W
Junction, Utah, U.S.A. 119 38 10N 112 15W
Junction B. 96 11 52 S 133 55 E
Junction City, Kans., U.S.A. 116 39 4N 96 55W
Junction City, Oreg., U.S.A. 118 44 14N 123 12W
Jundah 97 24 46 S 143 2 E
Jundiaí 125 24 30 S 47 0W
Juneau 104 58 20N 134 20W
Junee 97 34 53 S 147 35 E
Jungfrau 25 46 32N 7 58 E
Junggar Pendi 75 44 30N 86 0 E
Jungshahi 68 24 52N 67 44 E
Juniata → 112 40 30N 77 40W
Junín 124 34 33 S 60 57W
Junín de los Andes 128 39 45 S 71 0W
Jūniyah 64 33 59N 35 38 E
Junnar 70 19 12N 73 58 E
Junquera, La 32 42 25N 2 53 E
Junta, La 117 38 0N 103 30W
Juntura 118 43 44N 118 4W
Jupiter → 107 49 29N 63 37W
Jur, Nahr el → 87 8 45N 29 15 E
Jura, France 19 46 35N 6 5 E
Jura, U.K. 14 56 0N 5 50W
Jura □ 19 46 47N 5 45 E
Jura, Sd. of 14 55 57N 5 45W
Jura Suisse 25 47 10N 7 0 E
Jurado 126 7 7N 77 46W
Jurien B. 96 30 17 S 115 0 E
Jurilovca 46 44 46N 28 52 E
Juruá → 126 2 37 S 65 44W
Juruena → 126 7 20 S 58 3W
Juruti 127 2 9 S 56 4W
Jussey 19 47 50N 5 55 E
Justo Daract 124 33 52 S 65 12W
Jüterbog 24 52 0N 13 6 E
Juticalpa 121 14 40N 86 12W
Jutland = Jylland 8 56 25N 9 30 E
Juvigny-sous-Andaine 18 48 32N 0 30W
Juvisy 19 48 43N 2 23 E
Juwain 65 31 45N 61 30 E
Juzennecourt 19 48 10N 4 48 E
Jylland 8 56 25N 9 30 E
Jyväskylä 72 62 14N 25 50 E

K

K2 66 35 58N 76 32 E
Kaalasin 71 16 26N 103 30 E
Kaap die Goeie Hoop 92 34 24 S 18 30 E
Kaap Plato 92 28 30 S 24 0 E
Kaapkruis 92 21 43 S 14 0 E
Kaapstad = Cape Town 92 33 55 S 18 22 E
Kabaena 73 5 15 S 122 0 E
Kabala 84 9 38N 11 37W
Kabale 90 1 15 S 30 0 E
Kabalo 90 6 0 S 27 0 E
Kabambare 90 4 41 S 27 39 E
Kabango 91 8 35 S 28 30 E
Kabanjahe 72 3 6N 98 30 E
Kabara 84 16 40N 2 50W
Kabardinka 56 44 40N 37 57 E
Kabardino-Balkar-A.S.S.R. □ 57 43 30N 43 30 E
Kabare 73 0 4 S 130 58 E
Kabarega Falls 90 2 15N 31 30 E
Kabasalan 73 7 47N 122 44 E
Kabba 85 7 50N 6 3 E
Kabi 85 13 30N 12 35 E
Kabinakagami L. 106 48 54N 84 25W
Kabīr Kūh 64 33 0N 47 30 E
Kabīr, Zab al 64 36 0N 43 0 E
Kabkabīyah 81 13 50N 24 0 E
Kabna 86 19 6N 32 40 E
Kabompo 91 13 36 S 24 14 E
Kabompo → 89 14 10 S 23 11 E
Kabondo 91 8 58 S 25 40 E
Kabongo 90 7 22 S 25 33 E
Kabou 85 9 28N 0 55 E
Kaboudia, Rass 83 35 13N 11 10 E
Kabra 98 23 25 S 150 25 E
Kabūd Gonbad 65 37 5N 59 45 E
Kabul 66 34 28N 69 11 E
Kabúl □ 65 34 30N 69 0 E
Kabul → 66 33 55N 72 14 E
Kabunga 90 1 38 S 28 3 E
Kaburuang 73 3 50N 126 30 E
Kabushiya 87 16 54N 33 41 E
Kabwe 91 14 30 S 28 29 E
Kačanik 42 42 13N 21 12 E
Kachanovo 54 57 25N 27 38 E
Kachebera 91 13 50 S 32 50 E
Kachin □ 67 26 0N 97 30 E
Kachira, L. 90 0 40 S 31 7 E
Kachiry 58 53 10N 75 50 E
Kachisi 87 9 40N 37 50 E
Kackar 57 40 45N 41 10 E
Kadan Kyun 72 12 30N 98 20 E
Kadarkút 27 46 13N 17 39 E
Kadayanallur 70 9 3N 77 22 E
Kade 85 6 7N 0 56W
Kadi 68 23 18N 72 23 E
Kadina 97 34 0 S 137 43 E
Kadiri 70 14 12N 78 13 E
Kadirli 64 37 23N 36 5 E
Kadiyevka 57 48 35N 38 40 E
Kadoka 116 43 50N 101 31W
Kadom 55 54 37N 42 30 E
Kâdugli 81 11 0N 29 45 E
Kaduna 85 10 30N 7 21 E
Kaduna □ 85 11 0N 7 30 E
Kaédi 84 16 9N 13 28W
Kaelé 85 10 7N 14 27 E
Kaesŏng 76 37 58N 126 35 E
Kāf 64 31 25N 37 29 E
Kafakumba 88 9 38 S 23 46 E
Kafan 53 39 18N 46 15 E
Kafanchan 85 9 40N 8 20 E
Kafareti 85 10 25N 11 12 E
Kaffrine 84 14 8N 15 36W
Kafia Kingi 81 9 20N 24 25 E
Kafinda 91 12 32 S 30 20 E
Kafirévs, Ákra 45 38 9N 24 38 E
Kafr 'Ayn 62 32 3N 35 7 E
Kafr el Dauwâr 86 31 8N 30 8 E
Kafr el Sheikh 86 31 15N 30 50 E
Kafr Kammā 62 32 44N 35 26 E
Kafr Kannā 62 32 45N 35 20 E
Kafr Mālik 62 32 0N 35 18 E
Kafr Mandā 62 32 49N 35 15 E
Kafr Quaddūm 62 32 14N 35 7 E
Kafr Rā'ī 62 32 23N 35 9 E
Kafr Şīr 62 33 19N 35 23 E
Kafr Yāsīf 62 32 58N 35 10 E
Kafue 91 15 46 S 28 9 E
Kafue Flats 91 15 40 S 27 25 E
Kafulwe 91 9 0 S 29 1 E
Kaga Bandoro 88 7 0N 19 10 E
Kagan 58 39 43N 64 33 E
Kagawa □ 74 34 15N 134 0 E
Kagera → 90 0 57 S 31 47 E
Kağizman 64 40 5N 43 10 E
Kagoshima 74 31 35N 130 33 E
Kagoshima □ 74 31 30N 130 30 E
Kagoshima-Wan 74 31 25N 130 40 E
Kagul 56 45 50N 28 15 E
Kahajan → 72 3 40 S 114 0 E
Kahama 90 4 8 S 32 30 E
Kahama □ 90 3 50 S 32 0 E
Kahe 90 3 30 S 37 25 E
Kahemba 88 7 18 S 18 55 E
Kahil, Djebel bou 83 34 26N 4 0 E
Kahniah → 108 58 15N 120 55W
Kahnūj 65 27 55N 57 40 E
Kahoka 116 40 25N 91 42W
Kahoolawe 110 20 33N 156 35W
Kai Besar 73 5 35 S 133 0 E
Kai Kai 92 19 52 S 21 15 E
Kai, Kepulauan 73 5 55 S 132 45W
Kai-Ketjil 73 5 45 S 132 40 E
Kaiama 85 9 36N 4 1 E
Kaiapoi 101 42 24 S 172 40 E
Kaieteur Falls 126 5 1N 59 10W
Kaifeng 77 34 48N 114 21 E
Kaihua 77 29 12N 118 20 E
Kaiingveld 92 30 0 S 22 0 E
Kaikohe 101 35 25 S 173 49 E
Kaikoura 101 42 25 S 173 43 E
Kaikoura Pen. 101 42 25 S 173 43 E
Kaikoura Ra. 101 41 59 S 173 41 E
Kailahun 84 8 18N 10 39W
Kaili 77 26 33N 107 59 E
Kailu 76 43 38N 121 18 E
Kailua 110 19 39N 156 0W
Kaimana 73 3 39 S 133 45 E
Kaimanawa Mts. 101 39 15 S 175 56 E
Kaimganj 69 27 33N 79 24 E
Kaimur Hill 69 24 30N 82 0 E
Kainantu 98 6 18 S 145 52 E
Kaingaroa Forest 101 38 24 S 176 30 E
Kainji Res. 85 10 1N 4 40 E
Kaipara Harbour 101 36 25 S 174 14 E
Kaiping 77 22 23N 112 42 E
Kaipokok B. 107 54 54N 59 47W
Kairana 68 29 24N 77 15 E
Kaironi 73 0 47 S 133 40 E
Kairouan 83 35 45N 10 5 E
Kairuku 98 8 51 S 146 35 E
Kaiserslautern 25 49 30N 7 43 E
Kaitaia 101 35 8 S 173 17 E
Kaitangata 101 46 17 S 169 51 E
Kaithal 68 29 48N 76 26 E
Kaiwi Channel 110 21 13N 157 30W
Kaiyuan 76 42 28N 124 1 E
Kajaani 50 64 17N 27 46 E
Kajabbi 97 20 0 S 140 1 E
Kajan → 72 2 55N 117 35 E
Kajang 71 2 59N 101 48 E
Kajiado 90 1 53 S 36 48 E
Kajiado □ 90 2 0 S 36 30 E
Kajo Kaji 87 3 58N 31 40 E
Kajoa 73 0 1N 127 28 E
Kaka 81 10 38N 32 10 E
Kakabeka Falls 106 48 24N 89 37W
Kakamega 90 0 20N 34 46 E
Kakamega □ 90 0 20N 34 46 E
Kakanj 42 44 9N 18 7 E
Kakanui Mts. 101 45 10 S 170 30 E
Kakegawa 74 34 45N 138 1 E
Kakhib 57 42 28N 46 34 E
Kakhovka 56 46 40N 33 15 E
Kakhovskoye Vdkhr. 56 47 5N 34 16 E
Kakinada (Cocanada) 70 16 57N 82 11 E
Kakisa → 108 61 3N 118 10W
Kakisa L. 108 60 56N 117 43W
Kakwa → 108 54 37N 118 28W
Kala 85 12 2N 14 40 E
Kala Oya → 70 8 20N 79 45 E
Kalaa-Kebira 83 35 59N 10 32 E
Kalabagh 68 33 0N 71 28 E
Kalabahi 73 8 13 S 124 31 E
Kalabáka 44 39 42N 21 39 E
Kalabo 89 14 58 S 22 40 E
Kalach 55 50 22N 41 0 E
Kalach na Donu 57 48 43N 43 32 E
Kaladan → 67 20 20N 93 5 E
Kaladar 112 44 37N 77 5W
Kalahari 92 24 0 S 21 30 E
Kalahari Gemsbok Nat. Park 92 25 30 S 20 30 E
Kalahasti 70 13 45N 79 44 E
Kalakamati 93 20 40 S 27 25 E
Kalakan 59 55 15N 116 45 E
Kalama, U.S.A. 118 46 0N 122 55W
Kalama, Zaïre 90 2 52 S 28 35 E
Kalamariá 44 40 33N 22 55 E
Kalamata 45 37 3N 22 10 E
Kalamazoo 114 42 20N 85 35W
Kalamazoo → 114 42 40N 86 12W
Kalamb 70 18 3N 74 48 E
Kalambo Falls 91 8 37 S 31 35 E
Kálamos, Greece 45 38 37N 20 55 E
Kálamos, Greece 45 38 17N 23 52 E
Kalamoti 45 38 15N 26 4 E
Kalan 64 39 7N 39 32 E
Kalao 73 7 21 S 121 0 E
Kalaotoa 73 7 20 S 121 50 E
Kälarne 48 62 59N 16 8 E
Kalárovo 27 47 54N 18 0 E
Kalasin 71 16 26N 103 30 E
Kalat 66 29 8N 66 31 E
• Kalat □ 68 27 30N 66 0 E
Kálathos (Calato) 45 36 9N 28 8 E
Kalaus → 57 45 40N 44 7 E
Kalávrita 45 38 3N 22 8 E
Kalecik 56 40 4N 33 26 E
Kalegauk Kyun 67 15 33N 97 35 E
Kalehe 90 2 6 S 28 50 E
Kalema 90 1 12 S 31 55 E
Kalemie 90 5 55 S 29 9 E
Kalety 28 50 35N 18 52 E
Kalewa 67 23 10N 94 15 E
Kálfafellsstaður 50 64 11N 15 53W
Kalgan = Zhangjiakou 76 40 48N 114 55 E
Kalgoorlie 96 30 40 S 121 22 E
Kaliakra, Nos 43 43 21N 28 30 E
Kalianda 72 5 50 S 105 45 E
Kalibo 73 11 43N 122 22 E
Kaliganj Town 69 22 25N 89 8 E
Kalima 90 2 33 S 26 32 E
Kalimantan Barat □ 72 0 0 110 30 E
Kalimantan Selatan □ 72 2 30 S 115 30 E
Kalimantan Tengah □ 72 2 0 S 113 30 E
Kalimantan Timur □ 72 1 30N 116 30 E
Kálimnos 45 37 0N 27 0 E
Kalimpong 69 27 4N 88 35 E
Kalinadi → 70 14 50N 74 7 E
Kalinin 55 56 55N 35 55 E
Kaliningrad 54 54 42N 20 32 E
Kalinkovichi 54 52 12N 29 20 E
Kalinovik 42 43 31N 18 29 E
Kalipetrovo (Stančevo) 43 44 5N 27 14 E
Kaliro 90 0 56N 33 30 E
Kalirrákhi 44 40 40N 24 35 E
Kalispell 118 48 10N 114 22W
Kalisz 28 51 45N 18 8 E
Kalisz □ 28 51 30N 18 0 E
Kalisz Pomorski 28 53 17N 15 55 E
Kaliua 90 5 5 S 31 48 E
Kaliveli Tank 70 12 5N 79 50 E

• Now part of Baluchistan □

Kalix → 50 65 50N 23 11 E
Kalka 68 30 46N 76 57 E
Kalkaska 106 44 44N 85 11W
Kalkfeld 92 20 57 S 16 14 E
Kalkfontein 92 22 4 S 20 57 E
Kalkrand 92 24 1 S 17 35 E
Kallakurichi 70 11 44N 79 1 E
Kållandsö 49 58 40N 13 5 E
Kallia 62 31 46N 35 30 E
Kallidaikurichi 70 8 38N 77 31 E
Kallinge 49 56 15N 15 18 E
Kallithéa 45 37 55N 23 41 E
Kallmeti 44 41 51N 19 41 E
Kallonís, Kólpos 45 39 10N 26 10 E
Kallsjön 50 63 38N 13 0 E
Kalmalo 85 13 40N 5 20 E
Kalmar 49 56 40N 16 20 E
Kalmar län □ 49 57 25N 16 0 E
Kalmar sund 49 56 40N 16 25 E
Kalmyk A.S.S.R. □ 57 46 5N 46 1 E
Kalmykovo 57 49 0N 51 47 E
Kalna 69 23 13N 88 25 E
Kalo 98 10 1 S 147 48 E
Kalocsa 27 46 32N 19 0 E
Kalofer 43 42 37N 24 59 E
Kaloko 90 6 47 S 25 48 E
Kalol, Gujarat, India 68 23 15N 72 33 E
Kalol, Gujarat, India 68 22 37N 73 31 E
Kalolímnos 45 37 4N 27 8 E
Kalomo 91 17 0 S 26 30 E
Kaloneròn 45 37 20N 21 38 E
Kalpi 69 26 8N 79 47 E
Kalrayan Hills 70 11 45N 78 40 E
Kalsubai 70 19 35N 73 45 E
Kaltungo 85 9 48N 11 19 E
Kalu 68 25 5N 67 39 E
Kaluga 55 54 35N 36 10 E
Kalulushi 91 12 50 S 28 3 E
Kalundborg 49 55 41N 11 5 E
Kalush 54 49 3N 24 23 E
Kałuszyn 28 52 13N 21 52 E
Kalutara 70 6 35N 80 0 E
Kalwaria 27 49 53N 19 41 E
Kalya 52 60 15N 59 59 E
Kalyan 68 20 30N 74 3 E
Kalyazin 55 57 15N 37 55 E
Kam Keut 71 18 20N 104 48 E
Kama 90 3 30 S 27 5 E
Kama → 52 55 45N 52 0 E
Kamachumu 90 1 37 S 31 37 E
Kamaishi 74 39 20N 142 0 E
Kamalia 68 30 44N 72 42 E
Kamandorskiye Ostrava 59 55 0N 167 0 E
Kamapanda 91 12 5 S 24 0 E
Kamaran 63 15 21N 42 35 E
Kamativi 91 18 15 S 27 27 E
Kamba 85 11 50N 3 45 E
Kambam 70 9 45N 77 16 E
Kambar 68 27 37N 68 1 E
Kambarka 52 56 15N 54 11 E
Kambia 84 9 3N 12 53W
Kambolé 91 8 47 S 30 48 E
Kambove 91 10 51 S 26 33 E
Kamchatka, P-ov. 59 57 0N 160 0 E
Kamen 58 53 50N 81 30 E
Kamen Kashirskiy 54 51 39N 24 56 E
Kamenica, Srbija, Yugo. 42 44 25N 19 40 E
Kamenica, Srbija, Yugo. 42 43 27N 22 27 E
Kamenice 26 49 18N 15 2 E
Kamenjak, Rt 39 44 47N 13 55 E
Kamenka, R.S.F.S.R., U.S.S.R. 52 65 58N 44 0 E
Kamenka, R.S.F.S.R., U.S.S.R. 55 50 47N 39 20 E
Kamenka, R.S.F.S.R., U.S.S.R. 55 53 10N 44 5 E
Kamenka, Ukraine S.S.R., U.S.S.R. 56 49 3N 32 6 E
Kamenka Bugskaya 54 50 8N 24 16 E
Kamenka Dneprovskaya 56 47 29N 34 14 E
Kameno 43 42 34N 27 18 E
Kamenolomini 57 47 40N 40 14 E
Kamensk-Shakhtinskiy 57 48 23N 40 20 E
Kamensk Uralskiy 58 56 25N 62 2 E
Kamenskiy, R.S.F.S.R., U.S.S.R. 55 50 48N 45 25 E
Kamenskiy, R.S.F.S.R., U.S.S.R. 57 49 20N 41 15 E
Kamenskoye 59 62 45N 165 30 E
Kamenyak 43 43 24N 26 57 E
Kamenz 24 51 17N 14 7 E
Kami 44 42 17N 20 18 E
Kamiah 118 46 12N 116 2W
Kamień Krajeński 28 53 32N 17 32 E
Kamień Pomorski 28 53 57N 14 43 E
Kamienna → 28 51 6N 21 47 E
Kamienna Góra 28 50 47N 16 2 E
Kamiensk 28 51 12N 19 29 E
Kamilukuak, L. 109 62 22N 101 40W
Kamina 91 8 45 S 25 0 E
Kaminak L. 109 62 10N 95 0W
Kamituga 90 3 2 S 28 10 E
Kamloops 108 50 40N 120 20W
Kamloops L. 108 50 45N 120 40W
Kamnik 39 46 14N 14 37 E
Kamo 57 40 21N 45 7 E
Kamoke 68 32 4N 74 4 E
Kamp → 26 48 23N 15 42 E
Kampala 90 0 20N 32 30 E
Kampar 71 4 18N 101 9 E
Kampar → 72 0 30N 103 8 E
Kampen 16 52 33N 5 53 E
Kampolombo, L. 91 11 37 S 29 42 E
Kampot 71 10 36N 104 10 E
Kamptee 68 21 9N 79 19 E
Kampti 84 10 7N 3 25W
Kampuchea = Cambodia ■ 71 13 0N 105 0 E
Kampung → 73 5 44 S 138 24 E
Kampungbaru = Tolitoli 73 1 5N 120 50 E
Kamrau, Teluk 73 3 30 S 133 36 E
Kamsack 109 51 34N 101 54W
Kamskoye Ustye 55 55 10N 49 20 E
Kamskoye Vdkhr. 52 58 0N 56 0 E
Kamuchawie L. 109 56 18N 101 59W
Kamyshin 55 50 10N 45 24 E
Kamyzyak 57 46 4N 48 10 E
Kanaaupscow 106 54 2N 76 30W
Kanab 119 37 3N 112 29W
Kanab Creek 119 37 0N 112 40W
Kanagawa □ 74 35 20N 139 20 E
Kanairiktok → 107 55 2N 60 18W
Kanakapura 70 12 33N 77 28 E
Kanália 44 39 30N 22 53 E
Kananga 88 5 55 S 22 18 E
Kanarraville 119 37 34N 113 12W
Kanash 55 55 30N 47 32 E
Kanastraíon, Ákra 44 39 57N 23 45 E
Kanawha → 114 38 50N 82 8W
Kanazawa 74 36 30N 136 38 E
Kanchanaburi 71 14 2N 99 31 E
Kanchenjunga 69 27 50N 88 10 E
Kanchipuram (Conjeeveram) 70 12 52N 79 45 E
Kańczuga 27 49 59N 22 25 E
Kanda Kanda 88 6 52 S 23 48 E
Kandahar 65 31 32N 65 30 E
Kandalaksha 52 67 9N 32 30 E
Kandalakshkiy Zaliv 52 66 0N 35 0 E
Kandangan 72 2 50 S 115 20 E
Kandanos 45 35 19N 23 44 E
Kandhíla 45 37 46N 22 22 E
Kandhkot 68 28 16N 69 8 E
Kandhla 68 29 18N 77 19 E
Kandi, Benin 85 11 7N 2 55 E
Kandi, India 69 23 58N 88 5 E
Kandla 68 23 0N 70 10 E
Kandos 99 32 45 S 149 58 E
Kandukur 70 15 12N 79 57 E
Kandy 70 7 18N 80 43 E
Kane 114 41 39N 78 53W
Kane Bassin 4 79 30N 68 0W
Kanevskaya 57 46 3N 39 3 E
Kanfanar 39 45 7N 13 50 E
Kangaba 84 11 56N 8 25W
Kangar 71 6 27N 100 12 E
Kangaroo I. 97 35 45 S 137 0 E
Kangaroo Mts. 98 23 25 S 142 0 E
Kangavar 64 34 40N 48 0 E
Kangean, Kepulauan 72 6 55 S 115 23 E
Kangerdlugsuak 4 68 10N 32 20W
Kanggyee 76 41 0N 126 35 E
Kangnŭng 76 37 45N 128 54 E
Kango 88 0 11N 10 5 E
Kangto 67 27 50N 92 35 E
Kanhangad 70 12 21N 74 58 E
Kanheri 70 19 13N 72 50 E
Kani 84 8 29N 6 36W
Kaniama 90 7 30 S 24 12 E
Kaniapiskau → 107 56 40N 69 30W
Kaniapiskau L. 107 54 10N 69 55W
Kanin Nos, Mys 52 68 45N 43 20 E
Kanin, P-ov. 52 68 0N 45 0 E
Kanina 44 40 23N 19 30 E
Kaniva 99 36 22 S 141 18 E
Kanjiža 42 46 3N 20 4 E
Kankakee 114 41 6N 87 50W
Kankakee → 114 41 23N 88 16W
Kankan 84 10 23N 9 15W
Kanker 70 20 10N 81 40 E
Kankunskiy 59 57 37N 126 8 E
Kannapolis 115 35 32N 80 37W
Kannauj 69 27 3N 79 56 E
Kano 85 12 2N 8 30 E
Kano □ 85 11 45N 9 0 E
Kanoroba 84 9 7N 6 8W
Kanowit 72 2 14N 112 20 E
Kanowna 96 30 32 S 121 31 E
Kanoya 74 31 25N 130 50 E
Kanpetlet 67 21 10N 93 59 E
Kanpur 69 26 28N 80 20 E
Kansas □ 116 38 40N 98 0W
Kansas → 116 39 7N 94 36W
Kansas City, Kans., U.S.A. 116 39 0N 94 40W
Kansas City, Mo., U.S.A. 116 39 3N 94 30W
Kansenia 91 10 20 S 26 0 E
Kansk 59 56 20N 95 37 E
Kansu = Gansu □ 75 37 0N 103 0 E
Kantang 71 7 25N 99 31 E
Kantché 85 13 31N 8 30 E
Kanté 85 9 57N 1 3 E
Kantemirovka 57 49 43N 39 55 E
Kanturk 15 52 10N 8 55W
Kanuma 74 36 34N 139 42 E
Kanus 92 27 50 S 18 39 E
Kanye 92 25 0 S 25 28 E
Kanyu 92 20 7 S 24 37 E
Kanzenze 91 10 30 S 25 12 E
Kanzi, Ras 90 7 1 S 39 33 E
Kaohsiung = Gaoxiong 75 22 38N 120 18 E
Kaokoveld 92 18 20 S 13 37 E
Kaolack 84 14 5N 16 8W
Kapadvanj 68 23 5N 73 0 E
Kapanga 88 8 30 S 22 40 E
Kapchagai 58 43 50N 77 10 E
Kapéllo, Ákra 45 36 9N 23 3 E
Kapema 91 10 45 S 28 22 E
Kapfenberg 26 47 26N 15 18 E
Kapiri Mposhi 91 13 59 S 28 43 E
Kapisa □ 65 35 0N 69 20 E
Kapiskau → 106 52 47N 81 55W
Kapit 72 2 0N 112 55 E
Kapiti I. 101 40 50 S 174 56 E
Kaplice 26 48 42N 14 30 E
Kapoeta 87 4 50N 33 35 E
Kápolnásnyék 27 47 16N 18 41 E
Kapos → 27 46 44N 18 30 E
Kaposvár 27 46 25N 17 47 E
Kappeln 24 54 37N 9 56 E
Kapps 92 22 32 S 17 18 E
Kaprije 39 43 42N 15 43 E
Kapsukas 54 54 33N 23 19 E
Kapuas → 72 0 25 S 109 20 E
Kapuas Hulu, Pegunungan 72 1 30N 113 30 E
Kapulo 91 8 18 S 29 15 E
Kapunda 99 34 20 S 138 56 E
Kapurthala 68 31 23N 75 25 E
Kapuskasing 106 49 25N 82 30W
Kapuskasing → 106 49 49N 82 0W
Kapustin Yar 57 48 37N 45 40 E
Kaputir 90 2 5N 35 28 E

Name	Map	Lat.	Long.
Kapuvár	27	47 36N	17 1 E
Kara, Turkey	45	36 58N	27 30 E
Kara, U.S.S.R.	58	69 10N	65 0 E
Kara Bogaz Gol, Zaliv	53	41 0N	53 30 E
Kara Burun	45	38 41N	26 28 E
Kara Kalpak A.S.S.R. □	58	43 0N	60 0 E
Kara Sea	58	75 0N	70 0 E
Kara, Wadi	86	20 0N	41 25 E
Karabük	64	41 12N	32 37 E
Karaburuni	44	40 25N	19 20 E
Karabutak	58	49 59N	60 14 E
Karachala	57	39 45N	48 53 E
Karachayevsk	57	43 50N	42 0 E
Karachev	54	53 10N	35 5 E
Karachi	68	24 53N	67 0 E
Karachi □	68	25 30N	67 0 E
Karád	27	46 41N	17 51 E
Karad	70	17 15N	74 10 E
Karadeniz Boğazı	64	41 10N	29 10 E
Karaga	85	9 58N	0 28W
Karaganda	58	49 50N	73 10 E
Karagayly	58	49 26N	76 0 E
Karaginskiy, Ostrov	59	58 45N	164 0 E
Karagiye Depression	53	43 27N	51 45 E
Karagwe □	90	2 0S	31 0 E
Karaikkudi	70	10 0N	78 45 E
Karaitivu I.	70	9 45N	79 52 E
Karaitivu, I.	70	8 22N	79 47 E
Karaj	65	35 48N	51 0 E
Karakas	58	48 20N	83 30 E
Karakitang	73	3 14N	125 28 E
Karakoram Pass	66	35 33N	77 50 E
Karakoram Ra.	66	35 30N	77 0 E
Karakum, Peski	58	39 30N	60 0 E
Karalon	59	57 5N	115 50 E
Karaman	64	37 14N	33 13 E
Karamay	75	45 30N	84 58 E
Karambu	72	3 53S	116 6 E
Karamea Bight	101	41 22S	171 40 E
Karamoja □	90	3 0N	34 15 E
Karamsad	68	22 35N	72 50 E
Karanganjar	73	7 38S	109 37 E
Karanja	68	20 29N	77 31 E
Karasburg	92	28 0S	18 44 E
Karasino	58	66 50N	86 50 E
Karasjok	50	69 27N	25 30 E
Karasuk	58	53 44N	78 2 E
Karatau	58	43 10N	70 28 E
Karatau, Khrebet	58	43 30N	69 30 E
Karauli	68	26 30N	77 4 E
Karávi	45	36 49N	23 37 E
Karawanken	26	46 30N	14 40 E
Karazhal	58	48 2N	70 49 E
Karbalā	64	32 36N	44 3 E
Kårböle	48	61 59N	15 22 E
Karcag	27	47 19N	20 57 E
Karda	59	55 0N	103 16 E
Kardhámila	45	38 35N	26 5 E
Kardhítsa	44	39 23N	21 54 E
Kardhítsa □	44	39 15N	21 50 E
Kärdla	54	58 50N	22 40 E
Kareeberge	92	30 50S	22 0 E
Kareima	86	18 30N	31 49 E
Karelian A.S.S.R. □	52	65 30N	32 30 E
Karen	71	12 49N	92 53 E
Kargānrūd	64	37 55N	49 0 E
Kargasok	58	59 3N	80 53 E
Kargat	58	55 10N	80 15 E
Kargı	56	41 11N	34 30 E
Kargil	69	34 32N	76 12 E
Kargopol	52	61 30N	38 58 E
Kargowa	28	52 5N	15 51 E
Karguéri	85	13 27N	10 30 E
Karia ba Mohammed	82	34 22N	5 12W
Kariaí	44	40 14N	24 19 E
Kariba	91	16 28S	28 50 E
Kariba Gorge	91	16 30S	28 50 E
Kariba Lake	91	16 40S	28 25 E
Karibib	92	21 0S	15 56 E
Karikal	70	10 59N	79 50 E
Karimata, Kepulauan	72	1 25S	109 0 E
Karimata, Selat	72	2 0S	108 40 E
Karimnagar	70	18 26N	79 10 E
Karimunjawa, Kepulauan	72	5 50S	110 30 E
Karin	63	10 50N	45 52 E
Káristos	45	38 1N	24 29 E
Kariya	74	34 58N	137 1 E
Karkal	70	13 15N	74 56 E
Karkar I.	98	4 40S	146 0 E
Karkaralinsk	58	49 26N	75 30 E
Karkinitskiy Zaliv	56	45 56N	33 0 E
Karkur	62	32 29N	34 57 E
Karkur Tohl	86	22 5N	25 5 E
Karl Libknekht	54	51 40N	35 35 E
Karl-Marx-Stadt	24	50 50N	12 55 E
Karl-Marx-Stadt □	24	50 45N	13 0 E
Karla, L. = Voiviïs, L.	44	39 30N	22 45 E
Karlino	28	54 3N	15 53 E
Karlobag	39	44 32N	15 5 E
Karlovac	39	45 31N	15 36 E
Karlovka	56	49 29N	35 8 E
Karlovy Vary	26	50 13N	12 51 E
Karlsborg	49	58 33N	14 33 E
Karlshamn	49	56 10N	14 51 E
Karlskoga	48	59 22N	14 33 E
Karlskrona	49	56 10N	15 35 E
Karlsruhe	25	49 3N	8 23 E
Karlstad, Sweden	48	59 23N	13 30 E
Karlstad, U.S.A.	116	48 38N	96 30W
Karlstadt	25	49 57N	9 46 E
Karmøy	47	59 15N	5 15 E
Karnal	68	29 42N	77 2 E
Karnali →	69	29 0N	83 20 E
Karnaphuli Res.	67	22 40N	92 20 E
Karnataka □	70	14 15N	76 0 E
Karnes City	117	28 53N	97 53W
Karnische Alpen	26	46 36N	13 0 E
Kärnten □	26	46 52N	13 30 E
Karo	84	12 16N	3 18W
Karoi	91	16 48S	29 45 E
Karonga	91	9 57S	33 55 E
Karoonda	99	35 1S	139 59 E
Káros	45	36 54N	25 40 E
Karousádhes	44	39 47N	19 45 E
Kárpathos	45	35 37N	27 10 E
Karpáthos, Stenón	45	36 0N	27 30 E
Karpinsk	52	59 45N	60 1 E
Karpogory	52	63 59N	44 27 E
Karrebæk	49	55 12N	11 39 E
Kars, Turkey	64	40 40N	43 5 E
Kars, U.S.S.R.	56	40 36N	43 5 E
Karsakpay	58	47 55N	66 40 E
Karsha	57	49 45N	51 35 E
Karshi	58	38 53N	65 48 E
Karst	39	45 35N	14 0 E
Karsun	55	54 14N	46 57 E
Kartál Óros	44	41 15N	25 13 E
Kartaly	58	53 3N	60 40 E
Kartapur	68	31 27N	75 32 E
Karthaus	112	41 8N	78 9W
Kartuzy	28	54 22N	18 10 E
Karufa	73	3 50S	133 20 E
Karumba	98	17 31S	140 50 E
Karumo	90	2 25S	32 50 E
Karumwa	90	3 12S	32 38 E
Karungu	90	0 50S	34 10 E
Karup	49	56 19N	9 10 E
Karur	70	10 59N	78 2 E
Karviná	27	49 53N	18 25 E
Karwi	69	25 12N	80 57 E
Kas Kong	71	11 27N	102 12 E
Kasache	91	13 25S	34 20 E
Kasai →	88	3 30S	16 10 E
Kasai Oriental □	90	5 0S	24 30 E
Kasaji	91	10 25S	23 27 E
Kasama	91	10 16S	31 9 E
Kasane	92	17 34S	24 50 E
Kasanga	91	8 30S	31 10 E
Kasangulu	88	4 33S	15 15 E
Kasaragod	70	12 30N	74 58 E
Kasba L.	109	60 20N	102 10W
Kasba Tadla	82	32 36N	6 17W
Kasempa	91	13 30S	25 44 E
Kasenga	91	10 20S	28 45 E
Kasese	90	0 13N	30 3 E
Kasewa	91	14 28S	28 53 E
Kasganj	68	27 48N	78 42 E
Kashabowie	106	48 40N	90 26W
Kāshān	65	34 5N	51 30 E
Kashi	75	39 30N	76 2 E
Kashimbo	91	11 12S	26 19 E
Kashin	55	57 20N	37 36 E
Kashipur, Orissa, India	70	19 16N	83 3 E
Kashipur, Ut. P., India	68	29 15N	79 0 E
Kashira	55	54 45N	38 10 E
Kāshmar	65	35 16N	58 26 E
Kashmir	69	34 0N	76 0 E
Kashmor	68	28 28N	69 32 E
Kashpirovka	55	53 0N	48 30 E
Kashun Noerh = Gaxun Nur	75	42 22N	100 30 E
Kasimov	55	54 55N	41 20 E
Kasinge	90	6 15S	26 58 E
Kasiruta	73	0 25S	127 12 E
Kaskaskia →	116	37 58N	89 57W
Kaskattama →	109	57 3N	90 4W
Kaskinen	50	62 22N	21 15 E
Kaskö	50	62 22N	21 15 E
Kaslo	108	49 55N	116 55W
Kasmere L.	109	59 34N	101 10W
Kasongo	90	4 30S	26 33 E
Kasongo Lunda	88	6 35S	16 49 E
Kásos	45	35 20N	26 55 E
Kasos, Stenón	45	35 30N	26 30 E
Kaspi	57	41 54N	44 17 E
Kaspichan	43	43 18N	27 11 E
Kaspiysk	57	42 52N	47 40 E
Kaspiyskiy	57	45 22N	47 23 E
Kassab ed Doleib	87	13 30N	33 35 E
Kassaba	86	22 40N	29 55 E
Kassala	87	16 0N	36 0 E
Kassalâ □	87	15 20N	36 26 E
Kassándra	44	40 0N	23 30 E
Kassel	24	51 19N	9 32 E
Kassinga	89	15 5S	16 4 E
Kassinger	86	18 46N	31 51 E
Kassue	73	6 58S	139 21 E
Kastamonu	64	41 25N	33 43 E
Kastav	39	45 22N	14 20 E
Kastélli	45	35 29N	23 38 E
Kastéllion	45	35 12N	25 20 E
Kastellorizon = Megiste	35	36 8N	29 34 E
Kastellou, Ákra	45	35 30N	27 15 E
Kastlösa	49	56 26N	16 25 E
Kastóri	45	37 10N	22 17 E
Kastoría	44	40 30N	21 19 E
Kastoría □	44	40 30N	21 15 E
Kastorías, L.	44	40 30N	21 20 E
Kastornoye	55	51 55N	38 2 E
Kastós	45	38 35N	20 55 E
Kástron	44	39 50N	25 2 E
Kastrosikiá	44	39 6N	20 36 E
Kasulu	90	4 37S	30 5 E
Kasulu □	90	4 37S	30 5 E
Kasumkent	57	41 47N	48 15 E
Kasungu	91	13 0S	33 29 E
Kasur	68	31 5N	74 25 E
Kata	59	58 46N	102 40 E
Kataba	91	16 5S	25 10 E
Katako Kombe	90	3 25S	24 20 E
Katákolon	45	37 38N	21 19 E
Katale	90	4 52S	31 7 E
Katamatite	99	36 6S	145 41 E
Katanda, Zaïre	90	0 55S	29 21 E
Katanda, Zaïre	90	7 52S	24 13 E
Katangi	69	21 56N	79 50 E
Katangli	59	51 42N	143 14 E
Katanning	96	33 40S	117 33 E
Katastári	45	37 50N	20 45 E
Katavi Swamp	90	6 50S	31 10 E
Kateríni	44	40 18N	22 37 E
Katha	67	24 10N	96 30 E
Katherîna, Gebel	86	28 30N	33 57 E
Katherine	96	14 27S	132 20 E
Kathiawar	68	22 20N	71 0 E
Kati	84	12 41N	8 4W
Katiet	72	2 21S	99 54 E
Katihar	69	25 34N	87 36 E
Katima Mulilo	92	17 28S	24 13 E
Katimbira	91	12 40S	34 0 E
Katiola	84	8 10N	5 10W
Katkopberg	92	30 0S	20 0 E
Katlanovo	42	41 52N	21 40 E
Katmandu	69	27 45N	85 20 E
Kato Akhaïa	45	38 8N	21 33 E
Káto Stavros	44	40 39N	23 43 E
Katol	68	21 17N	78 38 E
Katompe	90	6 2S	26 23 E
Katonga →	90	0 34N	31 50 E
Katoomba	97	33 41S	150 19 E
Katowice	28	50 17N	19 5 E
Katowice □	28	50 10N	19 0 E
Katrine, L.	14	56 15N	4 30W
Katrineholm	48	59 9N	16 12 E
Katsepe	93	15 45S	46 15 E
Katsina Ala →	85	7 10N	9 20 E
Katsuura	74	35 10N	140 20 E
Kattawaz-Urgun □	65	32 10N	68 20 E
Kattegatt	49	57 0N	11 20 E
Katumba	90	7 40S	25 17 E
Katungu	90	2 55S	40 3 E
Katwa	69	23 30N	88 5 E
Katwijk-aan-Zee	16	52 12N	4 24 E
Katy	28	51 2N	16 45 E
Kauai	110	22 0N	159 30W
Kauai Chan.	110	21 45N	158 50W
Kaub	25	50 5N	7 46 E
Kaufbeuren	25	47 50N	10 37 E
Kaufman	117	32 35N	96 20W
Kaukauna	114	44 20N	88 13W
Kaukauveld	92	20 0S	20 15 E
Kaukonen	50	67 31N	24 53 E
Kauliranta	50	66 27N	23 41 E
Kaunas	54	54 54N	23 54 E
Kaura Namoda	85	12 37N	6 33 E
Kautokeino	50	69 0N	23 4 E
Kavacha	59	60 16N	169 51 E
Kavadarci	42	41 26N	22 3 E
Kavaja	44	41 11N	19 33 E
Kavali	70	14 55N	80 1 E
Kavála	44	40 57N	24 28 E
Kavála □	44	41 5N	24 30 E
Kavála Kólpos	44	40 50N	24 25 E
Kavarna	43	43 26N	28 22 E
Kavieng	98	2 36S	150 51 E
Kavkaz, Bolshoi	57	42 50N	44 0 E
Kavoúsi	45	35 7N	25 51 E
Kaw = Caux	127	4 30N	52 15W
Kawa	87	13 42N	32 34 E
Kawagama L.	112	45 18N	78 45W
Kawagoe	74	35 55N	139 29 E
Kawaguchi	74	35 52N	139 45 E
Kawaihae	110	20 3N	155 50W
Kawambwa	91	9 48S	29 3 E
Kawardha	69	22 0N	81 17 E
Kawasaki	74	35 35N	139 42 E
Kawene	106	48 45N	91 15W
Kawerau	101	38 7S	176 42 E
Kawhia Harbour	101	38 5S	174 51 E
Kawio, Kepulauan	73	4 30N	125 30 E
Kawnro	67	22 48N	99 8 E
Kawthaung	71	10 5N	98 36 E
Kawthoolei □ = Kawthule	67	18 0N	97 30 E
Kawthule □	67	18 0N	97 30 E
Kaya	85	13 4N	1 10W
Kayah □	67	19 15N	97 15 E
Kayangulam	70	9 10N	76 33 E
Kaycee	118	43 45N	106 46W
Kayeli	73	3 20S	127 10 E
Kayenta	119	36 46N	110 15W
Kayes	84	14 25N	11 30W
Kayima	84	8 54N	11 15W
Kayomba	91	13 11S	24 2 E
Kayoro	85	11 0N	1 28W
Kayrunnera	99	30 40S	142 30 E
Kaysatskoye	57	49 47N	46 49 E
Kayseri	64	38 45N	35 30 E
Kaysville	118	41 2N	111 58W
Kayuagung	72	3 24S	104 50 E
Kazachinskoye	59	56 16N	107 36 E
Kazachye	59	70 52N	135 58 E
Kazakh S.S.R. □	58	50 0N	70 0 E
Kazan	55	55 48N	49 3 E
Kazanlúk	43	42 38N	25 20 E
Kazanskaya	57	49 50N	41 10 E
Kazatin	56	49 45N	28 50 E
Kazbek	57	42 42N	44 30 E
Kāzerūn	65	29 38N	51 40 E
Kazi Magomed	57	40 3N	49 0 E
Kazimierz Dolny	28	51 19N	21 57 E
Kazimierza Wielka	28	50 15N	20 30 E
Kazincbarcika	27	48 17N	20 36 E
Kaztalovka	57	49 47N	48 43 E
Kazumba	88	6 25S	22 5 E
Kazym →	58	63 54N	65 50 E
Kcynia	28	53 0N	17 30 E
Ké-Macina	84	13 58N	5 22W
Kéa	45	37 35N	24 22 E
Kea	45	37 30N	24 22 E
Keams Canyon	119	35 53N	110 9W
Kearney	116	40 45N	99 3W
Keban	64	38 50N	38 50 E
Kébi	84	9 18N	6 37W
Kebili	83	33 47N	9 0 E
Kebnekaise	50	67 53N	18 33 E
Kebri Dehar	63	6 45N	44 17 E
Kebumen	73	7 42S	109 40 E
Kecel	27	46 31N	19 16 E
Kechika →	108	59 41N	127 12W
Kecskemét	27	46 57N	19 42 E
Kedada	87	5 25N	35 58 E
Kedah □	71	5 50N	100 40 E
Kedainiai	54	55 15N	24 2 E
Kedgwick	107	47 40N	67 20W
Kedia Hill	92	21 28S	24 37 E
Kediri	73	7 51S	112 1 E
Kédougou	84	12 35N	12 10W
Kedzierzyn	28	50 20N	18 12
Keefers	108	50 0N	121 40W
Keeley L.	109	54 54N	108 8W
Keeling Is. = Cocos Is.	94	12 12S	96 55
Keene	114	42 57N	72 17W
Keeper Hill	15	52 46N	8 17W
Keer-Weer, C.	97	14 0S	141 32
Keeseville	113	44 29N	73 30W
Keetmanshoop	92	26 35S	18 8
Keewatin	116	47 23N	93 0W
Keewatin □	109	63 20N	95 0W
Keewatin →	109	56 29N	100 46W
Kefa □	87	6 55N	36 30
Kefallinía	45	38 20N	20 30
Kefamenanu	73	9 28S	124 29
Kefar 'Eqron	62	31 52N	34 49
Kefar Ḥasīdim	62	32 47N	35 5
Kefar Naḥum	62	32 54N	35 34
Kefar Sava	62	32 11N	34 54
Kefar Szold	62	33 11N	35 39
Kefar Vitkin	62	32 22N	34 53
Kefar Yehezqel	62	32 34N	35 22
Kefar Yona	62	32 20N	34 54
Kefar Zekharya	62	31 43N	34 57
Kefar Zetim	62	32 48N	35 27
Keffi	85	8 55N	7 43
Keflavík	50	64 2N	22 35W
Keg River	108	57 54N	117 55W
Kegahka	107	50 9N	61 18W
Kegalla	70	7 15N	80 21
Kehl	25	48 34N	7 50
Keighley	12	53 52N	1 54W
Keimoes	92	28 41S	21 0
Keita	85	14 46N	5 56
Keith, Austral.	99	36 6S	140 20
Keith, U.K.	14	57 33N	2 58W
Keith Arm	104	64 20N	122 15W
Kekri	68	26 0N	75 10
Kël	59	69 30N	124 10
Kelamet	87	16 0N	38 30
Kelan	76	38 43N	111 31
Kelang	71	3 2N	101 26
Kelani Ganga →	70	6 58N	79 50
Kelantan □	71	5 10N	102 0
Kelantan →	71	6 13N	102 14
Këlcyra	44	40 22N	20 12
Kelheim	25	48 58N	11 57
Kelibia	83	36 50N	11 3
Kellé	88	0 8S	14 38
Keller	118	48 2N	118 44W
Kellerberrin	96	31 36S	117 38
Kellett C.	4	72 0N	126 0W
Kelleys I.	112	41 35N	82 42W
Kellogg	118	47 30N	116 5W
Kelloselkä	50	66 56N	28 53
Kells = Ceanannus Mor	15	53 42N	6 53W
Kélo	81	9 10N	15 45
Kelowna	108	49 50N	119 25W
Kelsey Bay	108	50 25N	126 0W
Kelso, N.Z.	101	45 54S	169 15
Kelso, U.K.	14	55 36N	2 27W
Kelso, U.S.A.	118	46 10N	122 57W
Keluang	71	2 3N	103 18
Kelvington	109	52 10N	103 30W
Kem	52	65 0N	34 38
Kem →	52	64 57N	34 41
Kem-Kem	82	30 40N	4 30W
Kema	73	1 22N	125 8
Kemah	64	39 32N	39 5
Kemano	108	53 35N	128 0W
Kembolcha	87	11 2N	39 42
Kemenets-Podolskiy	56	48 40N	26 40
Kemerovo	58	55 20N	86 5
Kemi	50	65 44N	24 34
Kemi älv = Kemijoki →	50	65 47N	24 32
Kemijärvi	50	66 43N	27 22
Kemijoki →	50	65 47N	24 32
Kemmerer	118	41 52N	110 30W
Kemp Coast	5	69 0S	55 0
Kemp L.	117	33 45N	99 15W
Kempsey	97	31 1S	152 50
Kempt, L.	106	47 25N	74 22W
Kempten	25	47 42N	10 18
Kemptville	106	45 0N	75 38W
Kenadsa	82	31 48N	2 26W
Kendal, Indon.	72	6 56S	110 14 E
Kendal, U.K.	12	54 19N	2 44W
Kendall	99	31 35S	152 44 E
Kendall →	98	14 4S	141 35 E
Kendallville	114	41 25N	85 15W
Kendari	73	3 50S	122 30 E
Kendawangan	72	2 32S	110 17 E
Kende	85	11 30N	4 12 E
Kendervicës, m. e.	44	40 15N	19 52 E
Kendrapara	69	20 35N	86 30 E
Kendrick	118	46 43N	116 41W
Kenedy	117	28 49N	97 51W
Kenema	84	7 50N	11 14W
Keng Tung	67	21 0N	99 30 E
Kenge	88	4 50S	17 4 E
Kengeja	90	5 26S	39 45 E
Kenhardt	92	29 19S	21 12 E
Kénitra (Port Lyautey)	82	34 15N	6 40W
Kenmare, Ireland	15	51 52N	9 35W
Kenmare, U.S.A.	116	48 40N	102 4W
Kenmare →	15	51 40N	10 0W
Kenmore	100	34 44S	149 45 E
Kenn Reef	97	21 12S	155 46 E
Kennebec	116	43 56N	99 54W
Kennedy	91	18 52S	27 10 E
Kennedy Taungdeik	67	23 15N	93 45 E
Kennet →	13	51 24N	0 58W
Kennett	117	36 7N	90 0W
Kennewick	118	46 11N	119 2W
Kénogami	107	48 25N	71 15W
Kenogami →	106	51 6N	84 28W
Kenora	109	49 47N	94 29W
Kenosha	114	42 33N	87 48W
Kensington, Can.	107	46 28N	63 34W
Kensington, U.S.A.	116	39 48N	99 2W
Kensington Downs	98	22 31S	144 19 E
Kent, Ohio, U.S.A.	114	41 8N	81 20W

Place	Page	Lat.	Long.
ent, Oreg., U.S.A.	118	45 11N	120 45W
ent, Tex., U.S.A.	117	31 5N	104 12W
ent □	13	51 12N	0 40 E
ent Group	99	39 30 S	147 20 E
ent Pen.	104	68 30N	107 0W
entau	58	43 32N	68 36 E
entland	114	40 45N	87 25W
enton	114	40 40N	83 35W
entucky □	114	37 20N	85 0W
entucky →	114	38 41N	85 11W
entucky Dam	114	37 2N	88 15W
entucky L.	115	36 25N	88 0W
entville	107	45 6N	64 29W
entwood	117	31 0N	90 30W
enya ■	90	1 0N	38 0 E
enya, Mt.	90	0 10 S	37 18 E
eokuk	116	40 25N	91 24W
ep-i-Gjuhës	44	40 28N	19 15 E
epi	73	6 32 S	139 19 E
epice	28	54 16N	16 51 E
ępno	28	51 18N	17 58 E
eppel B.	97	23 21 S	150 55 E
epsut	64	39 40N	28 9 E
erala □	70	11 0N	76 15 E
erang	97	35 40 S	143 55 E
eratéa	45	37 48N	23 58 E
eraudren, C.	99	19 58 S	119 45 E
eray	65	26 15N	57 30 E
erch	56	45 20N	36 20 E
erchenskiy Proliv	56	45 10N	36 30 E
erchoual	85	17 12N	0 20 E
erem Maharal	62	32 39N	34 59 E
erema	98	7 58 S	145 50 E
eren	87	15 45N	38 28 E
erewan	84	13 29N	16 10W
erguelen	3	48 15 S	69 10 E
eri	45	37 40N	20 49 E
eri Kera	87	12 21N	32 42 E
ericho	90	0 22 S	35 15 E
ericho □	90	0 30 S	35 15 E
erinci	72	1 40 S	101 15 E
erkenna, Iles	83	34 48N	11 11 E
erki	58	37 50N	65 12 E
erkinítis, Límni	44	41 12N	23 10 E
érkira	44	39 38N	19 50 E
erkrade	16	50 53N	6 4 E
erma	86	19 33N	30 32 E
ermadec Is.	94	30 0 S	178 15W
ermadec Trench	94	30 30 S	176 0W
ermān	65	30 15N	57 1 E
ermān □	65	30 0N	57 0 E
ermānshāh	64	34 23N	47 0 E
ermānshāhān □	64	34 0N	46 30 E
erme Körfezi	45	36 55N	27 50 E
ermen	43	42 30N	26 16 E
ermit	117	31 56N	103 3W
ern →	119	35 16N	119 18W
errobert	109	52 0N	109 11W
errville	117	30 1N	99 8W
erry □	15	52 7N	9 35W
erry Hd.	15	52 26N	9 56W
ersa	87	9 28N	41 48 E
erteminde	49	55 28N	10 39 E
ertosono	73	7 38 S	112 9 E
erulen →	75	48 48N	117 0 E
erzaz	82	29 29N	1 37W
esagami →	106	51 40N	79 45W
esagami L.	106	50 23N	80 15W
eşan	44	40 49N	26 38 E
eski-Suomen lääni □	50	62 0N	25 30 E
estell	93	28 17 S	28 42 E
estenga	52	66 0N	31 50 E
eswick	12	54 35N	3 9W
eszthely	27	46 50N	17 15 E
et →	58	58 55N	81 32 E
eta	85	5 49N	1 0 E
etapang	72	1 55 S	110 0 E
etchikan	104	55 25N	131 40W
etchum	118	43 41N	114 27W
ete Krachi	85	7 46N	0 1W
etef, Khalîg Umm el	86	23 40N	35 35 E
eti Bandar	68	24 8N	67 27 E
etri	68	28 1N	75 50 E
ętrzyn	28	54 7N	21 22 E
ettering	13	52 24N	0 44W
ettle →	109	56 40N	89 34W
ettle Falls	118	48 41N	118 2W
ety	27	49 51N	19 16 E
evin	118	48 45N	111 58W
ewanee	116	41 18N	89 55W
ewaunee	114	44 27N	87 30W
eweenaw B.	114	46 56N	88 23W
eweenaw Pen.	114	47 30N	88 0W
eweenaw Pt.	114	47 26N	87 40W
ey Harbour	106	45 50N	80 45W
ey West	121	24 33N	82 0W
eyport	113	40 26N	74 12W
eyser	114	39 26N	79 0W
eystone, S.D., U.S.A.	116	43 54N	103 27W
eystone, W. Va., U.S.A.	114	37 30N	81 30W
ezhma	59	58 59N	101 9 E
ežmarok	27	49 10N	20 28 E
habarovo	58	69 30N	60 30 E
habarovsk	59	48 30N	135 5 E
hābūr →	64	35 0N	40 30 E
hachmas	57	41 31N	48 42 E
hachraud	68	23 25N	75 20 E
hadari, W. el →	87	10 29N	27 15 E
hadro	68	26 11N	68 50 E
hadyzhensk	57	44 26N	39 32 E
hagaria	69	25 30N	86 32 E
haibar	86	25 49N	39 16 E
haipur, Bahawalpur, Pak.	68	29 34N	72 17 E
haipur, Hyderabad, Pak.	68	27 32N	68 49 E
hair	68	27 57N	77 46 E
hairabad	69	27 33N	80 47 E
hairagarh Raj	69	21 27N	81 2 E
hairpur □	68	27 20N	69 8 E
hakhea	92	24 48 S	23 22 E
halfallah	82	34 20N	0 16 E
halij-e-Fars □	65	28 20N	51 45 E
halilabad	69	26 48N	83 5 E
Khálki	44	39 36N	22 30 E
Khalkidhikí □	44	40 25N	23 20 E
Khalkís	45	38 27N	23 42 E
Khalmer-Sede = Tazovskiy	58	67 30N	78 30 E
Khalmer Yu	58	67 58N	65 1 E
Khalturin	55	58 40N	48 50 E
Khamaria	69	23 10N	80 52 E
Khamas Country	92	21 45 S	26 30 E
Khambhalia	68	22 14N	69 41 E
Khamgaon	68	20 42N	76 37 E
Khamilonísion	45	35 50N	26 15 E
Khamir	63	16 0N	44 0 E
Khammam	70	17 11N	80 6 E
Khān Yūnis	62	31 21N	34 18 E
Khānābād	65	36 45N	69 5 E
Khānaqīn	64	34 23N	45 25 E
Khandrá	45	35 3N	26 8 E
Khandwa	68	21 49N	76 22 E
Khandyga	59	62 42N	135 35 E
Khanewal	68	30 20N	71 55 E
• Khanh Hung	71	9 37N	105 50 E
Khaniá	45	35 30N	24 4 E
Khaniá □	45	35 30N	24 0 E
Khanion Kólpos	45	35 33N	23 55 E
Khanka, Oz.	59	45 0N	132 30 E
Khanna	68	30 42N	76 16 E
Khanpur	68	28 42N	70 35 E
Khanty-Mansiysk	58	61 0N	69 0 E
Khapcheranga	59	49 42N	112 24 E
Kharagpur	69	22 20N	87 25 E
Kharaij	86	21 25N	41 0 E
Kharan Kalat	66	28 34N	65 21 E
Kharānaq	65	32 20N	54 45 E
Kharda	70	18 40N	75 34 E
Khârga, El Wâhât el	86	25 10N	30 35 E
Khargon	68	21 45N	75 40 E
Kharit, Wadi el →	86	24 26N	33 3 E
Khārk, Jazireh	64	29 15N	50 28 E
Kharkov	56	49 58N	36 20 E
Kharmanli	43	41 55N	25 55 E
Kharovsk	55	59 56N	40 13 E
Kharsāniya	64	27 10N	49 10 E
Khartoum = El Khartûm	87	15 31N	32 35 E
Khasab	65	26 14N	56 15 E
Khasavyurt	57	43 16N	46 40 E
Khasebake	92	20 42 S	24 29 E
Khāsh	65	28 15N	61 15 E
Khashm el Girba	87	14 59N	35 58 E
Khashuri	57	41 58N	43 35 E
Khasi Hills	69	25 30N	91 30 E
Khaskovo	43	41 56N	25 30 E
Khatanga	59	72 0N	102 20 E
Khatanga →	59	72 55N	106 0 E
Khatangskiy, Saliv	4	66 0N	112 0 E
Khatauli	68	29 17N	77 43 E
Khatyrka	59	62 3N	175 15 E
Khavār □	64	37 20N	47 0 E
Khaybar, Harrat	64	25 45N	40 0 E
Khazzān Jabal el Awliyâ	87	15 24N	32 20 E
Khed, Maharashtra, India	70	17 43N	73 27 E
Khed, Maharashtra, India	70	18 51N	73 56 E
Khekra	68	28 52N	77 20 E
Khemelnik	56	49 33N	27 58 E
Khemis Miliana	82	36 11N	2 14 E
Khemissèt	82	33 50N	6 1W
Khemmarat	71	16 10N	105 15 E
Khenchela	83	35 28N	7 11 E
Khenifra	82	32 58N	5 46W
Kherrata	83	36 27N	5 13 E
Khérson	44	41 5N	22 47 E
Kherson	56	46 35N	32 35 E
Khersónisos Akrotíri	45	35 30N	24 10 E
Kheta →	59	71 54N	102 6 E
Khiliomódhion	45	37 48N	22 51 E
Khilok	59	51 30N	110 45 E
Khimki	55	55 50N	37 20 E
Khíos	45	38 27N	26 9 E
Khisar-Momina Banya	43	42 30N	24 44 E
Khiuma = Hiiumaa	54	58 50N	22 45 E
Khiva	58	41 30N	60 18 E
Khīyāv	64	38 30N	47 45 E
Khlebarovo	43	43 37N	26 15 E
Khlong →	71	15 30N	98 50 E
Khmelnitskiy	56	49 23N	27 0 E
Khmer Rep. = Cambodia ■	71	12 15N	105 0 E
Khojak P.	65	30 55N	66 30 E
Khokholskiy	55	51 35N	38 40 E
Kholm, Afghan.	65	36 45N	67 40 E
Kholm, U.S.S.R.	54	57 10N	31 15 E
Kholmsk	59	47 40N	142 5 E
Khomas Hochland	92	22 40 S	16 0 E
Khomeyn	64	33 40N	50 7 E
Khomo	92	21 7 S	24 35 E
Khon Kaen	71	16 30N	102 47 E
Khong	71	14 5N	105 56 E
Khong →	71	15 0N	106 50 E
Khonu	59	66 30N	143 12 E
Khoper →	55	49 30N	42 20 E
Khor el 'Atash	87	13 20N	34 15 E
Khóra	45	37 3N	21 42 E
Khóra Sfakion	45	35 15N	24 9 E
Khorāsān □	65	34 0N	58 0 E
Khorat = Nakhon Ratchasima	71	14 59N	102 12 E
Khorat, Cao Nguyen	71	15 30N	102 50 E
Khorb el Ethel	82	28 30N	6 17W
Khorixas	92	20 16 S	14 59 E
Khorog	58	37 30N	71 36 E
Khorol	56	49 48N	33 15 E
Khorramābād	64	33 30N	48 25 E
Khorramshahr	64	30 29N	48 15 E
Khotin	56	48 31N	26 27 E
Khouribga	82	32 58N	6 57W
Khowai	67	24 5N	91 40 E
Khoyniki	54	51 54N	29 55 E
Khrami →	57	41 30N	45 0 E
Khrenovoye	55	51 4N	40 16 E
Khristianá	45	36 14N	25 13 E
Khtapodhiá	45	37 24N	25 34 E
Khu Khan	71	14 42N	104 12 E
Khulna	69	22 45N	89 34 E
Khulo	57	41 33N	42 19 E
Khumago	92	20 26 S	24 32 E
Khunzakh	57	42 35N	46 42 E
Khūr	65	32 55N	58 18 E
Khurai	68	24 3N	78 23 E
Khurayş	64	24 55N	48 5 E
Khurja	68	28 15N	77 58 E
Khūryān Mūryān, Jazā 'ir	63	17 30N	55 58 E
Khushab	68	32 20N	72 20 E
Khuzdar	66	27 52N	66 30 E
Khūzetān □	64	31 0N	50 0 E
Khvalynsk	55	52 30N	48 2 E
Khvatovka	55	52 24N	46 32 E
Khvor	65	33 45N	55 0 E
Khvormūj	65	28 40N	51 30 E
Khvoy	64	38 35N	45 0 E
Khvoynaya	54	58 58N	34 28 E
Khyber Pass	66	34 10N	71 8 E
Kiabukwa	91	8 40 S	24 48 E
Kiadho →	70	19 37N	77 40 E
Kiama	99	34 40 S	150 50 E
Kiamba	73	6 2N	124 46 E
Kiambi	90	7 15 S	28 0 E
Kiambu	90	1 8 S	36 50 E
Kiangsi = Jiangxi □	75	27 30N	116 0 E
Kiangsu = Jiangsu □	75	33 0N	120 0 E
Kiáton	45	38 2N	22 43 E
Kibæk	49	56 2N	8 51 E
Kibanga Port	90	0 10N	32 58 E
Kibangou	88	3 26 S	12 22 E
Kibara	90	2 8 S	33 30 E
Kibare, Mts.	90	8 25 S	27 10 E
Kibombo	90	3 57 S	25 53 E
Kibondo	90	3 35 S	30 45 E
Kibondo □	90	4 0 S	30 55 E
Kibumbu	90	3 32 S	29 45 E
Kibungu	90	2 10 S	30 32 E
Kibuye, Burundi	90	3 39 S	29 59 E
Kibuye, Rwanda	90	2 3 S	29 21 E
Kibwesa	90	6 30 S	29 58 E
Kibwezi	90	2 27 S	37 57 E
Kičevo	42	41 34N	20 59 E
Kichiga	59	59 50N	163 5 E
Kicking Horse Pass	108	51 28N	116 16W
Kidal	85	18 26N	1 22 E
Kidderminster	13	52 24N	2 13W
Kidete	90	6 25 S	37 17 E
Kidira	84	14 28N	12 13W
Kidnappers, C.	101	39 38 S	177 5 E
Kidston	98	18 52 S	144 8 E
Kidugallo	90	6 49 S	38 15 E
Kiel	24	54 16N	10 8 E
Kiel Kanal = Nord-Ostee-Kanal	24	54 15N	9 40 E
Kielce	28	50 52N	20 42 E
Kielce □	28	50 40N	20 40 E
Kieler Bucht	24	54 30N	10 30 E
Kienge	91	10 30 S	27 30 E
Kiessé	85	13 29N	4 1 E
Kiev = Kiyev	54	50 30N	30 28 E
Kifār 'Aşyūn	62	31 39N	35 7 E
Kiffa	84	16 37N	11 24W
Kifisiá	45	38 4N	23 49 E
Kifissós →	45	38 35N	23 20 E
Kifrī	64	34 45N	45 0 E
Kigali	90	1 59 S	30 4 E
Kigarama	90	1 1 S	31 50 E
Kigoma □	90	5 0 S	30 0 E
Kigoma-Ujiji	90	4 55 S	29 36 E
Kigomasha, Ras	90	4 58 S	38 58 E
Kihee	99	27 23 S	142 37 E
Kii-Suidō	74	33 40N	135 0 E
Kikinda	42	45 50N	20 30 E
Kikládhes	45	37 20N	24 30 E
Kikládhes □	45	37 0N	25 0 E
Kikori	98	7 25 S	144 15 E
Kikori →	98	7 38 S	144 20 E
Kikwit	88	5 5 S	18 45 E
Kilafors	48	61 14N	16 36 E
Kilakarai	70	9 12N	78 47 E
Kilalki	45	36 15N	27 35 E
Kilauea Crater	110	19 24N	155 17W
Kilcoy	99	26 59 S	152 30 E
Kildare	15	53 10N	6 50W
Kildare □	15	53 10N	6 50W
Kilgore	117	32 22N	94 55W
Kilifi	90	3 40 S	39 48 E
Kilifi □	90	3 30 S	39 40 E
Kilimanjaro	90	3 7 S	37 20 E
Kilimanjaro □	90	4 0 S	38 0 E
Kilindini	90	4 4 S	39 40 E
Kilis	64	36 50N	37 10 E
Kiliya	56	45 28N	29 16 E
Kilju	76	40 57N	129 25 E
Kilkee	15	52 41N	9 40W
Kilkenny	15	52 40N	7 17W
Kilkenny □	15	52 35N	7 15W
Kilkieran B.	15	53 18N	9 45W
Kilkís	44	40 58N	22 57 E
Kilkís □	44	41 5N	22 50 E
Killala	15	54 13N	9 12W
Killala B.	15	54 20N	9 12W
Killaloe	15	52 48N	8 28W
Killaloe Sta.	112	45 33N	77 25W
Killam	108	52 47N	111 51W
Killarney, Can.	106	45 55N	81 30W
Killarney, Ireland	15	52 2N	9 30W
Killarney, Lakes of	15	52 0N	9 30W
Killary Harbour	15	53 38N	9 52W
Killdeer, Can.	109	49 6N	106 22W
Killdeer, U.S.A.	116	47 26N	102 48W
Killeen	117	31 7N	97 45W
Killiecrankie, Pass of	14	56 44N	3 46W
Killin	14	56 28N	4 20W
Killíni, Ilía, Greece	45	37 55N	21 8 E
Killíni, Korinthía, Greece	45	37 54N	22 25 E
Killybegs	15	54 38N	8 26W
Kilmarnock	14	55 36N	4 30W
Kilmez	55	56 58N	50 55 E
Kilmez →	55	56 58N	50 28 E
Kilmore	99	37 25 S	144 53 E
Kilondo	91	9 45 S	34 20 E
Kilosa	90	6 48 S	37 0 E
Kilosa □	90	6 48 S	37 0 E
Kilrush	15	52 39N	9 30W
Kilsmo	48	59 6N	15 35 E
Kilwa □	91	9 0 S	39 0 E
Kilwa Kisiwani	91	8 58 S	39 32 E
Kilwa Kivinje	91	8 45 S	39 25 E
Kilwa Masoko	91	8 55 S	39 30 E
Kim	117	37 18N	103 20W
Kimaam	73	7 58 S	138 53 E
Kimamba	90	6 45 S	37 10 E
Kimba	97	33 8 S	136 23 E
Kimball, Nebr., U.S.A.	116	41 17N	103 40W
Kimball, S.D., U.S.A.	116	43 47N	98 57W
Kimbe	98	5 33 S	150 11 E
Kimbe B.	98	5 15 S	150 30 E
Kimberley, Austral.	96	16 20 S	127 0 E
Kimberley, Can.	108	49 40N	115 59W
Kimberley, S. Afr.	92	28 43 S	24 46 E
Kimberly	118	42 33N	114 25W
Kimchaek	76	40 40N	129 10 E
Kimchŏn	76	36 11N	128 4 E
Kími	45	38 38N	24 6 E
Kimolos	45	36 48N	24 37 E
Kimovsk	55	54 0N	38 29 E
Kimparana	84	12 48N	5 0W
Kimry	55	56 55N	37 15 E
Kimsquit	108	52 45N	126 57W
Kimstad	49	58 35N	15 58 E
Kinabalu	72	6 0N	116 0 E
Kínaros	45	36 59N	26 15 E
Kinaskan L.	108	57 38N	130 8W
Kincaid	109	49 40N	107 0W
Kincardine	106	44 10N	81 40W
Kinda	91	9 18 S	25 4 E
Kindersley	109	51 30N	109 10W
Kindia	84	10 0N	12 52W
Kindu	90	2 55 S	25 50 E
Kinel	55	53 15N	50 40 E
Kineshma	55	57 30N	42 5 E
Kinesi	90	1 25 S	33 50 E
King City	119	36 11N	121 8W
King Cr. →	98	24 35 S	139 30 E
King Frederick VI Land = Kong Frederik VI.s. Kyst	4	63 0N	43 0W
King George B.	128	51 30 S	60 30W
King George I.	5	60 0 S	60 0W
King George Is.	105	57 20N	80 30W
King George Sd.	96	35 5 S	118 0 E
King I., Austral.	97	39 50 S	144 0 E
King I., Can.	108	52 10N	127 40W
King I. = Kadah Kyun	71	12 30N	98 20 E
King Leopold Ranges	96	17 30 S	125 45 E
King, Mt.	99	25 10 S	147 30 E
King Sd.	96	16 50 S	123 20 E
King William I.	104	69 10N	97 25W
King William's Town	92	32 51 S	27 22 E
Kingaroy	97	26 32 S	151 51 E
Kingfisher	117	35 50N	97 55W
Kingisepp	54	59 25N	28 40 E
Kingisepp (Kuressaare)	54	58 15N	22 30 E
Kingman, Ariz., U.S.A.	119	35 12N	114 2W
Kingman, Kans., U.S.A.	117	37 41N	98 9W
Kings →	119	36 10N	119 50W
Kings Canyon National Park	119	37 0N	118 35W
King's Lynn	12	52 45N	0 25 E
Kings Mountain	115	35 13N	81 20W
King's Peak	118	40 46N	110 27W
Kingsbridge	13	50 17N	3 46W
Kingsburg	119	36 35N	119 36W
Kingscote	99	35 40 S	137 38 E
Kingscourt	15	53 55N	6 48W
Kingsley	116	42 37N	95 58W
Kingsley Dam	116	41 20N	101 40W
Kingsport	115	36 33N	82 36W
Kingston, Can.	106	44 14N	76 30W
Kingston, Jamaica	121	18 0N	76 50W
Kingston, N.Z.	101	45 20 S	168 43 E
Kingston, N.Y., U.S.A.	114	41 55N	74 0W
Kingston, Pa., U.S.A.	114	41 19N	75 58W
Kingston, R.I., U.S.A.	113	41 29N	71 30W
Kingston South East	97	36 51 S	139 55 E
Kingston-upon-Thames	13	51 23N	0 20W
Kingstown	121	13 10N	61 10W
Kingstree	115	33 40N	79 48W
Kingsville, Can.	106	42 2N	82 45W
Kingsville, U.S.A.	117	27 30N	97 53W
Kingussie	14	57 5N	4 2W
Kinistino	109	52 57N	105 2W
Kinkala	88	4 18 S	14 49 E
Kinleith	101	38 20 S	175 56 E
Kinmount	112	44 48N	78 45W
Kinn	47	61 34N	4 45 E
Kinna	49	57 32N	12 42 E
Kinnaird	108	49 17N	117 39W
Kinnairds Hd.	14	57 40N	2 0W
Kinnared	49	57 2N	13 7 E
Kinneret	62	32 44N	35 34 E
Kinneret, Yam	62	32 45N	35 35 E
Kinoje →	106	52 8N	81 25W
Kinoni	90	0 41 S	30 28 E
Kinross	14	56 13N	3 25W
Kinsale	15	51 42N	8 31W
Kinsale, Old Hd. of	15	51 37N	8 32W
Kinsarvik	47	60 22N	6 43 E
Kinshasa	88	4 20 S	15 15 E
Kinsley	117	37 57N	99 30W
Kinston	115	35 18N	77 35W
Kintampo	85	8 5N	1 41W
Kintap	72	3 51 S	115 13 E
Kintyre	14	55 30N	5 35W
Kintyre, Mull of	14	55 17N	5 55W
Kinushseo →	106	55 15N	83 45W
Kinuso	108	55 20N	115 25W
Kinyangiri	90	4 25 S	34 37 E
Kinzig →	25	48 37N	7 49 E
Kinzua	112	41 52N	78 58W
Kinzua Dam	112	41 53N	79 0W
Kíoni	45	38 27N	20 41 E
Kiosk	106	46 6N	78 53W
Kiowa, Kans., U.S.A.	117	37 3N	98 30W
Kiowa, Okla., U.S.A.	117	34 45N	95 50W
Kipahigan L.	109	55 20N	101 55W
Kipanga	90	6 15 S	35 20 E
Kiparissía	45	37 15N	21 40 E

ow part of Sind □

• *Renamed Soc Trang*

Name	Page	Lat.	Long.
Kiparissiakós Kólpos	45	37 25N	21 25 E
Kipembawe	90	7 38S	33 27 E
Kipengere Ra.	91	9 12S	34 15 E
Kipili	90	7 28S	30 32 E
Kipini	90	2 30S	40 32 E
Kipling	109	50 6N	102 38W
Kippure	15	53 11N	6 23W
Kipushi	91	11 48S	27 12 E
Kirandul	70	18 33N	81 10 E
Kiratpur	68	29 32N	78 12 E
Kirchhain	24	50 49N	8 54 E
Kirchheim	25	48 38N	9 20 E
Kirchheim-Bolanden	25	49 40N	8 0 E
Kirchschlag	27	47 30N	16 19 E
Kirensk	59	57 50N	107 55 E
Kirgiz S.S.R. □	58	42 0N	75 0 E
Kirgiziya Steppe	53	50 0N	55 0 E
Kiri	88	1 29S	19 0 E
Kiribati ■	94	1 0N	176 0 E
Kiriburu	69	22 0N	85 0 E
Kırıkkale	64	39 51N	33 32 E
Kirillov	55	59 51N	38 14 E
Kirin = Jilin	76	43 55N	126 30 E
Kirin = Jilin □	76	44 0N	126 0 E
Kirindi →	70	6 15N	81 20 E
Kirishi	54	59 28N	31 59 E
Kirkcaldy	14	56 7N	3 10W
Kirkcudbright	14	54 50N	4 3W
Kirkee	70	18 34N	73 56 E
Kirkenær	47	60 27N	12 3 E
Kirkenes	50	69 40N	30 5 E
Kirkintilloch	14	55 57N	4 10W
Kirkjubæjarklaustur	50	63 47N	18 4W
Kirkland	119	34 29N	112 46W
Kirkland Lake	106	48 9N	80 2W
Kırklareli	43	41 44N	27 15 E
Kirksville	116	40 8N	92 35W
Kirkūk	64	35 30N	44 21 E
Kirkwall	14	58 59N	2 59W
Kirkwood	92	33 22S	25 15 E
Kirlampudi	70	17 12N	82 12 E
Kirn	25	49 46N	7 29 E
Kirov, R.S.F.S.R., U.S.S.R.	54	54 3N	34 20 E
Kirov, R.S.F.S.R., U.S.S.R.	58	58 35N	49 40 E
Kirovabad	57	40 45N	46 20 E
Kirovakan	57	40 48N	44 30 E
Kirovo-Chepetsk	55	58 28N	50 0 E
Kirovograd	56	48 35N	32 20 E
Kirovsk, R.S.F.S.R., U.S.S.R.	52	67 48N	33 50 E
Kirovsk, Turkmen S.S.R., U.S.S.R.	58	37 42N	60 23 E
Kirovsk, Ukraine S.S.R., U.S.S.R.	57	48 35N	38 30 E
Kirovski	57	45 51N	48 11 E
Kirovskiy	59	54 27N	155 42 E
Kirriemuir, Can.	109	51 56N	110 20W
Kirriemuir, U.K.	14	56 41N	3 0W
Kirsanov	55	52 35N	42 40 E
Kırşehir	64	39 14N	34 5 E
Kirstonia	92	25 30S	23 45 E
Kirtachi	85	12 52N	2 30 E
Kīrteh	65	32 15N	63 0 E
Kirthar Range	68	27 0N	67 0 E
Kiruna	50	67 52N	20 15 E
Kirundu	90	0 50S	25 35 E
Kirya	55	55 5N	46 45 E
Kiryū	74	36 24N	139 20 E
Kisa	49	58 0N	15 39 E
Kisaga	90	4 30S	34 23 E
Kisámou, Kólpos	45	35 30N	23 38 E
Kisanga	90	2 30N	26 35 E
Kisangani	90	0 35N	25 15 E
Kisar	73	8 5S	127 10 E
Kisaran	72	3 0N	99 37 E
Kisarawe	90	6 53S	39 0 E
Kisarawe □	90	7 3S	39 0 E
Kisarazu	74	35 23N	139 55 E
Kisbér	27	47 30N	18 0 E
Kiselevsk	58	54 5N	86 39 E
Kishanganj	69	26 3N	88 14 E
Kishangarh	68	27 50N	70 30 E
Kishi	85	9 1N	3 52 E
Kishinev	56	47 0N	28 50 E
Kishiwada	74	34 28N	135 22 E
Kishon	62	32 49N	35 2 E
Kishorganj	69	24 26N	90 40 E
Kishtwar	69	33 20N	75 48 E
Kisii	90	0 40S	34 45 E
Kisii □	90	0 40S	34 45 E
Kisiju	90	7 23S	39 19 E
Kısır, Dağ	57	41 0N	43 5 E
Kisizi	90	1 0S	29 58 E
Kiska I.	104	52 0N	177 30 E
Kiskatinaw →	108	56 8N	120 10W
Kiskittogisu L.	109	54 13N	98 20W
Kiskomárom = Zalakomár	27	46 33N	17 10 E
Kiskörös	27	46 37N	19 20 E
Kiskundorozsma	27	46 16N	20 5 E
Kiskunfelégyháza	27	46 42N	19 53 E
Kiskunhalas	27	46 28N	19 37 E
Kiskunmajsa	27	46 30N	19 48 E
Kislovodsk	57	43 50N	42 45 E
Kiso-Sammyaku	74	35 45N	137 45 E
Kisoro	90	1 17S	29 48 E
Kispest	27	47 27N	19 9 E
Kissidougou	84	9 5N	10 0W
Kissimmee	115	28 18N	81 22W
Kissimmee →	115	27 20N	80 55W
Kississing L.	109	55 10N	101 20W
Kistanje	39	43 58N	15 55 E
Kisterenye	27	48 3N	19 50 E
Kisújszállás	27	47 12N	20 50 E
Kisumu	90	0 3S	34 45 E
Kisvárda	27	48 14N	22 4 E
Kiswani	90	4 5S	37 57 E
Kiswere	91	9 27S	39 30 E
Kit Carson	116	38 48N	102 45W
Kita	84	13 5N	9 25W
Kitab	58	39 7N	66 52 E
Kitaibaraki	74	36 50N	140 45 E
Kitakami-Gawa →	74	38 25N	141 19 E
Kitakyūshū	74	33 50N	130 50 E
Kitale	90	1 0N	35 0 E
Kitangiri, L.	90	4 5S	34 20 E
Kitaya	91	10 38S	40 8 E
Kitchener	106	43 27N	80 29W
Kitega = Citega	90	3 30S	29 58 E
Kitengo	90	7 26S	24 8 E
Kiteto □	90	5 0S	37 0 E
Kitgum	90	3 17N	32 52 E
Kíthira	45	36 9N	23 0 E
Kíthnos	45	37 26N	24 27 E
Kitimat	108	54 3N	128 38W
Kitinen →	50	67 34N	26 40 E
Kitiyab	87	17 13N	33 35 E
Kítros	44	40 22N	22 34 E
Kittakittaooloo, L.	99	28 3S	138 14 E
Kittanning	114	40 49N	79 30W
Kittatinny Mts.	113	41 0N	75 0W
Kittery	114	43 7N	70 42W
Kitui	90	1 17S	38 0 E
Kitui □	90	1 30S	38 25 E
Kitwe	91	12 54S	28 13 E
Kitzbühel	26	47 27N	12 24 E
Kitzingen	25	49 44N	10 9 E
Kivalo	50	66 18N	26 0 E
Kivarli	68	24 33N	72 46 E
Kivotós	44	40 13N	21 26 E
Kivu □	90	3 10S	27 0 E
Kivu, L.	90	1 48S	29 0 E
Kiyev	54	50 30N	30 28 E
Kiyevskoye Vdkhr.	54	51 0N	30 0 E
Kizel	52	59 3N	57 40 E
Kiziguru	90	1 46S	30 23 E
Kızıl Irmak →	56	39 15N	36 0 E
Kizil Yurt	57	43 13N	46 54 E
Kızılcahamam	56	40 30N	32 30 E
Kizimkazi	90	6 28S	39 30 E
Kizlyar	57	43 51N	46 40 E
Kizyl-Arvat	58	38 58N	56 15 E
Kjellerup	49	56 17N	9 25 E
Kladanj	42	44 14N	18 42 E
Kladnica	42	43 23N	20 2 E
Kladno	26	50 10N	14 7 E
Kladovo	42	44 36N	22 33 E
Klagenfurt	26	46 38N	14 20 E
Klagshamn	49	55 32N	12 53 E
Klagstorp	49	55 22N	13 23 E
Klaipeda	54	55 43N	21 10 E
Klamath →	118	41 40N	124 4W
Klamath Falls	118	42 20N	121 50W
Klamath Mts.	118	41 20N	123 0W
Klanjec	39	46 3N	15 45 E
Klappan →	108	58 0N	129 43W
Klaten	73	7 43S	110 36 E
Klatovy	26	49 23N	13 18 E
Klawak	108	55 35N	133 0W
Klawer	92	31 44S	18 36 E
Kłecko	28	52 38N	17 25 E
Kleczew	28	52 22N	18 9 E
Kleena Kleene	108	52 0N	124 59W
Klein	118	46 26N	108 31W
Klein-Karas	92	27 33S	18 7 E
Klein Karoo	92	33 45S	21 30 E
Klekovača	39	44 25N	16 32 E
Klemtu	108	52 35N	128 55W
Klenovec, Czech.	27	48 36N	19 54 E
Klenovec, Yugo.	42	41 32N	20 49 E
Klerksdorp	92	26 51S	26 38 E
Kleszczele	28	52 35N	23 19 E
Kletnya	54	53 23N	33 12 E
Kletsk	54	53 5N	26 45 E
Kletskiy	57	49 20N	43 0 E
Kleve	24	51 46N	6 10 E
Klickitat	118	45 50N	121 10W
Klimovichi	54	53 36N	32 0 E
Klin	55	56 20N	36 48 E
Klinaklini →	108	51 21N	125 40W
Klintsey	54	52 50N	32 10 E
Klipplaat	92	33 0S	24 22 E
Klisura	43	42 40N	24 28 E
Klitmøller	49	57 3N	8 30 E
Kljajićevo	42	45 45N	19 17 E
Ključ	39	44 32N	16 48 E
Kłobuck	28	50 55N	18 55 E
Kłodawa	28	52 15N	18 55 E
Kłodzko	28	50 28N	16 38 E
Klondike	104	64 0N	139 26W
Klosi	44	41 28N	20 10 E
Klosterneuburg	27	48 18N	16 19 E
Klosters	25	46 52N	9 52 E
Klötze	24	52 38N	11 9 E
Klouto	85	6 57N	0 44 E
Kluane L.	104	61 15N	138 40W
Kluczbork	28	50 58N	18 12 E
Klyuchevskaya, Guba	59	55 50N	160 30 E
Knaresborough	12	54 1N	1 29W
Knee L., Man., Can.	109	55 3N	94 45W
Knee L., Sask., Can.	109	55 51N	107 0W
Kneïss, I.	83	34 22N	10 18 E
Knezha	43	43 30N	24 5 E
Knić	42	43 53N	20 45 E
Knight Inlet	108	50 45N	125 40W
Knighton	13	52 21N	3 2W
Knight's Landing	118	38 50N	121 43W
Knin	39	44 1N	16 17 E
Knittelfeld	26	47 13N	14 51 E
Knjaževac	42	43 35N	22 18 E
Knob, C.	96	34 32S	119 16 E
Knockmealdown Mts.	15	52 16N	8 0W
Knokke	16	51 20N	3 17 E
Knossos	45	35 16N	25 10 E
Knox	114	41 18N	86 36W
Knox, C.	108	54 11N	133 5W
Knox City	117	33 26N	99 49W
Knox Coast	5	66 30S	108 0 E
Knoxville, Iowa, U.S.A.	116	41 20N	93 5W
Knoxville, Tenn., U.S.A.	115	35 58N	83 57W
Knurów	27	50 13N	18 38 E
Knutshø	47	62 18N	9 41 E
Knysna	92	34 2S	23 2 E
Knyszyn	28	53 20N	22 56 E
Ko Chang	71	12 0N	102 20 E
Ko Kut	71	11 40N	102 32 E
Ko Phra Thong	71	9 6N	98 15 E
Ko Tao	71	10 6N	99 48 E
Koartac (Notre Dame de Koartac)	105	60 55N	69 40W
Koba, Aru, Indon.	73	6 37S	134 37 E
Koba, Bangka, Indon.	72	2 26S	106 14 E
Kobarid	39	46 15N	13 30 E
Kobayashi	74	31 56N	130 59 E
Kobdo = Hovd	75	48 2N	91 37 E
Kōbe	74	34 45N	135 10 E
Kobelyaki	56	49 11N	34 9 E
København	49	55 41N	12 34 E
Koblenz	25	50 21N	7 36 E
Kobo	87	12 2N	39 56 E
Kobrin	54	52 15N	24 22 E
Kobroor, Kepulauan	73	6 10S	134 30 E
Kobuleti	57	41 55N	41 45 E
Kobylin	28	51 43N	17 12 E
Kobyłka	28	52 21N	21 10 E
Kobylkino	55	54 8N	43 56 E
Kobylnik	54	54 58N	26 39 E
Kočane	42	43 12N	21 52 E
Kočani	42	41 55N	22 25 E
Koçarlı	45	37 45N	27 43 E
Koceljevo	42	44 28N	19 50 E
Kočevje	39	45 39N	14 50 E
Kochas	69	25 15N	83 56 E
Kocher →	25	49 14N	9 12 E
Kocheya	59	52 32N	120 42 E
Kōchi	74	33 30N	133 35 E
Kōchi □	74	33 40N	133 30 E
Kochiu = Gejiu	75	23 20N	103 10 E
Kock	28	51 38N	22 27 E
Koddiyar Bay	70	8 33N	81 15 E
Kodiak	104	57 30N	152 45W
Kodiak I.	104	57 30N	152 45W
Kodiang	71	6 21N	100 18 E
Kodinar	68	20 46N	70 46 E
Kodori →	57	42 47N	41 10 E
Koes	92	26 0S	19 15 E
Kofiau	73	1 11S	129 50 E
Köflach	26	47 4N	15 5 E
Koforidua	85	6 3N	0 17W
Kōfu	74	35 40N	138 30 E
Kogaluk →	107	56 12N	61 44W
Kogin Baba	85	7 55N	11 35 E
Koh-i-Bābā	65	34 30N	67 0 E
Kohat	66	33 40N	71 29 E
Kohima	67	25 35N	94 10 E
Kohler Ra.	5	77 0S	110 0W
Kohtla Järve	54	59 20N	27 20 E
Kojetin	27	49 21N	17 20 E
Koka	86	20 5N	30 35 E
Kokand	58	40 30N	70 57 E
Kokanee Glacier Prov. Park	108	49 47N	117 10W
Kokas	73	2 42S	132 26 E
Kokava	27	48 35N	19 50 E
Kokchetav	58	53 20N	69 25 E
Kokemäenjoki →	51	61 32N	21 44 E
Kokhma	55	56 55N	41 18 E
Kokkola (Gamlakarleby)	50	63 50N	23 8 E
Koko	85	11 28N	4 29 E
Koko Kyunzu	71	14 10N	93 25 E
Kokoda	98	8 54S	147 47 E
Kokolopozo	84	5 8N	6 5W
Kokomo	114	40 30N	86 6W
Kokonau	73	4 43S	136 26 E
Kokopo	98	4 22S	152 19 E
Kokoro	85	14 12N	0 55 E
Koksoak →	105	58 30N	68 10W
Kokstad	93	30 32S	29 29 E
Kokuora	59	71 35N	144 50 E
Kola, Indon.	73	5 35S	134 30 E
Kola, U.S.S.R.	52	68 45N	33 8 E
Kola Pen. = Kolskiy P-ov.	52	67 30N	38 0 E
Kolahun	84	8 15N	10 4W
Kolaka	73	4 3S	121 46 E
Kolar	70	13 12N	78 15 E
Kolar Gold Fields	70	12 58N	78 16 E
Kolari	50	67 20N	23 48 E
Kolarovgrad	43	43 18N	26 55 E
Kolašin	42	42 50N	19 31 E
Kolby Kås	49	55 48N	10 32 E
Kolchugino	55	56 17N	39 22 E
Kolda	84	12 55N	14 57W
Kolding	49	55 30N	9 29 E
Kole	88	3 16S	22 42 E
Koléa	82	36 38N	2 46 E
* Kolepom, Pulau	73	8 0S	138 30 E
Kolguyev, Ostrov	52	69 20N	48 30 E
Kolhapur	70	16 43N	74 15 E
Kolia	84	9 46N	6 28W
Kolín	26	50 2N	15 9 E
Kolind	49	56 21N	10 34 E
Kölleda	24	51 11N	11 14 E
Kollegal	70	12 9N	77 9 E
Kolleru L.	70	16 40N	81 10 E
Kolmanskop	92	26 45S	15 14 E
Köln	24	50 56N	6 58 E
Kolno	28	53 25N	21 56 E
Koło	28	52 14N	18 40 E
Kołobrzeg	28	54 10N	15 35 E
Kologriv	55	58 48N	44 25 E
Kolokani	84	13 35N	7 45W
Kolomna	55	55 8N	38 45 E
Kolomyya	56	48 31N	25 2 E
Kolondiéba	84	11 5N	6 54W
Kolonodale	73	2 3S	121 25 E
Kolosib	67	24 15N	92 45 E
Kolpashevo	58	58 20N	83 5 E
Kolpino	54	59 44N	30 39 E
Kolpny	55	52 12N	37 10 E
Kolskiy Poluostrov	52	67 30N	38 0 E
Kolskiy Zaliv	52	69 23N	34 0 E
Kolubara →	42	44 35N	20 15 E
Kolumna	28	51 36N	19 14 E
Koluszki	28	51 45N	19 46 E
Kolwezi	91	10 40S	25 25 E
Kolyberovo	55	55 15N	38 40 E
Kolyma →	59	69 30N	161 0 E
Kolymskoye, Okhotsko	59	63 0N	157 0 E
Kôm Ombo	86	24 25N	32 52 E
Komárno	27	47 49N	18 5
Komárom	27	47 43N	18 7
Komárom □	27	47 35N	18 20
Komarovo	54	58 38N	33 40
Komatipoort	93	25 25S	31 55
Kombissiri	85	12 4N	1 20
Kombori	84	13 26N	3 56
Kombóti	45	39 6N	21 5
Komen	39	45 49N	13 45
Komenda	85	5 4N	1 28
Komi A.S.S.R. □	52	64 0N	55 0
Komiža	39	43 3N	16 11
Komló	27	46 15N	18 16
Kommamur Canal	70	16 0N	80 25
Kommunarsk	57	48 30N	38 45
Kommunizma, Pik	58	39 0N	72 2
Komnes	47	59 30N	9 55
Komodo	73	8 37S	119 20
Komoé	84	5 12N	3 44
Komono	88	3 10S	13 20
Komoran, Pulau	73	8 18S	138 45
Komotini	44	41 9N	25 26
Komovi	42	42 41N	19 39
Kompong Cham	71	12 0N	105 30
Kompong Chhnang	71	12 20N	104 35
Kompong Speu	71	11 26N	104 32
Kompong Thom	71	12 35N	104 51
Komrat	56	46 18N	28 40
Komsberge	92	32 40S	20 45
Komsomolets, Ostrov	59	80 30N	95 0
Komsomolsk, R.S.F.S.R., U.S.S.R.	55	57 2N	40 20
Komsomolsk, R.S.F.S.R., U.S.S.R.	59	50 30N	137 0
Komsomolskaya	5	66 33S	93 1
Komsomolskiy	55	53 30N	49 30
Konakovo	55	56 52N	36 45
Konarhá □	65	35 30N	71 3
Konawa	117	34 59N	96 46
Kondagaon	70	19 35N	81 35
Kondakovo	59	69 36N	152 0
Konde	90	4 57S	39 45
Kondiá	44	39 49N	25 10
Kondoa	90	4 55S	35 50
Kondoa □	90	5 0S	36 0
Kondopaga	52	62 12N	34 17
Kondratyevo	59	57 22N	98 15
Konduga	85	11 35N	13 26
Konevo	52	62 8N	39 20
Kong	84	8 54N	4 36
Kong Christian IX.s Land	4	68 0N	36 0
Kong Christian X.s Land	4	74 0N	29 0
Kong Franz Joseph Fd.	4	73 20N	24 30
Kong Frederik IX.s Land	4	67 0N	52 0
Kong Frederik VI.s Kyst	4	63 0N	43 0
Kong Frederik VIII.s Land	4	78 30N	26 0
Kong, Koh	71	11 20N	103 0
Kong Oscar Fjord	4	72 20N	24 0
Konga	49	56 30N	15 6
Kongeå	49	55 24N	9 39
Kongju	76	36 30N	127 0
Konglu	67	27 13N	97 57
Kongolo, Kasai Or., Zaïre	90	5 26S	24 49
Kongolo, Shaba, Zaïre	90	5 22S	27 0
Kongor	81	7 1N	31 27
Kongoussi	85	13 19N	1 32
Kongsberg	47	59 39N	9 39
Kongsvinger	47	60 12N	12 2
Kongwa	90	6 11S	36 26
Koni	91	10 40S	27 11
Koni, Mts.	91	10 36S	27 10
Koniecpol	28	50 46N	19 40
Königsberg = Kaliningrad	54	54 42N	20 32
Königshofen	25	50 18N	10 29
Königslutter	24	52 14N	10 50
Königswusterhausen	24	52 19N	13 38
Konin	28	52 12N	18 15
Konin □	28	52 15N	18 30
Konispoli	44	39 42N	20 10
Kónitsa	44	40 5N	20 48
Konjic	42	43 42N	17 58
Konjice	39	46 20N	15 28
Konkouré →	84	9 50N	13 42
Könnern	24	51 40N	11 45
Konnur	70	16 14N	74 49
Kono	84	8 30N	11 5
Konongo	85	6 40N	1 15
Konosha	52	61 0N	40 5
Konotop	54	51 12N	33 7
Konqi He →	75	40 45N	90 10
Końskie	28	51 15N	20 23
Konsmo	47	58 16N	7 23
Konstantinovka	56	48 32N	37 39
Konstantinovski	57	47 33N	41 10
Konstantynów Łódźki	28	51 45N	19 20
Konstanz	25	47 39N	9 10
Kontagora	85	10 23N	5 27
Kontum	71	14 24N	108 0
Konya	64	37 52N	32 35
Konya Ovasi	64	38 30N	33 0
Konz	25	49 41N	6 36
Konza	90	1 45S	37 7
Koo-wee-rup	100	38 13S	145 28
Koolan I.	96	16 0S	123 45
Kooloonong	99	34 48S	143 10
Koondrook	99	35 33S	144 8
Koorawatha	99	34 2S	148 33
Kooskia	118	46 9N	115 59
Koostatak	109	51 26N	97 26
Kootenai →	118	49 15N	117 39
Kootenay L.	108	49 45N	116 50
Kootenay Nat. Park	108	51 0N	116 0
Kopanovka	57	47 28N	46 50
Kopaonik Planina	42	43 10N	21 50
Kopargaon	70	19 51N	74 28
Kópavogur	50	64 6N	21 55
Koper	39	45 31N	13 44
Kopervik	47	59 17N	5 17
Kopeysk	58	55 7N	61 37
Köping	48	59 31N	16 3
Kopiste	39	42 48N	16 42
Kopliku	44	42 15N	19 25

* *Renamed Yos Sudarso, P.*

öpmanholmen 48 63 10N 18 35 E
oppal 70 15 23N 76 5 E
oppang 47 61 34N 11 3 E
opparbergs län □ 48 61 20N 14 15 E
oppeh Dāgh 65 38 0N 58 0 E
opperå 47 63 24N 11 50 E
oppom 48 59 43N 12 10 E
oprivlen 43 41 36N 23 53 E
oprivnica 39 46 12N 16 45 E
oprivshtitsa 43 42 40N 24 19 E
opychintsy 54 49 7N 25 58 E
opys 54 54 20N 30 17 E
orab 42 41 44N 20 40 E
orakiána 44 39 42N 19 45 E
oraput 70 18 50N 82 40 E
orba 69 22 20N 82 45 E
orbach 24 51 17N 8 50 E
orça 44 40 37N 20 50 E
orça □ 44 40 40N 20 50 E
orčula 39 42 57N 17 8 E
orčulanski Kanal 39 43 3N 16 40 E
ordestan 64 35 30N 42 0 E
ordestān □ 64 36 0N 47 0 E
orea Bay 76 39 0N 124 0 E
oregaon 70 17 40N 74 10 E
orenevo 54 51 27N 34 55 E
orenovsk 57 45 30N 39 22 E
orets 54 50 40N 27 5 E
orgus 86 19 16N 33 29 E
orhogo 84 9 29N 5 28W
oribundu 84 7 41N 11 46W
orim 73 0 58 S 136 10 E
orinthia □ 45 37 50N 22 35 E
orinthiakós Kólpos 45 38 16N 22 30 E
órinthos 45 37 56N 22 55 E
orioumé 84 16 35N 3 0W
öriyama 74 37 24N 140 23 E
örmend 27 47 5N 16 35 E
ornat 39 43 50N 15 20 E
orneshty 56 47 21N 28 1 E
orneuburg 27 48 20N 16 20 E
ornsjø 47 58 57N 11 39 E
ornstad 47 62 59N 7 27 E
oro, Fiji 101 17 19 S 179 23 E
oro, Ivory C. 84 8 32N 7 30W
oro, Mali 84 14 1N 2 58W
oro Sea 101 17 30 S 179 45W
orocha 55 50 55N 37 30 E
orogwe 90 5 5 S 38 25 E
orogwe □ 90 5 0 S 38 20 E
oroit 99 38 18 S 142 24 E
oróni 45 36 48N 21 57 E
orónia, Limni 44 40 47N 23 37 E
oronis 45 37 12N 25 35 E
oronowo 28 53 19N 17 55 E
oror 73 7 20N 134 28 E
örös → 27 46 43N 20 12 E
öröstarcsa 27 46 53N 21 3 E
orosten 54 50 57N 28 25 E
orotoyak 55 51 1N 39 2 E
orraraika, Helodranon' i 93 17 45 S 43 57 E
orsakov 59 46 36N 142 42 E
orshunovo 59 58 37N 110 10 E
orsun Shevchenkovskiy 56 49 26N 31 16 E
orsze 28 54 11N 21 9 E
orti 86 18 6N 31 33 E
ortrijk 16 50 50N 3 17 E
orwai 68 24 7N 78 5 E
oryakskiy Khrebet 59 61 0N 171 0 E
os 45 36 50N 27 15 E
osa 87 7 50N 36 50 E
osaya Gora 55 54 10N 37 30 E
oschagyl 53 46 40N 54 0 E
ościan 28 52 5N 16 40 E
ościerzyna 28 54 8N 17 59 E
osciusko 117 33 3N 89 34W
osciusko I. 108 56 0N 133 40W
osciusko, Mt. 97 36 27 S 148 16 E
őszély → 27 47 25N 21 5 E
osgi 70 16 58N 77 43 E
osha 86 20 50N 30 30 E
'oshih = Kashi 75 39 30N 76 2 E
oshk-e Kohneh 65 34 55N 62 30 E
osi 68 27 48N 77 29 E
osi-meer 93 27 0 S 32 50 E
ošice 27 48 42N 21 15 E
osjerić 42 44 0N 19 55 E
oslan 52 63 28N 48 52 E
osŏng 76 38 40N 128 22 E
osovo, Pokrajina 42 42 40N 21 5 E
osovo, Soc. Aut. Pokrajina □ 42 42 30N 21 0 E
osovska-Mitrovica 42 42 54N 20 52 E
ostajnica 39 45 17N 16 30 E
ostamuksa 52 62 34N 32 44 E
ostanjevica 39 45 51N 15 27 E
ostelec 27 50 14N 16 35 E
ostenets 43 42 15N 23 52 E
oster 92 25 52 S 26 54 E
ostí 87 13 8N 32 43 E
ostolac 42 44 37N 21 15 E
ostopol 54 50 51N 26 22 E
ostroma 55 57 50N 40 58 E
ostromskoye Vdkhr. 55 57 52N 40 49 E
ostrzyn, Poland 28 52 24N 17 14 E
ostrzyn, Poland 28 52 35N 14 39 E
ostyukovichi 54 53 20N 32 4 E
oszalin 28 53 50N 16 8 E
oszalin □ 28 53 40N 16 10 E
őszeg 27 47 23N 16 33 E
ot Adu 68 30 30N 71 0 E
ot Moman 68 32 13N 73 0 E
ota 68 25 14N 75 49 E
ota Baharu 71 6 7N 102 14 E
ota Belud 72 6 21N 116 26 E
ota Kinabalu 72 6 0N 116 4 E
ota Tinggi 71 1 44N 103 53 E
otaagung 72 5 38 S 104 29 E
otabaru 72 3 20 S 116 20 E
otabumi 72 4 49 S 104 54 E
otagede 73 7 54 S 110 26 E
otamobagu 73 0 57N 124 31 E
otaneelee → 108 60 11N 123 42W
Kotawaringin 72 2 28 S 111 27 E
Kotcho L. 108 59 7N 121 12W
Kotel 43 42 52N 26 26 E
Kotelnich 55 58 20N 48 10 E
Kotelnikovo 57 47 38N 43 8 E
Kotelnyy, Ostrov 59 75 10N 139 0 E
Kothagudam 70 17 30N 80 40 E
Kothapet 70 19 21N 79 28 E
Köthen 24 51 44N 11 59 E
Kothi 69 24 45N 80 40 E
Kotiro 68 26 17N 67 13 E
Kotka 51 60 28N 26 58 E
Kotlas 52 61 15N 47 0 E
Kotlenska Planina 43 42 56N 26 30 E
Kotli 66 33 30N 73 55 E
Kotonkoro 85 11 3N 5 58 E
Kotor 42 42 25N 18 47 E
Kotor Varoš 42 44 38N 17 22 E
Kotoriba 39 46 23N 16 48 E
Kotovo 55 50 22N 44 45 E
Kotovsk 56 47 45N 29 35 E
Kotputli 68 27 43N 76 12 E
Kotri 68 25 22N 68 22 E
Kotri → 70 19 15N 80 35 E
Kótronas 45 36 38N 22 29 E
Kötschach-Mauthen 26 46 41N 13 1 E
Kottayam 70 9 35N 76 33 E
Kottur 70 10 34N 76 56 E
Kotuy → 59 71 54N 102 6 E
Kotzebue 104 66 50N 162 40W
Kouango 88 5 0N 20 10 E
Koudougou 84 12 10N 2 20W
Koufonísi 45 34 56N 26 8 E
Koufonísia 45 36 57N 25 35 E
Kougaberge 92 33 48 S 23 50 E
Kouibli 84 7 15N 7 14W
Kouilou → 88 4 10 S 12 5 E
Kouki 88 7 22N 17 3 E
Koula Moutou 88 1 15 S 12 25 E
Koulen 71 13 50N 104 40 E
Koulikoro 84 12 40N 7 50W
Koumala 98 21 38 S 149 15 E
Koumankou 84 11 58N 6 6W
Koumbia, Guin. 84 11 48N 13 29W
Koumbia, Upp. Vol. 84 11 10N 3 50W
Koumboum 84 10 25N 13 0W
Koumpenntoum 84 13 59N 14 34W
Koumra 81 8 50N 17 35 E
Koundara 84 12 29N 13 18W
Kounradskiy 58 46 59N 75 0 E
Kountze 117 30 20N 94 22W
Koupéla 85 12 11N 0 21W
Kourizo, Passe de 83 22 28N 15 27 E
Kouroussa 84 10 45N 9 45W
Koussané 84 14 53N 11 14W
Kousseri 81 12 0N 14 55 E
Koutiala 84 12 25N 5 23W
Kouto 84 9 53N 6 25W
Kouvé 85 6 25N 1 25 E
Kovačica 42 45 5N 20 38 E
Kovdor 52 67 34N 30 24 E
Kovel 54 51 10N 24 20 E
Kovilpatti 70 9 10N 77 50 E
Kovin 42 44 44N 20 59 E
Kovrov 55 56 25N 41 25 E
Kovur, Andhra Pradesh, India 70 17 3N 81 39 E
Kovur, Andhra Pradesh, India 70 14 30N 80 1 E
Kowal 28 52 32N 19 7 E
Kowalewo Pomorskie 28 53 10N 18 52 E
Kowkash 106 50 20N 87 12W
Kowloon 75 22 20N 114 15 E
Koyabuti 73 2 36 S 140 37 E
Koyan, Pegunungan 72 3 15N 114 30 E
Koyuk 104 64 55N 161 20W
Koyukuk → 104 64 56N 157 30W
Koyulhisar 56 40 20N 37 52 E
Koza 77 26 19N 127 46 E
Kozan 64 37 35N 35 50 E
Kozáni 44 40 19N 21 47 E
Kozáni □ 44 40 18N 21 45 E
Kozara 39 45 0N 17 0 E
Kozarac 39 44 58N 16 48 E
Kozelsk 54 54 2N 35 48 E
Kozhikode = Calicut 70 11 15N 75 43 E
Kozhva 52 65 10N 57 0 E
Koziegłowy 28 50 37N 19 8 E
Kozienice 28 51 35N 21 34 E
Kozje 39 46 5N 15 35 E
Kozle 28 50 20N 18 8 E
Kozloduy 43 43 45N 23 42 E
Kozlovets 43 43 30N 25 20 E
Koźmin 28 51 48N 17 27 E
Kozmodemyansk 55 56 20N 46 36 E
Kozuchów 28 51 45N 15 31 E
Kpabia 85 9 10N 0 20W
Kpalimé 85 6 57N 0 44 E
Kpandae 85 8 30N 0 2W
Kpessi 85 8 4N 1 16 E
Kra Buri 71 10 22N 98 46 E
Kra, Isthmus of = Kra, Kho Khot 71 10 15N 99 30 E
Kra, Kho Khot 71 10 15N 99 30 E
Kragan 73 6 43 S 111 38 E
Kragerø 47 58 52N 9 25 E
Kragujevac 42 44 2N 20 56 E
Krajenka 28 53 18N 16 59 E
Krakatau = Rakata, Pulau 72 6 10 S 105 20 E
Kraków 27 50 4N 19 57 E
Kraków □ 27 50 0N 20 0 E
Kraksaan 73 7 43 S 113 23 E
Kråkstad 47 59 39N 10 55 E
Králiky 27 50 6N 16 45 E
Kraljevo 42 43 44N 20 41 E
Kralovice 26 49 59N 13 29 E
Královský Chlmec 27 48 27N 22 0 E
Kralupy 26 50 13N 14 20 E
Kramatorsk 56 48 50N 37 30 E
Kramer 119 35 0N 117 38W
Kramfors 48 62 55N 17 48 E
Kramis, C. 82 36 26N 0 45 E
Krångede 48 63 9N 16 10 E
Kraniá 44 39 53N 21 18 E
Kranidhion 45 37 20N 23 10 E
Kranj 39 46 16N 14 22 E
Kranjska Gora 39 46 29N 13 48 E
Krapina 39 46 10N 15 52 E
Krapina → 39 45 50N 15 50 E
Krapivna 55 53 58N 37 10 E
Krapkowice 28 50 29N 17 56 E
Krasavino 52 60 58N 46 29 E
Kraskino 59 42 44N 130 48 E
Kraslice 26 50 19N 12 31 E
Krasnaya Gorbatka 55 55 52N 41 45 E
Krasnaya Polyana 57 43 40N 40 13 E
Kraśnik 28 50 55N 22 5 E
Kraśnik Fabryczny 28 50 58N 22 11 E
Krasnoarmeisk 56 48 18N 37 11 E
Krasnoarmeysk, R.S.F.S.R., U.S.S.R. 55 51 0N 45 42 E
Krasnoarmeysk, R.S.F.S.R., U.S.S.R. 57 48 30N 44 25 E
Krasnodar 57 45 5N 39 0 E
Krasnodon 57 48 17N 39 44 E
Krasnodonetskaya 57 48 5N 40 50 E
Krasnogorskiy 55 56 10N 48 28 E
Krasnograd 56 49 27N 35 27 E
Krasnogvardeyskoye 57 45 52N 41 33 E
Krasnogvardyesk 56 45 32N 34 16 E
Krasnokamsk 52 58 4N 55 48 E
Krasnokutsk 54 50 10N 34 50 E
Krasnoperekopsk 56 46 0N 33 54 E
Krasnoselkupsk 58 65 20N 82 10 E
Krasnoslobodsk, R.S.F.S.R., U.S.S.R. 55 54 25N 43 45 E
Krasnoslobodsk, R.S.F.S.R., U.S.S.R. 57 48 42N 44 33 E
Krasnoturinsk 58 59 46N 60 12 E
Krasnoufimsk 52 56 57N 57 46 E
Krasnouralsk 52 58 21N 60 3 E
Krasnovishersk 52 60 23N 57 3 E
Krasnovodsk 53 40 0N 52 52 E
Krasnoyarsk 59 56 8N 93 0 E
Krasnoye, Kalmyk A.S.S.R., U.S.S.R. 57 46 16N 45 0 E
Krasnoye, R.S.F.S.R., U.S.S.R. 55 59 15N 47 40 E
Krasnoye = Krasnyy 54 54 25N 31 30 E
Krasnozavodsk 55 56 27N 38 25 E
Krasny Liman 56 48 58N 37 50 E
Krasny Sulin 57 47 52N 40 8 E
Krasnystaw 28 50 57N 23 5 E
Krasnyy 54 54 25N 31 30 E
Krasnyy Kholm 55 58 10N 37 10 E
Krasnyy Kut 55 50 50N 47 0 E
Krasnyy Luch 57 48 13N 39 0 E
Krasnyy Profintern 55 57 45N 40 27 E
Krasnyy Yar, Kalmyk A.S.S.R., U.S.S.R. 57 46 43N 48 23 E
Krasnyy Yar, R.S.F.S.R., U.S.S.R. 55 53 30N 50 22 E
Krasnyy Yar, R.S.F.S.R., U.S.S.R. 55 50 42N 44 45 E
Krasnyye Baki 55 57 8N 45 10 E
Krasnyyoskolskoye Vdkhr. 56 49 30N 37 30 E
Kraszna → 27 48 0N 22 20 E
Kratie 71 12 32N 106 10 E
Kratovo 42 42 6N 22 10 E
Krau 73 3 19 S 140 5 E
Kravanh, Chuor Phnum 71 12 0N 103 32 E
Krawang 73 6 19N 107 18 E
Krefeld 24 51 20N 6 32 E
Krémaston, Límni 45 38 52N 21 30 E
Kremenchug 56 49 5N 33 25 E
Kremenchugskoye Vdkhr. 56 49 20N 32 30 E
Kremenets 56 50 8N 25 43 E
Kremenica 42 40 55N 21 25 E
Kremennaya 56 49 1N 38 10 E
Kremges = Svetlovodsk 56 49 5N 33 15 E
Kremikovtsi 43 42 46N 23 28 E
Kremmen 24 52 45N 13 1 E
Kremmling 118 40 10N 106 30W
Kremnica 27 48 45N 18 50 E
Krems 26 48 25N 15 36 E
Kremsmünster 26 48 3N 14 8 E
Kretinga 54 55 53N 21 15 E
Krettamia 82 28 47N 3 27W
Krettsy 54 58 15N 32 30 E
Kreuzberg 25 50 22N 9 58 E
Kribi 88 2 57N 9 56 E
Krichem 43 42 8N 24 28 E
Krichev 54 53 45N 31 50 E
Krim 39 45 53N 14 30 E
Krionéri 45 38 20N 21 35 E
Krishna → 70 15 57N 80 59 E
Krishnagiri 70 12 32N 78 16 E
Krishnanagar 69 23 24N 88 33 E
Krishnaraja Sagara 70 12 20N 76 30 E
Kristiansand 47 58 9N 8 1 E
Kristianstad 49 56 2N 14 9 E
Kristiansund 47 63 7N 7 45 E
Kristiinankaupunki 50 62 16N 21 21 E
Kristinehamn 48 59 18N 14 13 E
Kristinestad 50 62 16N 21 21 E
Kriti 45 35 15N 25 0 E
Kritsá 45 35 10N 25 41 E
Kriva → 42 42 5N 21 47 E
Kriva Palanka 42 42 11N 22 19 E
Krivaja → 42 44 27N 18 9 E
Krivelj 42 44 8N 22 5 E
Krivoy Rog 56 47 51N 33 20 E
Križevci 39 46 3N 16 32 E
Krk 39 45 8N 14 40 E
Krka → 39 45 50N 15 30 E
Krkonoše 26 50 50N 15 35 E
Krnov 27 50 5N 17 40 E
Krobia 28 51 47N 16 59 E
Kročehlavy 26 50 8N 14 9 E
Krøderen 47 60 9N 9 49 E
Krokawo 28 54 47N 18 9 E
Krokeaí 45 36 53N 22 32 E
Krokom 48 63 20N 14 30 E
Krolevets 54 51 35N 33 20 E
Kroměríz 27 49 18N 17 21 E
Krompachy 27 48 54N 20 52 E
Kromy 54 52 40N 35 48 E
Kronach 25 50 14N 11 19 E
Kronobergs län □ 49 56 45N 14 30 E
Kronprins Olav Kyst 5 69 0 S 42 0 E
Kronprinsesse Märtha Kyst 5 73 30 S 10 0 E
Kronshtadt 54 60 5N 29 45 E
Kroonstad 92 27 43 S 27 19 E
Kröpelin 24 54 4N 11 48 E
Kropotkin, R.S.F.S.R., U.S.S.R. 57 45 28N 40 28 E
Kropotkin, R.S.F.S.R., U.S.S.R. 59 59 0N 115 30 E
Kropp 24 54 24N 9 32 E
Krościenko 27 49 29N 20 25 E
Krośniewice 28 52 15N 19 11 E
Krosno 27 49 42N 21 46 E
Krosno □ 27 49 35N 22 0 E
Krosno Odrzańskie 28 52 3N 15 7 E
Krotoszyn 28 51 42N 17 23 E
Krraba 44 41 13N 20 0 E
Krško 39 45 57N 15 30 E
Krstača 42 42 57N 20 8 E
Kruger Nat. Park 93 24 0 S 31 40 E
Krugersdorp 93 26 5 S 27 46 E
Kruis, Kaap 92 21 55 S 13 57 E
Kruja 44 41 32N 19 46 E
Krulevshchina 54 55 5N 27 45 E
Kruma 44 42 14N 20 28 E
Krumbach 25 48 15N 10 22 E
Krumovgrad 43 41 29N 25 38 E
Krung Thep 71 13 45N 100 35 E
Krupanj 42 44 25N 19 22 E
Krupina 27 48 22N 19 5 E
Krupinica → 27 48 15N 18 52 E
Kruševac 42 43 35N 21 28 E
Kruševo 42 41 23N 21 19 E
Kruszwica 28 52 40N 18 20 E
Kruzof I. 108 57 10N 135 40W
Krylbo 48 60 7N 16 15 E
Krymsk Abinsk 56 44 50N 38 0 E
Krymskiy P-ov. 56 45 0N 34 0 E
Krynica 27 49 25N 20 57 E
Krynica Morska 28 54 23N 19 28 E
Krynki 28 53 17N 23 43 E
Krzepice 28 50 58N 18 50 E
Krzeszów 28 50 24N 22 21 E
Krzeszowice 27 50 8N 19 37 E
Krzna → 28 51 59N 22 47 E
Krzywiń 28 51 58N 16 50 E
Krzyz 28 52 52N 16 0 E
Ksabi 82 32 51N 4 13W
Ksar Chellala 82 35 13N 2 19 E
Ksar el Boukhari 82 35 51N 2 52 E
Ksar el Kebir 82 35 0N 6 0W
Ksar es Souk = Ar Rachidiya 82 31 58N 4 20W
Ksar Rhilane 83 33 0N 9 39 E
Ksiba, El 82 32 46N 6 0W
Ksour, Mts. des 82 32 45N 0 30W
Kstovo 55 56 12N 44 13 E
Kuala 72 2 55N 105 47 E
Kuala Kangsar 71 4 46N 100 56 E
Kuala Kerai 71 5 30N 102 12 E
Kuala Kubu Baharu 71 3 34N 101 39 E
Kuala Lipis 71 4 10N 102 3 E
Kuala Lumpur 71 3 9N 101 41 E
Kuala Sedili Besar 71 1 55N 104 5 E
Kuala Terengganu 72 5 20N 103 8 E
Kualakapuas 72 2 55 S 114 20 E
Kualakurun 72 1 10 S 113 50 E
Kualapembuang 72 3 14 S 112 38 E
Kualasimpang 72 4 17N 98 3 E
Kuandang 73 0 56N 123 1 E
Kuandian 76 40 45N 124 45 E
Kuangchou = Guangzhou 75 23 5N 113 10 E
Kuantan 71 3 49N 103 20 E
Kuba 57 41 21N 48 32 E
Kubak 66 27 10N 63 10 E
Kuban → 56 45 20N 37 30 E
Kubenskoye, Oz. 55 59 40N 39 25 E
Kuberle 57 47 0N 42 20 E
Kubrat 43 43 49N 26 31 E
Kučevo 42 44 30N 21 40 E
Kuchaman 68 27 13N 74 47 E
Kuchenspitze 26 47 7N 10 12 E
Kuching 72 1 33N 110 25 E
Kuçove = Qytet Stalin 44 40 47N 19 57 E
Kücük Kuyu 44 39 35N 26 27 E
Kudalier → 70 18 35N 79 48 E
Kudat 72 6 55N 116 55 E
Kudremukh, Mt. 70 13 15N 75 20 E
Kudus 73 6 48 S 110 51 E
Kudymkar 58 59 1N 54 39 E
Kueiyang = Guiyang 75 26 32N 106 40 E
Kufrinjah 62 32 20N 35 41 E
Kufstein 26 47 35N 12 11 E
Kugong I. 106 56 18N 79 50W
Kūh-e 'Alijūq 65 31 30N 51 41 E
Kūh-e Dīnār 65 30 40N 51 0 E
Kūh-e-Hazārān 65 29 35N 57 20 E
Kūh-e-Jebāl Bārez 65 29 0N 58 0 E
Kūh-e Sorkh 65 35 30N 58 45 E
Kūh-e Taftān 65 28 40N 61 0 E
Kūhak 65 27 12N 63 10 E
Kūhhā-ye-Bashākerd 65 26 45N 59 0 E
Kūhhā-ye Sabalān 64 38 15N 47 45 E
Kuhnsdorf 26 46 37N 14 38 E
Kūhpāyeh 65 32 44N 52 20 E
Kuile He → 76 49 32N 124 42 E
Kuito 89 12 22 S 16 55 E
Kukavica 42 42 48N 21 57 E
Kukawa 85 12 58N 13 27 E
Kukësi 44 42 5N 20 20 E
Kukësi □ 44 42 25N 20 15 E
Kukmor 55 56 11N 50 54 E
Kukvidze 55 50 40N 43 15 E
Kula, Bulg. 42 43 52N 22 36 E
Kula, Yugo. 42 45 37N 19 32 E
Kulai 71 1 44N 103 35 E
Kulal, Mt. 90 2 42N 36 57 E
Kulaly, O. 57 45 0N 50 0 E
Kulasekharapattanam 70 8 20N 78 0 E
Kuldiga 54 56 58N 21 59 E
Kuldja = Yining 75 43 58N 81 10 E
Kuldu 87 12 50N 28 30 E
Kulebaki 55 55 22N 42 25 E
Kulen Vakuf 39 44 35N 16 2 E

Kuli 57 42 2N 47 12 E
Küllük 45 37 12N 27 36 E
Kulm 116 46 22N 98 58W
Kulmbach 25 50 6N 11 27 E
Kulsary 58 46 59N 54 1 E
Kultay 57 45 5N 51 40 E
Kulti 69 23 43N 86 50 E
Kulunda 58 52 35N 78 57 E
Kulwin 99 35 0S 142 42 E
Kulyab 58 37 55N 69 50 E
Kum Tekei 58 43 10N 79 30 E
Kuma → 57 44 55N 47 0 E
Kumaganum 85 13 8N 10 38 E
Kumagaya 74 36 9N 139 22 E
Kumai 72 2 44 S 111 43 E
Kumamba, Kepulauan 73 1 36 S 138 45 E
Kumamoto 74 32 45N 130 45 E
Kumamoto □ 74 32 55N 130 55 E
Kumanovo 42 42 9N 21 42 E
Kumara 101 42 37 S 171 12 E
Kumasi 84 6 41N 1 38W
Kumba 88 4 36N 9 24 E
Kumbakonam 70 10 58N 79 25 E
Kumbarilla 99 27 15 S 150 55 E
Kumbo 85 6 15N 10 36 E
Kumbukkan Oya → 70 6 35N 81 40 E
Kumeny 55 58 10N 49 47 E
Kumertau 52 52 46N 55 47 E
Kumi 90 1 30N 33 58 E
Kumkale 44 40 0N 26 13 E
Kumla 48 59 8N 15 10 E
Kummerower See 24 53 47N 12 52 E
Kumo 85 10 1N 11 12 E
Kumon Bum 67 26 30N 97 15 E
Kumta 70 14 29N 74 25 E
Kumtorkala 57 43 2N 46 50 E
Kumylzhenskaya 57 49 51N 42 38 E
Kunágota 27 46 26N 21 3 E
Kunama 99 35 35 S 148 4 E
Kunashir, Ostrov 59 44 0N 146 0 E
Kunch 68 26 0N 79 10 E
Kunda 54 59 30N 26 34 E
Kundiawa 98 6 2 S 145 1 E
Kundla 68 21 21N 71 25 E
Kungala 99 29 58 S 153 7 E
Kungälv 49 57 53N 11 59 E
Kunghit I. 108 52 6N 131 3W
Kungrad 58 43 6N 58 54 E
Kungsbacka 49 57 30N 12 5 E
Kungur 52 57 25N 56 57 E
Kungurri 98 21 3 S 148 46 E
Kunhegyes 27 47 22N 20 36 E
Kuningan 73 6 59 S 108 29 E
Kunlong 67 23 20N 98 50 E
Kunlun Shan 75 36 0N 85 0 E
Kunmadaras 27 47 28N 20 45 E
Kunming 75 25 1N 102 41 E
Kunnamkulam 70 10 38N 76 7 E
Kunsan 76 35 59N 126 45 E
Kunshan 77 31 22N 120 58 E
Kunszentmárton 27 46 50N 20 20 E
Kununurra 96 15 40 S 128 50 E
Kunwarara 98 22 55 S 150 9 E
Kunya-Urgenoh 58 42 19N 59 10 E
Künzelsau 25 49 17N 9 41 E
Kuopio 50 62 53N 27 35 E
Kuopion lääni □ 50 63 25N 27 10 E
Kupa → 39 45 28N 16 24 E
Kupang 73 10 19 S 123 39 E
Kupres 42 44 1N 17 15 E
Kupyansk 56 49 52N 37 35 E
Kupyansk-Uzlovoi 56 49 45N 37 34 E
Kuqa 75 41 35N 82 30 E
Kura → 57 39 50N 49 20 E
Kuranda 98 16 48 S 145 35 E
Kurashiki 74 34 40N 133 50 E
Kurayoshi 74 35 26N 133 50 E
Kurduvadi 70 18 8N 75 29 E
Kŭrdzhali 43 41 38N 25 21 E
Kure 74 34 14N 132 32 E
Kuressaare = Kingisepp 54 58 15N 22 15 E
Kurgaldzhino 58 50 35N 70 20 E
Kurgan 58 55 26N 65 18 E
Kurganinsk 57 44 54N 40 34 E
Kurgannaya = Kurganinsk 57 44 54N 40 34 E
Kuria Maria I. = Khūryān Mūryān, Jazā 'ir 63 17 30N 55 58 E
Kurichchi 70 11 36N 77 35 E
Kuridala P.O 98 21 16 S 140 29 E
Kuril Is. = Kurilskiye Os. 59 45 0N 150 0 E
Kuril Trench 94 44 0N 153 0 E
Kurilsk 59 45 14N 147 53 E
Kurilskiye Ostrova 59 45 0N 150 0 E
Kuring Kuru 92 17 42 S 18 32 E
Kurkur 86 23 50N 32 0 E
Kurkūrah 83 31 30N 20 1 E
Kurla 70 19 5N 72 52 E
Kurlovskiy 55 55 25N 40 40 E
Kurmuk 87 10 33N 34 21 E
Kurnool 70 15 45N 78 0 E
Kurovskoye 55 55 35N 38 55 E
Kurow 101 44 44 S 170 29 E
Kurów 28 51 23N 22 12 E
Kurrajong 99 33 33 S 150 42 E
Kurri Kurri 99 32 50 S 151 28 E
Kursavka 57 44 29N 42 32 E
Kuršenai 54 56 1N 23 3 E
Kurseong 69 26 56N 88 18 E
Kursk 55 51 42N 36 11 E
Kuršumlija 42 43 9N 21 19 E
Kuršumlijska Banja 42 43 3N 21 11 E
Kuru (Chel), Bahr el 87 8 10N 26 50 E
Kuruktag 75 41 0N 89 0 E
Kuruman 92 27 28 S 23 28 E
Kurume 74 33 15N 130 30 E
Kurunegala 70 7 30N 80 23 E
Kurya 59 61 15N 108 10 E
Kuşada Körfezı 45 37 56N 27 0 E
Kuşadası 45 37 52N 27 15 E
Kusawa L. 108 60 20N 136 13W
Kusel 25 49 31N 7 25 E
Kushchevskaya 57 46 33N 39 35 E
Kushiro 74 43 0N 144 25 E
Kushiro → 74 42 59N 144 23 E
Kushka 58 35 20N 62 18 E
Kushtia 69 23 55N 89 5 E
Kushum → 57 49 0N 50 20 E
Kushva 52 58 18N 59 45 E
Kuskokwim → 104 60 17N 162 27W
Kuskokwim Bay 104 59 50N 162 56W
Kussharo-Ko 74 43 38N 144 21 E
Kustanay 58 53 10N 63 35 E
Kütahya 64 39 30N 30 2 E
Kutaisi 57 42 19N 42 40 E
Kutaraja = Banda Aceh 72 5 35N 95 20 E
Kutch, G. of 68 22 50N 69 15 E
Kutch, Rann of 68 24 0N 70 0 E
Kutina 39 45 29N 16 48 E
Kutiyana 68 21 36N 70 2 E
Kutjevo 42 45 23N 17 55 E
Kutkashen 57 40 58N 47 47 E
Kutná Hora 26 49 57N 15 16 E
Kutno 28 52 15N 19 23 E
Kuttabul 98 21 5 S 148 48 E
Kutu 88 2 40 S 18 11 E
Kutum 87 14 10N 24 40 E
Kúty 27 48 40N 17 3 E
Kuvshinovo 54 57 2N 34 11 E
Kuwait = Al Kuwayt 64 29 30N 47 30 E
Kuwait ■ 64 29 30N 47 30 E
Kuwana 74 35 0N 136 43 E
Kuybyshev 58 55 27N 78 19 E
Kuybyshev 58 53 8N 50 6 E
Kuybyshevskoye Vdkhr. 55 55 2N 49 30 E
Kūysanjaq 64 36 5N 44 38 E
Kuyto, Oz. 52 64 40N 31 0 E
Kuyumba 59 60 58N 96 59 E
Kuzey Anadolu Dağlari 64 41 30N 35 0 E
Kuzhithura 70 8 18N 77 11 E
Kuzmin 42 45 2N 19 25 E
Kuznetsk 55 53 12N 46 40 E
Kuzomen 52 66 22N 36 50 E
Kvænangen 50 70 5N 21 15 E
Kvam 47 61 40N 9 42 E
Kvamsøy 47 61 7N 6 28 E
Kvareli 57 41 27N 45 47 E
Kvarner 39 44 50N 14 10 E
Kvarnerič 39 44 43N 14 37 E
Kvernes 47 63 1N 7 44 E
Kvillsfors 49 57 24N 15 29 E
Kvine → 47 58 17N 6 56 E
Kvinesdal 47 58 19N 6 57 E
Kviteseid 47 59 24N 8 29 E
Kwabhaga 93 30 51 S 29 0 E
Kwadacha → 108 57 28N 125 38W
Kwakhanai 92 21 39 S 21 16 E
Kwakoegron 127 5 12N 55 25W
Kwale, Kenya 90 4 15 S 39 31 E
Kwale, Nigeria 85 5 46N 6 26 E
Kwale □ 90 4 15 S 39 10 E
Kwamouth 88 3 9 S 16 12 E
Kwando → 92 18 27 S 23 32 E
Kwangsi-Chuang = Guangxi Zhuangzu □ 75 24 0N 109 0 E
Kwangtung = Guangdong □ 75 23 0N 113 0 E
Kwara □ 85 8 0N 5 0 E
Kwataboahegan → 106 51 9N 80 50W
Kwatisore 73 3 18 S 134 50 E
Kweichow = Guizhou □ 75 27 0N 107 0 E
Kwidzyn 28 53 44N 18 55 E
Kwiguk 104 63 45N 164 35W
Kwimba □ 90 3 0S 33 0 E
Kwinana 96 32 15 S 115 47 E
Kwisa → 28 51 34N 15 24 E
Kwoka 73 0 31 S 132 27 E
Kyabé 81 9 30N 19 0 E
Kyabra Cr. → 99 25 36 S 142 55 E
Kyabram 99 36 19 S 145 4 E
Kyaikto 71 17 20N 97 3 E
Kyakhta 59 50 30N 106 25 E
Kyangin 67 18 20N 95 20 E
Kyaukpadaung 67 20 52N 95 8 E
Kyaukpyu 67 19 28N 93 30 E
Kyaukse 67 21 36N 96 10 E
Kyenjojo 90 0 40N 30 37 E
Kyle Dam 91 20 15 S 31 0 E
Kyle of Lochalsh 14 57 17N 5 43W
Kyll → 25 49 48N 6 42 E
Kyllburg 25 50 2N 6 35 E
Kyneton 99 37 10 S 144 29 E
Kynuna 98 21 37 S 141 55 E
Kyō-ga-Saki 74 35 45N 135 15 E
Kyoga, L. 90 1 35N 33 0 E
Kyogle 99 28 40 S 153 0 E
Kyongju 76 35 51N 129 14 E
Kyongpyaw 67 17 12N 95 10 E
Kyōto 74 35 0N 135 45 E
Kyōto □ 74 35 15N 135 45 E
Kyren 59 51 45N 101 45 E
Kyrenia 64 35 20N 33 20 E
Kyritz 24 52 57N 12 25 E
Kystatyam 59 67 20N 123 10 E
Kytal Ktakh 59 65 30N 123 40 E
Kyulyunken 59 64 10N 137 5 E
Kyunhla 67 23 25N 95 15 E
Kyuquot 108 50 3N 127 25W
Kyurdamir 57 40 25N 48 3 E
Kyūshū 74 33 0N 131 0 E
Kyūshū-Sanchi 74 32 35N 131 17 E
Kyustendil 42 42 16N 22 41 E
Kyusyur 59 70 39N 127 15 E
Kywong 99 34 58 S 146 44 E
Kyzyl 59 51 50N 94 30 E
Kyzyl-Kiya 58 40 16N 72 8 E
Kyzylkum, Peski 58 42 30N 65 0 E
Kzyl-Orda 58 44 48N 65 28 E

L

Laa 27 48 43N 16 23 E
Laaber → 25 49 0N 12 3 E
Laage 24 53 55N 12 21 E
Laasphe 24 50 56N 8 23 E
Laba → 57 45 11N 39 42 E
Labastide 20 43 28N 2 39 E
Labastide-Murat 20 44 39N 1 33 E
Labbézenga 85 15 2N 0 48 E
Labdah = Leptis Magna 83 32 40N 14 12 E
Labé 84 11 24N 12 16W
Labe = Elbe → 26 50 50N 14 12 E
Laberec → 27 48 37N 21 58 E
Laberge, L. 108 61 11N 135 12W
Labin 39 45 5N 14 8 E
Labinsk 57 44 40N 40 48 E
Labis 71 2 22N 103 2 E
Labiszyn 28 52 57N 17 54 E
Laboe 24 54 25N 10 13 E
Labouheyre 20 44 13N 0 55W
Laboulaye 124 34 10 S 63 30W
Labra, Peña 30 43 3N 4 26W
Labrador City 107 52 57N 66 55W
Labrador, Coast of □ 105 53 20N 61 0W
Lábrea 126 7 15 S 64 51W
Labrède 20 44 41N 0 32W
Labuan 72 5 21N 115 13 E
Labuha 73 0 30 S 127 30 E
Labuhan 73 6 26 S 105 50 E
Labuhanbajo 73 8 28 S 120 1 E
Labuk, Telok 72 6 10N 117 50 E
Labytnangi 58 66 39N 66 21 E
Łabżenica 28 53 18N 17 15 E
Lac Allard 107 50 33N 63 24W
Lac Bouchette 107 48 16N 72 11W
Lac du Flambeau 116 46 1N 89 51W
Lac Édouard 106 47 40N 72 16W
Lac la Biche 108 54 45N 111 58W
Lac la Martre 104 63 8N 117 16W
Lac-Mégantic 107 45 35N 70 53W
Lac Seul 109 50 28N 92 0W
Lacanau, Étang de 20 44 58N 1 7W
Lacanau-Médoc 20 44 59N 1 5W
Lacantúm → 120 16 36N 90 40W
Lacara → 31 38 55N 6 25W
Lacaune 20 43 43N 2 40 E
Lacaune, Mts. de 20 43 43N 2 50 E
Laccadive Is. = Lakshadweep Is. 60 10 0N 72 30 E
Lacepede B. 99 36 40 S 139 40 E
Lacepede Is. 96 16 55 S 122 0 E
Lacerdónia 91 18 3 S 35 35 E
Lachine 106 45 30N 73 40W
Lachlan → 97 34 22 S 143 55 E
Lachmangarh 68 27 50N 75 4 E
Lachute 106 45 39N 74 21W
Lackawanna 114 42 49N 78 50W
Lacolle 113 45 5N 73 22W
Lacombe 108 52 30N 113 44W
Lacona 113 43 37N 76 5W
Láconi 40 39 54N 9 4 E
Laconia 114 43 32N 71 30W
Lacq 20 43 25N 0 35W
Lacrosse 118 46 51N 117 58W
Ladakh Ra. 69 34 0N 78 0 E
Lądekzdrój 28 50 21N 16 53 E
Ládhon → 45 37 40N 21 50 E
Ladik 56 40 57N 35 58 E
Ladismith 92 33 28 S 21 15 E
Lādīz 65 28 55N 61 15 E
Ladnun 68 27 38N 74 25 E
Ladoga, L. = Ladozhskoye Oz. 52 61 15N 30 30 E
Ladon 19 48 0N 2 30 E
Ladozhskoye Ozero 52 61 15N 30 30 E
Lady Grey 92 30 43 S 27 13 E
Ladybrand 92 29 9 S 27 29 E
Ladysmith, Can. 108 49 0N 123 49W
Ladysmith, S. Afr. 93 28 32 S 29 46 E
Ladysmith, U.S.A. 116 45 27N 91 4W
Lae 94 6 40 S 147 2 E
Læsø 49 57 15N 10 53 E
Læsø Rende 49 57 20N 10 45 E
Lafayette, Colo., U.S.A. 116 40 0N 105 2W
Lafayette, Ga., U.S.A. 115 34 44N 85 15W
Lafayette, La., U.S.A. 117 30 18N 92 0W
Lafayette, Tenn., U.S.A. 115 36 35N 86 0W
Laferte → 108 61 53N 117 44W
Lafia 85 8 30N 8 34 E
Lafiagi 85 8 52N 5 20 E
Lafleche 109 49 45N 106 40W
Lafon 87 5 5N 32 29 E
Laforsen 48 61 56N 15 3 E
Lagan →, Sweden 49 56 56N 13 58 E
Lagan →, U.K. 15 54 35N 5 55W
Lagarfljót → 50 65 40N 14 18W
Lage, Ger. 24 52 0N 8 47 E
Lage, Spain 30 43 13N 9 0W
Lågen →, Oppland, Norway 47 61 8N 10 25 E
Lågen →, Vestfold, Norway 47 59 3N 10 5 E
Lägerdorf 24 53 53N 9 35 E
Laggers Pt. 99 30 52 S 153 4 E
Laghán □ 65 34 20N 70 0 E
Laghouat 82 33 50N 2 59 E
Lagnieu 21 45 55N 5 20 E
Lagny 19 48 52N 2 40 E
Lago 41 39 9N 16 8 E
Lagôa 31 37 8N 8 27W
Lagoaça 30 41 11N 6 44W
Lagodekhi 57 41 50N 46 22 E
Lagónegro 41 40 8N 15 45 E
Lagonoy Gulf 73 13 50N 123 50 E
Lagos, Nigeria 85 6 25N 3 27 E
Lagos, Port. 31 37 5N 8 41W
Lagos de Moreno 120 21 21N 101 55W
Lagrange 96 18 45 S 121 43 E
Laguardia 32 42 33N 2 35W
Laguépie 20 44 8N 1 57 E
Laguna, Brazil 125 28 30 S 48 50W
Laguna, U.S.A. 119 35 3N 107 28W
Laguna Beach 119 33 31N 117 52W
Laguna Dam 119 32 55N 114 30W
Laguna de la Janda 31 36 15N 5 45W
Laguna Limpia 124 26 32 S 59 45W
Laguna Madre 120 27 0N 97 20W
Lagunas, Chile 124 21 0S 69 45W
Lagunas, Peru 126 5 10 S 75 35W
Laha 76 48 12N 124 35 E
Lahad Datu 73 5 0N 118 20
Laharpur 69 27 43N 80 56
Lahat 72 3 45 S 103 30
Lahewa 72 1 22N 97 12
Lahijan 64 37 10N 50 6
Lahn → 25 50 52N 8 35
Laholm 49 56 30N 13 2
Laholmsbukten 49 56 30N 12 45
Lahontan Res. 118 39 28N 118 58
Lahore 68 31 32N 74 22
Lahore □ 68 31 55N 74 5
* Lahr 25 48 20N 7 52
Lahti 51 60 58N 25 40
Laï 81 9 25N 16 18
Lai Chau 71 22 5N 103 3
Laibin 75 23 42N 109 14
Laidley 99 27 39 S 152 20
Laifeng 77 29 27N 109 20
Laignes 19 47 50N 4 20
Laikipia □ 90 0 30N 36 30
Laingsburg 92 33 9 S 20 52
Lairg 14 58 1N 4 24
Lais 72 3 35 S 102 0
Laiyang 76 36 59N 120 45
Laizhou Wan 76 37 30N 119 30
Laja → 120 20 55N 100 46
Lajere 85 11 58N 11 25
Lajes 125 27 48 S 50 20
Lajkovac 42 44 27N 20 14
Lajosmizse 27 47 3N 19 32
Lakaband 68 31 2N 69 15
Lakar 73 8 15 S 128 17
Lake Andes 116 43 10N 98 32
Lake Anse 114 46 42N 88 25
Lake Arthur 117 30 8N 92 40
Lake Cargelligo 97 33 15 S 146 22
Lake Charles 117 30 15N 93 10
Lake City, Colo, U.S.A. 119 38 3N 107 27
Lake City, Fla., U.S.A. 115 30 10N 82 40
Lake City, Iowa, U.S.A. 116 42 12N 94 42
Lake City, Mich., U.S.A. 114 44 20N 85 10
Lake City, Minn., U.S.A. 116 44 28N 92 21
Lake City, Pa., U.S.A. 112 42 2N 80 20
Lake City, S.C., U.S.A. 115 33 51N 79 44
Lake George 113 43 25N 73 43
Lake Harbour 105 62 50N 69 50
Lake Havasu City 119 34 25N 114 29
Lake Lenore 109 52 24N 104 59
Lake Louise 108 51 30N 116 10
Lake Mead Nat. Rec. Area 119 36 0N 114 30
Lake Mills 116 43 23N 93 33
Lake Nash 98 20 57 S 138 0
Lake Providence 117 32 49N 91 12
Lake River 106 54 30N 82 31
Lake Superior Prov. Park 106 47 45N 84 45
Lake Village 117 33 20N 91 19
Lake Wales 115 27 55N 81 32
Lake Worth 115 26 36N 80 3
Lakefield 106 44 25N 78 16
Lakeland 115 28 0N 82 0
Lakemba 101 18 13 S 178 47
Lakes Entrance 99 37 50 S 148 0
Lakeside, Ariz., U.S.A. 119 34 12N 109 59
Lakeside, Nebr., U.S.A. 116 42 5N 102 24
Lakeview 118 42 15N 120 22
Lakewood, N.J., U.S.A. 114 40 5N 74 13
Lakewood, Ohio, U.S.A. 114 41 28N 81 50
Lakhaniá 45 35 58N 27 54
Lákhi 45 35 24N 23 57
Lakhpat 68 23 48N 68 47
Laki 50 64 4N 18 14
Lakin 117 37 58N 101 18
Lakitusaki → 106 54 21N 82 25
Lakonía □ 45 36 55N 22 30
Lakonikós Kólpos 45 36 40N 22 40
Lakota, Ivory C. 84 5 50N 5 30
Lakota, U.S.A. 116 48 0N 98 22
Laksefjorden 50 70 45N 26 50
Lakselv 50 70 2N 24 56
Lakshmi Kantapur 69 22 5N 88 20
Lala Ghat 67 24 30N 92 40
Lala Musa 68 32 40N 73 57
Lalago 90 3 28 S 33 58
Lalapanzi 91 19 20 S 30 15
Lalganj 69 25 52N 85 13
Lalibela 87 12 2N 39 2
Lalin 76 45 12N 127 0
Lalín 30 42 40N 8 5
Lalinde 20 44 50N 0 44
Lalitpur 68 24 42N 78 28
Lama Kara 85 9 30N 1 15
Lamaing 67 15 25N 97 53
Lamar, Colo., U.S.A. 116 38 9N 102 35
Lamar, Mo., U.S.A. 117 37 30N 94 20
Lamas 126 6 28 S 76 31
Lamastre 21 44 59N 4 35
Lambach 26 48 6N 13 51
Lamballe 18 48 29N 2 31
Lambaréné 88 0 41 S 10 12
Lambasa 101 16 30 S 179 10
Lambay I. 15 53 30N 6 0
Lambert 116 47 44N 104 39
Lambert Glacier 5 71 0 S 70 0
Lambesc 21 43 39N 5 16
Lambi Kyun (Sullivan I.) 71 10 50N 98 20
Lámbia 45 37 52N 21 53
Lambro → 38 45 8N 9 32
Lame 85 45 35N 106 40
Lame Deer 118 45 45N 106 40
Lamego 30 41 5N 7 52
Lamèque 107 47 45N 64 38
Lameroo 99 35 19 S 140 33
Lamesa 117 32 45N 101 57
Lamía 45 38 55N 22 26
† Lamitan 73 6 40N 122 10
Lammermuir Hills 14 55 50N 2 40
Lamoille 118 40 47N 115 31
Lamon Bay 73 14 30N 122 20
Lamont 108 53 46N 112 50
Lampa 126 15 22 S 70 22
Lampang, Thai. 71 18 18N 99 31
Lampang, Thai. 71 18 16N 99 32

* *Now part of Punjab* □

† *Renamed Isabela*

Lampasas 117 31 5N 98 10W
Lampaul 18 48 28N 5 7W
Lampazos de Naranjo 120 27 2N 100 32W
Lampedusa 36 35 36N 12 40 E
Lampeter 13 52 6N 4 6W
Lampione 83 35 33N 12 20 E
Lampman 109 49 25N 102 50W
Lamprechtshausen 26 48 0N 12 58 E
Lamprey 109 58 33N 94 8W
Lampung □ 72 5 30 S 104 30 E
Lamu 90 2 16 S 40 55 E
Lamu □ 90 2 0 S 40 45 E
Lamut, Tg. 72 3 50 S 105 58 E
Lamy 119 35 30N 105 58W
Lan Xian 76 38 15N 111 35 E
Lan Yu 77 22 5N 121 35 E
Lanai I. 110 20 50N 156 55W
Lanak La 69 34 27N 79 32 E
Lanak'o Shank'ou = Lanak La 69 34 27N 79 32 E
Lanao, L. 73 7 52N 124 15 E
Lanark, Can. 113 45 1N 76 22W
Lanark, U.K. 14 55 40N 3 48W
Lancashire □ 12 53 40N 2 30W
Lancaster, Can. 113 45 10N 74 30W
Lancaster, U.K. 12 54 3N 2 48W
Lancaster, Calif., U.S.A. 119 34 47N 118 8W
Lancaster, Ky., U.S.A. 114 37 40N 84 40W
Lancaster, N.H., U.S.A. 114 44 27N 71 33W
Lancaster, N.Y., U.S.A. 112 42 53N 78 43W
Lancaster, Pa., U.S.A. 114 40 4N 76 19W
Lancaster, S.C., U.S.A. 115 34 45N 80 47W
Lancaster, Wis., U.S.A. 116 42 48N 90 43W
Lancaster Sd. 4 74 13N 84 0W
Lancer 109 50 48N 108 53W
Lanchow = Lanzhou 76 36 1N 103 52 E
Lanciano 39 42 15N 14 22 E
Lancut 27 50 10N 22 13 E
Lândana 88 5 11 S 12 5 E
Landau, Bayern, Ger. 25 48 41N 12 41 E
Landau, Rhld-Pfz., Ger. 25 49 12N 8 7 E
Landeck 26 47 9N 10 34 E
Landen 16 50 45N 5 5 E
Lander 118 42 50N 108 49W
Landerneau 18 48 28N 4 17W
Landeryd 49 57 7N 13 15 E
Landes □ 20 43 57N 0 48W
Landes, Les 20 44 20N 1 0W
Landete 32 39 56N 1 25W
Landi Kotal 66 34 7N 71 6 E
Landivisiau 18 48 31N 4 6W
Landquart 25 46 58N 9 32 E
Landrecies 19 50 7N 3 40 E
Land's End 13 50 4N 5 43W
Landsberg 25 48 3N 10 52 E
Landsborough Cr. → 98 22 28 S 144 35 E
Landsbro 49 57 24N 14 56 E
Landshut 25 48 31N 12 10 E
Landskrona 49 55 53N 12 50 E
Landstuhl 25 49 25N 7 34 E
Landvetter 49 57 41N 12 17 E
Lanesboro 113 41 57N 75 34W
Lanett 115 33 0N 85 15W
Lang Bay 108 49 45N 124 21W
Lang Shan 76 41 0N 106 30 E
Lang Son 71 21 52N 106 42 E
La'nga Co 67 30 45N 81 15 E
Långadhás 44 40 46N 23 2 E
Langádhia 45 37 43N 22 1 E
Långan → 48 63 19N 14 44 E
Langara I. 108 54 14N 133 1W
Langdon 116 48 47N 98 24W
Langeac 20 45 7N 3 29 E
Langeais 18 47 20N 0 24 E
Langeb Baraka → 86 17 28N 36 50 E
Langeberge, C. Prov., S. Afr. 92 33 55 S 21 40 E
Langeberge, C. Prov., S. Afr. 92 28 15 S 22 33 E
Langeland 49 54 56N 10 48 E
Langen 25 49 59N 8 40 E
Langenburg 109 50 51N 101 43W
Langeness 24 54 34N 8 35 E
Langenlois 26 48 29N 15 40 E
Langeoog 24 53 44N 7 33 E
Langeskov 49 55 22N 10 35 E
Langesund 47 59 0N 9 45 E
Länghem 49 57 36N 13 14 E
Langhirano 38 44 39N 10 16 E
Langholm 14 55 9N 2 59W
Langjökull 50 64 39N 20 12W
Langkawi, P. 71 6 25N 99 45 E
Langkon 72 6 30N 116 40 E
Langlade 107 46 50N 56 20W
Langlois 118 42 54N 124 26W
Langnau 25 46 56N 7 47 E
Langogne 20 44 43N 3 50 E
Langon 20 44 33N 0 16W
Langøya 50 68 45N 14 50 E
Langpran, Gunong 72 1 0N 114 23 E
Langres 19 47 52N 5 20 E
Langres, Plateau de 19 47 45N 5 3 E
Langsa 72 4 30N 97 57 E
Långsele 48 63 12N 17 4 E
Långshyttan 48 60 27N 16 2 E
Langtry 117 29 50N 101 33W
Languedoc 20 43 58N 4 0 E
Langxiangzhen 76 39 43N 116 8 E
Langzhong 75 31 38N 105 58 E
Lanigan 109 51 51N 105 2W
Lankao 77 34 48N 114 50 E
Lannemezan 20 43 8N 0 23 E
Lannilis 18 48 35N 4 32W
Lannion 18 48 46N 3 29W
Lanouaille 20 45 24N 1 9 E
Lansdale 113 40 14N 75 18W
Lansdowne, Austral. 99 31 48 S 152 30 E
Lansdowne, Can. 113 44 24N 76 1W
Lansdowne House 106 52 14N 87 53W
Lansford 113 40 48N 75 55W
Lansing 114 42 47N 84 40W
Lanslebourg 21 45 17N 6 52 E
Lant, Pulau 72 4 10 S 116 0 E
Lanus 124 34 44 S 58 27W
Lanusei 40 39 53N 9 31 E
Lanxi 77 29 13N 119 28 E
Lanzarote 80 29 0N 13 40W
Lanzhou 76 36 1N 103 52 E
Lanzo Torinese 38 45 16N 7 29 E
Lao → 41 39 45N 15 45 E
Lao Cai 71 22 30N 103 57 E
Laoag 73 18 7N 120 34 E
Laoang 73 12 32N 125 8 E
Laoha He → 76 43 25N 120 35 E
Laois □ 15 53 0N 7 20W
Laon 19 49 33N 3 35 E
Laona 114 45 32N 88 41W
Laos ■ 71 17 45N 105 0 E
Lapa 125 25 46 S 49 44W
Lapalisse 20 46 15N 3 38 E
Laparan Cap 73 6 0N 120 0 E
Lapeer 114 43 3N 83 20W
Lapi □ 50 67 0N 27 0 E
Lapland = Lappland 50 68 7N 24 0 E
Laporte 113 41 27N 76 30W
Lapovo 42 44 10N 21 2 E
Lappland 50 68 7N 24 0 E
Laprairie 113 45 20N 73 30W
Laprida 124 37 34 S 60 45W
Laptev Sea 59 76 0N 125 0 E
Lapuş, Munţii 46 47 20N 23 50 E
Lapush 118 47 56N 124 33W
Lăpuşul → 46 47 25N 23 40 E
Łapy 28 52 59N 22 52 E
Lār 65 27 40N 54 14 E
Larabanga 84 9 16N 1 56W
Laracha 30 43 15N 8 35W
Larache 82 35 10N 6 5W
Laragne-Monteglin 21 44 18N 5 49 E
Laramie 116 41 20N 105 38W
Laramie Mts. 116 42 0N 105 30W
Laranjeiras do Sul 125 25 23 S 52 23W
Larantuka 73 8 21 S 122 55 E
Larap 73 14 18N 122 39 E
Larat 73 7 0 S 132 0 E
Lårdal 47 59 25N 8 10 E
Larde 91 16 28 S 39 43 E
Larder Lake 106 48 5N 79 40W
Lárdhos, Ákra 45 36 4N 28 10 E
Laredo, Spain 32 43 26N 3 28W
Laredo, U.S.A. 117 27 34N 99 29W
Laredo Sd. 108 52 30N 128 53W
Largentière 21 44 34N 4 18 E
Largs 14 55 48N 4 51W
Lari 38 43 34N 10 35 E
Lariang 73 1 26 S 119 17 E
Larimore 116 47 55N 97 35W
Larino 41 41 48N 14 54 E
Lárisa 44 39 49N 22 28 E
Lárisa □ 44 39 39N 22 24 E
Larkana 68 27 32N 68 18 E
Larkollen 47 59 20N 10 41 E
Larnaca 64 35 0N 33 35 E
Larne 15 54 52N 5 50W
Larned 116 38 15N 99 10W
Larrimah 96 15 35 S 133 12 E
Larsen Ice Shelf 5 67 0 S 62 0W
Larvik 47 59 4N 10 0 E
Laryak 58 61 15N 80 0 E
Larzac, Causse du 20 44 0N 3 17 E
Las Animas 117 38 8N 103 18W
Las Anod 63 8 26N 47 19 E
Las Blancos 33 37 38N 0 49W
Las Brenãs 124 27 5 S 61 7W
Las Cabezas de San Juan 31 37 0N 5 58W
Las Cascadas 120 9 5N 79 41W
Las Cruces 119 32 18N 106 50W
Las Flores 124 36 10 S 59 7W
Las Heras 124 32 51 S 68 49W
Las Khoreh 63 11 10N 48 20 E
Las Lajas 128 38 30 S 70 25W
Las Lomitas 124 24 43 S 60 35W
Las Marismas 31 37 5N 6 20W
Las Navas de la Concepción 31 37 56N 5 30W
Las Navas de Tolosa 31 38 18N 3 38W
Las Palmas, Argent. 124 27 8 S 58 45W
Las Palmas, Canary Is. 80 28 7N 15 26W
Las Palmas □ 80 28 10N 15 28W
Las Piedras 125 34 44 S 56 14W
Las Pipinas 124 35 30 S 57 19W
Las Plumas 128 43 40 S 67 15W
Las Rosas 124 32 30 S 61 35W
Las Tablas 121 7 49N 80 14W
Las Termas 124 27 29 S 64 52W
Las Varillas 124 31 50 S 62 50W
Las Vegas, N. Mex., U.S.A. 119 35 35N 105 10W
Las Vegas, Nev., U.S.A. 119 36 10N 115 5W
Lascano 125 33 35 S 54 12W
Lascaux 20 45 5N 1 10 E
Lashburn 109 53 10N 109 40W
Lashio 67 22 56N 97 45 E
Lashkar 68 26 10N 78 10 E
Łasin 28 53 30N 19 2 E
Lasíthi □ 45 35 5N 25 50 E
Lask 28 51 34N 19 8 E
Łaskarzew 28 51 48N 21 36 E
Laško 39 46 10N 15 16 E
Lassay 18 48 27N 0 30W
Lassen Pk. 118 40 29N 121 31W
Last Mountain L. 109 51 5N 105 14W
Lastoursville 88 0 55 S 12 38 E
Lastovo 39 42 46N 16 55 E
Lastovski Kanal 39 42 50N 17 0 E
Latacunga 126 0 50 S 78 35W
Latakia = Al Lādhiqīyah 64 35 30N 35 45 E
Latchford 106 47 20N 79 50W
Laterza 41 40 38N 16 47 E
Lathen 24 52 51N 7 21 E
Latiano 41 40 33N 17 43 E
Latina 40 41 26N 12 53 E
Latisana 39 45 47N 13 1 E
Latium = Lazio 39 42 10N 12 30 E
Latorica → 27 48 28N 21 50 E
Latouche Treville, C. 96 18 27 S 121 49 E
Latrobe 112 40 19N 79 21W
Latrônico 41 40 5N 16 0 E
Latrun 62 31 50N 34 58 E
Latur 70 18 25N 76 40 E
Latvian S.S.R. □ 54 56 50N 24 0 E
Lau (Eastern) Group 101 17 0 S 178 30W
Lauchhammer 24 51 35N 13 48 E
Laudal 47 58 15N 7 30 E
Lauenburg 24 53 23N 10 33 E
Lauffen 25 49 4N 9 9 E
Laugarbakki 50 65 20N 20 55W
Laujar 33 37 0N 2 54W
Launceston, Austral. 97 41 24 S 147 8 E
Launceston, U.K. 13 50 38N 4 21W
Laune → 15 52 5N 9 40W
Launglon Bok 71 13 50N 97 54 E
Laupheim 25 48 13N 9 53 E
Laura 97 15 32 S 144 32 E
Laureana di Borrello 41 38 28N 16 5 E
Laurel, Miss., U.S.A. 117 31 41N 89 9W
Laurel, Mont., U.S.A. 118 45 46N 108 49W
Laurencekirk 14 56 50N 2 30W
Laurens 115 34 32N 82 2W
Laurentian Plat. 107 52 0N 70 0W
Laurentides, Parc Prov. des 107 47 45N 71 15W
Lauria 41 40 3N 15 50 E
Laurie I. 5 60 44 S 44 37W
Laurie L. 109 56 35N 101 57W
Laurinburg 115 34 50N 79 25W
Laurium 114 47 14N 88 26W
Lausanne 25 46 32N 6 38 E
Laut, Kepulauan 72 4 45N 108 0 E
Laut Ketil, Kepulauan 72 4 45 S 115 40 E
Lauterbach 24 50 39N 9 23 E
Lauterecken 25 49 38N 7 35 E
Lautoka 101 17 37 S 177 27 E
Lauzon 107 46 48N 71 10W
Lava Hot Springs 118 42 38N 112 1W
Lavadores 30 42 14N 8 41W
Lavagna 38 44 18N 9 22 E
Laval 18 48 4N 0 48W
Lavalle 124 28 15 S 65 15W
Lavandou, Le 21 43 8N 6 22 E
Lávara 44 41 19N 26 22 E
Lavardac 20 44 12N 0 20 E
Lavaur 20 43 30N 1 49 E
Lavaveix 20 46 5N 2 8 E
Lavelanet 20 42 57N 1 51 E
Lavello 41 41 4N 15 47 E
Laverendrye Prov. Park 106 46 15N 17 15W
Laverne 117 36 43N 99 58W
Laverton 96 28 44 S 122 29 E
Lavi 62 32 47N 35 25 E
Lavik 47 61 6N 5 25 E
Lávkos 45 39 9N 23 14 E
Lavos 30 40 6N 8 49W
Lavras 125 21 20 S 45 0W
Lavre 31 38 46N 8 22W
Lavrentiya 59 65 35N 171 0W
Lávrion 45 37 40N 24 4 E
Lavumisa 93 27 20 S 31 55 E
Lawas 72 4 55N 115 25 E
Lawele 73 5 16 S 123 3 E
Lawn Hill 98 18 36 S 138 33 E
Lawng Pit 67 25 30N 97 25 E
Lawra 84 10 39N 2 51W
Lawrence, Kans., U.S.A. 116 39 0N 95 10W
Lawrence, Mass., U.S.A. 114 42 40N 71 9W
Lawrenceburg, Ind., U.S.A. 114 39 5N 84 50W
Lawrenceburg, Tenn., U.S.A. 115 35 12N 87 19W
Lawrenceville 115 33 55N 83 59W
Lawton 117 34 33N 98 25W
Lawu 73 7 40 S 111 13 E
Laxford, L. 14 58 25N 5 10W
Laxmeshwar 70 15 9N 75 28 E
Laylá 64 22 10N 46 40 E
Layon → 18 47 20N 0 45W
Laysan I. 95 25 30N 167 0W
Laytonville 118 39 44N 123 29W
Lazarevac 42 44 23N 20 17 E
Lazio □ 39 42 10N 12 30 E
Łazy 28 50 27N 19 24 E
Lea → 13 51 30N 0 10W
Lead 116 44 20N 103 40W
Leader 109 50 50N 109 30W
Leadhills 14 55 25N 3 47W
Leadville 119 39 17N 106 23W
Leaf → 117 31 0N 88 45W
Leakey 117 29 45N 99 45W
Leamington, Can. 106 42 3N 82 36W
Leamington, U.K. 13 52 18N 1 32W
Leamington, U.S.A. 118 39 37N 112 17W
Leandro Norte Alem 125 27 34 S 55 15W
Learmonth 96 22 13 S 114 10 E
Leask 109 53 5N 106 45W
Leavenworth, Mo., U.S.A. 116 39 25N 95 0W
Leavenworth, Wash., U.S.A. 118 47 44N 120 37W
Łeba 28 54 45N 17 32 E
Łeba → 28 54 46N 17 33 E
Lebak 73 6 32N 124 5 E
Lebane 42 42 56N 21 44 E
Lebanon, Ind., U.S.A. 114 40 3N 86 28W
Lebanon, Kans., U.S.A. 116 39 50N 98 35W
Lebanon, Ky., U.S.A. 114 37 35N 85 15W
Lebanon, Mo., U.S.A. 117 37 40N 92 40W
Lebanon, Oreg., U.S.A. 118 44 31N 122 57W
Lebanon, Pa., U.S.A. 114 40 20N 76 28W
Lebanon, Tenn., U.S.A. 115 36 15N 86 20W
Lebanon ■ 64 34 0N 36 0 E
Lebec 119 34 50N 118 59W
Lebedin 54 50 35N 34 30 E
Lebedyan 55 53 0N 39 10 E
Lebombo-berge 93 24 30 S 32 0 E
Lębork 28 54 33N 17 46 E
Lebrija 31 36 53N 6 5W
Łebsko, Jezioro 28 54 40N 17 25 E
Lebu 124 37 40 S 73 47W
Lecce 41 40 20N 18 10 E
Lecco 38 45 50N 9 27 E
Lecco, L. di. 38 45 51N 9 22 E
Lécera 32 41 13N 0 43W
Lech 26 47 13N 10 9 E
Lech → 25 48 44N 10 56 E
Lechang 77 25 10N 113 20 E
Lechtaler Alpen 26 47 15N 10 30 E
Lectoure 20 43 56N 0 38 E
Łęczna 28 51 18N 22 53 E
Łęczyca 28 52 5N 19 15 E
Ledbury 13 52 3N 2 25W
Ledeč 26 49 41N 15 18 E
Ledesma 30 41 6N 5 59W
Ledong 77 18 41N 109 5 E
Leduc 108 53 15N 113 30W
Ledyczek 28 53 33N 16 59 E
Lee, Mass., U.S.A. 113 42 17N 73 18W
Lee, Nev., U.S.A. 118 40 35N 115 36W
Lee → 15 51 50N 8 30W
Leech L. 116 47 9N 94 23W
Leedey 117 35 53N 99 24W
Leeds, U.K. 12 53 48N 1 34W
Leeds, U.S.A. 115 33 32N 86 30W
Leek 12 53 7N 2 2W
Leer 24 53 13N 7 29 E
Leesburg 115 28 47N 81 52W
Leesville 117 31 12N 93 15W
Leeton 97 34 33 S 146 23 E
Leetonia 112 40 53N 80 45W
Leeuwarden 16 53 15N 5 48 E
Leeuwin, C. 96 34 20 S 115 9 E
Leeward Is., Atl. Oc. 121 16 30N 63 30W
Leeward Is., Pac. Oc. 95 16 0 S 147 0W
Lefors 117 35 30N 100 50W
Lefroy, L. 96 31 21 S 121 40 E
Łeg → 28 50 42N 21 50 E
Legal 108 53 55N 113 35W
Legazpi 73 13 10N 123 45 E
Leghorn = Livorno 38 43 32N 10 18 E
Legion 91 21 25 S 28 30 E
Legionowo 28 52 25N 20 50 E
Legnago 39 45 10N 11 19 E
Legnano 38 45 35N 8 55 E
Legnica 28 51 12N 16 10 E
Legnica □ 28 51 30N 16 0 E
Legrad 39 46 17N 16 51 E
Legume 99 28 20 S 152 19 E
Leh 69 34 9N 77 35 E
Lehi 118 40 20N 111 51W
Lehighton 113 40 50N 75 44W
Lehliu 46 44 29N 26 20 E
Lehrte 24 52 22N 9 58 E
Lehututu 92 23 54 S 21 55 E
Leiah 68 30 58N 70 58 E
Leibnitz 26 46 47N 15 34 E
Leicester 13 52 39N 1 9W
Leicester □ 13 52 40N 1 10W
Leichhardt → 97 17 35 S 139 48 E
Leichhardt Ra. 98 20 46 S 147 40 E
Leiden 16 52 9N 4 30 E
Leie → 16 51 2N 3 45 E
Leigh Creek 97 30 28 S 138 24 E
Leikanger 47 61 10N 6 52 E
Leine → 24 52 20N 9 50 E
Leinster □ 15 53 0N 7 10W
Leinster, Mt. 15 52 38N 6 47W
Leipzig 24 51 20N 12 23 E
Leipzig □ 24 51 20N 12 30 E
Leiria 31 39 46N 8 53W
Leiria □ 31 39 46N 8 53W
Leith 14 55 59N 3 10W
Leith Hill 13 51 10N 0 23W
Leitha → 27 48 0N 16 35 E
Leitrim 15 54 0N 8 5W
Leitrim □ 15 54 8N 8 0W
Leiyang 77 26 27N 112 45 E
Leiza 32 43 5N 1 55W
Leizhou Bandao 77 21 0N 110 0 E
Leizhou Wan 77 20 50N 110 20 E
Lek → 16 52 0N 6 0 E
Lekáni 44 41 10N 24 35 E
Lekhainá 45 37 57N 21 16 E
Leksula 73 3 46 S 126 31 E
Leland 117 33 25N 90 52W
Leland Lakes 109 60 0N 110 59W
Leleque 128 42 28 S 71 0W
Lelystad 16 52 30N 5 25 E
Lema 85 12 58N 4 13 E
Léman, Lac 25 46 26N 6 30 E
Lemera 90 3 0 S 28 55 E
Lemery 73 13 51N 120 56 E
Lemgo 24 52 2N 8 52 E
Lemhi Ra. 118 44 30N 113 30W
Lemmer 16 52 51N 5 43 E
Lemmon 116 45 59N 102 10W
Lemoore 119 36 23N 119 46W
Lempdes 20 45 22N 3 17 E
Lemvig 49 56 33N 8 20 E
Lena → 59 72 52N 126 40 E
Lenartovce 27 48 18N 20 19 E
Lencloître 18 46 50N 0 20 E
Lendinara 39 45 4N 11 37 E
Lengau de Vaca, Pta. 124 30 14 S 71 38W
Lengerich 24 52 12N 7 50 E
Lenggong 71 5 6N 100 58 E
Lenggries 25 47 41N 11 34 E
Lengyeltóti 27 46 40N 17 40 E
Lenhovda 49 57 0N 15 16 E
Lenin 57 48 20N 40 56 E
Leninabad 58 40 17N 69 37 E
Leninakan 57 40 47N 43 50 E
Leningrad 54 59 55N 30 20 E
Lenino 56 45 17N 35 46 E
Leninogorsk 58 50 20N 83 30 E
Leninsk, R.S.F.S.R., U.S.S.R. 57 48 40N 45 15 E
Leninsk, R.S.F.S.R., U.S.S.R. 57 46 10N 43 46 E
Leninsk-Kuznetskiy 58 54 44N 86 10 E
Leninskaya Sloboda 55 56 7N 44 29 E
Leninskoye, R.S.F.S.R., U.S.S.R. 55 58 23N 47 3 E
Leninskoye, R.S.F.S.R., U.S.S.R. 59 47 56N 132 38 E
Lenk 25 46 27N 7 28 E
Lenkoran 53 39 45N 48 50 E
Lenmalu 73 1 45 S 130 15 E
Lenne → 24 51 25N 7 30 E
Lennoxville 113 45 22N 71 51W
Leno 38 45 24N 10 14 E
Lenoir 115 35 55N 81 36W
Lenoir City 115 35 40N 84 20W
Lenora 116 39 39N 100 1W

Lenore L. **109** 52 30N 104 59W
Lenox **113** 42 20N 73 18W
Lens **19** 50 26N 2 50 E
Lensk (Mukhtuya) **59** 60 48N 114 55 E
Lenskoye **56** 45 3N 34 1 E
Lenti **27** 46 37N 16 33 E
Lentini **41** 37 18N 15 0 E
Lentvaric **54** 54 39N 25 3 E
Lenzen **24** 53 6N 11 26 E
Léo **84** 11 3N 2 2W
Leoben **26** 47 22N 15 5 E
Leola **116** 45 47N 98 58W
Leominster, U.K. **13** 52 15N 2 43W
Leominster, U.S.A. **114** 42 32N 71 45W
Léon **20** 43 53N 1 18W
León, Mexico **120** 21 7N 101 30W
León, Nic. **121** 12 20N 86 51W
León, Spain **30** 42 38N 5 34W
Leon **116** 40 40N 93 40W
León □ **30** 42 40N 5 55W
León, Montañas de **30** 42 30N 6 18W
Leonardtown **114** 38 19N 76 39W
Leonforte **41** 37 39N 14 22 E
Leongatha **99** 38 30 S 145 58 E
Leonídhion **45** 37 9N 22 52 E
Leonora **96** 28 49 S 121 19 E
Léopold II, Lac = Mai-Ndombe **88** 2 0 S 18 20 E
Leopoldina **125** 21 28 S 42 40W
Leopoldsburg **16** 51 7N 5 13 E
Léopoldville = Kinshasa **88** 4 20 S 15 15 E
Leoti **116** 38 31N 101 19W
Leoville **109** 53 39N 107 33W
Lépa, L. do **92** 17 0 S 19 0 E
Lepe **31** 37 15N 7 12W
Lepel **54** 54 50N 28 40 E
Lepikha **59** 64 45N 125 55 E
Leping **77** 28 47N 117 7 E
Lepontino, Alpi **38** 46 22N 8 27 E
Lepsény **27** 47 0N 18 15 E
Leptis Magna **83** 32 40N 14 12 E
Lequeitio **32** 43 20N 2 32W
Lercara Friddi **40** 37 42N 13 36 E
Léré **81** 9 39N 14 13 E
Lere **85** 9 43N 9 18 E
Leribe **93** 28 51 S 28 3 E
Lérici **38** 44 4N 9 58 E
Lérida **32** 41 37N 0 39 E
Lérida □ **32** 42 6N 1 0 E
Lérins, Is. de **21** 43 31N 7 3 E
Lerma **30** 42 0N 3 47W
Léros **45** 37 10N 26 50 E
Lérouville **19** 48 50N 5 30 E
Lerwick **14** 60 10N 1 10W
Les **46** 46 58N 21 50 E
Lesbos, I. = Lésvos **45** 39 10N 26 20 E
Leshukonskoye **52** 64 54N 45 46 E
Lésina, L. di **39** 41 53N 15 25 E
Lesja **47** 62 7N 8 51 E
Lesjaverk **47** 62 12N 8 34 E
Lesko **27** 49 30N 22 23 E
Leskov I. **5** 56 0 S 28 0W
Leskovac **42** 43 0N 21 58 E
Leskoviku **44** 40 10N 20 34 E
Leslie **117** 35 50N 92 35W
Lesna **28** 51 0N 15 15 E
Lesneven **18** 48 35N 4 20W
Lešnica **42** 44 39N 19 20 E
Lesnoye **54** 58 15N 35 18 E
Lesotho ■ **93** 29 40 S 28 0 E
Lesozavodsk **59** 45 30N 133 29 E
Lesparre-Médoc **20** 45 18N 0 57W
Lessay **18** 49 14N 1 30W
Lesse → **16** 50 15N 4 54 E
Lesser Antilles **121** 15 0N 61 0W
Lesser Slave L. **108** 55 30N 115 25W
Lessines **16** 50 42N 3 50 E
Lestock **109** 51 19N 103 59W
Lésvos **45** 39 10N 26 20 E
Leszno **28** 51 50N 16 30 E
Leszno □ **28** 51 45N 16 30 E
Letchworth **13** 51 58N 0 13W
Letea, Ostrov **46** 45 18N 29 20 E
Lethbridge **108** 49 45N 112 45W
Leti **73** 8 10 S 127 40 E
Leti, Kepulauan **73** 8 10 S 128 0 E
Letiahau → **92** 21 16 S 24 0 E
Leticia **126** 4 9 S 70 0W
Leting **76** 39 23N 118 55 E
Letlhakeng **92** 24 0 S 24 59 E
Letpadan **67** 17 45N 95 45 E
Letpan **67** 19 28N 94 10 E
Letsôk-aw Kyun (Domel I.) **71** 11 30N 98 25 E
Letterkenny **15** 54 57N 7 42W
Leu **46** 44 10N 24 0 E
Leucate **20** 42 56N 3 3 E
Leucate, Étang de **20** 42 50N 3 0 E
Leuk **25** 46 19N 7 37 E
Leuser, G. **72** 3 46N 97 12 E
Leutkirch **25** 47 49N 10 1 E
Leuven (Louvain) **16** 50 52N 4 42 E
Leuze, Hainaut, Belg. **16** 50 36N 3 37 E
Leuze, Namur, Belg. **16** 50 33N 4 54 E
Lev Tolstoy **55** 53 13N 39 29 E
Levádhia **45** 38 27N 22 54 E
Levan **118** 39 37N 111 52W
Levanger **47** 63 45N 11 19 E
Levani **44** 40 40N 19 28 E
Levant, I. du **21** 43 3N 6 28 E
Lévanto **38** 44 10N 9 37 E
Levanzo **40** 38 0N 12 19 E
Levelland **117** 33 38N 102 23W
Leven **14** 56 12N 3 0W
Leven, L. **14** 56 12N 3 22W
Leven, Toraka **93** 12 30 S 47 45 E
Levens **21** 43 50N 7 12 E
Leveque C. **96** 16 20 S 123 0 E
Leverano **41** 40 16N 18 0 E
Leverkusen **24** 51 2N 6 59 E
Levet **19** 46 56N 2 22 E
Levice **27** 48 13N 18 35 E
Levick, Mt. **5** 75 0 S 164 0 E
Levico **39** 46 0N 11 18 E
Levie **21** 41 40N 9 7 E
Levier **19** 46 58N 6 8 E
Levin **101** 40 37 S 175 18 E
Lévis **107** 46 48N 71 9W
Levis, L. **108** 62 37N 117 58W
Levítha **45** 37 0N 26 28 E
Levittown, N.Y., U.S.A. **113** 40 41N 73 31W
Levittown, Pa., U.S.A. **113** 40 10N 74 51W
Levka **43** 41 52N 26 15 E
Lévka **45** 35 18N 24 3 E
Levkás **45** 38 40N 20 43 E
Levkimmi **44** 39 25N 20 3 E
Levkôsia = Nicosia **64** 35 10N 33 25 E
Levoča **27** 49 2N 20 35 E
Levroux **19** 47 0N 1 38 E
Levski **43** 43 21N 25 10 E
Levskigrad **43** 42 38N 24 47 E
Lewellen **116** 41 22N 102 5W
Lewes, U.K. **13** 50 53N 0 2 E
Lewes, U.S.A. **114** 38 45N 75 8W
Lewin Brzeski **28** 50 45N 17 37 E
Lewis **14** 58 10N 6 40W
Lewis, Butt of **14** 58 30N 6 12W
Lewis Ra. **118** 48 0N 113 15W
Lewisburg, Pa., U.S.A. **112** 40 57N 76 57W
Lewisburg, Tenn., U.S.A. **115** 35 29N 86 46W
Lewisporte **107** 49 15N 55 3W
Lewiston, Idaho, U.S.A. **118** 46 25N 117 0W
Lewiston, Utah, U.S.A. **118** 41 58N 111 56W
Lewistown, Mont., U.S.A. **118** 47 0N 109 25W
Lewistown, Pa., U.S.A. **112** 40 37N 77 33W
Lexington, Ill., U.S.A. **116** 40 37N 88 47W
Lexington, Ky., U.S.A. **114** 38 6N 84 30W
Lexington, Miss., U.S.A. **117** 33 8N 90 2W
Lexington, Mo., U.S.A. **116** 39 7N 93 55W
Lexington, N.C., U.S.A. **115** 35 50N 80 13W
Lexington, Nebr., U.S.A. **116** 40 48N 99 45W
Lexington, Ohio, U.S.A. **112** 40 39N 82 35W
Lexington, Oreg., U.S.A. **118** 45 29N 119 46W
Lexington, Tenn., U.S.A. **115** 35 38N 88 25W
Lexington Park **114** 38 16N 76 27W
Leyre → **20** 44 39N 1 1W
Leyte **73** 11 0N 125 0 E
Lezajsk **28** 50 16N 22 25 E
Lezay **20** 46 17N 0 0 E
Lezha **44** 41 47N 19 42 E
Lézignan-Corbières **20** 43 13N 2 43 E
Lezoux **20** 45 49N 3 21 E
Lgov **54** 51 42N 35 16 E
Lhasa **75** 29 25N 90 58 E
Lhazê **75** 29 5N 87 38 E
Lhokseumawe **72** 5 10N 97 10 E
Lhuntsi Dzong **67** 27 39N 91 10 E
Li Shui → **77** 29 24N 112 1 E
Li Xian, Gansu, China **77** 34 10N 105 5 E
Li Xian, Hunan, China **77** 29 36N 111 42 E
Liádhoi **45** 36 50N 26 11 E
Lianga **73** 8 38N 126 6 E
Liangdang **77** 33 56N 106 18 E
Lianhua **77** 27 3N 113 54 E
Lianjiang **77** 26 12N 119 27 E
Lianping **77** 24 26N 114 30 E
Lianshanguan **76** 40 53N 123 43 E
Lianyungang **77** 34 40N 119 11 E
Liao He → **76** 41 0N 121 50 E
Liaocheng **76** 36 28N 115 58 E
Liaodong Bandao **76** 40 0N 122 30 E
Liaodong Wan **76** 40 20N 121 10 E
Liaoning □ **76** 42 0N 122 0 E
Liaoyang **76** 41 15N 122 58 E
Liaoyuan **76** 42 58N 125 2 E
Liaozhong **76** 41 23N 122 50 E
Liapádhes **44** 39 42N 19 40 E
Liard → **108** 61 51N 121 18W
Libau = Liepaja **54** 56 30N 21 0 E
Libby **118** 48 20N 115 33W
Libenge **88** 3 40N 18 55 E
Liberal, Kans., U.S.A. **117** 37 4N 101 0W
Liberal, Mo., U.S.A. **117** 37 35N 94 30W
Liberec **26** 50 47N 15 7 E
Liberia **121** 10 40N 85 30W
Liberia ■ **84** 6 30N 9 30W
Liberty, Mo., U.S.A. **116** 39 15N 94 24W
Liberty, Tex., U.S.A. **117** 30 5N 94 50W
Libiaz **27** 50 7N 19 21 E
Libo **77** 25 22N 107 53 E
Libobo, Tanjung **73** 0 54 S 128 28 E
Libohava **44** 40 3N 20 10 E
Libonda **89** 14 28 S 23 12 E
Libourne **20** 44 55N 0 14W
Libramont **16** 49 55N 5 23 E
Librazhdi **44** 41 12N 20 22 E
Libreville **88** 0 25N 9 26 E
Libya ■ **81** 27 0N 17 0 E
Libyan Plateau = Ed-Déffa **86** 30 40N 26 30 E
Licantén **124** 35 55 S 72 0W
Licata **40** 37 6N 13 55 E
Lichfield **12** 52 40N 1 50W
Lichinga **91** 13 13 S 35 11 E
Lichtenburg **92** 26 8 S 26 8 E
Lichtenfels **25** 50 7N 11 4 E
Lichuan **77** 30 18N 108 57 E
Licosa, Punta **41** 40 15N 14 53 E
Lida, U.S.A. **119** 37 30N 117 30W
Lida, U.S.S.R. **54** 53 53N 25 15 E
Lidhult **49** 56 50N 13 27 E
Lidingö **48** 59 22N 18 8 E
Lidköping **49** 58 31N 13 14 E
Lido, Italy **39** 45 25N 12 23 E
Lido, Niger **85** 12 54N 3 44 E
Lido di Ostia **40** 41 44N 12 14 E
Lidzbark **28** 53 15N 19 49 E
Lidzbark Warminski **28** 54 7N 20 34 E
Liebenwalde **24** 52 51N 13 23 E
Lieberose **24** 51 59N 14 18 E
Liebling **42** 45 36N 21 20 E
Liechtenstein ■ **25** 47 8N 9 35 E
Liège **16** 50 38N 5 35 E
Liège □ **16** 50 32N 5 35 E
Liegnitz = Legnica **28** 51 12N 16 10 E
Lienart **90** 3 3N 25 31 E
Lienyünchiangshih = Lianyungang **77** 34 40N 119 11 E
Lienz **26** 46 50N 12 46 E
Liepaja **54** 56 30N 21 0 E
Lier **16** 51 7N 4 34 E
Liesta **46** 45 38N 27 34 E
Liévin **19** 50 24N 2 47 E
Lièvre → **106** 45 31N 75 26W
Liezen **26** 47 34N 14 15 E
Liffey → **15** 53 21N 6 20W
Lifford **15** 54 50N 7 30W
Liffré **18** 48 12N 1 30W
Lifjell **47** 59 27N 8 45 E
Lightning Ridge **99** 29 22 S 148 0 E
Lignano **39** 45 42N 13 8 E
Ligny-en-Barrois **19** 48 36N 5 20 E
Ligny-le-Châtel **19** 47 54N 3 45 E
Ligoúrion **45** 37 37N 23 2 E
Ligua, La **124** 32 30 S 71 16W
Ligueil **18** 47 2N 0 49 E
Liguria □ **38** 44 30N 9 0 E
Ligurian Sea **38** 43 20N 9 0 E
Lihir Group **98** 3 0 S 152 35 E
Lihou Reefs and Cays **97** 17 25 S 151 40 E
Lihue **110** 21 59N 159 24W
Lijiang **75** 26 55N 100 20 E
Likasi **91** 10 55 S 26 48 E
Likati **88** 3 20N 24 0 E
Likhoslavl **54** 57 12N 35 30 E
Likhovski **57** 48 10N 40 10 E
Likoma I. **91** 12 3 S 34 45 E
Likumburu **91** 9 43 S 35 8 E
Liling **77** 27 42N 113 29 E
Lille **19** 50 38N 3 3 E
Lille Bælt **49** 55 20N 9 45 E
Lillebonne **18** 49 30N 0 32 E
Lillehammer **47** 61 8N 10 30 E
Lillers **19** 50 35N 2 28 E
Lillesand **47** 58 15N 8 23 E
Lilleshall **13** 52 45N 2 22W
Lillestrøm **47** 59 58N 11 5 E
Lillo **32** 39 45N 3 20W
Lillooet → **108** 49 15N 121 57W
Lilongwe **91** 14 0 S 33 48 E
Liloy **73** 8 4N 122 39 E
Lim → **42** 43 0N 19 40 E
Lima, Indon. **73** 3 37 S 128 4 E
Lima, Peru **126** 12 0 S 77 0W
Lima, Sweden **48** 60 55N 13 20 E
Lima, Mont., U.S.A. **118** 44 41N 112 38W
Lima, Ohio, U.S.A. **114** 40 42N 84 5W
Lima → **30** 41 41N 8 50W
Limages **113** 45 20N 75 16W
Liman **57** 45 45N 47 12 E
Limanowa **27** 49 42N 20 22 E
Limassol **64** 34 42N 33 1 E
Limavady **15** 55 3N 6 58W
Limavady □ **15** 55 0N 6 55W
Limay → **128** 39 0 S 68 0W
Limay Mahuida **124** 37 10 S 66 45W
Limbang **72** 4 42N 115 6 E
Limbara, Monti **40** 40 50N 9 10 E
Limbdi **68** 22 34N 71 51 E
Limbri **99** 31 3 S 151 5 E
Limburg **25** 50 22N 8 4 E
Limburg □, Belg. **16** 51 2N 5 25 E
Limburg □, Neth. **16** 51 20N 5 55 E
Limedsforsen **48** 60 52N 13 25 E
Limeira **125** 22 35 S 47 28W
Limenária **44** 40 38N 24 32 E
Limerick **15** 52 40N 8 38W
Limerick □ **15** 52 30N 8 50W
Limestone **112** 42 2N 78 39W
Limestone → **109** 56 31N 94 7W
Limfjorden **49** 56 55N 9 0 E
Limia → **30** 41 41N 8 50W
Limmared **49** 57 34N 13 20 E
Limmen Bight **96** 14 40 S 135 35 E
Límni **45** 38 43N 23 18 E
Límnos **44** 39 50N 25 5 E
Limoeiro do Norte **127** 5 5 S 38 0W
Limoges **20** 45 50N 1 15 E
Limón **121** 10 0N 83 2W
Limon, Panama **120** 9 17N 79 45W
Limon, U.S.A. **116** 39 18N 103 38W
Limon B. **120** 9 22N 79 56W
Limone Piemonte **38** 44 12N 7 32 E
Limousin **20** 46 0N 1 0 E
Limousin, Plateaux du **20** 46 0N 1 0 E
Limoux **20** 43 4N 2 12 E
Limpopo → **93** 25 15 S 33 30 E
Limuru **90** 1 2 S 36 35 E
Linares, Chile **124** 35 50 S 71 40W
Linares, Mexico **120** 24 50N 99 40W
Linares, Spain **33** 38 10N 3 40W
Linares □ **124** 36 0 S 71 0W
Linas Mte. **40** 39 25N 8 38 E
Lincheng **76** 37 25N 114 30 E
Linchuan **75** 27 57N 116 15 E
Lincoln, Argent. **124** 34 55 S 61 30W
Lincoln, N.Z. **101** 43 38 S 172 30 E
Lincoln, U.K. **12** 53 14N 0 32W
Lincoln, Ill., U.S.A. **116** 40 10N 89 20W
Lincoln, Kans., U.S.A. **116** 39 6N 98 9W
Lincoln, Maine, U.S.A. **107** 45 27N 68 29W
Lincoln, N. Mex., U.S.A. **119** 33 30N 105 26W
Lincoln, N.H., U.S.A. **113** 44 3N 71 40W
Lincoln, Nebr., U.S.A. **116** 40 50N 96 42W
Lincoln □ **12** 53 14N 0 32W
Lincoln Sea **4** 84 0N 55 0W
Lincoln Wolds **12** 53 20N 0 5W
Lincolnton **115** 35 30N 81 15W
Lind **118** 47 0N 118 33W
Lindås, Norway **47** 60 44N 5 9 E
Lindås, Sweden **49** 56 38N 15 35 E
Lindau **25** 47 33N 9 41 E
Linden, Guyana **126** 6 0N 58 10W
Linden, U.S.A. **117** 33 0N 94 20W
Linderöd **49** 55 56N 13 47 E
Linderödsåsen **49** 55 53N 13 53 E
Lindesberg **48** 59 36N 15 15 E
Lindesnes **47** 57 58N 7 3 E
Lindi **91** 9 58 S 39 38 E
Lindi □ **91** 9 40 S 38 30 E
Lindi → **90** 0 33N 25 5 E
Lindian **76** 47 11N 124 52 E
Lindoso **30** 41 52N 8 11W
Lindow **24** 52 58N 12 58 E
Lindsay, Can. **106** 44 22N 78 43W
Lindsay, Calif., U.S.A. **119** 36 14N 119 6W
Lindsay, Okla., U.S.A. **117** 34 51N 97 37W
Lindsborg **116** 38 35N 97 40W
Línea de la Concepción, La **31** 36 15N 5 23W
Linfen **76** 36 3N 111 30 E
Ling Xian **76** 37 22N 116 30 E
Lingao **77** 19 56N 109 42 E
Lingayen **73** 16 1N 120 14 E
Lingayen G. **73** 16 10N 120 15 E
Lingchuan **77** 25 26N 110 21 E
Lingen **24** 52 32N 7 21 E
Lingga **72** 0 12 S 104 37 E
Lingga, Kepulauan **72** 0 10 S 104 30 E
Linghed **48** 60 48N 15 55 E
Lingle **116** 42 10N 104 18W
Lingling **77** 26 17N 111 37 E
Lingshan **77** 22 25N 109 18 E
Lingshi **76** 36 48N 111 48 E
Lingshui **77** 18 27N 110 0 E
Lingtai **77** 35 0N 107 40 E
Linguéré **84** 15 25N 15 5W
Lingyuan **76** 41 10N 119 15 E
Lingyun **75** 25 2N 106 35 E
Linh Cam **71** 18 31N 105 31 E
Linhai **75** 28 50N 121 8 E
Linhe **76** 40 48N 107 20 E
Linjiang **76** 41 50N 127 0 E
Linköping **49** 58 28N 15 36 E
Linkou **76** 45 15N 130 18 E
Linlithgow **14** 55 58N 3 38W
Linn, Mt. **118** 40 0N 123 0W
Linnhe, L. **14** 56 36N 5 25W
Linosa, I. **83** 35 51N 12 50 E
Linqing **76** 36 50N 115 42 E
Lins **125** 21 40 S 49 44W
Lintao **76** 35 18N 103 52 E
Linth → **25** 47 7N 9 7W
Linthal **25** 46 54N 9 0 E
Lintlaw **109** 52 4N 103 14W
Linton, Can. **107** 47 15N 72 16W
Linton, Ind., U.S.A. **114** 39 0N 87 10W
Linton, N. Dak., U.S.A. **116** 46 21N 100 12W
Linville **99** 26 50 S 152 11 E
Linwood **112** 43 35N 80 43W
Linwu **77** 25 19N 112 31 E
Linxe **20** 43 56N 1 13W
Linxi **76** 43 36N 118 2 E
Linxia **75** 35 36N 103 10 E
Linyanti → **92** 17 50 S 25 5 E
Linyi **77** 35 5N 118 21 E
Linz, Austria **26** 48 18N 14 18 E
Linz, Ger. **24** 50 33N 7 18 E
Lion-d'Angers, Le **18** 47 37N 0 43W
Lion, G. du **20** 43 0N 4 0 E
Lioni **41** 40 52N 15 10 E
Lion's Den **91** 17 15 S 30 5 E
Lion's Head **106** 44 58N 81 15W
Liozno **54** 55 0N 30 50 E
Lipali **91** 15 50 S 35 50 E
Lípari **41** 38 26N 14 58 E
Lípari, Is. **41** 38 30N 14 50 E
Lipetsk **55** 52 37N 39 35 E
Lipiany **28** 53 2N 14 58 E
Liping **77** 26 15N 109 7 E
Lipkany **56** 48 14N 26 48 E
Lipljan **42** 42 31N 21 7 E
Lipnik **27** 49 32N 17 36 E
Lipno **28** 52 49N 19 15 E
Lipova **42** 46 8N 21 42 E
Lipovets **56** 49 12N 29 1 E
Lippe → **24** 51 39N 6 38 E
Lippstadt **24** 51 40N 8 19 E
Lipscomb **117** 36 16N 100 16W
Lipsko **28** 51 9N 21 40 E
Lipsói **45** 37 19N 26 50 E
Liptovsky Svaty Milkulaš **27** 49 6N 19 35 E
Liptrap C. **99** 38 50 S 145 55 E
Lira **90** 2 17N 32 57 E
Liri → **40** 41 25N 13 52 E
Liria **32** 39 37N 0 35W
Lisala **88** 2 12N 21 38 E
Lisboa **31** 38 42N 9 10W
Lisboa □ **31** 39 0N 9 12W
Lisbon, N. Dak., U.S.A. **116** 46 30N 97 46W
Lisbon, N.H., U.S.A. **113** 44 13N 71 52W
Lisbon, Ohio, U.S.A. **112** 40 45N 80 42W
Lisbon = Lisboa **31** 38 42N 9 10W
Lisburn **15** 54 30N 6 9W
Lisburne, C. **104** 68 50N 166 0W
Liscannor, B. **15** 52 57N 9 24W
Liscia → **40** 41 11N 9 9 E
Lishi **76** 37 31N 111 8 E
Lishui **75** 28 28N 119 54 E
Lisianski I. **94** 26 2N 174 0W
Lisichansk **56** 48 55N 38 30 E
Lisieux **18** 49 10N 0 12 E
Lisle-sur-Tarn **20** 43 52N 1 49 E
Lismore, Austral. **97** 28 44 S 153 21 E
Lismore, Ireland **15** 52 8N 7 58W
Lisse **16** 52 16N 4 33 E
List **24** 55 1N 8 26 E
Lista **47** 58 7N 6 39 E
Lister, Mt. **5** 78 0 S 162 0 E
Liston **99** 28 39 S 152 6 E
Listowel, Can. **106** 43 44N 80 58W
Listowel, Ireland **15** 52 27N 9 30W
Lit-et-Mixe **20** 44 2N 1 15W
Litang, China **77** 23 12N 109 8 E
Litang, Malay. **73** 5 27N 118 31 E
Litani →, Leb. **62** 33 20N 35 14 E
Litani →, Surinam **62** 3 40N 54 0W
Litchfield, Conn., U.S.A. **113** 41 44N 73 12W
Litchfield, Ill., U.S.A. **116** 39 10N 89 40W
Litchfield, Minn., U.S.A. **116** 45 5N 94 31W
Liteni **46** 47 32N 26 32 E

ithgow 97 33 25 S 150 8 E
íthinon, Ákra 45 34 55N 24 44 E
ithuanian S.S.R. □ 54 55 30N 24 0 E
itija 39 46 3N 14 50 E
itókhoron 44 40 8N 22 34 E
itoměřice 26 50 33N 14 10 E
itomysl 27 49 52N 16 20 E
itschau 26 48 58N 15 4 E
ittle Abaco I. 121 26 50N 77 30W
ittle America 5 79 0S 160 0W
ittle Andaman I. 71 10 40N 92 15 E
ittle Barrier I. 101 36 12S 175 8 E
ittle Belt Mts. 118 46 50N 111 0W
ittle Blue → 116 39 41N 96 40W
ittle Bushman Land 92 29 10S 18 10 E
ittle Cadotte → 108 56 41N 117 6W
ittle Churchill → 109 57 30N 95 22W
ittle Colorado → 119 36 11N 111 48W
ittle Current 106 45 55N 82 0W
ittle Current → 106 50 57N 84 36W
ittle Falls, Minn., U.S.A. 116 45 58N 94 19W
ittle Falls, N.Y., U.S.A. 114 43 3N 74 50W
ittle Fork → 116 48 31N 93 35W
ittle Grand Rapids 109 52 0N 95 29W
ittle Humboldt → 118 41 0N 117 43W
ittle Inagua I. 121 21 40N 73 50W
ittle Lake 119 35 58N 117 58W
ittle Marais 116 47 24N 91 8W
ittle Minch 14 57 35N 6 45W
ittle Missouri → 116 47 30N 102 25W
ittle Namaqualand 92 29 0S 17 9 E
ittle Ouse → 13 52 25N 0 50 E
ittle Rann of Kutch 68 23 25N 71 25 E
ittle Red → 117 35 11N 91 27W
ittle River 101 43 45S 172 49 E
ittle Rock 117 34 41N 92 10W
ittle Ruaha → 90 7 57S 37 53 E
ittle Sable Pt. 114 43 40N 86 32W
ittle Sioux → 116 41 49N 96 4W
ittle Smoky → 108 54 44N 117 11W
ittle Snake → 118 40 27N 108 26W
ittle Valley 112 42 15N 78 48W
ittle Wabash → 114 37 54N 88 5W
ittlefield 117 33 57N 102 17W
ittlefork 116 48 24N 93 35W
ittlehampton 13 50 48N 0 32W
ittleton 114 44 19N 71 47W
iuba 77 33 38N 106 55 E
iucheng 77 24 38N 109 14 E
iukang Tenggaja 73 6 45S 118 50 E
iuli 91 11 3S 34 38 E
iuwa Plain 89 14 20S 22 30 E
iuyang 77 28 10N 113 37 E
iuzhou 75 24 22N 109 22 E
ivada 46 47 52N 23 5 E
ivadherón 44 40 2N 21 57 E
ivarot 18 49 0N 0 9 E
ive Oak 115 30 17N 83 0W
ivermore, Mt. 117 30 45N 104 8W
iverpool, Austral. 97 33 54S 150 58 E
iverpool, Can. 107 44 5N 64 41W
iverpool, U.K. 12 53 25N 3 0W
iverpool Plains 97 31 15S 150 15 E
iverpool Ra. 97 31 50S 150 30 E
ivingston, Guat. 120 15 50N 88 50W
ivingston, U.S.A. 118 45 40N 110 40W
ivingstone, U.S.A. 117 30 44N 94 54W
ivingstone, Zambia 91 17 46S 25 52 E
ivingstone I. 5 63 0S 60 15W
ivingstone Memorial 91 12 20S 30 18 E
ivingstone Mts. 91 9 40S 34 20 E
ivingstonia 91 10 38S 34 5 E
ivno 42 43 50N 17 0 E
ivny 55 52 30N 37 30 E
ivorno 38 43 32N 10 18 E
ivramento 125 30 55S 55 30W
ivron-sur-Drôme 21 44 46N 4 51 E
iwale 91 9 48S 37 58 E
iwale □ 91 9 0S 38 0 E
iwiec → 28 52 36N 21 34 E
ixoúrion 45 38 14N 20 24 E
izard I. 98 14 42S 145 30 E
izard Pt. 13 49 57N 5 11W
izzano 41 40 23N 17 25 E
jig 42 44 13N 20 18 E
jubija 39 44 55N 16 35 E
jubinje 42 42 58N 18 5 E
jubljana 39 46 4N 14 33 E
jubno 39 46 25N 14 46 E
jubovija 42 44 11N 19 22 E
jubuški 42 43 12N 17 34 E
jung 49 58 1N 13 3 E
jungan → 48 62 18N 17 23 E
jungaverk 48 62 30N 16 5 E
jungby 49 56 49N 13 55 E
jusdal 48 61 46N 16 3 E
jusnan → 48 61 12N 17 8 E
jusne 48 61 13N 17 7 E
jutomer 39 46 31N 16 11 E
lagostera 32 41 50N 2 54 E
lancanelo, Salina 124 35 40S 69 8W
landeilo 13 51 53N 4 0W
landovery 13 51 59N 3 49W
landrindod Wells 13 52 15N 3 23W
landudno 12 53 19N 3 51W
lanelli 13 51 41N 4 11W
lanes 30 43 25N 4 50W
langollen 12 52 58N 3 10W
lanidloes 13 52 28N 3 31W
lano 117 30 45N 98 41W
lano → 117 30 50N 98 25W
lano Estacado 117 34 0N 103 0W
lanos 126 5 0N 71 35W
lera 120 23 19N 99 1W
lerena 31 38 17N 6 0W
lico 124 34 46S 72 5W
lobregat → 32 41 19N 2 9 E
loret de Mar 32 41 41N 2 53 E
loyd B. 98 12 45S 143 27 E
loyd L. 109 57 22N 108 57W
loydminster 109 53 17N 110 0W
luchmayor 33 39 29N 2 53 E
Llullaillaco, volcán 124 24 43S 68 30W
Loa 119 38 18N 111 40W
Loa → 124 21 26S 70 41W
Loano 38 44 8N 8 14 E
Lobatse 92 25 12S 25 40 E
Löbau 24 51 5N 14 42 E
Lobenstein 24 50 25N 11 39 E
Lobería 124 38 10S 58 40W
Łobez 28 53 38N 15 39 E
Lobito 89 12 18S 13 35 E
Lobón, Canal de 31 38 50N 6 55W
Lobos 124 35 10S 59 0W
Lobos, I. 120 27 15N 110 30W
Lobos, Is. 122 6 57S 80 45W
Lobstick L. 107 54 0N 65 0W
Loc Binh 71 21 46N 106 54 E
Loc Ninh 71 11 50N 106 34 E
Locarno 25 46 10N 8 47 E
Lochaber 14 56 55N 5 0W
Lochcarron 14 57 25N 5 30W
Loche, La 109 56 29N 109 26W
Lochem 16 52 9N 6 26 E
Loches 18 47 7N 1 0 E
Lochgelly 14 56 7N 3 18W
Lochgilphead 14 56 2N 5 37W
Lochinver 14 58 9N 5 15W
Lochnagar, Austral. 98 23 33S 145 38 E
Lochnagar, U.K. 14 56 57N 3 14W
Łochów 28 52 33N 21 42 E
Lochy → 14 56 52N 5 3W
Lock 99 33 34S 135 46 E
Lock Haven 114 41 7N 77 31W
Lockeport 107 43 47N 65 4W
Lockerbie 14 55 7N 3 21W
Lockhart, Austral. 99 35 14S 146 40 E
Lockhart, U.S.A. 117 29 55N 97 40W
Lockney 117 34 7N 101 27W
Lockport 114 43 12N 78 42W
Locle, Le 25 47 3N 6 44 E
Locminé 18 47 54N 2 51W
Locri 41 38 14N 16 14 E
Locronan 18 48 7N 4 15W
Loctudy 18 47 50N 4 12W
Lod 62 31 57N 34 54 E
Lodalskåpa 47 61 47N 7 13 E
Loddon → 100 35 31S 143 51 E
Lodeinoye Pole 52 60 44N 33 33 E
Lodève 20 43 44N 3 19 E
Lodge Grass 118 45 21N 107 20W
Lodgepole 116 41 12N 102 40W
Lodgepole Cr. → 116 41 20N 104 30W
Lodhran 68 29 32N 71 30 E
Lodi, Italy 38 45 19N 9 30 E
Lodi, U.S.A. 118 38 12N 121 16W
Lodja 90 3 30S 23 23 E
Lodosa 32 42 25N 2 4W
Lödöse 49 58 2N 12 9 E
Lodwar 90 3 10N 35 40 E
Łódź 28 51 45N 19 27 E
Łódź □ 28 51 45N 19 27 E
Loengo 90 4 48S 26 30 E
Lofer 26 47 35N 12 41 E
Lofoten 50 68 30N 15 0 E
Lofsdalen 48 62 10N 13 20 E
Lofsen → 48 62 7N 13 57 E
Loftahammar 49 57 54N 16 41 E
Logan, Kans., U.S.A. 116 39 40N 99 35W
Logan, Ohio, U.S.A. 114 39 25N 82 22W
Logan, Utah, U.S.A. 118 41 45N 111 50W
Logan, W. Va., U.S.A. 114 37 51N 81 59W
Logan, Mt. 104 60 31N 140 22W
Logan Pass 108 48 41N 113 44W
Logansport, Ind., U.S.A. 114 40 45N 86 21W
Logansport, La., U.S.A. 117 31 58N 93 58W
Logar □ 65 34 0N 69 0 E
Logo 87 5 20N 30 18 E
Logroño 32 42 28N 2 27W
* Logroño □ 32 42 28N 2 27W
Logrosán 31 39 20N 5 32W
Løgstør 49 56 58N 9 14 E
Lohardaga 69 23 27N 84 45 E
Lohja 51 60 12N 24 5 E
Lohr 25 50 0N 9 35 E
Loi-kaw 67 19 40N 97 17 E
Loimaa 51 60 50N 23 5 E
Loir → 18 47 33N 0 32W
Loir-et-Cher □ 18 47 40N 1 20 E
Loire □ 21 45 40N 4 5 E
Loire → 18 47 16N 2 10W
Loire-Atlantique □ 18 47 25N 1 40W
Loiret □ 19 47 58N 2 10 E
Loitz 24 53 58N 13 8 E
Loja, Ecuador 126 3 59S 79 16W
Loja, Spain 31 37 10N 4 10W
Loji 73 1 38S 127 28 E
Loka 87 4 13N 31 0 E
Lokandu 90 2 30S 25 45 E
Løken 47 59 48N 11 29 E
Lokeren 16 51 6N 3 59 E
Lokhvitsa 54 50 25N 33 18 E
Lokichokio 90 4 19N 34 13 E
Lokitaung 90 4 12N 35 48 E
Lokka 50 67 49N 27 45 E
Løkken 49 57 22N 9 41 E
Løkkenverk 47 63 8N 9 45 E
Loknya 54 56 49N 30 4 E
Lokoja 85 7 47N 6 45 E
Lokolama 88 2 35S 19 50 E
Lokwei 77 19 5N 110 31 E
Lol → 87 9 13N 26 30 E
Lola 84 7 52N 8 29W
Lolibai, Gebel 87 3 50N 33 0 E
Lolimi 87 4 35N 34 0 E
Loliondo 90 2 2S 35 39 E
Lolland 49 54 45N 11 30 E
Lollar 24 50 39N 8 43 E
Lolo 118 46 50N 114 8W
Lolodorf 85 3 16N 10 49 E
Lom 43 43 48N 23 12 E
Lom → 42 43 45N 23 15 E
Loma 118 47 59N 110 29W
Lomami → 90 0 46N 24 16 E

* *Renamed La Rioja* □

Lomas de Zamóra 124 34 45S 58 25W
Lombard 118 46 7N 111 28W
Lombardia □ 38 45 35N 9 45 E
Lombardy = Lombardia 38 45 35N 9 45 E
Lombez 20 43 29N 0 55 E
Lomblen 73 8 30S 123 32 E
Lombok 72 8 45S 116 30 E
Lomé 85 6 9N 1 20 E
Lomela 88 2 19S 23 15 E
Lomela → 88 1 30S 22 50 E
Lomello 38 45 5N 8 46 E
Lometa 117 31 15N 98 25W
Lomié 88 3 13N 13 38 E
Lomma 49 55 43N 13 6 E
Lomond 108 50 24N 112 36W
Lomond, L. 14 56 8N 4 38W
Lomonosov 54 59 57N 29 53 E
Lompobatang 73 5 24S 119 56 E
Lompoc 119 34 41N 120 32W
Lomsegga 47 61 49N 8 21 E
Łomza 28 53 10N 22 2 E
Łomza □ 28 53 0N 22 30 E
Lonavla 70 18 46N 73 29 E
Loncoche 128 39 20S 72 50W
Londa 70 15 30N 74 30 E
Londe, La 21 43 8N 6 14 E
Londiani 90 0 10S 35 33 E
Londinières 18 49 50N 1 25 E
London, Can. 106 42 59N 81 15W
London, U.K. 13 51 30N 0 5W
London, Ky., U.S.A. 114 37 11N 84 5W
London, Ohio, U.S.A. 114 39 54N 83 28W
London, Greater □ 13 51 30N 0 5W
Londonderry 15 55 0N 7 20W
Londonderry □ 15 55 0N 7 20W
Londonderry, C. 96 13 45S 126 55 E
Londonderry, I. 128 55 0S 71 0W
Londrina 125 23 18S 51 10W
Lone Pine 119 36 35N 118 2W
Long Beach, Calif., U.S.A. 119 33 46N 118 12W
Long Beach, N.Y., U.S.A. 113 40 35N 73 40W
Long Beach, Wash., U.S.A. 118 46 20N 124 1W
Long Branch 114 40 19N 74 0W
Long Creek 118 44 43N 119 6W
Long Eaton 12 52 54N 1 16W
Long I., Austral. 98 22 8S 149 53 E
Long I., Bahamas 121 23 20N 75 10W
Long I., P.N.G. 98 5 20S 147 5 E
Long I., U.S.A. 114 40 50N 73 20W
Long I. Sd. 113 41 10N 73 0W
Long L. 106 49 30N 86 50W
Long Lake 113 43 57N 74 25W
Long Pine 116 42 33N 99 41W
Long Pt., Newf., Can. 107 48 47N 58 46W
Long Pt., Ont., Can. 112 42 35N 80 2W
Long Point B. 112 42 40N 80 10W
Long Range Mts. 107 49 30N 57 30W
Long Str. 4 70 0N 175 0 E
Long Xian 77 34 55N 106 55 E
Long Xuyen 71 10 19N 105 28 E
Longá 45 36 53N 21 55 E
Long'an 77 23 10N 107 40 E
Longarone 39 46 15N 12 18 E
Longchuan 77 24 5N 115 17 E
Longde 76 35 30N 106 20 E
Longeau 19 47 47N 5 20 E
Longford, Austral. 99 41 32S 147 3 E
Longford, Ireland 15 53 43N 7 50W
Longford □ 15 53 42N 7 45W
Longhua 76 41 18N 117 45 E
Longido 90 2 43S 36 42 E
Longiram 72 0 5S 115 45 E
Longjiang 76 47 20N 123 12 E
Longkou 76 37 40N 120 18 E
Longlac 106 49 45N 86 25W
Longlin 77 24 47N 105 20 E
Longmen 77 23 40N 114 18 E
Longmont 116 40 10N 105 4W
Longnan 77 24 55N 114 47 E
Longnawan 72 1 51N 114 55 E
Longobucco 41 39 27N 16 37 E
Longone → 81 10 0N 15 40 E
Longquan 77 28 7N 119 10 E
Longreach 97 23 28S 144 14 E
Longs Peak 118 40 20N 105 37W
Longshan 77 29 29N 109 25 E
Longsheng 77 25 48N 110 0 E
Longton 98 20 58S 145 55 E
Longtown 13 51 58N 2 59W
Longué 18 47 22N 0 8W
Longueau 19 49 52N 2 21 E
Longueuil 113 45 32N 73 28W
Longuyon 19 49 27N 5 35 E
Longview, Can. 108 50 32N 114 10W
Longview, Tex., U.S.A. 117 32 30N 94 45W
Longview, Wash., U.S.A. 118 46 9N 122 58W
Longwy 19 49 30N 5 45 E
Longxi 76 34 53N 104 40 E
Longzhou 77 22 22N 106 50 E
Lonigo 39 45 23N 11 22 E
Löningen 24 52 43N 7 44 E
Lonja → 39 45 30N 16 40 E
Lonoke 117 34 48N 91 57W
Lons-le-Saunier 19 46 40N 5 31 E
Lønstrup 49 57 29N 9 47 E
Looc 73 12 20N 112 5 E
Lookout, C., Can. 106 55 18N 83 56W
Lookout, C., U.S.A. 115 34 30N 76 30W
Loolmalasin 90 3 0S 35 53 E
Loon →, Alta., Can. 108 57 8N 115 3W
Loon →, Man., Can. 109 55 53N 101 59W
Loon Lake 109 54 2N 109 10W
Loop Hd. 15 52 34N 9 55W
Lop Nor = Lop Nur 75 40 20N 90 10 E
Lop Nur 75 40 20N 90 10 E
Lopare 42 44 39N 18 46 E
Lopatin 57 43 50N 47 35 E
Lopatina, G. 59 50 47N 143 10 E
Lopaye 87 6 37N 33 40 E
Lopera 31 37 56N 4 14W
Lopez, C. 88 0 47S 8 40 E
Lopphavet 50 70 27N 21 15 E
Lora →, Afghan. 65 32 0N 67 15 E
Lora →, Norway 47 62 8N 8 42 E
Lora del Río 31 37 39N 5 33W
Lora, Hamun-i- 66 29 38N 64 58 E
Lora, La 30 42 45N 4 0W
Lorain 114 41 28N 82 55W
Loralai 68 30 20N 68 41 E
Lorca 33 37 41N 1 42W
Lord Howe I. 94 31 33S 159 6 E
Lord Howe Ridge 94 30 0S 162 30 E
Lordsburg 119 32 22N 108 45W
Lorengau 98 2 1S 147 15 E
Loreto, Brazil 127 7 5S 45 10W
Loreto, Italy 39 43 26N 13 36 E
Loreto Aprutina 39 42 24N 13 59 E
Lorgues 21 43 28N 6 22 E
Lorient 18 47 45N 3 23W
Loristān □ 64 33 20N 47 0 E
Lorn 14 56 26N 5 10W
Lorn, Firth of 14 56 20N 5 40W
Lorne 99 38 33S 143 59 E
Lörrach 25 47 36N 7 38 E
Lorraine 19 49 0N 6 0 E
Lorrainville 106 47 21N 79 23W
Los Alamos 119 35 57N 106 17W
Los Andes 124 32 50S 70 40W
Los Angeles, Chile 124 37 28S 72 23W
Los Angeles, U.S.A. 119 34 0N 118 10W
Los Angeles Aqueduct 119 35 25N 118 0W
Los Banos 119 37 8N 120 56W
Los Barrios 31 36 11N 5 30W
Los Blancos 124 23 40S 62 30W
Los Gatos 119 37 15N 121 59W
Los Hermanos 126 11 45N 84 25W
Los, Îles de 84 9 30N 13 50W
Los Lamentos 120 30 36N 105 50W
Los Lunas 119 34 48N 106 47W
Los Mochis 120 25 45N 109 5W
Los Monegros 32 41 29N 0 13W
Los Olivos 119 34 40N 120 7W
Los Palacios y Villafranca 31 37 10N 5 55W
Los Roques 126 11 50N 66 45W
Los Santos de Maimona 31 38 27N 6 22W
Los Testigos 126 11 23N 63 6W
Los Vilos 124 32 10S 71 30W
Los Yébenes 31 39 36N 3 55W
Loshkalakh 59 62 45N 147 20 E
Łosice 28 52 13N 22 43 E
Lošinj 39 44 30N 14 30 E
Lossiemouth 14 57 43N 3 17W
Losuia 98 8 30S 151 4 E
Lot □ 20 44 39N 1 40 E
Lot → 20 44 18N 0 20 E
Lot-et-Garonne □ 20 44 22N 0 30 E
Lota 124 37 5S 73 10W
Løten 47 60 51N 11 21 E
Lothian □ 14 55 50N 3 0W
Lothiers 19 46 42N 1 33 E
Lotschbergtunnel 25 46 26N 7 43 E
Lottefors 48 61 25N 16 24 E
Loubomo 88 4 9S 12 47 E
Loudéac 18 48 11N 2 47W
Loudon 115 35 35N 84 22W
Loudonville 112 40 40N 82 15W
Loudun 18 47 0N 0 5 E
Loué 18 47 59N 0 9W
Loue → 19 47 1N 5 27 E
Louga 84 15 45N 16 5W
Loughborough 12 52 46N 1 11W
Loughrea 15 53 11N 8 33W
Loughros More B. 15 54 48N 8 30W
Louhans 21 46 38N 5 12 E
Louis Trichardt 93 23 0S 29 43 E
Louis XIV, Pte. 106 54 37N 79 45W
Louisa 114 38 5N 82 40W
Louisbourg 107 45 55N 60 0W
Louise I. 108 52 55N 131 50W
Louiseville 106 46 20N 72 56W
Louisiade Arch. 94 11 10S 153 0 E
Louisiana 116 39 25N 91 0W
Louisiana □ 117 30 50N 92 0W
Louisville, Ky., U.S.A. 114 38 15N 85 45W
Louisville, Miss., U.S.A. 117 33 7N 89 3W
Loulay 20 46 3N 0 30W
Loulé 31 37 9N 8 0W
Lount L. 109 50 10N 94 20W
Louny 26 50 20N 13 48 E
Loup City 116 41 19N 98 57W
Loupe, La 18 48 29N 1 1 E
Lourdes 20 43 6N 0 3W
Lourdes-du-Blanc-Sablon 107 51 24N 57 12W
Lourenço-Marques = Maputo 93 25 58S 32 32 E
Loures 31 38 50N 9 9W
Lourinhã 31 39 14N 9 17W
Louroux-Béconnais, Le 18 47 30N 0 55W
Lousã 30 40 7N 8 14W
Louth, Austral. 99 30 30S 145 8 E
Louth, Ireland 15 53 47N 6 33W
Louth, U.K. 12 53 23N 0 0W
Louth □ 15 53 55N 6 30W
Loutrá Aidhipsoú 45 38 54N 23 2 E
Loutráki 45 38 0N 22 57 E
Louvière, La 16 50 27N 4 10 E
Louviers 18 49 12N 1 10 E
Lovat → 54 58 14N 30 28 E
Lovćen 42 42 23N 18 51 E
Love 109 53 29N 104 10W
Lovech 43 43 8N 24 42 E
Loveland 116 40 27N 105 4W
Lovell 118 44 51N 108 20W
Lovelock 118 40 17N 118 25W
Lóvere 38 45 50N 10 4 E
Loviisa 51 60 28N 26 12 E
Loving 117 32 17N 104 4W
Lovington 117 33 0N 103 20W
Lovios 30 41 55N 8 4W
Lovisa 51 60 28N 26 12 E
Lovosice 26 50 30N 14 2 E
Lovran 39 45 18N 14 15 E
Lovrin 42 45 58N 20 48 E
Lövstabukten 48 60 35N 17 45 E
Low Rocky Pt. 97 42 59S 145 29 E

Lowa 90 1 25 S 25 47 E
Lowa → 90 1 24 S 25 51 E
Lowell 114 42 38N 71 19W
Lower Arrow L. 108 49 40N 118 5W
Lower Austria = Niederösterreich □ 26 48 25N 15 40 E
Lower Hutt 101 41 10 S 174 55 E
Lower L. 118 41 17N 120 3W
Lower Lake 118 38 56N 122 36W
Lower Neguac 107 47 20N 65 10W
Lower Post 108 59 58N 128 30W
Lower Red L. 116 47 58N 95 0W
Lower Saxony = Niedersachsen □ 24 52 45N 9 0 E
Lowestoft 13 52 29N 1 44 E
Łowicz 28 52 6N 19 55 E
Lowville 114 43 48N 75 30W
Loxton 97 34 28 S 140 31 E
Loyalty Is. = Loyauté, Is. 94 21 0 S 167 30 E
Loyang = Luoyang 77 34 40N 112 26 E
Loyev, U.S.S.R. 54 51 55N 30 40 E
Loyev, U.S.S.R. 54 51 56N 30 46 E
Loyoro 90 3 22N 34 14 E
Lož 39 45 43N 30 14 E
Lozère □ 20 44 35N 3 30 E
Loznica 42 44 32N 19 14 E
Lozovaya 56 49 0N 36 20 E
Luachimo 88 7 23 S 20 48 E
Luacono 88 11 15 S 21 37 E
Lualaba → 90 0 26N 25 20 E
Luampa 91 15 4 S 24 20 E
Lu'an 77 31 45N 116 29 E
Luan Chau 71 21 38N 103 24 E
Luan Xian 76 39 40N 118 40 E
Luanda 88 8 50 S 13 15 E
Luang Prabang 71 19 52N 102 10 E
Luangwa Valley 91 13 30 S 31 30 E
Luanping 76 40 53N 117 23 E
Luanshya 91 13 3 S 28 28 E
Luapula □ 91 11 0 S 29 0 E
Luapula → 91 9 26 S 28 33 E
Luarca 30 43 32N 6 32W
Luashi 91 10 50 S 23 36 E
Luau 88 10 40 S 22 10 E
Lubaczów 28 50 10N 23 8 E
Lubalo 88 9 10 S 19 15 E
Lubań 28 51 5N 15 15 E
Lubana, Ozero 54 56 45N 27 0 E
Lubang Is. 73 13 50N 120 12 E
Lubartów 28 51 28N 22 42 E
Lubawa 28 53 30N 19 48 E
Lübben 24 51 56N 13 54 E
Lübbenau 24 51 49N 13 59 E
Lubbock 117 33 40N 101 53W
Lübeck 24 53 52N 10 41 E
Lübecker Bucht 24 54 3N 11 0 E
Lubefu 90 4 47 S 24 27 E
Lubefu → 90 4 10 S 23 0 E
Lubero = Luofu 90 0 1 S 29 15 E
Lubicon L. 108 56 23N 115 56W
Lubień Kujawski 28 52 23N 19 9 E
Lubin 28 51 24N 16 11 E
Lublin 28 51 12N 22 38 E
Lublin □ 28 51 5N 22 30 E
Lubliniec 28 50 43N 18 45 E
Lubny 54 50 3N 32 58 E
Lubok Antu 72 1 3N 111 50 E
Lubon 28 52 21N 16 51 E
Lubongola 90 2 35 S 27 50 E
Lubotin 27 49 17N 20 53 E
Lubran 64 34 0N 36 0 E
Lubraniec 28 52 33N 18 50 E
Lubsko 28 51 45N 14 57 E
Lübtheen 24 53 18N 11 4 E
Lubuagan 73 17 21N 121 10 E
Lubudi → 91 9 0 S 25 35 E
Lubuklinggau 72 3 15 S 102 55 E
Lubuksikaping 72 0 10N 100 15 E
Lubumbashi 91 11 40 S 27 28 E
Lubunda 90 5 12 S 26 41 E
Lubungu 91 14 35 S 26 24 E
Lubutu 90 0 45 S 26 30 E
Luc-en-Diois 21 44 36N 5 28 E
Luc, Le 21 43 23N 6 21 E
Lucan 112 43 11N 81 24W
Lucca 38 43 50N 10 30 E
Luce Bay 14 54 45N 4 48W
Lucea 121 18 25N 78 10W
Lucedale 115 30 55N 88 34W
Lucena, Phil. 73 13 56N 121 37 E
Lucena, Spain 31 37 27N 4 31W
Lucena del Cid 32 40 9N 0 17W
Lučenec 27 48 18N 19 42 E
Lucera 41 41 30N 15 20 E
Lucerne = Luzern 25 47 3N 8 18 E
Luchena → 33 37 44N 1 50W
Lucheringo → 91 11 43 S 36 17 E
Lüchow 24 52 58N 11 8 E
Lucira 89 14 0 S 12 35 E
Luckau 24 51 50N 13 43 E
Luckenwalde 24 52 5N 13 11 E
Lucknow 69 26 50N 81 0 E
Luçon 20 46 28N 1 10W
Lüda 76 38 50N 121 40 E
Luda Kamchiya → 43 43 3N 27 29 E
Ludbreg 39 46 15N 16 38 E
Lüdenscheid 24 51 13N 7 37 E
Lüderitz 92 26 41 S 15 8 E
Ludewe □ 91 10 0 S 34 50 E
Ludhiana 68 30 57N 75 56 E
Lüdinghausen 24 51 46N 7 28 E
Ludington 114 43 58N 86 27W
Ludlow, U.K. 13 52 23N 2 42W
Ludlow, Calif., U.S.A. 119 34 43N 116 10W
Ludlow, Vt., U.S.A. 113 43 25N 72 40W
Ludus 46 46 29N 24 5 E
Ludvika 48 60 8N 15 14 E
Ludwigsburg 25 48 53N 9 11 E
Ludwigshafen 25 49 27N 8 27 E
Ludwigslust 24 53 19N 11 28 E
Ludza 54 56 32N 27 43 E
Luebo 88 5 21 S 21 23 E
Lueki 90 3 20 S 25 48 E
Luena, Zaïre 91 9 28 S 25 43 E
Luena, Zambia 91 10 40 S 30 25 E
Lüeyang 77 33 22N 106 10 E
Lufeng 77 22 57N 115 38 E
Lufkin 117 31 25N 94 40W
Lufupa 91 10 37 S 24 56 E
Luga 54 58 40N 29 55 E
Luga → 54 59 40N 28 18 E
Lugang 77 24 4N 120 23 E
Lugano 25 46 0N 8 57 E
Lugano, L. di 25 46 0N 9 0 E
Lugansk = Voroshilovgrad 57 48 35N 39 20 E
Lugard's Falls 90 3 6 S 38 41 E
Lugela 91 16 25 S 36 43 E
Lugenda → 91 11 25 S 38 33 E
Lugh Ganana 63 3 48N 42 34 E
Lugnaquilla 15 52 58N 6 28W
Lugnvik 48 62 56N 17 55 E
Lugo, Italy 39 44 25N 11 53 E
Lugo, Spain 30 43 2N 7 35W
Lugo □ 30 43 0N 7 30W
Lugoj 42 45 42N 21 57 E
Lugones 30 43 26N 5 50W
Lugovoy 58 42 54N 72 45 E
Luhe → 24 53 18N 10 11 E
Luiana 92 17 25 S 22 59 E
Luino 38 46 0N 8 42 E
Luís Correia 127 3 0 S 41 35W
Luitpold Coast 5 78 30 S 32 0W
Luize 88 7 40 S 22 30 E
Luizi 90 6 0 S 27 25 E
Luján 124 34 45 S 59 5W
Lukanga Swamps 91 14 30 S 27 40 E
Lukenie → 88 3 0 S 18 50 E
Lukhisaral 69 25 11N 86 5 E
Lūki 43 41 50N 24 43 E
Lukolela, Equateur, Zaïre 88 1 10 S 17 12 E
Lukolela, Kasai Or., Zaïre 90 5 23 S 24 32 E
Lukosi 91 18 30 S 26 30 E
Lukovit 43 43 13N 24 11 E
Łuków 28 51 55N 22 23 E
Lukoyanov 55 55 2N 44 29 E
Lule älv → 50 65 35N 22 10 E
Luleå 50 65 35N 22 10 E
Lüleburgaz 43 41 23N 27 22 E
Luling 117 29 45N 97 40W
Lulong 76 39 53N 118 51 E
Lulonga → 88 1 0N 19 0 E
Lulua → 88 6 30 S 22 50 E
Luluabourg = Kananga 88 5 55 S 22 26 E
Lumai 89 13 13 S 21 25 E
Lumajang 73 8 8 S 113 16 E
Lumbala 89 14 18 S 21 18 E
Lumberton, Miss., U.S.A. 117 31 4N 89 28W
Lumberton, N. Mex., U.S.A. 119 36 58N 106 57W
Lumberton, N.C., U.S.A. 115 34 37N 78 59W
Lumbres 19 50 40N 2 5 E
Lumbwa 90 0 12 S 35 28 E
Lumby 108 50 10N 118 50W
Lumsden 101 45 44 S 168 27 E
Lumut 71 4 13N 100 37 E
Lunavada 68 23 8N 73 37 E
Lunca 46 47 22N 25 1 E
Lund, Sweden 49 55 44N 13 12 E
Lund, U.S.A. 118 38 53N 115 0W
Lundazi 91 12 20 S 33 7 E
Lunde 47 59 17N 9 5 E
Lunderskov 49 55 29N 9 19 E
Lundi → 91 21 43 S 32 34 E
Lundu 72 1 40N 109 50 E
Lundy 13 51 10N 4 41W
Lune → 12 54 0N 2 51W
Lüneburg 24 53 15N 10 23 E
Lüneburg Heath = Lüneburger Heide 24 53 0N 10 0 E
Lüneburger Heide 24 53 0N 10 0 E
Lunel 21 43 39N 4 9 E
Lünen 24 51 36N 7 31 E
Lunenburg 107 44 22N 64 18W
Lunéville 19 48 36N 6 30 E
Lunga → 91 14 34 S 26 25 E
Lungi Airport 84 8 40N 13 17W
Lungleh 67 22 55N 92 45 E
Luni 68 26 0N 73 6 E
Lūni → 68 24 41N 71 14 E
Luninets 54 52 15N 26 50 E
Luning 118 38 30N 118 10W
Lunino 55 53 35N 45 6 E
Lunner 47 60 19N 10 35 E
Lunsemfwa → 91 14 54 S 30 12 E
Lunsemfwa Falls 91 14 30 S 29 6 E
Luo He → 77 34 35N 110 20 E
Luobei 76 47 35N 130 50 E
Luocheng 77 24 48N 108 53 E
Luochuan 76 35 45N 109 26 E
Luoding 77 22 45N 111 40 E
Luodong 77 24 41N 121 46 E
Luofu 90 0 10 S 29 15 E
Luoning 77 34 35N 111 40 E
Luoyang 77 34 40N 112 26 E
Luoyuan 77 26 28N 119 30 E
Luozi 88 4 54 S 14 0 E
Lupeni 46 45 21N 23 13 E
Łupków 27 49 15N 22 4 E
Luque, Parag. 124 25 19 S 57 25W
Luque, Spain 31 37 35N 4 16W
Luray 114 38 39N 78 26W
Lure 19 47 40N 6 30 E
Luremo 88 8 30 S 17 50 E
Lurgan 15 54 28N 6 20W
Lusaka 91 15 28 S 28 16 E
Lusambo 90 4 58 S 23 28 E
Lusangaye 90 4 54 S 26 0 E
Luseland 109 52 5N 109 24W
Lushan 77 33 45N 112 55 E
Lushih 77 34 3N 111 3 E
Lushnja 44 40 55N 19 41 E
Lushoto 90 4 47 S 38 20 E
Lushoto □ 90 4 45 S 38 20 E
Lüshun 76 38 45N 121 15 E
Lusignan 20 46 26N 0 8 E
Lusigny-sur-Barse 19 48 16N 4 15 E
Lusk 116 42 47N 104 27W
Lussac-les-Châteaux 20 46 24N 0 43 E
Luta = Lüda 76 38 50N 121 40 E
Luton 13 51 53N 0 24W
Lutong 72 4 30N 114 0 E
Lutsk 54 50 50N 25 15 E
Lütsow Holmbukta 5 69 10 S 37 30 E
Luverne 116 43 35N 96 12W
Luvua 91 8 48 S 25 17 E
Luwegu → 91 8 31 S 37 23 E
Luwuk 73 0 56 S 122 47 E
Luxembourg 16 49 37N 6 9 E
Luxembourg ■ 16 50 0N 6 0 E
Luxembourg □ 16 49 58N 5 30 E
Luxeuil-les-Bains 19 47 49N 6 24 E
Luxi 77 28 20N 110 7 E
Luxor = El Uqsur 86 25 41N 32 38 E
Luy → 20 43 39N 1 9W
Luy-de-Béarn → 20 43 39N 0 48W
Luy-de-France → 20 43 39N 0 48W
Luz-St-Sauveur 20 42 53N 0 1 E
Luza 52 60 39N 47 10 E
Luzern 25 47 3N 8 18 E
Luzern □ 25 47 2N 7 55 E
Luzhai 77 24 29N 109 42 E
Luzhou 75 28 52N 105 20 E
Luziânia 127 16 20 S 48 0W
Luzon 73 16 0N 121 0 E
Luzy 19 46 47N 3 58 E
Luzzi 41 39 28N 16 17 E
Lvov 54 49 50N 24 0 E
Lwówek 28 52 28N 16 10 E
Lwówek Śląski 28 51 7N 15 38 E
Lyakhovichi 54 53 2N 26 32 E
Lyakhovskiye, Ostrova 59 73 40N 141 0 E
Lyaki 57 40 34N 47 22 E
Lyallpur = Faisalabad 68 31 30N 73 5 E
Lyaskovets 43 43 6N 25 44 E
Lychen 24 53 13N 13 20 E
Lyckeby 49 56 12N 15 37 E
Lycksele 50 64 38N 18 40 E
Lycosura 45 37 20N 22 3 E
Lydda = Lod 62 31 57N 34 54 E
Lydenburg 93 25 10 S 30 29 E
Lyell 101 41 48 S 172 4 E
Lyell I. 108 52 40N 131 35W
Lyell Range 101 41 38 S 172 20 E
Lygnern 49 57 30N 12 15 E
Lykling 47 59 42N 5 12 E
Lyman 118 41 24N 110 15W
Lyme Regis 13 50 44N 2 57W
Lymington 13 50 46N 1 32W
Łyńa → 28 54 37N 21 14 E
Lynchburg 114 37 23N 79 10W
Lynd → 98 16 28 S 143 18 E
Lynd Ra. 99 25 30 S 149 20 E
Lynden, Can. 112 43 14N 80 9W
Lynden, U.S.A. 118 48 56N 122 32W
Lyndhurst 99 30 15 S 138 18 E
Lyndonville, N.Y., U.S.A. 112 43 19N 78 25W
Lyndonville, Vt., U.S.A. 113 44 32N 72 1W
Lyngdal, Aust-Agder, Norway 47 58 8N 7 7 E
Lyngdal, Buskerud, Norway 47 59 54N 9 32 E
Lynn 114 42 28N 70 57W
Lynn Canal 108 58 50N 135 20W
Lynn Lake 109 56 51N 101 3W
Lynton 13 51 14N 3 50W
Lyntupy 54 55 4N 26 23 E
Lynx L. 109 62 25N 106 15W
Lyø 49 55 3N 10 9 E
Lyon 21 45 46N 4 50 E
Lyonnais 21 45 45N 4 15 E
Lyons, Colo., U.S.A. 116 40 17N 105 15W
Lyons, Ga., U.S.A. 115 32 10N 82 15W
Lyons, Kans., U.S.A. 116 38 24N 98 13W
Lyons, N.Y., U.S.A. 114 43 3N 77 0W
Lyons = Lyon 21 45 46N 4 50 E
Lyrestad 49 58 48N 14 4 E
Lys → 19 50 39N 2 24 E
Lysá 26 50 11N 14 51 E
Lysekil 49 58 17N 11 26 E
Lyskovo 55 56 0N 45 3 E
Lysva 52 58 07N 57 49 E
Lysvik 48 60 1N 13 9 E
Lytle 117 29 14N 98 46W
Lyttelton 101 43 35 S 172 44 E
Lytton 108 50 13N 121 31W
Lyuban 54 59 16N 31 18 E
Lyubcha 54 53 46N 26 1 E
Lyubertsy 55 55 39N 37 50 E
Lyubim 55 58 20N 40 39 E
Lyubimets 43 41 50N 26 5 E
Lyuboml, U.S.S.R. 54 51 10N 24 2 E
Lyuboml, U.S.S.R. 54 51 11N 24 4 E
Lyubotin 56 50 0N 36 0 E
Lyubytino 54 58 50N 33 16 E
Lyudinovo 54 53 52N 34 28 E

M

Mā'ad 62 32 37N 35 36 E
Ma'alah 64 26 31N 47 20 E
Maamba 92 17 17 S 26 28 E
Ma'ann 64 30 12N 35 44 E
Ma'anshan 77 31 44N 118 29 E
Ma'arrat un Nu'man 64 35 38N 36 40 E
Maas → 16 51 45N 4 32 E
Maaseik 16 51 6N 5 45 E
Maassluis 16 51 56N 4 16 E
Maastricht 16 50 50N 5 40 E
Maave 93 21 4 S 34 47 E
Mabel L. 108 50 35N 118 43W
Mabenge 90 4 15N 24 12 E
Mablethorpe 12 53 21N 0 14 E
Maboma 90 2 30N 28 10 E
Mabrouk 85 19 29N 1 15W
Mabton 118 46 15N 120 12W
Mac Nutt 109 51 5N 101 36W
Mac Tier 112 45 9N 79 46W
Macachin 124 37 10 S 63 43
Macaé 125 22 20 S 41 43
McAlester 117 34 57N 95 46
McAllen 117 26 12N 98 15
Macallister → 100 38 2 S 146 59
Macamic 106 48 45N 79 0
Macão 31 39 35N 7 59
Macao = Macau ■ 75 22 16N 113 35
Macapá 127 0 5N 51 4
McArthur → 97 15 54 S 136 40
McArthur River 97 16 27 S 136 7
Macau 127 5 0 S 36 40
Macau ■ 75 22 16N 113 35
McBride 108 53 20N 120 19
McCall 118 44 55N 116 6
McCamey 117 31 8N 102 15
McCammon 118 42 41N 112 11
McCauley I. 108 53 40N 130 15
Macclesfield 12 53 16N 2 9
McClintock 109 57 50N 94 10
McCloud 118 41 14N 122 5
McClure 112 40 42N 77 20
McClure Str. 4 75 0N 119 0
McClusky 116 47 30N 100 31
McComb 117 31 13N 90 30
McCook 116 40 15N 100 35
McCusker → 109 55 32N 108 39
McDame 108 59 44N 128 59
McDermitt 118 42 0N 117 45
Macdonald → 100 33 22 S 151 0
McDonald Is. 3 54 0 S 73 0
Macdonald L. 96 23 30 S 129 0
Macdonnell Ranges 96 23 40 S 133 0
Macdougall L. 104 66 0N 98 27
MacDowell L. 106 52 15N 92 45
Macduff 14 57 40N 2 30
Maceda 30 42 16N 7 39
* Macedo de Cavaleiros 88 11 25 S 16 45
Macedonia = Makedhonía 44 40 39N 22 0
Macedonia = Makedonija 42 41 53N 21 40
Maceió 127 9 40 S 35 41
Maceira 31 39 41N 8 55
Macenta 84 8 35N 9 32
Macerata 39 43 19N 13 28
McFarlane → 109 59 12N 107 58
Macfarlane, L. 97 32 0 S 136 40
McGehee 117 33 40N 91 25
McGill 118 39 27N 114 50
Macgillycuddy's Reeks 15 52 2N 9 45
MacGregor 109 49 57N 98 48
McGregor, Iowa, U.S.A. 116 42 58N 91 15
McGregor, Minn., U.S.A. 116 46 37N 93 17
McGregor → 108 55 10N 122 0
McGregor Ra. 99 27 0 S 142 45
Mach 66 29 50N 67 20
Machado = Jiparana → 126 8 3 S 62 52
Machagai 124 26 56 S 60 2
Machakos 90 1 30 S 37 15
Machakos □ 90 1 30 S 37 15
Machala 126 3 20 S 79 57
Machanga 93 20 59 S 35 0
Machattie, L. 97 24 50 S 139 48
Machava 93 25 54 S 32 28
Machece 91 19 15 S 35 32
Machecoul 18 47 0N 1 49
Macheng 77 31 12N 115 2
Machevna 59 61 20N 172 20
Machezo 31 39 21N 4 20
Machias 107 44 40N 67 28
Machichaco, Cabo 32 43 28N 2 47
Machichi → 109 57 3N 92 6
Machilipatnam 70 16 12N 81 8
Machine, La 19 46 54N 3 27
Machiques 126 10 4N 72 34
Machupicchu 126 13 8 S 72 30
Machynlleth 13 52 36N 3 51
** Macias Nguema Biyoga 85 3 30N 8 40
Maciejowice 28 51 36N 21 26
McIlwraith Ra. 97 13 50 S 143 20
Măcin 46 45 16N 28 8
Macina 84 14 50N 5 0
McIntosh 116 45 57N 101 20
McIntosh L. 109 55 45N 105 0
Macintyre → 97 28 37 S 150 47
Macizo Galaico 30 42 30N 7 30
Mackay, Austral. 97 21 8 S 149 11
Mackay, U.S.A. 118 43 58N 113 37
Mackay → 108 57 10N 111 38
Mackay, L. 96 22 30 S 129 0
McKees Rock 112 40 27N 80 3
McKeesport 114 40 21N 79 50
Mackenzie 108 55 20N 123 05
McKenzie 115 36 10N 88 31
† Mackenzie □ 104 61 30N 115 0
Mackenzie →, Austral. 97 23 38 S 149 46
Mackenzie →, Can. 104 69 10N 134 20
McKenzie → 118 44 2N 123 6
Mackenzie City = Linden 126 6 0N 58 10
Mackenzie Highway 108 58 0N 117 15
Mackenzie Mts. 104 64 0N 130 0
Mackinaw City 114 45 47N 84 44
McKinlay 98 21 16 S 141 18
McKinlay → 98 20 50 S 141 28
McKinley, Mt. 104 63 2N 151 0
McKinley Sea 4 84 0N 10 0
McKinney 117 33 10N 96 40
Mackinnon Road 90 3 40 S 39 1
McKittrick 119 35 18N 119 39
Macksville 99 30 40 S 152 56
McLaughlin 116 45 50N 100 50
Maclean 97 29 26 S 153 16
McLean 117 35 15N 100 35
McLeansboro 116 38 5N 88 30
Maclear 93 31 2 S 28 23
Macleay → 97 30 56 S 153 0
McLennan 108 55 42N 116 50
MacLeod, B. 109 62 53N 110 0
McLeod L. 96 24 9 S 113 47
MacLeod Lake 108 54 58N 123 0
M'Clintock Chan. 104 72 0N 102 0
McLoughlin, Mt. 118 42 10N 122 19
McLure 108 51 2N 120 13

* *Renamed Andulo*
** *Renamed Bioko*
† *Now part of Fort Smith and Inuvik* □

:Mechen 112 39 57N 80 44W
:Millan L. 117 32 40N 104 20W
:Minnville, Oreg., U.S.A. 118 45 16N 123 11W
:Minnville, Tenn., U.S.A. 115 35 43N 85 45W
:Morran 109 51 19N 108 42W
:Murdo Sd. 5 77 0S 170 0 E
:Murray = Fort McMurray 108 56 45N 111 27W
:Nary 119 34 4N 109 53W
:Naughton L. 108 52 0N 118 10W
acodoene 93 23 32S 35 5 E
acomb 116 40 25N 90 40W
acomer 40 40 16N 8 48 E
icon 21 46 19N 4 50 E
acon, Ga., U.S.A. 115 32 50N 83 37W
acon, Miss., U.S.A. 115 33 7N 88 31W
acon, Mo., U.S.A. 116 39 40N 92 26W
acondo 89 12 37S 23 46 E
acossa 91 17 55S 33 56 E
acoun L. 109 56 32N 103 40W
acovane 93 21 30S 35 0 E
:Pherson 116 38 25N 97 40W
acpherson Ra. 99 28 15S 153 15 E
acquarie → 97 30 5S 147 30 E
acquarie Harbour 97 42 15S 145 23 E
acquarie Is. 94 54 36S 158 55 E
acquarie, L. 100 33 4S 151 36 E
acRobertson Coast 5 68 30S 63 0 E
acroom 15 51 54N 8 57W
acubela 91 16 53S 37 49 E
acugnaga 38 45 57N 7 58 E
acuiza 91 18 7S 34 29 E
acuse 91 17 45S 37 10 E
acuspana 120 17 46N 92 36W
acusse 92 17 48S 20 23 E
ícuzari, Presa 120 27 10N 109 10W
:Ville 116 47 46N 98 11W
adā 'in Salih 86 26 51N 37 58 E
adagali 85 10 56N 13 33 E
adagascar ■ 93 20 0S 47 0 E
adā'in Sālih 64 26 46N 37 57 E
adama 83 22 0N 13 40 E
adame I. 107 45 30N 60 58W
adan 43 41 30N 24 57 E
adanapalle 70 13 33N 78 28 E
adang 94 5 12S 145 49 E
adaoua 85 14 5N 6 27 E
adara 85 11 45N 10 35 E
adaripur 69 23 19N 90 15 E
adauk 67 17 56N 96 52 E
adawaska 112 45 30N 77 55W
adawaska → 106 45 27N 76 21W
adaya 67 22 12N 96 10 E
adbar 87 6 17N 30 45 E
addalena 40 41 15N 9 23 E
addalena, La 40 41 13N 9 25 E
addaloni 41 41 4N 14 23 E
adden Dam 120 9 13N 79 37W
adden Lake 120 9 20N 79 37W
adeira 80 32 50N 17 0W
adeira → 126 3 22S 58 45W
adeleine, Îs. de la 107 47 30N 61 40W
adera 119 37 0N 120 1W
adha 70 18 0N 75 30 E
adhubani 69 26 21N 86 7 E
adhya Pradesh □ 68 21 50N 81 0 E
adill 117 34 5N 96 49W
adimba 88 5 0S 15 0 E
adīnat ash Sha'b 63 12 50N 45 0 E
adingou 88 4 10S 13 33 E
adirovalo 93 16 26S 46 32 E
adison, Fla., U.S.A. 115 30 29N 83 39W
adison, Ind., U.S.A. 114 38 42N 85 20W
adison, Nebr., U.S.A. 116 41 53N 97 25W
adison, Ohio, U.S.A. 112 41 45N 81 4W
adison, S.D., U.S.A. 116 44 0N 97 8W
adison, Wis., U.S.A. 116 43 5N 89 25W
adison → 118 45 56N 111 30W
adison Junc. 118 44 42N 110 56W
adisonville, Ky., U.S.A. 114 37 20N 87 30W
adisonville, Tex., U.S.A. 117 30 57N 95 55W
dista 92 21 15S 25 6 E
diun 73 7 38S 111 32 E
dley 13 52 3N 2 51W
dol 87 9 3N 27 45 E
don → 19 48 36N 6 6 E
dona 54 56 53N 26 5 E
donie, Le 40 37 50N 13 50 E
dras, India 70 13 8N 80 19 E
dras, U.S.A. 118 44 40N 121 10W
dras = Tamil Nadu □ 70 11 0N 77 0 E
dre de Dios → 126 10 59S 66 8W
dre de Dios, I. 128 50 20S 75 10W
dre del Sur, Sierra 120 17 30N 100 0W
dre, Laguna, Mexico 120 25 0N 97 30W
dre, Laguna, U.S.A. 117 25 0N 97 40W
dre Occidental, Sierra 120 27 0N 107 0W
dre Oriental, Sierra 120 25 0N 100 0W
dre, Sierra, Mexico 120 16 0N 93 0W
dre, Sierra, Phil. 73 17 0N 122 0 E
dri 68 24 16N 73 32 E
drid 30 40 25N 3 45W
drid □ 30 40 30N 3 45W
dridejos 31 39 28N 3 33W
drigal de las Altas Torres 30 41 5N 5 0W
drona, Sierra 31 38 27N 4 16W
droñera 31 39 26N 5 42W
du 87 14 37N 26 4 E
dura, Selat 73 7 30S 113 20 E
durai 70 9 55N 78 10 E
durantakam 70 12 30N 79 50 E
dzhalis 57 42 9N 47 47 E
e Hong Son 71 19 16N 98 1 E
e Sot 71 16 43N 98 34 E
ebashi 74 36 24N 139 4 E
ella 32 41 8N 0 7 E
eruş 46 45 53N 25 31 E
esteg 13 51 36N 3 40W
estra, Sierra 121 20 15N 77 0W
estrazgo, Mts. del 32 40 30N 0 25W
evatanana 93 16 56N 46 49 E
'fan 83 25 56N 14 29 E
feking, Can. 109 52 40N 101 10W
• Mafeking, S. Afr. 92 25 50S 25 38 E
Maféré 84 5 30N 3 2W
Mafeteng 92 29 51S 27 15 E
Maffra 99 37 53S 146 58 E
Mafia 90 7 45S 39 50 E
Mafra, Brazil 125 26 10S 50 0W
Mafra, Port. 31 38 55N 9 20W
Mafungabusi Plateau 91 18 30S 29 8 E
Magadan 59 59 38N 150 50 E
Magadi 90 1 54S 36 19 E
Magadi, L. 90 1 54S 36 19 E
Magaliesburg 93 26 1S 27 32 E
Magallanes, Estrecho de 128 52 30S 75 0W
Magangué 126 9 14N 74 45W
Magaria 85 13 4N 9 5 E
Magburaka 84 8 47N 12 0W
Magdalena, Argent. 124 35 5S 57 30W
Magdalena, Boliv. 126 13 13S 63 57W
Magdalena, Malay. 72 4 25N 117 55 E
Magdalena, Mexico 120 30 50N 112 0W
Magdalena, U.S.A. 119 34 10N 107 20W
Magdalena →, Colomb. 126 11 6N 74 51W
Magdalena →, Mexico 120 30 40N 112 25W
Magdalena, B. 120 24 30N 112 10W
Magdalena, I. 120 24 40N 112 15W
Magdalena, Llano de la 120 25 0N 111 30W
Magdeburg 24 52 8N 11 36 E
Magdeburg □ 24 52 20N 11 30 E
Magdi'el 62 32 10N 34 54 E
Magdub 87 13 42N 25 5 E
Magee 117 31 53N 89 45W
Magee, I. 15 54 48N 5 44W
Magelang 73 7 29S 110 13 E
Magellan's Str. = Magallanes, Est. de 128 52 30S 75 0W
Magenta 38 45 28N 8 53 E
Maggia → 25 46 18N 8 36 E
Maggiorasca, Mte. 38 44 33N 9 29 E
Maggiore, L. 38 46 0N 8 35 E
Maghama 84 15 32N 12 57W
Maghār 62 32 54N 35 24 E
Magherafelt 15 54 44N 6 37W
Maghnia 82 34 50N 1 43W
Magione 39 43 10N 12 12 E
Maglaj 42 44 33N 18 7 E
Magliano in Toscana 39 42 36N 11 18 E
Máglie 41 40 8N 18 17 E
Magnac-Laval 20 46 13N 1 11 E
Magnetic Pole, 1976 (North) 4 76 12N 100 12W
Magnetic Pole, 1976 (South) 5 68 48S 139 30 E
Magnisía □ 44 39 15N 22 45 E
Magnitogorsk 52 53 27N 59 4 E
Magnolia, Ark., U.S.A. 117 33 18N 93 12W
Magnolia, Miss., U.S.A. 117 31 8N 90 28W
Magnor 47 59 56N 12 15 E
Magny-en-Vexin 19 49 9N 1 47 E
Magog 107 45 18N 72 9W
Magoro 90 1 45N 34 12 E
Magosa = Famagusta 64 35 8N 33 55 E
Magoye 91 16 1S 27 30 E
Magpie L. 107 51 0N 64 41W
Magrath 108 49 25N 112 50W
Magro → 33 39 11N 0 25W
Magrur, Wadi → 87 16 5N 26 30 E
Magu □ 90 2 31S 33 28 E
Maguarinho, C. 127 0 15S 48 30W
Maguse L. 109 61 40N 95 10W
Maguse Pt. 109 61 20N 93 50W
Magwe 67 20 10N 95 0 E
Mahābād 64 36 50N 45 45 E
Mahabaleshwar 70 17 58N 73 43 E
Mahabharat Lekh 69 28 30N 82 0 E
Mahabo 93 20 23S 44 40 E
Mahad 70 18 6N 73 29 E
Mahadeo Hills 68 22 20N 78 30 E
Mahadeopur 70 18 48N 80 0 E
Mahagi 90 2 20N 31 0 E
Mahajamba → 93 15 33S 47 8 E
Mahajamba, Helodranon' i 93 15 24S 47 5 E
Mahajan 68 28 48N 73 56 E
Mahajanga □ 93 17 0S 47 0 E
Mahajilo → 93 19 42S 45 22 E
Mahakam → 72 0 35S 117 17 E
Mahalapye 92 23 1S 26 51 E
Maḩallāt 65 33 55N 50 30 E
Mahanadi → 69 20 20N 86 25 E
Mahanoro 93 19 54S 48 48 E
Mahanoy City 113 40 48N 76 10W
Maharashtra □ 70 20 30N 75 30 E
Maharès 83 34 32N 10 29 E
Mahari Mts. 90 6 20S 30 0 E
Mahasolo 93 19 7S 46 22 E
Mahaweli → Ganga 70 8 30N 81 15 E
Mahboobabad 70 17 42N 80 2 E
Mahbubnagar 70 16 45N 77 59 E
Mahdia 83 35 28N 11 0 E
Mahé 70 11 42N 75 34 E
Mahendra Giri 70 8 20N 77 30 E
Mahenge 91 8 45S 36 41 E
Maheno 101 45 10S 170 50 E
Mahia Pen. 101 39 9S 177 55 E
Mahirija 82 34 0N 3 16W
Mahmiya 87 17 12N 33 43 E
Mahmud Kot 68 30 16N 71 0 E
Mahmudia 46 45 5N 29 5 E
Mahnomen 116 47 22N 95 57W
Mahoba 69 25 15N 79 55 E
Mahón 32 39 53N 4 16 E
Mahone Bay 107 44 39N 64 20W
Mahuta 85 11 32N 4 58 E
Mai-Ndombe, L. 88 2 0S 18 20 E
Maîche 19 47 16N 6 48 E
Maicurú → 127 2 14S 54 17W
Máida 41 38 51N 16 21 E
Maidenhead 13 51 31N 0 42W
Maidi 87 16 20N 42 45 E
Maidstone, Can. 109 53 5N 109 20W
Maidstone, U.K. 13 51 16N 0 31 E
Maiduguri 85 12 0N 13 20 E
Maignelay 19 49 32N 2 30 E
Maigudo 87 7 30N 37 8 E
Maijdi 69 22 48N 91 10 E
Maikala Ra. 69 22 0N 81 0 E
Mailly-le-Camp 19 48 41N 4 12 E
Mailsi 68 29 48N 72 15 E
Main →, Ger. 25 50 0N 8 18 E
Main →, U.K. 15 54 49N 6 20W
Main Centre 109 50 35N 107 21W
Mainburg 25 48 37N 11 49 E
Maine 18 48 0N 0 0 E
Maine □ 107 45 20N 69 0W
Maine → 15 52 10N 9 40W
Maine-et-Loire □ 18 47 31N 0 30W
Maïne-Soroa 85 13 13N 12 2 E
Maingkwan 67 26 15N 96 37 E
Mainit, L. 73 9 31N 125 30 E
Mainland, Orkney, U.K. 14 59 0N 3 10W
Mainland, Shetland, U.K. 14 60 15N 1 22W
Mainpuri 68 27 18N 79 4 E
Maintenon 19 48 35N 1 35 E
Maintirano 93 18 3S 44 1 E
Mainz 25 50 0N 8 17 E
Maipú 124 36 52S 57 50W
Maiquetía 126 10 36N 66 57W
Maira → 38 44 49N 7 38 E
Mairabari 67 26 30N 92 22 E
Maisi, Pta. de 121 20 10N 74 10W
Maisse 19 48 24N 2 21 E
Maitland, N.S.W., Austral. 97 32 33S 151 36 E
Maitland, S. Australia, Austral. 99 34 23S 137 40 E
Maitland → 112 43 45N 81 33W
Maiyema 85 12 5N 4 25 E
Maizuru 74 35 25N 135 22 E
Majalengka 73 6 55S 108 14 E
Majd el Kurūm 62 32 56N 35 15 E
Majene 73 3 38S 118 57 E
Majevica Planina 42 44 45N 18 50 E
Maji 87 6 12N 35 30 E
Major 109 51 52N 109 37W
Majorca, I. = Mallorca 32 39 30N 3 0 E
Maka 84 13 40N 14 10W
Makak 85 3 36N 11 0 E
Makale 73 3 6S 119 51 E
Makamba 90 4 8S 29 49 E
Makari 88 12 35N 14 28 E
Makarikari = Makgadikgadi Salt Pans 92 20 40S 25 45 E
Makarovo 59 57 40N 107 45 E
Makarska 42 43 20N 17 2 E
Makaryev 55 57 52N 43 50 E
Makasar = Ujung Pandang 73 5 10S 119 20 E
Makasar, Selat 73 1 0S 118 20 E
Makat 58 47 39N 53 19 E
Makedhonia □ 44 40 39N 22 0 E
Makedonija □ 42 41 53N 21 40 E
Makena 110 20 39N 156 27W
Makeni 84 8 55N 12 5W
Makeyevka 56 48 0N 38 0 E
Makgadikgadi Salt Pans 92 20 40S 25 45 E
Makhachkala 57 43 0N 47 30 E
Makhambet, U.S.S.R. 57 47 43N 51 40 E
Makhambet, U.S.S.R. 57 47 40N 51 35 E
Makharadze 57 41 55N 42 2 E
Makian 73 0 20N 127 20 E
• • Makin 94 3 30N 174 0 E
Makindu 90 2 18S 37 50 E
Makinsk 58 52 37N 70 26 E
Makkah 86 21 30N 39 54 E
Makkovik 107 55 10N 59 10W
† Maklakovo 59 58 16N 92 29 E
Makó 27 46 14N 20 33 E
Makokou 88 0 40N 12 50 E
Makongo 90 3 25N 26 17 E
Makoro 90 3 10N 29 59 E
Makoua 88 0 5S 15 50 E
Maków Mazowiecki 28 52 52N 21 6 E
Maków Podhal 27 49 43N 19 45 E
Makrá 45 36 15N 25 54 E
Makran 65 26 13N 61 30 E
Makran Coast Range 66 25 40N 64 0 E
Makrana 68 27 2N 74 46 E
Mákri 44 40 52N 25 40 E
Maksimkin Yar 58 58 42N 86 50 E
Maktar 83 35 48N 9 12 E
Mākū 64 39 15N 44 31 E
Makumbi 88 5 50S 20 43 E
Makunda 92 22 30S 20 7 E
Makurazaki 74 31 15N 130 20 E
Makurdi 85 7 43N 8 35 E
Makwassie 92 27 17S 26 0 E
Mal B. 15 52 50N 9 30W
Mal i Gjalicës së Lumës 44 42 2N 20 25 E
Mal i Gribës 44 40 17N 19 45 E
Mal i Nemërçkës 44 40 15N 20 15 E
Mal i Tomorit 44 40 42N 20 11 E
Mala Kapela 39 44 45N 15 30 E
Mala, Pta. 121 7 28N 80 2W
Malabang 73 7 36N 124 3 E
Malabar Coast 70 11 0N 75 0 E
Malacca, Str. of 71 3 0N 101 0 E
Malacky 27 48 27N 17 0 E
Malad City 118 42 10N 112 20 E
Málaga 31 36 43N 4 23W
Malaga 117 32 12N 104 2W
Málaga □ 31 36 38N 4 58W
Malagarasi 90 5 5S 30 50 E
Malagarasi → 90 5 12S 29 47 E
Malagón 31 39 11N 3 52W
Malagón → 31 37 35N 7 29W
Malaimbandy 93 20 20S 45 36 E
Malakâl 87 9 33N 31 40 E
Malakand 66 34 40N 71 55 E
Malakoff 117 32 10N 95 55W
Malamyzh 59 50 0N 136 50 E
Malang 73 7 59S 112 45 E
Malanje 88 9 36S 16 17 E
Mälaren 48 59 30N 17 10 E
Malargüe 124 35 32S 69 30W
Malartic 106 48 9N 78 9W
Malatya 64 38 25N 38 20 E
Malawi ■ 91 13 0S 34 0 E
Malawi, L. 91 12 30S 34 30 E
Malay Pen. 71 7 25N 100 0 E
• Malaya □ 71 4 0N 102 0 E
Malaya Belozërka 56 47 12N 34 56 E
Malaya Vishera 54 58 55N 32 25 E
Malaya Viska 56 48 39N 31 36 E
Malaybalay 73 8 5N 125 7 E
Malāyer 64 34 19N 48 51 E
Malaysia ■ 72 5 0N 110 0 E
Malazgirt 64 39 10N 42 33 E
Malbaie, La 107 47 40N 70 10W
Malbon 98 21 5S 140 17 E
Malbork 28 54 3N 19 1 E
Malcésine 38 45 46N 10 48 E
Malchin 24 53 43N 12 44 E
Malchow 24 53 29N 12 25 E
Malcolm 96 28 51S 121 25 E
Malczyce 28 51 14N 16 29 E
Maldegem 16 51 14N 3 26 E
Malden, Mass., U.S.A. 113 42 26N 71 5W
Malden, Mo., U.S.A. 117 36 35N 90 0W
Malden I. 95 4 3S 155 1W
Maldives ■ 60 7 0N 73 0 E
Maldonado 125 35 0S 55 0W
Maldonado, Punta 120 16 19N 98 35W
Malé 38 46 20N 10 55 E
Malé Karpaty 27 48 30N 17 20 E
Maléa, Ákra 45 36 28N 23 7 E
Malegaon 68 20 30N 74 38 E
Malei 91 17 12S 36 58 E
Malela 90 4 22S 26 8 E
Målerås 49 56 54N 15 34 E
Malerkotla 68 30 32N 75 58 E
Máles 45 35 6N 25 35 E
Malesherbes 19 48 15N 2 24 E
Maleshevska Planina 42 41 38N 23 7 E
Malestroit 18 47 49N 2 25W
Malfa 41 38 35N 14 50 E
Malgobek 57 43 30N 44 34 E
Malgomaj 50 64 40N 16 30 E
Malgrat 32 41 39N 2 46 E
Malha 81 15 8N 25 10 E
Malheur → 118 44 3N 116 59W
Malheur L. 118 43 19N 118 42W
Mali 84 12 10N 12 20W
Mali ■ 85 15 0N 2 0W
Mali → 67 25 40N 97 40 E
Mali Kanal 42 45 36N 19 24 E
Mali Kyun 71 13 0N 98 20 E
Malih → 62 32 20N 35 34 E
Malik 73 0 39S 123 16 E
Malili 73 2 42S 121 6 E
Malimba, Mts. 90 7 30S 29 30 E
Malin 54 50 46N 29 3 E
Malin Hd. 15 55 18N 7 24W
Malinau 72 3 35N 116 40 E
Malindi 90 3 12S 40 5 E
Maling 73 1 0N 121 0 E
Malingping 73 6 45S 106 2 E
Malinyi 91 8 56S 36 0 E
Maliqi 44 40 45N 20 48 E
Malita 73 6 19N 125 39 E
Maljenik 42 43 59N 21 55 E
Malkapur, Maharashtra, India 68 20 53N 73 58 E
Malkapur, Maharashtra, India 70 16 57N 73 58 E
Małkinia Górna 28 52 42N 22 5 E
Malko Tŭrnovo 43 41 59N 27 31 E
Mallacoota 100 37 40S 149 40 E
Mallacoota Inlet 97 37 34S 149 40 E
Mallaig 14 57 0N 5 50W
Mallawan 69 27 4N 80 12 E
Mallawi 86 27 44N 30 44 E
Mallemort 21 43 44N 5 11 E
Málles Venosta 38 46 42N 10 32 E
Mállia 45 35 17N 25 27 E
Mallorca 32 39 30N 3 0 E
Mallorytown 113 44 29N 75 53W
Mallow 15 52 8N 8 40W
Malmbäck 49 57 34N 14 28 E
Malmberget 50 67 11N 20 40 E
Malmédy 16 50 25N 6 2 E
Malmesbury 92 33 28S 18 41 E
Malmö 49 55 36N 12 59 E
Malmöhus län □ 49 55 45N 13 30 E
Malmslätt 49 58 27N 15 33 E
Malmyzh 55 56 35N 50 41 E
Malnaş 46 46 2N 25 49 E
Malo Konare 43 42 12N 24 24 E
Maloarkhangelsk 55 52 28N 36 30 E
Malolos 73 14 50N 120 49 E
Malombe L. 91 14 40S 35 15 E
Malomir 43 42 16N 26 30 E
Malone 114 44 50N 74 19W
Malorad 43 43 28N 23 41 E
Malorita 54 51 50N 24 3 E
Maloyaroslovets 55 55 2N 36 20 E
Malozemelskaya Tundra 52 67 0N 50 0 E
Malpartida 31 39 26N 6 30W
Malpelo 126 4 3N 81 35W
Malpica 30 43 19N 8 50W
Malprabha → 70 16 20N 76 5 E
Malta, Idaho, U.S.A. 118 42 15N 113 30W
Malta, Mont., U.S.A. 118 48 20N 107 55W
Malta ■ 36 35 50N 14 30 E
Malta Channel 40 36 40N 14 0 E
Malton, Can. 112 43 42N 79 38W
Malton, U.K. 12 54 9N 0 48W
Maluku 73 1 0S 127 0 E
Maluku □ 73 3 0S 128 0 E
Maluku, Kepulauan 73 3 0S 128 0 E
Malumfashi 85 11 48N 7 39 E
Malung 48 60 42N 13 44 E
Malvalli 70 12 28N 77 8 E
Malvan 70 16 2N 73 30 E
Malvern, U.K. 13 52 7N 2 19W
Malvern, U.S.A. 117 34 22N 92 50W
Malvern Hills 13 52 0N 2 19W
Malvérnia 93 22 6S 31 42 E
Malvik 47 63 25N 10 40 E
Malvinas, Is. = Falkland Is. 128 51 30S 59 0W
Malya 90 3 5S 33 38 E
Malyy Lyakhovskiy, Ostrov 59 74 7N 140 36 E
Mama 59 58 18N 112 54 E
Mamadysh 55 55 44N 51 23 E
Mamahatun 64 39 50N 40 23 E

• *Renamed Mafikeng*

• *Renamed Peninsular Malaysia*
† *Renamed Lesosibirsk*
• • *Renamed Butaritari*

Mamaia 46 44 18N 28 37 E
Mamanguape 127 6 50S 35 4W
Mamasa 73 2 55S 119 20 E
Mambasa 90 1 22N 29 3 E
Mamberamo → 73 2 0S 137 50 E
Mambilima 91 10 31S 28 45 E
Mambirima 91 11 25S 27 33 E
Mambo 90 4 52S 38 22 E
Mambrui 90 3 5S 40 5 E
Mamburao 73 13 13N 120 39 E
Mameigwess L. 106 52 35N 87 50W
Mamers 18 48 21N 0 22 E
Mamfe 85 5 50N 9 15 E
Mámmola 41 38 23N 16 13 E
Mammoth 119 32 46N 110 43W
Mamoré → 126 10 23S 65 53W
Mamou 84 10 15N 12 0W
Mampatá 84 11 54N 14 53W
Mampawah 72 0 30N 109 5 E
Mampong 85 7 6N 1 26W
Mamry, Jezioro 28 54 5N 21 50 E
Mamuju 73 2 41S 118 50 E
Man 84 7 30N 7 40W
Man → 70 17 31N 75 32 E
Man, I. of 12 54 15N 4 30W
Man Na 67 23 27N 97 19 E
Mana 127 5 45N 53 55W
Måna → 47 59 55N 8 50 E
Manaar, Gulf of 70 8 30N 79 0 E
Manacapuru 126 3 16S 60 37W
Manacor 32 39 34N 3 13 E
Manado 73 1 29N 124 51 E
Managua 121 12 6N 86 20W
Managua, L. 121 12 20N 86 30W
Manakara 93 22 8S 48 1 E
Manam I. 98 4 5S 145 0 E
Manamāh, Al 65 26 11N 50 35 E
Manambao → 93 17 35S 44 0 E
Manambato 93 13 43S 49 7 E
Manambolo → 93 19 18S 44 22 E
Manambolosy 93 16 2S 49 40 E
Mananara 93 16 10S 49 46 E
Mananara → 93 23 21S 47 42 E
Mananjary 93 21 13S 48 20 E
Manantenina 93 24 17S 47 19 E
Manaos = Manaus 126 3 0S 60 0W
Manapouri 101 45 34S 167 39 E
Manapouri, L. 101 45 32S 167 32 E
Manar → 70 18 50N 77 20 E
Manas 75 44 17N 85 56 E
Manasir 65 24 30N 51 10 E
Manaslu, Mt. 69 28 33N 84 33 E
Manasquan 113 40 7N 74 3W
Manassa 119 37 12N 105 58W
Manaung 67 18 45N 93 40 E
Manaus 126 3 0S 60 0W
Manawan L. 109 55 24N 103 14W
Manay 73 7 17N 126 33 E
Mancelona 114 44 54N 85 5W
Mancha, La 33 39 10N 2 54W
Mancha Real 31 37 48N 3 39W
Manche □ 18 49 10N 1 20W
Manchegorsk 52 67 40N 32 40 E
Manchester, U.K. 12 53 30N 2 15W
Manchester, Conn., U.S.A. 114 41 47N 72 30W
Manchester, Ga., U.S.A. 115 32 53N 84 32W
Manchester, Iowa, U.S.A. 116 42 28N 91 27W
Manchester, Ky., U.S.A. 114 37 9N 83 45W
Manchester, N.H., U.S.A. 114 42 58N 71 29W
Manchester, N.Y., U.S.A. 112 42 56N 77 16W
Manchester, Vt., U.S.A. 113 43 10N 73 5W
Manchester L. 109 61 28N 107 29W
Manciano 39 42 35N 11 30 E
Mancifa 87 6 53N 41 50 E
Mand → 65 28 20N 52 30 E
Manda, Chunya, Tanz. 90 6 51S 32 29 E
Manda, Ludewe, Tanz. 91 10 30S 34 40 E
Mandaguari 125 23 32S 51 42W
Mandal 47 58 2N 7 25 E
Mandalay 67 22 0N 96 4 E
Mandale = Mandalay 67 22 0N 96 4 E
Mandalī 64 33 43N 45 28 E
Mandalya Körfezi 45 37 15N 27 20 E
Mandan 116 46 50N 101 0W
Mandapeta 70 16 47N 81 56 E
Mandar, Teluk 73 3 35S 119 15 E
Mandas 40 39 40N 9 8 E
Mandasaur 68 24 3N 75 8 E
Mandasor = Mandasaur 68 24 3N 75 8 E
Mandawai (Katingan) → 72 3 30S 113 0 E
Mandelieu-la-Napoule 21 43 34N 6 57 E
Mandera 90 3 55N 41 53 E
Mandera □ 90 3 30N 41 0 E
Mandi 68 31 39N 76 58 E
Mandioli 73 0 40S 127 20 E
Mandla 69 22 39N 80 30 E
Mandø 49 55 18N 8 33 E
Mandoto 93 19 34S 46 17 E
Mandoúdhion 45 38 48N 23 29 E
Mandráki 45 36 36N 27 11 E
Mandrare → 93 25 10S 46 30 E
Mandritsara 93 15 50S 48 49 E
Mandúria 41 40 25N 17 38 E
Mandvi 68 22 51N 69 22 E
Mandya 70 12 30N 77 0 E
Mandzai 68 30 55N 67 6 E
Mané 85 12 59N 1 21W
Manengouba, Mts. 85 5 0N 9 50 E
Maner → 70 18 30N 79 40 E
Maneroo 98 23 22S 143 53 E
Maneroo Cr. → 98 23 21S 143 53 E
Manfalût 86 27 20N 30 52 E
Manfred 99 33 19S 143 45 E
Manfredónia 41 41 40N 15 55 E
Manfredónia, G. di 41 41 30N 16 10 E
Manga, Niger 85 15 0N 14 0 E
Manga, Upp. Vol. 85 11 40N 1 4W
Mangaia 101 21 55S 157 55W
Mangalagiri 70 16 26N 80 36 E
Mangalia 46 43 50N 28 35 E
Mangalore 70 12 55N 74 47 E
Manganeses 30 41 45N 5 43W
Mangaon 70 18 15N 73 20 E
Manger 47 60 38N 5 3 E
Manggar 72 2 50S 108 10 E
Manggawitu 73 4 8S 133 32 E
Mangkalihat, Tanjung 73 1 2N 118 59 E
Manglaur 68 29 44N 77 49 E
Mangnai 75 37 52N 91 43 E
Mango 85 10 20N 0 30 E
Mangoky → 93 21 29S 43 41 E
Mangole 73 1 50S 125 55 E
Mangombe 90 1 20S 26 48 E
Mangonui 101 35 1S 173 32 E
Mangualde 30 40 38N 7 48W
Mangueigne 81 10 30N 21 15 E
Mangueira, Lagoa da 125 33 0S 52 50W
Manguéni, Hamada 83 22 35N 12 40 E
Mangum 117 34 50N 99 30W
Mangyshlak P-ov. 57 44 30N 52 30 E
Mangyshlakskiy Zaliv 57 44 40N 50 50 E
Manhattan, Kans., U.S.A. 116 39 10N 96 40W
Manhattan, Nev., U.S.A. 119 38 31N 117 3W
Manhiça 93 25 23S 32 49 E
Manhuaçu 127 20 15S 42 2W
Mania → 93 19 42S 45 22 E
Maniago 39 46 11N 12 40 E
Manica e Sofala □ 93 19 10S 33 45 E
Manicaland □ 91 19 0S 32 30 E
Manicoré 126 5 48S 61 16W
Manicouagan → 107 49 30N 68 30W
Manicouagan L. 107 51 25N 68 15W
Manīfah 64 27 44N 49 0 E
Manigotagan 109 51 6N 96 18W
Manigotagan L. 109 50 52N 95 37W
Manihiki 95 10 24S 161 1W
Manika, Plat. de la 91 10 0S 25 5 E
Manila, Phil. 73 14 40N 121 3 E
Manila, U.S.A. 118 41 0N 109 44W
Manila B. 73 14 0N 120 0 E
Manilla 99 30 45S 150 43 E
Manimpé 84 14 11N 5 28W
Manipur □ 67 25 0N 94 0 E
Manipur → 67 23 45N 94 20 E
Manisa 64 38 38N 27 30 E
Manistee 114 44 15N 86 20W
Manistee → 114 44 15N 86 21W
Manistique 114 45 59N 86 18W
Manito L. 109 52 43N 109 43W
Manitoba □ 109 55 30N 97 0W
Manitoba, L. 109 51 0N 98 45W
Manitou 109 49 15N 98 32W
Manitou I. 106 47 22N 87 30W
Manitou Is. 114 45 8N 86 0W
Manitou L., Ont., Can. 109 49 15N 93 0W
Manitou L., Qué., Can. 107 50 55N 65 17W
Manitou Springs 116 38 52N 104 55W
Manitoulin I. 106 45 40N 82 30W
Manitowaning 106 45 46N 81 49W
Manitowoc 114 44 8N 87 40W
Manizales 126 5 5N 75 32W
Manja 93 21 26S 44 20 E
Manjakandriana 93 18 55S 47 47 E
Manjeri 70 11 7N 76 11 E
Manjhand 68 25 50N 68 10 E
Manjil 64 36 46N 49 30 E
Manjimup 96 34 15S 116 6 E
Manjra → 70 18 49N 77 52 E
Mankato, Kans., U.S.A. 116 39 49N 98 11W
Mankato, Minn., U.S.A. 116 44 8N 93 59W
Mankayana 93 26 38S 31 6 E
Mankono 84 8 1N 6 10W
Mankota 109 49 25N 107 5W
Manlleu 32 42 2N 2 17 E
Manly 99 33 48S 151 17 E
Manmad 70 20 18N 74 28 E
Manna 72 4 25S 102 55 E
Mannahill 99 32 25S 140 0 E
Mannar 70 9 1N 79 54 E
Mannar, G. of 70 8 30N 79 0 E
Mannar I. 70 9 5N 79 45 E
Mannargudi 70 10 45N 79 51 E
Mannheim 25 49 28N 8 29 E
Manning, Can. 108 56 53N 117 39W
Manning, U.S.A. 115 33 40N 80 9W
Manning → 100 31 52S 152 43 E
Manning Prov. Park 108 49 5N 120 45W
Mannington 114 39 35N 80 25W
Mannu → 40 39 15N 9 32 E
Mannu, C. 40 40 2N 8 24 E
Mannum 99 34 50S 139 20 E
Mano 84 8 3N 12 2W
Manokwari 73 0 54S 134 0 E
Manolás 45 38 4N 21 21 E
Manombo 93 22 57S 43 28 E
Manono 90 7 15S 27 25 E
Manosque 21 43 49N 5 47 E
Manouane L. 107 50 45N 70 45W
Manresa 32 41 48N 1 50 E
Mans, Le 18 48 0N 0 10 E
Mansa, Gujarat, India 68 23 27N 72 45 E
Mansa, Punjab, India 68 30 0N 75 27 E
Mansa, Zambia 91 11 13S 28 55 E
Mansel I. 105 62 0N 80 0W
Mansfield, Austral. 100 37 4S 146 6 E
Mansfield, U.K. 12 53 8N 1 12W
Mansfield, La., U.S.A. 117 32 2N 93 40W
Mansfield, Mass., U.S.A. 113 42 2N 71 12W
Mansfield, Ohio, U.S.A. 114 40 45N 82 30W
Mansfield, Pa., U.S.A. 112 41 48N 77 4W
Mansfield, Wash., U.S.A. 118 47 51N 119 44W
Mansilla de las Mulas 30 42 30N 5 25W
Mansle 20 45 52N 0 9 E
Mansoa 84 12 0N 15 20W
Manson Creek 108 55 37N 124 32W
Mansoura 83 36 1N 4 31 E
Manta 126 1 0S 80 40W
Mantalingajan, Mt. 72 8 55N 117 45 E
Mantare 90 2 42S 33 13 E
Manteca 119 37 50N 121 12W
Manteo 115 35 55N 75 41W
Mantes-la-Jolie 19 49 0N 1 41 E
Manthani 70 18 40N 79 35 E
Manthelan 18 47 9N 0 47 E
Manti 118 39 23N 111 32W
Mantiqueira, Serra da 125 22 0S 44 0W
Manton 114 44 23N 85 25W
Mantorp 49 58 21N 15 20 E
Mántova 38 45 20N 10 42 E
Mänttä 50 62 0N 24 40 E
Mantua = Mántova 38 45 20N 10 42 E
Manturovo 55 58 30N 44 30 E
Manu 126 12 10S 70 51W
Manua Is. 101 14 13S 169 35W
Manuel Alves → 127 11 19S 48 28W
Manui 73 3 35S 123 5 E
Manukan 73 8 14N 123 3 E
Manus I. 98 2 0S 147 0 E
Manvi 70 15 57N 76 59 E
Manville 116 42 48N 104 36W
Manwath 70 19 19N 76 32 E
Many 117 31 36N 93 28W
Manyane 92 23 21S 21 42 E
Manyara, L. 90 3 40S 35 50 E
Manych → 57 47 15N 40 0 E
Manych-Gudilo, Oz. 57 46 24N 42 38 E
Manyonga → 90 4 10S 34 15 E
Manyoni 90 5 45S 34 55 E
Manyoni □ 90 6 30S 34 30 E
Manzai 68 32 12N 70 15 E
Manzala, Bahra el 86 31 10N 31 56 E
Manzanares 33 39 0N 3 22W
Manzaneda, Cabeza de 30 42 12N 7 15W
Manzanillo, Cuba 121 20 20N 77 31W
Manzanillo, Mexico 120 19 0N 104 20W
Manzanillo, Pta. 121 9 30N 79 40W
Manzano Mts. 119 34 30N 106 45W
Manzhouli 75 49 35N 117 25 E
Manzini 93 26 30S 31 25 E
Mao 81 14 4N 15 19 E
Maoke, Pegunungan 73 3 40S 137 30 E
Maoming 75 21 50N 110 54 E
Mapam Yumco 75 30 45N 81 28 E
Mapia, Kepulauan 73 0 50N 134 20 E
Mapimí 120 25 50N 103 50W
Mapimí, Bolsón de 120 27 30N 104 15W
Mapinga 90 6 40S 39 12 E
Mapinhane 93 22 20S 35 0 E
Maple Creek 109 49 55N 109 29W
Mapleton 118 44 4N 123 58W
Maplewood 116 38 33N 90 18W
Maprik 98 3 44S 143 3 E
Mapuca 70 15 36N 73 46 E
Mapuera → 126 1 5S 57 2W
Maputo 93 25 58S 32 32 E
Maputo, B. de 93 25 50S 32 45 E
Maqnā 64 28 25N 34 50 E
Maquela do Zombo 88 6 0S 15 15 E
Maquinchao 128 41 15S 68 50W
Maquoketa 116 42 4N 90 40W
Mår → 47 59 59N 8 46 E
Mar Chiquita, L. 124 30 40S 62 50W
Mar del Plata 124 38 0S 57 30W
Mar Menor, L. 33 37 40N 0 45W
Mar, Serra do 125 25 30S 49 0W
Mara 90 1 30S 34 32 E
Mara □ 90 1 45S 34 20 E
Maraã 126 1 52S 65 25W
Marabá 127 5 20S 49 5W
Maracá, I. de 127 2 10N 50 30W
Maracaibo 126 10 40N 71 37W
Maracaibo, Lago de 126 9 40N 71 30W
Maracaju 125 21 38S 55 9W
Maracay 126 10 15N 67 28W
Marādah 83 29 15N 19 15 E
Maradi 85 13 29N 8 10 E
Maradun 85 12 35N 6 18 E
Marāgheh 64 37 30N 46 12 E
Marāh 64 25 0N 45 35 E
Marajó, Ilha de 127 1 0S 49 30W
Maralal 90 1 0N 36 38 E
Maralinga 96 30 13S 131 32 E
Marama 99 35 10S 140 10 E
Marampa 84 8 45N 12 28W
Maramureş □ 46 47 45N 24 0 E
Marana 119 32 30N 111 9W
Maranchón 32 41 6N 2 15W
Marand 64 38 30N 45 45 E
Marandellas 91 18 5S 31 42 E
Maranguape 127 3 55S 38 50W
Maranhão = São Luis 127 2 39S 44 15W
Maranhão □ 127 5 0S 46 0W
Marano, L. di 39 45 42N 13 13 E
Maranoa → 97 27 50S 148 37 E
Marañón → 126 4 30S 73 35W
Maraş 64 37 37N 36 53 E
Mărăşeşti 46 45 52N 27 14 E
Maratea 41 39 59N 15 43 E
Marateca 31 38 34N 8 40W
Marathókambos 45 37 43N 26 42 E
Marathon, Austral. 98 20 51S 143 32 E
Marathon, Can. 106 48 44N 86 23W
Marathón 45 38 11N 23 58 E
Marathon, N.Y., U.S.A. 113 42 25N 76 3W
Marathon, Tex., U.S.A. 117 30 15N 103 15W
Maratua 73 2 10N 118 35 E
Marbella 31 36 30N 4 57W
Marble Bar 96 21 9S 119 44 E
Marble Falls 117 30 30N 98 15W
Marblehead 113 42 29N 70 51W
Marburg 24 50 49N 8 36 E
Marby 48 63 7N 14 18 E
Marcal → 27 47 41N 17 32 E
Marcali 27 46 35N 17 25 E
Marcaria 38 45 7N 10 34 E
March 13 52 33N 0 5 E
Marchand = Rommani 82 33 20N 6 40W
Marché 20 46 0N 1 20 E
Marche □ 39 43 22N 13 10 E
Marche-en-Famenne 16 50 14N 5 19 E
Marchena 31 37 18N 5 23W
Marches = Marche 39 43 22N 13 10 E
Marciana Marina 38 42 44N 10 12 E
Marcianise 41 41 3N 14 16 E
Marcigny 21 46 17N 4 2 E
Marcillac-Vallon 20 44 29N 2 27 E
Marcillat 20 46 12N 2 38
Marck 19 50 57N 1 57
Marckolsheim 19 48 10N 7 30
Marcos Juárez 124 32 42S 62 5
Marcus 94 24 0N 153 45
Marcus Necker Ridge 94 20 0N 175 0
Marcy Mt. 113 44 7N 73 55
Mardin 64 37 20N 40 43
Maree L. 14 57 40N 5 30
Mareeba 97 16 59S 145 28
Marek 73 4 41S 120 24
Marek = Stanke Dimitrov 42 42 17N 23 9
Maremma 38 42 45N 11 15
Maréna 84 14 0N 7 20
Marenberg 39 46 38N 15 13
Marengo 116 41 42N 92 5
Marennes 20 45 49N 1 7
Marenyi 90 4 22S 39 8
Marerano 93 21 23S 44 52
Maréttimo 40 37 58N 12 5
Mareuil-sur-Lay 20 46 32N 1 14
Marfa 117 30 15N 104 0
Marganets 56 47 40N 34 40
Margao 70 15 12N 73 58
Margaret Bay 108 51 20N 126 35
Margaret L. 108 58 56N 115 25
Margarita 120 9 20N 79 55
Margarita, Isla de 126 11 0N 64 0
Margarítion 44 39 22N 20 26
Margate, S. Afr. 93 30 50S 30 20
Margate, U.K. 13 51 23N 1 24
Margeride, Mts. de la 20 44 43N 3 38
Margherita di Savola 41 41 25N 16 5
Marghita 46 47 22N 22 22
Margonin 28 52 58N 17 5
Marguerite 108 52 30N 122 25
Marhoum 82 34 27N 0 11
Mari, A.S.S.R. □ 55 56 30N 48 0
María Elena 124 22 18S 69 40
María Grande 124 31 45S 59 55
Maria I. 96 14 52S 135 45
Maria van Diemen, C. 101 34 29S 172 40
Mariager 49 56 40N 10 0
Mariager Fjord 49 56 42N 10 19
Mariakani 90 3 50S 39 27
Marian L. 108 63 0N 116 15
Mariana Is. 94 17 0N 145 0
Mariana Trench 94 13 0N 145 0
Marianao 121 23 8N 82 24
Marianna, Ark., U.S.A. 117 34 48N 90 48
Marianna, Fla., U.S.A. 115 30 45N 85 15
Mariannelund 49 57 37N 15 35
Mariánské Lázně 26 49 48N 12 41
Marias → 118 47 56N 110 30
Mariato, Punta 121 7 12N 80 52
Mariazell 26 47 47N 15 19
Ma'rib 63 15 25N 45 30
Maribo 49 54 48N 11 30
Maribor 39 46 36N 15 40
Marico → 92 23 35S 26 57
Maricopa, Ariz., U.S.A. 119 33 5N 112 2
Maricopa, Calif., U.S.A. 119 35 7N 119 27
Marîdî 87 4 55N 29 25
Maridi, Wadi → 87 6 15N 29 21
Marie-Galante 121 15 56N 61 16
Mariecourt 105 61 30N 72 0
Mariefred 48 59 15N 17 12
Mariehamn 51 60 5N 19 55
Marienberg, Ger. 24 50 40N 13 10
Marienberg, Neth. 16 52 30N 6 35
Marienbourg 16 50 6N 4 31
Mariental 92 24 36S 18 0
Marienville 112 41 27N 79 8
Mariestad 49 58 43N 13 50
Marietta, Ga., U.S.A. 115 34 0N 84 30
Marietta, Ohio, U.S.A. 114 39 27N 81 27
Marieville 113 45 26N 73 10
Marignane 21 43 25N 5 13
Mariinsk 58 56 10N 87 20
Mariinskiy Posad 55 56 10N 47 45
Marília 125 22 13S 50 0
Marín 30 42 23N 8 42
Marina di Cirò 41 39 22N 17 8
Mariña, La 30 43 30N 7 40
Marina Plains 98 14 37S 143 57
Marinduque 73 13 25N 122 0
Marine City 114 42 45N 82 29
Marinel, Le 91 10 25S 25 17
Marineo 40 37 57N 13 23
Marinette, Ariz., U.S.A. 119 33 41N 112 16
Marinette, Wis., U.S.A. 114 45 4N 87 40
Maringá 125 23 26S 52 2
Marinha Grande 31 39 45N 8 56
Marion, Ala., U.S.A. 115 32 33N 87 20
Marion, Ill., U.S.A. 117 37 45N 88 55
Marion, Ind., U.S.A. 114 40 35N 85 40
Marion, Iowa, U.S.A. 116 42 2N 91 36
Marion, Kans., U.S.A. 116 38 25N 97 2
Marion, Mich., U.S.A. 114 44 7N 85 8
Marion, N.C., U.S.A. 115 35 42N 82 0
Marion, Ohio, U.S.A. 114 40 38N 83 8
Marion, S.C., U.S.A. 115 34 11N 79 22
Marion, Va., U.S.A. 115 36 51N 81 29
Marion, L. 115 33 30N 80 15
Marion Reef 97 19 10S 152 17
Mariposa 119 37 31N 119 59
Mariscal Estigarribia 124 22 3S 60 40
Maritime Alps = Alpes Maritimes 38 44 10N 7 10
Maritsa 43 42 1N 25 50
Maritsá 45 36 22N 28 10
Maritsa → 43 42 15N 24 0
Mariyampole = Kapsukas 54 54 33N 23 19
Marka 86 18 14N 41 19
Markapur 70 15 44N 79 19
Markaryd 49 56 28N 13 35
Markdale 112 44 19N 80 39
Marked Tree 117 35 35N 90 24
Markelsdorfer Huk 24 54 33N 11 0
Marken 16 52 26N 5 12
Market Drayton 12 52 55N 2 30
Market Harborough 13 52 29N 0 55

Markham **112** 43 52N 79 16W
Markham → **98** 6 41 S 147 2 E
Markham I. **4** 84 0N 0 45W
Markham L. **109** 62 30N 102 35W
Markham Mt. **5** 83 0 S 164 0 E
Marki **28** 52 20N 21 2 E
Markoupoulon **45** 37 53N 23 57 E
Markovac **42** 44 14N 21 7 E
Markovo **59** 64 40N 169 40 E
Markoye **85** 14 39N 0 2 E
Marks **55** 51 45N 46 50 E
Marksville **117** 31 10N 92 2W
Markt Schwaben **25** 48 14N 11 49 E
Marktredwitz **25** 50 1N 12 2 E
Marlboro **113** 42 19N 71 33W
Marlborough **98** 22 46 S 149 52 E
Marlborough □ **101** 41 45 S 173 33 E
Marlborough Downs **13** 51 25N 1 55W
Marle **19** 49 43N 3 47 E
Marlin **117** 31 25N 96 50W
Marlow, Ger. **24** 54 8N 12 34 E
Marlow, U.S.A. **117** 34 40N 97 58W
Marmagao **70** 15 25N 73 56 E
Marmande **20** 44 30N 0 10 E
Marmara **56** 40 35N 27 38 E
Marmara Denizi **64** 40 45N 28 15 E
Marmara, Sea of = Marmara Denizi **64** 40 45N 28 15 E
Marmaris **64** 36 50N 28 14 E
Marmarth **116** 46 21N 103 52W
Marmion L. **106** 48 55N 91 20W
Marmolada, Mte. **39** 46 25N 11 55 E
Marmolejo **31** 38 3N 4 13W
Marmora **106** 44 28N 77 41W
Marnay **19** 47 20N 5 48 E
Marne **24** 53 57N 9 1 E
Marne □ **19** 49 0N 4 10 E
Marne → **19** 8 23N 18 36 E
Marnoo **100** 36 40 S 142 54 E
Marnueli **57** 41 30N 44 48 E
Maroala **93** 15 23 S 47 59 E
Maroantsetra **93** 15 26 S 49 44 E
Maromandia **93** 14 13 S 48 5 E
Maroni → **127** 4 0N 52 0W
Marónia **44** 40 53N 25 24 E
Maroochydore **99** 26 29 S 153 5 E
Maroona **99** 37 27 S 142 54 E
Maros → **27** 46 15N 20 13 E
Marosakoa **93** 15 26 S 46 38 E
Marostica **39** 45 44N 11 40 E
Maroua **85** 10 40N 14 20 E
Marovoay **93** 16 6 S 46 39 E
Marquard **92** 28 40 S 27 28 E
Marqueira **31** 38 41N 9 9W
Marquesas Is. **95** 9 30 S 140 0W
Marquette **114** 46 30N 87 21W
Marquise **19** 50 50N 1 40 E
Marra, Gebel **87** 7 20N 27 35 E
Marradi **39** 44 5N 11 37 E
Marrakech **82** 31 9N 8 0W
Marrawah **99** 40 55 S 144 42 E
Marree **97** 29 39 S 138 1 E
Marrimane **93** 22 58 S 33 34 E
Marronne → **20** 45 4N 1 56 E
Marroquí, Punta **31** 36 0N 5 37W
Marrowie Creek **99** 33 23 S 145 40 E
Marrubane **91** 18 0 S 37 0 E
Marrupa **91** 13 8 S 37 30 E
Mars, Le **116** 43 0N 96 0W
Marsa Brega **83** 30 24N 19 37 E
Marsá Susah **81** 32 52N 21 59 E
Marsabit **90** 2 18N 38 0 E
Marsabit □ **90** 2 45N 37 45 E
Marsala **40** 37 48N 12 25 E
Marsaxlokk (Medport) **36** 35 47N 14 32 E
Marsciano **39** 42 54N 12 20 E
Marsden **99** 33 47 S 147 32 E
Marseillan **20** 43 23N 3 31 E
Marseille **21** 43 18N 5 23 E
Marseilles = Marseille **21** 43 18N 5 23 E
Marsh I. **117** 29 35N 91 50W
Marsh L. **116** 45 5N 96 0W
Marshall, Liberia **84** 6 8N 10 22W
Marshall, Ark., U.S.A. **117** 35 58N 92 40W
Marshall, Mich., U.S.A. **114** 42 17N 84 59W
Marshall, Minn., U.S.A. **116** 44 25N 95 45W
Marshall, Mo., U.S.A. **116** 39 8N 93 15W
Marshall, Tex., U.S.A. **117** 32 29N 94 20W
Marshall Is. **94** 9 0N 171 0 E
Marshalltown **116** 42 5N 92 56W
Marshfield, Mo., U.S.A. **117** 37 20N 92 58W
Marshfield, Wis., U.S.A. **116** 44 42N 90 10W
Mársico Nuovo **41** 40 26N 15 43 E
Märsta **48** 59 37N 17 52 E
Marstal **49** 54 51N 10 30 E
Marstrand **49** 57 53N 11 35 E
Mart **117** 31 34N 96 51W
Marta → **39** 42 14N 11 42 E
Martaban **67** 16 30N 97 35 E
Martaban, G. of **67** 16 5N 96 30 E
Martagne **18** 46 59N 0 57W
Martano **41** 40 14N 18 18 E
Martapura, Kalimantan, Indon. **72** 3 22 S 114 47 E
Martapura, Sumatera, Indon. **72** 4 19 S 104 22 E
Marte **85** 12 23N 13 46 E
Martel **20** 44 57N 1 37 E
Martelange **16** 49 49N 5 43 E
Martés, Sierra **33** 39 20N 1 0W
Marthaguy Creek → **99** 30 16 S 147 35 E
Martha's Vineyard **114** 41 25N 70 35W
Martigné-Ferchaud **18** 47 50N 1 20W
Martigny **25** 46 6N 7 3 E
Martigues **21** 43 24N 5 4 E
Martil **82** 35 36N 5 15W
Martin, Czech. **27** 49 6N 18 48 E
Martin, S.D., U.S.A. **116** 43 11N 101 45W
Martin, Tenn., U.S.A. **117** 36 23N 88 51W
Martín → **32** 41 18N 0 19W
Martin, L. **115** 32 45N 85 50W
Martina Franca **41** 40 42N 17 20 E
Martinborough **101** 41 14 S 175 29 E
Martinique **121** 14 40N 61 0W
Martinique Passage **121** 15 15N 61 0W
Martínon **45** 38 35N 23 15 E
Martinópolis **125** 22 11 S 51 12W
Martins Ferry **113** 40 5N 80 46W
Martinsberg **26** 48 22N 15 9 E
Martinsburg, Pa., U.S.A. **112** 40 18N 78 21W
Martinsburg, W. Va., U.S.A. **114** 39 30N 77 57W
Martinsville, Ind., U.S.A. **114** 39 29N 86 23W
Martinsville, Va., U.S.A. **115** 36 41N 79 52W
Marton **101** 40 4 S 175 23 E
Martorell **32** 41 28N 1 56 E
Martos **31** 37 44N 3 58W
Martuni **57** 40 9N 45 10 E
Maru **85** 12 22N 6 22 E
Marudi **72** 4 10N 114 19 E
Ma'ruf **65** 31 30N 67 6 E
Marugame **74** 34 15N 133 40 E
Marúggio **41** 40 20N 17 33 E
Marulan **99** 34 43 S 150 3 E
Marunga **92** 17 28 S 20 2 E
Marungu, Mts. **90** 7 30 S 30 0 E
Mårvatn **47** 60 8N 8 14 E
Marvejols **20** 44 33N 3 19 E
Marwar **68** 25 43N 73 45 E
Mary **58** 37 40N 61 50 E
Mary Frances L. **109** 63 19N 106 13W
Mary Kathleen **97** 20 44 S 139 48 E
Maryborough, Queens., Austral. **97** 25 31 S 152 37 E
Maryborough, Vic., Austral. **97** 37 0 S 143 44 E
Maryfield **109** 49 50N 101 35W
Maryland □ **114** 39 10N 76 40W
Maryland Jc. **91** 17 45 S 30 31 E
Maryport **12** 54 43N 3 30W
Mary's Harbour **107** 52 18N 55 51W
Marystown **107** 47 10N 55 10W
Marysvale **119** 38 25N 112 17W
Marysville, Can. **108** 49 35N 116 0W
Marysville, Calif., U.S.A. **118** 39 14N 121 40W
Marysville, Kans., U.S.A. **116** 39 50N 96 49W
Marysville, Mich., U.S.A. **112** 42 55N 82 29W
Marysville, Ohio, U.S.A. **114** 40 15N 83 20W
Maryvale **99** 28 4 S 152 12 E
Maryville **115** 35 50N 84 0W
Marzūq **83** 25 53N 13 57 E
Masada = Mesada **62** 31 20N 35 19 E
Masahunga **90** 2 6 S 33 18 E
Masai Steppe **90** 4 30 S 36 30 E
Masaka **90** 0 21 S 31 45 E
Masalembo, Kepulauan **72** 5 35 S 114 30 E
Masalima, Kepulauan **72** 5 4 S 117 5 E
Masamba **73** 2 30 S 120 15 E
Masan **76** 35 11N 128 32 E
Masanasa **33** 39 25N 0 25W
Masandam, Ras **65** 26 30N 56 30 E
Masasi **91** 10 45 S 38 52 E
Masasi □ **91** 10 45 S 38 50 E
Masaya **121** 12 0N 86 7W
Masba **85** 10 35N 13 1 E
Masbate **73** 12 21N 123 36 E
Mascara **82** 35 26N 0 6 E
Mascota **120** 20 30N 104 50W
Masela **73** 8 9 S 129 51 E
Maseru **92** 29 18 S 27 30 E
Mashaba **91** 20 2 S 30 29 E
Mashābih **64** 25 35N 36 30 E
Mashan **77** 23 40N 108 11 E
Mashhad **65** 36 20N 59 35 E
Mashi **85** 13 0N 7 54 E
Mashike **74** 43 31N 141 30 E
Mashkel, Hamun-i- **66** 28 30N 63 0 E
Mashki Chah **66** 29 5N 62 30 E
Mashtaga **57** 40 35N 50 0 E
Masi **50** 69 26N 23 40 E
Masi Manimba **88** 4 40 S 17 54 E
Masindi **90** 1 40N 31 43 E
Masindi Port **90** 1 43N 32 2 E
Masisea **126** 8 35 S 74 22W
Masisi **90** 1 23 S 28 49 E
Masjed Soleyman **64** 31 55N 49 18 E
Mask, L. **15** 53 36N 9 24W
Maski **70** 15 56N 76 46 E
Maslen Nos **43** 42 18N 27 48 E
Maslinica **39** 43 24N 16 13 E
Masnou **32** 41 28N 2 20 E
Masoala, Tanjon' i **93** 15 59 S 50 13 E
Masoarivo **93** 19 3 S 44 19 E
Masohi **73** 3 2 S 128 15 E
Masomeloka **93** 20 17 S 48 37 E
Mason, S.D., U.S.A. **116** 45 12N 103 27W
Mason, Tex., U.S.A. **117** 30 45N 99 15W
Mason City, Iowa, U.S.A. **116** 43 9N 93 12W
Mason City, Wash., U.S.A. **118** 48 0N 119 0W
Masqat **65** 23 37N 58 36 E
Massa **38** 44 2N 10 7 E
Massa Maríttima **38** 43 3N 10 52 E
Massa, O. → **82** 30 2N 9 40W
Massachusetts □ **114** 42 25N 72 0W
Massachusetts B. **113** 42 30N 70 0W
Massada **62** 33 41N 35 36 E
Massafra **41** 40 35N 17 8 E
Massaguet **81** 12 28N 15 26 E
Massakory **81** 13 0N 15 49 E
Massangena **93** 21 34 S 33 0 E
Massarosa **38** 43 53N 10 17 E
Massat **20** 42 53N 1 21 E
Massawa = Mitsiwa **87** 15 35N 39 25 E
Massena **114** 44 52N 74 55W
Massénya **81** 11 21N 16 9 E
Masset **108** 54 2N 132 10W
Massiac **20** 45 15N 3 11 E
Massif Central **20** 45 30N 2 21 E
Massillon **114** 40 47N 81 30W
Massinga **93** 23 46 S 32 4 E
Masson **113** 45 32N 75 25W
Masson I. **5** 66 10 S 93 20 E
Mastaba **86** 20 52N 39 30 E
Mastanli = Momchilgrad **43** 41 33N 25 23 E
Masterton **101** 40 56 S 175 39 E
Mástikho, Ákra **45** 38 10N 26 2 E
Mastuj **69** 36 20N 72 36 E
Mastung **66** 29 50N 66 56 E
Mastura **86** 23 7N 38 52 E
Masuda **74** 34 40N 131 51 E
Maswa □ **90** 3 30 S 34 0 E
Matabeleland North □ **91** 19 0 S 28 0 E
Matabeleland South □ **91** 21 0 S 29 0 E
Mataboor **73** 1 41 S 138 3 E
Matachel → **31** 38 50N 6 17W
Matachewan **106** 47 56N 80 39W
Matad **75** 47 11N 115 27 E
Matadi **88** 5 52 S 13 31 E
Matagalpa **121** 13 0N 85 58W
Matagami **106** 49 45N 77 34W
Matagami, L. **106** 49 50N 77 40W
Matagorda **117** 28 43N 96 0W
Matagorda B. **117** 28 30N 96 15W
Matagorda I. **117** 28 10N 96 40W
Matak, P. **72** 3 18N 106 16 E
Matakana **99** 32 59 S 145 54 E
Matale **70** 7 30N 80 37 E
Matam **84** 15 34N 13 17W
Matameye **85** 13 26N 8 28 E
Matamoros, Coahuila, Mexico **120** 25 33N 103 15W
Matamoros, Puebla, Mexico **120** 18 2N 98 17W
Matamoros, Tamaulipas, Mexico **120** 25 50N 97 30W
Ma'tan as Sarra **81** 21 45N 22 0 E
Matandu → **91** 8 45 S 34 19 E
Matane **107** 48 50N 67 33W
Matankari **85** 13 46N 4 1 E
Matanuska **104** 61 39N 149 19W
Matanzas **121** 23 0N 81 40W
Matapan, C. = Taínaron, Akra **45** 36 22N 22 27 E
Matapédia **107** 48 0N 66 59W
Matara **70** 5 58N 80 30 E
Mataram **72** 8 41 S 116 10 E
Matarani **126** 77 0 S 72 10W
Mataranka **96** 14 55 S 133 4 E
Mataró **32** 41 32N 2 29 E
Matarraña → **32** 41 14N 0 22 E
Mataruška Banja **42** 43 40N 20 45 E
Matatiele **93** 30 20 S 28 49 E
Mataura **101** 46 11 S 168 51 E
Matehuala **120** 23 40N 100 40W
Mateke Hills **91** 21 48 S 31 0 E
Matélica **39** 43 15N 13 0 E
Matera **41** 40 40N 16 37 E
Mátészalka **27** 47 58N 22 20 E
Matetsi **91** 18 12 S 26 0 E
Mateur **83** 37 0N 9 40 E
Matfors **48** 62 21N 17 2 E
Matha **20** 45 52N 0 20W
Matheson Island **109** 51 45N 96 56W
Mathis **117** 28 4N 97 48W
Mathura **68** 27 30N 77 40 E
Mati **73** 6 55N 126 15 E
Mati → **44** 41 40N 20 0 E
Matías Romero **120** 16 53N 95 2W
Matibane **91** 14 49 S 40 45 E
Matima **92** 20 15 S 24 26 E
Matlock **12** 53 8N 1 32W
Matmata **83** 33 37N 9 59 E
Matna **87** 13 49N 35 10 E
Mato Grosso □ **127** 14 0 S 55 0W
Mato Grosso, Planalto do **127** 15 0 S 59 57W
Matochkin Shar **58** 73 10N 56 40 E
Matopo Hills **91** 20 36 S 28 20 E
Matopos **91** 20 20 S 28 29 E
Matosinhos **30** 41 11N 8 42W
Matour **21** 46 19N 4 29 E
Matrah **65** 23 37N 58 30 E
Matrûh **86** 31 19N 27 9 E
Matsena **85** 13 5N 10 5 E
Matsesta **57** 43 34N 39 51 E
Matsue **74** 35 25N 133 10 E
Matsumoto **74** 36 15N 138 0 E
Matsuyama **74** 33 45N 132 45 E
Mattagami → **106** 50 43N 81 29W
Mattancheri **70** 9 50N 76 15 E
Mattawa **106** 46 20N 78 45W
Mattawamkeag **107** 45 30N 68 21W
Matterhorn **25** 45 58N 7 39 E
Mattersburg **27** 47 44N 16 24 E
Matthew Town **121** 20 57N 73 40W
Matthew's Ridge **126** 7 37N 60 10W
Mattice **106** 49 40N 83 20W
Mattituck **113** 40 58N 72 32W
Mattmar **48** 63 18N 13 45 E
Matua **72** 2 58 S 110 46 E
Matuba **93** 24 28 S 32 49 E
Matucana **126** 11 55 S 76 25W
Matun **66** 33 22N 69 58 E
Maturín **126** 9 45N 63 11W
Matveyev Kurgan **57** 47 35N 38 47 E
Mau-é-ele **93** 24 18 S 34 2 E
Mau Escarpment **90** 0 40 S 36 0 E
Mau Ranipur **68** 25 16N 79 8 E
Maubeuge **19** 50 17N 3 57 E
Maubourguet **20** 43 29N 0 1 E
Maude **99** 34 29 S 144 18 E
Maudheim **5** 71 5 S 11 0W
Maudin Sun **67** 16 0N 94 30 E
Maués **126** 3 20 S 57 45W
Maui **110** 20 45N 156 20 E
Mauke **101** 20 09 S 157 20W
Maule □ **124** 36 5 S 72 30W
Mauléon-Licharre **20** 43 14N 0 54W
Maumee **114** 41 35N 83 40W
Maumee → **114** 41 42N 83 28W
Maumere **73** 8 38 S 122 13 E
Maun **92** 20 0 S 23 26 E
Mauna Kea **110** 19 50N 155 28W
Mauna Loa **110** 21 8N 157 10W
Maunath Bhanjan **69** 25 56N 83 33 E
Maungmagan Kyunzu **71** 14 0N 97 48 E
Maupin **118** 45 12N 121 9W
Maure-de-Bretagne **18** 47 53N 2 0W
Maurepas L. **117** 30 18N 90 35W
Maures **21** 43 15N 6 15 E
Mauriac **20** 45 13N 2 19 E
Maurice L. **96** 29 30 S 131 0 E
Mauritania ■ **80** 20 50N 10 0W
Mauritius ■ **3** 20 0 S 57 0 E
Mauron **18** 48 9N 2 18W
Maurs **20** 44 43N 2 12 E
Mauston **116** 43 48N 90 5W
Mauterndorf **26** 47 9N 13 40 E
Mauvezin **20** 43 44N 0 53 E
Mauzé-sur-le-Mignon **20** 46 12N 0 41W
Mavelikara **70** 9 14N 76 32 E
Mavinga **89** 15 50 S 20 21 E
Mavli **68** 24 45N 73 55 E
Mavqi'im **62** 31 38N 34 32 E
Mavrova **44** 40 26N 19 32 E
Mavuradonha Mts. **91** 16 30 S 31 30 E
Mawa **90** 2 45N 26 40 E
Mawana **68** 29 6N 77 58 E
Mawand **68** 29 33N 68 38 E
Mawk Mai **67** 20 14N 97 37 E
Mawson Base **5** 67 30 S 62 53 E
Max **116** 47 50N 101 20W
Maxcanú **120** 20 40N 92 0W
Maxhamish L. **108** 59 50N 123 17W
Maxixe **93** 23 54 S 35 17 E
Maxville **113** 45 17N 74 51W
Maxwelton **98** 20 43 S 142 41 E
May Downs **98** 22 38 S 148 55 E
May Glacier Tongue **5** 66 08 S 130 35 E
May Pen **121** 17 58N 77 15W
Maya **32** 43 12N 1 29W
Maya → **59** 54 31N 134 41 E
Maya Mts. **120** 16 30N 89 0W
Mayaguana **121** 22 30N 72 44W
Mayagüez **121** 18 12N 67 9W
Mayahi **85** 13 58N 7 40 E
Mayals **32** 41 22N 0 30 E
Mayarí **121** 20 40N 75 41W
Mayavaram = Mayuram **70** 11 3N 79 42 E
Maybell **118** 40 30N 108 4W
Maychew **87** 12 50N 39 31 E
Maydena **99** 42 45 S 146 30 E
Maydos **44** 40 13N 26 20 E
Mayen **25** 50 18N 7 10 E
Mayenne **18** 48 20N 0 38W
Mayenne □ **18** 48 10N 0 40W
Mayenne → **18** 47 30N 0 32W
Mayer **119** 34 28N 112 17W
Mayerthorpe **108** 53 57N 115 8W
Mayfield **115** 36 45N 88 40W
Mayhill **119** 32 58N 105 30W
Maykop **57** 44 35N 40 25 E
Maymyo **71** 22 2N 96 28 E
Maynooth **15** 53 22N 6 38W
Mayo **104** 63 38N 135 57W
Mayo □ **15** 53 47N 9 7W
Mayo → **120** 26 45N 109 47W
Mayo L. **104** 63 45N 135 0W
Mayon, Mt. **73** 13 15N 123 42 E
Mayor I. **101** 37 16 S 176 17 E
Mayorga **30** 42 10N 5 16W
Mayskiy **57** 43 47N 44 2 E
Mayson L. **109** 57 55N 107 10W
Maysville **114** 38 39N 83 46W
Maythalūn **62** 32 21N 35 16 E
Mayu **73** 1 30N 126 30 E
Mayuram **70** 11 3N 79 42 E
Mayville, N.D., U.S.A. **116** 47 30N 97 23W
Mayville, N.Y., U.S.A. **112** 42 14N 79 31W
Mayya **59** 61 44N 130 18 E
Mazabuka **91** 15 52 S 27 44 E
Mazagán = El Jadida **82** 33 11N 8 17W
Mazagão **127** 0 7 S 51 16W
Mazamet **20** 43 30N 2 20 E
Mazán **126** 3 30 S 73 0W
Mazan Deran □ **65** 36 30N 52 0 E
Mazar-e Sharīf **65** 36 41N 67 0 E
Mazar, O. → **82** 31 50N 1 36 E
Mazara del Vallo **40** 37 40N 12 34 E
Mazarredo **128** 47 10 S 66 50W
Mazarrón **33** 37 38N 1 19W
Mazarrón, Golfo de **33** 37 27N 1 19W
Mazaruni → **126** 6 25N 58 35W
Mazatenango **120** 14 35N 91 30W
Mazatlán **120** 23 10N 106 30W
Mažeikiai **54** 56 20N 22 20 E
Māzhān **65** 32 30N 59 0 E
Mazīnān **65** 36 19N 56 56 E
Mazoe, Mozam. **91** 16 42 S 33 7 E
Mazoe, Zimb. **91** 17 28 S 30 58 E
Mazrûb **87** 14 0N 29 20 E
Mazu Dao **77** 26 10N 119 55 E
Mazurian Lakes = Mazurski, Pojezierze **28** 53 50N 21 0 E
Mazurski, Pojezierze **28** 53 50N 21 0 E
Mazzarino **41** 37 19N 14 12 E
Mbaba **84** 14 59N 16 44W
Mbabane **93** 26 18 S 31 6 E
Mbagne **84** 16 6N 14 47W
M'bahiakro **84** 7 33N 4 19W
Mbaïki **88** 3 53N 18 1 E
Mbala **91** 8 46 S 31 24 E
Mbale **90** 1 8N 34 12 E
Mbalmayo **88** 3 33N 11 33 E
Mbamba Bay **91** 11 13 S 34 49 E
Mbandaka **88** 0 1N 18 18 E
Mbanga **85** 4 30N 9 33 E
Mbanza Congo **88** 6 18 S 14 16 E
Mbanza Ngungu **88** 5 12 S 14 53 E
Mbarara **90** 0 35 S 30 40 E
Mbatto **84** 6 28N 4 22W
Mbenkuru → **91** 9 25 S 39 50 E
Mberubu **85** 6 10N 7 38 E
Mbesuma **91** 10 0 S 32 2 E
Mbeya **91** 8 54 S 33 29 E
Mbeya □ **90** 8 15 S 33 30 E
Mbinga **91** 10 50 S 35 0 E
Mbinga □ **91** 10 50 S 35 0 E
Mbini = Rio Muni □ **88** 1 30N 10 0 E
Mboki **87** 5 19N 25 58 E
Mboro **84** 15 9N 16 54W
Mboune **84** 14 42N 13 34W
Mbour **84** 14 22N 16 54W
Mbout **84** 16 1N 12 38W
Mbozi □ **91** 9 0 S 32 50 E
Mbuji-Mayi **91** 6 9 S 23 40 E
Mbulu **90** 3 45 S 35 30 E
Mbulu □ **90** 3 52 S 35 33 E

Mburucuyá 124 28 1S 58 14W
Mcherrah 82 27 0N 4 30W
Mchinja 91 9 44S 39 45 E
Mchinji 91 13 47S 32 58 E
Mdennah 82 24 37N 6 0W
Mdina 36 35 51N 14 25 E
Mead, L. 119 36 1N 114 44W
Meade 117 37 18N 100 25W
Meadow Lake 109 54 10N 108 26W
Meadow Lake Prov. Park 109 54 27N 109 0W
Meadow Valley Wash → 119 36 39N 114 35W
Meadville 114 41 39N 80 9W
Meaford 106 44 36N 80 35W
Mealhada 30 40 22N 8 27W
Mealy Mts. 107 53 10N 58 0W
Meander River 108 59 2N 117 42W
Meares, C. 118 45 37N 124 0W
Mearim → 127 3 4S 44 35W
Meath □ 15 53 32N 6 40W
Meath Park 109 53 27N 105 22W
Meaulne 20 46 36N 2 36 E
Meaux 19 48 58N 2 50 E
Mecanhelas 91 15 12S 35 54 E
Mecca 119 33 37N 116 3W
Mecca = Makkah 86 21 30N 39 54 E
Mechanicsburg 112 40 12N 77 0W
Mechanicville 113 42 54N 73 41W
Mechara 87 8 36N 40 20 E
Mechelen 16 51 2N 4 29 E
Mecheria 82 33 35N 0 18W
Mechernich 24 50 35N 6 39 E
Mechetinskaya 57 46 45N 40 32 E
Mechra Benâbbou 82 32 39N 7 48W
Mecidiye 44 40 38N 26 32 E
Mecitözü 56 40 32N 35 17 E
Meconta 91 14 59S 39 50 E
Meda 30 40 57N 7 18W
Meda → 96 17 20S 123 50 E
Medak 70 18 1N 78 15 E
Medan 72 3 40N 98 38 E
Medanosa, Pta. 128 48 8S 66 0W
Medawachchiya 70 8 30N 80 30 E
Medéa 82 36 12N 2 50 E
Mededa 42 43 44N 19 15 E
Medellín 126 6 15N 75 35W
Medemblik 16 52 46N 5 8 E
Médenine 83 33 21N 10 30 E
Mederdra 84 17 0N 15 38W
Medford, Oreg., U.S.A. 118 42 20N 122 52W
Medford, Wis., U.S.A. 116 45 9N 90 21W
Medgidia 46 44 15N 28 19 E
Medi 87 5 4N 30 42 E
Media Agua 124 31 58S 68 25W
Media Luna 124 34 45S 66 44W
Mediaş 46 46 9N 24 22 E
Medical Lake 118 47 35N 117 42W
Medicina 39 44 29N 11 38 E
Medicine Bow 118 41 56N 106 11W
Medicine Bow Pk. 118 41 21N 106 19W
Medicine Bow Ra. 118 41 10N 106 25W
Medicine Hat 109 50 0N 110 45W
Medicine Lake 116 48 30N 104 30W
Medicine Lodge 117 37 20N 98 37W
Medina, N.D., U.S.A. 116 46 57N 99 20W
Medina, N.Y., U.S.A. 114 43 15N 78 27W
Medina, Ohio, U.S.A. 114 41 9N 81 50W
Medina = Al Madīnah 64 24 35N 39 35 E
Medina → 117 29 10N 98 20W
Medina de Ríoseco 30 41 53N 5 3W
Medina del Campo 30 41 18N 4 55W
Medina L. 117 29 35N 98 58W
Medina-Sidonia 31 36 28N 5 57W
Medinaceli 32 41 12N 2 30W
Mediterranean Sea 34 35 0N 15 0 E
Medjerda, O. → 83 37 7N 10 13 E
Medley 109 54 25N 110 16W
Médoc 20 45 10N 0 56W
Medstead 109 53 19N 108 5W
Medulin 39 44 49N 13 55 E
Medveda 42 42 50N 21 32 E
Medveditsa →, R.S.F.S.R., U.S.S.R. 55 49 35N 42 41 E
Medveditsa →, R.S.F.S.R., U.S.S.R. 55 57 5N 37 30 E
Medvedok 55 57 20N 50 1 E
Medvezhi, Ostrava 59 71 0N 161 0 E
Medvezhyegorsk 52 63 0N 34 25 E
Medway → 13 51 28N 0 45 E
Medyn 55 54 58N 35 52 E
Medzev 27 48 43N 20 55 E
Medzilaborce 27 49 17N 21 52 E
Meekatharra 96 26 32S 118 29 E
Meeker 118 40 1N 107 58W
Meerane 24 50 51N 12 30 E
Meersburg 25 47 42N 9 16 E
Meerut 68 29 1N 77 42 E
Meeteetse 118 44 10N 108 56W
Mega 87 3 57N 38 19 E
Megálo Khorío 45 36 27N 27 24 E
Megálo Petalí 45 38 0N 24 15 E
Megalópolis 45 37 25N 22 7 E
Meganísi 45 38 39N 20 48 E
Mégara 45 37 58N 23 22 E
Megarine 83 33 14N 6 2 E
Megdhova → 45 39 10N 21 45 E
Mégève 21 45 51N 6 37 E
Meghezez, Mt. 87 9 18N 39 26 E
Meghna → 69 22 50N 90 50 E
Megiddo 62 32 36N 35 11 E
Mégiscane, L. 106 48 35N 75 55W
Megiste 35 36 8N 29 34 E
Mehadia 46 44 56N 22 23 E
Mehaïguene, O. → 82 32 15N 2 59 E
Meharry, Mt. 96 22 59S 118 35 E
Mehedinţi □ 46 44 40N 22 45 E
Meheisa 86 19 38N 32 57 E
Mehndawal 69 26 58N 83 5 E
Mehsana 68 23 39N 72 26 E
Mehun-sur-Yèvre 19 47 10N 2 13 E
Mei Jiang → 77 24 25N 116 35 E
Mei Xian 75 24 16N 116 6 E
Meiganga 88 6 30N 14 25 E
Meiktila 67 20 53N 95 54 E
Meiningen 24 50 32N 10 25 E
Me'ir Shefeya 62 32 35N 34 58 E
Meira, Sierra de 30 43 15N 7 15W
Meiringen 25 46 43N 8 12 E
Meissen 24 51 10N 13 29 E
Meissner 24 51 13N 9 51 E
Meitan 77 27 45N 107 29 E
Méjean, Causse 20 44 15N 3 30 E
Mejillones 124 23 10S 70 30W
Mékambo 88 1 2N 13 50 E
Mekdela 87 11 24N 39 10 E
Mekele 87 13 33N 39 30 E
Meklong = Samut Songkhram 71 13 24N 100 1 E
Meknès 82 33 57N 5 33W
Meko 85 7 27N 2 52 E
Mekong → 71 9 30N 106 15 E
Mekongga 73 3 39S 121 15 E
Melagiri Hills 70 12 20N 77 30 E
Melah, Sebkhet el 82 29 20N 1 30W
Melaka 71 2 15N 102 15 E
Melaka □ 71 2 20N 102 15 E
Melalap 72 5 10N 116 5 E
Mélambes 45 35 8N 24 40 E
Melanesia 94 4 0S 155 0 E
Melapalaiyam 70 8 39N 77 44 E
Melbourne, Austral. 97 37 50S 145 0 E
Melbourne, U.S.A. 115 28 4N 80 35W
Melchor Múzquiz 120 27 50N 101 30W
Melchor Ocampo (San Pedro Ocampo) 120 24 52N 101 40W
Méldola 39 44 7N 12 3 E
Meldorf 24 54 5N 9 5 E
Mêle-sur-Sarthe, Le 18 48 31N 0 22 E
Melegnano 38 45 21N 9 20 E
Melenci 42 45 32N 20 20 E
Melenki 55 55 20N 41 37 E
Mélèzes → 105 57 30N 71 0W
Melfi, Chad 81 11 0N 17 59 E
Melfi, Italy 41 41 0N 15 33 E
Melfort, Can. 109 52 50N 104 37W
Melfort, Zimb. 91 18 0S 31 25 E
Melgaço 30 42 7N 8 15W
Melgar de Fernamental 30 42 27N 4 17W
Melhus 47 63 17N 10 18 E
Meligalá 45 37 15N 21 59 E
Melilla 82 35 21N 2 57W
Melilot 62 31 22N 34 37 E
Melipilla 124 33 42S 71 15W
Mélissa Óros 45 37 32N 26 4 E
Melita 109 49 15N 101 0W
Mélito di Porto Salvo 41 37 55N 15 47 E
Melitopol 56 46 50N 35 22 E
Melk 26 48 13N 15 20 E
Mellan-Fryken 48 59 45N 13 10 E
Mellansel 50 63 25N 18 17 E
Melle, France 20 46 14N 0 10W
Melle, Ger. 24 52 12N 8 20 E
Mellégue, O. → 83 36 32N 8 51 E
Mellen 116 46 19N 90 36W
Mellerud 49 58 41N 12 28 E
Mellette 116 45 11N 98 29W
Mellid 30 42 55N 8 1W
Mellish Reef 97 17 25S 155 50 E
Mellit 87 14 7N 25 34 E
Mellrichstadt 25 50 26N 10 19 E
Melnik 43 41 30N 23 25 E
Mělník 26 50 22N 14 23 E
Melo 125 32 20S 54 10W
Melolo 73 9 53S 120 40 E
Melovoye 57 49 25N 40 5 E
Melrhir, Chott 83 34 25N 6 24 E
Melrose, Austral. 99 32 42S 146 57 E
Melrose, U.K. 14 53 35N 2 44W
Melrose, U.S.A. 117 34 27N 103 33W
Melstone 118 46 36N 107 50W
Melsungen 24 51 8N 9 34 E
Melton Mowbray 12 52 46N 0 52W
Melun 19 48 32N 2 39 E
Melur 70 10 2N 78 23 E
Melut 87 10 30N 32 13 E
Melville 109 50 55N 102 50W
Melville B. 97 12 0S 136 45 E
Melville, C. 97 14 11S 144 30 E
Melville I., Austral. 96 11 30S 131 0 E
Melville I., Can. 4 75 30N 112 0W
Melville, L. 107 53 30N 60 0W
Melville Pen. 105 68 0N 84 0W
Melvin → 108 59 11N 117 31W
Mélykút 27 46 11N 19 25 E
Memaliaj 44 40 25N 19 58 E
Memba 91 14 11S 40 30 E
Memboro 73 9 30S 119 30 E
Membrilla 33 38 59N 3 21W
Memel 93 27 38S 29 36 E
Memel = Klaipeda 54 55 43N 21 10 E
Memmingen 25 47 59N 10 12 E
Memphis, Tenn., U.S.A. 117 35 7N 90 0W
Memphis, Tex., U.S.A. 117 34 45N 100 30W
Mena 117 34 40N 94 15W
Mena → 87 5 40N 40 50 E
Menai Strait 12 53 14N 4 10W
Ménaka 85 15 59N 2 18 E
Menan = Chao Phraya → 71 13 32N 100 36 E
Menarandra → 93 25 17S 44 30 E
Menard 117 30 57N 99 48W
Menasha 114 44 13N 88 27W
Menate 72 0 12S 113 3 E
Mendawai → 72 3 17S 113 21 E
Mende 20 44 31N 3 30 E
Mendebo Mts. 87 7 0N 39 22 E
Menderes → 64 37 25N 28 45 E
Mendi, Ethiopia 87 9 47N 35 4 E
Mendi, P.N.G. 98 6 11S 143 39 E
Mendip Hills 13 51 17N 2 40W
Mendocino 118 39 26N 123 50W
Mendocino Seascarp 95 41 0N 140 0W
Mendota, Calif., U.S.A. 119 36 46N 120 24W
Mendota, Ill., U.S.A. 116 41 35N 89 5W
Mendoza 124 32 50S 68 52W
Mendoza □ 124 33 0S 69 0W
Mene Grande 126 9 49N 70 56W
Menemen 64 38 34N 27 3 E
Menen 16 50 47N 3 7 E
Menfi 40 37 36N 12 57 E
Mengcheng 77 33 18N 116 31 E
Mengeš 39 46 24N 14 35 E
Menggala 72 4 30S 105 15 E
Mengíbar 31 37 58N 3 48W
Mengoub 82 29 49N 5 26W
Mengshan 77 24 14N 110 55 E
Mengzi 75 23 20N 103 22 E
Menihek L. 107 54 0N 67 0W
Menin = Menen 16 50 47N 3 7 E
Menindee 97 32 20S 142 25 E
Menindee, L. 99 32 20S 142 25 E
Meningie 99 35 35S 139 0 E
Menominee 114 45 9N 87 39W
Menominee → 114 45 5N 87 36W
Menomonie 116 44 50N 91 54W
Menongue 89 14 48S 17 52 E
Menorca 32 40 0N 4 0 E
Mentawai, Kepulauan 72 2 0S 99 0 E
Menton 21 43 50N 7 29 E
Mentor 112 41 40N 81 21W
Menzel-Bourguiba 83 39 9N 9 49 E
Menzel Chaker 83 35 0N 10 26 E
Menzel-Temime 83 36 46N 11 0 E
Menzelinsk 52 55 53N 53 1 E
Menzies 96 29 40S 120 58 E
Me'ona (Tarshiha) 62 33 1N 35 15 E
Mepaco 91 15 57S 30 48 E
Meppel 16 52 42N 6 12 E
Meppen 24 52 41N 7 20 E
Mequinenza 32 41 22N 0 17 E
Mer Rouge 117 32 47N 91 48W
Merabéllou, Kólpos 45 35 10N 25 50 E
Merak 73 5 56S 106 0 E
Meran = Merano 39 46 40N 11 10 E
Merano 39 46 40N 11 10 E
Merate 38 45 42N 9 23 E
Merauke 73 8 29S 140 24 E
Merbabu 73 7 30S 110 40 E
Merbein 99 34 10S 142 2 E
Merca 63 1 48N 44 50 E
Mercadal 32 39 59N 4 5 E
Mercara 70 12 30N 75 45 E
Mercato Saraceno 39 43 57N 12 11 E
Merced 119 37 18N 120 30W
Mercedes, Buenos Aires, Argent. 124 34 40S 59 30W
Mercedes, Corrientes, Argent. 124 29 10S 58 5W
Mercedes, San Luis, Argent. 124 33 40S 65 21W
Mercedes, Uruguay 124 33 12S 58 0W
Merceditas 124 28 20S 70 35W
Mercer, N.Z. 101 37 16S 175 5 E
Mercer, U.S.A. 112 41 14N 80 13W
Mercy C. 105 65 0N 63 30W
Merdrignac 18 48 11N 2 27W
Meredith C. 128 52 15S 60 40W
Meredith, L. 117 35 30N 101 35W
Merei 46 45 7N 26 43 E
Méréville 19 48 20N 2 5 E
Mergenevsky 57 49 59N 51 15 E
Mergui Arch. = Myeik Kyunzu 71 11 30N 97 30 E
Mérida, Mexico 120 20 9N 89 40W
Mérida, Spain 31 38 55N 6 25W
Mérida, Venez. 126 8 24N 71 8W
Meriden 114 41 33N 72 47W
Meridian, Idaho, U.S.A. 118 43 41N 116 25W
Meridian, Miss., U.S.A. 115 32 20N 88 42W
Meridian, Tex., U.S.A. 117 31 55N 97 37W
Mering 25 48 15N 11 0 E
Meringur 100 34 20S 141 19 E
Meriruma 127 1 15N 54 50W
Merkel 117 32 30N 100 0W
Merksem 16 51 16N 4 25 E
Merlebach 19 49 5N 6 52 E
Merlerault, Le 18 48 41N 0 16 E
Mern 49 55 3N 12 3 E
Merowe 86 18 29N 31 46 E
Merredin 96 31 28S 118 18 E
Merrick 14 55 8N 4 30W
Merrickville 113 44 55N 75 50W
Merrill, Oregon, U.S.A. 118 42 2N 121 37W
Merrill, Wis., U.S.A. 116 45 11N 89 41W
Merriman 116 42 55N 101 42W
Merritt 108 50 10N 120 45W
Merriwa 99 32 6S 150 22 E
Merriwagga 99 33 47S 145 43 E
Merry I. 106 55 29N 77 31W
Merrygoen 99 31 51S 149 12 E
Merryville 117 30 47N 93 31W
Mersa Fatma 87 14 57N 40 17 E
Mersch 16 49 44N 6 7 E
Merseburg 24 51 20N 12 0 E
Mersey → 12 53 20N 2 56W
Merseyside □ 12 53 25N 2 55W
Mersin 64 36 51N 34 36 E
Mersing 71 2 25N 103 50 E
Merta 68 26 39N 74 4 E
Merthyr Tydfil 13 51 45N 3 23W
Mértola 31 37 40N 7 40 E
Mertzon 117 31 17N 100 48W
Méru 19 49 13N 2 8 E
Meru, Kenya 90 0 3N 37 40 E
Meru, Tanz. 90 3 15S 36 46 E
Meru □ 90 0 3N 37 46 E
Merville 19 50 38N 2 38 E
Méry-sur-Seine 19 48 31N 3 54 E
Merzifon 56 40 53N 35 32 E
Merzig 25 49 26N 6 37 E
Merzouga, Erg Tin 83 24 0N 11 4 E
Mesa 119 33 20N 111 56W
Mesa, La, Calif., U.S.A. 119 32 48N 117 5W
Mesa, La, N. Mex., U.S.A. 119 32 6N 106 48W
Mesach Mellet 83 24 30N 11 30 E
Mesada 62 31 20N 35 19 E
Mesagne 41 40 34N 17 48 E
Mesaras, Kólpos 45 35 6N 24 47 E
Meschede 24 51 20N 8 17 E
Mesfinto 87 13 20N 37 22 E
Mesgouez, L. 106 51 20N 75 0W
Meshchovsk 54 54 22N 35 17 E
Meshed = Mashhad 65 36 20N 59 35 E
Meshoppen 113 41 36N 76 3W
Meshra er Req 81 8 25N 29 18 E
Mesick 114 44 24N 85 42W
Mesilinka → 108 56 6N 124 30W
Mesilla 119 32 20N 106 50W
Meslay-du-Maine 18 47 58N 0 33W
Mesocco 25 46 23N 9 12 E
Mesolóngion 45 38 21N 21 28 E
Mesopotamia = Al Jazirah 64 33 30N 44 0 E
Mesoraca 41 39 5N 16 47 E
Mésou Volímais 45 37 53N 20 35 E
Mess Cr. → 108 57 55N 131 14W
Messac 18 47 49N 1 50W
Messad 82 34 8N 3 30 E
Messalo → 91 12 25S 39 15 E
Méssaména 85 3 48N 12 49 E
Messeix 20 45 37N 2 33 E
Messeue 45 37 12N 21 58 E
Messina, Italy 41 38 10N 15 32 E
Messina, S. Afr. 93 22 20S 30 0 E
Messina, Str. di 41 38 5N 15 35 E
Messíni 45 37 4N 22 1 E
Messínia □ 45 37 10N 22 0 E
Messiniakós, Kólpos 45 36 45N 22 5 E
Messkirch 25 47 59N 9 7 E
Mesta → 43 41 30N 24 0 E
Mestà, Ákra 45 38 16N 25 53 E
Mestanza 31 38 35N 4 4W
Město Teplá 26 49 59N 12 52 E
Mestre 39 45 30N 12 13 E
Městys Zelezná Ruda 26 49 8N 13 15 E
Meta → 126 6 12N 67 28W
Metairie 117 29 59N 90 9W
Metalici, Munţii 42 46 15N 22 50 E
Metaline Falls 118 48 52N 117 22W
Metán 124 25 30S 65 0W
Metauro → 39 43 50N 13 3 E
Metema 87 12 56N 36 13 E
Metengobalame 91 14 49S 34 30 E
Méthana 45 37 35N 23 23 E
Methóni 45 36 49N 21 42 E
Methven 101 43 38S 171 40 E
Methy L. 109 56 28N 109 30W
Metkovets 43 43 37N 23 10 E
Metković 42 43 6N 17 39 E
Metlakatla 108 55 10N 131 33W
Metlaoui 83 34 24N 8 24 E
Metlika 39 45 40N 15 20 E
Metropolis 117 37 10N 88 47W
Métsovon 44 39 48N 21 12 E
Mettuppalaiyam 70 11 18N 76 59 E
Mettur 70 11 48N 77 47 E
Mettur Dam 70 11 45N 77 45 E
Metulla 62 33 17N 35 34 E
Metz 19 49 8N 6 10 E
Meulaboh 72 4 11N 96 3 E
Meulan 19 49 0N 1 52 E
Meung-sur-Loire 19 47 50N 1 40 E
Meureudu 72 5 19N 96 10 E
Meurthe → 19 48 47N 6 9 E
Meurthe-et-Moselle □ 19 48 52N 6 0 E
Meuse □ 19 49 8N 5 25 E
Meuse → 16 50 45N 5 41 E
Meuselwitz 24 51 3N 12 18 E
Mexborough 12 53 29N 1 18W
Mexia 117 31 38N 96 32W
Mexiana, I. 127 0 0 49 30W
Mexicali 120 32 40N 115 30W
México 120 19 20N 99 10W
Mexico, Me., U.S.A. 113 44 35N 70 30W
Mexico, Mo., U.S.A. 116 39 10N 91 55W
Mexico ■ 120 20 0N 100 0W
México □ 120 19 20N 99 10W
Mexico, G. of 120 25 0N 90 0W
Meyenburg 24 53 19N 12 15 E
Meymac 20 45 32N 2 10 E
Meymaneh 65 35 53N 64 38 E
Meyrargues 21 43 38N 5 32 E
Meyrueis 20 44 12N 3 27 E
Meyssac 20 45 3N 1 40 E
Mezdra 43 43 12N 23 42 E
Mèze 20 43 27N 3 36 E
Mezen 52 65 50N 44 20 E
Mézenc 21 44 55N 4 11 E
Mezeş, Munţii 46 47 5N 23 5 E
Mezha → 54 55 50N 31 45 E
Mézidon 18 49 5N 0 1W
Mézilhac 21 44 49N 4 21 E
Mézin 20 44 4N 0 16 E
Mezöberény 27 46 49N 21 3 E
Mezöfalva 27 46 55N 18 49 E
Mezöhegyes 27 46 19N 20 49 E
Mezökövácsháza 27 46 25N 20 57 E
Mezökövesd 27 47 49N 20 35 E
Mézos 20 44 5N 1 10W
Mezötúr 27 47 0N 20 41 E
Mezquital 120 23 29N 104 23W
Mezzolombardo 38 46 13N 11 5 E
Mgeta 91 8 22S 36 6 E
Mglin 54 53 2N 32 50 E
Mhlaba Hills 91 18 30S 30 30 E
Mhow 68 22 33N 75 50 E
Miahuatlán 120 16 21N 96 36W
Miajadas 31 39 9N 5 54W
Mialar 68 26 15N 70 20 E
Miallo 98 16 28S 145 22 E
Miami, Ariz., U.S.A. 119 33 25N 110 54W
Miami, Fla., U.S.A. 115 25 45N 80 15W
Miami, Tex., U.S.A. 117 35 44N 100 38W
Miami → 114 39 20N 84 40W
Miami Beach 115 25 49N 80 6W
Miamisburg 114 39 40N 84 11W
Mian Xian 77 33 10N 106 32 E
Mianchi 77 34 48N 111 48 E
Mīāndow āb 64 37 0N 46 5 E
Miandrivazo 93 19 31S 45 29 E
Mīāneh 64 37 30N 47 40 E
Mianwali 68 32 38N 71 28 E
Mianyang, Hubei, China 77 30 25N 113 25 E
Mianyang, Sichuan, China 77 31 22N 104 47 E
Miaoli 75 24 37N 120 49 E
Miarinarivo 93 18 57S 46 55 E

Place	Page	Lat.	Long.
Miass	**52**	54 59N	60 6 E
Miasteczko Kraj	**28**	53 7N	17 1 E
Miastko	**28**	54 0N	16 58 E
Micăsasa	**46**	46 7N	24 7 E
Michalovce	**27**	48 47N	21 58 E
Michelstadt	**25**	49 40N	9 0 E
Michigan □	**111**	44 40N	85 40W
Michigan City	**114**	41 42N	86 56W
Michigan, L.	**114**	44 0N	87 0W
Michipicoten	**106**	47 55N	84 55W
Michipicoten I.	**106**	47 40N	85 40W
Michoacan □	**120**	19 0N	102 0W
Michurin	**43**	42 9N	27 51 E
Michurinsk	**55**	52 58N	40 27 E
Miclere	**98**	22 34 S	147 32 E
Mico, Pta.	**121**	12 0N	83 30W
Micronesia	**94**	11 0N	160 0 E
Mid Glamorgan □	**13**	51 40N	3 25W
Mid-Indian Ridge	**94**	40 0 S	75 0 E
Mid-Oceanic Ridge	**94**	42 0 S	90 0 E
Midai, P.	**72**	3 0N	107 47 E
Midale	**109**	49 25N	103 20W
Midas	**118**	41 14N	116 48W
Middagsfjället	**48**	63 27N	12 19 E
Middelburg, Neth.	**16**	51 30N	3 36 E
Middelburg, C. Prov., S. Afr.	**92**	31 30 S	25 0 E
Middelburg, Trans., S. Afr.	**93**	25 49 S	29 28 E
Middelfart	**49**	55 30N	9 43 E
Middle Alkali L.	**118**	41 30N	120 3W
Middle Andaman I.	**71**	12 30N	92 30 E
Middle Loup →	**116**	41 17N	98 23W
Middleboro	**113**	41 56N	70 52W
Middleburg, N.Y., U.S.A.	**113**	42 36N	74 19W
Middleburg, Pa., U.S.A.	**112**	40 46N	77 5W
Middlebury	**113**	44 0N	73 9W
Middleport	**114**	39 0N	82 5W
Middlesboro	**115**	36 36N	83 43W
Middlesbrough	**12**	54 35N	1 14W
Middlesex	**113**	40 36N	74 30W
Middleton	**107**	44 57N	65 4W
Middleton Cr. →	**98**	22 35 S	141 51 E
Middleton P.O.	**98**	22 22 S	141 32 E
Middletown, Conn., U.S.A.	**114**	41 37N	72 40W
Middletown, N.Y., U.S.A.	**114**	41 28N	74 28W
Middletown, Ohio, U.S.A.	**114**	39 29N	84 25W
Middletown, Pa., U.S.A.	**113**	40 12N	76 44W
Midelt	**82**	32 46N	4 44W
Midi, Canal du	**20**	43 45N	1 21 E
Midi d'Ossau	**32**	42 50N	0 25W
Midland, Austral.	**96**	31 54 S	115 59 E
Midland, Can.	**106**	44 45N	79 50W
Midland, Mich., U.S.A.	**114**	43 37N	84 17W
Midland, Pa., U.S.A.	**112**	40 39N	80 27W
Midland, Tex., U.S.A.	**117**	32 0N	102 3W
Midlands □	**91**	19 40 S	29 0 E
Midleton	**15**	51 52N	8 12W
Midlothian	**117**	32 30N	97 0W
Midnapore	**69**	22 25N	87 21 E
Midongy Atsimo	**93**	23 35 S	47 1 E
Midongy, Tangorombohitr' i	**93**	23 30 S	47 0 E
Midour →	**20**	43 54N	0 30W
Midouze →	**20**	43 48N	0 51W
Midvale	**118**	40 39N	111 58W
Midway Is.	**94**	28 13N	177 22W
Midwest	**118**	43 27N	106 19W
Midyat	**64**	37 25N	41 23 E
Midzur	**42**	43 24N	22 40 E
Mie □	**74**	34 30N	136 10 E
Miechów	**28**	50 21N	20 5 E
Miedwie, Jezioro	**28**	53 17N	14 54 E
Międzybód	**28**	51 25N	17 34 E
Międzychód	**28**	52 35N	15 53 E
Międzylesie	**28**	50 8N	16 40 E
Międzyrzec Podlaski	**28**	51 58N	22 45 E
Międzyrzecz	**28**	52 26N	15 35 E
Międzyzdroje	**28**	53 56N	14 26 E
Miejska	**28**	51 39N	16 58 E
Miélan	**20**	43 27N	0 19 E
Mielec	**28**	50 15N	21 25 E
Mienga	**92**	17 12 S	19 48 E
Miercurea Ciuc	**46**	46 21N	25 48 E
Mieres	**30**	43 18N	5 48W
Mieroszów	**28**	50 40N	16 11 E
Mieso	**87**	9 15N	40 43 E
Mieszkowice	**28**	52 47N	14 30 E
Migdāl	**62**	32 51N	35 30 E
Migdal Afeq	**62**	32 5N	34 58 E
Migennes	**19**	47 58N	3 31 E
Migliarino	**39**	44 45N	11 56 E
Miguel Alemán, Presa	**120**	18 15N	96 40W
Miguel Alves	**127**	4 11 S	42 55W
Mihara	**74**	34 24N	133 5 E
Mijares →	**32**	39 55N	0 1W
Mijas	**31**	36 36N	4 40W
Mikese	**90**	6 48 S	37 55 E
Mikha-Tskhakaya	**57**	42 15N	42 7 E
Mikhailovka	**56**	47 36N	35 16 E
Mikhaylov	**55**	54 14N	39 0 E
Mikhaylovgrad	**43**	43 27N	23 16 E
Mikhaylovka, Azerbaijan, U.S.S.R.	**57**	41 31N	48 52 E
Mikhaylovka, R.S.F.S.R., U.S.S.R.	**55**	50 3N	43 5 E
Mikhnevo	**55**	55 4N	37 59 E
Mikínai	**45**	37 43N	22 46 E
Mikindani	**91**	10 15 S	40 2 E
Mikkeli	**51**	61 43N	27 15 E
Mikkeli □	**50**	62 0N	28 0 E
Mikkwa →	**108**	58 25N	114 46W
Mikniya	**87**	17 0N	33 45 E
Mikołajki	**28**	53 49N	21 37 E
Mikołów	**27**	50 10N	18 50 E
Míkonos	**45**	37 30N	25 25 E
Mikrí Préspa, Límni	**44**	40 47N	21 3 E
Mikrón Dhérion	**44**	41 19N	26 6 E
Mikstat	**28**	51 32N	17 59 E
Mikulov	**27**	48 48N	16 39 E
Mikumi	**90**	7 26 S	37 0 E
Mikun	**52**	62 20N	50 0 E
Mikura-Jima	**74**	33 52N	139 36 E
Milaca	**116**	45 45N	93 40W
Milagro	**126**	2 11 S	79 36W
Milan, Mo., U.S.A.	**116**	40 10N	93 5W
Milan, Tenn., U.S.A.	**115**	35 55N	88 45W
Milan = Milano	**38**	45 28N	9 10 E
Milange	**91**	16 3 S	35 45 E
Milano	**38**	45 28N	9 10 E
Milâs	**64**	37 20N	27 50 E
Milazzo	**41**	38 13N	15 13 E
Milbank	**116**	45 17N	96 38W
Milden	**109**	51 29N	107 32W
Mildmay	**112**	44 3N	81 7W
Mildura	**97**	34 13 S	142 9 E
Miléai	**44**	39 20N	23 9 E
Miles, Austral.	**97**	26 40 S	150 9 E
Miles, U.S.A.	**117**	31 39N	100 11W
Miles City	**116**	46 24N	105 50W
Milestone	**109**	49 59N	104 31W
Mileto	**41**	38 37N	16 3 E
Miletto, Mte.	**41**	41 26N	14 23 E
Miletus	**45**	37 20N	27 33 E
Milevsko	**26**	49 27N	14 21 E
Milford, Conn., U.S.A.	**113**	41 13N	73 4W
Milford, Del., U.S.A.	**114**	38 52N	75 27W
Milford, Mass., U.S.A.	**113**	42 8N	71 30W
Milford, Pa., U.S.A.	**113**	41 20N	74 47W
Milford, Utah, U.S.A.	**119**	38 20N	113 0W
Milford Haven	**13**	51 43N	5 2W
Milford Haven, B.	**13**	51 40N	5 10W
Milford Sd.	**101**	44 41 S	167 47 E
Milḩ, Baḩr al	**64**	32 40N	43 35 E
Milḩ, Ras al	**81**	31 54N	25 6 E
Miliana, Aïn Salah, Alg.	**82**	27 20N	2 32 E
Miliana, Médéa, Alg.	**82**	36 20N	2 15 E
Milicz	**28**	51 31N	17 19 E
Militello in Val di Catánia	**41**	37 16N	14 46 E
Milk →	**118**	48 5N	106 15W
Milk River	**108**	49 10N	112 5W
Milk, Wadi el →	**86**	17 55N	30 20 E
Mill City	**118**	44 45N	122 28W
Mill I.	**5**	66 0 S	101 30 E
Millau	**20**	44 8N	3 4 E
Millbridge	**112**	44 41N	77 36W
Millbrook	**112**	44 10N	78 29W
Mille	**115**	33 7N	83 15W
Mille Lacs, L.	**116**	46 10N	93 30W
Mille Lacs, L. des	**106**	48 45N	90 35W
Millen	**115**	32 50N	81 57W
Miller	**116**	44 35N	98 59W
Millerovo	**57**	48 57N	40 28 E
Millersburg, Ohio, U.S.A.	**112**	40 32N	81 52W
Millersburg, Pa., U.S.A.	**112**	40 32N	76 58W
Millerton	**113**	41 57N	73 32W
Millevaches, Plateau de	**20**	45 45N	2 0 E
Millicent	**97**	37 34 S	140 21 E
Millinocket	**107**	45 45N	68 45W
Millmerran	**99**	27 53 S	151 16 E
Mills L.	**108**	61 30N	118 20W
Millsboro	**112**	40 0N	80 0W
Milltown Malbay	**15**	52 51N	9 25W
Millville	**114**	39 22N	75 0W
Millwood Res.	**117**	33 45N	94 0W
Milly	**19**	48 24N	2 28 E
Milna	**39**	43 20N	16 28 E
Milne Inlet	**105**	72 30N	80 0W
Milnor	**116**	46 19N	97 29W
Milo	**108**	50 34N	112 53W
Mílos	**45**	36 44N	24 25 E
Miloševo	**42**	45 42N	20 20 E
Miłosław	**28**	52 12N	17 32 E
Milparinka P.O.	**99**	29 46 S	141 57 E
Miltenberg	**25**	49 41N	9 13 E
Milton, Can.	**112**	43 33N	79 53W
Milton, N.Z.	**101**	46 7 S	169 59 E
Milton, U.K.	**14**	57 18N	4 32W
Milton, Fla., U.S.A.	**115**	30 38N	87 0W
Milton, Pa., U.S.A.	**114**	41 0N	76 53W
Milton-Freewater	**118**	45 57N	118 24W
Milton Keynes	**13**	52 3N	0 42W
Miltou	**81**	10 14N	17 26 E
Milverton	**112**	43 34N	80 55W
Milwaukee	**114**	43 9N	87 58W
Milwaukie	**118**	45 27N	122 39W
Mim	**85**	6 57N	2 33W
Mimizan	**20**	44 12N	1 13W
Mimon	**26**	50 38N	14 43 E
Min Jiang →, Fujian, China	**75**	26 0N	119 35 E
Min Jiang →, Sichuan, China	**75**	28 45N	104 40 E
Min Xian	**77**	34 25N	104 0 E
Mina	**119**	38 21N	118 9W
Mina Pirquitas	**124**	22 40 S	66 30W
Mīnā Su'ud	**64**	28 45N	48 28 E
Mīnā'al Aḩmadī	**64**	29 5N	48 10 E
Mīnāb	**65**	27 10N	57 1 E
Minago →	**109**	54 33N	98 59W
Minaki	**109**	49 59N	94 40W
Minamata	**74**	32 10N	130 30 E
Minas	**125**	34 20 S	55 10W
Minas Basin	**107**	45 20N	64 12W
Minas de Rio Tinto	**31**	37 42N	6 35W
Minas de San Quintín	**31**	38 49N	4 23W
Minas Gerais □	**127**	18 50 S	46 0W
Minas, Sierra de las	**120**	15 9N	89 31W
Minatitlán	**120**	17 58N	94 35W
Minbu	**67**	20 10N	94 52 E
Mincio →	**38**	45 4N	10 59 E
Mindanao	**73**	8 0N	125 0 E
* Mindanao Sea	**73**	9 0N	124 0 E
Mindanao Trench	**73**	8 0N	128 0 E
Mindel →	**25**	48 31N	10 23 E
Mindelheim	**25**	48 4N	10 30 E
Minden, Can.	**112**	44 55N	78 43W
Minden, Ger.	**24**	52 18N	8 45 E
Minden, U.S.A.	**117**	32 40N	93 20W
Mindiptana	**73**	5 55 S	140 22 E
Mindona, L.	**100**	33 6 S	142 6 E
Mindoro	**73**	13 0N	121 0 E
Mindoro Strait	**73**	12 30N	120 30 E
Mindouli	**88**	4 12 S	14 28 E
Minehead	**13**	51 12N	3 29W
Mineola	**117**	32 40N	95 30W
Mineral Wells	**117**	32 50N	98 5W
Mineralnyye Vody	**57**	44 2N	43 8 E
Minersville, Pa., U.S.A.	**113**	40 11N	76 17W
Minersville, Utah, U.S.A.	**119**	38 14N	112 58W
Minerva	**112**	40 43N	81 8W
Minervino Murge	**41**	41 6N	16 4 E
Minetto	**113**	43 24N	76 28W
Mingan	**107**	50 20N	64 0W
Mingechaur	**57**	40 45N	47 0 E
Mingechaurskoye Vdkhr.	**57**	40 56N	47 20 E
Mingela	**98**	19 52 S	146 38 E
Mingera Cr. →	**98**	20 38 S	138 10 E
Minggang	**77**	32 24N	114 3 E
Mingin	**67**	22 50N	94 30 E
Minglanilla	**32**	39 34N	1 38W
Mingorria	**30**	40 45N	4 40W
Mingxi	**77**	26 18N	117 12 E
Miničevo	**42**	43 42N	22 18 E
Minidoka	**118**	42 47N	113 34W
Minigwal L.	**96**	29 31 S	123 14 E
Minipi, L.	**107**	52 25N	60 45W
Mink L.	**108**	61 54N	117 40W
Minna	**85**	9 37N	6 30 E
Minneapolis, Kans., U.S.A.	**116**	39 11N	97 40W
Minneapolis, Minn., U.S.A.	**116**	44 58N	93 20W
Minnedosa	**109**	50 14N	99 50W
Minnesota □	**116**	46 40N	94 0W
Minnesund	**47**	60 23N	11 14 E
Minnitaki L.	**106**	49 57N	92 10W
Miño →	**30**	41 52N	8 40W
Minoa	**45**	35 6N	25 45 E
Minorca = Menorca	**32**	40 0N	4 0 E
Minore	**99**	32 14 S	148 27 E
Minot	**116**	48 10N	101 15W
Minqing	**77**	26 15N	118 50 E
Minquiers, Les	**18**	48 58N	2 8W
Minsen	**24**	53 43N	7 58 E
Minsk	**54**	53 52N	27 30 E
Mińsk Mazowiecki	**28**	52 10N	21 33 E
Mintaka Pass	**69**	37 0N	74 58 E
Minto	**104**	64 55N	149 20W
Minton	**109**	49 10N	104 35W
Minturn	**118**	39 35N	106 25W
Minturno	**40**	41 15N	13 43 E
Minûf	**86**	30 26N	30 52 E
Minusinsk	**59**	53 50N	91 20 E
Minutang	**67**	28 15N	96 30 E
Minvoul	**88**	2 9N	12 8 E
Minya el Qamh	**86**	30 31N	31 21 E
Mionica	**42**	44 14N	20 6 E
Mir	**85**	14 5N	11 59 E
Mir-Bashir	**57**	40 20N	46 58 E
Mira, Italy	**39**	45 26N	12 9 E
Mira, Port.	**30**	40 26N	8 44W
Mira →	**31**	37 43N	8 47W
Mirabella Eclano	**41**	41 3N	14 59 E
Miraflores Locks	**120**	8 59N	79 36W
Miraj	**70**	16 50N	74 45 E
Miram	**98**	21 15 S	148 55 E
Miramar, Argent.	**124**	38 15 S	57 50W
Miramar, Mozam.	**93**	23 50 S	35 35 E
Miramas	**21**	43 33N	4 59 E
Mirambeau	**20**	45 23N	0 35W
Miramichi B.	**107**	47 15N	65 0W
Miramont-de-Guyenne	**20**	44 37N	0 21 E
Miranda	**127**	20 10 S	56 15W
Miranda de Ebro	**32**	42 41N	2 57W
Miranda do Corvo	**30**	40 6N	8 20W
Miranda do Douro	**30**	41 30N	6 16W
Mirande	**20**	43 31N	0 25 E
Mirandela	**30**	41 32N	7 10W
Mirando City	**117**	27 28N	98 59W
Mirandola	**38**	44 53N	11 2 E
Mirandópolis	**125**	21 9 S	51 6W
Mirango	**91**	13 32 S	34 58 E
Mirano	**39**	45 29N	12 6 E
Mirassol	**125**	20 46 S	49 28W
Mirbāţ	**63**	17 0N	54 45 E
Mirear	**86**	23 15N	35 41 E
Mirebeau, Côte-d'or, France	**19**	47 25N	5 20 E
Mirebeau, Vienne, France	**18**	46 49N	0 10 E
Mirecourt	**19**	48 20N	6 10 E
Mirgorod	**54**	49 58N	33 37 E
Miri	**72**	4 18N	114 0 E
Miriam Vale	**98**	24 20 S	151 33 E
Mirim, Lagoa	**125**	32 45 S	52 50W
Mirnyy, Antarct.	**5**	66 33 S	93 1 E
Mirnyy, U.S.S.R.	**59**	62 33N	113 53 E
Miroč	**42**	44 32N	22 16 E
Mirond L.	**109**	55 6N	102 47W
Mirosławiec	**28**	53 20N	16 5 E
Mirpur Bibiwari	**68**	28 33N	67 44 E
Mirpur Khas	**68**	25 30N	69 0 E
Mirpur Sakro	**68**	24 33N	67 41 E
Mirria	**85**	13 43N	9 7 E
Mirror	**108**	52 30N	113 7W
Mîrşani	**46**	44 1N	23 59 E
Mirsk	**28**	50 58N	15 23 E
Miryang	**76**	35 31N	128 44 E
Mirzaani	**57**	41 24N	46 5 E
Mirzapur-cum-Vindhyachal	**69**	25 10N	82 34 E
Miscou I.	**107**	47 57N	64 31W
Mish'āb, Ra'as al	**64**	28 15N	48 43 E
Mishan	**75**	45 37N	131 48 E
Mishawaka	**114**	41 40N	86 8W
Mishbih, Gebel	**86**	22 38N	34 44 E
Mishima	**74**	35 10N	138 52 E
Mishmar Ayyalon	**62**	31 52N	34 57 E
Mishmar Ha' Emeq	**62**	32 37N	35 7 E
Mishmar Ha Negev	**62**	31 22N	34 48 E
Mishmar Ha Yarden	**62**	33 0N	35 36 E
Misilmeri	**40**	38 2N	13 25 E
Misima I.	**98**	10 40 S	152 45 E
Misiones □, Argent.	**125**	27 0 S	55 0W
Misiones □, Parag.	**124**	27 0 S	56 0W
Miskīn	**65**	23 44N	56 52 E
Miskitos, Cayos	**121**	14 26N	82 50W
Miskolc	**27**	48 7N	20 50 E
Misoke	**90**	0 42 S	28 2 E
Misool	**73**	1 52 S	130 10 E
Misrātah	**83**	32 24N	15 3 E
Misrātah □	**83**	29 0N	16 0 E
Misriç	**64**	37 55N	41 40 E
Missanabie	**106**	48 20N	84 6W
Missinaibi →	**106**	50 43N	81 29W
Missinaibi L.	**106**	48 23N	83 40W
Mission, S.D., U.S.A.	**116**	43 21N	100 36W
Mission, Tex., U.S.A.	**117**	26 15N	98 20W
Mission City	**108**	49 10N	122 15W
Missisa L.	**106**	52 20N	85 7W
Mississagi →	**106**	46 15N	83 9W
Mississippi →	**117**	29 0N	89 15W
Mississippi, Delta of the	**117**	29 15N	90 30W
Mississippi L.	**113**	45 5N	76 10W
Mississippi □	**117**	33 25N	89 0W
Missoula	**118**	46 52N	114 0W
Missouri □	**116**	38 25N	92 30W
Missouri →	**116**	38 50N	90 8W
Missouri Valley	**116**	41 33N	95 53W
Mistake B.	**109**	62 8N	93 0W
Mistassini →	**107**	48 42N	72 20W
Mistassini L.	**106**	51 0N	73 30W
Mistastin L.	**107**	55 57N	63 20W
Mistatim	**109**	52 52N	103 22W
Mistelbach	**27**	48 34N	16 34 E
Misterbianco	**41**	37 32N	15 0 E
Mistretta	**41**	37 56N	14 20 E
Misty L.	**109**	58 53N	101 40W
Mît Ghamr	**86**	30 42N	31 12 E
Mitatib	**87**	15 59N	36 12 E
Mitchell, Austral.	**97**	26 29 S	147 58 E
Mitchell, Can.	**112**	43 28N	81 12W
Mitchell, Ind., U.S.A.	**114**	38 42N	86 25W
Mitchell, Nebr., U.S.A.	**116**	41 58N	103 45W
Mitchell, Oreg., U.S.A.	**118**	44 31N	120 8W
Mitchell, S.D., U.S.A.	**116**	43 40N	98 0W
Mitchell →	**97**	15 12 S	141 35 E
Mitchell, Mt.	**115**	35 40N	82 20W
Mitchelstown	**15**	52 16N	8 18W
Mitha Tiwana	**68**	32 13N	72 6 E
Mithimna	**44**	39 20N	26 12 E
Mitiaro, I.	**101**	19 49 S	157 43W
Mitilini	**45**	39 6N	26 35 E
Mitilinoí	**45**	37 42N	26 56 E
Mitla	**120**	16 55N	96 24W
Mito	**74**	36 20N	140 30 E
Mitsinjo	**93**	16 1 S	45 52 E
Mitsiwa	**87**	15 35N	39 25 E
Mitsiwa Channel	**87**	15 30N	40 0 E
Mitta Mitta →	**100**	36 14 S	147 10 E
Mittagong	**99**	34 28 S	150 29 E
Mittelland Kanal	**24**	52 23N	7 45 E
Mittenwalde	**24**	52 16N	13 33 E
Mitterteich	**25**	49 57N	12 15 E
Mittweida	**24**	50 59N	13 0 E
Mitú	**126**	1 8N	70 3W
Mitumba	**90**	7 8 S	31 2 E
Mitumba, Chaîne des	**90**	6 0 S	29 0 E
Mitwaba	**91**	8 2 S	27 17 E
Mityana	**90**	0 23N	32 2 E
Mitzic	**88**	0 45N	11 40 E
Mixteco →	**120**	18 11N	98 30W
Miyagi □	**74**	38 15N	140 45 E
Miyâh, W. el →	**86**	25 0N	33 23 E
Miyake-Jima	**74**	34 0N	139 30 E
Miyako	**74**	39 40N	141 59 E
Miyakonojō	**74**	31 40N	131 5 E
Miyazaki	**74**	31 56N	131 30 E
Miyazaki □	**74**	32 30N	131 30 E
Miyazu	**74**	35 35N	135 10 E
Miyet, Bahr el	**64**	31 30N	35 30 E
Miyun	**76**	40 28N	116 50 E
Mizal	**64**	23 59N	45 11 E
Mizamis = Ozamiz	**73**	8 15N	123 50 E
Mizdah	**83**	31 30N	13 0 E
Mizen Hd., Cork, Ireland	**15**	51 27N	9 50W
Mizen Hd., Wicklow, Ireland	**15**	52 52N	6 4W
Mizhi	**76**	37 47N	110 12 E
Mizil	**46**	44 59N	26 29 E
Mizoram □	**67**	23 30N	92 40 E
Mizpe Ramon	**62**	30 34N	34 49 E
Mjöbäck	**49**	57 28N	12 53 E
Mjölby	**49**	58 20N	15 10 E
Mjømna	**47**	60 55N	4 55 E
Mjörn	**49**	57 55N	12 25 E
Mjøsa	**47**	60 48N	11 0 E
Mkata	**90**	5 45 S	38 20 E
Mkokotoni	**90**	5 55 S	39 15 E
Mkomazi	**90**	4 40 S	38 7 E
Mkulwe	**91**	8 37 S	32 20 E
Mkumbi, Ras	**90**	7 38 S	39 55 E
Mkushi	**91**	14 25 S	29 15 E
Mkushi River	**91**	13 32 S	29 45 E
Mkuze →	**93**	27 45 S	32 30 E
Mladá Boleslav	**26**	50 27N	14 53 E
Mladenovac	**42**	44 28N	20 44 E
Mlala Hills	**90**	6 50 S	31 40 E
Mlange	**91**	16 2 S	35 33 E
Mlava →	**42**	44 45N	21 13 E
Mława	**28**	53 9N	20 25 E
Mlinište	**39**	44 15N	16 50 E
Mljet	**42**	42 43N	17 30 E
Mljetski Kanal	**42**	42 48N	17 35 E
Młynąry	**28**	54 12N	19 46 E
Mlynary	**28**	54 12N	19 43 E
Mme	**85**	6 18N	10 14 E
Mo	**47**	59 28N	7 50 E
Mo i Rana	**50**	66 15N	14 7 E
Moa	**73**	8 0 S	128 0 E
Moa →	**84**	6 59N	11 36 E
Moab	**119**	38 40N	109 35W
Moabi	**88**	2 24 S	10 59 E
Moala	**101**	18 36 S	179 53 E
Moalie Park	**99**	29 42 S	143 3 E
Moaña	**30**	42 18N	8 43W
Moapa	**119**	36 45N	114 37W
Moba	**90**	7 0 S	29 48 E
Mobaye	**88**	4 25N	21 5 E
Mobayi	**88**	4 15N	21 8 E
Moberley	**116**	39 25N	92 25W
Moberly →	**108**	56 12N	120 55W
Mobile	**115**	30 41N	88 3W
Mobile B.	**115**	30 30N	88 0W
Mobile, Pt.	**115**	30 15N	88 0W
Mobridge	**116**	45 31N	100 28W
Mobutu Sese Seko, L.	**90**	1 30N	31 0 E

* *Renamed Bohol Sea*

Place	Page	Lat.	Long.
Mocabe Kasari	91	9 58 S	26 12 E
Moçambique	91	15 3 S	40 42 E
Moçambique □	91	14 45 S	38 30 E
* Moçâmedes	89	15 7 S	12 11 E
* Moçâmedes □	92	16 35 S	12 30 E
Mochudi	92	24 27 S	26 7 E
Mocimboa da Praia	91	11 25 S	40 20 E
Mociu	46	46 46N	24 3 E
Möckeln	49	56 40N	14 15 E
Moclips	118	47 14N	124 10W
Mocoa	126	1 7N	76 35W
Mococa	125	21 28 S	47 0W
Mocorito	120	25 30N	107 53W
Moctezuma	120	29 50N	109 0W
Moctezuma →	120	21 59N	98 34W
Mocuba	91	16 54 S	36 57 E
Modalen	47	60 49N	5 48 E
Modane	21	45 12N	6 40 E
Modasa	68	23 30N	73 21 E
Modder →	92	29 2 S	24 37 E
Modderrivier	92	29 2 S	24 38 E
Módena	38	44 39N	10 55 E
Modena	119	37 55N	113 56W
Modesto	119	37 43N	121 0W
Módica	41	36 52N	14 45 E
Modigliana	39	44 9N	11 48 E
Modlin	28	52 24N	20 41 E
Mödling	27	48 5N	16 17 E
Modo	87	5 31N	30 33 E
Modra	27	48 19N	17 20 E
Modriča	42	44 57N	18 17 E
Moe	97	38 12 S	146 19 E
Moebase	91	17 3 S	38 41 E
Moei →	71	17 25N	98 10 E
Moëlan-sur-Mer	18	47 49N	3 38W
Moengo	127	5 45N	54 20W
Moffat	14	55 20N	3 27W
Moga	68	30 48N	75 8 E
Mogadishu = Muqdisho	63	2 2N	45 25 E
Mogador = Essaouira	82	31 32N	9 48W
Mogadouro	30	41 22N	6 47W
Mogami →	74	38 45N	140 0 E
Mogaung	67	25 20N	97 0 E
Møgeltønder	49	54 57N	8 48 E
Mogente	33	38 52N	0 45W
Mogho	87	4 54N	40 16 E
Mogi das Cruzes	125	23 31 S	46 11W
Mogi-Guaçu →	125	20 53 S	48 10W
Mogi-Mirim	125	22 29 S	47 0W
Mogielnica	28	51 42N	20 41 E
Mogilev	54	53 55N	30 18 E
Mogilev-Podolskiy	56	48 20N	27 40 E
Mogilno	28	52 39N	17 55 E
Mogincual	91	15 35 S	40 25 E
Mogliano Véneto	39	45 33N	12 15 E
Mogocha	59	53 40N	119 50 E
Mogoi	73	1 55 S	133 10 E
Mogok	67	23 0N	96 40 E
Mogollon	119	33 25N	108 48W
Mogollon Mesa	119	35 0N	111 0W
Moguer	31	37 15N	6 52W
Mohács	27	45 58N	18 41 E
Mohall	116	48 46N	101 30W
Moḩammadābād	65	37 52N	59 5 E
Mohammadia	82	35 33N	0 3 E
Mohammedia	82	33 44N	7 21W
Mohawk	119	32 45N	113 50W
Mohawk →	113	42 47N	73 42W
Mohe	76	53 28N	122 17 E
Moheda	49	57 1N	14 35 E
Möhne →	24	51 29N	7 57 E
Moholm	49	58 37N	14 5 E
Mohon	19	49 45N	4 44 E
Mohoro	90	8 6 S	39 8 E
Moia	87	5 3N	28 2 E
Moidart, L.	14	56 47N	5 40W
Moinabad	70	17 44N	77 16 E
Moineşti	46	46 28N	26 31 E
Mointy	58	47 10N	73 18 E
Moirans	21	45 20N	5 33 E
Moirans-en-Montagne	21	46 26N	5 43 E
Moires	45	35 4N	24 56 E
Moisakula	54	58 3N	25 12 E
Moisie	107	50 12N	66 1W
Moisie →	107	50 14N	66 5W
Moissac	20	44 7N	1 5 E
Moïssala	81	8 21N	17 46 E
Moita	31	38 38N	8 58W
Mojácar	33	37 6N	1 55W
Mojados	30	41 26N	4 40W
Mojave	119	35 8N	118 8W
Mojave Desert	119	35 0N	116 30W
Mojo, Boliv.	124	21 48 S	65 33W
Mojo, Ethiopia	87	8 35N	39 5 E
Mojo, Indon.	72	8 10 S	117 40 E
Mojokerto	73	7 29 S	112 25 E
Mokai	101	38 32 S	175 56 E
Mokambo	91	12 25 S	28 20 E
Mokameh	69	25 24N	85 55 E
Mokhós	45	35 16N	25 27 E
Mokhotlong	93	29 22 S	29 2 E
Moknine	83	35 35N	10 58 E
Mokokchung	67	26 15N	94 30 E
Mokra Gora	42	42 50N	20 30 E
Mokronog	39	45 57N	15 9 E
Moksha →	55	54 45N	41 53 E
Mokshan	55	53 25N	44 35 E
Mol	16	51 11N	5 5 E
Mola, C. de la	32	39 40N	4 20 E
Mola di Bari	41	41 3N	17 5 E
Moláoi	45	36 49N	22 56 E
Molat	39	44 15N	14 50 E
Molchanovo	58	57 40N	83 50 E
Mold	12	53 10N	3 10W
Moldava nad Bodvou	27	48 38N	21 0 E
Moldavia = Moldova	46	46 30N	27 0 E
Moldavian S.S.R. □	56	47 0N	28 0 E
Molde	47	62 45N	7 9 E
Moldova	46	46 30N	27 0 E
Moldova Nouă	42	44 45N	21 41 E
Moldoveanu	43	45 36N	24 45 E
Molepolole	92	24 28 S	25 28 E
Molfetta	41	41 12N	16 35 E
Molina de Aragón	32	40 46N	1 52W
Moline	116	41 30N	90 30W
Molinella	39	44 38N	11 40 E
Molinos	124	25 28 S	66 15W
Moliro	90	8 12 S	30 30 E
Molise □	39	41 45N	14 30 E
Moliterno	41	40 14N	15 50 E
Mollahat	69	22 56N	89 48 E
Mölle	49	56 17N	12 31 E
Molledo	30	43 8N	4 6W
Mollendo	126	17 0 S	72 0W
Mollerusa	32	41 37N	0 54 E
Mollina	31	37 8N	4 38W
Mölln	24	53 37N	10 41 E
Mölltorp	49	58 30N	14 26 E
Mölndal	49	57 40N	12 3 E
Molochansk	56	47 15N	35 35 E
Molochnaya →	56	47 0N	35 30 E
Molodechno	54	54 20N	26 50 E
Molokai	110	21 8N	157 0W
Moloma →	55	58 20N	48 15 E
Molong	99	33 5 S	148 54 E
Molopo →	92	28 30 S	20 13 E
Mólos	45	38 47N	22 37 E
Moloundou	88	2 8N	15 15 E
Molsheim	19	48 33N	7 29 E
Molson L.	109	54 22N	96 40W
Molteno	92	31 22 S	26 22 E
Molu	73	6 45 S	131 40 E
Molucca Sea	73	4 0 S	124 0 E
Moluccas = Maluku	73	1 0 S	127 0 E
Molusi	92	20 21 S	24 29 E
Moma, Mozam.	91	16 47 S	39 4 E
Moma, Zaïre	90	1 35 S	23 52 E
Momanga	92	18 7 S	21 41 E
Mombasa	90	4 2 S	39 43 E
Mombuey	30	42 3N	6 20W
Momchilgrad	43	41 33N	25 23 E
Momi	90	1 42 S	27 0 E
Mompós	126	9 14N	74 26W
Møn	49	54 57N	12 15 E
Mon →	67	20 25N	94 30 E
Mona, Canal de la	121	18 30N	67 45W
Mona, I.	121	18 5N	67 54W
Mona, Pta.	121	9 37N	82 36W
Mona, Punta	31	36 43N	3 45W
Monach Is.	14	57 32N	7 40W
Monaco ■	21	43 46N	7 23 E
Monadhliath Mts.	14	57 10N	4 4W
Monaghan	15	54 15N	6 58W
Monaghan □	15	54 10N	7 0W
Monahans	117	31 35N	102 50W
Monapo	91	14 56 S	40 19 E
Monarch Mt.	108	51 55N	125 57W
Monastier-sur-Gazeille, Le	20	44 57N	3 59 E
Monastir	83	35 50N	10 49 E
Monastyriska	54	49 8N	25 14 E
Moncada	32	39 30N	0 24W
Moncalieri	38	45 0N	7 40 E
Moncalvo	38	45 3N	8 15 E
Moncão	30	42 4N	8 27W
Moncarapacho	31	37 5N	7 46W
Moncayo, Sierra del	32	41 48N	1 50W
Mönchengladbach	24	51 12N	6 23 E
Monchique	31	37 19N	8 38W
Monclova	120	26 50N	101 30W
Moncontour	18	48 22N	2 38W
Moncoutant	18	46 43N	0 35W
Moncton	107	46 7N	64 51W
Mondego →	30	40 9N	8 52W
Mondego, Cabo	30	40 11N	8 54W
Mondeodo	73	3 34 S	122 9 E
Mondolfo	39	43 45N	13 8 E
Mondoñedo	30	43 25N	7 23W
Mondovì	38	44 23N	7 49 E
Mondovi	116	44 37N	91 40W
Mondragon	21	44 13N	4 44 E
Mondragone	40	41 8N	13 52 E
Monduli □	90	3 0 S	36 0 E
Monemvasía	45	36 41N	23 3 E
Monessen	114	40 9N	79 50W
Monesterio	31	38 6N	6 15W
Monestier-de-Clermont	21	44 55N	5 38 E
Monêtier-les-Bains, Le	21	44 58N	6 30 E
Monett	117	36 55N	93 56W
Monfalcone	39	45 49N	13 32 E
Monflanquin	20	44 32N	0 47 E
Monforte	31	39 6N	7 25W
Monforte de Lemos	30	42 31N	7 33W
Mong Cai	71	21 27N	107 54 E
Mong Hsu	67	21 54N	98 30 E
Mong Kung	67	21 35N	97 35 E
Mong Lang	71	21 29N	97 52 E
Mong Nai	67	20 32N	97 46 E
Mong Pawk	67	22 4N	99 16 E
Mong Ton	67	20 17N	98 45 E
Mong Wa	67	21 26N	100 27 E
Mong Yai	67	22 21N	98 3 E
Mongalla	87	5 8N	31 42 E
Mongers, L.	96	29 25 S	117 5 E
Monghyr	69	25 23N	86 30 E
Mongla	69	22 8N	89 35 E
Mongo	81	12 14N	18 43 E
Mongolia ■	75	47 0N	103 0 E
Mongonu	85	12 40N	13 32 E
Mongororo	81	12 3N	22 26 E
Mongu	89	15 16 S	23 12 E
Môngua	92	16 43 S	15 20 E
Monistrol	20	45 57N	3 38 E
Monistrol-St-Loire	21	45 17N	4 11 E
Monkey Bay	91	14 7 S	35 1 E
Mońki	28	53 23N	22 48 E
Monkira	98	24 46 S	140 30 E
Monkoto	88	1 38 S	20 35 E
Monmouth, U.K.	13	51 48N	2 43W
Monmouth, U.S.A.	116	40 50N	90 40W
Mono, L.	119	38 0N	119 9W
Monongahela	112	40 12N	79 56W
Monópoli	41	40 57N	17 18 E
Monor	27	47 21N	19 27 E
Monóvar	33	38 28N	0 53W
Monqoumba	88	3 33N	18 40 E
Monreal del Campo	32	40 47N	1 20W
Monreale	40	38 6N	13 16 E
Monroe, Ga., U.S.A.	115	33 47N	83 43W
Monroe, La., U.S.A.	117	32 32N	92 4W
Monroe, Mich., U.S.A.	114	41 55N	83 26W
Monroe, N.C., U.S.A.	115	35 2N	80 37W
Monroe, N.Y., U.S.A.	113	41 19N	74 11W
Monroe, Utah, U.S.A.	119	38 45N	112 5W
Monroe, Wis., U.S.A.	116	42 38N	89 40W
Monroe City	116	39 40N	91 40W
Monroeville	115	31 33N	87 15W
Monrovia, Liberia	84	6 18N	10 47W
Monrovia, U.S.A.	119	34 7N	118 1W
Mons	16	50 27N	3 58 E
Monsaraz	31	38 28N	7 22W
Monse	73	4 0 S	123 10 E
Monségur	20	44 38N	0 4 E
Monsélice	39	45 16N	11 46 E
Mont-de-Marsan	20	43 54N	0 31W
Mont d'Or, Tunnel	19	46 45N	6 18 E
Mont-Dore, Le	20	45 35N	2 50 E
Mont-Joli	107	48 37N	68 10W
Mont Laurier	106	46 35N	75 30W
Mont-sous-Vaudrey	19	46 58N	5 36 E
Mont-St-Michel, Le	18	48 40N	1 30W
Mont Tremblant Prov. Park	106	46 30N	74 30W
Montabaur	24	50 26N	7 49 E
Montagnac	20	43 29N	3 28 E
Montagnana	39	45 13N	11 29 E
Montagu	92	33 45 S	20 8 E
Montagu I.	5	58 25 S	26 20W
Montague, Can.	107	46 10N	62 39W
Montague, Calif., U.S.A.	118	41 47N	122 30W
Montague, Mass., U.S.A.	113	42 31N	72 33W
Montague, I.	120	31 40N	114 56W
Montague I.	104	60 0N	147 0W
Montague Sd.	96	14 28 S	125 20 E
Montaigu	18	46 59N	1 18W
Montalbán	32	40 50N	0 45W
Montalbano di Elicona	41	38 1N	15 0 E
Montalbano Iónico	41	40 17N	16 33 E
Montalbo	32	39 53N	2 42W
Montalcino	39	43 4N	11 30 E
Montalegre	30	41 49N	7 47W
Montalto di Castro	39	42 20N	11 36 E
Montalto Uffugo	41	39 25N	16 9 E
Montamarta	30	41 39N	5 49W
Montaña	126	6 0 S	73 0W
Montana □	110	47 0N	110 0W
Montánchez	31	39 15N	6 8W
Montargis	19	48 0N	2 43 E
Montauban	20	44 0N	1 21 E
Montauk	114	41 3N	71 57W
Montauk Pt.	113	41 4N	71 52W
Montbard	19	47 38N	4 20 E
Montbéliard	19	47 31N	6 48 E
Montblanch	32	41 23N	1 4 E
Montbrison	21	45 36N	4 3 E
Montcalm, Pic de	20	42 40N	1 25 E
Montceau-les-Mines	19	46 40N	4 23 E
Montchanin	38	46 47N	4 30 E
Montclair	113	40 53N	74 13W
Montcornet	19	49 40N	4 0 E
Montcuq	20	44 21N	1 13 E
Montdidier	19	49 38N	2 35 E
Monte Alegre	127	2 0 S	54 0W
Monte Azul	127	15 9 S	42 53W
Monte Bello Is.	96	20 30 S	115 45 E
Monte-Carlo	21	43 46N	7 23 E
Monte Caseros	124	30 10 S	57 50W
Monte Comán	124	34 40 S	67 53W
Monte Lindo →	124	23 56 S	57 12W
Monte Quemado	124	25 53 S	62 41W
Monte Redondo	30	39 53N	8 50W
Monte San Giovanni	40	41 39N	13 33 E
Monte San Savino	39	43 20N	11 42 E
Monte Sant' Ángelo	41	41 42N	15 59 E
Monte Santu, C. di	40	40 5N	9 42 E
Monte Vista	119	37 40N	106 8W
Monteagudo	125	27 14 S	54 8W
Montealegre	33	38 48N	1 17W
Montebello	106	45 40N	74 55W
Montebelluna	39	45 47N	12 3 E
Montebourg	18	49 30N	1 20W
Montecastrilli	39	42 40N	12 30 E
Montecatini Terme	38	43 55N	10 48 E
Montecristi	126	1 0 S	80 40W
Montecristo	38	42 20N	10 20 E
Montefalco	39	42 53N	12 38 E
Montefiascone	39	42 31N	12 2 E
Montefrío	31	37 20N	4 0W
Montego Bay	121	18 30N	78 0W
Montegranaro	39	43 13N	13 38 E
Montehanin	19	46 46N	4 44 E
Montejicar	33	37 33N	3 30W
Montélimar	21	44 33N	4 45 E
Montella	41	40 50N	15 0 E
Montellano	31	36 59N	5 36W
Montello	116	43 49N	89 21W
Montelupo Fiorentino	38	43 44N	11 2 E
Montemor-o-Novo	31	38 40N	8 12W
Montemor-o-Velho	30	40 11N	8 40W
Montemorelos	120	25 11N	99 42W
Montendre	20	45 16N	0 26W
Montenegro	125	29 39 S	51 29W
Montenegro = Crna Gora □	42	42 40N	19 20 E
Montenero di Bisaccia	39	42 0N	14 47 E
Montepuez	91	13 8 S	38 59 E
Montepuez →	91	12 32 S	40 27 E
Montepulciano	39	43 5N	11 46 E
Montereale	39	42 31N	13 13 E
Montereau	19	48 22N	2 57 E
Monterey	119	36 35N	121 57W
Montería	126	8 46N	75 53W
Monteros	124	27 11 S	65 30W
Monterotondo	39	42 3N	12 36 E
Monterrey	120	25 40N	100 30W
Montes Claros	127	16 30 S	43 50W
Montesano	118	47 0N	123 39W
Montesárchio	41	41 5N	14 37 E
Montescaglioso	41	40 34N	16 40 E
Montesilvano	39	42 30N	14 8 E
Montevarchi	39	43 30N	11 32 E
Montevideo	125	34 50 S	56 11W
Montezuma	116	41 32N	92 35W
Montfaucon, Haute-Loire, France	21	45 11N	4 20 E
Montfaucon, Meuse, France	19	49 16N	5 8 E
Montfort-l'Amaury	19	48 47N	1 49 E
Montfort-sur-Meu	18	48 8N	1 58W
Montgenèvre	21	44 56N	6 42 E
Montgomery, U.K.	13	52 34N	3 9W
Montgomery, Ala., U.S.A.	115	32 20N	86 20W
Montgomery, W. Va., U.S.A.	114	38 9N	81 21W
Montgomery = Sahiwal	68	30 45N	73 8 E
Montguyon	20	45 12N	0 12W
Monthey	25	46 15N	6 56 E
Monticelli d'Ongina	38	45 3N	9 56 E
Monticello, Ark., U.S.A.	117	33 40N	91 48W
Monticello, Fla., U.S.A.	115	30 35N	83 50W
Monticello, Ind., U.S.A.	114	40 40N	86 45W
Monticello, Iowa, U.S.A.	116	42 18N	91 12W
Monticello, Ky., U.S.A.	115	36 52N	84 50W
Monticello, Minn., U.S.A.	116	45 17N	93 52W
Monticello, Miss., U.S.A.	117	31 35N	90 8W
Monticello, N.Y., U.S.A.	113	41 37N	74 42W
Monticello, Utah, U.S.A.	119	37 55N	109 27W
Montichiari	38	45 28N	10 29 E
Montier	19	48 30N	4 45 E
Montignac	20	45 4N	1 10 E
Montigny-les-Metz	19	49 7N	6 10 E
Montigny-sur-Aube	19	47 57N	4 45 E
Montijo	31	38 52N	6 39W
Montijo, Presa de	31	38 55N	6 26W
Montilla	31	37 36N	4 40W
Montivideo	116	44 55N	95 40W
Montlhéry	19	48 39N	2 15 E
Montluçon	20	46 22N	2 36 E
Montmagny	107	46 58N	70 34W
Montmarault	20	46 19N	2 57 E
Montmartre	109	50 14N	103 27W
Montmédy	19	49 30N	5 20 E
Montmélian	21	45 30N	6 4 E
Montmirail	19	48 51N	3 30 E
Montmoreau-St-Cybard	20	45 23N	0 8 E
Montmorency	107	46 53N	71 11W
Montmorillon	20	46 26N	0 50 E
Montmort	19	48 55N	3 49 E
Monto	97	24 52 S	151 6 E
Montoire	18	47 45N	0 52 E
Montório al Vomano	39	42 35N	13 38 E
Montoro	31	38 1N	4 27W
Montour Falls	112	42 20N	76 51W
Montpelier, Idaho, U.S.A.	118	42 15N	111 20W
Montpelier, Ohio, U.S.A.	114	41 34N	84 40W
Montpelier, Vt., U.S.A.	114	44 15N	72 38W
Montpellier	20	43 37N	3 52 E
Montpezat-de-Quercy	20	44 15N	1 30 E
Montpon	20	45 2N	0 11 E
Montréal, Can.	106	45 31N	73 34W
Montréal, France	20	43 13N	2 8 E
Montreal L.	109	54 20N	105 45W
Montreal Lake	109	54 3N	105 46W
Montredon-Labessonniè	20	43 45N	2 18 E
Montréjeau	20	43 6N	0 35 E
Montrésor	18	47 10N	1 10 E
Montreuil	19	50 27N	1 45 E
Montreuil-Bellay	18	47 8N	0 9W
Montreux	25	46 26N	6 55 E
Montrevault	18	47 17N	1 2W
Montrevel-en-Bresse	21	46 21N	5 8 E
Montrichard	18	47 20N	1 10 E
Montrose, U.K.	14	56 43N	2 28W
Montrose, Col., U.S.A.	119	38 30N	107 52W
Montrose, Pa., U.S.A.	113	41 50N	75 55W
Monts, Pte des	107	49 20N	67 12W
Monts-sur-Guesnes	18	46 55N	0 13 E
Montsalvy	20	44 41N	2 30 E
Montsant, Sierra de	32	41 17N	1 0 E
Montsauche	19	47 13N	4 0 E
Montsech, Sierra del	32	42 0N	0 45 E
Montseny	32	41 55N	2 25W
Montserrat, Spain	32	41 36N	1 49 E
Montserrat, W. Indies	121	16 40N	62 10W
Montuenga	30	41 3N	4 38W
Montuiri	32	39 34N	2 59 E
Monveda	88	2 52N	21 30 E
Monywa	67	22 7N	95 11 E
Monza	38	45 35N	9 15 E
Monze	91	16 17 S	27 29 E
Monze, C.	66	24 47N	66 37 E
Monzón	32	41 52N	0 10 E
Moolawatana	99	29 55 S	139 45 E
Moonah →	98	22 3 S	138 33 E
Moonbeam	106	49 20N	82 10W
Moonie	99	27 46 S	150 20 E
Moonie →	97	29 19 S	148 43 E
Moonta	99	34 6 S	137 32 E
Mooraberree	99	25 13 S	140 54 E
Moorcroft	116	44 17N	104 58W
Moore, L.	96	29 50 S	117 35 E
Moorefield	114	39 5N	78 59W
Moores Res.	113	44 45N	71 50W
Mooresville	115	35 36N	80 45W
Moorfoot Hills	14	55 44N	3 8W
Moorhead	116	46 51N	96 44W
Mooroopna	99	36 25 S	145 22 E
Moorreesburg	92	33 6 S	18 38 E
Moosburg	25	48 28N	11 57 E
Moose →	106	51 20N	80 25W
Moose Factory	106	51 16N	80 32W
Moose I.	109	51 42N	97 10W
Moose Jaw	109	50 24N	105 30W
Moose Jaw Cr. →	109	50 34N	105 18W
Moose Lake, Can.	109	53 43N	100 20W
Moose Lake, U.S.A.	116	46 27N	92 48W
Moose Mountain Cr. →	109	49 13N	102 12W
Moose Mountain Prov. Park	109	49 48N	102 25W
Moose River	106	50 48N	81 17W
Moosehead L.	107	45 34N	69 40W
Moosomin	109	50 9N	101 40W
Moosonee	106	51 17N	80 39W
Moosup	113	41 44N	71 52W

* *Renamed Namibe*

Mopipi 92 21 6S 24 55 E
Mopoi 90 5 6N 26 54 E
Mopti 84 14 30N 4 0W
Moqatta 87 14 38N 35 50 E
Moquegua 126 17 15S 70 46W
Mór 27 47 25N 18 12 E
Móra 31 38 55N 8 10W
Mora, Sweden 48 61 2N 14 38 E
Mora, Minn., U.S.A. 116 45 52N 93 19W
Mora, N. Mex., U.S.A. 119 35 58N 105 21W
Mora de Ebro 32 41 6N 0 38 E
Mora de Rubielos 32 40 15N 0 45W
Mora la Nueva 32 41 7N 0 39 E
Morača → 42 42 20N 19 9 E
Moradabad 68 28 50N 78 50 E
Morafenobe 93 17 50S 44 53 E
Morąg 28 53 55N 19 56 E
Moral de Calatrava 33 38 51N 3 33W
Moraleja 30 40 6N 6 43W
Moran, Kans., U.S.A. 117 37 53N 94 35W
Moran, Wyo., U.S.A. 118 43 53N 110 37W
Morano Cálabro 41 39 51N 16 8 E
Morant Cays 121 17 22N 76 0W
Morant Pt. 121 17 55N 76 12W
Morar L. 14 56 57N 5 40W
Moratalla 33 38 14N 1 49W
Moratuwa 70 6 45N 79 55 E
Morava → 27 48 10N 16 59 E
Moravia 116 40 50N 92 50W
Moravian Hts. = Ceskemoravská V. 26 49 30N 15 40 E
Moravica → 42 43 52N 20 8 E
Moravice → 27 49 50N 17 43 E
Moravița 42 45 17N 21 14 E
Moravská Třebová 27 49 45N 16 40 E
Moravské Budějovice 26 49 4N 15 49 E
Morawhanna 126 8 30N 59 40W
Moray Firth 14 57 50N 3 30W
Morbach 25 49 48N 7 7 E
Morbegno 38 46 8N 9 34 E
Morbihan □ 18 47 55N 2 50W
Morcenx 20 44 0N 0 55W
Mordelles 18 48 5N 1 52W
Morden 109 49 15N 98 10W
Mordialloc 100 38 1S 145 6 E
Mordovian A.S.S.R. □ 55 54 20N 44 30 E
Mordovo 55 52 6N 40 50 E
Mordy 28 52 13N 22 31 E
Møre og Romsdal fylke □ 47 62 30N 8 0 E
Morea 9 37 45N 22 10 E
Moreau → 116 45 15N 100 43W
Morecambe 12 54 5N 2 52W
Morecambe B. 12 54 7N 3 0W
Moree 97 29 28S 149 54 E
Morehead 114 38 12N 83 22W
Morehead City 115 34 46N 76 44W
Morelia 120 19 40N 101 11W
Morella, Austral. 98 23 0S 143 52 E
Morella, Spain 32 40 35N 0 5W
Morelos □ 120 18 40N 99 10W
Morena, Sierra 31 38 20N 4 0W
Morenci 119 33 7N 109 20W
Moreni 46 44 59N 25 36 E
Moresby I. 108 52 30N 131 40W
Morestel 21 45 40N 5 28 E
Moret 19 48 22N 2 58 E
Moreton 98 12 22S 142 30 E
Moreton B. 97 27 10S 153 10 E
Moreton I. 97 27 10S 153 25 E
Moreuil 19 49 46N 2 30 E
Morez 21 46 31N 6 2 E
Morgan, Austral. 99 34 0S 139 35 E
Morgan, U.S.A. 118 41 3N 111 44W
Morgan City 117 29 40N 91 15W
Morganfield 114 37 40N 87 55W
Morganton 115 35 46N 81 48W
Morgantown 114 39 39N 79 58W
Morganville 99 25 10S 151 50 E
Morgat 18 48 15N 4 32W
Morgenzon 93 26 45S 29 36 E
Morges 25 46 31N 6 29 E
Morhange 19 48 55N 6 38 E
Mori 38 45 51N 10 59 E
Moriarty 119 35 3N 106 2W
Morice L. 108 53 50N 127 40W
Moriki 85 12 52N 6 30 E
Morinville 108 53 49N 113 41W
Morioka 74 39 45N 141 8 E
Morkalla 99 34 23S 141 10 E
Morlaàs 20 43 21N 0 18W
Morlaix 18 48 36N 3 52W
Mormanno 41 39 53N 15 59 E
Mormant 19 48 37N 2 52 E
Mornington 99 38 15S 145 5 E
Mornington I. 97 16 30S 139 30 E
Mornington, I. 128 49 50S 75 30W
Mórnos → 45 38 30N 22 0 E
Moro 87 10 50N 30 9 E
Moro G. 73 6 30N 123 0 E
Morobe 98 7 49S 147 38 E
Morocco ■ 82 32 0N 5 50W
Morococha 126 11 40S 76 5W
Morogoro 90 6 50S 37 40 E
Morogoro □ 90 8 0S 37 0 E
Moroleón 120 20 8N 101 32W
Morombe 93 21 45S 43 22 E
Moron 124 34 39S 58 37W
Morón 121 22 8N 78 39W
Mörön → 75 47 14N 110 37 E
Morón de Almazán 32 41 29N 2 27W
Morón de la Frontera 31 37 6N 5 28W
Morondava 93 20 17S 44 17 E
Morondo 84 8 57N 6 47W
Moronou 84 6 16N 4 59W
Morotai 73 2 10N 128 30 E
Moroto 90 2 28N 34 42 E
Moroto Summit 90 2 30N 34 43 E
Morozov (Bratan) 43 42 30N 25 10 E
Morozovsk 57 48 25N 41 50 E
Morpeth 12 55 11N 1 41W
Morphou 64 35 12N 32 59 E
Morrilton 117 35 10N 92 45W
Morrinhos 127 17 45S 49 10W
Morrinsville 101 37 40S 175 32 E
Morris, Can. 109 49 25N 97 22W
Morris, Ill., U.S.A. 114 41 20N 88 20W
Morris, Minn., U.S.A. 116 45 33N 95 56W
Morrisburg 106 44 55N 75 7W
Morrison 116 41 47N 90 0W
Morristown, Ariz., U.S.A. 119 33 54N 112 35W
Morristown, N.J., U.S.A. 113 40 48N 74 30W
Morristown, S.D., U.S.A. 116 45 57N 101 44W
Morristown, Tenn., U.S.A. 115 36 18N 83 20W
Morro Bay 119 35 27N 120 54W
Morro, Pta. 124 27 6S 71 0W
Morrosquillo, Golfo de 121 9 35N 75 40W
Mörrum 49 56 12N 14 45 E
Mors 49 56 50N 8 45 E
Morshansk 55 53 28N 41 50 E
Mörsil 48 63 19N 13 40 E
Mortagne 20 45 28N 0 49W
Mortagne → 19 48 33N 6 27 E
Mortagne-au-Perche 18 48 31N 0 33 E
Mortain 18 48 40N 0 57W
Mortara 38 45 15N 8 43 E
Morteau 19 47 3N 6 35 E
Morteros 124 30 50S 62 0W
Mortes, R. das → 127 11 45S 50 44W
Mortlake 99 38 5S 142 50 E
Morton, Tex., U.S.A. 117 33 39N 102 49W
Morton, Wash., U.S.A. 118 46 33N 122 17W
Morundah 99 34 57S 146 19 E
Moruya 99 35 58S 150 3 E
Morvan, Mts. du 19 47 5N 4 0 E
Morven 99 26 22S 147 5 E
Morvern 14 56 38N 5 44W
Morvi 68 22 50N 70 42 E
Morwell 97 38 10S 146 22 E
Moryn 28 52 51N 14 22 E
Morzhovets, Ostrov 52 66 44N 42 35 E
Mosalsk 54 54 30N 34 55 E
Mosbach 25 49 21N 9 9 E
Moščenice 39 45 17N 14 16 E
Mosciano Sant' Ángelo 39 42 42N 13 52 E
Moscos Is. 72 14 0N 97 30 E
Moscow 118 46 45N 116 59W
Moscow = Moskva 55 55 45N 37 35 E
Mosel → 16 50 22N 7 36 E
Moselle = Mosel → 16 50 22N 7 36 E
Moselle □ 19 48 59N 6 33 E
Moses Lake 118 47 9N 119 17W
Mosgiel 101 45 53S 170 21 E
Moshi 90 3 22S 37 18 E
Moshi □ 90 3 22S 37 18 E
Moshupa 92 24 46S 25 29 E
Mošina 28 52 15N 16 50 E
Mosjøen 50 65 51N 13 12 E
Moskenesøya 50 67 58N 13 0 E
Moskenstraumen 50 67 47N 12 45 E
Moskva 55 55 45N 37 35 E
Moskva → 55 55 5N 38 51 E
Moslavačka Gora 39 45 40N 16 37 E
Mosomane (Artesia) 92 24 2S 26 19 E
Mosonmagyaróvár 27 47 52N 17 18 E
Mošorin 42 45 19N 20 4 E
Mospino 56 47 52N 38 0 E
Mosquera 126 2 35N 78 24W
Mosquero 117 35 48N 103 57W
Mosqueruela 32 40 21N 0 27W
Mosquitos, Golfo de los 121 9 15N 81 10W
Moss 47 59 27N 10 40 E
Moss Vale 99 34 32S 150 25 E
Mossaka 88 1 15S 16 45 E
Mossbank 109 49 56N 105 56W
Mossburn 101 45 41S 168 15 E
Mosselbaai 92 34 11S 22 8 E
Mossendjo 88 2 55S 12 42 E
Mossgiel 99 33 15S 144 5 E
Mossman 97 16 21S 145 15 E
Mossoró 127 5 10S 37 15W
Møsstrand 47 59 51N 8 4 E
Mossuril 91 14 58S 40 42 E
Mossy → 109 54 5N 102 58W
Most 26 50 31N 13 38 E
Mostaganem 82 35 54N 0 5 E
Mostar 42 43 22N 17 50 E
Mostardas 125 31 2S 50 51W
Mostefa, Rass 83 36 55N 11 3 E
Mosterøy 47 59 5N 5 37 E
Mostiska 54 49 48N 23 4 E
Mosty 54 53 27N 24 38 E
Mosul = Al Mawșil 64 36 20N 43 5 E
Mosvatn 47 59 52N 8 5 E
Mota del Cuervo 32 39 30N 2 52W
Mota del Marqués 30 41 38N 5 11W
Motagua → 120 15 44N 88 14W
Motala 49 58 32N 15 1 E
Mothe-Achard, La 18 46 37N 1 40W
Motherwell 14 55 48N 4 0W
Motihari 69 26 30N 84 55 E
Motilla del Palancar 32 39 34N 1 55W
Motnik 39 46 14N 14 54 E
Motovun 39 45 20N 13 50 E
Motozintla de Mendoza 120 15 21N 92 14W
Motril 33 36 31N 3 37W
Motru → 46 44 44N 22 59 E
Mott 116 46 25N 102 29W
Motte-Chalançon, La 21 44 30N 5 21 E
Motte, La 21 44 20N 6 3 E
Móttola 41 40 38N 17 0 E
Motueka 101 41 7S 173 1 E
Motul 120 21 0N 89 20W
Mouanda 88 1 28S 13 7 E
Mouchalagane → 107 50 56N 68 41W
Moucontant 18 46 43N 0 36W
Moúdhros 44 39 50N 25 18 E
Moudjeria 84 17 50N 12 28W
Moudon 25 46 40N 6 49 E
Mouila 88 1 50S 11 0 E
Moulamein 99 35 3S 144 1 E
Moule 121 16 20N 61 22W
Moulins 20 46 35N 3 19 E
Moulmein 67 16 30N 97 40 E
Moulouya, O. → 82 35 5N 2 25W
Moulton 117 29 35N 97 8W
Moultrie 115 31 11N 83 47W
Moultrie, L. 115 33 25N 80 10W
Mound City, Mo., U.S.A. 116 40 2N 95 25W
Mound City, S.D., U.S.A. 116 45 46N 100 3W
Moúnda, Ákra 45 38 5N 20 45 E
Moundou 81 8 40N 16 10 E
Moundsville 114 39 53N 80 43W
Mount Airy 115 36 31N 80 37W
Mount Albert 112 44 8N 79 19W
Mount Angel 118 45 4N 122 46W
Mount Barker, S.A., Austral. 99 35 5S 138 52 E
Mount Barker, W.A., Austral. 96 34 38S 117 40 E
Mount Carmel, Ill., U.S.A. 114 38 20N 87 48W
Mount Carmel, Pa., U.S.A. 114 40 46N 76 25W
Mount Clemens 106 42 35N 82 50W
Mount Coolon 98 21 25S 147 25 E
Mount Darwin 91 16 45S 31 33 E
Mount Desert I. 107 44 15N 68 25W
Mount Dora 115 28 49N 81 32W
Mount Douglas 98 21 35S 146 50 E
Mount Edgecumbe 108 57 8N 135 22W
Mount Enid 96 21 42S 116 26 E
Mount Forest 106 43 59N 80 43W
Mount Gambier 97 37 50S 140 46 E
Mount Garnet 98 17 37S 145 6 E
Mount Hope 114 37 52N 81 9W
Mount Horeb 116 43 0N 89 42W
Mount Howitt 99 26 31S 142 16 E
Mount Isa 97 20 42S 139 26 E
Mount Larcom 98 23 48S 150 59 E
Mount Lofty Ra. 97 34 35S 139 5 E
Mount McKinley Nat. Park 104 64 0N 150 0W
Mount Magnet 96 28 2S 117 47 E
Mount Margaret 99 26 54S 143 21 E
Mount Maunganui 101 37 40S 176 14 E
Mount Morgan 97 23 40S 150 25 E
Mount Morris 114 42 43N 77 50W
Mount Mulligan 98 16 45S 144 47 E
Mount Nicholas 96 22 54S 120 27 E
Mount Oxide Mine 98 19 30S 139 29 E
Mount Pearl 107 47 31N 52 47W
Mount Perry 99 25 13S 151 42 E
Mount Pleasant, Iowa, U.S.A. 116 41 0N 91 35W
Mount Pleasant, Mich., U.S.A. 114 43 35N 84 47W
Mount Pleasant, Pa., U.S.A. 112 40 9N 79 31W
Mount Pleasant, S.C., U.S.A. 115 32 45N 79 48W
Mount Pleasant, Tenn., U.S.A. 115 35 31N 87 11W
Mount Pleasant, Tex., U.S.A. 117 33 5N 95 0W
Mount Pleasant, Ut., U.S.A. 118 39 40N 111 29W
Mount Pocono 113 41 8N 75 21W
Mount Rainier Nat. Park. 118 46 50N 121 43W
Mount Revelstoke Nat. Park 108 51 5N 118 30W
Mount Robson 108 52 56N 119 15W
Mount Robson Prov. Park 108 53 0N 119 0W
Mount Shasta 118 41 20N 122 18W
Mount Sterling, Ill., U.S.A. 116 40 0N 90 40W
Mount Sterling, Ky., U.S.A. 114 38 0N 84 0W
Mount Surprise 98 18 10S 144 17 E
Mount Union 112 40 22N 77 51W
Mount Vernon, Ind., U.S.A. 116 38 17N 88 57W
Mount Vernon, N.Y., U.S.A. 114 40 57N 73 49W
Mount Vernon, Ohio, U.S.A. 114 40 20N 82 30W
Mount Vernon, Wash., U.S.A. 108 48 25N 122 20W
Mount Whaleback 96 23 18S 119 44 E
Mountain City, Nev., U.S.A. 118 41 54N 116 0W
Mountain City, Tenn., U.S.A. 115 36 30N 81 50W
Mountain Grove 117 37 5N 92 20W
Mountain Home, Ark., U.S.A. 117 36 20N 92 25W
Mountain Home, Idaho, U.S.A. 118 43 11N 115 45W
Mountain Iron 116 47 30N 92 37W
Mountain Park. 108 52 50N 117 15W
Mountain View, Ark., U.S.A. 117 35 52N 92 10W
Mountain View, Calif., U.S.A. 119 37 26N 122 5W
Mountainair 119 34 35N 106 15W
Mountmellick 15 53 7N 7 20W
Moura, Austral. 98 24 35S 149 58 E
Moura, Brazil 126 1 32S 61 38W
Moura, Port. 31 38 7N 7 30W
Mourão 31 38 22N 7 22W
Mourdi Depression 81 18 10N 23 0 E
Mourdiah 84 14 35N 7 25W
Moure, La 116 46 27N 98 17W
Mourenx 20 43 23N 0 36W
Mouri 85 5 6N 1 14W
Mourilyan 98 17 35S 146 3 E
Mourmelon-le-Grand 19 49 8N 4 22 E
Mourne → 15 54 45N 7 39W
Mourne Mts. 15 54 10N 6 0W
Mouscron 16 50 45N 3 12 E
Moussoro 81 13 41N 16 35 E
Mouthe 19 46 44N 6 12 E
Moutier 25 47 16N 7 21 E
Moûtiers 21 45 29N 6 31 E
Moutong 73 0 28N 121 13 E
Mouy 19 49 18N 2 20 E
Mouzáki 44 39 25N 21 37 E
Moville 15 55 11N 7 3W
Moy → 15 54 5N 8 50W
Moyale, Ethiopia 87 3 34N 39 4 E
Moyale, Kenya 90 3 30N 39 0 E
Moyamba 84 8 4N 12 30W
Moyen Atlas 80 32 0N 5 0W
Moyle □ 15 55 10N 6 15W
Moyobamba 126 6 0S 77 0W
Moyyero → 59 68 44N 103 42 E
Mozambique = Moçambique 91 15 3S 40 42 E
Mozambique ■ 91 19 0S 35 0 E
Mozambique Chan. 93 20 0S 39 0 E
Mozdok 57 43 45N 44 48 E
Mozhaysk 55 55 30N 36 2 E
Mozhga 55 56 26N 52 15 E
Mozirje 39 46 22N 14 58 E
Mozyr 54 52 0N 29 15 E
Mpanda 90 6 23S 31 1 E
Mpanda □ 90 6 23S 31 40 E
Mpésoba 84 12 31N 5 39W
Mpika 91 11 51S 31 25 E
Mpulungu 91 8 51S 31 5 E
Mpwapwa 90 6 23S 36 30 E
Mpwapwa □ 90 6 30S 36 20 E
Mrągowo 28 53 52N 21 18 E
Mramor 42 43 20N 21 45 E
Mrimina 82 29 50N 7 9W
Mrkonjić Grad 42 44 26N 17 4 E
Mrkopalj 39 45 21N 14 52 E
Mrocza 28 53 16N 17 35 E
Msab, Oued en → 83 32 25N 5 20 E
Msaken 83 35 49N 10 33 E
Msambansovu 91 15 50S 30 3 E
M'sila 83 35 46N 4 30 E
Msta → 54 58 25N 31 20 E
Mstislavl 54 54 0N 31 50 E
Mszana Dolna 27 49 41N 20 5 E
Mszczonów 28 51 58N 20 33 E
Mtama 91 10 17S 39 21 E
Mtilikwe → 91 21 9S 31 30 E
Mtsensk 55 53 25N 36 30 E
Mtskheta 57 41 52N 44 45 E
Mtwara-Mikindani 91 10 20S 40 20 E
Mu Us Shamo 76 39 0N 109 0 E
Muaná 127 1 25S 49 15W
Muang Chiang Rai 71 19 52N 99 50 E
Muang Lamphun 71 18 40N 99 2 E
Muang Phichit 71 16 29N 100 21 E
Muar 71 2 3N 102 34 E
Muar → 71 2 15N 102 48 E
Muarabungo 72 1 28S 102 52 E
Muaradjuloi 72 0 12S 114 3 E
Muaraenim 72 3 40S 103 50 E
Muarakaman 72 0 2S 116 45 E
Muaratebo 72 1 30S 102 26 E
Muaratembesi 72 1 42S 103 8 E
Muaratewe 72 0 58S 114 52 E
Mubarakpur 69 26 6N 83 18 E
Mubende 90 0 33N 31 22 E
Mubi 85 10 18N 13 16 E
Mücheln 24 51 18N 11 49 E
Muchinga Mts. 91 11 30S 31 30 E
Muchkapskiy 55 51 52N 42 28 E
Muck 14 56 50N 6 15W
Muckadilla 99 26 35S 148 23 E
Mucuri 127 18 0S 39 36W
Mucusso 92 18 1S 21 25 E
Mudanjiang 76 44 38N 129 30 E
Mudanya 56 40 25N 28 50 E
Muddy → 119 38 0N 110 22W
Mudgee 97 32 32S 149 31 E
Mudjatik → 109 56 1N 107 36W
Muecate 91 14 55S 39 40 E
Muêda 91 11 36S 39 28 E
Muela, La 32 41 36N 1 7W
Muerto, Mar 120 16 10N 94 10W
Muertos, Punta de los 33 36 57N 1 54W
Mufindi □ 91 8 30S 35 20 E
Mufulira 91 12 32S 28 15 E
Mufumbiro Range 90 1 25S 29 30 E
Mugardos 30 43 27N 8 15W
Muge 31 39 3N 8 40W
Muge → 31 39 8N 8 44W
Múggia 39 45 36N 13 47 E
Mugia 30 43 3N 9 10W
Mugila, Mts. 90 7 0S 28 50 E
Muğla 64 37 15N 28 22 E
Mŭglizh 43 42 37N 25 32 E
Mugshin 63 19 35N 54 40 E
Mugu 69 29 45N 82 30 E
Muhammad Qol 86 20 53N 37 9 E
Muhammad Râs 86 27 42N 34 13 E
Muhammadabad 69 26 4N 83 25 E
Muharraqa = Sa'ad 62 31 28N 34 33 E
Muhesi → 90 7 0S 35 20 E
Muheza □ 90 5 0S 39 0 E
Mühldorf 25 48 14N 12 33 E
Mühlhausen 24 51 12N 10 29 E
Mühlig Hofmann fjella 5 72 30S 5 0 E
Muhutwe 90 1 35S 31 45 E
Mui Bai Bung 71 8 35N 104 42 E
Mui Ron 71 18 7N 106 27 E
Muikamachi 74 37 15N 138 50 E
Muine Bheag 15 52 42N 6 57W
Muiños 30 41 58N 7 59W
Mukachevo 54 48 27N 22 45 E
Mukah 72 2 55N 112 5 E
Mukawwa, Geziret 86 23 55N 35 53 E
Mukden = Shenyang 76 41 48N 123 27 E
Mukhtolovo 55 55 29N 43 15 E
Mukishi 91 8 30S 24 44 E
Mukomuko 72 2 30S 101 10 E
Mukomwenze 90 6 49S 27 15 E
Muktsar 68 30 30N 74 30 E
Mukur 66 32 50N 67 42 E
Mukutawa → 109 53 10N 97 24W
Mukwela 91 17 0S 26 40 E
Mula 33 38 3N 1 33W
Mula → 70 18 34N 74 21 E
Mulange 90 3 40S 27 10 E
• Mulatas, Arch. de las 121 9 50N 78 31W
Mulchén 124 37 45S 72 20W
Mulde → 24 51 10N 12 48 E
Mule Creek 116 43 19N 104 8W
Muleba 90 1 50S 31 37 E
Muleba □ 90 2 0S 31 30 E
Muleshoe 117 34 17N 102 42W
Mulgrave 107 45 38N 61 31W
Mulgrave I. 98 10 5S 142 10 E
Mulhacén 33 37 4N 3 20W
Mülheim 24 51 26N 6 53 E
Mulhouse 19 47 40N 7 20 E
Muling He → 76 45 53N 133 30 E
Mull 14 56 27N 6 0W
Mullaittvu 70 9 15N 80 49 E
Mullen 116 42 5N 101 0W
Mullengudgery 99 31 43S 147 23 E
Mullens 114 37 34N 81 22W
Muller, Pegunungan 72 0 30N 113 30 E
Mullet Pen. 15 54 10N 10 2W
Mullewa 96 28 29S 115 30 E
Müllheim 25 47 48N 7 37 E
Mulligan → 98 26 40S 139 0 E
Mullin 117 31 33N 98 38W
Mullingar 15 53 31N 7 20W
Mullins 115 34 12N 79 15W
Mullsjö 49 57 56N 13 55 E

• *Renamed San Blas, Arch. de*

Mullumbimby 99 28 30 S 153 30 E
Mulobezi 91 16 45 S 25 7 E
Mulshi L. 70 18 30N 73 48 E
Multai 68 21 50N 78 21 E
Multan 68 30 15N 71 36 E
• Multan □ 68 30 29N 72 29 E
Multrå 48 63 10N 17 24 E
Mulumbe, Mts. 91 8 40 S 27 30 E
Mulungushi Dam 91 14 48 S 28 48 E
Mulvane 117 37 30N 97 15W
Mulwad 86 18 45N 30 39 E
Mulwala 100 35 59 S 146 0 E
Mumra 57 45 45N 47 41 E
Mun → 71 15 17N 103 0 E
Muna 73 5 0 S 122 30 E
Munamagi 54 57 43N 27 4 E
Münchberg 25 50 11N 11 48 E
Muncheberg 24 52 30N 14 9 E
München 25 48 8N 11 33 E
Munchen-Gladbach = Mönchengladbach 24 51 12N 6 23 E
Muncho Lake 108 59 0N 125 50W
Muncie 114 40 10N 85 20W
Mundakayam 70 9 30N 76 50 E
Mundala, Puncak 73 4 30 S 141 0 E
Mundare 108 53 35N 112 20W
Munday 117 33 26N 99 39W
Münden 24 51 25N 9 42 E
Mundo → 33 38 30N 2 15W
Mundo Novo 127 11 50 S 40 29W
Mundra 68 22 54N 69 48 E
Munera 33 39 2N 2 29W
Muneru → 70 16 45N 80 3 E
Mungallala 99 26 28 S 147 34 E
Mungallala Cr. → 99 28 53 S 147 5 E
Mungana 98 17 8 S 144 27 E
Mungaoli 68 24 24N 78 7 E
Mungari 91 17 12 S 33 30 E
Mungbere 90 2 36N 28 28 E
Mungindi 97 28 58 S 149 1 E
Munhango 89 12 10 S 18 38 E
Munich = München 25 48 8N 11 33 E
Munising 114 46 25N 86 39W
Munjiye 86 18 47N 41 20 E
Munka-Ljungby 49 56 16N 12 58 E
Munkedal 49 58 28N 11 40 E
Munkfors 48 59 50N 13 30 E
Munku-Sardyk 59 51 45N 100 20 E
Münnerstadt 25 50 15N 10 11 E
Muñoz Gamero, Pen. 128 52 30 S 73 5 E
Munroe L. 109 59 13N 98 35W
Munster, France 19 48 2N 7 8 E
Munster, Ger. 24 52 59N 10 5 E
Münster 24 51 58N 7 37 E
Munster □ 15 52 20N 8 40W
Muntele Mare 46 46 30N 23 12 E
Muntok 72 2 5 S 105 10 E
Munyak 58 43 30N 59 15 E
Munyama 91 16 5 S 28 31 E
Muon Pak Beng 71 19 51N 101 4 E
Muonio 50 67 57N 23 40 E
Mupa 89 16 5 S 15 50 E
Muping 76 37 22N 121 36 E
Muqaddam, Wadi → 86 18 4N 31 30 E
Muqdisho 63 2 2N 45 25 E
Mur → 26 46 18N 16 53 E
Mur-de-Bretagne 18 48 12N 3 0W
Mura → 39 46 18N 16 53 E
Murallón, Cuerro 128 49 48 S 73 30W
Muranda 90 1 52 S 29 20 E
Murang'a 90 0 45 S 37 9 E
Murashi 55 59 30N 49 0 E
Murat 20 45 7N 2 53 E
Murau 26 47 6N 14 10 E
Muravera 40 39 25N 9 35 E
Murça 30 41 24N 7 28W
Murchison → 96 27 45 S 114 0 E
Murchison Falls = Kabarega Falls 90 2 15N 31 38 E
Murchison Ra. 96 20 0 S 134 10 E
Murchison Rapids 91 15 55 S 34 35 E
Murcia 33 38 20N 1 10W
Murcia □ 33 37 50N 1 30W
Murdo 116 43 56N 100 43W
Murdoch Pt. 98 14 37 S 144 55 E
Mure, La 21 44 55N 5 48 E
Mureş □ 46 46 45N 24 40 E
Mureş (Mureşul) → 46 46 15N 20 13 E
Muret 20 43 30N 1 20 E
Murfatlar 46 44 10N 28 26 E
Murfreesboro 115 35 50N 86 21W
Murg → 25 48 55N 8 10 E
Murgab 58 38 10N 74 2 E
Murgeni 46 46 12N 28 1 E
Murgon 97 26 15 S 151 54 E
Muriaé 125 21 8 S 42 23W
Murias de Paredes 30 42 52N 6 11W
Muriel Mine 91 17 14 S 30 40 E
Müritz see 24 53 25N 12 40 E
Murka 90 3 27 S 38 0 E
Murmansk 52 68 57N 33 10 E
Murnau 25 47 40N 11 11 E
Muro, France 21 42 34N 8 54 E
Muro, Spain 32 39 44N 3 3 E
Muro, C. de 21 41 44N 8 37 E
Muro Lucano 41 40 45N 15 30 E
Murom 55 55 35N 42 3 E
Muroran 74 42 25N 141 0 E
Muros 30 42 45N 9 5W
Muros y de Noya, Ría de 30 42 45N 9 0W
Muroto-Misaki 74 33 15N 134 10 E
Murowana Goślina 28 52 35N 17 0 E
Murphy 118 43 11N 116 33W
Murphysboro 117 37 50N 89 20W
Murrat 86 18 51N 29 33 E
Murray, Ky., U.S.A. 115 36 40N 88 20W
Murray, Utah, U.S.A. 118 40 41N 111 58W
Murray →, Austral. 97 35 20 S 139 22 E
Murray →, Can. 108 56 11N 120 45W
Murray Bridge 97 35 6 S 139 14 E
Murray Harbour 107 46 0N 62 28W
Murray, L., P.N.G. 98 7 0 S 141 35 E
Murray, L., U.S.A. 115 34 8N 81 30W
Murray Seascarp 95 30 0N 135 0W
Murraysburg 92 31 58 S 23 47 E
Murrayville 100 35 16 S 141 11 E
Murree 66 33 56N 73 28 E
Murrumbidgee → 97 34 43 S 143 12 E
Murrumburrah 99 34 32 S 148 22 E
Murrurundi 99 31 42 S 150 51 E
Mursala 72 1 41N 98 28 E
Murshid 86 21 40N 31 10 E
Murshidabad 69 24 11N 88 19 E
Murska Sobota 39 46 39N 16 12 E
Murtazapur 68 20 40N 77 25 E
Murtle L. 108 52 8N 119 38W
Murtoa 99 36 35 S 142 28 E
Murtosa 30 40 44N 8 40W
Murungu 90 4 12 S 31 10 E
Murwara 69 23 46N 80 28 E
Murwillumbah 97 28 18 S 153 27 E
Muryo 73 6 36 S 110 53 E
Mürz → 26 47 30N 15 25 E
Mürzzuschlag 26 47 36N 15 41 E
Muş 64 38 45N 41 30 E
Musa Khel Bazar 68 30 59N 69 52 E
Mûsá Qal'eh 65 32 20N 64 50 E
Musairik, Wadi → 86 19 30N 43 10 E
Musala 43 42 13N 23 37 E
Musan, Kor., N. 76 42 12N 129 12 E
Musan, Kor., N. 76 42 12N 129 12 E
Musangu 91 10 28 S 23 55 E
Musasa 90 3 25 S 31 30 E
Musay'id 65 25 0N 51 33 E
Muscat = Masqat 65 23 37N 58 36 E
Muscat & Oman = Oman ■ 63 23 0N 58 0 E
Muscatine 116 41 25N 91 5W
Musel 30 43 34N 5 42W
Musgrave Ras. 96 26 0 S 132 0 E
Mushie 88 2 56 S 16 55 E
Mushin 85 6 32N 3 21 E
Musi →, India 70 16 41N 79 40 E
Musi →, Indon. 72 2 20 S 104 56 E
Muskeg → 108 60 20N 123 20W
Muskegon 114 43 15N 86 17W
Muskegon → 114 43 25N 86 0W
Muskegon Hts. 114 43 12N 86 17W
Muskogee 117 35 50N 95 25W
Muskwa → 108 58 47N 122 48W
Musmar 86 18 13N 35 40 E
Musofu 91 13 30 S 29 0 E
Musoma 90 1 30 S 33 48 E
Musoma □ 90 1 50 S 34 30 E
Musquaro, L. 107 50 38N 61 5W
Musquodoboit Harbour 107 44 50N 63 9W
Musselburgh 14 55 57N 3 3W
Musselshell → 118 47 21N 107 58W
Mussidan 20 45 2N 0 22 E
Mussomeli 40 37 35N 13 43 E
Mussooree 68 30 27N 78 6 E
Mussuco 92 17 2 S 19 3 E
Mustang 69 29 10N 83 55 E
Musters, L. 128 45 20 S 69 25W
Muswellbrook 97 32 16 S 150 56 E
Muszyna 27 49 22N 20 55 E
Mût 86 25 28N 28 58 E
Mut 64 36 40N 33 28 E
Mutanda, Mozam. 93 21 0 S 33 34 E
Mutanda, Zambia 91 12 24 S 26 13 E
Mutaray 59 60 56N 101 0 E
Muting 73 7 23 S 140 20 E
Mutshatsha 91 10 35 S 24 20 E
Muttaburra 97 22 38 S 144 29 E
Mutuáli 91 14 55 S 37 0 E
Muvatupusha 70 9 53N 76 35 E
Muxima 88 9 33 S 13 58 E
Muy, Le 21 43 28N 6 34 E
Muya 59 56 27N 115 50 E
Muyinga 90 3 14 S 30 33 E
Muzaffarabad 69 34 25N 73 30 E
Muzaffargarh 68 30 5N 71 14 E
Muzaffarnagar 68 29 26N 77 40 E
Muzaffarpur 69 26 7N 85 23 E
Muzhi 58 65 25N 64 40 E
Muzillac 18 47 35N 2 30W
Muzon C. 108 54 40N 132 40W
Muztag 75 36 20N 87 28 E
Mvôlô 87 6 2N 29 53 E
Mwadui 90 3 26 S 33 32 E
Mwambo 91 10 30 S 40 22 E
Mwandi 91 17 30 S 24 51 E
Mwanza, Tanz. 90 2 30 S 32 58 E
Mwanza, Zaïre 90 7 55 S 26 43 E
Mwanza, Zambia 91 16 58 S 24 28 E
Mwanza □ 90 2 0 S 33 0 E
Mwaya 91 9 32 S 33 55 E
Mweelrea 15 53 37N 9 48W
Mweka 88 4 50 S 21 34 E
Mwenga 90 3 1 S 28 28 E
Mweru, L. 91 9 0 S 28 40 E
Mweza Range 91 21 0 S 30 0 E
Mwilambwe 90 8 7 S 25 0 E
Mwimbi 91 8 38 S 31 39 E
Mwinilunga 91 11 43 S 24 25 E
My Tho 71 10 29N 106 23 E
Mya, O. → 83 30 46N 4 54 E
Myall → 100 32 30 S 152 15 E
Myanaung 67 18 18N 95 22 E
Myaungmya 67 16 30N 94 40 E
Mycenae = Mikínai 45 37 43N 22 46 E
Myeik Kyunzu 71 11 30N 97 30 E
Myerstown 113 40 22N 76 18W
Myitkyina 67 25 24N 97 26 E
Myjava 27 48 41N 17 37 E
Mymensingh 69 24 45N 90 24 E
Myndus 45 37 3N 27 14 E
Mynydd ddu 13 51 45N 3 45W
Myrdal 47 60 43N 7 10 E
Mýrdalsjökull 50 63 40N 19 6W
Myrtle Beach 115 33 43N 78 50W
Myrtle Creek 118 43 0N 123 9W
Myrtle Point 118 43 0N 124 4W
Myrtleford 100 36 34 S 146 44 E
Mysen 47 59 33N 11 20 E
Myslenice 27 49 51N 19 57 E
Myślibórz 28 52 55N 14 50 E
Mysłowice 27 50 15N 19 12 E
Mysore 70 12 17N 76 41 E
Mysore □ = Karnataka 70 13 15N 77 0 E
Mystic 113 41 21N 71 58W
Mystishchi 55 55 50N 37 50 E
Myszków 28 50 45N 19 22 E
Myszyniec 28 53 23N 21 21 E
Myton 118 40 10N 110 2W
Mývatn 50 65 36N 17 0W
Mze → 26 49 46N 13 24 E
Mzimba 91 11 55 S 33 39 E
Mzimvubu → 93 31 38 S 29 33 E
Mzuzu 91 11 30 S 33 55 E

N

N' Dioum 84 16 31N 14 39W
Naab → 25 49 1N 12 2 E
Na'am 87 9 42N 28 27 E
Na'an 62 31 53N 34 52 E
Naantali 51 60 29N 22 2 E
Naas 15 53 12N 6 40W
Nababiep 92 29 36 S 17 46 E
Nabadwip 69 23 34N 88 20 E
Nabas 73 11 47N 122 6 E
Nabburg 25 49 27N 12 11 E
• Nabereznyje Celny 58 55 42N 52 19 E
Nabeul 83 36 30N 10 44 E
Nabha 68 30 26N 76 14 E
Nabire 73 3 15 S 135 26 E
Nabisar 68 25 8N 69 40 E
Nabisipi → 107 50 14N 62 13W
Nabiswera 90 1 27N 32 15 E
Nablus = Nābulus 62 32 14N 35 15 E
Naboomspruit 93 24 32 S 28 40 E
Nābulus 62 32 14N 35 15 E
Nacala-Velha 91 14 32 S 40 34 E
Nacaroa 91 14 22 S 39 56 E
Naches 118 46 48N 120 42W
Nachingwea 91 10 23 S 38 49 E
Nachingwea □ 91 10 30 S 38 30 E
Nachna 68 27 34N 71 41 E
Náchod 27 50 25N 16 8 E
Nacka 48 59 17N 18 12 E
Nackara 99 32 48 S 139 12 E
Naco 119 31 24N 109 58W
Nacogdoches 117 31 33N 94 39W
Nacozari 120 30 24N 109 39W
Nadi 86 18 40N 33 41 E
Nadiad 68 22 41N 72 56 E
Nădlac 42 46 10N 20 50 E
Nador 82 35 14N 2 58W
Nadūshan 65 32 2N 53 35 E
Nadvoitsy 52 63 52N 34 14 E
Nadvornaya 56 48 37N 24 30 E
Nadym 58 65 35N 72 42 E
Nadym → 58 66 12N 72 0 E
Nærbø 47 58 40N 5 39 E
Næstved 49 55 13N 11 44 E
Nafada 85 11 8N 11 20 E
Naft-e Shāh 64 34 0N 45 30 E
Nafūd ad Dahy 64 22 0N 45 0 E
Nafūsah, Jabal 83 32 12N 12 30 E
Nag Hammâdi 86 26 2N 32 18 E
Naga 73 13 38N 123 15 E
Naga, Kreb en 82 24 12N 6 0W
Nagagami → 106 49 40N 84 40W
Nagaland □ 67 26 0N 94 30 E
Nagano 74 36 40N 138 10 E
Nagano □ 74 36 15N 138 0 E
Nagaoka 74 37 27N 138 50 E
Nagappattinam 70 10 46N 79 51 E
Nagar Parkar 68 24 28N 70 46 E
Nagari Hills 70 13 3N 79 45 E
Nagarjuna Sagar 70 16 35N 79 17 E
Nagasaki 74 32 47N 129 50 E
Nagasaki □ 74 32 50N 129 40 E
Nagaur 68 27 15N 73 45 E
Nagbhil 70 20 34N 79 55 E
Nagercoil 70 8 12N 77 26 E
Nagina 68 29 30N 78 30 E
Nagîneh 65 34 20N 57 15 E
Nago 77 26 36N 128 0 E
Nagold 25 34 14N 57 2 E
Nagold → 25 48 52N 8 42 E
Nagoorin 98 24 17 S 151 15 E
Nagornyy 59 55 58N 124 57 E
Nagorsk 55 59 18N 50 48 E
Nagoya 74 35 10N 136 50 E
Nagpur 68 21 8N 79 10 E
Nagyatád 27 46 14N 17 22 E
Nagyecsed 27 47 53N 22 24 E
Nagykanizsa 27 46 28N 17 0 E
Nagykörös 27 47 5N 19 48 E
Nagyléta 27 47 23N 21 55 E
Naha 77 26 13N 127 42 E
Nahalal 62 32 41N 35 12 E
Nahanni Butte 108 61 2N 123 31W
Nahanni Nat. Park 108 61 15N 125 0W
Nahariyya 62 33 1N 35 5 E
Nahāvand 64 34 10N 48 22 E
Nahe → 25 49 58N 7 57 E
Nahf 62 32 56N 35 18 E
Nahîya, Wadi → 86 28 55N 31 0 E
Nahlin 108 58 55N 131 38W
Nahud 86 18 12N 41 40 E
Naicam 109 52 30N 104 30W
Nā'ifah 63 19 59N 50 46 E
Naila 25 50 19N 11 43 E
Nain 107 56 34N 61 40W
Nā'īn 65 32 54N 53 0 E
Naini Tal 69 29 30N 79 30 E
Naintré 18 46 46N 0 29 E
Naipu 46 44 12N 25 47 E
Naira 73 4 28 S 130 0 E
Nairn 14 57 35N 3 54W
Nairobi 90 1 17 S 36 48 E
Naivasha 90 0 40 S 36 30 E
Naivasha L. 90 0 48 S 36 20 E
Najac 20 44 14N 1 58 E
Najafābād 65 32 40N 51 15 E
Najd 64 26 30N 42 0 E
Nájera 32 42 26N 2 48W
Najerilla → 32 42 32N 2 48W
Najibabad 68 29 40N 78 20 E
Najin 76 42 12N 130 15 E
Nakalagba 90 2 50N 27 58 E
Nakamura 74 33 0N 133 0 E
Nakfa 87 16 40N 38 32 E
Nakhichevan A.S.S.R. □ 53 39 14N 45 30 E
Nakhl 86 29 55N 33 43 E
Nakhodka 59 42 53N 132 54 E
Nakhon Phanom 71 17 23N 104 43 E
Nakhon Ratchasima (Khorat) 71 14 59N 102 12 E
Nakhon Sawan 71 15 35N 100 10 E
Nakhon Si Thammarat 71 8 29N 100 0 E
Nakina, B.C., Can. 108 59 12N 132 52W
Nakina, Ont., Can. 106 50 10N 86 40W
Nakło nad Notecią 28 53 9N 17 38 E
Nakodar 68 31 8N 75 31 E
Nakskov 49 54 50N 11 8 E
Näkten 48 62 48N 14 38 E
Naktong → 76 35 7N 128 57 E
Nakuru 90 0 15 S 36 4 E
Nakuru □ 90 0 15 S 35 5 E
Nakuru, L. 90 0 23 S 36 5 E
Nakusp 108 50 20N 117 45W
Nal → 66 25 20N 65 30 E
Nalchik 57 43 30N 43 33 E
Nälden 48 63 21N 14 14 E
Näldsjön 48 63 25N 14 15 E
Nalerigu 85 10 35N 0 25W
Nalgonda 70 17 6N 79 15 E
Nalhati 69 24 17N 87 52 E
Nallamalai Hills 70 15 30N 78 50 E
Nalón → 30 43 32N 6 4W
Nālūt 83 31 54N 11 0 E
Nam Co 75 30 30N 90 45 E
Nam Dinh 71 20 25N 106 5 E
Nam-Phan 72 10 30N 106 0 E
Nam Phong 71 16 42N 102 52 E
Nam Tha 71 20 58N 101 30 E
Nama unde 92 17 18 S 15 50 E
Namak, Daryācheh-ye 65 34 30N 52 0 E
Namak, Kavir-e 65 34 30N 57 30 E
Namakkal 70 11 13N 78 13 E
Namaland 92 24 30 S 17 0 E
Namangan 58 41 0N 71 40 E
Namapa 91 13 43 S 39 50 E
Namaqualand 92 30 0 S 18 0 E
Namasagali 90 1 2N 33 0 E
Namatanai 98 3 40 S 152 29 E
Namber 73 1 2 S 134 49 E
Nambour 97 26 32 S 152 58 E
Nambucca Heads 99 30 37 S 153 0 E
Namche Bazar 69 27 51N 86 47 E
Namecunda 91 14 54 S 37 37 E
Nameh 72 2 34N 116 21 E
Nameponda 91 15 50 S 39 50 E
Náměšt' nad Oslavou 27 49 12N 16 10 E
Námestovo 27 49 24N 19 25 E
Nametil 91 15 40 S 39 21 E
Namew L. 109 54 14N 101 56W
Namib Desert = Namib Woestyn 92 22 30 S 15 0 E
Namib-Woestyn 92 22 30 S 15 0 E
Namibia ■ 92 22 0 S 18 9 E
Namlea 73 3 18 S 127 5 E
Namoi → 99 30 12 S 149 30 E
Namous, O. en → 82 31 0N 0 15W
Nampa 118 43 34N 116 34W
Nampula 91 15 6N 39 15 E
Namrole 73 3 46 S 126 46 E
Namse Shankou 67 30 0N 82 25 E
Namsen → 50 64 27N 11 42 E
Namsos 50 64 29N 11 30 E
Namtay 59 62 43N 129 37 E
Namtu 67 23 5N 97 28 E
Namtumbo 91 10 30 S 36 4 E
Namu 108 51 52N 127 50W
Namucha Shank'ou 69 30 0N 82 28 E
Namur 16 50 27N 4 52 E
Namur □ 16 50 17N 5 0 E
Namutoni 92 18 49 S 16 55 E
Namwala 91 15 44 S 26 30 E
Namysłów 28 51 6N 17 42 E
Nan 71 18 52N 100 42 E
Nana 46 44 17N 26 34 E
Nanaimo 108 49 10N 124 0W
Nanam 76 41 44N 129 40 E
Nanan 77 24 59N 118 21 E
Nanango 97 26 40 S 152 0 E
Nan'ao 77 23 28N 117 5 E
Nanao 74 37 0N 137 0 E
Nanbu 77 31 18N 106 3 E
Nanchang 75 28 42N 115 55 E
Nancheng 77 27 33N 116 35 E
Nanching = Nanjing 75 32 2N 118 47 E
Nanchong 75 30 43N 106 2 E
Nanchuan 77 29 9N 107 6 E
Nancy 19 48 42N 6 12 E
Nanda Devi 69 30 23N 79 59 E
Nandan 77 24 58N 107 29 E
Nander 70 19 10N 77 20 E
Nandewar Ra. 99 30 15 S 150 35 E
Nandi 101 17 42 S 177 20 E
Nandi □ 90 0 15N 35 0 E
Nandikotkur 70 15 52N 78 18 E
Nandura 68 20 52N 76 25 E
Nandurbar 68 21 20N 74 15 E
Nandyal 70 15 30N 78 30 E
Nanga-Eboko 88 4 41N 12 22 E
Nanga Parbat 69 35 10N 74 35 E
Nangade 91 11 5 S 39 36 E
Nangapinoh 72 0 20 S 111 44 E
Nangarhár □ 65 34 20N 70 0 E
Nangatayap 72 1 32 S 110 34 E
Nangeya Mts. 90 3 30N 33 30 E
Nangis 19 48 33N 3 0 E
Nanjangud 70 12 6N 76 43 E
Nanjeko 91 15 31 S 23 30 E

• *Now part of Punjab □*

• *Renamed Brezhnev*

anjiang 77 32 28N 106 51 E
anjing 75 32 2N 118 47 E
anjirinji 91 9 41S 39 5 E
ankana Sahib 68 31 27N 73 38 E
ankang 77 25 40N 114 45 E
anking = Nanjing 75 32 2N 118 47 E
annine 96 26 51S 118 18 E
anning 75 22 48N 108 20 E
anpara 69 27 52N 81 33 E
anpi 76 38 2N 116 45 E
anping 75 26 38N 118 10 E
anripe 91 13 52S 38 52 E
ansei-Shotō 74 26 0N 128 0 E
ansen Sd. 4 81 0N 91 0W
ansio 90 2 3S 33 4 E
ant 20 44 1N 3 18 E
antes 18 47 12N 1 33W
anteuil-le-Haudouin 19 49 9N 2 48 E
antiat 20 46 1N 1 11 E
anticoke 114 41 12N 76 1W
anton 108 50 21N 113 46W
antong 77 32 1N 120 52 E
antua 21 46 10N 5 35 E
antucket I. 102 41 16N 70 3W
anuque 127 17 50S 40 21W
anxiong 77 25 6N 114 15 E
anyang 75 33 11N 112 30 E
anyuan 76 39 44N 116 22 E
anyuki 90 0 2N 37 4 E
anzhang 77 31 45N 111 50 E
áo, C. de la 33 38 44N 0 14 E
aococane L. 107 52 50N 70 45W
aoetsu 74 37 12N 138 10 E
aogaon 69 24 52N 88 52 E
aoli He → 76 47 18N 134 9 E
áousa 44 40 42N 22 9 E
apa 118 38 18N 122 17W
apanee 106 44 15N 77 0W
apanoch 113 41 44N 74 22W
apier 101 39 30S 176 56 E
aples 115 26 10N 81 45W
aples = Nápoli 41 40 50N 14 17 E
apo → 126 3 20S 72 40W
apoleon, N. Dak., U.S.A. 116 46 32N 99 49W
apoleon, Ohio, U.S.A. 114 41 24N 84 7W
ápoli 41 40 50N 14 17 E
ápoli, G. di 41 40 40N 14 10 E
apopo 90 4 15N 28 0 E
appa Merrie 99 27 36S 141 7 E
aqâda 86 25 53N 32 42 E
ara, Japan 74 34 40N 135 49 E
ara, Mali 84 15 10N 7 20W
ara □ 74 34 30N 136 0 E
ara, Canal 68 24 30N 69 20 E
ara Visa 117 35 39N 103 10W
aracoorte 97 36 58S 140 45 E
aradhan 99 33 34S 146 17 E
arasapur 70 16 26N 81 40 E
arasaropet 70 16 14N 80 4 E
arathiwat 71 6 30N 101 48 E
arayanganj 69 23 40N 90 33 E
arayanpet 70 16 45N 77 30 E
arbonne 20 43 11N 3 0 E
arcea → 30 43 33N 6 44W
ardò 41 40 10N 18 0 E
arew 28 52 55N 23 31 E
arew → 28 52 26N 20 41 E
ari → 68 29 40N 68 0 E
arindra, Helodranon' i 93 14 55S 47 30 E
armada → 68 21 38N 72 36 E
arnaul 68 28 5N 76 11 E
arni 39 42 30N 12 30 E
aro, Ghana 84 10 22N 2 27W
aro, Italy 40 37 18N 13 48 E
aro Fominsk 55 55 23N 36 43 E
arodnaya, G. 52 65 5N 60 0 E
arok 90 1 55S 33 52 E
arok □ 90 1 20S 36 30 E
arón 30 43 32N 8 9W
arooma 99 36 14S 150 4 E
arowal 68 32 6N 74 52 E
arrabri 97 30 19S 149 46 E
arran → 99 28 37S 148 12 E
arrandera 97 34 42S 146 31 E
arraway → 108 55 44N 119 55W
arrogin 96 32 58S 117 14 E
arromine 97 32 12S 148 12 E
arsampet 70 17 57N 79 58 E
arsimhapur 68 22 54N 79 14 E
artkala 57 43 33N 43 51 E
arva 54 59 23N 28 12 E
arva → 54 59 27N 28 2 E
arvik 50 68 28N 17 26 E
arvskoye Vdkhr. 54 59 18N 28 14 E
arwana 68 29 39N 76 6 E
aryan-Mar 52 68 0N 53 0 E
aryilco 99 28 37S 141 53 E
arym 58 59 0N 81 30 E
arymskoye 58 49 10N 84 15 E
aryn 58 41 26N 75 58 E
asa 50 66 29N 15 23 E
asarawa 85 8 32N 7 41 E
ăsăud 46 47 19N 24 29 E
aseby 101 45 1S 170 10 E
sser, Buheirat en 86 23 0N 32 30 E
ashua, Iowa, U.S.A. 116 42 55N 92 34W
ashua, Mont., U.S.A. 118 48 10N 106 25W
ashua, N.H., U.S.A. 114 42 50N 71 25W
shville, Ark., U.S.A. 117 33 56N 93 50W
shville, Ga., U.S.A. 115 31 3N 83 15W
shville, Tenn., U.S.A. 115 36 12N 86 46W
šice 42 45 32N 18 4 E
sielsk 28 52 35N 20 50 E
sik 70 19 58N 73 50 E
sirabad 68 26 15N 74 45 E
skaupi → 107 53 47N 60 51W
so 41 38 8N 14 46 E
ss → 108 55 0N 129 40W
ssau, Bahamas 121 25 0N 77 20W
ssau, U.S.A. 113 42 30N 73 34W
ssau, Bahía 128 55 20S 68 0W
sser City = Kôm Ombo 86 24 25N 32 52 E
Nasser, L. = Naser, Buheiret en 86 23 0N 32 30 E
Nassian 84 8 28N 3 28W
Nässjö 49 57 39N 14 42 E
Nastopoka Is. 106 57 0N 77 0W
Näsum 49 56 10N 14 29 E
Näsviken 48 61 46N 16 52 E
Nat Kyizin 71 14 57N 97 59 E
Nata 92 20 12S 26 12 E
Natagaima 126 3 37N 75 6W
Natal, Brazil 127 5 47S 35 13W
Natal, Can. 108 49 43N 114 51W
Natal, Indon. 72 0 35N 99 7 E
Natal □ 93 28 30S 30 30 E
Natalinci 42 44 15N 20 49 E
Naṭanz 65 33 30N 51 55 E
Natashquan 107 50 14N 61 46W
Natashquan → 107 50 7N 61 50W
Natchez 117 31 35N 91 25W
Natchitoches 117 31 47N 93 4W
Nathalia 99 36 1S 145 13 E
Nathdwara 68 24 55N 73 50 E
Natick 113 42 16N 71 19W
Natih 65 22 25N 56 30 E
Natimuk 99 36 42S 142 0 E
Nation → 108 55 30N 123 32W
National City 119 32 39N 117 7W
Natitingou 85 10 20N 1 26 E
Natividad, I. 120 27 50N 115 10W
Natoma 116 39 14N 99 0W
Natron, L. 90 2 20S 36 0 E
Natrona 112 40 39N 79 43W
Natrûn, W. el. → 86 30 25N 30 13 E
Natuna Besar, Kepulauan 72 4 0N 108 15 E
Natuna Selatan, Kepulauan 72 2 45N 109 0 E
Natural Bridge 113 44 5N 75 30W
Naturaliste, C. 96 33 32S 115 0 E
Naturaliste C. 99 40 50S 148 15 E
Naturaliste Channel 96 25 20S 113 0 E
Naubinway 106 46 7N 85 27W
Naucelle 20 44 13N 2 20 E
Nauders 26 46 54N 10 30 E
Nauen 24 52 36N 12 52 E
Naugatuck 113 41 28N 73 4W
Naujoji Vilnia 54 54 48N 25 27 E
Naumburg 24 51 10N 11 48 E
Nauru 94 1 0S 166 0 E
Nauru Is. 94 0 32S 166 55 E
Nauta 126 4 31S 73 35W
Nautla 120 20 20N 96 50W
Nava del Rey 30 41 22N 5 6W
Navacerrada, Puerto de 30 40 47N 4 0W
Navahermosa 31 39 41N 4 28W
Navajo Res. 119 36 55N 107 30W
Navalcarnero 30 40 17N 4 5W
Navalmoral de la Mata 30 39 52N 5 33W
Navalvillar de Pela 31 39 9N 5 24W
Navan = An Uaimh 15 53 39N 6 40W
Navare 20 43 20N 1 20W
Navarino, I. 128 55 0S 67 40W
Navarra □ 32 42 40N 1 40W
Navarre, France 20 43 15N 1 20W
Navarre, U.S.A. 112 40 43N 81 31W
Navarrenx 20 43 20N 0 45W
Navas del Marqués, Las 30 40 36N 4 20W
Navasota 117 30 20N 96 5W
Navassa 121 18 30N 75 0W
Nave 38 45 35N 10 17 E
Naver → 14 58 34N 4 15W
Navia 30 43 35N 6 42W
Navia → 30 43 15N 6 50W
Navia de Suarna 30 42 58N 6 59W
Navidad 124 33 57S 71 50W
Navlya 54 52 53N 34 30 E
Navoi 58 40 9N 65 22 E
Navojoa 120 27 0N 109 30W
Navolok 52 62 33N 39 57 E
Návpaktos 45 38 23N 21 50 E
Návplion 45 37 33N 22 50 E
Navrongo 85 10 51N 1 3W
Navsari 68 20 57N 72 59 E
Nawa Kot 68 28 21N 71 24 E
Nawabganj, Bangla. 69 24 35N 88 14 E
Nawabganj, India 69 26 56N 81 14 E
Nawabganj, Bareilly 69 28 32N 79 40 E
Nawabshah 68 26 15N 68 25 E
Nawada 69 24 50N 85 33 E
Nawakot 69 27 55N 85 10 E
Nawalgarh 68 27 50N 75 15 E
Nawapara 69 20 46N 82 33 E
Nawāsīf, Harrat 64 21 20N 42 10 E
Nawi 86 18 32N 30 50 E
Náxos 45 37 8N 25 25 E
Nay 20 43 10N 0 18W
Nāy Band 65 27 20N 52 40 E
Nayakhan 59 61 56N 159 0 E
Nayarit □ 120 22 0N 105 0W
Nayé 84 14 28N 12 12W
Nazaré 31 39 36N 9 4W
Nazas 120 25 10N 104 6W
Nazas → 120 25 35N 103 25W
Naze, The 13 51 53N 1 19 E
Nazerat 62 32 42N 35 17 E
Nazir Hat 67 22 35N 91 49 E
Nazko 108 53 1N 123 37W
Nazko → 108 53 7N 123 34W
Nazret 87 8 32N 39 22 E
Nchanga 91 12 30S 27 49 E
Ncheu 91 14 50S 34 47 E
Ndala 90 4 45S 33 15 E
Ndalatando 88 9 12S 14 48 E
Ndali 85 9 50N 2 46 E
Ndareda 90 4 12S 35 30 E
Ndélé 81 8 25N 20 36 E
Ndendé 88 2 22S 11 23 E
Ndjamena 81 12 10N 14 59 E
Ndjolé 88 0 10S 10 45 E
Ndola 91 13 0S 28 34 E
Ndoto Mts. 90 2 0N 37 0 E
Nduguti 90 4 18S 34 41 E
Nea → 47 63 15N 11 0 E
Néa Epidhavros 45 37 40N 23 7 E
Néa Flippiás 44 39 12N 20 53 E
Néa Kallikrátia 44 40 21N 23 1 E
Néa Víssi 44 41 34N 26 33 E
Neagh, Lough 15 54 35N 6 25W
Neah Bay 118 48 25N 124 40W
Neamţ □ 46 47 0N 26 20 E
Neápolis, Kozan, Greece 44 40 20N 21 24 E
Neápolis, Lakonia, Greece 45 36 27N 23 8 E
Near Is. 104 53 0N 172 0 E
Neath 13 51 39N 3 49W
Nebbou 85 11 9N 1 51W
Nebine Cr. → 99 29 27S 146 56 E
Nebit Dag 58 39 30N 54 22 E
Nebolchy, U.S.S.R. 54 59 12N 32 58 E
Nebolchy, U.S.S.R. 54 59 8N 33 18 E
Nebraska □ 116 41 30N 100 0W
Nebraska City 116 40 40N 95 52W
Nébrodi, Monti 40 37 55N 14 50 E
Necedah 116 44 2N 90 7W
Nechako → 108 53 30N 122 44W
Neches → 117 29 55N 93 52W
Neckar → 25 49 31N 8 26 E
Necochea 124 38 30S 58 50W
Nedelišće 39 46 23N 16 22 E
Nédha → 45 37 25N 21 45 E
Nedroma 82 35 1N 1 45W
Nedstrand 47 59 21N 5 49 E
Needles 119 34 50N 114 35W
Needles, The 13 50 39N 1 35W
Ñeembucú □ 124 27 0S 58 0W
Neemuch (Nimach) 68 24 30N 74 56 E
Neenah 114 44 10N 88 30W
Neepawa 109 50 15N 99 30W
Nefta 83 33 53N 7 50 E
Neftah Sidi Boubekeur 82 35 1N 0 4 E
Neftegorsk 57 44 25N 39 45 E
Neftyannyye Kamni 53 40 20N 50 55 E
Negapatam = Nagappattinam 70 10 46N 79 50 E
Negaunee 114 46 30N 87 36W
Negba 62 31 40N 34 41 E
Negele 87 5 20N 39 36 E
Negeri Sembilan □ 71 2 50N 102 10 E
Negev = Hanegev 62 30 50N 35 0 E
Negoiu 46 45 35N 24 32 E
Negombo 70 7 12N 79 50 E
Negotin 42 44 16N 22 37 E
Negotino 42 41 29N 22 9 E
Negra, La 124 23 46S 70 18W
Negra, Peña 30 42 11N 6 30W
Negra Pt. 73 18 40N 120 50 E
Negreira 30 42 54N 8 45W
Negreşti 46 46 50N 27 30 E
Négrine 83 34 30N 7 30 E
Negro →, Argent. 128 41 2S 62 47W
Negro →, Brazil 126 3 0S 60 0W
Negro →, Uruguay 125 33 24S 58 22W
Negros 73 10 0N 123 0 E
Negru Vodă 46 43 47N 28 21 E
Nehbandān 65 31 35N 60 5 E
Neheim-Hüsten 24 51 27N 7 58 E
Nehoiaşu 46 45 24N 26 20 E
Nei Monggol Zizhiqu □ 76 42 0N 112 0 E
Neidpath 109 50 12N 107 20W
Neihart 118 47 0N 110 44W
Neijiang 75 29 35N 104 55 E
Neilton 118 17 24N 123 52W
Neira de Jusá 30 42 53N 7 14W
Neisse → 24 52 4N 14 46 E
Neiva 126 2 56N 75 18W
Neixiang 77 33 10N 111 52 E
Nejanilini L. 109 59 33N 97 48W
Nejo 87 9 30N 35 28 E
Nekemte 87 9 4N 36 30 E
Nêkheb 86 25 10N 32 48 E
Neksø 49 55 4N 15 8 E
Nelas 30 40 32N 7 52W
Nelaug 47 58 39N 8 40 E
Nelia 98 20 39S 142 12 E
Nelidovo 54 56 13N 32 49 E
Neligh 116 42 11N 98 2W
Nelkan 59 57 40N 136 4 E
Nellikuppam 70 11 46N 79 43 E
Nellore 70 14 27N 79 59 E
Nelma 59 47 39N 139 0 E
Nelson, Austral. 100 38 3S 141 2 E
Nelson, Can. 108 49 30N 117 20W
Nelson, N.Z. 101 41 18S 173 16 E
Nelson, U.K. 12 53 50N 2 14W
Nelson, Ariz., U.S.A. 119 35 35N 113 16W
Nelson, Nev., U.S.A. 119 35 46N 114 48W
Nelson □ 101 42 11S 172 15 E
Nelson → 109 54 33N 98 2W
Nelson, C., Austral. 99 38 26S 141 32 E
Nelson, C., P.N.G. 98 9 0S 149 20 E
Nelson, Estrecho 128 51 30S 75 0W
Nelson Forks 108 59 30N 124 0W
Nelson House 109 55 47N 98 51W
Nelson L. 109 55 48N 100 7W
Nelspruit 93 25 29S 30 59 E
Néma 84 16 40N 7 15W
Neman (Nemunas) → 54 55 25N 21 10 E
Neméa 45 37 49N 22 40 E
Nemeiben L. 109 55 20N 105 20W
Nemira 46 46 17N 26 19 E
Nemours 19 48 16N 2 40 E
Nemunas = Neman → 54 55 25N 21 10 E
Nemuro 74 43 20N 145 35 E
Nemuro-Kaikyō 74 43 30N 145 30 E
Nemuy 59 55 40N 136 9 E
Nen Jiang → 76 45 28N 124 30 E
Nenagh 15 52 52N 8 11W
Nenana 104 64 30N 149 20W
Nene → 12 52 38N 0 13 E
Nenjiang 75 49 10N 125 10 E
Neno 91 15 25S 34 40 E
Nenusa, Kepulauan 73 4 45N 127 1 E
Neodesha 117 37 30N 95 37W
Néon Petrítsi 44 41 16N 23 15 E
Neosho 117 36 56N 94 28W
Neosho → 117 35 59N 95 10W
Nepal ■ 69 28 0N 84 30 E
Nepalganj 69 28 5N 81 40 E
Nephi 118 39 43N 111 52W
Nephin 15 54 1N 9 21W
Nepomuk 26 49 29N 13 35 E
Neptune City 113 40 13N 74 4W
Néra → 42 44 48N 21 25 E
Nérac 20 44 8N 0 21 E
Nerchinsk 59 52 0N 116 39 E
Nerchinskiy Zavod 59 51 20N 119 40 E
Nereju 46 45 43N 26 43 E
Nerekhta 55 57 26N 40 38 E
Néret L. 107 54 45N 70 44W
Neretva → 42 43 1N 17 27 E
Neretvanski Kanal 42 43 7N 17 10 E
Neringa 54 55 30N 21 5 E
Nerja 31 36 43N 3 55W
Nerl → 55 56 11N 40 34 E
Nerokoúrou 45 35 29N 24 3 E
Nerpio 33 38 11N 2 16W
Nerva 31 37 42N 6 30W
Nes 50 65 53N 17 24W
Nes Ziyyona 62 31 56N 34 48W
Nesbyen 47 60 34N 9 35 E
Nesebŭr 43 42 41N 27 46 E
Nesflaten 47 59 38N 6 48 E
Neskaupstaður 50 65 9N 13 42W
Nesland 47 59 31N 7 59 E
Neslandsvatn 47 58 57N 9 10 E
Nesle 19 49 45N 2 53 E
Nesodden 47 59 48N 10 40 E
Nesque → 21 43 59N 4 59 E
Ness, Loch 14 57 15N 4 30W
Nestórion Óros 44 40 24N 21 5 E
Néstos → 44 41 20N 24 35 E
Nesttun 47 60 19N 5 21 E
Nesvizh 54 53 14N 26 38 E
Netanya 62 32 20N 34 51 E
Nète → 16 51 7N 4 14 E
Nether Stowey 13 51 0N 3 10W
Netherbury 13 50 46N 2 45W
Netherdale 97 21 10S 148 33 E
Netherlands ■ 16 52 0N 5 30 E
Netherlands Antilles □ 121 12 30N 68 0W
Netherlands Guiana = Surinam ■ 127 4 0N 56 0W
Neto → 41 39 13N 17 8 E
Netrakona 69 24 53N 90 47 E
Nettancourt 19 48 51N 4 57 E
Nettilling L. 105 66 30N 71 0W
Nettuno 40 41 29N 12 40 E
Netzahualcoyotl, Presa 120 17 10N 93 30W
Neu-Isenburg 25 50 3N 8 42 E
Neu-Ulm 25 48 23N 10 2 E
Neubrandenburg 24 53 33N 13 17 E
Neubrandenburg □ 24 53 30N 13 20 E
Neubukow 24 54 1N 11 40 E
Neuburg 25 48 43N 11 11 E
Neuchâtel 25 47 0N 6 55 E
Neuchâtel □ 25 47 0N 6 55 E
Neuchâtel, Lac de 25 46 53N 6 50 E
Neudau 26 47 11N 16 6 E
Neuenhaus 24 52 30N 6 55 E
Neuf-Brisach 19 48 0N 7 30 E
Neufahrn 25 48 44N 12 11 E
Neufchâteau, Belg. 16 49 50N 5 25 E
Neufchâteau, France 19 48 21N 5 40 E
Neufchâtel 19 49 43N 1 30 E
Neufchâtel-sur-Aisne 19 49 26N 4 0 E
Neuhaus 24 53 16N 10 54 E
Neuillé-Pont-Pierre 18 47 33N 0 33 E
Neuilly-St-Front 19 49 10N 3 15 E
Neukalen 24 53 49N 12 48 E
Neumarkt 25 49 16N 11 28 E
Neumarkt-Sankt Veit 25 48 22N 12 30 E
Neumünster 24 54 4N 9 58 E
Neung-sur-Beuvron 19 47 30N 1 50 E
Neunkirchen, Austria 26 47 43N 16 4 E
Neunkirchen, Ger. 25 49 23N 7 12 E
Neuquén 128 38 55S 68 0 E
Neuquén □ 124 38 0S 69 50W
Neuruppin 24 52 56N 12 48 E
Neuse → 115 35 5N 76 30W
Neusiedl 27 47 57N 16 50 E
Neusiedler See 27 47 50N 16 47 E
Neuss 24 51 12N 6 39 E
Neussargues-Moissac 20 45 9N 3 1 E
Neustadt, Baden-W., Ger. 25 47 54N 8 13 E
Neustadt, Bayern, Ger. 25 50 23N 11 0 E
Neustadt, Bayern, Ger. 25 49 42N 12 10 E
Neustadt, Bayern, Ger. 25 48 48N 11 47 E
Neustadt, Bayern, Ger. 25 49 34N 10 37 E
Neustadt, Gera, Ger. 24 50 45N 11 43 E
Neustadt, Hessen, Ger. 24 50 51N 9 9 E
Neustadt, Niedersachsen, Ger. 24 52 30N 9 30 E
Neustadt, Potsdam, Ger. 24 52 50N 12 27 E
Neustadt, Rhld-Pfz., Ger. 25 49 21N 8 10 E
Neustadt, Schleswig-Holstein, Ger. 24 54 6N 10 49 E
Neustrelitz 24 53 22N 13 4 E
Neuvic 20 45 23N 2 16 E
Neuville, Rhône, France 21 45 52N 4 51 E
Neuville, Vienne, France 18 46 41N 0 15 E
Neuville-aux-Bois 19 48 4N 2 3 E
Neuvy-le-Roi 18 47 36N 0 36 E
Neuvy-St-Sépulchure 20 46 35N 1 48 E
Neuvy-sur-Barangeon 19 47 20N 2 15 E
Neuwerk 24 53 55N 8 30 E
Neuwied 24 50 26N 7 29 E
Neva → 52 59 50N 30 30 E
Nevada 117 37 51N 94 22W
Nevada □ 118 39 20N 117 0W
Nevada City 118 39 20N 121 0W
Nevada de Sta. Marta, Sa. 126 10 55N 73 50W
Nevada, Sierra, Spain 33 37 3N 3 15W
Nevada, Sierra, U.S.A. 118 39 0N 120 30W
Nevado, Cerro 124 35 30S 68 32W
Nevanka 59 56 31N 98 55 E
Nevasa 70 19 34N 75 0 E
Nevel 54 56 0N 29 55 E
Nevers 19 47 0N 3 9 E
Nevertire 99 31 50S 147 44 E
Nevesinje 42 43 14N 18 6 E
Neville 109 49 58N 107 39W
Nevinnomyssk 57 44 40N 42 0 E
Nevis 121 17 0N 62 30W

Nevlunghavn **47** 55 58N 9 52 E
Nevrokop = Gotse Delchev **43** 41 33N 23 46 E
Nevşehir **64** 38 33N 34 40 E
Nevyansk **52** 57 30N 60 13 E
New Albany, Ind., U.S.A. **114** 38 20N 85 50W
New Albany, Miss., U.S.A. **117** 34 30N 89 0W
New Albany, Pa., U.S.A. **113** 41 35N 76 28W
New Amsterdam **126** 6 15N 57 36W
New Bedford **114** 41 40N 70 52W
New Bern **115** 35 8N 77 3W
New Bethlehem **112** 41 0N 79 22W
New Bloomfield **112** 40 24N 77 12W
New Boston **117** 33 27N 94 21W
New Braunfels **117** 29 43N 98 9W
New Brighton, N.Z. **101** 43 29 S 172 43 E
New Brighton, U.S.A. **112** 40 42N 80 19W
New Britain, P.N.G. **94** 5 50 S 150 20 E
New Britain, U.S.A. **114** 41 41N 72 47W
New Brunswick **114** 40 30N 74 28W
New Brunswick □ **107** 46 50N 66 30W
New Bussa **85** 9 53N 4 31 E
New Byrd **5** 80 0 S 120 0W
New Caledonia = Nouvelle-Calédonie **94** 21 0 S 165 0 E
New Castile = Castilla La Neuva **31** 39 45N 3 20W
New Castle, Ind., U.S.A. **114** 39 55N 85 23W
New Castle, Pa., U.S.A. **114** 41 0N 80 20W
New City **113** 41 8N 74 0W
New Cristóbal **120** 9 22N 79 40W
New Cumberland **112** 40 30N 80 36W
New Delhi **68** 28 37N 77 13 E
New Denver **108** 50 0N 117 25W
New England **116** 46 36N 102 47W
New England Ra. **97** 30 20 S 151 45 E
New Forest **13** 50 53N 1 40W
New Glasgow **107** 45 35N 62 36W
New Guinea **94** 4 0 S 136 0 E
New Hamburg **112** 43 23N 80 42W
New Hampshire □ **114** 43 40N 71 40W
New Hampton **116** 43 2N 92 20W
New Hanover, P.N.G. **98** 2 30 S 150 10 E
New Hanover, S. Afr. **93** 29 22 S 30 31 E
New Haven, Conn., U.S.A. **114** 41 20N 72 54W
New Haven, Mich., U.S.A. **112** 42 44N 82 46W
New Hazelton **108** 55 20N 127 30W
* New Hebrides **94** 15 0 S 168 0 E
New Iberia **117** 30 2N 91 54W
New Ireland **94** 3 20 S 151 50 E
New Jersey □ **114** 40 30N 74 10W
New Kensington **114** 40 36N 79 43W
New Lexington **114** 39 40N 82 15W
New Liskeard **106** 47 31N 79 41W
New London, Conn., U.S.A. **114** 41 23N 72 8W
New London, Minn., U.S.A. **116** 45 17N 94 55W
New London, Ohio, U.S.A. **112** 41 4N 82 25W
New London, Wis., U.S.A. **116** 44 23N 88 43W
New Madrid **117** 36 40N 89 30W
New Meadows **118** 45 0N 116 32W
New Mexico □ **110** 34 30N 106 0W
New Milford, Conn., U.S.A. **113** 41 35N 73 25W
New Milford, Pa., U.S.A. **113** 41 50N 75 45W
New Norfolk **97** 42 46 S 147 2 E
New Orleans **117** 30 0N 90 5W
New Philadelphia **114** 40 29N 81 25W
New Plymouth, N.Z. **101** 39 4 S 174 5 E
New Plymouth, U.S.A. **118** 43 58N 116 49W
New Providence **121** 25 25N 78 35W
New Radnor **13** 52 15N 3 10W
New Richmond **116** 45 6N 92 34W
New Roads **117** 30 43N 91 30W
New Rochelle **113** 40 55N 73 46W
New Rockford **116** 47 44N 99 7W
New Ross **15** 52 24N 6 58W
New Salem **116** 46 51N 101 25W
New Siberian Is. = Novosibirskiye Os. **59** 75 0N 142 0 E
New Smyrna Beach **115** 29 0N 80 50W
New South Wales □ **97** 33 0 S 146 0 E
New Town **116** 47 59N 102 30W
New Ulm **116** 44 15N 94 30W
New Waterford **107** 46 13N 60 4W
New Westminster **108** 49 13N 122 55W
New York □ **114** 42 40N 76 0W
New York City **114** 40 45N 74 0W
New Zealand ■ **94** 40 0 S 176 0 E
Newala **91** 10 58 S 39 18 E
Newala □ **91** 10 46 S 39 20 E
Newark, Del., U.S.A. **114** 39 42N 75 45W
Newark, N.J., U.S.A. **114** 40 41N 74 12W
Newark, N.Y., U.S.A. **114** 43 2N 77 10W
Newark, Ohio, U.S.A. **114** 40 5N 82 24W
Newark-on-Trent **12** 53 6N 0 48W
Newaygo **114** 43 25N 85 48W
Newberg **118** 45 22N 123 0W
Newberry, Mich., U.S.A. **114** 46 20N 85 32W
Newberry, S.C., U.S.A. **115** 34 17N 81 37W
Newbrook **108** 54 24N 112 57W
Newburgh **114** 41 30N 74 1W
Newbury, U.K. **13** 51 24N 1 19W
Newbury, U.S.A. **113** 44 7N 72 6W
Newburyport **114** 42 48N 70 50W
Newcastle, Austral. **97** 33 0 S 151 46 E
Newcastle, Can. **107** 47 1N 65 38W
Newcastle, S. Afr. **93** 27 45 S 29 58 E
Newcastle, U.K. **15** 54 13N 5 54W
Newcastle, U.S.A. **116** 43 50N 104 12W
Newcastle Emlyn **13** 52 2N 4 29W
Newcastle Ra. **97** 15 45 S 130 15 E
Newcastle-under-Lyme **12** 53 2N 2 15W
Newcastle-upon-Tyne **12** 54 59N 1 37W
Newcastle Waters **96** 17 30 S 133 28 E
Newdegate **96** 33 6 S 119 0 E
Newe Etan **62** 32 30N 35 32 E
Newe Sha'anan **62** 32 47N 34 59 E
Newe Zohar **62** 31 9N 35 21 E
Newell **116** 44 48N 103 25W
Newenham, C. **104** 58 40N 162 15W
Newfoundland **107** 48 30N 56 0W
Newfoundland □ **107** 53 0N 58 0W
Newhalem **108** 48 41N 121 16W
Newham **13** 51 31N 0 2 E
Newhaven **13** 50 47N 0 4 E
Newkirk **117** 36 52N 97 3W
Newman, Mt. **96** 23 20 S 119 34 E
Newmarket, Can. **112** 44 3N 79 28W
Newmarket, Ireland **15** 52 13N 9 0W
Newmarket, U.K. **13** 52 15N 0 23 E
Newmarket, U.S.A. **113** 43 4N 70 57W
Newnan **115** 33 22N 84 48W
Newnes **99** 33 9 S 150 16 E
Newport, Gwent, U.K. **13** 51 35N 3 0W
Newport, I. of W., U.K. **13** 50 42N 1 18W
Newport, Salop, U.K. **13** 52 47N 2 22W
Newport, Ark., U.S.A. **117** 35 38N 91 15W
Newport, Ky., U.S.A. **114** 39 5N 84 23W
Newport, N.H., U.S.A. **114** 43 23N 72 8W
Newport, Oreg., U.S.A. **118** 44 41N 124 2W
Newport, Pa., U.S.A. **112** 40 28N 77 8W
Newport, R.I., U.S.A. **114** 41 13N 71 19W
Newport, Tenn., U.S.A. **115** 35 59N 83 12W
Newport, Vt., U.S.A. **114** 44 57N 72 17W
Newport, Wash., U.S.A. **118** 48 11N 117 2W
Newport Beach **119** 33 40N 117 58W
Newport News **114** 37 2N 76 30W
Newquay **13** 50 24N 5 6W
Newry **15** 54 10N 6 20W
Newry & Mourne □ **15** 54 10N 6 15W
Newton, Iowa, U.S.A. **116** 41 40N 93 3W
Newton, Mass., U.S.A. **114** 42 21N 71 10W
Newton, Miss., U.S.A. **117** 32 19N 89 10W
Newton, N.C., U.S.A. **115** 35 42N 81 10W
Newton, N.J., U.S.A. **114** 41 3N 74 46W
Newton, Texas, U.S.A. **117** 30 54N 93 42W
Newton Abbot **13** 50 32N 3 37W
Newton Boyd **99** 29 45 S 152 16 E
Newton Stewart **14** 54 57N 4 30W
Newtonmore **14** 57 4N 4 7W
Newtown **13** 52 31N 3 19W
Newtownabbey **15** 54 40N 5 55W
Newtownabbey □ **15** 54 45N 6 0W
Newtownards **15** 54 37N 5 40W
Newville **112** 40 10N 77 24W
Nexon **20** 45 41N 1 11 E
Neya **55** 58 21N 43 49 E
Neyrīz **65** 29 15N 54 19 E
Neyshābūr **65** 36 10N 58 50 E
Neyyattinkara **70** 8 26N 77 5 E
Nezhin **54** 51 5N 31 55 E
Nezperce **118** 46 13N 116 15W
Ngabang **72** 0 23N 109 55 E
Ngabordamlu, Tanjung **73** 6 56 S 134 11 E
Ngambé **85** 5 48N 11 29 E
Ngami Depression **92** 20 30 S 22 46 E
Ngamo **91** 19 3 S 27 32 E
Nganglong Kangri **67** 33 0N 81 0 E
Nganjuk **73** 7 32 S 111 55 E
Ngaoundéré **88** 7 15N 13 35 E
Ngapara **101** 44 57 S 170 46 E
Ngara **90** 2 29 S 30 40 E
Ngara □ **90** 2 29 S 30 40 E
Ngau **101** 18 2 S 179 18 E
Ngawi **73** 7 24 S 111 26 E
Ngha Lo **71** 21 33N 104 28 E
Ngiva **92** 16 48 S 15 50 E
Ngoma **91** 13 8 S 33 45 E
Ngomahura **91** 20 26 S 30 43 E
Ngomba **91** 8 20 S 32 53 E
Ngop **87** 6 17N 30 9 E
Ngoring Hu **75** 34 55N 97 5 E
Ngorkou **84** 15 40N 3 41W
Ngorongoro **90** 3 11 S 35 32 E
Ngozi **90** 2 54 S 29 50 E
Ngudu **90** 2 58 S 33 25 E
Nguigmi **81** 14 20N 13 20 E
Ngunga **90** 3 37 S 33 37 E
Ngunza **88** 11 10 S 13 48 E
Nguru **85** 12 56N 10 29 E
Nguru Mts. **90** 6 0 S 37 30 E
Nha Trang **71** 12 16N 109 10 E
Nhacoongo **93** 24 18 S 35 14 E
Nhangutazi, L. **93** 24 0 S 34 30 E
Nhill **99** 36 18 S 141 40 E
Nia-nia **90** 1 30N 27 40 E
Niafounké **84** 16 0N 4 5W
Niagara **114** 45 45N 88 0W
Niagara Falls, Can. **106** 43 7N 79 5W
Niagara Falls, U.S.A. **114** 43 5N 79 0W
Niagara-on-the-Lake **112** 43 15N 79 4W
Niah **72** 3 58N 113 46 E
Nialia, L. **100** 33 20 S 141 42 E
Niamey **85** 13 27N 2 6 E
Nianforando **84** 9 37N 10 36W
Nianfors **48** 61 36N 16 46 E
Niangara **90** 3 42N 27 50 E
Nianzishan **76** 47 31N 122 53 E
Nias **72** 1 0N 97 30 E
Niassa □ **91** 13 30 S 36 0 E
Nibbiano **38** 44 54N 9 20 E
Nibe **49** 56 59N 9 38 E
Nibong Tebal **71** 5 10N 100 29 E
Nicaragua ■ **121** 11 40N 85 30W
Nicaragua, Lago de **121** 12 0N 85 30W
Nicastro **41** 39 0N 16 18 E
Nice **21** 43 42N 7 14 E
Niceville **115** 30 30N 86 30W
Nichinan **74** 31 38N 131 23 E
Nicholás, Canal **121** 23 30N 80 5W
Nicholasville **114** 37 54N 84 31W
Nichols **113** 42 1N 76 22W
Nicholson **113** 41 37N 75 47W
Nicobar Is. **60** 9 0N 93 0 E
Nicola **108** 50 12N 120 40W
Nicolet **106** 46 17N 72 35W
Nicolls Town **121** 25 8N 78 0W
Nicopolis **45** 39 2N 20 37 E
Nicosia, Cyprus **64** 35 10N 33 25 E
Nicosia, Italy **41** 37 45N 14 22 E
Nicótera **41** 38 33N 15 57 E
Nicoya, G. de **121** 10 0N 85 0W
Nicoya, Pen. de **121** 9 45N 85 40W
Nidd → **12** 54 1N 1 32W
Nidda **24** 50 24N 9 2 E
Nidda → **25** 50 6N 8 34 E
Nidzica **28** 53 25N 20 28 E
Niebüll **24** 54 47N 8 49 E
Nied → **19** 49 23N 6 40 E
Niederaula **24** 50 48N 9 37 E
Niederbronn **19** 48 57N 7 39 E
Niedere Tauern **26** 47 20N 14 0 E
Niedermarsberg **24** 51 28N 8 52 E
Niederösterreich □ **26** 48 25N 15 40 E
Niedersachsen □ **24** 52 45N 9 0 E
Niellé **84** 10 5N 5 38W
Niemba **90** 5 58 S 28 24 E
Niemcza **28** 50 42N 16 47 E
Niemodlin **28** 50 38N 17 38 E
Niemur **100** 35 17 S 144 9 E
Nienburg **24** 52 38N 9 15 E
Niepołomice **27** 50 3N 20 13 E
Niers → **24** 51 45N 5 58 E
Niesky **24** 51 18N 14 48 E
Nieszawa **28** 52 52N 18 50 E
Nieuw Amsterdam **127** 5 53N 55 5W
Nieuw Nickerie **127** 6 0N 56 59W
Nieuwpoort **16** 51 8N 2 45 E
Nieves **30** 42 7N 8 26W
Nièvre □ **19** 47 10N 3 40 E
Niğde **64** 38 0N 34 40 E
Nigel **93** 26 27 S 28 25 E
Niger ■ **85** 13 30N 10 0 E
Niger □ **85** 10 0N 5 0 E
Niger → **85** 5 33N 6 33 E
Nigeria ■ **85** 8 30N 8 0 E
Nightcaps **101** 45 57 S 168 2 E
Nigríta **44** 40 56N 23 29 E
Nihtaur **69** 29 20N 78 23 E
Nii-Jima **74** 34 20N 139 15 E
Niigata **74** 37 58N 139 0 E
Niigata □ **74** 37 15N 138 45 E
Niihama **74** 33 55N 133 16 E
Niihau **110** 21 55N 160 10W
Níjar **33** 36 53N 2 15W
Nijkerk **16** 52 13N 5 30 E
Nijmegen **16** 51 50N 5 52 E
Nijverdal **16** 52 22N 6 28 E
Nike **85** 6 26N 7 29 E
Nikel **50** 69 24N 30 12 E
Nikiniki **73** 9 49 S 124 30 E
Nikítas **44** 40 13N 23 34 E
Nikki **85** 9 58N 3 12 E
Nikkō **74** 36 45N 139 35 E
Nikolayev **56** 46 58N 32 0 E
Nikolayevsk **55** 50 0N 45 35 E
Nikolayevsk-na-Amur **59** 53 8N 140 44 E
Nikolsk **55** 59 30N 45 28 E
Nikolskoye **59** 55 12N 166 0 E
Nikopol, Bulg. **43** 43 43N 24 54 E
Nikopol, U.S.S.R. **56** 47 35N 34 25 E
Niksar **56** 40 31N 37 2 E
Nīkshahr **65** 26 15N 60 10 E
Nikšić **42** 42 50N 18 57 E
Nîl el Abyad → **87** 15 38N 32 31 E
Nîl el Azraq → **87** 15 38N 32 31 E
Nîl, Nahr en → **86** 30 10N 31 6 E
Niland **119** 33 16N 115 30W
Nile = Nîl, Nahr en → **86** 30 10N 31 6 E
Nile □ **90** 2 0N 31 30 E
Nile Delta **86** 31 40N 31 0 E
Niles **114** 41 8N 80 40W
Nilgiri Hills **70** 11 30N 76 30 E
Nimach = Neemuch **68** 24 30N 74 56 E
Nimbahera **68** 24 37N 74 45 E
Nîmes **21** 43 50N 4 23 E
Nimfaíon, Ákra- **44** 40 5N 24 20 E
Nimingarra **96** 20 31 S 119 55 E
Nimmitabel **99** 36 29 S 149 15 E
Nimneryskiy **59** 57 50N 125 10 E
Nimrod Glacier **5** 82 27 S 161 0 E
Nimule **87** 3 32N 32 3 E
Nin **39** 44 16N 15 12 E
Nindigully **99** 28 21 S 148 50 E
Ninemile **108** 56 0N 130 7W
Ninety Mile Beach, The **97** 38 15 S 147 24 E
Nineveh = Nīnawá **64** 36 25N 43 10 E
Ning'an **76** 44 22N 129 20 E
Ningbo **75** 29 51N 121 28 E
Ningde **75** 26 38N 119 23 E
Ningdu **77** 26 25N 115 59 E
Ningjin **76** 37 35N 114 57 E
Ningming **77** 22 8N 107 4 E
Ningpo = Ningbo **75** 29 51N 121 28 E
Ningqiang **77** 32 47N 106 15 E
Ningshan **77** 33 21N 108 21 E
Ningsia Hui A.R. = Ningxia Huizu Zizhiqu □ **76** 38 0N 106 0 E
Ningwu **76** 39 0N 112 18 E
Ningxia Huizu Zizhiqu □ **76** 38 0N 106 0 E
Ningxiang **77** 28 15N 112 30 E
Ningyuan **77** 25 37N 111 57 E
Ninh Binh **71** 20 15N 105 55 E
Ninove **16** 50 51N 4 2 E
Nioaque **125** 21 5 S 55 50W
Niobrara **116** 42 48N 97 59W
Niobrara → **116** 42 45N 98 0W
Niono **84** 14 15N 6 0W
Nioro du Rip **84** 13 40N 15 50W
Nioro du Sahel **84** 15 15N 9 30W
Niort **20** 46 19N 0 29W
Nipani **70** 16 20N 74 25 E
Nipawin **109** 53 20N 104 0W
Nipawin Prov. Park **109** 54 0N 104 37W
Nipigon **106** 49 0N 88 17W
Nipigon, L. **106** 49 50N 88 30W
Nipin → **109** 55 46N 108 35W
Nipishish L. **107** 54 12N 60 45W
Nipissing L. **106** 46 20N 80 0W
Nipomo **119** 35 4N 120 29W
Niquelândia **127** 14 33 S 48 23W
Nira → **70** 17 58N 75 8 E
Nirmal **70** 19 3N 78 20 E
Nirmali **69** 26 20N 86 35 E
Niš **42** 43 19N 21 58 E
Nisa **31** 39 30N 7 41W
Nişāb **63** 14 25N 46 29 E
Nišava → **42** 43 20N 21 46 E
Niscemi **41** 37 8N 14 21 E
Nishinomiya **74** 34 45N 135 20 E
Nísíros **45** 36 35N 27 12 E
Niskibi → **106** 56 29N 88 9W
Nisko **28** 50 35N 22 7 E
Nisporeny **46** 47 4N 28 10 E
Nissafors **49** 57 25N 13 37 E
Nissan → **49** 56 40N 12 51 E
Nissedal **47** 59 10N 8 30 E
Nisser **47** 59 7N 8 28 E
Nissum Fjord **49** 56 20N 8 11 E
Nisutlin → **108** 60 14N 132 34W
Niţā' **64** 27 15N 48 35 E
Nitchequon **107** 53 10N 70 58W
Niterói **125** 22 52 S 43 0W
Nith → **14** 55 20N 3 5W
Nitra **27** 48 19N 18 4 E
Nitra → **27** 47 46N 18 10 E
Nittedal **47** 60 1N 10 57 E
Nittendau **25** 49 12N 12 16 E
Niuafo'ou **101** 15 30 S 175 58W
Niue I. (Savage I.) **95** 19 2 S 169 54W
Niut **72** 0 55N 110 6 E
Nivelles **16** 50 35N 4 20 E
Nivernais **19** 47 0N 3 40 E
Nixon, Nev., U.S.A. **118** 39 54N 119 22W
Nixon, Tex., U.S.A. **117** 29 17N 97 45W
Nizam Sagar **70** 18 10N 77 58 E
Nizamabad **70** 18 45N 78 7 E
Nizamghat **67** 28 20N 95 45 E
Nizhne Kolymsk **59** 68 34N 160 55 E
Nizhne-Vartovskoye **58** 60 56N 76 38 E
Nizhneangarsk **59** 55 47N 109 30 E
Nizhnegorskiy **56** 45 27N 34 38 E
Nizhneudinsk **59** 54 54N 99 3 E
Nizhneyansk **59** 71 26N 136 4 E
Nizhniy Lomov **55** 53 34N 43 38 E
Nizhniy Novgorod = Gorkiy **55** 56 20N 44 0 E
Nizhniy Tagil **52** 57 55N 59 57 E
Nizhnyaya Tunguska → **59** 64 20N 93 0 E
Nizip **64** 37 5N 37 50 E
Nizké Tatry **27** 48 55N 20 0 E
Nizza Monferrato **38** 44 46N 8 22 E
Njakwa **91** 11 1 S 33 56 E
Njanji **91** 14 25 S 31 46 E
Njinjo **91** 8 48 S 38 54 E
Njombe **91** 9 20 S 34 50 E
Njombe □ **91** 9 20 S 34 49 E
Njombe → **90** 6 56 S 35 6 E
Nkambe **85** 6 35N 10 40 E
Nkana **91** 12 50 S 28 8
Nkawkaw **85** 6 36N 0 49W
Nkhota Kota **91** 12 56 S 34 15
Nkongsamba **88** 4 55N 9 55
Nkwanta **84** 6 10N 2 10W
Noatak **104** 67 32N 162 59W
Nobel **112** 45 25N 80 6W
Nobeoka **74** 32 36N 131 41 E
Noblejas **32** 39 58N 3 26W
Noblesville **114** 40 1N 85 59W
Noce → **38** 46 9N 11 4 E
Nocera Inferiore **41** 40 45N 14 37
Nocera Terinese **41** 39 2N 16 9
Nocera Umbra **39** 43 8N 12 47
Noci **41** 40 47N 17 7
Nockatunga **99** 27 42 S 142 42 E
Nocona **117** 33 48N 97 45W
Nocrich **46** 45 55N 24 26 E
Noel **117** 36 36N 94 29W
Nogales, Mexico **120** 31 20N 110 56W
Nogales, U.S.A. **119** 31 33N 110 56W
Nogat → **28** 54 17N 19 17 E
Nōgata **74** 33 48N 130 44 E
Nogent-en-Bassigny **19** 48 0N 5 20 E
Nogent-le-Rotrou **18** 48 20N 0 50 E
Nogent-sur-Seine **19** 48 30N 3 30 E
Noginsk, Moskva, U.S.S.R. **55** 55 50N 38 25 E
Noginsk, Sib., U.S.S.R. **59** 64 30N 90 50 E
Nogoa → **97** 23 40 S 147 55 E
Nogoyá **124** 32 24 S 59 48W
Nógrád □ **27** 48 0N 19 30 E
Nogueira de Ramuin **30** 42 21N 7 43W
Noguera Pallaresa → **32** 42 15N 1 0 E
Noguera Ribagorzana → **32** 41 40N 0 43 E
Nohar **68** 29 11N 74 49 E
Noi → **71** 14 50N 100 15 E
Noire, Mt. **18** 48 11N 3 40W
Noirétable **20** 45 48N 3 46
Noirmoutier **18** 47 0N 2 15W
Noirmoutier, Î. de **18** 46 58N 2 10W
Nojane **92** 23 15 S 20 14
Nok Kundi **66** 28 50N 62 45
Nokaneng **92** 19 40 S 22 17
Nokhtuysk **59** 60 0N 117 45
Nokomis **109** 51 35N 105 0W
Nokomis L. **109** 57 0N 103 0W
Nol **49** 57 56N 12 5
Nola, C. Afr. Rep. **88** 3 35N 16 4
Nola, Italy **41** 40 54N 14 29
Nolay **19** 46 58N 4 35
Noli, C. di **38** 44 12N 8 26
Nolinsk **55** 57 28N 49 57
Noma Omuramba → **92** 18 52 S 20 53
Noman L. **109** 62 15N 108 55W
Nome **104** 64 30N 165 24W
Nonacho L. **109** 61 42N 109 40W
Nonancourt **18** 48 47N 1 11
Nonant-le-Pin **18** 48 42N 0 12
Nonda **98** 20 40 S 142 28
Nong Khae **71** 14 29N 100 53
Nong Khai **71** 17 50N 102 46
Nong'an **76** 44 25N 125 5
Nonoava **120** 27 28N 106 44W
Nontron **20** 45 31N 0 40
Noonan **116** 48 51N 102 59W
Noondoo **99** 28 35 S 148 30
Noord Brabant □ **16** 51 40N 5 0
Noord Holland □ **16** 52 30N 4 45
Noordbeveland **16** 51 35N 3 50
Noordoostpolder **16** 52 45N 5 45
Noordwijk aan Zee **16** 52 14N 4 26
Nootka **108** 49 38N 126 38W
Nootka I. **108** 49 32N 126 42W

* *Renamed Vanuatu* ■

Name	Map	Lat.	Long.
Nóqui	**88**	5 55 S	13 30 E
Nora, Ethiopia	**87**	16 6N	40 4 E
Nora, Sweden	**48**	59 32N	15 2 E
Noranda	**106**	48 20N	79 0W
Norberg	**48**	60 4N	15 56 E
Nórcia	**39**	42 50N	13 5 E
Nord □	**19**	50 15N	3 30 E
Nord-Ostee Kanal	**24**	54 15N	9 40 E
Nord-Süd Kanal	**24**	53 0N	10 32 E
Nord-Trøndelag fylke □	**50**	64 20N	12 0 E
Nordagutu	**47**	59 25N	9 20 E
Nordaustlandet	**4**	79 14N	23 0 E
Nordborg	**49**	55 5N	9 50 E
Nordby, Arhus, Denmark	**49**	55 58N	10 32 E
Nordby, Ribe, Denmark	**49**	55 27N	8 24 E
Norddal	**47**	62 15N	7 14 E
Norddalsfjord	**47**	61 39N	5 23 E
Norddeich	**24**	53 37N	7 10 E
Nordegg	**108**	52 29N	116 5W
Norden	**24**	53 35N	7 12 E
Nordenham	**24**	53 29N	8 28 E
Norderhov	**47**	60 7N	10 17 E
Norderney	**24**	53 42N	7 15 E
Nordfjord	**47**	61 55N	5 30 E
Nordfriesische Inseln	**24**	54 40N	8 20 E
Nordhausen	**24**	51 29N	10 47 E
Nordhorn	**24**	52 27N	7 4 E
Nordjyllands Amtskommune □	**49**	57 0N	10 0 E
Nordkapp, Norway	**50**	71 10N	25 44 E
Nordkapp, Svalb.	**4**	80 31N	20 0 E
Nordkinn	**9**	71 8N	27 40 E
Nordland fylke □	**50**	65 40N	13 0 E
Nördlingen	**25**	48 50N	10 30 E
Nordrhein-Westfalen □	**24**	51 45N	7 30 E
Nordstrand	**24**	54 27N	8 50 E
Nordvik	**59**	74 2N	111 32 E
Nore	**47**	60 10N	9 0 E
Nore →	**15**	52 40N	7 20W
Norefjell	**47**	60 16N	9 29 E
Norembega	**106**	48 59N	80 43W
Noresund	**47**	60 11N	9 37 E
Norfolk, Nebr., U.S.A.	**116**	42 3N	97 25W
Norfolk, Va., U.S.A.	**114**	36 40N	76 15W
Norfolk □	**12**	52 39N	1 0 E
Norfolk Broads	**12**	52 30N	1 15 E
Norfolk I.	**94**	28 58 S	168 3 E
Norfork Res.	**117**	36 13N	92 15W
Norilsk	**59**	69 20N	88 6 E
Norley	**99**	27 45 S	143 48 E
Norma, Mt.	**98**	20 55 S	140 42 E
Normal	**116**	40 30N	89 0W
Norman	**117**	35 12N	97 30W
Norman →	**97**	17 28 S	140 49 E
Norman Wells	**104**	65 17N	126 51W
Normanby →	**97**	14 23 S	144 10 E
Normanby I.	**98**	10 55 S	151 5 E
Normandie	**18**	48 45N	0 10 E
Normandie, Collines de	**18**	48 55N	0 45W
Normandin	**106**	48 49N	72 31W
Normandy = Normandie	**18**	48 45N	0 10 E
Normanton	**97**	17 40 S	141 10 E
Norquay	**109**	51 53N	102 5W
Norquinco	**128**	41 51 S	70 55W
Norrahammar	**49**	57 43N	14 7 E
Norrbotten □	**50**	66 30N	22 30 E
Norrby	**50**	64 55N	18 15 E
Nørre Åby	**49**	55 27N	9 52 E
Nørre Nebel	**49**	55 47N	8 17 E
Nørresundby	**49**	57 5N	9 52 E
Norris	**118**	45 40N	111 40W
Norristown	**114**	40 9N	75 21W
Norrköping	**49**	58 37N	16 11 E
Norrland □	**50**	66 50N	18 0 E
Norrtälje	**48**	59 46N	18 42 E
Norsholm	**49**	58 31N	15 59 E
Norsk	**59**	52 30N	130 0 E
North Adams	**114**	42 42N	73 6W
North America	**102**	40 0N	100 0W
North Andaman I.	**71**	13 15N	92 40 E
North Atlantic Ocean	**6**	30 0N	50 0W
North Battleford	**109**	52 50N	108 17W
North Bay	**106**	46 20N	79 30W
North Belcher Is.	**106**	56 50N	79 50W
North Bend, Can.	**108**	49 50N	121 27W
North Bend, Oreg., U.S.A.	**118**	43 28N	124 14W
North Bend, Pa., U.S.A.	**112**	41 20N	77 42W
North Berwick, U.K.	**14**	56 4N	2 44W
North Berwick, U.S.A.	**113**	43 18N	70 43W
North Buganda □	**90**	1 0N	32 0 E
North Canadian →	**117**	35 17N	95 31W
North C., Antarct.	**5**	71 0S	166 0 E
North C., Can.	**107**	47 2N	60 20W
North C., N.Z.	**101**	34 23 S	173 4 E
North Caribou L.	**106**	52 50N	90 40W
North Carolina □	**115**	35 30N	80 0W
North Channel, Br. Is.	**14**	55 0N	5 30W
North Channel, Can.	**106**	46 0N	83 0W
North Chicago	**114**	42 19N	87 50W
North Dakota □	**116**	47 30N	100 0W
North Down □	**15**	54 40N	5 45W
North Downs	**13**	51 17N	0 30 E
North East	**112**	42 17N	79 50W
North East Frontier Agency = Arunachal Pradesh □	**67**	28 0N	95 0 E
North East Providence Chan.	**121**	26 0N	76 0W
North Eastern □	**90**	1 30N	40 0 E
North Esk →	**14**	56 44N	2 25W
North European Plain	**9**	55 0N	20 0 E
North Foreland	**13**	51 22N	1 28 E
North Frisian Is. = Nordfr'sche Inseln	**24**	54 50N	8 20 E
North Henik L.	**109**	61 45N	97 40W
North Horr	**90**	3 20N	37 8 E
North I., Kenya	**90**	4 5N	36 5 E
North I., N.Z.	**101**	38 0S	175 0 E
North Kingsville	**112**	41 53N	80 42W
North Knife →	**109**	58 53N	94 45W
North Koel →	**69**	24 45N	83 50 E
North Korea ■	**76**	40 0N	127 0 E
North Lakhimpur	**67**	27 14N	94 7 E
North Las Vegas	**119**	36 15N	115 6W
North Loup →	**116**	41 17N	98 23W

Name	Map	Lat.	Long.
North Mashonaland □	**91**	16 30 S	30 0 E
North Minch	**14**	58 5N	5 55W
North Nahanni →	**108**	62 15N	123 20W
North Ossetian A.S.S.R. □	**57**	43 30N	44 30 E
North Palisade	**119**	37 6N	118 32W
North Platte	**116**	41 10N	100 50W
North Platte →	**116**	41 15N	100 45W
North Pt.	**107**	47 5N	64 0W
North Pole	**4**	90 0N	0 0 E
North Portal	**109**	49 0N	102 33W
North Powder	**118**	45 2N	117 59W
North Ronaldsay	**14**	59 20N	2 30W
North Sea	**8**	56 0N	4 0 E
North Sentinel I.	**71**	11 35N	92 15 E
North Sporades = Voríai Sporádhes	**45**	39 15N	23 30 E
North Stradbroke I.	**97**	27 35 S	153 28 E
North Sydney	**107**	46 12N	60 15W
North Thompson →	**108**	50 40N	120 20W
North Tonawanda	**114**	43 5N	78 50W
North Troy	**113**	44 59N	72 24W
North Truchas Pk.	**119**	36 0N	105 30W
North Twin I.	**106**	53 20N	80 0W
North Tyne →	**12**	54 59N	2 7W
North Uist	**14**	57 40N	7 15W
North Vancouver	**108**	49 25N	123 3W
North Vernon	**114**	39 0N	85 35W
North Village	**121**	32 15N	64 45W
North Wabiskaw L.	**108**	56 0N	113 55W
North Walsham	**12**	52 49N	1 22 E
North West Basin	**96**	25 45 S	115 0 E
North West C.	**96**	21 45 S	114 9 E
North West Christmas I. Ridge	**95**	6 30N	165 0W
North West Highlands	**14**	57 35N	5 2W
North West Providence Channel	**121**	26 0N	78 0W
North West River	**107**	53 30N	60 10W
North Western □	**91**	13 30 S	25 30 E
North York Moors	**12**	54 25N	0 50W
North Yorkshire □	**12**	54 15N	1 25W
Northallerton	**12**	54 20N	1 26W
Northam	**96**	31 35 S	116 42 E
Northampton, Austral.	**96**	28 27 S	114 33 E
Northampton, U.K.	**13**	52 14N	0 54W
Northampton, Mass., U.S.A.	**114**	42 22N	72 31W
Northampton, Pa., U.S.A.	**113**	40 38N	75 24W
Northampton □	**13**	52 16N	0 55W
Northampton Downs	**98**	24 35 S	145 48 E
Northbridge	**113**	42 12N	71 40W
Northeim	**24**	51 42N	10 0 E
Northern □, Malawi	**91**	11 0S	34 0 E
Northern □, Uganda	**90**	3 5N	32 30 E
Northern □, Zambia	**91**	10 30 S	31 0 E
Northern Circars	**70**	17 30N	82 30 E
Northern Group	**101**	10 00 S	160 00W
Northern Indian L.	**109**	57 20N	97 20W
Northern Ireland □	**15**	54 45N	7 0W
Northern Light, L.	**106**	48 15N	90 39W
Northern Province □	**84**	9 15N	11 30W
Northern Territory □	**96**	16 0S	133 0 E
Northfield	**116**	44 30N	93 10W
Northome	**116**	47 53N	94 15W
Northport, Ala., U.S.A.	**115**	33 15N	87 35W
Northport, Mich., U.S.A.	**114**	45 8N	85 39W
Northport, Wash., U.S.A.	**118**	48 55N	117 48W
Northumberland □	**12**	55 12N	2 0W
Northumberland, C.	**97**	38 5 S	140 40 E
Northumberland Is.	**98**	21 30 S	149 50 E
Northumberland Str.	**107**	46 20N	64 0W
Northwest Territories □	**104**	65 0N	100 0W
Northwich	**12**	53 16N	2 30W
Northwood, Iowa, U.S.A.	**116**	43 27N	93 0W
Northwood, N.D., U.S.A.	**116**	47 44N	97 30W
Norton, U.S.A.	**116**	39 50N	99 53W
Norton, Zimb.	**91**	17 52 S	30 40 E
Norton Sd.	**104**	64 0N	164 0W
Nortorf	**24**	54 14N	9 47 E
Norwalk, Conn., U.S.A.	**114**	41 9N	73 25W
Norwalk, Ohio, U.S.A.	**114**	41 13N	82 38W
Norway	**114**	45 46N	87 57W
Norway House	**109**	53 59N	97 50W
Norwegian Dependency	**5**	66 0 S	15 0 E
Norwegian Sea	**6**	66 0N	1 0 E
Norwich, Can.	**112**	42 59N	80 36W
Norwich, U.K.	**12**	52 38N	1 17 E
Norwich, Conn., U.S.A.	**113**	41 33N	72 5W
Norwich, N.Y., U.S.A.	**114**	42 32N	75 30W
Norwood, Can.	**112**	44 23N	77 59W
Norwood, U.S.A.	**113**	42 10N	71 10W
Nosok	**58**	70 10N	82 20 E
Nosovka	**54**	50 50N	31 37 E
Noşratābād	**65**	29 55N	60 0 E
Noss Hd.	**14**	58 29N	3 4W
Nossebro	**49**	58 12N	12 43 E
Nossob →	**92**	26 55 S	20 37 E
Nosy Boraha	**93**	16 50 S	49 55 E
Nosy Varika	**93**	20 35 S	48 32 E
Noteć →	**28**	52 44N	15 26 E
Notigi Dam	**109**	56 40N	99 10W
Notikewin →	**108**	57 2N	117 38W
Notios Evvoïkos Kólpos	**45**	38 20N	24 0 E
Noto	**41**	36 52N	15 4 E
Noto, G. di	**41**	36 50N	15 10 E
Noto-Hanto	**74**	37 0N	137 0 E
Notodden	**47**	59 35N	9 17 E
Notre-Dame	**107**	46 18N	64 46W
Notre Dame B.	**107**	49 45N	55 30W
Notre Dame de Koartac	**105**	60 55N	69 40W
Notsé	**85**	7 0N	1 17 E
Nottaway →	**106**	51 22N	78 55W
Nøtterøy	**47**	59 14N	10 24 E
Nottingham	**12**	52 57N	1 10W
Nottingham □	**12**	53 10N	1 0W
Nottoway →	**114**	36 33N	76 55W
Notwani →	**92**	23 35 S	26 58 E
Nouâdhibou	**80**	20 54N	17 0W
Nouâdhibou, Ras	**80**	20 50N	17 0W
Nouakchott	**84**	18 9N	15 58W
Nouméa	**94**	22 17 S	166 30 E
Noupoort	**92**	31 10 S	24 57 E
Nouveau Comptoir (Paint Hills)	**106**	53 0N	78 49W
Nouvelle Calédonie	**94**	21 0S	165 0 E
Nouzonville	**19**	49 48N	4 44 E

Name	Map	Lat.	Long.
Nová Baňa	**27**	48 28N	18 39 E
Nová Bystřice	**26**	49 2N	15 8 E
† Nova Chaves	**88**	10 31 S	21 15 E
Nova Cruz	**127**	6 28 S	35 25W
Nova Esperança	**125**	23 8 S	52 24W
Nova Friburgo	**125**	22 16 S	42 30W
Nova Gaia	**88**	10 10 S	17 35 E
Nova Gradiška	**42**	45 17N	17 28 E
Nova Iguaçu	**125**	22 45 S	43 28W
Nova Iorque	**127**	7 0S	44 5W
Nova Lamego	**84**	12 19N	14 11W
Nova Lima	**125**	19 59 S	43 51W
Nova Lisboa = Huambo	**89**	12 42 S	15 44 E
Nova Lusitânia	**91**	19 50 S	34 34 E
Nova Mambone	**93**	21 0S	35 3 E
Nova Mesto	**39**	45 47N	15 12 E
Nova Paka	**26**	50 29N	15 30 E
Nova Scotia □	**107**	45 10N	63 0W
Nova Sofala	**93**	20 7 S	34 42 E
Nova Varoš	**42**	43 29N	19 48 E
Nova Venécia	**127**	18 45 S	40 24W
Nova Zagora	**43**	42 32N	25 59 E
Novaci, Romania	**46**	45 10N	23 42 E
Novaci, Yugo.	**42**	41 5N	21 29 E
Noval Iorque	**127**	6 48 S	44 0W
Novaleksandrovskaya	**57**	45 29N	41 17 E
Novannenskiy	**55**	50 32N	42 39 E
Novara	**38**	45 27N	8 36 E
Novaya Kakhovka	**56**	46 42N	33 27 E
Novaya Ladoga	**52**	60 7N	32 16 E
Novaya Lyalya	**58**	59 10N	60 35 E
Novaya Sibir, O.	**59**	75 10N	150 0 E
Novaya Zemlya	**58**	75 0N	56 0 E
Nové Město	**27**	48 45N	17 50 E
Nové Zámky	**27**	48 0N	18 8 E
Novelda	**33**	38 24N	0 45W
Novellara	**38**	44 50N	10 43 E
Noventa Vicentina	**39**	45 18N	11 30 E
Novgorod	**54**	58 30N	31 25 E
Novgorod-Severskiy	**54**	52 2N	33 10 E
Novi Bečej	**42**	45 36N	20 10 E
Novi Grad	**39**	45 19N	13 33 E
Novi Kneževa	**42**	46 4N	20 8 E
• Novi Krichim	**43**	42 8N	24 31 E
Novi Ligure	**38**	44 45N	8 47 E
Novi Pazar, Bulg.	**43**	43 25N	27 15 E
Novi Pazar, Yugo.	**42**	43 12N	20 28 E
Novi Sad	**42**	45 18N	19 52 E
Novi Vinodolski	**39**	45 10N	14 48 E
Novigrad	**39**	44 10N	15 32 E
Nôvo Hamburgo	**125**	29 37 S	51 7W
Novo-Zavidovskiy	**55**	56 32N	36 29 E
Novoakrainka	**56**	48 25N	31 30 E
Novoaltaysk	**58**	53 30N	84 0 E
Novoazovsk	**56**	47 15N	38 4 E
Novobelitsa	**54**	52 27N	31 2 E
Novobogatinskoye	**57**	47 20N	51 11 E
Novocherkassk	**57**	47 27N	40 5 E
Novodevichye	**55**	53 37N	48 50 E
Novograd-Volynskiy	**54**	50 34N	27 35 E
Novogrudok	**54**	53 40N	25 50 E
Novokayakent	**57**	42 30N	47 52 E
Novokazalinsk	**58**	45 48N	62 6 E
Novokhopersk	**55**	51 5N	41 39 E
Novokuybyshevsk	**55**	53 7N	49 58 E
Novokuznetsk	**58**	53 45N	87 10 E
Novomirgorod	**56**	48 45N	31 33 E
Novomoskovsk, R.S.F.S.R., U.S.S.R.	**55**	54 5N	38 15 E
Novomoskovsk, Ukraine, U.S.S.R.	**56**	48 33N	35 17 E
Novopolotsk	**54**	55 32N	28 37 E
Novorossiysk	**56**	44 43N	37 46 E
Novorybnoye	**59**	72 50N	105 50 E
Novorzhev	**54**	57 3N	29 25 E
Novoselitsa	**56**	48 14N	26 15 E
Novoshakhtinsk	**57**	47 46N	39 58 E
Novosibirsk	**58**	55 0N	83 5 E
Novosibirskiye Ostrava	**59**	75 0N	142 0 E
Novosil	**55**	52 58N	36 58 E
Novosokolniki	**54**	56 33N	30 5 E
Novotroitsk	**52**	51 10N	58 15 E
Novotulskiy	**55**	54 10N	37 43 E
Novouzensk	**55**	50 32N	48 17 E
Novovolynsk	**54**	50 45N	24 4 E
Novovyatsk	**55**	58 29N	49 44 E
Novozybkov	**54**	52 30N	32 0 E
Novska	**42**	45 19N	17 0 E
Novvy Port	**58**	67 40N	72 30 E
Novy Bug	**56**	47 34N	32 29 E
Nový Bydzov	**26**	50 14N	15 29 E
Nowy Dwór Mazowiecki	**28**	52 26N	20 44 E
Nový Jičín	**27**	49 30N	18 0 E
Novyy Afon	**57**	43 7N	40 50 E
Novyy Oskol	**55**	50 44N	37 55 E
Now Shahr	**65**	36 40N	51 30 E
Nowa Deba	**28**	50 26N	21 41 E
Nowa Huta	**27**	50 5N	20 30 E
Nowa Ruda	**28**	50 35N	16 30 E
Nowa Skalmierzyce	**28**	51 43N	18 0 E
Nowa Sól	**28**	51 48N	15 44 E
Nowe	**28**	53 41N	18 44 E
Nowe Miasteczko	**28**	51 42N	15 42 E
Nowe Miasto	**28**	51 38N	20 34 E
Nowe Miasto Lubawskie	**28**	53 27N	19 33 E
Nowe Warpno	**28**	53 42N	14 18 E
Nowgong	**67**	26 20N	92 50 E
Nowingi	**100**	34 33 S	142 15 E
Nowogard	**28**	53 41N	15 10 E
Nowogród	**28**	53 14N	21 53 E
Nowra	**97**	34 53 S	150 35 E
Nowy Dwór, Białystok, Poland	**28**	53 40N	23 30 E
Nowy Dwór, Gdansk, Poland	**28**	54 13N	19 7 E
Nowy Korczyn	**28**	50 19N	20 48 E
Nowy Sącz	**27**	49 40N	20 41 E
Nowy Sącz □	**27**	49 30N	20 30 E
Nowy Staw	**28**	54 13N	19 2 E
Nowy Tomyśl	**28**	52 19N	16 10 E
Noxen	**113**	41 25N	76 4W
Noxon	**118**	48 0N	115 43W
Noya	**30**	42 48N	8 53W
Noyant	**18**	47 30N	0 6 E

Name	Map	Lat.	Long.
Noyers	**19**	47 40N	4 0 E
Noyes I.	**108**	55 30N	133 40W
Noyon	**19**	49 34N	3 0 E
Nozay	**18**	47 34N	1 38W
Nsa, O. en →	**83**	32 28N	5 24 E
Nsanje	**91**	16 55 S	35 12 E
Nsawam	**85**	5 50N	0 24W
Nsomba	**91**	10 45 S	29 51 E
Nsukka	**85**	6 51N	7 29 E
Nuanetsi →	**91**	22 40 S	31 50 E
Nuba Mts. = Nubah, Jibalan	**87**	12 0N	31 0 E
Nubah, Jibalan	**87**	12 0N	31 0 E
Nûbîya, Es Sahrâ En	**86**	21 30N	33 30 E
Ñuble □	**124**	37 0S	72 0W
Nuboai	**73**	2 10 S	136 30 E
Nueces →	**117**	27 50N	97 30W
Nueima →	**62**	31 54N	35 25 E
Nueltin L.	**109**	60 30N	99 30W
Nueva Gerona	**121**	21 53N	82 49W
Nueva Imperial	**128**	38 45 S	72 58W
Nueva Palmira	**124**	33 52 S	58 20W
Nueva Rosita	**120**	28 0N	101 11W
Nueva San Salvador	**120**	13 40N	89 18W
Nuéve de Julio	**124**	35 30 S	61 0W
Nuevitas	**121**	21 30N	77 20W
Nuevo, Golfo	**128**	43 0S	64 30W
Nuevo Laredo	**120**	27 30N	99 30W
Nuevo León □	**120**	25 0N	100 0W
Nugget Pt.	**101**	46 27 S	169 50 E
Nugrus, Gebel	**86**	24 47N	34 35 E
Nuhaka	**101**	39 3S	177 45 E
Nuits	**19**	47 44N	4 12 E
Nuits-St-Georges	**19**	47 10N	4 56 E
Nukheila (Merga)	**86**	19 1N	26 21 E
Nuku'alofa	**101**	21 10 S	174 0W
Nukus	**58**	42 20N	59 7 E
Nulato	**104**	64 40N	158 10W
Nules	**32**	39 51N	0 9W
Nullagine	**96**	21 53 S	120 6 E
Nullarbor Plain	**96**	30 45 S	129 0 E
Numalla, L.	**99**	28 43 S	144 20 E
Numan	**85**	9 29N	12 3 E
Numata	**74**	36 45N	139 4 E
Numatinna →	**87**	7 38N	27 20 E
Numazu	**74**	35 7N	138 51 E
Numfoor	**73**	1 0S	134 50 E
Numurkah	**99**	36 5 S	145 26 E
Nunaksaluk I.	**107**	55 49N	60 20W
Nuneaton	**13**	52 32N	1 29W
Nungo	**91**	13 23 S	37 43 E
Nungwe	**90**	2 48 S	32 2 E
Nunivak	**104**	60 0N	166 0W
Nunkun	**69**	33 57N	76 2 E
Nunspeet	**16**	52 21N	5 45 E
Nuomin He →	**76**	46 45N	126 55 E
Nuoro	**40**	40 20N	9 20 E
Nuqayy, Jabal	**83**	23 11N	19 30 E
Nure →	**38**	45 3N	9 49 E
Nuremburg = Nürnberg	**25**	49 26N	11 5 E
Nuriootpa	**99**	34 27 S	139 0 E
Nurlat	**55**	54 29N	50 45 E
Nürnberg	**25**	49 26N	11 5 E
Nurran, L. = Terewah, L.	**99**	29 52 S	147 35 E
Nurri	**40**	39 43N	9 13 E
Nurzec →	**28**	52 37N	22 25 E
Nusa Barung	**73**	8 22 S	113 20 E
Nusa Kambangan	**73**	7 47 S	109 0 E
Nusa Tenggara Barat □	**72**	8 50 S	117 30 E
Nusa Tenggara Timur □	**73**	9 30 S	122 0 E
Nushki	**66**	29 35N	66 0 E
Nutak	**105**	57 28N	61 59W
Nuwakot	**69**	28 10N	83 55 E
Nuwara Eliya	**70**	6 58N	80 48 E
Nuweiba'	**86**	28 58N	34 40 E
Nuweveldberge	**92**	32 10 S	21 45 E
Nuyts Arch.	**96**	32 35 S	133 20 E
Nuyts, Pt.	**96**	35 4 S	116 38 E
Nuzvid	**70**	16 47N	80 53 E
Nxau-Nxau	**92**	18 57 S	21 4 E
Nyaake (Webo)	**84**	4 52N	7 37W
Nyabing	**96**	33 30 S	118 7 E
Nyack	**113**	41 5N	73 57W
Nyadal	**48**	62 48N	17 59 E
Nyah West	**100**	35 16 S	143 21 E
Nyahanga	**90**	2 20 S	33 37 E
Nyahua	**90**	5 25 S	33 23 E
Nyahururu	**90**	0 2N	36 27 E
Nyainqentanglha Shan	**75**	30 0N	90 0 E
Nyakanazi	**90**	3 2 S	31 10 E
Nyakrom	**85**	5 40N	0 50W
Nyâlâ	**87**	12 2N	24 58 E
Nyamandhlovu	**91**	19 55 S	28 16 E
Nyambiti	**90**	2 48 S	33 27 E
Nyamwaga	**90**	1 27 S	34 33 E
Nyandekwa	**90**	3 57 S	32 32 E
Nyanding →,	**87**	8 40N	32 41 E
Nyangana	**92**	18 0S	20 40 E
Nyanguge	**90**	2 30 S	33 12 E
Nyankpala	**85**	9 21N	0 58W
Nyanza, Burundi	**90**	4 21 S	29 36 E
Nyanza, Rwanda	**90**	2 20 S	29 42 E
Nyanza □	**90**	0 10 S	34 15 E
Nyarling →	**108**	60 41N	113 23W
Nyasa, L. = Malawi, L.	**91**	12 0S	34 30 E
Nyazepetrovsk	**52**	56 3N	59 36 E
Nyazwidzi →	**91**	20 0S	31 17 E
Nyborg	**49**	55 18N	10 47 E
Nybro	**49**	56 44N	15 55 E
Nyda	**58**	66 40N	72 58 E
Nyeri	**90**	0 23 S	36 56 E
Nyerol	**87**	8 41N	32 1 E
Nyhem	**48**	62 54N	15 37 E
Nyiel	**87**	6 9N	31 13 E
Nyinahin	**84**	6 43N	2 3W
Nyirbátor	**27**	47 49N	22 9 E
Nyíregyháza	**27**	47 58N	21 47 E
Nykarleby	**50**	63 22N	22 31 E
Nykøbing, Sjælland, Denmark	**49**	55 55N	11 40 E
Nykøbing, Storstrøm, Denmark	**49**	54 56N	11 52 E
Nykøbing, Viborg, Denmark	**49**	56 48N	8 51 E
Nyköping	**49**	58 45N	17 0 E

• *Renamed Stamboliyski*

† *Renamed Muconda*

Nykroppa 48 59 37N 14 18 E
Nykvarn 48 59 11N 17 25 E
Nyland 48 63 1N 17 45 E
Nylstroom 93 24 42 S 28 22 E
Nymagee 99 32 7 S 146 20 E
Nymburk 26 50 10N 15 1 E
Nynäshamn 48 58 54N 17 57 E
Nyngan 99 31 30 S 147 8 E
Nyon 25 46 23N 6 14 E
Nyong → 85 3 17N 9 54 E
Nyons 21 44 22N 5 10 E
Nyord 49 55 4N 12 13 E
Nyou 85 12 42N 2 1W
Nysa 28 50 30N 17 22 E
Nysa →, Poland/Poland 28 52 4N 14 46 E
Nysa →, Poland 28 50 49N 17 40 E
Nyssa 118 43 56N 117 2W
Nysted 49 54 40N 11 44 E
Nyunzu 90 5 57 S 27 58 E
Nyurba 59 63 17N 118 28 E
Nzega 90 4 10 S 33 12 E
Nzega □ 90 4 10 S 33 10 E
N'Zérékoré 84 7 49N 8 48W
Nzeto 88 7 10 S 12 52 E
Nzilo, Chutes de 91 10 18 S 25 27 E
Nzubuka 90 4 45 S 32 50 E

O

Oacoma 116 43 50N 99 26W
Oahe 116 44 33N 100 29W
Oahe Dam 116 44 28N 100 25W
Oahe Res. 116 45 30N 100 25W
Oahu 110 21 30N 158 0W
Oak Creek 118 40 15N 106 59W
Oak Harb. 118 48 20N 122 38W
Oak Hill 114 38 0N 81 7W
Oak Park 114 41 55N 87 45W
Oak Ridge 115 36 1N 84 12W
Oakbank 99 33 4 S 140 33 E
Oakdale, Calif., U.S.A. 119 46 14N 98 4W
Oakdale, La., U.S.A. 117 30 50N 92 38W
Oakengates 12 52 42N 2 29W
Oakes 116 46 14N 98 4W
Oakesdale 118 47 11N 117 15W
Oakey 99 27 25 S 151 43 E
Oakham 12 52 40N 0 43W
Oakland, Calif., U.S.A. 119 37 50N 122 18W
Oakland, Oreg., U.S.A. 118 43 23N 123 18W
Oakland City 114 38 20N 87 20W
Oakleigh 100 37 54 S 145 6 E
Oakley, Id., U.S.A. 118 42 14N 113 55W
Oakley, Kans., U.S.A. 116 39 8N 100 51W
Oakridge 118 43 47N 122 31W
Oakwood 117 31 35N 94 45W
Oamaru 101 45 5 S 170 59 E
Oates Coast 5 69 0 S 160 0 E
Oatman 119 35 1N 114 19W
Oaxaca 120 17 2N 96 40W
Oaxaca □ 120 17 0N 97 0W
Ob → 58 66 45N 69 30 E
Oba 106 49 4N 84 7W
Obala 85 4 9N 11 32 E
Oban, N.Z. 101 46 55 S 168 10 E
Oban, U.K. 14 56 25N 5 30W
Obbia 63 5 25N 48 30 E
Obed 108 53 30N 117 10W
Obera 125 27 21 S 55 2W
Oberammergau 25 47 35N 11 3 E
Oberdrauburg 26 46 44N 12 58 E
Oberengadin 25 46 35N 9 55 E
Oberhausen 24 51 28N 6 50 E
Oberkirch 25 48 31N 8 5 E
Oberlin, Kans., U.S.A. 116 39 52N 100 31W
Oberlin, La., U.S.A. 117 30 42N 92 42W
Oberlin, Ohio, U.S.A. 112 41 15N 82 10W
Obernai 19 48 28N 7 30 E
Oberndorf 25 48 17N 8 35 E
Oberon 99 33 45 S 149 52 E
Oberösterreich □ 26 48 10N 14 0 E
Oberpfälzer Wald 25 49 30N 12 25 E
Oberstdorf 25 47 25N 10 16 E
Obi, Kepulauan 73 1 23 S 127 45 E
Obiaruku 85 5 51N 6 9 E
Óbidos, Brazil 127 1 50 S 55 30W
Óbidos, Port. 31 39 19N 9 10W
Obihiro 74 42 56N 143 12 E
Obilatu 73 1 25 S 127 20 E
Obilnoye 57 47 32N 44 30 E
Obing 25 48 0N 12 25 E
Obisfelde 24 52 27N 10 57 E
Objat 20 45 16N 1 24 E
Obluchye 59 49 1N 131 4 E
Obninsk 55 55 8N 36 37 E
Obo, C. Afr. Rep. 90 5 20N 26 32 E
Obo, Ethiopia 87 3 46N 38 52 E
Oboa, Mt. 90 1 45N 34 45 E
Obock 87 12 0N 43 20 E
Oborniki 28 52 39N 16 50 E
Oborniki Śląskie 28 51 17N 16 53 E
Oboyan 55 51 13N 36 37 E
Obrenovac 42 44 40N 20 11 E
Obrovac 39 44 11N 15 41 E
Observatory Inlet 108 55 10N 129 54W
Obshchi Syrt 9 52 0N 53 0 E
Obskaya Guba 58 69 0N 73 0 E
Obuasi 85 6 17N 1 40W
Obubra 85 6 8N 8 20 E
Obzor 43 42 50N 27 52 E
Ocala 115 29 11N 82 5W
Ocampo 120 28 9N 108 24W
Ocaña 32 39 55N 3 30W
Ocanomowoc 116 43 7N 88 30W
Ocate 117 36 12N 104 59W
Occidental, Cordillera 126 5 0N 76 0W
Ocean City 114 39 18N 74 34W
Ocean, I. = Banaba 94 0 52 S 169 35 E
Ocean Park 118 46 30N 124 2W
Oceanlake 118 45 0N 124 0W
Oceanport 113 40 20N 74 3W
Oceanside 119 33 13N 117 26W
Ochagavia 32 42 55N 1 5W
Ochamchire 57 42 46N 41 32 E
Ochil Hills 14 56 14N 3 40W
Ochre River 109 51 4N 99 47W
Ochsenfurt 25 49 38N 10 3 E
Ochsenhausen 25 48 4N 9 57 E
Ocilla 115 31 35N 83 12W
Ockelbo 48 60 54N 16 45 E
Ocmulgee → 115 31 58N 82 32W
Ocna Mureş 46 46 23N 23 55 E
Ocna Sibiului 46 45 52N 24 2 E
Ocnele Mari 46 45 8N 24 18 E
Oconee → 115 31 58N 82 32W
Oconto 114 44 52N 87 53W
Oconto Falls 114 44 52N 88 10W
Ocotal 121 13 41N 86 31W
Ocotlán 120 20 21N 102 42W
Ocreza → 31 39 32N 7 50W
Ócsa 27 47 17N 19 15 E
Octave 119 34 10N 112 43W
Octeville 18 49 38N 1 40W
Ocumare del Tuy 126 10 7N 66 46W
Ocussi 73 9 20 S 124 23 E
Oda 85 5 50N 0 51W
Oda, Jebel 86 20 21N 36 39 E
Ódáðahraun 50 65 5N 17 0W
Ödåkra 49 56 7N 12 45 E
Odawara 74 35 20N 139 6 E
Odda 47 60 3N 6 35 E
Odder 49 55 58N 10 10 E
Oddur 63 4 11N 43 52 E
Ödeborg 49 58 32N 11 58 E
Odei → 109 56 6N 96 54W
Ödemira 31 37 35N 8 40W
Ödemiş 64 38 15N 28 0 E
Odendaalsrus 92 27 48 S 26 45 E
Odense 49 55 22N 10 23 E
Odenwald 25 49 40N 9 0 E
Oder → 24 53 33N 14 38 E
Oderzo 39 45 47N 12 29 E
Odessa, Can. 113 44 17N 76 43W
Odessa, Tex., U.S.A. 117 31 51N 102 23W
Odessa, Wash., U.S.A. 118 47 19N 118 35W
Odessa, U.S.S.R. 56 46 30N 30 45 E
Odiakwe 92 20 12 S 25 17 E
Odiel → 31 37 10N 6 55W
Odienné 84 9 30N 7 34W
Odobeşti 46 45 43N 27 4 E
Odolanów 28 51 34N 17 40 E
O'Donnell 117 33 0N 101 48W
Odorheiul Secuiesc 46 46 21N 25 21 E
Odoyevo 55 53 56N 36 42 E
Odra →, Poland 28 53 33N 14 38 E
Odra →, Spain 30 42 14N 4 17W
Odžaci 42 45 30N 19 17 E
Odžak 42 45 3N 18 18 E
Oeiras, Brazil 127 7 0 S 42 8W
Oeiras, Port. 31 38 41N 9 18W
Oelrichs 116 43 11N 103 14W
Oelsnitz 24 50 24N 12 11 E
Oelwein 116 42 41N 91 55W
Ofanto → 41 41 22N 16 13 E
Offa 85 8 13N 4 42 E
Offaly □ 15 53 15N 7 30W
Offenbach 25 50 6N 8 46 E
Offenburg 25 48 29N 7 56 E
Offerdal 48 63 28N 14 0 E
Offida 39 42 56N 13 40 E
Offranville 18 49 52N 1 0 E
Ofidhousa 45 36 33N 26 8 E
Ofotfjorden 50 68 27N 16 40 E
Oga-Hantō 74 39 58N 139 47 E
Ogahalla 106 50 6N 85 51W
Ōgaki 74 35 21N 136 37 E
Ogallala 116 41 12N 101 40W
Ogbomosho 85 8 1N 4 11 E
Ogden, Iowa, U.S.A. 116 42 3N 94 0W
Ogden, Utah, U.S.A. 118 41 13N 112 1W
Ogdensburg 114 44 40N 75 27W
Ogeechee → 115 31 51N 81 6W
Oglio → 38 45 2N 10 39 E
Ogmore 98 22 37 S 149 35 E
Ogna 47 58 31N 5 48 E
Ognon → 19 47 16N 5 28 E
Ogoja 85 6 38N 8 39 E
Ogoki → 106 51 38N 85 57W
Ogoki L. 106 50 50N 87 10W
Ogoki Res. 106 50 45N 88 15W
Ogooué → 88 1 0S 10 0 E
Ogosta → 43 43 48N 23 55 E
Ogowe = Ogooué → 88 1 0S 10 0 E
Ograźden 42 41 30N 22 50 E
Ogrein 86 17 55N 34 50 E
Ogulin 39 45 16N 15 16 E
Ogun □ 85 7 0N 3 0 E
Oguta 85 5 44N 6 44 E
Ogwashi-Uku 85 6 15N 6 30 E
Ogwe 85 5 0N 7 14 E
Ohai 101 44 55 S 168 0 E
Ohakune 101 39 24 S 175 24 E
Ohau, L. 101 44 15 S 169 53 E
Ohey 16 50 26N 5 8 E
O'Higgins □ 124 34 15 S 70 45W
Ohio □ 114 40 20N 14 10 E
Ohio → 114 38 0N 86 0W
Ohre →, Czech. 26 50 30N 14 10 E
Ohre →, Ger. 24 52 18N 11 47 E
Ohrid 42 41 8N 20 52 E
Ohridsko, Jezero 42 41 8N 20 52 E
Ohrigstad 93 24 19 S 30 36 E
Öhringen 25 49 11N 9 31 E
Oil City 114 41 26N 79 40W
Oinousa 45 38 33N 26 14 E
Oise □ 19 49 28N 2 30 E
Oise → 19 49 0N 2 4 E
Ōita 74 33 14N 131 36 E
Ōita □ 74 33 15N 131 30 E
Oiticica 127 5 3 S 41 5W
Ojai 119 34 28N 119 16W
Ojinaga 120 29 34N 104 25W
Ojos del Salado, Cerro 124 27 0 S 68 40W
Oka → 55 56 20N 43 59 E
Okaba 73 8 6 S 139 42 E
Okahandja 92 22 0 S 16 59 E
Okahukura 94 38 48 S 175 14 E
Okanagan L. 108 50 0N 119 30W
Okandja 88 0 35 S 13 45 E
Okanogan 118 48 6N 119 43W
Okanogan → 118 48 6N 119 43W
Okány 27 46 52N 21 21 E
Okaputa 92 20 5 S 17 0 E
Okara 68 30 50N 73 31 E
Okarito 101 43 15 S 170 9 E
Okavango Swamps 92 18 45 S 22 45 E
Okaya 74 36 0N 138 10 E
Okayama 74 34 40N 133 54 E
Okayama □ 74 35 0N 133 50 E
Okazaki 74 34 57N 137 10 E
Oke-Iho 85 8 1N 3 18 E
Okeechobee 115 27 16N 80 46W
Okeechobee L. 115 27 0N 80 50W
Okefenokee Swamp 115 30 50N 82 15W
Okehampton 13 50 44N 4 1W
Okene 85 7 32N 6 11 E
Oker → 24 52 30N 10 22 E
Okha 59 53 40N 143 0 E
Ókhi Óros 45 38 5N 24 25 E
Okhotsk 59 59 20N 143 10 E
Okhotsk, Sea of 59 55 0N 145 0 E
Okhotskiy Perevoz 59 61 52N 135 35 E
Okhotsko Kolymskoye 59 63 0N 157 0 E
Oki-Shotō 74 36 5N 133 15 E
Okiep 92 29 39 S 17 53 E
Okigwi 85 5 52N 7 20 E
Okija 85 5 54N 6 55 E
Okinawa □ 77 26 40N 128 0 E
Okitipupa 85 6 31N 4 50 E
Oklahoma □ 117 35 20N 97 30W
Oklahoma City 117 35 25N 97 30W
Okmulgee 117 35 38N 96 0W
Oknitsa 56 48 25N 27 30 E
Okolo 90 2 37N 31 8 E
Okolona 117 34 0N 88 45W
Okondeka 92 21 38 S 15 37 E
Okonek 28 53 32N 16 51 E
Okrika 85 4 40N 7 10 E
Oktabrsk 58 49 28N 57 25 E
Oktyabrsk 55 53 11N 48 40 E
Oktyabrskiy, Byelorussia, U.S.S.R. 54 52 38N 28 53 E
Oktyabrskiy, R.S.F.S.R., U.S.S.R. 52 54 28N 53 28 E
Oktyabrskoy Revolyutsii, Os. 59 79 30N 97 0 E
Oktyabrskoye 58 62 28N 66 3 E
Oktyabrskoye = Zhovtnevoye 56 47 54N 32 2 E
Okulovka 54 58 25N 33 19 E
Okuru 101 43 55 S 168 55 E
Okushiri-Tō 74 42 15N 139 30 E
Okuta 85 9 14N 3 12 E
Okwa → 92 22 30 S 23 0 E
Ola 117 35 2N 93 10W
Ólafsfjörður 50 66 4N 18 39W
Ólafsvík 50 64 53N 23 43W
Olancha 119 36 15N 118 1W
Olanchito 121 15 30N 86 30W
Öland 49 56 45N 16 38 E
Olargues 20 43 34N 2 53 E
Olary 99 32 18 S 140 19 E
Olascoaga 124 35 15 S 60 39W
Olathe 116 38 50N 94 50W
Olavarría 124 36 55 S 60 20W
Oława 28 50 57N 17 20 E
Ólbia 40 40 55N 9 30 E
Ólbia, G. di 40 40 55N 9 35 E
Old Bahama Chan. = Bahama, Canal Viejo de 121 22 10N 77 30W
Old Castile = Castilla la Vieja □ 30 41 55N 4 0W
Old Castle 15 53 46N 7 10W
Old Cork 98 22 57 S 141 52 E
Old Crow 104 67 30N 140 5 E
Old Dongola 86 18 11N 30 44 E
Old Forge, N.Y., U.S.A. 113 43 43N 74 58W
Old Forge, Pa., U.S.A. 113 41 20N 75 46W
Old Fort → 109 58 36N 110 24W
Old Shinyanga 90 3 33 S 33 27 E
Old Speckle, Mt. 113 44 35N 70 57W
Old Town 107 45 0N 68 41W
Old Wives L. 109 50 5N 106 0W
Oldbury 13 51 38N 2 30W
Oldeani 90 3 22 S 35 35 E
Oldenburg, Niedersachsen, Ger. 24 53 10N 8 10 E
Oldenburg, Schleswig-Holstein, Ger. 24 54 16N 10 53 E
Oldenzaal 16 52 19N 6 53 E
Oldham 12 53 33N 2 8W
Oldman → 108 49 57N 111 42W
Olds 108 51 50N 114 10W
Olean 114 42 8N 78 25W
Olecko 28 54 2N 22 31 E
Oléggio 38 45 36N 8 38 E
Oleiros 30 39 56N 7 56W
Olekma → 59 60 22N 120 42 E
Olekminsk 59 60 25N 120 30 E
Olenegorsk 52 68 9N 33 18 E
Olenek 59 68 28N 112 18 E
Olenek → 59 73 0N 120 10 E
Olenino 54 56 15N 33 30 E
Oléron, Île d' 20 45 55N 1 15W
Oleśnica 28 51 13N 17 22 E
Olesno 28 50 51N 18 26 E
Olevsk 54 51 12N 27 39 E
Olga 59 43 50N 135 14 E
Olga, L. 106 49 47N 77 15W
Olga, Mt. 96 25 20 S 130 50 E
Olgastretet 4 78 35N 25 0 E
Ølgod 49 55 49N 8 36 E
Olhão 31 37 3N 7 48W
Olib 39 44 23N 14 44 E
Olib, I. 39 44 23N 14 44 E
Oliena 40 40 18N 9 22 E
Oliete 32 41 1N 0 41W
Olifants → 93 24 5 S 31 20 E
Olifantshoek 92 27 57 S 22 42 E
Ólimbos 45 35 44N 27 11 E
Ólimbos, Óros 44 40 6N 22 23 E
Olímpia 125 20 44 S 48 54W
Olimpo □ 124 20 30 S 58 45W
Olite 32 42 29N 1 40W
Oliva, Argent. 124 32 0 S 63 38W
Oliva, Spain 33 38 58N 0 9W
Oliva de la Frontera 31 38 17N 6 54W
Oliva, Punta del 30 43 37N 5 28W
Olivares 32 39 46N 2 20W
Oliveira 127 20 39 S 44 50W
Oliveira de Azemeis 30 40 49N 8 29W
Olivença 91 11 47 S 35 13 E
Olivenza 31 38 41N 7 9W
Oliver 108 49 13N 119 37W
Oliver L. 109 56 56N 103 22W
Olkhovka 57 49 48N 44 32 E
Olkusz 28 50 18N 19 33 E
Ollagüe 124 21 15 S 68 10W
Olmedo 30 41 20N 4 43W
Olney, Ill., U.S.A. 114 38 40N 88 0W
Olney, Tex., U.S.A. 117 33 25N 98 45W
Olofström 49 56 17N 14 32 E
Oloma 85 3 29N 11 19 E
Olomane → 107 50 14N 60 37W
Olomouc 27 49 38N 17 12 E
Olonets 52 61 10N 33 0 E
Olongapo 73 14 50N 120 18 E
Oloron, Gave d' 20 43 33N 1 5W
Oloron-Ste-Marie 20 43 11N 0 38W
Olot 32 42 11N 2 30 E
Olovo 42 44 8N 18 35 E
Olovyannaya 59 50 58N 115 35 E
Oloy → 59 66 29N 159 29 E
Olpe 24 51 2N 7 50 E
Olshanka 56 48 16N 30 58 E
Olshany 56 50 3N 35 53 E
Olsztyn 28 53 48N 20 29 E
Olsztyn □ 28 54 0N 21 0 E
Olsztynek 28 53 34N 20 19 E
Olt □ 46 44 20N 24 30 E
Olt → 46 43 50N 24 40 E
Olten 25 47 21N 7 53 E
Olteniţa 46 44 7N 26 42 E
Olton 117 34 16N 102 7W
Oltu 64 40 35N 41 58 E
Olvega 32 41 47N 2 0W
Olvera 31 36 55N 5 18W
Olympia, Greece 45 37 39N 21 39 E
Olympia, U.S.A. 118 47 0N 122 58W
Olympic Mts. 118 47 50N 123 45W
Olympic Nat. Park 118 47 48N 123 30W
Olympus, Mt. 118 47 52N 123 40W
Olympus, Mt. = Ólimbos, Óros 44 40 6N 22 23 E
Olyphant 113 41 27N 75 36W
Om → 58 54 59N 73 22 E
Om Hajer 87 14 20N 36 41 E
Ōmachi 74 36 30N 137 50 E
Omagh 15 54 36N 7 20W
Omagh □ 15 54 35N 7 15W
Omaha 116 41 15N 96 0W
Omak 118 48 24N 119 31W
Oman ■ 63 23 0N 58 0 E
Oman, G. of 65 24 30N 58 30 E
Omaruru 92 21 26 S 16 0 E
Omaruru → 92 22 7 S 14 15 E
Omate 126 16 45 S 71 0W
Ombai, Selat 73 8 30 S 124 50 E
Ombo 47 59 18N 6 0 E
Omboué 88 1 35 S 9 15 E
Ombrone → 38 42 39N 11 0 E
Omchi 83 21 22N 17 53 E
Omdurmân 87 15 40N 32 28 E
Omegna 38 45 52N 8 23 E
Omeonga 90 3 40 S 24 22 E
Ometepe, Isla de 121 11 32N 85 35W
Ometepec 120 16 39N 98 23W
Omez 62 32 22N 35 0 E
Omineca → 108 56 3N 124 16W
Omiš 39 43 28N 16 40 E
Omišalj 39 45 13N 14 32 E
Omitara 92 22 16 S 18 2 E
Ōmiya 74 35 54N 139 38 E
Omme Å → 49 55 56N 8 32 E
Ommen 16 52 31N 6 26 E
Omo → 81 6 25N 36 10 E
Omolon → 59 68 42N 158 36 E
Omsk 58 55 0N 73 12 E
Omsukchan 59 62 32N 155 48 E
Omul, Vf. 46 45 27N 25 29 E
Omulew → 28 53 5N 21 33 E
Ōmura 74 32 56N 130 0 E
Omurtag 43 43 8N 26 26 E
Ōmuta 74 33 0N 130 26 E
Omutninsk 55 58 45N 52 4 E
Oña 32 42 43N 3 25W
Onaga 116 39 32N 96 12W
Onalaska 116 43 53N 91 14W
Onamia 116 46 4N 93 38W
Onancock 114 37 42N 75 49W
Onang 73 3 2 S 118 49 E
Onaping L. 106 47 3N 81 30W
Onarheim 47 59 57N 5 35 E
Oñate 32 43 3N 2 25W
Onavas 120 28 28N 109 30W
Onawa 116 42 2N 96 2W
Onaway 114 45 21N 84 11W
Oncesti 46 43 56N 25 52 E
Oncócua 92 16 30 S 13 25 E
Onda 32 39 55N 0 17W
Ondangua 92 17 57 S 16 4 E
Ondárroa 32 43 19N 2 25W
Ondava → 27 48 27N 21 48 E
Ondo 85 7 4N 4 47 E
Ondo □ 85 7 0N 5 0 E
Öndörhaan 75 47 19N 110 39 E
Öndverðarnes 50 64 52N 24 0W
Onega 52 64 0N 38 10 E
Onega → 52 63 58N 37 55 E
Onega, G. of = Onezhskaya G. 52 64 30N 37 0 E
Onega, L. = Onezhskoye Oz. 52 62 0N 35 30 E
Onehunga 101 36 55 S 174 48 E

neida 114 43 5N 75 40W
neida L. 114 43 12N 76 0W
'Neill 116 42 30N 98 38W
nekotan, Ostrov 59 49 25N 154 45 E
nema 90 4 35 S 24 30 E
neonta, Ala., U.S.A. 115 33 58N 86 29W
neonta, N.Y., U.S.A. 114 42 26N 75 5W
nezhskaya Guba 52 64 30N 37 0 E
nezhskoye Ozero 52 62 0N 35 30 E
ngarue 101 38 42 S 175 19 E
ngniud Qi 76 43 0N 118 38 E
ngoka 90 1 20 S 26 0 E
ngole 70 15 33N 80 2 E
nguren 59 53 38N 107 36 E
ni 57 42 33N 43 26 E
nida 116 44 42N 100 5W
nilahy → 93 23 34 S 43 45 E
nitsha 85 6 6N 6 42 E
noda 74 34 2N 131 25 E
ns, Islas d' 30 42 23N 8 55W
nsala 49 57 26N 12 0 E
nslow 96 21 40 S 115 12 E
nslow B. 115 34 20N 77 20W
nstwedde 16 53 2N 7 4 E
ntake-San 74 35 53N 137 29 E
ntaneda 30 43 12N 3 57W
ntario, Calif., U.S.A. 119 34 2N 117 40W
ntario, Oreg., U.S.A. 118 44 1N 117 1W
ntario □ 106 52 0N 88 10W
ntario, L. 106 43 40N 78 0W
nteniente 33 38 50N 0 35W
ntonagon 116 46 52N 89 19W
ntur 33 38 38N 1 29W
odnadatta 96 27 33 S 135 30 E
oldea 96 30 27 S 131 50 E
ona River 108 53 57N 130 16W
orindi 98 20 40 S 141 1 E
ost-Vlaanderen □ 16 51 5N 3 50 E
ostende 16 51 15N 2 50 E
osterhout 16 51 39N 4 47 E
osterschelde 16 51 33N 4 0 E
otacamund 70 11 30N 76 44 E
otsa L. 108 53 50N 126 2W
otsi 92 25 2 S 25 45 E
paka 43 43 28N 26 10 E
pala, U.S.S.R. 59 51 58N 156 30 E
pala, Zaïre 88 0 40 S 24 20 E
palenica 28 52 18N 16 24 E
pan 43 42 13N 25 41 E
panake 70 6 35N 80 40 E
pasatika 106 49 30N 82 50W
pasquia 109 53 16N 93 34W
patija 39 45 21N 14 17 E
patów 28 50 50N 21 27 E
pava 27 49 57N 17 58 E
pelousas 117 30 35N 92 7W
pémisca L. 106 50 0N 75 0W
pheim 118 48 52N 106 30W
phir 104 63 10N 156 40W
phthalmia Ra. 96 23 15 S 119 30 E
pi 85 6 36N 7 28 E
pinaca → 106 52 15N 78 2W
pinaca L. 106 52 39N 76 20W
piskotish, L. 107 53 10N 67 50W
pobo 85 4 35N 7 34 E
pochka 54 56 42N 28 45 E
poczno 28 51 22N 20 18 E
pole 28 50 42N 17 58 E
pole □ 28 50 40N 17 56 E
porto = Porto 30 41 8N 8 40W
potiki 101 38 1 S 177 19 E
pp 115 31 19N 86 13W
ppegård 47 59 48N 10 48 E
ppenheim 25 49 50N 8 22 E
pido Mamertina 41 38 16N 15 59 E
pland fylke □ 47 61 15N 9 40 E
pstad 47 60 17N 11 40 E
rtalj 39 45 23N 13 50 E
ua 101 35 19 S 174 9 E
punake 101 39 26 S 173 52 E
puzen 42 43 1N 17 34 E
r Yehuda 62 32 2N 34 50 E
ra, Israel 62 30 55N 35 1 E
ra, Italy 39 46 20N 11 19 E
racle 119 32 36N 110 46W
radea 46 47 2N 21 58 E
ræfajökull 50 64 2N 16 39W
rahovac 42 42 24N 20 40 E
rahovica 42 45 35N 17 52 E
rai 69 25 58N 79 30 E
raison 21 43 55N 5 55 E
ran, Alg. 82 35 45N 0 39W
ran, Argent. 124 23 10 S 64 20W
range, Austral. 97 33 15 S 149 7 E
range, France 21 44 8N 4 47 E
range, Mass., U.S.A. 113 42 35N 72 15W
range, Tex., U.S.A. 117 30 10N 93 50W
range, Va., U.S.A. 114 38 17N 78 5W
range, C. 127 4 20N 51 30W
range Free State = Oranje Vrystaat □ 92 28 30 S 27 0 E
range Grove 117 27 57N 97 57W
range Walk 120 18 6N 88 33W
rangeburg 115 33 35N 80 53W
rangeville 106 43 55N 80 5W
ranienburg 24 52 45N 13 15 E
ranje → 92 28 41 S 16 28 E
ranje Vrystaat □ 92 28 30 S 27 0 E
ranjemund 92 28 38 S 16 29 E
r'Aquiva 62 32 30N 34 54 E
ras 73 12 9N 125 28 E
rašje 42 45 1N 18 42 E
răştie 46 45 50N 23 10 E
raşul Stalin = Braşov 46 45 38N 25 35 E
ava → 27 49 24N 19 20 E
avita 42 45 2N 21 43 E
b → 20 43 17N 3 17 E
ba → 38 44 53N 8 37 E
bæk 49 55 17N 10 39 E
be 25 46 43N 6 32 E
bec 18 49 1N 0 23 E
rbetello 39 42 26N 11 11 E
Órbigo → 30 42 5N 5 42W
Orbost 97 37 40 S 148 29 E
Örbyhus 48 60 15N 17 43 E
Orce 33 37 44N 2 28W
Orce → 33 37 44N 2 28W
Orchies 19 50 28N 3 14 E
Orchila, Isla 126 11 48N 66 10W
Orco → 38 45 10N 7 52 E
Ord → 96 15 33 S 138 15 E
Ord, Mt. 96 17 20 S 125 34 E
Ordenes 30 43 5N 8 29W
Orderville 119 37 18N 112 43W
Ordos = Mu Us Shamo 76 39 0N 109 0 E
Ordu 64 40 55N 37 53 E
Orduña, Álava, Spain 32 42 58N 2 58 E
Orduña, Granada, Spain 33 37 20N 3 30W
Ordway 116 38 15N 103 42W
Ordzhonikidze, R.S.F.S.R., U.S.S.R. 57 43 0N 44 43 E
Ordzhonikidze, Ukraine S.S.R., U.S.S.R. 56 47 39N 34 3 E
Ore, Sweden 48 61 8N 15 10 E
Ore, Zaïre 90 3 17N 29 30 E
Ore Mts. = Erzgebirge 24 50 25N 13 0 E
Orebić 42 43 0N 17 11 E
Örebro 48 59 20N 15 18 E
Örebro län □ 48 59 27N 15 0 E
Oregon 116 42 1N 89 20W
Oregon □ 118 44 0N 121 0W
Oregon City 118 45 21N 122 35W
Öregrund 48 60 21N 18 30 E
Öregrundsgrepen 48 60 25N 18 15 E
Orekhov 56 47 30N 35 48 E
Orekhovo-Zuyevo 55 55 50N 38 55 E
Orel 55 52 57N 36 3 E
Orel → 56 48 30N 34 54 E
Orellana, Canal de 31 39 2N 6 0W
Orellana la Vieja 31 39 1N 5 32W
Orellana, Pantano de 31 39 5N 5 10W
Orem 118 40 20N 111 45W
Oren 45 37 3N 27 57 E
Orenburg 52 51 45N 55 6 E
Orense 30 42 19N 7 55W
Orense □ 30 42 15N 7 51W
Orepuki 101 46 19 S 167 46 E
Orestiás 44 41 30N 26 33 E
Øresund 49 55 45N 12 45 E
Orford Ness 13 52 6N 1 31 E
Orgaña 32 42 13N 1 20 E
Orgaz 31 39 39N 3 53W
Orgeyev 56 47 24N 28 50 E
Orgon 21 43 47N 5 3 E
Orgūn 65 32 55N 69 12 E
Orhon Gol → 75 49 30N 106 0 E
Ória 41 40 30N 17 38 E
Orient 99 28 7 S 142 50 E
Oriental, Cordillera 126 6 0N 73 0W
Oriente 124 38 44 S 60 37W
Origny-Ste-Benoîte 19 49 50N 3 30 E
Orihuela 33 38 7N 0 55W
Orihuela del Tremedal 32 40 33N 1 39W
Oriku 44 40 20N 19 30 E
Orinoco → 126 9 15N 61 30W
Orissa □ 69 20 0N 84 0 E
Oristano 40 39 54N 8 35 E
Oristano, Golfo di 40 39 50N 8 22 E
Orizaba 120 18 50N 97 10W
Orizare 43 42 44N 27 39 E
Ørje 47 59 29N 11 39 E
Orjen 42 42 35N 18 34 E
Orjiva 33 36 53N 3 24W
Orkanger 47 63 18N 9 52 E
Orkelljunga 49 56 17N 13 17 E
Örkény 27 47 9N 19 26 E
Orkla → 47 63 18N 9 51 E
Orkney 92 26 58 S 26 40 E
Orkney □ 14 59 0N 3 0W
Orkney Is. 14 59 0N 3 0W
Orla 28 52 42N 23 20 E
Orland 118 39 46N 122 12W
Orlando 115 28 30N 81 25W
Orlando, C. d' 41 38 10N 14 43 E
Orléanais 19 48 0N 2 0 E
Orléans 19 47 54N 1 52 E
Orleans 113 44 49N 72 10W
Orléans, Î. d' 107 46 54N 70 58W
Orlice → 26 50 5N 16 10 E
Orlické Hory 27 50 15N 16 30 E
Orlik 59 52 30N 99 55 E
Orlov 27 49 17N 20 51 E
Orlov Gay 55 50 56N 48 19 E
Orlovat 42 45 14N 20 33 E
Ormara 66 25 16N 64 33 E
Ormea 38 44 9N 7 54 E
Ormília 44 40 16N 23 39 E
Ormoc 73 11 0N 124 37 E
Ormond, N.Z. 101 38 33 S 177 56 E
Ormond, U.S.A. 115 29 13N 81 5W
Ormož 39 46 25N 16 10 E
Ormstown 113 45 8N 74 0W
Ornans 19 47 7N 6 10 E
Orne □ 18 48 40N 0 5 E
Orne → 18 49 18N 0 15W
Orneta 28 54 8N 20 9 E
Ørnhøj 49 56 13N 8 34 E
Ornö 48 59 4N 18 24 E
Örnsköldsvik 48 63 17N 18 40 E
Oro → 120 25 35N 105 2W
Orocué 126 4 48N 71 20W
Orodo 85 5 34N 7 4 E
Orogrande 119 32 20N 106 4W
Orol 30 43 34N 7 39W
Oromocto 107 45 54N 66 29W
Oron 85 4 48N 8 14 E
Orono 112 43 59N 78 37W
Oropesa 30 39 57N 5 10W
Oroqen Zizhiqi 76 50 34N 123 43 E
Oroquieta 73 8 32N 123 44 E
Orós 127 6 15 S 38 55W
Orosei, G. di 40 40 15N 9 40 E
Orosháza 27 46 32N 20 42 E
Orotukan 59 62 16N 151 42 E
Oroville, Calif., U.S.A. 118 39 31N 121 30W
Oroville, Wash., U.S.A. 118 48 58N 119 30W
Orrefors 49 56 50N 15 45 E
Orroroo 99 32 43 S 138 38 E
Orrville 112 40 50N 81 46W
Orsa 48 61 7N 14 37 E
Orsara di Púglia 41 41 17N 15 16 E
Orsasjön 48 61 7N 14 37 E
Orsha 54 54 30N 30 25 E
Orsk 52 51 12N 58 34 E
Ørslev 49 55 3N 11 56 E
Orsogna 39 42 13N 14 17 E
Orşova 46 44 41N 22 25 E
Ørsted 49 56 30N 10 20 E
Orta, L. d' 38 45 48N 8 21 E
Orta Nova 41 41 20N 15 40 E
Orte 39 42 28N 12 23 E
Ortegal, C. 30 43 43N 7 52W
Orthez 20 43 29N 0 48W
Ortigueira 30 43 40N 7 50W
Ortles 38 46 31N 10 33 E
Ortón → 126 10 50 S 67 0W
Ortona 39 42 21N 14 24 E
Orune 40 40 25N 9 20 E
Oruro 126 18 0 S 67 9W
Orust 49 58 10N 11 40 E
Orūzgān □ 65 33 30N 66 0 E
Orvault 18 47 17N 1 38W
Orvieto 39 42 43N 12 8 E
Orwell 112 41 32N 80 52W
Orwell → 13 52 2N 1 12 E
Oryakhovo 43 43 40N 23 57 E
Orzinuovi 38 45 24N 9 55 E
Orzyc → 28 52 46N 21 14 E
Orzysz 28 53 50N 21 58 E
Os 47 60 9N 5 30 E
Osa 52 57 17N 55 26 E
Osa → 28 53 33N 18 46 E
Osa, Pen. de 121 8 0N 84 0W
Osage, Iowa, U.S.A. 116 43 15N 92 50W
Osage, Wyo., U.S.A. 116 43 59N 104 25W
Osage → 116 38 35N 91 57W
Osage City 116 38 43N 95 51W
Ōsaka 74 34 40N 135 30 E
Osaka □ 74 34 30N 135 30 E
Osawatomie 116 38 30N 94 55W
Osborne 116 39 30N 98 45W
Osby 49 56 23N 13 59 E
Osceola, Ark., U.S.A. 117 35 40N 90 0W
Osceola, Iowa, U.S.A. 116 41 0N 93 20W
Oschatz 24 51 17N 13 8 E
Oschersleben 24 52 2N 11 13 E
Oschiri 40 40 43N 9 7 E
Oscoda 114 44 26N 83 20W
Oscoda-Au-Sable 112 44 26N 83 20W
Osečina 42 44 23N 19 34 E
Ösel = Saaremaa 54 58 30N 22 30W
Osëry 55 54 52N 38 28 E
Osh 58 40 37N 72 49 E
Oshawa 106 43 50N 78 50W
ŌShima 74 34 44N 139 24 E
Oshkosh, Nebr., U.S.A. 116 41 27N 102 20W
Oshkosh, Wis., U.S.A. 116 44 3N 88 35W
Oshmyany 54 54 26N 25 52 E
Oshogbo 85 7 48N 4 37 E
Oshwe 88 3 25 S 19 28 E
Osica de Jos 46 44 14N 24 20 E
Osieczna 28 51 55N 16 40 E
Osijek 42 45 34N 18 41 E
Ōsilo 40 40 45N 8 41 E
Osimo 39 43 28N 13 30 E
Osintorf 54 54 40N 30 39 E
Osipenko = Berdyansk 56 46 45N 36 50 E
Osipovichi 54 53 19N 28 33 E
Oskaloosa 116 41 18N 92 40W
Oskarshamn 49 57 15N 16 27 E
Oskélanéo 106 48 5N 75 15W
Oskol → 55 49 6N 37 25 E
Oslo 47 59 55N 10 45 E
Oslob 73 9 31N 123 26 E
Oslofjorden 47 59 20N 10 35 E
Osmanabad 70 18 5N 76 10 E
Osmancık 56 40 45N 34 47 E
Osmaniye 64 37 5N 36 10 E
Ösmo 48 58 58N 17 55 E
Osnabrück 24 52 16N 8 2 E
Ośno Lubuskie 28 52 28N 14 51 E
Osobláha 27 50 17N 17 44 E
Osogovska Planina 42 42 10N 22 30 E
Osor 38 44 42N 14 24 E
Osorio 125 29 53 S 50 17W
Osorno, Chile 128 40 25 S 73 0W
Osorno, Spain 30 42 24N 4 22W
Osoyoos 108 49 0N 119 30W
Ospika → 108 56 20N 124 0W
Osprey Reef 97 13 52 S 146 36 E
Oss 16 51 46N 5 32 E
Ossa de Montiel 33 38 58N 2 45W
Ossa, Mt. 97 41 52 S 146 3 E
Ossa, Oros 44 39 47N 22 42 E
Ossabaw I. 115 31 45N 81 8W
Osse → 20 44 7N 0 17 E
Ossining 114 41 9N 73 50W
Ossipee 113 43 41N 71 9W
Ossokmanuan L. 107 53 25N 65 0W
Ossora 59 59 20N 163 13 E
Ostashkov 54 57 4N 33 2 E
Oste → 24 53 30N 9 12 E
Ostend = Oostende 16 51 15N 2 50 E
Oster 54 50 57N 30 53 E
Osterburg 24 52 47N 11 44 E
Osterburken 25 49 26N 9 25 E
Österbybruk 48 60 13N 17 55 E
Österbymo 49 57 49N 15 15 E
Östergötlands län □ 49 58 35N 15 45 E
Osterholz-Scharmbeck 24 53 14N 8 48 E
Østerild 49 57 2N 8 51 E
Österkorsberga 49 57 18N 15 6 E
Osterøya 47 60 32N 5 30 E
Östersund 48 63 10N 14 38 E
Østfold fylke □ 47 59 25N 11 25 E
Ostfriesland 24 53 20N 7 30 E
Ostfriesische Inseln 24 53 45N 7 15 E
Óstia, Lido di (Lido di Roma) 40 41 43N 12 17 E
Ostiglia 39 45 4N 11 9 E
Ostra 39 43 40N 13 5 E
Ostrava 27 49 51N 18 18 E
Ostróda 28 53 42N 19 58 E
Ostrog 54 50 20N 26 30 E
Ostrogozhsk 55 50 55N 39 7 E
Ostrogróg Sźamotuły 28 52 37N 16 33 E
Ostrołeka 28 53 4N 21 32 E
Ostrołeka □ 28 53 0N 21 30 E
Ostrov, Bulg. 43 43 40N 24 9 E
Ostrov, Romania 46 44 6N 27 24 E
Ostrov, U.S.S.R. 54 57 25N 28 20 E
Ostrów Lubelski 28 51 29N 22 51 E
Ostrów Mazowiecka 28 52 50N 21 51 E
Ostrów Wielkopolski 28 51 36N 17 44 E
Ostrowiec-Świętokrzyski 28 50 55N 21 22 E
Ostrozac 42 43 43N 17 49 E
Ostrzeszów 28 51 25N 17 52 E
Ostseebad-Külungsborn 24 54 10N 11 40 E
Ostuni 41 40 44N 17 34 E
Ōsum → 43 43 40N 24 50 E
Ōsumi → 44 40 40N 20 10 E
Ōsumi-Kaikyō 74 30 55N 131 0 E
Osuna 31 37 14N 5 8W
Oswego 114 43 29N 76 30W
Oswestry 12 52 52N 3 3W
Oświecim 27 50 2N 19 11 E
Otago □ 101 44 44 S 169 10 E
Otago Harb. 101 45 47 S 170 42 E
Ōtake 74 34 12N 132 13 E
Otaki 101 40 45 S 175 10 E
Otaru 74 43 10N 141 0 E
Otava → 26 49 26N 14 12 E
Otavalo 126 0 13N 78 20W
Otavi 92 19 40 S 17 24 E
Otchinjau 92 16 30 S 13 56 E
Otelec 42 45 36N 20 50 E
Otero de Rey 30 43 6N 7 36W
Othello 118 46 53N 119 8W
Othonoí 44 39 52N 19 22 E
Óthris, Óros 45 39 4N 22 42 E
Otira Gorge 101 42 53 S 171 33 E
Otis 116 40 12N 102 58W
Otjiwarongo 92 20 30 S 16 33 E
Otmuchów 28 50 28N 17 10 E
Otočac 39 44 53N 15 12 E
Otorohanga 101 38 12 S 175 14 E
Otoskwin → 106 52 13N 88 6W
Otosquen 109 53 17N 102 1W
Otra → 47 58 8N 8 1 E
Otranto 41 40 9N 18 28 E
Otranto, C. d' 41 40 7N 18 30 E
Otranto, Str. of 41 40 15N 18 40 E
Ōtsu 74 35 0N 135 50 E
Otta 47 61 46N 9 32 E
Otta → 47 61 46N 9 31 E
Ottapalam 70 10 46N 76 23 E
Ottawa, Can. 106 45 27N 75 42W
Ottawa, Ill., U.S.A. 116 41 20N 88 55W
Ottawa, Kans., U.S.A. 116 38 40N 95 6W
Ottawa = Outaouais → 106 45 27N 74 8W
Ottawa Is. 105 59 35N 80 10W
Ottélé 85 3 38N 11 19 E
Ottenby 49 56 15N 16 24 E
Otter L. 109 55 35N 104 39W
Otter Rapids, Ont., Can. 106 50 11N 81 39W
Otter Rapids, Sask., Can. 109 55 38N 104 44W
Otterberg 25 49 30N 7 46 E
Otterndorf 24 53 47N 8 52 E
Ottersheim 26 48 21N 14 12 E
Otterup 49 55 30N 10 22 E
Otterville 112 42 55N 80 36W
Otto Beit Bridge 91 15 59 S 28 56 E
Ottosdal 92 26 46 S 25 59 E
Ottoshoop 92 25 45 S 25 58 E
Ottsjö 48 63 13N 13 2 E
Ottumwa 116 41 0N 92 25W
Otu 85 8 14N 3 22 E
Otukpa (Al Owuho) 85 7 9N 7 41 E
Oturkpo 85 7 16N 8 8 E
Otway, Bahía 128 53 30 S 74 0W
Otway, C. 97 38 52 S 143 30 E
Otwock 28 52 5N 21 20 E
Ötz 26 47 13N 10 53 E
Ötz → 26 47 14N 10 50 E
Ötztaler Alpen 26 46 45N 11 0 E
Ou → 71 20 4N 102 13 E
Ou-Sammyaku 74 39 20N 140 35 E
Ouachita → 117 31 38N 91 49W
Ouachita, L. 117 34 40N 93 25W
Ouachita Mts. 117 34 50N 94 30W
Ouadâne 80 20 50N 11 40W
Ouadda 81 8 15N 22 20 E
Ouagadougou 85 12 25N 1 30W
Ouahigouya 84 13 31N 2 25W
Ouahila 82 27 50N 5 0W
Ouahran = Oran 82 35 49N 0 39W
Oualâta 84 17 20N 6 55W
Ouallene 82 24 41N 1 11 E
Ouanda Djallé 81 8 55N 22 53 E
Ouango 88 4 19N 22 30 E
Ouargla 83 31 59N 5 16 E
Ouarkziz, Djebel 82 28 50N 8 0W
Ouarzazate 82 30 55N 6 50W
Ouatagouna 85 15 11N 0 43 E
Oubangi → 88 1 0N 17 50 E
Oubarakai, O. → 83 27 20N 9 0 E
Ouche → 19 47 6N 5 16 E
Ouddorp 16 51 50N 3 57 E
Oude Rijn → 16 52 12N 4 24 E
Oudenaarde 16 50 50N 3 37 E
Oudon 18 47 22N 1 19W
Oudon → 18 47 38N 1 18 E
Oudtshoorn 92 33 35 S 22 14 E
Oued Zem 82 32 52N 6 34W
Ouellé 84 7 26N 4 1W
Ouenza 83 35 57N 8 4 E
Ouessa 84 11 4N 2 47W
Ouessant, Île d' 18 48 28N 5 6W
Ouesso 88 1 37N 16 5 E

Ouest, Pte. 107 49 52N 64 40W
Ouezzane 82 34 51N 5 35W
Ouidah 85 6 25N 2 0 E
Ouistreham 18 49 17N 0 18W
Oujda 82 34 41N 1 55W
Oujeft 80 20 2N 13 0W
Ould Yenjé 84 15 38N 12 16W
Ouled Djellal 83 34 28N 5 2 E
Ouled Naïl, Mts. des 82 34 30N 3 30 E
Oulmès 82 33 17N 6 0W
Oulu 50 65 1N 25 29 E
Oulu □ 50 65 10N 27 20 E
Oulujärvi 50 64 25N 27 15 E
Oulujoki → 50 65 1N 25 30 E
Oulx 38 45 2N 6 49 E
Oum Chalouba 81 15 48N 20 46 E
Oum-el-Bouaghi 83 35 55N 7 6 E
Oum el Ksi 82 29 4N 6 59W
Oum-er-Rbia, O. → 82 33 19N 8 21W
Oumè 84 6 21N 5 27W
Ounane, Dj. 83 25 4N 7 19 E
Ounguati 92 21 54 S 15 46 E
Ounianga-Kébir 81 19 4N 20 29 E
Ounianga Sérir 81 18 54N 19 51 E
Our → 16 49 55N 6 5 E
Ouray 119 38 3N 107 40W
Ourcq → 19 49 1N 3 1 E
Oureg, Oued el → 82 32 34N 2 10 E
Ouricuri 127 7 53 S 40 5W
Ourinhos 125 23 0 S 49 54W
Ourique 31 37 38N 8 16W
Ouro Fino 125 22 16 S 46 25W
Ouro Prêto 125 20 20 S 43 30W
Ouro Sogui 84 15 36N 13 19W
Oursi 85 14 41N 0 27W
Ourthe → 16 50 29N 5 35 E
Ouse 99 42 38 S 146 42 E
Ouse →, Sussex, U.K. 13 50 43N 0 3 E
Ouse →, Yorks., U.K. 12 54 3N 0 7 E
Oust 20 42 52N 1 13 E
Oust → 18 47 35N 2 6W
Outaouais → 106 45 27N 74 8W
Outardes → 107 49 24N 69 30W
Outat Oulad el Haj 82 33 22N 3 42W
Outer Hebrides 14 57 30N 7 40W
Outer I. 107 51 10N 58 35W
Outes 30 42 52N 8 55W
Outjo 92 20 5 S 16 7 E
Outlook, Can. 109 51 30N 107 0W
Outlook, U.S.A. 116 48 53N 104 46W
Outreau 19 50 40N 1 36 E
Ouvèze → 21 43 59N 4 51 E
Ouyen 97 35 1 S 142 22 E
Ouzouer-le-Marché 18 47 54N 1 32 E
Ovada 38 44 39N 8 40 E
Ovalau 101 17 40 S 178 48 E
Ovalle 124 30 33 S 71 18W
Ovar 30 40 51N 8 40W
Ovens → 100 36 2 S 146 12 E
Over Flakkee 16 51 45N 4 5 E
Overijssel □ 16 52 25N 6 35 E
Overpelt 16 51 12N 5 20 E
Overton 119 36 32N 114 31W
Övertorneå 50 66 23N 23 38 E
Overum 49 58 0N 16 20 E
Ovid 116 41 0N 102 17W
Ovidiopol 56 46 15N 30 30 E
Oviedo 30 43 25N 5 50W
Oviedo □ 30 43 20N 6 0W
Oviken 48 63 0N 14 23 E
Oviksfjällen 48 63 0N 13 49 E
Ovoro 85 5 26N 7 16 E
Övre Sirdal 47 58 48N 6 43 E
Ovruch 54 51 25N 28 45 E
Owaka 101 46 27 S 169 40 E
Owambo 92 17 20 S 16 30 E
Owase 74 34 7N 136 12 E
Owatonna 116 44 3N 93 10W
Owbeh 65 34 28N 63 10 E
Owego 114 42 6N 76 17W
Owen Falls 90 0 30N 33 5 E
Owen Sound 106 44 35N 80 55W
Owen Stanley Range 98 8 30 S 147 0 E
Owendo 88 0 17N 9 30 E
Owens L. 119 36 20N 118 0W
Owensboro 114 37 40N 87 5W
Owensville 116 38 20N 91 30W
Owerri 85 5 29N 7 0 E
Owl → 109 57 51N 92 44W
Owo 85 7 10N 5 39 E
Owosso 114 43 0N 84 10W
Owyhee 118 42 0N 116 3W
Owyhee → 118 43 46N 117 2W
Owyhee Res. 118 43 40N 117 16W
Ox Mts. 15 54 6N 9 0W
Oxberg 48 61 7N 14 11 E
Oxelösund 49 58 43N 17 15 E
Oxford, N.Z. 101 43 18 S 172 11 E
Oxford, U.K. 13 51 45N 1 15W
Oxford, Miss., U.S.A. 117 34 22N 89 30W
Oxford, N.C., U.S.A. 115 36 19N 78 36W
Oxford, Ohio, U.S.A. 114 39 30N 84 40W
Oxford □ 13 51 45N 1 15W
Oxford L. 109 54 51N 95 37W
Oxía 45 38 16N 21 5 E
Oxílithos 45 38 35N 24 7 E
Oxley 99 34 11 S 144 6 E
Oxnard 119 34 10N 119 14W
Oya 72 2 55N 111 55 E
Oyem 88 1 34N 11 31 E
Oyen 109 51 22N 110 28W
Öyeren 47 59 50N 11 15 E
Oykel → 14 57 55N 4 26W
Oymyakon 59 63 25N 142 44 E
Oyo 85 7 46N 3 56 E
Oyo □ 85 8 0N 3 30 E
Oyonnax 21 46 16N 5 40 E
Oyster B. 113 40 52N 73 32W
Øystese 47 60 22N 6 9 E
Ozamis (Mizamis) 73 8 15N 123 50 E
Ozark, Ala., U.S.A. 115 31 29N 85 39W
Ozark, Ark., U.S.A. 117 35 30N 93 50W
Ozark, Mo., U.S.A. 117 37 0N 93 15W
Ozark Plateau 117 37 20N 91 40W
Ozarks, L. of 116 38 10N 92 40W
Ózd 27 48 14N 20 15 E
Ozieri 40 40 35N 9 0 E
Ozimek 28 50 41N 18 11 E
Ozona 117 30 43N 101 11W
Ozorków 28 51 57N 19 16 E
Ozren 42 43 55N 18 29 E
Ozuluama 120 21 40N 97 50W
Ozun 46 45 47N 25 50 E

P

Pa 84 11 33N 3 19W
Pa-an 67 16 51N 97 40 E
Pa Sak → 71 15 30N 101 0 E
Paar → 25 48 13N 10 59 E
Paarl 92 33 45 S 18 56 E
Paatsi → 50 68 55N 29 0 E
Paauilo 110 20 3N 155 22W
Pab Hills 66 26 30N 66 45 E
Pabianice 28 51 40N 19 20 E
Pabna 69 24 1N 89 18 E
Pabo 90 3 1N 32 10 E
Pacaja → 127 1 56 S 50 50W
Pacaraima, Sierra 126 4 0N 62 30W
Pacasmayo 126 7 20 S 79 35W
Pacaudière, La 20 46 11N 3 52 E
Paceco 40 37 59N 12 32 E
Pachhar 68 24 40N 77 42 E
Pachino 41 36 43N 15 4 E
Pachora 68 20 38N 75 29 E
Pachuca 120 20 10N 98 40W
Pacific 108 54 48N 128 28W
Pacific-Antarctic Basin 95 46 0 S 95 0W
Pacific-Antarctic Ridge 95 43 0 S 115 0W
Pacific Grove 119 36 38N 121 58W
Pacific Ocean 94 10 0N 140 0W
Pacitan 73 8 12 S 111 7 E
Pacofi 108 53 0N 132 30W
Pacov 26 49 27N 15 0 E
Pacsa 27 46 44N 17 2 E
Paczków 28 50 28N 17 0 E
Padaido, Kepulauan 73 1 5 S 138 0 E
Padalarang 73 7 50 S 107 30 E
Padang 72 1 0 S 100 20 E
Padangpanjang 72 0 40 S 100 20 E
Padangsidempuan 72 1 30N 99 15 E
Padborg 49 54 49N 9 21 E
Paddockwood 109 53 30N 105 30W
Paderborn 24 51 42N 8 44 E
Padeşul 46 45 40N 22 22 E
Padina 46 44 50N 27 8 E
Padloping Island 105 67 0N 62 50W
Padmanabhapuram 70 8 16N 77 17 E
Pádova 39 45 24N 11 52 E
Padra 68 22 15N 73 7 E
Padrauna 69 26 54N 83 59 E
Padre I. 117 27 0N 97 20W
Padrón 30 42 41N 8 39W
Padstow 12 50 33N 4 57W
Padua = Pádova 39 45 24N 11 52 E
Paducah, Ky., U.S.A. 114 37 0N 88 40W
Paducah, Tex., U.S.A. 117 34 3N 100 16W
Padul 31 37 1N 3 38W
Padula 41 40 20N 15 40 E
Padwa 70 18 27N 82 47 E
Paeroa 101 37 23 S 175 41 E
Paesana 38 44 40N 7 18 E
Pag 39 44 30N 14 50 E
Paga 85 11 1N 1 8W
Pagadian 73 7 55N 123 30 E
Pagai Selatan 72 3 0 S 100 15W
Pagai Utara 72 2 35 S 100 0 E
Pagalu = Annobón 79 1 25 S 5 36 E
Pagastikós Kólpos 44 39 15N 23 0 E
Pagatan 72 3 33 S 115 59 E
Page, Ariz., U.S.A. 119 36 57N 111 27W
Page, N.D., U.S.A. 116 47 11N 97 37W
Paglieta 39 42 10N 14 30 E
Pagny-sur-Moselle 19 48 59N 6 2 E
Pago Pago 101 14 16 S 170 43W
Pagosa Springs 119 37 16N 107 4W
Pagwa River 106 50 2N 85 14W
Pahala 110 19 12N 155 25W
Pahang □ 71 3 40N 102 20 E
Pahang → 71 3 30N 103 9 E
Pahiatua 101 40 27 S 175 50 E
Pahokee 115 26 50N 80 40W
Pahrump 119 36 15N 116 0W
Paia 110 20 54N 156 22W
Paide 54 58 57N 25 31 E
Paignton 13 50 26N 3 33W
Päijänne, L. 51 61 30N 25 30 E
Pailin 71 12 46N 102 36 E
Paimbœuf 18 47 17N 2 0W
Paimpol 18 48 48N 3 4W
Painan 72 1 21 S 100 34 E
Painesville 114 41 42N 81 18W
Paint I. 109 55 28N 97 57W
Paint Rock 117 31 30N 99 56W
Painted Desert 119 36 0N 111 30W
Paintsville 114 37 50N 82 50W
Paisley, Can. 112 44 18N 81 16W
Paisley, U.K. 14 55 51N 4 27W
Paisley, U.S.A. 118 42 43N 120 40W
Paita 126 5 11 S 81 9W
Paiva → 30 41 4N 8 16W
Pajares 30 43 1N 5 46W
Pajares, Puerto de 30 43 0N 5 46W
Pajeczno 28 51 10N 19 0 E
Pak Lay 71 18 15N 101 27 E
Pakala 70 13 29N 79 8 E
Pakanbaru 72 0 30N 101 15 E
Pakaraima Mts. 126 6 0N 60 0W
Pakistan ■ 66 30 0N 70 0 E
Pakistan, East = Bangladesh ■ 67 24 0N 90 0 E
Pakokku 67 21 20N 95 0 E
Pakosc 28 52 48N 18 6 E
Pakpattan 68 30 25N 73 27 E
Pakrac 42 45 27N 17 12 E
Paks 27 46 38N 18 55 E
Pakse 71 15 5N 105 52 E
Paktīā □ 65 33 0N 69 15 E
Pakwach 90 2 28N 31 27 E
Pala, Chad 81 9 25N 15 5 E
Pala, Zaïre 90 6 45 S 29 30 E
Palabek 90 3 22N 32 33 E
Palacios 117 28 44N 96 12W
Palafrugell 32 41 55N 3 10 E
Palagiano 41 40 35N 17 0 E
Palagonía 41 37 20N 14 43 E
Palagruža 39 42 24N 16 15 E
Palaiokastron 45 35 12N 26 18 E
Palaiokhóra 45 35 16N 23 39 E
Pálairos 45 38 45N 20 51 E
Palais, Le 18 47 20N 3 10W
Palakol 70 16 31N 81 46 E
Palam 70 19 0N 77 0 E
Palamás 44 39 26N 22 4 E
Palamós 32 41 50N 3 10 E
Palampur 68 32 10N 76 30 E
Palana, Austral. 99 39 45 S 147 55 E
Palana, U.S.S.R. 59 59 10N 159 59 E
Palanan 73 17 8N 122 29 E
Palanan Pt. 73 17 17N 122 30 E
Palangkaraya 72 2 16 S 113 56 E
Palanpur 68 24 10N 72 25 E
Palapye 92 22 30 S 27 7 E
Palar → 70 12 27N 80 13 E
Palatka, U.S.A. 115 29 40N 81 40W
Palatka, U.S.S.R. 59 60 6N 150 54 E
* Palau Is. 94 7 30N 134 30 E
Palauig 73 15 26N 119 54 E
Palauk 71 13 10N 98 40 E
Palavas 20 43 32N 3 56 E
Palawan 72 9 30N 118 30 E
Palayancottai 70 8 45N 77 45 E
Palazzo San Gervásio 41 40 53N 15 58 E
Palazzolo Acreide 41 37 4N 14 54 E
Paldiski 54 59 23N 24 9 E
Pale 42 43 50N 18 38 E
Paleleh 73 1 10N 121 50 E
Palembang 72 3 0 S 104 50 E
Palencia 30 42 1N 4 34W
Palencia □ 30 42 31N 4 33W
Palermo, Italy 40 38 8N 13 20 E
Palermo, U.S.A. 118 39 30N 121 37W
Palestine, Asia 62 32 0N 35 0 E
Palestine, U.S.A. 117 31 42N 95 35W
Palestrina 40 41 50N 12 52 E
Paletwa 67 21 10N 92 50 E
Palghat 70 10 46N 76 42 E
Pali 68 25 50N 73 20 E
Palinuro, C. 41 40 1N 15 14 E
Palisade 116 40 21N 101 10W
Palitana 68 21 32N 71 49 E
Palizada 120 18 18N 92 8W
Palizzi 41 37 58N 15 59 E
Palk Bay 70 9 30N 79 15 E
Palk Strait 70 10 0N 79 45 E
Palkonda 70 18 36N 83 48 E
Palkonda Ra. 70 13 50N 79 20 E
Pallanza = Verbánia 38 45 50N 8 55 E
Pallasovka 55 50 4N 47 0 E
Palleru → 70 16 45N 80 2 E
Pallisa 90 1 12N 33 43 E
Pallu 68 28 59N 74 14 E
Palm Beach 115 26 46N 80 0W
Palm Is. 97 18 40 S 146 35 E
Palm Springs 119 33 51N 116 35W
Palma, Canary Is. 8 28 40N 17 50W
Palma, Mozam. 91 10 46 S 40 29 E
Palma → 127 12 33 S 47 52W
Palma, B. de 33 39 30N 2 39 E
Palma de Mallorca 32 39 35N 2 39 E
Palma del Río 31 37 43N 5 17W
Palma di Montechiaro 40 37 12N 13 46 E
Palma, La, Canary Is. 80 28 40N 17 50W
Palma, La, Panama 121 8 15N 78 0W
Palma, La, Spain 31 37 21N 6 38W
Palma Soriano 121 20 15N 76 0W
Palmahim 62 31 56N 34 44 E
Palmanova 39 45 54N 13 18 E
Palmares 127 8 41 S 35 28W
Palmarola 40 40 57N 12 50 E
Palmas 125 26 29 S 52 0W
Palmas, C. 84 4 27N 7 46W
Pálmas, G. di 40 39 0N 8 30 E
Palmdale 119 34 36N 118 7W
Palmeira dos Índios 127 9 25 S 36 37W
Palmeirinhas, Pta. das 88 9 2 S 12 57 E
Palmela 31 38 32N 8 57W
Palmer, Alaska, U.S.A. 104 61 35N 149 10W
Palmer, Mass., U.S.A. 113 42 9N 72 21W
Palmer →, N. Terr., Austral. 96 24 46 S 133 25 E
Palmer →, Queens., Austral. 98 15 34 S 142 26 E
Palmer Arch 5 64 15 S 65 0W
Palmer Lake 116 39 10N 104 52W
Palmer Land 5 73 0 S 60 0W
Palmerston 112 43 50N 80 51W
Palmerston, C. 97 21 32 S 149 29 E
Palmerston North 101 40 21 S 175 39 E
Palmerton 113 40 47N 75 36W
Palmetto 115 27 33N 82 33W
Palmi 41 38 21N 15 51 E
Palmira, Argent. 124 32 59 S 68 34W
Palmira, Colomb. 126 3 32N 76 16W
Palms 112 43 37N 82 47W
Palmyra, Mo., U.S.A. 116 39 45N 91 30W
Palmyra, N.Y., U.S.A. 112 42 5N 77 18W
Palmyra = Tudmur 64 34 30N 37 17 E
Palmyra Is. 95 5 52N 162 6W
Palni 70 10 30N 77 30 E
Palni Hills 70 10 14N 77 33 E
Palo Alto 119 37 25N 122 8W
Palo del Colle 41 41 4N 16 43 E
Paloma, La 124 30 35 S 71 0W
Palombara Sabina 39 42 4N 12 45 E
Palopo 73 3 0 S 120 16 E
Palos, Cabo de 33 37 38N 0 40W
Palouse 118 46 59N 117 5W
Palparara 98 24 47 S 141 28 E
Pålsboda 49 59 3N 15 22 E
Palu, Indon. 73 1 0 S 119 52 E
Palu, Turkey 64 38 45N 40 0 E
Paluan 73 13 26N 120 29 E
Palwal 68 28 8N 77 19 E
Pama 85 11 19N 0 44 E
Pamamaroo, L. 100 32 17 S [illegible] 28 E
Pamanukan 73 6 16 S 107 49 E
Pamban I. 70 9 15N 79 20 E
Pamekasan 73 7 10 S 113 29 E
Pameungpeuk 73 7 38 S 107 44 E
Pamiers 20 43 7N 1 39 E
Pamir 58 37 40N 73 0 E
Pamlico → 115 35 25N 76 30W
Pamlico Sd. 115 35 20N 76 0W
Pampa 117 35 35N 100 58W
Pampa de las Salinas 124 32 1 S 66 58W
Pampa, La □ 124 36 50 S 66 0W
Pampanua 73 4 16 S 120 8 E
Pamparato 38 44 16N 7 54 E
Pampas, Argent. 124 35 0 S 63 0W
Pampas, Peru 126 12 20 S 74 50W
Pamplona, Colomb. 126 7 23N 72 39W
Pamplona, Spain 32 42 48N 1 38W
Pampoenpoort 92 31 3 S 22 40 E
Pana 116 39 25N 89 10W
Panaca 119 37 51N 114 23W
Panagyurishte 43 42 30N 24 15 E
Panaitan 73 6 35 S 105 10 E
Panaji (Panjim) 70 15 25N 73 50 E
Panamá 121 9 0N 79 25W
Panama ■ 121 8 48N 79 55W
Panama Canal 121 9 10N 79 37W
Panama City 115 30 10N 85 41W
Panamá, Golfo de 121 8 4N 79 20W
Panamint Mts. 119 36 30N 117 20W
Panão 126 9 55 S 75 55W
Panarea 41 38 38N 15 3 E
Panaro → 38 44 55N 11 25 E
Panarukan 73 7 40 S 113 52 E
Panay 73 11 10N 122 30 E
Panay, G. 73 11 0N 122 30 E
Pancake Ra. 119 38 30N 116 0W
Pančevo 42 44 52N 20 41 E
Panciu 46 45 54N 27 8 E
Panco 73 8 42 S 118 40 E
Pancorbo, Paso 32 42 32N 3 5W
Pandan 73 11 45N 122 10 E
Pandeglang 73 6 25 S 106 0 E
Pandharpur 70 17 41N 75 20 E
Pandhurna 68 21 36N 78 35 E
Pandilla 32 41 32N 3 43W
Pando 125 34 44 S 56 0W
Pando, L. = Hope L. 99 28 24 S 139 18 E
Panevezys 54 55 42N 24 25 E
Panfilov 58 44 10N 80 0 E
Panfilovo 55 50 25N 42 46 E
Pang-Long 67 23 11N 98 45 E
Pang-Yang 67 22 7N 98 48 E
Panga 90 1 52N 26 18 E
Pangaíon Óros 44 40 50N 24 0 E
Pangalanes, Canal des 93 22 48 S 47 50 E
Pangani 90 5 25 S 38 58 E
Pangani □ 90 5 25 S 39 0 E
Pangani → 90 5 26 S 38 58 E
Pangfou = Bengbu 77 32 56N 117 20 E
Pangil 90 3 10 S 26 35 E
Pangkah, Tanjung 73 6 51 S 112 33 E
Pangkalanberandan 72 4 1N 98 20 E
Pangkalanbuun 72 2 41 S 111 37 E
Pangkalansusu 72 4 2N 98 13 E
Pangkoh 72 3 5 S 114 8 E
Pangnirtung 105 66 8N 65 54W
Pangrango 73 6 46 S 107 1 E
Panguitch 119 37 52N 112 30W
Pangutaran Group 73 6 18N 120 34 E
Panhandle 117 35 23N 101 23W
Pani Mines 68 22 29N 73 50 E
Pania-Mutombo 90 5 11 S 23 51 E
Panipat 68 29 25N 77 2 E
Panjal Range 68 32 30N 76 50 E
Panjgur 66 27 0N 64 5 E
Panjim = Panaji 70 15 25N 73 50 E
Panjinad Barrage 65 29 22N 71 15 E
Pankajene 73 4 46 S 119 34 E
Pankalpinang 72 2 0 S 106 0 E
Pankshin 85 9 16N 9 25 E
Panna 69 24 40N 80 15 E
Panna Hills 69 24 40N 81 15 E
Pannuru 70 16 5N 80 34 E
Panorama 125 21 21 S 51 51W
Panruti 70 11 46N 79 35 E
Panshan 76 41 3N 122 2 E
Panshi 76 42 58N 126 5 E
Pantano 119 32 0N 110 32W
Pantar 73 8 28 S 124 10 E
Pantelleria 40 36 52N 12 0 E
Pantón 30 42 31N 7 37W
Pánuco 120 22 0N 98 15W
Panyam 85 9 27N 9 8 E
Panyu 77 22 51N 113 20 E
Páola 41 39 21N 16 2 E
Paola 116 38 36N 94 50W
Paonia 119 38 56N 107 37W
Paoting = Baoding 76 38 50N 115 28 E
Paot'ou = Baotou 76 40 32N 110 2 E
Paoua 88 7 9N 16 20 E
Papá 27 47 22N 17 30 E
Papagayo → 120 16 36N 99 43W
Papagayo, Golfo de 121 10 30N 85 50W
Papagni → 70 15 35N 77 45 E
Papakura 101 37 4 S 174 59 E
Papantla 120 20 30N 97 30W
Papar 72 5 45N 116 0 E
Pápas, Ákra 45 38 13N 21 20 E
Papenburg 24 53 7N 7 25 E
Papigochic → 120 29 9N 109 40W
Paposo 124 25 0 S 70 30W
Papua, Gulf of 98 9 0 S 144 50 E
Papua New Guinea ■ 94 8 0 S 145 0 E

* Renamed Belau

apuča 39 44 22N 15 30 E
apudo 124 32 29 S 71 27W
apuk 42 45 30N 17 30 E
apun 67 18 0N 97 30 E
ará = Belém 127 1 20 S 48 30W
ará □ 127 3 20 S 52 0W
arábita 41 40 3N 18 8 E
araburdoo 96 23 14 S 117 32 E
aracatu 127 17 10 S 46 50W
arachilna 99 31 10 S 138 21 E
arachinar 66 33 55N 70 5 E
araćin 42 43 54N 21 27 E
aradas 31 37 18N 5 29W
aradela 30 42 44N 7 37W
aradip 69 20 15N 86 35 E
aradise 118 47 27N 114 17W
aradise → 107 53 27N 57 19W
aradise Valley 118 41 30N 117 28W
arado 73 8 42 S 118 30 E
aradyz 28 51 19N 20 2 E
aragould 117 36 5N 90 30W
aragua → 126 6 55N 62 55W
aragua, La 126 6 50N 63 20W
araguaçu → 127 12 45 S 38 54W
araguaçu Paulista 125 22 22 S 50 35W
araguaná, Pen. de 126 12 0N 70 0W
araguarí 124 25 36 S 57 0W
araguarí □ 124 26 0 S 57 10W
araguay ■ 124 23 0 S 57 0W
araguay → 124 27 18 S 58 38W
araíba = João Pessoa 127 7 10 S 35 0W
araíba □ 127 7 0 S 36 0W
araíba do Sul → 125 21 37 S 41 3W
arainen 51 60 18N 22 18 E
arakhino Paddubye 54 58 26N 33 10 E
arakou 85 9 25N 2 40 E
arálion-Astrous 45 37 25N 22 45 E
aramagudi 70 9 31N 78 39 E
aramaribo 127 5 50N 55 10W
aramithiá 44 39 30N 20 35 E
aramushir, Ostrov 59 50 24N 156 0 E
aran → 62 30 20N 35 10 E
araná 124 31 45 S 60 30W
aranã 127 12 30 S 47 48W
araná □ 125 24 30 S 51 0W
araná → 124 33 43 S 59 15W
aranaguá 125 25 30 S 48 30W
aranaíba → 127 20 6 S 51 4W
aranapanema → 125 22 40 S 53 9W
aranapiacaba, Serra do 125 24 31 S 48 35W
aranavaí 125 23 4 S 52 56W
arang, Jolo, Phil. 73 5 55N 120 54 E
arang, Mindanao, Phil. 73 7 23N 124 16 E
arapóla 45 36 55N 23 27 E
araspóri, Ákra 45 35 55N 27 15 E
aratinga 127 12 40 S 43 10W
aratoo 99 32 42 S 139 40 E
arattah 99 42 22 S 147 23 E
aray-le-Monial 21 46 27N 4 7 E
arbati → 68 25 50N 76 30 E
arbhani 68 19 8N 76 52 E
archim 24 53 25N 11 50 E
arczew 28 51 40N 22 52 E
ardes Hanna 32 32 28N 34 57 E
ardilla 30 41 33N 3 43W
ardo →, Bahia, Brazil 127 15 40 S 39 0W
ardo →, Mato Grosso, Brazil 125 21 46 S 52 9W
ardo →, São Paulo, Brazil 127 20 10 S 48 38W
ardubice 26 50 3N 15 45 E
are 73 7 43 S 112 12 E
are □ 90 4 10 S 38 0 E
are Mts. 90 4 0 S 37 45 E
arecis, Serra dos 126 13 0 S 60 0W
aredes de Nava 30 42 9N 4 42W
aren 59 62 30N 163 15 E
arent 106 47 55N 74 35W
arent, Lac. 106 48 31N 77 1W
arentis-en-Born 20 44 21N 1 4W
arepare 73 4 0 S 119 40 E
arfino 54 57 59N 31 34 E
arfuri 93 22 28 S 31 17 E
arguba 52 62 20N 34 27 E
arham 113 44 39N 76 43W
ariaguán 126 8 51N 64 34W
ariaman 72 0 47 S 100 11 E
aricutín, Cerro 120 19 28N 102 15W
arigi, Java, Indon. 73 7 42 S 108 29 E
arigi, Sulawesi, Indon. 73 0 50 S 120 5 E
arika 126 6 50N 58 20W
arima, Serra 126 2 30N 64 0W
arinari 126 4 35 S 74 25W
arincea 46 46 27N 27 9 E
arîng 46 45 20N 23 37 E
arintins 127 2 40 S 56 50W
ariparit Kyun 67 14 55 S 93 45 E
aris, Can. 106 43 12N 80 25W
aris, France 19 48 50N 2 20 E
aris, Idaho, U.S.A. 118 42 13N 111 30W
aris, Ky., U.S.A. 114 38 12N 84 12W
aris, Tenn., U.S.A. 115 36 20N 88 20W
aris, Tex., U.S.A. 117 33 40N 95 30W
aris, Ville de □ 19 48 50N 2 20 E
arish 113 43 24N 76 9W
ariti 73 10 15 S 123 45 E
ark City 118 40 42N 111 35W
ark Falls 116 45 58N 90 27W
ark Range 118 40 0N 106 30W
ark Rapids 116 46 56N 95 0W
ark River 116 48 25N 97 43W
ark Rynie 93 30 25 S 30 45 E
ark View 119 36 45N 106 37W
arker, Ariz., U.S.A. 119 34 8N 114 16W
arker, S.D., U.S.A. 116 43 25N 97 7W
arker Dam 119 34 13N 114 5W
arkersburg 114 39 18N 81 31W
arkerview 109 51 21N 103 18W
arkes, A.C.T., Austral. 97 35 18 S 149 8 E
arkes, N.S.W., Austral. 97 33 9 S 148 11 E
arkside 109 53 10N 106 33W
arkston 116 43 25N 98 0W
arksville 108 49 20N 124 21W
arlakimedi 70 18 45N 84 5 E
Parma, Italy 38 44 50N 10 20 E
Parma, Idaho, U.S.A. 118 43 49N 116 59W
Parma, Ohio, U.S.A. 112 41 25N 81 42W
Parma → 38 44 56N 10 26 E
Parnaguá 127 10 10 S 44 38W
Parnaíba, Piauí, Brazil 127 2 54 S 41 47W
Parnaíba, São Paulo, Brazil 127 19 34 S 51 14W
Parnaíba → 127 3 0 S 41 50W
Parnassós 45 38 35N 22 30 E
Párnis 45 38 14N 23 45 E
Párnon Óros 45 37 15N 22 45 E
Pärnu 54 58 28N 24 33 E
Parola 68 20 47N 75 7 E
Paroo → 97 31 28 S 143 32 E
Paroo Chan. 97 30 50 S 143 35 E
Páros, Greece 45 37 5N 25 9 E
Páros, Greece 45 37 5N 25 12 E
Parowan 119 37 54N 112 56W
Parpaillon 21 44 30N 6 40 E
Parral 124 36 10 S 71 52W
Parramatta 99 33 48 S 151 1 E
Parras 120 25 30N 102 20W
Parrett → 13 51 7N 2 58W
Parris I. 115 32 20N 80 30W
Parrsboro 107 45 30N 64 25W
Parry Is. 4 77 0N 110 0W
Parry Sound 106 45 20N 80 0W
Parsberg 25 49 10N 11 43 E
Parseta → 28 54 11N 15 34 E
Parshall 116 47 56N 102 11W
Parsnip → 108 55 10N 123 2W
Parsons 117 37 20N 95 17W
Partabpur 70 20 0N 80 42 E
Partanna 40 37 43N 12 51 E
Partapgarh 68 24 2N 74 40 E
Parthenay 18 46 38N 0 16W
Partinico 40 38 3N 13 6 E
Partur 70 19 40N 76 14 E
Paru → 127 1 33 S 52 38W
Parur 70 10 13N 76 14 E
Paruro 126 13 45 S 71 50W
Parván □ 65 35 0N 69 0 E
Parvatipuram 70 18 50N 83 25 E
Parys 92 26 52 S 27 29 E
Pas-de-Calais □ 19 50 30N 2 30 E
Pasadena, Calif., U.S.A. 119 34 5N 118 9W
Pasadena, Tex., U.S.A. 117 29 45N 95 14W
Pasaje 126 3 23 S 79 50W
Pasaje → 124 25 39 S 63 56W
Pascagoula 117 30 21N 88 30W
Pascagoula → 117 30 21N 88 35W
Paşcani 46 47 14N 26 45 E
Pasco 118 46 10N 119 0W
Pasco, Cerro de 126 10 45 S 76 10W
Pasewalk 24 53 30N 14 0 E
Pasfield L. 109 58 24N 105 20W
Pasha → 54 60 29N 32 55 E
Pashmakli = Smolyan 43 41 36N 24 38 E
Pasing 25 48 9N 11 27 E
Pasir Mas 71 6 2N 102 8 E
Pasir Puteh 71 5 50N 102 24 E
Pasirian 73 8 13 S 113 8 E
Pasłeka → 28 54 26N 19 46 E
Pasley, C. 96 33 52 S 123 35 E
Pašman 39 43 58N 15 20 E
Pasni 66 25 15N 63 27 E
Paso de Indios 128 43 55 S 69 0W
Paso de los Libres 124 29 44 S 57 10W
Paso de los Toros 124 32 45 S 56 30W
Paso Robles 119 35 40N 120 45W
Paspébiac 107 48 3N 65 17W
Pasrur 68 32 16N 74 43 E
Passage West 15 51 52N 8 20W
Passaic 113 40 50N 74 8W
Passau 25 48 34N 13 27 E
Passero, C. 41 36 42N 15 8 E
Passo Fundo 125 28 10 S 52 20W
Passos 127 20 45 S 46 37W
Passow 24 53 13N 14 10 E
Passy 21 45 55N 6 41 E
Pastaza → 126 4 50 S 76 52W
Pastęk 28 54 3N 19 41 E
Pasto 126 1 13N 77 17W
Pastrana 32 40 27N 2 53W
Pasuruan 73 7 40 S 112 44 E
Pasym 28 53 48N 20 49 E
Pásztó 27 47 52N 19 43 E
Patagonia, Argent. 128 45 0 S 69 0W
Patagonia, U.S.A. 119 31 35N 110 45W
Patan, Gujarat, India 70 17 22N 73 57 E
Patan, Maharashtra, India 68 23 54N 72 14 E
Patani 73 0 20N 128 50 E
Pataudi 68 28 18N 76 48 E
Patay 19 48 2N 1 40 E
Patchewollock 99 35 22 S 142 12 E
Patchogue 114 40 46N 73 1W
Patea 101 39 45 S 174 30 E
Pategi 85 8 50N 5 45 E
Patensie 92 33 46 S 24 49 E
Paternò 41 37 34N 14 53 E
Paternoster, Kepulauan 72 7 5 S 118 15 E
Pateros 118 48 4N 119 58W
Paterson, Austral. 100 32 37 S 151 39 E
Paterson, U.S.A. 114 40 55N 74 10W
Pathankot 68 32 18N 75 45 E
Pathfinder Res. 118 42 30N 107 0W
Pati 73 6 45 S 111 3 E
Patiala 68 30 23N 76 26 E
Patine Kouka 84 12 45N 13 45W
Patkai Bum 67 27 0N 95 30 E
Pátmos 45 37 21N 26 36 E
Patna 69 25 35N 85 12 E
Patonga 90 2 45N 33 15 E
Patos de Minas 127 18 35 S 46 32W
Patos, Lag. dos 125 31 20 S 51 0 E
Patosi 44 40 42N 19 38 E
Patquia 124 25 30N 102 11W
Pátrai 45 38 14N 21 47 E
Pátraikós, Kólpos 45 38 17N 21 30 E
Patrocínio 127 18 57 S 47 0W
Patta 90 2 10 S 41 0 E
Pattada 40 40 35N 9 7 E
Pattanapuram 70 9 6N 76 50 E
Pattani 71 6 48N 101 15 E
Patten 107 45 59N 68 28W
Patterson, Calif., U.S.A. 119 37 30N 121 9W
Patterson, La., U.S.A. 117 29 44N 91 20W
Patti, India 68 31 17N 74 54 E
Patti, Italy 41 38 8N 14 57 E
Pattoki 68 31 5N 73 52 E
Patton 112 40 38N 78 40W
Pattukkottai 70 10 25N 79 20 E
Patuakhali 69 22 20N 90 25 E
Patuca → 121 15 50N 84 18W
Patuca, Punta 121 15 49N 84 14W
Pátzcuaro 120 19 30N 101 40W
Pau 20 43 19N 0 25W
Pau, Gave de 20 43 33N 1 12W
Pauillac 20 45 11N 0 46W
Pauini → 126 1 42 S 62 50W
Pauk 67 21 27N 94 30 E
Paul I. 107 56 30N 61 20W
Paulhan 20 43 33N 3 28 E
Paulis = Isiro 90 2 47N 27 37 E
Paulistana 127 8 9 S 41 9W
Paullina 116 42 55N 95 40W
Paulo Afonso 127 9 21 S 38 15W
Paulpietersburg 93 27 23 S 30 50 E
Pauls Valley 117 34 40N 97 17W
Pauni 69 20 48N 79 40 E
Pavelets 55 53 49N 39 14 E
Pavia 38 45 10N 9 10 E
Pavlikeni 43 43 14N 25 20 E
Pavlodar 58 52 33N 77 0 E
Pavlograd 56 48 30N 35 52 E
Pavlovo, Gorkiy, U.S.S.R. 55 55 58N 43 5 E
Pavlovo, Yakut A.S.S.R., U.S.S.R. 59 63 5N 115 25 E
Pavlovsk 55 50 26N 40 5 E
Pavlovskaya 57 46 17N 39 47 E
Pavlovskiy-Posad 55 55 47N 38 42 E
Pavullo nel Frignano 38 44 20N 10 50 E
Pawhuska 117 36 40N 96 25W
Pawling 113 41 35N 73 37W
Pawnee 117 36 24N 96 50W
Pawnee City 116 40 8N 96 10W
Pawtucket 114 41 51N 71 22W
Paximádhia 45 35 0N 24 35 E
Paxoí 44 39 14N 20 12 E
Paxton, Ill., U.S.A. 114 40 25N 88 7W
Paxton, Nebr., U.S.A. 116 41 12N 101 27W
Paya Bakri 71 2 3N 102 44 E
Payakumbah 72 0 20 S 100 35 E
Payerne 25 46 49N 6 56 E
Payette 118 44 0N 117 0W
Paymogo 31 37 44N 7 21W
Payne L. 105 59 30N 74 30W
Paynesville, Liberia 84 6 20N 10 45W
Paynesville, U.S.A. 116 45 21N 94 44W
Pays Basque 20 43 15N 1 0W
Paysandú 124 32 19 S 58 8W
Payson, Ariz., U.S.A. 119 34 17N 111 15W
Payson, Utah, U.S.A. 118 40 8N 111 41W
Paz → 120 13 44N 90 10W
Paz, Bahía de la 120 24 15N 110 25W
Paz, La, Entre Ríos, Argent. 124 30 50 S 59 45W
Paz, La, San Luis, Argent. 124 33 30 S 67 20W
Paz, La, Boliv. 126 16 20 S 68 10W
Paz, La, Hond. 120 14 20N 87 47W
Paz, La, Mexico 120 24 10N 110 20W
Pazar 64 41 10N 40 50 E
Pazardzhik 43 42 12N 24 20 E
Pazin 39 45 14N 13 56 E
Pčinja → 42 41 50N 21 45 E
Pe Ell 118 46 30N 123 18W
Peabody 113 42 31N 70 56W
Peace → 108 59 0N 111 25W
Peace Point 108 59 7N 112 27W
Peace River 108 56 15N 117 18W
Peach Springs 119 35 36N 113 30W
Peak Downs 98 22 14 S 148 0 E
Peak Hill 99 32 47 S 148 11 E
Peak Range 97 22 50 S 148 20 E
Peak, The 12 53 24N 1 53W
Peake 99 35 25 S 140 0 E
Peale Mt. 119 38 25N 109 12W
Pearce 119 31 57N 109 56W
Pearl → 117 30 23N 89 45W
Pearl Banks 70 8 45N 79 45 E
Pearl City 110 21 24N 158 0W
Pearsall 117 28 55N 99 8W
Pearse I. 108 54 52N 130 14W
Peary Land 4 82 40N 33 0W
Pease → 117 34 12N 99 7W
Pebane 91 17 10 S 38 8 E
Pebas 126 3 10 S 71 46W
Peč 42 42 40N 20 17 E
Péccioli 38 43 32N 10 43 E
Pechea 46 45 36N 27 49 E
Pechenezhin 56 48 30N 24 48 E
Pechenga 52 69 30N 31 25 E
Pechnezhskoye Vdkhr. 55 50 0N 37 10 E
Pechora → 52 68 13N 54 15 E
Pechorskaya Guba 52 68 40N 54 0 E
Pechory 54 57 48N 27 40 E
Pecica 42 46 10N 21 3 E
Pečka 42 44 18N 19 33 E
Pécora, C. 40 39 28N 8 23 E
Pecos 117 31 25N 103 35W
Pecos → 117 29 42N 102 30W
Pécs 27 46 5N 18 15 E
Peddapalli 70 18 40N 79 24 E
Peddapuram 70 17 6N 8 13 E
Pedra Azul 127 16 2 S 41 17W
Pedreiras 127 4 32 S 44 40W
Pedrera, La 126 1 18 S 69 43W
Pedro Afonso 127 9 0 S 48 10W
Pedro Cays 121 17 5N 77 48W
Pedro de Valdivia 124 22 55 S 69 38W
Pedro Juan Caballero 125 22 30 S 55 40W
Pedro Miguel Locks 120 9 1N 79 36W
Pedro Muñoz 33 39 25N 2 56W
Pedrógão Grande 30 39 55N 8 9W
Peduyim 62 31 20N 34 37 E
Peebinga 99 34 52 S 140 57 E
Peebles 14 55 40N 3 12W
Peekskill 114 41 18N 73 57W
Peel 12 54 14N 4 40W
Peel →, Austral. 99 30 50 S 150 29 E
Peel →, Can. 104 67 0N 135 0W
Peene → 24 54 9N 13 46 E
Peera Peera Poolanna L. 99 26 30 S 138 0 E
Peers 108 53 40N 116 0W
Pegasus Bay 101 43 20 S 173 10 E
Peggau 26 47 12N 15 21 E
Pegnitz 25 49 45N 11 33 E
Pegnitz → 25 49 29N 10 59 E
Pego 33 38 51N 0 8W
Pegu Yoma 67 19 0N 96 0 E
Pehčevo 42 41 41N 22 55 E
Pehuajó 124 35 45 S 62 0W
Peine, Chile 124 23 45 S 68 8W
Peine, Ger. 24 52 19N 10 12 E
Peip'ing = Beijing 76 39 55N 116 20 E
Peiss 25 47 58N 11 47 E
Peissenberg 25 47 48N 11 4 E
Peitz 24 51 50N 14 23 E
Peixe 127 12 0 S 48 40W
Pek → 42 44 45N 21 29 E
Pekalongan 73 6 53 S 109 40 E
Pekan 71 3 30N 103 25 E
Pekin 116 40 35N 89 40W
Peking = Beijing 76 39 55N 116 20 E
Pelabuhan Ratu, Teluk 73 7 5 S 106 30 E
Pelabuhanratu 73 7 0 S 106 32 E
Pélagos 44 39 17N 24 4 E
Pelaihari 72 3 55 S 114 45 E
Pelat, Mont 21 44 16N 6 42 E
Pełczyce 28 53 3N 15 16 E
Peleaga 46 45 22N 22 55 E
Pelee I. 106 41 47N 82 40W
Pelée, Mt. 121 14 48N 61 0W
Pelee, Pt. 106 41 54N 82 31W
Pelekech, mt. 90 3 52N 35 8 E
Peleng 73 1 20 S 123 30 E
Pelham 115 31 5N 84 6W
Pelhřimov 26 49 24N 15 12 E
Pelican L. 109 52 28N 100 20W
Pelican Narrows 109 55 10N 102 56W
Pelican Portage 108 55 51N 112 35W
Pelican Rapids 109 52 45N 100 42W
Peljesac 42 42 55N 17 25 E
Pelkosenniemi 50 67 6N 27 28 E
Pella, Greece 44 40 46N 22 23 E
Pella, U.S.A. 116 41 30N 93 0W
Pélla □ 44 40 52N 22 0 E
Péllaro 41 38 1N 15 40 E
Pellworm 24 54 30N 8 40 E
Pelly → 104 62 47N 137 19W
Pelly Bay 105 68 38N 89 50W
Pelly L. 104 66 0N 102 0W
Peloponnes = Pelóponnisos □ 45 37 10N 22 0 E
Pelopónnisos □ 45 37 10N 22 0 E
Peloritani, Monti 41 38 2N 15 25 E
Peloro, C. 41 38 15N 15 40 E
Pelorus Sound 101 40 59 S 173 59 E
Pelotas 125 31 42 S 52 23W
Pelòvo 43 43 26N 24 17 E
Pelvoux, Massif de 21 44 52N 6 20 E
Pemalang 73 6 53 S 109 23 E
Pematang 72 0 12 S 102 4 E
Pematangsiantar 72 2 57N 99 5 E
Pemba, Mozam. 91 12 58 S 40 30 E
Pemba, Tanz. 90 5 0 S 39 45 E
Pemba, Zambia 91 16 30 S 27 28 E
Pemba Channel 90 5 0 S 39 37 E
Pemberton, Austral. 96 34 30 S 116 0 E
Pemberton, Can. 108 50 25N 122 50W
Pembina 108 49 58N 97 15W
Pembina → 109 49 0N 98 12W
Pembine 114 45 38N 87 59W
Pembino 116 48 58N 97 15W
Pembroke, Can. 106 45 50N 77 7W
Pembroke, U.K. 13 51 41N 4 57W
Pembroke, U.S.A. 115 32 5N 81 32W
Pen-y-Ghent 12 54 10N 2 15W
Peña de Francia, Sierra de 30 40 32N 6 10W
Peña, Sierra de la 32 42 32N 0 45W
Penafiel 30 41 12N 8 17W
Peñafiel 30 41 35N 4 7W
Peñaflor 31 37 43N 5 21W
Peñalara, Pico 30 40 51N 3 57W
Penamacôr 30 40 10N 7 10W
Penang = Pinang 71 5 25N 100 15 E
Penápolis 125 21 30 S 50 0W
Peñaranda de Bracamonte 30 40 53N 5 13W
Peñarroya-Pueblonuevo 31 38 19N 5 16W
Peñas, C. de 30 43 42N 5 52W
Peñas de San Pedro 33 38 44N 2 0W
Penas, G. de 128 47 0 S 75 0W
Peñausende 30 41 17N 5 52W
Pench'i = Benxi 76 41 20N 123 48 E
Pend Oreille → 118 49 4N 117 37W
Pend Oreille, L. 118 48 0N 116 30W
Pendálofon 44 40 14N 21 12 E
Pendelikón 45 38 10N 23 53 E
Pendembu 84 9 7N 12 14W
Pendleton 118 45 35N 118 50W
Penedo 127 10 15 S 36 36W
Penetanguishene 106 44 50N 79 55W
Pengalengan 73 7 9 S 107 30 E
Penge, Kasai Oriental, Congo 90 5 30 S 24 33 E
Penge, Kivu, Congo 90 4 27 S 28 25 E
Penglai 76 37 48N 120 42 E
Pengshui 77 29 17N 108 12 E
Penguin 99 41 8 S 146 6 E
Penhalonga 91 18 52 S 32 40 E
Peniche 31 39 19N 9 22W
Penicuik 14 55 50N 3 14W
Penida 72 8 45 S 115 30 E
Peñíscola 32 40 22N 0 24 E
Penmarch 18 47 49N 4 21W
Penmarch, Pte. de 18 47 48N 4 22W
Pennabilli 39 43 50N 12 17 E
Pennant 109 50 32N 108 14W
Penne 39 42 28N 13 56 E

Pennel Glacier **5** 69 20 S 157 27 E
Penner → **70** 14 35N 80 10 E
Pennine, Alpi **38** 46 4N 7 30 E
Pennines **12** 54 50N 2 20W
Pennino, Mte. **39** 43 6N 12 54 E
Pennsylvania □ **114** 40 50N 78 0W
Penny **108** 53 51N 121 20W
Pennyan **114** 42 39N 77 7W
Peno **54** 57 2N 32 49 E
Penola **97** 37 25 S 140 21 E
Penong **96** 31 59 S 133 5 E
Penonomé **121** 8 31N 80 21W
Penrhyn Is. **95** 9 0 S 158 30W
Penrith, Austral. **97** 33 43 S 150 38 E
Penrith, U.K. **12** 54 40N 2 45W
Pensacola **115** 30 30N 87 10W
Pensacola Mts. **5** 84 0 S 40 0W
Pense **109** 50 25N 104 59W
Penshurst **99** 37 49 S 142 20 E
Penticton **108** 49 30N 119 38W
Pentland **97** 20 32 S 145 25 E
Pentland Firth **14** 58 43N 3 10W
Pentland Hills **14** 55 48N 3 25W
Penukonda **70** 14 5N 77 38 E
Penylan L. **109** 61 50N 106 20W
Penza **55** 53 15N 45 5 E
Penzance **13** 50 7N 5 32W
Penzberg **25** 47 46N 11 23 E
Penzhino **59** 63 30N 167 55 E
Penzhinskaya Guba **59** 61 30N 163 0 E
Penzlin **24** 53 32N 13 6 E
Peoria, Ariz., U.S.A. **119** 33 40N 112 15W
Peoria, Ill., U.S.A. **116** 40 40N 89 40W
Pepperwood **118** 40 23N 124 0W
Peqini **44** 41 4N 19 44 E
Pera Hd. **98** 12 55 S 141 37 E
Perabumilih **72** 3 27 S 104 15 E
Perak → **71** 5 10N 101 4 E
Perakhóra **45** 38 2N 22 56 E
Perales de Alfambra **32** 40 38N 1 0W
Perales del Puerto **30** 40 10N 6 40W
Peralta **32** 42 21N 1 49W
Pérama **45** 35 20N 24 40 E
Perast **42** 42 31N 18 47 E
Percé **107** 48 31N 64 13W
Perche **18** 48 31N 1 1 E
Perche, Collines du **18** 48 30N 0 40 E
Percy **18** 48 55N 1 11W
Percy Is. **98** 21 39 S 150 16 E
Pereira **126** 4 49N 75 43W
Perekerten **99** 34 55 S 143 40 E
Perekop **56** 46 10N 33 42 E
Pereslavi-Zalesskiy **55** 56 45N 38 50 E
Pereyaslav Khmelnitskiy **54** 50 3N 31 28 E
Pérez, I. **120** 22 24N 89 42W
Perg **26** 48 15N 14 38 E
Pergamino **124** 33 52 S 60 30W
Pérgine Valsugano **39** 46 4N 11 15 E
Pérgola **39** 43 35N 12 50 E
Perham **116** 46 36N 95 36W
Perhentian, Kepulauan **71** 5 54N 102 42 E
Periam **42** 46 2N 20 59 E
Péribonca → **107** 48 45N 72 5W
Péribonca, L. **107** 50 1N 71 10W
Perico **124** 24 20 S 65 5W
Pericos **120** 25 3N 107 42W
Périers **18** 49 11N 1 25W
Périgord **20** 45 0N 0 40 E
Périgueux **20** 45 10N 0 42 E
Perijá, Sierra de **126** 9 30N 73 3W
Peristéra **45** 39 15N 23 58 E
Periyakulam **70** 10 5N 77 30 E
Periyar → **70** 10 15N 76 10 E
Periyar, L. **70** 9 25N 77 10 E
Perkam, Tg. **73** 1 35 S 137 50 E
Perković **39** 43 41N 16 10 E
Perlas, Arch. de las **121** 8 41N 79 7W
Perlas, Punta de **121** 12 30N 83 30W
Perleberg **24** 53 5N 11 50 E
Perlevka **55** 51 48N 38 57 E
Perlez **42** 45 11N 20 22 E
Perlis □ **71** 6 30N 100 15 E
Perm (Molotov) **52** 58 0N 57 10 E
Përmeti **44** 40 15N 20 21 E
Pernambuco = Recife **127** 8 0 S 35 0W
Pernambuco □ **127** 8 0 S 37 0W
Pernik **42** 42 35N 23 2 E
Péronne **19** 49 55N 2 57 E
Perosa Argentina **38** 44 57N 7 11 E
Perow **108** 54 35N 126 10W
Perpendicular Pt. **99** 31 37 S 152 52 E
Perpignan **20** 42 42N 2 53 E
Perros-Guirec **18** 48 49N 3 28W
Perry, Fla., U.S.A. **115** 30 9N 83 40W
Perry, Ga., U.S.A. **115** 32 25N 83 41W
Perry, Iowa, U.S.A. **116** 41 48N 94 5W
Perry, Maine, U.S.A. **115** 44 59N 67 20W
Perry, Okla., U.S.A. **117** 36 20N 97 20W
Perryton **117** 36 28N 100 48W
Perryville **117** 37 42N 89 50W
Persberg **48** 59 47N 14 15 E
Persepolis **65** 29 55N 52 50 E
Persia = Iran ■ **65** 35 0N 50 0 E
Persian Gulf **65** 27 0N 50 0 E
Perstorp **49** 56 10N 13 25 E
Perth, Austral. **96** 31 57 S 115 52 E
Perth, Can. **106** 44 55N 76 15W
Perth, U.K. **14** 56 24N 3 27W
Perth Amboy **114** 40 31N 74 16W
Perthus, Le **20** 42 30N 2 53 E
Pertuis **21** 43 42N 5 30 E
Peru, Ill., U.S.A. **116** 41 18N 89 12W
Peru, Ind., U.S.A. **114** 40 42N 86 0W
Peru ■ **126** 8 0 S 75 0W
Peru-Chile Trench **95** 20 0 S 72 0W
Perúgia **39** 43 6N 12 24 E
Perušić **39** 44 40N 15 22 E
Pervomaysk, R.S.F.S.R., U.S.S.R. **55** 54 56N 43 58 E
Pervomaysk, Ukraine S.S.R., U.S.S.R. **56** 48 10N 30 46 E
Pervouralsk **52** 56 55N 60 0 E
Pésaro **39** 43 55N 12 53 E
Pescara **39** 42 28N 14 13 E
Pescara → **39** 42 28N 14 13 E
Peschanokopskoye **57** 46 14N 41 4 E
Péscia **38** 43 54N 10 40 E
Pescina **39** 42 0N 13 39 E
Peshawar **66** 34 2N 71 37 E
* Peshawar □ **66** 33 30N 71 20 E
Peshkopia **44** 41 41N 20 25 E
Peshtera **43** 42 2N 24 18 E
Peshtigo **114** 45 4N 87 46W
Peski **55** 51 14N 42 29 E
Peskovka **55** 59 23N 52 20 E
Pêso da Régua **30** 41 10N 7 47W
Pesqueira **127** 8 20 S 36 42W
Pesqueria → **120** 25 54N 99 11W
Pessac **20** 44 48N 0 37W
Pest □ **27** 47 29N 19 5 E
Pestovo **54** 58 33N 35 42 E
Pestravka **55** 52 28N 49 57 E
Péta **45** 39 10N 21 2 E
Petah Tiqwa **62** 32 6N 34 53 E
Petalidhion **45** 36 57N 21 55 E
Petaling Jaya **71** 3 4N 101 42 E
Petaluma **118** 38 13N 122 39W
Petange **16** 49 33N 5 55 E
Petatlán **120** 17 31N 101 16W
Petauke **91** 14 14 S 31 20 E
Petawawa **106** 45 54N 77 17W
Petén Itzá, Lago **120** 16 58N 89 50W
Peter 1st, I. **5** 69 0 S 91 0W
Peter Pond L. **109** 55 55N 108 44W
Peterbell **106** 48 36N 83 21W
Peterborough, Austral. **97** 32 58 S 138 51 E
Peterborough, Can. **112** 44 20N 78 20W
Peterborough, U.K. **13** 52 35N 0 14W
Peterborough, U.S.A. **113** 42 55N 71 59W
Peterhead **14** 57 30N 1 49W
Petersburg, Alas., U.S.A. **108** 56 50N 133 0W
Petersburg, Ind., U.S.A. **114** 38 30N 87 15W
Petersburg, Va., U.S.A. **114** 37 17N 77 26W
Petersburg, W. Va., U.S.A. **114** 38 59N 79 10W
Petford **98** 17 20 S 144 58 E
Petília Policastro **41** 39 7N 16 48 E
Petit Bois I. **115** 30 16N 88 25W
Petit-Cap **107** 48 3N 64 30W
Petit Goâve **121** 18 27N 72 51W
Petit-Quevilly, Le **18** 49 26N 1 0 E
Petit Saint Bernard, Col du **38** 45 40N 6 52 E
Petitcodiac **107** 45 57N 65 11W
Petite Baleine → **106** 55 50N 77 0W
Petite Saguenay **107** 48 15N 70 4W
Petitsikapau, L. **107** 54 37N 66 25W
Petlad **68** 22 30N 72 45 E
Peto **120** 20 10N 88 53W
Petone **101** 41 13 S 174 53 E
Petoskey **106** 45 22N 84 57W
Petra, Jordan **62** 30 20N 35 22 E
Petra, Spain **32** 39 37N 3 6 E
Petra, Ostrova **4** 76 15N 118 30 E
Petralia **41** 37 49N 14 4 E
Petrel **33** 38 30N 0 46W
Petrich **43** 41 24N 23 13 E
Petrijanec **39** 46 23N 16 17 E
Petrikov **54** 52 11N 28 29 E
Petrila **46** 45 29N 23 29 E
Petrinja **39** 45 28N 16 18 E
Petrolândia **127** 9 5 S 38 20W
Petrolia **106** 42 54N 82 9W
Petrolina **127** 9 24 S 40 30W
Petromagoúla **45** 38 31N 23 0 E
Petropavlovsk **58** 54 53N 69 13 E
Petropavlovsk-Kamchatskiy **59** 53 3N 158 43 E
Petrópolis **125** 22 33 S 43 9W
Petroşeni **46** 45 28N 23 20 E
Petroskey **114** 45 22N 84 57W
Petrova Gora **39** 45 15N 15 45 E
Petrovac, Crna Gora, Yugo. **42** 42 13N 18 57 E
Petrovac, Srbija, Yugo. **42** 44 22N 21 26 E
Petrovaradin **42** 45 16N 19 55 E
Petrovsk **55** 52 22N 45 19 E
Petrovsk-Zabaykalskiy **59** 51 20N 108 55 E
Petrovskoye = Svetlograd **57** 45 25N 42 58 E
Petrozavodsk **52** 61 41N 34 20 E
Petrus Steyn **93** 27 38 S 28 8 E
Petrusburg **92** 29 4 S 25 26 E
Petukhovka **54** 53 42N 30 54 E
Peumo **124** 34 21 S 71 12W
Peureulak **72** 4 48N 97 45 E
Pevek **59** 69 41N 171 19 E
Peveragno **38** 44 20N 7 37 E
Peyrehorade **20** 43 34N 1 7W
Peyruis **21** 44 1N 5 56 E
Pézenas **20** 43 28N 3 24 E
Pezinok **27** 48 17N 17 17 E
Pfaffenhofen **25** 48 31N 11 31 E
Pfarrkirchen **25** 48 25N 12 57 E
Pfeffenhausen **25** 48 40N 11 58 E
Pforzheim **25** 48 53N 8 43 E
Pfullendorf **25** 47 55N 9 15 E
Pfungstadt **25** 49 47N 8 36 E
Phala **92** 23 45 S 26 50 E
Phalodi **68** 27 12N 72 24 E
Phalsbourg **19** 48 46N 7 15 E
Phan Rang **71** 11 34N 109 0 E
Phan Thiet **71** 11 1N 108 9 E
Phanae **45** 38 8N 25 87 E
Phangan, Ko **71** 9 45N 100 0 E
Phangnga **71** 8 28N 98 30 E
Phanh Bho Ho Chi Minh **71** 10 58N 106 40 E
Pharenda **69** 27 5N 83 17 E
Phatthalung **71** 7 39N 100 6 E
Phelps, N.Y., U.S.A. **112** 42 57N 77 5W
Phelps, Wis., U.S.A. **116** 46 2N 89 2W
Phelps L. **109** 59 15N 103 15W
Phenix City **115** 32 30N 85 0W
Phetchabun **71** 16 25N 101 8 E
Phetchabun, Thiu Khao **71** 16 0N 101 20 E
Phetchaburi **71** 13 1N 99 55 E
Phichai **71** 17 22N 100 10 E
Philadelphia, Miss., U.S.A. **117** 32 47N 89 5W
Philadelphia, N.Y., U.S.A. **113** 44 9N 75 40W
Philadelphia, Pa., U.S.A. **114** 40 0N 75 10W
Philip **116** 44 4N 101 42W
Philippeville **16** 50 12N 4 33 E
Philippi **44** 41 1N 24 16 E
Philippi L. **98** 24 20 S 138 55 E
Philippines ■ **73** 12 0N 123 0 E
Philippolis **92** 30 15 S 25 16 E
Philippopolis = Plovdiv **43** 42 8N 24 44 E
Philipsburg, Mont., U.S.A. **118** 46 20N 113 21W
Philipsburg, Pa., U.S.A. **112** 40 53N 78 10W
Philipstown **92** 30 28 S 24 30 E
Phillip **97** 38 30 S 145 12 E
Phillips, Texas, U.S.A. **117** 35 48N 101 17W
Phillips, Wis., U.S.A. **116** 45 41N 90 22W
Phillipsburg, Kans., U.S.A. **116** 39 48N 99 20W
Phillipsburg, Pa., U.S.A. **113** 40 43N 75 12W
Phillott **99** 27 53 S 145 50 E
Philmont **113** 42 14N 73 37W
Philomath **118** 44 28N 123 21W
Phitsanulok **71** 16 50N 100 12 E
Phnom Dangrek **71** 14 20N 104 0 E
Phnom Penh **71** 11 33N 104 55 E
Phnom Thbeng **71** 13 50N 104 56 E
Phoenix, Ariz., U.S.A. **119** 33 30N 112 10W
Phoenix, N.Y., U.S.A. **113** 43 13N 76 18W
Phoenix Is. **94** 3 30 S 172 0W
Phoenixville **113** 40 12N 75 29W
Phong Saly **71** 21 42N 102 9 E
Phra Chedi Sam Ong **71** 15 16N 98 23 E
Phra Nakhon Si Ayutthaya **71** 14 25N 100 30 E
Phrae **71** 18 7N 100 9 E
Phrao **71** 19 23N 99 15 E
Phu Doan **71** 21 40N 105 10 E
Phu Loi **71** 20 14N 103 14 E
Phu Ly **71** 20 35N 105 50 E
Phu Qui **71** 19 20N 105 20 E
Phuket **71** 7 52N 98 22 E
Phulera (Phalera) **68** 26 52N 75 16 E
† Phuoc Le **71** 10 30N 107 10 E
Piacenza **38** 45 2N 9 42 E
Piádena **38** 45 8N 10 22 E
Pialba **97** 25 20 S 152 45 E
Pian Cr. → **99** 30 2 S 148 12 E
Piana **21** 42 15N 8 34 E
Pianella **39** 42 24N 14 5 E
Pianoro **39** 44 20N 11 20 E
Pianosa, Puglia, Italy **39** 42 12N 15 44 E
Pianosa, Toscana, Italy **38** 42 36N 10 4 E
Piapot **109** 49 59N 109 8W
Piare → **39** 45 32N 12 44 E
Pias **31** 38 1N 7 29W
Piaseczno **28** 52 5N 21 2 E
Piaski **28** 51 8N 22 52 E
Piastów **28** 52 12N 20 48 E
Piatra **46** 43 51N 25 9 E
Piatra Neamţ **46** 46 56N 26 21 E
Piatra Olt **46** 44 22N 24 16 E
Piauí □ **127** 7 0 S 43 0W
Piave → **39** 45 32N 12 44 E
Piazza Armerina **41** 37 21N 14 20 E
Pibor → **87** 7 35N 33 0 E
Pibor Post **87** 6 47N 33 3 E
Pica **126** 20 35 S 69 25W
Picardie **19** 50 0N 2 15 E
Picardie, Plaine de **19** 50 0N 2 0 E
Picardy = Picardie **19** 50 0N 2 15 E
Picayune **117** 30 31N 89 40W
Picerno **41** 40 40N 15 37 E
Pichilemu **124** 34 22 S 72 0W
Pickerel L. **106** 48 40N 91 25W
Pickle Lake **106** 51 30N 90 12W
Pico **8** 38 28N 28 18W
Pico Truncado **128** 46 40 S 68 0W
Picos Ancares, Sierra de **30** 42 51N 6 52W
Picquigny **19** 49 56N 2 10 E
Picton, Austral. **99** 34 12 S 150 34 E
Picton, Can. **106** 44 1N 77 9W
Picton, N.Z. **101** 41 18 S 174 3 E
Pictou **107** 45 41N 62 42W
Picture Butte **108** 49 55N 112 45W
Picún Leufú **128** 39 30 S 69 5W
Pidurutalagala **70** 7 10N 80 50 E
Piedad, La **120** 20 20N 102 1W
Piedicavallo **38** 45 41N 7 57 E
Piedmont **115** 33 55N 85 39W
Piedmont = Piemonte **38** 45 0N 7 30 E
Piedmont Plat. **115** 34 0N 81 30W
Piedmonte d'Alife **41** 41 22N 14 22 E
Piedra → **32** 41 18N 1 47W
Piedrabuena **31** 39 0N 4 10W
Piedrahita **30** 40 28N 5 23W
Piedras Blancas Pt. **119** 35 45N 121 18W
Piedras Negras **120** 28 35N 100 35W
Piedras, R. de las → **126** 12 30 S 69 15W
Piemonte □ **38** 45 0N 7 30 E
Piensk **28** 51 16N 15 2 E
Pierce **118** 46 29N 115 53W
Piercefield **113** 44 13N 74 35W
Piería □ **44** 40 13N 22 25 E
Pierre, France **19** 46 54N 5 13 E
Pierre, U.S.A. **116** 44 23N 100 20W
Pierre Benite, Barrage **21** 45 42N 4 49 E
Pierrefeu **21** 43 8N 6 9 E
Pierrefonds **19** 49 20N 3 0 E
Pierrefontaine **19** 47 14N 6 32 E
Pierrefort **20** 44 55N 2 50 E
Pierrelatte **21** 44 23N 4 43 E
Pieštany **27** 48 38N 17 55 E
Piesting → **27** 48 6N 16 40 E
Pieszyce **28** 50 43N 16 33 E
Piet Retief **93** 27 1 S 30 50 E
Pietarsaari **50** 63 40N 22 43 E
Pietermaritzburg **93** 29 35 S 30 25 E
Pietersburg **93** 23 54 S 29 25 E
Pietraperzia **41** 37 26N 14 8 E
Pietrasanta **38** 43 57N 10 12 E
Pietrosu **46** 47 12N 25 8 E
Pietrosul **46** 47 35N 24 43 E
Pieve di Cadore **39** 46 25N 12 22 E
Pieve di Teco **38** 44 3N 7 54 E
Pievepélago **38** 44 12N 10 35 E
Pigádhia **45** 35 30N 27 12 E
Pigadhítsa **44** 39 59N 21 23
Pigeon **114** 43 50N 83 17W
Pigeon I. **70** 14 2N 74 20
Piggott **117** 36 20N 90 10W
Pigna **38** 43 57N 7 40
Pigüe **124** 37 36 S 62 25W
Pihani **69** 27 36N 80 15
Pikalevo **54** 59 37N 34 0
Pikes Peak **116** 38 50N 105 10W
Piketberg **92** 32 55 S 18 40
Pikeville **114** 37 30N 82 30W
Pikwitonei **109** 55 35N 97 9W
Piła **28** 53 10N 16 48
Pila **33** 38 16N 1 11W
Piła □ **28** 53 0N 17 0
Pilaía **44** 40 32N 22 59
Pilani **68** 28 22N 75 33
Pilar, Brazil **127** 9 36 S 35 56W
Pilar, Parag. **124** 26 50 S 58 20W
Pilas **73** 6 39N 121 37
Pilawa **28** 51 57N 21 32
Pilbara **96** 21 15 S 118 16
Pilcomayo → **124** 25 21 S 57 42W
Pili **45** 36 50N 27 15
Pilibhit **69** 28 40N 79 50
Pilica → **28** 51 52N 21 17
Pilion **44** 39 27N 23 7
Pilis **27** 47 17N 19 35
Pilisvörösvár **27** 47 38N 18 56
Pilkhawa **68** 28 43N 77 42
Pilos **45** 36 55N 21 42
Pilot Mound **109** 49 15N 98 54W
Pilot Point **117** 33 26N 97 0W
Pilot Rock **118** 45 30N 118 50W
Pilsen = Plzen **26** 49 45N 13 22
Pilštanj **39** 46 8N 15 39
Pilzno **27** 50 0N 21 16
Pima **119** 32 54N 109 50W
Pimba **97** 31 18 S 136 46
Pimenta Bueno **126** 11 35 S 61 10W
Pimentel **126** 6 45 S 79 55W
Pina **32** 41 29N 0 33W
Pinang **71** 5 25N 100 15
Pinar del Río **121** 22 26N 83 40W
Pinaroo **97** 35 17 S 140 53
Pincehely **27** 46 41N 18 27
Pincher Creek **108** 49 30N 113 57W
Pinchi L. **108** 54 38N 124 30W
Pinckneyville **116** 38 5N 89 20W
Pîncota **42** 46 20N 21 45
Pińczów **28** 50 32N 20 32
Pind Dadan Khan **68** 32 36N 73 7
Pindiga **85** 9 58N 10 53
Pindos Óros **44** 40 0N 21 0
Pindus Mts. = Pindos Óros **44** 40 0N 21 0
Pine **119** 34 27N 111 30W
Pine → **109** 58 50N 105 38W
Pine Bluff **117** 34 10N 92 0W
Pine, C. **107** 46 37N 53 32W
Pine City **116** 45 46N 93 0W
Pine Creek **96** 13 50 S 132 10
Pine Falls **109** 50 34N 96 11W
Pine, La **118** 43 40N 121 30W
Pine Pass **108** 55 25N 122 42W
Pine Point **108** 60 50N 114 28W
Pine Ridge **116** 43 0N 102 35W
Pine River, Can. **109** 51 45N 100 30W
Pine River, U.S.A. **116** 46 43N 94 24W
Pinedale **119** 34 23N 110 16W
Pinega → **52** 64 8N 46 54
Pinehill **98** 23 38 S 146 57
Pinerolo **38** 44 47N 7 21
Pineto **39** 42 36N 14 4
Pinetop **119** 34 10N 109 57W
Pinetown **93** 29 48 S 30 54
Pinetree **118** 43 42N 105 52W
Pineville, Ky., U.S.A. **115** 36 42N 83 42W
Pineville, La., U.S.A. **117** 31 22N 92 30W
Piney **19** 48 22N 4 21 E
Ping → **71** 15 42N 100 9 E
Pingding **76** 37 47N 113 38
Pingdingshan **77** 33 43N 113 27
Pingdong **75** 22 39N 120 30
Pingdu **76** 36 42N 119 59 E
Pingguo **77** 23 19N 107 36
Pinghe **77** 24 17N 117 21 E
Pingjiang **77** 28 45N 113 36
Pingle **77** 24 40N 110 40
Pingliang **76** 35 35N 106 31
Pingluo **76** 38 52N 106 30
Pingnan **77** 23 33N 110 22
Pingtan Dao **77** 25 29N 119 47
Pingwu **75** 32 25N 104 30
Pingxiang, Guangxi Zhuangzu, China **75** 22 6N 106 46
Pingxiang, Jiangxi, China **77** 27 43N 113 48
Pingyao **76** 37 12N 112 10
Pinhal **125** 22 10 S 46 46W
Pinhel **30** 40 50N 7 1W
Pini **72** 0 10N 98 40
Piniós →, Ilia, Greece **45** 37 48N 21 20
Piniós →, Trikkala, Greece **44** 39 55N 22 10
Pinjarra **96** 32 37 S 115 52
Pink → **109** 56 50N 103 50W
Pinkafeld **27** 47 22N 16 9 E
Pinneberg **24** 53 39N 9 48
Pinos **120** 22 20N 101 40W
Pinos, I. de **121** 21 40N 82 40W
Pinos Pt. **119** 36 38N 121 57W
Pinos Puente **31** 37 15N 3 45W
Pinrang **73** 3 46 S 119 41
Pinsk **54** 52 10N 26 1
Pintados **126** 20 35 S 69 40W
Pinyang **77** 27 42N 120 31
Pinyug **52** 60 5N 48 0
Pinzolo **38** 46 9N 10 45
Pioche **119** 38 0N 114 35W
Piombino **38** 42 54N 10 30
Piombino, Canale di **38** 42 50N 10 25
Pioner, Os. **59** 79 50N 92 0
Pionki **28** 51 29N 21 28
Piorini, L. **126** 3 15 S 62 35W

* *Now part of North West Frontier □*

† *Renamed Ba Ria*

Name	Page	Lat.	Long.
iotrków Trybunalski	28	51 23N	19 43 E
iotrków Trybunalski □	28	51 30N	19 45 E
iove di Sacco	39	45 18N	12 1 E
ip	65	26 45N	60 10 E
ipar	68	26 25N	73 31 E
ipariya	68	22 45N	78 23 E
ipéri	44	39 20N	24 19 E
ipestone	116	44 0N	96 20W
ipestone →	106	52 53N	89 23W
ipestone Cr. →	109	49 42N	100 45W
ipmuacan, Rés.	107	49 45N	70 30W
ipriac	18	47 49N	1 58W
iqua	114	40 10N	84 10W
iquiri →	125	24 3 S	54 14W
iracicaba	125	22 45 S	47 40W
iracuruca	127	3 50 S	41 50W
iræus = Piraiévs	45	37 57N	23 42 E
iraiévs	45	37 57N	23 42 E
iraiévs □	45	37 0N	23 30 E
iráino	41	38 10N	14 52 E
irajuí	125	21 59 S	49 29W
iran (Pirano)	39	45 31N	13 33 E
irané	124	25 42 S	59 6W
irapora	127	17 20 S	44 56W
irdop	43	42 40N	24 10 E
irganj	69	25 51N	88 24 E
irgos, Ilía, Greece	45	37 40N	21 27 E
írgos, Messinia, Greece	45	36 50N	22 16 E
irgovo	43	43 44N	25 43 E
iriac-sur-Mer	18	47 22N	2 33W
iribebuy	124	25 26 S	57 2W
irin Planina	43	41 40N	23 30 E
irineos	32	42 40N	1 0 E
iripiri	127	4 15 S	41 46W
irmasens	25	49 12N	7 30 E
irna	24	50 57N	13 57 E
irojpur	69	22 35N	90 1 E
irot	42	43 9N	22 39 E
irtleville	119	31 25N	109 35W
iru	73	3 4 S	128 12 E
iryatin	54	50 15N	32 25 E
iryí	45	38 13N	25 59 E
isa	38	43 43N	10 23 E
isa →	28	53 14N	21 52 E
isagua	126	19 40 S	70 15W
isarovina	39	45 35N	15 50 E
isciotta	41	40 7N	15 12 E
isco	126	13 50 S	76 12W
iscu	46	45 30N	27 43 E
isek	26	49 19N	14 10 E
ishan	75	37 30N	78 33 E
ising	73	5 8 S	121 53 E
issos	20	44 19N	0 49W
isticci	41	40 24N	16 33 E
istóia	38	43 57N	10 53 E
istol B.	109	62 25N	92 37W
isuerga →	30	41 33N	4 52W
isz	28	53 38N	21 49 E
itarpunga, L.	99	34 24 S	143 30 E
itcairn I.	95	25 5 S	130 5W
ite älv →	50	65 20N	21 25 E
iteå	50	65 20N	21 25 E
iterka	55	50 41N	47 29 E
iteşti	46	44 52N	24 54 E
ithapuram	70	17 10N	82 15 E
ithion	44	41 24N	26 40 E
ithiviers	19	48 10N	2 13 E
itigliano	39	42 38N	11 40 E
itlochry	14	56 43N	3 43W
itt I.	108	53 30N	129 50W
ittsburg, Calif., U.S.A.	118	38 1N	121 50W
ittsburg, Kans., U.S.A.	117	37 21N	94 43W
ittsburg, Tex., U.S.A.	117	32 59N	94 58W
ittsburgh	114	40 25N	79 55W
ittsfield, Ill., U.S.A.	116	39 35N	90 46W
ittsfield, Mass., U.S.A.	114	42 28N	73 17W
ittsfield, N.H., U.S.A.	113	43 17N	71 18W
ittston	114	41 19N	75 50W
ittsworth	99	27 41 S	151 37 E
ituri →	98	22 35 S	138 30 E
iura	126	5 15 S	80 38W
iva →	42	43 20N	18 50 E
iwniczna	27	49 27N	20 42 E
iyai	44	39 17N	21 25 E
izzo	41	38 44N	16 10 E
lacentia	107	47 20N	54 0W
lacentia B.	107	47 0N	54 40W
lacerville	118	38 47N	120 51W
lacetas	121	22 15N	79 44W
lačkovica	42	41 45N	22 30 E
lain Dealing	117	32 56N	93 41W
lainfield	114	40 37N	74 28W
lains, Kans., U.S.A.	117	37 20N	100 35W
lains, Mont., U.S.A.	118	47 27N	114 57W
lains, Tex., U.S.A.	117	33 11N	102 50W
lainview, Nebr., U.S.A.	116	42 25N	97 48W
lainview, Tex., U.S.A.	117	34 10N	101 40W
lainville	116	39 18N	99 19W
lainwell	114	42 28N	85 40W
laisance	20	43 36N	0 3 E
láka	44	40 0N	25 24 E
lakenska Planina	42	41 14N	21 2 E
lakhino	58	67 45N	86 5 E
laná	26	49 50N	12 44 E
lancoët	18	48 32N	2 13W
landište	42	45 16N	21 10 E
lanina, Slovenija, Yugo.	39	46 10N	15 20 E
lanina, Slovenija, Yugo.	39	45 47N	14 19 E
lankinton	116	43 45N	98 27W
lano	117	33 0N	96 45W
lant City	115	28 0N	82 8W
lant, La	116	45 11N	100 40W
laquemine	117	30 20N	91 15W
lasencia	30	40 3N	6 8W
laški	39	45 4N	15 22 E
lassen	48	61 9N	12 30 E
laster Rock	107	46 53N	67 22W
lata, La	124	35 0 S	57 55W
lata, Río de la	124	34 45 S	57 30W
latani →	40	37 23N	13 16 E
lateau	5	79 55 S	40 0 E
lateau □	85	8 0N	8 30 E
Plateau du Coteau du Missouri	116	47 9N	101 5W
Platí, Ákra-	44	40 27N	24 0 E
Plato	126	9 47N	74 47W
Platte	116	43 28N	98 50W
Platte →	116	39 16N	94 50W
Platteville	116	40 18N	104 47W
Plattling	25	48 46N	12 53 E
Plattsburg	114	44 41N	73 30W
Plattsmouth	116	41 0N	95 50W
Plau	24	53 27N	12 16 E
Plauen	24	50 29N	12 9 E
Plav	42	42 38N	19 57 E
Plavinas	54	56 35N	25 46 E
Plavnica	42	42 20N	19 13 E
Plavsk	55	53 40N	37 18 E
Playgreen L.	109	54 0N	98 15W
Pleasant Bay	107	46 51N	60 48W
Pleasant Hill	116	38 48N	94 14W
Pleasanton	117	29 0N	98 30W
Pleasantville	114	39 25N	74 30W
Pléaux	20	45 8N	2 13 E
Pleiku (Gia Lai)	71	13 57N	108 0 E
Plélan-le-Grand	18	48 0N	2 7W
Plémet	18	48 11N	2 36W
Pléneuf-Val-André	18	48 35N	2 32W
Pleniţa	46	44 14N	23 10 E
Plenty, Bay of	101	37 45 S	177 0 E
Plentywood	116	48 45N	104 35W
Plesetsk	52	62 40N	40 10 E
Plessisville	107	46 14N	71 47W
Plestin-les-Grèves	18	48 40N	3 39W
Pleszew	28	51 53N	17 47 E
Pleternica	42	45 17N	17 48 E
Pletipi L.	107	51 44N	70 6W
Pleven	43	43 26N	24 37 E
Plevlja	42	43 21N	19 21 E
Ploče	42	43 4N	17 26 E
Płock	28	52 32N	19 40 E
Płock □	28	52 30N	19 45 E
Plöcken Passo	39	46 37N	12 57 E
Ploëmeur	18	47 44N	3 26W
Ploërmel	18	47 55N	2 26W
Ploieşti	46	44 57N	26 5 E
Plomárion	45	38 58N	26 24 E
Plomb du Cantal	20	45 2N	2 48 E
Plombières	19	47 59N	6 27 E
Plomin	39	45 8N	14 10 E
Plön	24	54 8N	10 22 E
Plöner See	24	45 10N	10 22 E
Plonge, Lac La	109	55 8N	107 20W
Płońsk	28	52 37N	20 21 E
Płoty	28	53 48N	15 18 E
Plouaret	18	48 37N	3 28W
Plouay	18	47 55N	3 21W
Ploučnice →	26	50 46N	14 13 E
Ploudalmézeau	18	48 34N	4 41W
Plougasnou	18	48 42N	3 49W
Plouha	18	48 41N	2 57W
Plouhinec	18	48 0N	4 29W
Plovdiv	43	42 8N	24 44 E
Plum I.	113	41 10N	72 12W
Plummer	118	47 21N	116 59W
Plumtree	91	20 27 S	27 55 E
Plunge	54	55 53N	21 59 E
Pluvigner	18	47 46N	3 1W
Plymouth, U.K.	13	50 23N	4 9W
Plymouth, Ind., U.S.A.	114	41 20N	86 19W
Plymouth, Mass., U.S.A.	113	41 58N	70 40W
Plymouth, N.C., U.S.A.	115	35 54N	76 46W
Plymouth, N.H., U.S.A.	113	43 44N	71 41W
Plymouth, Pa., U.S.A.	113	41 17N	76 0W
Plymouth, Wis., U.S.A.	114	43 42N	87 58W
Plymouth Sd.	13	50 20N	4 10W
Plynlimon = Pumlumon Fawr	13	52 29N	3 47W
Plyussa	54	58 40N	29 20 E
Plyussa →	54	58 40N	29 0 E
Plzen	26	49 45N	13 22 E
Pniewy	28	52 31N	16 16 E
Pô	85	11 14N	1 5W
Po →	38	44 57N	12 4 E
Po, Foci del	39	44 55N	12 30 E
Po Hai = Bo Hai	76	39 0N	120 0 E
Pobé	85	7 0N	2 56 E
Pobeda	59	65 12N	146 12 E
Pobedino	59	49 51N	142 49 E
Pobedy Pik	58	40 45N	79 58 E
Pobiedziska	28	52 29N	17 11 E
Pobla de Lillet, La	32	42 16N	1 59 E
Pobla de Segur	32	42 15N	0 58 E
Pobladura de Valle	30	42 6N	5 44W
Pocahontas, Arkansas, U.S.A.	117	36 18N	91 0W
Pocahontas, Iowa, U.S.A.	116	42 41N	94 42W
Pocatello	118	42 50N	112 25W
Počátky	26	49 15N	15 14 E
Pochep	54	52 58N	33 29 E
Pochinki	55	54 41N	44 59 E
Pochinok	54	54 28N	32 29 E
Pöchlarn	26	48 12N	15 12 E
Pochontas	108	53 10N	117 51W
Pochutla	120	15 50N	96 31W
Pocomoke City	114	38 4N	75 32W
Poços de Caldas	125	21 50 S	46 33W
Poddebice	28	51 54N	18 58 E
Poděbrady	26	50 9N	15 8 E
Podensac	20	44 40N	0 22W
Podgorač	42	45 27N	18 13 E
Podgorica = Titograd	42	42 30N	19 19 E
Podkamennaya Tunguska →	59	61 50N	90 13 E
Podlapac	39	44 37N	15 47 E
Podmokly	26	50 48N	14 10 E
Podoleni	46	46 46N	26 39 E
Podolínec	27	49 16N	20 31 E
Podolsk	55	55 25N	37 30 E
Podor	84	16 40N	15 2W
Podporozhy	52	60 55N	34 2 E
Podravska Slatina	42	45 42N	17 45 E
Podu Turcului	46	46 11N	27 25 E
Podujevo	42	42 54N	21 10 E
Poel	24	54 0N	11 25 E
Pofadder	92	29 10 S	19 22 E
Pogamasing	106	46 55N	81 50W
Poggiardo	41	40 3N	18 21 E
Poggibonsi	39	43 27N	11 8 E
Pogoanele	46	44 55N	27 0 E
Pogorzela	28	51 50N	17 12 E
Pogradeci	44	40 57N	20 37 E
Poh	73	0 46 S	122 51 E
Pohang	76	36 1N	129 23 E
Pohorelá	27	48 50N	20 2 E
Pohořelice	27	48 59N	16 31 E
Pohorje	39	46 30N	15 20 E
Poiana Mare	46	43 57N	23 5 E
Poiana Ruscăi, Munţii	46	45 45N	22 25 E
Poinsett, C.	5	65 42 S	113 18 E
Point Edward	106	43 0N	82 30W
Point Pedro	70	9 50N	80 15 E
Point Pleasant, U.S.A.	113	40 5N	74 4W
Point Pleasant, W. Va., U.S.A.	114	38 50N	82 7W
Pointe-à-la Hache	117	29 35N	89 55W
Pointe-à-Pitre	121	16 10N	61 30W
Pointe Noire	88	4 48 S	11 53 E
Poirino	38	44 55N	7 50 E
Poissy	19	48 55N	2 0 E
Poitiers	18	46 35N	0 20 E
Poitou, Plaines et Seuil du	20	46 30N	0 1W
Poix	19	49 47N	2 0 E
Poix-Terron	19	49 38N	4 38 E
Pojoaque	119	35 55N	106 0W
Pokataroo	99	29 30 S	148 36 E
Poko, Sudan	87	5 41N	31 55 E
Poko, Zaïre	90	3 7N	26 52 E
Pokrov	55	55 55N	39 7 E
Pokrovsk	59	61 29N	126 12 E
Pol	30	43 9N	7 20W
Pola de Allande	30	43 16N	6 37W
Pola de Gordón, La	30	42 51N	5 41W
Pola de Lena	30	43 10N	5 49W
Pola de Siero	30	43 24N	5 39W
Pola de Somiedo	30	43 5N	6 15W
Polacca	119	35 52N	110 25W
Polan	65	25 30N	61 10 E
Poland ■	28	52 0N	20 0 E
Polanów	28	54 7N	16 41 E
Polar Sub-Glacial Basin	5	85 0 S	110 0 E
Polcura	124	37 17 S	71 43W
Połczyn Zdrój	28	53 47N	16 5 E
Polden Hills	13	51 7N	2 50W
Polessk	54	54 50N	21 8 E
Polevskoy	52	56 26N	60 11 E
Polewali, Sulawesi, Indon.	73	4 8 S	119 43 E
Polewali, Sulawesi, Indon.	73	3 21 S	119 23 E
Polgar	27	47 54N	21 6 E
Poli	88	8 34N	13 15 E
Poliaigos	45	36 45N	24 38 E
Policastro, Golfo di	41	39 55N	15 35 E
Police	28	53 33N	14 33 E
Polička	27	49 43N	16 15 E
Polignano a Mare	41	41 0N	17 12 E
Poligny	19	46 50N	5 42 E
Políkhnitas	45	39 4N	26 10 E
Polillo Is.	73	14 56N	122 0 E
Polístena	41	38 25N	16 4 E
Políyiros	44	40 23N	23 25 E
Polk	112	41 22N	79 57W
Polkowice	28	51 29N	16 3 E
Polla	41	40 31N	15 27 E
Pollachi	70	10 35N	77 0 E
Pollensa	32	39 54N	3 1 E
Pollensa, B. de	32	39 53N	3 8 E
Póllica	41	40 13N	15 3 E
Pollino, Mte.	41	39 54N	16 13 E
Pollock	116	45 58N	100 18W
Polna	54	58 31N	28 0 E
Polnovat	58	63 50N	65 54 E
Polo	116	42 0N	89 38W
Pologi	56	47 29N	36 15 E
Polonnoye	54	50 6N	27 30 E
Polotsk	54	55 30N	28 50 E
Polski Trŭmbesh	43	43 20N	25 38 E
Polsko Kosovo	43	43 23N	25 38 E
Polson	118	47 45N	114 12W
Poltava	56	49 35N	34 35 E
Polunochnoye	52	60 52N	60 25 E
Polur	70	12 32N	79 11 E
Polyanovgrad	43	42 39N	26 59 E
Polyarny	52	69 8N	33 20 E
Polynesia	95	10 0 S	162 0W
Pomarance	38	43 18N	10 51 E
Pomarico	41	40 31N	16 33 E
Pombal, Brazil	127	6 45 S	37 50W
Pombal, Port.	30	39 55N	8 40W
Pómbia	45	35 0N	24 51 E
Pomeroy, Ohio, U.S.A.	114	39 0N	82 0W
Pomeroy, Wash., U.S.A.	118	46 30N	117 33W
Pomona	119	34 2N	117 49W
Pomorie	43	42 32N	27 41 E
Pomoshnaya	56	48 13N	31 36 E
Pompano Beach	115	26 12N	80 6W
Pompei	41	40 45N	14 30 E
Pompey	19	48 50N	6 2 E
Pompeys Pillar	118	46 0N	108 0W
Ponape	94	6 55N	158 10 E
Ponask, L.	106	54 0N	92 41W
Ponass L.	109	52 16N	103 58W
Ponca	116	42 38N	96 41W
Ponca City	117	36 40N	97 5W
Ponce	121	18 1N	66 37W
Ponchatoula	117	30 27N	90 25W
Poncheville, L.	106	50 10N	76 55W
Poncin	21	46 6N	5 25 E
Pond Inlet	105	72 40N	77 0W
Pondicherry	70	11 59N	79 50 E
Pondoland	93	31 10 S	29 30 E
Ponds, I. of	107	53 27N	55 52W
Ponferrada	30	42 32N	6 35W
Pongo, Wadi →	87	8 42N	27 40 E
Poniatowa	28	51 11N	22 3 E
Poniec	28	51 48N	16 50 E
Ponikva	39	46 16N	15 26 E
Ponnaiyar →	70	11 50N	79 45 E
Ponnani	70	10 45N	75 59 E
Ponneri	70	13 20N	80 15 E
Ponnyadaung	67	22 0N	94 10 E
Ponoi	52	67 0N	41 0 E
Ponoi →	52	66 59N	41 17 E
Ponoka	108	52 42N	113 40W
Ponorogo	73	7 52 S	111 29 E
Pons, France	20	45 35N	0 34W
Pons, Spain	32	41 55N	1 12 E
Ponsul →	31	39 40N	7 31W
Pont-à-Mousson	19	48 54N	6 1 E
Pont-Audemer	18	49 21N	0 30 E
Pont-Aven	18	47 51N	3 47W
Pont Canavese	38	45 24N	7 33 E
Pont-de-Roide	19	47 23N	6 45 E
Pont-de-Salars	20	44 18N	2 44 E
Pont-de-Vaux	19	46 26N	4 56 E
Pont-de-Veyle	21	46 17N	4 53 E
Pont-l'Abbé	18	47 52N	4 15W
Pont-l'Évêque	18	49 18N	0 11 E
Pont-St-Esprit	21	44 16N	4 40 E
Pont-sur-Yonne	19	48 18N	3 10 E
Ponta Grossa	125	25 7 S	50 10W
Ponta Pora	125	22 20 S	55 35W
Pontacq	20	43 11N	0 8W
Pontailler	19	47 18N	5 24 E
Pontarlier	19	46 54N	6 20 E
Pontassieve	39	43 47N	11 25 E
Pontaubault	18	48 40N	1 20W
Pontaumur	20	45 52N	2 40 E
Pontcharra	21	45 26N	6 1 E
Pontchartrain, L.	117	30 12N	90 0W
Pontchâteau	18	47 25N	2 5W
Ponte da Barca	30	41 48N	8 25W
Ponte de Sor	31	39 17N	7 57W
Ponte dell 'Olio	38	44 52N	9 39 E
Ponte di Legno	38	46 15N	10 30 E
Ponte do Lima	30	41 46N	8 35W
Ponte do Pungué	91	19 30 S	34 33 E
Ponte Leccia	21	42 28N	9 13 E
Ponte Macassar	73	9 30 S	123 58 E
Ponte nell' Alpi	39	46 10N	12 18 E
Ponte Nova	125	20 25 S	42 54W
Ponte San Martino	38	45 36N	7 47 E
Ponte San Pietro	38	45 42N	9 35 E
Pontebba	39	46 30N	13 17 E
Pontecorvo	40	41 28N	13 40 E
Pontedera	38	43 40N	10 37 E
Pontefract	12	53 42N	1 19W
Ponteix	109	49 46N	107 29W
Pontelandolfo	41	41 17N	14 41 E
Pontevedra	30	42 26N	8 40W
Pontevedra □	30	42 25N	8 39W
Pontevedra, R. de →	30	42 22N	8 45W
Pontevico	38	45 16N	10 6 E
Pontiac, Ill., U.S.A.	116	40 50N	88 40W
Pontiac, Mich., U.S.A.	114	42 40N	83 20W
Pontian Kechil	71	1 29N	103 23 E
Pontianak	72	0 3 S	109 15 E
Pontine Is. = Ponziane, Isole	40	40 55N	13 0 E
Pontine Mts. = Karadeniz D.	64	41 30N	35 0 E
Pontínia	40	41 25N	13 2 E
Pontivy	18	48 5N	3 0W
Pontoise	19	49 3N	2 5 E
Ponton →	108	58 27N	116 11W
Pontorson	18	48 34N	1 30W
Pontrémoli	38	44 22N	9 52 E
Pontrieux	18	48 42N	3 10W
Ponts-de-Cé, Les	18	47 25N	0 30W
Pontypool, Can.	112	44 6N	78 38W
Pontypool, U.K.	13	51 42N	3 1W
Pontypridd	13	51 36N	3 21W
Ponza	40	40 55N	12 57 E
Ponziane, Isole	40	40 55N	13 0 E
Poole	13	50 42N	1 58W
Pooley I.	108	52 45N	128 15W
Poona = Pune	70	18 29N	73 57 E
Poonamallee	70	13 3N	80 10 E
Pooncarie	99	33 22 S	142 31 E
Poopelloe, L.	99	31 40 S	144 0 E
Poopó, Lago de	126	18 30 S	67 35W
Popayán	126	2 27N	76 36W
Poperinge	16	50 51N	2 42 E
Popigay	59	72 1N	110 39 E
Popilta, L.	99	33 10 S	141 42 E
Popina	43	44 7N	26 57 E
Popio, L.	99	33 10 S	141 52 E
Poplar	116	48 3N	105 9W
Poplar →, Man., Can.	109	53 0N	97 19W
Poplar →, N.W.T., Can.	108	61 22N	121 52W
Poplar Bluff	117	36 45N	90 22W
Poplarville	117	30 55N	89 30W
Popocatepetl	120	19 10N	98 40W
Popokabaka	88	5 41 S	16 40 E
Pópoli	39	42 12N	13 50 E
Popondetta	98	8 48 S	148 17 E
Popovača	39	45 30N	16 41 E
Popovo	43	43 21N	26 18 E
Poprád	27	49 3N	20 18 E
Poprád →	27	49 38N	20 42 E
Porbandar	68	21 44N	69 43 E
Porcher I.	108	53 50N	130 30W
Porcuna	31	37 52N	4 11W
Porcupine →, Can.	109	59 11N	104 46W
Porcupine →, U.S.A.	104	66 35N	145 15W
Pordenone	39	45 58N	12 40 E
Pordim	43	43 23N	24 51 E
Poreč	39	45 14N	13 36 E
Poretskoye	55	55 9N	46 21 E
Pori	51	61 29N	21 48 E
Porí	45	35 58N	23 13 E
Porjus	50	66 57N	19 50 E
Porkhov	54	57 45N	29 38 E
Porkkala	51	59 59N	24 26 E
Porlamar	126	10 57N	63 51W
Porlezza	38	46 2N	9 8 E
Porma →	30	42 49N	5 28W
Pornic	18	47 7N	2 5W
Poronaysk	59	49 13N	143 0 E
Póros	45	37 30N	23 30 E
Poroshiri-Dake	74	42 41N	142 52 E
Poroszló	27	47 39N	20 40 E
Poroto Mts.	91	9 0 S	33 30 E
Porquerolles, Îles de	21	43 0N	6 13 E
Porrentruy	25	47 25N	7 6 E
Porreras	32	39 31N	3 2 E

Place	Page	Lat.	Long.
Porretta, Passo di	38	44 2N	10 56 E
Porsangen	50	70 40N	25 40 E
Porsgrunn	47	59 10N	9 40 E
Port	19	47 43N	6 4 E
Port Adelaide	99	34 46 S	138 30 E
Port Alberni	108	49 40N	124 50W
Port Albert	100	38 42 S	146 42 E
Port Albert Victor	68	21 0N	71 30 E
Port Alfred, Can.	107	48 18N	70 53W
Port Alfred, S. Afr.	92	33 36 S	26 55 E
Port Alice	108	50 20N	127 25W
Port Allegany	114	41 49N	78 17W
Port Allen	117	30 30N	91 15W
Port Alma	98	23 38 S	150 53 E
Port Angeles	118	48 7N	123 30W
Port Antonio	121	18 10N	76 30W
Port Aransas	117	27 49N	97 4W
Port Arthur, Austral.	97	43 7 S	147 50 E
Port Arthur, U.S.A.	117	30 0N	94 0W
Port au Port B.	107	48 40N	58 50W
Port-au-Prince	121	18 40N	72 20W
Port Augusta	97	32 30 S	137 50 E
Port Augusta West	97	32 29 S	137 29 E
Port Austin	106	44 3N	82 59W
Port Bell	90	0 18N	32 35 E
Port Bergé Vaovao	93	15 33 S	47 40 E
Port Blair	71	11 40N	92 30 E
Port Blandford	107	48 20N	54 10W
Port Bolivar	117	29 20N	94 40W
Port Bou	32	42 25N	3 9 E
Port Bouët	84	5 16N	3 57W
Port Bradshaw	97	12 30 S	137 20 E
Port Broughton	99	33 37 S	137 56 E
Port Burwell	106	42 40N	80 48W
Port-Cartier	107	50 2N	66 50W
Port Chalmers	101	45 49 S	170 30 E
Port Chester	114	41 0N	73 41W
Port Clements	108	53 40N	132 10W
Port Clinton	114	41 30N	82 58W
Port Colborne	106	42 50N	79 10W
Port Coquitlam	108	49 15N	122 45W
Port Credit	112	43 33N	79 35W
Port Dalhousie	112	43 13N	79 16W
Port Darwin, Austral.	96	12 24 S	130 45 E
Port Darwin, Falk. Is.	128	51 50 S	59 0W
Port Davey	97	43 16 S	145 55 E
Port-de-Bouc	21	43 24N	4 59 E
Port-de-Paix	121	19 50N	72 50W
Port Dickson	71	2 30N	101 49 E
Port Douglas	98	16 30 S	145 30 E
Port Dover	112	42 47N	80 12W
Port Edward	108	54 12N	130 10W
Port Elgin	106	44 25N	81 25W
Port Elizabeth	92	33 58 S	25 40 E
Port Ellen	14	55 38N	6 10W
Port-en-Bessin	18	49 21N	0 45W
Port Erin	12	54 5N	4 45W
Port Etienne = Nouâdhibou	80	20 54N	17 0W
Port Fairy	97	38 22 S	142 12 E
Port Fouâd = Bûr Fuad	86	31 15N	32 20 E
Port-Gentil	88	0 40 S	8 50 E
Port Gibson	117	31 57N	91 0W
Port Glasgow	14	55 57N	4 40W
Port Harcourt	85	4 40N	7 10 E
Port Hardy	108	50 41N	127 30W
Port Harrison	105	58 25N	78 15W
Port Hawkesbury	107	45 36N	61 22W
Port Hedland	96	20 25 S	118 35 E
Port Henry	114	44 0N	73 30W
Port Hood	107	46 0N	61 32W
Port Hope	106	43 56N	78 20W
Port Huron	114	43 0N	82 28W
Port Isabel	117	26 4N	97 9W
Port Jackson	97	33 50 S	151 18 E
Port Jefferson	114	40 58N	73 5W
Port Jervis	113	41 22N	74 42W
Port-Joinville	18	46 45N	2 23W
Port Katon	57	46 52N	38 46 E
Port Kelang	71	3 0N	101 23 E
Port Kembla	99	34 52 S	150 49 E
Port-la-Nouvelle	20	43 1N	3 3 E
Port Laoise	15	53 2N	7 20W
Port Lavaca	117	28 38N	96 38W
Port-Leucate-Barcarès	20	42 53N	3 3 E
Port Lincoln	96	34 42 S	135 52 E
Port Loko	84	8 48N	12 46W
Port Louis	18	47 42N	3 22W
Port Lyautey = Kenitra	82	34 15N	6 40W
Port Macdonnell	99	38 0 S	140 48 E
Port Macquarie	97	31 25 S	152 25 E
Port Maria	121	18 25N	77 5W
Port Mellon	108	49 32N	123 31W
Port-Menier	107	49 51N	64 15W
Port Moresby	94	9 24 S	147 8 E
Port Mouton	107	43 58N	64 50W
Port Musgrave	97	11 55 S	141 50 E
Port-Navalo	18	47 34N	2 54W
Port Nelson	109	57 3N	92 36W
Port Nolloth	92	29 17 S	16 52 E
Port Nouveau-Québec (George River)	105	58 30N	65 59W
Port O'Connor	117	28 26N	96 24W
Port of Spain	121	10 40N	61 31W
Port Orchard	118	47 31N	122 38W
Port Oxford	118	42 45N	124 28W
Port Pegasus	101	47 12 S	167 41 E
Port Perry	106	44 6N	78 56W
Port Phillip B.	97	38 10 S	144 50 E
Port Pirie	97	33 10 S	138 1 E
Port Pólnocny	28	54 25N	18 42 E
Port Radium = Echo Bay	104	66 10N	117 40W
Port Renfrew	108	48 30N	124 20W
Port Rowan	106	42 40N	80 30W
Port Safaga = Bûr Safâga	86	26 43N	33 57 E
Port Said = Bûr Sa'îd	86	31 16N	32 18 E
Port St. Joe	115	29 49N	85 20W
Port St. Louis	93	13 7 S	48 48 E
Port-St-Louis-du-Rhône	21	43 23N	4 49 E
Port Sanilac	106	43 26N	82 33W
Port Saunders	107	50 40N	57 18W
Port Severn	112	44 48N	79 43W
Port Shepstone	93	30 44 S	30 28 E
Port Simpson	108	54 30N	130 20W
Port Stanley	106	42 40N	81 10W
Port Stephens	97	32 38 S	152 12 E
Port Sudan = Bûr Sûdân	86	19 32N	37 9 E
Port Talbot	13	51 35N	3 48W
Port Taufiq = Bûr Taufiq	86	29 54N	32 32 E
Port Townsend	118	48 7N	122 50W
Port-Vendres	20	42 32N	3 8 E
Port Vladimir	52	69 25N	33 6 E
Port Washington	114	43 25N	87 52W
Port Weld	71	4 50N	100 38 E
Portachuelo	126	17 10 S	63 20W
Portadown	15	54 27N	6 26W
Portage	116	43 31N	89 25W
Portage La Prairie	109	49 58N	98 18W
Portageville	117	36 25N	89 40W
Portalegre	31	39 19N	7 25W
Portalegre □	31	39 20N	7 40W
Portales	117	34 12N	103 25W
Portarlington	15	53 10N	7 10W
Porte, La	114	41 36N	86 43W
Portel	31	38 19N	7 41W
Porter L., N.W.T., Can.	109	61 41N	108 5W
Porter L., Sask., Can.	109	56 20N	107 20W
Porterville, S. Afr.	92	33 0 S	18 57 E
Porterville, U.S.A.	119	36 5N	119 0W
Porthcawl	13	51 28N	3 42W
Porthill	118	49 0N	116 30W
Portile de Fier	46	44 42N	22 30 E
Portimão	31	37 8N	8 32W
Portland, N.S.W., Austral.	99	33 20 S	150 0 E
Portland, Victoria, Austral.	97	38 20 S	141 35 E
Portland, Can.	113	44 42N	76 12W
Portland, Conn., U.S.A.	113	41 34N	72 39W
Portland, Me., U.S.A.	107	43 40N	70 15W
Portland, Mich., U.S.A.	114	42 52N	84 58W
Portland, Oreg., U.S.A.	118	45 35N	122 40W
Portland B.	99	38 15 S	141 45 E
Portland, Bill of	13	50 31N	2 27W
Portland, C.	97	40 46 S	148 0 E
Portland, I. of	13	50 32N	2 25W
Portland Prom.	105	58 40N	78 33W
Portneuf	107	46 43N	71 55W
Porto	30	41 8N	8 40W
Porto □	30	41 8N	8 20W
Pôrto Alegre	125	30 5 S	51 10W
Porto Alexandre	92	15 55 S	11 55 E
Porto Amboim = Gunza	88	10 50 S	13 50 E
Porto Argentera	38	44 15N	7 27 E
Porto Azzurro	38	42 46N	10 24 E
Porto Botte	40	39 3N	8 33 E
Porto Civitanova	39	43 19N	13 44 E
Pôrto de Móz	127	1 41 S	52 13W
Porto Empédocle	40	37 18N	13 30 E
Pôrto Esperança	126	19 37 S	57 29W
Pôrto Franco	127	6 20 S	47 24W
Porto Garibaldi	39	44 41N	12 14 E
Porto, G. de	21	42 17N	8 34 E
Pórto Lágo	44	40 58N	25 6 E
Pôrto Mendes	125	24 30 S	54 15W
Pôrto Murtinho	126	21 45 S	57 55W
Pôrto Nacional	127	10 40 S	48 30W
Porto Novo, Benin	85	6 23N	2 42 E
Porto Novo, India	70	11 30N	79 38 E
Porto Recanati	39	43 26N	13 40 E
Porto San Giórgio	39	43 11N	13 49 E
Porto Santo	80	33 45N	16 25W
Porto Santo Stefano	38	42 26N	11 7 E
Pôrto São José	125	22 43 S	53 10W
Pôrto Seguro	127	16 26 S	39 5W
Porto Tolle	39	44 57N	12 20 E
Porto Tórres	40	40 50N	8 23 E
Pôrto União	125	26 10 S	51 10W
Pôrto Válter	126	8 15 S	72 40W
Porto-Vecchio	21	41 35N	9 16 E
Pôrto Velho	126	8 46 S	63 54W
Portoferráio	38	42 50N	10 20 E
Portogruaro	39	45 47N	12 50 E
Portola	118	39 49N	120 28W
Portomaggiore	39	44 41N	11 47 E
Portoscuso	40	39 12N	8 22 E
Portovénere	38	44 2N	9 50 E
Portoviejo	126	1 7 S	80 28W
Portpatrick	14	54 50N	5 7W
Portree	14	57 25N	6 11W
Portrush	15	55 13N	6 40W
Portsall	18	48 37N	4 45W
Portsmouth, Domin.	121	15 34N	61 27W
Portsmouth, U.K.	13	50 48N	1 6W
Portsmouth, N.H., U.S.A.	114	43 5N	70 45W
Portsmouth, Ohio, U.S.A.	114	38 45N	83 0W
Portsmouth, R.I., U.S.A.	113	41 35N	71 15W
Portsmouth, Va., U.S.A.	114	36 50N	76 20W
Portsoy	14	57 41N	2 41W
Porttipahta	50	68 5N	26 40 E
Portugal ■	30	40 0N	7 0W
Portugalete	32	43 19N	3 4W
Portuguese-Guinea = Guinea-Bissau ■	84	12 0N	15 0W
Portuguese Timor □ = Timor	73	8 0 S	126 30 E
Portumna	15	53 5N	8 12W
Portville	112	42 3N	78 21W
Porvenir	128	53 10 S	70 16W
Porvoo	51	60 24N	25 40 E
Porzuna	31	39 9N	4 9W
Posada →	40	40 40N	9 45 E
Posadas, Argent.	125	27 30 S	55 50W
Posadas, Spain	31	37 47N	5 11W
Poschiavo	25	46 19N	10 4 E
Posets	32	42 39N	0 25 E
Poshan = Boshan	76	36 28N	117 49 E
Posídhion, Ákra	44	39 57N	23 30 E
Posidium	45	35 30N	27 10 E
Poso	73	1 20 S	120 55 E
Posse	127	14 4 S	46 18W
Possel	88	5 5N	19 10 E
Possession I.	5	72 4 S	172 0 E
Pössneck	24	50 42N	11 34 E
Post	117	33 13N	101 21W
Post Falls	118	47 46N	116 59W
Postavy	54	55 4N	26 50 E
Poste Maurice Cortier (Bidon 5)	82	22 14N	1 2 E
Postmasburg	92	28 18 S	23 5 E
Postojna	39	45 46N	14 12 E
Potamós, Andikíthira, Greece	45	36 18N	22 58 E
Potamós, Kíthira, Greece	45	36 15N	22 58 E
Potchefstroom	92	26 41 S	27 7 E
Potcoava	46	44 30N	24 39 E
Poteau	117	35 5N	94 37W
Poteet	117	29 4N	98 35W
Potelu, Lacul	46	43 44N	24 20 E
Potenza	41	40 40N	15 50 E
Potenza →	39	43 27N	13 38 E
Potenza Picena	39	43 22N	13 37 E
Poteriteri, L.	101	46 5 S	167 10 E
Potes	30	43 15N	4 42W
Potgietersrus	93	24 10 S	28 55 E
Poti	57	42 10N	41 38 E
Potiskum	85	11 39N	11 2 E
Potlogi	46	44 34N	25 34 E
Potomac →	114	38 0N	76 23W
Potosí	126	19 38 S	65 50W
Pototan	73	10 54N	122 38 E
Potrerillos	124	26 30 S	69 30W
Potsdam, Ger.	24	52 23N	13 4 E
Potsdam, U.S.A.	114	44 40N	74 59W
Potsdam □	24	52 40N	12 50 E
Pottenstein	25	49 46N	11 25 E
Potter	116	41 15N	103 20W
Pottery Hill = Abu Ballas	86	24 26N	27 36 E
Pottstown	114	40 17N	75 40W
Pottsville	114	40 39N	76 12W
Pouancé	18	47 44N	1 10W
Pouce Coupé	108	55 40N	120 10W
Poughkeepsie	114	41 40N	73 57W
Pouilly	19	47 18N	2 57 E
Poulaphouca Res.	15	53 8N	6 30W
Pouldu, Le	18	47 41N	3 36W
Poulsbo	118	47 45N	122 39W
Pourri, Mont	21	45 32N	6 52 E
Pouso Alegre, Mato Grosso, Brazil	127	11 46 S	57 16W
Pouso Alegre, Minas Gerais, Brazil	125	22 14 S	45 57W
Pouzages	20	46 40N	0 50W
Pouzauges	18	46 47N	0 50W
Povenets	52	62 50N	34 50 E
Poverty Bay	101	38 43 S	178 2 E
Povlen	42	44 9N	19 44 E
Póvoa de Lanhosa	30	41 33N	8 15W
Póvoa de Varzim	30	41 25N	8 46W
Povorino	55	51 12N	42 5 E
Powassan	106	46 5N	79 25W
Powder →	116	46 47N	105 12W
Powder River	118	43 5N	107 0W
Powell	118	44 45N	108 45W
Powell Creek	96	18 6 S	133 46 E
Powell, L.	119	37 25N	110 45W
Powell River	108	49 50N	124 35W
Powers, Mich., U.S.A.	114	45 40N	87 32W
Powers, Oreg., U.S.A.	118	42 53N	124 2W
Powers Lake	116	48 37N	102 38W
Powys □	13	52 20N	3 20W
Poyang Hu	75	29 5N	116 20 E
Poyarkovo	59	49 36N	128 41 E
Poysdorf	27	48 40N	16 37 E
Poza de la Sal	32	42 35N	3 31W
Poza Rica	120	20 33N	97 27W
Požarevac	42	44 35N	21 18 E
Požega	42	43 53N	20 2 E
Poznań	28	52 25N	16 55 E
Poznań □	28	52 50N	17 0 E
Pozo Alcón	33	37 42N	2 56W
Pozo Almonte	126	20 10 S	69 50W
Pozo Colorado	124	23 30 S	58 45W
Pozoblanco	31	38 23N	4 51W
Pozzallo	41	36 44N	14 52 E
Pozzuoli	41	40 46N	14 6 E
Pra →	85	5 1N	1 37W
Prabuty	28	53 47N	19 15 E
Prača	42	43 47N	18 43 E
Prachatice	26	49 1N	14 0 E
Prachin Buri	71	14 0N	101 25 E
Prachuap Khiri Khan	71	11 49N	99 48 E
Pradelles	20	44 46N	3 52 E
Prades	20	42 38N	2 23 E
Prado	127	17 20 S	39 13W
Prado del Rey	31	36 48N	5 33W
Præstø	49	55 8N	12 2 E
Pragersko	39	46 27N	15 42 E
Prague = Praha	26	50 5N	14 22 E
Praha	26	50 5N	14 22 E
Prahecq	20	46 19N	0 26W
Prahita →	70	19 0N	79 55 E
Prahova □	46	45 10N	26 0 E
Prahova →	46	44 50N	25 50 E
Prahovo	42	44 18N	22 39 E
Praid	46	46 32N	25 10 E
Prainha, Amazonas, Brazil	126	7 10 S	60 30W
Prainha, Pará, Brazil	127	1 45 S	53 30W
Prairie	98	20 50 S	144 35 E
Prairie →	117	34 30N	99 23W
Prairie City	118	44 27N	118 44W
Prairie du Chien	116	43 1N	91 9W
Praja	72	8 39 S	116 17 E
Pramánda	44	39 32N	21 8 E
Prang	85	8 1N	0 56W
Prapat	72	2 41N	98 58 E
Praszka	28	51 5N	18 31 E
Prata	127	19 25 S	48 54W
Prática di Mare	40	41 40N	12 26 E
Prato	38	43 53N	11 5 E
Prátola Peligna	39	42 7N	13 51 E
Pratovécchio	39	43 44N	11 43 E
Prats-de-Mollo	20	42 25N	2 27 E
Pratt	117	37 40N	98 45W
Prattville	115	32 30N	86 28W
Pravara →	70	19 35N	74 45 E
Pravdinsk	55	56 29N	43 28 E
Pravia	30	43 30N	6 12W
Pré-en-Pail	18	48 28N	0 12W
Pré St. Didier	38	45 45N	7 0 E
Precordillera	124	30 0 S	69 1W
Predáppio	39	44 7N	11 58 E
Predazzo	39	46 19N	11 37 E
Predejane	42	42 51N	22 9 E
Preeceville	109	51 57N	102 40W
Préfailles	18	47 9N	2 11W
Pregrada	39	46 11N	15 45 E
Preko	39	44 7N	15 14 E
Prelate	109	50 51N	109 24W
Prelog	39	46 18N	16 32 E
Premier	108	56 4N	129 56W
Premier Downs	96	30 30 S	126 30 E
Premont	117	27 19N	98 8W
Premuda	39	44 20N	14 36 E
Prenj	42	43 33N	17 53 E
Prenjasi	44	41 6N	20 32 E
Prentice	116	45 31N	90 19W
Prenzlau	24	53 19N	13 51 E
Prepansko Jezero	44	40 55N	21 0 E
Preparis North Channel	71	15 12N	93 40 E
Preparis South Channel	71	14 36N	93 40 E
Přerov	27	49 28N	17 27 E
Presanella	38	46 13N	10 40 E
Prescott, Can.	106	44 45N	75 30W
Prescott, Ariz., U.S.A.	119	34 35N	112 30W
Prescott, Ark., U.S.A.	117	33 49N	93 22W
Preservation Inlet	101	46 8 S	166 35 E
Preševo	42	42 19N	21 39 E
Presho	116	43 56N	100 4W
Presicce	41	39 53N	18 13 E
Presidencia de la Plaza	124	27 0 S	29 50W
Presidencia Roque Saenz Peña	124	26 45 S	60 30W
Presidente Epitácio	127	21 56 S	52 6W
Presidente Hayes □	124	24 0 S	59 0W
Presidente Hermes	126	11 17 S	61 55W
Presidente Prudente	125	22 5 S	51 25W
Presidio	117	29 30N	104 20W
Preslav	43	43 10N	26 52 E
Preslavska Planina	43	43 10N	26 45 E
Prešov	27	49 0N	21 15 E
Prespa	43	41 44N	24 55 E
Prespa, L. = Prepansko Jezero	44	40 55N	21 0 E
Presque Isle	107	46 40N	68 0W
Presseger See	26	46 37N	13 26 E
Prestbury	13	51 54N	2 2W
Prestea	84	5 22N	2 7W
Presteigne	13	52 17N	3 0W
Přeštice	26	49 34N	13 20 E
Preston, Can.	112	43 23N	80 21W
Preston, U.K.	12	53 46N	2 42W
Preston, Idaho, U.S.A.	118	42 10N	111 55W
Preston, Minn., U.S.A.	116	43 39N	92 3W
Preston, Nev., U.S.A.	118	38 59N	115 2W
Preston, C.	96	20 51 S	116 12 E
Prestonpans	14	55 58N	3 0W
Prestwick	14	55 30N	4 38W
Pretoria	93	25 44 S	28 12 E
Preuilly-sur-Claise	18	46 51N	0 56 E
Préveza	45	38 57N	20 47 E
Préveza □	44	39 20N	20 40 E
Prey-Veng	71	11 35N	105 29 E
Priazovskoye	56	46 44N	35 40 E
Pribilof Is.	4	56 0N	170 0W
Priboj	42	43 35N	19 32 E
Pribram	26	49 41N	14 2 E
Price	118	39 40N	110 48W
Price I.	108	52 23N	128 41W
Prichalnaya	57	48 57N	44 33 E
Priego	32	40 26N	2 21W
Priego de Córdoba	31	37 27N	4 12W
Priekule	54	57 27N	21 45 E
Prien	25	47 52N	12 20 E
Prieska	92	29 40 S	22 42 E
Priest L.	118	48 30N	116 55W
Priest River	118	48 11N	116 55W
Priestly	108	54 8N	125 20W
Prievidza	27	48 46N	18 36 E
Prijedor	39	44 58N	16 41 E
Prijepolje	42	43 27N	19 40 E
Prikaspiyskaya Nizmennost	57	47 0N	48 0 E
Prikumsk	56	44 50N	44 10 E
Prilep	42	41 21N	21 37 E
Priluki	54	50 30N	32 24 E
Primorsko	43	42 15N	27 44 E
Primorsko-Akhtarsk	56	46 2N	38 10 E
Primorskoye	56	47 10N	37 38 E
Primrose L.	109	54 55N	109 45W
Prince Albert	109	53 15N	105 50W
Prince Albert Mts.	5	76 0 S	161 30 E
Prince Albert Nat. Park	109	54 0N	106 25W
Prince Albert Pen.	104	72 30N	116 0W
Prince Albert Sd.	104	70 25N	115 0W
Prince Alfred C.	4	74 20N	124 40W
Prince Charles I.	105	67 47N	76 12W
Prince Charles Mts.	5	72 0 S	67 0 E
Prince Edward I. □	107	46 20N	63 20W
Prince Edward Is.	3	45 15 S	39 0 E
Prince George	108	53 55N	122 50W
Prince of Wales I.	104	55 30N	133 0W
Prince of Wales Is.	97	10 40 S	142 10 E
Prince Patrick I.	4	77 0N	120 0W
Prince Regent Inlet	4	73 0N	90 0W
Prince Rupert	108	54 20N	130 20W
Princess Charlotte B.	97	14 25 S	144 0 E
Princess Royal I.	108	53 0N	128 40W
Princeton, Can.	108	49 27N	120 30W
Princeton, Ill., U.S.A.	116	41 25N	89 25W
Princeton, Ind., U.S.A.	114	38 20N	87 35W
Princeton, Ky., U.S.A.	114	37 6N	87 55W
Princeton, Mo., U.S.A.	116	40 23N	93 35W
Princeton, N.J., U.S.A.	114	40 18N	74 40W
Princeton, W. Va., U.S.A.	114	37 21N	81 8W
Principe Chan.	108	53 28N	130 0W
Principe da Beira	126	12 20 S	64 30W
Principe, I. de	79	1 37N	7 27 E
Prineville	118	44 17N	120 50W
Prins Albert	92	33 12 S	22 2 E
Prins Harald Kyst	5	70 0 S	35 1 E
Prinsesse Astrid Kyst	5	70 45 S	12 30 E
Prinsesse Ragnhild Kyst	5	70 15 S	27 30 E
Prior, C.	30	43 34N	8 17W
Priozersk	52	61 2N	30 7 E
Pripet = Pripyat →	54	51 20N	30 9 E
Pripet Marshes = Polesye	54	52 0N	28 10 E

Pripyat → 54 51 20N 30 9 E
Prislop, Pasul 46 47 37N 25 15 E
Pristen 55 51 15N 36 44 E
Priština 42 42 40N 21 13 E
Pritchard 115 30 47N 88 5W
Pritzwalk 24 53 10N 12 11 E
Privas 21 44 45N 4 37 E
Priverno 40 41 29N 13 10 E
Privolzhsk 55 57 23N 41 16 E
Privolzhskaya Vozvyshennost 55 51 0N 46 0 E
Privolzhskiy 55 51 25N 46 3 E
Privolzhye 55 52 52N 48 33 E
Priyutnoye 57 46 12N 43 40 E
Prizren 42 42 13N 20 45 E
Prizzi 40 37 44N 13 24 E
Prnjavor 42 44 52N 17 43 E
Probolinggo 73 7 46 S 113 13 E
Prochowice 28 51 17N 16 20 E
Procida 40 40 46N 14 0 E
Proddatur 70 14 45N 78 30 E
Proença-a-Nova 31 39 45N 7 54W
Progreso 120 21 20N 89 40W
Prokhladnyy 57 43 50N 44 2 E
Prokletije 44 42 30N 19 45 E
Prokopyevsk 58 54 0N 86 45 E
Prokuplje 42 43 16N 21 36 E
Proletarskaya 57 46 42N 41 50 E
Prome = Pyè 67 18 45N 95 30 E
Prophet → 108 58 48N 122 40W
Propriá 127 10 13 S 36 51W
Propriano 21 41 41N 8 52 E
Proserpine 97 20 21 S 148 36 E
Prosna 28 51 1N 18 30 E
Prosser 118 46 11N 119 52W
Prostějov 27 49 30N 17 9 E
Prostki 28 53 42N 22 25 E
Proston 99 26 8 S 151 32 E
Proszowice 27 50 13N 20 16 E
Protection 117 37 16N 99 30W
Próti 45 37 5N 21 32 E
Provadiya 43 43 12N 27 30 E
Provence 21 43 40N 5 46 E
Providence, Ky., U.S.A. 114 37 25N 87 46W
Providence, R.I., U.S.A. 114 41 50N 71 28W
Providence Bay 106 45 41N 82 15W
Providence Mts. 119 35 0N 115 30W
Providencia, I. de 121 13 25N 81 26W
Provideniya 59 64 23N 173 18W
Provins 19 48 33N 3 15 E
Provo 118 40 16N 111 37W
Provost 109 52 25N 110 20W
Prozor 42 43 50N 17 34 E
Prud'homme 109 52 20N 105 54W
Prudnik 28 50 20N 17 38 E
Prüm 25 50 14N 6 22 E
Pruszcz Gd. 28 54 17N 18 40 E
Pruszków 28 52 9N 20 49 E
Prut → 46 46 3N 28 10 E
Pruzhany 54 52 33N 24 28 E
Prvič 39 44 55N 14 47 E
Prydz B. 5 69 0 S 74 0 E
Pryor 117 36 17N 95 20W
Przasnysz 28 53 2N 20 45 E
Przedbórz 28 51 6N 19 53 E
Przedecz 28 52 20N 18 53 E
Przemyśl 27 49 50N 22 45 E
Przeworsk 27 50 6N 22 32 E
Przewóz 28 51 28N 14 57 E
Przhevalsk 58 42 30N 78 20 E
Przysuchla 28 51 22N 20 38 E
Psakhná 45 38 34N 23 35 E
Psará 45 38 37N 25 38 E
Psathoúra 44 39 30N 24 12 E
Psel → 56 49 5N 33 20 E
Pserimos 45 36 56N 27 12 E
Pskov 54 57 50N 28 25 E
Psunj 42 45 25N 17 19 E
Pszczyna 27 49 59N 18 58 E
Pteleón 45 39 3N 22 57 E
Ptich → 54 52 9N 28 52 E
Ptolemaís 44 40 30N 21 43 E
Ptuj 39 46 28N 15 50 E
Ptujska Gora 39 46 23N 15 47 E
Puán 124 37 30 S 62 45W
Pucallpa 126 8 25 S 74 30W
Pucheng 77 27 59N 118 31 E
Pucheni 46 45 12N 25 17 E
Pučišće 39 43 22N 16 43 E
Puck 28 54 45N 18 23 E
Pucka, Zatoka 28 54 30N 18 40 E
Pudozh 52 61 48N 36 32 E
Pudukkottai 70 10 28N 78 47 E
Puebla 120 19 0N 98 10W
Puebla □ 120 18 30N 98 0W
Puebla de Alcocer 31 38 59N 5 14W
Puebla de Cazalla, La 31 37 10N 5 20W
Puebla de Don Fadrique 33 37 58N 2 25W
Puebla de Don Rodrigo 31 39 5N 4 37W
Puebla de Guzmán 31 37 37N 7 15W
Puebla de los Infantes, La 31 37 47N 5 24W
Puebla de Montalbán, La 30 39 52N 4 22W
Puebla de Sanabria 30 42 4N 6 38W
Puebla de Trives 30 42 20N 7 10W
Puebla del Caramiñal 30 42 37N 8 56W
Puebla, La 32 39 46N 3 1 E
Pueblo 116 38 20N 104 40W
Pueblo Bonito 119 36 4N 107 57W
Pueblo Hundido 124 26 20 S 70 5W
Puelches 124 38 5 S 65 51W
Puelén 124 37 32 S 67 38W
Puente Alto 124 33 32 S 70 35W
Puente del Arzobispo 30 39 48N 5 10W
Puente-Genil 31 37 22N 4 47W
Puente la Reina 32 42 40N 1 49W
Puenteareas 30 42 10N 8 28W
Puentedeume 30 43 24N 8 10W
Puentes de Garcia Rodriguez 30 43 27N 7 50W
Puerco → 119 34 22N 107 50W
Puerta, La 33 38 22N 2 45W
Puerto Aisén 128 45 27 S 73 0W
Puerto Armuelles 121 8 20N 82 51W
Puerto Ayacucho 126 5 40N 67 35W
Puerto Barrios 120 15 40N 88 32W
Puerto Bermejo 124 26 55 S 58 34W
Puerto Bermúdez 126 10 20 S 75 0W
Puerto Bolívar 126 3 19 S 79 55W
Puerto Cabello 126 10 28N 68 1W
Puerto Cabezas 121 14 0N 83 30W
Puerto Capaz = Jebba 82 35 11N 4 43W
Puerto Carreño 126 6 12N 67 22W
Puerto Castilla 121 16 0N 86 0W
Puerto Chicama 126 7 45 S 79 20W
Puerto Coig 128 50 54 S 69 15W
Puerto Cortes 121 8 55N 84 0W
Puerto Cortés 120 15 51N 88 0W
Puerto Cumarebo 126 11 29N 69 30W
Puerto de Santa María 31 36 36N 6 13W
Puerto del Rosario 80 28 30N 13 52W
Puerto Deseado 128 47 55 S 66 0W
Puerto Heath 126 12 34 S 68 39W
Puerto Juárez 120 21 11N 86 49W
Puerto La Cruz 126 10 13N 64 38W
Puerto Leguízamo 126 0 12 S 74 46W
Puerto Libertad 120 29 55N 112 41W
Puerto Lobos 128 42 0 S 65 3W
Puerto Lumbreras 33 37 34N 1 48W
Puerto Madryn 128 42 48 S 65 4W
Puerto Maldonado 126 12 30 S 69 10W
Puerto Mazarrón 33 37 34N 1 15W
Puerto Montt 128 41 28 S 73 0W
Puerto Morelos 120 20 49N 86 52W
Puerto Natales 128 51 45 S 72 15W
Puerto Padre 121 21 13N 76 35W
Puerto Páez 126 6 13N 67 28W
Puerto Peñasco 120 31 20N 113 33W
Puerto Pinasco 124 22 36 S 57 50W
Puerto Pirámides 128 42 35 S 64 20W
Puerto Plata 121 19 48N 70 45W
Puerto Princesa 73 9 46N 118 45 E
Puerto Quellón 128 43 7 S 73 37W
Puerto Quepos 121 9 29N 84 6W
Puerto Real 31 36 33N 6 12W
Puerto Rico ■ 121 18 15N 66 45W
Puerto Sastre 124 22 2 S 57 55W
Puerto Suárez 126 18 58 S 57 52W
Puerto Vallarta 120 20 36N 105 15W
Puerto Wilches 126 7 21N 73 54W
Puertollano 31 38 43N 4 7W
Puertomarín 30 42 48N 7 36W
Pueyrredón, L. 128 47 20 S 72 0W
Pugachev 55 52 0N 48 49 E
Puge 90 4 45 S 33 11 E
Puget Sd. 118 47 15N 122 30W
Puget-Théniers 21 43 58N 6 53 E
Púglia □ 41 41 0N 16 30 E
Pugu 90 6 55 S 39 4 E
Pui 46 45 30N 23 4 E
Puieşti 46 46 25N 27 33 E
Puig Mayor, Mte. 32 39 48N 2 47 E
Puigcerdá 32 42 24N 1 50 E
Puigmal 32 42 23N 2 7 E
Puisaye, Collines de 19 47 34N 3 18 E
Puiseaux 19 48 11N 2 30 E
Puka 44 42 2N 19 53 E
Pukaki L. 101 44 4 S 170 1 E
Pukatawagan 109 55 45N 101 20W
Pukekohe 101 37 12 S 174 55 E
Pukou 77 32 7N 118 38 E
Pula 40 39 0N 9 0 E
Pula (Pola) 39 44 54N 13 57 E
Pulaski, N.Y., U.S.A. 114 43 32N 76 9W
Pulaski, Tenn., U.S.A. 115 35 10N 87 0W
Pulaski, Va., U.S.A. 114 37 4N 80 49W
Pulawy 28 51 23N 21 59 E
Pulgaon 68 20 44N 78 21 E
Pulicat, L. 70 13 40N 80 15 E
Puliyangudi 70 9 11N 77 24 E
Pullman 118 46 49N 117 10W
Pulog, Mt. 73 16 40N 120 50 E
Puloraja 72 4 55N 95 24 E
Pułtusk 28 52 43N 21 6 E
Pumlumon Fawr 13 52 29N 3 47W
Puna 126 19 45 S 65 28W
Puná, I. 126 2 55 S 80 5W
Punakha 69 27 42N 89 52 E
Punalur 70 9 0N 76 56 E
Punasar 68 27 6N 73 6 E
Punata 126 17 32 S 65 50W
Punch 69 33 48N 74 4 E
Pune 70 18 29N 73 57 E
Pungue, Ponte de 91 19 0 S 34 0 E
Puning 77 23 20N 116 12 E
Punjab □ 68 31 0N 76 0 E
Puno 126 15 55 S 70 3W
Punta Alta 128 38 53 S 62 4W
Punta Arenas 128 53 10 S 71 0W
Punta de Díaz 124 28 0 S 70 45W
Punta Gorda, Belize 120 16 10N 88 45W
Punta Gorda, U.S.A. 115 26 55N 82 0W
Puntarenas 121 10 0N 84 50W
Punto Fijo 126 11 50N 70 13W
Punxsutawney 114 40 56N 79 0W
Puqi 77 29 40N 113 50 E
Puquio 126 14 45 S 74 10W
Pur → 58 67 31N 77 55 E
Purace, Vol. 126 2 21N 76 23W
Puračić 42 44 33N 18 28 E
Purari → 98 7 49 S 145 0 E
Purbeck, Isle of 13 50 40N 2 5W
Purcell 117 35 0N 97 25W
Purchena Tetica 33 37 21N 2 21W
Puri 69 19 50N 85 58 E
Purli 68 18 50N 76 35 E
Purmerend 16 52 30N 4 58 E
Purna → 70 19 6N 77 2 E
Purnea 69 25 45N 87 31 E
Pursat 71 12 34N 103 50 E
Purukcahu 72 0 35 S 114 35 E
Purulia 69 23 17N 86 24 E
Purus → 126 3 42 S 61 28W
Pŭrvomay 43 42 8N 25 17 E
Purwakarta 73 6 35 S 107 29 E
Purwodadi, Jawa, Indon. 73 7 51 S 110 0 E
Purwodadi, Jawa, Indon. 73 7 7 S 110 55 E
Purwokerto 73 7 25 S 109 14 E
Purworedjo 73 7 43 S 110 2 E
Pus → 70 19 55N 77 55 E
Pusad 70 19 56N 77 36 E
Pusan 76 35 5N 129 0 E
Pushchino 59 54 10N 158 0 E
Pushkin 54 59 45N 30 25 E
Pushkino, R.S.F.S.R., U.S.S.R. 55 51 16N 47 0 E
Pushkino, R.S.F.S.R., U.S.S.R. 55 56 2N 37 49 E
Püspökladány 27 47 19N 21 6 E
Pustoshka 54 56 20N 29 30 E
Puszczykowo 28 52 18N 16 49 E
Putahow L. 109 59 54N 100 40W
Putao 67 27 28N 97 30 E
Putaruru 101 38 2 S 175 50 E
Putbus 24 54 19N 13 29 E
Puţeni 46 45 49N 27 42 E
Puthein Myit → 67 15 56N 94 18 E
Putian 77 25 23N 119 0 E
Putignano 41 40 50N 17 5 E
Puting, Tanjung 72 3 31 S 111 46 E
Putlitz 24 53 15N 12 3 E
Putna 46 47 50N 25 33 E
Putna → 46 45 42N 27 26 E
Putnam 113 41 55N 71 55W
Putnok 27 48 18N 20 26 E
Putorana, Gory 59 69 0N 95 0 E
Puttalam Lagoon 70 8 15N 79 45 E
Putten 16 52 16N 5 36 E
Puttgarden 24 54 28N 11 15 E
Puttur 70 12 46N 75 12 E
Putumayo → 126 3 7 S 67 58W
Putussibau 72 0 50N 112 56 E
Puy-de-Dôme 20 45 46N 2 57 E
Puy-de-Dôme □ 20 45 47N 3 0 E
Puy-de-Sancy 20 45 32N 2 48 E
Puy-Guillaume 20 45 57N 3 29 E
Puy, Le 20 45 3N 3 52 E
Puy l'Êvêque 20 44 31N 1 9 E
Puyallup 118 47 10N 122 22W
Puyang 76 35 40N 115 1 E
Puylaurens 20 43 35N 2 0 E
Puyôo 20 43 33N 0 56W
Pwani □ 90 7 0 S 39 0 E
Pweto 91 8 25 S 28 51 E
Pwllheli 12 52 54N 4 26W
Pya-ozero 52 66 5N 30 58 E
Pyana → 55 55 30N 46 0 E
Pyapon 67 16 20N 95 40 E
Pyasina → 59 73 30N 87 0 E
Pyatigorsk 57 44 2N 43 6 E
Pyatikhatki 56 48 28N 33 38 E
Pydna 44 40 20N 22 34 E
Pyinmana 67 19 45N 96 12 E
Pyŏngyang 76 39 0N 125 30 E
Pyote 117 31 34N 103 5W
Pyramid L. 118 40 0N 119 30W
Pyramids 86 29 58N 31 9 E
Pyrénées 20 42 45N 0 18 E
Pyrenees = Pyrénées 20 42 45N 0 18 E
Pyrénées-Atlantiques □ 20 43 15N 1 0W
Pyrénées-Orientales □ 20 42 35N 2 26 E
Pyrzyce 28 53 10N 14 55 E
Pyshchug 55 58 57N 45 47 E
Pytalovo 54 57 5N 27 55 E
Pyttegga 47 62 13N 7 42 E
Pyu 67 18 30N 96 28 E
Pyzdry 28 52 11N 17 42 E

Q

Qabalān 62 32 8N 35 17 E
Qabātiyah 62 32 25N 35 16 E
Qaidam Pendi 75 37 0N 95 0 E
Qa'iya 64 24 33N 43 15 E
Qal' at Shajwa 86 25 2N 38 57 E
Qala-i-Jadid (Spin Baldak) 68 31 1N 66 25 E
Qalāt 65 32 15N 66 58 E
Qal'at al Akhḍar 64 28 0N 37 10 E
Qal'at al Mu'azzam 64 27 45N 37 31 E
Qal'at Saura 86 26 10N 38 40 E
Qal'eh-ye Now 65 35 0N 63 5 E
Qalqīlya 62 32 12N 34 58 E
Qalyūb 86 30 12N 31 11 E
Qam 62 32 36N 35 43 E
Qamar, Ghubbat al 63 16 20N 52 30 E
Qamruddin Karez 68 31 45N 68 20 E
Qāna 62 33 12N 35 17 E
Qâra 86 29 38N 26 30 E
Qarachuk 64 37 0N 42 2 E
Qārah 64 29 55N 40 3 E
Qardud 87 10 20N 29 56 E
Qarqan 75 38 5N 85 20 E
Qarqan He → 75 39 30N 88 30 E
Qarrasa 87 14 38N 32 5 E
Qasim 64 26 0N 43 0 E
Qāsim 62 32 59N 36 2 E
Qaşr Bū Hadi 83 31 1N 16 45 E
Qaşr-e Qand 65 26 15N 60 45 E
Qasr Farâfra 86 27 0N 28 1 E
Qatar ■ 65 25 30N 51 15 E
Qattâra 86 30 12N 27 3 E
Qattâra Depression = Qattâra, Munkhafed el 86 29 30N 27 30 E
Qattâra, Munkhafed el 86 29 30N 27 30 E
Qāyen 65 33 40N 59 10 E
Qazvin 64 36 15N 50 0 E
Qena 86 26 10N 32 43 E
Qena, Wadi → 86 26 12N 32 44 E
Qeshm 65 26 55N 56 10 E
Qezi'ot 62 30 52N 34 26 E
Qian Xian 77 34 31N 108 15 E
Qianshan 77 30 37N 116 35 E
Qianxi 77 27 3N 106 3 E
Qianyang 77 27 18N 110 10 E
Qijiang 77 28 57N 106 35 E
Qila Safed 66 29 0N 61 30 E
Qila Saifulla 68 30 45N 68 17 E
Qilian Shan 75 38 30N 96 0 E
Qin Ling = Qinling Shandi 77 33 50N 108 10 E
Qin'an 77 34 48N 105 40 E
Qingdao 76 36 5N 120 20 E
Qinghai □ 75 36 0N 98 0 E
Qinghai Hu 75 36 40N 100 10 E
Qingjiang, Jiangsu, China 77 33 30N 119 2 E
Qingjiang, Jiangxi, China 77 28 4N 115 29 E
Qingliu 77 26 11N 116 48 E
Qingshuihe 76 39 55N 111 35 E
Qingyang 76 36 2N 107 55 E
Qingyuan 77 23 40N 112 59 E
Qinhuangdao 76 39 56N 119 30 E
Qinling Shandi 77 33 50N 108 10 E
Qinyang 77 35 7N 112 57 E
Qinyuan 76 36 29N 112 20 E
Qinzhou 75 21 58N 108 38 E
Qiongshan 77 19 51N 110 26 E
Qiongzhou Haixia 77 20 10N 110 15 E
Qiqihar 75 47 26N 124 0 E
Qiryat 'Anavim 62 31 49N 35 7 E
Qiryat Ata 62 32 47N 35 6 E
Qiryat Bialik 62 32 50N 35 5 E
Qiryat Gat 62 31 32N 34 46 E
Qiryat Ḥayyim 62 32 49N 35 4 E
Qiryat Mal'akhi 62 31 44N 34 44 E
Qiryat Shemona 62 33 13N 35 35 E
Qiryat Yam 62 32 51N 35 4 E
Qishan 77 22 52N 120 25 E
Qishon → 62 32 49N 35 2 E
Qishrān 86 20 14N 40 2 E
Qitai 75 44 2N 89 35 E
Qiyahe 76 53 0N 120 35 E
Qiyang 77 26 35N 111 50 E
Qizan 87 16 57N 42 34 E
Qizān 63 17 0N 42 20 E
Qom 65 34 40N 51 0 E
Qomolangma Feng (Mt. Everest) 75 28 0N 86 45 E
Qondūz 65 36 50N 68 50 E
Qondūz □ 65 36 50N 68 50 E
Qu Jiang → 77 30 1N 106 24 E
Qu Xian, Sichuan, China 77 30 48N 106 58 E
Qu Xian, Zhejiang, China 75 28 57N 118 54 E
Quackenbrück 24 52 40N 7 59 E
Quakertown 113 40 27N 75 20W
Quambatook 99 35 49 S 143 34 E
Quambone 99 30 57 S 147 53 E
Quan Long = Ca Mau 71 9 7N 105 8 E
Quanan 117 34 20N 99 45W
Quandialla 99 34 1 S 147 47 E
Quang Ngai 71 15 13N 108 58 E
Quang Yen 71 20 56N 106 52 E
Quantock Hills 13 51 8N 3 10W
Quanzhou, Fujian, China 75 24 55N 118 34 E
Quanzhou, Guangxi Zhuangzu, China 77 25 57N 111 5 E
Quaraí 124 30 15 S 56 20W
Quarré-les-Tombes 19 47 21N 4 0 E
Quartu Sant' Elena 40 39 15N 9 10 E
Quartzsite 119 33 44N 114 16W
Quatsino 108 50 30N 127 40W
Quatsino Sd. 108 50 25N 127 58W
Qubab = Mishmar Ayyalon 62 31 52N 34 57 E
Qūchān 65 37 10N 58 27 E
† Que Que 91 18 58 S 29 48 E
Queanbeyan 97 35 17 S 149 14 E
Québec 107 46 52N 71 13W
Québec □ 107 50 0N 70 0W
Quedlinburg 24 51 47N 11 9 E
Queen Alexandra Ra. 5 85 0 S 170 0 E
Queen Charlotte 108 53 15N 132 2W
Queen Charlotte Is. 108 53 20N 132 10W
Queen Charlotte Str. 108 51 0N 128 0W
Queen Elizabeth Is. 102 76 0N 95 0W
Queen Elizabeth Nat. Park 90 0 0 S 30 0 E
Queen Mary Coast 5 70 0 S 95 0 E
Queen Maud G. 104 68 15N 102 30W
Queen Maud Ra. 5 86 0 S 160 0W
Queens Chan. 96 15 0 S 129 30 E
Queenscliff 97 38 16 S 144 39 E
Queensland □ 97 22 0 S 142 0 E
Queenstown, Austral. 97 42 4 S 145 35 E
Queenstown, N.Z. 101 45 1 S 168 40 E
Queenstown, S. Afr. 92 31 52 S 26 52 E
Queguay Grande → 124 32 9 S 58 9W
Queimadas 127 11 0 S 39 38W
Quela 88 9 10 S 16 56 E
Quelimane 91 17 53 S 36 58 E
Quelpart = Cheju Do 77 33 29N 126 34 E
Quemado, N. Mex., U.S.A. 119 34 17N 108 28W
Quemado, Tex., U.S.A. 117 28 58N 100 35W
Quemú-Quemú 124 36 3 S 63 36W
Quequén 124 38 30 S 58 30W
Querétaro 120 20 40N 100 23W
Querétaro □ 120 20 30N 100 0W
Querfurt 24 51 22N 11 33 E
Querqueville 18 49 40N 1 42W
Quesada 33 37 51N 3 4W
Queshan 77 32 55N 114 2 E
Quesnel 108 53 0N 122 30W
Quesnel → 108 52 58N 122 29W
Quesnel L. 108 52 30N 121 20W
Quesnoy, Le 19 50 15N 3 38 E
Questa 119 36 45N 105 35W
Questembert 18 47 40N 2 28W
Quetico Prov. Park 106 48 30N 91 45W
Quetta 66 30 15N 66 55 E
• Quetta □ 66 30 15N 66 55 E
Quezaltenango 120 14 50N 91 30W
Quezon City 73 14 38N 121 0 E
Qui Nhon 71 13 40N 109 13 E
Quiaca, La 124 22 5 S 65 35W
Quibaxe 88 8 24 S 14 27 E
Quibdo 126 5 42N 76 40W
Quiberon 18 47 29N 3 9W
Quick 108 54 36N 126 54W
Quickborn 24 53 42N 9 52 E
Quiet L. 108 61 5N 133 5W
Quiindy 124 25 58 S 57 14W
Quilán, C. 128 43 15 S 74 30W
Quilengues 89 14 12 S 14 12 E
Quilimarí 124 32 5 S 71 30W
Quilino 124 30 14 S 64 29W
Quillabamba 126 12 50 S 72 50W

• *Now part of Baluchistan* □

† *Renamed Kwekwe*

Quillagua 124 21 40 S 69 40W
Quillaicillo 124 31 17 S 71 40W
Quillan 20 42 53N 2 10 E
Quillebeuf 18 49 28N 0 30 E
Quillota 124 32 54 S 71 16W
Quilmes 124 34 43 S 58 15W
Quilon 70 8 50N 76 38 E
Quilpie 97 26 35 S 144 11 E
Quilpué 124 33 5 S 71 33W
Quilua 91 16 17 S 39 54 E
Quimili 124 27 40 S 62 30W
Quimper 18 48 0N 4 9W
Quimperlé 18 47 53N 3 33W
Quincy, Calif., U.S.A. 118 39 56N 121 0W
Quincy, Fla., U.S.A. 115 30 34N 84 34W
Quincy, Ill., U.S.A. 116 39 55N 91 20W
Quincy, Mass., U.S.A. 114 42 14N 71 0W
Quincy, Wash., U.S.A. 118 47 22N 119 56W
Quines 124 32 13 S 65 48W
Quinga 91 15 49 S 40 15 E
Quingey 19 47 7N 5 52 E
Quintana de la Serena 31 38 45N 5 40W
Quintana Roo □ 120 19 0N 88 0W
Quintanar de la Orden 32 39 36N 3 5W
Quintanar de la Sierra 32 41 57N 2 55W
Quintanar del Rey 33 39 21N 1 56W
Quintero 124 32 45 S 71 30W
Quintin 18 48 26N 2 56W
Quinto 32 41 25N 0 32W
Quinyambie 99 30 15 S 141 0 E
Quipar → 33 38 15N 1 40W
Quirihue 124 36 15 S 72 35W
Quirindi 99 31 28 S 150 40 E
Quiroga 30 42 28N 7 18W
Quissac 21 43 55N 4 0 E
Quissanga 91 12 24 S 40 28 E
Quitilipi 124 26 50 S 60 13W
Quitman, Ga., U.S.A. 115 30 49N 83 35W
Quitman, Miss., U.S.A. 115 32 2N 88 42W
Quitman, Tex., U.S.A. 117 32 48N 95 25W
Quito 126 0 15 S 78 35W
Quixadá 127 4 55 S 39 0W
Quixaxe 91 15 17 S 40 4 E
Qul'ân, Jazâ'ir 86 24 22N 35 31 E
Qumrân 62 31 43N 35 27 E
Quneitra 62 33 7N 35 48 E
Quoin Pt. 92 34 46 S 19 37 E
Quondong 99 33 6 S 140 18 E
Quorn 97 32 25 S 138 0 E
Qurein 87 13 30N 34 50 E
Qûs 86 25 55N 32 50 E
Quseir 86 26 7N 34 16 E
Qusrah 62 32 5N 35 20 E
Quthing 93 30 25 S 27 36 E
Qytet Stalin (Kuçove) 44 40 47N 19 57 E

R

Râå 49 56 0N 12 45 E
Raab 26 48 21N 13 39 E
Raahe 50 64 40N 24 28 E
Ra'ananna 62 32 12N 34 52 E
Raasay 14 57 25N 6 4W
Raasay, Sd. of 14 57 30N 6 8W
Rab 39 44 45N 14 45 E
Raba 73 8 36 S 118 55 E
Rába → 27 47 38N 17 38 E
Raba → 27 50 8N 20 30 E
Rabaçal → 30 41 30N 7 12W
Rabah 85 13 5N 5 30 E
Rabai 90 3 50 S 39 31 E
Rabastens, Hautes-Pyrénées, France 20 43 25N 0 10 E
Rabastens, Tarn, France 20 43 50N 1 43 E
Rabat, Malta 36 35 53N 14 25 E
Rabat, Moroc. 82 34 2N 6 48W
Rabaul 94 4 24 S 152 18 E
Rabbit → 108 59 41N 127 12W
Rabbit Lake 109 53 8N 107 46W
Rabbitskin → 108 61 47N 120 42W
Râbigh 64 22 50N 39 5 E
Rabka 27 49 37N 19 59 E
Rača 42 44 14N 21 0 E
Răcale 41 39 57N 18 6 E
Racalmuto 40 37 25N 13 41 E
Răcășdia 42 44 59N 21 36 E
Racconigi 38 44 47N 7 41 E
Race, C. 107 46 40N 53 5W
Rach Gia 71 10 5N 105 5 E
Raciąż 28 52 46N 20 10 E
Racibórz 27 50 7N 18 18 E
Racine 114 42 41N 87 51W
Radama, Nosy 93 14 0 S 47 47 E
Radama, Saikanosy 93 14 16 S 47 53 E
Radan 42 42 59N 21 29 E
Rădăuţi 46 47 50N 25 59 E
Radbuza → 26 49 35N 13 5 E
Räde 47 59 21N 10 53 E
Radeburg 24 51 6N 13 55 E
Radeče 39 46 5N 15 14 E
Radekhov 54 50 25N 24 32 E
Radew → 28 54 2N 15 52 E
Radford 114 37 8N 80 32W
Radhanpur 68 23 50N 71 38 E
Radhwa, Jabal 64 24 34N 38 18 E
Radiska → 42 41 38N 20 37 E
Radisson 109 52 30N 107 20W
Radium Hill 97 32 30 S 140 42 E
Radium Hot Springs 108 50 35N 116 2W
Radja, Kepulauan 73 0 30 S 130 00 E
Radków 28 50 30N 16 24 E
Radlin 27 50 3N 18 29 E
Radna 42 46 7N 21 41 E
Radnevo 43 42 17N 25 58 E
Radnice 26 49 51N 13 35 E
Radnor Forest 13 52 17N 3 10W
Radolfzell 25 47 44N 8 58 E
Radom 28 51 23N 21 12 E
Radom □ 28 51 30N 21 0 E
Radomir 42 42 37N 23 4 E
Radomka → 28 51 31N 21 11 E
Radomsko 28 51 5N 19 28 E
Radomyshl 54 50 30N 29 12 E
Radomysl Wielki 27 50 14N 21 15 E
Radoszyce 28 51 4N 20 15 E
Radoviš 42 41 38N 22 28 E
Radovljica 39 46 22N 14 12 E
Radstadt 26 47 24N 13 28 E
Radstock 13 51 17N 2 25W
Răducăneni 46 46 58N 27 54 E
Raduša 42 42 7N 21 15 E
Radviliškis 54 55 49N 23 33 E
Radville 109 49 30N 104 15W
Radymno 27 49 59N 22 52 E
Radzanów 28 52 56N 20 8 E
Radziejów 28 52 40N 18 30 E
Radzymin 28 52 25N 21 11 E
Radzyń Chełmiński 28 53 23N 18 55 E
Radzyń Podlaski 28 51 47N 22 37 E
Rae 108 62 50N 116 3W
Rae Bareli 69 26 18N 81 20 E
Rae Isthmus 105 66 40N 87 30W
Raeren 16 50 41N 6 7 E
Raeside, L. 96 29 20 S 122 0 E
Raetihi 101 39 25 S 175 17 E
Rafaela 124 31 10 S 61 30W
Rafah 86 31 18N 34 14 E
Rafai 90 4 59N 23 58 E
Raffadali 40 37 23N 13 29 E
Rafḥā 64 29 35N 43 35 E
Rafsanjān 65 30 30N 56 5 E
Ragag 87 10 59N 24 40 E
Raglan, Austral. 98 23 42 S 150 49 E
Raglan, N.Z. 101 37 55 S 174 55 E
Ragunda 48 63 6N 16 23 E
Ragusa 41 36 56N 14 42 E
Raha 73 4 55 S 123 0 E
Rahad al Bardī 81 11 20N 23 40 E
Rahad, Nahr ed → 87 14 28N 33 31 E
Rahden 24 52 26N 8 36 E
Raheita 87 12 46N 43 4 E
Rahimyar Khan 68 28 30N 70 25 E
Raichur 70 16 10N 77 20 E
Raiganj 69 25 37N 88 10 E
Raigarh, Madhya Pradesh, India 69 21 56N 83 25 E
Raigarh, Orissa, India 70 19 51N 82 6 E
Raiis 64 23 33N 38 43 E
Raijua 73 10 37 S 121 36 E
Railton 99 41 25 S 146 28 E
Rainbow Lake 108 58 30N 119 23W
Rainier 118 46 4N 123 0W
Rainier, Mt. 118 46 50N 121 50W
Rainy L. 109 48 42N 93 10W
Rainy River 109 48 43N 94 29W
Raipur 69 21 17N 81 45 E
Raja, Kepulauan 73 0 30 S 129 40 E
Raja, Ujung 72 3 40N 96 25 E
Rajahmundry 70 17 1N 81 48 E
Rajang → 72 2 30N 112 0 E
Rajapalaiyam 70 9 25N 77 35 E
Rajasthan □ 68 26 45N 73 30 E
Rajasthan Canal 68 28 0N 72 0 E
Rajbari 69 23 47N 89 41 E
Rajgarh, Mad. P., India 68 24 2N 76 45 E
Rajgarh, Raj., India 68 28 40N 75 25 E
Rajgród 28 53 42N 22 42 E
Rajhenburg 39 46 1N 15 29 E
Rajkot 68 22 15N 70 56 E
Rajmahal Hills 69 24 30N 87 30 E
Rajnandgaon 69 21 5N 81 5 E
Rajojooseppi 50 68 25N 28 30 E
Rajpipla 68 21 50N 73 30 E
Rajpura 68 30 25N 76 32 E
Rajshahi 69 24 22N 88 39 E
Rajshahi □ 69 25 0N 89 0 E
Rakaia 101 43 45 S 172 1 E
Rakaia → 101 43 36 S 172 15 E
Rakan, Ra's 65 26 10N 51 20 E
Rakaposhi 69 36 10N 74 25 E
Rakha 86 18 25N 41 30 E
Rakhni 68 30 4N 69 56 E
Rakitovo 43 41 59N 24 5 E
Rakkestad 47 59 25N 11 21 E
Rakoniewice 28 52 10N 16 16 E
Rakops 92 21 1 S 24 28 E
Rákospalota 27 47 30N 19 5 E
Rakov 54 53 58N 26 59 E
Rakovica 39 44 59N 15 38 E
Rakovník 26 50 6N 13 42 E
Rakovski 43 42 21N 24 57 E
Rakvere 54 59 30N 26 25 E
Raleigh 115 35 47N 78 39W
Raleigh B. 115 34 50N 76 15W
Ralja 42 44 33N 20 34 E
Ralls 117 33 40N 101 20W
Ram → 108 62 1N 123 41W
Râm Allâh 62 31 55N 35 10 E
Rama 62 32 56N 35 21 E
Ramacca 41 37 24N 14 40 E
Ramachandrapuram 70 16 50N 82 4 E
Ramales de la Victoria 32 43 15N 3 28W
Ramanathapuram 70 9 25N 78 55 E
Ramanetaka, B. de 93 14 13 S 47 52 E
Ramas C. 70 15 5N 73 55 E
Ramat Gan 62 32 4N 34 48 E
Ramat HaSharon 62 32 7N 34 50 E
Ramatlhabama 92 25 37 S 25 33 E
Rambervillers 19 48 20N 6 38 E
Rambipuji 73 8 12 S 113 37 E
Rambla, La 31 37 37N 4 45W
Rambouillet 19 48 40N 1 48 E
Ramdurg 70 15 58N 75 22 E
Rame Hd. 99 37 47 S 149 30 E
Ramea 107 47 28N 57 4W
Ramechhap 69 27 25N 86 10 E
Ramelau 73 8 55 S 126 22 E
Ramenskoye 55 55 32N 38 15 E
Ramgarh, Bihar, India 69 23 40N 85 35 E
Ramgarh, Rajasthan, India 68 27 16N 75 14 E
Ramgarh, Rajasthan, India 68 27 30N 70 36 E
Rāmhormoz 64 31 15N 49 35 E
Ramla 62 31 55N 34 52 E
Ramlat Zalṭan 83 28 30N 19 30 E
Ramlu 87 13 32N 41 40 E
Ramme 49 56 30N 8 11 E
Rammūn 62 31 55N 35 17 E
Ramnad = Ramanathapuram 70 9 25N 78 55 E
Ramnäs 48 59 46N 16 12 E
Ramon 55 51 55N 39 21 E
Ramon, Har 62 30 30N 34 38 E
Ramona 119 33 1N 116 56W
Ramore 106 48 30N 80 25W
Ramos → 120 25 35N 105 3W
Ramoutsa 92 24 50 S 25 52 E
Rampart 104 65 0N 150 15W
Rampur, H.P., India 68 31 26N 77 43 E
Rampur, Mad. P., India 68 23 25N 73 53 E
Rampur, Orissa, India 69 21 48N 83 58 E
Rampur, U.P., India 68 28 50N 79 5 E
Rampura 68 24 30N 75 27 E
Rampurhat 69 24 10N 87 50 E
Ramree Kyun 67 19 0N 94 0 E
Ramsey, Can. 106 47 25N 82 20W
Ramsey, U.K. 12 54 20N 4 21W
Ramsgate 13 51 20N 1 25 E
Ramsjö 48 62 11N 15 37 E
Ramtek 69 21 20N 79 15 E
Ramu → 98 4 0 S 144 41 E
Ramvik 48 62 49N 17 51 E
Ranaghat 69 23 15N 88 35 E
Ranahu 68 25 55N 69 45 E
Ranau 72 6 2N 116 40 E
Rancagua 124 34 10 S 70 50W
Rance → 18 48 34N 1 59W
Rance, Barrage de la 18 48 30N 2 3W
Rancheria → 108 60 13N 129 7W
Ranchester 118 44 57N 107 12W
Ranchi 69 23 19N 85 27 E
Rancu 46 44 32N 24 15 E
Rand 100 35 33 S 146 32 E
Randan 20 46 2N 3 21 E
Randazzo 41 37 53N 14 56 E
Randers 49 56 29N 10 1 E
Randers Fjord 49 56 37N 10 20 E
Randfontein 93 26 8 S 27 45 E
Randolph, Mass., U.S.A. 113 42 10N 71 3W
Randolph, N.Y., U.S.A. 112 42 10N 78 59W
Randolph, Utah, U.S.A. 118 41 43N 111 10W
Randolph, Vt., U.S.A. 113 43 55N 72 39W
Randsburg 119 35 22N 117 44W
Randsfjorden 47 60 15N 10 25 E
Råne älv → 50 65 50N 22 20 E
Rangaunu B. 101 34 51 S 173 15 E
Rångedala 49 57 47N 13 9 E
Rangeley 114 44 58N 70 33W
Rangely 118 40 3N 108 53W
Ranger 117 32 30N 98 42W
Rangia 67 26 28N 91 38 E
Rangiora 101 43 19 S 172 36 E
Rangitaiki → 101 37 54 S 176 49 E
Rangitata → 101 43 45 S 171 15 E
Rangkasbitung 73 6 22 S 106 16 E
Rangon → 67 16 28N 96 40 E
Rangoon 67 16 45N 96 20 E
Ranibennur 70 14 35N 75 30 E
Raniganj 69 23 40N 87 5 E
Ranipet 70 12 56N 79 23 E
Rankin 117 31 16N 101 56W
Rankin Inlet 104 62 30N 93 0W
Rankins Springs 99 33 49 S 146 14 E
Rannoch, L. 14 56 41N 4 20W
Rannoch Moor 14 56 38N 4 48W
Ranobe, Helodranon' i 93 23 3 S 43 33 E
Ranohira 93 22 29 S 45 24 E
Ranomafana, Tamatave, Madag. 93 18 57 S 48 50 E
Ranomafana, Tuléar, Madag. 93 24 34 S 47 0 E
Ranong 71 9 56N 98 40 E
Ransiki 73 1 30 S 134 10 E
Rantau 72 2 56 S 115 9 E
Rantauprapat 72 2 15N 99 50 E
Rantemario 73 3 15 S 119 57 E
Rantīs 62 32 4N 35 3 E
Rantoul 114 40 18N 88 10W
Ranum 49 56 54N 9 14 E
Ranwanlenau 92 19 37 S 22 49 E
Raohe 76 46 47N 134 0 E
Raon l'Étape 19 48 24N 6 50 E
Raoui, Erg er 82 29 0N 2 0W
Rapa Iti 95 27 35 S 144 20W
Rapallo 38 44 21N 9 12 E
Rapang 73 3 45 S 119 55 E
Rāpch 65 25 40N 59 15 E
Rapid → 108 59 15N 129 5W
Rapid City 116 44 0N 103 0W
Rapid River 114 45 55N 87 0W
Rapides des Joachims 106 46 13N 77 43W
Rapla 54 59 1N 24 52 E
Rarotonga 95 21 30 S 160 0W
Ra's al Khaymah 65 25 50N 56 5 E
Ra's al-Unuf 83 30 25N 18 15 E
Ras Bânâs 81 23 57N 35 59 E
Ras Dashen 87 13 8N 38 26 E
Ras el Ma 82 34 26N 0 50W
Ras Mallap 86 29 18N 32 50 E
Ra's Tannūrah 64 26 40N 50 10 E
Râs Timirist 84 19 21N 16 30W
Rasa, Punta 128 40 50 S 62 15W
Raseiniai 54 55 25N 23 5 E
Rashad 87 11 55N 31 0 E
Rashîd 86 31 21N 30 22 E
Rashîd, Masabb 86 31 22N 30 17 E
Rasht 64 37 20N 49 40 E
Rasipuram 70 11 30N 78 15 E
Raška 42 43 19N 20 39 E
Rason, L. 96 28 45 S 124 25 E
Raşova 46 44 15N 27 55 E
Rasovo 43 43 42N 23 17 E
Rasra 69 25 50N 83 50 E
Rass el Oued 83 35 57N 5 2 E
Rasskazovo 55 52 35N 41 50 E
Rastatt 25 48 50N 8 12 E
Rastu 46 43 53N 23 16 E
Raszków 28 51 43N 17 40 E
Rat Buri 71 13 30N 99 54 E
Rat Is. 104 51 50N 178 15 E
Rat River 108 61 7N 112 36W
Ratangarh 68 28 5N 74 35 E
Rath 69 25 36N 79 37 E
Rath Luirc (Charleville) 15 52 21N 8 40W
Rathdrum, Ireland 15 52 57N 6 13W
Rathdrum, U.S.A. 118 47 50N 116 58W
Rathenow 24 52 38N 12 23 E
Rathkeale 15 52 32N 8 57W
Rathlin I. 15 55 18N 6 14W
Rathlin O'Birne I. 15 54 40N 8 50W
Ratibor = Racibórz 27 50 7N 18 18 E
Rätikon 26 47 0N 9 55 E
Ratlam 68 23 20N 75 0 E
Ratnagiri 70 16 57N 73 18 E
Ratnapura 70 6 40N 80 20 E
Raton 117 37 0N 104 30W
Ratten 26 47 28N 15 44 E
Rattray Hd. 14 57 38N 1 50W
Rättvik 48 60 52N 15 7 E
Ratz, Mt. 108 57 23N 132 12W
Ratzeburg 24 53 41N 10 46 E
Raub 71 3 47N 101 52 E
Rauch 124 36 45 S 59 5W
Raufarhöfn 50 66 27N 15 57W
Raufoss 47 60 44N 10 37 E
Raukumara Ra. 101 38 5 S 177 55 E
Rauland 47 59 43N 8 0 E
Rauma 51 61 10N 21 30 E
Rauma → 47 62 34N 7 43 E
Raundal 47 60 40N 6 37 E
Raung 73 8 8 S 114 4 E
Raurkela 69 22 14N 84 50 E
Rava Russkaya 54 50 15N 23 42 E
Ravanusa 40 37 16N 13 58 E
Rāvar 65 31 20N 56 51 E
Ravena 113 42 28N 73 49W
Ravenna, Italy 39 44 28N 12 15 E
Ravenna, Nebr., U.S.A. 116 41 3N 98 58W
Ravenna, Ohio, U.S.A. 112 41 11N 81 15W
Ravensburg 25 47 48N 9 38 E
Ravenshoe 97 17 37 S 145 29 E
Ravensthorpe 96 33 35 S 120 2 E
Ravenswood, Austral. 98 20 6 S 146 54 E
Ravenswood, U.S.A. 114 38 58N 81 47W
Ravi → 68 30 35N 71 49 E
Ravna Gora 39 45 24N 14 50 E
Ravna Reka 42 43 59N 21 35 E
Rawa Mazowiecka 28 51 46N 20 12 E
Rawalpindi 66 33 38N 73 8 E
Rawāndūz 64 36 40N 44 30 E
Rawang 71 3 20N 101 35 E
Rawdon 106 46 3N 73 40W
Rawene 101 35 25 S 173 32 E
Rawicz 28 51 36N 16 52 E
Rawka → 28 52 9N 20 8 E
Rawlinna 96 30 58 S 125 28 E
Rawlins 118 41 50N 107 20W
Rawlinson Range 96 24 40 S 128 30 E
Rawson 128 43 15 S 65 0W
Ray 116 48 21N 103 6W
Ray, C. 107 47 33N 59 15W
Rayachoti 70 14 4N 78 50 E
Rayadrug 70 14 40N 76 50 E
Rayagada 70 19 15N 83 20 E
Raychikhinsk 59 49 46N 129 25 E
Raymond, Can. 108 49 30N 112 35W
Raymond, U.S.A. 118 46 45N 123 48W
Raymondville 117 26 30N 97 50W
Raymore 109 51 25N 104 31W
Rayne 117 30 16N 92 16W
Rayong 71 12 40N 101 20 E
Rayville 117 32 30N 91 45W
Raz, Pte. du 18 48 2N 4 47W
Ražana 42 44 6N 19 55 E
Ražanj 42 43 40N 21 31 E
Razdelna 43 43 13N 27 41 E
Razdel'naya 56 46 50N 30 2 E
Razdolnoye 56 45 46N 33 29 E
Razelm, Lacul 46 44 50N 29 0 E
Razgrad 43 43 33N 26 34 E
Razlog 43 41 53N 23 28 E
Razmak 68 32 45N 69 50 E
Razole 70 16 36N 81 48 E
Ré, Île de 20 46 12N 1 30W
Reading, U.K. 13 51 27N 0 57W
Reading, U.S.A. 114 40 20N 75 53W
Realicó 124 35 0 S 64 15W
Réalmont 20 43 48N 2 10 E
Ream 71 10 34N 103 39 E
Rebais 19 48 50N 3 10 E
Rebi 73 6 23 S 134 7 E
Rebiana 81 24 12N 22 10 E
Rebun-Tō 74 45 23N 141 2 E
Recanati 39 43 24N 13 32 E
Recaş 42 45 46N 21 30 E
Recherche, Arch. of the 96 34 15 S 122 50 E
Rechitsa 54 52 13N 30 15 E
Recife 127 8 0 S 35 0W
Recklinghausen 24 51 36N 7 10 E
Reconquista 124 29 10 S 59 45W
Recreo 124 29 25 S 65 10W
Recz 28 53 16N 15 31 E
Red →, Can. 109 50 24N 96 48W
Red →, Minn., U.S.A. 116 48 10N 97 0W
Red →, Tex., U.S.A. 117 31 0N 91 40W
Red Bank 113 40 21N 74 4W
Red Bay 107 51 44N 56 25W
Red Bluff 118 40 11N 122 11W
Red Bluff L. 117 31 59N 103 58W
Red Cloud 116 40 8N 98 33W
Red Deer 108 52 20N 113 50W
Red Deer →, Alta., Can. 109 50 58N 110 0W
Red Deer →, Man., Can. 109 52 53N 101 1W
Red Deer L. 109 52 55N 101 20W
Red Indian L. 107 48 35N 57 0W
Red Lake 109 51 3N 93 49W
Red Lake Falls 116 47 54N 96 15W
Red Lodge 118 45 10N 109 10W
Red Oak 116 41 0N 95 10W
Red Rock 106 48 55N 88 15W
Red Rock, L. 116 41 30N 93 15W

Red Sea 63 25 0N 36 0 E
Red Sucker L 109 54 9N 93 40W
Red Tower Pass = Turnu Rosu P. 46 45 33N 24 17 E
Red Wing 116 44 32N 92 35W
Reda 28 54 40N 18 19 E
Redbridge 13 51 35N 0 7 E
Redcar 12 54 37N 1 4W
Redcliff 109 50 10N 110 50W
Redcliffe 99 27 12 S 153 0 E
Reddersburg 92 29 41 S 26 10 E
Redding 118 40 30N 122 25W
Redditch 13 52 18N 1 57W
Redfield 116 45 0N 98 30W
Redknife → 108 61 14N 119 22W
Redlands 119 34 0N 117 11W
Redmond 118 44 19N 121 11W
Redon 18 47 40N 2 6W
Redonda 121 16 58N 62 19W
Redondela 30 42 15N 8 38W
Redondo 31 38 39N 7 37W
Redondo Beach 119 33 52N 118 26W
Redrock Pt. 108 62 11N 115 2W
Redruth 13 50 14N 5 14W
Redvers 109 49 35N 101 40W
Redwater 108 53 55N 113 6W
Redwood 113 44 18N 75 48W
Redwood City 119 37 30N 122 15W
Redwood Falls 116 44 30N 95 2W
Ree, L. 15 53 35N 8 0W
Reed City 114 43 52N 85 30W
Reed, L 109 54 38N 100 30W
Reeder 116 46 7N 102 52W
Reedley 119 36 36N 119 27W
Reedsburg 116 43 34N 90 5W
Reedsport 118 43 45N 124 4W
Reefton 101 42 6 S 171 51 E
Reftele 49 57 11N 13 35 E
Refugio 117 28 18N 97 17W
Rega → 28 54 10N 15 18 E
Regalbuto 41 37 40N 14 38 E
Regavim 62 32 32N 35 2 E
Regen 25 48 58N 13 9 E
Regen → 25 49 2N 12 6 E
Regensburg 25 49 1N 12 7 E
Réggio di Calábria 41 38 7N 15 38 E
Réggio nell' Emilia 38 44 42N 10 38 E
Regina 109 50 27N 104 35W
Registro 125 24 29 S 47 49W
Reguengos de Monsaraz 31 38 25N 7 32W
Rehar → 69 23 55N 82 40 E
Rehoboth 92 23 15 S 17 4 E
Rehovot 62 31 54N 34 48 E
Rei-Bouba 81 8 40N 14 15 E
Reichenbach 24 50 36N 12 19 E
Reid River 98 19 40 S 146 48 E
Reidsville 115 36 21N 79 40W
Reigate 13 51 14N 0 11W
Reillo 32 39 54N 1 53W
Reims 19 49 15N 4 0 E
Reina 62 32 43N 35 18 E
Reina Adelaida, Arch. 128 52 20 S 74 0W
Reinbeck 116 42 18N 92 0W
Reindeer → 109 55 36N 103 11W
Reindeer I. 109 52 30N 98 0W
Reindeer L. 109 57 15N 102 15W
Reine, La 32 48 50N 79 30W
Reinga, C. 101 34 25 S 172 43 E
Reinosa 30 43 2N 4 15W
Reinosa, Paso 30 42 56N 4 10W
Reitz 93 27 48 S 28 29 E
Reivilo 92 27 36 S 24 8 E
Rejmyra 49 58 50N 15 55 E
Rejowiec Fabryczny 28 51 5N 23 17 E
Reka → 39 45 40N 14 0 E
Rekinniki 59 60 51N 163 40 E
Rekovac 42 43 51N 21 3 E
Reliance 109 63 0N 109 20W
Remad, Oued → 82 33 28N 1 20W
Rémalard 18 48 26N 0 47 E
Remanso 127 9 41 S 42 4W
Remarkable, Mt. 99 32 48 S 138 10 E
Rembang 73 6 42 S 111 21 E
Remchi 82 35 2N 1 26W
Remeshk 65 26 55N 58 50 E
Remetea 46 46 45N 25 29 E
Remich 16 49 32N 6 22 E
Remiremont 19 48 0N 6 36 E
Remo 87 6 48N 41 20 E
Remontnoye 57 46 34N 43 37 E
Remoulins 21 43 55N 4 35 E
Remscheid 24 51 11N 7 12 E
Rena 47 61 8N 11 20 E
Rena → 47 61 8N 11 23 E
Rende 41 39 19N 16 11 E
Rendina 45 39 4N 21 58 E
Rendsburg 24 54 18N 9 41 E
Rene 59 66 2N 179 25W
Renfrew, Can. 106 45 30N 76 40W
Renfrew, U.K. 14 55 52N 4 24W
Rengat 72 0 30 S 102 45 E
Rengo 124 34 24 S 70 50W
Renhuai 77 27 48N 106 24 E
Reni 56 45 28N 28 15 E
Renigunta 70 13 38N 79 30 E
Renk 81 11 50N 32 50 E
Renkum 16 51 58N 5 43 E
Renmark 97 34 11 S 140 43 E
Rennell Sd. 108 53 23N 132 35W
Renner Springs T.O. 96 18 20 S 133 47 E
Rennes 18 48 7N 1 41W
Rennes, Bassin de 18 48 12N 1 33W
Rennesøy 47 59 6N 5 43 E
Reno 118 39 30N 119 50W
Reno → 39 44 37N 12 17 E
Renovo 114 41 20N 77 47W
Rensselaer, Ind., U.S.A. 114 40 57N 87 10W
Rensselaer, N.Y., U.S.A. 113 42 38N 73 41W
Renteria 32 43 19N 1 54W
Renton 118 47 30N 122 9W
Réo 84 12 28N 2 35W
Réole, La 20 44 35N 0 1W
Reotipur 69 25 33N 83 45 E
Repalle 70 16 2N 80 45 E
Répcelak 27 47 24N 17 1 E
Republic, Mich., U.S.A. 114 46 25N 87 59W
Republic, Wash., U.S.A. 118 48 38N 118 42W
Republican → 116 39 3N 96 48W
Republican City 116 40 9N 99 20W
Repulse B., Antarct. 5 64 30 S 99 30 E
Repulse B., Austral. 97 20 31 S 148 45 E
Repulse Bay 105 66 30N 86 30W
Requena, Peru 126 5 5 S 73 52W
Requena, Spain 33 39 30N 1 4W
Resele 48 63 20N 17 5 E
Resen 42 41 5N 21 0 E
Reserve, Can. 109 52 28N 102 39W
Reserve, U.S.A. 119 33 50N 108 54W
Resht = Rasht 64 37 20N 49 40 E
Resistencia 124 27 30 S 59 0W
Reşiţa 42 45 18N 21 53 E
Resko 28 53 47N 15 25 E
Resolution I., Can. 105 61 30N 65 0W
Resolution I., N.Z. 101 45 40 S 166 40 E
Ressano Garcia 93 25 25 S 32 0 E
Reston 109 49 33N 101 6W
Reszel 28 54 4N 21 10 E
Retalhuleu 120 14 33N 91 46W
Reteag 46 47 10N 24 0 E
Retenue, Lac de 91 11 0 S 27 0 E
Rethel 19 49 30N 4 20 E
Rethem 24 52 47N 9 25 E
Réthimnon 45 35 18N 24 30 E
Réthimnon □ 45 35 23N 24 28 E
Rétiers 18 47 55N 1 25W
Retortillo 30 40 48N 6 21W
Rétság 27 47 58N 19 10 E
Réunion 3 22 0 S 56 0 E
Reus 32 41 10N 1 5 E
Reuss → 25 47 16N 8 24 E
Reuterstadt Stavenhagen 24 53 41N 12 54 E
Reutlingen 25 48 28N 9 13 E
Reutte 26 47 29N 10 42 E
Reval = Tallinn 54 59 29N 24 58 E
Revda 52 56 48N 59 57 E
Revel 20 43 28N 2 0 E
Revelganj 69 25 50N 84 40 E
Revelstoke 108 51 0N 118 10W
Reventazón 126 6 10 S 81 0W
Revigny 19 48 50N 5 0 E
Revilla Gigedo, Is. 95 18 40N 112 0W
Revillagigedo I. 108 55 50N 131 20W
Revin 19 49 55N 4 39 E
Revuè → 91 19 50 S 34 0 E
Rewa 69 24 33N 81 25 E
Rewari 68 28 15N 76 40 E
Rexburg 118 43 55N 111 50W
Rey Malabo 88 3 45N 8 50 E
Rey, Rio del → 85 4 30N 8 48 E
Reykjahlið 50 65 40N 16 55W
Reykjanes 50 63 48N 22 40W
Reykjavík 50 64 10N 21 57 E
Reynolds 109 49 40N 95 55W
Reynolds Ra. 96 22 30 S 133 0 E
Reynoldsville 112 41 5N 78 58W
Reynosa 120 26 5N 98 18W
Rezā'īyeh 64 37 40N 45 0 E
Rezā'īyeh, Daryācheh-ye 64 37 50N 45 30 E
Rezekne 54 56 30N 27 17 E
Rezovo 43 42 0N 28 0 E
Rgotina 42 44 1N 22 17 E
Rhamnus 45 38 12N 24 3 E
Rharis, O. → 83 26 0N 5 4 E
Rhayader 13 52 19N 3 30W
Rheden 16 52 0N 6 3 E
Rhein 109 51 25N 102 15W
Rhein → 24 51 52N 6 20 E
Rhein-Main-Donau-Kanal 25 49 1N 11 27 E
Rheinbach 24 50 38N 6 54 E
Rheine 24 52 17N 7 25 E
Rheinland-Pfalz □ 25 50 0N 7 0 E
Rheinsberg 24 53 6N 12 52 E
Rheriss, Oued → 82 30 50N 4 34W
Rheydt 24 51 10N 6 24 E
Rhin = Rhein → 24 51 52N 6 20 E
Rhinau 19 48 19N 7 43 E
Rhine = Rhein → 24 51 52N 6 20 E
Rhinelander 116 45 38N 89 29W
Rhino Camp 90 3 0N 31 22 E
Rhir, Cap 82 30 38N 9 54W
Rho 38 45 31N 9 2 E
Rhode Island □ 114 41 38N 71 37W
Rhodes = Ródhos 45 36 15N 28 10 E
Rhodes' Tomb 91 20 30 S 28 30 E
Rhodesia = Zimbabwe ■ 91 20 0 S 30 0 E
Rhodope Mts. = Rhodopi Planina 43 41 40N 24 20 E
Rhodopi Planina 43 41 40N 24 20 E
Rhondda 13 51 39N 3 30W
Rhône □ 21 45 54N 4 35 E
Rhône → 21 43 28N 4 42 E
Rhum 14 57 0N 6 20W
Rhumney 13 51 32N 3 7W
Rhyl 12 53 19N 3 29W
Ri-Aba 85 3 28N 8 40 E
Riachão 127 7 20 S 46 37W
Riaño 30 42 59N 5 0W
Rians 21 43 37N 5 44 E
Riansares → 32 39 32N 3 18W
Riasi 69 33 10N 74 50 E
Riau □ 72 0 0 102 35 E
Riau, Kepulauan 72 0 30N 104 20 E
Riaza 32 41 18N 3 30W
Riaza → 32 41 42N 3 55W
Riba de Saelices 32 40 55N 2 17W
Ribadavia 30 42 17N 8 8W
Ribadeo 30 43 35N 7 5W
Ribadesella 30 43 30N 5 7W
Ribas 32 42 19N 2 15 E
Ribble → 12 54 13N 2 20W
Ribe 49 55 19N 8 44 E
Ribeauvillé 19 48 10N 7 20 E
Ribécourt 19 49 30N 2 55 E
Ribeira 30 42 36N 8 58W
Ribeirão Prêto 125 21 10 S 47 50W
Ribemont 19 49 47N 3 27 E
Ribera 40 37 30N 13 13 E
Ribérac 20 45 15N 0 20 E
Riberalta 126 11 0 S 66 0W
Ribnica 39 45 45N 14 45 E
Ribnitz-Damgarten 24 54 14N 12 24 E
Ričany 26 50 0N 14 40 E
Riccarton 101 43 32 S 172 37 E
Riccia 41 41 30N 14 50 E
Riccione 39 44 0N 12 39 E
Rice L. 112 44 12N 78 10W
Rice Lake 116 45 30N 91 42W
Riceys, Les 19 47 59N 4 22 E
Rich 82 32 16N 4 30W
Rich Hill 117 38 5N 94 22W
Richards Bay 93 28 48 S 32 6 E
Richards L. 109 59 10N 107 10W
Richardson → 108 58 25N 111 14W
Richardton 116 46 56N 102 22W
Richelieu 18 47 0N 0 20 E
Richey 116 47 42N 105 5W
Richfield, Idaho, U.S.A. 118 43 2N 114 5W
Richfield, Utah, U.S.A. 119 38 50N 112 0W
Richford 113 45 0N 72 40W
Richibucto 107 46 42N 64 54W
Richland, Ga., U.S.A. 115 32 7N 84 40W
Richland, Oreg., U.S.A. 118 44 49N 117 9W
Richland, Wash., U.S.A. 118 46 15N 119 15W
Richland Center 116 43 21N 90 22W
Richlands 114 37 7N 81 49W
Richmond, N.S.W., Austral. 100 33 35 S 150 42 E
Richmond, Queens., Austral. 97 20 43 S 143 8 E
Richmond, N.Z. 101 41 20 S 173 12 E
Richmond, S. Afr. 93 29 51 S 30 18 E
Richmond, N. Yorks., U.K. 12 54 24N 1 43W
Richmond, Surrey, U.K. 13 51 28N 0 18W
Richmond, Calif., U.S.A. 118 37 58N 122 21W
Richmond, Ind., U.S.A. 114 39 50N 84 50W
Richmond, Ky., U.S.A. 114 37 40N 84 20W
Richmond, Mich., U.S.A. 112 42 47N 82 45W
Richmond, Mo., U.S.A. 116 39 15N 93 58W
Richmond, Tex., U.S.A. 117 29 32N 95 42W
Richmond, Utah, U.S.A. 118 41 55N 111 48W
Richmond, Va., U.S.A. 114 37 33N 77 27W
Richmond, Ra. 99 29 0 S 152 45 E
Richton 115 31 23N 88 58W
Richwood 114 38 17N 80 32W
Ricla 32 41 31N 1 24W
Riddarhyttan 48 59 49N 15 33 E
Ridgedale 109 53 0N 104 10W
Ridgeland 115 32 30N 80 58W
Ridgelands 98 23 16 S 150 17 E
Ridgetown 106 42 26N 81 52W
Ridgewood 113 40 59N 74 7W
Ridgway 114 41 25N 78 43W
Riding Mt. Nat. Park 109 50 50N 100 0W
Ried 26 48 14N 13 30 E
Riedlingen 25 48 9N 9 28 E
Rienza → 39 46 49N 11 47 E
Riesa 24 51 19N 13 19 E
Riesi 41 37 16N 14 4 E
Rieti 39 42 23N 12 50 E
Rieupeyroux 20 44 19N 2 12 E
Riez 21 43 49N 6 6 E
Rifle 118 39 40N 107 50W
Rifstangi 50 66 32N 16 12W
Rift Valley □ 90 0 20N 36 0 E
Rig Rig 81 14 13N 14 25 E
Riga 54 56 53N 24 8 E
Riga, G. of = Rīgas Jūras Līcis 54 57 40N 23 45 E
Rigas Jūras Līcis 54 57 40N 23 45 E
Rigaud 113 45 29N 74 18W
Rigby 118 43 41N 111 58W
Rīgestān □ 65 30 15N 65 0 E
Riggins 118 45 29N 116 26W
Rignac 20 44 25N 2 16 E
Rigolet 107 54 10N 58 23W
Riihimäki 51 60 45N 24 48 E
Riiser-Larsen-halvøya 5 68 0 S 35 0 E
Rijau 85 11 8N 5 17 E
Rijeka 39 45 20N 14 21 E
Rijeka Crnojevica 42 42 24N 19 1 E
Rijn → 16 52 12N 4 21 E
Rijssen 16 52 19N 6 30 E
Rijswijk 16 52 4N 4 22 E
Rike 87 10 50N 39 53 E
Rila 43 42 7N 23 7 E
Rila Planina 42 42 10N 23 0 E
Riley 118 43 35N 119 33W
Rilly 19 49 11N 4 3 E
Rima → 85 13 4N 5 10 E
Rimah, Wadi ar → 64 26 5N 41 30 E
Rimavská Sobota 27 48 22N 20 2 E
Rimbey 108 52 35N 114 15W
Rimbo 48 59 44N 18 21 E
Rimforsa 49 58 6N 15 43 E
Rimi 85 12 58N 7 43 E
Rimini 39 44 3N 12 33 E
Rîmna → 46 45 36N 27 3 E
Rîmnicu Sărat 46 45 26N 27 3 E
Rîmnicu Vîlcea 46 45 9N 24 21 E
Rimouski 107 48 27N 68 30W
Rinca 73 8 45 S 119 35 E
Rinconada 124 22 26 S 66 10W
Rineanna 15 52 42N 85 7W
Ringarum 49 58 21N 16 26 E
Ringe 49 55 13N 10 28 E
Ringim 85 12 13N 9 10 E
Ringkøbing 49 56 5N 8 15 E
Ringling 118 46 16N 110 56W
Ringsaker 47 60 54N 10 45 E
Ringsjön 49 55 55N 13 30 E
Ringsted 49 55 25N 11 46 E
Ringvassøy 50 69 56N 19 15 E
Rinía 45 37 23N 25 13 E
Rinjani 72 8 24 S 116 28 E
Rinteln 24 52 11N 9 3 E
Rio Branco 126 9 58 S 67 49W
Río Branco 125 32 40 S 53 40W
Rio Brilhante 125 21 48 S 54 33W
Rio Claro, Brazil 125 22 19 S 47 35W
Rio Claro, Trin. 121 10 20N 61 25W
Río Colorado 128 39 0 S 64 0W
Río Cuarto 124 33 10 S 64 25W
Rio das Pedras 93 23 8 S 35 28 E
Rio de Janeiro 125 23 0 S 43 12W
Rio de Janeiro □ 125 22 50 S 43 0W
Rio do Sul 125 27 13 S 49 37W
Río Gallegos 128 51 35 S 69 15W
Río Grande 128 53 50 S 67 45W
Rio Grande 125 32 0 S 52 20W
Rio Grande → 117 25 57N 97 9W
Rio Grande City 117 26 23N 98 49W
Río Grande del Norte → 110 26 0N 97 0W
Rio Grande do Norte □ 127 5 40 S 36 0W
Rio Grande do Sul □ 125 30 0 S 53 0W
Rio Largo 127 9 28 S 35 50W
Rio Maior 31 39 19N 8 57W
Rio Marina 38 42 48N 10 25 E
Río Mulatos 126 19 40 S 66 50W
Río Muni □ 88 1 30N 10 0 E
Rio Negro 125 26 0 S 50 0W
Rio Pardo 125 30 0 S 52 30W
Río, Punta del 33 36 49N 2 24W
Rio Segundo 124 31 40 S 63 59W
Rio Tercero 124 32 15 S 64 8W
Rio Tinto 30 41 11N 8 34W
Rio Verde 127 17 50 S 51 0W
Río Verde 120 21 56N 99 59W
Rio Vista 118 38 11N 121 44W
Ríobamba 126 1 50 S 78 45W
Ríohacha 126 11 33N 72 55W
Rioja, La, Argent. 124 29 20 S 67 0W
Rioja, La, Spain 32 42 20N 2 20W
Rioja, La □ 124 29 30 S 67 0W
Riom 20 45 54N 3 7 E
Riom-ès-Montagnes 20 45 17N 2 39 E
Rion-des-Landes 20 43 55N 0 56W
Rionero in Vúlture 41 40 55N 15 40 E
Rioni → 57 42 5N 41 50 E
Rios 30 41 58N 7 16W
Riosucio 126 5 30N 75 40W
Ríosucio 126 7 27N 77 7W
Riou L. 109 59 7N 106 25W
Rioz 19 47 25N 6 04 E
Riparia, Dora → 38 45 7N 7 24 E
Ripatransone 39 43 0N 13 45 E
Ripley, Can. 112 44 4N 81 35W
Ripley, N.Y., U.S.A. 112 42 16N 79 44W
Ripley, Tenn., U.S.A. 117 35 43N 89 34W
Ripoll 32 42 15N 2 13 E
Ripon, U.K. 12 54 8N 1 31W
Ripon, U.S.A. 114 43 51N 88 50W
Riposto 41 37 44N 15 12 E
Risan 42 42 32N 18 42 E
Riscle 20 43 39N 0 5W
Rishiri-Tō, Japan 74 45 11N 141 15 E
Rishiri-Tō, Japan 74 45 11N 141 15 E
Rishon le Ziyyon 62 31 58N 34 48 E
Rishpon 62 32 12N 34 49 E
Risle → 18 49 26N 0 23 E
Rîşnov 46 45 35N 25 27 E
Rison 117 33 57N 92 11W
Risør 47 58 43N 9 13 E
Ritchies Archipelago 71 12 5N 94 0 E
Riti 85 7 57N 9 41 E
Rittman 112 40 57N 81 48W
Ritzville 118 47 10N 118 21W
Riva Bella 18 49 17N 0 18W
Riva del Garda 38 45 53N 10 50 E
Rivadavia, Buenos Aires, Argent. 124 35 29 S 62 59W
Rivadavia, Mendoza, Argent. 124 33 13 S 68 30W
Rivadavia, Salta, Argent. 124 24 5 S 62 54W
Rivadavia, Chile 124 29 57 S 70 35W
Rivarolo Canavese 38 45 20N 7 42 E
Rivas 121 11 30N 85 50W
Rive-de-Gier 21 45 32N 4 37 E
River Cess 84 5 30N 9 32W
Rivera 125 31 0 S 55 50W
Riverdsale 92 34 7 S 21 15 E
Riverhead 114 40 53N 72 40W
Riverhurst 109 50 55N 106 50W
Riverina 97 35 30 S 145 20 E
Rivers 109 50 2N 100 14W
Rivers □ 85 5 0N 6 30 E
Rivers Inl. 108 51 40N 127 20W
Rivers, L. of the 109 49 49N 105 44W
Riverside, Calif., U.S.A. 119 34 0N 117 22W
Riverside, Wyo., U.S.A. 118 41 12N 106 57W
Riversleigh 98 19 5 S 138 40 E
Riverton, Austral. 99 34 10 S 138 46 E
Riverton, Can. 109 51 1N 97 0W
Riverton, N.Z. 101 46 21 S 168 0 E
Riverton, U.S.A. 118 43 1N 108 27W
Rives 21 45 21N 5 31 E
Rivesaltes 20 42 47N 2 50 E
Riviera 38 44 0N 8 30 E
Riviera di Levante 36 44 23N 9 15 E
Riviera di Ponente 36 43 50N 7 58 E
Rivière-à-Pierre 107 46 59N 72 11W
Rivière-au-Renard 107 48 59N 64 23W
Rivière-du-Loup 107 47 50N 69 30W
Rivière-Pentecôte 107 49 57N 67 1W
Rívoli 38 45 3N 7 31 E
Rivoli B. 99 37 32 S 140 3 E
Riyadh = Ar Riyāḍ 64 24 41N 46 42 E
Rize 64 41 0N 40 30 E
Rizhao 77 35 25N 119 30 E
Rizzuto, C. 41 38 54N 17 5 E
Rjukan 47 59 54N 8 33 E
Rjuven 47 59 9N 7 8 E
Roa, Norway 47 60 17N 10 37 E
Roa, Spain 30 41 41N 3 56W
Roag, L. 14 58 10N 6 55W
Roanne 21 46 3N 4 4 E
Roanoke, Ala., U.S.A. 115 33 9N 85 23W
Roanoke, Va., U.S.A. 114 37 19N 79 55W
Roanoke → 115 35 56N 76 43W
Roanoke I. 115 35 55N 75 40W
Roanoke Rapids 115 36 28N 77 42W
Roatán 121 16 18N 86 35W
Robbins I. 99 40 42 S 145 0 E
Robe → 15 53 38N 9 10W
Robe, Mt. 100 31 40 S 141 20 E
Röbel 24 53 24N 12 37 E

Robert Lee 117 31 55N 100 26W
Roberts 118 43 44N 112 8W
Robertsganj 69 24 44N 83 4 E
Robertson 92 33 46 S 19 50 E
Robertson I. 5 65 15 S 59 30W
Robertsport 84 6 45N 11 26W
Robertstown 99 33 58 S 139 5 E
Roberval 107 48 32N 72 15W
Robeson Ch. 4 82 0N 61 30W
Robinson Crusoe I. 95 33 38 S 78 52W
Robinson Ranges 96 25 40 S 119 0 E
Robinvale 99 34 40 S 142 45 E
Robla, La 30 42 50N 5 41W
Roblin 109 51 14N 101 21W
Roboré 126 18 10 S 59 45W
Robson, Mt. 108 53 10N 119 10W
Robstown 117 27 47N 97 40W
Roc, Pointe du 18 48 50N 1 37W
Roca, C. da 31 38 40N 9 31W
Rocas, I. 127 4 0 S 34 1W
Rocca d'Aspidé 41 40 27N 15 10 E
Rocca San Casciano 39 44 3N 11 45 E
Roccalbegna 39 42 47N 11 30 E
Roccastrada 39 43 0N 11 10 E
Roccella Iônica 41 38 20N 16 24 E
Rocha 125 34 30 S 54 25W
Rochdale 12 53 36N 2 10W
Roche-Bernard, La 18 47 31N 2 19W
Roche-Canillac, La 20 45 12N 1 57 E
Roche, La 21 46 4N 6 19 E
Roche-sur-Yon, La 18 46 40N 1 25W
Rochechouart 20 45 50N 0 49 E
Rochefort, Belg. 16 50 9N 5 12 E
Rochefort, France 20 45 56N 0 57W
Rochefort-en-Terre 18 47 42N 2 22W
Rochefoucauld, La 20 45 44N 0 24 E
Rochelle 116 41 55N 89 5W
Rochelle, La 20 46 10N 1 9W
Rocher River 108 61 23N 112 44W
Rocheservière 18 46 57N 1 30W
Rochester, Austral. 100 36 22 S 144 41 E
Rochester, Can. 108 54 22N 113 27W
Rochester, U.K. 13 51 22N 0 30 E
Rochester, Ind., U.S.A. 114 41 5N 86 15W
Rochester, Minn., U.S.A. 116 44 1N 92 28W
Rochester, N.H., U.S.A. 114 43 19N 70 57W
Rochester, N.Y., U.S.A. 114 43 10N 77 40W
Rochester, Pa., U.S.A. 112 40 41N 80 17W
Rociana 31 37 19N 6 35W
Rociu 46 44 43N 25 2 E
Rock → 108 60 7N 127 7W
Rock Hill 115 34 55N 81 2W
Rock Island 116 41 30N 90 35W
Rock Port 116 40 26N 95 30W
Rock Rapids 116 43 25N 96 10W
Rock River 118 41 49N 106 0W
Rock Sound 121 24 54N 76 12W
Rock Sprs., Ariz., U.S.A. 119 34 2N 112 11W
Rock Sprs., Mont., U.S.A. 118 46 55N 106 11W
Rock Sprs., Tex., U.S.A. 117 30 2N 100 11W
Rock Sprs., Wyo., U.S.A. 118 41 40N 109 10W
Rock Valley 116 43 10N 96 17W
Rockall 8 57 37N 13 42W
Rockdale 117 30 40N 97 0W
Rockefeller Plat. 5 80 0 S 140 0W
Rockford 116 42 20N 89 0W
Rockglen 109 49 11N 105 57W
Rockhampton 97 23 22 S 150 32 E
Rockingham B. 98 18 5 S 146 10 E
Rockingham Forest 13 52 28N 0 42W
Rocklake 116 48 50N 99 13W
Rockland, Can. 113 45 33N 75 17W
Rockland, Idaho, U.S.A. 118 42 37N 112 57W
Rockland, Me., U.S.A. 107 44 6N 69 6W
Rockland, Mich., U.S.A. 116 46 40N 89 10W
Rocklands Reservoir 100 37 15 S 142 5 E
Rockmart 115 34 1N 85 2W
Rockport 117 28 2N 97 3W
Rockville, Conn., U.S.A. 113 41 51N 72 27W
Rockville, Md., U.S.A. 114 39 7N 77 10W
Rockwall 117 32 55N 96 30W
Rockwell City 116 42 20N 94 35W
Rockwood 115 35 52N 84 40W
Rocky Ford 116 38 7N 103 45W
Rocky Lane 108 58 31N 116 22W
Rocky Mount 115 35 55N 77 48W
Rocky Mountain House 108 52 22N 114 55W
Rocky Mts. 108 55 0N 121 0W
Rocky Pt. 96 33 30 S 123 57 E
Rocky River 112 41 30N 81 40W
Rockyford 108 51 14N 113 10W
Rocroi 19 49 55N 4 30 E
Rod 66 28 10N 63 5 E
Roda, La, Albacete, Spain 33 39 13N 2 15W
Roda, La, Sevilla, Spain 31 37 12N 4 46W
Rødberg 47 60 17N 8 56 E
Rødby 49 54 41N 11 23 E
Rødbyhavn 49 54 39N 11 22 E
Roddickton 107 50 51N 56 8W
Rødding 49 55 23N 9 3 E
Rødekro 49 55 4N 9 20 E
Rødenes 47 59 35N 11 34 E
Rodenkirchen 24 53 24N 8 26 E
Roderick I. 108 52 38N 128 22W
Rodez 20 44 21N 2 33 E
Rodholívas 44 40 55N 24 0 E
Rodhópi □ 44 41 5N 25 30 E
Ródhos 45 36 15N 28 10 E
Rodi Garganico 41 41 55N 15 53 E
Rodna 46 47 25N 24 50 E
Rodnei, Munţii 46 47 35N 24 35 E
Rodney 112 42 34N 81 41W
Rodney, C. 101 36 17 S 174 50 E
Rodniki 55 57 7N 41 47 E
Rodriguez 3 19 45 S 63 20 E
Rodstock, C. 96 33·12 S 134 20 E
Roe → 15 55 10N 6 59W
Roebling 113 40 7N 74 45W
Roebourne 96 20 44 S 117 9 E
Roebuck B. 96 18 5 S 122 20 E
Roermond 16 51 12N 6 0 E
Roes Welcome Sd. 105 65 0N 87 0W
Roeselare 16 50 57N 3 7 E
Rogachev 54 53 8N 30 5 E
Rogaçica 42 44 4N 19 40 E
Rogagua, L. 126 13 43 S 66 50W
Rogaland fylke □ 47 59 12N 6 20 E
Rogaška Slatina 39 46 15N 15 42 E
Rogatec 39 46 15N 15 46 E
Rogatica 42 43 47N 19 0 E
Rogatin 54 49 24N 24 36 E
Rogers 117 36 20N 94 5W
Rogers City 114 45 25N 83 49W
Rogerson 118 42 10N 114 40W
Rogersville 115 36 27N 83 1W
Roggan 106 54 25N 79 32W
Roggeveldberge 92 32 10 S 20 10 E
Roggiano Gravina 41 39 37N 16 9 E
Rogliano, France 21 42 57N 9 30 E
Rogliano, Italy 41 39 11N 16 20 E
Rogoaguado, L. 126 13 0 S 65 30W
Rogowo 28 52 43N 17 38 E
Rogozno 28 52 45N 16 59 E
Rogue → 118 42 30N 124 0W
Rohan 18 48 4N 2 45W
Rohrbach 19 49 3N 7 15 E
Rohri 68 27 45N 68 51 E
Rohri Canal 68 26 15N 68 27 E
Rohtak 68 28 55N 76 43 E
Roi Et 71 16 4N 103 40 E
Roisel 19 49 58N 3 6 E
Rojas 124 34 10 S 60 45W
Rojo, C. 120 21 33N 97 20W
Rokan → 72 2 0N 100 50 E
Rokeby 98 13 39 S 142 40 E
Rokiskis 54 55 55N 25 35 E
Rokitno 54 50 57N 35 56 E
Rokycany 26 49 43N 13 35 E
Rolândia 125 23 18 S 51 23W
Røldal 47 59 47N 6 50 E
Rolette 116 48 42N 99 50W
Rolla, Kansas, U.S.A. 117 37 10N 101 40W
Rolla, Mo., U.S.A. 117 37 56N 91 42W
Rolla, N. Dak., U.S.A. 116 48 50N 99 36W
Rollag 47 60 2N 9 18 E
Rolleston 98 24 28 S 148 35 E
Rollingstone 98 19 2 S 146 24 E
Rom 87 9 54N 32 16 E
Roma, Austral. 97 26 32 S 148 49 E
Roma, Italy 40 41 54N 12 30 E
Roman, Bulg. 43 43 8N 23 54 E
Roman, Romania 46 46 57N 26 55 E
Roman, U.S.S.R. 59 66 4N 112 14 E
Roman-Kosh, Gora 56 44 37N 34 15 E
Romana, La 121 18 27N 68 57W
Romanche → 21 45 5N 5 43 E
Romang 73 7 30 S 127 20 E
Români 86 30 59N 32 38 E
Romania ■ 46 46 0N 25 0 E
Romanija Planina 42 43 50N 18 45 E
Romano, Cayo 121 22 0N 77 30W
Romano di Lombardia 38 45 32N 9 45 E
Romanovka = Bessarabka 56 46 21N 28 58 E
Romans 21 45 3N 5 3 E
Romanshorn 25 47 33N 9 22 E
Romblon 73 12 33N 122 17 E
Rombo □ 90 3 10 S 37 30 E
Rome, Ga., U.S.A. 115 34 20N 85 0W
Rome, N.Y., U.S.A. 114 43 14N 75 29W
Rome = Roma 40 41 54N 12 30 E
Romeleåsen 49 55 34N 13 33 E
Romenay 21 46 30N 5 1 E
Romerike 47 60 7N 11 10 E
Romilly 19 48 31N 3 44 E
Romîni 46 44 59N 24 11 E
Rommani 82 33 31N 6 40W
Romney 114 39 21N 78 45W
Romney Marsh 13 51 0N 1 0 E
Romny 54 50 48N 33 28 E
Rømø 49 55 10N 8 30 E
Romodan 54 50 0N 33 15 E
Romodanovo 55 54 26N 45 23 E
Romont 25 46 42N 6 54 E
Romorantin-Lanthenay 19 47 21N 1 45 E
Romsdalen 47 62 25N 8 0 E
Rona 14 57 33N 6 0W
Ronan 118 47 30N 114 6W
Roncador, Cayos 121 13 32N 80 4W
Roncador, Serra do 127 12 30 S 52 30W
Roncesvalles, Paso 32 43 1N 1 19W
Ronceverte 114 37 45N 80 28W
Ronciglione 39 42 18N 12 12 E
Ronco → 39 44 24N 12 12 E
Ronda 31 36 46N 5 12W
Ronda, Serranía de 31 36 44N 5 3W
Rondane 47 61 57N 9 50 E
Rondônia □ 126 11 0 S 63 0W
Rondonópolis 127 16 28 S 54 38W
Rong, Koh 71 10 45N 103 15 E
Rong Xian 77 29 23N 104 22 E
Rong'an 77 25 14N 109 22 E
Ronge, L. la 109 55 6N 105 17W
Ronge, La 109 55 5N 105 20W
Rongshui 77 25 5N 109 12 E
Ronne Land 5 83 0 S 70 0W
Ronneby 49 56 12N 15 17 E
Ronse 16 50 45N 3 35 E
Roof Butte 119 36 29N 109 5W
Roorkee 68 29 52N 77 59 E
Roosendaal 16 51 32N 4 29 E
Roosevelt, Minn., U.S.A. 116 48 51N 95 2W
Roosevelt, Utah, U.S.A. 118 40 19N 110 1W
Roosevelt I. 5 79 30 S 162 0W
Roosevelt, Mt. 108 58 26N 125 20W
Roosevelt Res. 119 33 46N 111 0W
Ropczyce 27 50 4N 21 38 E
Roper → 96 14 43 S 135 27 E
Ropesville 117 33 25N 102 10W
Roque Pérez 124 35 25 S 59 24W
Roquebrou, La 20 44 58N 2 12 E
Roquefort 20 44 2N 0 20W
Roquefort-sur-Soulzon 20 43 58N 2 59 E
Roquemaure 21 44 3N 4 48 E
Roquetas 32 40 50N 0 30 E
Roquevaire 21 43 20N 5 36 E
Roraima □ 126 2 0N 61 30W
Roraima, Mt. 126 5 10N 60 40W
Rorketon 109 51 24N 99 35W
Røros 47 62 35N 11 23 E
Rorschach 25 47 28N 9 30 E
Rosa 91 9 33 S 31 15 E
Rosa, C. 83 37 0N 8 16 E
Rosa, Monte 25 45 57N 7 53 E
Rosal 30 41 57N 8 51W
Rosal de la Frontera 31 37 59N 7 13W
Rosalia 118 47 14N 117 25W
Rosans 21 44 24N 5 29 E
Rosario 124 33 0 S 60 40W
Rosário 127 3 0 S 44 15W
Rosario, Baja Calif. N., Mexico 120 30 0N 115 50W
Rosario, Durango, Mexico 120 26 30N 105 35W
Rosario, Sinaloa, Mexico 120 23 0N 105 52W
Rosario, Parag. 124 24 30 S 57 35W
Rosario de la Frontera 124 25 50 S 65 0W
Rosario de Lerma 124 24 59 S 65 35W
Rosario del Tala 124 32 20 S 59 10W
Rosário do Sul 125 30 15 S 54 55W
Rosarno 41 38 29N 15 59 E
Rosas 32 42 19N 3 10 E
Roscoe 116 45 27N 99 20W
Roscoff 18 48 44N 4 0W
Roscommon, Ireland 15 53 38N 8 11W
Roscommon, U.S.A. 114 44 27N 84 35W
Roscommon □ 15 53 40N 8 15W
Roscrea 15 52 58N 7 50W
Rose Blanche 107 47 38N 58 45W
Rose Harbour 108 52 15N 131 10W
Rose Pt. 108 54 11N 131 39W
Rose Valley 109 52 19N 103 49W
Roseau, Domin. 121 15 20N 61 24W
Roseau, U.S.A. 116 48 51N 95 46W
Rosebery 99 41 46 S 145 33 E
Rosebud, Austral. 100 38 21 S 144 54 E
Rosebud, U.S.A. 117 31 5N 97 0W
Roseburg 118 43 10N 123 20W
Rosedale, Austral. 98 24 38 S 151 53 E
Rosedale, U.S.A. 117 33 51N 91 0W
Rosemary 108 50 46N 112 5W
Rosenberg 117 29 30N 95 48W
Rosendaël 19 51 3N 2 24 E
Rosenheim 25 47 51N 12 9 E
Roseto degli Abruzzi 39 42 40N 14 2 E
Rosetown 109 51 35N 107 59W
Rosetta = Rashîd 86 31 21N 30 22 E
Roseville 118 38 46N 121 17W
Rosewood 99 27 38 S 152 36 E
Rosh Haniqra, Kefar 62 33 5N 35 5 E
Rosh Pinna 62 32 58N 35 32 E
Rosières 19 49 49N 2 43 E
Rosignano Marittimo 38 43 23N 10 28 E
Rosignol 126 6 15N 57 30W
Roşiori de Vede 46 44 9N 25 0 E
Rositsa 43 43 57N 27 57 E
Rositsa → 43 43 10N 25 30 E
Roskilde 49 55 38N 12 3 E
Roskilde Amtskommune □ 49 55 35N 12 5 E
Roskilde Fjord 49 55 50N 12 2 E
Roslavl 54 53 57N 32 55 E
Roslyn 99 34 29 S 149 37 E
Rosmaninhal 31 39 44N 7 5W
Røsnæs 49 55 44N 10 55 E
Rosolini 41 36 49N 14 58 E
Rosporden 18 47 57N 3 50W
Ross, Austral. 99 42 2 S 147 30 E
Ross, N.Z. 101 42 53 S 170 49 E
Ross Dependency □ 5 70 0 S 170 5W
Ross I. 5 77 30 S 168 0 E
Ross Ice Shelf 5 80 0 S 180 0W
Ross L. 118 48 50N 121 5W
Ross on Wye 13 51 55N 2 34W
Ross Sea 5 74 0 S 178 0 E
Rossan Pt. 15 54 42N 8 47W
Rossano Cálabro 41 39 36N 16 39 E
Rossburn 109 50 40N 100 49W
Rosseau 112 45 16N 79 39W
Rossignol, L., N.S., Can. 107 44 12N 65 10W
Rossignol, L., Qué., Can. 106 52 43N 73 40W
Rossland 108 49 6N 117 50W
Rosslare 15 52 17N 6 23W
Rosslau 24 51 52N 12 15 E
Rosso 84 16 40N 15 45W
Rossosh 57 50 15N 39 28 E
Rossport 106 48 50N 87 30W
Røssvatnet 50 65 45N 14 5 E
Rossville 98 15 48 S 145 15 E
Rosthern 109 52 40N 106 20W
Rostock 24 54 4N 12 9 E
Rostock □ 24 54 10N 12 30 E
Rostov, Don, U.S.S.R. 57 47 15N 39 45 E
Rostov, Moskva, U.S.S.R. 55 57 14N 39 25 E
Rostrenen 18 48 14N 3 21W
Roswell 117 33 26N 104 32W
Rosyth 14 56 2N 3 26W
Rota 31 36 37N 6 20W
Rotälven → 48 61 15N 14 3 E
Rotan 117 32 52N 100 30W
Rotenburg 24 53 6N 9 24 E
Roth 25 49 15N 11 6 E
Rothaargebirge 22 51 0N 8 20 E
Rothenburg ob der Tauber 25 49 21N 10 11 E
Rother → 13 50 59N 0 40 E
Rotherham 12 53 26N 1 21W
Rothes 14 57 31N 3 12W
Rothesay, Can. 107 45 23N 66 0W
Rothesay, U.K. 14 55 50N 5 3W
Roti 73 10 50 S 123 0 E
Roto 97 33 0 S 145 30 E
Rotondella 41 40 10N 16 30 E
Rotoroa, L. 101 41 55 S 172 39 E
Rotorua 101 38 9 S 176 16 E
Rotorua, L. 101 38 5 S 176 18 E
Rott → 25 48 26N 13 26 E
Rottenburg 25 48 28N 8 56 E
Rottenmann 26 47 31N 14 22 E
Rotterdam 16 51 55N 4 30 E
Rottumeroog 16 53 33N 6 34 E
Rottweil 25 48 9N 8 38 E
Rotuma 94 12 25 S 177 5 E
Roubaix 19 50 40N 3 10 E
Roudnice 26 50 25N 14 15 E
Rouen 18 49 27N 1 4 E
Rouillac 20 45 47N 0 4W
Rouleau 109 50 10N 104 56W
Round Mt. 97 30 26 S 152 16 E
Round Mountain 118 38 46N 117 3W
Roundup 118 46 25N 108 35W
Rousay 14 59 10N 3 2W
Rouses Point 113 44 58N 73 22W
Rousse, L'Île 21 42 37N 8 57 E
Roussillon, Isère, France 21 45 24N 4 49 E
Roussillon, Pyrénées-Or., France 20 42 30N 2 35 E
Rouxville 92 30 25 S 26 50 E
Rouyn 106 48 20N 79 0W
Rovaniemi 50 66 29N 25 41 E
Rovato 38 45 34N 10 0 E
Rovenki 57 48 5N 39 21 E
Rovereto 38 45 53N 11 3 E
Rovigo 39 45 4N 11 48 E
Rovinari 46 44 56N 23 10 E
Rovinj 39 45 5N 13 40 E
Rovno 54 50 40N 26 10 E
Rovnoye 55 50 52N 46 3 E
Rovuma → 91 10 29 S 40 28 E
Rowena 99 29 48 S 148 55 E
Rowley Shoals 96 17 30 S 119 0 E
Roxa 84 11 15N 15 45W
Roxas 73 11 36N 122 49 E
Roxboro 115 36 24N 78 59W
Roxborough Downs 98 22 30 S 138 45 E
Roxburgh 101 45 33 S 169 19 E
Roxen 49 58 30N 15 40 E
Roy, Mont., U.S.A. 118 47 17N 109 0W
Roy, N. Mex., U.S.A. 117 35 57N 104 8W
Roy, Le 117 38 8N 95 35W
Roya, Peña 32 40 25N 0 40W
Royal Oak 114 42 30N 83 5W
Royan 20 45 37N 1 2W
Roye 19 49 42N 2 48 E
Røyken 47 59 45N 10 23 E
Rožaj 42 42 50N 20 15 E
Rózan 28 52 52N 21 25 E
Rozay 19 48 40N 2 56 E
Rozhishche 54 50 54N 25 15 E
Rozier, Le 20 44 13N 3 12 E
Rǒžnava 27 48 37N 20 35 E
Rozogi 28 53 48N 21 9 E
Rozoy-sur-Serre 19 49 40N 4 8 E
Rozwadów 28 50 37N 22 2 E
Rrësheni 44 41 47N 19 49 E
Rrogozhino 44 41 2N 19 50 E
Rtanj 42 43 45N 21 50 E
Rtishchevo 55 55 16N 43 50 E
Rúa 30 42 24N 7 6W
Ruacaná 92 17 20 S 14 12 E
Ruahine Ra. 101 39 55 S 176 2 E
Ruapehu 101 39 17 S 175 35 E
Ruapuke I. 101 46 46 S 168 31 E
Ruaus, Wadi → 83 30 26N 15 24 E
Rubeho Mts. 90 6 50 S 36 25 E
Rubezhnoye 56 49 6N 38 25 E
Rubh a' Mhail 14 55 55N 6 10W
Rubha Hunish 14 57 42N 6 20W
Rubicone → 39 44 8N 12 28 E
Rubino 84 6 4N 4 18W
Rubio 126 7 43N 72 22W
Rubtsovsk 58 51 30N 81 10 E
Ruby 104 64 40N 155 35W
Ruby L. 118 40 10N 115 28W
Ruby Mts. 118 40 30N 115 30W
Rubyvale 98 23 25 S 147 45 E
Rucava 54 56 9N 21 12 E
Ruciane-Nida 28 53 40N 21 32 E
Rud 47 60 1N 10 1 E
Ruda 49 57 6N 16 7 E
Ruda Śląska 28 50 16N 18 50 E
Ruden 24 54 13N 13 47 E
Rüdersdorf 24 52 28N 13 48 E
Rudewa 91 10 7 S 34 40 E
Rudkøbing 49 54 56N 10 41 E
Rudna 28 51 30N 16 17 E
Rudnichnyy 52 59 38N 52 26 E
Rudnik, Bulg. 43 42 36N 27 30 E
Rudnik, Poland 28 50 26N 22 15 E
Rudnik, Yugo. 42 44 8N 20 30 E
Rudnik, Yugo. 43 44 7N 20 35 E
Rudnogorsk 59 57 15N 103 42 E
Rudnya 54 54 55N 31 7 E
Rudnyy 58 52 57N 63 7 E
Rudo 42 43 41N 19 23 E
Rudolf, Ostrov 58 81 45N 58 30 E
Rudolstadt 24 50 44N 11 20 E
Rudozem 43 41 29N 24 51 E
Rudyard 114 46 14N 84 35W
Rue 19 50 15N 1 40 E
Ruelle 20 45 41N 0 14 E
Rufa'a 87 14 44N 33 22 E
Ruffec-Charente 20 46 2N 0 12 E
Rufiji □ 90 8 0 S 38 30 E
Rufiji → 90 7 50 S 39 15 E
Rufino 124 34 20 S 62 50W
Rufisque 84 14 40N 17 15W
Rufunsa 91 15 4 S 29 34 E
Rugao 77 32 23N 120 31 E
Rugby, U.K. 13 52 23N 1 16W
Rugby, U.S.A. 116 48 21N 100 0W
Rügen 24 54 22N 13 25 E
Rugles 18 48 50N 0 40 E
Ruhama 62 31 31N 34 43 E
Ruhengeri 90 1 30 S 29 36 E
Ruhla 24 50 53N 10 21 E
Ruhland 24 51 27N 13 52 E
Ruhr → 24 51 25N 6 44 E
Ruhuhu → 91 10 31 S 34 34 E
Rui'an 77 27 47N 120 40 E
Ruidosa 117 29 59N 104 39W
Ruidoso 119 33 19N 105 39W
Ruj 42 42 52N 22 42 E
Rujen 42 42 9N 22 30 E

Ruk 68 27 50N 68 42 E
Rukwa □ 90 7 0 S 31 30 E
Rukwa L. 90 8 0 S 32 20 E
Rum Cay 121 23 40N 74 58W
Rum Jungle 96 13 0 S 130 59 E
Ruma 42 45 0N 19 50 E
Rumāḥ 64 25 29N 47 10 E
Rumania = Romania ■ 46 46 0N 25 0 E
Rumbêk 87 6 54N 29 37 E
Rumburk 26 50 57N 14 32 E
Rumford 114 44 30N 70 30W
Rumia 28 54 37N 18 25 E
Rumilly 21 45 53N 5 56 E
Rumoi 74 43 56N 141 39W
Rumonge 90 3 59 S 29 26 E
Rumsey 108 51 51N 112 48W
Rumula 98 16 35 S 145 20 E
Rumuruti 90 0 17N 36 32 E
Runan 77 33 0N 114 30 E
Runanga 101 42 25 S 171 15 E
Runaway, C. 101 37 32 S 178 2 E
Runcorn 12 53 20N 2 44W
Rungwa 90 6 55 S 33 32 E
Rungwa → 90 7 36 S 31 50 E
Rungwe 91 9 11 S 33 32 E
Rungwe □ 91 9 25 S 33 32 E
Runka 85 12 28N 7 20 E
Runn 48 60 30N 15 40 E
Ruoqiang 75 38 55N 88 10 E
Rupa 67 27 15N 92 21 E
Rupar 68 31 2N 76 38 E
Rupat 72 1 45N 101 40 E
Rupea 46 46 2N 25 13 E
Rupert → 106 51 29N 78 45W
Rupert House = Fort Rupert 106 51 30N 78 40W
Rupsa 69 21 44N 89 30 E
Rur → 24 51 20N 6 0 E
Rurrenabaque 126 14 30 S 67 32W
Rus → 33 39 30N 2 30W
Rusambo 91 16 30 S 32 4 E
Rusape 91 18 35 S 32 8 E
Ruschuk = Ruse 43 43 48N 25 59 E
Ruse 43 43 48N 25 59 E
Ruşeţu 46 44 57N 27 14 E
Rushden 13 52 17N 0 37W
Rushford 116 43 48N 91 46W
Rushville, Ill., U.S.A. 116 40 6N 90 35W
Rushville, Ind., U.S.A. 114 39 38N 85 22W
Rushville, Nebr., U.S.A. 116 42 43N 102 28W
Rushworth 100 36 32 S 145 1 E
Rusken 49 57 15N 14 20 E
Russas 127 4 55 S 37 50W
Russell, Can. 109 50 50N 101 20W
Russell, N.Z. 101 35 16 S 174 10 E
Russell, U.S.A. 116 38 56N 98 55W
Russell L., Man., Can. 109 56 15N 101 30W
Russell L., N.W.T., Can. 108 63 5N 115 44W
Russellkonda 69 19 57N 84 42 E
Russellville, Ala., U.S.A. 115 34 30N 87 44W
Russellville, Ark., U.S.A. 117 35 15N 93 8W
Russellville, Ky., U.S.A. 115 36 50N 86 50W
Russi 39 44 21N 12 1 E
Russian S.F.S.R. □ 59 62 0N 105 0 E
Russkaya Polyana 58 53 47N 73 53 E
Russkoye Ustie 4 71 0N 149 0 E
Rust 27 47 49N 16 42 E
Rustavi 57 41 30N 45 0 E
Rustenburg 92 25 41 S 27 14 E
Ruston 117 32 30N 92 58W
Rutana 90 3 55 S 30 0 E
Rute 31 37 19N 4 23W
Ruteng 73 8 35 S 120 30 E
Ruth, Mich., U.S.A. 112 43 42N 82 45W
Ruth, Nev., U.S.A. 118 39 15N 115 1W
Rutherglen, Austral. 100 36 5 S 146 29 E
Rutherglen, U.K. 14 55 50N 4 11W
Rutigliano 41 41 1N 17 0 E
Rutland I. 71 11 25N 92 40 E
Rutland Plains 98 15 38 S 141 43 E
Rutledge → 109 61 4N 112 0W
Rutledge L. 109 61 33N 110 47W
Rutshuru 90 1 13 S 29 25 E
Ruurlo 16 52 5N 6 24 E
Ruvo di Púglia 41 41 7N 16 27 E
Ruvu 90 6 49 S 38 43 E
Ruvu → 90 6 23 S 38 52 E
Ruvuma □ 91 10 20 S 36 0 E
Ruwenzori 90 0 30N 29 55 E
Ruyigi 90 3 29 S 30 15 E
Ruzayevka 55 54 4N 45 0 E
Rûzhevo Konare 43 42 23N 24 46 E
Ružomberok 27 49 3N 19 17 E
Rwanda ■ 90 2 0 S 30 0 E
Ry 49 56 5N 9 45 E
Ryakhovo 43 44 0N 26 18 E
Ryan, L. 14 55 0N 5 2W
Ryazan 55 54 40N 39 40 E
Ryazhsk 55 53 45N 40 3 E
Rybache 58 46 40N 81 20 E
Rybachiy Poluostrov 52 69 43N 32 0 E
Rybinsk 55 58 5N 38 50 E
Rybinskoye Vdkhr. 55 58 30N 38 25 E
Rybnik 27 50 6N 18 32 E
Rybnitsa 56 47 45N 29 0 E
Rybnoye 55 54 45N 39 30 E
Rychwał 28 52 4N 18 10 E
Ryd 49 56 27N 14 42 E
Ryde 13 50 44N 1 9W
Rydöbruk 49 56 58N 13 7 E
Rydsnäs 49 57 47N 15 9 E
Rydułtowy 27 50 4N 18 23 E
Rydzyna 28 51 47N 16 39 E
Rye 13 50 57N 0 46 E
Rye → 12 54 12N 0 53W
Rye Patch Res. 118 40 38N 118 20W
Ryegate 118 46 21N 109 15W
Ryki 28 51 38N 21 56 E
Rylsk 54 51 36N 34 43 E
Rylstone 99 32 46 S 149 58 E
Rymanów 27 49 35N 21 51 E
Ryn 28 53 57N 21 34 E
Rypin 28 53 3N 19 25 E
Ryūkyū Is. = Nansei-Shotō 74 26 0N 128 0 E
Rzepin 28 52 20N 14 49 E
Rzeszów 27 50 5N 21 58 E
Rzeszów □ 27 50 0N 22 0 E
Rzhev 54 56 20N 34 20 E

S

Sa Dec 71 10 20N 105 46 E
Sa'ad (Muharraqa) 62 31 28N 34 33 E
Sa'ādatābād 65 30 10N 53 5 E
Saale → 24 51 57N 11 56 E
Saaler Bodden 24 54 20N 12 25 E
Saalfeld 24 50 39N 11 21 E
Saalfelden 26 47 25N 12 51 E
Saane → 25 46 23N 7 18 E
Saar (Sarre) → 19 49 42N 6 34 E
Saarbrücken 25 49 15N 6 58 E
Saarburg 25 49 36N 6 32 E
Saaremaa 54 58 30N 22 30 E
Saariselkä 50 68 16N 28 15 E
Saarland □ 25 49 15N 7 0 E
Saarlouis 25 49 19N 6 45 E
Saba 121 17 42N 63 26W
Šabac 42 44 48N 19 42 E
Sabadell 32 41 28N 2 7 E
Sabagalet 72 1 36 S 98 40 E
Sabah □ 72 6 0N 117 0 E
Sábana de la Mar 121 19 7N 69 24W
Sábanalarga 126 10 38N 74 55W
Sabang 72 5 50N 95 15 E
Sabará 127 19 55 S 43 46W
Sabarania 73 2 5 S 138 18 E
Sabari → 70 17 35N 81 16 E
Sabasṭiyah 62 32 17N 35 12 E
Sabattis 113 44 6N 74 40W
Sabáudia 40 41 17N 13 2 E
Sabhah 83 27 9N 14 29 E
Sabhah □ 83 26 0N 14 0 E
Sabie 93 25 10 S 30 48 E
Sabinal, Mexico 120 30 58N 107 25W
Sabinal, U.S.A. 117 29 20N 99 27W
Sabinal, Punta del 33 36 43N 2 44W
Sabinas 120 27 50N 101 10W
Sabinas Hidalgo 120 26 33N 100 10W
Sabine 117 29 42N 93 54W
Sabine → 117 30 0N 93 35W
Sabine L. 117 29 50N 93 50W
Sabinov 27 49 6N 21 5 E
Sabirabad 57 40 5N 48 30 E
Sabkhat Tāwurghā' 83 31 48N 15 30 E
Sablayan 73 12 50N 120 50 E
Sable, C., Can. 107 43 29N 65 38W
Sable, C., U.S.A. 121 25 13N 81 0W
Sable I. 107 44 0N 60 0W
Sablé-sur-Sarthe 18 47 50N 0 20W
Sables-d'Olonne, Les 20 46 30N 1 45W
Sabolev 59 54 20N 155 30 E
Sabor → 30 41 10N 7 7W
Sabou 84 12 1N 2 15W
Sabrātah 83 32 47N 12 29 E
Sabria 83 33 22N 8 45 E
Sabrina Coast 5 68 0 S 120 0 E
Sabugal 30 40 20N 7 5W
Sabzevār 65 36 15N 57 40 E
Sabzvārān 65 28 45N 57 50 E
Sac City 116 42 26N 95 0W
Sacedón 32 40 29N 2 41W
Sachigo → 106 55 6N 88 58W
Sachigo, L. 106 53 50N 92 12W
Sachkhere 57 42 25N 43 28 E
Sacile 39 45 58N 12 30 E
Sackets Harbor 113 43 56N 76 7W
Säckingen 25 47 34N 7 56 E
Saco, Me., U.S.A. 115 43 30N 70 27W
Saco, Mont., U.S.A. 118 48 28N 107 19W
Sacramento 118 38 33N 121 30 E
Sacramento → 118 38 3N 121 56W
Sacramento Mts. 119 32 30N 105 30W
Sacratif, Cabo 33 36 42N 3 28W
Săcueni 46 47 20N 22 5 E
Sada 30 43 22N 8 15W
Sádaba 32 42 19N 1 12W
Sadani 90 5 58 S 38 35 E
Sadao 71 6 38N 100 26 E
Sadasivpet 70 17 38N 77 59 E
Sadd el Aali 86 23 54N 32 54 E
Sade 85 11 22N 10 45 E
Sadimi 91 9 25 S 23 32 E
Sado 74 38 0N 138 25 E
Sado → 31 38 29N 8 55W
Sado, Shima 74 38 15N 138 30 E
Sadon, Burma 67 25 28N 98 0 E
Sadon, U.S.S.R. 57 42 52N 43 58 E
Sæby 49 57 21N 10 30 E
Saegerstown 112 41 42N 80 10W
Saelices 32 39 55N 2 49W
Safaga 86 26 42N 34 0 E
Şafaha 86 26 25N 39 0 E
Šafárikovo 27 48 25N 20 20 E
Säffle 48 59 8N 12 55 E
Safford 119 32 50N 109 43W
Saffron Walden 13 52 2N 0 15 E
Safi 82 32 18N 9 20W
Safīd Kūh 65 34 45N 63 0 E
Safonovo 54 55 4N 33 16 E
Safranbolu 56 41 15N 32 41 E
Sag Harbor 113 40 59N 72 17W
Saga 73 2 40 S 132 55 E
Saga □ 74 33 15N 130 20 E
Sagala 84 14 9N 6 38W
Sagara 70 14 14N 75 6 E
Sagara, L. 90 5 20 S 31 0 E
Saghīr, Zab al 64 35 10N 43 20 E
Sagil 75 50 15N 91 15 E
Saginaw 114 43 26N 83 55W
Saginaw B. 106 43 50N 83 40W
Sagleipie 84 7 0N 8 52W
Saglouc (Sugluk) 105 62 10N 74 40W
Sagone 21 42 7N 8 42 E
Sagone, G. de 21 42 4N 8 40 E
Sagra, La > 33 37 57N 2 35W
Sagres 31 37 0N 8 58W
Sagua la Grande 121 22 50N 80 10W
Saguache 119 38 10N 106 10W
Saguenay → 107 48 22N 71 0W
Sagunto 32 39 42N 0 18W
Sahaba 86 18 57N 30 25 E
Sahagún 30 42 18N 5 2W
Saham 62 32 42N 35 46 E
Saḥam al Jawlān 62 32 45N 35 55 E
Sahand, Kūh-e 64 37 44N 46 27 E
Sahara 82 23 0N 5 0 E
Saharanpur 68 29 58N 77 33 E
Saharien Atlas 82 33 30N 1 0 E
Sahasinaka 93 21 49 S 47 49 E
Sahaswan 68 28 5N 78 45 E
Sahel, Canal du 84 14 20N 6 0W
Sahibganj 69 25 12N 87 40 E
Sahiwal 68 30 45N 73 8 E
Sahtaneh → 108 59 2N 122 28W
Sahuaripa 120 29 0N 109 13W
Sahuarita 119 31 58N 110 59W
Sahuayo 120 20 4N 102 43W
Sahy 27 48 4N 18 55 E
Saibai I. 98 9 25 S 142 40 E
Sa'id Bundas 81 8 24N 24 48 E
Saïda 82 34 50N 0 11 E
Saīdābād 65 29 30N 55 45 E
Saïdia 82 35 5N 2 14W
Saidu 69 34 43N 72 24 E
Saignes 20 45 20N 2 31 E
Saigon = Phanh Bho Ho Chi Minh 71 10 46N 106 40 E
Saih-al-Malih 65 23 37N 58 31 E
Saijō 74 33 55N 133 11 E
Saikhoa Ghat 67 27 50N 95 40 E
Saiki 74 32 58N 131 51 E
Saillans 21 44 42N 5 12 E
Sailolof 73 1 7 S 130 46 E
St. Abb's Head 14 55 55N 2 10W
St. Aegyd 26 47 52N 15 33 E
St-Affrique 20 43 57N 2 53 E
St-Agrève 21 45 0N 4 23 E
St-Aignan 18 47 16N 1 22 E
St. Alban's 107 47 51N 55 50W
St. Albans, U.K. 13 51 44N 0 19W
St. Albans, Vt., U.S.A. 114 44 49N 73 7W
St. Albans, W. Va., U.S.A. 114 38 21N 81 50W
St. Alban's Head 13 50 34N 2 3W
St. Albert 108 53 37N 113 32W
St-Amand 19 50 25N 3 26 E
St-Amand-en-Puisaye 19 47 32N 3 5 E
St-Amand-Mont-Rond 20 46 43N 2 30 E
St-Amarin 19 47 54N 7 0 E
St-Amour 21 46 26N 5 21 E
St-André-de-Cubzac 20 44 59N 0 26W
St-André-de-l'Eure 18 48 54N 1 16 E
St-André-les-Alpes 21 43 58N 6 30 E
St. André, Tanjona 93 16 11 S 44 27 E
St. Andrew's 107 47 45N 59 15W
St. Andrews 14 56 20N 2 48W
St-Anicet 113 45 8N 74 22W
St. Ann B. 107 46 22N 60 25W
St. Anne 18 49 43N 2 11W
St. Anthony, Can. 107 51 22N 55 35W
St. Anthony, U.S.A. 118 44 0N 111 40W
St-Antonin-Noble-Val 20 44 10N 1 45 E
St. Arnaud 99 36 40 S 143 16 E
St. Arthur 107 47 33N 67 46W
St. Asaph 12 53 15N 3 27W
St-Astier 20 45 8N 0 31 E
St-Aubin-du-Cormier 18 48 15N 1 26W
St. Augustin 93 23 33 S 43 46 E
St-Augustin-Saguenay 107 51 13N 58 38W
St. Augustine 115 29 52N 81 20W
St. Austell 13 50 20N 4 48W
St-Avold 19 49 6N 6 43 E
St.-Barthélemy, I. 121 17 50N 62 50W
St. Bee's Hd. 12 54 30N 3 38 E
St-Benoît-du-Sault 20 46 26N 1 24 E
St. Bernard, Col du Grand 25 45 53N 7 11 E
St. Boniface 109 49 53N 97 5W
St-Bonnet 21 44 40N 6 5 E
St-Brévin-les-Pins 18 47 14N 2 10W
St-Brice-en-Coglès 18 48 25N 1 22W
St. Bride's 107 46 56N 54 10W
St. Bride's B. 13 51 48N 5 15W
St-Brieuc 18 48 30N 2 46W
St-Calais 18 47 55N 0 45 E
St-Cast 18 48 37N 2 18W
St. Catharines 106 43 10N 79 15W
St. Catherines I. 115 31 35N 81 10W
St. Catherine's Pt. 13 50 34N 1 18W
St-Céré 20 44 51N 1 54 E
St.-Cergue 25 46 27N 6 10 E
St-Cernin 20 45 5N 2 25 E
St-Chamond 21 45 28N 4 31 E
St. Charles, Ill., U.S.A. 114 41 55N 88 21W
St. Charles, Mo., U.S.A. 116 38 46N 90 30W
St-Chély-d'Apcher 20 44 48N 3 17 E
St-Chinian 20 43 25N 2 56 E
St. Christopher (St. Kitts) 121 17 20N 62 40W
St-Ciers-sur-Gironde 20 45 17N 0 37W
St. Clair, Mich, U.S.A. 112 42 47N 82 27W
St. Clair, Pa., U.S.A. 113 40 42N 76 12W
St. Clair, L. 106 42 30N 82 45W
St. Clairsville 112 40 5N 80 53W
St-Claud 20 45 54N 0 28 E
St. Claude 109 49 40N 98 20W
St-Claude 21 46 22N 5 52 E
St-Cloud 18 48 51N 2 12 E
St. Cloud, Fla., U.S.A. 115 28 15N 81 15W
St. Cloud, Minn., U.S.A. 116 45 30N 94 11W
St-Coeur de Marie 107 48 39N 71 43W
St. Croix 121 17 45N 64 45W
St. Croix → 116 44 45N 92 50W
St. Croix Falls 116 45 18N 92 22W
St-Cyprien 20 42 37N 3 0 E
St-Cyr 21 43 11N 5 43 E
St. David's, Can. 107 48 12N 58 52W
St. David's, U.K. 13 51 54N 5 16W
St. David's Head 13 51 55N 5 16W
St-Denis 19 48 56N 2 22 E
St-Denis-d'Orques 18 48 2N 0 17W
St-Dié 19 48 17N 6 56 E
St-Dizier 19 48 40N 5 0 E
St-Egrève 21 45 14N 5 41 E
St. Elias, Mt. 104 60 14N 140 50W
St Elias Mts. 108 60 33N 139 28W
St-Éloy-les-Mines 20 46 10N 2 51 E
St-Émilion 20 44 53N 0 9W
St-Étienne 21 45 27N 4 22 E
St-Étienne-de-Tinée 21 44 16N 6 56 E
St. Eugène 113 45 30N 74 28W
St. Eustatius 121 17 20N 63 0W
St-Félicien 106 48 40N 72 25W
St-Florent 21 42 41N 9 18 E
St-Florent-sur-Cher 19 46 59N 2 15 E
St-Florentin 19 48 0N 3 45 E
St-Flour 20 45 2N 3 6 E
St-Fons 21 45 42N 4 52 E
St. Francis 116 39 48N 101 47W
St. Francis → 117 34 38N 90 36W
St. Francis, C. 92 34 14 S 24 49 E
St-Francis, L. 113 45 10N 74 22W
St. Francisville 117 30 48N 91 22W
St-Fulgent 18 46 50N 1 10W
St-Gabriel-de-Brandon 106 46 17N 73 24W
St-Gaudens 20 43 6N 0 44 E
St-Gengoux-le-National 21 46 37N 4 40 E
St-Geniez-d'Olt 20 44 27N 2 58 E
St. George, Austral. 97 28 1 S 148 30 E
St. George, Berm. 121 32 24N 64 42W
St. George, Can. 107 45 11N 66 50W
St. George, S.C., U.S.A. 115 33 13N 80 37W
St. George, Utah, U.S.A. 119 37 10N 113 35W
St. George, C., Can. 107 48 30N 59 16W
St. George, C., U.S.A. 115 29 36N 85 2W
St-Georges 16 50 37N 5 20 E
St. George's 107 48 26N 58 31W
St. Georges 106 46 42N 72 35W
St-Georges 107 46 8N 70 40W
St. Georges 127 4 0N 52 0W
St. George's 121 12 5N 61 43W
St. George's B. 107 48 24N 58 53W
Saint George's Channel 98 4 10 S 152 20 E
St. George's Channel 11 52 0N 6 0W
St-Georges-de-Didonne 20 45 36N 1 0W
St. Georges Head 100 35 12 S 150 42 E
St-Germain 19 48 53N 2 5 E
St-Germain-Lembron 20 45 27N 3 14 E
St-Germain-de-Calberte 20 44 13N 3 48 E
St-Germain-des-Fossés 20 46 12N 3 26 E
St-Germain-du-Plain 19 46 42N 4 58 E
St-Germain-Laval 21 45 50N 4 1 E
St-Gers 20 45 18N 0 37W
St-Gervais, Haute Savoie, France 21 45 53N 6 42 E
St-Gervais, Puy de Dôme, France 20 46 4N 2 50 E
St-Gildas, Pte. de 18 47 8N 2 14W
St-Gilles-Croix-de-Vie 18 46 41N 1 55W
St-Gilles-du-Gard 21 43 40N 4 26 E
St-Girons 20 42 59N 1 8 E
St. Goar 25 50 12N 7 43 E
St-Gualtier 18 46 39N 1 26 E
St-Guénolé 18 47 49N 4 23W
St. Helena, Atl. Oc. 7 15 55 S 5 44W
St. Helena, U.S.A. 118 38 29N 122 30W
St. Helenabaai 92 32 40 S 18 10 E
St. Helens, U.K. 12 53 28N 2 44W
St. Helens, U.S.A. 118 45 55N 122 50W
St. Helier 18 49 11N 2 6W
St-Hilaire 18 48 35N 1 7W
St-Hippolyte 19 47 20N 6 50 E
St-Hippolyte-du-Fort 20 43 58N 3 52 E
St-Honoré 19 46 54N 3 50 E
St-Hubert 16 50 2N 5 23 E
St-Hyacinthe 106 45 40N 72 58W
St. Ignace 114 45 53N 84 43W
St. Ignace I. 106 48 45N 88 0W
St. Ignatius 118 47 19N 114 8W
St-Imier 25 47 9N 6 58 E
St. Ives, Cambs., U.K. 13 52 20N 0 5W
St. Ives, Cornwall, U.K. 13 50 13N 5 29W
St-James 18 48 31N 1 20W
St. James 116 43 57N 94 40W
St. Jean 106 45 20N 73 20W
St-Jean 21 45 30N 5 10 E
St-Jean → 107 50 17N 64 20W
St. Jean Baptiste 109 49 15N 97 20W
St-Jean-d'Angély 20 45 57N 0 31W
St-Jean-de-Maurienne 21 45 16N 6 21 E
St-Jean-de-Luz 20 43 23N 1 39W
St-Jean-de-Monts 18 46 47N 2 4W
St-Jean-du-Gard 20 44 7N 3 52 E
St-Jean-en-Royans 21 45 1N 5 18 E
St-Jean, L. 107 48 40N 72 0W
St-Jean-Port-Joli 107 47 15N 70 13W
St-Jérôme, Qué., Can. 106 45 47N 74 0W
St-Jérôme, Qué., Can. 107 48 26N 71 53W
St. John, Can. 107 45 20N 66 8W
St. John, Kans., U.S.A. 117 37 59N 98 45W
St. John, N.D., U.S.A. 116 48 58N 99 40W
St. John → 107 45 15N 66 4W
St. John, C. 107 50 0N 55 32W
St. John's, Antigua 121 17 6N 61 51W
St. John's, Can. 107 47 35N 52 40W
St. Johns, Ariz., U.S.A. 119 34 31N 109 26W
St. Johns, Mich., U.S.A. 114 43 0N 84 31W
St. John's → 115 30 20N 81 30W
St. Johnsbury 114 44 25N 72 1W
St. Johnsville 113 43 0N 74 43W
St. Joseph, La., U.S.A. 117 31 55N 91 15W
St. Joseph, Mich., U.S.A. 114 42 5N 86 30W
St. Joseph, Mo., U.S.A. 116 39 46N 94 50W
St. Joseph → 114 42 7N 86 30W
St. Joseph, I. 106 46 12N 83 58W
St. Joseph, L. 106 51 10N 90 35W
St-Jovite 106 46 8N 74 38W
St-Juéry 20 43 55N 2 12 E
St-Julien 21 46 8N 6 5 E
St-Julien-Chapteuil 21 45 2N 4 4 E
St-Julien-du-Sault 19 48 1N 3 17 E
St-Junien 20 45 53N 0 55 E

Place	Page	Lat.	Long.
St-Just-en-Chaussée	19	49 30N	2 25 E
St-Just-en-Chevalet	20	45 55N	3 50 E
St-Justin	20	43 59N	0 14W
St. Kilda, N.Z.	101	45 53 S	170 31 E
St. Kilda, U.K.	8	57 9N	8 34W
St. Kitts-Nevis ■	121	17 20N	62 40W
St. Laurent	109	50 25N	97 58W
St-Laurent	127	5 29N	54 3W
St-Laurent-du-Pont	21	45 23N	5 45 E
St-Laurent-en-Grandvaux	21	46 35N	5 58 E
St. Lawrence	107	46 54N	55 23W
St. Lawrence →	107	49 30N	66 0W
St. Lawrence, Gulf of	107	48 25N	62 0W
St. Lawrence I.	104	63 0N	170 0W
St. Leonard	107	47 12N	67 58W
St-Léonard-de-Noblat	20	45 49N	1 29 E
St. Lewis →	107	52 26N	56 11W
St-Lô	18	49 7N	1 5W
St-Louis	84	16 8N	16 27W
St. Louis, Mich., U.S.A.	114	43 27N	84 38W
St. Louis, Mo., U.S.A.	116	38 40N	90 12W
St. Louis →	116	47 15N	92 45W
St-Loup-sur-Semouse	19	47 53N	6 16 E
St. Lucia ■	121	14 0N	60 50W
St. Lucia, C.	93	28 32 S	32 29 E
St. Lucia Channel	121	14 15N	61 0W
St. Lucia, Lake	93	28 5 S	32 30 E
St. Lunaire-Griquet	107	51 31N	55 28W
St. Maarten	121	18 0N	63 5W
St-Maixent-l'École	20	46 24N	0 12W
St-Malo	18	48 39N	2 1W
St-Malo, G. de	18	48 50N	2 30W
St-Mandrier	21	43 4N	5 56 E
St-Marc	121	19 10N	72 41W
St-Marcellin	21	45 9N	5 20 E
St-Marcouf, Îs.	18	49 30N	1 10W
St. Maries	118	47 17N	116 34W
St-Martin, Charente-M., France	20	46 12N	1 22W
St-Martin, Pas-de-Calais, France	19	50 42N	1 38 E
St-Martin, I.	121	18 0N	63 0W
St. Martin L.	109	51 40N	98 30W
St-Martin-Vésubie	21	44 4N	7 15 E
St. Martins	107	45 22N	65 34W
St. Martinsville	117	30 10N	91 50W
St-Martory	20	43 9N	0 56 E
St. Mary B.	107	46 50N	53 50W
St. Mary Is.	70	13 20N	74 35 E
St. Mary Pk.	97	31 32 S	138 34 E
St. Marys, Austral.	97	41 35 S	148 11 E
St. Marys, Can.	112	43 20N	81 10W
St. Mary's, U.K.	13	49 55N	6 17W
St. Mary's, U.S.A.	114	40 33N	84 20W
St. Marys	114	41 27N	78 33W
St. Marys Bay	107	44 25N	66 10W
St. Mary's, C.	107	46 50N	54 12W
St. Mathews I. = Zadetkyi Kyun	71	10 0N	98 25 E
St-Mathieu, Pte. de	18	48 20N	4 45W
St-Maur-des-Fossés	19	48 48N	2 30 E
St-Maurice →	106	46 21N	72 31W
St-Médard-de-Guizières	20	45 1N	0 4W
St-Méen-le-Grand	18	48 11N	2 12W
St. Michaels	119	35 38N	109 5W
St. Michael's Mt.	13	50 7N	5 30W
St-Michel	21	45 15N	6 29 E
St-Mihiel	19	48 54N	5 30 E
St-Nazaire	18	47 17N	2 12W
St. Neots	13	52 14N	0 16W
St-Nicolas-de-Port	19	48 38N	6 18 E
St-Omer	19	50 45N	2 15 E
St. Ouen	19	48 50N	2 20 E
St-Ouen	19	50 2N	2 7 E
St-Pacome	107	47 24N	69 58W
St-Palais	20	45 40N	1 8W
St-Pamphile	107	46 58N	69 48W
St-Pardoux-la-Rivière	20	45 29N	0 45 E
St. Pascal	107	47 32N	69 48W
St. Paul, Can.	108	54 0N	111 17W
St. Paul, Ind. Oc.	3	30 40 S	77 34 E
St. Paul, Minn., U.S.A.	116	44 54N	93 5W
St. Paul, Nebr., U.S.A.	116	41 15N	98 30W
St-Paul-de-Fenouillet	20	42 50N	2 28 E
St. Paul, I.	107	47 12N	60 9W
St-Péray	21	44 57N	4 50 E
St-Père-en-Retz	18	47 11N	2 2W
St. Peter	116	44 21N	93 57W
St. Peter Port	18	49 27N	2 31W
St. Peters, N.S., Can.	107	45 40N	60 53W
St. Peters, P.E.I., Can.	107	46 25N	62 35W
St. Petersburg	115	27 45N	82 40W
St-Philbert-de-Grand-Lieu	18	47 2N	1 39W
St Pierre	107	46 46N	56 12W
St-Pierre-d'Oléron	20	45 57N	1 19W
St-Pierre-Église	18	49 40N	1 24W
St-Pierre-en-Port	18	49 48N	0 30 E
St-Pierre et Miquelon □	107	46 55N	56 10W
St-Pierre, L.	106	46 12N	72 52W
St-Pierre-le-Moûtier	19	46 47N	3 7 E
St.-Pierre-sur-Dives	18	49 2N	0 1W
St.-Pol	19	50 21N	2 20 E
St-Pol-de-Léon	18	48 41N	4 0W
St-Pol-sur-Mer	19	51 1N	2 20 E
St-Pons	20	43 30N	2 45 E
St-Pourçain-sur-Sioule	20	46 18N	3 18 E
St-Quay-Portrieux	18	48 39N	2 51W
St-Quentin	19	49 50N	3 16 E
St-Rambert-d'Albon	21	45 17N	4 49 E
St-Raphaël	21	43 25N	6 46 E
St. Regis, Mont., U.S.A.	118	47 20N	115 3W
St. Regis, N.Y., U.S.A.	113	44 39N	74 34W
St-Rémy-de-Provence	21	43 48N	4 50 E
St-Renan	18	48 26N	4 37W
St-Saëns	18	49 41N	1 16 E
St-Sauveur-en-Puisaye	19	47 37N	3 12 E
St-Sauveur-le-Vicomte	18	49 23N	1 32W
St-Savin	20	46 34N	0 50 E
St-Savinien	20	45 53N	0 42W
St. Sebastien, Tanjon' i	93	12 26 S	48 44 E
St-Seine-l'Abbaye	19	47 26N	4 47 E
St-Sernin	20	43 54N	2 35 E
St-Servan-sur-Mer	18	48 38N	2 0W
St-Sever	20	43 46N	0 34W
St-Sever-Calvados	18	48 50N	1 3W
St-Siméon	107	47 51N	69 54W
St. Stephen	107	45 16N	67 17W
St-Sulpice-Laurière	20	46 3N	1 29 E
St-Sulpice-la-Pointe	20	43 46N	1 41 E
St-Thégonnec	18	48 31N	3 57W
St. Thomas, Can.	106	42 45N	81 10W
St. Thomas, W. Indies	121	18 21N	64 55W
St-Tite	106	46 45N	72 34W
St-Tropez	21	43 17N	6 38 E
St. Troud = Sint Truiden	16	50 48N	5 10 E
St-Vaast-la-Hougue	18	49 35N	1 17W
St-Valéry	19	50 10N	1 38 E
St-Valéry-en-Caux	18	49 52N	0 43 E
St-Vallier	21	45 11N	4 50 E
St-Vallier-de-Thiey	21	43 42N	6 51 E
St-Varent	18	46 53N	0 13W
St. Vincent	6	18 0N	26 1W
St. Vincent ■	121	13 10N	61 10W
St-Vincent-de-Tyrosse	20	43 39N	1 18W
St. Vincent, G.	97	35 0 S	138 0 E
St. Vincent Passage	121	13 30N	61 0W
St. Vincent, Tanjona	93	21 58 S	43 20 E
St-Vith	16	50 17N	6 9 E
St-Yrieux-la-Perche	20	45 31N	1 12 E
Ste-Adresse	18	49 31N	0 5 E
Ste-Agathe-des-Monts	106	46 3N	74 17W
Ste Anne de Beaupré	107	47 2N	70 58W
Ste-Anne-des-Monts	107	49 8N	66 30W
Ste-Énimie	20	44 22N	3 26 E
Ste-Foy-la-Grande	20	44 50N	0 13 E
Ste. Genevieve	116	37 59N	90 2W
Ste-Hermine	20	46 32N	1 4W
Ste-Livrade-sur-Lot	20	44 24N	0 36 E
Ste-Marguerite →	107	50 9N	66 36W
Ste Marie	121	14 48N	61 1W
Ste-Marie-aux-Mines	19	48 10N	7 12 E
Ste-Marie de la Madeleine	107	46 26N	71 0W
Ste-Maure-de-Touraine	18	47 7N	0 37 E
Ste-Maxime	21	43 19N	6 39 E
Ste-Menehould	19	49 5N	4 54 E
Ste-Mère-Église	18	49 24N	1 19W
Ste-Rose	121	16 20N	61 45W
Ste.-Rose du lac	109	51 4N	99 30W
Saintes	20	45 45N	0 37W
Saintes, Île des	121	15 50N	61 35W
Saintes-Maries-de-la-Mer	21	43 26N	4 26 E
Saintonge	20	45 40N	0 50W
Sairang	67	23 50N	92 45 E
Sairecábur, Cerro	124	22 43 S	67 54W
Saitama □	74	36 25N	139 30 E
Sajama	126	18 7 S	69 0W
Sajan	42	45 50N	20 20 E
Sajószentpéter	27	48 12N	20 44 E
Sakai	74	34 30N	135 30 E
Sakākah	64	30 0N	40 8 E
Sakami, L.	106	53 15N	77 0W
Sâkâne, 'Erg i-n	82	20 30N	1 30W
Sakania	91	12 43 S	28 30 E
Sakarya →	56	41 7N	30 39 E
Sakata	74	38 55N	139 50 E
Sakeny →	93	20 0 S	45 25 E
Sakété	85	6 40N	2 45 E
Sakhalin, Ostrov	59	51 0N	143 0 E
Sakhi Gopal	69	19 58N	85 50 E
Sakhnīn	62	32 52N	35 12 E
Saki	56	45 9N	33 34 E
Sakiai	54	54 59N	23 0 E
Sakołow Małopolski	28	50 10N	22 9 E
Sakon Nakhon	71	17 10N	104 9 E
Sakrand	68	26 10N	68 15 E
Sakri	68	21 2N	74 20 E
Sakskøbing	49	54 49N	11 39 E
Sal →	57	47 31N	40 45 E
Šal'a	27	48 10N	17 50 E
Sala	48	59 58N	16 35 E
Sala Consilina	41	40 23N	15 35 E
Sala-y-Gómez	95	26 28 S	105 28W
Salaberry-de-Valleyfield	106	45 15N	74 8W
Saladas	124	28 15 S	58 40W
Saladillo	124	35 40 S	59 55W
Salado →, Buenos Aires, Argent.	124	35 44 S	57 22W
Salado →, La Pampa, Argent.	128	37 30 S	67 0W
Salado →, Santa Fe, Argent.	124	31 40 S	60 41W
Salado →, Mexico	120	26 52N	99 19W
Salaga	85	8 31N	0 31W
Sălaj □	46	47 15N	23 0 E
Salala, Liberia	84	6 42N	10 7W
Salala, Sudan	86	21 17N	36 16 E
Salālah	63	16 56N	53 59 E
Salamanca, Chile	124	31 46 S	70 59W
Salamanca, Spain	30	40 58N	5 39W
Salamanca, U.S.A.	114	42 10N	78 42W
Salamanca □	30	40 57N	5 40W
Salamis	45	37 56N	23 30 E
Salar de Atacama	124	23 30 S	68 25W
Salar de Uyuni	126	20 30 S	67 45W
Sălard	46	47 12N	22 3 E
Salas	30	43 25N	6 15W
Salas de los Infantes	32	42 2N	3 17W
Salatiga	73	7 19 S	110 30 E
Salavat	52	53 21N	55 55 E
Salaverry	126	8 15 S	79 0W
Salawati	73	1 7 S	130 52 E
Salayar	73	6 7 S	120 30 E
Salazar →	32	42 40N	1 20W
Salbris	19	47 25N	2 3 E
Salcia	46	43 56N	24 55 E
Salcombe	13	50 14N	3 47W
Saldaña	30	42 32N	4 48W
Saldanha	92	33 0 S	17 58 E
Saldanhabaai	92	33 6 S	18 0 E
Saldus	54	56 38N	22 30 E
Sale	97	38 6 S	147 6 E
Salé	82	34 3N	6 48W
Sale	12	53 26N	2 19W
Salebabu	73	3 55N	126 40 E
Salekhard	58	66 30N	66 35 E
Salem, India	70	11 40N	78 11 E
Salem, Ind., U.S.A.	114	38 38N	86 6W
Salem, Mass., U.S.A.	114	42 29N	70 53W
Salem, Mo., U.S.A.	117	37 40N	91 30W
Salem, N.J., U.S.A.	114	39 34N	75 29W
Salem, Ohio, U.S.A.	114	40 52N	80 50W
Salem, Oreg., U.S.A.	118	45 0N	123 0W
Salem, S.D., U.S.A.	116	43 44N	97 23W
Salem, Va., U.S.A.	114	37 19N	80 8W
Salemi	40	37 49N	12 47 E
Salernes	21	43 34N	6 15 E
Salerno	41	40 40N	14 44 E
Salerno, G. di	41	40 35N	14 45 E
Salfīt	62	32 5N	35 11 E
Salford	12	53 30N	2 17W
Salgir →	56	45 38N	35 1 E
Salgótarján	27	48 5N	19 47 E
Salies-de-Béarn	20	43 28N	0 56W
Salina, Italy	41	38 35N	14 50 E
Salina, U.S.A.	116	38 50N	97 40W
Salina Cruz	120	16 10N	95 10W
Salinas, Brazil	127	16 10 S	42 10W
Salinas, Chile	124	23 31 S	69 29W
Salinas, Ecuador	126	2 10 S	80 58W
Salinas, U.S.A.	119	36 40N	121 41W
Salinas →, Mexico	120	16 28N	90 31W
Salinas →, U.S.A.	119	36 45N	121 48W
Salinas Ambargasta	124	29 0 S	65 0W
Salinas, B. de	121	11 4N	85 45W
Salinas, C. de	33	39 16N	3 4 E
Salinas (de Hidalgo)	120	22 30N	101 40W
Salinas Grandes	124	30 0 S	65 0W
Salinas, Pampa de las	124	31 58 S	66 42W
Saline →, Ark., U.S.A.	117	33 10N	92 8W
Saline →, Kans., U.S.A.	116	38 51N	97 30W
Salinópolis	127	0 40 S	47 20W
Salins	19	46 57N	5 53 E
Salins-les-Bains	19	46 58N	5 52 E
Salir	31	37 14N	8 2W
Salisbury, Austral.	99	34 46 S	138 40 E
Salisbury, U.K.	13	51 4N	1 48W
Salisbury, Md., U.S.A.	114	38 20N	75 38W
Salisbury, N.C., U.S.A.	115	35 20N	80 29W
* Salisbury, Zimb.	91	17 43 S	31 2 E
Salisbury Plain	13	51 13N	1 50W
Sălişte	46	45 45N	23 56 E
Salka	85	10 20N	4 58 E
Salle, La	116	41 20N	89 6W
Sallent	32	41 49N	1 54 E
Salles-Curan	20	44 11N	2 48 E
Salling	49	56 40N	8 55 E
Sallisaw	117	35 26N	94 45W
Sallom Junction	86	19 17N	37 6 E
Salmerón	32	40 33N	2 29W
Salmo	108	49 10N	117 20W
Salmon	118	45 12N	113 56W
Salmon →, Can.	108	54 3N	122 40W
Salmon →, U.S.A.	118	45 51N	116 46W
Salmon Arm	108	50 40N	119 15W
Salmon Falls	118	42 48N	114 59W
Salmon Res.	107	48 05N	56 00W
Salmon River Mts.	118	45 0N	114 30W
Salo	51	60 22N	23 10 E
Salò	38	45 37N	10 32 E
Salobreña	31	36 44N	3 35W
Salome	119	33 51N	113 37W
Salon-de-Provence	21	43 39N	5 6 E
Salonica = Thessaloníki	44	40 38N	22 58 E
Salonta	46	46 49N	21 42 E
Salop = Shropshire □	13	52 36N	2 45W
Salor →	31	39 39N	7 3W
Salou, Cabo	32	41 3N	1 10 E
Salsacate	124	31 20 S	65 5W
Salses	20	42 50N	2 55 E
Salsette I.	70	19 5N	72 50 E
Salsk	57	46 28N	41 30 E
Salso →	41	37 6N	13 55 E
Salsomaggiore	38	44 48N	9 59 E
Salt →, Can.	108	60 0N	112 25W
Salt →, U.S.A.	119	33 23N	112 18W
Salt Creek	99	36 8 S	139 38 E
Salt Fork →	117	36 37N	97 7W
Salt Lake City	118	40 45N	111 58W
Salt Range	68	32 30N	72 25 E
Salta	124	24 57 S	65 25W
Salta □	124	24 48 S	65 30W
Saltcoats	14	55 38N	4 47W
Saltee Is.	15	52 7N	6 37W
Saltfjorden	50	67 15N	14 10 E
Saltholm	49	55 38N	12 43 E
Salthólmavík	50	65 24N	21 57W
Saltillo	120	25 30N	100 57W
Salto, Argent.	124	34 20 S	60 15W
Salto, Uruguay	124	31 27 S	57 50W
Salton Sea	119	33 20N	115 50W
Saltpond	85	5 15N	1 3W
Saltsjöbaden	49	59 15N	18 20 E
Saltspring	108	48 54N	123 37W
Saltville	114	36 53N	81 46W
Saluda →	115	34 0N	81 4W
Salûm	86	31 31N	25 7 E
Salûm, Khâlig el	86	31 30N	25 9 E
Salur	70	18 27N	83 18 E
Saluzzo	38	44 39N	7 29 E
Salvador, Brazil	127	13 0 S	38 30W
Salvador, Can.	109	52 10N	109 32W
Salvador, L.	117	29 46N	90 16W
Salvaterra de Magos	31	39 1N	8 47W
Sálvora, Isla	30	42 30N	8 58W
Salwa	65	24 45N	50 55 E
Salween →	67	16 31N	97 37 E
Salyany	53	39 10N	48 50 E
Salyersville	114	37 45N	83 4W
Salza →	26	47 40N	14 43 E
Salzach →	26	48 12N	12 56 E
Salzburg	26	47 48N	13 2 E
Salzburg □	26	47 15N	13 0 E
Salzgitter	24	52 13N	10 22 E
Salzwedel	24	52 50N	11 11 E
Sam Neua	71	20 29N	104 0 E
Sam Ngao	71	17 18N	99 0 E
Sam Rayburn Res.	117	31 15N	94 20W
Sama	58	60 12N	60 22 E
Sama de Langreo	30	43 18N	5 40W
Samagaltai	59	50 36N	95 3 E
Samales Group	73	6 0N	122 0 E
Samalkot	70	17 3N	82 13 E
Samâlût	86	28 20N	30 42
Samana	68	30 10N	76 13
Samanga	91	8 20 S	39 13
Samangán □	65	36 15N	68 3
Samangwa	90	4 23 S	24 10
Samar	73	12 0N	125 0
Samarai	98	10 39 S	150 41
Samaria = Shōmrōn	62	32 15N	35 13
Samarinda	72	0 30 S	117 9
Samarkand	58	39 40N	66 55
Sāmarrā"	64	34 16N	43 55
Samastipur	69	25 50N	85 50
Samatan	20	43 29N	0 55
Samba	90	4 38 S	26 22
Sambalpur	69	21 28N	84 4
Sambar, Tanjung	72	2 59 S	110 19
Sambas	72	1 20N	109 20
Sambava	93	14 16 S	50 10
Sambawizi	91	18 24 S	26 13
Sambhal	68	28 35N	78 37
Sambhar	68	26 52N	75 6
Sambiase	41	38 58N	16 16
Sambonifacio	38	45 24N	11 16
Sambor, Camb.	71	12 46N	106 0
Sambor, U.S.S.R.	54	49 30N	23 10
Sambre →	16	50 27N	4 52
Sambuca di Sicilia	40	37 39N	13 6
Samburu □	90	1 10N	37 0
Samchŏk	76	37 30N	129 10
Same	90	4 2 S	37 38
Samer	19	50 38N	1 44
Samfya	91	11 22 S	29 31
Sámi	45	38 15N	20 39
Samna	86	25 12N	37 17
Samnū	83	27 15N	14 55
Samo Alto	124	30 22 S	71 0W
Samobor	39	45 47N	15 44
Samoëns	21	46 5N	6 45
Samokov	43	42 18N	23 35
Samoorombón, Bahía	124	36 5 S	57 20W
Samorogouan	84	11 21N	4 57W
Sámos	45	37 45N	26 50
Samos	30	42 44N	7 20W
Samoš	42	45 13N	20 49
Samothráki	44	39 48N	19 31
Samothráki	44	40 28N	25 28
Samoylovka	55	51 12N	43 43
Sampa	84	8 0N	2 36W
Sampacho	124	33 20 S	64 50W
Sampang	73	7 11 S	113 13
Samper de Calanda	32	41 11N	0 28W
Sampit	72	2 34 S	113 0
Sampit, Teluk	72	3 5 S	113 3
Samra	64	25 35N	41 0
Samsø	49	55 50N	10 35
Samsø Bælt	49	55 45N	10 45
Samsun	64	41 15N	36 22
Samsun Dağı	45	37 45N	27 10
Samtredia	57	42 7N	42 24
Samui, Ko	71	9 30N	100 0
Samur →	57	41 53N	48 32
Samusole	91	10 2 S	24 0
Samut Prakan	71	13 32N	100 40
Samut Sakhon	71	13 31N	100 13
Samut Songkhram (Mekong)	71	13 24N	100 1
Samwari	68	28 30N	66 46
San	84	13 15N	4 57W
San →	27	50 45N	21 51
San Adrián, C. de	30	43 21N	8 50W
San Agustin, C.	73	6 20N	126 13
San Agustín de Valle Fértil	124	30 35 S	67 30W
San Ambrosio	95	26 28 S	79 53W
San Andreas	118	38 0N	120 39W
San Andrés, I. de	121	12 42N	81 46W
San Andres Mts.	119	33 0N	106 45W
San Andrés Tuxtla	120	18 30N	95 20W
San Angelo	117	31 30N	100 30W
San Antonio, Chile	124	33 40 S	71 40W
San Antonio, N. Mex., U.S.A.	119	33 58N	106 57W
San Antonio, Tex., U.S.A.	117	29 30N	98 30W
San Antonio →	117	28 30N	96 50W
San Antonio Abad	33	38 59N	1 19
San Antonio, C., Argent.	124	36 15 S	56 40W
San Antonio, C., Cuba	121	21 50N	84 57W
San Antonio, C. de	33	38 48N	0 12
San Antonio de los Baños	121	22 54N	82 31W
San Antonio de los Cobres	124	24 10 S	66 17W
San Antonio Oeste	128	40 40 S	65 0W
San Augustine	117	31 30N	94 7W
San Bartolomeo in Galdo	41	41 23N	15 2
San Benedetto	38	45 2N	10 57
San Benedetto del Tronto	39	42 57N	13 52
San Benito	117	26 5N	97 39W
San Bernardino	119	34 7N	117 18W
San Bernardino Str.	73	13 0N	125 0
San Bernardo	124	33 40 S	70 50W
San Bernardo, I. de	126	9 45N	75 50W
San Blas	120	26 4N	108 46W
San Blas, C.	115	29 40N	85 12W
San Borja	126	14 50 S	66 52W
San Buenaventura	120	27 5N	101 32W
San Carlos, Argent.	124	33 50 S	69 0W
San Carlos, Chile	124	36 10 S	72 0W
San Carlos, Mexico	120	29 0N	100 54W
San Carlos, Nic.	121	11 12N	84 50W
San Carlos, Phil.	73	10 29N	123 25
San Carlos, Uruguay	125	34 46 S	54 58W
San Carlos, U.S.A.	119	33 24N	110 27W
San Carlos, Amazonas, Venez.	126	1 55N	67 4W
San Carlos, Cojedes, Venez.	126	9 40N	68 36W
San Carlos = Butuku-Luba	85	3 29N	8 33
San Carlos de Bariloche	128	41 10 S	71 25W
San Carlos de la Rápita	32	40 37N	0 35
San Carlos del Zulia	126	9 1N	71 55W
San Carlos L.	119	33 15N	110 25W
San Cataldo	40	37 30N	13 58
San Celoni	32	41 42N	2 30
San Clemente, Chile	124	35 30 S	71 29W
San Clemente, Spain	33	39 24N	2 25W
San Clemente, U.S.A.	119	33 29N	117 36W
San Clemente I.	119	32 53N	118 30W
San Constanzo	39	43 46N	13 5

* *Renamed Harare*

an Cristóbal, Argent. 124 30 20S 61 10W
an Cristóbal, Dom. Rep. 121 18 25N 70 6W
an Cristóbal, Venez. 126 16 50N 92 40W
an Cristóbal de las Casas 120 16 50N 92 33W
an Damiano d'Asti 38 44 51N 8 4 E
an Daniele del Friuli 39 46 10N 13 0 E
an Demétrio Corone 41 39 34N 16 22 E
an Diego, Calif., U.S.A. 119 32 43N 117 10W
an Diego, Tex., U.S.A. 117 27 47N 98 15W
an Diego, C. 128 54 40S 65 10W
an Donà di Piave 39 45 38N 12 34 E
an Elpídio a Mare 39 43 16N 13 41 E
an Estanislao 124 24 39S 56 26W
an Esteban de Gormaz 32 41 34N 3 13W
an Felice sul Panaro 38 44 51N 11 9 E
an Felipe, Chile 124 32 43S 70 42W
an Felipe, Mexico 120 31 0N 114 52W
an Felipe, Venez. 126 10 20N 68 44W
an Feliu de Guíxols 32 41 45N 3 1 E
an Feliu de Llobregat 32 41 23N 2 2 E
an Félix 95 26 23S 80 0W
an Fernando, Chile 124 34 30S 71 0W
an Fernando, Mexico 120 30 0N 115 10W
an Fernando, Luzon, Phil. 73 16 40N 120 23 E
an Fernando, Luzon, Phil. 73 15 5N 120 37 E
an Fernando, Spain 31 36 28N 6 17W
an Fernando, Trin. 121 10 20N 61 30W
an Fernando, U.S.A. 119 34 15N 118 29W
an Fernando → 120 24 55N 98 10W
an Fernando de Apure 126 7 54N 67 15W
an Fernando de Atabapo 126 4 3N 67 42W
an Fernando di Púglia 41 41 18N 16 5 E
an Francisco, Argent. 124 31 30S 62 5W
an Francisco, U.S.A. 119 37 47N 122 30W
an Francisco → 119 32 59N 109 22W
an Francisco de Macorís 121 19 19N 70 15W
an Francisco del Monte de Oro 124 32 36S 66 8W
an Francisco del Oro 120 26 52N 105 50W
an Francisco Javier 33 38 42N 1 26 E
an Francisco, Paso de 124 27 0S 68 0W
an Fratello 41 38 1N 14 33 E
an Gavino Monreale 40 39 33N 8 47 E
an Gil 126 6 33N 73 8W
an Gimignano 38 43 28N 11 3 E
an Giórgio di Nogaro 39 45 50N 13 13 E
an Giórgio Iónico 41 40 27N 17 23 E
an Giovanni Bianco 38 45 52N 9 40 E
an Giovanni in Fiore 41 39 16N 16 42 E
an Giovanni in Persiceto 39 44 39N 11 12 E
an Giovanni Rotondo 41 41 41N 15 42 E
an Giovanni Valdarno 39 43 32N 11 30 E
an Giuliano Terme 38 43 45N 10 26 E
an Gottardo, Paso del 25 46 33N 8 33 E
an Grcángelo 40 40 14N 16 14 E
an Gregorio 125 32 37S 55 40W
an Guiseppe Iato 40 37 57N 13 11 E
an Ignacio, Boliv. 126 16 20S 60 55W
an Ignacio, Parag. 124 26 52S 57 3W
an Ignacio, Laguna 120 26 50N 113 11W
an Ildefonso, C. 73 16 0N 122 1 E
an Isidro 124 34 29S 58 31W
an Javier, Misiones, Argent. 125 27 55S 55 5W
an Javier, Santa Fe, Argent. 124 30 40S 59 55W
an Javier, Boliv. 126 16 18S 62 30W
an Javier, Chile 124 35 40S 71 45W
an Javier, Spain 33 37 49N 0 50W
an Joaquin → 119 37 4N 121 51W
an Jorge 124 31 54S 61 50W
an Jorge, Bahía de 120 31 20N 113 20W
an Jorge, Golfo 128 46 0S 66 0W
an Jorge, G. de 32 40 50N 0 55W
an José, Boliv. 126 17 53S 60 50W
an José, C. Rica 121 10 0N 84 2W
an José, Guat. 120 14 0N 90 50W
an José, Mexico 120 25 0N 110 50W
an Jose, Luzon, Phil. 73 15 45N 120 55 E
an Jose, Mindoro, Phil. 73 12 27N 121 4 E
an Jose, Panay, Phil. 73 10 50N 122 5 E
an José 33 38 55N 1 18 E
an Jose, Calif., U.S.A. 119 37 20N 121 53W
an Jose, N. Mex., U.S.A. 119 35 26N 105 30W
an Jose → 119 34 58N 106 7W
an José de Feliciano 124 30 26S 58 46W
an José de Jáchal 124 30 15S 68 46W
an José de Mayo 124 34 27S 56 40W
an José de Ocune 126 4 15N 70 20W
an José del Cabo 120 23 0N 109 40W
an José del Guaviare 126 2 35N 72 38W
an Juan, Argent. 124 31 30S 68 30W
an Juan, Dom. Rep. 121 18 45N 72 45W
an Juan, Mexico 120 21 20N 102 50W
an Juan, Phil. 73 8 25N 126 20 E
an Juan, Pto. Rico 121 18 28N 66 8W
an Juan □ 124 31 9S 69 0W
an Juan →, Argent. 124 32 20S 67 25W
an Juan →, Nic. 121 10 56N 83 42W
an Juan →, U.S.A. 119 37 20N 110 20W
an Juan Bautista, Parag. 124 26 37S 57 6W
an Juan Bautista, Spain 33 39 5N 1 31 E
an Juan, C. 88 1 5N 9 20 E
an Juan Capistrano 119 33 29N 117 40W
an Juan de los Morros 126 9 55N 67 21W
an Juan del Norte, B. de 121 11 0N 83 40W
an Juan del Puerto 31 37 20N 6 50W
an Juan del Río 120 20 25N 100 0W
an Juan del Sur 121 11 20N 85 51W
an Juan Mts. 119 38 30N 108 30W
an Julián 128 49 15S 67 45W
an Just, Sierra de 32 40 45N 0 49W
an Justo 124 30 47S 60 30W
an Lázaro, C. 120 24 50N 112 18W
an Lázaro, Sa. de 120 23 25N 110 0W
an Leandro 119 37 40N 122 6W
an Leonardo 32 41 51N 3 5W
an Lorenzo, Argent. 124 32 45S 60 45W
an Lorenzo, Ecuador 126 1 15N 78 50W
an Lorenzo, Parag. 124 25 20S 57 32W
an Lorenzo → 120 24 15N 107 24W
an Lorenzo de la Parrilla 32 39 51N 2 22W
an Lorenzo de Morunys 32 42 8N 1 35 E
an Lorenzo, I., Mexico 120 28 35N 112 50W
an Lorenzo, I., Peru 126 12 7S 77 15W
San Lorenzo, Mt. 128 47 40S 72 20W
San Lucas, Boliv. 126 20 5S 65 7W
San Lucas, Mexico 120 27 10N 112 14W
San Lucas, C. de 120 22 50N 110 0W
San Lúcido 41 39 18N 16 3 E
San Luis, Argent. 124 33 20S 66 20W
San Luis, U.S.A. 119 37 3N 105 26W
San Luis □ 124 34 0S 66 0W
San Luis de la Paz 120 21 19N 100 32W
San Luis, I. 120 29 58N 114 26W
San Luis Obispo 119 35 21N 120 38W
San Luis Potosí 120 22 9N 100 59W
San Luis Potosí □ 120 22 10N 101 0W
San Luis Río Colorado 120 32 29N 114 58W
San Luis, Sierra de 124 32 30S 66 10W
San Marco Argentano 41 39 34N 16 8 E
San Marco dei Cavoti 41 41 20N 14 50 E
San Marco in Lámis 41 41 43N 15 38 E
San Marcos, Guat. 120 14 59N 91 52W
San Marcos, Mexico 120 27 13N 112 6W
San Marcos, U.S.A. 117 29 53N 98 0W
San Marino 39 43 56N 12 25 E
San Marino ■ 39 43 56N 12 25 E
San Martín 124 33 5S 68 28W
San Martín de Valdeiglesias 30 40 21N 4 24W
San Martín, L. 128 48 50S 72 50W
San Martino de Calvi 38 45 57N 9 41 E
San Mateo, Spain 32 40 28N 0 10 E
San Mateo, U.S.A. 119 37 32N 122 19W
San Matías 126 16 25S 58 20W
San Matías, Golfo 128 41 30S 64 0W
San Matias, G. of 122 41 30S 64 0W
San Miguel, El Sal. 120 13 30N 88 12W
San Miguel, Spain 33 39 3N 1 26 E
San Miguel, U.S.A. 119 35 45N 120 42W
San Miguel → 126 13 52S 63 56W
San Miguel de Salinas 33 37 59N 0 47W
San Miguel de Tucumán 124 26 50S 65 20W
San Miguel del Monte 124 35 23S 58 50W
San Miniato 38 43 40N 10 50 E
San Narciso 73 15 2N 120 3 E
San Nicolás de los Arroyas 124 33 25S 60 10W
San Nicolas I. 119 33 16N 119 30W
San Pablo 124 21 43S 66 38W
San Paolo di Civitate 41 41 44N 15 16 E
San Pedro, Buenos Aires, Argent. 125 26 30S 54 10W
San Pedro, Jujuy, Argent. 124 24 12S 64 55W
San-Pédro 84 4 50N 6 33W
San Pedro □ 124 24 0S 57 0W
San Pedro →, Chihuahua, Mexico 120 28 20N 106 10W
San Pedro →, Nayarit, Mexico 120 21 45N 105 30W
San Pedro →, U.S.A. 119 33 0N 110 50W
San Pedro de Atacama 124 22 55S 68 15W
San Pedro de Jujuy 124 24 12S 64 55W
San Pedro de las Colonias 120 25 50N 102 59W
San Pedro de Lloc 126 7 15S 79 28W
San Pedro de Macorís 121 18 30N 69 18W
San Pedro del Paraná 124 26 43S 56 13W
San Pedro del Pinatar 33 37 50N 0 50W
San Pedro Mártir, Sierra 120 31 0N 115 30W
San Pedro Mixtepec 120 16 2N 97 7W
San Pedro Ocampo = Melchor Ocampo 120 24 52N 101 40W
San Pedro, Pta. 124 25 30S 70 38W
San Pedro, Sierra de 31 39 18N 6 40W
San Pedro Sula 120 15 30N 88 0W
San Pedro,Pta. 124 25 30S 70 38W
San Pietro, I. 40 39 9N 8 17 E
San Pietro Vernótico 41 40 28N 18 0 E
San Quintín 73 16 1N 120 56 E
San Rafael, Argent. 124 34 40S 68 21W
San Rafael, Calif., U.S.A. 118 37 59N 122 32W
San Rafael, N. Mex., U.S.A. 119 35 6N 107 58W
San Ramón de la Nueva Orán 124 23 10S 64 20W
San Remo 38 43 48N 7 47 E
San Roque, Argent. 124 28 25S 58 45W
San Roque, Spain 31 36 17N 5 21W
San Rosendo 124 37 16S 72 43W
San Saba 117 31 12N 98 45W
San Salvador 120 13 40N 89 10W
San Salvador de Jujuy 124 24 10S 64 48W
San Salvador I. 121 24 0N 74 32W
San Sebastián, Argent. 128 53 10S 68 30W
San Sebastián, Spain 32 43 17N 1 58W
San Serverino Marche 39 43 13N 13 10 E
San Simon 119 32 14N 109 16W
San Stéfano di Cadore 39 46 34N 12 33 E
San Valentin, Mte. 128 46 30S 73 30W
San Vicente de Alcántara 31 39 22N 7 8W
San Vicente de la Barquera 30 43 23N 4 29W
San Vincenzo 38 43 6N 10 29 E
San Vito 40 39 26N 9 32 E
San Vito al Tagliamento 39 45 55N 12 50 E
San Vito, C. 40 38 11N 12 41 E
San Vito Chietino 39 42 19N 14 27 E
San Vito dei Normanni 41 40 40N 17 40 E
San Ygnacio 117 27 6N 99 24W
Sana' 63 15 27N 44 12 E
Sana → 39 45 3N 16 23 E
Sanaba 84 12 25N 3 47W
Sanabria, La 30 42 0N 6 30W
Sanâfir 86 27 55N 34 37 E
Sanaga → 88 3 35N 9 38 E
Sanak I. 104 53 30N 162 30W
Sanana 73 2 5S 125 59 E
Sanand 68 22 59N 72 25 E
Sanandaj 64 35 18N 47 1 E
Sanandita 124 21 40S 63 45W
Sanary 21 43 7N 5 48 E
Sanawad 68 22 11N 76 5 E
Sancergues 19 47 10N 2 54 E
Sancerre 19 47 20N 2 50 E
Sancerrois, Coll. du 19 47 20N 2 40 E
Sancha He → 77 26 48N 106 7 E
Sanchor 68 24 45N 71 55 E
Sanco, Pt. 73 8 15N 126 24 E
Sancoins 19 46 47N 2 55 E
Sancti-Spíritus 121 21 52N 79 33W
Sand → 93 22 25S 30 5 E
Sand Springs 117 36 12N 96 5W
Sandah 86 20 35N 39 32 E
Sandakan 72 5 53N 118 4 E
Sandan 71 12 46N 106 0 E
Sandanski 43 41 35N 23 16 E
Sandaré 84 14 40N 10 15W
Sanday 14 59 15N 2 30W
Sande, Möre og Romsdal, Norway 47 62 15N 5 27 E
Sande, Sogn og Fjordane, Norway 47 61 20N 5 47 E
Sandefjord 47 59 10N 10 15 E
Sandeid 47 59 33N 5 52 E
Sanders 119 35 12N 109 25W
Sanderson 117 30 5N 102 30W
Sandfly L. 109 55 43N 106 6W
Sandgate 99 27 18S 153 3 E
Sandia 126 14 10S 69 30W
Sandıklı 64 38 30N 30 20 E
Sandnes 47 58 50N 5 45 E
Sandness 14 60 18N 1 38W
Sandoa 88 9 41S 23 0 E
Sandomierz 28 50 40N 21 43 E
Sandover → 97 21 43S 136 32 E
Sandoway 67 18 20N 94 30 E
Sandpoint 118 48 20N 116 34W
Sandringham 12 52 50N 0 30 E
Sandslån 48 63 2N 17 49 E
Sandspit 108 53 14N 131 49W
Sandstone 96 27 59S 119 16 E
Sandusky, Mich., U.S.A. 106 43 26N 82 50W
Sandusky, Ohio, U.S.A. 114 41 25N 82 40W
Sandvig 49 55 18N 14 48 E
Sandviken 48 60 38N 16 46 E
Sandwich B., Can. 107 53 40N 57 15W
Sandwich B., S. Afr. 92 23 25S 14 20 E
Sandwich, C. 98 18 14S 146 18 E
Sandwich Group 5 57 0S 27 0W
Sandwip Chan. 67 22 35N 91 35 E
Sandy C., Queens., Austral. 97 24 42S 153 15 E
Sandy C., Tas., Austral. 97 41 25S 144 45 E
Sandy Cr. → 118 41 15N 109 47W
Sandy L. 106 53 2N 93 0W
Sandy Lake 106 53 0N 93 15W
Sandy Narrows 109 55 5N 103 4W
Sanford, Fla., U.S.A. 115 28 45N 81 20W
Sanford, Me., U.S.A. 113 43 28N 70 47W
Sanford, N.C., U.S.A. 115 35 30N 79 10W
Sanford → 96 27 22S 115 53 E
Sanford Mt. 104 62 30N 143 0W
Sanga 91 12 22S 35 21 E
Sanga → 88 1 5S 17 0 E
Sanga-Tolon 59 61 50N 149 40 E
Sangamner 70 19 37N 74 15 E
Sangar 59 64 2N 127 31 E
Sangasanga 72 0 36S 117 13 E
Sange 90 6 58S 28 21 E
Sangeang 73 8 12S 119 6 E
Sanger 119 36 41N 119 35W
Sangerhausen 24 51 28N 11 18 E
Sanggan He → 76 38 12N 117 15 E
Sanggau 72 0 5N 110 30 E
Sangihe, Kepulauan 73 3 0N 126 0 E
Sangihe, P. 73 3 45N 125 30 E
Sangkapura 72 5 52S 112 40 E
Sangli 70 16 55N 74 33 E
Sangmélina 88 2 57N 12 1 E
Sangonera → 33 37 59N 1 4W
Sangre de Cristo Mts. 117 37 0N 105 0W
Sangro → 39 42 14N 14 32 E
Sangudo 108 53 50N 114 54W
Sangüesa 32 42 37N 1 17W
Sanguinaires, Îs. 21 41 51N 8 36 E
Sangzhi 77 29 25N 110 12 E
Sanhala 84 10 3N 6 51W
Sanish 116 48 0N 102 30W
Sanje 90 0 49S 31 30 E
Sanjiang 77 25 48N 109 37 E
Sankaranayinarkovil 70 9 10N 77 35 E
Sankeshwar 70 16 23N 74 32 E
Sankt Andra 26 46 46N 14 50 E
Sankt Blasien 25 47 47N 8 7 E
Sankt Gallen 25 47 26N 9 22 E
Sankt Gallen □ 25 47 25N 9 22 E
Sankt Gotthard P. = San Gottardo, Paso del 25 46 33N 8 33 E
Sankt Ingbert 25 49 16N 7 6 E
Sankt Johann, Salzburg, Austria 26 47 22N 13 12 E
Sankt Johann, Tirol, Austria 26 47 30N 12 25 E
Sankt Moritz 25 46 30N 9 50 E
Sankt Olof 49 55 37N 14 8 E
Sankt Pölten 26 48 12N 15 38 E
Sankt Valentin 26 48 11N 14 33 E
Sankt Veit 26 46 54N 14 22 E
Sankt Wendel 25 49 27N 7 9 E
Sankt Wolfgang 26 47 43N 13 27 E
Sankuru → 88 4 17S 20 25 E
Sanlúcar de Barrameda 31 36 46N 6 21W
Sanlúcar la Mayor 31 37 26N 6 18W
Sanluri 40 39 35N 8 55 E
Sanmenxia 77 34 47N 111 12 E
Sannaspos 92 29 6S 26 34 E
Sannicandro Gargánico 41 41 50N 15 34 E
Sannidal 47 58 55N 9 15 E
Sannieshof 92 26 30S 25 47 E
Sanok 27 49 35N 22 10 E
Sanquhar 14 55 21N 3 56W
Sansanding Dam 84 13 48N 6 0W
Sansepolcro 39 43 34N 12 8 E
Sanshui 75 23 10N 112 56 E
Sanski Most 39 44 46N 16 40 E
Sant' Ágata de Goti 41 41 6N 14 30 E
Sant' Ágata di Militello 41 38 2N 14 8 E
Santa Ana, Boliv. 126 13 50S 65 40W
Santa Ana, Ecuador 126 1 16S 80 20W
Santa Ana, El Sal. 120 14 0N 89 31W
Santa Ana, Mexico 120 30 31N 111 8W
Santa Ana, U.S.A. 119 33 48N 117 55W
Sant' Ángelo Lodigiano 38 45 14N 9 25 E
Sant' Antíoco 40 39 2N 8 30 E
Sant' Arcángelo di Romagna 39 44 4N 12 26 E
Santa Bárbara, Mexico 120 26 48N 105 50W
Santa Bárbara, Spain 32 40 42N 0 29 E
Santa Barbara 119 34 25N 119 40W
Santa Bárbara, Mt. 33 37 23N 2 50W
Santa Catalina 120 25 40N 110 50W
Santa Catalina, G. of 119 33 0N 118 0W
Santa Catalina I. 119 33 20N 118 30W
Santa Catarina □ 125 27 25S 48 30W
Santa Catarina, I. de 125 27 30S 48 40W
Santa Caterina Villarmosa 41 37 37N 14 1 E
Santa Cecília 125 26 56S 50 18W
Santa Clara, Cuba 121 22 20N 80 0W
Santa Clara, Calif., U.S.A. 119 37 21N 122 0W
Santa Clara, Utah, U.S.A. 119 37 10N 113 38W
Santa Clara de Olimar 125 32 50S 54 54W
Santa Clara Pk. 119 35 58N 106 45W
Santa Clotilde 126 2 33S 73 45W
Santa Coloma de Farnés 32 41 50N 2 39 E
Santa Coloma de Gramanet 32 41 27N 2 13 E
Santa Comba 30 43 2N 8 49W
Santa Croce Camerina 41 36 50N 14 30 E
Santa Croce di Magliano 41 41 43N 14 59 E
Santa Cruz, Argent. 128 50 0S 68 32W
Santa Cruz, Boliv. 126 17 43S 63 10W
Santa Cruz, Chile 124 34 38S 71 27W
Santa Cruz, C. Rica 121 10 15N 85 35W
Santa Cruz, Phil. 73 14 20N 121 24 E
Santa Cruz, Calif., U.S.A. 119 36 55N 122 1W
Santa Cruz, N. Mexico, U.S.A. 119 35 59N 106 1W
Santa Cruz □ 126 17 43S 63 10W
Santa Cruz → 128 50 10S 68 20W
Santa Cruz de Mudela 33 38 39N 3 28W
Sta. Cruz de Tenerife 80 28 28N 16 15W
Santa Cruz del Retamar 30 40 8N 4 14W
Santa Cruz del Sur 121 20 44N 78 0W
Santa Cruz do Rio Pardo 125 22 54S 49 37W
Santa Cruz do Sul 125 29 42S 52 25W
Santa Cruz I. 119 34 0N 119 45W
Santa Cruz, Is. 94 10 30S 166 0 E
Santa Domingo, Cay 121 21 25N 75 15W
Santa Elena, Argent. 124 30 58S 59 47W
Santa Elena, Ecuador 126 2 16S 80 52W
Santa Elena, C. 121 10 54N 85 56W
Sant' Eufémia, Golfo di 41 38 50N 16 10 E
Santa Eulalia 33 38 59N 1 32 E
Santa Fe, Argent. 124 31 35S 60 41W
Santa Fe, Spain 31 37 11N 3 43W
Santa Fe, U.S.A. 119 35 40N 106 0W
Santa Fé □ 124 31 50S 60 55W
Santa Filomena 127 9 6S 45 50W
Santa Genoveva 120 23 18N 109 52W
Santa Inés 31 38 32N 5 37W
Santa Inés, I. 128 54 0S 73 0W
Santa Isabel, Argent. 124 36 10S 66 54W
Santa Isabel, Brazil 127 11 45S 51 30W
Santa Isabel = Rey Malabo 85 3 45N 8 50 E
Santa Isabel, Pico 85 3 36N 8 49 E
Santa Lucía, Corrientes, Argent. 124 28 58S 59 5W
Santa Lucía, San Juan, Argent. 124 31 30S 68 30W
Santa Lucía, Spain 33 37 35N 0 58W
Santa Lucia 124 34 27S 56 24W
Santa Lucia Range 119 36 0N 121 20W
Santa Margarita, Argent. 124 38 28S 61 35W
Santa Margarita, Mexico 120 24 30N 111 50W
Santa Margherita 38 44 20N 9 11 E
Santa Maria 124 26 40S 66 0W
Santa Maria, Brazil 125 29 40S 53 48W
Santa Maria, Spain 32 39 38N 2 47 E
Santa Maria, U.S.A. 119 34 58N 120 29W
Santa Maria, Zambia 91 11 5S 29 58 E
Santa María → 120 31 0N 107 14W
Santa María, Bahía de 120 25 10N 108 40W
Santa Maria, Cabo de 31 36 58N 7 53W
Santa Maria Capua Vetere 41 41 3N 14 15 E
Santa Maria da Vitória 127 13 24S 44 12W
Santa Maria del Oro 120 25 58N 105 20W
Santa Maria di Leuca, C. 41 39 48N 18 20 E
Santa María la Real de Nieva 30 41 4N 4 24W
Santa Marta, Colomb. 126 11 15N 74 13W
Santa Marta, Spain 31 38 37N 6 39W
Santa Marta Grande, C. 125 28 43S 48 50W
Santa Marta, Ría de 30 43 44N 7 45W
Santa Marta, Sierra Nevada de 126 10 55N 73 50W
Santa Maura = Levkás 45 38 40N 20 43 E
Santa Monica 119 34 0N 118 30W
Santa Olalla, Huelva, Spain 31 37 54N 6 14W
Santa Olalla, Toledo, Spain 30 40 2N 4 25W
Sant' Onofrio 41 38 42N 16 10 E
Santa Paula 119 34 20N 119 2W
Santa Pola 33 38 13N 0 35W
Santa Rita 119 32 50N 108 0W
Santa Rosa, La Pampa, Argent. 124 36 40S 64 17W
Santa Rosa, San Luis, Argent. 124 32 21S 65 10W
Santa Rosa, Boliv. 126 10 36S 67 20W
Santa Rosa, Brazil 125 27 52S 54 29W
Santa Rosa, Calif., U.S.A. 118 38 26N 122 43W
Santa Rosa, N. Mexico, U.S.A. 117 34 58N 104 40W
Santa Rosa de Copán 120 14 47N 88 46W
Santa Rosa de Río Primero 124 31 8S 63 20W
Santa Rosa I., Calif., U.S.A. 119 34 0N 120 6W
Santa Rosa I., Fla., U.S.A. 115 30 23N 87 0W
Santa Rosa Mts. 118 41 45N 117 30W
Santa Rosalía 120 27 20N 112 20W
Santa Sofia 39 43 57N 11 55 E
Santa Sylvina 124 27 50S 61 10W
Santa Tecla = Nueva San Salvador 120 13 40N 89 25W
Santa Teresa 124 33 25S 60 47W
Santa Teresa di Riva 41 37 58N 15 21 E
Santa Teresa Gallura 40 41 14N 9 12 E
Santa Vitória do Palmar 125 33 32S 53 25W
Santadi 40 39 5N 8 42 E
Santai 75 31 5N 104 58 E
Santana, Coxilha de 125 30 50S 55 35W
Santana do Livramento 125 30 55S 55 30W
Santanayi 33 39 20N 3 5 E
Santander 30 43 27N 3 51W
Santander □ 30 43 25N 4 0W
Santander Jiménez 120 24 11N 98 29W
Santaquin 118 40 0N 111 51W
Santarém, Brazil 127 2 25S 54 42W
Santarém, Port. 31 39 12N 8 42W
Santarém □ 31 39 10N 8 40W
Santaren Channel 121 24 0N 79 30W
Santéramo in Colle 41 40 48N 16 45 E

Santerno → 39 44 10N 11 38 E
Santhia 38 45 20N 8 10 E
Santiago, Brazil 125 29 11 S 54 52W
Santiago, Chile 124 33 24 S 70 40W
Santiago, Panama 121 8 0N 81 0W
Santiago □ 124 33 30 S 70 50W
Santiago de Compostela 30 42 52N 8 37W
Santiago de Cuba 121 20 0N 75 49W
Santiago de los Cabelleros 121 19 30N 70 40W
Santiago del Estero 124 27 50 S 64 15W
Santiago del Estero □ 124 27 40 S 63 15W
Santiago do Cacém 31 38 1N 8 42W
Santiago Ixcuintla 120 21 50N 105 11W
Santiago Papasquiaro 120 25 0N 105 20W
Santiago, Punta de 85 3 12N 8 40 E
Santiaguillo, L. de 120 24 50N 104 50W
Santillana del Mar 30 43 24N 4 6W
Santipur 69 23 17N 88 25 E
Santisteban del Puerto 33 38 17N 3 15W
Santo Amaro 127 12 30 S 38 43W
Santo Anastácio 125 21 58 S 51 39W
Santo André 125 23 39 S 46 29W
Santo Ângelo 125 28 15 S 54 15W
Santo Antonio 127 15 50 S 56 0W
Santo Corazón 126 18 0 S 58 45W
Santo Domingo, Dom. Rep. 121 18 30N 64 54W
Santo Domingo, Baja Calif. N., Mexico 120 30 43N 116 2W
Santo Domingo, Baja Calif. S., Mexico 120 25 32N 112 2W
Santo Domingo, Nic. 121 12 14N 84 59W
Santo Domingo de la Calzada 32 42 26N 2 57W
Santo Stéfano di Camastro 41 38 1N 14 22 E
Santo Stino di Livenza 39 45 45N 12 40 E
Santo Tirso 30 41 21N 8 28W
Santo Tomás 126 14 26 S 72 8W
Santo Tomé 125 28 40 S 56 5W
Santo Tomé de Guayana 126 8 22N 62 40W
Santoña 30 43 29N 3 27W
Santos 125 24 0 S 46 20W
Santos Dumont 125 22 55 S 43 10W
Santos, Sierra de los 31 38 7N 5 12W
Şanūr 62 32 22N 35 15 E
Sanvignes-les-Mines 19 46 40N 4 18 E
Sanyuan 77 34 35N 108 58 E
Sanza Pombo 88 7 18 S 15 56 E
São Anastácio 125 22 0 S 51 40W
São Bartolomeu de Messines 31 37 15N 8 17W
São Borja 125 28 39 S 56 0W
São Bras d'Alportel 31 37 8N 7 37W
São Carlos 125 22 0 S 47 50W
São Cristóvão 127 11 1 S 37 15W
São Domingos 127 13 25 S 46 19W
São Francisco 127 16 0 S 44 50W
São Francisco → 127 10 30 S 36 24W
São Francisco do Sul 125 26 15 S 48 36W
São Gabriel 125 30 20 S 54 20W
São Gonçalo 125 22 48 S 43 5W
Sao Hill 91 8 20 S 35 12 E
São João da Boa Vista 125 22 0 S 46 52W
São João da Pesqueira 30 41 8N 7 24W
São João del Rei 125 21 8 S 44 15W
São João do Araguaia 127 5 23 S 48 46W
São João do Piauí 127 8 21 S 42 15W
São José do Rio Prêto 125 20 50 S 49 20W
São José dos Campos 125 23 7 S 45 52W
São Leopoldo 125 29 50 S 51 10W
São Lourenço 125 22 7 S 45 3W
São Lourenço → 127 17 53 S 57 27W
São Luís Gonzaga 125 28 25 S 55 0W
São Luís (Maranhão) 127 2 39 S 44 15W
São Marcos → 127 18 15 S 47 37W
São Marcos, B. de 127 2 0 S 44 0W
São Martinho 30 40 18N 8 8W
São Mateus 127 18 44 S 39 50W
São Miguel 8 37 33N 25 27W
São Paulo 125 23 32 S 46 37W
São Paulo □ 125 22 0 S 49 0W
Sao Paulo, I. 6 0 50N 31 40W
São Pedro do Sul 30 40 46N 8 4W
São Roque, C. de 127 5 30 S 35 16W
São Sebastião do Paraíso 125 20 54 S 46 59W
São Sebastião, I. de 125 23 50 S 45 18W
São Teotónio 31 37 30N 8 42W
São Tomé 79 0 10N 6 39 E
São Tomé, C. de 125 22 0 S 40 59W
São Vicente 125 23 57 S 46 23W
São Vicente, Cabo de 31 37 0N 9 0W
Saona, I. 121 18 10N 68 40W
Saône → 19 45 44N 4 50 E
Saône-et-Loire □ 19 46 25N 4 50 E
Saonek 73 0 22 S 130 55 E
Saoura, O. → 82 29 0N 0 55W
Sápai 44 41 2N 25 43 E
Saparua 73 3 33 S 128 40 E
Sapele 85 5 50N 5 40 E
Sapelo I. 115 31 28N 81 15W
Sapiéntza 45 36 45N 21 43 E
Sapone 85 12 3N 1 35W
Saposoa 126 6 55 S 76 45W
Sapozhok 55 53 59N 40 41 E
Sapphire Mts. 118 46 20N 113 45W
Sapporo 74 43 0N 141 21 E
Sapri 41 40 5N 15 37 E
Sapudi 73 7 2 S 114 17 E
Sapulpa 117 36 0N 96 0W
Saqqez 64 36 15N 46 20 E
Sar-e Pol 65 36 10N 66 0 E
Sar Planina 42 42 10N 21 0 E
Sara 84 11 40N 3 53W
Sarāb 64 38 0N 47 30 E
Saragossa = Zaragoza 32 41 39N 0 53W
Saraguro 126 3 35 S 79 16W
Saraipalli 69 21 20N 82 59 E
Sarajevo 42 43 52N 18 26 E
Saralu 46 44 43N 28 10 E
Saran 86 19 35N 40 30 E
Saran, G. 72 0 30 S 111 25 E
Saranac Lake 114 44 20N 74 10W
Saranda, Alb. 44 39 52N 19 55 E
Saranda, Tanz. 90 5 45 S 34 59 E
Sarandí del Yi 125 33 18 S 55 38W
Sarandí Grande 124 33 44 S 56 20W
Sarangani B. 73 6 0N 125 13 E
Sarangani Is. 73 5 25N 125 25 E
Sarangarh 69 21 30N 83 5 E
Saransk 55 54 10N 45 10 E
Sarapul 52 56 28N 53 48 E
Sarasota 115 27 20N 82 30W
Saratoga 118 41 30N 106 48W
Saratoga Springs 114 43 5N 73 47W
Saratov 55 51 30N 46 2 E
Saravane 71 15 43N 106 25 E
Sarawak □ 72 2 0N 113 0 E
Saraya 84 12 50N 11 45W
Sarbāz 65 26 38N 61 19 E
Sarbīsheh 65 32 30N 59 40 E
Sârbogård 27 46 50N 18 40 E
Sarca → 38 45 52N 10 52 E
Sardalas 83 25 50N 10 34 E
Sardarshahr 68 28 30N 74 29 E
Sardegna 40 39 57N 9 0 E
Sardhana 68 29 9N 77 39 E
Sardinia = Sardegna 40 39 57N 9 0 E
Šarengrad 42 45 14N 19 16 E
Saréyamou 84 16 7N 3 10W
Sargasso Sea 6 27 0N 72 0W
Sargent 116 41 42N 99 24W
Sargodha 68 32 10N 72 40 E
* Sargodha □ 68 31 50N 72 0 E
Sarh 81 9 5N 18 23 E
Sarhro, Djebel 82 31 6N 5 0W
Sārī 65 36 30N 53 4 E
Sária 45 35 54N 27 17 E
Sarida → 62 32 4N 34 45 E
Sarikamiş 64 40 22N 42 35 E
Sarikei 72 2 8N 111 30 E
Sarina 97 21 22 S 149 13 E
Sariñena 32 41 47N 0 10W
Sarīr Tibasti 83 22 50N 18 30 E
Sarita 117 27 14N 97 49W
Sariyer 43 41 10N 29 3 E
Sark 18 49 25N 2 20W
Sarkad 27 46 47N 21 23 E
Sarlat-la-Canéda 20 44 54N 1 13 E
Sarles 116 48 58N 99 0W
Sărmaşu 46 46 45N 24 13 E
Sarmi 73 1 49 S 138 44 E
Sarmiento 128 45 35 S 69 5W
Särna 48 61 41N 13 8 E
Sarnano 39 43 2N 13 17 E
Sarnen 25 46 53N 8 13 E
Sarnia 106 42 58N 82 23W
Sarno 41 40 48N 14 35 E
Sarnowa 28 51 39N 16 53 E
Sarny 54 51 17N 26 40 E
Särö 49 57 31N 11 57 E
Sarolangun 72 2 19 S 102 42 E
Saronikós Kólpos 45 37 45N 23 45 E
Saronno 38 45 38N 9 2 E
Saros Körfezi 44 40 30N 26 15 E
Sárospatak 27 48 18N 21 33 E
Sarosul Românesc 42 45 34N 21 43 E
Sarova 55 54 55N 43 19 E
Sarpsborg 47 59 16N 11 12 E
Sarracín 32 42 15N 3 45W
Sarralbe 19 48 55N 7 1 E
Sarre = Saar → 19 49 7N 7 4 E
Sarre, La 106 48 45N 79 15W
Sarre-Union 19 48 55N 7 4 E
Sarrebourg 19 48 43N 7 3 E
Sarreguemines 19 49 1N 7 4 E
Sarriá 30 42 49N 7 29W
Sarrión 32 40 9N 0 49W
Sarro 84 13 40N 5 15W
Sarstedt 24 52 13N 9 50 E
Sartène 21 41 38N 8 58 E
Sarthe □ 18 47 58N 0 10 E
Sarthe → 18 47 33N 0 31W
Sartilly 18 48 45N 1 28W
Sartynya 58 63 22N 63 11 E
Sarum 86 21 11N 39 10 E
Sarūr 65 23 17N 58 4 E
Sárvár 27 47 15N 16 56 E
Sarvestān 65 29 20N 53 10 E
Särvfjallet 48 62 42N 13 30 E
Sárviz → 27 46 24N 18 41 E
Sary-Tash 58 39 44N 73 15 E
Sarych, Mys. 56 44 25N 33 45 E
Saryshagan 58 46 12N 73 38 E
Sarzana 38 44 5N 9 59 E
Sarzeau 18 47 31N 2 48W
Sasa 62 33 2N 35 23 E
Sasabeneh 63 7 59N 44 43 E
Sasaram 69 24 57N 84 5 E
Sasca Montană 42 44 50N 21 45 E
Sasebo 74 33 10N 129 43 E
Saser Mt. 69 34 50N 77 50 E
Saskatchewan □ 109 54 40N 106 0W
Saskatchewan → 109 53 37N 100 40W
Saskatoon 109 52 10N 106 38W
Saskylakh 59 71 55N 114 1 E
Sasnovka 55 56 20N 51 4 E
Sasolburg 93 26 46 S 27 49 E
Sasovo 55 54 25N 41 55 E
Sassandra 84 5 0N 6 8W
Sassandra → 84 4 58N 6 5W
Sássari 40 40 44N 8 33 E
Sassnitz 24 54 29N 13 39 E
Sasso Marconi 39 44 22N 11 12 E
Sassocorvaro 39 43 47N 12 30 E
Sassoferrato 39 43 26N 12 51 E
Sassuolo 38 44 31N 10 47 E
Sástago 32 41 19N 0 21W
Sastown 84 4 45N 8 27W
Sasumua Dam 90 0 45 S 36 40 E
Sasyk, Ozero 46 45 45N 30 0 E
Sata-Misaki 74 30 59N 130 40 E
Satadougou 84 12 25N 11 25W
Satanta 117 37 30N 101 0W
Satara 70 17 44N 73 58 E
Satilla → 115 30 59N 81 28W
Satka 52 55 3N 59 1 E
Satkhira 69 22 43N 89 8 E
Satmala Hills 70 20 15N 74 40 E
Satna 69 24 35N 80 50 E
Sator 39 44 11N 16 37 E
Sátoraljaújhely 27 48 25N 21 41 E
Satpura Ra. 68 21 25N 76 10 E
Satrup 24 54 39N 9 38 E
Sattenapalle 70 16 25N 80 6 E
Satu Mare 46 47 46N 22 55 E
Satui 72 3 50 S 115 27 E
Satumare □ 46 47 45N 23 0 E
Satun 71 6 43N 100 2 E
Saturnina → 126 12 15 S 58 10W
Sauce 124 30 5 S 58 46W
Saucillo 120 28 1N 105 17W
Sauda 47 59 40N 6 20 E
Sauðarkrókur 50 65 45N 19 40W
Saudi Arabia ■ 64 26 0N 44 0 E
Sauerland 24 51 0N 8 0 E
Saugeen → 112 44 30N 81 22W
Saugerties 114 42 4N 73 58W
Saugues 20 44 58N 3 32 E
Sauherad 47 59 25N 9 15 E
Saujon 20 45 41N 0 55W
Sauk Center 116 45 42N 94 56W
Sauk Rapids 116 45 35N 94 10W
Saulgau 25 48 4N 9 32 E
Saulieu 19 47 17N 4 14 E
Sault 21 44 6N 5 24 E
Sault Ste. Marie, Can. 106 46 30N 84 20W
Sault Ste. Marie, U.S.A. 114 46 27N 84 22W
Saumlaki 73 7 55 S 131 20 E
Saumur 18 47 15N 0 5W
Saunders C. 101 45 53 S 170 45 E
Saunders I. 5 57 48 S 26 28W
Saurbær, Borgarfjarðarsýsla, Iceland 50 64 24N 21 35W
Saurbær, Eyjafjarðarsýsla, Iceland 50 65 27N 18 13W
Sauri 85 11 42N 6 44 E
Saurimo 88 9 40 S 20 12 E
Sauveterre 20 43 25N 0 57W
Sauzé-Vaussais 20 46 8N 0 8 E
Sava 39 40 28N 17 32 E
Sava → 39 44 50N 20 26 E
Savage 116 47 27N 104 20W
Savai'i 101 13 28 S 172 24W
Savalou 85 7 57N 1 58 E
Savane 91 19 37 S 35 8 E
Savanna 116 42 5N 90 10W
Savanna la Mar 121 18 10N 78 10W
Savannah, Ga., U.S.A. 115 32 4N 81 4W
Savannah, Mo., U.S.A. 116 39 55N 94 46W
Savannah, Tenn., U.S.A. 115 35 12N 88 18W
Savannah → 115 32 2N 80 53W
Savannakhet 71 16 30N 104 49 E
Savant L. 106 50 16N 90 44W
Savant Lake 106 50 14N 90 40W
Savantvadi 70 15 55N 73 54 E
Savanur 70 14 59N 75 21 E
Savda 68 21 9N 75 56 E
Savé 85 8 2N 2 29 E
Save → 20 43 47N 1 17 E
Sāveh 64 35 2N 50 20 E
Savelugu 85 9 38N 0 54W
Savenay 18 47 20N 1 55W
Saverdun 20 43 14N 1 34 E
Saverne 19 48 39N 7 20 E
Savigliano 38 44 39N 7 40 E
Savigny-sur-Braye 18 47 53N 0 49 E
Saviñao 30 42 35N 7 38W
Savio → 39 44 19N 12 20 E
Šavnik 42 42 59N 19 10 E
Savoie □ 21 45 26N 6 35 E
Savona 38 44 19N 8 29 E
Savonlinna 52 61 52N 28 53 E
Sävsjö 49 57 20N 14 40 E
Sävsjøström 49 57 1N 15 25 E
Sawahlunto 72 0 40 S 100 52 E
Sawai 73 3 0 S 129 5 E
Sawai Madhopur 68 26 0N 76 25 E
Sawara 74 35 55N 140 30 E
Sawatch Mts. 119 38 30N 106 30W
Sawdā, Jabal as 83 28 51N 15 12 E
Sawel, Mt. 15 54 48N 7 5W
Sawfajjin, W. 83 31 46N 14 30 E
Sawknah 81 29 4N 15 47 E
Sawmills 91 19 30 S 28 2 E
Sawu 73 10 35 S 121 50 E
Sawu Sea 73 9 30 S 121 50 E
Sawyerville 113 45 20N 71 34W
Saxby → 98 18 25 S 140 53 E
Saxony, Lower = Niedersachsen □ 24 52 45N 9 0 E
Saxton 112 40 12N 78 18W
Say 85 13 8N 2 22 E
Saya 85 9 30N 3 18 E
Sayabec 107 48 35N 67 41W
Sayán 126 11 8 S 77 12W
Sayan, Vostochnyy 59 54 0N 96 0 E
Sayan, Zapadnyy 59 52 30N 94 0 E
Sayasan 57 42 56N 46 15 E
Saydā 64 33 35N 35 25 E
Şayghān 65 35 10N 67 55 E
Sayḩut 63 15 12N 51 10 E
Saynshand 75 44 55N 110 11 E
Sayre, Okla., U.S.A. 117 35 20N 99 40W
Sayre, Pa., U.S.A. 114 42 0N 76 30W
Sayula 120 19 50N 103 40W
Sayville 113 40 45N 73 7W
Sazan 44 40 30N 19 20 E
Sázava → 26 49 53N 14 24 E
Sazin 69 35 35N 73 30 E
Sazlika → 43 41 59N 25 50 E
Sbeïtla 83 35 12N 9 7 E
Scaër 18 48 2N 3 42W
Scafell Pikes 12 54 26N 3 14W
Scalea 41 39 49N 15 47 E
Scalpay 14 57 51N 6 40W
Scandia 108 50 20N 112 0W
Scandiano 38 44 36N 10 40 E
Scandinavia 9 64 0N 12 0 E
Scansano 39 42 40N 11 20 E
Scapa Flow 14 58 52N 3 6W
Scarborough, Trin. 121 11 11N 60 42W
Scarborough, U.K. 12 54 17N 0 24W
Scarpe → 19 50 31N 3 27 E
Śćedro 39 43 6N 16 43 E
Scenic 116 43 49N 102 32W
Schaal See 24 53 40N 10 57 E
Schaffhausen □ 25 47 42N 8 36 E
Schagen 16 52 49N 4 48 E
Schärding 26 48 27N 13 27 E
Scharhörn 24 53 58N 8 24 E
Scharnitz 26 47 23N 11 15
Scheessel 24 53 10N 9 33
Schefferville 107 54 48N 66 50W
Scheibbs 26 48 1N 15 9 E
Schelde → 16 51 15N 4 16 E
Schenectady 114 42 50N 73 58W
Scherfede 24 51 32N 9 2 E
Schesslitz 25 49 59N 11 2 E
Scheveningen 16 52 6N 4 16 E
Schiedam 16 51 55N 4 25 E
Schiermonnikoog 16 53 30N 6 15 E
Schifferstadt 25 49 22N 8 23 E
Schiltigheim 19 48 35N 7 45 E
Schio 39 45 42N 11 21
Schirmeck 19 48 29N 7 12 E
Schladming 26 47 23N 13 41 E
Schlei → 24 54 45N 9 52 E
Schleiden 24 50 32N 6 26 E
Schleiz 24 50 35N 11 49 E
Schleswig 24 54 32N 9 34 E
Schleswig-Holstein □ 24 54 10N 9 40 E
Schlüchtern 25 50 20N 9 32 E
Schmalkalden 24 50 43N 10 28 E
Schmölin 24 50 54N 12 22 E
Schmölln 24 53 15N 14 6 E
Schneeberg, Austria 26 47 47N 15 48 E
Schneeberg, Ger. 24 50 35N 12 39 E
Schofield 116 44 54N 89 39W
Schönberg, Rostock, Ger. 24 53 50N 10 55 E
Schönberg, Schleswig-Holstein, Ger. 24 54 23N 10 20 E
Schönebeck 24 52 2N 11 42 E
Schongau 25 47 49N 10 54 E
Schöningen 24 52 8N 10 57 E
Schortens 24 53 37N 7 51 E
Schouten I. 99 42 20 S 148 20 E
Schouten, Kepulauan 73 1 0 S 136 0 E
Schouwen 16 51 43N 3 45 E
Schramberg 25 48 12N 8 24 E
Schrankogl 26 47 3N 11 7 E
Schreiber 106 48 45N 87 20W
Schrobenhausen 25 48 33N 11 16 E
Schruns 26 47 5N 9 56 E
Schuler 109 50 20N 110 6W
Schumacher 106 48 30N 81 16W
Schurz 118 38 57N 118 48W
Schuyler 116 41 30N 97 3W
Schuylkill Haven 113 40 37N 76 11W
Schwabach 25 49 19N 11 3 E
Schwäbisch Gmünd 25 48 49N 9 48 E
Schwäbisch Hall 25 49 7N 9 45 E
Schwäbische Alb 25 48 30N 9 30 E
Schwabmünchen 25 48 11N 10 45 E
Schwandorf 25 49 20N 12 7 E
Schwarmstedt 24 52 41N 9 37 E
Schwarzach → 26 46 56N 12 35 E
Schwärze 24 52 50N 13 49 E
Schwarzenberg 24 50 31N 12 49 E
Schwarzwald 25 48 0N 8 0 E
Schwaz 26 47 20N 11 44 E
Schwedt 24 53 4N 14 18 E
Schweinfurt 25 50 3N 10 12 E
Schweizer Reneke 92 27 11 S 25 18 E
Schwerin 24 53 37N 11 22 E
Schwerin □ 24 53 35N 11 20 E
Schweriner See 24 53 45N 11 26 E
Schwetzingen 25 49 22N 8 35 E
Schwyz 25 47 2N 8 39 E
Schwyz □ 25 47 2N 8 39 E
Sciacca 40 37 30N 13 3 E
Scicli 41 36 48N 14 41 E
Scie, La 107 49 57N 55 36W
Scilla 41 38 18N 15 44 E
Scilly, Isles of 13 49 55N 6 15W
Ścinawa 28 51 25N 16 26 E
Scione 44 39 57N 23 36 E
Scioto → 114 38 44N 83 0W
Scobey 116 48 47N 105 30W
Scone, Austral. 99 32 5 S 150 52 E
Scone, U.K. 14 56 25N 3 26W
Scordia 41 37 19N 14 50 E
Scoresbysund 4 70 20N 23 0W
Scorno, Punta dello 40 41 7N 8 23 E
Scotia, Calif., U.S.A. 118 40 36N 124 4W
Scotia, N.Y., U.S.A. 113 42 50N 73 58W
Scotia Sea 5 56 5 S 56 0W
Scotland 116 43 10N 97 45W
Scotland □ 13 57 0N 4 0W
Scotland Neck 115 36 6N 77 32W
Scott 5 77 0 S 165 0 E
Scott, C. 5 71 30 S 168 0 E
Scott City 116 38 30N 100 52W
Scott Glacier 5 66 15 S 100 5 E
Scott I. 5 67 0 S 179 0 E
Scott Inlet 105 71 0N 71 0W
Scott Is. 108 50 48N 128 40W
Scott L. 109 59 55N 106 18W
Scott Reef 96 14 0 S 121 50 E
Scottburgh 93 30 15 S 30 47 E
Scottdale 112 40 8N 79 35W
Scottsbluff 116 41 55N 103 35W
Scottsboro 115 34 40N 86 0W
Scottsburg 114 38 40N 85 46W
Scottsdale 97 41 9 S 147 31 E
Scottsville, Ky., U.S.A. 115 36 48N 86 10W
Scottsville, N.Y., U.S.A. 112 43 2N 77 47W
Scottville, Austral. 98 20 33 S 147 49 E
Scottville, U.S.A. 114 43 57N 86 18W
Scranton 114 41 22N 75 41W
Scugog, L. 112 44 10N 78 55W
Scunthorpe 12 53 35N 0 38W

* *Now part of Punjab* □

Name	Page	Lat.	Long.
Scusciuban	**63**	10 18N	50 12 E
Sea Breeze	**112**	43 12N	77 32W
Seaford, Austral.	**100**	38 10 S	145 11 E
Seaford, U.S.A.	**114**	38 37N	75 36W
Seaforth	**106**	43 35N	81 25W
Seagraves	**117**	32 56N	102 30W
Seal →	**109**	58 50N	97 30W
Seal Cove	**107**	49 57N	56 22W
Seal L.	**107**	54 20N	61 30W
Sealy	**117**	29 46N	96 9W
Searchlight	**119**	35 31N	114 55W
Searcy	**117**	35 15N	91 45W
Searles L.	**119**	35 47N	117 17W
Seaside	**118**	45 59N	123 55W
Seaspray	**99**	38 25 S	147 15 E
Seattle	**118**	47 41N	122 15W
Seaview Ra.	**97**	18 40 S	145 45 E
Sebastián Vizcaíno, Bahía	**120**	28 0N	114 30W
Sebastopol	**118**	38 24N	122 49W
Sebastopol = Sevastopol	**56**	44 35N	33 30 E
Sebderat	**87**	15 26N	36 42 E
Sebdou	**82**	34 38N	1 19W
Sebeş	**46**	45 58N	23 34 E
Sebeşului, Munţii	**46**	45 36N	23 40 E
Sebewaing	**114**	43 45N	83 27W
Sebezh	**54**	56 14N	28 22 E
Sébi	**84**	15 50N	4 12W
Sebinkarahisar	**56**	40 22N	38 28 E
Sebiş	**46**	46 23N	22 13 E
Sebkhet Te-n-Dghâmcha	**84**	18 30N	15 55W
Sebkra Azzel Mati	**82**	26 10N	0 43 E
Sebkra Mekerghene	**82**	26 21N	1 30 E
Sebnitz	**24**	50 58N	14 17 E
Sebou, Oued →	**82**	34 16N	6 40W
Sebring, Fla., U.S.A.	**115**	27 30N	81 26W
Sebring, Ohio, U.S.A.	**112**	40 55N	81 2W
Sebringville	**112**	43 24N	81 4W
Sebta = Ceuta	**82**	35 52N	5 19W
Sebuku	**72**	3 30 S	116 25 E
Sebuku, Teluk	**72**	4 0N	118 10 E
Sečanj	**42**	45 25N	20 47 E
Secchia →	**38**	44 4N	11 0 E
Sechelt	**108**	49 25N	123 42W
Sechura, Desierto de	**126**	6 0 S	80 30W
Seclin	**19**	50 33N	3 2 E
Secondigny	**18**	46 37N	0 26W
Sečovce	**27**	48 42N	21 40 E
Secretary I.	**101**	45 15 S	166 56 E
Secunderabad	**70**	17 28N	78 30 E
Sedalia	**116**	38 40N	93 18W
Sedan, Austral.	**99**	34 34 S	139 19 E
Sedan, France	**19**	49 43N	4 57 E
Sedan, U.S.A.	**117**	37 10N	96 11W
Sedano	**32**	42 43N	3 49W
Seddon	**101**	41 40 S	174 7 E
Seddonville	**101**	41 33 S	172 1 E
Sede Ya'aqov	**62**	32 43N	35 7 E
Sedgewick	**108**	52 48N	111 41W
Sedhiou	**84**	12 44N	15 30W
Sedičany	**26**	49 40N	14 25 E
Sedico	**39**	46 8N	12 6 E
Sedienie	**43**	42 16N	24 33 E
Sedley	**109**	50 10N	104 0W
Sedom	**62**	31 5N	35 20 E
Sedova, Pik	**58**	73 29N	54 58 E
Sedrata	**83**	36 7N	7 31 E
Sedro Woolley	**118**	48 30N	122 15W
Seduva	**54**	55 45N	23 45 E
Sedziszów Małapolski	**27**	50 5N	21 45 E
Seebad Ahlbeck	**24**	53 56N	14 10 E
Seefeld	**26**	47 19N	11 13 E
Seehausen	**24**	52 52N	11 43 E
Seeheim	**92**	26 50 S	17 45 E
Seekoe →	**92**	30 18 S	25 1 E
Seelaw	**24**	52 32N	14 22 E
Se'elim, Nahal	**62**	31 21N	35 24 E
Sées	**18**	48 38N	0 10 E
Seesen	**24**	51 53N	10 10 E
Sefadu	**84**	8 35N	10 58W
Séfeto	**84**	14 8N	9 49W
Sefrou	**82**	33 52N	4 52W
Sefwi Bekwai	**84**	6 10N	2 25W
Seg-ozero	**54**	63 0N	33 10 E
Segamat	**71**	2 30N	102 50 E
Segarcea	**46**	44 6N	23 43 E
Segbwema	**84**	8 0N	11 0W
Seget	**73**	1 24 S	130 58 E
Segezha	**52**	63 44N	34 19 E
Seggueur, O. →	**82**	32 4N	2 4 E
Segid	**87**	16 55N	42 0 E
Segonzac	**20**	45 36N	0 14W
Segorbe	**32**	39 50N	0 30W
Ségou	**84**	13 30N	6 16W
Segovia	**30**	40 57N	4 10W
Segovia = Coco →	**121**	15 0N	83 8W
Segovia □	**30**	40 55N	4 10W
Segré	**18**	47 40N	0 52W
Segre →	**32**	41 40N	0 43 E
Séguéla	**84**	7 55N	6 40W
Seguin	**117**	29 34N	97 58W
Segundo	**117**	37 12N	104 50W
Segundo →	**124**	30 53 S	62 44W
Segura →	**33**	38 6N	0 54W
Segura, Sierra de	**33**	38 5N	2 45W
Sehore	**68**	23 10N	77 5 E
Sehwan	**68**	26 28N	67 53 E
Seica Mare	**46**	46 1N	24 7 E
Seiland	**50**	70 25N	23 15 E
Seiling	**117**	36 10N	98 56W
Seille →, Moselle, France	**19**	49 7N	6 11 E
Seille →, Saône-et-Loire, France	**21**	46 31N	4 57 E
Sein, Î. de	**18**	48 2N	4 52W
Seinäjoki →	**50**	62 40N	22 45 E
Seine →	**18**	49 26N	0 26 E
Seine, B. de la	**18**	49 40N	0 40W
Seine-et-Marne □	**19**	48 45N	3 0 E
Seine-Maritime □	**18**	49 40N	1 0 E
Seine-Saint-Denis □	**19**	48 58N	2 24 E
Seini	**46**	47 44N	23 21 E
Seistan	**65**	30 50N	61 0 E
Seistan-Balūchestān □	**65**	27 0N	62 0 E
Sejerø	**49**	55 54N	11 9 E
Sejerø Bugt	**49**	55 53N	11 15 E
Sejny	**28**	54 6N	23 21 E
Seka	**87**	8 10N	36 52 E
Sekayu	**72**	2 51 S	103 51 E
Seke	**90**	3 20 S	33 31 E
Sekenke	**90**	4 18 S	34 11 E
Sekiu	**118**	48 16N	124 18W
Sekken Veøy	**47**	62 45N	7 30 E
Sekondi-Takoradi	**84**	4 58N	1 45W
Sekuma	**92**	24 36 S	23 50 E
Selah	**118**	46 44N	120 30W
Selama	**71**	5 12N	100 42 E
Selangor □	**71**	3 20N	101 30 E
Selárgius	**40**	39 14N	9 14 E
Selaru	**73**	8 9 S	131 0 E
Selb	**25**	50 9N	12 9 E
Selby, U.K.	**12**	53 47N	1 5W
Selby, U.S.A.	**116**	45 34N	100 2W
Selca	**39**	43 20N	16 50 E
Selden	**116**	39 33N	100 39W
Seldovia	**104**	59 30N	151 45W
Sele →	**41**	40 27N	14 58 E
Selemdzha →	**59**	51 42N	128 53 E
Selenge →	**75**	49 25N	103 59 E
Selenica	**44**	40 33N	19 39 E
Selenter See	**24**	54 19N	10 26 E
Sélestat	**19**	48 16N	7 26 E
Seletan, Tg.	**72**	4 10 S	114 40 E
Seletin	**46**	47 50N	25 12 E
Selevac	**42**	44 28N	20 52 E
Selfridge	**116**	46 3N	100 57W
Sélibabi	**84**	15 10N	12 15W
Seliger, Oz.	**54**	57 15N	33 0 E
Seligman	**119**	35 17N	112 56W
Şelim	**57**	40 30N	42 46 E
Selîma, El Wâhât el	**86**	21 22N	29 19 E
Selinda Spillway	**92**	18 35 S	23 10 E
Selinoús	**45**	37 35N	21 37 E
Selizharovo	**54**	56 51N	33 27 E
Selje	**47**	62 3N	5 22 E
Seljord	**47**	59 30N	8 40 E
Selkirk, Can.	**109**	50 10N	96 55W
Selkirk, U.K.	**14**	55 33N	2 50W
Selkirk I.	**109**	53 20N	99 6W
Selkirk Mts.	**108**	51 15N	117 40W
Selles-sur-Cher	**19**	47 16N	1 33 E
Sellières	**19**	46 50N	5 32 E
Sells	**119**	31 57N	111 57W
Sellye	**27**	45 52N	17 51 E
Selma, Ala., U.S.A.	**115**	32 30N	87 0W
Selma, Calif., U.S.A.	**119**	36 39N	119 39W
Selma, N.C., U.S.A.	**115**	35 32N	78 15W
Selmer	**115**	35 9N	88 36W
Selo	**44**	41 10N	25 53 E
Selongey	**19**	47 36N	5 10 E
Selowandoma Falls	**91**	21 15 S	31 50 E
Selpele	**73**	0 1 S	130 5 E
Selsey Bill	**13**	50 44N	0 47W
Seltz	**19**	48 48N	8 4 E
Selu	**73**	7 32 S	130 55 E
Selukwe	**91**	19 40 S	30 0 E
Sélune →	**18**	48 38N	1 22W
Selva, Argent.	**124**	29 50 S	62 0W
Selva, Italy	**39**	46 33N	11 46 E
Selva, Spain	**32**	41 13N	1 8 E
Selva, La	**32**	42 0N	2 45 E
Selvas	**126**	6 30 S	67 0W
Selwyn L.	**109**	60 0N	104 30W
Selwyn P.O.	**97**	21 32 S	140 30 E
Selwyn Ra.	**97**	21 10 S	140 0 E
Seman →	**44**	40 45N	19 50 E
Semara	**82**	26 48N	11 41W
Semarang	**73**	7 0 S	110 26 E
Semau	**73**	10 13 S	123 22 E
Sembabule	**90**	0 4 S	31 25 E
Sémé	**84**	15 4N	13 41W
Semeih	**87**	12 43N	30 53 E
Semenov	**55**	56 43N	44 30 E
Semenovka, Ukraine S.S.R., U.S.S.R.	**54**	52 8N	32 36 E
Semenovka, Ukraine S.S.R., U.S.S.R.	**56**	49 37N	33 10 E
Semeru	**73**	8 4 S	112 55 E
Semiluki	**55**	51 41N	39 2 E
Seminoe Res.	**118**	42 0N	107 0W
Seminole, Okla., U.S.A.	**117**	35 15N	96 45W
Seminole, Tex., U.S.A.	**117**	32 41N	102 38W
Semiozernoye	**58**	52 22N	64 8 E
Semipalatinsk	**58**	50 30N	80 10 E
Semirara Is.	**73**	12 0N	121 20 E
Semisopochnoi	**104**	52 0N	179 40W
Semitau	**72**	0 29N	111 57 E
Semiyarskoye	**58**	50 55N	78 23 E
Semmering Pass	**26**	47 41N	15 45 E
Semnān	**65**	35 55N	53 25 E
Semnān □	**65**	36 0N	54 0 E
Semois →	**16**	49 53N	4 44 E
Semporna	**73**	4 30N	118 33 E
Semuda	**72**	2 51 S	112 58 E
Semur-en-Auxois	**19**	47 30N	4 20 E
Sen →	**71**	13 45N	105 12 E
Sena	**91**	17 25 S	35 0 E
Sena Madureira	**126**	9 5 S	68 45W
Senador Pompeu	**127**	5 40 S	39 20W
Senai	**71**	1 38N	103 38 E
Senaja	**72**	6 45N	117 3 E
Senanga	**92**	16 2 S	23 14 E
Senatobia	**117**	34 38N	89 57W
Sendafa	**87**	9 11N	39 3 E
Sendai, Kagoshima, Japan	**74**	31 50N	130 20 E
Sendai, Miyagi, Japan	**74**	38 15N	140 53 E
Sendamangalam	**70**	11 17N	78 17 E
Sendeling's Drift	**92**	28 12 S	16 52 E
Sendenhorst	**24**	51 50N	7 49 E
Sendurjana	**68**	21 32N	78 17 E
Senec	**27**	48 12N	17 23 E
Seneca, Oreg., U.S.A.	**118**	44 10N	119 2W
Seneca, S.C., U.S.A.	**115**	34 43N	82 59W
Seneca Falls	**114**	42 55N	76 50W
Seneca L.	**114**	42 40N	76 58W
Senegal ■	**84**	14 30N	14 30W
Senegal →	**84**	15 48N	16 32W
Senekal	**93**	28 30 S	27 36 E
Senftenberg	**24**	51 30N	14 1 E
Senga Hill	**91**	9 19 S	31 11 E
Senge Khambab (Indus) →	**68**	28 40N	70 10 E
Sengerema □	**90**	2 10 S	32 20 E
Sengiley	**55**	53 58N	48 46 E
Sengkang	**73**	4 8 S	120 1 E
Sengua →	**91**	17 7 S	28 5 E
Senhor-do-Bonfim	**127**	10 30 S	40 10W
Senica	**27**	48 41N	17 25 E
Senigállia	**39**	43 42N	13 12 E
Senio →	**39**	44 35N	12 15 E
Senise	**40**	40 6N	16 15 E
Senj	**39**	45 0N	14 58 E
Senja	**50**	69 25N	17 30 E
Senlis	**19**	49 13N	2 35 E
Senmonorom	**71**	12 27N	107 12 E
Sennâr	**87**	13 30N	33 35 E
Senneterre	**106**	48 25N	77 15W
Senniquelle	**84**	7 19N	8 38W
Senno	**54**	54 45N	29 43 E
Sennori	**40**	40 49N	8 36 E
Senonches	**18**	48 34N	1 2 E
Senorbì	**40**	39 33N	9 8 E
Senožeče	**39**	45 43N	14 3 E
Sens	**19**	48 11N	3 15 E
Senta	**42**	45 55N	20 3 E
Sentein	**20**	42 53N	0 58 E
Sentery	**90**	5 17 S	25 42 E
Sentinel	**119**	32 45N	113 13W
Sentolo	**73**	7 55 S	110 13 E
Senya Beraku	**85**	5 28N	0 31W
Seo de Urgel	**32**	42 22N	1 23 E
Seohara	**68**	29 15N	78 33 E
Seoni	**69**	22 5N	79 30 E
Seoriuarayan	**69**	21 45N	82 34 E
Seoul = Sŏul	**76**	37 31N	127 6 E
Separation Point	**107**	53 37N	57 25W
Sepik →	**98**	3 49 S	144 30 E
Sępólno Krajeńskie	**28**	53 26N	17 30 E
Sepone	**71**	16 45N	106 13 E
Sepopa	**92**	18 49 S	22 12 E
Sepopol	**28**	54 16N	21 2 E
Sept-Îles	**107**	50 13N	66 22W
Septemvri	**43**	42 13N	24 6 E
Septimus	**98**	21 13 S	148 47 E
Sepúlveda	**30**	41 18N	3 45W
Sequeros	**30**	40 31N	6 2W
Sequim	**118**	48 3N	123 9W
Sequoia Nat. Park	**119**	36 30N	118 30W
Serafimovich	**57**	49 36N	42 43 E
Seraing	**16**	50 35N	5 32 E
Seram	**73**	3 10 S	129 0 E
Seram Sea	**73**	2 30 S	128 30 E
Serampore	**69**	22 44N	88 21 E
Serang	**73**	6 8 S	106 10 E
Serasan	**72**	2 29N	109 4 E
Seravezza	**38**	43 59N	10 13 E
Serbia = Srbija	**42**	43 30N	21 0 E
Sercaia	**46**	45 49N	25 9 E
Serdo	**87**	11 56N	41 14 E
Serdobsk	**55**	52 28N	44 10 E
Seredka	**54**	58 12N	28 10 E
Seregno	**38**	45 40N	9 12 E
Seremban	**71**	2 43N	101 53 E
Serena, La, Chile	**124**	29 55 S	71 10W
Serena, La, Spain	**31**	38 45N	5 40W
Serengeti □	**90**	2 0 S	34 30 E
Serengeti Plain	**90**	2 40 S	35 0 E
Sereth = Siret →	**46**	47 58N	26 5 E
Sergach	**55**	55 30N	45 30 E
Serge →	**32**	41 54N	0 50 E
Sergino	**58**	62 30N	65 38 E
Sergipe □	**127**	10 30 S	37 30W
Seria	**72**	4 37N	114 23 E
Serian	**72**	1 10N	110 31 E
Seriate	**38**	45 42N	9 43 E
Seribu, Kepulauan	**72**	5 36 S	106 33 E
Sérifontaine	**19**	49 20N	1 45 E
Sérifos	**45**	37 9N	24 30 E
Sérignan	**20**	43 17N	3 17 E
Sermaize-les-Bains	**19**	48 47N	4 54 E
Sermata	**73**	8 15 S	128 50 E
Sérmide	**39**	45 0N	11 17 E
Sernovodsk	**55**	53 54N	51 16 E
Serny Zavod	**58**	39 59N	58 50 E
Serock	**28**	52 31N	21 4 E
Serón	**33**	37 20N	2 29W
Serós	**32**	41 27N	0 24 E
Serov	**58**	59 29N	60 35 E
Serowe	**92**	22 25 S	26 43 E
Serpa	**31**	37 57N	7 38 E
Serpeddi, Punta	**40**	39 19N	9 18 E
Serpentara	**40**	39 8N	9 38 E
Serpis →	**33**	38 59N	0 9W
Serpukhov	**55**	54 55N	37 28 E
Serra San Bruno	**41**	38 31N	16 23 E
Serracapriola	**41**	41 47N	15 12 E
Serradilla	**30**	39 50N	6 9W
Sérrai	**44**	41 5N	23 31 E
Sérrai □	**44**	41 5N	23 37 E
Serramanna	**40**	39 26N	8 56 E
Serrat, C.	**83**	37 14N	9 10 E
Serre-Poncon, Barrage de	**21**	44 22N	6 20 E
Serres	**21**	44 26N	5 43 E
Serrezuela	**124**	30 40 S	65 20W
Serrinha	**127**	11 39 S	39 0W
Sersale	**41**	39 1N	16 44 E
Sertã	**30**	39 48N	8 6W
Sertânia	**127**	8 5 S	37 20W
Sertanópolis	**125**	23 4 S	51 2W
Serua	**73**	6 18 S	130 1 E
Serui	**73**	1 53 S	136 10 E
Serule	**92**	21 57 S	27 20 E
Sérvia	**44**	40 9N	21 58 E
Sese Is.	**90**	0 20 S	32 20 E
Sesepe	**73**	1 30 S	127 59 E
Sesfontein	**92**	19 7 S	13 39 E
Sesheke	**92**	17 29 S	24 13 E
Sesia →	**38**	45 5N	8 37 E
Sesimbra	**31**	38 28N	9 6W
Sessa Aurunca	**40**	41 14N	13 55 E
Sestao	**32**	43 18N	3 0W
Sesto S. Giovanni	**38**	45 32N	9 14 E
Sestos	**44**	40 16N	26 23 E
Sestri Levante	**38**	44 17N	9 22 E
Sestrières	**38**	44 58N	6 56 E
Sestrunj	**39**	44 10N	15 0 E
Sestu	**40**	39 18N	9 6 E
Sète	**20**	43 25N	3 42 E
Sete Lagôas	**127**	19 27 S	44 16W
Sétif	**83**	36 9N	5 26 E
Setonaikai	**74**	34 20N	133 30 E
Settat	**82**	33 0N	7 40W
Setté-Cama	**88**	2 32 S	9 45 E
Séttimo Tor	**38**	45 9N	7 46 E
Setting L.	**109**	55 0N	98 38W
Settle	**12**	54 5N	2 18W
Settlement Pt.	**115**	26 40N	79 0W
Setto Calende	**38**	45 44N	8 37 E
Setúbal	**31**	38 30N	8 58W
Setúbal □	**31**	38 25N	8 35W
Setúbal, B. de	**31**	38 40N	8 56W
Seugne →	**20**	45 42N	0 32W
Seul, Lac-Rés.	**106**	50 25N	92 30W
Seulimeum	**72**	5 27N	95 15 E
Sevan	**57**	40 33N	44 56 E
Sevan, Ozero	**57**	40 30N	45 20 E
Sevastopol	**56**	44 35N	33 30 E
Seven Sisters	**108**	54 56N	128 10W
Sever →	**31**	39 40N	7 32W
Sévérac-le-Château	**20**	44 20N	3 5 E
Severn →, Can.	**106**	56 2N	87 36W
Severn →, U.K.	**13**	51 35N	2 38W
Severn L.	**106**	53 54N	90 48W
Severnaya Zemlya	**59**	79 0N	100 0 E
Severnyye Uvaly	**52**	58 0N	48 0 E
Severo-Kurilsk	**59**	50 40N	156 8 E
Severo-Yeniseyskiy	**59**	60 22N	93 1 E
Severočeský □	**26**	50 30N	14 0 E
Severodinsk	**52**	64 27N	39 58 E
Severodonetsk	**57**	48 58N	38 30 E
Severomoravský □	**27**	49 38N	17 40 E
Severomorsk	**52**	69 5N	33 27 E
Severouralsk	**52**	60 9N	59 57 E
Sevier	**119**	38 39N	112 11W
Sevier →	**119**	39 10N	113 6W
Sevier L.	**118**	39 0N	113 20W
Sevilla	**31**	37 23N	6 0W
Sevilla □	**31**	37 25N	5 30W
Seville = Sevilla	**31**	37 23N	6 0W
Sevlievo	**43**	43 2N	25 3 E
Sevnica	**39**	46 2N	15 19 E
Sèvre-Nantaise →	**18**	47 12N	1 33W
Sèvre Niortaise →	**20**	46 18N	1 8W
Sevsk	**54**	52 10N	34 30 E
Seward, Alaska, U.S.A.	**104**	60 6N	149 26W
Seward, Nebr., U.S.A.	**116**	40 55N	97 6W
Seward Pen.	**104**	65 0N	164 0W
Sewell	**124**	34 10 S	70 23W
Sewer	**73**	5 53 S	134 40 E
Sewickley	**112**	40 33N	80 12W
Sexsmith	**108**	55 21N	118 47W
Seychelles ■	**3**	5 0 S	56 0 E
Seyðisfjörður	**50**	65 16N	14 0W
Seym →	**54**	51 27N	32 34 E
Seymchan	**59**	62 54N	152 30 E
Seymour, Austral.	**99**	37 0 S	145 10 E
Seymour, Conn., U.S.A.	**113**	41 23N	73 5W
Seymour, Ind., U.S.A.	**114**	39 0N	85 50W
Seymour, Tex., U.S.A.	**117**	33 35N	99 18W
Seymour, Wis., U.S.A.	**114**	44 30N	88 20W
Seyne	**21**	44 21N	6 22 E
Seyne-sur-Mer, La	**21**	43 7N	5 52 E
Seyssel	**21**	45 57N	5 50 E
Sežana	**39**	45 43N	13 41 E
Sézanne	**19**	48 40N	3 40 E
Sezze	**40**	41 30N	13 3 E
Sfax	**83**	34 49N	10 48 E
Sfintu Gheorghe	**46**	45 52N	25 48 E
Sha Xian	**77**	26 23N	117 45 E
Shaanxi □	**77**	35 0N	109 0 E
Shaba	**90**	8 0 S	25 0 E
† Shabani	**91**	20 17 S	30 2 E
Shabla	**43**	43 31N	28 32 E
Shabunda	**90**	2 40 S	27 16 E
Shache	**75**	38 20N	77 10 E
Shackleton	**5**	78 30 S	36 1W
Shackleton Ice Shelf	**5**	66 0 S	100 0 E
Shackleton Inlet	**5**	83 0 S	160 0 E
Shaddad	**86**	21 25N	40 2 E
Shadrinsk	**58**	56 5N	63 32 E
Shaffa	**85**	10 30N	12 6 E
Shafter, Calif., U.S.A.	**119**	35 32N	119 14W
Shafter, Tex., U.S.A.	**117**	29 49N	104 18W
Shaftesbury	**13**	51 0N	2 12W
Shagamu	**85**	6 51N	3 39 E
Shah Bunder	**68**	24 13N	67 56 E
* Shah Faisalabad	**68**	31 30N	73 5 E
Shahabad, Andhra Pradesh, India	**70**	17 10N	76 54 E
Shahabad, Punjab, India	**68**	30 10N	76 55 E
Shahabad, Raj., India	**68**	25 15N	77 11 E
Shahabad, Ut. P., India	**69**	27 36N	79 56 E
Shāhābād, Kermānshāhān, Iran	**64**	34 10N	46 30 E
Shāhābād, Khorāsān, Iran	**65**	37 40N	56 50 E
Shahada	**68**	21 33N	74 30 E
Shahadpur	**68**	25 55N	68 35 E
Shahapur	**70**	15 50N	74 34 E
Shahdād	**65**	30 30N	57 40 E
Shahdadkot	**68**	27 50N	67 55 E
Shahganj	**69**	26 3N	82 44 E
Shaḫḫāt	**81**	32 48N	21 54 E
Shāhī	**65**	36 30N	52 55 E
Shahjahanpur	**69**	27 54N	79 57 E
Shahpur, Mad. P., India	**68**	22 12N	77 58 E
Shahpur, Mysore, India	**70**	16 40N	76 48 E
Shahpūr	**64**	38 12N	44 45 E
Shahpur	**68**	28 46N	68 27 E
Shahpura	**69**	23 10N	80 45 E
Shahr Kord	**65**	32 15N	50 55 E
Shahrezā	**65**	32 0N	51 55 E
Shahrig	**68**	30 15N	67 40 E
Shāhrūd	**65**	36 30N	55 0 E

* *Renamed Faisalabad*

† *Renamed Zvishavane*

Shahsād, Namakzār-e 65 30 20N 58 20 E
Shahsavār 65 36 45N 51 12 E
Shaibara 86 25 26N 36 47 E
Shaikhabad 66 34 2N 68 45 E
Shajapur 68 23 27N 76 21 E
Shakargarh 68 32 17N 75 10 E
Shakawe 92 18 28 S 21 49 E
Shaker Heights 112 41 29N 81 36W
Shakhty 57 47 40N 40 16 E
Shakhunya 55 57 40N 46 46 E
Shaki 85 8 41N 3 21 E
Shakopee 116 44 45N 93 30W
Shala, L. 87 7 30N 38 30 E
Shallow Lake 112 44 36N 81 5W
Sham, J. ash 65 23 10N 57 5 E
Shamâl Dârfûr □ 87 15 0N 25 0 E
Shamâl Kordofân □ 87 15 0N 30 0 E
Shamattawa 109 55 51N 92 5W
Shamattawa → 106 55 1N 85 23W
Shambe 87 7 8N 30 46 E
Shambu 87 9 32N 37 3 E
Shamgong Dzong 69 27 13N 90 35 E
Shamīl 65 27 30N 56 55 E
Shamkhor 57 40 50N 46 0 E
Shamli 68 29 32N 77 18 E
Shammar, Jabal 64 27 40N 41 0 E
Shamo, L. 87 5 45N 37 30 E
Shamokin 114 40 47N 76 33W
Shamrock 117 35 15N 100 15W
Shan □ 67 21 30N 98 30 E
Shanan → 87 8 0N 40 20 E
Shanchengzhen 76 42 20N 125 20 E
Shandong □ 76 36 0N 118 0 E
Shang Xian 77 33 50N 109 58 E
Shangalowe 91 10 50 S 26 30 E
Shangani 91 19 41 S 29 20 E
Shangani → 91 18 41 S 27 10 E
Shangbancheng 76 40 50N 118 1 E
Shangcheng 77 31 47N 115 26 E
Shangchuan Dao 77 21 40N 112 50 E
Shangdu 76 41 30N 113 30 E
Shanggao 77 28 17N 114 55 E
Shanghai 75 31 15N 121 26 E
Shangqiu 77 34 26N 115 36 E
Shangrao 75 28 25N 117 59 E
Shangshui 77 33 42N 114 35 E
Shangsi 77 22 8N 107 58 E
Shangyou 77 25 48N 114 32 E
Shangzhi 76 45 22N 127 56 E
Shani 85 10 14N 12 2 E
Shaniko 118 45 0N 120 50W
Shannon, Greenl. 4 75 10N 18 30W
Shannon, N.Z. 101 40 33 S 175 25 E
Shannon → 15 52 35N 9 30W
Shansi = Shanxi □ 76 37 0N 112 0 E
Shantar, Ostrov Bolshoy 59 55 9N 137 40 E
Shantou 75 23 18N 116 40 E
Shantung = Shandong □ 76 36 0N 118 0 E
Shanxi □ 76 37 0N 112 0 E
Shanyang 77 33 31N 109 55 E
Shaoguan 75 24 48N 113 35 E
Shaowu 75 27 22N 117 28 E
Shaoxing 75 30 0N 120 35 E
Shaoyang 75 27 14N 111 25 E
Shapinsay 14 59 2N 2 50W
Shaqrā', Si. Arab. 64 25 15N 45 16 E
Shaqrā', Yemen, S. 63 13 22N 45 44 E
Sharafa (Ogr) 87 11 59N 27 7 E
Sharavati → 70 14 20N 74 25 E
Sharbot Lake 113 44 46N 76 41W
Shark B. 96 25 55 S 113 32 E
Sharm el Sheikh 86 27 53N 34 15 E
Sharon, Mass., U.S.A. 113 42 5N 71 11W
Sharon, Pa., U.S.A. 114 41 18N 80 30W
Sharon, Plain of = Hasharon 62 32 12N 34 49 E
Sharon Springs 116 38 54N 101 45W
Sharp Pt. 98 10 58 S 142 43 E
Sharpe L. 109 54 5N 93 40W
Sharpsville 112 41 16N 80 28W
Shary 64 27 14N 43 29 E
Sharya 55 58 22N 45 20 E
Shasha 87 6 29N 35 59 E
Shashemene 87 7 13N 38 33 E
Shashi 75 30 25N 112 14 E
Shashi → 91 21 14 S 29 20 E
Shasta, Mt. 118 41 30N 122 12W
Shasta Res. 118 40 50N 122 15W
Shatsk 55 54 0N 41 45 E
Shattuck 117 36 17N 99 55W
Shatura 55 55 34N 39 31 E
Shaumyani 57 41 22N 41 45 E
Shaunavon 109 49 35N 108 25W
Shaw → 96 20 21 S 119 17 E
Shaw I. 98 20 30 S 149 2 E
Shawan 75 44 34N 85 50 E
Shawanaga 112 45 31N 80 17W
Shawano 114 44 45N 88 38W
Shawinigan 106 46 35N 72 50W
Shawnee 117 35 15N 97 0W
Shayib el Banat, Bebel 86 26 59N 33 29 E
Shchekino 55 54 1N 37 34 E
Shcherbakov = Rybinsk 55 58 5N 38 50 E
Shchigri 55 51 55N 36 58 E
Shchors 54 51 48N 31 56 E
Shchuchiosk 58 52 56N 70 12 E
She Xian 77 29 50N 118 25 E
Shebekino 55 50 28N 36 54 E
Shebele, Wabi → 87 2 0N 44 0 E
Sheboygan 114 43 46N 87 45W
Shechem 62 32 13N 35 21 E
Shediac 107 46 14N 64 32W
Sheelin, Lough 15 53 48N 7 20W
Sheep Haven 15 55 12N 7 55W
Sheerness 13 51 26N 0 47 E
Sheet Harbour 107 44 56N 62 31W
Shefar'am 62 32 48N 35 10 E
Sheffield, U.K. 12 53 23N 1 28W
Sheffield, Ala., U.S.A. 115 34 45N 87 42W
Sheffield, Mass., U.S.A. 113 42 6N 73 23W
Sheffield, Pa., U.S.A. 112 41 42N 79 3W
Sheffield, Tex., U.S.A. 117 30 42N 101 49W
Shegaon 68 20 48N 76 47 E
Sheho 109 51 35N 103 13W
Shehojele 87 10 40N 35 9 E
Sheikhpura 69 25 9N 85 53 E
Shek Hasan 87 12 5N 35 58 E
Shekhupura 68 31 42N 73 58 E
Sheki 57 41 10N 47 5 E
Sheksna → 55 59 0N 38 30 E
Shelburne, N.S., Can. 107 43 47N 65 20W
Shelburne, Ont., Can. 106 44 4N 80 15W
Shelburne, U.S.A. 113 44 23N 73 15W
Shelburne B. 97 11 50 S 142 50 E
Shelburne Falls 113 42 36N 72 45W
Shelby, Mich., U.S.A. 114 43 34N 86 27W
Shelby, Mont., U.S.A. 118 48 30N 111 52W
Shelby, N.C., U.S.A. 115 35 18N 81 34W
Shelby, Ohio, U.S.A. 112 40 52N 82 40W
Shelbyville, Ill., U.S.A. 116 39 25N 88 45W
Shelbyville, Ind., U.S.A. 114 39 30N 85 42W
Shelbyville, Tenn., U.S.A. 115 35 30N 86 25W
Sheldon 116 43 6N 95 40W
Sheldrake 107 50 20N 64 51W
Shelikhova, Zaliv 59 59 30N 157 0 E
Shell Creek Ra. 118 39 15N 114 30W
Shell Lake 109 53 19N 107 2W
Shellbrook 109 53 13N 106 24W
Shellharbour 97 34 31 S 150 51 E
Shelling Rocks 15 51 45N 10 35W
Shelon → 54 58 10N 30 30 E
Shelton, Conn., U.S.A. 113 41 18N 73 7W
Shelton, Wash., U.S.A. 118 47 15N 123 6W
Shemakha 57 40 38N 48 37 E
Shenandoah, Iowa, U.S.A. 116 40 50N 95 25W
Shenandoah, Pa., U.S.A. 114 40 49N 76 13W
Shenandoah, Va., U.S.A. 114 38 30N 78 38W
Shenandoah → 114 39 19N 77 44W
Shenchi 76 39 8N 112 10 E
Shencottah 70 8 59N 77 18 E
Shendam 85 8 49N 9 30 E
Shendî 87 16 46N 33 22 E
Shendurni 70 20 39N 75 36 E
Sheng Xian 77 29 35N 120 50 E
Shëngjergji 44 41 17N 20 10 E
Shëngjini 44 41 50N 19 35 E
Shenmëria 44 42 7N 20 13 E
Shenmu 76 38 50N 110 29 E
Shenqiucheng 77 33 24N 115 2 E
Shensi = Shaanxi □ 77 35 0N 109 0 E
Shenyang 76 41 48N 123 27 E
Shepetovka 54 50 10N 27 10 E
Shephelah = Hashefela 62 31 30N 34 43 E
Shepparton 97 36 23 S 145 26 E
Sheqi 77 33 12N 112 57 E
Sherada 87 7 18N 36 30 E
Sherborne 13 50 56N 2 31W
Sherbro I. 84 7 30N 12 40W
Sherbrooke 107 45 28N 71 57W
Sherda 83 20 7N 16 46 E
Shereik 86 18 44N 33 47 E
Sheridan, Ark., U.S.A. 117 34 20N 92 25W
Sheridan, Col., U.S.A. 116 39 44N 105 3W
Sheridan, Wyo., U.S.A. 118 44 50N 107 0W
Sherkot 68 29 22N 78 35 E
Sherman 117 33 40N 96 35W
Sherpur 69 25 0N 90 0 E
Sherridon 109 55 8N 101 5W
Sherwood, N.D., U.S.A. 116 48 59N 101 36W
Sherwood, Tex., U.S.A. 117 31 18N 100 45W
Sherwood Forest 12 53 5N 1 5W
Sheslay 108 58 17N 131 52W
Sheslay → 108 58 48N 132 5W
Shethanei L. 109 58 48N 97 50W
Shetland □ 14 60 30N 1 30W
Shetland Is. 14 60 30N 1 30W
Shevaroy Hills 70 11 58N 78 12 E
Shewa □ 87 9 33N 38 10 E
Shewa Gimira 87 7 4N 35 51 E
Sheyenne 116 47 52N 99 8W
Sheyenne → 116 47 5N 96 50W
Shibâm 63 16 0N 48 36 E
Shibîn El Kôm 86 30 31N 30 55 E
Shibîn el Qanâtir 86 30 19N 31 19 E
Shibogama L. 106 53 35N 88 15W
Shibushi 74 31 25N 131 8 E
Shidao 76 36 50N 122 25 E
Shiel, L. 14 56 48N 5 32W
Shiga □ 74 35 20N 136 0 E
Shigaib 81 15 5N 23 35 E
Shiguaigou 76 40 52N 110 15 E
Shihchiachuangi = Shijiazhuang 76 38 2N 114 28 E
Shijaku 44 41 21N 19 33 E
Shijiazhuang 76 38 2N 114 28 E
Shikarpur, India 68 28 17N 78 7 E
Shikarpur, Pak. 68 27 57N 68 39 E
Shikoku 74 33 30N 133 30 E
Shikoku □ 74 33 30N 133 30 E
Shikoku-Sanchi 74 33 30N 133 30 E
Shilabo 63 6 22N 44 32 E
Shilka 59 52 0N 115 55 E
Shilka → 59 53 20N 121 26 E
Shillelagh 15 52 46N 6 32W
Shillong 67 25 35N 91 53 E
Shilo 62 32 4N 35 18 E
Shilong 75 23 5N 113 52 E
Shilovo 55 54 25N 40 57 E
Shimabara 74 32 48N 130 20 E
Shimada 74 34 49N 138 10 E
Shimane □ 74 35 0N 132 30 E
Shimanovsk 59 52 15N 127 30 E
Shimizu 74 35 0N 138 30 E
Shimodate 74 36 20N 139 55 E
Shimoga 70 13 57N 75 32 E
Shimoni 90 4 38 S 39 20 E
Shimonoseki 74 33 58N 131 0 E
Shimpuru Rapids 92 17 45 S 19 55 E
Shimsha → 70 13 15N 77 10 E
Shimsk 54 58 15N 30 50 E
Shin, L. 14 58 7N 4 30W
Shin-Tone → 74 35 44N 140 51 E
Shinano → 74 36 50N 138 30 E
Shīndand 65 33 12N 62 8 E
Shingleton 106 46 25N 86 33W
Shingū 74 33 40N 135 55 E
Shinkafe 85 13 8N 6 29 E
Shinyanga 90 3 45 S 33 27 E
Shinyanga □ 90 3 50 S 34 0 E
Shio-no-Misaki 74 33 25N 135 45 E
Ship I. 117 30 16N 88 55W
Shipehenski Prokhod 43 42 45N 25 15 E
Shippegan 107 47 45N 64 45W
Shippensburg 114 40 4N 77 32W
Shiprock 119 36 51N 108 45W
Shiqian 77 27 32N 108 13 E
Shiqma, N. → 62 31 37N 34 30 E
Shiquan 77 33 5N 108 15 E
Shīr Kūh 65 31 39N 54 3 E
Shīrāz 65 29 42N 52 30 E
Shirbin 86 31 11N 31 32 E
Shire → 91 17 42 S 35 19 E
Shiretoko-Misaki 74 44 21N 145 20 E
Shiringushi 55 53 51N 42 46 E
Shiriya-Zaki 74 41 25N 141 30 E
Shirol 70 16 47N 74 41 E
Shirpur 68 21 21N 74 57 E
Shīrvān 65 37 30N 57 50 E
Shishmanova 43 42 58N 23 12 E
Shisur 63 17 30N 54 0 E
Shitai 77 30 12N 117 25 E
Shivali (Sirkali) 70 11 15N 79 41 E
Shivpuri 68 25 26N 77 42 E
Shivta 62 30 53N 34 40 E
Shiwei 76 51 19N 119 55 E
Shixing 77 24 46N 114 5 E
Shiyata 86 29 25N 25 7 E
Shizuishan 76 39 15N 106 50 E
Shizuoka 74 35 0N 138 24 E
Shizuoka □ 74 35 15N 138 40 E
Shklov 54 54 16N 30 15 E
Shkoder = Shkodra 44 42 6N 19 1 E
Shkodra 44 42 6N 19 20 E
Shkodra □ 44 42 25N 19 20 E
Shkumbini → 44 41 5N 19 50 E
Shmidt, O. 59 81 0N 91 0 E
Shoal Lake 109 50 30N 100 35W
Shoalhaven → 100 34 54 S 150 42 E
Shoeburyness 13 51 31N 0 49 E
Sholapur 70 17 43N 75 56 E
Shologontsy 59 66 13N 114 0 E
Shomera 62 33 4N 35 17 E
Shōmrōn 62 32 15N 35 13 E
Shongopovi 119 35 49N 110 37W
Shoranur 70 10 46N 76 19 E
Shorapur 70 16 31N 76 48 E
Shoshone 118 43 0N 114 27W
Shoshone L. 118 44 30N 110 40W
Shoshone Mts. 118 39 30N 117 30W
Shoshong 92 22 56 S 26 31 E
Shoshoni 118 43 13N 108 5W
Shostka 54 51 57N 33 32 E
Shouyang 76 37 54N 113 8 E
Show Low 119 34 16N 110 0W
Shpola 56 49 1N 31 30 E
Shreveport 117 32 30N 93 50W
Shrewsbury 12 52 42N 2 45W
Shrivardhan 70 18 4N 73 3 E
Shropshire □ 13 52 36N 2 45W
Shuangcheng 76 45 20N 126 15 E
Shuangliao 76 43 29N 123 30 E
Shuangyashan 75 46 28N 131 5 E
Shucheng 77 31 28N 116 57 E
Shu'eib, Wadi 62 31 54N 35 38 E
Shuguri Falls 91 8 33 S 37 22 E
Shujalpur 68 23 18N 76 46 E
Shulan 76 44 28N 127 0 E
Shule 75 39 25N 76 3 E
Shumagin Is. 104 55 0N 159 0W
Shumerlya 55 55 30N 46 25 E
Shumikha 58 55 10N 63 15 E
Shunchang 77 26 54N 117 48 E
Shunde 77 22 42N 113 14 E
Shungay 57 48 30N 46 45 E
Shungnak 104 66 55N 157 10W
Shuo Xian 76 39 20N 112 33 E
Shūr → 65 28 30N 55 0 E
Shurma 55 56 58N 50 21 E
Shūsf 65 31 50N 60 5 E
Shūshtar 64 32 0N 48 50 E
Shuswap L. 108 50 55N 119 3W
Shuwaykah 62 32 20N 35 1 E
Shuya 55 56 50N 41 28 E
Shwebo 67 22 30N 95 45 E
Shwegu 67 24 15N 96 26 E
Shweli → 67 23 45N 96 45 E
Shyok 69 34 15N 78 12 E
Shyok → 69 35 13N 75 53 E
Si Kiang = Xi Jiang → 75 22 5N 113 20 E
Si Racha 71 13 10N 100 48 E
Siah 64 22 0N 47 0 E
Siahan Range 66 27 30N 64 40 E
Siaksrinderapura 72 0 51N 102 0 E
Sialkot 68 32 32N 74 30 E
Siam = Thailand ■ 71 16 0N 102 0 E
Siam, G. of 71 11 30N 101 0 E
Sian = Xi'an 77 34 15N 109 0 E
Siantan, P. 72 3 10N 106 15 E
Sīāreh 65 28 5N 60 14 E
Siargao 73 9 52N 126 3 E
Siasi 73 5 34N 120 50 E
Siátista 44 40 15N 21 33 E
Siau 73 2 50N 125 25 E
Siauliai 54 55 56N 23 15 E
Siaya □ 90 0 0N 34 20 E
Siazan 57 41 3N 49 10 E
Sibâi, Gebel el 86 25 45N 34 10 E
Sibari 41 39 47N 16 27 E
Sibay 52 52 42N 58 39 E
Sibaya, L. 93 27 20 S 32 45 E
Šibenik 39 43 48N 15 54 E
Siberia 60 60 0N 100 0 E
Siberut 72 1 30 S 99 0 E
Sibi 68 29 30N 67 54 E
Sibil 73 4 59 S 140 35 E
Sibiti 88 3 38 S 13 19 E
Sibiu 46 45 45N 24 9 E
Sibiu □ 46 45 50N 24 15 E
Sibley, Iowa, U.S.A. 116 43 21N 95 43W
Sibley, La., U.S.A. 117 32 34N 93 16W
Sibolga 72 1 42N 98 45 E
Sibsagar 67 27 0N 94 36 E
Sibu 72 2 18N 111 49 E
Sibuco 73 7 20N 122 10 E
Sibuguey B. 73 7 50N 122 45 E
Sibutu 73 4 45N 119 30 E
Sibutu Passage 73 4 50N 120 0 E
Sibuyan 73 12 25N 122 40 E
Sibuyan Sea 73 12 30N 122 20 E
Sicamous 108 50 49N 119 0W
Siccus → 99 31 42 S 139 25 E
Sichuan □ 75 31 0N 104 0 E
Sicilia 41 37 30N 14 30 E
Sicilia, Canale di 40 37 25N 12 30 E
Sicilian Channel = Sicilia, Canale di 40 37 25N 12 30 E
Sicily = Sicilia 41 37 30N 14 30 E
Sicuani 126 14 21 S 71 10W
Siculiana 40 37 20N 13 23 E
Šid 42 45 8N 19 14 E
Sidamo □ 87 5 0N 37 50 E
Sidaouet 85 18 34N 8 3 E
Siddipet 70 18 0N 78 51 E
Sidéradougou 84 10 42N 4 12W
Siderno Marina 41 38 16N 16 17 E
Sidheros, Ákra 45 35 19N 26 19 E
Sidhirókastron 44 41 13N 23 24 E
Sidhpur 68 23 56N 72 25 E
Sîdi Abd el Rahmân 86 30 55N 29 44 E
Sîdi Barrâni 86 31 38N 25 58 E
Sidi-bel-Abbès 82 35 13N 0 39W
Sidi Bennour 82 32 40N 8 25W
Sidi Haneish 86 31 10N 27 35 E
Sidi Kacem 82 34 11N 5 49W
Sidi Moussa, O. → 82 26 58N 3 54 E
Sidi Omar 86 31 24N 24 57 E
Sidi Slimane 82 34 16N 5 56W
Sidi Smaïl 82 32 50N 8 31W
Sidlaw Hills 14 56 32N 3 10W
Sidley, Mt. 5 77 2 S 126 2W
Sidmouth 13 50 40N 3 13W
Sidmouth, C. 98 13 25 S 143 36 E
Sidney, Can. 108 48 39N 123 24W
Sidney, Mont., U.S.A. 116 47 42N 104 7W
Sidney, N.Y., U.S.A. 114 42 18N 75 20W
Sidney, Ohio, U.S.A. 114 40 18N 84 6W
Sidoarjo 73 7 30 S 112 46 E
Sidra, G. of = Khalīj Surt 35 31 40N 18 30 E
Siedlce 28 52 10N 22 20 E
Siedlce □ 28 52 0N 22 0 E
Sieg → 24 50 46N 7 7 E
Siegburg 24 50 48N 7 12 E
Siegen 24 50 52N 8 2 E
Siem Reap 71 13 20N 103 52 E
Siena 39 43 20N 11 20 E
Sieniawa 27 50 11N 22 38 E
Sieradź 28 51 37N 18 41 E
Sieraków 28 52 39N 16 2 E
Sierck-les-Bains 19 49 26N 6 20 E
Sierpc 28 52 55N 19 43 E
Sierra Blanca, N. Mex., U.S.A. 119 33 20N 105 54W
Sierra Blanca, Tex., U.S.A. 119 31 11N 105 17W
Sierra City 118 39 34N 120 42W
Sierra Colorada 128 40 35 S 67 50W
Sierra de Yeguas 31 37 7N 4 52W
Sierra Gorda 124 22 50 S 69 15W
Sierra Leone ■ 84 9 0N 12 0W
Sierra Mojada 120 27 19N 103 42W
Sierre 25 46 17N 7 31 E
Sif Fatima 83 31 6N 8 41 E
Sífnos 45 37 0N 24 45 E
Sifton 109 51 21N 100 8W
Sifton Pass 108 57 52N 126 15W
Sig 82 35 32N 0 12W
Sigdal 47 60 4N 9 38 E
Sigean 20 43 2N 2 58 E
Sighetul Marmatiei 46 47 57N 23 52 E
Sighişoara 46 46 12N 24 50 E
Sigli 72 5 25N 96 0 E
Siglufjörður 50 66 12N 18 55W
Sigma 73 11 29N 122 40 E
Sigmaringen 25 48 5N 9 13 E
Signakhi 57 41 40N 45 57 E
Signy I. 5 60 45 S 45 56W
Signy-l'Abbaye 19 49 40N 4 25 E
Sigsig 126 3 0 S 78 50W
Sigtuna 48 59 36N 17 44 E
Sigüenza 32 41 3N 2 40W
Siguiri 84 11 31N 9 10W
Sigulda 54 57 10N 24 55 E
Sigurd 119 38 49N 112 0W
Sihanoukville = Kompong Som 71 10 40N 103 30 E
Sihui 77 23 20N 112 40 E
Si'ir 62 31 35N 35 9 E
Siirt 64 37 57N 41 55 E
Sijarira Ra. 91 17 36 S 27 45 E
Sikar 68 27 33N 75 10 E
Sikasso 84 11 18N 5 35W
Sikeston 117 36 52N 89 35W
Sikhote Alin, Khrebet 59 46 0N 136 0 E
Sikiá. 44 40 2N 23 56 E
Síkinos 45 36 40N 25 8 E
Sikkani Chief → 108 57 47N 122 15W
Sikkim □ 69 27 50N 88 30 E
Siklós 27 45 50N 18 19 E
Sil → 30 42 27N 7 43W
Sila, La 41 39 15N 16 35 E
Silandro 38 46 38N 10 48 E
Sīlat az Ẓahr 62 32 19N 35 11 E
Silba 39 44 24N 14 41 E
Silchar 67 24 49N 92 48 E
Silcox 109 57 12N 94 10W
Siler City 115 35 44N 79 30W
Sileru → 70 17 49N 81 24 E
Silesia = Slask 22 51 0N 16 30 E
Silet 82 22 44N 4 37 E
Silgarhi Doti 69 29 15N 81 0 E
Silghat 67 26 35N 93 0 E
Silifke 64 36 22N 33 58 E
Siliguri 69 26 45N 88 25 E

Siling Co 75 31 50N 89 20 E
Siliqua 40 39 20N 8 49 E
Silistra 43 44 6N 27 19 E
Siljan, L. 48 60 55N 14 45 E
Silkeborg 49 56 10N 9 32 E
Sillajhuay, Cordillera 126 19 46 S 68 40W
Sillé-le-Guillaume 18 48 10N 0 8W
Siloam Springs 117 36 15N 94 31W
Silogui 72 1 10 S 9 0 E
Silsbee 117 30 20N 94 8W
Silute 54 55 21N 21 33 E
Silva Porto = Bié 89 12 22 S 16 55 E
Silver City, Panama 120 9 19N 79 53W
Silver City, N. Mex., U.S.A. 119 32 50N 108 18W
Silver City, Nev., U.S.A. 118 39 15N 119 48W
Silver Cr. → 118 43 16N 119 13W
Silver Creek 114 42 33N 79 9W
Silver Lake 118 43 9N 121 4W
Silverton, Austral. 100 31 52 S 141 10 E
Silverton, Colo., U.S.A. 119 37 51N 107 45W
Silverton, Tex., U.S.A. 117 34 30N 101 16W
Silves 31 37 11N 8 26W
Silvi 39 42 32N 14 5 E
Silvies → 118 43 22N 118 48W
Silvretta Gruppe 25 46 50N 10 6 E
Silwa Bahari 86 24 45N 32 55 E
Silwâd 62 31 59N 35 15 E
Silz 26 47 16N 10 56 E
Sim, C. 82 31 26N 9 51W
Simanggang 72 1 15N 111 32 E
Simard, L. 106 47 40N 78 40W
Sîmărtin 46 46 19N 25 58 E
Simba 90 2 10 S 37 36 E
Simbach 25 48 16N 13 3 E
Simbo 90 4 51 S 29 41 E
Simcoe 106 42 50N 80 20W
Simcoe, L. 106 44 25N 79 20W
Simenga 59 62 42N 108 25 E
Simeto → 41 37 25N 15 10 E
Simeulue 72 2 45N 95 45 E
Simferopol 56 44 55N 34 3 E
Sími 45 36 35N 27 50 E
Simikot 69 30 0N 81 50 E
Simitli 42 41 52N 23 7 E
Simla 68 31 2N 77 9 E
Şimleu-Silvaniei 46 47 17N 22 50 E
Simmern 25 49 59N 7 32 E
Simmie 109 49 56N 108 6W
Simojärvi 50 66 5N 27 3 E
Simojoki → 50 65 35N 25 1 E
Simonette → 108 55 9N 118 15W
Simonstown 92 34 14 S 18 26 E
Simontornya 27 46 45N 18 33 E
Simpang, Indon. 72 1 16 S 104 5 E
Simpang, Malay. 71 4 50N 100 40 E
Simplon Pass 25 46 15N 8 0 E
Simplon Tunnel 25 46 15N 8 7 E
Simpson Des. 97 25 0 S 137 0 E
Simrishamn 49 55 33N 14 22 E
Simunjan 72 1 25N 110 45 E
Simushir, Ostrov 59 46 50N 152 30 E
Sina → 70 17 30N 75 55 E
Sinabang 72 2 30N 96 24 E
Sinadogo 63 5 50N 47 0 E
Sinai = Es Sînâ' 86 29 0N 34 0 E
Sinai, Mt. = Mûsa, G. 86 28 32N 33 59 E
Sinaia 46 45 21N 25 38 E
Sinaloa 120 25 50N 108 20W
Sinaloa □ 120 25 0N 107 30W
Sinalunga 39 43 12N 11 43 E
Sinan 77 27 56N 108 13 E
Sînandrei 46 45 52N 21 13 E
Sînâwan 83 31 0N 10 37 E
Sincelejo 126 9 18N 75 24W
Sinclair 118 41 47N 107 10W
Sinclair Mills 108 54 5N 121 40W
Sincorá, Serra do 127 13 30 S 41 0W
Sind 68 26 0N 68 30 E
Sind Sagar Doab 68 32 0N 71 30 E
Sindal 49 57 28N 10 10 E
Sindangan 73 8 10N 123 5 E
Sindangbarang 73 7 27 S 107 1 E
Sinde 91 17 28 S 25 51 E
Sinegorski 57 48 0N 40 52 E
Sinelnikovo 56 48 25N 35 30 E
Sines 31 37 56N 8 51W
Sines, Cabo de 31 37 58N 8 53W
Sineu 32 39 38N 3 1 E
Sinfra 84 6 35N 5 56W
Singa 87 13 10N 33 57 E
Singanallur 70 11 2N 77 1 E
Singaparna 73 7 23 S 108 4 E
Singapore ■ 71 1 17N 103 51 E
Singapore, Straits of 71 1 15N 104 0 E
Singaraja 72 8 6 S 115 10 E
Singen 25 47 45N 8 50 E
Singida 90 4 49 S 34 48 E
Singida □ 90 6 0 S 34 30 E
Singitikós Kólpos 44 40 6N 24 0 E
Singkaling Hkamti 67 26 0N 95 39 E
Singkawang 72 1 0N 108 57 E
Singkep 72 0 30 S 104 20 E
Singleton 97 32 33 S 151 0 E
Singleton, Mt. 96 29 27 S 117 15 E
Singö 48 60 12N 18 45 E
Singoli 68 25 0N 75 22 E
Siniátsikon, Óros 44 40 25N 21 35 E
Siniscóla 40 40 35N 9 40 E
Sinj 39 43 42N 16 39 E
Sinjai 73 5 7 S 120 20 E
Sinjajevina, Planina 42 42 57N 19 22 E
Sinjār 64 36 19N 41 52 E
Sinjil 62 32 3N 35 15 E
Sinkat 86 18 55N 36 49 E
Sinkiang Uighur = Xinjiang Uygur □ 75 42 0N 86 0 E
Sinnai 40 39 18N 9 13 E
Sinnar 70 19 48N 74 0 E
Sinni → 41 40 9N 16 42 E
Sînnicolau Maré 42 46 5N 20 39 E
Sinnuris 86 29 26N 30 31 E
Sinoe, L. 46 44 35N 28 50 E
Sinoia 91 17 20 S 30 8 E
Sinop 64 42 1N 35 11 E
Sinskoye 59 61 8N 126 48 E
Sint Maarten 121 18 0N 63 5W
Sint Niklaas 16 51 10N 4 9 E
Sint Truiden 16 50 48N 5 10 E
Sîntana 46 46 20N 21 30 E
Sintang 72 0 5N 111 35 E
Sinton 117 28 1N 97 30W
Sintra 31 38 47N 9 25W
Sinŭiju 76 40 5N 124 24 E
Sinyukha → 56 48 3N 30 51 E
Siocon 73 7 40N 122 10 E
Siófok 27 46 39 S 23 36 E
Sioma 92 16 25 S 23 28 E
Sion 25 46 14N 7 20 E
Sioux City 116 42 32N 96 25W
Sioux Falls 116 43 35N 96 40W
Sioux Lookout 106 50 10N 91 50W
Šipan 42 42 45N 17 52 E
Siping 76 43 8N 124 21 E
Sipiwesk L. 109 55 5N 97 35W
Sipora 72 2 18 S 99 40 E
Siquia → 121 12 10N 84 20W
Siquijor 73 9 12N 123 35 E
Sir Edward Pellew Group 97 15 40 S 137 10 E
Sira 70 13 41N 76 49 E
Siracusa 41 37 4N 15 17 E
Sirajganj 69 24 25N 89 47 E
Sirakoro 84 12 41N 9 14W
Sirasso 84 9 16N 6 6W
Siret 46 47 55N 26 5 E
Siret → 46 47 58N 26 5 E
Şiria 42 46 16N 21 38 E
Sirino, Monte 41 40 7N 15 50 E
Sirkali (Shivali) 70 11 15N 79 41 E
Sirna. 45 36 22N 26 42 E
Sirohi 68 24 52N 72 53 E
Široki Brijeg 42 43 21N 17 36 E
Sironj 68 24 5N 77 39 E
Síros 45 37 28N 24 57 E
Sirsa 68 29 33N 75 4 E
Sirsi 70 14 40N 74 49 E
Siruela 31 38 58N 5 3W
Sisak 39 45 30N 16 21 E
Sisaket 71 15 8N 104 23 E
Sisante 33 39 25N 2 12W
Sisargas, Islas 30 43 21N 8 50W
Sishen 92 27 47 S 22 59 E
Sishui 77 34 48N 113 15 E
Sisipuk L. 109 55 45N 101 50W
Sisophon 71 13 38N 102 59 E
Sisseton 116 45 43N 97 3W
Sissonne 19 49 34N 3 51 E
Sistema Central 30 40 40N 5 55W
Sistema Iberico 32 41 0N 2 10W
Sisteron 21 44 12N 5 57 E
Sisters 118 44 21N 121 32W
Sitamarhi 69 26 37N 85 30 E
Sitapur 69 27 38N 80 45 E
Siteki 93 26 32 S 31 58 E
Sitges 32 41 17N 1 47 E
Sithoniá 44 40 0N 23 45 E
Sitía 45 35 13N 26 6 E
Sitka 104 57 9N 135 20W
Sitoti 92 23 15 S 23 40 E
Sitra 86 28 40N 26 53 E
Sittang → 67 17 10N 96 58 E
Sittang Myit → 67 17 20N 96 45 E
Sittard 16 51 0N 5 52 E
Sittensen 24 53 17N 9 32 E
Sittona 87 14 25N 37 23 E
Situbondo 73 7 45 S 114 0 E
Sivaganga 70 9 50N 78 28 E
Sivagiri 70 9 16N 77 26 E
Sivakasi 70 9 24N 77 47 E
Sivana 68 28 37N 78 6 E
Sīvand 65 30 5N 52 55 E
Sivas 64 39 43N 36 58 E
Siverek 64 37 50N 39 19 E
Sivomaskinskiy 52 66 40N 62 35 E
Sivrihisar 64 39 30N 31 35 E
Sîwa 86 29 11N 25 31 E
Sîwa, El Wâhât es 86 29 10N 25 30 E
Siwalik Range 69 28 0N 83 0 E
Siwan 69 26 13N 84 21 E
Siyâl, Jazâ'ir 86 22 49N 35 12 E
Sizewell 13 52 13N 1 38 E
Sjælland 49 55 30N 11 30 E
Sjællands Odde 49 56 0N 11 15 E
Själevad 48 63 18N 18 36 E
Sjarinska Banja 42 42 45N 21 38 E
Sjenica 42 43 16N 20 0 E
Sjoa 47 61 41N 9 33 E
Sjöbo 49 55 37N 13 45 E
Sjösa 49 58 47N 17 4 E
Skadarsko Jezero 42 42 10N 19 20 E
Skadovsk 56 46 17N 32 52 E
Skagafjörður 50 65 54N 19 35W
Skagastølstindane 47 61 28N 7 52 E
Skagen 49 57 43N 10 35 E
Skagern 49 59 0N 14 20 E
Skagerrak 49 57 30N 9 0 E
Skagway 104 59 23N 135 20W
Skaidi 50 70 26N 24 30 E
Skala Podolskaya 56 48 50N 26 15 E
Skalat 54 49 23N 25 55 E
Skalbmierz 28 50 20N 20 25 E
Skalica 27 48 50N 17 15 E
Skalni Dol = Kamenyak 43 43 24N 26 57 E
Skals 49 56 34N 9 24 E
Skanderborg 49 56 2N 9 55 E
Skånevik 47 59 43N 5 53 E
Skänninge 49 58 24N 15 5 E
Skanör 49 55 24N 12 50 E
Skantzoúra 45 39 5N 24 6 E
Skara 49 58 25N 13 30 E
Skaraborgs län □ 49 58 20N 13 30 E
Skardu 69 35 20N 75 44 E
Skarrild 49 55 58N 8 53 E
Skarszewy 28 54 4N 18 25 E
Skaryszew 28 51 19N 21 15 E
Skarzysko Kamienna 28 51 7N 20 52 E
Skattungbyn 48 61 10N 14 56 E
Skebokvarn 48 59 7N 16 45 E
Skeena → 108 54 9N 130 5W
Skeena Mts. 108 56 40N 128 30W
Skegness 12 53 9N 0 20 E
Skeldon 126 5 55N 57 20W
Skellefte älv → 50 64 45N 21 10 E
Skellefteå 50 64 45N 20 58 E
Skelleftehamn 50 64 47N 20 59 E
Skender Vakuf 42 44 29N 17 22 E
Skene 49 57 30N 12 37 E
Skerries, The 12 53 27N 4 40W
Skhíza 45 36 41N 21 40 E
Skhoinoúsa 45 36 53N 25 31 E
Skhwaner, Pegunungan 72 1 0 S 112 30 E
Ski 47 59 43N 10 52 E
Skíathos 45 39 12N 23 30 E
Skibbereen 15 51 33N 9 16W
Skiddaw 12 54 39N 3 9W
Skien 47 59 12N 9 35 E
Skierniewice 28 51 58N 20 10 E
Skierniewice □ 28 52 0N 20 10 E
Skikda 83 36 50N 6 58 E
Skillingaryd 49 57 27N 14 5 E
Skillinge 49 55 30N 14 16 E
Skillingmark 48 59 48N 12 1 E
Skinári, Ákra 45 37 56N 20 40 E
Skipton, Austral. 99 37 39 S 143 40 E
Skipton, U.K. 12 53 57N 2 1W
Skiropoúla 45 38 50N 24 21 E
Skíros 45 38 55N 24 34 E
Skivarp 49 55 26N 13 34 E
Skive 49 56 33N 9 2 E
Skjåk 47 61 52N 8 22 E
Skjálfandafljót → 50 65 59N 17 25W
Skjálfandi 50 66 5N 17 30W
Skjeberg 47 59 12N 11 12 E
Skjern 49 55 57N 8 30 E
Skoczów 27 49 49N 18 45 E
Skodje 47 62 30N 6 43 E
Škofja Loka 39 46 9N 14 19 E
Skoghall 48 59 20N 13 30 E
Skoki 28 52 40N 17 11 E
Skole 54 49 3N 23 30 E
Skópelos 45 39 9N 23 47 E
Skopin 55 53 55N 39 32 E
Skopje 42 42 1N 21 32 E
Skórcz 28 53 47N 18 30 E
Skottfoss 47 59 12N 9 30 E
Skovorodino 59 54 0N 125 0 E
Skowhegan 107 44 49N 69 40W
Skownan 109 51 58N 99 35W
Skradin 39 43 52N 15 53 E
Skreanäs 49 56 52N 12 35 E
Skrwa → 28 52 35N 19 32 E
Skull 15 51 32N 9 40W
Skultorp 49 58 24N 13 51 E
Skunk → 116 40 42N 91 7W
Skuodas 54 56 21N 21 45 E
Skurup 49 55 28N 13 30 E
Skutskär 49 60 37N 17 25 E
Skvira 56 49 44N 29 40 E
Skwierzyna 28 52 33N 15 30 E
Skye 14 57 15N 6 10W
Skykomish 118 47 43N 121 16W
Skyros = Skíros 45 38 52N 24 37 E
Slagelse 49 55 23N 11 19 E
Slamet, G. 72 7 16 S 109 8 E
Slaney → 15 52 52N 6 45W
Slangerup 49 55 50N 12 11 E
Slănic 46 45 14N 25 58 E
Slankamen 42 45 8N 20 15 E
Slano 42 42 48N 17 53 E
Slantsy 54 59 7N 28 5 E
Slany 26 50 13N 14 6 E
Slask 22 51 0N 16 30 E
Slate Is. 106 48 40N 87 0W
Slatina 46 44 28N 24 22 E
Slaton 117 33 27N 101 38W
Slave → 108 61 18N 113 39W
Slave Coast 85 6 0N 2 30 E
Slave Lake 108 55 17N 114 43W
Slave Pt. 108 61 11N 115 56W
Slavgorod 58 53 1N 78 37 E
Slavinja 42 43 9N 22 50 E
Slavkov (Austerlitz) 27 49 10N 16 52 E
Slavnoye 54 54 24N 29 15 E
Slavonska Požega 42 45 20N 17 40 E
Slavonski Brod 42 45 11N 18 0 E
Slavuta 54 50 15N 27 2 E
Slavyansk 56 48 55N 37 36 E
Slavyansk-na-Kubani 56 45 15N 38 11 E
Sława 28 51 52N 16 2 E
Sławno 28 54 20N 16 41 E
Sławoborze 28 53 55N 15 42 E
Sleaford 12 53 0N 0 22W
Sleat, Sd. of 14 57 5N 5 47W
Sleeper Is. 105 58 30N 81 0W
Sleepy Eye 116 44 15N 94 45W
Sleman 73 7 40 S 110 20 E
Slemon L. 108 63 13N 116 4W
Ślesin 28 52 22N 18 14 E
Slidell 117 30 20N 89 48W
Sliedrecht 16 51 50N 4 45 E
Slieve Aughty 15 53 4N 8 30W
Slieve Bloom 15 53 4N 7 40W
Slieve Donard 15 54 10N 5 57W
Slieve Gullion 15 54 8N 6 26W
Slieve Mish 15 52 12N 9 50W
Slievenamon 15 52 25N 7 37W
Sligo 15 54 17N 8 28W
Sligo □ 15 54 10N 8 35W
Sligo B. 15 54 20N 8 40W
Slite 51 57 42N 18 48 E
Sliven 43 42 42N 26 19 E
Slivnitsa 42 42 50N 23 0 E
Sljeme 39 45 57N 15 58 E
Sloansville 113 42 45N 74 22W
Slobodskoy 52 58 40N 50 6 E
Slobozia, Ialomiţa, Romania 46 44 34N 27 23 E
Slobozia, Valahia, Romania 46 44 30N 25 14 E
Slocan 108 49 48N 117 28W
Slochteren 16 53 12N 6 48 E
Slöinge 49 56 51N 12 42 E
Słomniki 28 50 16N 20 4 E
Slonim 54 53 4N 25 19 E
Slough 13 51 30N 0 35W
Slovakia = Slovensko 27 48 30N 19 0 E
Slovakian Ore Mts. = Slovenské Rudohorie 27 48 45N 20 0 E
Slovenia = Slovenija 39 45 58N 14 30 E
Slovenija □ 39 45 58N 14 30 E
Slovenj Gradec 39 46 31N 15 5 E
Slovenska Bistrica 39 46 24N 15 35 E
Slovenská Socialisticka Republika □ 27 48 30N 10 0 E
Slovenské Rudohorie 27 48 45N 20 0 E
Slovensko □ 27 48 30N 19 0 E
Słubice 28 52 22N 14 35 E
Sluch → 54 51 37N 26 38 E
Sluis 16 51 18N 3 23 E
Slunchev Bryag 43 42 40N 27 41 E
Slunj 39 45 6N 15 33 E
Słupca 28 52 15N 17 52 E
Słupia → 28 54 35N 16 51 E
Słupsk 28 54 30N 17 3 E
Słupsk □ 28 54 15N 17 30 E
Slurry 92 25 49 S 25 42 E
Slutsk 54 53 2N 27 31 E
Slyne Hd. 15 53 25N 10 10W
Slyudyanka 59 51 40N 103 40 E
Smålandsfarvandet 49 55 10N 11 20 E
Smalandsstenar 49 57 9N 13 24 E
Smalltree L. 109 61 0N 105 0W
Smallwood Reservoir 107 54 20N 63 10W
Smarje 39 46 15N 15 34 E
Smart Syndicate Dam 92 30 45 S 23 10 E
Smeaton 109 53 30N 104 49W
Smederevo 42 44 40N 20 57 E
Smederevska Palanka 42 44 22N 20 58 E
Smela 56 49 15N 31 58 E
Smethport 112 41 50N 78 28W
Smidovich 59 48 36N 133 49 E
Smigiel 28 52 1N 16 32 E
Smiley 109 51 38N 109 29W
Smilyan 43 41 29N 24 46 E
Smith 108 55 10N 114 0W
Smith → 108 59 34N 126 30W
Smith Arm 104 66 15N 123 0W
Smith Center 116 39 50N 98 50W
Smith Sund 4 78 30N 74 0W
Smithburne → 98 17 3 S 140 57 E
Smithers 108 54 45N 127 10W
Smithfield, Madag. 93 30 9 S 26 30 E
Smithfield, N.C., U.S.A. 115 35 31N 78 16W
Smithfield, Utah, U.S.A. 118 41 50N 111 50W
Smiths Falls 106 44 55N 76 0W
Smithton 99 40 53 S 145 6 E
Smithtown 99 30 58 S 152 48 E
Smithville, Can. 112 43 6N 79 33W
Smithville, U.S.A. 117 30 2N 97 12W
Smoky → 108 56 10N 117 21W
Smoky Falls 106 50 4N 82 10W
Smoky Hill → 116 39 3N 96 48W
Smoky Lake 108 54 10N 112 30W
Smøla 47 63 23N 8 3 E
Smolensk 54 54 45N 32 0 E
Smolikas, Óros 44 40 9N 20 58 E
Smolník 27 48 43N 20 44 E
Smolyan 43 41 36N 24 38 E
Smooth Rock Falls 106 49 17N 81 37W
Smoothstone L. 109 54 40N 106 50W
Smorgon 54 54 20N 26 24 E
Smulţi 46 45 57N 27 44 E
Smyadovo 43 43 2N 27 1 E
Smyrna = İzmir 64 38 25N 27 8 E
Snaefell 12 54 18N 4 26W
Snaefellsjökull 50 64 45N 23 46W
Snake → 118 46 12N 119 2W
Snake I. 99 38 47 S 146 33 E
Snake L. 109 55 32N 106 35W
Snake Ra. 118 39 0N 114 30W
Snake River 118 44 10N 110 42W
Snake River Plain 118 43 13N 113 0W
Snarum 47 60 1N 9 54 E
Snedsted 49 56 55N 8 32 E
Sneek 16 53 2N 5 40 E
Snejbjerg 49 56 8N 8 54 E
Snezhnoye 57 48 0N 38 58 E
Sněžka 26 50 41N 15 50 E
Snežnik 39 45 36N 14 35 E
Sniadowo 28 53 2N 22 0 E
Sniardwy, Jezioro 28 53 48N 21 50 E
Snigirevka 56 47 2N 32 49 E
Snina 27 49 0N 22 9 E
Snizort, L. 14 57 33N 6 28W
Snøhetta 47 62 19N 9 16 E
Snohomish 118 47 53N 122 6W
Snonuten 47 59 31N 6 50 E
Snow Hill 114 38 10N 75 21W
Snow Lake 109 54 52N 100 3W
Snowbird L. 109 60 45N 103 0W
Snowdon 12 53 4N 4 8W
Snowdrift 109 62 24N 110 44W
Snowdrift → 109 62 24N 110 44W
Snowflake 119 34 30N 110 4W
Snowshoe Pk. 118 48 13N 115 41W
Snowtown 99 33 46 S 138 14 E
Snowville 118 41 59N 112 47W
Snowy → 97 37 46 S 148 30 E
Snowy Mts. 99 36 30 S 148 20 E
Snyatyn 56 48 30N 25 50 E
Snyder, Okla., U.S.A. 117 34 40N 99 0W
Snyder, Tex., U.S.A. 117 32 45N 100 57W
Soahanina 93 18 42 S 44 13 E
Soalala 93 16 6 S 45 20 E
Soanierana-Ivongo 93 16 55 S 49 35 E
Soap Lake 118 47 23N 119 31W
Sobat, Nahr → 87 9 22N 31 33 E
Soběslav 26 49 16N 14 45 E
Sobhapur 68 22 47N 78 17 E
Sobinka 55 56 0N 40 0 E
Sobótka 28 50 54N 16 44 E

Sobrado 30 43 2N 8 2W
Sobral 127 3 50S 40 20W
Sobreira Formosa 31 39 46N 7 51W
Soča → 39 46 20N 13 40 E
Sochaczew 28 52 15N 20 13 E
Soch'e = Shache 75 38 20N 77 10 E
Sochi 57 43 35N 39 40 E
Société, Is. de la 95 17 0S 151 0W
Society Is. = Société, Is. de la 95 17 0S 151 0W
Socompa, Portezuelo de 124 24 27S 68 18W
Socorro, Colomb. 126 6 29N 73 16W
Socorro, U.S.A. 119 34 4N 106 54W
Socotra 63 12 30N 54 0 E
Socúellmos 33 39 16N 2 47W
Soda L. 119 35 7N 116 2W
Soda Plains 69 35 30N 79 0 E
Soda Springs 118 42 40N 111 40W
Söderfors 48 60 23N 17 25 E
Söderhamn 48 61 18N 17 10 E
Söderköping 48 58 31N 16 20 E
Södermanlands län □ 48 59 10N 16 30 E
Södertälje 48 59 12N 17 39 E
Sodiri 81 14 27N 29 0 E
Sodo 87 7 0N 37 41 E
Södra Vi 49 57 45N 15 45 E
Sodražica 39 45 45N 14 39 E
Sodus 112 43 13N 77 5W
Soekmekaar 93 23 30S 29 55 E
Soest, Ger. 24 51 34N 8 7 E
Soest, Neth. 16 52 9N 5 19 E
Sofádhes 44 39 20N 22 4 E
Sofara 84 13 59N 4 9W
Sofia = Sofiya 43 42 45N 23 20 E
Sofia → 93 15 27S 47 23 E
Sofievka 56 48 6N 33 55 E
Sofiiski 59 52 15N 133 59 E
Sofikón 45 37 47N 23 3 E
Sofiya 43 42 45N 23 20 E
Sogad 73 10 30N 125 0 E
Sogakofe 85 6 2N 0 39 E
Sogamoso 126 5 43N 72 56W
Sögel 24 52 50N 7 32 E
Sogn og Fjordane fylke □ 47 61 40N 6 0 E
Sognefjorden 47 61 10N 5 50 E
Sohâg 86 26 33N 31 43 E
Soignies 16 50 35N 4 5 E
Soira, Mt. 87 14 45N 39 30 E
Soissons 19 49 25N 3 19 E
Sōja 74 34 40N 133 45 E
Sojat 68 25 55N 73 45 E
Sok → 55 53 24N 50 8 E
Sokal 54 50 31N 24 15 E
Söke 45 37 48N 27 28 E
Sokelo 91 9 55S 24 36 E
Sokhós 44 40 48N 23 22 E
Sokki, Oued In → 82 29 30N 3 42 E
Sokna 47 60 16N 9 50 E
Soknedal 47 62 57N 10 13 E
Soko Banja 42 43 40N 21 51 E
Sokodé 85 9 0N 1 11 E
Sokol 55 59 30N 40 5 E
Sokolac 42 43 56N 18 48 E
Sokółka 28 53 25N 23 30 E
Sokolo 84 14 53N 6 8W
Sokolov 26 50 12N 12 40 E
Sokołów Małpolski 27 50 12N 22 7 E
Sokołów Podlaski 28 52 25N 22 15 E
Sokoły 28 52 59N 22 42 E
Sokoto 85 13 2N 5 16 E
Sokoto □ 85 12 30N 5 0 E
Sokoto → 85 11 20N 4 10 E
Sol Iletsk 52 51 10N 55 0 E
Sola 47 58 53N 5 36 E
Sola → 27 50 4N 19 15 E
Solai 90 0 2N 36 12 E
Solana, La 33 38 59N 3 14W
Solano 73 16 31N 121 15 E
Solares 30 43 23N 3 43W
Solberga 49 57 45N 14 43 E
Solca 46 47 40N 25 50 E
Solec Kujawski 28 53 5N 18 14 E
Soledad, U.S.A. 119 36 27N 121 16W
Soledad, Venez. 126 8 10N 63 34W
Solent, The 13 50 45N 1 25W
Solenzara 21 41 53N 9 23 E
Solesmes 19 50 10N 3 30 E
Solfonn 47 60 2N 6 57 E
Soligalich 55 59 5N 42 10 E
Soligorsk 54 52 51N 27 27 E
Solikamsk 58 59 38N 56 50 E
Solila 93 21 25S 46 37 E
Solimões → = Amazonas → 126 2 15S 66 30W
Solingen 24 51 10N 7 4 E
Sollebrunn 49 58 8N 12 32 E
Sollefteå 48 63 12N 17 20 E
Sollentuna 48 59 26N 17 56 E
Söller 32 39 46N 2 43 E
Solling 24 51 44N 9 36 E
Solna 48 59 22N 18 1 E
Solnechnogorsk 55 56 10N 36 57 E
Sologne 19 47 40N 2 0 E
Solok 72 0 45S 100 40 E
Sololá 120 14 49N 91 10 E
Solomon Is. ■ 94 6 0S 155 0 E
Solomon, N. Fork → 116 39 29N 98 26W
Solomon Sea 98 7 0S 150 0 E
Solomon, S. Fork → 116 39 25N 99 12W
Solomon's Pools = Birak Sulaymān 62 31 42N 35 7 E
Solon 75 46 32N 121 10 E
Solon Springs 116 46 19N 91 47W
Solor 73 8 27S 123 0 E
Solotcha 55 54 48N 39 53 E
Solothurn 25 47 13N 7 32 E
Solothurn □ 25 47 18N 7 40 E
Solsona 32 42 0N 1 31 E
Solt 27 46 45N 19 1 E
Solta 39 43 24N 16 15 E
Soltānābād 65 36 29N 58 5 E
Soltānīyeh 64 36 20N 48 55 E
Soltau 24 52 59N 9 50 E
Soltsy 54 58 10N 30 30 E
Solund 47 61 5N 4 50 E
Solunska Glava 42 41 44N 21 31 E
Solvay 114 43 5N 76 17W
Sölvesborg 49 56 5N 14 35 E
Solvychegodsk 52 61 21N 46 56 E
Solway Firth 12 54 45N 3 38W
Solwezi 91 12 11S 26 21 E
Somali Rep. ■ 63 7 0N 47 0 E
Sombe Dzong 69 27 13N 89 8 E
Sombernon 19 47 20N 4 40 E
Sombor 42 45 46N 19 9 E
Sombra 112 42 43N 82 29W
Sombrerete 120 23 40N 103 40W
Sombrero 121 18 37N 63 30W
Somers 118 48 4N 114 18W
Somerset, Berm. 121 32 16N 64 55W
Somerset, Can. 109 49 25N 98 39W
Somerset, Colo., U.S.A. 119 38 55N 107 30W
Somerset, Ky., U.S.A. 114 37 5N 84 40W
Somerset, Mass., U.S.A. 113 41 45N 71 10W
Somerset, Pa., U.S.A. 112 40 1N 79 4W
Somerset □ 13 51 9N 3 0W
Somerset East 92 32 42S 25 35 E
Somerset I. 104 73 30N 93 0W
Somerset West 92 34 8S 18 50 E
Somersworth 113 43 15N 70 51W
Somerton 119 32 35N 114 47W
Somerville 113 40 34N 74 36W
Someş → 46 47 15N 23 45 E
Someşul Mare → 46 47 18N 24 30 E
Somma Lombardo 38 45 41N 8 42 E
Somma Vesuviana 41 40 52N 14 23 E
Sommariva 99 26 24S 146 36 E
Sommatino 40 37 20N 14 0 E
Somme □ 19 50 0N 2 20 E
Somme, B. de la 18 50 14N 1 33 E
Sommen 49 58 12N 15 0 E
Sommen, L. 49 58 0N 15 15 E
Sommepy-Tahure 19 49 15N 4 31 E
Sömmerda 24 51 10N 11 8 E
Sommesous 19 48 44N 4 12 E
Sommières 21 43 47N 4 6 E
Somogy □ 27 46 19N 17 30 E
Somogyszob 27 46 18N 17 20 E
Sompolno 28 52 26N 18 30 E
Somport, Paso 32 42 48N 0 31W
Somport, Puerto de 32 42 48N 0 31W
Son, Norway 47 59 32N 10 42 E
Son, Spain 30 42 43N 8 58W
Son La 71 21 20N 103 50 E
Sonamukhi 69 23 18N 87 27 E
Soncino 38 45 24N 9 52 E
Sondags → 92 33 44S 25 51 E
Sóndalo 38 46 20N 10 20 E
Sønder Omme 49 55 50N 8 54 E
Sønder Ternby 49 57 31N 9 58 E
Sønderborg 49 54 55N 9 49 E
Sonderjyllands Amtskommune □ 49 55 10N 9 10 E
Sondershausen 24 51 22N 10 50 E
Sóndrio 38 46 10N 9 53 E
Sone 91 17 23S 34 55 E
Sonepat 68 29 0N 77 5 E
Sonepur 69 20 55N 83 50 E
Song Cau 71 13 27N 109 18 E
Song Xian 77 34 12N 112 8 E
Songea 91 10 40S 35 40 E
Songea □ 91 10 30S 36 0 E
Songeons 19 49 32N 1 50 E
Songhua Hu 76 43 35N 126 50 E
Songhua Jiang → 75 47 45N 132 30 E
Songjiang 77 31 1N 121 12 E
Songkhla 71 7 13N 100 37 E
Songling 76 48 2N 121 9 E
Songpan 75 32 40N 103 30 E
Songtao 77 28 11N 109 10 E
Songwe 90 3 20S 26 16 E
Songwe → 91 9 44S 33 58 E
Songzi 77 30 12N 111 45 E
Sonkovo 55 57 50N 37 5 E
Sonmiani 66 25 25N 66 40 E
Sonnino 40 41 25N 13 13 E
Sono → 127 9 58S 48 11W
Sonora, Calif., U.S.A. 119 37 59N 120 27W
Sonora, Texas, U.S.A. 117 30 33N 100 37W
Sonora □ 120 29 0N 111 0W
Sonora → 120 28 50N 111 33W
Sonora P. 118 38 17N 119 35W
Sonsomate 120 13 43N 89 44W
Sonthofen 25 47 31N 10 16 E
Soo Junction 114 46 20N 85 14W
Soochow = Suzhou 75 31 19N 120 38 E
Sopi 73 2 34N 128 28 E
Sopo, Nahr → 87 8 40N 26 30 E
Sopot, Poland 28 54 27N 18 31 E
Sopot, Yugo. 42 44 29N 20 30 E
Sopotnica 42 41 23N 21 13 E
Sopron 27 47 45N 16 32 E
Sop's Arm 107 49 46N 56 56W
Sør-Rondane 5 72 0S 25 0 E
Sør-Trøndelag fylke □ 47 63 0N 10 0 E
Sora 40 41 45N 13 36 E
Sorada 70 19 45N 84 26 E
Sorah 68 27 13N 68 56 E
Söråker 48 62 30N 17 32 E
Sorano 39 42 40N 11 42 E
Sorata 126 15 50S 68 40W
Sorbas 33 37 6N 2 7W
Sorel 106 46 0N 73 10W
Sorento 99 38 22S 144 47 E
Soreq, N. → 62 31 57N 34 43 E
Soresina 38 45 17N 9 51 E
Sorgono 40 40 01N 9 06 E
Sorgues 21 44 1N 4 53 E
Soria 32 41 43N 2 32W
Soria □ 32 41 46N 2 28W
Soriano 124 33 24S 58 19W
Soriano nel Cimino 39 42 25N 12 14 E
Sorkh, Kuh-e 65 35 40N 58 30 E
Sorø 49 55 26N 11 32 E
Soro 84 10 9N 9 48W
Sorocaba 125 23 31S 47 27W
Sorochinsk 52 52 26N 53 10 E
Soroki 56 48 8N 28 12 E
Soroksár 27 47 24N 19 9 E
Soron 68 27 55N 78 45 E
Sorong 73 0 55S 131 15 E
Soroti 90 1 43N 33 35 E
Sørøya 50 70 40N 22 30 E
Sørøyane 47 62 25N 5 32 E
Sørøysundet 50 70 25N 23 0 E
Sorraia → 31 38 55N 8 53W
Sorrento 41 40 38N 14 23 E
Sorris Sorris 92 21 0S 14 46 E
Sorsele 50 65 31N 17 30 E
Sorso 40 40 50N 8 34 E
Sorsogon 73 13 0N 124 0 E
Sortavala 52 61 42N 30 41 E
Sortino 41 37 9N 15 1 E
Sorvizhi 55 57 52N 48 32 E
Sos 32 42 30N 1 13W
Soscumica, L. 106 50 15N 77 27W
Sosna → 55 52 42N 38 55 E
Sosnogorsk 52 63 37N 53 51 E
Sosnovka, R.S.F.S.R., U.S.S.R. 55 53 13N 41 24 E
Sosnovka, R.S.F.S.R., U.S.S.R. 59 54 9N 109 35 E
Sosnowiec 28 50 20N 19 10 E
Sospel 21 43 52N 7 27 E
Šoštanj 39 46 23N 15 4 E
Sosva 52 59 10N 61 50 E
Soto la Marina → 120 23 40N 97 40W
Soto y Amío 30 42 46N 5 53W
Sotteville-lès-Rouen 18 49 24N 1 5 E
Sotuta 120 20 29N 89 43W
Souanké 88 2 10N 14 3 E
Soúdhas, Kólpos 45 35 25N 24 10 E
Souflíon 44 41 12N 26 18 E
Souillac 20 44 53N 1 29 E
Souk-Ahras 83 36 23N 7 57 E
Souk el Arba du Rharb 82 34 43N 5 59W
Sŏul 76 37 31N 126 58 E
Soulac-sur-Mer 20 45 30N 1 7W
Soultz 19 48 57N 7 52 E
Soúnion, Ákra 45 37 37N 24 1 E
Sour el Ghozlane 83 36 10N 3 45 E
Sources, Mt. aux 93 28 45S 28 50 E
Sourdeval 18 48 43N 0 55W
Soure, Brazil 127 0 35S 48 30W
Soure, Port. 30 40 4N 8 38W
Souris, Man., Can. 109 49 40N 100 20W
Souris, P.E.I., Can. 107 46 21N 62 15W
Souris → 109 49 40N 99 34W
Soúrpi 45 39 6N 22 54 E
Sousa 127 6 45S 38 10W
Sousel, Brazil 127 2 38S 52 29W
Sousel, Port. 31 38 57N 7 40W
Souss, O. → 82 30 27N 9 31W
Sousse 83 35 50N 10 38 E
Soustons 20 43 45N 1 19W
Souterraine, La 20 46 15N 1 30 E
South Africa, Rep. of, ■ 89 32 0S 17 0 E
South America 122 10 0S 60 0W
South Atlantic Ocean 7 20 0S 10 0W
South Aulatsivik I. 107 56 45N 61 30W
South Australia □ 96 32 0S 139 0 E
South Baldy, Mt. 119 34 6N 107 27W
South Bend, Ind., U.S.A. 114 41 38N 86 20W
South Bend, Wash., U.S.A. 118 46 44N 123 52W
South Boston 115 36 42N 78 58W
South Branch 107 47 55N 59 2W
South Brook 107 49 26N 56 5W
South Buganda □ 90 0 15S 31 30 E
South Carolina □ 115 33 45N 81 0W
South Charleston 114 38 20N 81 40W
South China Sea 71 10 0N 113 0 E
South Dakota □ 116 45 0N 100 0W
South Downs 13 50 53N 0 10W
South East C. 97 43 40S 146 50 E
South-East Indian Rise 94 43 0S 80 0 E
South Esk → 14 56 44N 3 3W
South Foreland 13 51 7N 1 23 E
South Fork → 118 47 54N 113 15W
South Gamboa 120 9 4N 79 40W
South Georgia 5 54 30S 37 0W
South Glamorgan □ 13 51 30N 3 20W
South Grafton 99 29 41S 152 57 E
South Haven 114 42 22N 86 20W
South Henik, L. 109 61 30N 97 30W
South Honshu Ridge 94 23 0N 143 0 E
South Horr 90 2 12N 36 56 E
South I., Kenya 90 2 35N 36 35 E
South I., N.Z. 101 44 0S 170 0 E
South Invercargill 101 46 26S 168 23 E
South Knife → 109 58 55N 94 37W
South Korea ■ 76 36 0N 128 0 E
South Loup → 116 41 4N 98 40W
South Mashonaland □ 91 18 0S 31 30 E
South Milwaukee 114 42 50N 87 52W
South Molton 13 51 1N 3 50W
South Nahanni → 108 61 3N 123 21W
South Negril Pt. 121 18 14N 78 30W
South Orkney Is. 5 63 0S 45 0W
South Pass 118 42 20N 108 58W
South Passage 96 26 07S 113 09 E
South Pines 115 35 10N 79 25W
South Pittsburg 115 35 1N 85 42W
South Platte → 116 41 7N 100 42W
South Pole 5 90 0S 0 0 E
South Porcupine 106 48 30N 81 12W
South River, Can. 106 45 52N 79 23W
South River, U.S.A. 113 40 27N 74 23W
South Ronaldsay 14 58 46N 2 58W
South Sandwich Is. 7 57 0S 27 0W
South Saskatchewan → 109 53 15N 105 5W
South Seal → 109 58 48N 98 8W
South Sentinel I. 71 11 1N 92 16 E
South Shetland Is. 5 62 0S 59 0W
South Shields 12 54 59N 1 26W
South Sioux City 116 42 30N 96 24W
South Taranaki Bight 101 39 40S 174 5 E
South Thompson → 108 50 40N 120 20W
South Twin I. 106 53 7N 79 52W
South Tyne → 12 54 46N 2 25W
South Uist 14 57 20N 7 15W
South West Africa = Namibia ■ 92 22 0S 18 9 E
South West C. 99 43 34S 146 3
South Yemen ■ 63 15 0N 48 0
South Yorkshire □ 12 53 30N 1 20W
Southampton, Can. 106 44 30N 81 25W
Southampton, U.K. 13 50 54N 1 23W
Southampton, U.S.A. 114 40 54N 72 22W
Southampton I. 105 64 30N 84 0W
Southbridge, N.Z. 101 43 48S 172 16
Southbridge, U.S.A. 113 42 4N 72 2W
Southeast Pacific Basin 95 16 30S 92 0W
Southend 109 56 19N 103 22W
Southend-on-Sea 13 51 32N 0 42
Southern □, Malawi 91 15 0S 35 0
Southern □, S. Leone 84 8 0N 12 30W
Southern □, Zambia 91 16 20S 26 20
Southern Alps 101 43 41S 170 11
Southern Cross 96 31 12S 119 15
Southern Indian L. 109 57 10N 98 30W
Southern Ocean 5 62 0S 60 0
Southern Uplands 14 55 30N 3 3W
Southington 113 41 37N 72 53W
Southold 113 41 4N 72 26W
Southport, Austral. 97 27 58S 153 25
Southport, U.K. 12 53 38N 3 1W
Southport, U.S.A. 115 33 55N 78 0W
Southwestern Pacific Basin 94 42 0S 170 0W
Southwold 13 52 19N 1 41
Soutpansberge 93 23 0S 29 30
Souvigny 20 46 33N 3 10
Sovata 46 46 35N 25 3
Sovetsk, Lithuania, U.S.S.R. 54 55 6N 21 50
Sovetsk, R.S.F.S.R., U.S.S.R. 55 57 38N 48 53
Sovetskaya 57 49 1N 42 7
Sovetskaya Gavan 59 48 50N 140 0
Sovicille 39 43 16N 11 12
Sovra 42 42 44N 17 34
Sōya-Misaki 74 45 30N 142 0
Soyo 88 6 13S 12 20
Sozh → 54 51 57N 30 48
Sozopol 43 42 23N 27 42
Spa 16 50 29N 5 53
Spain ■ 29 40 0N 5 0W
Spalding, Austral. 99 33 30S 138 37
Spalding, U.K. 12 52 47N 0 9W
Spalding, U.S.A. 116 41 45N 98 27W
Spangereid 47 58 3N 7 9
Spangler 112 40 39N 78 48W
Spaniard's Bay 107 47 38N 53 20W
Spanish 106 46 12N 82 20W
Spanish Fork 118 40 10N 111 37W
Spanish Town 121 18 0N 76 57W
Sparks 118 39 30N 119 45W
Sparta, Ga., U.S.A. 115 33 18N 82 59W
Sparta, Wis., U.S.A. 116 43 55N 90 47W
Sparta = Spárti 45 37 5N 22 25
Spartanburg 115 35 0N 82 0W
Spartansburg 112 41 48N 79 43W
Spartel, C. 82 35 47N 5 56W
Spárti 45 37 5N 22 25
Spartivento, C., Calabria, Italy 41 37 56N 16 4
Spartivento, C., Sard., Italy 40 38 52N 8 50
Spas-Demensk 54 54 20N 34 0
Spas-Klepiki 55 55 10N 40 10
Spassk-Dalniy 59 44 40N 132 48
Spassk-Ryazanskiy 55 54 24N 40 25
Spátha, Ákra 45 35 42N 23 43
Spatsizi → 108 57 42N 128 7W
Spearfish 116 44 32N 103 52W
Spearman 117 36 15N 101 10W
Speers 109 52 43N 107 34W
Speightstown 121 13 15N 59 39W
Speke Gulf 90 2 20S 32 50
Spenard 104 61 11N 149 50W
Spence Bay 104 69 32N 93 32W
Spencer, Idaho, U.S.A. 118 44 18N 112 8W
Spencer, Iowa, U.S.A. 116 43 5N 95 19W
Spencer, N.Y., U.S.A. 113 42 14N 76 30W
Spencer, Nebr., U.S.A. 116 42 52N 98 43W
Spencer, W. Va., U.S.A. 114 38 47N 81 24W
Spencer B. 92 25 30S 14 47
Spencer, C. 97 35 20S 136 53
Spencer G. 97 34 0S 137 20
Spencerville 113 44 51N 75 33W
Spences Bridge 108 50 25N 121 20W
Spenser Mts. 101 42 15S 172 45
Sperkhiós → 45 38 57N 22 3
Sperrin Mts. 15 54 50N 7 0W
Spessart 25 50 10N 9 20
Spétsai 45 37 15N 23 10
Spey → 14 57 26N 3 25W
Speyer 25 49 19N 8 26
Speyer → 25 49 19N 8 27
Spézia, La 38 44 8N 9 50
Spezzano Albanese 41 39 41N 16 19
Spiekeroog 24 53 45N 7 42
Spielfeld 39 46 43N 15 38
Spiez 25 46 40N 7 40
Spili 45 35 13N 24 31
Spilimbergo 39 46 7N 12 53
Spinazzola 41 40 58N 16 5
Spind 47 58 6N 6 53
Spineni 46 44 43N 24 37
Spirit Lake 118 47 56N 116 56W
Spirit River 108 55 45N 118 50W
Spiritwood 109 53 24N 107 33W
Spišská Nová Ves 27 48 58N 20 34
Spišské Podhradie 27 49 0N 20 48
Spital 26 47 42N 14 18
Spithead 13 50 43N 1 5W
Spittal 26 46 48N 13 31
Spitzbergen = Svalbard 4 78 0N 17 0
Split 39 43 31N 16 26
Split L. 109 56 8N 96 15W
Splitski Kanal 39 43 31N 16 20
Splügenpass 25 46 30N 9 20
Spoffard 117 29 10N 100 27W
Spokane 118 47 45N 118 25W
Spoleto 39 42 46N 12 47
Spooner 116 45 49N 91 51W
Sporádhes 45 39 0N 24 30
Sporyy Navolok, Mys 58 75 50N 68 40
Spragge 106 46 15N 82 40W

Sprague 118 47 18N 117 59W
Sprague River 118 42 28N 121 31W
Spratly, I. 72 8 20N 112 0 E
Spray 118 44 50N 119 46W
Spree → 24 52 32N 13 13 E
Spring City 118 39 31N 111 28W
Spring Mts. 119 36 20N 115 43W
Spring Valley, Minn., U.S.A. 116 43 40N 92 23W
Spring Valley, N.Y., U.S.A. 113 41 7N 74 4W
Springbok 92 29 42S 17 54 E
Springburn 101 43 40S 171 32 E
Springdale, Can. 107 49 30N 56 6W
Springdale, Ark., U.S.A. 117 36 10N 94 5W
Springdale, Wash., U.S.A. 118 48 1N 117 50W
Springe 24 52 12N 9 35 E
Springer 117 36 22N 104 36W
Springerville 119 34 10N 109 16W
Springfield, Can. 112 42 50N 80 56W
Springfield, N.Z. 101 43 19S 171 56 E
Springfield, Colo., U.S.A. 117 37 26N 102 40W
Springfield, Ill., U.S.A. 116 39 48N 89 40W
Springfield, Mass., U.S.A. 114 42 8N 72 37W
Springfield, Mo., U.S.A. 117 37 15N 93 20W
Springfield, Ohio, U.S.A. 114 39 58N 83 48W
Springfield, Oreg., U.S.A. 118 44 2N 123 0W
Springfield, Tenn., U.S.A. 115 36 35N 86 55W
Springfield, Vt., U.S.A. 113 43 20N 72 30W
Springfontein 92 30 15S 25 40 E
Springhill 107 45 40N 64 4W
Springhouse 108 51 56N 122 7W
Springhurst 99 36 10S 146 31 E
Springs 93 26 13S 28 25 E
Springsure 97 24 8S 148 6 E
Springvale, Austral. 98 23 33S 140 42 E
Springvale, U.S.A. 113 43 28N 70 48W
Springville, N.Y., U.S.A. 114 42 31N 78 41W
Springville, Utah, U.S.A. 118 40 14N 111 35W
Springwater 109 51 58N 108 23W
Spruce-Creek 112 40 36N 78 9W
Spur 117 33 28N 100 50W
Spurn Hd. 12 53 34N 0 8 E
Spuž 42 42 32N 19 10 E
Spuzzum 108 49 37N 121 23W
Squam L. 113 43 45N 71 32W
Squamish 108 49 45N 123 10W
Square Islands 107 52 47N 55 47W
Squillace, Golfo di 41 38 43N 16 35 E
Squinzano 41 40 27N 18 1 E
Sragen 73 7 28S 110 59 E
Srbac 42 45 7N 17 30 E
Srbija □ 42 43 30N 21 0 E
Srbobran 42 45 32N 19 48 E
Sre Umbell 71 11 8N 103 46 E
Srebrnica 42 44 10N 19 18 E
Sredinnyy Khrebet 59 57 0N 160 0 E
Središče 39 46 24N 16 17 E
Sredna Gora 43 42 40N 24 20 E
Sredne Tambovskoye 59 50 55N 137 45 E
Srednekolymsk 59 67 27N 153 40 E
Srednevilyuysk 59 63 50N 123 5 E
Średni Rodopi 43 41 40N 24 45 E
Śrem 28 52 6N 17 2 E
Sremska Mitrovica 42 44 59N 19 33 E
Sremski Karlovci 42 45 12N 19 56 E
Sretensk 59 52 10N 117 40 E
Sri Lanka ■ 70 7 30N 80 50 E
Sriharikota, I. 70 13 40N 80 20 E
Srikakulam 70 18 14N 83 58 E
Srinagar 66 34 5N 74 50 E
Sripur 69 24 14N 90 30 E
Srirangam 70 10 54N 78 42 E
Srirangapatnam 70 12 26N 76 43 E
Srivilliputtur 70 9 31N 77 40 E
Środa Śląska 28 51 10N 16 36 E
Środa Wielkopolski 28 52 15N 17 19 E
Srokowo 28 54 13N 21 31 E
Srpska Crnja 42 45 38N 20 44 E
Srpska Itabej 42 45 35N 20 44 E
Staaten → 98 16 24S 141 17 E
Staberhuk 24 54 23N 11 18 E
Stade 24 53 35N 9 31 E
Staðarhólskirkja 50 65 23N 21 58W
Städjan 48 61 56N 12 52 E
Stadlandet 47 62 10N 5 10 E
Stadskanaal 16 53 4N 6 55 E
Stadthagen 24 52 20N 9 14 E
Stadtlohn 24 52 0N 6 52 E
Stadtroda 24 50 51N 11 44 E
Stafafell 50 64 25N 14 52W
Staffa 14 56 26N 6 21W
Stafford, U.K. 12 52 49N 2 9W
Stafford, U.S.A. 117 38 0N 98 35W
Stafford □ 12 52 53N 2 10W
Stafford Springs 113 41 58N 72 20W
Stagnone 40 37 50N 12 28 E
Staines 13 51 26N 0 30W
Stainz 26 46 53N 15 17 E
Stalač 42 43 43N 21 28 E
Stalingrad = Volgograd 57 48 40N 44 25 E
Staliniri = Tskhinvali 57 42 14N 44 1 E
Stalino = Donetsk 56 48 0N 37 45 E
Stalinogorsk = Novomoskovsk 55 54 5N 38 15 E
Stalowa Wola 28 50 34N 22 3 E
Stalybridge 12 53 29N 2 4W
Stamford, Austral. 98 21 15S 143 46 E
Stamford, U.K. 13 52 39N 0 29W
Stamford, Conn., U.S.A. 114 41 5N 73 30W
Stamford, Tex., U.S.A. 117 32 58N 99 50W
Stamps 117 33 22N 93 30W
Stanberry 116 40 12N 94 32W
Standerton 93 26 55S 29 7 E
Standish 114 43 58N 83 57W
Stanford 118 47 11N 110 10W
Stange 47 60 43N 11 5 E
Stanger 93 29 27S 31 14 E
Stanišić 42 45 56N 19 10 E
Stanislav = Ivano-Frankovsk 54 49 0N 24 40 E
Stanisławów 28 52 18N 21 33 E
Stanke Dimitrov 42 42 17N 23 9 E
Stanley, Austral. 99 40 46S 145 19 E
Stanley, N.B., Can. 107 46 20N 66 44W
Stanley, Sask., Can. 109 55 24N 104 22W
Stanley, Falk. Is. 128 51 40S 59 51W
Stanley, Idaho, U.S.A. 118 44 10N 114 59W
Stanley, N.D., U.S.A. 116 48 20N 102 23W
Stanley, N.Y., U.S.A. 112 42 48N 77 6W
Stanley, Wis., U.S.A. 116 44 57N 91 0W
Stanley Res. 70 11 50N 77 40 E
Stann Creek 120 17 0N 88 13W
Stanovoy Khrebet 59 55 0N 130 0 E
Stanthorpe 97 28 36S 151 59 E
Stanton 117 32 8N 101 45W
Staples 116 46 21N 94 48W
Stapleton 116 41 30N 100 31W
Staporków 28 51 9N 20 31 E
Star City 109 52 50N 104 20W
Stara-minskaya 57 46 33N 39 0 E
Stara Moravica 42 45 50N 19 30 E
Stara Pazova 42 45 0N 20 10 E
Stara Planina 43 43 15N 23 0 E
Stara Zagora 43 42 26N 25 39 E
Starachowice 28 51 3N 21 2 E
Starashcherbinovskaya 57 46 40N 38 53 E
Staraya Russa 54 57 58N 31 23 E
Starbuck I. 95 5 37S 155 55W
Stargard 24 53 29N 13 19 E
Stargard Szczeciński 28 53 20N 15 0 E
Stari Bar 42 42 7N 19 13 E
Stari Trg 39 45 29N 15 7 E
Staritsa 54 56 33N 35 0 E
Starke 115 30 0N 82 10W
Starkville, Colo., U.S.A. 117 37 10N 104 31W
Starkville, Miss., U.S.A. 115 33 26N 88 48W
Starnberg 25 48 0N 11 20 E
Starnberger See 25 47 55N 11 20 E
Starobelsk 57 49 16N 39 0 E
Starodub 54 52 30N 32 50 E
Starogard 28 53 59N 18 30 E
Starokonstantinov 56 49 48N 27 10 E
Starosielce 28 53 8N 23 5 E
Start Pt. 13 50 13N 3 38W
Stary Sącz 27 49 33N 20 35 E
Staryy Biryuzyak 57 44 46N 46 50 E
Staryy Chartoriysk 54 51 15N 25 54 E
Staryy Kheydzhan 59 60 0N 144 50 E
Staryy Krym 56 45 3N 35 8 E
Staryy Oskol 55 51 19N 37 55 E
Stassfurt 24 51 51N 11 34 E
Staszów 28 50 33N 21 10 E
State College 114 40 47N 77 49W
Staten I. 113 40 35N 74 10W
Staten, I. = Los Estados, I. de 128 54 40S 64 30W
Statesboro 115 32 26N 81 46W
Statesville 115 35 48N 80 51W
Staunton, Ill., U.S.A. 116 39 0N 89 49W
Staunton, Va., U.S.A. 114 38 7N 79 4W
Stavanger 47 58 57N 5 40 E
Stavelot 16 50 23N 5 55 E
Staveren 16 52 53N 5 22 E
Stavern 47 59 0N 10 1 E
Stavre 48 62 51N 15 19 E
Stavropol 57 45 5N 42 0 E
Stavroúpolis 44 41 12N 24 45 E
Stawell 97 37 5S 142 47 E
Stawell → 98 20 20S 142 55 E
Stawiski 28 53 22N 22 9 E
Stawiszyn 28 51 56N 18 4 E
Stayner 112 44 25N 80 5W
Steamboat Springs 118 40 30N 106 50W
Stębark 28 53 30N 20 10 E
Stebleva 44 41 18N 20 33 E
Steele 116 46 56N 99 52W
Steelton 114 40 17N 76 50W
Steelville 117 37 57N 91 21W
Steen River 108 59 40N 117 12W
Steenvoorde 19 50 48N 2 33 E
Steenwijk 16 52 47N 6 7 E
Steep Pt. 96 26 08S 113 8 E
Steep Rock 109 51 30N 98 48W
Ştefăneşti 46 47 44N 27 15 E
Stefanie L. = Chew Bahir 87 4 40N 36 50 E
Stefansson Bay 5 67 20S 59 8 E
Stege 49 55 0N 12 18 E
Steiermark □ 26 47 26N 15 0 E
Steigerwald 25 49 45N 10 30 E
Steinbach 109 49 32N 96 40W
Steinfort 16 49 39N 5 55 E
Steinheim 24 51 50N 9 6 E
Steinhuder Meer 24 52 48N 9 20 E
Steinkjer 50 63 59N 11 31 E
Stellaland 92 26 45S 24 50 E
Stellarton 107 45 32N 62 30W
Stellenbosch 92 33 58S 18 50 E
Stemshaug 47 63 19N 8 44 E
Stendal 24 52 36N 11 50 E
Stensele 50 65 3N 17 8 E
Stenstorp 49 58 17N 13 45 E
Stepanakert 53 39 40N 46 25 E
Stephan 116 48 30N 96 53W
Stephens Creek 99 31 50S 141 30 E
Stephens I. 108 54 10N 130 45W
Stephenville, Can. 107 48 31N 58 35W
Stephenville, U.S.A. 117 32 12N 98 12W
Stepnica 28 53 38N 14 36 E
Stepnoi = Elista 57 46 16N 44 14 E
Stepnyak 58 52 50N 70 50 E
Steppe 60 50 0N 50 0 E
Stereá Ellas □ 45 38 50N 22 0 E
Sterkstroom 92 31 32S 26 32 E
Sterling, Colo., U.S.A. 116 40 40N 103 15W
Sterling, Ill., U.S.A. 116 41 45N 89 45W
Sterling, Kans., U.S.A. 116 38 17N 98 13W
Sterling City 117 31 50N 100 59W
Sterling Run 112 41 25N 78 12W
Sterlitamak 52 53 40N 56 0 E
Sternberg 24 53 42N 11 48 E
Šternberk 27 49 45N 17 15 E
Stettin = Szczecin 28 53 27N 14 27 E
Stettiner Haff 24 53 50N 14 25 E
Stettler 108 52 19N 112 40W
Steubenville 114 40 21N 80 39W
Stevens Port 116 44 32N 89 34W
Stevenson L. 109 53 55N 96 0W
Stevns Klint 49 55 17N 12 28 E
Stewart, B.C., Can. 108 55 56N 129 57W
Stewart, N.W.T., Can. 104 63 19N 139 26W
Stewart, I. 128 54 50S 71 15W
Stewart I. 101 46 58S 167 54 E
Stewiacke 107 45 9N 63 22W
Steynsburg 92 31 15S 25 49 E
Steyr 26 48 3N 14 25 E
Steyr → 26 48 17N 14 15 E
Steytlerville 92 33 17S 24 19 E
Stia 39 43 48N 11 41 E
Stigler 117 35 19N 95 6W
Stigliano 41 40 24N 16 13 E
Stigsnæs 49 55 13N 11 18 E
Stigtomta 49 58 47N 16 48 E
Stikine → 104 56 40N 132 30W
Stilfontein 92 26 50S 26 50 E
Stilís 45 38 55N 22 47 E
Stillwater, Minn., U.S.A. 116 45 3N 92 47W
Stillwater, N.Y., U.S.A. 113 42 55N 73 41W
Stillwater, Okla., U.S.A. 117 36 5N 97 3W
Stillwater Mts. 118 39 45N 118 6W
Stilwell 117 35 52N 94 36W
Stimfalías, L. 45 37 51N 22 27 E
Štip 42 41 42N 22 10 E
Stíra 45 38 9N 24 14 E
Stiring-Wendel 19 49 12N 6 57 E
Stirling, Austral. 98 17 12S 141 35 E
Stirling, Can. 108 49 30N 112 30W
Stirling, U.K. 14 56 7N 3 57W
Stirling Ra. 96 34 23S 118 0 E
Stittsville 113 45 15N 75 55W
Stockach 25 47 51N 9 01 E
Stockaryd 49 57 19N 14 36 E
Stockerau 27 48 24N 16 12 E
Stockett 118 47 23N 111 7W
Stockholm 48 59 20N 18 3 E
Stockholms län □ 48 59 30N 18 20 E
Stockinbingal 100 34 30S 147 53 E
Stockport 12 53 25N 2 11W
Stockton, Austral. 100 32 50S 151 47 E
Stockton, Calif., U.S.A. 119 38 0N 121 20W
Stockton, Kans., U.S.A. 116 39 30N 99 20W
Stockton, Mo., U.S.A. 117 37 40N 93 48W
Stockton-on-Tees 12 54 34N 1 20W
Stockvik 48 62 17N 17 23 E
Stoczek Łukowski 28 51 58N 22 0 E
Stöde 48 62 28N 16 35 E
Stogovo 42 41 31N 20 38 E
Stoke-on-Trent 12 53 1N 2 11W
Stokes Bay 106 45 0N 81 28W
Stokes Pt. 99 40 10S 143 56 E
Stokkseyri 50 63 50N 21 2W
Stokksnes 50 64 14N 14 58W
Stolac 42 43 8N 17 59 E
Stolberg 24 50 48N 6 13 E
Stolbovaya, R.S.F.S.R., U.S.S.R. 55 55 10N 37 32 E
Stolbovaya, R.S.F.S.R., U.S.S.R. 59 64 50N 153 50 E
Stolbovoy, Ostrov 59 56 44N 163 14 E
Stolbtsy 54 53 30N 26 43 E
Stolin 54 51 53N 26 50 E
Stolnici 46 44 31N 24 48 E
Ston 42 42 51N 17 43 E
Stonehaven 14 56 58N 2 11W
Stonehenge 98 24 22S 143 17 E
Stonewall 109 50 10N 97 19W
Stonington I. 5 68 11S 67 0W
Stony L., Man., Can. 109 58 51N 98 40W
Stony L., Ont., Can. 112 44 30N 78 0W
Stony Rapids 109 59 16N 105 50W
Stony Tunguska = Tunguska, Nizhnyaya → 59 65 48N 88 4 E
Stopnica 28 50 27N 20 57 E
Stora Gla 48 59 30N 12 30 E
Stora Karlsö 49 57 17N 17 59 E
Stora Lulevatten 50 67 10N 19 30 E
Stora Sjöfallet 50 67 29N 18 40 E
Storavan 50 65 45N 18 10 E
Stordal 47 63 28N 10 56 E
Store Bælt 49 55 20N 11 0 E
Store Creek 99 32 54S 149 6 E
Store Heddinge 49 55 18N 12 23 E
Støren 47 63 3N 10 18 E
Storfjorden 47 62 25N 6 30 E
Storm B. 97 43 10S 147 30 E
Storm Lake 116 42 35N 95 11W
Stormberg 92 31 16S 26 17 E
Stormsrivier 92 33 59S 23 52 E
Stornoway 14 58 12N 6 23W
Storozhinets 56 48 14N 25 45 E
Storsjö 48 62 49N 13 5 E
Storsjöen, Hedmark, Norway 47 60 20N 11 40 E
Storsjöen, Hedmark, Norway 47 61 30N 11 14 E
Storsjön, Gävleborg, Sweden 48 60 35N 16 45 E
Storsjön, Jämtland, Sweden 48 62 50N 13 8 E
Storstrøms Amt. □ 49 54 50N 11 45 E
Storuman 50 65 5N 17 10 E
Storuman,sjö 50 65 13N 16 50 E
Storvik 48 60 35N 16 33 E
Stoughton 109 49 40N 103 0W
Stour →, Dorset, U.K. 13 50 48N 2 7W
Stour →, Here. & Worcs., U.K. 13 52 25N 2 13W
Stour →, Suffolk, U.K. 13 51 55N 1 5 E
Stour (Gt. Stour) → 13 51 15N 1 20 E
Stourbridge 13 52 28N 2 8W
Stout, L. 109 52 0N 94 40W
Stowmarket 13 52 11N 1 0 E
Strabane 15 54 50N 7 28W
Strabane □ 15 54 45N 7 25W
Stracin 42 42 13N 22 2 E
Stradella 38 45 4N 9 20 E
Strahan 97 42 9S 145 20 E
Strakonice 26 49 15N 13 53 E
Straldzha 43 42 35N 26 40 E
Stralsund 24 54 17N 13 5 E
Strand, Norway 47 61 17N 11 17 E
Strand, S. Afr. 92 34 9S 18 48 E
Stranda 47 62 19N 6 58 E
Strandebarm 47 60 17N 6 0 E
Strandvik 47 60 9N 5 41 E
Strangford, L. 15 54 30N 5 37W
Strängnäs 48 59 23N 17 2 E
Stranraer 14 54 54N 5 0W
Strasbourg, Can. 109 51 4N 104 55W
Strasbourg, France 19 48 35N 7 42 E
Strasburg, Ger. 24 53 30N 13 44 E
Strasburg, U.S.A. 116 46 12N 100 9W
Stratford, Austral. 100 37 59S 147 7 E
Stratford, Can. 106 43 23N 81 0W
Stratford, N.Z. 101 39 20S 174 19 E
Stratford, Calif., U.S.A. 119 36 10N 119 49W
Stratford, Conn., U.S.A. 113 41 13N 73 8W
Stratford, Tex., U.S.A. 117 36 20N 102 3W
Stratford-on-Avon 13 52 12N 1 42W
Strath Spey 14 57 15N 3 40W
Strathalbyn 99 35 13S 138 53 E
Strathclyde □ 14 56 0N 4 50W
Strathcona Prov. Park 108 49 38N 125 40W
Strathmore, Austral. 98 17 50S 142 35 E
Strathmore, Can. 108 51 5N 113 18W
Strathmore, U.K. 14 56 40N 3 4W
Strathnaver 108 53 20N 122 33W
Strathpeffer 14 57 35N 4 32W
Strathroy 106 42 58N 81 38W
Strathy Pt. 14 58 35N 4 0W
Stratton, U.K. 12 51 41N 1 45W
Stratton, U.S.A. 116 39 20N 102 36W
Straubing 25 48 53N 12 35 E
Straumnes 50 66 26N 23 8W
Strausberg 24 52 40N 13 52 E
Strawberry Res. 118 40 10N 111 7W
Strawn 117 32 36N 98 30W
Strážnice 27 48 54N 17 19 E
Streaky Bay 96 32 48S 134 13 E
Streator 116 41 9N 88 52W
Středočeský □ 26 49 55N 14 30 E
Středoslovenský □ 27 48 30N 19 15 E
Streeter 116 46 39N 99 21W
Streetsville 112 43 35N 79 42W
Strehaia 46 44 37N 23 10 E
Strelcha 43 42 25N 24 19 E
Strelka 59 58 5N 93 3 E
Strésa 38 45 52N 8 28 E
Strezhevoy 58 60 42N 77 34 E
Stříbro 26 49 44N 13 0 E
Strickland → 98 7 35S 141 36 E
Strimón → 44 40 46N 23 51 E
Strimonikós Kólpos 44 40 33N 24 0 E
Strofádhes 45 37 15N 21 0 E
Strombacka 48 61 58N 16 44 E
Strómboli 41 38 48N 15 12 E
Stromeferry 14 57 20N 5 33W
Stromness 14 58 58N 3 18W
Ströms vattudal 50 64 15N 14 55 E
Strömsnäsbruk 49 56 35N 13 45 E
Strömstad 48 58 55N 11 15 E
Strömsund 50 63 51N 15 33 E
Stróngoli 41 39 16N 17 2 E
Stronsay 14 59 8N 2 38W
Stronsburg 116 41 7N 97 36W
Stropkov 27 49 13N 21 39 E
Stroud 13 51 44N 2 12W
Stroud Road 99 32 18S 151 57 E
Stroudsberg 113 40 59N 75 15W
Struer 49 56 30N 8 35 E
Struga 42 41 13N 20 44 E
Strugi Krasnyye 54 58 21N 29 1 E
Strumica 42 41 28N 22 41 E
Strumica → 42 41 20N 22 22 E
Struthers, Can. 106 48 41N 85 51W
Struthers, U.S.A. 114 41 6N 80 38W
Stryama 43 42 16N 24 54 E
Stryi 54 49 16N 23 48 E
Stryker 108 48 40N 114 44W
Stryków 28 51 55N 19 33 E
Strzegom 28 50 58N 16 20 E
Strzelce Krajeńskie 28 52 52N 15 33 E
Strzelce Opolskie 28 50 31N 18 18 E
Strzelecki Cr. → 97 29 37S 139 59 E
Strzelin 28 50 46N 17 2 E
Strzelno 28 52 35N 18 9 E
Strzybnica 28 50 28N 18 48 E
Strzyżów 27 49 52N 21 47 E
Stuart, Fla., U.S.A. 115 27 11N 80 12W
Stuart, Nebr., U.S.A. 116 42 39N 99 8W
Stuart → 108 54 0N 123 35W
Stuart L. 108 54 30N 124 30W
Stuart Range 96 29 10S 134 56 E
Stuart Town 100 32 44S 149 4 E
Stubbekøbing 49 54 53N 12 9 E
Stuben 26 47 10N 10 8 E
Studen Kladenets, Yazovir 43 41 37N 25 30 E
Stugun 48 63 10N 15 40 E
Stühlingen 25 47 44N 8 26 E
Stull, L. 109 54 24N 92 34W
Stung Treng 71 13 31N 105 58 E
Stupart → 109 56 0N 93 25W
Stupino 55 54 57N 38 2 E
Sturgeon B. 109 52 0N 97 50W
Sturgeon Bay 114 44 52N 87 20W
Sturgeon Falls 106 46 25N 79 57W
Sturgeon L., Alta., Can. 108 55 6N 117 32W
Sturgeon L., Ont., Can. 106 50 0N 90 45W
Sturgeon L., Ont., Can. 112 44 28N 78 43W
Sturgis, Mich., U.S.A. 114 41 50N 85 25W
Sturgis, S.D., U.S.A. 116 44 25N 103 30W
Sturkö 49 56 5N 15 42 E
Štúrovo 27 47 48N 18 41 E
Sturt Cr. → 96 20 8S 127 24 E
Stutterheim 92 32 33S 27 28 E
Stuttgart, Ger. 25 48 46N 9 10 E
Stuttgart, U.S.A. 117 34 30N 91 33W
Stuyvesant 113 42 23N 73 45W
Stykkishólmur 50 65 2N 22 40W
Styr → 54 52 7N 26 35 E
Styria = Steiermark □ 26 47 26N 15 0 E
Su Xian 77 33 41N 116 59 E
Suakin 86 19 8N 37 20 E
Suaqui 120 29 12N 109 41W
Subang 73 6 34S 107 45 E
Subi 72 2 58N 108 50 E
Subiaco 39 41 56N 13 5 E
Subotica 42 46 6N 19 49 E
Success 109 50 28N 108 6W
Suceava 46 47 38N 26 16 E

Suceava □ 46 47 37N 25 40 E
Suceava → 46 47 38N 26 16 E
Sucha-Beskidzka 27 49 44N 19 35 E
Suchan 28 53 18N 15 18 E
Suchedniów 28 51 3N 20 49 E
Suchitoto 120 13 56N 89 0W
Suchou = Suzhou 75 31 18N 120 36 E
Süchow = Xuzhou 77 34 18N 117 10 E
Suchowola 28 53 33N 23 3 E
Suck → 15 53 17N 8 18W
Suckling, Mt. 98 9 49 S 148 53 E
Sucre 126 19 0 S 65 15W
Sućuraj 39 43 10N 17 8 E
Sud-Ouest, Pte. du 107 49 23N 63 36W
Sud, Pte. 107 49 3N 62 14W
Suda → 55 59 0N 37 40 E
Sudair 64 26 0N 45 0 E
Sudak 56 44 51N 34 57 E
Sudan 117 34 4N 102 32W
Sudan ■ 81 15 0N 30 0 E
Suday 55 59 0N 43 0 E
Sudbury 106 46 30N 81 0W
Sûdd 87 8 20N 30 0 E
Süderbrarup 24 54 38N 9 47 E
Süderlügum 24 54 50N 8 55 E
Süderoog-Sand 24 54 27N 8 30 E
Sudetan Mts. = Sudety 27 50 20N 16 45 E
Sudety 27 50 20N 16 45 E
Sudi 91 10 11 S 39 57 E
Sudirman, Pegunungan 73 4 30 S 137 0 E
Sudiţi 46 44 35N 27 38 E
Sudogda 55 55 55N 40 50 E
Sudr 86 29 40N 32 42 E
Sudzha 54 51 14N 35 17 E
Sueca 33 39 12N 0 21W
Suedala 49 55 30N 13 15 E
Sueur, Le 116 44 25N 93 52W
Suez = El Suweis 86 28 40N 33 0 E
Suez Canal = Suweis, Qanâl es 86 31 0N 33 20 E
Sūf 62 32 19N 35 49 E
Şufaynah 64 23 6N 40 33 E
Suffield 109 50 12N 111 10W
Suffolk 114 36 47N 76 33W
Suffolk □ 13 52 16N 1 0 E
Sufuk 65 23 50N 51 50 E
Şugag 46 45 47N 23 37 E
Sugar City 116 38 18N 103 38W
Sugluk = Sagloue 105 62 30N 74 15W
Suhaia, L. 46 43 45N 25 15 E
Suhār 65 24 20N 56 40 E
Suhbaatar 75 50 17N 106 10 E
Suhl 24 50 35N 10 40 E
Suhl □ 24 50 37N 10 43 E
Sui Xian, Henan, China 77 34 25N 115 2 E
Sui Xian, Henan, China 77 31 42N 113 24 E
Suichang 77 28 29N 119 15 E
Suichuan 77 26 20N 114 32 E
Suide 76 37 30N 110 12 E
Suifenhe 76 44 25N 131 10 E
Suihua 75 46 32N 126 55 E
Suining, Hunan, China 77 26 35N 110 10 E
Suining, Sichuan, China 77 30 26N 105 35 E
Suiping 77 33 10N 113 59 E
Suippes 19 49 8N 4 30 E
Suir → 15 52 15N 7 10W
Suixi 77 21 19N 110 18 E
Suizhong 76 40 21N 120 20 E
Sujangarh 68 27 42N 74 31 E
Sujica 42 43 52N 17 11 E
Sukabumi 73 6 56 S 106 50 E
Sukadana, Kalimantan, Indon. 72 1 10 S 110 0 E
Sukadana, Sumatera, Indon. 72 5 5 S 105 33 E
Sukaradja 72 2 28 S 110 25 E
Sukarnapura = Jayapura 73 2 37 S 140 38 E
Sukhindol 43 43 11N 25 10 E
Sukhinichi 54 54 8N 35 10 E
Sukhona → 52 60 30N 45 0 E
Sukhumi 57 43 0N 41 0 E
Sukkur 68 27 42N 68 54 E
Sukkur Barrage 68 27 40N 68 50 E
Sukma 70 18 24N 81 45 E
Sukovo 42 43 4N 22 37 E
Sukunka → 108 55 45N 121 15W
Sula → 54 49 40N 32 41 E
Sula, Kepulauan 73 1 45 S 125 0 E
Sulaiman Range 68 30 30N 69 50 E
Sulak → 57 43 20N 47 34 E
Sulam Tsor 62 33 4N 35 6 E
Sulawesi □ 73 2 0 S 120 0 E
Sulechów 28 52 5N 15 40 E
Sulęcin 28 52 26N 15 10 E
Sulejów 28 51 26N 19 53 E
Sulejówek 28 52 13N 21 17 E
Sulima 84 6 58N 11 32W
Sulina 46 45 10N 29 40 E
Sulingen 24 52 41N 8 47 E
Suliţa 46 47 39N 26 59 E
Sulitälma 50 67 17N 17 28 E
Sulitjelma 50 67 9N 16 3 E
Sułkowice 27 49 50N 19 49 E
Sullana 126 4 52 S 80 39W
Sullivan, Ill., U.S.A. 116 39 40N 88 40W
Sullivan, Ind., U.S.A. 114 39 5N 87 26W
Sullivan, Mo., U.S.A. 116 38 10N 91 10W
Sullivan Bay 108 50 55N 126 50W
Sully-sur-Loire 19 47 45N 2 20 E
Sulmierzyce 28 51 37N 17 32 E
Sulmona 39 42 3N 13 55 E
Sulphur, La., U.S.A. 117 30 13N 93 22W
Sulphur, Okla., U.S.A. 117 34 35N 97 0W
Sulphur Pt. 108 60 56N 114 48W
Sulphur Springs 117 33 5N 95 36W
Sulphur Springs, Cr. → 117 32 12N 101 36W
Sultan 106 47 36N 82 47W
Sultanpur 69 26 18N 82 4 E
Sultsa 52 63 27N 46 2 E
Sulu Arch. 73 6 0N 121 0 E
Sulu Sea 73 8 0N 120 0 E
Sululta 87 9 10N 38 43 E
Suluq 83 31 44N 20 14 E
Sulzbach 25 49 18N 7 4 E
Sulzbach-Rosenberg 25 49 30N 11 46 E
Sumalata 73 1 0N 122 31 E
Sumampa 124 29 25 S 63 29W
Sumatera □ 72 0 40N 100 20 E
Sumatera Barat □ 72 1 0 S 100 0 E
Sumatera Selatan □ 72 3 30 S 104 0 E
Sumatera Utara □ 72 2 0N 99 0 E
Sumatra 118 46 38N 107 31W
Sumatra = Sumatera □ 72 0 40N 100 20 E
Sumba 73 9 45 S 119 35 E
Sumba, Selat 73 9 0 S 118 40 E
Sumbawa 72 8 26 S 117 30 E
Sumbawa Besar 72 8 30 S 117 26 E
Sumbawanga □ 90 8 0 S 31 30 E
Sumbing 73 7 19 S 110 3 E
Sumburgh Hd. 14 59 52N 1 17W
Sumedang 73 6 49 S 107 56 E
Sümeg 27 46 59N 17 20 E
Sumenep 73 7 3 S 113 51 E
Sumgait 57 40 34N 49 38 E
Summer L. 118 42 50N 120 50W
Summerland 108 49 32N 119 41W
Summerside 107 46 24N 63 47W
Summerville, Ga., U.S.A. 115 34 30N 85 20W
Summerville, S.C., U.S.A. 115 33 2N 80 11W
Summit Lake 108 54 20N 122 40W
Summit Pk. 119 37 20N 106 48W
Sumner 116 42 49N 92 7W
Sumperk 27 49 59N 17 0 E
Sumter 115 33 55N 80 22W
Sumy 54 50 57N 34 50 E
Sunart, L. 14 56 42N 5 43W
Sunburst 118 48 56N 111 59W
Sunbury, Austral. 99 37 35 S 144 44 E
Sunbury, U.S.A. 114 40 50N 76 46W
Sunchales 124 30 58 S 61 35W
Suncho Corral 124 27 55 S 63 27W
Sunchon 77 34 52N 127 31 E
Suncook 113 43 8N 71 27W
Sunda Is. 94 5 0 S 105 0 E
Sunda Kecil, Kepulauan 72 7 30 S 117 0 E
Sunda, Selat 72 6 20 S 105 30 E
Sundance 116 44 27N 104 27W
Sundarbans, The 69 22 0N 89 0 E
Sundargarh 69 22 4N 84 5 E
Sundays = Sondags → 92 33 44 S 25 51 E
Sundbyberg 48 59 22N 17 58 E
Sunderland, Can. 112 44 16N 79 4W
Sunderland, U.K. 12 54 54N 1 22W
Sunderland, U.S.A. 113 42 27N 72 36W
Sundre 108 51 49N 114 38W
Sundridge 106 45 45N 79 25W
Sunds 49 56 13N 9 1 E
Sundsjö 48 62 59N 15 9 E
Sundsvall 48 62 23N 17 17 E
Sungaigerong 72 2 59 S 104 52 E
Sungailiat 72 1 51 S 106 8 E
Sungaipakning 72 1 19N 102 0 E
Sungaipenuh 72 2 1 S 101 20 E
Sungaitiram 72 0 45 S 117 8 E
Sungari = Songhua Jiang → 76 47 45N 132 30 E
Sungei Patani 71 5 38N 100 29 E
Sungei Siput 71 4 51N 101 6 E
Sungguminasa 73 5 17 S 119 30 E
Sunghua Chiang = Songhua Jiang → 76 47 45N 132 30 E
Sungikai 87 12 20N 29 51 E
Sungtao Hu 77 19 20N 109 35 E
Sungurlu 56 40 12N 34 21 E
Sunja 39 45 21N 16 35 E
Sunndalsøra 47 62 40N 8 33 E
Sunne 48 59 52N 13 5 E
Sunnfjord 47 61 25N 5 18 E
Sunnyside, Utah, U.S.A. 118 39 34N 110 24W
Sunnyside, Wash., U.S.A. 118 46 24N 120 2W
Sunray 117 36 1N 101 47W
Sunshine 100 37 48 S 144 52 E
Suntar 59 62 15N 117 30 E
Sunyani 84 7 21N 2 22W
Suoyarvi 52 62 12N 32 23 E
Supai 119 36 14N 112 44W
Supaul 69 26 10N 86 40 E
Superior, Ariz., U.S.A. 119 33 19N 111 9W
Superior, Mont., U.S.A. 118 47 15N 114 57W
Superior, Nebr., U.S.A. 116 40 3N 98 2W
Superior, Wis., U.S.A. 116 46 45N 92 5W
Superior, L. 111 47 40N 87 0W
Supetar 39 43 25N 16 32 E
Suphan Buri 71 14 14N 100 10 E
Suphan Dağı 64 38 54N 42 48 E
Suprasl 28 53 13N 23 19 E
Suq al Jum'ah 83 32 58N 13 12 E
Sūq ash Shūyukh 64 30 53N 46 28 E
Suqian 77 33 54N 118 8 E
Sūr, Leb. 62 33 19N 35 16 E
Sūr, Oman 65 22 34N 59 32 E
Sur, Pt. 119 36 18N 121 54W
Sura → 55 56 6N 46 0 E
Surabaja = Surabaya 73 7 17 S 112 45 E
Surabaya 73 7 17 S 112 45 E
Surahammar 48 59 43N 16 13 E
Suraia 46 45 40N 27 25 E
Surakarta 73 7 35 S 110 48 E
Surakhany 57 40 25N 50 1 E
Surandai 70 8 58N 77 26 E
Šurany 27 48 6N 18 10 E
Surat, Austral. 99 27 10 S 149 6 E
Surat, India 68 21 12N 72 55 E
Surat Thani 71 9 6N 99 20 E
Suratgarh 68 29 18N 73 55 E
Suraz 28 52 57N 22 57 E
Surazh, Byelorussia, U.S.S.R. 54 55 25N 30 44 E
Surazh, R.S.F.S.R., U.S.S.R. 54 53 5N 32 27 E
Surduc 46 47 15N 23 25 E
Surduc Pasul 46 45 21N 23 23 E
Surdulica 42 42 41N 22 11 E
Sûre → 16 49 44N 6 31 E
Surendranagar 68 22 45N 71 40 E
Surgères 20 46 7N 0 47W
Surgut 58 61 14N 73 20 E
Suri 69 23 50N 87 34 E
Surianu 46 45 33N 23 31 E
Suriapet 70 17 10N 79 40 E
Şurīf 62 31 40N 35 4 E
Surigao 73 9 47N 125 29 E
Surin 71 14 50N 103 34 E
Surinam ■ 127 4 0N 56 0W
Suriname → 127 5 50N 55 15W
Surmene 57 41 0N 40 1 E
Surovikino 57 48 32N 42 55 E
Surprise L. 108 59 40N 133 15W
Surrey □ 13 51 16N 0 30W
Sursee 25 47 11N 8 6 E
Sursk 55 53 3N 45 40 E
Surt 83 31 11N 16 39 E
Surt, Al Hammadah al 83 30 0N 17 50 E
Surt, Khalīj 83 31 40N 18 30 E
Surtsey 50 63 20N 20 30W
Suruga-Wan 74 34 45N 138 30 E
Susa 38 45 8N 7 3 E
Suså → 49 55 20N 11 42 E
Sušac 39 42 46N 16 30 E
Susak 39 44 30N 14 18 E
Süsangerd 64 31 35N 48 6 E
Susanino 59 52 50N 140 14 E
Susanville 118 40 28N 120 40W
Sušice 26 49 17N 13 30 E
Susquehanna → 114 39 33N 76 5W
Susquehanna Depot 113 41 55N 75 36W
Susques 124 23 35 S 66 25W
Sussex, Can. 107 45 45N 65 37W
Sussex, U.S.A. 113 41 12N 74 38W
Sussex, E. □ 13 51 0N 0 20 E
Sussex, W. □ 13 51 0N 0 30W
Sustut → 108 56 20N 127 30W
Susuman 59 62 47N 148 10 E
Susunu 73 3 20 S 133 25 E
Susz 28 53 44N 19 20 E
Şuţeşti 46 45 13N 27 27 E
Sutherland, S. Afr. 92 32 33 S 20 40 E
Sutherland, U.S.A. 116 41 12N 101 11W
Sutherland Falls 101 44 48 S 167 46 E
Sutherland Pt. 97 28 15 S 153 35 E
Sutherlin 118 43 28N 123 16W
Sutivan 39 43 23N 16 30 E
Sutlej → 68 29 23N 71 3 E
Sutton, Can. 113 45 6N 72 37W
Sutton, U.S.A. 116 40 40N 97 50W
Sutton → 106 55 15N 83 45W
Sutton-in-Ashfield 12 53 7N 1 20W
Suttor → 98 21 36 S 147 2 E
Suva 94 18 6 S 178 30 E
Suva Gora 42 41 45N 21 3 E
Suva Planina 42 43 10N 22 5 E
Suva Reka 42 42 21N 20 50 E
Suvo Rudïste 42 43 17N 20 49 E
Suvorov 55 54 7N 36 30 E
Suvorov Is. = Suwarrow Is. 95 13 15 S 163 30W
Suvorovo 43 43 20N 27 35 E
Suwałki 28 54 8N 22 59 E
Suwałki □ 28 54 0N 22 30 E
Suwannee → 115 29 18N 83 9W
Suwanose Jima 74 29 26N 129 30 E
Suwarrow Is. 95 15 0 S 163 0W
Suweis, Khalîg el 86 28 40N 33 0 E
Suweis, Qanâl es 86 31 0N 32 20 E
Suwŏn 76 37 17N 127 1 E
Suzdal 55 56 29N 40 26 E
Suze, La 18 47 54N 0 2 E
Suzhou 75 31 19N 120 38 E
Suzu-Misaki 74 37 31N 137 21 E
Suzuka 74 34 55N 136 36 E
Suzzara 38 45 0N 10 45 E
Svalbard 4 78 0N 17 0 E
Svalbarð 50 66 12N 15 43W
Svalöv 49 55 57N 13 8 E
Svanvik 50 69 25N 30 3 E
Svappavaara 50 67 40N 21 03 E
Svarstad 47 59 27N 9 56 E
Svartisen 50 66 40N 13 50 E
Svartvik 48 62 19N 17 24 E
Svatovo 56 49 35N 38 11 E
Svay Rieng 71 11 9N 105 45 E
Sveio 47 59 33N 5 23 E
Svendborg 49 55 4N 10 35 E
Svene 47 59 45N 9 31 E
Svenljunga 49 57 29N 13 5 E
Svenstrup 49 56 58N 9 50 E
Sverdlovsk, R.S.F.S.R., U.S.S.R. 52 56 50N 60 30 E
Sverdlovsk, Ukraine S.S.R., U.S.S.R. 57 48 5N 39 37 E
Sverdrup Is. 4 79 0N 97 0W
Svetac 39 43 3N 15 43 E
Sveti Ivan Zelina 39 45 57N 16 16 E
Sveti Jurij 39 46 14N 15 24 E
Sveti Lenart 39 46 36N 15 48 E
Sveti Nikola, Prokhad 42 43 27N 22 6 E
Sveti Nikole 42 41 51N 21 56 E
Sveti Rok 39 40 1N 9 6 E
Sveti Trojica 39 46 37N 15 50 E
Svetlogorsk 54 52 38N 29 46 E
Svetlograd 57 45 25N 42 58 E
Svetlovodsk 54 49 2N 33 13 E
Svetozarevo 42 44 5N 21 15 E
Svidník 27 49 20N 21 37 E
Svilaja Pl. 39 43 49N 16 31 E
Svilajnac 42 44 15N 21 11 E
Svilengrad 43 41 49N 26 12 E
Svir → 52 60 30N 32 48 E
Svishtov 43 43 36N 25 23 E
Svisloch 54 53 3N 24 2 E
Svitava → 27 49 30N 16 37 E
Svitavy 27 49 47N 16 28 E
Svobodnyy 59 51 20N 128 0 E
Svoge 43 42 59N 23 23 E
Svolvær 50 68 15N 14 34 E
Svratka → 27 49 11N 16 38 E
Svrljig 42 43 25N 22 6 E
Swabian Alps = Schäbischer Alb 25 48 30N 9 30 E
Swain Reefs 97 21 45 S 152 20 E
Swainsboro 115 32 38N 82 22W
Swakopmund 92 22 37 S 14 30 E
Swale → 12 54 5N 1 20W
Swan → 96 32 3 S 115 45 E
Swan Hill 97 35 20 S 143 33 E
Swan Hills 108 54 42N 115 24
Swan Islands 121 17 22N 83 57
Swan L. 109 52 30N 100 40
Swan River 109 52 10N 101 16
Swanage 13 50 36N 1 59
Swansea, Austral. 99 33 3 S 151 35
Swansea, U.K. 13 51 37N 3 57
Swartberge 92 33 20 S 22 0
Swartruggens 92 25 39 S 26 42
Swarzędz 28 52 25N 17 4
Swastika 106 48 7N 80 6
Swatow = Shantou 76 23 18N 116 40
Swaziland ■ 93 26 30 S 31 30
Sweden ■ 50 67 0N 15 0
Swedru 85 5 32N 0 41
Sweet Home 118 44 26N 122 25
Sweetwater 117 32 30N 100 28
Sweetwater → 118 42 31N 107 2
Swellendam 92 34 1 S 20 26
Swider → 28 52 6N 21 14
Świdnica 28 50 50N 16 30
Świdnik 28 51 13N 22 39
Świdwin 28 53 47N 15 49
Świebodzice 28 50 51N 16 20
Świebodzin 28 52 15N 15 31
Świecie 28 53 25N 18 30
Świętokrzyskie, Góry 28 51 0N 20 30
Swift Current 109 50 20N 107 45
Swiftcurrent → 109 50 38N 107 44
Swilly, L. 15 55 12N 7 35
Swindle, I. 108 52 30N 128 35
Swindon 13 51 33N 1 47
Świnemünde = Świnoujście 28 53 54N 14 16
Świnoujście 28 53 54N 14 16
Switzerland ■ 25 46 30N 8 0
Swords 15 53 27N 6 15
Syasstroy 54 60 5N 32 15
Sychevka 54 55 59N 34 16
Syców 28 51 19N 17 40
Sydney, Austral. 97 33 53 S 151 10
Sydney, Can. 107 46 7N 60 7
Sydney, U.S.A. 116 41 12N 103 0
Sydney Mines 107 46 18N 60 15
Sydprøven 4 60 30N 45 35
Sydra G. of = Surt, Khalīj 35 31 40N 18 30
Syke 24 52 55N 8 50
Syktyvkar 52 61 45N 50 40
Sylacauga 115 33 10N 86 15
Sylarna 50 63 2N 12 13
Sylhet 67 24 54N 91 52
Sylt 24 54 50N 8 20
Sylvan Lake 108 52 20N 114 03
Sylvania 115 32 45N 81 37
Sylvester 115 31 31N 83 50
Sym 58 60 20N 88 18
Syracuse, Kans., U.S.A. 117 38 0N 101 46
Syracuse, N.Y., U.S.A. 114 43 4N 76 11
Syrdarya → 58 46 3N 61 0
Syria ■ 64 35 0N 38 0
Syriam 69 16 44N 96 19
Syrian Desert 60 31 0N 40 0
Syul'dzhyukyor 59 63 14N 113 32
Syutkya 43 41 50N 24 16
Syzran 55 53 12N 48 30
Szabolcs-Szatmár □ 27 48 2N 21 45
Szamocin 28 53 2N 17 7
Szamos → 27 48 7N 22 20
Szaraz → 27 46 28N 20 44
Szarvas 27 46 50N 20 38
Százhalombatta 27 47 20N 18 58
Szczawnica 27 49 26N 20 30
Szczebrzeszyn 28 50 42N 22 59
Szczecin 28 53 27N 14 27
Szczecin □ 28 53 25N 14 32
Szczecinek 28 53 43N 16 41
Szczekocimy 28 50 38N 19 48
Szczucin 28 50 18N 21 4
Szczuczyn 28 53 36N 22 19
Szczytno 28 53 33N 21 0
Szechwan = Sichuan □ 75 31 0N 104 0
Szécsény 27 48 7N 19 30
Szeged 27 46 16N 20 10
Szeghalom 27 47 1N 21 10
Székesfehérvár 27 47 15N 18 25
Szekszárd 27 46 22N 18 42
Szendrö 27 48 24N 20 41
Szentendre 27 47 39N 19 4
Szentes 27 46 39N 20 21
Szentgotthárd 27 46 58N 16 19
Szentlörinc 27 46 3N 18 1
Szerencs 27 48 10N 21 12
Szigetvár 27 46 3N 17 46
Szikszó 27 48 12N 20 56
Szkwa → 28 53 11N 21 43
Szlichtyngowa 28 51 42N 16 15
Szob 27 47 48N 18 53
Szolnok 27 47 10N 20 15
Szolnok □ 27 47 15N 20 30
Szombathely 27 47 14N 16 38
Szprotawa 28 51 33N 15 35
Sztum 28 53 55N 19 1
Sztutowo 28 54 20N 19 15
Szubin 28 53 1N 17 45
Szydłowiec 28 51 15N 20 51
Szypliszki 28 54 17N 23 2

T

Tabacal 124 23 15 S 64 15W
Tabaco 73 13 22N 123 44 E
Tabagné 84 7 59N 3 4W
Ţābah 64 26 55N 42 38 E
Tabar Is. 98 2 50 S 152 0 E
Tabarca, Isla de 33 38 17N 0 30W
Tabarka 83 36 56N 8 46 E
Ţabas, Khorāsān, Iran 65 33 35N 56 55 E
Ţabas, Khorāsān, Iran 65 32 48N 60 12 E
Tabasará, Serranía de 121 8 35N 81 40W
Tabasco □ 120 17 45N 93 30W
Tabatinga, Serra da 127 10 30 S 44 0W

Tabelbala, Kahal de 82 28 47N 2 0W
Tabelkaza 80 29 50N 0 55 E
Taber 108 49 47N 112 8W
Tabernas 33 37 4N 2 26W
Tabernes de Valldigna 33 39 5N 0 13W
Tablas 73 12 25N 122 2 E
Table B. 107 53 40N 56 25W
Table Mt. 92 34 0S 18 22 E
Table Top, Mt. 98 23 24S 147 11 E
Tábor 26 49 25N 14 39 E
Tabor 62 32 42N 35 24 E
Tabora 90 5 2S 32 50 E
Tabora □ 90 5 0S 33 0 E
Tabou 84 4 30N 7 20W
Tabrīz 64 38 7N 46 20 E
Tabuenca 32 41 42N 1 33W
Tabūk 64 28 23N 36 36 E
Tacheng 75 46 40N 82 58 E
Tach'ing Shan = Daqing Shan 76 40 40N 111 0 E
Tachov 26 49 47N 12 39 E
Tácina → 41 38 57N 16 55 E
Tacloban 73 11 15N 124 58 E
Tacna 126 18 0S 70 20W
Tacoma 118 47 15N 122 30W
Tacuarembó 125 31 45S 56 0W
Tademaït, Plateau du 82 28 30N 2 30 E
Tadent, O. → 83 22 25N 6 40 E
Tadjerdjeri, O. → 83 26 0N 8 0W
Tadjerouna 82 33 31N 2 3 E
Tadjettaret, O. → 83 21 20N 7 22 E
Tadjmout, Atlas, Alg. 82 33 52N 2 30 E
Tadjmout, Sahara, Alg. 82 25 37N 3 48 E
Tadjoura 87 11 50N 42 55 E
Tadjoura, Golfe de 87 11 50N 43 0 E
Tadmor 101 41 27S 172 45 E
Tadoule, L. 109 58 36N 98 20W
Tadoussac 107 48 11N 69 42W
Tadzhik S.S.R. □ 58 35 30N 70 0 E
Taegu 76 35 50N 128 37 E
Taejŏn 76 36 20N 127 28 E
Tafalla 32 42 30N 1 41W
Tafar 87 6 52N 28 15 E
Ţafas 62 32 44N 36 5 E
Tafassasset, O. → 83 22 0N 9 57 E
Tafelbaai 92 33 35S 18 25 E
Tafelney, C. 82 31 3N 9 51W
Tafermaar 73 6 47S 134 10 E
Taffermit 82 29 37N 9 15W
Tafí Viejo 124 26 43S 65 17W
Tafiré 84 9 4N 5 4W
Tafnidilt 82 28 47N 10 58W
Tafraoute 82 29 50N 8 58W
Taft, Phil. 73 11 57N 125 30 E
Taft, Calif., U.S.A. 119 35 9N 119 28W
Taft, Tex., U.S.A. 117 27 58N 97 23W
Taga Dzong 69 27 5N 89 55 E
Taganrog 57 47 12N 38 50 E
Taganrogskiy Zaliv 56 47 0N 38 30 E
Tagânt 84 18 20N 11 0W
Tagbilaran 73 9 39N 123 51 E
Tággia 38 43 52N 7 50 E
Taghrifat 83 29 5N 17 26 E
Taghzout 82 33 30N 4 49W
Tagish 108 60 19N 134 16W
Tagish L. 104 60 10N 134 20W
Tagliacozzo 39 42 4N 13 13 E
Tagliamento → 39 45 38N 13 5 E
Táglio di Po 39 45 0N 12 12 E
Tagomago, I. de 33 39 2N 1 39 E
Taguatinga 127 12 16S 42 26W
Tagula I. 98 11 30S 153 30 E
Tagum (Hijo) 73 7 33N 125 53 E
Tagus = Tajo → 29 39 44N 5 50W
Tahakopa 101 46 30S 169 23 E
Tahala 82 34 0N 4 28W
Tahan, Gunong 71 4 34N 102 17 E
Tahat 83 23 18N 5 33 E
Tāherī 65 27 43N 52 20 E
Tahiti 95 17 37S 149 27W
Tahoe City 118 39 12N 120 9W
Tahoe, L. 118 39 0N 120 9W
Tahoua 85 14 57N 5 16 E
Tahta 86 26 44N 31 32 E
Tahulandang 73 2 27N 125 23 E
Tahuna 73 3 38N 125 30 E
Taï 84 5 55N 7 30W
Tai Hu 75 31 5N 120 10 E
Tai Shan 76 36 25N 117 20 E
Tai'an 76 36 12N 117 8 E
Taibei 75 25 4N 121 29 E
Taibus Qi 76 41 54N 115 22 E
T'aichung = Taizhong 75 24 10N 120 38 E
Taidong 75 22 43N 121 9 E
Taieri → 101 46 3S 170 12 E
Taiga Madema 83 23 46N 15 25 E
Taigu 76 37 28N 112 30 E
Taihang Shan 76 36 0N 113 30 E
Taihape 101 39 41S 175 48 E
Taihe 77 26 47N 114 52 E
Taihu 77 30 22N 116 20 E
Taijiang 77 26 39N 108 21 E
Taikang, Heilongjiang, China 76 46 50N 124 25 E
Taikang, Henan, China 77 34 5N 114 50 E
Taikkyi 69 17 20N 96 0 E
Tailai 76 46 23N 123 24 E
Tailem Bend 99 35 12S 139 29 E
Tailfingen 25 48 15N 9 1 E
Taimyr = Taymyr 59 75 0N 100 0 E
Taimyr, Oz. 59 74 20N 102 0 E
Tain 14 57 49N 4 4W
Tainan 77 23 17N 120 18 E
Tainaron, Ákra 45 36 22N 22 27 E
Taining 77 26 54N 117 9 E
T'aipei = Taibei 75 25 4N 121 29 E
Taiping 71 4 51N 100 44 E
Taishan 77 22 14N 112 41 E
Taishun 77 27 30N 119 42 E
Taita □ 90 4 0S 38 30 E
Taita Hills 90 3 25S 38 15 E
Taitao, Pen. de 128 46 30S 75 0W
Taivalkoski 50 65 33N 28 12 E
Taiwan ■ 75 24 0N 121 0 E
Taÿetos Óros 45 37 0N 22 23 E
Taiyib → 62 31 55N 35 17 E
Taiyiba 62 32 36N 35 27 E
Taiyuan 76 37 52N 112 33 E
Taizhong 77 24 12N 120 35 E
Taizhou 77 32 28N 119 55 E
Ta'izz 63 13 35N 44 2 E
Tajarḥī 83 24 21N 14 28 E
Tajo → 31 38 40N 9 24W
Tajumulco, Volcán de 120 15 2N 91 50W
Tājūrā 83 32 51N 13 21 E
Tak 71 16 52N 99 8 E
Takada 74 37 7N 138 15 E
Takaka 101 40 51S 172 50 E
Takamatsu 74 34 20N 134 5 E
Takanabe 74 32 8N 131 30 E
Takaoka 74 36 47N 137 0 E
Takapuna 101 36 47S 174 47 E
Takasaki 74 36 20N 139 0 E
Takatsuki 74 34 51N 135 37 E
Takaungu 90 3 38S 39 52 E
Takayama 74 36 18N 137 11 E
Takefu 74 35 50N 136 10 E
Takengeun 72 4 45N 96 50 E
Takeo 71 10 59N 104 47 E
Tåkern 49 58 22N 14 45 E
Tākestān 64 36 0N 49 40 E
Takhar □ 65 36 40N 70 0 E
Takla L. 108 55 15N 125 45W
Takla Landing 108 55 30N 125 50W
Takla Makan 60 39 0N 83 0 E
Takla Makan = Taklimakan Shamo 75 38 0N 83 0 E
Taklimakan Shamo 75 38 0N 83 0 E
Taku → 108 58 30N 133 50W
Takua Pa 71 7 18N 9 59 E
Takum 85 7 18N 9 36 E
Tala 125 34 21S 55 46W
Talagante 124 33 40S 70 50W
Talaïnt 82 29 41N 9 40W
Talak 85 18 0N 5 0 E
Talamanca, Cordillera de 121 9 20N 83 20W
Talara 126 4 38S 81 18 E
Talas 58 42 30N 72 13 E
Talasea 98 5 20S 150 2 E
Talata Mafara 85 12 38N 6 4 E
Talaud, Kepulauan 73 4 30N 127 10 E
Talavera de la Reina 30 39 55N 4 46W
Talayan 73 6 52N 124 24 E
Talbert, Sillon de 18 48 53N 3 5W
Talbot, C. 96 13 48S 126 43 E
Talbragar → 99 32 12S 148 37 E
Talca 124 35 28S 71 40W
Talca □ 124 35 20S 71 46W
Talcahuano 124 36 40S 73 10W
Talcher 69 21 0N 85 18 E
Talcho 85 14 44N 3 28 E
Taldy Kurgan 58 45 10N 78 45 E
Ţalesh, Kūhhā-ye 64 39 0N 48 30 E
Talfit 62 32 5N 35 17 E
Talguharai 86 18 19N 35 56 E
Tali Post 87 5 55N 30 44 E
Taliabu 73 1 45S 125 0 E
Talibon 73 10 9N 124 20 E
Talihina 117 34 45N 95 1W
Talikoti 70 16 29N 76 17 E
Taling Sung 71 15 5N 99 11 E
Taliwang 72 8 50S 116 55 E
Talkeetna 104 62 20N 150 9W
Tall 62 33 0N 35 6 E
Tall 'Afar 64 36 22N 42 27 E
Tall 'Asūr 62 31 59N 35 17 E
Talla 86 28 5N 30 43 E
Talladega 115 33 28N 86 2W
Tallahassee 115 30 25N 84 15W
Tallangatta 99 36 15S 147 19 E
Tallarook 99 37 5S 145 6 E
Tällberg 48 60 51N 15 2 E
Tallering Pk. 96 28 6S 115 37 E
Tallinn 54 59 22N 24 48 E
Tallulah 117 32 25N 91 12W
Ţallūzā 62 32 17N 35 18 E
Tălmaciu 46 45 38N 24 19 E
Talmest 82 31 48N 9 21W
Talmont 20 46 27N 1 37W
Talnoye 56 48 50N 30 44 E
Taloda 68 21 34N 74 11 E
Talodi 87 10 35N 30 22 E
Talovaya 55 51 6N 40 45 E
Talsi 54 57 10N 22 30 E
Talsinnt 82 32 33N 3 27W
Taltal 124 25 23S 70 33W
Taltson → 108 61 24N 112 46W
Taltson L. 109 61 30N 110 15W
Talwood 99 28 29S 149 29 E
Talyawalka Cr. → 99 32 28S 142 22 E
Tama 116 41 56N 92 37W
Tamale 85 9 22N 0 50W
Taman 56 45 14N 36 41 E
Tamanar 82 31 1N 9 46W
Tamano 74 34 29N 133 59 E
Tamanrasset 83 22 50N 5 30 E
Tamanrasset, O. → 82 22 0N 2 0 E
Tamaqua 113 40 46N 75 58W
Tamar → 13 50 33N 4 15W
Tamarite de Litera 32 41 52N 0 25 E
Tamási 27 46 40N 18 18 E
Tamaské 85 14 49N 5 43 E
Tamaulipas □ 120 24 0N 99 0W
Tamaulipas, Sierra de 120 23 30N 98 20W
Tamazula 120 24 55N 106 58W
Tamba-Dabatou 84 11 50N 10 40W
Tambacounda 84 13 45N 13 40W
Tambelan, Kepulauan 72 1 0N 107 30 E
Tambo 98 24 54S 146 14 E
Tambo de Mora 126 13 30S 76 8W
Tambohorano 93 17 30S 43 58 E
Tambora 72 8 12S 118 5 E
Tambov 55 52 45N 41 28 E
Tambre → 30 42 49N 8 53W
Tambuku 73 7 8S 113 40 E
Tamburâ 87 5 40N 27 25 E
Tâmchekket 84 17 25N 10 40W
Tamega → 30 41 5N 8 21W
Tamelelt 82 31 50N 7 32W
Tamenglong 67 25 0N 93 35 E
Tamerza 83 34 23N 7 58 E
Tamgak, Mts. 80 19 12N 8 35 E
Tamiahua, Laguna de 120 21 30N 97 30W
Tamil Nadu □ 70 11 0N 77 0 E
Tamluk 69 22 18N 87 58 E
Tammerfors = Tampere 51 61 30N 23 50 E
Tammisaari 51 60 0N 23 26 E
Ţammūn 62 32 18N 35 23 E
Tämnaren 48 60 10N 17 25 E
Tamo Abu, Pegunungan 72 3 10N 115 0 E
Tampa 115 27 57N 82 38W
Tampa B. 115 27 40N 82 40W
Tampere 51 61 30N 23 50 E
Tampico 120 22 20N 97 50W
Tampin 71 2 28N 102 13 E
Tamri 82 30 49N 9 50W
Tamrida = Hadibu 63 12 35N 54 2 E
Tamsagbulag 75 47 14N 117 21 E
Tamsalu 54 59 11N 26 8 E
Tamsweg 26 47 7N 13 49 E
Tamu 67 24 13N 94 12 E
Tamuja → 31 39 38N 6 29W
Tamworth, Austral. 97 31 7S 150 58 E
Tamworth, U.K. 13 52 38N 1 41W
Tan-tan 82 28 29N 11 1W
Tana 50 70 26N 28 14 E
Tana →, Kenya 90 2 32S 40 31 E
Tana →, Norway 50 70 30N 28 23 E
Tana, L. 87 13 5N 37 30 E
Tana River 90 2 0S 39 30 E
Tanafjorden 50 70 45N 28 25 E
Tanagro → 41 40 35N 15 25 E
Tanahbala 72 0 30S 98 30 E
Tanahgrogot 72 1 55S 116 15 E
Tanahjampea 73 7 10S 120 35 E
Tanahmasa 72 0 12S 98 39 E
Tanahmerah 73 6 5S 140 16 E
Tanakura 74 37 10N 140 20 E
Tanami Des. 96 18 50S 132 0 E
Tanana 104 65 10N 152 15W
Tanana → 104 65 9N 151 55W
Tananarive = Antananarivo 93 18 55S 47 35 E
Tanannt 82 31 54N 6 56W
Tânaro → 38 45 1N 8 47 E
Tanaunella 40 40 42N 9 45 E
Tancarville 18 49 29N 0 28 E
Tanchŏn 76 40 27N 128 54 E
Tanda, U.P., India 68 28 57N 78 56 E
Tanda, U.P., India 69 26 33N 82 35 E
Tanda, Ivory C. 84 7 48N 3 10W
Tandag 73 9 4N 126 9 E
Tandaia 91 9 25S 34 15 E
Tăndărei 46 44 39N 27 40 E
Tandaué 92 16 58S 18 5 E
Tandil 124 37 15S 59 6W
Tandil, Sa. del 124 37 30S 59 0W
Tandlianwala 68 31 3N 73 9 E
Tando Adam 68 25 45N 68 40 E
Tandou L. 99 32 40S 142 5 E
Tandsbyn 48 63 0N 14 45 E
Tandur 70 19 11N 79 30 E
Tane-ga-Shima 74 30 30N 131 0 E
Taneatua 101 38 4S 177 1 E
Tanen Tong Dan 67 16 30N 98 30 E
Tanew → 28 50 29N 22 16 E
Tanezrouft 82 23 9N 0 11 E
Tanga 88 5 5S 39 2 E
Tanga □ 90 5 20S 38 0 E
Tanga Is. 98 3 20S 153 15 E
Tangail 69 24 15N 89 55 E
Tanganyika, L. 90 6 40S 30 0 E
Tanger 82 35 50N 5 49W
Tangerang 73 6 12S 106 39 E
Tangerhütte 24 52 26N 11 50 E
Tangermünde 24 52 32N 11 57 E
Tanggu 76 39 2N 117 40 E
Tanggula Shan 75 32 40N 92 10 E
Tanghe 77 32 47N 112 50 E
Tangier = Tanger 82 35 50N 5 49W
Tangkak 71 2 18N 102 34 E
Tangorin P.O. 98 21 47S 144 12 E
Tangshan 76 39 38N 118 10 E
Tanguiéta 85 10 35N 1 21 E
Tanimbar, Kepulauan 73 7 30S 131 30 E
Taninges 21 46 7N 6 36 E
Tanjay 73 9 30N 123 5 E
Tanjore = Thanjavur 70 10 48N 79 12 E
Tanjung 72 2 10S 115 25 E
Tanjungbalai 72 2 55N 99 44 E
Tanjungbatu 72 2 23N 118 3 E
Tanjungkarang 72 5 20S 105 10 E
Tanjungpandan 72 2 43S 107 38 E
Tanjungpinang 72 1 5N 104 30 E
Tanjungpriok 73 6 8S 106 55 E
Tanjungredeb 72 2 9N 117 29 E
Tanjungselor 72 2 55N 117 25 E
Tank 68 32 14N 70 25 E
Tänndalen 48 62 33N 12 18 E
Tannis Bugt 49 57 40N 10 15 E
Tannu-Ola 59 51 0N 94 0 E
Tano → 84 5 7N 2 56W
Tanout 85 14 50N 8 55 E
Tanta 86 30 45N 30 57 E
Tantoyuca 120 21 21N 98 10W
Tantung = Dandong 76 40 10N 124 20 E
Tantūra = Dor 62 32 37N 34 55 E
Tanuku 70 16 45N 81 44 E
Tanumshede 49 58 42N 11 20 E
Tanunda 99 34 30S 139 0 E
Tanur 70 11 1N 75 52 E
Tanus 20 44 8N 2 19 E
Tanzania ■ 90 6 40S 34 0 E
Tanzilla → 108 58 8N 130 43W
Tao'an 76 45 22N 122 40 E
Taormina 41 37 52N 15 16 E
Taos 119 36 28N 105 35W
Taoudenni 82 22 40N 3 55W
Taoudrart, Adrar 82 24 25N 2 24 E
Taounate 82 34 25N 4 41W
Taourirt, Alg. 82 26 37N 0 20 E
Taourirt, Moroc. 82 34 25N 2 53W
Taouz 82 30 53N 4 0W
Taoyuan, China 77 28 55N 111 16 E
Taoyuan, Taiwan 77 25 0N 121 13 E
Tapa 54 59 15N 25 50 E
Tapa Shan = Daba Shan 75 31 50N 109 20 E
Tapachula 120 14 54N 92 17W
Tapah 71 4 12N 101 15 E
Tapajós → 127 2 24S 54 41W
Tapaktuan 72 3 15N 97 10 E
Tapanui 101 45 56S 169 18 E
Tapauá → 126 5 40S 64 21W
Tapeta 84 6 29N 8 52W
Tapia 30 43 34N 6 56W
Tápiószele 27 47 25N 19 55 E
Tapirapecó, Serra 126 1 10N 65 0W
Tapolca 27 46 53N 17 29 E
Tappahannock 114 37 56N 76 50W
Tapti → 68 21 8N 72 41 E
Tapuaenuku, Mt. 101 42 0S 173 39 E
Tapul Group 73 5 35N 120 50 E
Taquara 125 29 36S 50 46W
Taquari → 126 19 15S 57 17W
Tar Island 108 57 03N 111 40W
Tara, Austral. 99 27 17S 150 31 E
Tara, Can. 112 44 28N 81 9W
Tara, U.S.S.R. 58 56 55N 74 24 E
Tara, Zambia 91 16 58S 26 45 E
Tara →, U.S.S.R. 58 56 42N 74 36 E
Tara →, Yugo. 42 43 21N 18 51 E
Tarabagatay, Khrebet 58 48 0N 83 0 E
Tarābulus, Leb. 64 34 31N 35 50 E
Tarābulus, Libya 83 32 49N 13 7 E
Tarahouahout 83 22 41N 5 59 E
Tarakan 72 3 20N 117 35 E
Tarakit, Mt. 90 2 2N 35 10 E
Taralga 99 34 26S 149 52 E
Taranagar 68 28 43N 74 50 E
Taranaki □ 101 39 5S 174 51 E
Tarancón 32 40 1N 3 1W
Taranga 68 23 56N 72 43 E
Taranga Hill 68 24 0N 72 40 E
Táranto 41 40 30N 17 11 E
Táranto, G. di 41 40 0N 17 15 E
Tarapacá 126 2 56S 69 46W
Tarapacá □ 124 20 45S 69 30W
Tarare 21 45 54N 4 26 E
Tararua Range 101 40 45S 175 25 E
Tarascon, Ariège, France 20 42 50N 1 37 E
Tarascon, Bouches-du-Rhône, France 21 43 48N 4 39 E
Tarashcha 56 49 30N 30 31 E
Tarat 80 25 55N 9 3 E
Tarat, Bj. 83 26 13N 9 18 E
Tarauacá 126 8 6S 70 48W
Tarauacá → 126 6 42S 69 48W
Taravo → 21 41 42N 8 49 E
Tarawera 101 39 2S 176 36 E
Tarawera L. 101 38 13S 176 27 E
Tarazona 32 41 55N 1 43W
Tarazona de la Mancha 33 39 16N 1 55W
Tarbat Ness 14 57 52N 3 48W
Tarbert, Strathclyde, U.K. 14 55 55N 5 25W
Tarbert, W. Isles, U.K. 14 57 54N 6 49W
Tarbes 20 43 15N 0 3 E
Tarboro 115 35 55N 77 30W
Tarbrax 98 21 7S 142 26 E
Tarbū 83 26 0N 15 5 E
Tarcento 39 46 12N 13 12 E
Tarcoola 96 30 44S 134 36 E
Tarcoon 99 30 15S 146 43 E
Tardets-Sorholus 20 43 8N 0 52W
Tardoire → 20 45 52N 0 14 E
Taree 97 31 50S 152 30 E
Tarentaise 21 45 30N 6 35 E
Tarf, Ras 82 35 40N 5 11W
Tarf Shaqq al Abd 86 26 50N 36 6 E
Tarfa, Wadi el → 86 28 25N 30 50 E
Tarfaya 80 27 55N 12 55W
Targon 20 44 44N 0 16W
Targuist 82 34 59N 4 14W
Tărhăus 46 46 40N 26 8 E
Tărhăus, Munţii 46 46 39N 26 7 E
Tarhbalt 82 30 39N 5 20W
Tarhit 82 30 58N 2 0W
Tarhūnah 83 32 27N 13 36 E
Tarib, Wadi → 86 18 30N 43 23 E
Tarifa 31 36 1N 5 36W
Tarija 124 21 30S 64 40W
Tarija □ 124 21 30S 63 30W
Tariku → 73 2 55S 138 26 E
Tarim He → 75 39 30N 88 30 E
Tarim Pendi 75 40 0N 84 0 E
Tarime □ 90 1 15S 34 0 E
Taritatu → 73 2 54S 138 27 E
Tarka → 92 32 10S 26 0 E
Tarkastad 92 32 0S 26 16 E
Tarkhankut, Mys 56 45 25N 32 30 E
Tarko Sale 58 64 55N 77 50 E
Tarkwa 84 5 20N 2 0W
Tarlac 73 15 29N 120 35 E
Tarm 49 55 56N 8 31 E
Tarma 126 11 25S 75 45W
Tarn □ 20 43 49N 2 8 E
Tarn → 20 44 5N 1 6 E
Tarn-et-Garonne □ 20 44 8N 1 20 E
Tarna → 27 47 31N 19 59 E
Tårnby 49 55 37N 12 36 E
Tarnica 27 49 4N 22 44 E
Tarnobrzeg 28 50 35N 21 41 E
Tarnobrzeg □ 28 50 40N 22 0 E
Tarnogród 28 50 22N 22 45 E
Tarnów 27 50 3N 21 0 E
Tarnów □ 27 50 0N 21 0 E
Tarnowskie Góry 28 50 27N 18 54 E
Tåro → 38 45 0N 10 15 E
Tarong 99 26 47S 151 51 E
Taroom 97 25 36S 149 48 E
Taroudannt 82 30 30N 8 52W
Tarp 24 54 40N 9 25 E

Tarpon Springs 115 28 8N 82 42W
Tarquinia 39 42 15N 11 45 E
Tarqūmiyah 62 31 35N 35 1 E
Tarragona 32 41 5N 1 17 E
Tarragona □ 32 41 0N 1 0 E
Tarrasa 32 41 34N 2 1 E
Tárrega 32 41 39N 1 9 E
Tarrytown 113 41 5N 73 52W
Tarshiha = Me'ona 62 33 1N 35 15 E
Tarso Emissi 83 21 27N 18 36 E
Tarso Ourari 83 21 27N 17 27 E
Tarsus 64 36 58N 34 55 E
Tartagal 124 22 30 S 63 50W
Tartas 20 43 50N 0 49W
Tartna Point 99 32 54 S 142 24 E
Tartu 54 58 20N 26 44 E
Tarţūs 64 34 55N 35 55 E
Tarussa 55 54 44N 37 10 E
Tarutao, Ko 71 6 33N 99 40 E
Tarutung 72 2 0N 98 54 E
Tarvisio 39 46 31N 13 35 E
Tarz Ulli 83 25 32N 10 8 E
Tasāwah 83 26 0N 13 30 E
Taschereau 106 48 40N 78 40W
Taseko → 108 52 4N 123 9W
Tasgaon 70 17 2N 74 39 E
Tash-Kumyr 58 41 40N 72 10 E
Ta'shan 87 16 31N 42 33 E
Tashauz 58 41 49N 59 58 E
Tashi Chho Dzong = Thimphu 69 27 31N 89 45 E
Tashkent 58 41 20N 69 10 E
Tashtagol 58 52 47N 87 53 E
Tasikmalaya 73 7 18 S 108 12 E
Tåsjön 50 64 15N 16 0 E
Taskan 59 62 59N 150 20 E
Taskopru 56 41 30N 34 15 E
Tasman B. 101 40 59 S 173 25 E
Tasman Mts. 101 41 3 S 172 25 E
Tasman Pen. 97 43 10 S 148 0 E
Tasman Sea 94 36 0 S 160 0 E
Tasmania □ 97 42 0 S 146 30 E
Tăşnad 46 47 30N 22 33 E
Tassil Tin-Rerhoh 82 20 5N 3 55 E
Tassili n-Ajjer 83 25 47N 8 1 E
Tassili-Oua-n-Ahaggar 83 20 41N 5 30 E
Tasu Sd. 108 52 47N 132 2W
Tata, Hung. 27 47 37N 18 19 E
Tata, Moroc. 82 29 46N 7 56W
Tatabánya 27 47 32N 18 25 E
Tatahouine 83 32 57N 10 29 E
Tatar A.S.S.R. □ 52 55 30N 51 30 E
Tatarbunary 56 45 50N 29 39 E
Tatarsk 58 55 14N 76 0 E
* Tatarskiy Proliv 59 54 0N 141 0 E
Tateyama 74 35 0N 139 50 E
Tathlina L. 108 60 33N 117 39W
Tathra 99 36 44 S 149 59 E
Tatinnai L. 109 60 55N 97 40W
Tatnam, C. 109 57 16N 91 0W
Tatra = Tatry 27 49 20N 20 0 E
Tatry 27 49 20N 20 0 E
Tatta 68 24 42N 67 55 E
Tatuī 125 23 25 S 47 53W
Tatum 117 33 16N 103 16W
Tat'ung = Datong 76 40 6N 113 12 E
Tatura 100 36 29 S 145 16 E
Tatvan 64 38 31N 42 15 E
Taubaté 125 23 0 S 45 36W
Tauberbischofsheim 25 49 37N 9 40 E
Taucha 24 51 22N 12 31 E
Tauern 26 47 15N 12 40 E
Tauern-tunnel 26 47 0N 13 12 E
Taufikia 87 9 24N 31 37 E
Taumarunui 101 38 53 S 175 15 E
Taumaturgo 126 8 54 S 72 51W
Taung 92 27 33 S 24 47 E
Taungdwingyi 67 20 1N 95 40 E
Taunggyi 67 20 50N 97 0 E
Taungup 67 18 51N 94 14 E
Taungup Pass 67 18 40N 94 45 E
Taunsa Barrage 68 30 42N 70 50 E
Taunton, U.K. 13 51 1N 3 7W
Taunton, U.S.A. 114 41 54N 71 6W
Taunus 25 50 15N 8 20 E
Taupo 101 38 41 S 176 7 E
Taupo, L. 101 38 46 S 175 55 E
Taurage 54 55 14N 22 16 E
Tauranga 101 37 42 S 176 11 E
Tauranga Harb. 101 37 30 S 176 5 E
Taurianova 41 38 22N 16 1 E
Taurus Mts. = Toros Dağlari 64 37 0N 35 0 E
Tauste 32 41 58N 1 18W
Tauz 57 41 0N 45 40 E
Tavda 58 58 7N 65 8 E
Tavda → 58 59 20N 63 28 E
Taverny 19 49 2N 2 13 E
Taveta 90 3 23 S 37 37 E
Taveuni 101 16 51 S 179 58W
Tavignano → 21 42 7N 9 33 E
Tavira 31 37 8N 7 40W
Tavistock, Can. 112 43 19N 80 50W
Tavistock, U.K. 13 50 33N 4 9W
Tavolara 40 40 55N 9 40 E
Távora → 30 41 8N 7 35W
Tavoy 71 14 2N 98 12 E
Taw → 13 17 37 S 177 55 E
Tawas City 114 44 16N 83 31W
Tawau 72 4 20N 117 55 E
Tawitawi 73 5 10N 120 0 E
Tāwurgha' 83 32 1N 15 2 E
Tay → 14 56 37N 3 38W
Tay, Firth of 14 56 25N 3 8W
Tay, L. 14 56 30N 4 10W
Tay Ninh 71 11 20N 106 5 E
Tayabamba 126 8 15 S 77 16W
Taylakovy 58 59 13N 74 0 E
Taylor, Can. 108 56 13N 120 40W
Taylor, Ariz., U.S.A. 119 34 28N 110 5W
Taylor, Nebr., U.S.A. 116 41 46N 99 23W
Taylor, Pa., U.S.A. 113 41 23N 75 43W
Taylor, Tex., U.S.A. 117 30 30N 97 30W
Taylor Mt. 119 35 16N 107 36W
Taylorville 116 39 32N 89 20W
Taymā' 64 27 35N 38 45 E
Taymyr, P-ov. 59 75 0N 100 0 E
Tayport 14 56 27N 2 52W
Ţayr Zibnā 62 33 14N 35 23 E
Tayshet 59 55 58N 98 1 E
Tayside □ 14 56 25N 3 30W
Taytay 73 10 45N 119 30 E
Taz → 58 67 32N 78 40 E
Taza 82 34 16N 4 6W
Tazenakht 82 30 35N 7 12W
Tazin → 109 60 26N 110 45W
Tazin L. 109 59 44N 108 42W
Tazoult 83 35 29N 6 11 E
Tazovskiy 58 67 30N 78 44 E
Tbilisi (Tiflis) 57 41 43N 44 50 E
Tchad (Chad) ■ 81 12 30N 17 15 E
Tchad, L. 81 13 30N 14 30 E
Tch'ang-k'ing = Changqing 75 29 35N 106 35 E
Tchaourou 85 8 58N 2 40 E
Tch'eng-tou = Chengdu 75 30 38N 104 2 E
Tchentlo L. 108 55 15N 125 0W
Tchibanga 88 2 45 S 11 0 E
Tchin Tabaraden 85 15 58N 5 56 E
Tczew 28 54 8N 18 50 E
Te Anau, L. 101 45 15 S 167 45 E
Te Aroha 101 37 32 S 175 44 E
Te Awamutu 101 38. 1 S 175 20 E
Te Kuiti 101 38 20 S 175 11 E
Te Puke 101 37 46 S 176 22 E
Te Waewae B. 101 46 13 S 167 33 E
Teaca 46 46 55N 24 30 E
Teague 117 31 40N 96 20W
Teano 41 41 15N 14 1 E
Teapa 120 18 35N 92 56W
Teba 31 36 59N 4 55W
Tebakang 72 1 6N 110 30 E
Teberda 57 43 30N 41 46 E
Tébessa 83 35 22N 8 8 E
Tebicuary → 124 26 36 S 58 16W
Tebingtinggi, Bengkulu, Indon. 72 3 38 S 103 9 E
Tebingtinggi, Sumatera Utara, Indon. 72 3 20N 99 9 E
Tébourba 83 36 49N 9 51 E
Téboursouk 83 36 29N 9 10 E
Tebulos 57 42 36N 45 17 E
Tech → 20 42 36N 3 3 E
Techiman 84 7 35N 1 58W
Techirghiol 46 44 4N 28 32 E
Tecuala 120 22 23N 105 27W
Tecuci 46 45 51N 27 27 E
Tecumseh 114 42 1N 83 59W
Tedzhen 58 37 23N 60 31 E
Tees → 12 54 36N 1 25W
Teesside 12 54 37N 1 13W
Teeswater 112 43 59N 81 17W
Tefé 126 3 25 S 64 50W
Tegal 73 6 52 S 109 8 E
Tegelen 16 51 20N 6 9 E
Tegernsee 25 47 43N 11 46 E
Teggiano 41 40 24N 15 32 E
Teghra 69 25 30N 85 34 E
Tegid, L. 12 52 53N 3 38W
Tegina 85 10 5N 6 11 E
Tegucigalpa 121 14 5N 87 14W
Tehachapi 119 35 11N 118 29W
Tehachapi Mts. 119 35 0N 118 40W
Tehamiyam 86 18 20N 36 32 E
Tehilla 86 17 42N 36 6 E
Téhini 84 9 39N 3 40W
Tehrān 65 35 44N 51 30 E
Tehrān □ 65 35 0N 49 30 E
Tehuacán 120 18 30N 97 30W
Tehuantepec 120 16 21N 95 13W
Tehuantepec, Golfo de 120 15 50N 95 0W
Tehuantepec, Istmo de 120 17 0N 94 30W
Teich, Le 20 44 38N 0 59W
Teifi → 13 52 4N 4 14W
Teign → 13 50 41N 3 42W
Teignmouth 13 50 33N 3 30W
Teil, Le 21 44 33N 4 40 E
Teilleul, Le 18 48 32N 0 53W
Teiuş 46 46 12N 23 40 E
Teixeira Pinto 84 12 3N 16 0W
Tejo → 31 38 40N 9 24W
Tekamah 116 41 48N 96 22W
Tekapo, L. 101 43 53 S 170 33 E
Tekax 120 20 11N 89 18W
Tekeli 58 44 50N 79 0 E
Tekeze → 87 14 20N 35 50 E
Tekija 42 44 42N 22 26 E
Tekirdağ 64 40 58N 27 30 E
Tekkali 70 18 37N 84 15 E
Tekoa 118 47 19N 117 4W
Tekouiât, O. → 82 22 25N 2 35 E
Tel Adashim 62 32 30N 35 17 E
Tel Aviv-Yafo 62 32 4N 34 48 E
Tel Lakhish 62 31 34N 34 51 E
Tel Megiddo 62 32 35N 35 11 E
Tel Mond 62 32 15N 34 56 E
Tela 120 15 40N 87 28W
Télagh 82 34 51N 0 32W
Telanaipura = Jambi 72 1 38 S 103 37 E
Telavi 57 42 0N 45 30 E
Telciu 46 47 25N 24 24 E
Telegraph Cr. 108 58 0N 131 10W
Telekhany 54 52 30N 25 46 E
Telemark fylke □ 47 59 25N 8 30 E
Telén 124 36 15 S 65 31W
Teleneshty 46 47 35N 28 24 E
Teleño 30 42 23N 6 22W
Teleorman □ 46 44 0N 25 0 E
Teleorman → 46 44 15N 25 20 E
Teles Pires → 126 7 21 S 58 3W
Telescope Peak 119 36 6N 117 7W
Teletaye 85 16 31N 1 30 E
Telford 12 52 42N 2 31W
Telfs 26 47 19N 11 4 E
Telgte 24 51 59N 7 46 E
Télimélé 84 10 54N 13 2W
Telkwa 108 54 41N 127 5W
Tell City 114 38 0N 86 44W
Tellicherry 70 11 45N 75 30 E
Telluride 119 37 58N 107 48W
Telok Anson 71 4 3N 101 0 E
Telom → 71 4 20N 101 46 E
Telpos Iz 52 63 35N 57 30 E
Telsen 128 42 30 S 66 50W
Telšiai 54 55 59N 22 14 E
Teltow 24 52 24N 13 15 E
Telukbetung 72 5 29 S 105 17 E
Telukbutun 72 4 13N 108 12 E
Telukdalem 72 0 33N 97 50 E
Tema 85 5 41N 0 0 E
Temanggung 73 7 18 S 110 10 E
Temax 120 21 10N 88 50W
Tembe 90 0 16 S 28 14 E
Tembeling → 71 4 20N 102 23 E
Tembleque 32 39 41N 3 30W
Tembuland 93 31 35 S 28 0 E
Teme → 13 52 23N 2 15W
Temecula 119 33 26N 117 6W
Temerloh 71 3 27N 102 25 E
Temir 58 49 21N 57 3 E
Temirtau, Kazakh, U.S.S.R. 58 50 5N 72 56 E
Temirtau, R.S.F.S.R., U.S.S.R. 58 53 10N 87 30 E
Témiscaming 106 46 44N 79 5W
Temma 99 41 12 S 144 48 E
Temnikov 55 54 40N 43 11 E
Temo → 40 40 20N 8 30 E
Temora 99 34 30 S 147 30 E
Temosachic 120 28 58N 107 50W
Tempe 119 33 26N 111 59W
Tempino 72 1 42 S 103 30 E
Témpio Pausania 40 40 53N 9 6 E
Temple 117 31 5N 97 22W
Temple B. 97 12 15 S 143 3 E
Templemore 15 52 48N 7 50W
Templeton → 98 21 0 S 138 40 E
Templin 24 53 8N 13 31 E
Temryuk 56 45 15N 37 24 E
Temska → 42 43 17N 22 33 E
Temuco 128 38 45 S 72 40W
Temuka 101 44 14 S 171 17 E
Tenabo 120 20 2N 90 12W
Tenaha 117 31 57N 94 25W
Tenali 70 16 15N 80 35 E
Tenancingo 120 19 0N 99 33W
Tenango 120 19 7N 99 33W
Tenasserim 71 12 6N 99 3 E
Tenasserim □ 71 14 0N 98 30 E
Tenay 21 45 55N 5 30 E
Tenby 13 51 40N 4 42W
Tendaho 87 11 48N 40 54 E
Tende 21 44 5N 7 35 E
Tende, Col de 21 44 9N 7 32 E
Tendelti 87 13 1N 31 55 E
Tendjedi, Adrar 83 23 41N 7 32 E
Tendrara 82 33 3N 1 58W
Teneida 86 25 30N 29 19 E
Ténéré 85 19 0N 10 30 E
Tenerife 80 28 15N 16 35W
Ténès 82 36 31N 1 14 E
Teng → 71 20 30N 98 10 E
Teng Xian, Guangxi Zhuangzu, China 77 23 21N 110 56 E
Teng Xian, Shandong, China 77 35 5N 117 10 E
Tengah □ 73 2 0 S 122 0 E
Tengah Kepulauan 72 7 5 S 118 15 E
Tengchong 75 25 0N 98 28 E
Tenggara □ 73 3 0 S 122 0 E
Tenggarong 72 0 24 S 116 58 E
Tengiz, Ozero 58 50 30N 69 0 E
Tenille 115 32 58N 82 50W
Tenkasi 70 8 55N 77 20 E
Tenke, Congo 91 11 22 S 26 40 E
Tenke, Zaïre 91 10 32 S 26 7 E
Tenkodogo 85 11 54N 0 19W
Tenna → 39 43 12N 13 47 E
Tennant Creek 96 19 30 S 134 15 E
Tennessee □ 111 36 0N 86 30W
Tennessee → 114 34 30N 86 20W
Tennsift, Oued → 82 32 3N 9 28W
Tenom 72 5 4N 115 57 E
Tenosique 120 17 30N 91 24W
Tenryū-Gawa → 74 35 39N 137 48 E
Tent L. 109 62 25N 107 54W
Tenterfield 97 29 0 S 152 0 E
Teófilo Otoni 127 17 50 S 41 30W
Teotihuacán 120 19 44N 98 50W
Tepa 73 7 52 S 129 31 E
Tepalcatepec → 120 18 35N 101 59W
Tepelena 44 40 17N 20 2 E
Tepic 120 21 30N 104 54W
Teplice 26 50 40N 13 48 E
Tepoca, C. 120 30 20N 112 25W
Tequila 120 20 54N 103 47W
Ter → 32 42 0N 3 12 E
Ter Apel 16 52 53N 7 5 E
Téra 85 14 0N 0 45 E
Tera → 30 41 54N 5 44W
Téramo 39 42 40N 13 40 E
Terang 99 38 15 S 142 55 E
Terazit, Massif de 83 20 2N 8 30 E
Terceira 8 38 43N 27 13W
Tercero → 124 32 58 S 61 47W
Terdal 70 16 33N 75 3 E
Terebovlya 54 49 18N 25 44 E
Teregova 46 45 10N 22 16 E
Terek →, U.S.S.R. 56 43 55N 47 30 E
Terek →, U.S.S.R. 57 44 0N 47 30 E
Terembone Cr. → 99 30 25 S 148 50 E
Terengganu □ 71 4 55N 103 0 E
Tereshka → 55 51 48N 46 26 E
Teresina 127 5 9 S 42 45W
Terespol 28 52 5N 23 37 E
Terewah L. 99 29 52 S 147 35 E
Terges → 31 37 49N 7 41W
Tergnier 19 49 40N 3 17 E
Terhazza 82 23 38N 5 22W
Terlizzi 41 41 8N 16 32 E
Terme 56 41 11N 37 0 E
Termez 58 37 15N 67 15 E
Términi Imerese 40 37 58N 13 42 E
Términos, Laguna de 120 18 35N 91 30W
Térmoli 39 42 0N 15 0 E
Ternate 73 0 45N 127 25 E
Terneuzen 16 51 20N 3 50 E
Terney 59 45 3N 136 37 E
Terni 39 42 34N 12 38 E
Ternitz 26 47 43N 16 2 E
Ternopol 54 49 30N 25 40 E
Terra Nova B. 5 74 50 S 164 40 E
Terrace 108 54 30N 128 35W
Terrace Bay 106 48 47N 87 5W
Terracina 40 41 17N 13 12 E
Terralba 40 39 42N 8 38 E
Terranuova Bracciolini 39 43 31N 11 35 E
Terrasini Favarotta 40 38 10N 13 4 E
Terrasson 20 45 7N 1 19 E
Terre Haute 114 39 28N 87 24W
Terrebonne B. 117 29 15N 90 28W
Terrecht 82 20 10N 0 10W
Terrell 117 32 44N 96 19W
Terrenceville 107 47 40N 54 44W
Terrick Terrick 98 24 44 S 145 5 E
Terry 116 46 47N 105 20W
Terschelling 16 53 25N 5 20 E
Terter → 57 40 35N 47 22 E
Teruel 32 40 22N 1 8W
Teruel □ 32 40 48N 1 0W
Tervel 43 43 45N 27 28 E
Tervola 50 66 6N 24 49 E
Teryaweyna L. 99 32 18 S 143 22 E
Tešanj 42 44 38N 17 59 E
Teseney 87 15 5N 36 42 E
Tesha → 55 55 38N 42 9 E
Teshio-Gawa → 74 44 53N 141 45 E
Tešica 42 43 27N 21 45 E
Tesiyn Gol → 75 50 40N 93 20 E
Teslić 42 44 37N 17 54 E
Teslin 104 60 10N 132 43W
Teslin → 108 61 34N 134 35W
Teslin L. 108 60 15N 132 57W
Tessalit 85 20 12N 1 0 E
Tessaoua 85 13 47N 7 56 E
Tessin 24 54 2N 12 28 E
Tessit 85 15 13N 0 18 E
Test → 13 51 7N 1 30W
Testa del Gargano 41 41 50N 16 10 E
Teste, La 20 44 37N 1 8W
Tét 27 47 30N 17 33 E
Têt → 20 42 44N 3 2 E
Tetachuck L. 108 53 18N 125 55W
Tetas, Pta. 124 23 31 S 70 38W
Tete 91 16 13 S 33 33 E
Tete □ 91 15 15 S 32 40 E
Teterev → 54 51 1N 30 5 E
Teterow 24 53 45N 12 34 E
Teteven 43 42 58N 24 17 E
Tethul → 108 60 35N 112 12W
Tetiyev 56 49 22N 29 38 E
Teton → 118 47 58N 111 0W
Tétouan 82 35 35N 5 21W
Tetovo 42 42 1N 21 2 E
Tetuán = Tétouan 82 35 30N 5 25W
Tetyushi 55 54 55N 48 49 E
Teuco → 124 25 35 S 60 11W
Teulada 40 38 59N 8 47 E
Teulon 109 50 23N 97 16W
Teun 73 6 59 S 129 8 E
Teutoburger Wald 22 52 5N 8 20 E
Tevere → 39 41 44N 12 14 E
Teverya 62 32 47N 35 32 E
Teviot → 14 55 21N 2 51W
Tewantin 99 26 27 S 153 3 E
Tewkesbury 13 51 59N 2 8W
Texada I. 108 49 40N 124 25W
Texarkana, Ark., U.S.A. 117 33 25N 94 0W
Texarkana, Tex., U.S.A. 117 33 25N 94 3W
Texas 99 28 49 S 151 9 E
Texas □ 117 31 40N 98 30W
Texas City 117 29 20N 94 55W
Texel 16 53 5N 4 50 E
Texhoma 117 36 32N 101 47W
Texline 117 36 26N 103 0W
Texoma L. 117 34 0N 96 38W
Teykovo 55 56 55N 40 30 E
Teyvareh 65 33 30N 64 24 E
Teza → 55 56 32N 41 53 E
Teziutlán 120 19 50N 97 22W
Tezpur 67 26 40N 92 45 E
Tezzeron L. 108 54 43N 124 30W
Tha-anne → 109 60 31N 94 37W
Tha Nun 71 8 12N 98 17 E
Thaba Putsoa 93 29 45 S 28 0 E
Thabana Ntlenyana 93 29 30 S 29 16 E
Thabazimbi 93 24 40 S 27 21 E
Thabor, Mt. 21 45 7N 6 34 E
Thai Nguyen 71 21 35N 105 55 E
Thailand (Siam) ■ 71 16 0N 102 0 E
Thakhek 71 17 25N 104 45 E
Thal 66 33 28N 70 33 E
Thal Desert 68 31 10N 71 30 E
Thala 83 35 35N 8 40 E
Thala La 67 28 25N 97 23 E
Thallon 99 28 39 S 148 49 E
Thalwil 25 47 17N 8 35 E
Thame → 13 51 35N 1 8W
Thames 101 37 7 S 175 34 E
Thames →, Can. 106 42 20N 82 25W
Thames →, U.K. 13 51 30N 0 35 E
Thames →, U.S.A. 113 41 18N 72 9W
Thamesford 112 43 4N 81 0W
Thamesville 112 42 33N 81 59W
Thāmit, W. 83 30 51N 16 14 E
Thana 70 19 12N 72 59 E
Thanesar 68 30 1N 76 52 E
Thanet, I. of 13 51 21N 1 20 E
Thang Binh 71 15 50N 108 20 E
Thangool 98 24 38 S 150 42 E
Thanh Hoa 71 19 48N 105 46 E
Thanjavur (Tanjore) 70 10 48N 79 12 E
Thanlwin Myit → 67 20 0N 98 0 E
Thann 19 47 48N 7 5 E
Thaon 19 48 15N 6 25 E

* *Renamed Sakhalinskiy Zaliv*

Thar (Great Indian) Desert 68 28 0N 72 0 E
Tharad 68 24 30N 71 44 E
Thargomindah 97 27 58 S 143 46 E
Tharrawaddy 67 17 38N 95 48 E
Thasopoúla 44 40 49N 24 45 E
Thásos, Greece 44 40 50N 24 42 E
Thásos, Greece 44 40 40N 24 40 E
Thatcher, Ariz., U.S.A. 119 32 54N 109 46W
Thatcher, Colo., U.S.A. 117 37 38N 104 6W
Thaton 67 16 55N 97 22 E
Thau, Étang de 20 43 23N 3 36 E
Thaungdut 67 24 30N 94 40 E
Thayer 117 36 34N 91 34W
Thayetmyo 67 19 20N 95 10 E
Thazi 67 21 0N 96 5 E
The Bight 121 24 19N 75 24W
The Dalles 118 45 40N 121 11W
The English Company's Is. 97 11 50 S 136 32 E
The Flatts 121 32 16N 64 45W
The Frome → 99 29 8 S 137 54 E
The Granites 96 20 35 S 130 21 E
The Grenadines, Is. 121 12 40N 61 20W
The Hague = 's-Gravenhage 16 52 7N 4 14 E
The Hamilton → 96 26 40 S 135 19 E
The Johnston Lakes 96 32 25 S 120 30 E
The Macumba → 97 27 52 S 137 12 E
The Pas 109 53 45N 101 15W
The Range 91 19 2 S 31 2 E
The Rock 99 35 15 S 147 2 E
The Salt Lake 99 30 6 S 142 8 E
The Warburton → 99 28 4 S 137 28 E
Thebes 86 25 40N 32 35 E
Thebes = Thívai 45 38 19N 23 19 E
Thedford, Can. 112 43 9N 81 51W
Thedford, U.S.A. 116 41 59N 100 31W
Theebine 99 25 57 S 152 34 E
Theil, Le 18 48 16N 0 42 E
Thekulthili L. 109 61 3N 110 0W
Thelon → 109 62 35N 104 3W
Thénezay 18 46 44N 0 2W
Thenia 83 36 44N 3 33 E
Thenon 20 45 9N 1 4 E
Theodore 97 24 55 S 150 3 E
Thérain → 19 49 15N 2 27 E
Theresa 113 44 13N 75 50W
Thermaïkos Kólpos 44 40 15N 22 45 E
Thermopolis 118 43 35N 108 10W
Thermopylae P. 45 38 48N 22 35 E
Thesprotía □ 44 39 27N 20 22 E
Thessalía □ 44 39 30N 22 0 E
Thessalon 106 46 20N 83 30W
Thessaloníki 44 40 38N 22 58 E
Thessaloníki □ 44 40 45N 23 0 E
Thessaly = Thessalía 44 39 30N 22 0 E
Thetford 13 52 25N 0 44 E
Thetford Mines 107 46 8N 71 18W
Theunissen 92 28 26 S 26 43 E
Thiámis → 44 39 15N 20 6 E
Thiberville 18 49 8N 0 27 E
Thibodaux 117 29 48N 90 49W
Thicket Portage 109 55 19N 97 42W
Thief River Falls 116 48 15N 96 48W
Thiel Mts. 5 85 15 S 91 0W
Thiene 39 45 42N 11 29 E
Thiérache 19 49 51N 3 45 E
Thiers 20 45 52N 3 33 E
Thies 84 14 50N 16 51W
Thiet 87 7 37N 28 49 E
Thika 90 1 1 S 37 5 E
Thikombia 101 15 44 S 179 55W
Thille-Boubacar 84 16 31N 15 5W
Thillot, Le 19 47 53N 6 46 E
Thimphu (Tashi Chho Dzong) 69 27 31N 89 45 E
Þingvallavatn 50 64 11N 21 9W
Thionville 19 49 20N 6 10 E
Thíra 45 36 23N 25 27 E
Thirasía 45 36 26N 25 21 E
Thirsk 12 54 15N 1 20W
Thistle I. 96 35 0 S 136 8 E
Thívai 45 38 19N 23 19 E
Thiviers 20 45 25N 0 54 E
Thizy 21 46 2N 4 18 E
Þjórsá → 50 63 47N 20 48W
Thlewiaza →, Man., Can. 109 59 43N 100 5W
Thlewiaza →, N.W.T., Can. 109 60 29N 94 40W
Thoa → 109 60 31N 109 47W
Thoissey 21 46 12N 4 48 E
Thomas, Okla., U.S.A. 117 35 48N 98 48W
Thomas, W. Va., U.S.A. 114 39 10N 79 30W
Thomas, L. 99 26 4 S 137 58 E
Thomaston 115 32 54N 84 20W
Thomasville, Ala., U.S.A. 115 31 55N 87 42W
Thomasville, Ga., U.S.A. 115 30 50N 84 0W
Thomasville, N.C., U.S.A. 115 35 55N 80 4W
Thompson 109 55 45N 97 52W
Thompson →, Can. 108 50 15N 121 24W
Thompson →, U.S.A. 116 39 46N 93 37W
Thompson Falls 118 47 37N 115 20W
Thompson Landing 109 62 56N 110 40W
Thompson Pk. 118 41 0N 123 3W
Thompsons 119 39 0N 109 50W
Thompsonville 113 42 0N 72 37W
Thomson → 97 25 11 S 142 53 E
Thomson's Falls = Nyahururu 90 0 2N 36 27 E
Thon Buri 71 13 43N 100 29 E
Thônes 21 45 54N 6 18 E
Thonon-les-Bains 21 46 22N 6 29 E
Thorez 57 48 4N 38 34 E
Þórisvatn 50 64 20N 18 55W
Þorlákshöfn 50 63 51N 21 22W
Thornaby on Tees 12 54 36N 1 19W
Thornbury 112 44 34N 80 26W
Thorne Glacier 5 87 30 S 150 0W
Thorold 112 43 7N 79 12W
Þórshöfn 50 66 12N 15 20W
Thouarcé 18 47 17N 0 30W
Thouars 18 46 58N 0 15W
Thrace = Thráki □ 44 41 10N 25 30 E
Thráki □ 44 41 9N 25 30 E
Thrakikón Pélagos 44 40 30N 25 0 E
Three Forks 118 45 55N 111 32W
Three Hills 108 51 43N 113 15W
Three Hummock I. 99 40 25 S 144 55 E
Three Lakes 116 45 48N 89 10W
Three Points, C. 84 4 42N 2 6W
Three Rivers 117 28 30N 98 10W
Three Sisters, Mt. 118 44 10N 121 46W
Throssell Ra. 96 22 3 S 121 43 E
Thrun Pass 26 47 20N 12 25 E
Thubun Lakes 109 61 30N 112 0W
Thuddungra 100 34 8 S 148 8 E
Thueyts 21 44 41N 4 9 E
Thuin 16 50 20N 4 17 E
Thuir 20 42 38N 2 45 E
Thule, Antarct. 5 59 27 S 27 19W
Thule, Greenl. 4 77 40N 69 0W
Thun 25 46 45N 7 38 E
Thunder B. 114 45 0N 83 20W
Thunder Bay 106 48 20N 89 15W
Thunersee 25 46 43N 7 39 E
Thung Song 71 8 10N 99 40 E
Thunkar 69 27 55N 91 0 E
Thur → 25 47 32N 9 10 E
Thurgau □ 25 47 34N 9 10 E
Thüringer Wald 24 50 35N 11 0 E
Thurles 15 52 40N 7 53W
Thurloo Downs 99 29 15 S 143 30 E
Thurn P. 25 47 20N 12 25 E
Thursday I. 97 10 30 S 142 3 E
Thurso, Can. 106 45 36N 75 15W
Thurso, U.K. 14 58 34N 3 31W
Thurston I. 5 72 0 S 100 0W
Thury-Harcourt 18 49 0N 0 30W
Thutade L. 108 57 0N 126 55W
Thyborøn 49 56 42N 8 12 E
Thylungra 99 26 4 S 143 28 E
Thyolo 91 16 7 S 35 5 E
Thysville = Mbanza Ngungu 88 5 12 S 14 53 E
Ti-n-Barraouene, O. → 85 18 40N 4 5 E
Ti-n-Medjerdam, O. → 82 25 45N 1 30 E
Ti-n-Tarabine, O. → 83 21 0N 7 25 E
Ti-n-Zaouatène 82 20 0N 2 55 E
Tia 99 31 10 S 150 34 E
Tian Shan 75 43 0N 84 0 E
Tiandu 77 18 18N 109 36 E
Tian'e 77 25 1N 107 9 E
Tianhe 77 24 48N 108 40 E
Tianjin 76 39 8N 117 10 E
Tiankoura 84 10 47N 3 17W
Tianshui 77 34 32N 105 40 E
Tianyang 77 23 42N 106 53 E
Tianzhen 76 40 24N 114 5 E
Tiaret 82 35 20N 1 21 E
Tiassalé 84 5 58N 4 57W
Tibagi 125 24 30 S 50 24W
Tibagi → 125 22 47 S 51 1W
Tibati 85 6 22N 12 30 E
Tiber = Tevere → 39 41 44N 12 14 E
Tiber Res. 118 48 20N 111 15W
Tiberias, L. = Kinneret, Yam 62 32 45N 35 35 E
Tibesti 83 21 0N 17 30 E
Tibet = Xizang □ 75 32 0N 88 0 E
Tibiri 85 13 34N 7 4 E
Ţibleş 46 47 32N 24 15 E
Tibnîn 62 33 12N 35 24 E
Tibooburra 97 29 26 S 142 1 E
Tibro 49 58 28N 14 10 E
Tiburón 120 29 0N 112 30W
Tîchît 84 18 21N 9 29W
Ticho 87 7 50N 39 32 E
Ticino □ 25 46 20N 8 45 E
Ticino → 38 45 9N 9 14 E
Ticonderoga 114 43 50N 73 28W
Ticul 120 20 20N 89 31W
Tidaholm 49 58 12N 13 55 E
Tiddim 67 23 28N 93 45 E
Tideridjaouine, Adrar 82 23 0N 2 15 E
Tidikelt 82 26 58N 1 30 E
Tidjikja 84 18 29N 11 35W
Tidore 73 0 40N 127 25 E
Tiébissou 84 7 9N 5 10W
Tiéboro 83 21 20N 17 7 E
Tiel, Neth. 16 51 53N 5 26 E
Tiel, Senegal 84 14 55N 15 5W
Tieling 76 42 20N 123 55 E
Tielt 16 51 0N 3 20 E
Tien Shan = Tian Shan 65 42 0N 80 0 E
Tien-tsin = Tianjin 75 39 8N 117 10 E
T'iench'ing = Tianjin 76 39 8N 117 10 E
Tienen 16 50 48N 4 57 E
Tiénigbé 84 8 11N 5 43W
Tientsin = Tianjin 76 39 8N 117 10 E
Tierp 48 60 20N 17 30 E
Tierra Amarilla, Chile 124 27 28 S 70 18W
Tierra Amarilla, U.S.A. 119 36 42N 106 33W
Tierra de Barros 31 38 40N 6 30W
Tierra de Campos 30 42 10N 4 50W
Tierra del Fuego, I. Gr. de 128 54 0 S 69 0W
Tiétar → 30 39 50N 6 1W
Tieté → 125 20 40 S 51 35W
Tifarit 82 26 9N 10 33W
Tiffin 114 41 8N 83 10W
Tiflèt 82 33 54N 6 20W
Tiflis = Tbilisi 57 41 43N 44 50 E
Tifrah 62 31 19N 34 42 E
Tifton 115 31 28N 83 32W
Tifu 73 3 39 S 126 24 E
Tigil 59 57 49N 158 40 E
Tignish 107 46 58N 64 2W
Tigre □ 87 13 35N 39 15 E
Tigre → 126 4 30 S 74 10W
Tigris = Dijlah, Nahr → 64 31 0N 47 25 E
Tiguentourine 83 27 52N 9 8 E
Tigveni 46 45 10N 24 31 E
Tigyaing 67 23 45N 96 10 E
Tigzerte, O. → 82 28 10N 9 37W
Tîh, Gebel el 86 29 32N 33 26 E
Tihama 64 22 0N 39 0 E
Tihodaine, Dunes de 83 25 15N 7 15 E
Tijesno 39 43 48N 15 39 E
Tîjî 83 32 0N 11 18 E
Tijuana 120 32 30N 117 10W
Tikal 120 17 13N 89 24W
Tikamgarh 68 24 44N 78 50 E
Tikhoretsk 57 45 56N 40 5 E
Tikhvin 54 59 35N 33 30 E
Tikkadouine, Adrar 82 24 28N 1 30 E
Tiko 85 4 4N 9 20 E
Tikrīt 64 34 35N 43 37 E
Tiksi 59 71 40N 128 45 E
Tilamuta 73 0 32N 122 23 E
Tilburg 16 51 31N 5 6 E
Tilbury, Can. 106 42 17N 82 23W
Tilbury, U.K. 13 51 27N 0 24 E
Tilcara 124 23 36 S 65 23W
Tilden, Nebr., U.S.A. 116 42 3N 97 45W
Tilden, Tex., U.S.A. 117 28 28N 98 33W
Tilemses 85 15 37N 4 44 E
Tilemsi, Vallée du 85 17 42N 0 15 E
Tilhar 69 28 0N 79 45 E
Tilia, O. → 82 27 32N 0 55 E
Tilichiki 59 60 27N 166 5 E
Tiligul → 56 47 4N 30 57 E
Tililane 82 27 49N 0 6W
Tílissos 45 35 2N 25 0 E
Till → 12 55 35N 2 3W
Tillabéri 85 14 28N 1 28 E
Tillamook 118 45 29N 123 55W
Tillberga 48 59 52N 16 39 E
Tillia 85 16 8N 4 47 E
Tillsonburg 106 42 53N 80 44W
Tílos 45 36 27N 27 27 E
Tilpa 99 30 57 S 144 24 E
Tilrhemt 82 33 9N 3 22 E
Tilsit = Sovetsk 54 55 6N 21 50 E
Tilt → 14 56 50N 3 50W
Tilton 113 43 25N 71 36W
Timagami L. 106 47 0N 80 10W
Timanskiy Kryazh 52 65 58N 50 5 E
Timaru 101 44 23 S 171 14 E
Timashevsk 57 45 35N 39 0 E
Timau, Italy 39 46 35N 13 0 E
Timau, Kenya 90 0 4N 37 15 E
Timbákion 45 35 4N 24 45 E
Timbedgha 84 16 17N 8 16W
Timber Lake 116 45 29N 101 6W
Timboon 99 38 30 S 142 58 E
Timbuktu = Tombouctou 84 16 50N 3 0W
Timdjaouine 82 21 37N 4 30 E
Timellouline 83 29 22N 8 55 E
Timétrine Montagnes 85 19 25N 1 0W
Timfi Óros 44 39 59N 20 45 E
Timfristós, Óros 45 38 57N 21 50 E
Timhadit 82 33 15N 5 4W
Timia 85 18 4N 8 40 E
Timimoun 82 29 14N 0 16 E
Timimoun, Sebkha de 82 28 50N 0 46 E
Timiş □ 42 45 40N 21 30 E
Timiş → 46 45 30N 21 0 E
Timişoara 42 45 43N 21 15 E
Timmins 106 48 28N 81 25W
Timok → 42 44 10N 22 40 E
Timon 127 5 8 S 42 52W
Timor 73 9 0 S 125 0 E
Timor □ 73 9 0 S 125 0 E
Timor Sea 97 10 0 S 127 0 E
Tin Alkoum 83 24 42N 10 17 E
Tin Gornai 85 16 38N 0 38W
Tin Gornaï → 85 20 30N 4 35 E
Tîna, Khalîg el 86 31 20N 32 42 E
Tinaca Pt. 73 5 30N 125 25 E
Tinafak, O. → 83 27 10N 7 0 E
Tinca 46 46 46N 21 58 E
Tinchebray 18 48 47N 0 45W
Tindivanam 70 12 15N 79 41 E
Tindouf 82 27 42N 8 10W
Tinee → 21 43 55N 7 11 E
Tineo 30 43 21N 6 27W
Tinerhir 82 31 29N 5 31W
Tinfouchi 82 28 52N 5 49W
Tinglev 49 54 57N 9 13 E
Tingo Maria 126 9 10 S 75 54W
Tingsryd 49 56 31N 15 0 E
Tinjoub 82 29 45N 5 40W
Tinnoset 47 59 55N 9 3 E
Tinnsjø 47 59 55N 8 54 E
Tinogasta 124 28 5 S 67 32W
Tínos 45 37 33N 25 8 E
Tiñoso, C. 33 37 32N 1 6W
Tintina 124 27 2 S 62 45W
Tintinara 99 35 48 S 140 2 E
Tinto → 31 37 12N 6 55W
Tioga 112 41 54N 77 9W
Tioman, Pulau 71 2 50N 104 10 E
Tione di Trento 38 46 3N 10 44 E
Tionesta 112 41 29N 79 28W
Tior 87 6 26N 31 11 E
Tioulilin 82 27 1N 0 2W
Tipongpani 67 27 20N 95 55 E
Tipperary 15 52 28N 8 10W
Tipperary □ 15 52 37N 7 55W
Tipton, U.K. 13 52 32N 2 4W
Tipton, Calif., U.S.A. 119 36 3N 119 19W
Tipton, Ind., U.S.A. 114 40 17N 86 0W
Tipton, Iowa, U.S.A. 116 41 45N 91 12W
Tiptonville 117 36 22N 89 30W
Tiptur 70 13 15N 76 26 E
Tirahart, O. 82 23 45N 3 10 E
Tirān 65 32 45N 51 8 E
Tirân 86 27 56N 34 45 E
Tirana 44 41 18N 19 49 E
Tirana-Durrësi □ 44 41 35N 20 0 E
Tirano 38 46 13N 10 11 E
Tiraspol 56 46 55N 29 35 E
Tirat Karmel 62 32 46N 34 58 E
Tirat Yehuda 62 32 1N 34 56 E
Tirat Zevi 62 32 26N 35 31 E
Tiratimine 82 25 56N 3 37 E
Tirdout 85 16 7N 1 5W
Tire 64 38 5N 27 50 E
Tirebolu 64 40 58N 38 45 E
Tiree 14 56 31N 6 55W
Tîrgovişte 46 44 55N 25 27 E
Tîrgu Frumos 46 47 12N 27 2 E
Tîrgu-Jiu 46 45 5N 23 19 E
Tîrgu Mureş 46 46 31N 24 38 E
Tîrgu Neamţ 46 47 12N 26 25 E
Tîrgu Ocna 46 46 16N 26 39 E
Tîrgu Secuiesc 46 46 0N 26 10 E
Tirich Mir 66 36 15N 71 55 E
Tiriola 41 38 57N 16 32 E
Tirna → 70 18 4N 76 57 E
Tîrnava Mare → 46 46 15N 24 30 E
Tîrnava Mică → 46 46 17N 24 30 E
Tîrnăveni 46 46 19N 24 13 E
Tírnavos 44 39 45N 22 18 E
Tîrnova 46 45 23N 22 1 E
Tirodi 69 21 40N 79 44 E
Tirol □ 26 47 3N 10 43 E
Tirschenreuth 25 49 51N 12 20 E
Tirso → 40 39 52N 8 33 E
Tirso, L. del 40 40 8N 8 56 E
Tiruchchirappalli 70 10 45N 78 45 E
Tiruchendur 70 8 30N 78 11 E
Tiruchengodu 70 11 23N 77 56 E
Tirumangalam 70 9 49N 77 58 E
Tirunelveli (Tinnevelly) 70 8 45N 77 45 E
Tirupati 70 13 39N 79 25 E
Tiruppattur 70 12 30N 78 30 E
Tiruppur 70 11 5N 77 22 E
Tiruturaipundi 70 10 32N 79 41 E
Tiruvadaimarudur 70 11 2N 79 27 E
Tiruvallar 70 13 9N 79 57 E
Tiruvannamalai 70 12 15N 79 5 E
Tiruvarur 70 10 46N 79 38 E
Tiruvatipuram 70 12 39N 79 33 E
Tiruvottiyur 70 13 10N 80 22 E
Tisa → 42 45 15N 20 17 E
Tisdale 109 52 50N 104 0W
Tishomingo 117 34 14N 96 38W
Tisjön 48 60 56N 13 0 E
Tisnaren 48 58 58N 15 56 E
Tišnov 27 49 21N 16 25 E
Tisovec 27 48 41N 19 56 E
Tissemsilt 82 35 35N 1 50 E
Tissint 82 29 57N 7 16W
Tissø 49 55 35N 11 18 E
Tista → 69 25 23N 89 43 E
Tisza → 27 46 8N 20 2 E
Tiszaföldvár 27 47 0N 20 14 E
Tiszafüred 27 47 38N 20 50 E
Tiszalök 27 48 0N 21 10 E
Tiszavasvári 27 47 58N 21 18 E
Tit, Ahaggar, Alg. 83 23 0N 5 10 E
Tit, Tademait, Alg. 82 27 0N 1 29 E
Tit-Ary 59 71 55N 127 2 E
Titaguas 32 39 53N 1 6W
Titel 42 45 10N 20 18 E
Titicaca, L. 126 15 30 S 69 30W
Titilagarh 70 20 15N 83 11 E
Titiwa 85 12 14N 12 53 E
Titograd 42 42 30N 19 19 E
Titov Veles 42 41 46N 21 47 E
Titova Korenica 39 44 45N 15 41 E
Titovo Uzice 42 43 55N 19 50 E
Titule 90 3 15N 25 31 E
Titusville, Fla., U.S.A. 115 28 37N 80 49W
Titusville, Pa., U.S.A. 114 41 35N 79 39W
Tivaouane 84 14 56N 16 45W
Tivat 42 42 28N 18 43 E
Tiveden 49 58 50N 14 30 E
Tiverton 13 50 54N 3 30W
Tívoli 39 41 58N 12 45 E
Tiwī 65 22 45N 59 12 E
Tiyo 87 14 41N 40 15 E
Tizga 82 32 1N 5 9W
Ti'zi N'Isli 82 32 28N 5 47W
Tizi-Ouzou 83 36 42N 4 3 E
Tizimín 120 21 0N 88 1W
Tiznit 82 29 48N 9 45W
Tjeggelvas 50 66 37N 17 45 E
Tjirebon = Cirebon 73 6 45 S 108 32 E
Tjöme 47 59 8N 10 26 E
Tjörn 49 58 0N 11 35 E
Tkibuli 57 42 26N 43 0 E
Tkvarcheli 57 42 47N 41 42 E
Tlahualilo 120 26 20N 103 30W
Tlaxcala 120 19 20N 98 14W
Tlaxcala □ 120 19 30N 98 20W
Tlaxiaco 120 17 18N 97 40W
Tlell 108 53 34N 131 56W
Tlemcen 82 34 52N 1 21W
Tleta Sidi Bouguedra 82 32 16N 9 59W
Tlumach, U.S.S.R. 54 48 46N 25 0 E
Tlumach, U.S.S.R. 56 48 51N 25 0 E
Tłuszcz 28 52 25N 21 25 E
Tlyarata 57 42 9N 46 26 E
Tmassah 83 26 19N 15 51 E
Tnine d'Anglou 82 29 50N 9 50W
Toad → 108 59 25N 124 57W
Toala 73 1 30 S 121 40 E
Toamasina 93 18 10 S 49 25 E
Toamasina □ 93 18 0 S 49 0 E
Toay 124 36 43 S 64 38W
Toba 74 34 30N 136 51 E
Toba, Danau 72 2 40N 98 50 E
Toba Kakar 68 31 30N 69 0 E
Toba Tek Singh 68 30 55N 72 25 E
Tobago 121 11 10N 60 30W
Tobarra 33 38 37N 1 44W
Tobelo 73 1 45N 127 56 E
Tobermorey 98 22 12 S 137 51 E
Tobermory, Can. 106 45 12N 81 40W
Tobermory, U.K. 14 56 37N 6 4W
Tobin L. 109 53 35N 103 30W
Toboali 72 3 0 S 106 25 E
Tobol 58 52 40N 62 39 E
Toboli 73 0 38 S 120 5 E
Tobolsk 58 58 15N 68 10 E
Tobruk = Tubruq 81 32 7N 23 55 E
Tobyhanna 113 41 10N 75 25W
Tocantinópolis 127 6 20 S 47 25W
Tocantins → 127 1 45 S 49 10W
Toccoa 115 34 32N 83 17W
Toce → 38 45 56N 8 29 E
Tochigi 74 36 25N 139 45 E
Tochigi □ 74 36 45N 139 45 E
Tocina 31 37 37N 5 44W

Tocopilla 124 22 5S 70 10W
Tocumwal 99 35 51S 145 31 E
Tocuyo → 126 11 3N 68 23W
Todeli 73 1 38S 124 34 E
Todenyang 90 4 35N 35 56 E
Todi 39 42 47N 12 24 E
Todos os Santos, Baía de 127 12 48S 38 38W
Todos Santos 120 23 27N 110 13W
Todtnau 25 47 50N 7 56 E
Toecé 85 11 50N 1 16W
Tofield 108 53 25N 112 40W
Tofino 108 49 11N 125 55W
Töfsingdalens nationalpark 48 62 15N 12 44 E
Toftlund 49 55 11N 9 2 E
Tofua 101 19 45S 175 05W
Togba 84 17 26N 10 12W
Togian, Kepulauan 73 0 20S 121 50 E
Togliatti 55 53 32N 49 24 E
Togo ■ 85 6 15N 1 35 E
Togtoh 76 40 15N 111 10 E
Toinya 87 6 17N 29 46 E
Tojo 73 1 20S 121 15 E
Tokaj 27 48 8N 21 27 E
Tōkamachi 74 37 8N 138 43 E
Tokanui 101 46 34S 168 56 E
Tokar 81 18 27N 37 56 E
Tokara Kaikyō 74 30 0N 130 0 E
Tokarahi 101 44 56S 170 39 E
Tokat 64 40 22N 36 35 E
Tokelau Is. ■ 94 9 0S 171 45W
Tokmak 58 42 49N 75 15 E
Toko Ra. 98 23 5S 138 20 E
Tokong 71 5 27N 100 23 E
Tokushima 74 34 4N 134 34 E
Tokushima □ 74 34 15N 134 0 E
Tokuyama 74 34 3N 131 50 E
Tōkyō 74 35 45N 139 45 E
Tōkyō □ 74 35 40N 139 30 E
Tolbukhin 43 43 37N 27 49 E
Toledo, Spain 30 39 50N 4 2W
Toledo, Ohio, U.S.A. 114 41 37N 83 33W
Toledo, Oreg., U.S.A. 118 44 40N 123 59W
Toledo, Wash., U.S.A. 118 46 29N 122 51W
Toledo, Montes de 31 39 33N 4 20W
Tolentino 39 43 12N 13 17 E
Tolga, Alg. 83 34 40N 5 22 E
Tolga, Norway 47 62 26N 11 1 E
Toliara 93 23 21S 43 40 E
Toliara □ 93 21 0S 45 0 E
Tolima, Vol. 126 4 40N 75 19W
Tolitoli 73 1 5N 120 50 E
Tolkmicko 28 54 19N 19 31 E
Tollarp 49 55 55N 13 58 E
Tolleson 119 33 29N 112 10W
Tolmachevo 54 58 56N 29 51 E
Tolmezzo 39 46 23N 13 0 E
Tolmin 39 46 11N 13 45 E
Tolna 27 46 25N 18 48 E
Tolna □ 27 46 30N 18 30 E
Tolo 88 2 55S 18 34 E
Tolo, Teluk 73 2 20S 122 10 E
Tolochin 54 54 25N 29 42 E
Tolosa 32 43 8N 2 5W
Tolox 31 36 41N 4 54W
Toluca 120 19 20N 99 40W
Tom Burke 93 23 5S 28 4 E
Tom Price 96 22 40S 117 48 E
Tomah 116 43 59N 90 30W
Tomahawk 116 45 28N 89 40W
Tomar 31 39 36N 8 25W
Tómaros Óros 44 39 29N 20 48 E
Tomaszów Mazowiecki 28 51 30N 19 57 E
Tombé 87 5 53N 31 40 E
Tombigbee → 115 31 4N 87 58W
Tombouctou 84 16 50N 3 0W
Tombstone 119 31 40N 110 4W
Tomé 124 36 36S 72 57W
Tomelilla 49 55 33N 13 58 E
Tomelloso 33 39 10N 3 2W
Tomingley 99 32 6S 148 16 E
Tomini 73 0 30N 120 30 E
Tomini, Teluk 73 0 10S 122 0 E
Tominian 84 13 17N 4 35W
Tomiño 30 41 59N 8 46W
Tommot 59 59 4N 126 20 E
Tomnavoulin 14 57 19N 3 18W
Toms River 113 39 59N 74 12W
Tomsk 58 56 30N 85 5 E
Tomtabacken 49 57 30N 14 30 E
Tonalá 120 16 8N 93 41W
Tonale, Passo del 38 46 15N 10 34 E
Tonalea 119 36 17N 110 58W
Tonantins 126 2 45S 67 45W
Tonasket 118 48 45N 119 30W
Tonawanda 114 43 0N 78 54W
Tonbridge 13 51 12N 0 18 E
Tondano 73 1 35N 124 54 E
Tondela 30 40 31N 8 5W
Tønder 49 54 58N 8 50 E
Tondi 70 9 45N 79 4 E
Tondi Kiwindi 85 14 28N 2 02 E
Tondibi 85 16 39N 0 14W
Tong Xian 76 39 55N 116 35 E
Tonga ■ 101 19 50S 174 30W
Tonga Trench 94 18 0S 175 0W
Tongaat 93 29 33S 31 9 E
Tongaland 93 27 0S 32 0 E
Tongareva 95 9 0S 158 0W
Tongatapu 101 21 10S 174 0W
Tongcheng 77 31 4N 116 56 E
Tongchuan 77 35 6N 109 3 E
Tongdao 77 26 10N 109 42 E
Tongeren 16 50 47N 5 28 E
Tongguan 77 34 40N 110 25 E
Tonghua 76 41 42N 125 58 E
Tongio 99 37 14S 147 44 E
Tongjiang, Heilongjiang, China 75 47 40N 132 27 E
Tongjiang, Sichuan, China 77 31 58N 107 11 E
Tongking = Tonkin, G. of 71 20 0N 108 0 E
Tongliao 76 43 38N 122 18 E
Tongling 77 30 55N 117 48 E
Tonglu 77 29 45N 119 37 E
Tongnan 77 30 9N 105 50 E
Tongobory 93 23 32S 44 20 E
Tongoy 124 30 16S 71 31W
Tongren 75 27 43N 109 11 E
Tongres = Tongeren 16 50 47N 5 28 E
Tongue 14 58 29N 4 25W
Tongue → 116 46 24N 105 52W
Tongyu 76 44 45N 123 4 E
Tongzi 77 28 9N 106 49 E
Tonj 87 7 20N 28 44 E
Tonk 68 26 6N 75 54 E
Tonkawa 117 36 44N 97 22W
Tonkin = Bac-Phan 71 22 0N 105 0 E
Tonlé Sap 71 13 0N 104 0 E
Tonnay-Charente 20 45 56N 0 55W
Tonneins 20 44 23N 0 19 E
Tonnerre 19 47 51N 3 59 E
Tönning 24 54 18N 8 57 E
Tonopah 119 38 4N 117 12W
Tønsberg 47 59 19N 10 25 E
Tonstad 47 58 40N 6 45 E
Tonto Basin 119 33 56N 111 27W
Tooele 118 40 30N 112 20W
Toompine 99 27 15S 144 19 E
Toonpan 98 19 28S 146 48 E
Toora 99 38 39S 146 23 E
Toora-Khem 59 52 28N 96 17 E
Toowoomba 97 27 32S 151 56 E
Top-ozero 52 65 35N 32 0 E
Topalu 46 44 31N 28 3 E
Topeka 116 39 3N 95 40W
Topki 58 55 20N 85 35 E
Topl'a → 27 48 45N 21 45 E
Topley 108 54 49N 126 18W
Toplica → 42 43 15N 21 49 E
Toplița 46 46 55N 25 20 E
Topocalma, Pta. 124 34 10S 72 2W
Topock 119 34 46N 114 29W
Topola 42 44 17N 20 41 E
Topolčani 42 41 14N 21 56 E
Topolčany 27 48 35N 18 12 E
Topoli 57 47 59N 51 38 E
Topolnitsa → 43 42 11N 24 18 E
Topolobampo 120 25 40N 109 4W
Topolovgrad 43 42 5N 26 20 E
Topolvătu Mare 42 45 46N 21 41 E
Toppenish 118 46 27N 120 16W
Topusko 39 45 18N 15 59 E
Tor Bay 96 35 5S 117 50 E
Torá 32 41 49N 1 25 E
Tora Kit 87 11 2N 32 36 E
Toraka Vestale 93 16 20S 43 58 E
Torata 126 17 23S 70 1W
Torbat-e Ḥeydārīyeh 65 35 15N 59 12 E
Torbat-e Jām 65 35 16N 60 35 E
Torbay, Can. 107 47 40N 52 42W
Torbay, U.K. 13 50 26N 3 31W
Tørdal 47 59 10N 8 45 E
Tordesillas 30 41 30N 5 0W
Tordoya 30 43 6N 8 36W
Töreboda 49 58 41N 14 7 E
Torey 59 50 33N 104 50 E
Torfajökull 50 63 54N 19 0W
Torgau 24 51 32N 13 0 E
Torgelow 24 53 40N 13 59 E
Torhout 16 51 5N 3 7 E
Tori 87 7 53N 33 35 E
Torigni-sur-Vire 18 49 3N 0 58W
Torija 32 40 44N 3 2W
Torin 120 27 33N 110 15W
Toriñana, C. 30 43 3N 9 17W
Torino 38 45 4N 7 40 E
Torit 87 4 27N 32 31 E
Torkovichi 54 58 51N 30 21 E
Tormac 42 45 30N 21 30 E
Tormentine 107 46 6N 63 46W
Tormes → 30 41 18N 6 29W
Tornado Mt. 108 49 55N 114 40W
Torne älv → 50 65 50N 24 12 E
Torneträsk 50 68 24N 19 15 E
Tornio 50 65 50N 24 12 E
Tornionjoki → 50 65 50N 24 12 E
Tornquist 124 38 8S 62 15W
Toro 30 41 35N 5 24W
Torö 49 58 48N 17 50 E
Toro, Cerro del 124 29 10S 69 50W
Toro, Pta. 120 9 22N 79 57W
Törökszentmiklós 27 47 11N 20 27 E
Toroníios Kólpos 44 40 5N 23 30 E
Toronto, Austral. 99 33 0S 151 30 E
Toronto, Can. 106 43 39N 79 20W
Toronto, U.S.A. 114 40 27N 80 36W
Toronto, L. 120 27 40N 105 30W
Toropets 54 56 30N 31 40 E
Tororo 90 0 45N 34 12 E
Toros Dağlari 64 37 0N 35 0 E
Torpshammar 48 62 29N 16 20 E
Torquay, Can. 109 49 9N 103 30W
Torquay, U.K. 13 50 27N 3 31W
Torquemada 30 42 2N 4 19W
Torralba de Calatrava 31 39 1N 3 44W
Torrão 31 38 16N 8 11W
Torre Annunziata 41 40 45N 14 26 E
Tôrre de Moncorvo 30 41 12N 7 8W
Torre del Greco 41 40 47N 14 22 E
Torre del Mar 31 36 44N 4 6W
Torre-Pacheco 33 37 44N 0 57W
Torre Pellice 38 44 49N 7 13 E
Torreblanca 32 40 14N 0 12 E
Torrecampo 31 38 29N 4 41W
Torrecilla en Cameros 32 42 15N 2 38W
Torredembarra 32 41 9N 1 24 E
Torredonjimeno 31 37 46N 3 57W
Torrejoncillo 30 39 54N 6 28W
Torrelaguna 32 40 50N 3 38W
Torrelavega 30 43 20N 4 5W
Torremaggiore 41 41 42N 15 17 E
Torremolinos 31 36 38N 4 30W
Torrens Cr. → 98 22 23S 145 9 E
Torrens Creek 98 20 48S 145 3 E
Torrens, L. 97 31 0S 137 50 E
Torrente 33 39 27N 0 28W
Torrenueva 33 38 38N 3 22W
Torréon 120 25 33N 103 25W
Torreperogil 33 38 2N 3 17W
Torres 120 28 46N 110 47W
Torres Novas 31 39 27N 8 33W
Torres Strait 97 9 50S 142 20 E
Torres Vedras 31 39 5N 9 15W
Torrevieja 33 37 59N 0 42W
Torrey 119 38 18N 111 25W
Torridge → 13 50 51N 4 10W
Torridon, L. 14 57 35N 5 50W
Torrijos 30 39 59N 4 18W
Torrington, Conn., U.S.A. 114 41 50N 73 9W
Torrington, Wyo., U.S.A. 116 42 5N 104 8W
Torroella de Montgrí 32 42 2N 3 8 E
Torrox 31 36 46N 3 57W
Torsås 49 56 24N 16 0 E
Torsby 48 60 7N 13 0 E
Torsö 49 58 48N 13 45 E
Tortola 121 18 19N 65 0W
Tórtoles de Esgueva 30 41 49N 4 2W
Tortona 38 44 53N 8 54 E
Tortoreto 39 42 50N 13 55 E
Tortorici 41 38 2N 14 48 E
Tortosa 32 40 49N 0 31 E
Tortosa, C. 32 40 41N 0 52 E
Tortosendo 30 40 15N 7 31W
Tortue, Î. de la 121 20 5N 72 57W
Tortuga, La 126 11 0N 65 22W
Torūd 65 35 25N 55 5 E
Toruń 28 53 0N 18 39 E
Toruń □ 28 53 20N 19 0 E
Torup, Denmark 49 57 5N 9 5 E
Torup, Sweden 49 56 57N 13 5 E
Tory I. 15 55 17N 8 12W
Torysa → 27 48 39N 21 21 E
Torzhok 54 57 5N 34 55 E
Tosa-Wan 74 33 15N 133 30 E
Toscana 38 43 30N 11 5 E
Toscano, Arcipelago 38 42 30N 10 30 E
Tosno 54 59 38N 30 46 E
Tossa 32 41 43N 2 56 E
Tostado 124 29 15S 61 50W
Tostedt 24 53 17N 9 42 E
Tosya 64 41 1N 34 2 E
Toszek 28 50 27N 18 32 E
Totak 47 59 40N 7 45 E
Totana 33 37 45N 1 30W
Toten 47 60 37N 10 53 E
Toteng 92 20 22S 22 58 E
Tôtes 18 49 41N 1 3 E
Tótkomlós 27 46 24N 20 45 E
Totma 55 60 0N 42 40 E
Totnes 13 50 26N 3 41W
Totonicapán 120 14 58N 91 12W
Totten Glacier 5 66 45S 116 10 E
Tottenham, Austral. 99 32 14S 147 21 E
Tottenham, Can. 112 44 1N 79 49W
Tottori 74 35 30N 134 15 E
Tottori □ 74 35 30N 134 12 E
Touat 82 27 27N 0 30 E
Touba 84 8 22N 7 40W
Toubkal, Djebel 82 31 0N 8 0W
Toucy 19 47 44N 3 15 E
Tougan 84 13 11N 2 58W
Touggourt 83 33 10N 6 0 E
Tougué 84 11 25N 11 50W
Toukmatine 83 24 49N 7 11 E
Toul 19 48 40N 5 53 E
Toulepleu 84 6 32N 8 24W
Toulon 21 43 10N 5 55 E
Toulouse 20 43 37N 1 27 E
Toummo 83 22 45N 14 8 E
Toummo Dhoba 83 22 30N 14 31 E
Toumodi 84 6 32N 5 4W
Tounassine, Hamada 82 28 48N 5 0W
Toungoo 67 19 0N 96 30 E
Touques → 18 49 22N 0 8 E
Touquet-Paris-Plage, Le 19 50 30N 1 36 E
Tour-du-Pin, La 21 45 33N 5 27 E
Touraine 18 47 20N 0 30 E
Tourcoing 19 50 42N 3 10 E
Tournai 16 50 35N 3 25 E
Tournan-en-Brie 19 48 44N 2 46 E
Tournay 20 43 13N 0 13 E
Tournon 21 45 4N 4 50 E
Tournon-St-Martin 18 46 45N 0 58 E
Tournus 21 46 35N 4 54 E
Tours 18 47 22N 0 40 E
Touside, Pic 83 21 1N 16 29 E
Touwsrivier 92 33 20S 20 0 E
Tovarkovskiy 55 53 40N 38 14 E
Tovdal 47 58 47N 8 10 E
Tovdalselva → 47 58 15N 8 5 E
Towamba 99 37 6S 149 43 E
Towanda 114 41 46N 76 30W
Towang 67 27 37N 91 50 E
Tower 116 47 49N 92 17W
Towerhill Cr. → 98 22 28S 144 35 E
Towner 116 48 25N 100 26W
Townsend 118 46 25N 111 32W
Townshend, C. 97 22 18S 150 30 E
Townshend I. 97 22 10S 150 31 E
Townsville 97 19 15S 146 45 E
Towson 114 39 26N 76 34W
Towyn 13 52 36N 4 5W
Toyah 117 31 20N 103 48W
Toyahvale 117 30 58N 103 45W
Toyama 74 36 40N 137 15 E
Toyama □ 74 36 45N 137 30 E
Toyama-Wan 74 37 0N 137 30 E
Toyohashi 74 34 45N 137 25 E
Toyokawa 74 34 48N 137 27 E
Toyonaka 74 34 50N 135 28 E
Toyooka 74 35 35N 134 48 E
Toyota 74 35 3N 137 7 E
Tozeur 83 33 56N 8 8 E
Trabancos → 30 41 36N 5 15W
Traben Trarbach 25 49 57N 7 7 E
Trabzon 64 41 0N 39 45 E
Tracadie 107 47 30N 64 55W
Tracy, Calif., U.S.A. 119 37 46N 121 27W
Tracy, Minn., U.S.A. 116 44 12N 95 38W
Tradate 38 45 43N 8 54 E
Trafalgar 100 38 14S 146 12 E
Trafalgar, C. 31 36 10N 6 2W
Trâghân 83 26 0N 14 30 E
Traian 46 45 2N 28 15 E
Trail 108 49 5N 117 40W
Trainor L. 108 60 24N 120 17W
Tralee 15 52 16N 9 42W
Tralee B. 15 52 17N 9 55W
Tramore 15 52 10N 7 10W
Tran Ninh, Cao Nguyen 71 19 30N 103 10 E
Tranås 49 58 3N 14 59 E
Trancas 124 26 11S 65 20W
Tranche, La 20 46 20N 1 26W
Tranche-sur-Mer, La 18 46 20N 1 27W
Trancoso 30 40 49N 7 21W
Tranebjerg 49 55 51N 10 36 E
Tranemo 49 57 30N 13 20 E
Trang 71 7 33N 99 38 E
Trangahy 93 19 7S 44 31 E
Trangan 73 6 40S 134 20 E
Trangie 99 32 4S 148 0 E
Trångsviken 48 63 19N 14 0 E
Trani 41 41 17N 16 24 E
Tranoroa 93 24 42S 45 4 E
Tranquebar 70 11 1N 79 54 E
Tranqueras 125 31 13S 55 45W
Trans Nzoia □ 90 1 0N 35 0 E
Transcona 109 49 55N 97 0W
Transilvania 46 46 19N 25 0 E
Transkei □ 93 32 15S 28 15 E
Transtrand 48 61 6N 13 20 E
Transvaal □ 92 25 0S 29 0 E
Transylvania = Transilvania 46 46 19N 25 0 E
Transylvanian Alps 46 45 30N 25 0 E
Trápani 40 38 1N 12 30 E
Trapper Peak 118 45 56N 114 29W
Traralgon 97 38 12S 146 34 E
Traryd 49 56 35N 13 45 E
Trarza □ 84 17 30N 15 0W
Trasacco 39 41 58N 13 30 E
Trăscău, Munţii 46 46 14N 23 14 E
Trasimeno, L. 39 43 10N 12 5 E
Trat 71 12 14N 102 33 E
Traun 26 48 14N 14 15 E
Traunsee 26 47 55N 13 50 E
Traunstein 25 47 52N 12 40 E
Trävad 49 58 15N 13 5 E
Traveller's L. 99 33 20S 142 0 E
Travemünde 24 53 58N 10 52 E
Travers, Mt. 101 42 1S 172 45 E
Traverse City 114 44 45N 85 39W
Traverse Is. 5 57 0S 28 0W
Travnik 42 44 17N 17 39 E
Trazo 30 43 0N 8 30W
Trbovlje 39 46 12N 15 5 E
Trébbia → 38 45 4N 9 41 E
Trebel → 24 53 55N 13 1 E
Třebíč 26 49 14N 15 55 E
Trebinje 42 42 44N 18 22 E
Trebisacce 41 39 52N 16 32 E
Trebišnica → 42 42 47N 18 8 E
Trebišov 27 48 38N 21 41 E
Trebižat → 42 43 15N 17 30 E
Trebnje 39 45 54N 15 1 E
Třeboň 26 48 59N 14 48 E
Trebujena 31 36 52N 6 11W
Trecate 38 45 26N 8 42 E
Tredegar 13 51 47N 3 16W
Tregaron 13 52 14N 3 56W
Trégastel-Plage 18 48 49N 3 31W
Tregnago 39 45 31N 11 10 E
Tréguier 18 48 47N 3 16W
Trégune 18 47 51N 3 51W
Treherne 109 49 38N 98 42W
Tréia 39 43 20N 13 20 E
Treignac 20 45 32N 1 48 E
Treinta y Tres 125 33 16S 54 17W
Treis 25 50 9N 7 19 E
Treklyano 42 42 33N 22 36 E
Trekveld 92 30 35S 19 45 E
Trelde Næs 49 55 38N 9 53 E
Trelew 128 43 10S 65 20W
Trelissac 20 45 11N 0 47 E
Trelleborg 49 55 20N 13 10 E
Trélon 19 50 5N 4 6 E
Tremblade, La 20 45 46N 1 8W
Tremiti 39 42 8N 15 30 E
Tremonton 118 41 45N 112 10W
Tremp 32 42 10N 0 52 E
Trenary 114 46 12N 86 59W
Trenche → 106 47 46N 72 53W
Trenčín 27 48 52N 18 4 E
Trenggalek 73 8 5S 111 38 E
Trenque Lauquen 124 36 5S 62 45W
Trent → 12 53 33N 0 44W
Trentino-Alto Adige □ 38 46 30N 11 0 E
Trento 38 46 5N 11 8 E
Trenton, Can. 106 44 10N 77 34W
Trenton, Mo., U.S.A. 116 40 5N 93 37W
Trenton, N.J., U.S.A. 114 40 15N 74 41W
Trenton, Nebr., U.S.A. 116 40 14N 101 4W
Trenton, Tenn., U.S.A. 117 35 58N 88 57W
Trepassey 107 46 43N 53 25W
Tréport, Le 18 50 3N 1 20 E
Trepuzzi 41 40 26N 18 4 E
Tres Arroyos 124 38 26S 60 20W
Três Corações 125 21 44S 45 15W
Três Lagoas 127 20 50S 51 43W
Tres Marías 120 21 25N 106 28W
Tres Montes, C. 128 46 50S 75 30W
Três Pontas 125 21 23S 45 29W
Tres Puentes 124 27 50S 70 15W
Tres Puntas, C. 128 47 0S 66 0W
Três Rios 125 22 6S 43 15W
Treska → 42 42 0N 21 20 E
Treskavika Planina 42 43 40N 18 20 E
Trespaderne 32 42 47N 3 24W
Trets 21 43 27N 5 41 E
Treuchtlingen 25 48 58N 10 55 E
Treuenbrietzen 24 52 6N 12 51 E

Treviglio 38 45 31N 9 35 E
Trevinca, Peña 30 42 15N 6 46W
Treviso 39 45 40N 12 15 E
Trévoux 21 45 57N 4 47 E
Treysa 24 50 55N 9 12 E
Trgovište 42 42 20N 22 10 E
Triabunna 99 42 30 S 147 55 E
Triánda 45 36 25N 28 10 E
Triaucourt-en-Argonne 19 48 59N 5 2 E
Tribsees 24 54 4N 12 46 E
Tribulation, C. 97 16 5 S 145 29 E
Tribune 116 38 30N 101 45W
Tricárico 41 40 37N 16 9 E
Tricase 41 39 56N 18 20 E
Trichinopoly = Tiruchchirappalli 70 10 45N 78 45 E
Trichur 70 10 30N 76 18 E
Trida 99 33 1 S 145 1 E
Trier 25 49 45N 6 37 E
Trieste 39 45 39N 13 45 E
Trieste, G. di 39 45 37N 13 40 E
Trieux → 18 48 50N 3 3W
Triggiano 41 41 4N 16 58 E
Triglav 39 46 21N 13 50 E
Trigno → 39 42 4N 14 48 E
Trigueros 31 37 24N 6 50W
Tríkeri 45 39 6N 23 5 E
Tríkhonis, Límni 45 38 34N 21 30 E
Tríkkala 44 39 34N 21 47 E
Tríkkala □ 44 39 41N 21 30 E
Trikora, Puncak 73 4 15 S 138 45 E
Trilj 39 43 38N 16 42 E
Trillo 32 40 42N 2 35W
Trim 15 53 34N 6 48W
Trincomalee 70 8 38N 81 15 E
Trindade, I. 7 20 20 S 29 50W
Trinidad, Boliv. 126 14 46 S 64 50W
Trinidad, Colomb. 126 5 25N 71 40W
Trinidad, Cuba 121 21 48N 80 0W
Trinidad, Uruguay 124 33 30 S 56 50W
Trinidad, U.S.A. 117 37 15N 104 30W
Trinidad, W. Indies 121 10 30N 61 15W
Trinidad & Tobago ■ 121 10 30N 61 20W
Trinidad → 120 17 49N 95 9W
Trinidad, I. 128 39 10 S 62 0W
Trinitápoli 41 41 22N 16 5 E
Trinity, Can. 107 48 59N 53 55W
Trinity, U.S.A. 117 30 59N 95 25W
Trinity →, Calif., U.S.A. 118 41 11N 123 42W
Trinity →, Tex., U.S.A. 117 30 30N 95 0W
Trinity B., Austral. 97 16 30 S 146 0 E
Trinity B., Can. 107 48 20N 53 10W
Trinity Mts. 118 40 20N 118 50W
Trinkitat 81 18 45N 37 51 E
Trino 38 45 10N 8 18 E
Trion 115 34 35N 85 18W
Trionto C. 41 39 38N 16 47 E
Triora 38 44 0N 7 46 E
Tripoli = Tarābulus, Leb. 64 34 31N 35 50 E
Tripoli = Tarābulus, Libya 83 32 58N 13 12 E
Trípolis 45 37 31N 22 25 E
Tripp 116 43 16N 97 58W
Tripura □ 67 24 0N 92 0 E
Trischen 24 54 3N 8 32 E
Tristan da Cunha 7 37 6 S 12 20W
Trivandrum 70 8 41N 77 0 E
Trivento 41 41 48N 14 31 E
Trnava 27 48 23N 17 35 E
Trobriand Is. 98 8 30 S 151 0 E
Trochu 108 51 50N 113 13W
Trodely I. 106 52 15N 79 26W
Troezen 45 37 25N 23 15 E
Trogir 39 43 32N 16 15 E
Troglav 39 43 56N 16 36 E
Trøgstad 47 59 37N 11 16 E
Tróia 41 41 22N 15 19 E
Troilus, L. 106 50 50N 74 35W
Troina 41 37 47N 14 34 E
Trois Fourches, Cap des 82 35 26N 2 58W
Trois-Pistoles 107 48 5N 69 10W
Trois-Rivières 106 46 25N 72 34W
Troitsk 58 54 10N 61 35 E
Troitsko Pechorsk 52 62 40N 56 10 E
Trölladyngja 50 64 54N 17 16W
Trollhättan 49 58 17N 12 20 E
Trollheimen 47 62 46N 9 1 E
Troms fylke □ 50 68 56N 19 0 E
Tromsø 50 69 40N 18 56 E
Tronador 128 41 10 S 71 50W
Trondheim 47 63 36N 10 25 E
Trondheimsfjorden 47 63 35N 10 30 E
Trönninge 49 56 37N 12 51 E
Trönö 48 61 22N 16 54 E
Tronto → 39 42 54N 13 55 E
Troon 14 55 33N 4 40W
Tropea 41 38 40N 15 53 E
Tropic 119 37 36N 112 4W
Tropoja 44 42 23N 20 10 E
Trossachs, The 14 56 14N 4 24W
Trostan 15 55 4N 6 10W
Trostberg 25 48 2N 12 33 E
Trostyanets 54 50 33N 34 59 E
Trotternish 14 57 32N 6 15W
Troup 117 32 10N 95 3W
Trout → 108 61 19N 119 51W
Trout L., N.W.T., Can. 108 60 40N 121 40W
Trout L., Ont., Can. 109 51 20N 93 15W
Trout Lake 106 46 10N 85 2W
Trout River 107 49 29N 58 8W
Trouville 18 49 21N 0 5 E
Trowbridge 13 51 18N 2 12W
Troy, Turkey 44 39 57N 26 12 E
Troy, Turkey 64 39 55N 26 20 E
Troy, Ala., U.S.A. 115 31 50N 85 58W
Troy, Idaho, U.S.A. 118 46 44N 116 46W
Troy, Kans., U.S.A. 116 39 47N 95 2W
Troy, Mo., U.S.A. 116 38 56N 90 59W
Troy, Montana, U.S.A. 118 48 30N 115 58W
Troy, N.Y., U.S.A. 114 42 45N 73 39W
Troy, Ohio, U.S.A. 114 40 0N 84 10W
Troyan 43 42 57N 24 43 E
Troyes 19 48 19N 4 3 E
Trpanj 42 43 1N 17 15 E
Trstena 27 49 21N 19 37 E
Trstenik 42 43 36N 21 0 E
Trubchevsk 54 52 33N 33 47 E
Trucial States = United Arab Emirates ■ 65 24 0N 54 30 E
Truckee 118 39 20N 120 11W
Trujillo, Hond. 121 16 0N 86 0W
Trujillo, Peru 126 8 6 S 79 0W
Trujillo, Spain 31 39 28N 5 55W
Trujillo, U.S.A. 117 35 34N 104 44W
Trujillo, Venez. 126 9 22N 70 38W
Truk 94 7 25N 151 46 E
Trumann 117 35 42N 90 32W
Trumbull, Mt. 119 36 25N 113 8W
Trun 42 42 51N 22 38 E
Trun 18 48 50N 0 2 E
Trundle 99 32 53 S 147 35 E
Trung-Phan 72 16 0N 108 0 E
Truro, Can. 107 45 21N 63 14W
Truro, U.K. 13 50 17N 5 2W
Trustrup 49 56 20N 10 46 E
Truth or Consequences 119 33 9N 107 16W
Trutnov 26 50 37N 15 54 E
Truyère → 20 44 38N 2 34 E
Tryavna 43 42 54N 25 25 E
Tryon 115 35 15N 82 16W
Tryonville 112 41 42N 79 48W
Trzcianka 28 53 3N 16 25 E
Trzciel 28 52 23N 15 50 E
Trzcińsko Zdrój 28 52 58N 14 35 E
Trzebiatów 28 54 3N 15 18 E
Trzebiez 28 53 38N 14 31 E
Trzebinia-Siersza 27 50 11N 19 18 E
Trzebnica 28 51 20N 17 1 E
Trzemeszno 28 52 33N 17 48 E
Tržič 39 46 22N 14 18 E
Tsageri 57 42 39N 42 46 E
Tsamandás 44 39 46N 20 21 E
Tsaratanana 93 16 47 S 47 39 E
Tsaratanana, Mt. de 93 14 0 S 49 0 E
Tsarevo = Michurin 43 42 9N 27 51 E
Tsarichanka 56 48 55N 34 30 E
Tsaritsáni 44 39 53N 22 14 E
Tsau 92 20 8 S 22 22 E
Tsebrikovo 56 47 9N 30 10 E
Tselinograd 58 51 10N 71 30 E
Tsetserleg 75 47 36N 101 32 E
Tshabong 92 26 2 S 22 29 E
Tshane 92 24 5 S 21 54 E
Tshela 88 4 57 S 13 4 E
Tshesebe 93 21 51 S 27 32 E
Tshibeke 90 2 40 S 28 35 E
Tshibinda 90 2 23 S 28 43 E
Tshikapa 88 6 28 S 20 48 E
Tshilenge 90 6 17 S 23 48 E
Tshinsenda 91 12 20 S 28 0 E
Tshofa 90 5 13 S 25 16 E
Tshwane 92 22 24 S 22 1 E
Tsigara 92 20 22 S 25 54 E
Tsihombe 93 25 18 S 45 29 E
Tsimlyansk 57 47 40N 42 6 E
Tsimlyanskoye Vdkhr. 57 48 0N 43 0 E
Tsinan = Jinan 76 36 38N 117 1 E
Tsineng 92 27 05 S 23 05 E
Tsinga 44 41 23N 24 44 E
Tsinghai = Qinghai □ 75 36 0N 98 0 E
Tsingtao = Qingdao 76 36 5N 120 20 E
Tsinjomitondraka 93 15 40 S 47 8 E
Tsiroanomandidy 93 18 46 S 46 2 E
Tsivilsk 55 55 50N 47 25 E
Tsivory 93 24 4 S 46 5 E
Tskhinali 53 42 22N 43 52 E
Tskhinvali 57 42 14N 44 1 E
Tsna → 55 54 55N 41 58 E
Tsodilo Hill 92 18 49 S 21 43 E
Tsu 74 34 45N 136 25 E
Tsu L. 108 60 40N 111 52W
Tsuchiura 74 36 5N 140 15 E
Tsugaru-Kaikyō 74 41 35N 141 0 E
Tsumeb 92 19 9 S 17 44 E
Tsumis 92 23 39 S 17 29 E
Tsuruga 74 35 45N 136 2 E
Tsushima 74 34 20N 129 20 E
Tsvetkovo 56 49 8N 31 33 E
Tua → 30 41 13N 7 26W
Tual 73 5 38 S 132 44 E
Tuam 15 53 30N 8 50W
Tuamotu Arch. 95 17 0 S 144 0W
Tuamotu Ridge 95 20 0 S 138 0W
Tuao 73 17 55N 122 22 E
Tuapse 57 44 5N 39 10 E
Tuatapere 101 46 8 S 167 41 E
Tuba City 119 36 8N 111 18W
Tubac 119 31 37N 111 20W
Tuban 73 6 54 S 112 3 E
Tubarão 125 28 30 S 49 0W
Tūbās 62 32 20N 35 22 E
Tubau 72 3 10N 113 40 E
Tübingen 25 48 31N 9 4 E
Tubja, W. → 86 25 27N 38 45 E
Tubruq 81 32 7N 23 55 E
Tubuai Is. 95 25 0 S 150 0W
Tucacas 126 10 48N 68 19W
Tuchodi → 108 58 17N 123 42W
Tuchola 28 53 33N 17 52 E
Tuchów 27 49 54N 21 1 E
Tucker's Town 121 32 17N 64 43W
Tucson 119 32 14N 110 59W
Tucumán □ 124 26 48 S 66 2W
Tucumcari 117 35 12N 103 45W
Tucupita 126 9 2N 62 3W
Tucuruí 127 3 42 S 49 44W
Tuczno 28 53 13N 16 10 E
Tudela 32 42 4N 1 39W
Tudela de Duero 30 41 37N 4 39W
Tudmur 64 34 36N 38 15 E
Tudor, Lac 107 55 50N 65 25W
Tudora 46 47 31N 26 45 E
Tuella → 30 41 30N 7 12W
Tufi 98 9 8 S 149 19 E
Tuguegarao 73 17 35N 121 42 E
Tugur 59 53 44N 136 45 E
Tukangbesi, Kepulauan 73 6 0 S 124 0 E
Tukarak I. 106 56 15N 78 45W
Tūkh 86 30 21N 31 12 E
Tukobo 84 5 1N 2 47W
Tūkrah 83 32 30N 20 37 E
Tuktoyaktuk 104 69 27N 133 2W
Tukums 54 57 2N 23 10 E
Tukuyu 91 9 17 S 33 35 E
Tula, Hidalgo, Mexico 120 20 0N 99 20W
Tula, Tamaulipas, Mexico 120 23 0N 99 40W
Tula, Nigeria 85 9 51N 11 27 E
Tula, U.S.S.R. 55 54 13N 37 38 E
Tulak 65 33 55N 63 40 E
Tulancingo 120 20 5N 99 22W
Tulare 119 36 15N 119 26W
Tulare Lake 119 36 0N 119 53W
Tularosa 119 33 4N 106 1W
Tulbagh 92 33 16 S 19 6 E
Tulcán 126 0 48N 77 43W
Tulcea 46 45 13N 28 46 E
Tulcea □ 46 45 0N 29 0 E
Tulchin 56 48 41N 28 49 E
Tulemalu L. 109 62 58N 99 25W
Tulgheş 46 46 58N 25 45 E
Tuli, Indon. 73 1 24 S 122 26 E
Tuli, Zimb. 91 21 58 S 29 13 E
Ţūlkarm 62 32 19N 35 2 E
Tulla 117 34 35N 101 44W
Tullahoma 115 35 23N 86 12W
Tullamore, Austral. 99 32 39 S 147 36 E
Tullamore, Ireland 15 53 17N 7 30W
Tulle 20 45 16N 1 46 E
Tullibigeal 99 33 25 S 146 44 E
Tullins 21 45 18N 5 29 E
Tulln 26 48 20N 16 4 E
Tullow 15 52 48N 6 45W
Tullus 87 11 7N 24 31 E
Tully 98 17 56 S 145 55 E
Ţulmaythah 81 32 40N 20 55 E
Tulmur 98 22 40 S 142 20 E
Tulnici 46 45 51N 26 38 E
Tulovo 43 42 33N 25 32 E
Tulsa 117 36 10N 96 0W
Tulsequah 108 58 39N 133 35W
Tulu Milki 87 9 55N 38 20 E
Tulu Welel 87 8 56N 34 47 E
Tulua 126 4 6N 76 11W
Tulun 59 54 32N 100 35 E
Tulungagung 72 8 5 S 111 54 E
Tum 73 3 36 S 130 21 E
Tuma 55 55 10N 40 30 E
Tuma → 121 13 6N 84 35W
Tumaco 126 1 50N 78 45W
Tumatumari 126 5 20N 58 55W
Tumba 48 59 12N 17 48 E
Tumba, L. 88 0 50 S 18 0 E
Tumbarumba 99 35 44 S 148 0 E
Tumbaya 124 23 50 S 65 26W
Túmbes 126 3 37 S 80 27W
Tumbwe 91 11 25 S 27 15 E
Tumen 76 43 0N 129 50 E
Tumen Jiang → 76 42 20N 130 35 E
Tumeremo 126 7 18N 61 30W
Tumkur 70 13 18N 77 6 E
Tummel, L. 14 56 43N 3 55W
Tump 66 26 7N 62 16 E
Tumpat 71 6 11N 102 10 E
Tumsar 69 21 26N 79 45 E
Tumu 84 10 56N 1 56W
Tumucumaque, Serra 127 2 0N 55 0W
Tumut 97 35 16 S 148 13 E
Tumwater 118 47 0N 122 58W
Tunas de Zaza 121 21 39N 79 34W
Tunbridge Wells 13 51 7N 0 16 E
Tuncurry 99 32 17 S 152 29 E
Tunduru 91 11 8 S 37 25 E
Tunduru □ 91 11 5 S 37 22 E
Tundzha → 43 41 40N 26 35 E
Tune 47 59 16N 11 2 E
Tunga → 70 15 0N 75 50 E
Tunga Pass 67 29 0N 94 14 E
Tungabhadra → 70 15 57N 78 15 E
Tungabhadra Dam 70 15 0N 75 50 E
Tungaru 81 10 9N 30 52 E
Tungla 121 13 24N 84 21W
Tungnafellsjökull 50 64 45N 17 55W
Tungsten, Can. 108 61 57N 128 16W
Tungsten, U.S.A. 118 40 50N 118 10W
Tunguska, Nizhnyaya → 59 65 48N 88 4 E
Tunguska, Podkamennaya → 59 61 36N 90 18 E
Tuni 70 17 22N 82 36 E
Tunica 117 34 43N 90 23W
Tunis 83 36 50N 10 11 E
Tunis, Golfe de 83 37 0N 10 30 E
Tunisia ■ 83 33 30N 9 10 E
Tunja 126 5 33N 73 25W
Tunkhannock 113 41 32N 75 46W
Tunliu 76 36 13N 112 52 E
Tunnsjøen 50 64 45N 13 25 E
Tunungayualok I. 107 56 0N 61 0W
Tunuyán 124 33 35 S 69 0W
Tunuyán → 124 33 33 S 67 30W
Tunxi 75 29 42N 118 25 E
Tuolumne 119 37 59N 120 16W
Tuoy-Khaya 59 62 32N 111 25 E
Tupã 125 21 57 S 50 28W
Tupelo 115 34 15N 88 42W
Tupik, U.S.S.R. 54 55 42N 33 22 E
Tupik, U.S.S.R. 59 54 26N 119 57 E
Tupinambaranas 126 3 0 S 58 0W
Tupiza 124 21 30 S 65 40W
Tupižnica 42 43 43N 22 10 E
Tupper 108 55 32N 120 1W
Tupper L. 114 44 18N 74 30W
Tupungato, Cerro 124 33 15 S 69 50W
Tuquan 76 45 18N 121 38 E
Túquerres 126 1 5N 77 37W
Tura, India 69 25 30N 90 16 E
Tura, U.S.S.R. 59 64 20N 100 17 E
Turaba, Wadi → 86 21 15N 41 32 E
Turabah 64 28 20N 43 15 E
Turaiyur 70 11 9N 78 38 E
Tūrān 65 35 39N 56 42 E
Turan 59 51 55N 95 0 E
Turayf 64 31 41N 38 39 E
Turbacz 27 49 30N 20 8 E
Turbe 42 44 15N 17 35 E
Turda 46 46 34N 23 47 E
Turégano 30 41 9N 4 1W
Turek 28 52 3N 18 30 E
Turfan = Turpan 75 43 58N 89 10 E
Turfan Depression = Turpan Hami 75 42 40N 89 25 E
Tŭrgovishte 43 43 17N 26 38 E
Turgutlu 64 38 30N 27 48 E
Turhal 56 40 24N 36 5 E
Turia → 33 39 27N 0 19W
Turiaçu 127 1 40 S 45 19W
Turiaçu → 127 1 36 S 45 19W
Turiec → 27 49 07N 18 55 E
Turin 108 49 47N 112 24W
Turin = Torino 38 45 3N 7 40 E
Turka 54 49 10N 23 2 E
Turkana □ 90 3 0N 35 30 E
Turkana, L. 90 3 30N 36 5 E
Turkestan 58 43 17N 68 16 E
Türkeve 27 47 6N 20 44 E
Turkey ■ 64 39 0N 36 0 E
Turki 55 52 0N 43 15 E
Turkmen S.S.R. □ 58 39 0N 59 0 E
Turks Is. 121 21 20N 71 20W
Turks Island Passage 121 21 30N 71 30W
Turku 51 60 30N 22 19 E
Turkwe → 90 3 6N 36 6 E
Turlock 119 37 30N 120 55W
Turnagain → 108 59 12N 127 35W
Turnagain, C. 101 40 28 S 176 38 E
Turneffe Is. 120 17 20N 87 50W
Turner 118 48 52N 108 25W
Turner Valley 108 50 40N 114 17W
Turners Falls 113 42 36N 72 34W
Turnhout 16 51 19N 4 57 E
Türnitz 26 47 55N 15 29 E
Turnor L. 109 56 35N 108 35W
Turnov 26 50 34N 15 10 E
Tŭrnovo 43 43 5N 25 41 E
Turnovo 43 43 5N 25 41 E
Turnu Măgurele 46 43 46N 24 56 E
Turnu Rosu Pasul 46 45 33N 24 17 E
Turnu-Severin 46 44 39N 22 41 E
Turobin 28 50 50N 22 44 E
Turon 117 37 48N 98 27W
Turpan 75 43 58N 89 10 E
Turpan Hami 75 42 40N 89 25 E
Turrës, Kalaja e 44 41 10N 19 28 E
Turriff 14 57 32N 2 28W
Tursha 55 56 55N 47 36 E
Tursi 41 40 15N 16 27 E
Turtle Hd. I. 98 10 56 S 142 37 E
Turtle L., Can. 109 53 36N 108 38W
Turtle L., U.S.A. 116 45 22N 92 10W
Turtle Lake 116 47 30N 100 55W
Turtleford 109 53 23N 108 57W
Turukhansk 59 65 21N 88 5 E
Turun ja Porin lääni □ 51 60 27N 22 15 E
Turzovka 27 49 25N 18 35 E
Tuscaloosa 115 33 13N 87 31W
Tuscánia 39 42 25N 11 53 E
Tuscany = Toscana 38 43 28N 11 15 E
Tuscola, Ill., U.S.A. 114 39 48N 88 15W
Tuscola, Tex., U.S.A. 117 32 15N 99 48W
Tuscumbia 115 34 42N 87 42W
Tuskar Rock 15 52 12N 6 10W
Tuskegee 115 32 24N 85 39W
Tustna 47 63 10N 8 5 E
Tuszyn 28 51 39N 19 33 E
Tutayev 55 57 53N 39 32 E
Tuticorin 70 8 50N 78 12 E
Tutin 42 43 0N 20 20 E
Tutóia 127 2 45 S 42 20W
Tutong 72 4 47N 114 40 E
Tutova → 46 46 20N 27 30 E
Tutrakan 43 44 2N 26 40 E
Tutshi L. 108 59 56N 134 30W
Tuttle 116 47 9N 100 00W
Tuttlingen 25 47 59N 8 50 E
Tutuala 73 8 25 S 127 15 E
Tutuila 101 14 19 S 170 50W
Tuva A.S.S.R. □ 59 51 30N 95 0 E
Tuvalu ■ 94 8 0 S 178 0 E
Tuxpan 120 20 58N 97 23W
Tuxtla Gutiérrez 120 16 50N 93 10W
Tuy 30 42 3N 8 39W
Tuy Hoa 71 13 5N 109 10 E
Tuya L. 108 59 7N 130 35W
Tuyen Hoa 71 17 50N 106 10 E
Tuz Gölü 64 38 45N 33 30 E
Ţūz Khurmātū 64 34 56N 44 38 E
Tuzla 42 44 34N 18 41 E
Tuzlov → 57 47 28N 39 45 E
Tvååker 49 57 4N 12 25 E
Tvedestrand 47 58 38N 8 58 E
Tvŭrditsa 43 42 42N 25 53 E
Twardogóra 28 51 23N 17 28 E
Tweed 112 44 29N 77 19W
Tweed → 14 55 42N 2 10W
Tweedsmuir Prov. Park 108 53 0N 126 20W
Twentynine Palms 119 34 10N 116 4W
Twillingate 107 49 42N 54 45W
Twin Bridges 118 45 33N 112 23W
Twin Falls 118 42 30N 114 30W
Twin Valley 116 47 18N 96 15W
Twisp 118 48 21N 120 5W
Twistringen 24 52 48N 8 38 E
Two Harbors 116 47 1N 91 40W
Two Hills 108 53 43N 111 52W
Two Rivers 114 44 10N 87 31W
Twofold B. 97 37 8 S 149 59 E
Tychy 27 50 9N 18 59 E
Tyczyn 27 49 58N 22 2 E
Tydal 47 63 4N 11 34 E
Tykocin 28 53 13N 22 46 E
Tyldal 47 62 8N 10 48 E

Tyler, Minn., U.S.A. **116** 44 18N 96 8W
Tyler, Tex., U.S.A. **117** 32 18N 95 18W
Týn nad Vltavou **26** 49 13N 14 26 E
Tynda **59** 55 10N 124 43 E
Tyne & Wear □ **12** 54 55N 1 35W
Tyne → **12** 54 58N 1 28W
Tynemouth **12** 55 1N 1 27W
Tynset **47** 62 17N 10 47 E
Tyre = Sûr **62** 33 12N 35 11 E
Tyrifjorden **47** 60 2N 10 8 E
Tyringe **49** 56 9N 13 35 E
Tyristrand **47** 60 5N 10 5 E
Tyrnyauz **57** 43 21N 42 45 E
Tyrol = Tirol **26** 47 3N 10 43 E
Tyrone **112** 40 39N 78 10W
Tyrrell → **100** 35 26 S 142 51 E
Tyrrell Arm **109** 62 27N 97 30W
Tyrrell, L. **99** 35 20 S 142 50 E
Tyrrell L. **109** 63 7N 105 27W
Tyrrhenian Sea **34** 40 0N 12 30 E
Tysfjorden **50** 68 7N 16 25 E
Tysnes **47** 60 1N 5 30 E
Tysnesøy **47** 60 0N 5 35 E
Tyssedal **47** 60 7N 6 35 E
Tystberga **49** 58 51N 17 15 E
Tyub Karagan, M. **57** 44 40N 50 19 E
Tyuleniy **57** 44 28N 47 30 E
Tyulgan **52** 52 22N 56 12 E
Tyumen **58** 57 11N 65 29 E
Tywi → **13** 51 48N 4 20W
Tzaneen **93** 23 47 S 30 9 E
Tzermiadhes Neápolis **46** 35 11N 25 29 E
Tzoumérka, Óros **44** 39 30N 21 26 E
Tzukong = Zigong **75** 29 15N 104 48 E

U

Uad Erni, O. → **82** 26 45N 10 47W
Uanda **98** 21 37 S 144 55 E
Uarsciek **63** 2 28N 45 55 E
Uasin □ **90** 0 30N 35 20 E
Uato-Udo **73** 9 7 S 125 36 E
Uatumã → **126** 2 26 S 57 37W
Uaupés **126** 0 8 S 67 5W
Ub **42** 44 28N 20 6 E
Ubá **125** 21 8 S 43 0W
Ubaitaba **127** 14 18 S 39 20W
Ubangi = Oubangi → **88** 1 0N 17 50 E
Ubauro **68** 28 15N 69 45 E
Ubaye → **21** 44 28N 6 18 E
Ube **74** 33 56N 131 15 E
Ubeda **33** 38 3N 3 23W
Uberaba **127** 19 50 S 47 55W
Uberlândia **127** 19 0 S 48 20W
Überlingen **25** 47 46N 9 10 E
Ubiaja **85** 6 41N 6 22 E
Ubombo **93** 27 31 S 32 4 E
Ubon Ratchathani **71** 15 15N 104 50 E
Ubondo **90** 0 55 S 25 42 E
Ubort → **54** 52 6N 28 30 E
Ubrique **31** 36 41N 5 27W
Ubundu **90** 0 22 S 25 30 E
Ucayali → **126** 4 30 S 73 30W
Uchi Lake **109** 51 5N 92 35W
Uchiura-Wan **74** 42 25N 140 40 E
Uchte **24** 52 29N 8 52 E
Uchur → **59** 58 48N 130 35 E
Ucluelet **108** 48 57N 125 32W
Ucuriş **46** 46 41N 21 58 E
Uda → **59** 54 42N 135 14 E
Udaipur **68** 24 36N 73 44 E
Udaipur Garhi **69** 27 0N 86 35 E
Udamalpet **70** 10 35N 77 15 E
Udbina **39** 44 31N 15 47 E
Uddeholm **48** 60 1N 13 38 E
Uddevalla **49** 58 21N 11 55 E
Uddjaur **50** 65 25N 21 15 E
Udgir **70** 18 25N 77 5 E
Udi **85** 6 23N 7 21 E
Udine **39** 46 5N 13 10 E
Udipi **70** 13 25N 74 42 E
Udmurt A.S.S.R. □ **52** 57 30N 52 30 E
Udon Thani **71** 17 29N 102 46 E
Udvoy Balkan **43** 42 50N 26 50 E
Udzungwa Range **91** 9 30 S 35 10 E
Ueckermünde **24** 53 45N 14 1 E
Ueda **74** 36 24N 138 16 E
Uedineniya, Os. **4** 78 0N 85 0 E
Uelen **59** 66 10N 170 0W
Uelzen **24** 53 0N 10 33 E
Uere → **88** 3 45N 24 45 E
Ufa **52** 54 45N 55 55 E
Ufa → **52** 54 40N 56 0 E
Uffenheim **25** 49 32N 10 15 E
Ugalla → **90** 5 8 S 30 42 E
Uganda ■ **90** 2 0N 32 0 E
Ugento **41** 39 55N 18 10 E
Ugep **85** 5 53N 8 2 E
Ugie **93** 31 10 S 28 13 E
Ugijar **33** 36 58N 3 7W
Ugine **21** 45 45N 6 25 E
Ugla **86** 25 40N 37 42 E
Uglegorsk **59** 49 5N 142 2 E
Uglich **55** 57 33N 38 20 E
Ugljane **39** 43 35N 16 46 E
Ugolyak **59** 64 33N 120 30 E
Ugra → **54** 54 30N 36 7 E
Ugûrchin **43** 43 6N 24 26 E
Uh → **27** 48 7N 21 25 E
Uherske Hradiště **27** 49 4N 17 30 E
Uhersky Brod **27** 49 1N 17 40 E
Úhlava → **26** 49 45N 13 24 E
Uhrichsville **114** 40 23N 81 22W
Uige **88** 7 30 S 14 40 E
Uiju **76** 40 15N 124 35 E
Uinta Mts. **118** 40 45N 110 30W
Uitenhage **92** 33 40 S 25 28 E
Uithuizen **16** 53 24N 6 41 E
Újfehértó **27** 47 49N 21 41 E
Ujhani **68** 28 0N 79 6 E
Ujjain **68** 23 9N 75 43 E
Újpest **27** 47 32N 19 6 E
Újszász **27** 47 19N 20 7 E
Ujung Pandang **73** 5 10 S 119 20 E
Uka **59** 57 50N 162 0 E
Ukara I. **90** 1 50 S 33 0 E
Ukerewe □ **90** 2 0 S 32 30 E
Ukerewe I. **90** 2 0 S 33 0 E
Ukholovo **55** 53 47N 40 30 E
Ukhrul **67** 25 10N 94 25 E
Ukhta **52** 63 55N 54 0 E
Ukiah **118** 39 10N 123 9W
Ukmerge **54** 55 15N 24 45 E
Ukrainian S.S.R. □ **56** 49 0N 32 0 E
Ukwi **92** 23 29 S 20 30 E
Ulaanbaatar **75** 47 54N 106 52 E
Ulaangom **75** 50 0N 92 10 E
Ulamba **91** 9 3 S 23 38 E
Ulan Bator = Ulaanbaatar **75** 47 54N 106 52 E
Ulan Ude **59** 51 45N 107 40 E
Ulanga □ **91** 8 40 S 36 50 E
Ulanów **28** 50 30N 22 16 E
Ulaya, Morogoro, Tanz. **90** 7 3 S 36 55 E
Ulaya, Tabora, Tanz. **90** 4 25 S 33 30 E
Ulcinj **42** 41 58N 19 10 E
Ulco **92** 28 21 S 24 15 E
Ulefoss **47** 59 17N 9 16 E
Ulëza **44** 41 46N 19 57 E
Ulfborg **49** 56 16N 8 20 E
Ulhasnagar **70** 19 15N 73 10 E
Uljma **42** 45 2N 21 10 E
Ulla → **30** 42 39N 8 44W
Ulladulla **99** 35 21 S 150 29 E
Ullånger **48** 62 58N 18 10 E
Ullapool **14** 57 54N 5 10W
Ullared **49** 57 8N 12 42 E
Ulldecona **32** 40 36N 0 20 E
Ullswater **12** 54 35N 2 52W
Ullung-do **76** 37 30N 130 30 E
Ulm **25** 48 23N 10 0 E
Ulmarra **99** 29 37 S 153 4 E
Ulmeni **46** 45 4N 26 40 E
Ulricehamn **49** 57 46N 13 26 E
Ulsberg **47** 62 45N 9 59 E
Ulsteinvik **47** 62 21N 5 53 E
Ulster □ **15** 54 35N 6 30W
Ulstrem **43** 42 1N 26 27 E
Ulubaria **69** 22 31N 88 4 E
Uluguru Mts. **90** 7 15 S 37 40 E
Ulungur He **75** 47 1N 87 24 E
Ulutau **58** 48 39N 67 1 E
Ulverston **12** 54 13N 3 7W
Ulverstone **97** 41 11 S 146 11 E
Ulvik **47** 60 35N 6 54 E
Ulya **59** 59 10N 142 0 E
Ulyanovsk **55** 54 20N 48 25 E
Ulyasutay (Javhlant) **75** 47 56N 97 28 E
Ulysses **117** 37 39N 101 25W
Umag **39** 45 26N 13 31 E
Umala **126** 17 25 S 68 5W
Uman **56** 48 40N 30 12 E
Umarkhed **70** 19 37N 77 46 E
Umatilla **118** 45 58N 119 17W
Umba **52** 66 50N 34 20 E
Umbertide **39** 43 18N 12 20 E
Umboi I. **98** 5 40 S 148 0 E
Umbrella Mts. **101** 45 35 S 169 5 E
Umbria □ **39** 42 53N 12 30 E
Ume älv → **50** 63 45N 20 20 E
Umeå **50** 63 45N 20 20 E
Umera **73** 0 12 S 129 37 E
Umfuli → **91** 17 30 S 29 23 E
Umgusa **91** 19 29 S 27 52 E
Umka **42** 44 40N 20 19 E
Umkomaas **93** 30 13 S 30 48 E
Umm al Arānib **83** 26 10N 14 43 E
Umm al Qaywayn **65** 25 30N 55 35 E
Umm Arda **87** 15 17N 32 31 E
Umm az Zamul **65** 22 42N 55 18 E
Umm Bel **87** 13 35N 28 0 E
Umm Dubban **87** 15 23N 32 52 E
Umm el Fahm **62** 32 31N 35 9 E
Umm Koweika **87** 13 10N 32 16 E
Umm Lajj **64** 25 0N 37 23 E
Umm Merwa **86** 18 4N 32 30 E
Umm Qays **62** 32 40N 35 41 E
Umm Rumah **86** 25 50N 36 30 E
Umm Ruwaba **87** 12 50N 31 20 E
Umm Sidr **87** 14 29N 25 10 E
Ummanz **24** 54 29N 13 9 E
Umnak **104** 53 20N 168 20W
Umniati → **91** 16 49 S 28 45 E
Umpang **71** 16 3N 98 54 E
Umpqua → **118** 43 42N 124 3W
Umrer **68** 20 51N 79 18 E
Umreth **68** 22 41N 73 4 E
Umshandige Dam **91** 20 10 S 30 40 E
• Umtali **91** 18 58 S 32 38 E
Umtata **93** 31 36 S 28 49 E
Umuahia **85** 5 33N 7 29 E
Umvukwe Ra. **91** 16 45 S 30 45 E
Umvukwes **91** 17 0 S 30 57 E
Umvuma **91** 19 16 S 30 30 E
Umzimvubu **93** 31 38 S 29 33 E
Umzingwane → **91** 22 12 S 29 56 E
Umzinto **93** 30 15 S 30 45 E
Una **68** 20 46N 71 8 E
Una → **39** 45 16N 16 55 E
Unac → **39** 44 30N 16 9 E
Unadilla **113** 42 20N 75 17W
Unalaska **104** 53 40N 166 40W
Uncastillo **32** 42 21N 1 8W
Uncía **126** 18 25 S 66 40W
Uncompahgre Pk. **119** 38 5N 107 32W
Unden **49** 58 45N 14 25 E
Underbool **99** 35 10 S 141 51 E
Undersaker **48** 63 19N 13 21 E
Undersvik **48** 61 36N 16 20 E
Undredal **47** 60 57N 7 6 E
Unecha **54** 52 50N 32 37 E
Ungarie **99** 33 38 S 146 56 E
Ungava B. **105** 59 30N 67 30W
Ungeny **56** 47 11N 27 51 E
Unggi **76** 42 16N 130 28 E
Ungwatiri **87** 16 52N 36 10 E
Uni **55** 56 44N 51 47 E
União da Vitória **125** 26 13 S 51 5W
Uniejów **28** 51 59N 18 46 E
Unije **39** 44 40N 14 15 E
Unimak **104** 55 0N 164 0W
Unimak Pass. **104** 53 30N 165 15W
Union, Miss, U.S.A. **117** 32 34N 89 14W
Union, Mo., U.S.A. **116** 38 25N 91 0W
Union, S.C., U.S.A. **115** 34 43N 81 39W
Union City, N.J., U.S.A. **113** 40 47N 74 5W
Union City, Ohio, U.S.A. **114** 40 11N 84 49W
Union City, Pa., U.S.A. **112** 41 53N 79 50W
Union City, Tenn., U.S.A. **117** 36 25N 89 0W
Union Gap **118** 46 38N 120 29W
Unión, La, Chile **128** 40 10 S 73 0W
Unión, La, El Sal. **120** 13 20N 87 50W
Unión, La, Spain **33** 37 38N 0 53W
Union, Mt. **119** 34 34N 112 21W
Union of Soviet Socialist Republics ■ **59** 60 0N 100 0 E
Union Springs **115** 32 9N 85 44W
Uniondale **92** 33 39 S 23 7 E
Uniontown **114** 39 54N 79 45W
Unionville **116** 40 29N 93 1W
Unirea **46** 44 15N 27 35 E
United Arab Emirates ■ **65** 23 50N 54 0 E
United Kingdom ■ **11** 55 0N 3 0W
United States of America ■ **111** 37 0N 96 0W
United States Trust Terr. of the Pacific Is. **94** 10 0N 160 0 E
Unity **109** 52 30N 109 5W
Universales, Mtes. **32** 40 18N 1 33W
Unjha **68** 23 46N 72 24 E
Unnao **69** 26 35N 80 30 E
Uno, Ilha **84** 11 15N 16 13W
Unst **14** 60 50N 0 55W
Unstrut → **24** 51 10N 11 48 E
Unuk → **108** 56 5N 131 3W
Ünye **56** 41 5N 37 15 E
Unzha **55** 58 0N 44 0 E
Unzha → **55** 57 30N 43 40 E
Upa → **27** 50 35N 16 15 E
Upata **126** 8 1N 62 24W
Upemba, L. **91** 8 30 S 26 20 E
Upernavik **4** 72 49N 56 20W
Upington **92** 28 25 S 21 15 E
Upleta **68** 21 46N 70 16 E
Upolu **101** 13 58 S 172 0W
Upper Alkali Lake **118** 41 47N 120 8W
Upper Arrow L. **108** 50 30N 117 50W
Upper Austria = Oberösterreich **26** 48 10N 14 0 E
Upper Foster L. **109** 56 47N 105 20W
Upper Hutt **101** 41 8 S 175 5 E
Upper Klamath L. **118** 42 16N 121 55W
Upper L. Erne **15** 54 14N 7 22W
Upper Lake **118** 39 10N 122 55W
Upper Musquodoboit **107** 45 10N 62 58W
Upper Red L. **116** 48 0N 95 0W
Upper Sandusky **114** 40 50N 83 17W
Upper Taimyr → **59** 74 15N 99 48 E
Upper Volta ■ **84** 12 0N 1 0W
Upphärad **49** 58 9N 12 19 E
Uppsala **48** 59 53N 17 38 E
Uppsala län □ **48** 60 0N 17 30 E
Upstart, C. **98** 19 41 S 147 45 E
Upton **116** 44 8N 104 35W
Ur **64** 30 55N 46 25 E
Uracara **126** 2 20 S 57 50W
Urach **25** 48 29N 9 25 E
Urad Qianqi **76** 40 40N 108 30 E
Ural → **58** 47 0N 51 48 E
Ural, Mt. **99** 33 21 S 146 12 E
Ural Mts. = Uralskie Gory **52** 60 0N 59 0 E
Uralla **99** 30 37 S 151 29 E
Uralsk **52** 51 20N 51 20 E
Uralskie Gory **52** 60 0N 59 0 E
Urambo **90** 5 4 S 32 0 E
Urambo □ **90** 5 0 S 32 0 E
Urana **100** 35 15 S 146 21 E
Urandangie **97** 21 32 S 138 14 E
Uranium City **109** 59 34N 108 37W
Uravakonda **70** 14 57N 77 12 E
Urawa **74** 35 50N 139 40 E
Uray **58** 60 5N 65 15 E
Urbana, Ill., U.S.A. **114** 40 7N 88 12W
Urbana, Ohio, U.S.A. **114** 40 9N 83 44W
Urbana, La **126** 7 8N 66 56W
Urbánia **39** 43 40N 12 31 E
Urbel → **32** 42 21N 3 40W
Urbino **39** 43 43N 12 38 E
Urbión, Picos de **32** 42 1N 2 52W
Urcos **126** 13 40 S 71 38W
Urda, Spain **31** 39 25N 3 43W
Urda, U.S.S.R. **57** 48 52N 47 23 E
Urdinarrain **124** 32 37 S 58 52W
Urdos **20** 42 51N 0 35W
Urdzhar **58** 47 5N 81 38 E
Ure → **12** 54 20N 1 25W
Uren **55** 57 35N 45 55 E
Urengoy **58** 65 58N 28 25 E
Ures **120** 29 30N 110 30W
Urfa **64** 37 12N 38 50 E
Urfahr **26** 48 19N 14 17 E
Urgench **58** 41 40N 60 41 E
Uri □ **25** 46 43N 8 35 E
Uribia **126** 11 43N 72 16W
Urim **62** 31 18N 34 32 E
Uriondo **124** 21 41 S 64 41W
Urique → **120** 26 29N 107 58W
Urk **16** 52 39N 5 36 E
Urla **64** 38 20N 26 47 E
Urlati **46** 44 59N 26 15 E
Urmia = Rezā'īyeh **64** 37 40N 45 0 E
Urmia, L. = Rezā'īyeh, Daryācheh-ye **64** 37 30N 45 30 E
Uroševac **42** 42 23N 21 10 E
Urshult **49** 56 31N 14 50 E
Ursus **28** 52 12N 20 53 E
Uruana **127** 15 30 S 49 41W
Uruapan **120** 19 30N 102 0W
Urubamba **126** 13 20 S 72 10W
Urubamba → **126** 10 43 S 73 48W
Uruçuí **127** 7 20 S 44 28W
Uruguai → **125** 26 0 S 53 30W
Uruguaiana **124** 29 50 S 57 0W
Uruguay ■ **124** 32 30 S 56 30W
Uruguay → **124** 34 12 S 58 18W
Urumchi = Ürümqi **75** 43 45N 87 45 E
Ürümqi **75** 43 45N 87 45 E
Urup → **57** 46 0N 41 10 E
Urup, Os. **59** 46 0N 151 0 E
Uryung-Khaya **59** 72 48N 113 23 E
Uryupinsk **55** 50 45N 41 58 E
Urzhum **55** 57 10N 49 56 E
Urziceni **46** 44 40N 26 42 E
Usa → **52** 65 67N 56 55 E
Uşak **64** 38 43N 29 28 E
Usakos **92** 22 0 S 15 31 E
Ušče **42** 43 30N 20 39 E
Usedom **24** 53 50N 13 55 E
Usfan **86** 21 58N 39 27 E
Ush-Tobe **58** 45 16N 78 0 E
Ushakova, O. **4** 82 0N 80 0 E
Ushant = Ouessant, Île d' **18** 48 25N 5 5W
Ushashi **90** 1 59 S 33 57 E
Ushat **87** 7 59N 29 28 E
Ushuaia **128** 54 50 S 68 23W
Ushumun **59** 52 47N 126 32 E
Usk → **13** 51 37N 2 56W
Uskedal **47** 59 56N 5 53 E
Üsküdar **64** 41 0N 29 5 E
Uslar **24** 51 39N 9 39 E
Usman **55** 52 5N 39 48 E
Usoke **90** 5 7 S 32 19 E
Usolye Sibirskoye **59** 52 48N 103 40 E
Usoro **85** 5 33N 6 11 E
Uspallata, P. de **124** 32 37 S 69 22W
Uspenskiy **58** 48 41N 72 43 E
Ussel **20** 45 32N 2 18 E
Ussuriysk **59** 43 48N 131 59 E
Ust-Aldan = Batamay **59** 63 30N 129 15 E
Ust Amginskoye = Khandyga **59** 62 42N 135 0 E
Ust-Bolsheretsk **59** 52 50N 156 15 E
Ust Buzulukskaya **55** 50 8N 42 11 E
Ust chaun **59** 68 47N 170 30 E
Ust-Donetskiy **57** 47 35N 40 55 E
Ust'-Ilga **59** 55 5N 104 55 E
Ust Ilimpeya = Yukti **59** 63 20N 105 0 E
Ust-Ilimsk **59** 58 3N 102 39 E
Ust Ishim **58** 57 45N 71 10 E
Ust-Kamchatsk **59** 56 10N 162 28 E
Ust-Kamenogorsk **58** 50 0N 82 36 E
Ust-Karenga **59** 54 25N 116 30 E
Ust Khayryuzova **59** 57 15N 156 45 E
Ust-Kut **59** 56 50N 105 42 E
Ust Kuyga **59** 70 1N 135 43 E
Ust-Labinsk **57** 45 15N 39 41 E
Ust Luga **54** 59 35N 28 20 E
Ust Maya **59** 60 30N 134 28 E
Ust-Mil **59** 59 40N 133 11 E
Ust-Nera **59** 64 35N 143 15 E
Ust-Nyukzha **59** 56 34N 121 37 E
Ust Olenek **59** 73 0N 119 48 E
Ust-Omchug **59** 61 9N 149 38 E
Ust Port **58** 69 40N 84 26 E
Ust Tsilma **52** 65 25N 52 0 E
Ust-Tungir **59** 55 25N 120 36 E
Ust Urt = Ustyurt, Plato **58** 44 0N 55 0 E
Ust Usa **52** 66 0N 56 30 E
Ust Vorkuta **58** 67 24N 64 0 E
Ustaoset **47** 60 30N 8 2 E
Ustaritz **20** 43 24N 1 27W
Uste **55** 59 35N 39 40 E
Ústí nad Labem **26** 50 41N 14 3 E
Ústí nad Orlicí **27** 49 58N 16 24 E
Ustica **40** 38 42N 13 10 E
Ustka **28** 54 35N 16 55 E
Ustroń **27** 49 43N 18 48 E
Ustrzyki Dolne **27** 49 27N 22 40 E
Ustye **59** 57 46N 94 37 E
Ustyurt, Plato **58** 44 0N 55 0 E
Ustyuzhna **55** 58 50N 36 32 E
Usu **75** 44 27N 84 40 E
Usuki **74** 33 8N 131 49 E
Usulután **120** 13 25N 88 28W
Usumacinta → **120** 17 0N 91 0W
Usure **90** 4 40 S 34 22 E
Uta **73** 4 33 S 136 0 E
Utah □ **118** 39 30N 111 30W
Utah, L. **118** 40 10N 111 58W
Ute Cr. **117** 35 21N 103 45W
Utena **54** 55 27N 25 40 E
Ütersen **24** 53 40N 9 40 E
Utete **90** 8 0 S 38 45 E
Uthai Thani **71** 15 22N 100 3 E
Utiariti **126** 13 0 S 58 10W
Utica, N.Y., U.S.A. **114** 43 5N 75 18W
Utica, Ohio, U.S.A. **112** 40 13N 82 26W
Utiel **32** 39 37N 1 11W
Utik L. **109** 55 15N 96 0W
Utikuma L. **108** 55 50N 115 30W
Utrecht, Neth. **16** 52 5N 5 8 E
Utrecht, S. Afr. **93** 27 38 S 30 20 E
Utrecht □ **16** 52 6N 5 7 E
Utrera **31** 37 12N 5 48W
Utsjoki **50** 69 51N 26 59 E
Utsunomiya **74** 36 30N 139 50 E
Uttar Pradesh □ **69** 27 0N 80 0 E
Uttaradit **71** 17 36N 100 5 E
Uttoxeter **12** 52 53N 1 50W
Ütze **24** 52 28N 10 11 E
Uusikaarlepyy **50** 63 32N 22 31 E
Uusikaupunki **51** 60 47N 21 25 E
Uva **52** 56 59N 52 13 E
Uvac → **42** 43 35N 19 40 E
Uvalde **117** 29 15N 99 48W
Uvarovo **55** 51 59N 42 14 E
Uvat **58** 59 5N 68 50 E
Uvinza **90** 5 5 S 30 24 E
Uvira **90** 3 22 S 29 3 E

• *Renamed Mutare*

Uvs Nuur 75 50 20N 92 30 E
Uwajima 74 33 10N 132 35 E
Uweinat, Jebel 86 21 54N 24 58 E
Uxbridge 112 44 6N 79 7W
Uxin Qi 76 38 50N 109 5 E
Uxmal 120 20 22N 89 46W
Uyandi 59 69 19N 141 0 E
Uyo 85 5 1N 7 53 E
Uyuni 126 20 28 S 66 47W
Uzbek S.S.R. □ 58 41 30N 65 0 E
Uzen 53 43 27N 53 10 E
Uzen, Bol. → 55 50 0N 49 30 E
Uzen, Mal. → 55 50 0N 48 30 E
Uzerche 20 45 25N 1 34 E
Uzès 21 44 1N 4 26 E
Uzh → 54 51 15N 30 12 E
Uzhgorod 54 48 36N 22 18 E
Uzlovaya 55 54 0N 38 5 E
Uzunköprü 43 41 16N 26 43 E

V

Vaal → 92 29 4 S 23 38 E
Vaaldam 93 27 0 S 28 14 E
Vaalwater 93 24 15 S 28 8 E
Vaasa 50 63 6N 21 38 E
Vaasan lääni □ 50 63 2N 22 50 E
Vabre 20 43 42N 2 24 E
Vác 27 47 49N 19 10 E
Vacaria 125 28 31 S 50 52W
Vacaville 118 38 21N 122 0W
Vaccarès, Étang de 21 43 32N 4 34 E
Vach → 58 60 45N 76 45 E
Vache, Î.-à- 121 18 2N 73 35W
Väddö 48 59 55N 18 50 E
Vadnagar 68 23 47N 72 40 E
Vado Lígure 38 44 16N 8 26 E
Vadodara 68 22 20N 73 10 E
Vadsø 50 70 3N 29 50 E
Vadstena 49 58 28N 14 54 E
Vaduz 25 47 8N 9 31 E
Værøy 50 67 40N 12 40 E
Vagney 19 48 1N 6 43 E
Vagnhärad 48 58 57N 17 33 E
Vagos 30 40 33N 8 42W
Váh → 27 47 55N 18 0 E
Vahsel B. 5 75 0 S 35 0W
Vaigach 58 70 10N 59 0 E
Vaigai → 70 9 15N 79 10 E
Vaiges 18 48 2N 0 30W
Vaihingen 25 48 55N 8 58 E
Vaijapur 70 19 58N 74 45 E
Vaikam 70 9 45N 76 25 E
Vailly Aisne 19 49 25N 3 30 E
Vaippar → 70 9 0N 78 25 E
Vaison 21 44 14N 5 4 E
Vajpur 68 21 24N 73 17 E
Vakarel 43 42 35N 23 40 E
Vaksdal 47 60 29N 5 45 E
Vál 27 47 22N 18 40 E
Val-d'Ajol, Le 19 47 55N 6 30 E
Val-de-Marne □ 19 48 45N 2 28 E
Val-d'Oise □ 19 49 5N 2 10 E
Val d'Or 106 48 7N 77 47W
Val Marie 109 49 15N 107 45W
Valadares 30 41 5N 8 38W
Valahia 46 44 35N 25 0 E
Valais □ 25 46 12N 7 45 E
Valandovo 42 41 19N 22 34 E
Valašské Meziříčí 27 49 29N 17 59 E
Valáxa 45 38 50N 24 29 E
Vălcani 42 46 0N 20 26 E
Valcheta 128 40 40 S 66 8W
Valdagno 39 45 38N 11 18 E
Valdahon, Le 19 47 8N 6 20 E
Valday 54 57 58N 33 9 E
Valdayskaya Vozvyshennost 54 57 0N 33 30 E
Valdeazogues → 31 38 45N 4 55W
Valdemarsvik 49 58 14N 16 40 E
Valdepeñas, Ciudad Real, Spain 31 38 43N 3 25W
Valdepeñas, Jaén, Spain 31 37 33N 3 47W
Valderaduey → 30 41 31N 5 42W
Valderrobres 32 40 53N 0 9 E
Valdés, Pen. 128 42 30 S 63 45W
Valdez 104 61 14N 76 17W
Valdivia 128 39 50 S 73 14W
Valdobbiádene 39 45 53N 12 0 E
Valdosta 115 30 50N 83 20W
Valdoviño 30 43 36N 8 8W
Valdres 47 60 55N 9 28 E
Vale, U.S.A. 118 44 0N 117 15W
Vale, U.S.S.R. 57 41 30N 42 58 E
Valea lui Mihai 46 47 32N 22 11 E
Valença, Brazil 127 13 20 S 39 5W
Valença, Port. 30 42 1N 8 34W
Valença do Piauí 127 6 20 S 41 45W
Valençay 19 47 9N 1 34 E
Valence 21 44 57N 4 54 E
Valence-d'Agen 20 44 8N 0 54 E
Valencia, Spain 33 39 27N 0 23W
Valencia, Venez. 126 10 11N 68 0W
Valencia □ 33 39 20N 0 40W
Valencia, Albufera de 33 39 20N 0 27W
Valencia de Alcántara 31 39 25N 7 14W
Valencia de Don Juan 30 42 17N 5 31W
Valencia del Ventoso 31 38 15N 6 29W
Valencia, G. de 33 39 30N 0 20 E
Valenciennes 19 50 20N 3 34 E
Văleni 46 44 15N 24 45 E
Valensole 21 43 50N 5 59 E
Valentia Hr. 15 51 56N 10 17W
Valentia I. 15 51 54N 10 22W
Valentim, Sa. do 127 6 0 S 43 30W
Valentine, Nebr., U.S.A. 116 42 50N 100 35W
Valentine, Tex., U.S.A. 117 30 36N 104 28W
Valenza 38 45 2N 8 39 E
Våler 47 60 41N 11 50 E
Valera 126 9 19N 70 37W
Valga 54 57 44N 26 0 E
Valguarnera Caropepe 41 37 30N 14 22 E
Valier 118 48 25N 112 9W
Valinco, G. de 21 41 40N 8 52 E
Valjevo 42 44 18N 19 53 E
Valkenswaard 16 51 21N 5 29 E
Vall de Uxó 32 39 49N 0 15W
Valla 48 59 2N 16 20 E
Valladolid, Mexico 120 20 40N 88 11W
Valladolid, Spain 30 41 38N 4 43W
Valladolid □ 30 41 38N 4 43W
Vallata 41 41 3N 15 16 E
Valldemosa 32 39 43N 2 37 E
Valle 47 59 13N 7 33 E
Valle d'Aosta □ 38 45 45N 7 22 E
Valle de Arán 32 42 50N 0 55 E
Valle de Cabuérniga 30 43 14N 4 18W
Valle de la Pascua 126 9 13N 66 0W
Valle de Santiago 120 20 25N 101 15W
Valle Fértil, Sierra del 124 30 20 S 68 0W
Valle Hermoso 120 25 35N 97 40W
Vallecas 30 40 23N 3 41W
Vallejo 118 38 12N 122 15W
Vallenar 124 28 30 S 70 50W
Valleraugue 20 44 6N 3 39 E
Vallet 18 47 10N 1 15W
Valletta 36 35 54N 14 30 E
Valley City 116 46 57N 98 0W
Valley Falls 118 42 33N 120 16W
Valleyview 108 55 5N 117 17W
Valli di Comácchio 39 44 40N 12 15 E
Vallimanca, Arroyo 124 35 40 S 59 10W
Vallo della Lucánia 41 40 14N 15 16 E
Vallon 21 44 25N 4 23 E
Vallorbe 25 46 42N 6 20 E
Valls 32 41 18N 1 15 E
Vallsta 48 61 31N 16 22 E
Valmaseda 32 43 11N 3 12W
Valmiera 54 57 37N 25 29 E
Valmont 18 49 45N 0 30 E
Valmontone 40 41 48N 12 55 E
Valmy 19 49 5N 4 45 E
Valnera, Mte. 32 43 9N 3 40W
Valognes 18 49 30N 1 28W
Valona = Vlóra 44 40 32N 19 28 E
Valongo 30 41 8N 8 30W
Valpaços 30 41 36N 7 17W
Valparaíso, Chile 124 33 2 S 71 40W
Valparaíso, Mexico 120 22 50N 103 32W
Valparaiso 114 41 27N 87 2W
Valparaíso □ 124 33 2 S 71 40W
Valpovo 42 45 39N 18 25 E
Valréas 21 44 24N 5 0 E
Vals 25 46 39N 9 11 E
Vals → 92 27 23 S 26 30 E
Vals-les-Bains 21 44 42N 4 24 E
Vals, Tanjung 73 8 26 S 137 25 E
Valsbaai 92 34 15 S 18 40 E
Valskog 48 59 27N 15 57 E
Válta 44 40 3N 23 25 E
Valtellina 38 46 9N 9 55 E
Valuyki 55 50 10N 38 5 E
Valverde del Camino 31 37 35N 6 47W
Valverde del Fresno 30 40 15N 6 51W
Vama 46 47 34N 25 42 E
Vámos 45 35 24N 24 13 E
Vamsadhara → 70 18 21N 84 8 E
Van 64 38 30N 43 20 E
Van Alstyne 117 33 25N 96 36W
Van Bruyssel 107 47 56N 72 9W
Van Buren, Can. 107 47 10N 67 55W
Van Buren, Ark., U.S.A. 117 35 28N 94 18W
Van Buren, Me., U.S.A. 115 47 10N 68 1W
Van Buren, Mo., U.S.A. 117 37 0N 91 0W
Van der Kloof Dam 92 30 04 S 24 40 E
Van Diemen, C. 97 16 30 S 139 46 E
Van Diemen G. 96 11 45 S 132 0 E
Van Gölü 64 38 30N 43 0 E
Van Horn 117 31 3N 104 55W
Van Reenen P. 93 28 22 S 29 27 E
Van Rees, Pegunungan 73 2 35 S 138 15 E
Van Tassell 116 42 40N 104 3W
Van Tivu 70 8 51N 78 15 E
Van Wert 114 40 52N 84 31W
Vanavara 59 60 22N 102 16 E
Vancouver, Can. 108 49 15N 123 10W
Vancouver, U.S.A. 118 45 44N 122 41W
Vancouver I. 108 49 50N 126 0W
Vandalia, Ill., U.S.A. 116 38 57N 89 4W
Vandalia, Mo., U.S.A. 116 39 18N 91 30W
Vandeloos Bay 70 8 0N 81 45 E
Vanderbijlpark 93 26 42 S 27 54 E
Vandergrift 114 40 36N 79 33W
Vanderhoof 108 54 0N 124 0W
Vanderlin I. 97 15 44 S 137 2 E
Vandyke 98 24 10 S 147 51 E
Vänern 49 58 47N 13 30 E
Vänersborg 49 58 26N 12 19 E
Vang Vieng 71 18 58N 102 32 E
Vanga 90 4 35 S 39 12 E
Vangaindrano 93 23 21 S 47 36 E
Vanguard 109 49 55N 107 20W
Vanier 106 45 27N 75 40W
Vanimo 98 2 42 S 141 21 E
Vanivilasa Sagara 70 13 45N 76 30 E
Vaniyambadi 70 12 46N 78 44 E
Vankarem 59 67 51N 175 50 E
Vankleek Hill 106 45 32N 74 40W
Vänna 50 70 6N 19 50 E
Vännäs 50 63 58N 19 48 E
Vannes 18 47 40N 2 47W
Vanoise, Massif de la 21 45 25N 6 40 E
Vanrhynsdorp 92 31 36 S 18 44 E
Vanrook 98 16 57 S 141 57 E
Vans, Les 21 44 25N 4 7 E
Vansbro 48 60 32N 14 15 E
Vanse 47 58 6N 6 41 E
Vansittart B. 96 14 3 S 126 17 E
Vanthli 68 21 28N 70 25 E
Vanua Levu 101 16 33 S 179 15 E
Vanua Mbalavu 101 17 40 S 178 57W
Vanwyksvlei 92 30 18 S 21 49 E
Vanylven 47 62 5N 5 33 E
Vapnyarka 56 48 32N 28 45 E
Var □ 21 43 27N 6 18 E
Var → 21 43 39N 7 12 E
Vara 49 58 16N 12 55 E
Varada → 70 15 0N 75 40 E
Varades 18 47 25N 1 1W
Varaita → 38 44 49N 7 36 E
Varaldsoøy 47 60 6N 5 59 E
Varallo 38 45 50N 8 13 E
Varanasi (Benares) 69 25 22N 83 0 E
Varangerfjorden 50 70 3N 29 25 E
Varazdin 39 46 20N 16 20 E
Varazze 38 44 21N 8 36 E
Varberg 49 57 6N 12 20 E
Vardar → 42 40 35N 22 50 E
Varde 49 55 38N 8 29 E
Varde Å 49 55 35N 8 19 E
Varel 24 53 23N 8 9 E
Varena 54 54 12N 24 30 E
Varennes-sur-Allier 20 46 19N 3 24 E
Vareš 42 44 12N 18 23 E
Varese 38 45 49N 8 50 E
Varese Ligure 38 44 22N 9 33 E
Vårgårda 49 58 2N 12 49 E
Varginha 125 21 33 S 45 25W
Vargön 49 58 22N 12 20 E
Varhaug 47 58 37N 5 41 E
Variadero 117 35 43N 104 17W
Varillas 124 24 0 S 70 10W
Väring 49 58 30N 14 0 E
Värmeln 48 59 35N 12 54 E
Värmlands län □ 48 60 0N 13 20 E
Varna 43 43 13N 27 56 E
Varna → 70 16 48N 74 32 E
Värnamo 49 57 10N 14 3 E
Varnsdorf 26 50 55N 14 35 E
Värö 49 57 16N 12 11 E
Vars 113 45 21N 75 21W
Varteig 47 59 23N 11 12 E
Varvarin 42 43 43N 21 20 E
Varzaneh 65 32 25N 52 40 E
Varzi 38 44 50N 9 12 E
Varzo 38 46 12N 8 15 E
Varzy 19 47 22N 3 20 E
Vas □ 27 47 10N 16 55 E
Vasa 50 63 6N 21 38 E
Vasa Barris → 127 11 10 S 37 10W
Vásárosnamény 27 48 9N 22 19 E
Vascão → 31 37 31N 7 31W
Vaşcău 46 46 28N 22 30 E
Vascongadas 32 42 50N 2 45W
Väse 48 59 23N 13 52 E
Vasht = Khāsh 65 28 14N 61 14 E
Vasilevichi 54 52 15N 29 50 E
Vasilikón 45 38 25N 23 40 E
Vasilkov 54 50 7N 30 15 E
Vaslui 46 46 38N 27 42 E
Vaslui □ 46 46 30N 27 45 E
Väsman 48 60 9N 15 5 E
Vassar, Can. 109 49 10N 95 55W
Vassar, U.S.A. 114 43 23N 83 33W
Västerås 49 59 37N 16 38 E
Västerbottens län □ 50 64 58N 18 0 E
Västernorrlands län □ 48 63 30N 17 30 E
Västervik 49 57 43N 16 43 E
Västmanlands län □ 48 59 45N 16 20 E
Vasto 39 42 8N 14 40 E
Vasvár 27 47 3N 16 47 E
Vatan 19 47 4N 1 50 E
Vathí, Itháki, Greece 45 38 18N 20 40 E
Vathí, Sámos, Greece 45 37 46N 27 1 E
Váthia 45 36 29N 22 29 E
Vatican City ■ 39 41 54N 12 27 E
Vaticano, C. 40 38 40N 15 48 E
Vatin 42 45 12N 21 20 E
Vatnajökull 50 64 30N 16 48W
Vatnås 47 59 58N 9 37 E
Vatne 47 62 33N 6 38 E
Vatneyri 50 65 35N 24 0W
Vatoa 101 19 50 S 178 13W
Vatoloha, Mt. 93 17 52 S 47 48 E
Vatomandry 93 19 20 S 48 59 E
Vatra-Dornei 46 47 22N 25 22 E
Vättern 49 58 25N 14 30 E
Vaucluse □ 21 44 3N 5 10 E
Vaucouleurs 19 48 37N 5 40 E
Vaud □ 25 46 35N 6 30 E
Vaughan 119 34 37N 105 12W
Vaughn 118 47 37N 111 36W
Vaupés → 126 0 2N 67 16W
Vauvert 21 43 42N 4 17 E
Vauxhall 108 50 5N 112 9W
Vava'u 101 18 36 S 174 0W
Vavincourt 19 48 49N 5 12 E
Vavoua 84 7 23N 6 29W
Vaxholm 48 59 25N 18 20 E
Växjö 49 56 52N 14 50 E
Vaygach, Ostrov 58 70 0N 60 0 E
Vazovgrad 43 42 39N 24 45 E
Vechta 24 52 47N 8 18 E
Vechte → 16 52 34N 6 6 E
Vecilla, La 30 42 51N 5 27W
Vecsés 27 47 26N 19 19 E
Vedaraniam 70 10 25N 79 50 E
Veddige 49 57 17N 12 20 E
Vedea → 46 44 0N 25 20 E
Vedia 124 34 30 S 61 31W
Vedra, I. del 33 38 52N 1 12 E
Veendam 16 53 5N 6 52 E
Veenendaal 16 52 2N 5 34 E
Vefsna → 50 65 48N 13 10 E
Vega, Norway 50 65 40N 11 55 E
Vega, U.S.A. 117 35 18N 102 26W
Vega, La 121 19 20N 70 30W
Vegadeo 30 43 27N 7 4W
Vegafjorden 50 65 37N 12 0 E
Vegesack 24 53 10N 8 38 E
Veggli 47 60 3N 9 9 E
Veghel 16 51 37N 5 32 E
Vegorritis, Límni 44 40 45N 21 45 E
Vegreville 108 53 30N 112 5W
Vegusdal 47 58 32N 8 10 E
Veii 39 42 0N 12 24 E
Vejen 49 55 30N 9 9 E
Vejer de la Frontera 31 36 15N 5 59W
Vejle 49 55 43N 9 30 E
Vejle Fjord 49 55 40N 9 50 E
Vela Luka 39 42 59N 16 44 E
Velanai I. 70 9 45N 79 45 E
Velarde 119 36 11N 106 1W
Velasco 117 29 0N 95 20W
Velasco, Sierra de. 124 29 20 S 67 10W
Velay, Mts. du 20 45 0N 3 40 E
Velddrif 92 32 42 S 18 11 E
Velebit Planina 39 44 50N 15 20 E
Velebitski Kanal 39 44 45N 14 55 E
Veleka → 43 42 4N 27 58 E
Velenje 39 46 23N 15 8 E
Velestínon 44 39 23N 22 43 E
Veleta, La 31 37 1N 3 22W
Vélez 126 6 1N 73 41W
Velež 42 43 19N 18 2 E
Vélez Blanco 33 37 41N 2 5W
Vélez Málaga 31 36 48N 4 5W
Vélez Rubio 33 37 41N 2 5W
Velhas → 127 17 13 S 44 49W
Velika 42 45 27N 17 40 E
Velika Gorica 39 45 44N 16 5 E
Velika Gradište 42 44 46N 21 29 E
Velika Kapela 39 45 10N 15 5 E
Velika Kladuša 39 45 11N 15 48 E
Velika Morava → 42 44 43N 21 3 E
Velika Plana 42 44 20N 21 1 E
Velikaya → 54 57 48N 28 20 E
Velikaya Lepetikha 56 47 2N 33 58 E
Veliké Kapušany 27 48 34N 22 5 E
Velike Lašče 39 45 49N 14 45 E
Veliki Backa Kanal 42 45 45N 19 15 E
Veliki Jastrebac 42 43 25N 21 30 E
Veliki Popović 42 44 8N 21 18 E
Velikiy Ustyug 52 60 47N 46 20 E
Velikiye Luki 54 56 25N 30 32 E
Velikonda Range 70 14 45N 79 10 E
Velikoye, Oz. 55 55 15N 40 10 E
Velingrad 43 42 4N 23 58 E
Velino, Mte. 39 42 10N 13 20 E
Velizh 54 55 36N 31 11 E
Velké Karlovice 27 49 20N 18 17 E
Velke Meziřici 26 49 21N 16 1 E
Vel'ký ostrov Žitný 27 48 5N 17 20 E
Vellar → 70 11 30N 79 36 E
Velletri 40 41 43N 12 43 E
Vellinge 49 55 29N 13 0 E
Vellore 70 12 57N 79 10 E
Velsen-Noord 16 52 27N 4 40 E
Velsk 52 61 10N 42 5 E
Velten 24 52 40N 13 11 E
Velva 116 48 6N 100 56W
Velvendós 44 40 15N 22 6 E
Vembanad Lake 70 9 36N 76 15 E
Veme 47 60 14N 10 7 E
Ven 49 55 55N 12 45 E
Vena 49 57 31N 16 0 E
Venado 120 22 56N 101 10W
Venado Tuerto 124 33 50 S 62 0W
Venafro 41 41 28N 14 3 E
Venarey-les-Laumes 19 47 32N 4 26 E
Venaria 38 45 6N 7 39 E
Venčane 42 44 24N 20 28 E
Vence 21 43 43N 7 6 E
Vendas Novas 31 38 39N 8 27W
Vendée □ 18 46 50N 1 35W
Vendée → 18 46 20N 1 10W
Vendée, Collines de 18 46 35N 0 45W
Vendeuvre-sur-Barse 19 48 14N 4 28 E
Vendôme 18 47 47N 1 3 E
Vendrell 32 41 10N 1 30 E
Vendsyssel 49 57 22N 10 0 E
Véneta, Laguna 39 45 23N 12 25 E
Véneto □ 39 45 40N 12 0 E
Venev 55 54 22N 38 17 E
Venézia 39 45 27N 12 20 E
Venézia, Golfo di 39 45 20N 13 0 E
Venezuela ■ 126 8 0N 65 0W
Venezuela, Golfo de 126 11 30N 71 0W
Vengurla 70 15 53N 73 45 E
Vengurla Rocks 70 15 55N 73 22 E
Venice = Venézia 39 45 27N 12 20 E
Vénissieux 21 45 43N 4 53 E
Venkatagiri 70 14 0N 79 35 E
Venkatapuram 70 18 20N 80 30 E
Venlo 16 51 22N 6 11 E
Vennesla 47 58 15N 8 0 E
Venraij 16 51 31N 6 0 E
Venta de Cardeña 31 38 16N 4 20W
Venta de San Rafael 30 40 42N 4 12W
Ventana, Punta de la 120 24 4N 109 48W
Ventana, Sa. de la 124 38 0 S 62 30W
Ventersburg 92 28 7 S 27 9 E
Ventimíglia 38 43 50N 7 39 E
Ventnor 13 50 35N 1 12W
Ventotene 40 40 48N 13 25 E
Ventoux 21 44 10N 5 17 E
Ventspils 54 57 25N 21 32 E
Ventuarí → 126 3 58N 67 2W
Ventura 119 34 16N 119 18W
Vera, Argent. 124 29 30 S 60 20W
Vera, Spain 33 37 15N 1 51W
Veracruz 120 19 10N 96 10W
Veracruz □ 120 19 0N 96 15W
Veraval 68 20 53N 70 27 E
Verbánia 38 45 56N 8 43 E
Verbicaro 41 39 46N 15 54 E
Vercelli 38 45 19N 8 25 E
Verchovchevo 56 48 32N 34 10 E
Verdalsøra 50 63 48N 11 30 E
Verde →, Argent. 128 41 56 S 65 5W
Verde →, Chihuahua, Mexico 120 26 29N 107 58W
Verde →, Oaxaca, Mexico 120 15 59N 97 50W
Verde →, Veracruz, Mexico 120 21 10N 102 50W
Verde →, Parag. 124 23 9 S 57 37W
Verde, Cay 121 23 0N 75 5W
Verden 24 52 58N 9 18 E
Verdhikoúsa 44 39 47N 21 59 E
Verdigre 116 42 38N 98 0W

Verdon → 21 43 43N 5 46 E
Verdon-sur-Mer, Le 20 45 33N 1 4W
Verdun 19 49 12N 5 24 E
Verdun-sur-le Doubs 19 46 54N 5 0 E
Vereeniging 93 26 38 S 27 57 E
Vérendrye, Parc Prov. de la 106 47 20N 76 40W
Verga, C. 84 10 30N 14 10W
Vergara 32 43 9N 2 28W
Vergato 38 44 18N 11 8 E
Vergemont 98 23 33 S 143 1 E
Vergemont Cr. → 98 24 16 S 143 16 E
Vergennes 113 44 9N 73 15W
Vergt 20 45 2N 0 43 E
Verín 30 41 57N 7 27W
Veriña 30 43 32N 5 43W
Verkhnedvinsk 54 55 45N 27 58 E
Verkhnevilyuysk 59 63 27N 120 18 E
Verkhneye Kalinino 59 59 54N 108 8 E
Verkhniy Baskunchak 57 48 14N 46 44 E
Verkhovye 55 52 55N 37 15 E
Verkhoyansk 59 67 35N 133 25 E
Verkhoyanskiy Khrebet 59 66 0N 129 0 E
Verlo 109 50 19N 108 35W
Verma 47 62 21N 8 3 E
Vermenton 19 47 40N 3 42 E
Vermilion 109 53 20N 110 50W
Vermilion →, Alta., Can. 109 53 22N 110 51W
Vermilion →, Qué., Can. 106 47 38N 72 56W
Vermilion, B. 117 29 45N 91 55W
Vermilion Bay 109 49 51N 93 34W
Vermilion Chutes 108 58 22N 114 51W
Vermilion L. 116 47 53N 92 25W
Vermillion 116 42 50N 96 56W
Vermont □ 114 43 40N 72 50W
Vernal 118 40 28N 109 35W
Verner 106 46 25N 80 8W
Verneuil-sur-Avre 18 48 45N 0 55 E
Vernon, Can. 108 50 20N 119 15W
Vernon, France 18 49 5N 1 30 E
Vernon, U.S.A. 117 34 10N 99 20W
Vero Beach 115 27 39N 80 23W
Véroia 44 40 34N 22 12 E
Verolanuova 38 45 20N 10 5 E
Véroli 40 41 43N 13 24 E
Verona 38 45 27N 11 0 E
Veropol 59 65 15N 168 40 E
Versailles 19 48 48N 2 8 E
Vert, C. 84 14 45N 17 30W
Vertou 18 47 10N 1 28W
Vertus 19 48 54N 4 0 E
Verulam 93 29 38 S 31 2 E
Verviers 16 50 37N 5 52 E
Vervins 19 49 50N 3 53 E
Verwood 109 49 30N 105 40W
Verzej 39 46 34N 16 13 E
Veselí nad Lužnicí 26 49 12N 14 43 E
Veseliye 43 42 18N 27 38 E
Veselovskoye Vdkhr. 57 47 0N 41 0 E
Veshenskaya 57 49 35N 41 44 E
Vesle → 19 49 23N 3 38 E
Vesoul 19 47 40N 6 11 E
Vessigebro 49 56 58N 12 40 E
Vest-Agder fylke □ 47 58 30N 7 15 E
Vestby 47 59 37N 10 45 E
Vestfjorden 50 67 55N 14 0 E
Vestfold fylke □ 47 59 15N 10 0 E
Vestmannaeyjar 50 63 27N 20 15W
Vestmarka 47 59 56N 11 59 E
Vestnes 47 62 39N 7 5 E
Vestone 38 45 43N 10 25 E
Vestsjællands Amtskommune □ 49 55 30N 11 20 E
Vestspitsbergen 4 78 40N 17 0 E
Vestvågøy 50 68 18N 13 50 E
Vesuvio 41 40 50N 14 22 E
Vesuvius, Mt. = Vesuvio 41 40 50N 14 22 E
Vesyegonsk 55 58 40N 37 16 E
Veszprém 27 47 8N 17 57 E
Veszprém □ 27 47 5N 17 55 E
Vésztő 27 46 55N 21 16 E
Vetapalem 70 15 47N 80 18 E
Vetlanda 49 57 24N 15 3 E
Vetluga 55 57 53N 45 45 E
Vetluzhskiy 55 57 17N 45 12 E
Vetovo 43 43 42N 26 16 E
Vetralia 39 42 20N 12 2 E
Vetren 43 42 15N 24 3 E
Vettore, Monte 39 42 49N 13 16 E
Veurne 16 51 5N 2 40 E
Vevey 25 46 28N 6 51 E
Vévi 44 40 47N 21 38 E
Veynes 21 44 32N 5 49 E
Veys 64 31 30N 49 0 E
Vézelise 19 48 30N 6 5 E
Vézère → 20 44 53N 0 53 E
Vezhen 43 42 50N 24 20 E
Viacha 126 16 39 S 68 18W
Viadana 38 44 55N 10 30 E
Viana, Brazil 127 3 13 S 45 0W
Viana, Spain 32 42 31N 2 22W
Viana del Bollo 30 42 11N 7 6W
Viana do Alentejo 31 38 17N 7 59W
Viana do Castelo 30 41 42N 8 50W
Vianna do Castelo □ 30 41 50N 8 30W
Vianópolis 127 16 40 S 48 35W
Viar → 31 37 36N 5 50W
Viaréggio 38 43 52N 10 13 E
Viaur → 20 44 8N 1 58 E
Vibank 109 50 20N 103 56W
Vibo Valéntia 41 38 40N 16 5 E
Viborg 49 56 27N 9 23 E
Vibraye 18 48 3N 0 44 E
Vic-en-Bigorre 20 43 24N 0 3 E
Vic-Fézensac 20 43 47N 0 19 E
Vic-sur-Cère 20 44 59N 2 38 E
Vic-sur-Seille 19 48 45N 6 33 E
Vicenza 39 45 32N 11 31 E
Vich 32 41 58N 2 19 E
Vichuga 55 57 12N 41 55 E
Vichy 20 46 9N 3 26 E
Vicksburg, Mich., U.S.A. 114 42 10N 85 30W
Vicksburg, Miss., U.S.A. 117 32 22N 90 56W
Vico del Gargaro 41 41 54N 15 57 E
Vico, L. di 39 42 20N 12 10 E
Viçosa 127 9 28 S 36 14W
Victor, Colo., U.S.A. 116 38 43N 105 7W
Victor, N.Y., U.S.A. 112 42 58N 77 24W
Victor Harbour 97 35 30 S 138 37 E
Victoria, Argent. 124 32 40 S 60 10W
Victoria, Camer. 88 4 1N 9 10 E
Victoria, Can. 108 48 30N 123 25W
Victoria, Chile 128 38 13 S 72 20W
Victoria, Guin.* 84 10 50N 14 32W
Victoria, H. K. 75 22 16N 114 15 E
Victoria, Malay. 72 5 20N 115 14 E
Victoria, Kans., U.S.A. 116 38 52N 99 8W
Victoria, Tex., U.S.A. 117 28 50N 97 0W
Victoria □, Austral. 97 37 0 S 144 0 E
Victoria □, Zimb. 91 21 0 S 31 30 E
Victoria → 96 15 10 S 129 40 E
Victoria Beach 109 50 40N 96 35W
Victoria de las Tunas 121 20 58N 76 59W
Victoria Falls 91 17 58 S 25 52 E
Victoria, Grand L. 106 47 31N 77 30W
Victoria Harbour 106 44 45N 79 45W
Victoria I. 104 71 0N 111 0W
Victoria, L. 90 1 0 S 33 0 E
Victoria Ld. 5 75 0 S 160 0 E
Victoria, Mt. 98 8 55 S 147 32 E
Victoria Nile → 90 2 14N 31 26 E
Victoria Res. 107 48 20N 57 27W
Victoria River Downs 96 16 25 S 131 0 E
Victoria Taungdeik 67 21 15N 93 55 E
Victoria West 92 31 25 S 23 4 E
Victoriaville 107 46 4N 71 56W
Victorica 124 36 20 S 65 30W
Victorville 119 34 32N 117 18W
Vicuña 124 30 0 S 70 50W
Vicuña Mackenna 124 33 53 S 64 25W
Vidalia 115 32 13N 82 25W
Vidauban 21 43 25N 6 27 E
Vidigueira 31 38 12N 7 48W
Vidin 42 43 59N 22 50 E
Vidio, Cabo 30 43 35N 6 14W
Vidisha (Bhilsa) 68 23 28N 77 53 E
Vidöstern 49 57 5N 14 0 E
Vidra 46 45 56N 26 55 E
Viduša 42 42 55N 18 21 E
Vidzy 54 55 23N 26 37 E
Viechtach 25 49 5N 12 53 E
Viedma 128 40 50 S 63 0W
Viedma, L. 128 49 30 S 72 30W
Vieira 30 41 38N 8 8W
Viella 32 42 43N 0 44 E
Vien Pou Kha 71 20 45N 101 5 E
Vienenburg 24 51 57N 10 35 E
Vienna 117 37 29N 88 54W
Vienna = Wien 27 48 12N 16 22 E
Vienne 21 45 31N 4 53 E
Vienne □ 20 46 30N 0 42 E
Vienne → 18 47 13N 0 5 E
Vientiane 71 17 58N 102 36 E
Vientos, Paso de los 121 20 0N 74 0W
Viersen 24 51 15N 6 23 E
Vierwaldstättersee 25 47 0N 8 30 E
Vierzon 19 47 13N 2 5 E
Vieste 40 41 52N 16 14 E
Vietnam ■ 71 19 0N 106 0 E
Vieux-Boucau-les-Bains 20 43 48N 1 23W
Vif 21 45 5N 5 41 E
Vigan 73 17 35N 120 28 E
Vigan, Le 20 44 0N 3 36 E
Vigévano 38 45 18N 8 50 E
Vigia 127 0 50 S 48 5W
Vignacourt 19 50 1N 2 15 E
Vignemale, Pic du 20 42 47N 0 10W
Vigneulles 19 48 59N 5 40 E
Vignola 38 44 29N 11 0 E
Vigo 30 42 12N 8 41W
Vigo, Ría de 30 42 15N 8 45W
Vihiers 18 47 10N 0 30W
Vijayadurg 70 16 30N 73 25 E
Vijayawada (Bezwada) 70 16 31N 80 39 E
Vikedal 47 59 30N 5 55 E
Viken 49 58 39N 14 20 E
Vikersund 47 59 58N 10 2 E
Viking 108 53 7N 111 50W
Vikna 50 64 55N 10 58 E
Vikramasingapuram 70 8 40N 76 47 E
Viksjö 48 62 45N 17 26 E
Vikulovo 58 56 50N 70 40 E
Vila Aiferes Chamusca 93 24 27 S 33 0 E
Vila Caldas Xavier 91 14 28 S 33 0 E
Vila Coutinho 91 14 37 S 34 19 E
Vila da Maganja 91 17 18 S 37 30 E
Vila de João Belo = Xai-Xai 93 25 6 S 33 31 E
Vila de Junqueiro 91 15 25 S 36 58 E
Vila de Manica 91 18 58 S 32 59 E
Vila de Rei 31 39 41N 8 9W
Vila do Bispo 31 37 5N 8 53W
Vila do Chibuto 93 24 40 S 33 33 E
Vila do Conde 30 41 21N 8 45W
Vila Fontes 91 17 51 S 35 24 E
Vila Franca de Xira 31 38 57N 8 59W
Vila Gamito 91 14 12 S 33 0 E
Vila Gomes da Costa 93 24 20 S 33 37 E
Vila Luisa 93 25 45 S 32 35 E
Vila Machado 91 19 15 S 34 14 E
Vila Mouzinho 91 14 48 S 34 25 E
Vila Nova de Foscôa 30 41 5N 7 9W
Vila Nova de Ourém 31 39 40N 8 35W
Vila Novo de Gaia 30 41 4N 8 40W
Vila Paiva de Andrada 91 18 44 S 34 2 E
Vila Pouca de Aguiar 30 41 30N 7 38W
Vila Real 30 41 17N 7 48W
Vila Real de Santo António 31 37 10N 7 28W
Vila Vasco da Gama 91 14 54 S 32 14 E
Vila Velha 125 20 20 S 40 17W
Vila Veríssimo Sarmento 88 8 7 S 20 38 E
Vila Viçosa 31 38 45N 7 27W
Vilaboa 30 42 21N 8 39W
Vilaine → 18 47 30N 2 27W
Vilanculos 93 22 1 S 35 17 E
Vilar Formosa 30 40 38N 6 45W
Vilareal □ 30 41 36N 7 35W
Vilaseca-Salou 32 41 7N 1 9 E
Vilcea □ 46 45 0N 24 10 E
Vileyka 54 54 30N 26 53 E
Vilhelmina 50 64 35N 16 39 E
Vilhena 126 12 40 S 60 5W
Viliga 59 61 36N 156 56 E
Viliya → 54 55 54N 23 53 E
Viljandi 54 58 28N 25 30 E
Vilkovo 56 45 28N 29 32 E
Villa Abecia 124 21 0 S 68 18W
Villa Ahumada 120 30 38N 106 30W
Villa Ana 124 28 28 S 59 40W
Villa Ángela 124 27 34 S 60 45W
Villa Bella 126 10 25 S 65 22W
Villa Bens = Tarfaya 80 27 55N 12 55W
Villa Cañás 124 34 0 S 61 35W
Villa Cisneros = Dakhla 80 23 50N 15 53W
Villa Colón 124 31 38 S 68 20W
Villa Constitución 124 33 15 S 60 20W
Villa de María 124 29 55 S 63 43W
Villa Dolores 124 31 58 S 65 15W
Villa Guillermina 124 28 15 S 59 29W
Villa Hayes 124 25 0 S 57 20W
Villa Iris 124 38 12 S 63 12W
Villa María 124 32 20 S 63 10W
Villa Mazán 124 28 40 S 66 30W
Villa Minozzo 38 44 21N 10 30 E
Villa Montes 124 21 10 S 63 30W
Villa Ocampo 124 28 30 S 59 20W
Villa Ojo de Agua 124 29 30 S 63 44W
Villa San Giovanni 41 38 13N 15 38 E
Villa San José 124 32 12 S 58 15W
Villa San Martín 124 28 15 S 64 9W
Villa Santina 39 46 25N 12 55 E
Villablino 30 42 57N 6 19W
Villacañas 32 39 38N 3 20W
Villacarlos 32 39 53N 4 17 E
Villacarriedo 32 43 14N 3 48W
Villacarrillo 33 38 7N 3 3W
Villacastín 30 40 46N 4 25W
Villach 26 46 37N 13 51 E
Villaciado 40 39 27N 8 45 E
Villada 30 42 15N 4 59W
Villadiego 30 42 31N 4 1W
Villadóssola 38 46 4N 8 16 E
Villafeliche 32 41 10N 1 30W
Villafranca 32 42 17N 1 46W
Villafranca de los Barros 31 38 35N 6 18W
Villafranca de los Caballeros 33 39 26N 3 21W
Villafranca del Bierzo 30 42 38N 6 50W
Villafranca del Cid 32 40 26N 0 16W
Villafranca del Panadés 32 41 21N 1 40 E
Villafranca di Verona 38 45 20N 10 51 E
Villagarcía de Arosa 30 42 34N 8 46W
Villagrán 120 24 29N 99 29W
Villaguay 124 32 0 S 59 0W
Villaharta 31 38 9N 4 54W
Villahermosa, Mexico 120 18 0N 92 50W
Villahermosa, Spain 33 38 46N 2 52W
Villaines-la-Juhel 18 48 21N 0 20W
Villajoyosa 33 38 30N 0 12W
Villalba 30 43 26N 7 40W
Villalba de Guardo 30 42 42N 4 49W
Villalcampo, Pantano de 30 41 31N 6 0W
Villalón de Campos 30 42 5N 5 4W
Villalpando 30 41 51N 5 25W
Villaluenga 30 40 2N 3 54W
Villamanán 30 42 19N 5 35W
Villamartín 31 36 52N 5 38W
Villamayor 32 39 50N 2 59W
Villamblard 20 45 2N 0 32 E
Villanova Monteleone 40 40 30N 8 28 E
Villanueva 119 35 16N 105 23W
Villanueva de Castellón 33 39 5N 0 31W
Villanueva de Córdoba 31 38 20N 4 38W
Villanueva de la Fuente 33 38 42N 2 42W
Villanueva de la Serena 31 38 59N 5 50W
Villanueva de la Sierra 30 40 12N 6 24W
Villanueva de los Castillejos 31 37 30N 7 15W
Villanueva del Arzobispo 33 38 10N 3 0W
Villanueva del Duque 31 38 20N 5 0W
Villanueva del Fresno 31 38 23N 7 10W
Villanueva y Geltrú 32 41 13N 1 40 E
Villaodrid 30 43 20N 7 11W
Villaputzu 40 39 28N 9 33 E
Villar del Arzobispo 32 39 44N 0 50W
Villar del Rey 31 39 7N 6 50W
Villarcayo 32 42 56N 3 34W
Villard-Bonnet 21 45 14N 5 53 E
Villard-de-Lans 21 45 3N 5 33 E
Villarino de los Aires 30 41 18N 6 23W
Villarosa 41 37 36N 14 9 E
Villarramiel 30 42 2N 4 55W
Villarreal 32 39 55N 0 3W
Villarrica, Chile 128 39 15 S 72 15W
Villarrica, Parag. 124 25 40 S 56 30W
Villarrobledo 33 39 18N 2 36W
Villarroya de la Sierra 32 41 27N 1 46W
Villarrubia de los Ojos 33 39 14N 3 36W
Villars 21 46 0N 5 2 E
Villarta de San Juan 33 39 15N 3 25W
Villasayas 32 41 24N 2 39W
Villaseca de los Gamitos 30 41 2N 6 7W
Villastar 32 40 17N 1 9W
Villatobas 32 39 54N 3 20W
Villavicencio, Argent. 124 32 28 S 69 0W
Villavicencio, Colomb. 126 4 9N 73 37W
Villaviciosa 30 43 32N 5 27W
Villazón 124 22 0 S 65 35W
Ville-Marie 106 47 20N 79 30W
Ville Platte 117 30 45N 92 17W
Villedieu 18 48 50N 1 12W
Villefort 20 44 28N 3 56 E
Villefranche 19 47 19N 1 46 E
Villefranche-de-Lauragais 20 43 25N 1 44 E
Villefranche-de-Rouergue 20 44 21N 2 2 E
Villefranche-du-Périgord 20 44 38N 1 5 E
Villefranche-sur-Saône 21 45 59N 4 43 E
Villel 32 40 14N 1 12W
Villemaur 19 48 14N 3 40 E
Villemur-sur-Tarn 20 43 51N 1 31 E
Villena 33 38 39N 0 52W
Villenauxe 19 48 36N 3 30 E
Villenave 20 44 46N 0 33W
Villeneuve, France 19 48 42N 2 25 E
Villeneuve, Italy 38 45 40N 7 10 E
Villeneuve-l'Archevêque 19 48 14N 3 32 E
Villeneuve-lès-Avignon 21 43 57N 4 49 E
Villeneuve-sur-Allier 20 46 40N 3 13 E
Villeneuve-sur-Lot 20 44 24N 0 42 E
Villeréal 20 44 38N 0 45 E
Villers-Bocage 18 49 3N 0 40W
Villers-Bretonneux 19 49 50N 2 30 E
Villers-Cotterêts 19 49 15N 3 4 E
Villers-Outreaux 19 50 2N 3 18 E
Villers-sur-Mer 18 49 21N 0 2W
Villersexel 19 47 33N 6 26 E
Villerupt 19 49 28N 5 55 E
Villerville 18 49 26N 0 5 E
Villiers 93 27 2 S 28 36 E
Villingen 25 48 4N 8 28 E
Villingen-Schwenningen 25 48 3N 8 29 E
Villisca 116 40 55N 94 59W
Villupuram 70 11 59N 79 31 E
Vilna 108 54 7N 111 55W
Vilnius 54 54 38N 25 19 E
Vils 26 47 33N 10 37 E
Vils → 25 48 38N 13 11 E
Vilsbiburg 25 48 27N 12 23 E
Vilshofen 25 48 38N 13 11 E
Vilskutskogo, Proliv 59 78 0N 103 0 E
Vilusi 42 42 44N 18 34 E
Vilvoorde 16 50 56N 4 26 E
Vilyuy → 59 64 24N 126 26 E
Vilyuysk 59 63 40N 121 35 E
Vimercate 38 45 38N 9 25 E
Vimiosa 30 41 35N 6 31W
Vimmerby 49 57 40N 15 55 E
Vimoutiers 18 48 57N 0 10 E
Vimperk 26 49 3N 13 46 E
Viña del Mar 124 33 0 S 71 30W
Vinaroz 32 40 30N 0 27 E
Vincennes 114 38 42N 87 29W
Vinchina 124 28 45 S 68 15W
Vindel älven → 50 63 55N 19 50 E
Vindeln 50 64 12N 19 43 E
Vinderup 49 56 29N 8 45 E
Vindhya Ra. 68 22 50N 77 0 E
Vineland 114 39 30N 75 0W
Vinga 42 46 0N 21 14 E
Vingnes 47 61 7N 10 26 E
Vinh 71 18 45N 105 38 E
Vinhais 30 41 50N 7 0W
Vinica, Hrvatska, Yugo. 39 46 20N 16 9 E
Vinica, Slovenija, Yugo. 39 45 28N 15 16 E
Vinita 117 36 40N 95 12W
Vinkovci 42 45 19N 18 48 E
Vinnitsa 56 49 15N 28 30 E
Vinson Massif 5 78 35 S 85 25W
Vinstra 47 61 37N 9 44 E
Vinton, Iowa, U.S.A. 116 42 8N 92 1W
Vinton, La., U.S.A. 117 30 13N 93 35W
Vinţu de Jos 46 46 0N 23 30 E
Viöl 24 54 32N 9 12 E
Vipava 39 45 51N 13 58 E
Vipiteno 39 46 55N 11 25 E
Viqueque 73 8 52 S 126 23 E
Vir 39 44 17N 15 3 E
Virac 73 13 30N 124 20 E
Virago Sd. 108 54 0N 132 30W
Virajpet 70 12 10N 75 50 E
Viramgam 68 23 5N 72 0 E
Viranansehir 64 37 13N 39 45 E
Virarajendrapet = Virajpet 70 12 10N 75 50 E
Viravanallur 70 8 40N 77 30 E
Virden 109 49 50N 100 56W
Vire 18 48 50N 0 53W
Vire → 18 49 20N 1 7W
Vírgenes, C. 128 52 19 S 68 21W
Virgin →, Can. 109 57 2N 108 17W
Virgin →, U.S.A. 119 36 50N 114 10W
Virgin Gorda 121 18 30N 64 26W
Virgin Is. 121 18 40N 64 30W
Virginia, S. Afr. 92 28 8 S 26 55 E
Virginia, U.S.A. 116 47 30N 92 32W
Virginia □ 114 37 45N 78 0W
Virginia Beach 114 36 54N 75 58W
Virginia City, Mont., U.S.A. 118 45 18N 111 58W
Virginia City, Nev., U.S.A. 118 39 19N 119 39W
Virginia Falls 108 61 38N 125 42W
Virginiatown 106 48 9N 79 36W
Virieu-le-Grand 21 45 51N 5 39 E
Virje 42 46 4N 16 59 E
Viroqua 116 43 33N 90 57W
Virovitica 42 45 51N 17 21 E
Virpazar 42 42 14N 19 6 E
Virserum 49 57 20N 15 35 E
Virton 16 49 35N 5 32 E
Virtsu 54 58 32N 23 33 E
Virudunagar 70 9 30N 78 0 E
Vis 39 43 0N 16 10 E
Vis Kanal 39 43 4N 16 5 E
Visalia 119 36 25N 119 18W
Visayan Sea 73 11 30N 123 30 E
Visby 49 57 37N 18 18 E
Viscount Melville Sd. 4 74 10N 108 0W
Visé 16 50 44N 5 41 E
Višegrad 42 43 47N 19 17 E
Viseu, Brazil 127 1 10 S 46 5W
Viseu, Port. 30 40 40N 7 55W
Viseu □ 30 40 40N 7 55W
Vişeu de Sus 46 47 45N 24 25 E
Vishakhapatnam 70 17 45N 83 20 E
Vishnupur 69 23 8N 87 20 E
Visikoi I. 5 56 43 S 27 15W
Visingsö 49 58 2N 14 20 E
Viskafors 49 57 37N 12 50 E
Vislanda 49 56 46N 14 30 E
Vislinskil Zaliv (Zalew Wislany) 28 54 20N 19 50 E
Visnagar 68 23 45N 72 32 E
Višnja Gora 39 45 58N 14 45 E
Viso del Marqués 33 38 32N 3 34W
Viso, Mte. 38 44 38N 7 5 E
Visoko 42 43 58N 18 10 E

* *Renamed Limbe*

Name	Page	Lat.	Long.
sp	**25**	46 17N	7 52 E
sselhövede	**24**	52 59N	9 36 E
stonikos, Ormos	**44**	41 0N	25 7 E
stula = Wisła →	**28**	54 22N	18 55 E
t →	**43**	43 30N	24 30 E
tanje	**39**	46 25N	15 18 E
tebsk	**54**	55 10N	30 15 E
terbo	**39**	42 25N	12 8 E
ti Levu	**101**	17 30 S	177 30 E
tiaz Str.	**98**	5 40 S	147 10 E
tigudino	**30**	41 1N	6 26W
tim	**59**	59 28N	112 35 E
tim →	**59**	59 26N	112 34 E
tína	**45**	37 40N	22 10 E
tina	**42**	43 17N	17 29 E
tória	**127**	20 20 S	40 22W
toria	**32**	42 50N	2 41W
tória da Conquista	**127**	14 51 S	40 51W
tória de São Antão	**127**	8 10 S	35 20W
tré	**18**	48 8N	1 12W
try-le-François	**19**	48 43N	4 33 E
tsi, Óros	**44**	40 40N	21 25 E
tteaux	**19**	47 24N	4 30 E
ttel	**19**	48 12N	5 57 E
ttória	**41**	36 58N	14 30 E
ttório Véneto	**39**	45 59N	12 18 E
tu Is.	**98**	4 50 S	149 25 E
ver	**32**	39 55N	0 36W
vero	**30**	43 39N	7 38W
viers	**21**	44 30N	4 40 E
vonne	**20**	46 25N	0 15 E
zcaíno, Desierto de	**120**	27 40N	113 50W
zcaíno, Sierra	**120**	27 30N	114 0W
zcaya □	**32**	43 15N	2 45W
zianagaram	**70**	18 6N	83 30 E
zille	**21**	45 5N	5 46 E
zinada	**39**	45 20N	13 46 E
ziru	**46**	45 0N	27 43 E
zovice	**27**	49 12N	17 56 E
zzini	**41**	37 9N	14 43 E
josa →	**44**	40 37N	19 42 E
aardingen	**16**	51 55N	4 21 E
ădeasa	**46**	46 47N	22 50 E
adicin Han	**42**	42 42N	22 1 E
adimir	**55**	56 15N	40 30 E
adimir Volynskiy	**54**	50 50N	24 18 E
adimirci	**42**	44 36N	19 45 E
adimirovac	**42**	45 1N	20 53 E
adimirovka, R.S.F.S.R., U.S.S.R.	**57**	48 27N	46 10 E
adimirovka, R.S.F.S.R., U.S.S.R.	**57**	44 45N	44 41 E
adimirovo	**43**	43 32N	23 22 E
adislavovka	**56**	45 15N	35 15 E
adivostok	**59**	43 10N	131 53 E
asenica	**42**	44 11N	18 59 E
ašić	**42**	44 19N	17 37 E
ašim	**26**	49 40N	14 53 E
asinsko Jezero	**42**	42 44N	22 22 E
asotinci	**42**	42 59N	22 7 E
ieland	**16**	53 16N	4 55 E
issingen	**16**	51 26N	3 34 E
óra	**44**	40 32N	19 28 E
óra □	**44**	40 12N	20 0 E
orës, Gjiri i	**44**	40 29N	19 27 E
tava →	**26**	50 21N	14 30 E
obarno	**38**	45 38N	10 30 E
oćin	**42**	45 37N	17 33 E
öcklabruck	**26**	48 1N	13 39 E
odice	**39**	43 47N	15 47 E
odňany	**26**	49 9N	14 11 E
odnjan	**39**	44 59N	13 52 E
ogelkop = Doberai, Jazirah	**73**	1 25 S	133 0 E
ogelsberg	**24**	50 37N	9 15 E
oghera	**38**	44 59N	9 1 E
ohibinany	**93**	18 49 S	49 4 E
ohimarina	**93**	13 25 S	50 0 E
ohimena, Tanjon' i	**93**	25 36 S	45 8 E
ohipeno	**93**	22 22 S	47 51 E
oi	**90**	3 25 S	38 32 E
oid	**19**	48 40N	5 36 E
oineşti, Iaşi, Romania	**46**	47 5N	27 27 E
oineşti, Prahova, Romania	**46**	45 5N	25 14 E
oiotía □	**45**	38 20N	23 0 E
oiron	**21**	45 22N	5 35 E
oisey B.	**107**	56 15N	61 50W
oitsberg	**26**	47 3N	15 9 E
oiviïs Límni	**44**	39 30N	22 45 E
ojens	**49**	55 16N	9 18 E
ojmsjön	**50**	64 55N	16 40 E
ojnik	**38**	46 18N	15 19 E
ojnió	**39**	45 19N	15 43 E
ojvodina, Auton. Pokrajina □	**42**	45 20N	20 0 E
okhma	**55**	59 0N	46 45 E
okhma →	**55**	56 20N	46 20 E
okhtoga	**55**	58 46N	41 8 E
olary	**26**	48 54N	13 52 E
olborg	**116**	45 50N	105 44W
olcano Is.	**94**	25 0N	141 0 E
olchansk	**55**	50 17N	36 58 E
olchayevka	**59**	48 40N	134 30 E
olchya →	**56**	48 0N	37 0 E
olda	**47**	62 9N	6 5 E
olga	**55**	57 58N	38 16 E
olga →	**57**	48 30N	46 0 E
olga Hts. = Privolzhskaya V. S.	**53**	51 0N	46 0 E
olgodonsk	**57**	47 33N	42 5 E
olgograd	**57**	48 40N	44 25 E
olgogradskoye Vdkhr.	**55**	50 0N	45 20 E
olgorechensk	**55**	57 28N	41 14 E
olissós	**45**	38 29N	25 54 E
olkach	**25**	49 52N	10 14 E
ölkermarkt	**26**	46 39N	14 39 E
olkhov	**54**	59 55N	32 15 E
olkhov →	**54**	60 8N	32 20 E
ölklingen	**25**	49 15N	6 50 E
olkovysk	**54**	53 9N	24 30 E
olksrust	**93**	27 24 S	29 53 E
'ollenhove	**16**	52 40N	5 58 E
'ol'n'ansk	**56**	47 55N	35 29 E
'olnovakha	**56**	47 35N	37 30 E
'olochanka	**59**	71 0N	94 28 E
Volodarsk	**55**	56 12N	43 15 E
Vologda	**55**	59 10N	40 0 E
Volokolamsk	**55**	56 5N	35 57 E
Volokonovka	**55**	50 33N	37 52 E
Vólos	**44**	39 24N	22 59 E
Volosovo	**54**	59 27N	29 32 E
Volozhin	**54**	54 3N	26 30 E
Volsk	**55**	52 5N	47 22 E
Volta →	**85**	5 46N	0 41 E
Volta, L.	**85**	7 30N	0 15 E
Volta Redonda	**125**	22 31 S	44 5W
Volterra	**38**	43 24N	10 50 E
Voltri	**38**	44 25N	8 43 E
Volturara Áppula	**41**	41 30N	15 2 E
Volturno →	**41**	41 1N	13 55 E
Volubilis	**82**	34 2N	5 33W
Volujak	**42**	43 53N	17 47 E
Vólvi, L.	**44**	40 40N	23 34 E
Volzhsk	**55**	55 57N	48 23 E
Volzhskiy	**57**	48 56N	44 46 E
Vondrozo	**93**	22 49 S	47 20 E
Vónitsa	**45**	38 53N	20 58 E
Voorburg	**16**	52 5N	4 24 E
Vopnafjörður	**50**	65 45N	14 40W
Vorarlberg □	**26**	47 20N	10 0 E
Vóras Óros	**44**	40 57N	21 45 E
Vorbasse	**49**	55 39N	9 6 E
Vorderrhein →	**25**	46 49N	9 25 E
Vordingborg	**49**	55 0N	11 54 E
Voreppe	**21**	45 18N	5 39 E
Voríai Sporádhes	**45**	39 15N	23 30 E
Vórios Evvoïkos Kólpos	**45**	38 45N	23 15 E
Vorkuta	**52**	67 48N	64 20 E
Vorma →	**47**	60 9N	11 27 E
Vorona →	**55**	51 22N	42 3 E
Voronezh, R.S.F.S.R., U.S.S.R.	**55**	51 40N	39 10 E
Voronezh, Ukraine, U.S.S.R.	**54**	51 47N	33 28 E
Voronezh →	**55**	51 56N	37 17 E
Vorontsovo-Aleksandrovskoye = Zelenokumsk	**57**	44 30N	44 1 E
Voroshilovgrad	**57**	48 38N	39 15 E
Vorovskoye	**59**	54 30N	155 50 E
Vorskla →	**56**	48 50N	34 10 E
Vöru	**54**	57 48N	26 54 E
Vorupør	**49**	56 58N	8 22 E
Vosges	**19**	48 20N	7 10 E
Vosges □	**19**	48 12N	6 20 E
Voskopoja	**44**	40 40N	20 33 E
Voskresensk	**55**	55 19N	38 43 E
Voskresenskoye	**55**	56 51N	45 30 E
Voss	**47**	60 38N	6 26 E
Vostochnyy Sayan	**59**	54 0N	96 0 E
Vostok I.	**95**	10 5 S	152 23W
Votice	**26**	49 38N	14 39 E
Votkinsk	**52**	57 0N	53 55 E
Votkinskoye Vdkhr.	**52**	57 30N	55 0 E
Vouga →	**30**	40 41N	8 40W
Vouillé	**18**	46 38N	0 10 E
Voulte-sur-Rhône, La	**21**	44 48N	4 46 E
Vouvray	**18**	47 25N	0 48 E
Voúxa, Ákra	**45**	35 37N	23 32 E
Vouzela	**30**	40 43N	8 7W
Vouziers	**19**	49 22N	4 40 E
Voves	**19**	48 15N	1 38 E
Voxna	**48**	61 20N	15 40 E
Vozhe Oz.	**52**	60 45N	39 0 E
Vozhgaly	**55**	58 9N	50 11 E
Voznesenka	**59**	56 40N	95 3 E
Voznesensk	**56**	47 35N	31 21 E
Voznesenye	**52**	61 0N	35 45 E
Vráble	**27**	48 15N	18 16 E
Vraćevšnica	**42**	44 2N	20 34 E
Vrådal	**47**	59 20N	8 25 E
Vraka	**44**	42 8N	19 28 E
Vrakhnéïka	**45**	38 10N	21 40 E
Vrancea □	**46**	45 50N	26 45 E
Vrancei, Munţii	**46**	46 0N	26 30 E
Vrangelya, Ostrov	**59**	71 0N	180 0 E
Vranica	**42**	43 55N	17 50 E
Vranje	**42**	42 34N	21 54 E
Vranjska Banja	**42**	42 34N	22 1 E
Vranov	**27**	48 53N	21 40 E
Vransko	**39**	46 17N	14 58 E
Vratsa	**43**	43 13N	23 30 E
Vrbas	**42**	45 40N	19 40 E
Vrbas →	**42**	45 8N	17 29 E
Vrbnik	**39**	45 4N	14 40 E
Vrbovec	**39**	45 53N	16 28 E
Vrbovsko	**39**	45 24N	15 5 E
Vrchlabí	**26**	50 38N	15 37 E
Vrede	**93**	27 24 S	29 6 E
Vredefort	**92**	27 0 S	26 22 E
Vredenburg	**92**	32 51 S	18 0 E
Vredendal	**92**	31 41 S	18 35 E
Vrena	**49**	58 54N	16 41 E
Vrgorac	**42**	43 12N	17 20 E
Vrhnika	**39**	45 58N	14 15 E
Vriddhachalam	**70**	11 30N	79 20 E
Vrïdi	**84**	5 15N	4 3W
Vrindaban	**68**	27 37N	77 40 E
Vrnograč	**39**	45 10N	15 57 E
Vrondádhes	**45**	38 25N	26 7 E
Vrpolje	**42**	45 13N	18 24 E
Vršac	**42**	45 8N	21 18 E
Vrsacki Kanal	**42**	45 15N	21 0 E
Vryburg	**92**	26 55 S	24 45 E
Vryheid	**93**	27 45 S	30 47 E
Vsetín	**27**	49 20N	18 0 E
Vucha →	**43**	42 10N	24 26 E
Vučitrn	**42**	42 49N	20 59 E
Vught	**16**	51 38N	5 20 E
Vukovar	**42**	45 21N	18 59 E
Vulcan, Can.	**108**	50 25N	113 15W
Vulcan, Romania	**46**	45 23N	23 17 E
Vulcan, U.S.A.	**114**	45 46N	87 51W
Vulcano	**41**	38 25N	14 58 E
Vŭlchedruma	**43**	43 42N	23 27 E
Vulci	**39**	42 23N	11 37 E
Vulkaneshty	**56**	45 35N	28 30 E
Vunduzi →	**91**	18 56 S	34 1 E
Vung Tau	**71**	10 21N	107 4 E
Vŭrbitsa	**43**	42 59N	26 40 E
Vurshets	**43**	43 15N	23 23 E
Vutcani	**46**	46 26N	27 59 E
Vuyyuru	**70**	16 28N	80 50 E
Vyara	**68**	21 8N	73 28 E
Vyasniki	**55**	56 10N	42 10 E
Vyatka →	**52**	56 30N	51 0 E
Vyatskiye Polyany	**52**	56 5N	51 0 E
Vyazemskiy	**59**	47 32N	134 45 E
Vyazma	**54**	55 10N	34 15 E
Vyborg	**52**	60 43N	28 47 E
Vychegda →	**52**	61 18N	46 36 E
Vychodné Beskydy	**27**	49 30N	22 0 E
Východočeský □	**26**	50 20N	15 45 E
Východoslovenský □	**27**	48 50N	21 0 E
Vyg-ozero	**52**	63 30N	34 0 E
Vyksa	**55**	55 19N	42 11 E
Vypin	**70**	10 10N	76 15 E
Vyrnwy, L.	**12**	52 48N	3 30W
Vyshniy Volochek	**54**	57 30N	34 30 E
Vyškov	**27**	49 17N	17 0 E
Vysoké Mýto	**27**	49 58N	10 10 E
Vysokovsk	**55**	56 22N	36 30 E
Vysotsk	**54**	51 43N	26 32 E
Vyšší Brod	**26**	48 37N	14 19 E
Vytegra	**52**	61 0N	36 27 E

W

Name	Page	Lat.	Long.
W.A.C. Bennett Dam	**108**	56 2N	122 6W
Wa	**84**	10 7N	2 25W
Waal →	**16**	51 59N	4 30 E
Wabakimi L.	**106**	50 38N	89 45W
Wabana	**107**	47 40N	53 0W
Wabasca	**108**	55 57N	113 56W
Wabash	**114**	40 48N	85 46W
Wabash →	**114**	37 46N	88 2W
Wabeno	**114**	45 25N	88 40W
Wabi →	**87**	7 45N	40 50 E
Wabigoon L.	**109**	49 44N	92 44W
Wabowden	**109**	54 55N	98 38W
Wąbrzeźno	**28**	53 16N	18 57 E
Wabuk Pt.	**106**	55 20N	85 5W
Wabush	**107**	52 55N	66 52W
Wabuska	**118**	39 9N	119 13W
Wächtersbach	**25**	50 16N	9 18 E
Waco	**117**	31 33N	97 5W
Waconichi, L.	**106**	50 8N	74 0W
Wad Ban Naqa	**87**	16 32N	33 9 E
Wad Banda	**87**	13 10N	27 56 E
Wad el Haddad	**87**	13 50N	33 30 E
Wad en Nau	**87**	14 10N	33 34 E
Wad Hamid	**87**	16 30N	32 45 E
Wâd Medanî	**87**	14 28N	33 30 E
Waddān	**83**	29 9N	16 10 E
Waddān, Jabal	**83**	29 0N	16 15 E
Waddeneilanden	**16**	53 25N	5 10 E
Waddenzee	**16**	53 6N	5 10 E
Waddington	**113**	44 51N	75 12W
Waddington, Mt.	**108**	51 23N	125 15W
Waddy Pt.	**99**	24 58 S	153 21 E
Wadena, Can.	**109**	51 57N	103 47W
Wadena, U.S.A.	**116**	46 25N	95 8W
Wädenswil	**25**	47 14N	8 40 E
Wadesboro	**115**	35 2N	80 2W
Wadhams	**108**	51 30N	127 30W
Wādī ash Shāţi'	**83**	27 30N	15 0 E
Wādī Banī Walīd	**83**	31 49N	14 0 E
Wadi Gemâl	**86**	24 35N	35 10 E
Wadi Halfa	**86**	21 53N	31 19 E
Wadi Masila	**63**	16 30N	49 0 E
Wadi Şabāḩ	**64**	23 50N	48 30 E
Wadlew	**28**	51 31N	19 23 E
Wadowice	**27**	49 52N	19 30 E
Wadsworth	**118**	39 38N	119 22W
Wafrah	**64**	28 33N	47 56 E
Wageningen	**16**	51 58N	5 40 E
Wager B.	**105**	65 26N	88 40W
Wager Bay	**105**	65 56N	90 49W
Wagga Wagga	**97**	35 7 S	147 24 E
Waghete	**73**	4 10 S	135 50 E
Wagin	**96**	33 17 S	117 25 E
Wagon Mound	**117**	36 1N	104 44W
Wagoner	**117**	36 0N	95 20W
Wagrowiec	**28**	52 48N	17 11 E
Wahai	**73**	2 48 S	129 35 E
Wahiawa	**110**	21 30N	158 2W
Wahoo	**116**	41 15N	96 35W
Wahpeton	**116**	46 20N	96 35W
Wai	**70**	17 56N	73 57 E
Waiau →	**101**	42 47 S	173 22 E
Waiawe Ganga →	**70**	6 15N	81 0 E
Waibeem	**73**	0 30 S	132 59 E
Waiblingen	**25**	48 49N	9 20 E
Waidhofen, Niederösterreich, Austria	**26**	48 49N	15 17 E
Waidhofen, Niederösterreich, Austria	**26**	47 57N	14 46 E
Waigeo	**73**	0 20 S	130 40 E
Waihi	**101**	37 23 S	175 52 E
Waihou →	**101**	37 15 S	175 40 E
Waika	**90**	2 22 S	25 42 E
Waikabubak	**73**	9 45 S	119 25 E
Waikaremoana	**101**	38 42 S	177 12 E
Waikari	**101**	42 58 S	172 41 E
Waikato →	**101**	37 23 S	174 43 E
Waikerie	**99**	34 9 S	140 0 E
Waikokopu	**101**	39 3 S	177 52 E
Waikouaiti	**101**	45 36 S	170 41 E
Waimate	**101**	44 45 S	171 3 E
Wainganga →	**69**	18 50N	79 55 E
Waingapu	**73**	9 35 S	120 11 E
Wainwright, Can.	**109**	52 50N	110 50W
Wainwright, U.S.A.	**104**	70 39N	160 1W
Waiouru	**101**	39 28 S	175 41 E
Waipara	**101**	43 3 S	172 46 E
Waipawa	**101**	39 56 S	176 38 E
Waipiro	**101**	38 2 S	178 22 E
Waipu	**101**	35 59 S	174 29 E
Waipukurau	**101**	40 1 S	176 33 E
Wairakei	**101**	38 37 S	176 6 E
Wairarapa, L.	**101**	41 14 S	175 15 E
Wairoa	**101**	39 3 S	177 25 E
Waitaki →	**101**	44 56 S	171 7 E
Waitara	**101**	38 59 S	174 15 E
Waitsburg	**118**	46 15N	118 0W
Waiuku	**101**	37 15 S	174 45 E
Wajima	**74**	37 30N	137 0 E
Wajir	**90**	1 42N	40 5 E
Wajir □	**90**	1 42N	40 20 E
Wakasa-Wan	**74**	35 40N	135 30 E
Wakatipu, L.	**101**	45 5 S	168 33 E
Wakaw	**109**	52 39N	105 44W
Wakayama	**74**	34 15N	135 15 E
Wakayama-ken □	**74**	33 50N	135 30 E
Wake Forest	**115**	35 58N	78 30W
Wake I.	**94**	19 18N	166 36 E
Wakefield, N.Z.	**101**	41 24 S	173 5 E
Wakefield, U.K.	**12**	53 41N	1 31W
Wakefield, Mass., U.S.A.	**113**	42 30N	71 3W
Wakefield, Mich., U.S.A.	**116**	46 28N	89 53W
Wakema	**67**	16 30N	95 11 E
Wakkanai	**74**	45 28N	141 35 E
Wakkerstroom	**93**	27 24 S	30 10 E
Wakool	**99**	35 28 S	144 23 E
Wakool →	**99**	35 5 S	143 33 E
Wakre	**73**	0 19 S	131 5 E
Wakuach L.	**107**	55 34N	67 32W
Walamba	**91**	13 30 S	28 42 E
Wałbrzych	**28**	50 45N	16 18 E
Walbury Hill	**13**	51 22N	1 28W
Walcha	**99**	30 55 S	151 31 E
Walcheren	**16**	51 30N	3 35 E
Walcott	**118**	41 50N	106 55W
Wałcz	**28**	53 17N	16 27 E
Wald	**25**	47 17N	8 56 E
Waldbröl	**24**	50 52N	7 36 E
Waldeck	**24**	51 12N	9 4 E
Walden, Colo., U.S.A.	**118**	40 47N	106 20W
Walden, N.Y., U.S.A.	**113**	41 32N	74 13W
Waldport	**118**	44 30N	124 2W
Waldron, Can.	**109**	50 53N	102 35W
Waldron, U.S.A.	**117**	34 52N	94 4W
Waldshut	**25**	47 37N	8 12 E
Walembele	**84**	10 30N	1 58W
Wales □	**11**	52 30N	3 30W
Walewale	**85**	10 21N	0 50W
Walgett	**97**	30 0 S	148 5 E
Walgreen Coast	**5**	75 15 S	105 0W
Walhalla, Austral.	**99**	37 56 S	146 29 E
Walhalla, U.S.A.	**109**	48 55N	97 55W
Walker	**116**	47 4N	94 35W
Walker L., Man., Can.	**109**	54 42N	95 57W
Walker L., Qué., Can.	**107**	50 20N	67 11W
Walker L., U.S.A.	**118**	38 56N	118 46W
Walkerston	**98**	21 11 S	149 8 E
Walkerton	**112**	44 10N	81 10W
Wall	**116**	44 0N	102 14W
Walla Walla	**118**	46 3N	118 25W
Wallabadah	**98**	17 57 S	142 15 E
Wallace, Idaho, U.S.A.	**118**	47 30N	116 0W
Wallace, N.C., U.S.A.	**115**	34 44N	77 59W
Wallace, Nebr., U.S.A.	**116**	40 51N	101 12W
Wallaceburg	**106**	42 34N	82 23W
Wallachia = Valahia	**46**	44 35N	25 0 E
Wallal	**99**	26 32 S	146 7 E
Wallaroo	**97**	33 56 S	137 39 E
Wallasey	**12**	53 26N	3 2W
Walldürn	**25**	49 34N	9 23 E
Wallerawang	**99**	33 25 S	150 4 E
Wallingford, U.K.	**12**	51 40N	1 15W
Wallingford, U.S.A.	**113**	41 27N	72 50W
Wallis Arch.	**94**	13 18 S	176 10W
Wallowa	**118**	45 40N	117 35W
Wallowa, Mts.	**118**	45 20N	117 30W
Wallsend, Austral.	**99**	32 55 S	151 40 E
Wallsend, U.K.	**12**	54 59N	1 30W
Wallula	**118**	46 3N	118 59W
Wallumbilla	**99**	26 33 S	149 9 E
Walmer	**92**	33 57 S	25 35 E
Walmsley, L.	**109**	63 25N	108 36W
Walney, Isle of	**12**	54 5N	3 15W
Walnut Ridge	**117**	36 7N	90 58W
Walsall	**13**	52 36N	1 59W
Walsenburg	**117**	37 42N	104 45W
Walsh	**117**	37 28N	102 15W
Walsh →	**98**	16 31 S	143 42 E
Walsh P.O.	**98**	16 40 S	144 0 E
Walsrode	**24**	52 51N	9 37 E
Waltair	**70**	17 44N	83 23 E
Walterboro	**115**	32 53N	80 40W
Walters	**117**	34 25N	98 20W
Waltershausen	**24**	50 53N	10 33 E
Waltham	**113**	42 22N	71 12W
Waltham Sta.	**106**	45 57N	76 57W
Waltman	**118**	43 8N	107 15W
Walton	**113**	42 12N	75 9W
Walvisbaai	**92**	23 0 S	14 28 E
Wamba, Kenya	**90**	0 58N	37 19 E
Wamba, Zaïre	**90**	2 10N	27 57 E
Wamego	**116**	39 14N	96 22W
Wamena	**73**	4 4 S	138 57 E
Wampsville	**113**	43 4N	75 42W
Wamsasi	**73**	3 27 S	126 7 E
Wana	**68**	32 20N	69 32 E
Wanaaring	**99**	29 38 S	144 9 E
Wanaka L.	**101**	44 33 S	169 7 E
Wan'an	**77**	26 26N	114 49 E
Wanapiri	**73**	4 30 S	135 59 E
Wanapitei L.	**106**	46 45N	80 40W
Wanbi	**99**	34 46 S	140 17 E
Wanda Shan	**76**	46 0N	132 0 E
Wanderer	**91**	19 36 S	30 1 E
Wandiwash	**70**	12 30N	79 30 E
Wandoan	**97**	26 5 S	149 55 E
Wang Kai (Ghâbat el Arab)	**87**	9 3N	29 23 E
Wang Saphung	**71**	17 18N	101 46 E
Wanga	**90**	2 58N	29 12 E
Wangal	**73**	6 8 S	134 9 E
Wanganella	**99**	35 6 S	144 49 E
Wanganui	**101**	39 56 S	175 3 E
Wangaratta	**97**	36 21 S	146 19 E
Wangdu	**76**	38 40N	115 7 E

Wangerooge 24 53 47N 7 52 E
Wangi 90 1 58 S 40 58 E
Wangiwangi 73 5 22 S 123 37 E
Wangjiang 77 30 10N 116 42 E
Wangqing 76 43 12N 129 42 E
Wankaner 68 22 35N 71 0 E
• Wankie 91 18 18 S 26 30 E
• Wankie Nat. Park 92 19 0 S 26 30 E
Wanless 109 54 11N 101 21W
Wanning 77 18 48N 110 22 E
Wannon → 100 37 38 S 141 25 E
Wanquan 76 40 50N 114 40 E
Wanxian 75 30 42N 108 20 E
Wanyuan 77 32 4N 108 3 E
Wanzai 77 28 7N 114 30 E
Wapakoneta 114 40 35N 84 10W
Wapato 118 46 30N 120 25W
Wapawekka L. 109 54 55N 104 40W
Wappingers Falls 113 41 35N 73 56W
Wapsipinicon → 116 41 44N 90 19W
Waranga Res. 100 36 32 S 145 5 E
Warangal 70 17 58N 79 35 E
Waratah 99 41 30 S 145 30 E
Waratah B. 99 38 54 S 146 5 E
Warburg 24 51 29N 9 10 E
Warburton 99 37 47 S 145 42 E
Warburton → 97 28 4 S 137 28 E
Ward 101 41 49 S 174 11 E
Ward → 99 26 28 S 146 6 E
Ward Cove 108 55 25N 132 43W
Ward Hunt, C. 98 8 2 S 148 10 E
Wardak □ 65 34 0N 68 0 E
Warden 93 27 50 S 29 0 E
Wardha 68 20 45N 78 39 E
Wardlow 108 50 56N 111 31W
Ware, Can. 108 57 26N 125 41W
Ware, U.S.A. 113 42 16N 72 15W
Wareham 113 41 45N 70 44W
Waren 24 53 30N 12 41 E
Warendorf 24 51 57N 8 0 E
Warialda 97 29 29 S 150 33 E
Wariap 73 1 30 S 134 5 E
Warka 28 51 47N 21 12 E
Warkopi 73 1 12 S 134 9 E
Warley 13 52 30N 2 0W
Warm Springs, Mont., U.S.A. 118 46 11N 112 48W
Warm Springs, Nev., U.S.A. 119 38 16N 116 32W
Warman 109 52 19N 106 30W
Warmbad, Namibia 92 28 25 S 18 42 E
Warmbad, S. Afr. 93 24 51 S 28 19 E
Warmeriville 19 49 20N 4 13 E
Warnambool Downs 98 22 48 S 142 52 E
Warnemünde 24 54 9N 12 5 E
Warner 108 49 17N 112 12W
Warner Range, Mts. 118 41 30 S 120 20W
Warner Robins 115 32 41N 83 36W
Warnow → 24 54 6N 12 9 E
Warora 70 20 14N 79 1 E
Warracknabeal 100 36 9 S 142 26 E
Warragul 99 38 10 S 145 58 E
Warrego → 97 30 24 S 145 21 E
Warrego Ra. 97 24 58 S 146 0 E
Warren, Austral. 99 31 42 S 147 51 E
Warren, Ark., U.S.A. 117 33 35N 92 3W
Warren, Minn., U.S.A. 116 48 12N 96 46W
Warren, Ohio, U.S.A. 114 41 18N 80 52W
Warren, Pa., U.S.A. 114 41 52N 79 10W
Warrenpoint 15 54 7N 6 15W
Warrensburg 116 38 45N 93 45W
Warrenton, S. Afr. 92 28 9 S 24 47 E
Warrenton, U.S.A. 118 46 11N 123 59W
Warrenville 99 25 48 S 147 22 E
Warri 85 5 30N 5 41 E
Warrina 96 28 12 S 135 50 E
Warrington, U.K. 12 53 25N 2 38W
Warrington, U.S.A. 115 30 22N 87 16W
Warrnambool 97 38 25 S 142 30 E
Warroad 116 48 54N 95 19W
Warsa 73 0 47 S 135 55 E
Warsaw, Ind., U.S.A. 114 41 14N 85 50W
Warsaw, N.Y., U.S.A. 112 42 46N 78 10W
Warsaw, Ohio, U.S.A. 112 40 20N 82 0W
Warsaw = Warszawa 28 52 13N 21 0 E
Warstein 24 51 26N 8 20 E
Warszawa 28 52 13N 21 0 E
Warszawa □ 28 52 30N 21 0 E
Warta 28 51 43N 18 38 E
Warta → 28 52 35N 14 39 E
Waru 73 3 30 S 130 36 E
Warud 68 21 30N 78 16 E
Warwick, Austral. 97 28 10 S 152 1 E
Warwick, U.K. 13 52 17N 1 36W
Warwick, U.S.A. 114 41 43N 71 25W
Warwick □ 13 52 20N 1 30W
Wasa 108 49 45N 115 50W
Wasaga Beach 112 44 31N 80 1W
Wasatch, Ra. 118 40 30N 111 15W
Wasbank 93 28 15 S 30 9 E
Wasco, Calif., U.S.A. 119 35 37N 119 16W
Wasco, Oreg., U.S.A. 118 45 36N 120 46W
Waseca 116 44 3N 93 31W
Wasekamio L. 109 56 45N 108 45W
Wash, The 12 52 58N 0 20 E
Washago 112 44 45N 79 20W
Washburn, N.D., U.S.A. 116 47 17N 101 0W
Washburn, Wis., U.S.A. 116 46 38N 90 55W
Washington, D.C., U.S.A. 114 38 52N 77 0W
Washington, Ga., U.S.A. 115 33 45N 82 45W
Washington, Ind., U.S.A. 114 38 40N 87 8W
Washington, Iowa, U.S.A. 116 41 20N 91 45W
Washington, Mo, U.S.A. 116 38 35N 91 1W
Washington, N.C., U.S.A. 115 35 35N 77 1W
Washington, N.J., U.S.A. 113 40 45N 74 59W
Washington, Pa., U.S.A. 114 40 10N 80 20W
Washington, Utah, U.S.A. 119 37 10N 113 30W
Washington □ 118 47 45N 120 30W
† Washington I., Pac. Oc. 95 4 43N 160 25W
Washington I., U.S.A. 114 45 24N 86 54W
Washington Mt. 114 44 15N 71 18W
Wasian 73 1 47 S 133 19 E
Wasilków 28 53 12N 23 13 E
Wasior 73 2 43 S 134 30 E
Waskaiowaka, L. 109 56 33N 96 23W
Waskesiu Lake 109 53 55N 106 5W
Wasm 86 18 2N 41 32 E
Wassenaar 16 52 8N 4 24 E
Wasserburg 25 48 4N 12 15 E
Wasserkuppe 24 50 30N 9 56 E
Wassy 19 48 30N 4 58 E
Waswanipi 106 49 40N 76 29W
Waswanipi, L. 106 49 35N 76 40W
Watangpon 73 4 29 S 120 25 E
Water Park Pt. 98 22 56 S 150 47 E
Water Valley 117 34 9N 89 38W
Waterberg, Namibia 92 20 30 S 17 18 E
Waterberg, S. Afr. 93 24 14 S 28 0 E
Waterbury, Conn., U.S.A. 114 41 32N 73 0W
Waterbury, Vt., U.S.A. 113 44 22N 72 44W
Waterbury L. 109 58 10N 104 22W
Waterdown 112 43 20N 79 53W
Waterford, Can. 112 42 56N 80 17W
Waterford, Ireland 15 52 16N 7 8W
Waterford □ 15 52 10N 7 40W
Waterford Harb. 15 52 10N 6 58W
Waterhen L., Man., Can. 109 52 10N 99 40W
Waterhen L., Sask., Can. 109 54 28N 108 25W
Waterloo, Belg. 16 50 43N 4 25 E
Waterloo, Ont., Can. 106 43 30N 80 32W
Waterloo, Qué., Can. 113 45 22N 72 32W
Waterloo, S. Leone 84 8 26N 13 8W
Waterloo, Ill., U.S.A. 116 38 22N 90 6W
Waterloo, Iowa, U.S.A. 116 42 27N 92 20W
Waterloo, N.Y., U.S.A. 112 42 54N 76 53W
Watersmeet 116 46 15N 89 12W
Waterton Lakes Nat. Park 108 49 5N 114 15W
Watertown, Conn., U.S.A. 113 41 36N 73 7W
Watertown, N.Y., U.S.A. 114 43 58N 75 57W
Watertown, S.D., U.S.A. 116 44 57N 97 5W
Watertown, Wis., U.S.A. 116 43 15N 88 45W
Waterval-Boven 93 25 40 S 30 18 E
Waterville, Can. 113 45 16N 71 54W
Waterville, Me., U.S.A. 107 44 35N 69 40W
Waterville, N.Y., U.S.A. 113 42 56N 75 23W
Waterville, Pa., U.S.A. 112 41 19N 77 21W
Waterville, Wash., U.S.A. 118 47 38N 120 1W
Watervliet 114 42 46N 73 43W
Wates 73 7 53 S 110 6 E
Watford, Can. 112 42 57N 81 53W
Watford, U.K. 13 51 38N 0 23W
Watford City 116 47 50N 103 23W
Wathaman → 109 57 16N 102 59W
Watkins Glen 112 42 25N 76 55W
Watling I. = San Salvador 121 24 0N 74 40W
Watonga 117 35 51N 98 24W
Watrous, Can. 109 51 40N 105 25W
Watrous, U.S.A. 117 35 50N 104 55W
Watsa 90 3 4N 29 30 E
Watseka 114 40 45N 87 45W
Watson 109 52 10N 104 30W
Watson Lake 104 60 6N 128 49W
Watsonville 119 36 55N 121 49W
Wattwil 25 47 18N 9 6 E
Watuata = Batuata 73 6 12 S 122 42 E
Watubela, Kepulauan 73 4 28 S 131 35 E
Wau 98 7 21 S 146 47 E
Waubamik 112 45 27N 80 1W
Waubay 116 45 22N 97 17W
Waubra 99 37 21 S 143 39 E
Wauchope 99 31 28 S 152 45 E
Wauchula 115 27 35N 81 50W
Waugh 109 49 40N 95 11W
Waukegan 114 42 22N 87 54W
Waukesha 114 43 0N 88 15W
Waukon 116 43 14N 91 33W
Wauneta 116 40 27N 101 25W
Waupaca 116 44 22N 89 8W
Waupun 116 43 38N 88 44W
Waurika 117 34 12N 98 0W
Wausau 116 44 57N 89 40W
Wautoma 116 44 3N 89 20W
Wauwatosa 114 43 6N 87 59W
Wave Hill 96 17 32 S 131 0 E
Waveney → 13 52 24N 1 20 E
Waverley 101 39 46 S 174 37 E
Waverly, Iowa, U.S.A. 116 42 40N 92 30W
Waverly, N.Y., U.S.A. 114 42 0N 76 33W
Wavre 16 50 43N 4 38 E
Wâw 87 7 45N 28 1 E
Wâw al Kabîr 81 25 20N 17 20 E
Wāw al Kabīr 83 25 20N 16 43 E
Wāw an Nāmūs 83 24 55N 17 46 E
Wawa, Can. 106 47 59N 84 47W
Wawa, Nigeria 85 9 54N 4 27 E
Wawa, Sudan 86 20 30N 30 22 E
Wawanesa 109 49 36N 99 40W
Wawoi → 98 7 48 S 143 16 E
Waxahachie 117 32 22N 96 53W
Waxweiler 25 50 6N 6 22 E
Wayabula Rau 73 2 29N 128 17 E
Wayatinah 99 42 19 S 146 27 E
Waycross 115 31 12N 82 25W
Wayi 87 5 8N 30 10 E
Wayne, Nebr., U.S.A. 116 42 16N 97 0W
Wayne, W. Va., U.S.A. 114 38 15N 82 27W
Waynesboro, Ga., U.S.A. 115 33 6N 82 1W
Waynesboro, Miss., U.S.A. 115 31 40N 88 39W
Waynesboro, Pa., U.S.A. 114 39 46N 77 32W
Waynesboro, Va., U.S.A. 114 38 4N 78 57W
Waynesburg 114 39 54N 80 12W
Waynesville 115 35 31N 83 0W
Waynoka 117 36 38N 98 53W
Wāzin 83 31 58N 10 40 E
Wazirabad 68 32 30N 74 8 E
Wda → 28 53 25N 18 29 E
We 72 5 51N 95 18 E
Weald, The 13 51 7N 0 9 E
Wear → 12 54 55N 1 22W
Weatherford, Okla., U.S.A. 117 35 30N 98 45W
Weatherford, Tex., U.S.A. 117 32 45N 97 48W
Weaverville 118 40 44N 122 56W
Webb City 117 37 9N 94 30W
Webster, Mass., U.S.A. 113 42 4N 71 54W
Webster, N.Y., U.S.A. 112 43 11N 77 27W
Webster, S.D., U.S.A. 116 45 24N 97 33W
Webster, Wis., U.S.A. 116 45 53N 92 25W
Webster City 116 42 30N 93 50W
Webster Green 116 38 38N 90 20W
Webster Springs 114 38 30N 80 25W
Weda 73 0 21N 127 50 E
Weda, Teluk 73 0 30N 127 50 E
Weddell I. 128 51 50 S 61 0W
Weddell Sea 5 72 30 S 40 0W
Wedderburn 99 36 26 S 143 33 E
Wedge I. 96 30 50 S 115 11 E
Wedgeport 107 43 44N 65 59W
Wedza 91 18 40 S 31 33 E
Wee Waa 99 30 11 S 149 26 E
Weed 118 41 29N 122 22W
Weedsport 113 43 3N 76 35W
Weedville 112 41 17N 78 28W
Weemelah 99 29 2 S 149 15 E
Weenen 93 28 48 S 30 7 E
Weener 24 53 10N 7 23 E
Weert 16 51 15N 5 43 E
Wegierska-Gorka 27 49 36N 19 7 E
Wegliniec 28 51 18N 15 10 E
Węgorzewo 28 54 13N 21 43 E
Węgrów 28 52 24N 22 0 E
Wei He →, Hebei, China 76 36 10N 115 45 E
Wei He →, Shaanxi, China 77 34 38N 110 15 E
Weida 24 50 47N 12 3 E
Weiden 25 49 40N 12 10 E
Weifang 76 36 44N 119 7 E
Weihai 76 37 30N 122 6 E
Weilburg 24 50 28N 8 17 E
Weilheim 25 47 50N 11 9 E
Weimar 24 51 0N 11 20 E
Weinan 77 34 31N 109 29 E
Weingarten 25 47 49N 9 39 E
Weinheim 25 49 33N 8 40 E
Weipa 97 12 40 S 141 50 E
Weir →, Austral. 99 28 20 S 149 50 E
Weir →, Can. 109 56 54N 93 21W
Weir River 109 56 49N 94 6W
Weirton 112 40 23N 80 35W
Weiser 118 44 10N 117 0W
Weishan 77 34 47N 117 5 E
Weissenburg 25 49 2N 10 58 E
Weissenfels 24 51 11N 12 0 E
Weisswasser 24 51 30N 14 36 E
Wéitra 26 48 41N 14 54 E
Weiyuan 76 35 7N 104 10 E
Weiz 26 47 13N 15 39 E
Weizhou Dao 77 21 0N 109 5 E
Wejherowo 28 54 35N 18 12 E
Wekusko 109 54 30N 99 45W
Wekusko L. 109 54 40N 99 50W
Welby 109 50 33N 101 29W
Welch 114 37 29N 81 36W
Weldya 87 11 50N 39 34 E
Welega □ 87 9 25N 34 20 E
Welkite 87 8 15N 37 42 E
Welkom 92 28 0 S 26 50 E
Welland 106 43 0N 79 15W
Welland → 12 52 43N 0 10W
Wellesley Is. 97 16 42 S 139 30 E
Wellin 16 50 5N 5 6 E
Wellingborough 13 52 18N 0 41W
Wellington, Austral. 97 32 35 S 148 59 E
Wellington, Can. 106 43 57N 77 20W
Wellington, N.Z. 101 41 19 S 174 46 E
Wellington, S. Afr. 92 33 38 S 18 57 E
Wellington, U.K. 13 50 58N 3 13W
Wellington, Col., U.S.A. 116 40 43N 105 0W
Wellington, Kans., U.S.A. 117 37 15N 97 25W
Wellington, Nev., U.S.A. 118 38 47N 119 28W
Wellington, Ohio, U.S.A. 112 41 9N 82 12W
Wellington, Tex., U.S.A. 117 34 55N 100 13W
Wellington □ 101 40 8 S 175 36 E
Wellington, I. 128 49 30 S 75 0W
Wellington, L. 99 38 6 S 147 20 E
Wellington (Telford) 12 52 42N 2 31W
Wells, Norfolk, U.K. 12 52 57N 0 51 E
Wells, Somerset, U.K. 13 51 12N 2 39W
Wells, Me., U.S.A. 113 43 18N 70 35W
Wells, Minn., U.S.A. 116 43 44N 93 45W
Wells, Nev., U.S.A. 118 41 8N 115 0W
Wells Gray Prov. Park 108 52 30N 120 15W
Wells L. 96 26 44 S 123 15 E
Wells River 113 44 9N 72 4W
Wellsboro 114 41 45N 77 20W
Wellsburg 112 40 15N 80 36W
Wellsville, Mo., U.S.A. 116 39 4N 91 30W
Wellsville, N.Y., U.S.A. 114 42 9N 77 53W
Wellsville, Ohio, U.S.A. 114 40 36N 80 40W
Wellsville, Utah, U.S.A. 118 41 35N 111 59W
Wellton 119 32 39N 114 6W
Welmel, Wabi → 87 5 38N 40 47 E
Wełna → 28 52 46N 17 32 E
Welo □ 87 11 50N 39 48 E
Wels 26 48 9N 14 1 E
Welshpool 13 52 40N 3 9W
Welwyn 109 50 20N 101 30W
Wem 12 52 52N 2 45W
Wembere → 90 4 10 S 34 15 E
Wen Xian 77 32 43N 104 36 E
Wenatchee 118 47 30N 120 17W
Wenchang 77 19 38N 110 42 E
Wenchi 84 7 46N 2 8W
Wenchow = Wenzhou 75 28 0N 120 38 E
Wendell 118 42 50N 114 42W
Wendeng 76 37 15N 122 5 E
Wendesi 73 2 30 S 134 17 E
Wendo 87 6 40N 38 27 E
Wendover 118 40 49N 114 1W
Wengcheng 77 24 22N 113 50 E
Wenlock 98 13 6 S 142 58 E
Wenlock → 97 12 2 S 141 55 E
Wensu 75 41 15N 80 10 E
Wentworth 97 34 2 S 141 54 E
Wenut 73 3 11 S 133 19 E
Wenxi 77 35 20N 111 10 E
Wenzhou 75 28 0N 120 38 E
Weott 118 40 19N 123 56W
Wepener 92 29 42 S 27 3 E
Werda 92 25 24 S 23 15 E
Werdau 24 50 45N 12 20 E
Werder, Ethiopia 63 6 58N 45 1 E
Werder, Ger. 24 52 23N 12 56 E
Werdohl 24 51 15N 7 47 E
Wereilu 87 10 40N 39 28 E
Weri 73 3 10 S 132 38 E
Werne 24 51 38N 7 38 E
Werneck 25 49 59N 10 6 E
Wernigerode 24 51 49N 10 45 E
Werra → 24 51 26N 9 39 E
Werribee 99 37 54 S 144 40 E
Werrimull 99 34 25 S 141 38 E
Werris Creek 99 31 18 S 150 38 E
Wersar 73 1 30 S 131 55 E
Wertach → 25 48 24N 10 53 E
Wertheim 25 49 44N 9 32 E
Wertingen 25 48 33N 10 41 E
Wesel 24 51 39N 6 34 E
Weser → 24 53 33N 8 30 E
Wesiri 73 7 30 S 126 30 E
Wesleyville, Can. 107 49 8N 53 36W
Wesleyville, U.S.A. 112 42 9N 80 1W
Wessel Is. 97 11 10 S 136 45 E
Wesselburen 24 54 11N 8 53 E
Wessington 116 44 30N 98 40W
Wessington Springs 116 44 10N 98 35W
West 117 31 50N 97 5W
West B. 117 29 5N 89 27W
West Bend 114 43 25N 88 10W
West Bengal □ 69 23 0N 88 0 E
West Branch 114 44 16N 84 13W
West Bromwich 13 52 32N 2 1W
West Chazy 113 44 49N 73 28W
West Chester 114 39 58N 75 36W
West Columbia 117 29 10N 95 38W
West Des Moines 116 41 30N 93 45W
West Falkland 128 51 40 S 60 0W
West Frankfurt 116 37 56N 89 0W
West Germany ■ 24 52 0N 9 0 E
West Glamorgan □ 13 51 40N 3 55W
West Hartford 113 41 45N 72 45W
West Haven 113 41 18N 72 57W
West Helena 117 34 30N 90 40W
West Ice Shelf 5 67 0 S 85 0 E
West Indies 121 15 0N 70 0W
West Looe 13 50 21N 4 29W
West Lorne 112 42 36N 81 36W
West Lunga → 91 13 6 S 24 39 E
West Magpie → 107 51 2N 64 42W
West Memphis 117 35 5N 90 11W
West Midlands □ 13 52 30N 1 55W
West Monroe 117 32 32N 92 7W
West Moors 12 50 49N 1 50W
West Newton 112 40 14N 79 46W
West Nicholson 91 21 2 S 29 20 E
West Palm Beach 115 26 44N 80 3W
West Pittston 113 41 19N 75 49W
West Plains 117 36 45N 91 50W
West Point, Ga., U.S.A. 115 32 54N 85 10W
West Point, Miss., U.S.A. 115 33 36N 88 38W
West Point, Nebr., U.S.A. 116 41 50N 96 43W
West Point, Va., U.S.A. 114 37 35N 76 47W
West Pokot □ 90 1 30N 35 15 E
West Road → 108 53 18N 122 53W
West Rutland 114 43 38N 73 0W
West Schelde → = Westerschelde 16 51 25N 3 25 E
West Siberian Plain 60 62 0N 75 0 E
West Sussex □ 13 50 55N 0 30W
West-Terschelling 16 53 22N 5 13 E
West Virginia □ 114 39 0N 81 0W
West-Vlaanderen □ 16 51 0N 3 0 E
West Wyalong 100 33 56 S 147 10 E
West Yellowstone 118 44 47N 111 4W
West Yorkshire □ 12 53 45N 1 40W
Westbrook, Maine, U.S.A. 115 43 40N 70 22W
Westbrook, Tex., U.S.A. 117 32 25N 101 0W
Westbury 99 41 30 S 146 51 E
Westby 116 48 52N 104 3W
Westerland 24 54 51N 8 20 E
Western □, Kenya 90 0 30N 34 30 E
Western □, Uganda 90 1 45N 31 30 E
Western □, Zambia 91 15 15 S 24 30 E
Western Australia □ 96 25 0 S 118 0 E
Western Ghats 70 14 0N 75 0 E
Western Isles □ 14 57 30N 7 10W
Western Samoa ■ 101 14 0 S 172 0W
Westernport 114 39 30N 79 5W
Westerschelde → 16 51 25N 3 25 E
Westerstede 24 53 15N 7 55 E
Westerwald 24 50 39N 8 0 E
Westfield, Mass., U.S.A. 113 42 9N 72 49W
Westfield, N.Y., U.S.A. 112 42 20N 79 38W
Westfield, Pa., U.S.A. 112 41 54N 77 32W
Westhope 116 48 55N 101 0W
Westland □ 101 43 33 S 169 59 E
Westland Bight 101 42 55 S 170 5 E
Westlock 108 54 9N 113 55W
Westmeath □ 15 53 30N 7 30W
Westminster 114 39 34N 77 1W
Westmorland 119 33 2N 115 42W
Weston, Malay. 72 5 10N 115 35 E
Weston, Oreg., U.S.A. 118 45 50N 118 30W
Weston, W. Va., U.S.A. 114 39 3N 80 29W
Weston I. 106 52 33N 79 36W
Weston-super-Mare 13 51 20N 2 59W
Westport, Can. 113 44 40N 76 25W
Westport, Ireland 15 53 44N 9 31W
Westport, N.Z. 101 41 46 S 171 37 E
Westport, U.S.A. 118 46 48N 124 4W
Westray, Can. 109 53 36N 101 24W
Westray, U.K. 14 59 18N 3 0W
Westree 106 47 26N 81 34W
Westview 108 49 50N 124 31W
Westville, Ill., U.S.A. 114 40 3N 87 36W
Westville, Okla., U.S.A. 117 36 0N 94 33W
Westwood 118 40 26N 121 0W
Wetar 73 7 30 S 126 30 E
Wetaskiwin 108 52 55N 113 24W
Wethersfield 113 41 43N 72 40W
Wetteren 16 51 0N 3 53 E
Wetzlar 24 50 33N 8 30 E

• *Renamed Hwange*
† *Renamed Teraina*

Wewak **98** 3 38 S 143 41 E
Wewaka **117** 35 10N 96 35W
Wexford **15** 52 20N 6 28W
Wexford □ **15** 52 20N 6 25W
Wexford Harb. **15** 52 20N 6 25W
Weyburn **109** 49 40N 103 50W
Weyburn L. **108** 63 0N 117 59W
Weyer **26** 47 51N 14 40 E
Weyib → **87** 7 15N 40 15 E
Weymouth, Can. **107** 44 30N 66 1W
Weymouth, U.K. **13** 50 36N 2 28W
Weymouth, U.S.A. **113** 42 13N 70 53W
Weymouth, C. **97** 12 37 S 143 27 E
Whakatane **101** 37 57 S 177 1 E
Whale → **107** 58 15N 67 40W
Whale Cove **104** 62 11N 92 36W
Whales, B. of **5** 78 0 S 165 0W
Whalsay **14** 60 22N 1 0W
Whangamomona **101** 39 8 S 174 44 E
Whangarei **101** 35 43 S 174 21 E
Whangarei Harbour **101** 35 45 S 174 28 E
Wharfe → **12** 53 55N 1 30W
Wharfedale **12** 54 7N 2 4W
Wharton, N.J., U.S.A. **113** 40 53N 74 36W
Wharton, Pa., U.S.A. **112** 41 31N 78 1W
Wharton, Tex., U.S.A. **117** 29 20N 96 6W
Wheatland **116** 42 4N 104 58W
Wheatley **112** 42 6N 82 27W
Wheaton **116** 45 50N 96 29W
Wheeler, Oreg., U.S.A. **118** 45 50N 123 57W
Wheeler, Tex., U.S.A. **117** 35 29N 100 15W
Wheeler → **109** 57 25N 105 30W
Wheeler Pk., N. Mex., U.S.A. **119** 36 34N 105 25W
Wheeler Pk., Nev., U.S.A. **119** 38 57N 114 15W
Wheeling **114** 40 2N 80 41W
Whernside **12** 54 14N 2 24W
Whidbey I. **108** 48 15N 122 40W
Whidbey Is. **96** 34 30 S 135 3 E
Whiskey Gap **108** 49 0N 113 3W
Whiskey Jack L. **109** 58 23N 101 55W
Whistler **115** 30 50N 88 10W
Whitby, Can. **112** 43 52N 78 56W
Whitby, U.K. **12** 54 29N 0 37W
White →, Ark., U.S.A. **117** 33 53N 91 3W
White →, Colo., U.S.A. **118** 40 8N 109 41W
White →, Ind., U.S.A. **114** 38 25N 87 44W
White →, S.D., U.S.A. **116** 43 45N 99 30W
White B. **107** 50 0N 56 35W
White Bear Res. **107** 48 10N 57 5W
White Bird **118** 45 46N 116 21W
White Butte **116** 46 23N 103 19W
White City **116** 38 50N 96 45W
White Cliffs **99** 30 50 S 143 10 E
White Deer **117** 35 30N 101 8W
White Hall **116** 39 25N 90 27W
White Haven **113** 41 3N 75 47W
White I. **101** 37 30 S 177 13 E
White L., Can. **113** 45 18N 76 31W
White L., U.S.A. **117** 29 45N 92 30W
White Mts., Calif., U.S.A. **119** 37 30N 118 15W
White Mts., N.H., U.S.A. **113** 44 15N 71 15W
White Nile = Nîl el Abyad → **87** 15 38N 32 31 E
White Nile Dam **87** 15 24N 32 30 E
White Otter L. **106** 49 5N 91 55W
White Pass **104** 59 40N 135 3W
White Plains **113** 41 2N 73 44W
White River, Can. **106** 48 35N 85 20W
White River, S. Afr. **93** 25 20 S 31 00 E
White River, U.S.A. **116** 43 34N 100 45W
White River Junc. **113** 43 38N 72 20W
White Russia = Byelorussian S.S.R. □ **54** 53 30N 27 0 E
White Sea = Beloye More **52** 66 30N 38 0 E
White Sulphur Springs, Mont., U.S.A. **118** 46 35N 110 54W
White Sulphur Springs, W. Va., U.S.A. **114** 37 50N 80 16W
White Volta (Volta Blanche) → **85** 9 10N 1 15W
Whitecliffs **101** 43 26 S 171 55 E
Whitecourt **108** 54 10N 115 45W
Whiteface **117** 33 35N 102 40W
Whitefield **113** 44 23N 71 37W
Whitefish **118** 48 25N 114 22W
Whitefish L. **109** 62 41N 106 48W
Whitefish Pt. **114** 46 45N 85 0W
Whitegull, L. **107** 55 27N 64 17W
Whitehall, Mich., U.S.A. **114** 43 21N 86 20W
Whitehall, Mont., U.S.A. **118** 45 52N 112 4W
Whitehall, N.Y., U.S.A. **114** 43 32N 73 28W
Whitehall, Wis., U.S.A. **116** 44 20N 91 19W
Whitehaven **12** 54 33N 3 35W
Whitehorse **104** 60 43N 135 3W
Whitehorse, Vale of **13** 51 37N 1 30W
Whiteman Ra. **98** 5 55 S 150 0 E
Whitemark **99** 40 7 S 148 3 E
Whitemouth **109** 49 57N 95 58W
Whiteplains **84** 6 28N 10 40W
Whitesail, L. **108** 53 35N 127 45W
Whitesboro, N.Y., U.S.A. **113** 43 8N 75 20W
Whitesboro, Tex., U.S.A. **117** 33 40N 96 58W
Whiteshell Prov. Park **109** 50 0N 95 40W
Whitetail **116** 48 54N 105 15W
Whiteville **115** 34 20N 78 40W
Whitewater **114** 42 50N 88 45W
Whitewater Baldy, Mt. **119** 33 20N 108 44W
Whitewater L. **106** 50 50N 89 10W
Whitewood, Austral. **98** 21 28 S 143 30 E
Whitewood, Can. **109** 50 20N 102 20W
Whitfield **99** 36 42 S 146 24 E
Whithorn **14** 54 44N 4 25W
Whitianga **101** 36 47 S 175 41 E
Whitman **113** 42 4N 70 55W
Whitmire **115** 34 33N 81 40W
Whitney **106** 45 31N 78 14W
Whitney, Mt. **119** 36 35N 118 14W
Whitney Pt. **113** 42 19N 75 59W
Whitstable **13** 51 21N 1 2 E
Whitsunday I. **97** 20 15 S 149 4 E
Whittier **104** 60 46N 148 48W
Whittlesea **99** 37 27 S 145 9 E
Whitwell **115** 35 15N 85 30W
Wholdaia L. **109** 60 43N 104 20W
Whyalla **97** 33 2 S 137 30 E
Whyjonta **99** 29 41 S 142 28 E
Wiarton **106** 44 40N 81 10W
Wiawso **84** 6 10N 2 25W
Wiazów **28** 50 50N 17 10 E
Wibaux **116** 47 0N 104 13W
Wichita **117** 37 40N 97 20W
Wichita Falls **117** 33 57N 98 30W
Wick **14** 58 26N 3 5W
Wickenburg **119** 33 58N 112 45W
Wickett **117** 31 37N 102 58W
Wickham, C. **99** 39 35 S 143 57 E
Wickliffe **112** 41 36N 81 29W
Wicklow **15** 53 0N 6 2W
Wicklow □ **15** 52 59N 6 25W
Wicklow Hd. **15** 52 59N 6 3W
Wicklow Mts. **15** 53 0N 6 30W
Widawa **28** 51 27N 18 51 E
Widawka **28** 51 7N 19 36 E
Widnes **12** 53 22N 2 44W
Więcbork **28** 53 21N 17 30 E
Wiedenbrück **24** 51 52N 8 15 E
Wiek **24** 54 37N 13 17 E
Wielbark **28** 53 24N 20 55 E
Wielén **28** 52 53N 16 9 E
Wieliczka **27** 50 0N 20 5 E
Wieluń **28** 51 15N 18 34 E
Wien **27** 48 12N 16 22 E
Wiener Neustadt **27** 47 49N 16 16 E
Wieprz →, Koszalin, Poland **28** 54 26N 16 35 E
Wieprz →, Lublin, Poland **28** 51 34N 21 49 E
Wierden **16** 52 22N 6 35 E
Wieruszów **28** 51 19N 18 9 E
Wiesbaden **25** 50 7N 8 17 E
Wiesental **25** 49 15N 8 30 E
Wigan **12** 53 33N 2 38W
Wiggins, Colo., U.S.A. **116** 40 16N 104 3W
Wiggins, Miss., U.S.A. **117** 30 53N 89 9W
Wight, I. of **13** 50 40N 1 20W
Wigry, Jezioro **28** 54 2N 23 8 E
Wigtown **14** 54 52N 4 27W
Wigtown B. **14** 54 46N 4 15W
Wil **25** 47 28N 9 3 E
Wilamowice **27** 49 55N 19 9 E
Wilber **116** 40 34N 96 59W
Wilberforce **112** 45 2N 78 13W
Wilberforce, C. **97** 11 54 S 136 35 E
Wilburton **117** 34 55N 95 15W
Wilcannia **97** 31 30 S 143 26 E
Wilcox **112** 41 34N 78 43W
Wildbad **25** 48 44N 8 32 E
Wildeshausen **24** 52 54N 8 25 E
Wildon **26** 46 52N 15 31 E
Wildrose **116** 48 36N 103 11W
Wildspitze **26** 46 53N 10 53 E
Wildwood **114** 38 59N 74 46W
Wilga → **28** 51 52N 21 18 E
Wilhelm II Coast **5** 68 0 S 90 0 E
Wilhelm Mt. **98** 5 50 S 145 1 E
Wilhelm-Pieck-Stadt Guben **24** 51 59N 14 48 E
Wilhelmsburg, Austria **26** 48 6N 15 36 E
Wilhelmsburg, Ger. **24** 53 28N 10 1 E
Wilhelmshaven **24** 53 30N 8 9 E
Wilhelmstal **92** 21 58 S 16 21 E
Wilkes Barre **114** 41 15N 75 52W
Wilkes Land **5** 69 0 S 120 0 E
Wilkes Sub-Glacial Basin **5** 75 0 S 130 0 E
Wilkesboro **115** 36 10N 81 9W
Wilkie **109** 52 27N 108 42W
Wilkinsburg **112** 40 26N 79 50W
Willamina **118** 45 9N 123 32W
Willandra Billabong Creek → **99** 33 22 S 145 52 E
Willapa, B. **118** 46 44N 124 0W
Willard, N. Mex., U.S.A. **119** 34 35N 106 1W
Willard, Utah, U.S.A. **118** 41 28N 112 1W
Willcox **119** 32 13N 109 53W
Willemstad **121** 12 5N 69 0W
William → **109** 59 8N 109 19W
Williams **119** 35 16N 112 11W
Williams Lake **108** 52 10N 122 10W
Williamsburg, Ky., U.S.A. **115** 36 45N 84 10W
Williamsburg, Pa., U.S.A. **112** 40 27N 78 14W
Williamsburg, Va., U.S.A. **114** 37 17N 76 44W
Williamson, N.Y., U.S.A. **112** 43 14N 77 15W
Williamson, W. Va., U.S.A. **114** 37 46N 82 17W
Williamsport **114** 41 18N 77 1W
Williamston **115** 35 50N 77 5W
Williamstown, Austral. **99** 37 51 S 144 52 E
Williamstown, Mass., U.S.A. **113** 42 41N 73 12W
Williamstown, N.Y., U.S.A. **113** 43 25N 75 54W
Williamsville **117** 37 0N 90 33W
Willimantic **113** 41 45N 72 12W
Williston, S. Afr. **92** 31 20 S 20 53 E
Williston, Fla., U.S.A. **115** 29 25N 82 28W
Williston, N.D., U.S.A. **116** 48 10N 103 35W
Williston L. **108** 56 0N 124 0W
Willits **118** 39 28N 123 17W
Willmar **116** 45 5N 95 0W
Willoughby **112** 41 38N 81 26W
Willow Bunch **109** 49 20N 105 35W
Willow L. **108** 62 10N 119 8W
Willow Lake **116** 44 40N 97 40W
Willow River **108** 54 6N 122 28W
Willow Springs **117** 37 0N 92 0W
Willowlake → **108** 62 42N 123 8W
Willowmore **92** 33 15 S 23 30 E
Willows, Austral. **98** 23 39 S 147 25 E
Willows, U.S.A. **118** 39 30N 122 10W
Wills Cr. → **98** 22 43 S 140 2 E
Wills Pt. **117** 32 42N 95 57W
Willunga **99** 35 15 S 138 30 E
Wilmette **114** 42 6N 87 44W
Wilmington, Austral. **99** 32 39 S 138 7 E
Wilmington, Del., U.S.A. **114** 39 45N 75 32W
Wilmington, Ill., U.S.A. **114** 41 19N 88 10W
Wilmington, N.C., U.S.A. **115** 34 14N 77 54W
Wilmington, Ohio, U.S.A. **114** 39 27N 83 50W
Wilpena Cr. → **99** 31 25 S 139 29 E
Wilsall **118** 45 59N 110 40W
Wilson **115** 35 44N 77 54W
Wilson → **99** 27 38 S 141 24 E
Wilson, Mt. **119** 37 55N 108 3W
Wilson's Promontory **97** 38 55 S 146 25 E
Wilster **24** 53 55N 9 23 E
Wilton, U.K. **13** 51 5N 1 52W
Wilton, U.S.A. **116** 47 12N 100 47W
Wiltshire □ **13** 51 20N 2 0W
Wiltz **16** 49 57N 5 55 E
Wiluna **96** 26 36 S 120 14 E
Wimereux **19** 50 45N 1 37 E
Wimmera **97** 36 30 S 142 0 E
Wimmera → **99** 36 8 S 141 56 E
Winam G. **90** 0 20 S 34 15 E
Winburg **92** 28 30 S 27 2 E
Winchendon **113** 42 40N 72 3W
Winchester, U.K. **13** 51 4N 1 19W
Winchester, Conn., U.S.A. **113** 41 53N 73 9W
Winchester, Idaho, U.S.A. **118** 46 11N 116 32W
Winchester, Ind., U.S.A. **114** 40 10N 84 56W
Winchester, Ky., U.S.A. **114** 38 0N 84 8W
Winchester, Mass., U.S.A. **113** 42 28N 71 10W
Winchester, N.H., U.S.A. **113** 42 47N 72 22W
Winchester, Tenn., U.S.A. **115** 35 11N 86 8W
Winchester, Va., U.S.A. **114** 39 14N 78 8W
Wind → **118** 43 8N 108 12W
Wind River Range **118** 43 0N 109 30W
Windber **114** 40 14N 78 50W
Windermere, L. **12** 54 20N 2 57W
Windfall **108** 54 12N 116 13W
Windflower L. **108** 62 52N 118 30W
Windhoek **92** 22 35 S 17 4 E
Windischgarsten **26** 47 42N 14 21 E
Windom **116** 43 48N 95 3W
Windorah **97** 25 24 S 142 36 E
Window Rock **119** 35 47N 109 4W
Windrush → **13** 51 48N 1 35W
Windsor, Austral. **99** 33 37 S 150 50 E
Windsor, N.S., Can. **107** 44 59N 64 5W
Windsor, Newf., Can. **107** 48 57N 55 40W
Windsor, Ont., Can. **106** 42 18N 83 0W
Windsor, U.K. **13** 51 28N 0 36W
Windsor, Col., U.S.A. **116** 40 33N 104 45W
Windsor, Conn., U.S.A. **113** 41 50N 72 40W
Windsor, Mo., U.S.A. **116** 38 32N 93 31W
Windsor, N.Y., U.S.A. **113** 42 5N 75 37W
Windsor, Vt., U.S.A. **114** 43 30N 72 25W
Windsorton **92** 28 16 S 24 44 E
Windward Is., Atl. Oc. **121** 13 0N 63 0W
Windward Is., Pac. Oc. **95** 18 0 S 149 0W
Windward Passage = Vientos, Paso de los **121** 20 0N 74 0W
Windy L. **109** 60 20N 100 2W
Winefred L. **109** 55 30N 110 30W
Winejok **87** 9 1N 27 30 E
Winfield **117** 37 15N 97 0W
Wingen **99** 31 54 S 150 54 E
Wingham, Austral. **99** 31 48 S 152 22 E
Wingham, Can. **106** 43 55N 81 20W
Winifred **118** 47 30N 109 28W
Winisk **106** 55 20N 85 15W
Winisk → **106** 55 17N 85 5W
Winisk L. **106** 52 55N 87 22W
Wink **117** 31 49N 103 9W
Winkler **109** 49 10N 97 56W
Winklern **26** 46 52N 12 52 E
Winlock **118** 46 29N 122 56W
Winneba **85** 5 25N 0 36W
Winnebago **116** 43 43N 94 8W
Winnebago L. **114** 44 0N 88 20W
Winnemucca **118** 41 0N 117 45W
Winnemucca, L. **118** 40 25N 119 21W
Winner **116** 43 23N 99 52W
Winnetka **114** 42 8N 87 46W
Winnett **118** 47 2N 108 21W
Winnfield **117** 31 57N 92 38W
Winnibigoshish L. **116** 47 25N 94 12W
Winnipeg **109** 49 54N 97 9W
Winnipeg → **109** 50 38N 96 19W
Winnipeg Beach **109** 50 30N 96 58W
Winnipeg, L. **109** 52 0N 97 0W
Winnipegosis **109** 51 39N 99 55W
Winnipegosis L. **109** 52 30N 100 0W
Winnipesaukee, L. **113** 43 38N 71 21W
Winnsboro, La., U.S.A. **117** 32 10N 91 41W
Winnsboro, S.C., U.S.A. **115** 34 23N 81 5W
Winnsboro, Tex., U.S.A. **117** 32 56N 95 15W
Winokapau, L. **107** 53 15N 62 50W
Winona, Miss., U.S.A. **117** 33 30N 89 42W
Winona, Wis., U.S.A. **116** 44 2N 91 39W
Winooski **114** 44 31N 73 11W
Winschoten **16** 53 9N 7 3 E
Winsen **24** 53 21N 10 11 E
Winslow **119** 35 2N 110 41W
Winsted **113** 41 55N 73 5W
Winston-Salem **115** 36 7N 80 15W
Winter Garden **115** 28 33N 81 35W
Winter Haven **115** 28 0N 81 42W
Winter Park **115** 28 34N 81 19W
Winterberg **24** 51 12N 8 30 E
Winters **117** 31 58N 99 58W
Winterset **116** 41 18N 94 0W
Wintersville **112** 40 22N 80 38W
Winterswijk **16** 51 58N 6 43 E
Winterthur **25** 47 30N 8 44 E
Winthrop, Minn., U.S.A. **116** 44 31N 94 25W
Winthrop, Wash., U.S.A. **118** 48 27N 120 6W
Winton, Austral. **97** 22 24 S 143 3 E
Winton, N.Z. **101** 46 8 S 168 20 E
Winton, N.C., U.S.A. **115** 36 25N 76 58W
Winton, Pa., U.S.A. **113** 41 27N 75 33W
Wintzenheim **19** 48 4N 7 17 E
Wipper → **24** 51 17N 11 10 E
Wirral **12** 53 25N 3 0W
Wisbech **12** 52 39N 0 10 E
Wisconsin □ **116** 44 30N 90 0W
Wisconsin → **116** 43 0N 91 15W
Wisconsin Dells **116** 43 38N 89 45W
Wisconsin Rapids **116** 44 25N 89 50W
Wisdom **118** 45 37N 113 27W
Wishaw **14** 55 46N 3 55W
Wishek **116** 46 20N 99 35W
Wisła **27** 49 38N 18 53 E
Wisła → **28** 54 22N 18 55 E
Wisłok → **27** 50 13N 22 32 E
Wisłoka → **27** 50 27N 21 23 E
Wismar **24** 53 53N 11 23 E
Wisner **116** 42 0N 96 46W
Wissant **19** 50 52N 1 40 E
Wissembourg **19** 49 2N 7 57 E
Wistoka → **27** 49 50N 21 28 E
Wisznice **28** 51 48N 23 13 E
Witbank **93** 25 51 S 29 14 E
Witdraai **92** 26 58 S 20 48 E
Witham → **12** 53 3N 0 8W
Withernsea **12** 53 43N 0 2 E
Witkowo **28** 52 26N 17 45 E
Witney **13** 51 47N 1 29W
Witnossob → **92** 26 55 S 20 37 E
Wittdün **24** 54 38N 8 23 E
Witten **24** 51 26N 7 19 E
Wittenberg **24** 51 51N 12 39 E
Wittenberge **24** 53 0N 11 44 E
Wittenburg **24** 53 30N 11 4 E
Wittenoom **96** 22 15 S 118 20 E
Wittingen **24** 52 43N 10 43 E
Wittlich **25** 50 0N 6 54 E
Wittmund **24** 53 39N 7 45 E
Wittow **24** 54 37N 13 21 E
Wittstock **24** 53 10N 12 30 E
Witzenhausen **24** 51 20N 9 50 E
Wkra → **28** 52 27N 20 44 E
Władysławowo **28** 54 48N 18 25 E
Wlen **28** 51 0N 15 39 E
Wlingi **73** 8 5 S 112 25 E
Włocławek □ **28** 52 50N 19 10 E
Włocławek **28** 52 40N 19 3 E
Włodawa **28** 51 33N 23 31 E
Włoszczowa **28** 50 50N 19 55 E
Woburn **113** 42 31N 71 7W
Wodonga **99** 36 5 S 146 50 E
Wodzisław Śląski **27** 50 1N 18 26 E
Woerth **19** 48 57N 7 45 E
Woëvre, Plaine de la **19** 49 15N 5 45 E
Wokam **73** 5 45 S 134 28 E
Woking **108** 55 35N 118 50W
Wolbrom **28** 50 24N 19 45 E
Wołczyn **28** 51 1N 18 3 E
Woldegk **24** 53 27N 13 35 E
Wolf → **108** 60 17N 132 33W
Wolf Creek **118** 47 1N 112 2W
Wolf L. **108** 60 24N 131 40W
Wolf Point **116** 48 6N 105 40W
Wolfe I. **106** 44 7N 76 20W
Wolfenbüttel **24** 52 10N 10 33 E
Wolfenden **108** 52 0N 119 25W
Wolfsberg **26** 46 50N 14 52 E
Wolfsburg **24** 52 27N 10 49 E
Wolgast **24** 54 3N 13 46 E
Wolhusen **25** 47 4N 8 4 E
Wolin, Poland **28** 53 50N 14 37 E
Wolin, Poland **28** 54 0N 14 40 E
Wollaston, Islas **128** 55 40 S 67 30W
Wollaston L. **109** 58 7N 103 10W
Wollaston Pen. **104** 69 30N 115 0W
Wollondilly → **100** 34 12 S 150 18 E
Wollongong **97** 34 25 S 150 54 E
Wolmaransstad **92** 27 12 S 26 13 E
Wolmirstedt **24** 52 15N 11 35 E
Wołomin **28** 52 19N 21 15 E
Wołów **28** 51 20N 16 38 E
Wolseley, Austral. **99** 36 23 S 140 54 E
Wolseley, Can. **109** 50 25N 103 15W
Wolseley, S. Afr. **92** 33 26 S 19 7 E
Wolstenholme Fjord **4** 76 0N 70 0W
Wolsztyn **28** 52 8N 16 5 E
Wolvega **16** 52 52N 6 0 E
Wolverhampton **13** 52 35N 2 6W
Wondai **97** 26 20 S 151 49 E
Wonder Gorge **91** 14 40 S 29 0 E
Wongalarroo L. **99** 31 32 S 144 0 E
Wŏnju **76** 37 22N 127 58 E
Wonosari **73** 7 58 S 110 36 E
Wŏnsan **76** 39 11N 127 27 E
Wonthaggi **97** 38 37 S 145 37 E
Woocalla **99** 31 42 S 137 12 E
Wood Buffalo Nat. Park **108** 59 0N 113 41W
Wood L. **109** 55 17N 103 17W
Wood Lake **116** 42 38N 100 14W
Woodbridge **112** 43 47N 79 36W
Woodburn **99** 29 6 S 153 23 E
Woodend **99** 37 20 S 144 33 E
Woodland **118** 38 40N 121 50W
Woodlark I. **98** 9 10 S 152 50 E
Woodpecker **108** 53 30N 122 40W
Woodridge **109** 49 20N 96 9W
Woodroffe, Mt. **96** 26 20 S 131 45 E
Woodruff, Ariz., U.S.A. **119** 34 51N 110 1W
Woodruff, Utah, U.S.A. **118** 41 30N 111 4W
Woods, L., Austral. **96** 17 50 S 133 30 E
Woods, L., Can. **107** 54 30N 65 13W
Woods, L. of the **109** 49 15N 94 45W
Woodside **100** 38 31 S 146 52 E
Woodstock, Austral. **98** 19 35 S 146 50 E
Woodstock, N.B., Can. **107** 46 11N 67 37W
Woodstock, Ont., Can. **106** 43 10N 80 45W
Woodstock, U.K. **13** 51 51N 1 20W
Woodstock, Ill., U.S.A. **116** 42 17N 88 30W
Woodstock, Vt., U.S.A. **113** 43 37N 72 31W
Woodsville **114** 44 10N 72 0W
Woodville, N.Z. **101** 40 20 S 175 53 E
Woodville, U.S.A. **117** 30 45N 94 25W
Woodward **117** 36 24N 99 28W
Woolamai, C. **99** 38 30 S 145 23 E
Woombye **99** 26 40 S 152 55 E
Woomera **97** 31 30 S 137 10 E
Woonona **100** 34 21 S 150 54 E
Woonsocket **114** 42 0N 71 30W
Woonsockett **116** 44 5N 98 15W
Wooramel → **96** 25 47 S 114 10 E
Wooster **114** 40 48N 81 55W
Worcester, S. Afr. **92** 33 39 S 19 27 E
Worcester, U.K. **13** 52 12N 2 12W
Worcester, Mass., U.S.A. **114** 42 14N 71 49W
Worcester, N.Y., U.S.A. **113** 42 35N 74 45W
Wörgl **26** 47 29N 12 3 E
Workington **12** 54 39N 3 34W

Worksop 12 53 19N 1 9W
Workum 16 52 59N 5 26 E
Worland 118 44 0N 107 59W
Wormhoudt 19 50 52N 2 28 E
Worms 25 49 37N 8 21 E
Wörth 25 49 1N 12 24 E
Wortham 117 31 48N 96 27W
Wörther See 26 46 37N 14 10 E
Worthing 13 50 49N 0 21W
Worthington 116 43 35N 95 36W
Wosi 73 0 15 S 128 0 E
Wou-han = Wuhan 75 30 31N 114 18 E
Wour 83 21 14N 16 0 E
Wowoni 73 4 5 S 123 5 E
Wozniki 28 50 35N 19 4 E
Wrangell 104 56 30N 132 25W
Wrangell, I. 108 56 20N 132 10W
Wrangell Mts. 104 61 40N 143 30W
Wrath, C. 14 58 38N 5 0W
Wray 116 40 8N 102 18W
Wrekin, The 12 52 41N 2 35W
Wrens 115 33 13N 82 23W
Wrexham 12 53 5N 3 0W
Wriezen 24 52 43N 14 9 E
Wright, Can. 108 51 52N 121 40W
Wright, Phil. 73 11 42N 125 2 E
Wrightson, Mt. 119 31 43N 110 56W
Wrigley 104 63 16N 123 37W
Wrocław 28 51 5N 17 5 E
Wrocław □ 28 51 0N 17 0 E
Wronki 28 52 41N 16 21 E
Września 28 52 21N 17 36 E
Wschowa 28 51 48N 16 20 E
Wu Jiang → 75 29 40N 107 20 E
Wuchang 76 44 55N 127 5 E
Wuchuan 77 28 25N 108 3 E
Wuding He → 76 37 2N 110 23 E
Wugang 77 26 44N 110 35 E
Wugong Shan 77 27 30N 114 0 E
Wuhan 75 30 31N 114 18 E
Wuhsi = Wuxi 75 31 33N 120 18 E
Wuhu 75 31 22N 118 21 E
Wukari 85 7 51N 9 42 E
Wulehe 85 8 39N 0 0
Wuliaru 73 7 27 S 131 0 E
Wulumuchi = Ürümqi 75 43 45N 87 45 E
Wum 85 6 24N 10 2 E
Wuning 77 29 17N 115 5 E
Wunnummin L. 106 52 55N 89 10W
Wunsiedel 25 50 2N 12 0 E
Wunstorf 24 52 26N 9 29 E
Wuntho 67 23 55N 95 45 E
Wuping 77 25 5N 116 5 E
Wuppertal, Ger. 24 51 15N 7 8 E
Wuppertal, S. Afr. 92 32 13 S 19 12 E
Wuqing 76 39 23N 117 4 E
Wurung 98 19 13 S 140 38 E
Würzburg 25 49 46N 9 55 E
Wurzen 24 51 21N 12 45 E
Wushan 77 31 7N 109 54 E
Wustrow 24 54 4N 11 33 E
Wutach → 25 47 37N 8 15 E
Wutongqiao 75 29 22N 103 50 E
Wuwei, Anhui, China 77 31 18N 117 54 E
Wuwei, Gansu, China 75 37 57N 102 34 E
Wuxi, Jiangsu, China 75 31 33N 120 18 E
Wuxi, Sichuan, China 77 31 23N 109 35 E
Wuxing 77 30 51N 120 8 E
Wuyi, Hebei, China 76 37 46N 115 56 E
Wuyi, Zhejiang, China 77 28 52N 119 50 E
Wuyi Shan 75 27 0N 117 0 E
Wuying 76 47 53N 129 56 E
Wuyo 85 10 23N 11 50 E
Wuyuan 76 41 2N 108 20 E
Wuzhai 76 38 54N 111 48 E
Wuzhi Shan 75 18 45N 109 45 E
Wuzhong 76 38 2N 106 12 E
Wuzhou 75 23 30N 111 18 E
Wyaaba Cr. → 98 16 27 S 141 35 E
Wyalusing 113 41 40N 76 16W
Wyandotte 114 42 14N 83 13W
Wyandra 97 27 12 S 145 56 E
Wyangala Res. 100 33 54 S 149 0 E
Wyara, L. 99 28 42 S 144 14 E
Wycheproof 99 36 0 S 143 17 E
Wye → 13 51 36N 2 40W
Wyk 24 54 41N 8 33 E
Wymondham 13 52 45N 0 42W
Wymore 116 40 10N 96 40W
Wynberg 92 34 2 S 18 28 E
Wyndham, Austral. 96 15 33 S 128 3 E
Wyndham, N.Z. 101 46 20 S 168 51 E
Wyndmere 116 46 23N 97 7W
Wynne 117 35 15N 90 50W
Wynnum 99 27 27 S 153 9 E
Wynyard 109 51 45N 104 10W
Wyoming □ 110 42 48N 109 0W
Wyong 99 33 14 S 151 24 E
Wyrzysk 28 53 10N 17 17 E
Wysoka 28 53 13N 17 2 E
Wysokie 28 50 55N 22 40 E
Wysokie Mazowieckie 28 52 55N 22 30 E
Wyszków 28 52 36N 21 25 E
Wyszogród 28 52 23N 20 9 E
Wytheville 114 37 0N 81 3W

X

Xai-Xai 93 25 6 S 33 31 E
Xainza 75 30 58N 88 35 E
Xangongo 92 16 45 S 15 0 E
Xanten 24 51 40N 6 27 E
Xánthi 44 41 10N 24 58 E
Xánthi □ 44 41 10N 24 58 E
Xapuri 126 10 35 S 68 35W
Xau, L. 92 21 15 S 24 44 E
Xavantina 125 21 15 S 52 48W
Xenia 114 39 42N 83 57W
Xi Jiang → 75 22 5N 113 20 E
Xi Xian 76 36 41N 110 58 E
Xiachengzi 76 44 40N 130 18 E
Xiachuan Dao 77 21 40N 112 40 E
Xiaguan 75 25 32N 100 16 E
Xiajiang 77 27 30N 115 10 E
Xiamen 75 24 25N 118 4 E
Xi'an 77 34 15N 109 0 E
Xianfeng 77 29 40N 109 8 E
Xiang Jiang → 75 28 55N 112 50 E
Xiangfan 75 32 2N 112 8 E
Xiangning 76 35 58N 110 50 E
Xiangtan 75 27 51N 112 54 E
Xiangxiang 77 27 43N 112 28 E
Xiangyang 75 32 1N 112 8 E
Xiangyin 77 28 38N 112 54 E
Xiangzhou 77 23 58N 109 40 E
Xianju 77 28 51N 120 44 E
Xianyang 77 34 20N 108 40 E
Xiao Hinggan Ling 75 49 0N 127 0 E
Xiaogan 77 30 52N 113 55 E
Xiapu 75 26 54N 119 59 E
Xichang 75 27 51N 102 19 E
Xichuan 77 33 0N 111 30 E
Xieng Khouang 71 19 17N 103 25 E
Xifeng 77 27 7N 106 42 E
Xigazê 75 29 5N 88 45 E
Xihe 77 34 2N 105 20 E
Xiliao He → 76 43 32N 123 35 E
Xilin 77 24 30N 105 6 E
Xilókastron 45 38 4N 22 43 E
Xin Xian 76 38 22N 112 46 E
Xinavane 93 25 2 S 32 47 E
Xinbin 76 41 40N 125 2 E
Xincheng 77 24 5N 108 39 E
Xinfeng 77 25 27N 114 58 E
Xing'an 75 25 38N 110 40 E
Xingan 77 27 46N 115 20 E
Xingcheng 76 40 40N 120 45 E
Xingguo 77 26 21N 115 21 E
Xinghua 77 32 58N 119 48 E
Xinghua Wan 77 25 15N 119 20 E
Xingning 77 24 3N 115 42 E
Xingren 75 25 24N 105 11 E
Xingshan 77 31 15N 110 45 E
Xingtai 76 37 3N 114 32 E
Xingu → 127 1 30 S 51 53W
Xingyang 77 34 45N 112 52 E
Xinhua 77 27 42N 111 13 E
Xiniás, L. 45 39 2N 22 12 E
Xining 75 36 34N 101 40 E
Xinjiang 76 35 34N 111 11 E
Xinjiang Uygur Zizhiqu □ 75 42 0N 86 0 E
Xinjin 76 39 25N 121 58 E
Xinle 76 38 25N 114 40 E
Xinmin 76 41 59N 122 50 E
Xinning 77 26 28N 110 50 E
Xinxiang 77 35 18N 113 50 E
Xinyang 75 32 6N 114 3 E
Xinzheng 77 34 20N 113 45 E
Xinzhou 77 19 43N 109 17 E
Xinzhu 75 24 49N 120 57 E
Xiongyuecheng 76 40 12N 122 5 E
Xiping 77 33 22N 114 0 E
Xique-Xique 127 10 50 S 42 40W
Xiuyan 76 40 18N 123 11 E
Xixabangma Feng 67 28 20N 85 40 E
Xixiang 77 33 0N 107 44 E
Xizang □ 75 32 0N 88 0 E
Xuancheng 77 30 56N 118 43 E
Xuan'en 77 30 0N 109 30 E
Xuanhan 77 31 18N 107 38 E
Xuanhua 76 40 40N 115 2 E
Xuchang 77 34 2N 113 48 E
Xuguit Qi 76 49 17N 120 44 E
Xunke 76 49 35N 128 27 E
Xupu 77 27 53N 110 32 E
Xuwen 77 20 20N 110 10 E
Xuyong 77 28 10N 105 22 E
Xuzhou 77 34 18N 117 10 E

Y

Ya 'Bad 62 32 27N 35 10 E
Yaamba 98 23 8 S 150 22 E
Ya'an 75 29 58N 103 5 E
Yaapeet 99 35 45 S 142 3 E
Yabassi 85 4 30N 9 57 E
Yabelo 87 4 50N 38 8 E
Yablanitsa 43 43 2N 24 5 E
Yablonovy Khrebet 59 53 0N 114 0 E
Yabrīn 64 23 17N 48 58 E
Yacheng 77 18 22N 109 6 E
Yacuiba 124 22 0 S 63 43W
Yadgir 70 16 45N 77 5 E
Yadkin → 115 35 23N 80 3W
Yadrin 55 55 57N 46 12 E
Yagaba 85 10 14N 1 20W
Yagodnoye 59 62 33N 149 40 E
Yagoua 88 10 20N 15 13 E
Yagur 62 32 45N 35 4 E
Yahila 90 0 13N 24 28 E
Yahk 108 49 6N 116 10W
Yahuma 88 1 0N 23 10 E
Yajua 85 11 27N 12 49 E
Yakima 118 46 42N 120 30W
Yakima → 118 47 0N 120 30W
Yako 84 12 59N 2 15W
Yakoruda 43 42 1N 23 29 E
Yakut A.S.S.R. □ 59 62 0N 130 0 E
Yakutat 104 59 29N 139 44W
Yakutsk 59 62 5N 129 50 E
Yala 71 6 33N 101 18 E
Yalabusha → 117 33 30N 90 12W
Yalboroo 98 20 50 S 148 40 E
Yale 112 43 9N 82 47W
Yalgoo 96 28 16 S 116 39 E
Yalinga 88 6 33N 23 10 E
Yalkubul, Punta 120 21 32N 88 37W
Yalleroi 98 24 3 S 145 42 E
Yallourn 97 38 10 S 146 18 E
Yalong Jiang → 75 26 40N 101 55 E
Yalpukh, Oz. 46 45 30N 28 41 E
Yalta 56 44 30N 34 10 E
Yalu Chiang → 76 41 30N 126 30 E
Yalu He → 76 46 56N 123 30 E
Yalu Jiang → 76 40 0N 124 22 E
Yalutorovsk 58 56 41N 66 12 E
Yam Kinneret 62 32 45N 35 35 E
Yamagata 74 38 15N 140 15 E
Yamagata □ 74 38 30N 140 0 E
Yamaguchi 74 34 10N 131 32 E
Yamaguchi □ 74 34 20N 131 40 E
Yamal, Poluostrov 58 71 0N 70 0 E
Yamama 64 24 5N 47 30 E
Yamanashi □ 74 35 40N 138 40 E
Yamantau 52 54 20N 57 40 E
Yamantau, Gora 52 54 15N 58 6 E
Yamba 99 29 26 S 153 23 E
Yâmbiô 87 4 35N 28 16 E
Yambol 43 42 30N 26 36 E
Yamdena 73 7 45 S 131 20 E
Yamil 85 12 53N 8 4 E
Yamma-Yamma, L. 97 26 16 S 141 20 E
Yampa → 118 40 37N 108 59W
Yampi Sd. 96 16 8 S 123 38 E
Yampol 56 48 15N 28 15 E
Yamrat 85 10 11N 9 55 E
Yamrukchal 43 42 44N 24 52 E
Yamuna (Jumna) → 68 25 30N 81 53 E
Yamzho Yumco 75 28 48N 90 35 E
Yan 85 10 5N 12 11 E
Yan → 70 9 0N 81 10 E
Yana → 59 71 30N 136 0 E
Yanac 99 36 8 S 141 25 E
Yanai 74 33 58N 132 7 E
Yanam 70 16 47N 82 15 E
Yan'an 76 36 35N 109 26 E
Yanaul 52 56 25N 55 0 E
Yanbu 'al Baḥr 64 24 0N 38 5 E
Yancannia 99 30 12 S 142 35 E
Yanchang 76 36 43N 110 1 E
Yancheng, Henan, China 77 33 35N 114 0 E
Yancheng, Jiangsu, China 77 33 23N 120 8 E
Yanchi 76 37 48N 107 20 E
Yanchuan 76 36 51N 110 10 E
Yanco 100 34 38 S 146 27 E
Yandaran 98 24 43 S 152 6 E
Yanfolila 84 11 11N 8 9W
Yangambi 90 0 47N 24 20 E
Yangch'ü = Taiyuan 76 37 52N 112 33 E
Yangchun 75 22 11N 111 48 E
Yanggao 76 40 21N 113 55 E
Yangi-Yer 58 40 17N 68 48 E
Yangjiang 75 21 50N 110 59 E
Yangquan 76 37 58N 113 31 E
Yangshan 77 24 30N 112 40 E
Yangshuo 77 24 48N 110 29 E
Yangtze Kiang = Chang Jiang → 75 31 20N 121 52 E
Yangxin 77 29 50N 115 12 E
Yangzhou 77 32 21N 119 26 E
Yanhee Res. 71 17 30N 98 45 E
Yanji 76 42 59N 129 30 E
Yankton 116 42 55N 97 25W
Yanna 99 26 58 S 146 0 E
Yanonge 90 0 35N 24 38 E
Yanqi 75 42 5N 86 35 E
Yanqing 76 40 30N 115 58 E
Yanshan 77 28 15N 117 41 E
Yantabulla 99 29 21 S 145 0 E
Yantai 76 37 34N 121 22 E
Yanting 77 31 11N 105 24 E
Yantra → 43 43 40N 25 37 E
Yanzhou 76 35 35N 116 49 E
Yao 81 12 56N 17 33 E
Yaoundé 88 3 50N 11 35 E
Yap 94 9 31N 138 6 E
Yapen 73 1 50 S 136 0 E
Yapen, Selat 73 1 20 S 136 10 E
Yappar → 98 18 22 S 141 16 E
Yaqui → 120 27 37N 110 39W
Yar 55 58 14N 52 5 E
Yar-Sale 58 66 50N 70 50 E
Yaraka 97 24 53 S 144 3 E
Yarangüme 64 37 35N 29 8 E
Yaransk 55 57 22N 47 49 E
Yaratishky 54 54 3N 26 0 E
Yare → 13 52 36N 1 28 E
Yarensk 52 61 10N 49 8 E
Yarfa 86 24 40N 38 35 E
Yarí → 126 0 20 S 72 20W
Yarkand = Shache 75 38 20N 77 10 E
Yarker 113 44 23N 76 46W
Yarkhun → 69 36 17N 72 30 E
Yarmouth 107 43 50N 66 7W
Yarmuk → 62 32 38N 35 34 E
Yarmūk → 62 32 42N 35 40 E
Yaroslavl 55 57 35N 39 55 E
Yarra → 100 37 50 S 144 53 E
Yarram 99 38 29 S 146 9 E
Yarraman 99 26 50 S 152 0 E
Yarranvale 99 26 50 S 145 20 E
Yarras 99 31 25 S 152 20 E
Yarrawonga 100 36 0 S 146 0 E
Yartsevo, R.S.F.S.R., U.S.S.R. 54 55 6N 32 43 E
Yartsevo, R.S.F.S.R., U.S.S.R. 59 60 20N 90 0 E
Yasawa Group 101 17 00 S 177 23 E
Yaselda → 54 52 7N 26 28 E
Yashi 85 12 23N 7 54 E
Yasinovataya 56 48 7N 37 57 E
Yasinski, L. 106 53 16N 77 35W
Yasothon 71 15 50N 104 10 E
Yass 97 34 49 S 148 54 E
Yas'ur 62 32 54N 35 10 E
Yatağn 45 37 20N 28 10 E
Yates Center 117 37 53N 95 45W
Yathkyed L. 109 62 40N 98 0W
Yatsushiro 74 32 30N 130 40 E
Yatta Plateau 90 2 0 S 38 0 E
Yaṭṭah 62 31 27N 35 6 E
Yauyos 126 12 19 S 75 50W
Yaval 68 21 10N 75 42 E
Yavari → 126 4 21 S 70 2W
Yavne 62 31 52N 34 45 E
Yavorov 54 49 55N 23 20 E
Yawatahama 74 33 27N 132 24 E
Yawri B. 84 8 22N 13 0W
Yazd (Yezd) 65 31 55N 54 27 E
Yazdān 65 33 30N 60 50 E
Yazoo → 117 32 35N 90 50W
Yazoo City 117 32 48N 90 28W
Ybbs 26 48 12N 15 4 E
Ye Xian 76 37 8N 119 57 E
Yebbi-Souma 83 21 7N 17 54 E
Yebyu 67 14 15N 98 13 E
Yecla 33 38 35N 1 5W
Yedintsy 56 48 9N 27 18 E
Yefremov 55 53 8N 38 3 E
Yegorlyk → 57 46 33N 41 40 E
Yegorlykskaya 57 46 35N 40 35 E
Yegoryevsk 55 55 27N 38 55 E
Yegros 124 26 20 S 56 25W
Yehuda, Midbar 62 31 35N 35 15 E
Yei 87 4 9N 30 40 E
Yei, Nahr → 87 6 15N 30 13 E
Yelabuga 52 55 45N 52 4 E
Yelan 55 50 55N 43 43 E
Yelan-Kolenovski 55 51 16N 41 4 E
Yelandur 70 12 6N 77 0 E
Yelanskoye 59 61 25N 128 0 E
Yelarbon 99 28 33 S 150 38 E
Yelatma 55 55 0N 41 45 E
Yelets 55 52 40N 38 30 E
Yélimané 84 15 9N 10 34W
Yell 14 60 35N 1 5W
Yell Sd. 14 60 33N 1 15W
Yellamanchilli (Elamanchili) 70 17 33N 82 50 E
Yellow Mt. 100 32 31 S 146 52 E
Yellow Sea 76 35 0N 123 0 E
Yellowhead P. 108 52 53N 118 25W
Yellowknife 108 62 27N 114 29W
Yellowknife → 104 62 31N 114 19W
Yellowstone → 116 47 58N 103 59W
Yellowstone L. 118 44 30N 110 20W
Yellowstone National Park 118 44 35N 110 0W
Yellowtail Res. 118 45 6N 108 8W
Yelnya 54 54 35N 33 15 E
Yelsk 54 51 50N 29 10 E
Yelvertoft 98 20 13 S 138 45 E
Yelwa 85 10 49N 4 41 E
Yemen ■ 63 15 0N 44 0 E
Yenakiyevo 56 48 15N 38 15 E
Yenangyaung 67 20 30N 95 0 E
Yenda 99 34 13 S 146 14 E
Yendéré 84 10 12N 4 59W
Yendi 85 9 29N 0 1W
Yenisaía 44 41 1N 24 57 E
Yenisey → 58 71 50N 82 40 E
Yeniseysk 59 58 27N 92 13 E
Yeniseyskiy Zaliv 58 72 20N 81 0 E
Yenne 21 45 43N 5 44 E
Yenotayevka 57 47 15N 47 0 E
Yenyuka 59 57 57N 121 15 E
Yeo, L. 96 28 0 S 124 30 E
Yeola 70 20 0N 74 30 E
Yeotmal 70 20 20N 78 15 E
Yeovil 13 50 57N 2 38W
Yepes 32 39 55N 3 39W
Yeppoon 97 23 5 S 150 47 E
Yeráki 45 37 0N 22 42 E
Yerbent 58 39 30N 58 50 E
Yerbogachen 59 61 16N 108 0 E
Yerevan 57 40 10N 44 31 E
Yerla → 70 16 50N 74 30 E
Yermak 58 52 2N 76 55 E
Yermakovo 59 52 25N 126 20 E
Yermo 119 34 58N 116 50W
Yerofey Pavlovich 59 54 0N 122 0 E
Yershov 55 51 22N 48 16 E
Yerushalayim 62 31 47N 35 10 E
Yerville 18 49 40N 0 53 E
Yes Tor 13 50 41N 3 59W
Yesnogorsk 55 54 32N 37 38 E
Yeso 117 34 29N 104 37W
Yessentuki 57 44 0N 42 53 E
Yessey 59 68 29N 102 10 E
Yeste 33 38 22N 2 19W
Yeu, I. d' 18 46 42N 2 20W
Yevlakh 57 40 39N 47 7 E
Yevpatoriya 56 45 15N 33 20 E
Yevstratovskiy 55 50 11N 39 45 E
Yeya → 57 46 40N 38 40 E
Yeysk 56 46 40N 38 12 E
Yhati 124 25 45 S 56 35W
Yhú 125 25 0 S 56 0W
Yi → 124 33 7 S 57 8W
Yi Xian 76 41 30N 121 22 E
Yiali 45 36 41N 27 11 E
Yi'allaq, G. 86 30 21N 33 31 E
Yiáltra 45 38 51N 22 59 E
Yiannisádhes 45 35 20N 26 10 E
Yiannitsa 44 40 46N 22 24 E
Yibin 75 28 45N 104 32 E
Yichang 75 30 40N 111 20 E
Yicheng 76 35 42N 111 40 E
Yichuan 76 36 2N 110 10 E
Yichun, Heilongjiang, China 75 47 44N 128 52 E
Yichun, Jiangxi, China 77 27 48N 114 22 E
Yidhá 44 40 35N 22 53 E
Yidu 76 36 43N 118 28 E
Yihuang 77 27 30N 116 12 E
Yijun 76 35 28N 109 8 E
Yilan, China 76 46 19N 129 34 E
Yilan, Taiwan 75 24 51N 121 44 E
Yilehuli Shan 76 51 20N 124 20 E
Yimianpo 76 45 7N 128 2 E
Yinchuan 76 38 30N 106 15 E
Ying He → 77 32 30N 116 30 E
Ying Xian 76 39 32N 113 10 E
Yingcheng 77 30 56N 113 35 E
Yingde 77 24 10N 113 25 E
Yingkou 76 40 37N 122 18 E
Yingshan 77 30 41N 115 32 E
Yingshang 77 32 38N 116 12 E
Yingtan 75 28 12N 117 0 E
Yining 75 43 58N 81 10 E

Yinjiang 77 28 1N 108 21 E
Yinkanie 99 34 22 S 140 17 E
Yinnietharra 96 24 39 S 116 12 E
Yioúra, Greece 44 39 23N 24 10 E
Yioúra, Greece 45 37 32N 24 40 E
Yipinglang 75 25 10N 101 52 E
Yirga Alem 87 6 48N 38 22 E
Yirshi 76 47 18N 119 49 E
Yishan 75 24 28N 108 38 E
Yithion 45 36 46N 22 34 E
Yitong 76 43 13N 125 20 E
Yitulihe 76 50 38N 121 34 E
Yixing 77 31 21N 119 48 E
Yiyang, Henan, China 77 34 27N 112 10 E
Yiyang, Hunan, China 75 28 35N 112 18 E
Yizhang 77 25 27N 112 57 E
Yizre'el 62 32 34N 35 19 E
Ylitornio 50 66 19N 23 39 E
Ylivieska 50 64 4N 24 28 E
Yngaren 49 58 50N 16 35 E
Ynykchanskiy 59 60 15N 137 35 E
Yoakum 117 29 20N 97 20W
Yog Pt. 73 14 6N 124 12 E
Yogan 85 6 23N 1 30 E
Yogyakarta 73 7 49 S 110 22 E
Yoho Nat. Park 108 51 25N 116 30W
Yojoa, L. de 120 14 53N 88 0W
Yokadouma 88 3 26N 15 6 E
Yokkaichi 74 35 0N 136 38 E
Yoko 85 5 32N 12 20 E
Yokohama 74 35 27N 139 28 E
Yokosuka 74 35 20N 139 40 E
Yola 85 9 10N 12 29 E
Yolaina, Cordillera de 121 11 30N 84 0W
Yonago 74 35 25N 133 19 E
Yong Peng 71 2 0N 103 3 E
Yong'an 77 25 59N 117 25 E
Yongchun 77 25 16N 118 20 E
Yongding 77 24 43N 116 45 E
Yongfeng 77 27 20N 115 22 E
Yongfu 77 24 59N 109 59 E
Yonghe 76 36 46N 110 38 E
Yongji 77 34 52N 110 28 E
Yongshun 77 29 2N 109 51 E
Yongxin 77 26 58N 114 15 E
Yongxing 77 26 9N 113 8 E
Yongxiu 77 29 2N 115 42 E
Yonibana 84 8 30N 12 19W
Yonkers 114 40 57N 73 51W
Yonne □ 19 47 50N 3 40 E
Yonne → 19 48 23N 2 58 E
Yoqne'am 62 32 40N 35 6 E
York, Austral. 96 31 52 S 116 47 E
York, U.K. 12 53 58N 1 7W
York, Ala., U.S.A. 115 32 30N 88 18W
York, Nebr., U.S.A. 116 40 55N 97 35W
York, Pa., U.S.A. 114 39 57N 76 43W
York, C. 97 10 42 S 142 31 E
York, Kap 4 75 55N 66 25W
York Sd. 96 14 50 S 125 5 E
Yorke Pen. 97 34 50 S 137 40 E
Yorkshire Wolds 12 54 0N 0 30W
Yorkton 109 51 11N 102 28W
Yorktown 117 29 0N 97 29W
Yosemite National Park 119 38 0N 119 30W
Yoshkar Ola 55 56 38N 47 55 E
Yŏsu 77 34 47N 127 45 E
Yotvata 62 29 55N 35 2 E
You Jiang → 75 23 22N 110 3 E
Youbou 108 48 53N 124 13W
Youghal 15 51 58N 7 51W
Youghal B. 15 51 55N 7 50W
Youkounkoun 84 12 35N 13 11W
Young, Austral. 97 34 19 S 148 18 E
Young, Can. 109 51 47N 105 45W
Young, Uruguay 124 32 44 S 57 36W
Young, U.S.A. 119 34 9N 110 56W
Younghusband Pen. 99 36 0 S 139 25 E
Youngstown, Can. 109 51 35N 111 10W
Youngstown, N.Y., U.S.A. 112 43 16N 79 2W
Youngstown, Ohio, U.S.A. 114 41 7N 80 41W
Youngsville 112 41 51N 79 21W
Youssoufia 82 32 16N 8 31W
Youyang 77 28 47N 108 42 E
Youyu 76 40 10N 112 20 E
Yozgat 64 39 51N 34 47 E
Ypané → 124 23 29 S 57 19W
Yport 18 49 45N 0 15 E
Ypres = Ieper 16 50 51N 2 53 E
Ypsilanti 114 42 18N 83 40W
Yreka 118 41 44N 122 40W
Ysleta 119 31 45N 106 24W
Yssingeaux 21 45 9N 4 8 E
Ystad 49 55 26N 13 50 E
Ythan → 14 57 26N 2 12W
Ytterhogdal 48 62 12N 14 56 E
Ytyk-Kel 59 62 30N 133 45 E
Yu Shan 75 23 30N 120 58 E
Yu Xian, Hebei, China 76 39 50N 114 35 E
Yu Xian, Henan, China 77 34 10N 113 28 E
Yuan Jiang → 75 28 55N 111 50 E
Yuanling 75 28 29N 110 22 E
Yuanyang 75 23 10N 102 43 E
Yuba City 118 39 12N 121 37W
Yucatán □ 120 21 30N 86 30W
Yucatán, Canal de 121 22 0N 86 30W
Yucca 119 34 56N 114 6W
Yucheng 76 36 55N 116 32 E
Yuci 76 37 42N 112 46 E
Yudino, R.S.F.S.R., U.S.S.R. 55 55 51N 48 55 E
Yudino, R.S.F.S.R., U.S.S.R. 58 55 10N 67 55 E
Yudu 77 25 59N 115 30 E
Yueqing 77 28 9N 120 59 E
Yueyang 77 29 21N 113 5 E
Yugan 77 28 43N 116 37 E
Yugoslavia ■ 37 44 0N 20 0 E
Yuhuan 77 28 9N 121 12 E
Yujiang 77 28 10N 116 43 E
Yukhnov 54 54 44N 35 15 E
Yukon Territory □ 104 63 0N 135 0W
Yukti 59 63 26N 105 42 E
Yule → 96 20 41 S 118 17 E
Yuli 85 9 44N 10 12 E
Yülin 77 18 10N 109 31 E
Yulin, Guangxi Zhuangzu, China 77 22 40N 110 8 E
Yulin, Shaanxi, China 76 38 20N 109 30 E
Yuma, Ariz., U.S.A. 119 32 45N 114 37W
Yuma, Colo., U.S.A. 116 40 10N 102 43W
Yuma, B. de 121 18 20N 68 35W
Yumbe 90 3 28N 31 15 E
Yumbi 90 1 12 S 26 15 E
Yumen 75 39 50N 97 30 E
Yun Xian 75 32 50N 110 46 E
Yungas 126 17 0 S 66 0W
Yungay 124 37 10 S 72 5W
Yunhe 77 28 8N 119 33 E
Yunlin 77 23 42N 120 30 E
Yunnan □ 75 25 0N 102 0 E
Yunquera de Henares 32 40 47N 3 11W
Yunta 99 32 34 S 139 36 E
Yunxiao 77 23 59N 117 18 E
Yur 59 59 52N 137 41 E
Yurgao 58 55 42N 84 51 E
Yuribei 58 71 8N 76 58 E
Yurimaguas 126 5 55 S 76 7W
Yurya 55 59 1N 49 13 E
Yuryev-Polskiy 55 56 30N 39 40 E
Yuryevets 55 57 25N 43 2 E
Yuscarán 121 13 58N 86 45W
Yushu, Jilin, China 76 44 43N 126 38 E
Yushu, Qinghai, China 75 33 5N 96 55 E
Yuyao 77 30 3N 121 10 E
Yuzha 55 56 34N 42 1 E
Yuzhno-Sakhalinsk 59 46 58N 142 45 E
Yvelines □ 19 48 40N 1 45 E
Yverdon 25 46 47N 6 39 E
Yvetot 18 49 37N 0 44 E

Z

Zaandam 16 52 26N 4 49 E
Zab, Monts du 83 34 55N 5 0 E
Žabalj 42 45 21N 20 5 E
Žabari 42 44 22N 21 15 E
Zabarjad 86 23 40N 36 12 E
Zabaykalskiy 59 49 40N 117 25 E
Zabid 63 14 0N 43 10 E
Ząbkowice Śląskie 28 50 35N 16 50 E
Žabljak 42 43 18N 19 7 E
Zabłudów 28 53 0N 23 19 E
Žabno 27 50 9N 20 53 E
Zābol 65 31 0N 61 32 E
Zābolī 65 27 10N 61 35 E
Zabré 85 11 12N 0 36W
Zabrze 28 50 18N 18 50 E
Zabul □ 65 32 0N 67 0 E
Zacapa 120 14 59N 89 31W
Zacatecas 120 22 49N 102 34W
Zacatecas □ 120 23 30N 103 0W
Zacatecoluca 120 13 29N 88 51W
Zacoalco 120 20 14N 103 33W
Zadar 39 44 8N 15 14 E
Zadawa 85 11 33N 10 19 E
Zadetkyi Kyun 72 10 0N 98 25 E
Zadonsk 55 52 25N 38 56 E
Zafora 45 36 5N 26 24 E
Zafra 31 38 26N 6 30W
Zafriya 62 31 59N 34 51 E
Żagań 28 51 39N 15 22 E
Zagazig 86 30 40N 31 30 E
Zaghouan 83 36 23N 10 10 E
Zaglivérion 44 40 36N 23 15 E
Zaglou 82 27 17N 0 3W
Zagnanado 85 7 18N 2 28 E
Zagorá 44 39 27N 23 6 E
Zagora 82 30 22N 5 51W
Zagórów 28 52 10N 17 54 E
Zagorsk 55 56 20N 38 10 E
Zagórz 27 49 30N 22 14 E
Zagreb 39 45 50N 16 0 E
Zāgros, Kudhā-ye 65 33 45N 47 0 E
Žagubica 42 44 15N 21 47 E
Zaguinaso 84 10 1N 6 14W
Zagyva → 27 47 5N 20 4 E
Zāhedān 65 29 30N 60 50 E
Zahirabad 70 17 43N 77 37 E
Zahlah 64 33 52N 35 50 E
Zahna 24 51 54N 12 47 E
Zahrez Chergui 82 35 0N 3 30 E
Zahrez Rharbi 82 34 50N 2 55 E
Zaïr 82 29 47N 5 51W
Zaïre → 88 6 4 S 12 24 E
Zaïre, Rep. of ■ 88 3 0 S 23 0 E
Zaječar 42 43 53N 22 18 E
Zakamensk 59 50 23N 103 17 E
Zakataly 57 41 38N 46 35 E
Zakavkazye 57 42 0N 44 0 E
Zākhū 64 37 10N 42 50 E
Zákinthos 45 37 47N 20 57 E
Zaklików 28 50 46N 22 7 E
Zakopane 27 49 18N 19 57 E
Zakroczym 28 52 26N 20 38 E
Zala □ 27 46 42N 16 50 E
Zala → 27 46 43N 17 16 E
Zalaegerszeg 27 46 53N 16 47 E
Zalakomár 27 46 33N 17 10 E
Zalalövö 27 46 51N 16 35 E
Zalamea de la Serena 31 38 40N 5 38W
Zalamea la Real 31 37 41N 6 38W
Zalău 46 47 12N 23 3 E
Zalazna 55 58 39N 52 31 E
Žalec 39 46 16N 15 10 E
Zaleshchiki 56 48 45N 25 45 E
Zalewo 28 53 50N 19 41 E
Zalingei 81 12 51N 23 29 E
Zalṭan, Jabal 83 28 46N 19 45 E
Zambeke 90 2 8N 25 17 E
Zambeze → 91 18 55 S 36 4 E
Zambezi 89 13 30 S 23 15 E
Zambezi = Zambeze → 91 18 55 S 36 4 E
Zambezia □ 91 16 15 S 37 30 E
Zambia ■ 89 15 0 S 28 0 E
Zamboanga 73 6 59N 122 3 E
Zambrów 28 52 59N 22 14 E
Zametchino 55 53 30N 42 30 E
Zamora, Mexico 120 20 0N 102 21W
Zamora, Spain 30 41 30N 5 45W
Zamora □ 30 41 30N 5 46W
Zamość 28 50 43N 23 15 E
Zamość □ 28 50 40N 23 10 E
Zamzam, W. 83 31 0N 14 30 E
Zan 85 9 26N 0 17W
Zanaga 88 2 48 S 13 48 E
Záncara → 33 39 18N 3 18W
Zandvoort 16 52 22N 4 32 E
Zanesville 114 39 56N 82 2W
Zangue → 91 17 50 S 35 21 E
Zanjan 64 36 40N 48 35 E
Zannone 40 40 58N 13 2 E
Zante = Zákinthos 45 37 47N 20 54 E
Zanthus 96 31 2 S 123 34 E
Zanzibar 90 6 12 S 39 12 E
Zanzūr 83 32 55N 13 1 E
Zaouiet El-Kala = Bordj Omar Driss 83 28 4N 6 40 E
Zaouiet Reggane 82 26 32N 0 3 E
Zapadna Morava → 42 43 38N 21 30 E
Zapadnaya Dvina 54 56 15N 32 3 E
Zapadnaya Dvina → 54 57 4N 24 3 E
Západné Beskydy 27 49 30N 19 0 E
Zapadni Rodopi 43 41 50N 24 0 E
Západočeský □ 26 49 35N 13 0 E
Západoslovenský □ 27 48 30N 17 30 E
Zapala 128 39 0 S 70 5W
Zapaleri, Cerro 124 22 49 S 67 11W
Zapata 117 26 56N 99 17W
Zapatón → 31 39 0N 6 49W
Zapodnyy Sayan 59 52 30N 94 0 E
Zapolyarnyy 52 69 26N 30 51 E
Zaporozhye 56 47 50N 35 10 E
Zapponeta 41 41 27N 15 57 E
Zara 64 39 58N 37 43 E
Zaragoza, Coahuila, Mexico 120 28 30N 101 0W
Zaragoza, Nuevo León, Mexico 120 24 0N 99 46W
Zaragoza, Spain 32 41 39N 0 53W
Zaragoza □ 32 41 35N 1 0W
Zarand 65 30 46N 56 34 E
Zărandului, Munţii 46 46 14N 22 7 E
Zaranj 65 30 55N 61 55 E
Zarasai 54 55 40N 26 20 E
Zarate 124 34 7 S 59 0W
Zaraysk 55 54 48N 38 53 E
Zarembo I. 108 56 20N 132 50W
Zaria 85 11 0N 7 40 E
Zarisberge 92 24 30 S 16 15 E
Zárkon 44 39 38N 22 6 E
Żarów 28 50 56N 16 29 E
Zarqā' → 62 32 10N 35 37 E
Zaruma 126 3 40 S 79 38W
Żary 28 51 37N 15 10 E
Zarza de Alange 31 38 49N 6 13W
Zarza de Granadilla 30 40 14N 6 3W
Zarza, La 31 37 42N 6 51W
Zarzaïtine 83 28 15N 9 34 E
Zarzis 83 33 31N 11 2 E
Zas 30 43 4N 8 53W
Zashiversk 59 67 25N 142 40 E
Zaskar Mountains 69 33 15N 77 30 E
Zastron 92 30 18 S 27 7 E
Žatec 26 50 20N 13 32 E
Zator 27 49 59N 19 28 E
Zavala 42 42 50N 17 59 E
Zavarāh 65 33 29N 52 28 E
Zavetnoye 57 47 13N 43 50 E
Zavidovići 42 44 27N 18 13 E
Zavitinsk 59 50 10N 129 20 E
Zavodoski 5 56 0 S 27 45W
Zavolzhsk 55 57 30N 42 10 E
Zavolzhye 55 56 37N 43 26 E
Zawadzkie 28 50 37N 18 28 E
Zawichost 28 50 48N 21 51 E
Zawidów 28 51 1N 15 1 E
Zawiercie 28 50 30N 19 24 E
Zāwiyat al Bayḍā 81 32 30N 21 40 E
Zawyet Shammâs 86 31 30N 26 37 E
Zâwyet Um el Rakham 86 31 18N 27 1 E
Zâwyet Ungeîla 86 31 23N 26 42 E
Zāyandeh → 65 32 35N 52 0 E
Zayarsk 59 56 12N 102 55 E
Zaysan 58 47 28N 84 52 E
Zaysan, Oz. 58 48 0N 83 0 E
Zaytā 62 32 23N 35 2 E
Zāzamt, W. 83 30 29N 14 30 E
Zazir, O. → 83 22 0N 5 40 E
Zázrivá 27 49 16N 19 7 E
Zbarazh 54 49 43N 25 44 E
Zbąszyń 28 52 14N 15 56 E
Zbąszynek 28 52 16N 15 51 E
Zblewo 28 53 56N 18 19 E
Zdolbunov 54 50 30N 26 15 E
Ždrelo 42 44 16N 21 28 E
Zduńska Wola 28 51 37N 18 59 E
Zduny 28 51 39N 17 21 E
Zeballos 108 49 59N 126 50W
Zebediela 93 24 20 S 19 7 E
Zeebrugge 16 51 19N 3 12 E
Zeehan 97 41 52 S 145 25 E
Zeeland □ 16 51 30N 3 50 E
Ze'elim 62 31 13N 34 32 E
Zeerust 92 25 31 S 26 4 E
Zefat 62 32 58N 35 29 E
Zegdou 82 29 51N 4 45W
Zege 87 11 43N 37 18 E
Zégoua 84 10 32N 5 35W
Zehdenick 24 52 59N 13 20 E
Zeila 63 11 21N 43 30 E
Zeist 16 52 5N 5 15 E
Zeitz 24 51 3N 12 9 E
Żelechów 28 51 49N 21 54 E
Zelengora 42 43 22N 18 30 E
Zelenika 42 42 27N 18 37 E
Zelenodolsk 55 55 55N 48 30 E
Zelenogradsk 54 54 53N 20 29 E
Zelenokumsk 57 44 24N 43 53 E
Zelënyy 57 48 6N 50 45 E
Zeleznik 42 44 43N 20 23 E
Zell, Baden, Ger. 25 47 42N 7 50 E
Zell, Rhld-Pfz., Ger. 25 50 2N 7 11 E
Zell am See 26 47 19N 12 47 E
Zella Mehlis 24 50 40N 10 41 E
Zelów 28 51 28N 19 14 E
Zelzate 16 51 13N 3 47 E
Zembra, I. 83 37 5N 10 56 E
Zémio 90 5 2N 25 5 E
Zemlya Frantsa Iosifa 4 81 0N 55 0 E
Zemmora 82 35 44N 0 51 E
Zemoul, O. → 82 29 15N 7 0W
Zemun 42 44 51N 20 25 E
Zengbe 85 5 46N 13 4 E
Zenica 42 44 10N 17 57 E
Zenina 82 34 30N 2 37 E
Žepče 42 44 28N 18 2 E
Zeraf, Bahr ez → 87 9 42N 30 52 E
Zerbst 24 51 59N 12 8 E
Zerhamra 82 29 58N 2 30W
Żerków 28 52 4N 17 32 E
Zermatt 25 46 2N 7 46 E
Zernez 25 46 42N 10 7 E
Zernograd 57 46 52N 40 19 E
Zerqani 44 41 30N 20 20 E
Zestafoni 57 42 6N 43 0 E
Zetel 24 53 25N 7 57 E
Zeulenroda 24 50 39N 12 0 E
Zeven 24 53 17N 9 19 E
Zévio 38 45 23N 11 10 E
Zeya 59 53 48N 127 14 E
Zeya → 59 53 13N 127 35 E
Zêzere → 31 39 28N 8 20W
Zgierz 28 51 50N 19 27 E
Zgorzelec 28 51 10N 15 0 E
Zhabinka 54 52 13N 24 2 E
Zhailma 58 51 37N 61 33 E
Zhangguangcai Ling 76 45 0N 129 0 E
Zhanghua 75 24 6N 120 29 E
Zhangjiakou 76 40 48N 114 55 E
Zhangping 77 25 17N 117 23 E
Zhangpu 77 24 8N 117 35 E
Zhangwu 76 42 43N 123 52 E
Zhangye 75 38 50N 100 23 E
Zhangzhou 75 24 30N 117 35 E
Zhanhua 76 37 40N 118 8 E
Zhanjiang 75 21 15N 110 20 E
Zhanyi 75 25 38N 103 48 E
Zhanyu 76 44 30N 122 30 E
Zhao Xian 76 37 43N 114 45 E
Zhao'an 77 23 41N 117 10 E
Zhaoping 77 24 11N 110 48 E
Zhaoqing 77 23 0N 112 20 E
Zhaotong 75 27 20N 103 44 E
Zhaoyuan 76 37 20N 120 23 E
Zharkovskiy 54 55 56N 32 19 E
Zhashkov 56 49 15N 30 5 E
Zhdanov 56 47 5N 37 31 E
Zhecheng 77 34 7N 115 20 E
Zhejiang □ 75 29 0N 120 0 E
Zheleznodorozhny 52 62 35N 50 55 E
Zheleznogorsk 54 52 22N 35 23 E
Zheleznogorsk-Ilimskiy 59 56 34N 104 8 E
Zheltyye Vody 56 48 21N 33 31 E
Zhen'an 77 33 27N 109 9 E
Zhenfeng 77 25 22N 105 40 E
Zheng'an 77 28 32N 107 27 E
Zhengding 76 38 8N 114 32 E
Zhenghe 77 27 20N 118 50 E
Zhengyang 77 32 37N 114 22 E
Zhengyangguan 77 32 30N 116 29 E
Zhengzhou 77 34 45N 113 34 E
Zhenjiang 75 32 11N 119 26 E
Zhenlai 76 45 50N 123 5 E
Zhenning 77 26 4N 105 45 E
Zhenyuan, Gansu, China 76 35 35N 107 30 E
Zhenyuan, Guizhou, China 75 27 4N 108 21 E
Zherdevka 55 51 56N 41 29 E
Zhigansk 59 66 48N 123 27 E
Zhigulevsk 55 53 28N 49 30 E
Zhijiang 75 27 27N 109 42 E
Zhirnovsk 55 50 57N 44 49 E
Zhitomir 54 50 20N 28 40 E
Zhizdra 54 53 45N 34 40 E
Zhlobin 54 52 55N 30 0 E
Zhmerinka 56 49 2N 28 2 E
Zhodino 54 54 5N 28 17 E
Zhokhova, Ostrov 59 76 4N 152 40 E
Zhong Xian 77 30 21N 108 1 E
Zhongdian 75 27 48N 99 42 E
Zhongshan 77 22 26N 113 20 E
Zhongwei 76 37 30N 105 12 E
Zhongxiang 77 31 12N 112 34 E
Zhoushan Dao 77 28 5N 122 10 E
Zhouzhi 77 34 10N 108 12 E
Zhovtnevoye 56 46 54N 32 3 E
Zhuanghe 76 39 40N 123 0 E
Zhucheng 76 36 0N 119 27 E
Zhugqu 77 33 40N 104 30 E
Zhuji 77 29 40N 120 10 E
Zhukovka 54 53 35N 33 50 E
Zhumadian 75 32 59N 114 2 E
Zhuo Xian 76 39 28N 115 58 E
Zhupanovo 59 53 40N 159 52 E
Zhushan 77 32 15N 110 13 E
Zhuxi 77 32 25N 109 40 E
Zhuzhou 75 27 49N 113 12 E
Ziarat 68 30 25N 67 49 E
Zibo 76 36 47N 118 3 E
Zidarovo 43 42 20N 27 24 E
Ziębice 28 50 37N 17 2 E
Zielona Góra 28 51 57N 15 31 E
Zielona Góra □ 28 51 57N 15 30 E
Zierikzee 16 51 40N 3 55 E
Ziesar 24 52 16N 12 19 E
Zifta 86 30 43N 31 14 E
Zigey 81 14 43N 15 50 E
Zigong 75 29 15N 104 48 E
Zigui 75 31 0N 110 40 E
Ziguinchor 84 12 35N 16 20W
Zikhron Ya'Aqov 62 32 34N 34 56 E

Zile 64 40 15N 35 52 E
Žilina 27 49 12N 18 42 E
Zillah 83 28 30N 17 33 E
Zillertaler Alpen 26 47 6N 11 45 E
Zima 59 54 0N 102 5 E
Zimane, Adrar in 82 22 10N 4 30 E
Zimapán 120 20 54N 99 20W
Zimba 91 17 20S 26 11 E
Zimbabwe 91 20 16S 30 54 E
Zimbabwe ■ 91 20 0S 30 0 E
Zimnicea 46 43 40N 25 22 E
Zimovniki 57 47 10N 42 25 E
Zinder 85 13 48N 9 0 E
Zinga 91 9 16S 38 49 E
Zingst 24 54 24N 12 45 E
Ziniaré 85 12 35N 1 18W
Zinjibār 63 13 5N 45 23 E
Zinkgruvan 49 58 50N 15 6 E
Zinnowitz 24 54 5N 13 54 E
Zion Nat. Park 119 37 25N 112 50W
Zipaquirá 126 5 0N 74 0W
Zippori 62 32 45N 35 16 E
Zirc 27 47 17N 17 42 E
Žiri 39 46 5N 14 5 E
Žirje 39 43 39N 15 42 E
Zirko 65 25 0N 53 40 E
Zirl 26 47 17N 11 14 E
Zisterdorf 27 48 33N 16 45 E
Zitácuaro 120 19 28N 100 21W
Zitava → 27 48 14N 18 21 E
Žitište 42 45 30N 20 32 E
Zítsa 44 39 47N 20 40 E
Zittau 24 50 54N 14 47 E
Zitundo 93 26 48S 32 47 E
Živinice 42 44 27N 18 36 E
Ziway, L. 87 8 0N 38 50 E
Zixi 77 27 45N 117 4 E
Ziyang 77 32 32N 108 31 E
Ziz, Oued → 82 31 40N 4 15W
Zizhong 77 29 48N 104 47 E
Zlarin 39 43 42N 15 49 E
Zlatar, Hrvatska, Yugo. 39 46 5N 16 3 E
Zlatar, Srbija, Yugo. 42 43 25N 19 47 E
Zlataritsa 43 43 2N 25 55 E
Zlatibor 42 43 45N 19 43 E
Zlatitsa 43 42 41N 24 7 E
Zlatna 46 46 8N 23 11 E
Zlatograd 43 41 22N 25 7 E
Zlatoust 52 55 10N 59 40 E
Zletovo 42 41 59N 22 17 E
Zlītan 83 32 32N 14 35 E
Złocieniec 28 53 30N 16 1 E
Złoczew 28 51 24N 18 35 E
Zlot 42 44 1N 22 0 E
Złotoryja 28 51 8N 15 55 E
Złotów 28 53 22N 17 2 E
Złoty Stok 28 50 27N 16 53 E
Zmeinogorsk 58 51 10N 82 13 E
Żmigród 28 51 28N 16 53 E
Zmiyev 56 49 39N 36 27 E
Znamenka 56 48 45N 32 30 E
Znamensk 54 54 37N 21 17 E
Żnin 28 52 51N 17 44 E
Znojmo 26 48 50N 16 2 E
Zoar 92 33 30S 21 26 E
Zobia 90 3 0N 25 59 E
Zogno 38 45 49N 9 41 E
Zolochev 54 49 45N 24 51 E
Zolotonosha 56 49 39N 32 5 E
Zomba 91 15 22S 35 19 E
Zongo 88 4 20N 18 35 E
Zonguldak 56 41 28N 31 50 E
Zorgo 85 12 15N 0 35W
Zorita 31 39 17N 5 39W
Zorleni 46 46 14N 27 44 E
Zornitsa 43 42 23N 26 58 E
Zorra Island 120 9 18N 79 52W
Zorritos 126 3 43S 80 40W
Zory 27 50 3N 18 44 E
Zorzor 84 7 46N 9 28W
Zossen 24 52 13N 13 28 E
Zou Xiang 77 35 30N 116 58 E
Zouar 83 20 30N 16 32 E
Zouérate 80 22 44N 12 21W
Zousfana, O. → 82 31 28N 2 17W
Zoutkamp 16 53 20N 6 18 E
Zrenjanin 42 45 22N 20 23 E
Zuarungu 85 10 49N 0 46W
Zuba 85 9 11N 7 12 E
Zubair, Jazāir 87 15 0N 42 10 E
Zubia 31 37 8N 3 33W
Zubtsov 54 56 10N 34 34 E
Zuénoula 84 7 34N 6 3W
Zuera 32 41 51N 0 49W
Zuetina 83 30 58N 20 7 E
Zufar 63 17 40N 54 0 E
Zug 25 47 10N 8 31 E
Zugdidi 57 42 30N 41 55 E
Zugersee 25 47 7N 8 35 E
Zugspitze 25 47 25N 10 59 E
Zuid-Holland □ 16 52 0N 4 35 E
Zuidhorn 16 53 15N 6 23 E
Zújar 33 37 34N 2 50W
Zújar → 31 39 1N 5 47W
Zújar, Pantano del 31 38 55N 5 35W
Zula 87 15 17N 39 40 E
Zulpich 24 50 41N 6 38 E
Zululand 93 43 19N 2 15 E
Zumaya 32 43 19N 2 15W
Zumbo 91 15 35S 30 26 E
Zummo 85 9 51N 12 59 E
Zungeru 85 9 48N 6 8 E
Zunhua 76 40 18N 117 58 E
Zuni 119 35 7N 108 57W
Zunyi 75 27 42N 106 53 E
Županja 42 45 4N 18 43 E
Zuqar 87 14 0N 42 40 E
Žur 42 42 13N 20 34 E
Zürich 25 47 22N 8 32 E
Zürich □ 25 47 26N 8 40 E
Zürichsee 25 47 18N 8 40 E
Zuromin 28 53 4N 19 51 E
Zuru 85 11 20N [illegible] 11 E
Žut 39 43 52N 5 17 E
Zutphen 16 52 9N 6 12 E
Zuwārah 83 32 58N 12 1 E
Zuyevka 55 58 25N 51 10 E
Žužemberk 39 45 52N 14 56 E
Zvenigorodka 56 49 4N 30 56 E
Zverinogolovskoye 58 54 23N 64 40 E
Zvezdets 43 42 6N 27 26 E
Zvolen 27 48 33N 19 10 E
Zvonce 42 42 57N 22 34 E
Zvornik 42 44 26N 19 7 E
Zwedru (Tchien) 84 5 59N 8 15W
Zweibrücken 25 49 15N 7 20 E
Zwenkau 24 51 13N 12 19 E
Zwettl 26 48 35N 15 9 E
Zwickau 24 50 43N 12 30 E
Zwiesel 25 49 1N 13 14 E
Zwischenahn 24 53 12N 8 1 E
Zwoleń 28 51 21N 21 36 E
Zwolle, Neth. 16 52 31N 6 6 E
Zwolle, U.S.A. 117 31 38N 93 38W
Żychlin 28 52 15N 19 37 E
Zymoetz → 108 54 33N 128 31W
Żyrardów 28 52 3N 20 28 E
Zyrya 57 40 20N 50 15 E
Zyryanka 59 65 45N 150 51 E
Zyryanovsk 58 49 43N 84 20 E
Żywiec 27 49 42N 19 10 E

Recent Place Name Changes

The following place name changes have recently occurred.
The new names are on the maps but the former names are in the index.

India

Former name	New name
Ambarnath	Amarnath
Arrah	Ara
Aruppukottai	Aruppukkottai
Barrackpur	Barakpur
Berhampore	Baharampur
Bokharo Steel City	Bokaro
Budge Budge	Baj Baj
Burdwam	Barddhaman
Chapra	Chhapra
Cooch Behar	Koch Bihar
Dohad	Dahod
Dhulia	Dhule
English Bazar	Ingraj Bazar
Farrukhabad-cum-Fatehgarh	Fategarh
Ferozepore	Firozpur
Gadag-Batgeri	Gadag
Gudiyatam	Gudiyattam
Hardwar	Haridwar
Hooghly-Chinsura	Chunchura
Howrah	Haora
Hubli-Dharwar	Dharwad
Kadayanallur	Kadaiyanallur
Manaar, Gulf of	Mannar, Gulf of
Maunath Bhanjan	Mau
Mehsana	Mahesana
Midnapore	Medinipur
Monghyr	Munger
Morvi	Morbi
Nabadwip	Navadwip
Nander	Nanded
Palayancottai	Palayankottai
Purnea	Purnia
Rajnandgaon	Raj Nandgaon
Santipur	Shantipur
Serampore	Shrirampur
Siliguri	Shiliguri
Sonepat	Sonipat
South Suburban	Behala

Iran

Former name	New name
Bandar-e Pahlavi	Bandar-e Anzalī
Bandar-e Shāh	Bandar-e Torkeman
Bandar-e Shahpur	Bandar-e Khomeynī
Dezh Shāhpūr	Marīvan
Gach Sārān	Gachsāran
Herowābād	Khalkhāl
Kermānshāh	Qahremānshahr
Naft-e Shāh	Naftshahr
Rezā'īyeh	Orūmīyeh
Rezā'īyeh, Daryācheh-ye	Orūmīyeh, Daryācheh-ye
Shāhābād	Āshkhāneh
Shāhābād	Eslāmābād-e Gharb
Shāhī	Qā 'emshahr
Shahrezā	Qomsheh
Shāhrud	Emāmrūd
Shahsavār	Tonekābon
Solṭāniyeh	Sa'īdīyeh

Mozambique

Former name	New name
Augusto Cardosa	Metangula
Entre Rios	Malema
Malvérnia	Chicualacuala
Miranda	Macalogue
Olivença	Lupilichi
Vila Alferes Chamusca	Guijá
Vila Caldas Xavier	Muende
Vila Coutinho	Ulonguè
Vila Fontes	Caia
Vila de Junqueiro	Gurué
Vila Luísa	Marracuene
Vila Paiva de Andrada	Gorongoza

Zimbabwe

Former name	New name
Balla Balla	Mbalabala
Belingwe	Mberengwa
Chipinga	Chipinge
Dett	Dete
Enkeldoorn	Chivhu
Essexvale	Esigodini
Fort Victoria	Masvingo
Gwelo	Gweru
Hartley	Chegutu
Gatooma	Kadoma
Inyazura	Nyazura
Marandellas	Marondera
Mashaba	Mashava
Melsetter	Chimanimani
Mrewa	Murewa
Mtoko	Mutoko
Nuanetsi	Mwenezi
Que Que	Kwekwe
Salisbury	Harare
Selukwe	Shurugwi
Shabani	Zvishavane
Sinoia	Chinhoyi
Somabula	Somabhula
Tjolotjo	Tsholotsho
Umvuma	Mvuma
Umtali	Mutare.
Wankie	Hwange

Maps, Illustrations and Index printed in Great Britain by George Philip Printers Ltd., London